Antislavery
Newspapers and Periodicals

Reference Publications in Afro-American Studies

Professor Charles T. Davis, Editor
Director of Afro-American Studies, Yale University

Professor Henry-Louis Gates, Jr., Assistant Editor
Department of Afro-American Studies, Yale University

Advisory Board

Antislavery
Newspapers and Periodicals

Volume II
(1835–1865)

Annotated Index of Letters in the
Liberator, Anti-Slavery Record,
Human Rights, **and the** *Observer*

Edited by
John W. Blassingame and Mae G. Henderson

G.K. HALL & CO. BOSTON, MASSACHUSETTS

The preparation of this volume of the *Antislavery Newspapers and Periodicals: Annotated Index of Letters* **was made possible through grants from the Research Tools Program of the National Endowment for the Humanities and Yale University.**

Library of Congress Cataloging in Publication Data
Main entry under title:
Antislavery newspapers and periodicals.
  (Reference publications in Afro-American studies)
  Includes indexes.
  CONTENTS: v. 1. Annotated index of letters in the Philanthropist, Emancipator, Genius of universal emancipation, Abolition intelligencer, African observer, and the Liberator, 1817–1845.—v. 2. Annotated index. of letters in the Liberator, Anti-slavery record, St. Louis/Alton Observer, and Human rights, 1835–1865.
  1. Afro-American newspapers—Indexes. 2. Afro-American periodicals—Indexes. 3. American newspapers—Indexes. 4. American periodicals—Indexes. 5. Newspapers—Sections, columns, etc.—Letters to the editor. 6. Social problems—Indexes. 7. Slavery in the United States—Anti-slavery movements—Periodicals—Indexes. I. Blassingame, John W., 1940–   II. Henderson, Mae. III. Series.
AI3.A54   016.051   79-20230
ISBN 0-8161-8163-2 (v. 1)
ISBN 0-8161-8434-8 (v. 2)

This publication is printed on permanent/durable acid-free paper.
MANUFACTURED IN THE UNITED STATES OF AMERICA

To the Antislavery Editors

The trials incident to the editorship of a newspaper are many and peculiar, and can be adequately known only to those who have been made acquainted with them by experience. And these trials will be abundantly enhanced in the case of every Editor who ventures to maintain his independence at the risk of his popularity. Of all guides the most uncertain, perhaps, and variable is popular opinion. He who trims his sail to catch the popular breeze, may have a pleasant voyage, perhaps, for a season, that is, supposing him to have thrown conscience and principle overboard. But he will quickly find his bark veering about to every possible point of the compass, and when the tempest—which sooner or later is sure to arise—shall come upon him, he will then find himself destitute of the only pilot that could have safely guided his vessel to land. Look back upon the shores of past time, and behold the innumerable wrecks that testify to the truth of this observation. Principle—Eternal Truth—alone can guide erring man through the straits and over the shallows and quicksands of mortal life, and bring him at last to rest, unharmed, to the haven of endless bliss.

Shall the press dare to speak out freely, or shall it be muzzled? We make it our request that all who feel an interest in this subject, in any way, would communicate with the Editor, with as little delay as possible. We ask that those who approve, as well as those who disapprove of our course, would inform us of their sentiments.—

Elijah P. Lovejoy

Contents

Illustrations

Preface

Most scholars agree that Charles Sainte-Beuve stated the obvious when he observed: "The details of history, in truth, can only be gathered from a study of the immense and varied surface which the literature of newspapers presents." At the same time, most scholars view newspapers and magazines, especially those from the nineteenth century, as labyrinths without a clue because there are no comprehensive journal indexes. We set out in the fall of 1977 to provide some clues to an extensive body of newspaper literature by establishing the Black and Reform Newspaper Indexing Project.

Funded by the National Endowment for the Humanities, the objective of the Project was the preparation of a multivolumed annotated list of letters appearing in selected nineteenth-century abolitionist, black, and reform journals. Unfortunately, we were only able to complete work on abolitionist newspapers and magazines. We chose to concentrate on letters because we felt they contained more of the personal details of history than did editorials, signed articles, book reviews, advertisements, and the like.

The letters in the journals reflect the spirit of the times, the fluctuating interests of blacks, reformers, and others, and represent a valuable tool in reconstructing the past. Until the first decades of the twentieth century Americans were addicted to writing letters to newspapers and magazines. As a result, nineteenth-century black and reform-oriented journals generally filled one-fifth of their columns with letters. Reports of conventions and social affairs, extended debates and discussions of controversial issues, accounts of foreign travel, and narratives of political campaigns were frequent. The body of the letters constitute an incomparable source for genealogists, historians, and students of nineteenth-century American literature, black life and culture, the abolitionist movement, women's rights, music, education, social problems, urbanization, folklore, health and science, social mobility, alcoholism and temperance, pacifism, electoral politics, religion, migration, marriage and family life, immigration, slavery, the Civil War and Reconstruction, interracial violence, prisons and prison reform, emigration, drama, journalism, Indian life and culture, labor, agriculture, and diplomacy.

This published list of letters in newspapers and magazines gives scholars a key to the correspondence of individuals needed for writing biographies. It elucidates many of the intellectual, social, and political currents of the nineteenth century and expands the data available for studying local communities. A surprisingly large number of nineteenth-century journals contained correspondence from all parts of the United States. Often, the only extant letters either written by antebellum blacks or containing descriptions of Afro-Americans in widely scattered cities in the United States were printed in abolitionist newspapers.

Although focussing primarily on their own constituencies, abolitionist journals reprinted letters of correspondents catholic in their interests. Abolitionist newspapers frequently contained letters from Greece, Great Britain, Haiti, Russia, France, Latin America, Africa, and other parts of the world. Famous politicians, stung by editorial attacks, published letters on various topics in the journals. Generally not found in manuscript collections, but often published in abolitionist journals, the letters of such individuals become more accessible to their biographers through the publication of this annotated list.

An overwhelming majority of the correspondents are obscure individuals. Collectively, however, their letters provide a perspective on an almost unlimited range of topics and simplify the task of writing collective sketches, compiling biographical encyclopedias and directories of such groups as nineteenth-century women, abolitionists, Southern and Northern black politicians, novelists, poets, musicians, educators, and others.

Nineteenth-century abolitionist journals are among the most elusive of sources. Standard bibliographies and general histories of American journalism furnish few clues to either the number of journals published or the location of extant copies. There are no central repositories for the journals. Consequently, systematic research is required even to compile a list of nineteenth-century abolitionist periodicals. While some of the titles we discovered have been more elusive than others, we made a concerted effort to locate all of the extant issues of the journals we indexed. Because of the large number and historical dispersion of abolitionist and reform journals published in the nineteenth century, we were unable to locate all of the potential titles. We did, however, search systematically for them. Given limited resources, we tried to index all of the key abolitionist journals, while attempt to ensure geographical and ideological representativeness.

As important as abolitionist journals were during the nineteenth century, contemporary Americans know little about their editors, the financial struggles involved in keeping the journals afloat, or how frequently mobs destroyed them. The story of these journals is an exciting but neglected chapter of American journalism. Although their combined circulation figure was higher than that of such better known contemporaries as the *New York Times* in the nineteenth century, it is the *Times* which has attracted historians and student of journalism. Dozens of histories of the *Times* have been published; there is not only no book-length study of an abolitionist newspaper, but even articles on them are rare. Because so little is known about these journals, it is necessary for us to explain briefly why we concentrated on certain categories of newspapers and magazines.

We were interested in compiling an index of abolitionist newspapers and periodicals because, in few general interest journals can the black and reform angle of vision on the nineteenth century be found. All too often when Afro-Americans and reformers sent letters to metropolitan newspapers they were rejected. Willis Hodges, a New York black, narrated a typical experience in the 1840's when he objected to an article in the New York *Sun* attacking Afro-Americans:

> I prepared a reply to this article and took it to the editor of the *Sun,* but he would not publish it unless I paid him $15. He then put my article away down in the corner out of the sight of nine out of ten of the readers. I went to him and demanded to know why? He said because it was "a paid advertisement." I then said, "Well, you told me that you would not put it in unless I paid you, and I, therefore, expected to see it in some other part of the paper. You are only giving light on one side of the case, and your paper says that it 'shines for all.'"
>
> [The editor replied:] "The *Sun* shines for all white men, not black men. You must get up a paper of your own if you want to tell your side of the story to the public. Good morning."

The editors of practically all other nineteenth-century abolitionist journals included a "Correspondents" section in their papers to insure that the sun would also shine on the oppressed, black and white.

Even the most liberal papers carried relatively few communications from blacks because their letters often lacked literary polish. In contrast, black and reform journals often published the letters of the semiliterate in an effort to encourage the development of literary skills in the black community. One correspondent in *Frederick Douglass' Paper,* for instance, observed in 1851 that "it should not be forgotten, that *Frederick Douglass' Paper* has afforded the most extensive opportunity for a free and full expression of sentiments by the illiterate as well as the learned." A year later, Douglass stated an editorial position on publishing letters which was typical of nineteenth-century black and reform editors:

> We sometimes publish letters, which, when viewed apart from the writers, do very little credit to the literary character of our paper. The motive for such publication is to en-

courage those for whose special development and elevation this paper was established. Our readers must bear with them and give *our people* a chance to be great as well as themselves.

Open to a much broader spectrum of the reading public than general interest journals edited by whites, abolitionist periodicals contain an indispensable record of nineteenth-century Afro-American life and culture. Many blacks who rarely sent missives to general interest newspapers published dozens of letters in abolitionist newspapers and periodicals.

The early reform journals have been included in the index because they differed in many ways from those published after 1830. Abolitionist editors in the 1820's, for instance, were far more tolerant and less militant than their successors. Published in Tennessee, Missouri, Kentucky, and Maryland, the early journals reflected the gradualist antislavery stance of many Southern abolitionists. John Finley Crowe's 1822 editorial declaration in the Shelbyville (Ky.) *Abolition Intelligencer* that the aim of the paper was "to *prepare* the public mind for taking the necessary *preparatory* measures for the *gradual* abolition of slavery," contrasted sharply with the objectives of William Lloyd Garrison's *Liberator*. Writing in his first issue in 1831, Garrison asserted:

> I shall strenuously contend for the immediate enfranchisement of our slave population. . . . I am aware that many object to the severity of my language; but is there not cause for severity? I *will* be as harsh as truth, and as uncompromising as justice. On this subject, I do not wish to think or speak, or write, with moderation. No! no! Tell a man whose house is on fire to give a moderate alarm; tell him to moderately rescue his wife from the hands of the ravisher; tell the mother to gradually extricate her babe from the fire into which it has fallen;—but urge me not to use moderation in a cause like the present.

Slaveholders appeared in the *Liberator* as sinners; in the earlier journals they were often depicted as ordinary men saddled with a complex social problem by their forefathers. The *Liberator* rejected African colonization; many of the earlier abolitionist journals contended that the only way blacks could obtain equality was by leaving the United States.

Because many of the early abolitionist journals were more moderate in tone than the later ones and were published in the South and Southwest (Tennessee, Missouri, Maryland, and Kentucky) they contain many letters from Southern reformers, colonizationists, and slaveholders. Confronting slavery as a reality rather than an abstraction, Southern correspondents publishing letters in periodicals between 1817 and 1830 present a portrait of the peculiar institution differing in many ways from that drawn by many historians. Southern planters appeared, for instance, quite ready to acknowledge guilt over holding slaves. Southern interest in temperance and other reforms also emerges in letters published in such journals as the *Genius of Universal Emancipation* and the *Abolition Intelligencer*.

We begin by publishing indexes of the letters in abolitionist and reform journals which started publication between 1817 and 1831. The newspapers and magazines indexed in Volume One were published in Tennessee, Maryland, Kentucky, Washington, D.C., Pennsylvania, Ohio, Illinois, and Massachusetts and include the Mount Pleasant (Oh.) *Philanthropist*, 1817-18: Tennessee *Emancipator*, 1820; Shelbyville (Ky.) *Abolition Intelligencer*, 1822-23; *Genius of Univeral Emancipation*, 1821-39; *African Observer*, 1827-28 and the Boston (Ma.) *Liberator*, 1831-65. The index of each journal is presented in its entirety with the exception of the long-running *Liberator*. Volume One includes the first fifteen years of the *Liberator*, 1831-45. Volume Two includes the second part of the *Liberator*, 1846-65; New York *Anti-Slavery Record*, 1835-38; New York *Human Rights*, 1835-38; and the Alton (Il.) *Observer*, 1835-38.

The annotated list of letters is presented chronologically by date of appearance in each journal and the entries are numbered consecutively throughout the volume. The list of letters in each journal is published in its entirety before beginning those appearing in another. A journal data sheet appears before the list of letters in each journal and presents its history in capsule form: including places where issues are located, whether or not there is a microform, names of editor(s), and place(s) of publication. Whenever they could be located, we have reprinted prospectuses of the journals to give readers some sense of their purpose. For the same reasons, we have included short biographical sketches, autobiographical statements, and reminiscences of the editors, the people who inevitably put their stamp on the journals. We have drawn these sketches, whenever possible, from nineteenth-century newspapers, books, pamphlets, and periodicals because biographies written by contemporaries and associates frequently include little known and especially revealing personal anecdotes and facts.

As a general rule, we attempted to present a rough characterization of the letters in as brief a form as was consistent with clarity and utility. Though we would have like to publish a more detailed précis of each letter, we have to be realistic about the economics of research and printing. Consequently, we sought entries of manageable compactness and clarity. When the material being summarized is from an extract of a letter, this fact is noted. Boldface type is used to denote senders and recipients, dates and places of letters. Each entry has been assigned a number to facilitate indexing.

The entries vary in character and detail and partially reflect the different styles of several dozen graduate and undergraduate students who did the basic research. We tried throughout the project to have researchers write précis of between fifteen and twenty-five words. But as researchers became more familiar with the topics explored by correspondents (or bored with their repetitiveness), they began writing extremely short summaries. In some instances, they were originally so cryptic that we had to expand them during our proofreading and copy-editing. Often a cryptic entry will appear because the annotated letter was part of a series in which the earlier entries give fuller detail. On the other hand, some of our researchers consistently wrote such long "abstracts" that we spent a great deal of time at the copyediting stage trying to reduce them to manageable size. Undoubtedly we have not always succeeded in our search for uniformity.

Despite our best efforts, we occasionally ended up with microfilm of journals where issues were illegible. We have indicated in our summaries those letters which were partially illegible. Illegible issues were much easier for us to handle than those rare instances when we began annotating a journal only to find months later than an entire reel of microfilm was illegible. In such cases we first explored the possibility of a second photocopying of the run. Secondly, when the original newspaper was so faded that we could not obtain a readable microfilm, we tried to locate other repositories having runs that we could photocopy. Finally, when we had exhausted all of the possibilities without being able to obtain complete runs, we decided to include the index of the partial run of such journals. We will note those journals with incomplete runs.

While perfection is perhaps more devoutly to be wished for in a reference tool than in any other work a scholar does, it is also the most difficult of tasks. In the final analysis, we can only tell readers how we tried to ensure accuracy and comprehensiveness and beg their indulgence for any errors of commission or omission.

People indexing newspapers and magazines eventually reach the point where they feel they are the object of the "error conspiracy." Nineteenth-century printers were notorious for mutilating names; inevitably their errors are replicated by researchers. Even with a minimum of errors in the journals being indexed, our typists sometimes fought a losing battle in trying to decipher the script of dozens of researchers. The frequent resort to pseudonyms and initials by nineteenth-century correspondents and the idiosyncratic recording of place names made it impossible to verify certain items by turning to other sources.

Generally, we have recorded personal and place names as they appeared in the journals rather than trying to standardize or to modernize them. However strange such spellings as "Porto Rico" and "Mohamet" may appear to contemporary readers, they were acceptable according to nineteenth-century usage. Since we generally recorded names as they appeared in the newspapers and magazines, we have rarely used "*sic*" in our entries.

Occasionally newspapers and magazines committed errors in dating issues and enumerating pages. To indicate such errors, we have normally cited the dates and page numbers as they appeared in the journal and then added the correct information in brackets.

Many of the letters we have annotated covered two or more columns or pages in a journal. Our entries indicate only where each letter begins. Some letters were so long that they were printed in part in one issue of a journal and concluded in another one. We have usually noted when a letter continues from one issue to another.

In a number of cases, correspondents wrote long letters themselves while enclosing other letters which they suggested that an editor also publish. The editors did not always follow such suggestions. Consequently, some of our entries may indicate that a correspondent enclosed a letter while we have no précis of the enclosure.

Nineteenth-century newspapers and magazines were inconsistent in how they defined and treated letters. Letters often appeared in columns labelled "Correspondence," "Exchanges," or with headlines, with and without salutations, and were frequently clipped from other journals. Many editors favored the use of initials by correspondents while others adopted such typographic practices that it was often difficult to separate letters from signed articles. Whatever the practices of the editors, we tried to err on the side of generosity in our annotation of the newspapers and magazines by adopting a broad definition of what constituted a "letter."

In an effort to ensure as high a degree of accuracy as possible, we first proofread the typescripts against the notecards and secondly against the journals. Systematically proofreading our original entries against the newspapers and magazines, we verified the names of correspondents and places, dates, page and column numbers, and the completeness and adequacy of annotations.

The entries are most reliable and useful as guides to the public letters written by individuals to the newspapers and magazines included in these volumes. Although we were unable to expand all of the cryptic entries, they can still often provide useful clues to the creative researcher. For example, it is frequently the case that entries preceding and following a cryptic one will provide enough detail to shed light on it. Thus, an entry on "nonresistance" might be followed by others indicating correspondents' reactions to a recent meeting of the New England Non-Resistance Society. In other words, those readers interested in specific subjects rather than individuals would be well served by checking those cryptic entries indicating larger categories under which their more limited topic might have been subsumed.

In order to avoid confusion, we should say a word about the index. Different correspondents who used the same initials and pseudonyms or who had identical names are included in the same entries in the index. It was, unfortunately, impossible to separate them with and confidence solely on the basis of data appearing in the journals.

The Black and Reform Newspaper Indexing Project was singularly fortunate in being able to build upon the work done by the staff of the Frederick Douglass Papers project between 1973 and 1977. By the latter date, the Douglass staff had compiled more than 60,000 notecards in the course of their search for Douglass letters and speeches published in nineteenth-century journals. Between 1973 and 1977, Yale undergraduates Donald Woodall, Mitchell Crusto, Wendy Jones, Marcia Finkelstein, James Singleton, Peter Bollier, Bart Steinfeld, Teresa McAlpine, Michelle Anderson, Ruth Good, Devon Miller, Carter Eskew, Marsha Moseley, Joanne Payton, Bruce Piersawl, Brent Raulerson, Kenneth Noble, Judith Hall, Phyllis Eckhaus, Christine Eng, Mark Gallego, Elizabeth Hillyer, Nan Helm, and Klara Glowczewski set the tone for dedication and accuracy. Patricia Bates of Spelman College and Yale graduate students Harold Cooke, Glenn May, Carla Carr, Julie Jones, Horace Porter, and Barbara Riley also spent part of their summers annotating letters in nineteenth-century journals. In October 1977 the voluminous periodical files of the Douglass staff were turned over to the Black and Reform Newspaper Indexing Project. It was the work of these researchers which created the foundation upon which the Black and Reform Newspaper Indexing Project was built.

We were blessed throughout the life of the Black and Reform Newspaper Indexing Project with a remarkably talented and committed group of researchers. Jennifer Pruett of the University of New Mexico, David Curtis of Harvard University, Joan Reiss of New Haven, and Kurt Kaboth of Yale were the quintessential researchers during the first year of the project. Our Assistants in Research during the latter stages of the project, Amy Mantell, David Barnett, Richard Kramer, Lois Jameson, Carolyn Cott, Diane Peterson, John Caulfield, Jessica Dunn, Joel Cornwell, Roy Nirschel, LaTanya Bailey, Michael Betz, Delgra Childs, and Ronald Matz, proofed, copyedited, and indexed the volumes. Their work substantially improved the accuracy and consistency of the entries. Our undergraduate researchers spent several months helping us to complete the research begun by the Douglass staff. The work of Stephen Schwanauer, Amy Wierczorowski, Maria Celichowski, Neeka Harris, Joseph

Liken, Daryl Warder, Ruth Copeland, Patricia Granger, Eric Koranteng, Peter Eckerstrom, Michael Cutler, Carlos McDade, Peter Borten, Steven Morris, Jefferson Morley, Cephas Ocloo, and Dorothy Trench helped to make the project more comprehensive than it was originally.

We owe special thanks to Dorothy Trench and Jessica Dunn for translating and proofing French-language newspapers and magazines.

Carl Mallard of Philadelphia contributed greatly to the project with his fine reproductions of our photographs of editors.

The penetrating questions raised by the staff of the Research Tools Division of the National Endowment for the Humanities, especially George Farr, Cathy Fuller, and Maben Herring, forced us to entertain alternative perspectives and to examine our priorities in a more systematic fashion than we otherwise would have. We gained much from critiques of the project by Arthur Link of Princeton University and Joel Myerson of the University of South Carolina. Our editors at G. K. Hall encouraged our efforts to make the project comprehensive, and utilitarian. Ultimately, they saved us from making many mistakes in design and execution of our research.

Our typists, Eileen Bell, Sharon Adams, Delgra Childs, Robert Reilly, Ruth Krigbaum, Anne Granger, Pamela Y. Price, Fabienne Moore, Katherine Harris, Kim Caron, and Jacqueline Shea did yeoman service in standardizing the entries and maintaining a remarkably high level of accuracy in transcribing thousands of notecards. Janet Giarratano's cheerfulness as she kept track of all of our drafts and addenda and in the face of our impossible demands inspired all of us.

No large-scale newspaper project can achieve even minimal success without the cooperation of thousands of librarians. We gratefully acknowledge all of those who graciously answered our letters seeking information on nineteenth-century journals, suggested unlikely repositories we might contact, and cheered us on by their enthusiasm for our project. Susan Steinberg of the Yale University Library deserves much of the credit for the success of the project. Suggesting research strategies, warning us of pitfalls in our attempts to locate elusive journals, and acquiring many obscure periodicals, Susan was our best critic, friend, and booster.

Because of the large commitment of time and energy which such projects demand, we must give the greatest credit to our friends and families for their patience and understanding in the face of the long hours we had to devote to the Black and Reform Newspaper Indexing Project. We hope that their sacrifice has helped to provide scholars with some clues to the details of history in nineteenth-century abolitionist newspapers and magazines.

JOHN W. BLASSINGAME
MAE G. HENDERSON
New Haven
May 1979

List of Symbols

AA	Anti-Slavery Association
AAS	American Anti-Slavery Society
ACS	American Colonization Society
AS	Anti-Slavery Society
ASS	Anti-Slavery Societies
CS	Colonization Society
CSS	Colonization Societies
n.p.	no place
n.n.	no name
n.d.	no date
(*)	Whenever printing errors which are not self-correcting result in a repeated page number, an asterisk (*) is placed next to the misleading pagination. The asterisk is used both for a single repeating page number and throughout a series.

State Abbreviations

Alabama—Al.
Alaska—Ak.
Arizona—Az.
Arkansas—Ar.
California—Ca.
Colorado—Co.
Connecticut—Ct.
Delaware—De.
Florida—Fl.
Georgia—Ga.
Hawaii—Hi.
Idaho—Id.
Illinois—Il.
Indiana—In.
Iowa—Ia.
Kansas—Ks.
Kentucky—Ky.
Louisiana—La.
Maine—Me.
Maryland—Md.
Massachusetts—Ma.
Michigan—Mi.
Minnesota—Mn.
Mississippi—Ms.
Missouri—Mo.

Montana—Mt.
Nebraska—Ne.
Nevada—Nv.
New Hampshire—N. H.
New Jersey—N. J.
New Mexico—N. M.
New York—N. Y.
North Carolina—N. C.
North Dakota—N. D.
Ohio—Oh.
Oklahoma—Ok.
Oregon—Or.
Pennsylvania—Pa.
Rhode Island—R. I.
South Carolina—S. C.
South Dakota—S. D.
Tennessee—Tn.
Texas—Tx.
Utah—Ut.
Vermont—Vt.
Virginia—Va.
Washington—Wa.
West Virginia—W. V.
Wisconsin—Wi.
Wyoming—Wy.

Boston *Liberator*, 1846–1865

NOTE: See Volume I for introductory material to the *Liberator*.

[1846]

1 H. C. WRIGHT *to* **MARY [HIS DAUGHTER]. 30 July 1844. Brussels.** Discusses the religion and history of Brussels. 2 January 1846. p.1, c2.

2 THOMAS CLARKSON *to* **MRS. H. G. CHAPMAN. [from the** *Liberty Bell***] 3 October 1845. Ipswich.** Regrets that he will not be able to attend the anti-slavery fair; discusses the memoirs of the King of Haiti. 2 January 1846. p.1, c3.

3 C. *to* **MESSRS. EDITORS. [from the** *New York Tribune***] 12 December 1845. Mobile, Al.** Relates his opinions and impressions of Haiti and Dominica. 2 January 1846. p.2, c4.

4 n.n. *to* **FRIEND [H. C. WRIGHT]. 9 November 1845. n.p.** Praises Wright's letter to James Haughton; advocates dissolution of the Union. 2 January 1846. p.3, c3.

5 H. C. WRIGHT *to* **FRIEND GARRISON. 27 November 1845. Glasgow.** Donates pamphlets for the anti-slavery fair. 2 January 1846. p.3, c3.

6 n.n. *to* **FRIEND [H. C. WRIGHT]. 27 November 1845. n.p.** Advocates the dissolution of the Union. 2 January 1846. p.3, c3.

7 E. D. HUDSON *to* **FRIEND [W. L. GARRISON]. 28 December 1845. Springfield.** Claims that the Liberty Party and the Church are pro-slavery. 2 January 1846. p.3, c4.

8 A FRIEND TO LIBERTY *to* **FRIEND GARRISON. n.d. n.p.** Reports on Frederick Douglass' anti-slavery speech on board the *Cambria*. 2 January 1846. p.3, c4.

9 C. B. STEARNS *to* **MR. EDITOR [W. L. GARRISON]. 19 December 1845. Boston.** Regrets that not everyone benefited by the free discussion in the *Liberator*; notes that bigots still remain. 2 January 1846. p.4, c3.

10 H. C. WRIGHT *to* **E. L. B. WRIGHT [HIS WIFE]. 31 July 1844. Waterloo.** Describes Waterloo. 9 January 1846. p.5, c2.

11 JAMES MITCHELL *to* **WM. LLOYD GARRISON. 19 December 1845. Boston.** Attacks Garrison's view that the poor of England and the slaves in the United States cannot be compared. 9 January 1846. p.6, c4.

12 CHAS F. HOVEY *to* **FRIEND GARRISON. n.d. n.p.** Forwards an article on white slavery in England. 9 January 1846. p.6, c6.

13 STEPHEN S. HARDING *to* **WM. LLOYD GARRISON. 13 December 1845. Milan, In.** States that he is a Liberty Party man who supports the *Liberator*. 9 January 1846. p.7, c3.

14 CLAYMORE *to* **FRIEND GARRISON. n.d. n.p.** Forwards the notebook of an anti-slavery agent. 9 January 1846. p.7, c4.

15 T. P. LOCKE *to* **BRO. GARRISON. 29 December 1845. Westminster.** Believes that the Constitution has become a tool of tyranny. 9 January 1846. p.7, c4.

16 DISUNION *to* **THE EDITOR OF THE** *LIBERATOR* **[W. L. GARRISON]. n.d. n.p.** Advocates disunion. 9 January 1846. p.7, c5.

17 SEWARD MITCHELL *to* **MR. GARRISON. 15 December 1845. Boston.** States that he was excommunicated from his pro-slavery church. 9 January 1846. p.8, c3.

18 HENRY C. WRIGHT *to* **n.n. 1 August 1844. Brussels.** Describes his travels in Europe. 16 January 1846. p.9, c2.

19 FREDERICK DOUGLASS *to* **THURLOW WEED. 1 December 1845. Dublin.** Thanks Weed for his defense of Frederick Douglass' conduct on the *Cambria*. 16 January 1846. p.9, c5.

20 R[ALPH] W[ALDO] EMERSON *to* **W. J. ROTCH. 17 November 1845. Concord.** Protests Concord Lyceum's exclusion of blacks. 16 January 1846. p.10, c6.

21 CHARLES SUMNER *to* **W. J. ROTCH. 29 November 1845. Boston.** Protests Concord Lyceum's exclusion of blacks. 16 January 1846. p.10, c6.

22 J. McC. *to* **MR. GARRISON. 7 January 1846. Georgetown.** Compares the poor of England with the American slave. 16 January 1846. p.11, c3.

23 JOSEPH NOYES *to* **MR. GARRISON. 12 January 1846. Boston.** Feels that the clergy is pro-slavery. 16 January 1846. p.11, c4.

24 EDWARD CURTIS, E. C. BENEDICT, R. M. BLATCHFORD, JOHN INMAN, EDWARD DAYTON, HENRY W. BELLOWS, ISAAC T. HOPPER, ORVILLE DEWEY, HIRAM KETCHUM, JAMES HARPER, HORACE GREELEY, DAVID B. OGDEN AND JOHN JAY *to* **CASSIUS M. CLAY. [from the** *New York Tribune***] 9 January 1846. New York.** Ask Clay to give a speech. 23 January 1846. p.13, c1.

25 C. M. CLAY *to* **EDWARD CURTIS, ORVILLE DEWEY, E. C. BENEDICT, HIRAM KETCHUM, R. M. BLATCHFORD, JAMES HARPER, JOHN INMAN, HORACE GREELEY, EDWARD DAYTON, DAVID B. OGDEN, HENRY BELLOWS, JOHN JAY, AND ISAAC T. HOPPER. [from the** *New York Tribune***] 9 January 1846. n.p.** Accepts their invitation to speak. 23 January 1846. p.13, c1.

26 JASON BARTON *to* **MRS. MARIA W. CHAPMAN. 23 December 1845. Middle Haddam, Ct.** Sends a donation for the anti-slavery fair. 23 January 1846. p.14, c5.

27 n.n. *to* **THE COMMITTEE OF THE ANTI-SLAVERY FAIR. 8 December 1845. St. Louis, Mo.** Sends a donation for the anti-slavery fair. 23 January 1846. p.14, c5.

28 W. H. CHANNING *to* **THE ANTI-SLAVERY FAIR. 19 December 1845. Boston.** Expresses his regret that he cannot be with them. 23 January 1846. p.14, c6.

29 C. M. CLAY *to* **THE EDITORS OF THE** *NEW YORK TRIBUNE***. 14 January 1846. Astor House.** Claims that the central government has no power over slavery. 23 January 1846. p.15, c3.

30 E. J. *to* **THE EDITOR OF THE** *LIBERATOR* **[W. L. GARRISON]. n.d. n.p.** Discusses the expulsion of a reverend from the pulpit by the Hollis Street Society. 23 January 1846. p.15, c4.

31 MINORITY OF THE [HOLLIS STREET] SOCIETY *to* **REV. DAVID FOSDICK. 15 January 1846. Boston.** State reasons why they have invited Fosdick to be a pastor. 23 January 1846. p.15, c4.

32 DAVID MERRITT *to* **FRIEND GARRISON. January 1846. Salem.** Forwards the memoirs of Robert Robinson. 23 January 1846. p.15, c5.

33 NATHAN EVANS *to* **FRIEND GARRISON. December 1845. Willistown.** States what he believes to be the rights of God. 23 January 1846. p.16, c2.

34 JOHN M. HOGARTH *to* **n.n. [from the** *Pennsylvania Freeman*] **5 December 1845. Port Republican.** Accuses American papers of misrepresenting Haiti. 23 January 1846. p.16, c5.

35 SAMUEL AARON *to* **THE EDITORS OF THE** *PENNSYLVANIA FREEMAN.* **30 December 1845. Norristown, Pa.** Discontinues his subscription to the paper because of its anti-slavery stand. 30 January 1846. p.17, c1.

36 WILLIAM SHORTT *to* **THE PREACHERS, STEWARDS, AND LEADERS OF THE WESLEYAN METHODIST SOCIETY, DUBLIN. 16 December 1845. Dublin.** States that the Wesleyan Methodist Society denied Frederick Douglass the use of its preaching house. 30 January 1846. p.17, c6.

37 ABBOTT LAWRENCE *to* **W. C. RIVES. 7 January 1846. Boston.** Discusses the development of resources in Virginia. 30 January 1846. p.18, c1.

38 EDMUND JACKSON *to* **ABBOTT LAWRENCE. n.d. n.p.** Declares that Lawrence's plan for Virginia cannot succeed. 30 January 1846. p.19, c1.

39 FREDERICK DOUGLASS *to* **FRIEND GARRISON. 1 January 1846. Belfast.** Notes the difference between America's and Europe's reception of Frederick Douglass. 30 January 1846. p.19, c2.

40 HENRY VINCENT *to* **HENRY C. WRIGHT. 1 December 1845. London.** Argues that slavery in America has strengthened despotism throughout the world. 30 January 1846. p.19, c3.

41 HENRY C. WRIGHT *to* **FRIEND GARRISON. 7 December 1845. Kirlentilloch.** Feels ashamed that "slavery is the cornerstone of the Republican Institutions of America." 30 January 1846. p.19, c3.

42 JAMES WOTHERSPOON *to* **HENRY C. WRIGHT. 7 December 1845. Kirkaldy.** Believes that dissolution of the Union is a necessity. 30 January 1846. p.19, c4.

43 n.n. *to* **HENRY C. WRIGHT. 12 December 1845. Bristol.** Calls for dissociation from slaveholders; attacks Reverends Chalmers, Cunningham, and Candlish. 30 January 1846. p.19, c5.

44 DAVID YOUNG *to* **H. C. WRIGHT. 25 December 1845. Pennsylvania.** Declares that the American Union is a scandal to civilization and to Christianity. 30 January 1846. p.19, c5.

45 JOHN NEWLANDS *to* **H. C. WRIGHT. 20 December 1845. Perth.** Declares that the Constitution helps to uphold slavery. 30 January 1846. p.19, c5.

46 C. W. *to* **MR. GARRISON. n.d. n.p.** Corrects a printed error concerning the first anti-slavery fair. 30 January 1846. p.19, c6.

47 ALPHEUS COWLES *to* **WM. LLOYD GARRISON. 14 January 1846. Geneva, Oh.** Declares that the *Liberator* is the best abolitionist paper published. 30 January 1846. p.20, c2.

48 E. R. *to* **FRIEND GARRISON. n.d. n.p.** Discusses what he feels are the rights of God. 30 January 1846. p.20, c3.

49 S. M. *to* **SIR. [from the** *Christian World*] **n.d. n.p.** Discusses national support for a pro-slavery Constitution. 6 February 1846. p.21, c6.

50 C. M. CLAY *to* **THE EDITOR OF THE** *SUNDAY VISITOR.* **26 January 1846. Baltimore.** States that the federal government cannot abolish slavery in the states where it already exists. 6 February 1846. p.22, c2.

51 A FRIEND IN WORCESTER COUNTY *to* **W. L. GARRISON. [extract] n.d. Worcester County.** Quotes remarks of a friend of Joseph Sturge concerning John Scoble's visit. 6 February 1846. p.23, c2.

52 LORING MOODY *to* **THE MEMBERS AND FRIENDS OF THE MASSACHUSETTS AS. n.d. n.p.** Reports on anti-slavery lectures in Massachusetts. 6 February 1846. p.23, c3.

53 G. W. S. *to* **[W. L.] GARRISON. 21 January 1846. Milford.** Praises the work of anti-slavery agents. 6 February 1846. p.23, c3.

54 S. M. *to* **MR. GARRISON. 19 January 1846. Leicester.** Introduces letter from W. Douglass, an emancipated West Indian slave. 6 February 1846. p.23, c4.

55 W. DOUGLASS *to* **GENTLEMEN [MERCHANTS OF BRISTOL, ENGLAND]. 12 September 1845. St. Kitts.** Expresses gratitude for their concern for his emancipation. 6 February 1846. p.23, c4.

56 JAMES HAUGHTON *to* **H. C. WRIGHT. 11 December 1845. Dublin.** Approves of the stand of independent congregations who uphold "no fellowship with slaveholders." 6 February 1846. p.23, c5.

57 n.n. *to* **W. L. GARRISON. [extract] n.d. Bristol, England.** Reports on two sermons recently heard; expresses the desire of people of Bristol to learn more of slavery. 6 February 1846. p.23, c5.

58 HENRY C. WRIGHT *to* **[W. L.] GARRISON. 26 December 1846. Dunsinane.** Comments on the chaos in England due to the "coming revolution." 6 February 1846. p.23, c5.

59 ANTI-CHRISTIAN *to* **THE** *BOSTON INVESTIGATOR.* **n.d. n.p.** Believes that the Christian religion sanctions and encourages war. 6 February 1846. p.24, c4.

60 H. C. WRIGHT *to* **n.n. n.d. n.p.** Concludes the journal of his travels. 13 February 1846. p.25, c2.

61 C. M. CLAY *to* **N. W. COFFIN. 17 January 1846. Philadelphia.** Regrets that he cannot accept speaking invitation. 13 February 1846. p.25, c5.

62 H. W. *to* **FRIEND SCHOULER. n.d. n.p.** Reports on Boston anti-slavery meetings. 13 February 1846. p.26, c2.

63 THOMAS CLARKSON *to* **H. C. WRIGHT. 9 December 1845. Playford Hall.** States that he has been laboring for reform for thirty-one years. 13 February 1846. p.26, c5.

64 EDMUND QUINCY *to* **WILLIAM LLOYD GARRISON. 7 February 1846. Boston.** Gives an account of the attendance at the Massachusetts AS Convention. 13 February 1846. p.26, c6.

65 SAMUEL J. MAY *to* **[W. L.] GARRISON. 3 February 1846. Syracuse.** Praises the *Liberator.* 13 February 1846. p.27, c2.

66 JAMES MITCHELL *to* **WILLIAM LLOYD GARRISON. 23 January 1846. Nantucket.** Replies to Garrison's criticism. 13 February 1846. p.27, c2.

67 W. H. WILLICOTT *to* **FRIEND GARRISON. 18 January 1846. New York.** Discusses his surprise at the comparison of slaves in America with the poor of England. 13 February 1846. p.27, c4.

68 A SUBSCRIBER *to* **FRIEND GARRISON. n.d. n.p.** Praises the *Liberator*. 13 February 1846. p.28, c2.

69 H. C. WRIGHT *to* **[W. L.] GARRISON. 28 December 1846. Scone.** Describes his travels in Scotland. 13 February 1846. p.28, c2.

70 ABEL WILDER *to* **MR. GARRISON. 3 February 1846. Blackstone, Ma.** Praises freedom of speech in the *Liberator*. 13 February 1846. p.28, c2.

71 MR. AULD [F. DOUGLASS' FORMER MASTER] *to* **n.n. [extract] n.d. n.p.** Refutes Frederick Douglass' claim that Auld beat him. 20 February 1846. p.29, c4.

72 DR. A. C. THOMPSON *to* **A.C.C. THOMPSON. [extract] n.d. Cambridge, Md.** Considers Thomas Auld, Frederick Douglass' former master, a worthy and pious man. 20 February 1846. p.29, c4.

73 DR. JAMES DAWSON *to* **A.C.C. THOMPSON. [extract] n.d. Talbot County, Md.** Declares that Frederick Douglass' account of the character of Mr. Thomas Auld is a base and villainous fabrication. 20 February 1846. p.29, c4.

74 THOMAS GRAHAM *to* **A.C.C. THOMPSON. n.d. Talbot County, Md.** Believes that statements by Frederick Douglass regarding Mr. Thomas Auld's treatment of his servants are false. 20 February 1846. p.29, c4.

75 L. DODSON *to* **A.C.C. THOMPSON. n.d. Talbot County, Md.** Claims that Frederick Douglass' charges against Thomas Auld are false. 20 February 1846. p.29, c4.

76 A.C.C. THOMPSON *to* **THE PROPRIETOR OF THE** *ALBANY PATRIOT*. **12 January 1846. Wilmington, De.** Asserts that Frederick Douglass' narrative is false. 20 February 1846. p.29, c4.

77 SETH SPRAGUE *to* **FRIENDS [STATE AS]. 11 February 1846. Duxbury.** Claims he is too old to be influential in the question of disunion. 20 February 1846. p.30, c5.

78 HENRY W. WILLIAMS *to* **THE BOARD OF MANAGERS OF THE MASSA-CHUSETTS AS. 14 February 1846. Boston.** Resigns from the board because of illness. 20 February 1846. p.30, c6.

79 R. *to* **[W. L.] GARRISON. 11 February 1846. New Bedford.** Reports on gains by liberals in Nantucket. 20 February 1846. p.31, c2.

80 N. H. WHITING *to* **FRIEND GARRISON. 30 January 1846. Marshfield.** Wonders whether intemperance or slavery is the greater evil. 20 February 1846. p.31, c3.

81 HOMO. *to* **CHARLES C. KENT. 25 January 1846. n.p.** Refutes the assertion by the members of the South Marshfield Lyceum that intemperance is worse than slavery. 20 February 1846. p.31, c3.

82 [DR.] E. D. HUDSON *to* **GARRISON. 2 February 1846. Springfield.** Reports on the anti-slavery effort in Massachusetts. 20 February 1846. p.31, c4.

83 JONATHAN WALKER *to* **WILLIAM L. GARRISON. 16 February 1846. n.p.** Thanks Garrison for sums collected for himself and family. 20 February 1846. p.31, c5.

84 A NEW BEDFORD ABOLITIONIST *to* **FRIEND GARRISON. 7 February 1846. New Bedford.** Gives an account of the peace convention held in New Bedford. 20 February 1846. p.32, c2.

85 ADDISON DAVIS *to* **FRIEND GARRISON. n.d. n.p.** Criticizes the views of Cheever and Lewis on capital punishment. 20 February 1846. p.32, c3.

86 EUGENE CLIFFORD *to* **MR. EDITOR [W. L. GARRISON]. February 1846. Groton, Ma.** States that the days of the Odd Fellows are numbered. 20 February 1846. p.32, c4.

87 N. C. FLETCHER *to* **HENRY BACON, SEBASTIAN STREETER, SYLVANUS COBB, LUCIUS R. PAIGE, AND EDWIN H. CHAPIN. [from the** *Gospel* **(Universalist)** *Banner***] 9 February 1846. Thomaston, Me.** Explains why he denied their request to sign his name to circular protesting slavery. 27 February 1846. p.33, c1.

88 MARY J. TORREY *to* **THE GOV. OF MARYLAND. n.d. n.p.** Reports that Rev. Charles T. Torrey was convicted of aiding in the escape of slaves. 27 February 1846. p.33, c5.

89 EX-GOVERNOR DAVIS, LINCOLN, ET AL. *to* **GOV. OF MARYLAND. n.d. n.p.** State that they do not condone the actions of Charles Torrey. 27 February 1846. p.33, c5.

90 n.n. *to* **ABBOTT LAWRENCE. 4 February 1846. Boston.** Inquires whether Lawrence is opposed to slavery. 27 February 1846. p.34, c1.

91 WALTER SAVAGE LANDOR *to* **MR. [DANIEL] WEBSTER. [from the** *London Daily News***] n.d. London.** Presents both sides of the argument concerning Oregon. 27 February 1846. p.34, c3.

92 H. C. WRIGHT *to* **THE EDITOR OF THE [***LONDON***]** *NONCONFORMIST***. n.d. n.p.** Inquires whether slaveholders will be admitted to the upcoming meeting of the Evangelical Alliance. 27 February 1846. p.34, c4.

93 A UNITARIAN CLERGYMAN *to* **n.n. n.d. n.p.** Discusses Rev. David Fosdick's view that the duty of Northern ministers is to leave the issue of slavery alone. 27 February 1846. p.35, c1.

94 A PERSON IN THE TOWN OF STERLING *to* **n.n. n.d. n.p.** Discusses the views of Rev. David Fosdick regarding temperance and slavery. 27 February 1846. p.35, c2.

95 G. W. S. *to* **GARRISON. 13 February 1846. Milford.** Praises free discussion in the *Liberator.* 27 February 1846. p.35, c2.

96 FREDERICK DOUGLASS *to* **THE EDITOR OF THE** *LIBERATOR* **[W. L. GARRISON]. 27 January 1846. Perth, Scotland.** Replies to A. C. C. Thompson, who seeks to discredit Frederick Douglass' narrative. 27 February 1846. p.35, c3.

97 H. C. WRIGHT *to* **FRIEND GARRISON. 26 January 1846. Auchterarder.** Describes the town of Auchterarder; reports on the anti-slavery meetings in Perth at which Frederick Douglass and J. Buffum lectured. 27 February 1846. p.35, c4.

98 H. C. WRIGHT *to* **FRIEND [W. L. GARRISON]. n.d. n.p.** Forwards correspondence from J. P. Mursell, Duncan McKerchar, and John Newlands. 27 February 1846. p.35, c5.

99 J. P. MURSELL *to* **H. C. WRIGHT. 18 January 1846. Leicester.** Advocates dissolution of the Union. 27 February 1846. p.35, c5.

100 DUNCAN McKERCHAR *to* **H. C. WRIGHT. 14 January 1846. Stronfernon.** Condemns slavery and hopes for the dissolution of the Union. 27 February 1846. p.35, c5.

101 JOHN NEWLANDS *to* **H. C. WRIGHT. 20 December 1845. Craigie, Perth.** Believes that disunion might still be avoided. 27 February 1846. p.35, c5.

102 T.C.B. *to* **FRIEND GARRISON. 9 February 1846. Pulaski.** Praises free discussion in the *Liberator*, the "refuge of truth." 27 February 1846. p.36, c2.

103 CHANDLER ROBBINS AND EZRA S. GANNETT *to* **REV. JOHN PIERPONT. 4 November 1845. Boston.** Send "unfeigned wishes of health and happiness" to Pierpont from the Boston Association of Congregational Ministers. 27 February 1846. p.36, c2.

104 JOHN PIERPONT *to* **REV. CHANDLER ROBBINS AND REV. E. S. GANNETT, D.D. 25 November 1845. Boston.** Thanks the Association of Congregational Ministers for its kindness. 27 February 1846. p.36, c2.

105 H.C.B. *to* **ELIHU BURRITT. [from the** *Christian Citizen***] 6 February 1846. Providence.** Reports that the free colored population of Providence is learning to read and write. 27 February 1846. p.36, c4.

106 JONATHAN WALKER *to* **WM. L. GARRISON. 3 March 1846. Chelsea.** Discusses the release of Rev. Charles Torrey from prison. 6 March 1846. p.39, c3.

107 N. S. *to* **MR. EDITOR [W. L. GARRISON]. 15 February 1846. Springfield.** Criticizes Boston newspapers for not giving the news of the day more fully. 6 March 1846. p.39, c3.

108 G.W.F. MELLEN *to* **MR. GARRISON. n.d. n.p.** States that he will not support dissolution of the Union. 6 March 1846. p.39, c4.

109 ROSS WILKINS *to* **REV. JOHN M. BROWN. 9 February 1846. Detroit.** Forwards money donated to a colored congregation in Detroit. 6 March 1846. p.39, c5.

110 G. *to* **FRIEND GARRISON. n.d. n.p.** States that the *New York Express* seems to be pro-slavery. 6 March 1846. p.39, c5.

111 ONE WHO IS NOT AN ODD FELLOW *to* **MR. EDITOR [W. L. GARRISON]. 24 February 1846. Milford.** Believes that Eugene Clifford should substantiate his charges against Odd Fellows. 6 March 1846. p.39, c5.

112 W. McKERRONE AND PEOPLE OF MANCHESTER, ENGLAND *to* **CITIZENS OF THE UNITED STATES. 2 February 1846. n.p.** Feel that war between England and America must be avoided. 6 March 1846. p.40, c3.

113 PEOPLE OF PLYMOUTH, ENGLAND *to* **PEOPLE OF AMERICA. 27 January 1846. n.p.** Beg Americans not to allow the controversy over the Oregon Territory to lead to war. 6 March 1846. p.40, c3.

114 THEOBALD MATHEW *to* **FRIENDS. [extract] 10 January 1846. Cork.** Praises universal brotherhood. 6 March 1846. p.40, c3.

115 n.n. *to* **n.n. [extract] n.d. Boston.** Supports the movement to prevent war between the United States and Great Britain over Oregon. 6 March 1846. p.40, c4.

116 JOHN BOWRING *to* **n.n. [extract] 14 January 1846. London.** Concurs with the promotion of universal peace. 6 March 1846. p.40, c4.

117 n.n. *to* **n.n. [extract] n.d. Worcester.** Supports peaceful settlement of the conflict over the Oregon Territory. 6 March 1846. p.40, c4.

118 n.n. *to* **n.n. [extract] n.d. Sheffield.** Supports peace among nations. 6 March 1846. p.40, c4.

119 DOUGLAS JERROLD *to* **SIR. [extract] 9 January 1846. n.p.** Favors a resolution of peace between the United States and Great Britain. 6 March 1846. p.40, c4.

120 E. HEALY *to* **n.n. [extract] n.d. n.p.** Affirms peace as a divine attribute of Christianity. 6 March 1846. p.40, c4.

121 WILLIAM HINCKS *to* **n.n. [extract] n.d. n.p.** Expresses support for the cause of peace. 6 March 1846. p.40, c4.

122 THOMAS CLARKSON *to* **FRIEND. [extract] 18 January 1846. Playford Hall.** Opposes war between England and the United States. 6 March 1846. p.40, c4.

123 AUGUSTUS F. BOYLE *to* **WM. LLOYD GARRISON. 27 February 1846. Providence.** Comments on the success of efforts to teach free colored persons to read. 6 March 1846. p.40, c5.

124 NOAH JACKMAN *to* **BRO. GARRISON. 15 February 1846. North Attleboro, Ma.** Praises the *Liberator* as a free press; feels it is wasted on clergy and politicians who only ignore it. 6 March 1846. p.40, c5.

125 J. F. DORVELAS DORVAL *to* **THE AAS. 20 November 1845. Port-au-Prince, Hayti.** Expresses gratitude to the AAS for a medal presented to him in recognition of his philanthropic efforts. 13 March 1846. p.43, c1.

126 J. F. DORVELAS DORVAL *to* **MR. GARRISON. November 1845. Port-au-Prince.** Sends a cover letter for Dorval's speech to his fellow Haitians. 13 March 1846. p.43, c1.

127 RICHARD ALLEN *to* **W. L. GARRISON. 3 February 1846. Dublin.** Discusses Frederick Douglass and his anti-slavery efforts in Ireland. 13 March 1846. p.43, c2.

128 JOHN M. FISK *to* **FRIEND GARRISON. 9 March 1846. West Brookfield.** Gives an account of a meeting of the Worcester County South Division AS. 13 March 1846. p.43, c3.

129 LORING MOODY *to* **THE ABOLITIONISTS OF MASSACHUSETTS. n.d. n.p.** Reports on a meeting of the Massachusetts AS. 13 March 1846. p.43, c4.

130 CHARLES SPEAR *to* **WM. LLOYD GARRISON. n.d. Boston.** Discusses the treatment of criminals. 13 March 1846. p.43, c4.

131 ALEXANDER WILDER *to* **MR. EDITOR [W. L. GARRISON]. n.d. Verona, N.Y.** Quotes from the Bible in order to refute the popular belief that the Levitical laws are God-given. 13 March 1846. p.44, c2.

132 J. TAYLOR *to* **FRIEND GARRISON. 1 March 1846. Walpole.** Charges that the *Liberator* tends to subvert Christianity for its own ends. 13 March 1846. p.44, c2.

133 C. *to* **FRIEND GARRISON. n.d. n.p.** Questions C. B. Stearns' view of God. 13 March 1846. p.44, c2.

134 BENJAMIN RIDER *to* **THE EDITOR OF THE** *LIBERATOR* **[W. L. GARRISON].** **29 January 1846. n.p.** Requests further information from the *Liberator* concerning the murder of a man named Rider by Cherokees. 13 March 1846. p.44, c2.

135 GEO. W. STACY *to* **[W. L.] GARRISON. n.d. n.p.** Offers his opinions of the Worcester County South Division AS Meeting. 20 March 1846. p.45, c2.

136 JOHN BAILEY *to* **FRIEND GARRISON. 28 February 1846. New Bedford.** Discusses the state of the fugitive slaves residing in New Bedford. 20 March 1846. p.45, c3.

137 EZEKIEL HUMPHREY *to* **COUSIN JOE. [from the** *Christian Citizen***] n.d. n.p.** Advises cousin to keep his eyes open for opportunities to criticize England. 20 March 1846. p.45, c6.

138 H. H. BRIGHAM *to* **WILLIAM LLOYD GARRISON. 14 March 1846. South Abington.** Praises the anti-slavery work of the *Liberator*, the *Christian Citizen*, and Nathaniel Colver. 20 March 1846. p.47, c1.

139 C. *to* **W. L. GARRISON. 9 March 1845. Manhattan.** Reports on lectures he attended concerning the death penalty and war. 20 March 1846. p.47, c2.

140 GEORGE WEBB *to* **MR. W. L. GARRISON. 9 March 1846. Middletown, Ct.** Praises the abolitionist clergyman Rev. E. Chapin. 20 March 1846. p.47, c2.

141 C. B. STEARNS *to* **MR. WM. LLOYD GARRISON. 10 March 1846. Boston.** Compares the poor in England to slaves in the South. 20 March 1846. p.47, c3.

142 H. I. BOWDITCH *to* **FRIEND GARRISON. n.d. n.p.** Corrects printed statement that Capt. Small has had to pay for the release of Capt. Walker from prison. 20 March 1846. p.47, c3.

143 E. CLIFFORD *to* **MR. EDITOR [W. L. GARRISON]. 11 March 1846. Groton.** Forwards an editorial published by the Odd Fellows. 20 March 1846. p.47, c4.

144 GEORGE MESSENGER *to* **H. BACON, S. STREETER, S. COBB, L. R. PAIGE, AND E. H. CHAPIN. 25 January 1846. Ravenna, Oh.** "Respectfully declines" to sign a protest against American slavery. 27 March 1846. p.49, c1.

145 DAVID TRUESDELL *to* **THE EDITOR OF THE** *BOSTON INVESTIGATOR***. [extract] n.d. Charleston, S.C.** States his concern for the consequences of abolitionism. 27 March 1846. p.49, c1.

146 A. *to* **BROTHER GARRISON. n.d. n.p.** Worries about critical anti-slavery lectures. 27 March 1846. p.49, c3.

147 AMASA WALKER *to* **FRIEND GARRISON. 16 March 1846. North Brookfield.** Clarifies his earlier remarks on the Constitution and political and moral revolution. 27 March 1846. p.49, c4.

148 AMASA WALKER *to* **FRIEND CLAPP. 8 February 1846. North Brookfield.** Criticizes abolitionists for being "too combative, too belligerent, and too impetuous." 27 March 1846. p.49, c6.

149 BELA MARSH *to* **MR. GARRISON. 19 March 1846. Boston.** Forwards testimonials concerning Spooner's pamphlet on the unconstitutionality of slavery. 27 March 1846. p.50, c3.

150 FREDERICK DOUGLASS *to* **FRIEND GARRISON. 26 February 1846. Montrose, Scotland.** Describes poverty in Dublin. 27 March 1846. p.50, c6.

151 JOHN McNEILL *to* **MR. GARRISON. 3 March 1846. Belfast.** Praises Garrison, Wright, and Frederick Douglass. 27 March 1846. p.51, c1.

152 GEORGE B. WATSON *to* **SIR [H. C. WRIGHT]. 22 December 1845. Methuen.** Welcomes Wright to Methuen. 27 March 1846. p.51, c1.

153 M. M. MUNROE *to* **H. C. WRIGHT. 25 December 1845. Enfield, England.** Praises Wright's pamphlet on disunion. 27 March 1846. p.51, c1.

154 HENRY C. WRIGHT *to* **W. L. GARRISON. 6 February 1845. Glammis.** Believes that the American Republic is a great liar. 27 March 1846. p.51, c1.

155 EDWARD SEARCH *to* **W. L. GARRISON. 24 February 1846. London.** Opposes the Corn Laws. 27 March 1846. p.51, c2.

156 EDWARD SEARCH *to* **W. L. GARRISON. 3 March 1846. n.p.** Opposes the Corn Laws. 27 March 1846. p.51, c2.

157 DAVID BALL, AND REVERENDS PERRY, COOK, JACKSON, BAKER, BUD-DINGTON, ALBRO, BENNET, FAY, AND EMERSON *to* **THE COUNCIL AT SOUTH PARISH, READING. 17 March 1846. Reading.** State that no one would listen to their remarks refuting the charges that Rev. Mr. Pickett neglected his duty. 27 March 1846. p.51, c3.

158 ROBERT JOHNSTON *to* **WILLIAM LLOYD GARRISON. 26 February 1846. Dublin.** Criticizes the *Liberator* for printing lies while claiming to be a free press. 27 March 1846. p.52, c2.

159 C. B. STEARNS *to* **THE EDITOR OF THE** *LIBERATOR* **[W. L. GARRISON]. 13 March 1846. Boston.** Clarifies his previous remarks on the character of God and the sacredness of life. 27 March 1846. p.52, c4.

160 H. C. WRIGHT *to* **FRIEND [W. L. GARRISON]. 2 February 1846. Kinross.** Describes arguments in the Free Church of Scotland concerning slavery. 3 April 1846. p.53, c2.

161 H. C. WRIGHT *to* **FRIEND [W. L. GARRISON]. 12 February 1846. Carnaustic.** Encloses correspondence from James Wise. 3 April 1846. p.53, c3.

162 JAMES WISE *to* **HENRY C. WRIGHT [extract] 7 January 1846. Auchtermuchty.** Praises Wright's letter on the Free church and slavery. 3 April 1846. p.53, c3.

163 H. C. WRIGHT *to* **[W. L.] GARRISON. 2 March 1846. Glasgow.** Discusses his activities in Scotland and the continuing debate over abolition of the Corn Laws. 3 April 1846. p.53, c4.

164 CHARLES H. BELL *to* **SIR. 16 December 1845. Africa.** Gives an account of the capture of the slave ship *Pons*. 3 April 1846. p.53, c6.

165 A. A. PHELPS *to* **SIR [CHARLES TORREY'S LAWYER]. 22 August 1845. New York.** Claims that he can raise the money needed to release Torrey from prison. 3 April 1846. p.54, c4.

166 A. A. PHELPS AND C. D. CLEVELAND *to* **THOMAS G. PRATT. 20 March 1846. Philadelphia.** Announce that they seek the release of Rev. Charles Torrey; express concern for his family. 3 April 1846. p.54, c4.

167 D. LEWIS *to* **FRIEND GARRISON. 19 March 1846. Auburn, N.Y.** Laments the return of a fugitive slave to Virginia. 3 April 1846. p.55, c1.

168 THEODORE P. LOCKE *to* **BRO. GARRISON. 14 March 1846. Westminster.** Reports on resolutions of the Worcester North Division AS. 3 April 1846. p.55, c3.

169 E. D. HUDSON *to* **BRO. GARRISON. 23 March 1846. Palmer Depot.** Charges the Connecticut clergy with helping to uphold slavery. 3 April 1846. p.55, c4.

170 PARKER PILLSBURY *to* **FRIEND ELA. [from the** *Herald of Freedom***] n.d. n.p.** Relates a discussion of slavery and religion held at a meeting at the Andover Theological Seminary. 10 April 1846. p.57, c2.

171 Q. F. ATKINS *to* **FRIEND RICE. 14 March 1846. n.p.** Reports on the condition of slaves belonging to Henry Clay. 10 April 1846. p.57, c3.

172 DANIEL MANN *to* **MR. GARRISON. n.d. n.p.** Requests further information regarding Garrison's views of the Liberty Party. 10 April 1846. p.58, c6.

173 J. P. *to* **FRIEND GARRISON. n.d. n.p.** Forwards a letter which is a reply to an article in the *Christian Freeman.* 10 April 1846. p.59, c1.

174 J. PRINCE *to* **BROTHER COBB. 30 March 1846. South Danvers.** Defends Theodore Parker against charges of duplicity made by Cobb. 10 April 1846. p.59, c1.

175 A BALTIMOREAN *to* **THE EDITOR OF THE** *LIBERATOR* **[W. L. GARRISON]. 12 March 1846. Baltimore.** Criticizes Park Benjamin's defense of slavery; notes that Charles Torrey may soon die of consumption in prison. 10 April 1846. p.59, c2.

176 JAMES WESTON *to* **THE HONORABLE COUNCIL [READING, SOUTH PARISH, MA.]. 5 March 1846. Reading, Ma.** Criticizes the council's dismissal of Rev. Pickett from the parish. 10 April 1846. p.59, c3.

177 HIRAM WILSON *to* **FRIEND [W. L. GARRISON]. 6 April 1846. Salem.** Discusses Canadian efforts to end slavery. 10 April 1846. p.59, c5.

178 LAOCOON *to* **MR. EDITOR [W. L. GARRISON]. n.d. n.p.** Condemns the Odd Fellows for their secrecy. 10 April 1846. p.60, c2.

179 ISAAC STEARNS *to* **FRIEND GARRISON. 31 April 1846. Mansfield.** Inquires about the *Liberator*'s stance on the right of God to take lives. 17 April 1846. p.61, c2.

180 ALFRED WELLS *to* **WM. L. GARRISON. 6 February 1846. Colosse, N.Y.** Withdraws from everything except his religion. 17 April 1846. p.61, c2.

181 A. STETSON *to* **FRIEND GARRISON. 10 April 1846. Duxbury.** Reports on the Plymouth County AS meeting. 17 April 1846. p.63, c2.

182 GEO. SELBERBAUER *to* **SIR [W. L. GARRISON]. 27 January 1846. Cape Town.** Claims that the *Shipping and Mercantile Gazette* is devoted to the abolition of slavery. 17 April 1846. p.63, c2.

183 G. *to* **THE EDITOR OF THE** *LIBERATOR* **[W. L. GARRISON]. April 1846. Boston.** Notes that Benedict Arnold was a Freemason and escaped as a result of this association. 17 April 1846. p.63, c3.

184 JAMES WESTON *to* **REV. GARDNER B. PERRY. 10 April 1846. Boston.** Discusses the dismissal of Rev. Pickett from the parish. 17 April 1846. p.63, c3.

185 S. COBB *to* **FRIEND GARRISON. 14 April 1846. Boston.** Claims that the letter from John Prince erroneously accuses Cobb of slandering T. Parker. 17 April 1846. p.63, c4.

186 JOHN L. LORD *to* **FRIEND GARRISON. 2 April 1846. Newburyport.** Criticizes the Odd Fellows for their treatment of colored people. 17 April 1846. p.64, c2.

187 FATHER HENRY *to* **BROTHER GARRISON. April 1846. Palmer.** Discusses Gov. Briggs' proclamation of a state fast. 17 April 1846. p.64, c2.

188 HENRY RICHARDS CRUMMELL *to* **MR. EDITOR. [from the** *National Anti-Slavery Standard***] 28 February 1846. Upton, Ma.** Praises the good people of the Northampton community; discusses D. Ruggles and the water cure. 17 April 1846. p.64, c4.

189 L. S. IVES *to* **GEORGE W. FREEMAN. 30 November 1836. Raleigh.** Opposes a new abolitionist publication. 24 April 1846. p.65, c3.

190 VOX AFRICANI *to* **THE EDITOR OF THE** *MORNING JOURNAL.* **n.d. n.p.** Discusses the possibility of an English-American war. 24 April 1846. p.65, c6.

191 AN AMERICAN SOLDIER *to* **FATHER. 30 March 1846. Point Isabel.** Discusses the probability of an invasion of Mexico by the United States. 24 April 1846. p.66, c4.

192 JOHN MURRAY AND WILLIAM SMEAL *to* **FRIEND WM. LLOYD GARRISON. 30 March 1846. Glasgow.** Praise anti-slavery efforts of Henry Wright and Frederick Douglass in Scotland. 24 April 1846. p.67, c1.

193 ANDREW PATON *to* **MR. WM. L. GARRISON. 2 April 1846. Glasgow.** Praises H. C. Wright. 24 April 1846. p.67, c1.

194 H. C. WRIGHT *to* **ANDREW PATON. 19 March 1846. Coldstream.** Praises Rev. Adam Thompson. 24 April 1846. p.67, c1.

195 E. D. HUDSON *to* **GARRISON. 4 April 1846. Northfield.** Reports on anti-slavery activity in Franklin County. 24 April 1846. p.67, c3.

196 S. L. L. *to* **MR. GARRISON. n.d. Newport.** Laments the murder of Rev. C. T. Torrey. 24 April 1846. p.67, c5.

197 H. C. WRIGHT *to* **FRIEND [W. L. GARRISON]. 8 March 1846. Scotland.** Forwards letters from James Miller and others. 1 May 1846. p.69, c2.

198 JAMES MILLER *to* **MR. [H. C.] WRIGHT. 26 January 1846. Perth.** Praises Wright's pamphlet, "Dissolution of the American Union." 1 May 1846. p.69, c2.

199 H. C. WRIGHT *to* **W. L. GARRISON. 11 March 1846. Teviotdale.** Introduces a letter from A. Pollack Black. 1 May 1846. p.69, c3.

200 A. POLLACK BLACK *to* **BROTHER IN THE COMMON CAUSE OF FREEDOM [H. C. WRIGHT]. 6 January 1846. Abernetry.** Opposes slavery; advocates disunion. 1 May 1846. p.69, c3.

201 H. C. WRIGHT *to* **W. L. GARRISON. 14 March 1846. Tweeddale, Scotland.** Introduces a letter by Phillip Carpenter. 1 May 1846. p.69, c3.

202 PHILLIP P. CARPENTER *to* **H. C. WRIGHT. 16 January 1846. Stand [near Manchester].** Expresses surprise upon learning of the state of the Union; condemns slavery. 1 May 1846. p.69, c3.

203 H. C. WRIGHT *to* **W. L. GARRISON. 16 March 1846. Jedburgh.** Introduces a letter by Abraham Duncan. 1 May 1846. p.69, c4.

204 ABRAHAM DUNCAN *to* **H. C. WRIGHT. 2 January 1846. Arbroath.** Sends encouraging words to Wright for his stance on the dissolution of the Union and American slavery. 1 May 1846. p.69, c4.

205 H. C. WRIGHT *to* **W. L. GARRISON. 19 March 1846. Tweeddale.** Introduces a letter from G. C. Morrison. 1 May 1846. p.69, c4.

206 G. C. MORRISON *to* **H. C. WRIGHT. 4 February 1846. Fifeshire.** Believes that he has learned a great deal from reading "Dissolution of the American Union." 1 May 1846. p.69, c4.

207 H. C. WRIGHT *to* **W. L. GARRISON. 22 March 1846. Berwick, on the Tweed.** Introduces a letter from H. C. Howells. 1 May 1846. p.69, c5.

208 H. C. HOWELLS *to* **H. C. WRIGHT. 1846. Bristol.** Praises the Evangelical Alliance. 1 May 1846. p.69, c5.

209 H. C. WRIGHT *to* **W. L. GARRISON. 28 March 1846. Melrose.** Encloses a letter from Robert Michie. 1 May 1846. p.69, c5.

210 ROBERT MICHIE *to* **H. C. WRIGHT. 4 March 1846. Hawick.** Discusses the opposition Wright's lectures have sparked among leaders of the Free church. 1 May 1846. p.69, c6.

211 HENRY C. WRIGHT *to* **W. L. GARRISON. 30 March 1846. Galashiel.** Encloses letters from Wm. Halket and Wm. M. L. 1 May 1846. p.70, c1.

212 WM. HALKET *to* **HENRY C. WRIGHT. 7 March 1846. Dundee.** Discusses Frederick Douglass' lectures in Scotland; reports meetings of the Free church to discuss slavery. 1 May 1846. p.70, c1.

213 WM. M. L. *to* **HENRY C. WRIGHT. 25 March 1846. Berwick.** Denounces Wright for his criticism of the Free church. 1 May 1846. p.70, c2.

214 JAMES N. BUFFUM *to* **FRIEND GARRISON. 31 March 1846. Bowling Bay, near Glasgow.** Gives account of Buffum's and Frederick Douglass' stay in Scotland. 1 May 1846. p.70, c2.

215 EDWARD SEARCH *to* **WM. LLOYD GARRISON. 3 March 1846. London.** Believes that war between England and the United States is likely. 1 May 1846. p.70, c2.

216 J. PRINCE *to* **BROTHER GARRISON. n.d. South Danvers, Ma.** States that his criticism of S. Cobb was friendly. 1 May 1846. p.71, c2.

217 S. COBB *to* **BRO. PRINCE. 31 March 1846. Boston.** States that he cannot publish Cobb's vindication of Theodore Parker. 1 May 1846. p.71, c2.

218 PRUDENCE C. PHILLEO *to* **WM. LLOYD GARRISON. 22 April 1846. Boston.** Informs him of a phonotypic school. 1 May 1846. p.71, c3.

219 SAUNDERS KENYEQUHAE *to* **THE EDITOR OF THE** *MONTROSE* **[SCOT-TISH]** *STANDARD*. **March 1846. Links.** States that he heard Douglass speak. 1 May 1846. p.72, c1.

220 B. H. DAVIS *to* **FRIEND GARRISON. 13 April 1846. Milford.** Defends the Odd Fellowship. 1 May 1846. p.72, c2.

221 J. T. E. *to* **FRIEND GARRISON. n.d. n.p.** Reports on a lecture of the American Peace Society. 8 May 1846. p.76, c3.

222 H. H. BRIGHAM *to* **FRIEND GARRISON. 24 April 1846. South Abington.** Reports on a revival of the Baptist church in Abington. 8 May 1846. p.76, c4.

223 W. H. H. CLAFIN *to* **FRIEND GARRISON. 12 April 1846. West Brookfield, Vt.** Relates a conversation he had with a "reverend neckbreaker." 8 May 1846. p.76, c4.

224 E. W. FARNHAM *to* **J. W. EDMONDS. 11 April 1846. Sing Sing.** Discusses the progress of prison reform. 8 May 1846. p.76, c4.

225 E. SMITH *to* **BROTHER LEE. 15 April 1846. Pittsburgh.** Praises the anti-slavery work of Stephen Foster and Abby Kelley. 15 May 1846. p.77, c1.

226 C. K. W. *to* **THE EDITOR OF THE** *BOSTON COURIER*. **n.d. n.p.** Condemns the Methodist Episcopal church for its pro-slavery stance. 15 May 1846. p.78, c3.

227 CHARLES WOODHOUSE *to* **B. R. COBB. 16 April 1846. East Clarendon.** Adds his name to the list of those protesting American slavery. 15 May 1846. p.78, c3.

228 A BALTIMOREAN *to* **THE EDITOR OF THE** *LIBERATOR* **[W. L. GARRISON]. 10 May 1846. Baltimore.** Reports the death of Charles T. Torrey. 15 May 1846. p.78, c5.

229 FREDERICK DOUGLASS *to* **WM. LLOYD GARRISON. 16 April 1846. Glasgow.** States that his former master wants to re-enslave him for revenge; declares that Scotland is ablaze with anti-slavery agitation. 15 May 1846. p.78, c6.

230 EDWARD SEARCH *to* **WM. L. GARRISON. 4 April 1846. London.** Believes in the power of public opinion to subdue freedom. 15 May 1846. p.78, c6.

231 JAMES N. BUFFUM *to* **FRIEND GARRISON. 14 April 1846. Bowling Bay, Scotland.** Discusses the state of anti-slavery in Scotland; discusses Douglass' and Buffum's lectures. 15 May 1846. p.79, c1.

232 n.n. *to* **THE EDITOR OF THE** *LIBERATOR*. **[extract] n.d. n.p.** Condemns the Odd Fellowship. 1 May 1846. p.72, c3.

233 n.n. *to* **WM. LLOYD GARRISON. April 1846. Baltimore.** Defends slavery. 8 May 1846. p.73, c1.

234 WM. CHALMERS *to* **THE EDITORS OF THE** *EDINBURGH WITNESS*. **15 May 1845. London.** Explains his absence from the anniversary meeting of the AAS. 8 May 1846. p.73, c1.

235 WM. LLOYD GARRISON *to* **WM. CHALMERS. 27 April 1844. Boston.** Invites him to address the anniversary meeting of the AAS. 8 May 1846. p.73, c2.

236 WM. CHALMERS *to* **W. L. GARRISON. 1 May 1844. Boston.** Declines Garrison's invitation to address the anniversary meeting of the AAS. 8 May 1846. p.73, c2.

237 S. M. *to* **MR. C. M. CLAY. 2 April 1846. Richmond, Ky.** Defends slavery. 8 May 1846. p.73, c4.

238 L. MOODY *to* **FRIEND GARRISON. n.d. n.p.** Reports on a meeting of the Worcester County North Division AS. 8 May 1846. p.73, c6.

239 C[HARLES] C. BURLEIGH *to* **FRIEND MOODY. 29 April 1846. n.p.** Discusses Burleigh's activities in the anti-slavery cause. 8 May 1846. p.74, c6.

240 H. C. WRIGHT *to* **[W. L.] GARRISON. 15 April 1846. Selkirk.** Praises Frederick Douglass' work in Scotland. 8 May 1846. p.75, c4.

241 H. C. WRIGHT *to* **[W. L.] GARRISON. 10 April 1846. Melrose.** Discusses changes in the world. 8 May 1846. p.75, c4.

242 ELIZABETH PEASE *to* **FRIEND [H. C. WRIGHT]. 26 May 1846. Darlington.** Relates the "dying advice" of her father. 8 May 1846. p.75, c4.

243 W. M. FERNALD *to* **FRIEND GARRISON. n.d. n.p.** Forwards an article which the *Christian Freeman* refused to print. 8 May 1846. p.76, c2.

244 JAMES BARNABY *to* **WM. L. GARRISON. 6 April 1846. Salem, Oh.** Reports on the Ohio AAS meeting. 15 May 1846. p.79, c2.

245 DAVID LEE CHILD *to* **THE EXECUTIVE COMMITTEE OF THE AAS. 10 May 1846. Northampton.** Gives an optimistic overview of the state of anti-slavery in America. 22 May 1846. p.82, c2.

246 C. F. HOVEY *to* **FRIEND GARRISON. 17 May 1846. Gloucester.** Thanks him for his "noble appeal to the people, on the pro-slavery war with Mexico." 22 May 1846. p.83, c5.

247 MICAJAH T. JOHNSON *to* **FRIEND GARRISON. 22 March 1846. Short Creek, Oh.** Criticizes the stance of the non-resistants. 22 May 1846. p.84, c2.

248 G. B. STEBBINS *to* **W. L. GARRISON. 5 May 1846. Boston.** Discusses the evils of slavery. 22 May 1846. p. 84, c2.

249 S. PRESTON *to* **FRIEND GARRISON. 10 May 1846. Lancaster County, Pa.** Praises phonotypy. 22 May 1846. p.84, c3.

250 H. C. WRIGHT *to* **[W. L.] GARRISON. 30 April 1846. Edinburgh.** Reports on the Glasgow Emancipation Society; notes anti-slavery activity in Scotland. 29 May 1846. p. 87, c3.

251 H. C. WRIGHT *to* **[W. L.] GARRISON. 1 May 1846. Edinburgh.** Reports on the Glasgow Emancipation Society; notes anti-slavery activity in Scotland. 29 May 1846. p.87, c3.

252 JOHN MURRAY AND WILLIAM SMEAL *to* **WM. LLOYD GARRISON. 2 May 1846. Glasgow.** Forward a copy of a resolution of the Glasgow Emancipation Society. 29 May 1846. p.87, c4.

253 THOMAS EARLE *to* **THE AAS. 18 May 1846. Philadelphia.** Recommends the use of petitions and constitutional amendments. 29 May 1846. p.88, c4.

254 MACON B. ALLEN *to* **MR. GARRISON. 1 June 1846. Boston.** Explains why he did not sign the petition circulated at the convention of the New England AS. 5 June 1846. p.91, c5.

255 HENRY C. WRIGHT *to* **[W. L.] GARRISON. 2 May 1846. Edinburgh.** Forwards resolutions from a Scottish church on slavery, religion, and accepting money from slaveholders. 12 June 1846. p.93, c1.

256 THOS. VAN RENSSELAER *to* **FRIEND GARRISON. 19 May 1846. New York.** Reports on the anniversary of the AAS; condemns the Union because it upholds slavery. 12 June 1846. p.93, c2.

257 ADAM THOMPSON *to* **HENRY C. WRIGHT. 20 April 1846. Coldstream.** Expresses disappointment in the Glasgow Anti-Slavery Committee for not condemning every form of slavery. 12 June 1846. p.93, c2.

258 SAMUEL W. WHEELER *to* **FRIEND GARRISON. 26 May 1846. Providence.** Declares his support for the AAS. 12 June 1846. p.93, c3.

259 JAMES HAUGHTON *to* **THE EDITOR OF THE** *DUBLIN FREEMAN.* **27 April 1846. n.p.** Condemns the imprisonment of British subjects in America. 12 June 1846. p.93, c4.

260 ANDREW PATON *to* **WM. L. GARRISON. 16 May 1846. Glasgow.** Outlines the position of ecclesiastical bodies in Scotland regarding the question of non-fellowship with slaveholders. 12 June 1846. p.94, c4.

261 CASSIUS M. CLAY *to* **THE MASSACHUSETTS SENATE. [from the** *True American***] n.d. n.p.** Denounces the lack of courage among Northerners who are reluctant to speak out against slavery for fear of economic reprisals. 12 June 1846. p.94, c4.

262 WHILOM, A LIBERTY PARTY MAN *to* **FRIEND GARRISON. n.d. n.p.** Notes a remark made by Origen Bacheler at a Liberty Party meeting stating that if slavery is to be abolished, men must attack the Church and force it to preach a new religion. 12 June 1846. p.95, c4.

263 HIRAM WILSON *to* **FRIEND [W. L. GARRISON]. 20 May 1846. Canada West.** Comments on the state of refugees from slavery residing in Canada. 12 June 1846. p.95, c4.

264 JUNIPER HEDGEHOG *to* **EBENEEZER PRUNE. [from Douglas Jerrold's** *Shilling Magazine***] n.d. n.p.** Satirical letter supports the war. 12 June 1846. p.96, c2.

265 SAMUEL J. MAY *to* **MR. EDITOR. [from the** *Syracuse Star***] n.d. n.p.** Criticizes the paper's support of war. 12 June 1846. p.96, c2.

266 HENRY C. WRIGHT *to* **[W. L.] GARRISON. 16 May 1846. Edinburgh.** States that the Free Church of Scotland has characterized George Thompson, Garrison, and himself as infidels. 19 June 1846. p.97, c2.

267 GEORGE THOMPSON *to* **HENRY C. WRIGHT. 7 May 1846. London.** Discusses slavery in relation to religion. 19 June 1846. p.97, c2.

268 VIATOR *to* **MR. EDITOR [W. L. GARRISON]. n.d. n.p.** Inquires into the truth of statements about Mexican "perfidy" towards American government. 19 June 1846. p.97, c3.

269 R. B. ROGERS *to* **BROTHER GARRISON. 9 June 1846. Chelsea.** States that he made an anti-war pledge. 19 June 1846. p.97, c4.

270 LYNN A.S.S. CIRCLE *to* **BROTHER GARRISON. 5 May 1846. Lynn.** Praises J. N. Buffum; encloses letter received from him for publication. 19 June 1846. p.97, c4.

271 JAMES N. BUFFUM *to* **THE LADIES' ANTI-SLAVERY SEWING CIRCLE IN LYNN. 24 March 1846. Ayr, Scotland.** Expresses affection for the Lynn Circle and exhorts them to persevere in the cause of the slave. 19 June 1846. p.97, c4.

272 n.n. *to* **W. L. GARRISON. [extract] n.d. Dublin.** Reports on recent debates and lectures in Ireland concerning the anti-slavery cause. 19 June 1846. p.99, c3.

273 JAMES ROBERTS *to* **SIR [HIS MASTER]. 1 January 1793. Portsmouth.** Informs his former master that he has left and gained his freedom. 19 June 1846. p.99, c3.

274 ABBOTT LAWRENCE *to* **JOSEPH HYDE. 24 April 1846. Boston.** Sends his donation for the Bible Society. 19 June 1846. p.100, c3.

275 FREDERICK DOUGLASS *to* **MR. GREELEY. [from the** *New York Tribune***] 15 April 1846. Glasgow.** Thanks him for printing his previous letter; admires Greeley's "deep and lively" interest in the anti-slavery cause. 26 June 1846. p.101, c2.

276 JOHN B. PIERCE *to* **W. L. GARRISON. 22 June 1846. Salem.** Sends words of encouragement for Garrison's trip to England. 26 June 1846. p.102, c3.

277 CHRISTOPHER ROBINSON *to* **THE READERS OF THE** *LYNN PIONEER***. 17 June 1846. Lynn.** Claims that Garrison's attack on the editor of the *Pioneer* was false and slanderous. 26 June 1846. p.102, c5.

278 HENRY C. WRIGHT *to* **W. L. GARRISON. 31 May 1846. Edinburgh.** Discusses controversy between anti-slavery factions and the Free Church of Scotland. 26 June 1846. p.102, c6.

279 JAMES N. BUFFUM *to* **BROTHER GARRISON. 1 June 1846. Edinburgh.** Feels that the controversy with the Free church has served to improve popular opinion of the anti-slavery cause in Scotland. 26 June 1846. p.102, c6.

280 GEORGE THOMPSON *to* **BROTHER GARRISON. 1 June 1846. Edinburgh.** Praises Garrison's efforts in behalf of American anti-slavery. 26 June 1846. p.102, c6.

281 FREDERICK DOUGLASS *to* **WM. LLOYD GARRISON. 23 May 1846. London.** Reports on a meeting of the British and Foreign AS; praises George Thompson for exposing the corruption of the East India Company. 26 June 1846. p.103, c1.

282 PARKER PILLSBURY *to* **FRIEND GARRISON. 22 June 1846. Salem, Oh.** Reports on anti-slavery activity in Ohio. 3 July 1846. p.106, c6.

283 OLD SCHOOL ABOLITIONIST *to* **BRO. GARRISON. 25 June 1846. Providence.** Expresses disappointment with J. C. Lovejoy's discourse on the death of Charles Torrey. 3 July 1846. p.107, c1.

284 G. W. F. MELLEN *to* **MR. GARRISON. n.d. n.p.** States that he does not uphold slavery. 3 July 1846. p.107, c1.

285 WENDELL PHILLIPS *to* **GARRISON. 27 June 1846. Natick.** Criticizes the state legislature for not advancing the abolition of capital punishment; notes the progress of the women's rights movement. 3 July 1846. p.107, c2.

286 HENRY W. WILLIAMS *to* **FRIEND [W. L. GARRISON]. 22 May 1846. Paris.** Describes his travels in France. 10 July 1846. p.111, c5.

287 L. L. ALLEN *to* **MESSRS EDITORS. 24 May 1846. New Orleans.** Requests donations of Bibles for the soldiers in Mexico. 17 July 1846. p.113, c5.

288 A. BAER, JR. *to* **FRIENDS. [from the** *Ohio Anti-Slavery Bugle***] 22 June 1846. Crawford County, Oh.** Comments on anti-slavery activity in Ohio. 17 July 1846. p.114, c2.

289 n.n. *to* **FRIENDS. 12 July 1846. Boston.** Reflects upon his duty to God and country to do all he can for the deliverance of American slaves. 17 July 1846. p.114, c5.

290 C. M. CLAY *to* **MRS. CHAPMAN. 30 June 1846. Louisville, Ky.** Declares his support for the AS. 17 July 1846. p.114, c5.

291 JOHN PERKINS *to* **FRIEND GARRISON. 4 July 1846. Franklin, Oh.** Describes Methodist action concerning slavery. 17 July 1846. p.115, c1.

292 JOHN SMITH *to* **BROTHER GARRISON. 24 June 1846. Mecca, Oh.** Likens the present day struggles with slavery to tribulations during the time of Christ. 17 July 1846. p.115, c2.

293 PARKER PILLSBURY *to* **FRIEND GARRISON. 4 July 1846. Hartford, Oh.** Discusses the dishonesty of the third party in Ohio. 17 July 1846. p.115, c4.

294 MICAJAH T. JOHNSON *to* **FRIEND GARRISON. July 1846. Short Creek, Oh.** Upholds the purpose of Garrison's visit to England; opposes war with Mexico and C. M. Clay's support of the war. 17 July 1846. p.115, c5.

295 FREDERICK DOUGLASS *to* **A FRIEND. [extract from the** *Albany Evening Journal***] 23 April 1846. n.p.** Describes Ayr, the birthplace of Robert Burns. 17 July 1846. p.116, c4.

296 WENDELL PHILLIPS *to* **FRIEND SPEAR. [from the** *Prisoner's Friend***] n.d. n.p.** Encloses letters by J. Lawrie and Richard Cobden. 17 July 1846. p.116, c5.

297 JOHN LAWRIE *to* **THE EDITOR. [from the** *Prisoner's Friend***] 24 March 1846. Hyde Park Place, London.** Urges that houses be established to prevent released prisoners from committing further crimes. 17 July 1846. p.116, c5.

298 RICHARD COBDEN *to* **MR. SHERIFF [JOHN] LAWRIE. [from the** *Prisoner's Friend***] 21 March 1846. Portman Square, London.** Endorses Lawrie's support for establishing an institution for discharged prisoners. 17 July 1846. p.116, c5.

299 WM. T. ALLEN *to* **BRO. EASTMAN. [from the** *Western Citizen***] 7 June 1846. Geneseo.** Notes pro-slavery sentiment in the legislature of Illinois. 24 July 1846. p.117, c5.

300 OWEN LOVEJOY *to* **MR. EDITOR. [from the** *Western Citizen***] 10 June 1846. Vermillion County.** Believes that America has contracted war fever. 24 July 1846. p.117, c5.

301 J. B. P. *to* **EDMUND QUINCY. 13 July 1846. Salem.** Comments on the installation of Thomas Stone as pastor of First Church in Salem. 24 July 1846. p.120, c2.

302 C. B. STEARNS *to* **MR. WM. LLOYD GARRISON. 5 July 1846. Boston.** Believes that abolitionists come closest to realizing Christian ideals. 24 July 1846. p.120, c2.

303 A SUBSCRIBER *to* **MR. GARRISON. 9 July 1846. New Bedford.** Describes the Fourth of July activities in New Bedford. 31 July 1846. p.121, c6.

304 J. R. GIDDINGS *to* **GENTLEMEN. [extract] 3 June 1846. Washington.** States that slaveholders have usurped power in Congress. 31 July 1846. p.122, c2.

305 HENRY C. WRIGHT *to* **[W. L.] GARRISON. 28 June 1846. Peaton Cottage, Roseneath, Scotland.** Believes that those who defend the Union and the Constitution are fighting the will of God. 31 July 1846. p.123, c3.

306 EDMUND QUINCY *to* **JOHN T. COLES. 6 July 1846. Dedham.** Cancels his subscription to the *Washingtonian.* 31 July 1846. p.123, c3.

307 CHAS. SPEAR *to* **ADIN BALLOU. n.d. n.p.** Comments on Ballou's book on non-resistance. 31 July 1846. p.124, c2.

308 M. HARDING *to* **THE EDITOR OF THE** *LIBERATOR.* **17 July 1846. Stowe.** Forwards an article on slavery from the *Boston Recorder.* 7 August 1846. p.125, c1.

309 SAGITTA *to* **ABBOTT LAWRENCE. 19 July 1846. Boston.** Criticizes Lawrence's letters to W. M. C. Rives for suppressing the facts about slavery. 7 August 1846. p.125, c4.

310 SAGITTA *to* **ABBOTT LAWRENCE. 29 June 1846. Boston.** Believes Lawrence has suppressed the facts about slavery because of fear of the consequences if he told the truth. 7 August 1846. p.125, c4.

311 WM. LLOYD GARRISON *to* **EDMUND QUINCY. 19 July 1846. Halifax.** Criticizes the pro-slavery, intemperate people with whom he will have to associate; praises T. Parker's "Sermon on War." 7 August 1846. p.126, c3.

312 WM. LLOYD GARRISON *to* **WIFE. 18 July 1846. n.p.** Describes the journey to Halifax. 7 August 1846. p.126, c4.

313 MARIA WESTON CHAPMAN *to* **C. M. CLAY. 25 July 1846. Weymouth.** Criticizes Clay for siding with slaveholders. 7 August 1846. p.126, c5.

314 n.n. *to* **THE EDITOR OF THE** *LIBERATOR.* **n.d. n.p.** Gives an account of a successful anti-slavery assembly held at Concord. 14 August 1846. p.127, c2.

315 SAGITTA *to* **ABBOTT LAWRENCE. 3 July 1846. Boston.** Criticizes Lawrence for saying nothing about slavery in his letters. 14 August 1846. p.129, c6.

316 J. H. HOWE *to* **ELIPHALET MILLS. 30 June 1846. Unionville.** Announces his intention to attend a meeting the following day. 14 August 1846. p.130, c2.

317 S. S. FOSTER *to* **THE EDITORS OF THE** *ANTI-SLAVERY BUGLE.* **10 July 1846. Mentor.** Mentions Lake County officials who harrassed S. S. Foster and Abby K. Foster. 14 August 1846. p.130, c2.

318 JOHN PRINCE *to* **BROTHER COBB. 25 June 1846. South Danvers.** Claims that he was misrepresented in the *Freeman.* 14 August 1846. p.132, c2.

319 S. COBB *to* **BRO. PRINCE. 29 June 1846. Boston.** Claims that he did not misrepresent Prince. 14 August 1846. p.132, c2.

320 J. PRINCE *to* **BRO. COBB. 2 July 1846. South Danvers.** Defends himself and Theodore Parker against Cobb's misrepresentations. 14 August 1846. p.132, c2.

321 L. S. IVES *to* **REV. GEORGE W. FREEMAN. 30 November 1846. Raleigh.** Defends slavery as it exists. 28 August 1846. p.139, c3.

322 WILLIAM WEST *to* **GENTLEMEN. 19 August 1846. New York City.** Praises the National Reform Association, which advocates land reforms; considers their principles to be more sound than those of non-resistants. 28 August 1846. p.140, c2.

323 GEO. C. BECKWITH *to* **JAMES K. POLK. 27 July 1849. Boston.** Urges an end to the war with Mexico. 28 August 1846. p.140, c2.

324 WENDELL PHILLIPS *to* **GEORGE H. EVANS. 7 August 1846. Boston.** Discusses an article in *Young America* about the distribution of public lands. 4 September 1846. p.143, c3.

325 AMARANCY PAINE *to* **EDMUND QUINCY. 25 July 1846. Providence.** Forwards anti-slavery circular for publication in the *Liberator*. 11 September 1846. p.146, c2.

326 EDMUND QUINCY *to* **MISS AMARANCY PAINE. 6 August 1846. Dedham.** Refuses to advertise Paine's fair in the *Liberator*. 11 September 1846. p.146, c2.

327 AMARANCY PAINE *to* **MR. EDMUND QUINCY. 6 August 1846. Providence.** Notes the division in the anti-slavery movement between Garrisonians and anti-Garrisonians. 11 September 1846. p.146, c2.

328 WM. LLOYD GARRISON *to* **[EDMUND] QUINCY. 1 August 1846. Liverpool.** Announces his arrival in Liverpool; requests that H. C. Wright and G. Thompson write reports on the failure of the World's Temperance Convention. 11 September 1846. p.146, c4.

329 WM. LLOYD GARRISON *to* **[EDMUND] QUINCY. 18 August 1846. London.** Announces the formation of the London Anti-Slavery League; gives an account of a public meeting at which Frederick Douglass, J. Haughton, G. Thompson, E. Quincy, and others were praised for their anti-slavery work. 11 September 1846. p.146, c5.

330 WM. LLOYD GARRISON *to* **[EDMUND] QUINCY. 14 August 1846. London.** Informs him of his intentions while in England; discusses his interview with Douglas Jerrold. 11 September 1846. p.146, c5.

331 MR. GARRISON *to* **HIS WIFE. [extract] 4 August 1846. London.** Criticizes the lack of free discussion at the World's Temperance Convention. 11 September 1846. p.147, c1.

332 WENDELL PHILLIPS *to* **THE EDITOR OF THE** *DAILY ADVERTISER.* **2 September 1846. Nahant.** Defends his evaluation of Judge Story. 11 September 1846. p.147, c3.

333 G. W. BARNES *to* **THEOPHILIUS FREEMAN. 16 November 1839. Halifax, N.C.** Discusses the domestic slave trade. 18 September 1846. p.145*, c2.

334 PARKER PILLSBURY *to* **FRIEND QUINCY. n.d. n.p.** Gives an account of mob violence at Sterling. 18 September 1846. p.147*, c2.

335 HENRY C. WRIGHT *to* **FRIEND [EDMUND QUINCY]. 11 August 1846. London.** Reports on the World's Temperance Convention; states that the principal speakers were Frederick Douglass, Garrison, Thompson, Vincent, Webb, and himself; notes that the topic of slavery was discussed often during the convention. 18 September 1846. p.147*, c3.

336 HENRY C. WRIGHT *to* **[EDMUND QUINCY]. 15 August 1846. Enfield.** Reports on the World's Temperance Convention; notes the formation of the Anti-Slavery League in Britain to co-operate with the AAS; denounces the British and Foreign AS. 18 September 1846. p.147*, c3.

337 HENRY C. WRIGHT *to* **FRIEND [EDMUND QUINCY]. 18 August 1846. London.** Reports on a meeting of the newly-formed Anti-Slavery League in London. 18 September 1846. p.147*, c4.

338 VALENTINE NICHOLSON *to* **C. B. STEARNS. n.d. n.p.** Denies Stearns' earlier statement that reformers, or "comeouters," lack spirituality. 18 September 1846. p.148*, c2.

339 D. S. GRANDIN *to* **SIR. n.d. n.p.** Discusses the rights of the poor. 18 September 1846. p.148*, c4.

340 PHILANDER CHASE *to* **RIGHT REV. SAMUEL, LORD BISHOP OF OXFORD, ENGLAND. 1 August 1846. Illinois.** Criticizes the abolitionist view that emancipation is essential to the teaching of the gospel. 25 September 1846. p.149, c1.

341 W. L. GARRISON *to* **n.n. [extract] 11 August 1846. London.** Notes that Frederick Douglass was with him in Bristol. 25 September 1846. p.151, c3.

342 W. L. GARRISON *to* **n.n. 3 September 1846. London.** Notes that Frederick Douglass was with him in Bristol. 25 September 1846. p.151, c3.

343 WM. LLOYD GARRISON *to* **QUINCY. 29 August 1846. London.** Submits a letter by W. H. Ashurst. 25 September 1846. p.151, c4.

344 W. H. ASHURST *to* **W. L. GARRISON. 11 August 1846. Worthing.** Praises Garrison, G. Thompson, and the anti-slavery effort in England. 25 September 1846. p.151, c4.

345 GEO. THOMPSON *to* **EDMUND QUINCY. 3 September 1846. London.** Announces the founding of an Anti-Slavery League in London; reports a conflict within the Evangelical Alliance on the question of slavery and forthcoming addresses by Garrison. 25 September 1846. p.151, c5.

346 WILLIAM WEST *to* **MR. E[DMUND] Q[UINCY]. 14 September 1846. Boston.** Warns of the dangers that accompany slavery. 25 September 1846. p.152, c2.

347 EDWARD SEARCH *to* **SIR. August 1846. England.** Believes that oppression is universally injurious. 9 October 1846. p.161, c3.

348 n.n. *to* **WM. LLOYD GARRISON. 10 August 1846. Islington.** Relates his observations on the Anti-Slavery League. 9 October 1846. p.161, c4.

349 JOHN BAILEY *to* **FRIEND GARRISON. 24 July 1846. Peoria County, Il.** Reports having met Abby Kelley and Stephen Foster en route to Illinois; discusses anti-slavery in Illinois. 9 October 1846. p.161, c4.

350 WM. LLOYD GARRISON *to* **[EDMUND] QUINCY. 18 September 1846. London.** States his travel itinerary; notes that the Evangelical Alliance has been unable to resolve the slavery question. 9 October 1846. p.162, c3.

351 GEO. THOMPSON *to* **EDMUND QUINCY. n.d. n.p.** Denounces pro-slavery American clergymen who undermine the abolitionist cause in Britain; reflects upon the fragmented state of the Evangelical Alliance. 9 October 1846. p.162, c4.

352 LUKE J. HANSARD *to* **MESSRS. HOWE. 15 September 1846. London.** Donates money for the Christian Emancipation Society. 9 October 1846. p.162, c4.

353 R. SMITH *to* **THE EDITOR OF THE** *LIBERATOR* **[EDMUND QUINCY]. 18 September 1846. London.** Comments on the Evangelical Alliance and anti-slavery in England; notes that Frederick Douglass spoke against slavery at an Evangelical Alliance meeting. 9 October 1846. p.162, c4.

354 A. W. QUIMBY *to* **EDMUND QUINCY. 24 August 1846. Hanover County, Va.** Believes that it is treason to advocate dissolution of the Union. 9 October 1846. p.163, c2.

355 SIMON SHACKLE *to* **THE GOV. OF SOUTH CAROLINA. n.d. n.p.** Proposes a law to enslave all Jews in the state. 9 October 1846. p.163, c3.

356 G. W. S. *to* **FRIEND QUINCY. 22 September 1846. Milford.** States his thoughts on community enterprise. 9 October 1846. p.164, c2.

357 JOHN FENWICK *to* **REV. MR. OSBORNE. [from the** *London Non-Conformist***] 4 September 1846. England.** Comments on the Evangelical Alliance. 16 October 1846. p.166, c4.

358 W. H. C. *to* **CHAS. SUMNER. 28 September 1846. Brattleboro.** Accuses Sumner of twisting Dr. Channing's statements on the Union and the anti-slavery cause. 16 October 1846. p.166, c5.

359 R. C. *to* **MR. EDITOR [EDMUND QUINCY]. 5 October 1846. Cambridge, Ma.** Informs that J. R. Lowell authored the lines "We will speak out—we will be heard." 16 October 1846. p.167, c4.

360 EDWARD SEARCH *to* **n.n. 1 September 1846. England.** Addresses the injustice of the present system by which land is held and managed in Ireland; notes the importance of Irish independence from England. 23 October 1846. p.169, c2.

361 EDWARD SEARCH *to* **[W. L.] GARRISON. 13 September 1846. London.** Praises Garrison for not allowing the Evangelical Alliance to weaken the anti-slavery cause. 23 October 1846. p.169, c3.

362 W. SHORTT *to* **REV. ROBERT NEWTON. [from the** *Christian Penny Record***] 15 August 1846. n.p.** Discusses the "North" and "South" divisions of the Methodist Episcopal Church of America. 23 October 1846. p.170, c1.

363 B. TRESENRIDER *to* **BROTHER LEE. [from the** *True Wesleyan***] September 1846. Jamestown, Oh.** Criticizes the pro-slavery stand of participants at the Ohio Conference of the Methodist Episcopal Church. 23 October 1846. p.170, c2.

364 J. HARDY *to* **BROTHER LEE. [from the** *True Wesleyan***] 12 September 1846. New Haven.** Reports on the meeting of the American Board of Commissioners for Foreign Missions; relates discussions of polygamy and slavery. 23 October 1846. p.170, c2.

365 JNO. H. PEARSON *to* **THE EDITOR OF THE** *COURIER.* **14 October 1841. Boston.** States that S. C. Phillips denounced Pearson as one who would return a fugitive slave. 23 October 1846. p.170, c3.

366 JAMES W. HANNUM *to* **THE EDITORS OF THE** *NEW ORLEANS PICAYUNE.* **11 September 1846. Boston.** Describes his futile attempt to help a fugitive slave leave the country. 23 October 1846. p.170, c3.

367 JAMES W. HANNUM *to* **THE EDITORS OF THE** *NEW ORLEANS PICAYUNE.* **22 September 1846. Boston.** Reports that abolitionists put Hannum in jail. 23 October 1846. p.170, c3.

368 JNO. H. PEARSON *to* **S. C. PHILLIPS. 14 October 1846. Boston.** Explains why he advised Capt. Harrison to return a fugitive slave. 23 October 1846. p.170, c3.

369 L. D. SMITH *to* **FRIEND QUINCY. 29 October 1846. Stoneham.** Gives an account of the Middlesex County Anti-Slavery Convention. 23 October 1846. p.171, c2.

370 PARKER PILLSBURY *to* **FRIEND QUINCY. n.d. n.p.** Reports on the anti-slavery meeting at East Randolph. 23 October 1846. p.171, c3.

371 PARKER PILLSBURY *to* **QUINCY. n.d. n.p.** Forwards extract of a letter from Mr. and Mrs. Foster. 23 October 1846. p.171, c4.

372 MR. AND MRS. FOSTER *to* **PARKER PILLSBURY. [extract] n.d. n.p.** Reports on the progress of the abolitionist cause in Ohio. 23 October 1846. p.171, c4.

373 J. S. E. *to* **MR. EDITOR. [from the** *Christian Register***] n.d. n.p.** Believes that Christian spirit and war are incompatible. 23 October 1846. p.171, c4.

374 JOSIAH BUTLER *to* **E. MERRIAM. 26 August 1846. South Deerfield, N.H.** Notes strange explosions in Deerfield. 23 October 1846. p.172, c4.

375 GEO. THOMPSON *to* **THE EDITOR OF THE** *LONDON PATRIOT.* **n.d. n.p.** Forwards article by Thomas Clarkson in which he discusses slavery and dissolution of the Union. 30 October 1846. p.173, c4.

376 WM. LLOYD GARRISON *to* **n.n. 3 October 1846. Belfast.** Discusses his activities in Ireland. 30 October 1846. p.174, c3.

377 ANDREW PATON *to* **EDMUND QUINCY. 2 October 1846. Glasgow.** Reports on Garrison's itinerary in Scotland. 30 October 1846. p.174, c4.

378 JAMES ROBERTSON *to* **EDMUND QUINCY. n.d. Edinburgh.** Praises Garrison and Frederick Douglass' efforts in Scotland. 30 October 1846. p.174, c5.

379 WILLIAM SMEAL *to* **FRIEND [EDMUND QUINCY]. 2 October 1846. Glasgow.** Forwards a manuscript from Garrison; declares that Garrison's visit has done much to further the cause. 30 October 1846. p.174, c6.

380 AN ESSEX NORTH WHIG ABOLITIONIST *to* **MR. QUINCY. 15 October 1846. Haverhill.** Discusses the nomination of Deacon Abbott to Congress. 30 October 1846. p.175, c2.

381 AUGUSTUS R. POPE *to* **PLYMOUTH COLONY AS. 30 September 1846. Kingston.** Reports he cannot attend a meeting in Marlborough; affirms his support for the anti-slavery cause. 30 October 1846. p.175, c3.

382 CHARLES SUMNER *to* **ROBERT C. WINTHROP. [from the** *Boston Daily Whig***] n.d. n.p.** Criticizes Winthrop's vote on the Mexican War Bill. 6 November 1846. p.177, c2.

383 R. SMITH *to* **SIR. [from the** *London Patriot***] 28 September 1846. London.** Affirms the Anti-Slavery League's support of the AAS. 6 November 1846. p.177, c6.

384 S. C. PHILLIPS *to* **THE EDITOR. [from the** *Boston Courier***] 17 October 1846. Salem.** Comments on the alleged kidnapping of a slave by Capt. Hannum. 6 November 1846. p.178, c1.

385 EDWARD SEARCH *to* **THE EDITOR OF THE** *LIBERATOR* **[EDMUND QUINCY]. 29 September 1846. London.** Declares that Garrison's visit and the "faltering" of the Evangelical Alliance have made the British aware of "our danger from the slave spirit." 6 November 1846. p.178, c5.

386 A. *to* **FRIEND QUINCY. 28 October 1846. New Bedford.** Reports on a meeting of "the sectarians" at which Rev. Kirk spoke on the Evangelical Alliance; adds that the Friends and anti-slavery were also discussed. 6 November 1846. p.178, c6.

387 JAMES N. BUFFUM *to* **FRIEND QUINCY. n.d. n.p.** Reports on his interview with Thomas Clarkson. 6 November 1846. p.179, c3.

388 JAS. HAUGHTON *to* **THE EDITOR OF THE** *FREEMAN***. 15 September 1846. n.p.** Claims that he does not advocate the use of physical force. 6 November 1846. p.180, c2.

389 T. M. RAY *to* **JAMES HAUGHTON. 10 September 1846. Dublin.** States that the Loyal National Repeal Association refuses to work with the Young Ireland Party. 6 November 1846. p.180, c2.

390 JAS. HAUGHTON *to* **THE COMMITTEE OF THE LOYAL NATIONAL REPEAL ASSOCIATION. n.d. n.p.** Compares the Young Ireland Party to the Old Ireland Party. 6 November 1846. p.180, c2.

391 JAS. HAUGHTON *to* **T. M. RAY. 11 September 1846. Dublin.** Asks that the matter of the Young Ireland Party be debated. 6 November 1846. p.180, c2.

392 ISAAC T. HOPPER *to* **MESSRS. WALTER CHANNING, & C. 20 October 1846. New York.** Regrets he cannot attend a public meeting held to discuss the reformation of criminals. 6 November 1846. p.180, c3.

393 FRANK P. APPLETON *to* **THE EDITORS OF THE** *PRISONER'S FRIEND***. 21 October 1846. Danvers.** Supports their work with prisoners. 6 November 1846. p.180, c3.

394 LEVI D. SMITH *to* **FRIEND QUINCY. n.d. n.p.** Reports on the activities of the Middlesex County AS. 13 November 1846. p.183, c1.

395 PARKER PILLSBURY *to* **FRIEND QUINCY. 3 November 1846. Marlboro'.** Discusses third party activities. 13 November 1846. p.183, c2.

396 BERIAH GREEN *to* **RUFUS ANDERSON. 16 October 1846. Whitesboro'.** Terminates his connections with the American Board. 13 November 1846. p.183, c3.

397 DR. COX *to* **MESSRS. EDITORS. [from the** *New York Evangelist***] 8 August 1846. London.** Notes the closing of the Grand Temperance Convention; gives an account of a large public meeting at which Frederick Douglass denounced the American temperance movement. 20 November 1846. p.185, c1.

398 WM. BROCK *to* **THE EDITOR OF THE** *LONDON NONCONFORMIST.* **n.d. n.p.** Comments on the Evangelical Alliance and American slavery. 20 November 1846. p.185, c5.

399 J.V. HIMES *to* **SIR. [from the** *London Patriot***] 4 September 1846. London.** Justifies his vote against receiving slaveholders into the Evangelical Alliance. 20 November 1846. p.185, c6.

400 GERRIT SMITH *to* **STEPHEN C. PHILLIPS. 23 October 1846. Peterboro'.** Enumerates Massachusetts' anti-slavery "blusters", including the imprisonment of fugitive slave George Latimer, the support of Clay in the annexation of Texas, and the exoneration of Capt. Hannum; questions Phillips' earnestness as a defendant of the slave. 20 November 1846. p.186, c1.

401 EDMUND QUINCY *to* **GERRIT SMITH. 12 November 1846. Dedham, Ma.** Concurs with Smith's condemnation of Massachusetts, but attributes the state's guilt to different causes. 20 November 1846. p.186, c4.

402 W.L. GARRISON *to* **n.n. 20 October 1846. Liverpool.** Claims that George Thompson inspired people more than either Garrison or Douglass. 20 November 1846. p.187, c2.

403 FREDERICK DOUGLASS *to* **SAMUEL HANSON COX. 30 October 1846. Edinburgh.** Answers Cox's attack on Frederick Douglass. 27 November 1846. p.189, c2.

404 HENRY C. WRIGHT *to* **GARRISON. 4 November 1846. Liverpool.** Hopes the Union will be dissolved by the time he returns home; praises Garrison's efforts. 27 November 1846. p.190, c4.

405 EDWARD SEARCH *to* **GARRISON. 19 October 1846. England.** Praises Garrison, Wright, and Douglass for enlightening the British on the subjects of clerical hypocrisy and anti-slavery. 27 November 1846. p.190, c5.

406 EDWARD SEARCH *to* **W. L. GARRISON. 21 October 1846. London.** Praises Garrison and his efforts in behalf of the abolitionist cause. 27 November 1846. p.190, c5.

407 WM. LLOYD GARRISON *to* **THE EDITOR OF THE** *CHRISTIAN WITNESS.* **n.d. n.p.** Answers the editor's complaint that he is "not exactly at ease" with Garrison by comparing him to slaveholders who share the same sentiments. 4 December 1846. p.193, c2.

408 EDWARD SEARCH *to* **[W. L.] GARRISON. 2 November 1846. London.** Condemns the *Christian Witness* for slandering Garrison; criticizes the ministry's attack on Garrison. 4 December 1846. p.193, c5.

409 STEPHEN S. FOSTER *to* **FRIEND GARRISON. [extract] n.d. n.p.** Notes upcoming anti-slavery meetings in Worcester. 4 December 1846. p.194, c5.

410 JOHN QUINCY ADAMS *to* **SIR [A GENTLEMAN OF ALEXANDRIA]. 9 November 1846. Quincy.** Declares that he considers the retrocession of the county of Alexandria to Virginia unconstitutional and void. 4 December 1846. p.194, c5.

411 SAMUEL J. MAY *to* **BROTHER [W. L. GARRISON]. 26 November 1846. Syracuse.** Welcomes Garrison home. 4 December 1846. p.194, c6.

412 S. W. W. *to* **FRIEND GARRISON. 20 November 1846. Providence.** Comments on the attendance at the peace and anti-slavery convention. 4 December 1846. p.195, c2.

413 EDWARD SEARCH *to* **W. L. GARRISON. October 1846. London.** Criticizes the decision of his parson to forbid travel by coach on the Sabbath; adds that this prevents those who are not in his parish from attending their own places of worship. 4 December 1846. p.195, c2.

414 D. S. GRANDIN *to* **BROTHER GARRISON. 29 November 1846. Boston.** Announces the formation of the Workingmen's Protective Union. 4 December 1846. p.195, c3.

415 W. H. A. *to* **REV. R. BURGESS. November 1843. Hornsey.** Criticizes his decision to forbid travel by coach on the Sabbath. 4 December 1846. p.196, c2.

416 G[EORGE] B[RADBURN] *to* **n.n. [extract from the** *Boston Chronotype***] n.d. Cleveland.** Appreciates the "sober second thought" afforded abolitionists by the paper's republication of Elizur Wright's "streak letter" to Henry Stanton. 11 December 1846. p.197, c2.

417 T. MATLACK *to* **WILLIAM FINDLEY. 11 January 1817. Philadelphia.** Discusses the abolition of slavery in Pennsylvania. 11 December 1846. p.197, c3.

418 HENRY C. WRIGHT *to* **[W. L.] GARRISON. 6 November 1846. Manchester.** Criticizes the Evangelical Alliance. 11 December 1846. p.199, c2.

419 E. SEARCH *to* **[W. L.] GARRISON. n.d. n.p.** Reports on the effects of Garrison's visit to Europe. 11 December 1846. p.199, c4.

420 CHARLES SPEAR *to* **FRIEND GARRISON. 10 December 1846. Boston.** Notes approaching anniversary of the Massachusetts Society for Abolition of Capital Punishment. 11 December 1846. p.199, c4.

421 GEO. BUSH *to* **THE EDITOR OF THE** *NEW YORK TRIBUNE.* **n.d. n.p.** Discusses "magnetic marvels" and the clairvoyant Mr. David. 11 December 1846. p.200, c2.

422 L. *to* **MR. EDITOR [W. L. GARRISON]. n.d. n.p.** Criticizes current lack of meetings and speeches by agents of the Massachusetts AS. 18 December 1846. p.203, c1.

423 EDWARD SEARCH *to* **THE EDITOR OF THE** *LIBERATOR* **[W. L. GARRISON]. 1 November 1846. London.** Recounts progress made by abolitionists and non-resistants. 18 December 1846. p.203, c2.

424 R. SMITH *to* **THE EDITOR OF THE** *LIBERATOR* **[W. L. GARRISON]. 19 November 1846. London.** Discusses anti-slavery meetings held in England since Garrison's departure. 18 December 1846. p.203, c3.

425 F[RANCIS] J[ACKSON] *to* **THE EDITOR OF THE** *LIBERATOR* **[W. L. GARRISON]. n.d. n.p.** Forwards a letter from the president of the Massachusetts AS. 18 December 1846. p.203, c4.

426 JOHN KENRICK *to* **[FRANCIS JACKSON]. 17 March 1829. Newton.** Predicts the dissolution of the Union. 18 December 1846. p.203, c4.

427 E. A. S. SMITH *to* **MRS. CHAPMAN. n.d. n.p.** Offers suggestions for the Massachusetts Anti-Slavery Bazaar. 18 December 1846. p.203, c6.

428 EDWARD SEARCH *to* **[W. L. GARRISON]. 5 November 1846. London.** Believes that society has no right to punish those whom it has not educated. 18 December 1846. p.120 [204], c3.

429 N. D. ANDERSON *to* **THE EDITORS OF THE** *ELIZABETHTOWN REGISTER*. **14 November 1846. Brandenberg, Ky.** Reports proceedings of public meeting held to discuss the formation of an anti-abolition society. 25 December 1846. p.205, c1.

430 C. W. BEARD *to* **THE EDITORS OF THE** *ELIZABETHTOWN REGISTER*. **n.d. n.p.** Forwards proceedings of meeting held to discuss the formation of an anti-abolition society. 25 December 1846. p.205, c1.

431 WM. LLOYD GARRISON *to* **MARCUS MORTON. 27 November 1846. Boston.** Questions the tax imposed on a silver tea service. 25 December 1846. p.206, c1.

432 EDMUND QUINCY *to* **GERRIT SMITH. 11 December 1846. Dedham.** Denies that his use of the term "Third Party" implied opprobrium or reproach. 25 December 1846. p.206, c2.

433 EDWARD SEARCH *to* **THE EDITOR OF THE** *LIBERATOR* **[W. L. GARRISON]. 1 November 1846. London.** Praises the late Mr. Clarkson and his efforts for the anti-slavery cause. 25 December 1846. p.206, c5.

434 HENRY C. WRIGHT *to* **A MEMBER OF THE EVANGELICAL ALLIANCE. 20 November 1846. Wakefield.** Denounces the Evangelical Alliance's refusal to pronounce judgement upon Christianity as practiced by slaveholders. 25 December 1846. p.207, c3.

435 A MEMBER OF THE EVANGELICAL ALLIANCE *to* **H. C. WRIGHT. 25 November 1846. n.p.** Explains that the majority of the Evangelical Alliance abhors slavery, despite the organization's refusal to question the ethics of professing Christian slaveholders. 25 December 1846. p.207, c3.

436 HENRY C. WRIGHT *to* **WM. LLOYD GARRISON. 25 November 1846. n.p.** Maintains that members of the Evangelical Alliance are apologists for slavery. 25 December 1846. p.207, c3.

437 CAPT. C. W. BULLEN *to* **n.n. [extract from the** *Louisville Journal***] n.d. n.p.** Provides a front-line account of the war with Mexico. 25 December 1846. p. 208, c2.

438 JAMES S. JACKSON *to* **n.n. [extract] 23 September 1846. Texas.** A soldier describes the poor state of his regiment. 25 December 1846. p.208, c2.

439 CAPT. HARPER *to* **n.n. [extract from the** *Louisville Journal***] n.d. n.p.** Reports heavy casualties on both sides in the Mexican War. 25 December 1846. p.208, c3.

[1847]

440 RICHARD WEBB *to* **MARIA W. CHAPMAN. 17 November 1846. Dublin.** Laments the death of N. P. Rogers. 1 January 1847. p.1, c2.

441 WM. DENTON *to* **MR. EDITOR. [from the** *Boston Atlas***] 19 December 1846. n.p.** Refuses to support the Mexican War. 1 January 1847. p.2, c3.

442 P. P. *to* **FRIEND GARRISON. n.d. n.p.** Recommends the *Lectures of Rev. John Prince*. 1 January 1847, p.3, c3.

443 EDWARD SEARCH *to* **WM. LLOYD GARRISON. 5 November 1846. London.** Discusses England and the famine in Ireland. 1 January 1847. p.3, c4.

444 BENJAMIN CHASE *to* **MR. GARRISON. December 1846. Auburn, N.Y.** Recounts his recent visit with George Washington's slaves. 1 January 1847. p.3, c4.

445 T. P. LOCKE *to* **BRO. GARRISON. n.d. n.p.** Gives account of a meeting of the Worcester County North Division AS; lists officers. 1 January 1847. p.3, c5.

446 J. R. R. *to* **THE EDITOR OF THE** *LONDON INQUIRER.* **4 November 1846. Devizer.** Praises Garrison. 8 January 1847. p.5, c5.

447 S. *to* **FRIEND GARRISON. n.d. n.p.** Encloses letter from the files of the *Dartmouth Chronicle.* 8 January 1846. p.7, c4.

448 GUSTAVUS *to* **THE PRINTERS OF** *CONNECTICUT COURANT.* **August 1797. New London County.** Discusses objections to the division of the United States over slavery. 8 January 1847. p.7, c4.

449 J. T. EVERETT *to* **MR. EDITOR [W. L. GARRISON]. 1846. Princeton, Ma.** Discusses the position of American Whigs on the war with Mexico. 8 January 1847. p.7, c5.

450 EDWARD SEARCH *to* **THE EDITOR OF THE** *LIBERATOR* **[W. L. GARRISON]. November 1846. London.** A supporter of the Church of England accuses ministers of the Free church of "preaching for hire." 8 January 1847. p.8, c2.

451 THOMAS PECK *to* **THE EDITOR OF THE** *LIBERATOR* **[W. L. GARRISON]. 26 October 1846. London.** Congratulates him on his trip to England and his struggles with the Evangelical Alliance. 15 January 1847. p.11, c1.

452 INCREASE SMITH *to* **THE EDITOR OF THE** *LIBERATOR* **[W. L. GARRISON]. 9 January 1847. Dorchester.** Discusses the purchase of Frederick Douglass' freedom. 15 January 1847. p.11, c3.

453 J. SEXTON *to* **BROTHER GARRISON. 11 January 1847. Fall River.** Comments on the purchase of Frederick Douglass' freedom. 15 January 1847. p.11, c3.

454 E. SEARCH *to* **THE EDITOR OF THE** *LIBERATOR* **[W. L. GARRISON]. 1 December 1846. London.** Discusses various reforms in England. 15 January 1847. p.12, c2.

455 EDWARD SEARCH *to* **WM. LLOYD GARRISON. 3 November 1846. London.** Notes the progress of phonotypy; discusses the possibility of a universal language. 22 January 1847. p.13, c2.

456 C. M. CLAY *to* **THE** *NEW YORK TRIBUNE.* **19 December 1846. Camargo, Mexico.** Discusses motives governing his involvement in the war with Mexico. 22 January 1847. p.13, c6.

457 ALPHEUS COWLES *to* **FRIEND GARRISON. 6 January 1847. Geneva, Oh.** Encourages Garrison in his efforts; notes that Christ was also denounced in his time; criticizes Goodell's "ridiculous" attempt to prove the Constitution anti-slavery. 22 January 1847. p.15, c2.

458 J. T. EVERETT *to* **BROTHER GARRISON. 10 January 1847. Princeton.** States that he has found four new subscribers for the *Liberator.* 22 January 1847. p.15, c3.

459 MARY WELSH *to* **THE SECRETARY OF WORLD'S TEMPERANCE CONVENTION. 8 October 1846. Edinburgh.** Reports on pro-slavery attitudes of American ministers at the convention. 22 January 1847. p.15, c4.

460 A. B. *to* **THE EDITOR OF THE *LIBERATOR* [W. L. GARRISON]. n.d. n.p.** Objects to Garrison's attack on Church and clergy; asserts that the Church should not involve itself with temporal affairs. 22 January 1847. p.16, c2.

461 J. A. M. *to* **[W. L.] GARRISON. 18 December 1846. Princeton.** Discusses Thanksgiving Day. 22 January 1847. p.16, c2.

462 HENRY TREND *to* **THE MGRS. OF ANTI-SLAVERY BAZAAR, BOSTON. 5 October 1846. England.** States that ladies of his congregation support the anti-slavery bazaar. 29 January 1847. p.17, c2.

463 H. C. WRIGHT *to* **FREDERICK DOUGLASS. 12 December 1846. Doncaster.** Believes that Frederick Douglass should not have allowed his freedom to be bought. 29 January 1847. p.18, c1.

464 FREDERICK DOUGLASS *to* **HENRY C. WRIGHT. 22 December 1846. Manchester.** Claims that in order to be of use to the anti-slavery cause he must be in the United States, and that in order to be in the United States he must be free. 29 January 1847. p.18, c1.

465 HENRY C. WRIGHT *to* **GARRISON. 2 January 1847. Newcastle-on-Tyne.** Forwards news of anti-slavery in England; criticizes anti-clerical statements by Dr. Campbell as too strong; lists his coming speaking engagements. 29 January 1847. p.18, c4.

466 FREDERICK DOUGLASS *to* **FRIEND [W. L. GARRISON]. 2 January 1847. Carlisle, England.** States that his anti-slavery efforts in Europe will keep him there until summer. 29 January 1847. p.18, c5.

467 R. SMITH *to* **WM. LLOYD GARRISON. 2 January 1847. Newcastle.** Expresses satisfaction with anti-slavery progress in Newcastle; reports that he and Douglass have given several lectures. 29 January 1847. p.18, c5.

468 R. KEMP PHILP *to* **WM. LLOYD GARRISON. 2 January 1847. Office of the** *People's Journal.* Forwards "Proposal for a National Remonstrance against Slavery." 29 January 1847. p.18, c6.

469 JAMES N. BUFFUM *to* **FRIEND GARRISON. n.d. n.p.** Criticizes the Liberty Party. 29 January 1847. p.19, c1.

470 C. STEARNS *to* **MR. GARRISON. 22 January 1847. Boston.** Comments on the hypocrisy displayed at a recent meeting of an anti-slavery religious congregation. 29 January 1847. p.19, c3.

471 S. S. FOSTER *to* **GARRISON. 25 January 1847. Abington.** Reports on the Liberty Party State Convention. 29 January 1847. p.19, c4.

472 n.n. *to* **THE EDITORS OF THE *JOURNAL OF COMMERCE*. 5 January 1847. Charleston, S. C.** A New Englander claims that Southerners have been slandered by Northerners. 5 February 1847. p.21, c1.

473 GEORGE BRADBURN *to* **THE** *BOSTON CHRONOTYPE*. **[extract] n.d. n.p.** Expresses his disappointment with Garrison's depiction of American anti-slavery during his visit to England. 5 February 1847. p.21, c1.

474 J. W. WALKER *to* **FRIENDS [WESLEYANS]. January 1847. Cleveland, Oh.** Withdraws from the church because of his anti-slavery convictions. 5 February 1847. p.21, c5.

475 RICHARD ALLEN *to* **[W. L.] GARRISON. 3 January 1847. Dublin.** Discusses the famine in Ireland. 5 February 1847. p.23, c1.

476 STEPHEN S. FOSTER *to* **FRIEND GARRISON. January 1847. Boston.** Criticizes the Christian Conference on Slavery and its managers, prominent clerical Liberty Party men. 5 February 1847. p.23, c2.

477 H. H. BRIGHAM *to* **FRIEND GARRISON. 30 January 1847. South Abington.** Claims that anti-slavery lectures lead to mob violence. 5 February 1847. p.23, c4.

478 H. C. WRIGHT *to* **[W. L.] GARRISON. 1 January 1847. Hexham, England.** Criticizes Dr. Campbell and the American delegates to the World Temperance Convention; remembers the needy Irish. 5 February 1847. p.23, c4.

479 LYMAN CROWL *to* **WM. LLOYD GARRISON. 2 January 1847. Ohio City.** Informs him that charges of stealing the "streak letter" of Elizur Wright to Henry B. Stanton are being reviewed. 5 February 1847. p.24, c2.

480 EDWARD J. FULLER *to* **MR. GARRISON. 11 January 1847. Brooklyn, Oh.** Considers charges of stealing the "streak letter" absurd. 5 February 1847. p.24, c2.

481 C. STEARNS *to* **MR. GARRISON. 14 January 1847. Boston.** Examines the morality of association with or benefit from the actions of evil men. 5 February 1847. p.24, c3.

482 EDWARD SEARCH *to* **[W. L.] GARRISON. December 1846. London.** Discusses implications of the marriage of the Spanish queen. 5 February 1847. p.24, c4.

483 W. GOODELL *to* **WILLIAM LLOYD GARRISON. 20 January 1847. Ontario County, N.Y.** Criticizes W. L. Garrison's anti-slavery platform for being too broad. 12 February 1847. p.25, c3.

484 J. *to* **THE EDITOR OF THE** *LIBERATOR* **[W. L. GARRISON]. 1 February 1847. Boston.** Discusses emancipation; reports that Jonathan Jackson freed his slave, Pomp. 12 February 1847. p.25, c4.

485 L. *to* **W. L. GARRISON. n.d. n.p.** Denounces C. M. Clay's involvement in the war with Mexico as an attempt to gain popularity in his home state. 12 February 1847. p.25, c5.

486 JONATHAN WALKER *to* **FRIEND W. L. GARRISON. 1 February 1847. Great Falls, N.Y.** Thanks Garrison for gifts he has received. 12 February 1847. p.25, c5.

487 B. W. RICHMOND *to* **MR. RICE. 28 December 1847. Burton.** States that anti-slavery spirit is not dead in Burton. 12 February 1847. p.25, c6.

488 S. W. W. *to* **FRIEND EDITOR [W. L. GARRISON]. n.d. n.p.** Reports on proceedings of the Rhode Island legislature. 12 February 1847. p.27, c2.

489 ISAAC STEARNS *to* **FRIEND GARRISON. 3 February 1847. Mansfield.** Compliments lecture on slavery by Addison Davis. 12 February 1847. p.27, c3.

490 ANTI-EVIL *to* **FRIEND GARRISON. 3 February 1847. Worcester.** Discusses the secession of Massachusetts. 12 February 1847. p.27, c3.

491 EDWARD SEARCH *to* **WM. LLOYD GARRISON. 3 December 1846. London.** Forwards an article on the policy of peace. 12 February 1847. p.28, c2.

492 JOHN M. FISK *to* **FRANCIS JACKSON. 24 February 1847. West Brookfield.** Discusses the secession of Massachusetts from the Union. 19 February 1847. p.31, c2.

493 S. S. FOSTER *to* **R. HILDRETH, JOHN G. WHITTIER, AND WILLIAM H. BREWSTER. 4 February 1847. Boston.** Corrects their report of Foster's actions at the Liberty Party Convention. 19 February 1847. p.31, c2.

494 LEA H. GAUSE, ELIZABETH GAUSE, JOHN BUSHONG, GEO. PEIRCE, AND ELIZABETH BUSHONG *to* **FRIEND [W. L. GARRISON]. 24 January 1847. Bart, Pa.** Discuss the position of Garrisonians on slave labor. 19 February 1847. p.31, c4.

495 C. W. LEFFINGWELL *to* **FRIEND GARRISON. 19 January 1847. Franklin, Oh.** Reviews stages of his anti-slavery career. 19 February 1847. p.31, c4.

496 FRANCIS JACKSON *to* **THE EDITOR OF THE** *LIBERATOR* **[W. L. GARRISON]. 16 February 1847. Boston.** Discusses the famine in Ireland. 19 February 1847. p.31, c5.

497 EDWARD SEARCH *to* **SIR [W. L. GARRISON]. December 1846. London.** Informs him that abolitionists are putting the Free church to shame. 19 February 1847. p.32. c2.

498 C. K. W. *to* **FRIEND GARRISON. n.d. n.p.** Criticizes the exploitation of the popular child dancers from Vienna. 19 February 1847. p.32, c2.

499 J. P. DURBIN *to* **THE EDITORS OF THE** *NEW YORK OBSERVER.* **n.d. n.p.** Discusses his article on slavery in the United States. 26 February 1847. p.33, c1.

500 EDWARD SEARCH *to* **[W. L.] GARRISON. January 1847. London.** States that peasants in England are oppressed by class legislation. 26 February 1847. p.33, c2.

501 WM. ENDICOTT *to* **FRIEND GARRISON. 15 February 1847. Danvers.** Reports on an Essex County AS meeting. 26 February 1847. p.33, c3.

502 ALEXANDER FRASER *to* **THE EDITOR. [from the** *True Wesleyan***] n.d. n.p.** Reports that some Englishmen dislike Dr. Cox. 26 February 1847. p.33, c5.

503 RICHARD ALLEN *to* **[W. L.] GARRISON. 3 February 1847. Dublin.** Discusses the famine in Ireland. 26 February 1847. p.34, c6.

504 A. *to* **MR. GARRISON. n.d. n.p.** Criticizes the Unitarians. 26 February 1847. p.34, c6.

505 ELIZA WIGHAM *to* **FRIEND [W. L. GARRISON]. 30 January 1847. Edinburgh.** Discusses anti-slavery efforts and the Free Church of Scotland. 26 February 1847. p.35, c1.

506 n.n. *to* **MR. GARRISON. 16 January 1847. Edinburgh.** Praises the *Liberator*; criticizes the Free church for its connection with slaveholding churches in America. 26 February 1847. p.35, c1.

507 JAMES McDONALD *to* **SIR [W. L. GARRISON]. 18 January 1847. Dundee.** Reports on anti-slavery activity in Scotland. 26 February 1847. p.35, c2.

508 JAMES ROSE *to* **WM. LLOYD GARRISON. 20 January 1847. Belfast.** Encloses a copy of a letter which was rejected by the *London Christian Witness.* 26 February 1847. p.35, c3.

509 JAMES ROSE, ROBERT WORKMAN, PETER DALE, WILLIAM DALE, AND JAMES SHAW *to* **THE EDITOR OF THE** *CHRISTIAN WITNESS.* **19 November 1846. Belfast.** Defend W. L. Garrison against the *Christian Witness'* attack on his conduct and opinions. 26 February 1847. p.35, c3.

510 FRANCIS BISHOP *to* **WM. LLOYD GARRISON. December 1846. Exeter.** States that Dr. Campbell has been influenced by bigots; praises lecture by Henry Clapp, Jr.; encourages the Anti-Slavery League. 26 February 1847. p.35, c4.

511 MARY BRADY *to* **FRIEND [W. L. GARRISON]. 31 January 1847. Sheffield.** Discusses the activities of H. C. Wright and Frederick Douglass. 26 February 1847. p.35, c5.

512 PARKER PILLSBURY *to* **FRIEND GARRISON. n.d. n.p.** Reports on an anti-slavery revival in Worcester. 5 March 1847. p.37, c4.

513 SAMUEL MAY *to* **SIR [W. L. GARRISON]. 28 February 1847. Brooklyn, Ct.** Discusses the Unitarians' stance on slavery. 5 March 1847. p.39, c2.

514 JONATHAN WALKER *to* **FRIEND GARRISON. 27 February 1847. Plymouth.** Discusses the boycott of slave-labor produce. 5 March 1847. p.39, c2.

515 H. *to* **FRIEND GARRISON. 23 February 1847. Worcester.** Supports the buying of Frederick Douglass' freedom. 5 March 1847. p.39, c4.

516 J. T. CARTER *to* **SIR [W. L. GARRISON]. 17 February 1847. Franklin City.** Forwards a dissolution petition for signatures. 5 March 1847. p.39, c4.

517 EDWARD SEARCH *to* **THE EDITOR OF THE** *LIBERATOR* **[W. L. GARRISON]. 20 January 1847. London.** Discusses the famine in Ireland. 5 March 1847. p.40, c2.

518 GEORGE COMBE *to* **MR. EBEN. AVERY. 25 November 1846. Edinburgh.** Discusses the problems of the working class. 5 March 1847. p.40, c3.

519 F[RANCIS] J[ACKSON] *to* **THE EDITOR OF THE** *BOSTON COURIER.* **n.d. n.p.** Forwards a letter from John Calkins. 12 March 1847. p.42, c3.

520 JOHN CALKINS *to* **FRANCIS JACKSON. 1 March 1847. South Wilbraham.** Forwards a donation for the people in Ireland. 12 March 1847. p.42, c3.

521 AN ADMIRER OF TRUE BRAVERY *to* **MR. GARRISON. 8 March 1847. Boston.** Donates five dollars for Loring Moody. 12 March 1847. p.42, c5.

522 J. FULTON, JR. *to* **W. L. GARRISON. 15 February 1847. Chester County, Pa.** States that both C. M. Clay and Dr. G. Bailey have been misrepresented in the *Liberator.* 12 March 1847. p.42, c6.

523 WILLIAM GOODELL *to* **MR. 'OLD FRIEND' GARRISON. 1 March 1847. Ontario County, N. Y.** Discusses the Constitution in relation to slavery. 12 March 1847. p.43, c1.

524 S. S. FOSTER *to* **[W. L.] GARRISON. 1 March 1847. Fall River.** Replies to an article in the *Cincinnati Morning Herald* concerning the Liberty Party in Ohio. 12 March 1847. p.43, c3.

525 A. *to* **MR. GARRISON. n.d. n.p.** Discusses the Unitarians' stance on slavery. 12 March 1847. p.43, c4.

526 SAMUEL MAY *to* **MR. GARRISON. n.d. n.p.** Corrects and explains his article on Unitarianism and slavery. 12 March 1847. p.43, c5.

527 DANIEL E. STEPHENS *to* **THE** *LONDON TIMES.* **26 January 1847. Essex.** Reports on the starving people in Ireland. 12 March 1847. p.44, c2.

528 EDWARD SEARCH *to* **THE EDITOR OF THE** *LIBERATOR* **[W. L. GARRISON]. 27 January 1847. London.** Discusses starvation and land distribution in Ireland. 12 March 1847. p.44, c2.

529 MICAJAH T. JOHNSON *to* **FRIEND GARRISON. 11 February 1847. Short Creek, Oh.** Replies to C. Stearns that conscience should govern one's actions. 12 March 1847. p.44, c3.

530 F. *to* **SIR. [from the** *London Inquirer***] n.d. n.p.** Describes the coarse behavior of members of the Evangelical Alliance. 12 March 1847. p.44, c4.

531 GEORGE ARMSTRONG *to* **FREDERICK DOUGLASS. [from the** *Bristol Mercury***] 17 January 1847. Bristol.** Presents Frederick Douglass with a silver inkstand and eighteen sovereigns; rejoices in Douglass' newly-purchased freedom; asks God's blessing upon all who labor in behalf of the poor. 12 March 1847. p.46, c1.

532 FREDERICK DOUGLASS *to* **GEORGE ARMSTRONG. [from the** *Bristol Mercury***] 19 January 1847. Manchester.** Expresses gratitude for the gift of a silver inkstand. 12 March 1847. p.46, c1.

533 J. C. CALLOWAY *to* **MESSRS. EDITORS. [from the** *Western Citizen***] n.d. n.p.** Condemns Rev. G. Moore for having traded a woman and child for a jackass. 19 March 1847. p.46, c2.

534 H. H. B. *to* **FRIEND GARRISON. n.d. n.p.** Notes that 173 Abington voters favor the dissolution of the Union. 19 March 1847. p.46, c4.

535 n.n. *to* **n.n. [extract] n.d. Iowa.** Feels that popular sentiment in Iowa opposes slavery, although both congressional representatives voted to extend it. 19 March 1847. p.47, c1.

536 EDWARD SEARCH *to* **GARRISON. 10 January 1847. London.** Comments on labors of George Thompson; assails the "pharasaic" Evangelical Alliance. 19 March 1847. p.47, c1.

537 Q. *to* **THE EDITOR OF THE** *LIBERATOR* **[W. L. GARRISON]. n.d. n.p.** Criticizes a naive article on the Slave Power by the editor of the *Courier*; emphasizes that the benefits of slavery are enjoyed by the North as well as the South. 19 March 1847. p.47, c3.

538 JOHN BAILEY *to* **FRIEND GARRISON. 17 March 1847. New Bedford.** Suggests a convention of anti-slavery delegates. 19 March 1847. p.47, c4.

539 H. *to* **FRIEND GARRISON. 16 March 1847. Worcester.** Sends a donation for Loring Moody. 19 March 1847. p.47, c5.

540 DISUNION *to* **MR. GARRISON. 14 February 1847. Boston.** Notes the inconsistency of non-resistants who oppose political action in voting, yet favor political separation of slave and free states. 26 March 1847. p.49, c3.

541 A. *to* **MR. GARRISON. n.d. n.p.** Encloses article from the fictitious *Nicht-zu-Finden Truth-Teller* satirizing reformists of the day. 26 March 1847. p.49, c4.

542 EDWARD SEARCH *to* **THE EDITOR OF THE** *LIBERATOR* **[W. L. GARRISON]. 30 January 1847. London.** Reports that Douglas Jerrold's paper, *Punch,* is banned in France, and that Edward Miall has established the Anti-State Church Society in London; laments unfair treatment of the Hutchinsons by Philadelphia authorities. 26 March 1847. p.49, c5.

543 GEORGE COMBE *to* **MRS. MARIA W. CHAPMAN. [from the** *Liberty Bell***] 22 November 1846. Edinburgh.** Condemns American slavery. 26 March 1847. p.50, c1.

544 R. KEMP PHILP *to* **WM. LLOYD GARRISON. 1 March 1847. Liverpool.** Discusses plans for a national remonstrance against slavery; welcomes Garrison's support. 26 March 1847. p.51, c1.

545 WM. LOVETT *to* **WILLIAM LLOYD GARRISON. 1 March 1847. London.** Reports that he met Frederick Douglass; esteems W. L. Garrison. 26 March 1847. p.51, c1.

546 ELIZABETH PEASE *to* **WM. LLOYD GARRISON. 17 February 1847. Darlington.** Praises Frederick Douglass. 26 March 1847. p.51, c2.

547 HENRY C. WRIGHT *to* **WM. LLOYD GARRISON. 27 February 1847. Dublin.** States that Garrison will be hearing from Frederick Douglass on the progress of anti-slavery in Dublin; also comments on Wright's illness and the famine in Ireland. 26 March 1847. p.51, c3.

548 ELIZA WIGHAM *to* **FRIEND [W. L. GARRISON]. 27 February 1847. Edinburgh.** Discusses the Free church and slavery. 26 March 1847. p.51, c3.

549 ELI HAMBLETON *to* **FRIEND GARRISON. 23 January 1847. Chester County, Pa.** Discusses the ransom of Frederick Douglass. 26 March 1847. p.51, c4.

550 S. W. W. *to* **BRO. GARRISON. 15 March 1847. Providence.** Gives account of a non-resistance meeting. 26 March 1847. p.52, c2.

551. A. B. SMOLNIKAR *to* **THE EDITOR OF THE** *LIBERATOR* **[W. L. GARRISON]. 26 February 1847. Cincinnati.** Forwards his article entitled ''Convention of Christ's Messengers'' for publication. 26 March 1847. p.52, c3.

552 VALENTINE NICHOLSON *to* **MARTHA D. COX, CATHARINE A. COX, HARRIET SHULDHAM, ANNA MARIA GILBRAITH, ISABELA SULLIVAN, AND ELLEN JAGOE OF CORK COUNTY, IRELAND. 13 March 1847. Warren County, Oh.** Asks whether they truly believe that God is responsible for either the famine in Ireland or slavery in America. 2 April 1847. p.53, c1.

553 WILLIAM WEST *to* **WILLIAM LLOYD GARRISON. 20 March 1847. Boston.** Refutes Garrison's argument that wage slaves are far better off than chattel slaves; cites the example of Ireland. 2 April 1847. p.53, c3.

554 EDWARD SEARCH *to* **GARRISON. n.d. n.p.** Notes indications of progress of knowledge and human liberty throughout the world. 2 April 1847. p.53, c4.

555 R. *to* **FRIEND GARRISON. March 1847. New Bedford.** Quotes from a letter to a fugitive slave in New Bedford. 2 April 1847. p.55, c5.

556 S. M. *to* **MR. GARRISON. n.d. n.p.** Discusses relief for Ireland. 2 April 1847. p.55, c6.

557 ELIHU BURRITT *to* **FRIENDS OF HUMANITY. [from Burritt's** *Christian Citizen***] 23 February 1847. Ireland.** Asks for help for the starving people in Ireland. 2 April 1847. p.56, c3.

558 S. *to* **WM. LLOYD GARRISON. 16 March 1847. Chicago.** Forwards a letter from Seth Paine terminating his association with the Liberty Party. 9 April 1847. p.57, c2.

559 SETH PAINE *to* **MR. EASTMAN. n.d. n.p.** Details his reasons for choosing, and now leaving, the Liberty Party. 9 April 1847. p.57, c2.

560 JONATHAN WALKER *to* **FRIEND S. H. GAY. 3 March 1847. Plymouth.** Discusses his activities with the Massachusetts AS. 9 April 1847. p.57, c5.

561 ANTONIO LOPEZ DE SANTA ANNA *to* **HIS EXCELLENCY THE MINISTER OF WAR. 23 February 1847. Near Buena Vista.** Gives an account of casualties incurred during a two-day battle with the United States Army at Agua Nueva; declares that a campaign cannot be carried on without adequate supplies. 9 April 1847. p.58, c2.

562 JUAN MORALES *to* **COMPATRIOTS. 5 March 1847. Vera Cruz.** States that he has seen the enemy squadron enter the port; declares that superior numbers are never a match for discipline and valor. 9 April 1847. p.58, c2.

563 SOUTH SHORE *to* **MR. GARRISON. n.d. n.p.** Objects to both the Liberty Party and disunion. 9 April 1847. p.59, c2.

564 ELKANAH NICKERSON *to* **[W. L.] GARRISON. 30 March 1847. Harwich.** Expresses "hurt and surprise" at *Liberator*'s criticism of A. B. Smolnickar and its opposition to mystical aspects of religion. 9 April 1847. p.60, c2.

565 G. F. TALBOT *to* **MR. GARRISON. 3 April 1847. East Machias, Me.** Comments on the *Christian Mirror*'s reporting of a recent anti-slavery convention. 16 April 1847. p.61, c2.

566 JABEZ BURNS *to* **THE FREE-WILL BAPTISTS OF AMERICA. [from the** *Daily Morning Star***] 3 March 1847. London.** Affirms his support of the American Free-Will Baptists; expresses hope that the American branch of the Evangelical Alliance will remain free of the taint of slavery. 16 April 1847. p.61, c5.

567 ABM. H. HOWLAND *to* **LORING MOODY. 25 March 1847. House of Representatives.** Forwards money to L. Moody for an act of bravery. 16 April 1847. p.62, c5.

568 LORING MOODY *to* **A. HOWLAND. 6 April 1847. Boston.** Sends thanks for the donation. 16 April 1847. p.62, c5.

569 SOUTH SHORE *to* **MR. GARRISON. n.d. n.p.** Discusses the dissolution of the Union. 16 April 1847. p.62, c6.

570 ANNE W. WESTON *to* **MESSRS. HANSON, BATES, AND WHITE. 13 February 1847. Weymouth.** Members of the Weymouth Female AS ask for use of a meetinghouse. 16 April 1847. p.63, c1.

571 H. H. BRIGHAM *to* **FRIEND GARRISON. 6 April 1847. South Abington.** Notes that South Abington voted to allow Abby Kelley to speak. 16 April 1847. p.63, c2.

572 PARKER PILLSBURY *to* **FRIEND GARRISON. 30 March 1847. Fall River.** Criticizes the Church. 16 April 1847. p.63, c5.

573 n.n. *to* **W. L. GARRISON. n.d. n.p.** Encloses a letter from a Protestant divine to an Irish woman. 16 April 1847. p.63, c5.

574 n.n. *to* **n.n. [from the** *Bristol Mirror***] 18 December 1846. Skibereen.** A Protestant divine describes famine conditions and the oppressive tax structure in Ireland; foresees violence. 16 April 1847. p.63, c5.

575 CHARLES GLADDING *to* **FRIEND GARRISON. 4 April 1847. Upton.** Questions the moral principles of secret societies. 16 April 1847. p.64, c2.

576 SPECTATOR *to* **MR. EDITOR. [from the** *Charleston* **(S.C.)** *Mercury***] n.d. n.p.** Discusses the principle of Southern slavery. 23 April 1847. p.67, c1.

577 WILLIAM WEST *to* **WILLIAM LLOYD GARRISON. 5 April 1847. Boston.** Continues his argument that wage slaves are as oppressed as chattel slaves. 23 April 1847. p.67, c2.

578 D. S. GRANDIN *to* **BRO. GARRISON. n.d. n.p.** Discusses the Workingmen's Protective Union. 23 April 1847. p.68, c2.

579 JOHN L. LORD *to* **BRO. GARRISON. 11 April 1847. Newburyport.** Questions the admissions policy of the Sons of Temperance. 23 April 1847. p.68, c2.

580 JAMES ROBERTSON *to* **FRIEND [W. L. GARRISON]. 2 April 1847. Edinburgh.** Comments on the Evangelical Alliance; regrets that Frederick Douglass must return to the United States. 23 April 1847. p.68, c3.

581 WATCHMAN *to* **SIR [W. L. GARRISON]. 1 April 1847. Glasgow.** Expresses sorrow that Frederick Douglass is leaving Scotland. 23 April 1847. p.68, c3.

582 H. C. WRIGHT *to* **[W. L.] GARRISON. 26 March 1847. Dublin.** Discloses that many of the funds of the Central Relief Committee of the Society of Friends in Dublin were obtained in slaveholding areas. 23 April 1847. p.68, c4.

583 WM. CAIRD *to* **THE EDITOR OF THE** *LIBERATOR* **[W. L. GARRISON]. 31 March 1847. Glasgow.** Praises American reformers in Scotland and Frederick Douglass. 23 April 1847. p.68, c5.

584 M.B. *to* **FRIEND [W. L. GARRISON]. 31 March 1847. Sheffield.** Comments on an appearance by Frederick Douglass at an anti-slavery meeting. 23 April 1847. p.68, c6.

585 E. W. *to* **FRIEND [W. L. GARRISON]. 30 March 1847. Newcastle-on-Tyne.** Expresses sorrow at the departure of Frederick Douglass. 23 April 1847. p.68, c6.

586 PARKER PILLSBURY *to* **FRIEND GARRISON. n.d. n.p.** Cites examples of clerical hypocrisy. 23 April 1847. p.69, c2.

587 R. *to* **GARRISON. 12 April 1847. New Bedford.** Pities "Poor Calhoun," who seems unable to keep his darling institution of slavery from falling. 23 April 1847. p.69, c3.

588 SIR WILLIAM BERKELEY *to* **THE GOV. OF NEW ENGLAND. 12 June 1644. Virginia.** Requests assistance for Mr. John Chew in recapturing his fugitive slaves. 23 April 1847. p.69, c3.

589 BENJAMIN EMERSON *to* **FRIEND GARRISON. 16 April 1847. Haverhill.** Favors disunion. 23 April 1847. p.69, c3.

590 J. F. DORVELAS DORVAL *to* **FRIENDS. n.d. Port-au-Prince, Hayti.** Praises abolitionists' work; anticipates the glorious day of universal emancipation. 30 April 1847. p.69*, c1.

591 J. F. DORVELAS DORVAL *to* **MR. WILLIAM LLOYD GARRISON. 3 March 1847. Hayti.** Reports the death of President Riche of Haiti. 30 April 1847. p.69*, c1.

592 ADDISON DAVIS *to* **[W. L.] GARRISON. 19 April 1847. Leicester.** Discusses books purchased from the Massachusetts AS. 30 April 1847. p.69*, c1.

593 W. SHORTT *to* **THE** *CHRISTIAN PENNY RECORD.* **22 February 1847. Dublin.** Comments on the much-improved opinions of the Rev. James Caughey, who now condemns slaveholders. 30 April 1847. p.69*, c6.

594 THEOBALD MATHEW *to* **MR. WEED. [from the** *Albany Evening Journal***] 31 March 1847. Cork.** Discusses famine in Ireland. 30 April 1847. p.70, c2.

595 FREDERICK DOUGLASS *to* **FRIEND [W. L. GARRISON]. 21 April 1847. Lynn.** Discusses his passage home; mentions discrimination on the ship. 30 April 1847. p.70, c4.

596 JOHN SPRATT, JAMES HAUGHTON AND 881 OTHERS *to* **IRISHMEN IN AMERICA. February 1847. Dublin.** Discuss the famine in Ireland. 30 April 1847. p.70, c6.

597 R. SMITH *to* **SIR [W. L. GARRISON]. 3 March 1847. London.** Discusses the progress of the Anti-Slavery League. 30 April 1847. p.71, c1.

598 RICHARD D. WEBB *to* **FRIEND FRANCIS JACKSON. 28 March 1847. Dublin.** Discusses the appropriation of money. 30 April 1847. p.71, c2.

599 JAMES HAUGHTON *to* **FRIEND [W. L. GARRISON]. 31 March 1847. Dublin.** Expresses appreciation of Frederick Douglass' efforts in Ireland; encourages American abolitionists. 30 April 1847. p.71, c3.

600 WM. SHORTT *to* **FRIEND W. L. GARRISON. 2 April 1847. Dublin.** Opposes the Friends' acceptance of slaveholder money for Ireland; requests Garrison's opinion on the matter. 30 April 1847. p.71, c4.

601 JOHN HART *to* **BROTHER. 29 January 1847. Cork.** Describes the famine in Ireland. 30 April 1847. p.71, c4.

602 RICHARD ALLEN *to* **[W. L.] GARRISON. 3 April 1847. Dublin.** Discusses American response to Ireland's suffering. 30 April 1847. p.71, c4.

603 HENRY C. WRIGHT *to* **[W. L.] GARRISON. 1 April 1847. Dublin.** Comments on anti-slavery in America. 30 April 1847. p.71, c4.

604 BENJ. S. WHITING *to* **MR. GARRISON. 23 April 1847. South Hingham.** Comments on Andrew Hunter, a fugitive slave who bought his wife's freedom. 30 April 1847. p.71, c5.

605 MELANCTHON *to* **THE** *LIBERATOR.* **n.d. n.p.** Inquires whether the object of the organization is to effect a dissolution of the Union, how this would be accomplished, and whether this is truly the best way to overthrow the sin of slavery. 7 May 1847. p.74, c6.

606 J. FULTON, JR. *to* **FRIEND GARRISON. 25 April 1847. Ercildoun, Pa.** Expresses dismay at the *Liberator*'s harsh language used in reference to Gamaliel Bailey's inconsistency on the war question. 7 May 1847. p.75, c1.

607 DAVID TILTON *to* **W. L. GARRISON. 1 May 1847. Gloucester.** Answers Parker Pillsbury's letter in the *Liberator* of 23 April; denies his account of their confrontation at Cape Ann lecture. 7 May 1847. p.75, c2.

608 DAVID TILTON *to* **MR. GARRISON. 1 May 1847. Gloucester.** Comments on the ministry of Cape Ann. 7 May 1847. p.75, c2.

609 JOSEPH MERRILL *to* **FRIEND GARRISON. 4 May 1847. Danvers, New Mills.** Corrects an article in the *Liberator*; states that he did not donate money for Ireland. 7 May 1847. p.75, c4.

610 A. *to* **W. L. GARRISON. n.d. n.p.** Expresses disappointment at H. C. Wright's decision that the Irish relief fund should not accept contributions from slaveholders. 14 May 1847. p.77, c1.

611 J. W. C. *to* **FRIEND GARRISON. 19 April 1847. Windham, Me.** Reports on the antislavery cause in Maine. 14 May 1847. p.77, c1.

612 B. *to* **FRIEND GARRISON. 4 May 1847. Worcester.** Laments the plight of those who have given up "the blessings of slavery," in a sarcastic reply to William West. 14 May 1847. p.77, c2.

613 WILLIAM BEVAN *to* **THE EDITORS OF THE** *LIVERPOOL MERCURY.* **n.d. n.p.** Relates that Frederick Douglass informed him of the facts connected with the "outward passage" in the *Cambria.* 14 May 1847. p.78, c1.

614 CHARLES M. BURROP *to* **THE EDITOR OF THE** *TIMES.* **8 April 1847. Berkshire.** Discusses the treatment of Frederick Douglass on board the *Cambria.* 14 May 1847. p.78, c3.

615 F. R. *to* **THE EDITOR. [from** *Jerrold's Magazine***] 14 April 1847. Bristol.** Discusses the treatment of Frederick Douglass on board the *Cambria.* 14 May 1847. p.78, c4.

616 CHAS. M'IVER *to* **THE EDITORS OF THE** *LIVERPOOL MERCURY.* **12 April 1847. Liverpool.** Discusses his meeting with Frederick Douglass on board the *Cambria*; contradicts Frederick Douglass' account of their conversation. 14 May 1847. p.78, c4.

617 JOSEPH LUPTON AND THOS. HARVEY *to* **THE EDITORS OF THE** *LEEDS MERCURY.* **n.d. n.p.** Discuss the treatment of Frederick Douglass on board the *Cambria.* 14 May 1847. p.78, c4.

618 FAIR PLAY *to* **THE EDITOR OF THE** *MORNING CHRONICLE.* **12 April 1847. London.** Discusses the treatment of Frederick Douglass on the *Cambria.* 14 May 1847. p.79, c1.

619 E. H. K. *to* **THE EDITOR OF THE** *MANCHESTER EXAMINER.* **7 April 1847. Stockport.** Condemns the treatment of Frederick Douglass on board the *Cambria.* 14 May 1847. p.79, c2.

620 S. CUNARD *to* **THE EDITOR OF THE** *TIMES.* **13 April 1847. London.** Regrets the treatment of Frederick Douglass on board the *Cambria.* 14 May 1847. p.79, c2.

621 WM. LLOYD GARRISON *to* **n. n. 11 April 1847. New York.** Comments on the speech by Frederick Douglass at New York anniversary. 14 May 1847. p.79, c3.

622 E. *to* **BRO. GARRISON. 19 April 1847. Bristol.** Praises Frederick Douglass' work in England. 14 May 1847. p.79, c5.

623 WILLIAM LOGAN *to* **WM. LLOYD GARRISON. 17 April 1847. Rochdale.** Relates having met Frederick Douglass in England. 14 May 1847. p.79, c5.

624 ALEXANDER WILDER *to* **BRO. GARRISON. 27 April 1847. Vernons, N.Y.** Defends voluntary associations. 14 May 1847. p.80, c2.

625 WENDELL PHILLIPS *to* **OLIVER DYER. 14 May 1847. New York.** Compliments the coverage of a speech given by Phillips and recorded by Dyer. 21 May 1847. p.83, c4.

626 PARKER PILLSBURY *to* **W. L. GARRISON. n.d. n.p.** Responds to David Tilton's letter in the *Liberator* of 7 May; asserts that Tilton has, in fact, confirmed Pillsbury's charges by denying Pillsbury's initial account of their confrontation at Cape Ann. 21 May 1847. p.83, c5.

627 H. C. WRIGHT *to* **GARRISON. 10 April 1847. Wexham.** Discusses his travels in Ireland; relates his debate with Scotch Presbyterians, who claimed that the Bible sanctions war and slavery. 28 May 1847. p.86, c4.

628 H. C. WRIGHT *to* **GARRISON, 1 May 1847. Wexham.** Condemns the hypocritical Free church; reports on a debate about the education bill and land reform; notes that the alliance between English and American Evangelicals is dissolved. 28 May 1847. p.86, c4.

629 H. C. WRIGHT *to* **W. L. GARRISON. n.d. Wrexham, Wales.** Forwards an epitaph copied from the tomb of Elihu Yale, buried in Wrexham; accuses Dr. S. H. Cox of hypocrisy. 28 May 1847. p.86, c5.

630 JAMES McDONALD *to* **WM. L. GARRISON. 1 May 1847. Dundee.** Reports on the progress of the anti-slavery cause in Dundee; praises the "noble work" of the Free Church AS. 28 May 1847. p.86, c5.

631 M. B. *to* **FRIEND [W. L. GARRISON]. 17 April 1847. Sheffield.** Discusses the treatment of Frederick Douglass on board the *Cambria*. 28 May 1847. p.86, c6.

632 RICHARD THURROW *to* **FRIEND [W. L. GARRISON]. 1 May 1847. Edinburgh.** Cites the hypocrisy of the Free church. 28 May 1847. p.86, c6.

633 ELIZABETH PEASE *to* **FRIEND. [extract] 17 April 1847. Darlington.** On the exclusion of Frederick Douglass from a cabin on the *Cambria*. 28 May 1847. p.87, c1.

634 RICHARD ALLEN *to* **[W. L. GARRISON]. 3 May 1847. Dublin.** Discusses the famine in Ireland. 28 May 1847. p.87, c1.

635 JOHN M. FISK *to* **MR. GARRISON. 23 May 1847. West Brookfield.** Reports on the Worcester County South Division AS. 28 May 1847. p.87, c2.

636 A. *to* **MR. GARRISON. n.d. n.p.** Sends an extract of a sermon by Rev. Samuel Johnson. 28 May 1847. p.87, c3.

637 H. CARPENTER *to* **SIR [W. L. GARRISON]. 17 May 1847. Upton.** Reports on Rev. William Bates' refusal to read the notice of a speech by Solomon Bond, a former slave, from the church pulpit. 28 May 1847. p.87, c4.

638 ANDREW PATON *to* **SIR [W. L. GARRISON]. 1 May 1847. Glasgow.** Reports on a controversy concerning the Sabbath in Scotland. 28 May 1847. p.88, c2.

639 W. *to* **FRIEND [W. L. GARRISON]. 1 January 1847. Paris.** Describes Paris. 28 May 1847. p.88, c3.

640 C. A. JOHNSON *to* **A. J. SCOTT. 6 April 1847. Utica.** Invites him to volunteer for the army. 28 May 1847. p.88, c4.

641 A. J. SCOTT *to* **C. A. JOHNSON. 7 April 1847. Oriskany.** Refuses to volunteer for the army. 28 May 1847. p.88, c4.

642 CHAS. LOWELL *to* **THE EDITOR OF THE** *BOSTON COURIER.* **17 May 1847. n.p.** States that slavery in Massachusetts was abolished intentionally rather than accidentally. 4 June 1847. p.90, c2.

643 P. *to* **W. L. GARRISON. n.d. n.p.** Compliments the *People's Journal*; affirms that slaves suffer more than other laboring classes. 4 June 1847. p.90, c6.

644 JOHN L. LORD *to* **BRO. GARRISON. 31 May 1847. Newburyport.** Notes that a supposed fugitive, Andrew Hunter, is abusing Frederick Douglass. 4 June 1847. p.90, c6.

645 S. M. *to* **MR. GARRISON. n.d. n.p.** Notes the presence of slaveholders in the American Unitarian Association. 4 June 1847. p.91, c5.

646 FREDERICK DOUGLASS *to* **SIR. [from the** *New York Ram's Horn***] 18 May 1847. Lynn, Ma.** Ridicules an article in the *New York Sun* attacking himself; discusses freedom of speech. 4 June 1847. p.92, c4.

647 EDWARD SEARCH *to* **GARRISON. 6 March 1847. London.** Reports the formation of a "People's International League" to promote "the cause of national love and universal progress." 11 June 1847. p.93, c2.

648 R. SMITH *to* **SIR [W. L. GARRISON]. 30 April 1847. London.** Forwards a list of individuals at Frederick Douglass' farewell dinner in London; comments on Frederick Douglass in Europe and on the *Cambria*; reports on the British and Foreign AS. 11 June 1847. p.93, c2.

649 n.n. *to* **FRIEND [W. L. GARRISON]. 27 May 1847. Edinburgh.** Reports on the Free Church AS; notes that Frederick Douglass has returned safely to America. 11 June 1847. p.93, c3.

650 J. P. PARKER AND A. F. PRIDGEON *to* **MEMBERS OF TEMPERANCE SOCIETIES IN THE UNITED STATES. n.d. n.p.** Comment on colored people in temperance societies. 11 June 1847. p.94, c3.

651 SAMUEL MAY, JR. *to* **ROBERT F. WALLCUT. 8 June 1847. Leicester.** Accepts the position as general agent of Massachusetts AS. 11 June 1847. p.94, c5.

652 SAMUEL MAY *to* **THE ABOLITIONISTS OF MASSACHUSETTS. 8 June 1847. Leicester.** Begins work as general agent for the Massachusetts AS immediately. 11 June 1847. p.94, c5.

653 FREDERICK DOUGLASS *to* **FRIEND [W. L. GARRISON]. 4 June 1847. Lynn, Ma.** Answers charges that he had adjoining rooms with a white woman on a Hudson River steamer. 11 June 1847. p.95, c1.

654 H. C. WRIGHT *to* **[W. L.] GARRISON. 16 May 1847. London.** Discusses the free suffrage question and the controversy over observance of the Sabbath. 11 June 1847. p.95, c2.

655 PARKER PILLSBURY *to* **FRIEND GARRISON. 6 June 1847. Concord, N.H.** Reports on the New Hampshire AS. 11 June 1847. p.95, c3.

656 E. W. *to* **MR. EDITOR [W. L. GARRISON]. 9 June 1847. Boston.** Notes a service of worship to Mars at which Rev. William Parsons Lunt presided. 11 June 1847. p.95, c4.

657 E. W. *to* **FRIEND GARRISON. 1 June 1847. Brooklyn, Ct.** Reports that Rev. George Tillotson refused to read a notice of a speech by William Brown, a colored man, to his congregation. 11 June 1847. p.95, c5.

658 JOSEPH A. DUGDALE *to* **W. LLOYD GARRISON. 1 June 1847. Near Selma, Oh.** Forwards an address adopted by the Green Plain Quarterly Meeting of Friends. 18 June 1847. p.97, c2.

659 A SUBSCRIBER *to* **MR. GARRISON. 8 June 1847. New Bedford.** Comments on the anti-slavery convention. 18 June 1847. p.97, c3.

660 S. M. *to* **MR. CHANNING. [from the** *Boston Christian World***] n.d. n.p.** Compliments the candor of the editors of the *New York Evangelist* in printing articles by those whose opinions differ from theirs. 18 June 1847. p.97, c6.

661 WM. LLOYD GARRISON *to* **REV. HEMAN HUMPHREY. 15 June 1847. Boston.** Denounces the CS. 18 June 1847. p.98, c4.

662 O. F. HARRIS *to* **FRIEND GARRISON. 13 June 1847. Worcester.** Reports on the Worcester AS convention. 18 June 1847. p.99, c2.

663 CULLING EARDLEY SMITH *to* **REV. S. H. COX. 24 December 1846. Torquay.** Comments on the Evangelical Alliance. 18 June 1847. p.100, c3.

664 SAMUEL HANSON COX *to* **SIR C. E. SMITH. 29 January 1847. Brooklyn, N. Y.** Affirms his faith in the Evangelical Alliance. 18 June 1847. p.100, c3.

665 EDWARD SEARCH *to* **[W. L.] GARRISON. April 1847. London.** Discusses proposals for starting an International League. 25 June 1847. p.101, c2.

666 ROBERT LOCKHART *to* **WM. LLOYD GARRISON. 31 May 1847. Scotland.** Reports on efforts to raise funds for the purchase of a printing press for Frederick Douglass. 25 June 1847. p.101, c3.

667 W. L. GARRISON *to* **THE REV. HEMAN HUMPHREY. n.d. n.p.** Denounces the work of the ACS, of which Humphrey is an agent. 25 June 1847. p.106 [102], c5.

668 HENRY BIBB *to* **MR. EDITOR [W. L. GARRISON]. 6 June 1847. Albany.** Favors giving slaves the Bible. 25 June 1847. p.107 [103], c1.

669 HENRY BIBB *to* **MESSRS. EDITORS. [from the** *Emancipator***] 21 May 1847. New York.** Criticizes Douglass, Garrison, and others who voted against giving Bibles to the slaves. 25 June 1847. p.107 [103], c1.

670 H. C. WRIGHT *to* **[W. L.] GARRISON. 1 June 1847. Edinburgh.** Comments on the deaths of Rev. Thomas Chalmers and Daniel O'Connell. 25 June 1847. p.107 [103], c2.

671 RICHARD THURROW *to* **FRIEND [W. L. GARRISON]. 2 June 1847. Edinburgh.** Reports that Congregationalists in Dundee voted to deny fellowship to slaveholders; reports on the Free Church AS. 25 June 1847. p.107 [103], c2.

672 H. C. WRIGHT *to* **GARRISON. 1 June 1847. Edinburgh.** Criticizes Rev. Dr. Cunningham and the Free church. 2 July 1847. p.105, c4.

673 EDWARD SEARCH *to* **GARRISON. May 1847. London.** Discusses two means of oppression: chattel slavery and land monopoly. 2 July 1847. p.105, c4.

674 FRANCIS JACKSON, EDMUND QUINCY, AND ROBERT WALCUTT *to* **JAMES K. POLK. 29 June 1847. Boston.** The Massachusetts AS appeals to the president of the United States to set his slaves free. 2 July 1847. p.106, c3.

675 RICHARD D. WEBB *to* **FRANCIS JACKSON. 1 June 1847. Dublin.** Discusses famine in Ireland. 2 July 1847. p.107, c1.

676 H. WHITCHER *to* **BRO. BAILEY. [from the** *Liberty Press***] 11 June 1847. Boston.** Reports on the presidential nominating convention of the Liberty League, including a debate over a choice of name, and the adoption of the *Albany Patriot* as their organ. 2 July 1847. p.112 [108], c5.

677 EDWARD SEARCH *to* **GARRISON. May 1847. London.** Appeals for donations to the anti-slavery cause. 9 July 1847. p.109, c2.

678 ELLIS GRAY LORING *to* **GARRISON. 28 June 1847. Boston.** Insists that non-resistance principles should be upheld until expunged from the AS constitution. 9 July 1847. p.109, c3.

679 LIBERTAS *to* **MR. EDITOR [W. L. GARRISON]. 26 June 1847. Boston.** Discusses an anti-slavery journal to be edited by Frederick Douglass. 9 July 1847. p.109, c4.

680 FREDERICK DOUGLASS *to* **MR. EDITOR. [from the** *Boston Daily Whig***] 27 June 1847. Lynn, Ma.** States that he has given up his intention of publishing a paper because three colored journals have already come into existence. 9 July 1847. p.109, c4.

681 RICHARD D. WEBB *to* **n.n. [extract from the** *Anti-Slavery Standard***] n.d. n.p.** Denounces the Roman Catholic clergy of Ireland for their conduct throughout the famine. 9 July 1847. p.109, c5.

682 WM. LLOYD GARRISON *to* **REV. DR. HUMPHREY. n.d. n.p.** Assails Humphrey for advocating colonization. 9 July 1847. p.110, c5.

683 E. W. *to* **FRIEND [W. L. GARRISON]. 15 June 1847. Edinburgh.** Criticizes the hypocrisy of the Free church and the Evangelical Alliance. 9 July 1847. p.111, c1.

684 RICHARD THURROW *to* **FRIEND [W. L. GARRISON]. 17 June 1847. Edinburgh.** Condemns Dr. Chalmers, a supporter of slavery; notes a public appearance by M. M. Clarke, a colored minister whom he considers mercenary; reports on a meeting of the Evangelical Alliance. 9 July 1847. p.111, c2.

685 n.n. *to* **FRIEND WALLCUT. 16 June 1847. New York.** Declares that Jacob Williams, a fugitive slave, is an impostor. 9 July 1847. p.111, c3.

686 J. M. ALDRICH *to* **FRIEND GARRISON. 3 July 1847. Fall River.** Declares that the fugitive slave from New Orleans is an imposter. 9 July 1847. p.111, c3.

687 CLAUDIUS BRADFORD *to* **SAMUEL MAY, JR. 4 July 1847. Bridgewater.** Comments on the fugitive slave Jacob Williams. 9 July 1847. p.111, c3.

688 SETH PAINE *to* **[W. L.] GARRISON. 12 June 1847. Lake Zurich.** Criticizes the Liberty Party in the West. 9 July 1847. p.111, c4.

689 JOHN BAILEY *to* **FRIEND GARRISON. 3 July 1847. New Bedford.** Corrects the *Liberator*'s report on the Bristol County AS meeting. 9 July 1847. p.111, c4.

690 LIBERTY *to* **THE EDITOR. n.d. n.p.** Denounces the Rev. Thomas F. Norris' publication, the *Olive Branch*, for its abuse of Frederick Douglass. 16 July 1847. p.113, c2.

691 J. B. ESTLIN *to* **REV. EDWARD TAGART. 7 June 1847. Bristol.** Comments on English Unitarians and American slavery. 16 July 1847. p.114, c1.

692 J. M. *to* **THE** *NATIONAL ERA.* **26 June 1847. Baltimore.** Requests that the *National Era* no longer be sent to him. 16 July 1847. p.114, c5.

693 ISAAC STEARNS *to* **FRIEND GARRISON. 13 July 1847. Mansfield.** Notes that Frederick Douglass has decided not to accept a printing press from his British abolition friends. 16 July 1847. p.114, c6.

694 GEORGE FILER *to* **SIR [W. L. GARRISON]. 12 July 1847. Belchertown.** Discusses means of abolishing slavery; argues that slave labor is more expensive than free labor. 16 July 1847. p.115, c1.

695 F. H. D. *to* **FRIEND GARRISON. 6 July 1847. Leominster.** Praises W. W. Brown; reports on the Women's County AS. 16 July 1847. p.115, c1.

696 J. B. *to* **FRIEND GARRISON. 9 July 1847. New Bedford.** Reports on the Yearly Meeting of Society of Friends. 16 July 1847. p.115, c2.

697 SAMUEL DYER *to* **FRIEND GARRISON. 11 July 1847. S. Abington.** Encloses resolutions of the Old Colony AS. 16 July 1847. p.115, c3.

698 JOSEPH MERRILL *to* **BRO. GARRISON. 27 June 1847. Danvers, Ma.** Opposes Mike Walsh as head of the working-men's party in New York. 16 July 1847. p.115, c3.

669 QUERO *to* **MR. EDITOR [W. L. GARRISON]. 29 June 1847. n.p.** Questions Masonic traditions. 16 July 1847. p.116, c2.

700 SAMUEL FESSENDEN *to* **THE EDITOR OF THE** *LIBERATOR* **[W. L. GARRISON]. 13 July 1847. Portland.** Clarifies his statements about the Liberty Party. 23 July 1847. p.117, c2.

701 J. SMITH *to* **GARRISON. 19 May 1847. Mecca, Oh.** Encourages Garrison in his work. 23 July 1847. p.117, c2.

702 FREDERICK DOUGLASS *to* **WM. LLOYD GARRISON. 18 July 1847. Lynn, Ma.** Apologizes that his decision not to publish a newspaper at the present time has brought criticism on W. L. Garrison. 23 July 1847. p.118, c3.

703 J. B. COLTHURST *to* **SIR [W. L. GARRISON]. 7 October 1846. Cork.** Congratulates W. L. Garrison for exposing the Evangelical Alliance. 23 July 1847. p.118, c6.

704 EDWARD SEARCH *to* **THE EDITOR OF THE** *LIBERATOR* **[W. L. GARRISON].** **June 1847. London.** Opposes returning slaveholders' contributions for the suffering in Ireland. 23 July 1847. p.119, c3.

705 J. C. CALHOUN *to* **SAMUEL A. WALES. 27 June 1847. Fort Hill.** Expresses appreciation for the Putnam Whigs' support of the bill he introduced in the Senate in opposition to the Wilmot Proviso. 30 July 1847. p.122, c1.

706 n. n. *to* **MR. [W. W.] BROWN. 6 July 1847. West Newton.** Comments on the impact of Brown's speech. 30 July 1847. p.122, c5.

707 EDMUND QUINCY *to* **WILLIAM W. BROWN. 1 July 1847. Dedham.** Praises Brown's slave narrative. 30 July 1847. p.122, c5.

708 B. *to* **MR. EDITOR [W. L. GARRISON]. 1 July 1847. Hingham.** Discusses the impact of W. W. Brown at Hingham. 30 July 1847. p.122, c6.

709 EDWARD SEARCH *to* **[W. L.] GARRISON. June 1847. London.** Comments on T. Parker's "Sermon of Merchants," W. J. Fox, and the anti-slavery cause in general. 30 July 1847. p.123, c3.

710 SAMUEL MAY, JR. *to* **MR. GARRISON. 20 July 1847. Boston.** Encloses a letter to the *Christian Examiner.* 30 July 1847. p.124, c2.

711 SAMUEL MAY, JR. *to* **THE** *CHRISTIAN EXAMINER.* **8 July 1847. Leicester.** Corrects the paper's statement on the New England Convention. 30 July 1847. p.124, c2.

712 JOSEPH A. DUGDALE *to* **WILLIAM LLOYD GARRISON. 17 July 1847. Selma, Oh.** Comments on his improved health and strengthened faith. 30 July 1847. p.124, c3.

713 A. W. QUIMBY *to* **WILLIAM LLOYD GARRISON. July 1847. County of Hanover, Va.** Describes unpleasant consequences of the abolition of slavery. 6 August 1847. p.125, c1.

714 ROBERT SMITH *to* **SIR [W. L. GARRISON]. 4 July 1847. Islington.** Reports on anti-slavery in England; mentions Frederick Douglass. 6 August 1847. p.126, c3.

715 H. C. WRIGHT *to* **[W. L.] GARRISON. 15 July 1847. Dublin.** Describes poverty and famine in Ireland. 6 August 1847. p. 126, c4.

716 H. C. WRIGHT *to* **[W. L.] GARRISON. 16 July 1847. Dublin.** Describes poverty and famine in Ireland; encloses a letter from James Haughton. 6 August 1847. p.126, c4.

717 JAMES HAUGHTON *to* **H. C. WRIGHT. 15 July 1847. Dublin.** Justifies commercial and social interaction with American slaveholders. 6 August 1847. p.126, c4.

718 W. C. N. *to* **FRIEND GARRISON. 28 July 1847. Boston.** Discusses the value of mental and moral advancement. 6 August 1847. p.126, c6.

719 WM. F. WOOD *to* **[W. L.] GARRISON. 20 July 1847. Fall River.** Defends the anti-slavery record of the New England Yearly Meeting of Friends. 6 August 1847. p.127, c1.

720 LORING MOODY *to* **THE ABOLITIONISTS OF MASSACHUSETTS. n.d. n.p.** Requests money for the Massachusetts AS. 6 August 1847. p.127, c2.

721 SAMUEL ADAMS *to* **MR. EDITOR. [from the** *Christian World***] n.d. n.p.** States his reaction to the hospitality of South Carolina. 13 August 1847. p.120 [130], c1.

722 n.n. *to* **THE** *BOSTON WHIG.* **[extract] 22 July 1847. Richmond.** A New Yorker praises the city of Richmond; criticizes abolitionists for giving a false impression of Northern sentiments toward the people of the South. 13 August 1847. p.120 [130], c3.

723 LORING MOODY *to* **MASSACHUSETTS ABOLITIONISTS. n.d. n.p.** Appeals for funds on behalf of the Massachusetts AS. 13 August 1847. p.121 [131], c3.

724 WM. LLOYD GARRISON *to* **n.n. 7 August 1847. Philadelphia.** Reports on W. L. Garrison and Frederick Douglass in Pennsylvania. 20 August 1847. p.135, c1.

725 WM. LLOYD GARRISON *to* **n.n. 9 August 1847. Harrisburg.** Reports on W. L. Garrison and Frederick Douglass in Pennsylvania; comments on violence in Harrisburg. 20 August 1847. p.135, c1.

726 NATH. A. BORDEN *to* **EDMUND QUINCY. 4 August 1847. New Bedford.** Discusses plans to celebrate the anniversary of British West India emancipation. 20 August 1847. p.135, c3,

727 A PHILANTHROPIST *to* **REV. CHARLES BRIGGS. [from the** *Christian Register***] n.d. n.p.** Comments on anti-game laws in England. 27 August 1847. p.137, c1.

728 CAROLINE W. H. DALL *to* **MR. EDITOR. 7 August 1847. E. Needham, Ma.** Discusses the popular condemnation of acceptance of slaveholder contributions for the starving people in Ireland. 27 August 1847. p.139, c1.

729 H. C. WRIGHT *to* **GARRISON. 1 August 1847. London.** Relates discussions held with Douglas Jerrold Mazzini, Robert Owen, and James H. Webb. 27 August 1847. p.139, c2.

730 H. C. WRIGHT *to* **W. L. GARRISON. 3 August 1847. London.** Details his visit to Epping Forest. 27 August 1847. p.139, c2.

731 ROBERT SMITH *to* **FRIEND. 3 August 1847. Islington.** Comments on George Thompson and the Anti-Corn Law League. 27 August 1847. p.139, c3.

732 n.n. *to* **MR. EDITOR. [from the** *Baltimore Patriot***] n.d. n.p.** Relates the story of a man convicted on circumstantial evidence of murder, who died in prison before the true murderer confessed to the crime. 27 August 1847. p.140, c2.

733 ORVILLE DEWEY *to* **THE EDITORS OF THE** *NEW YORK CHRISTIAN IN-QUIRER.* **20 July 1847. Sheffield.** Refutes statement by Rev. Dr. Hutton that he is apathetic toward abolition. 3 September 1847. p.141, c1.

734 SAMUEL MAY *to* **REV. GEORGE ARMSTRONG. 30 June 1847. Boston.** Discusses the position of the British and Foreign Unitarian Association on slavery. 3 September 1847. p.141, c6.

735 WM. W. BROWN *to* **FRIEND MAY. 9 August 1847. Fitchburg.** Reports on a meeting at New Bedford and the anti-slavery cause in general. 3 September 1847. p.143, c5.

736 HENRY C. WRIGHT *to* **COMMITTEE OF THE GLASGOW EMANCIPATION SOCIETY. 4 July 1847. Roseneath.** Sends his farewell to the Glasgow Emancipation Society. 10 September 1847. p.145, c4.

737 WM. LLOYD GARRISON *to* **n.n. 25 August 1847. Richfield, Oh.** Praises Frederick Douglass' speech on Southern religion; notes Frederick Douglass' illness on 20 August 1847 in New Lyme, Ohio. 10 September 1847. p.146, c6.

738 PARKER PILLSBURY *to* **FRIEND QUINCY. n.d. n.p.** Encloses proposals to England adopted at the First of August celebration urging England to discontinue relations with America. 10 September 1847. p.147, c2.

739 C. M. CLAY *to* **THE EDITORS OF THE** *NEW ORLEANS PICAYUNE.* **15 July 1847. City of Mexico.** Discusses the Mexican War. 10 September 1847. p.148, c3.

740 RESIDENTS OF BRIDGEWATER, ENGLAND *to* **INHABITANTS OF BRIDGE-WATER, MASSACHUSETTS. September 1846. n.p.** Express happiness that the name of Bridgewater is not disgraced by being affixed to a residence of slaveholders; urge the residents to be instruments of the delivery of slaves from bondage. 17 September 1847. p.150, c1.

741 INHABITANTS OF BRIDGEWATER, MASSACHUSETTS *to* **RESIDENTS OF BRIDGEWATER, ENGLAND. 10 February 1847. Bridgewater.** Reply to a letter of September 1846; extend wishes of good-will and prosperity; explain the American system of state governments, which renders the abolition of slavery impossible to any except the residents of a given slave state; also share the hope of universal emancipation. 17 September 1847. p.150, c2.

742 n.n. *to* **n.n. 26 August 1847. n.p.** Comments on Lucretia Mott. 17 September 1847. p.150, c6.

743 H. C. WRIGHT *to* **[W. L.] GARRISON. 5 September 1847. Philadelphia.** Announces his arrival in the United States. 17 September 1847. p.151, c2.

744 RICHARD ALLEN *to* **[W. L.] GARRISON. 18 August 1847. Dublin.** Notes Henry Wright's departure. 17 September 1847. p.151, c2.

745 EDWARD SEARCH *to* **SIR. August 1847. London.** Discusses democracy, means of production, and progress. 17 September 1847. p.151, c3.

746 H. H. BRIGHAM *to* **FRIEND QUINCY. 5 September 1847. South Abington.** Claims that the Orthodox church at Abington opposes temperance. 17 September 1847. p.152, c2.

747 JOHN B. COLTHURST *to* **F. BEDDINGFELD. 16 November 1836. n.p.** Discusses technicalities of appraising and discharging apprentices in the West Indies. 24 September 1847. p.153, c5.

748 E. RICHMOND *to* **MR. EDITOR. 6 September 1847. Abington.** Reports on the Old Colony Association of Universalists. 24 September 1847. p.155, c3.

749 LEANDER EATON *to* **n.n. September 1847. Worcester, Ma.** Protests the Mexican War. 24 September 1847. p.156, c2.

750 JOHN T. BARRY *to* **THE EDITORS OF THE** *BRITISH FRIEND.* **24 July 1847. London.** Reports on English elections. 24 September 1847. p.156, c3.

751 JOHN CARGILL, ROBERT HERRIOT, AND ROBERT LOCKHART *to* **THE EDITOR OF THE** *EDINBURGH WEEKLY JOURNAL.* **30 August 1847. Kirkaldy.** Note the hypocrisy of A. Campbell regarding slavery. 24 September 1847. p.158, c1.

752 E. N. SAWTELL *to* **MESSRS. EDITORS. [from the** *New York Observer***] 20 March 1847. New Orleans.** Discusses misunderstood facts concerning slavery in the South. 1 October 1847. p.157*, c1.

753 L. *to* **WM. LLOYD GARRISON. 15 August 1847. Kirkcaldy.** Comments on the election of George Thompson to Parliament. 1 October 1847. p.157*, c3.

754 RICHARD THURROW *to* **FRIEND [W. L. GARRISON]. 17 August 1847. Edinburgh.** Notes anti-slavery activity in Scotland. 1 October 1847. p.157*, c4.

755 JAMES BUCHANAN *to* **CHARLES KESSLER, GEO. F. SPAYD, AND JACOB LIVENGOOD. [from the** *Pennsylvanian***] 25 August 1847. Washington.** Discusses the Wilmot Proviso. 1 October 1847. p.158*, c2.

756 SIMMONS COATES *to* **FRIEND [W. L. GARRISON]. 31 August 1847. Gap, Pa.** Forwards resolutions of Clarkson County AS. 1 October 1847. p.159, c1.

757 P. *to* **THE EDITOR OF THE** *LIBERATOR* **[W. L. GARRISON]. August 1847. Lowell, Ma.** Protests against slavery. 1 October 1847. p.159, c2.

758 GEORGE WILSON McCREE *to* **W. L. GARRISON. 2 September 1847. Nottingham, England.** Condemns slavery in America; admires H. C. Wright. 8 October 1847. p.161, c3.

759 JOHN BUNKER *to* **FRIEND GARRISON. 15 September 1847. Fairhaven.** Notes the progress of the anti-slavery cause. 8 October 1847. p.162, c6.

760 EDGEWORTH *to* **THE** *HARBINGER.* **n.d. n.p.** Advocates an alternative to immediate emancipation of slaves. 15 October 1847. p.165, c1.

761 COLORED CITIZENS OF TORONTO *to* **THE ATTORNEY GENERAL OF CANADA EAST. 24 August 1847. Toronto.** Express thanks for the courteous reception given to Rev. Samuel Young of New York. 15 October 1847. p.165, c3.

762 HIRAM WILSON *to* **FRIEND GARRISON. 22 December 1847. Canada West.** Comments on the death of Samuel Young. 15 October 1847. p.165, c3.

763 JAMES HAUGHTON *to* **THE EDITOR OF THE** *NORTHERN WHIG.* **n.d. n.p.** Forwards a letter to Dr. Montgomery. 15 October 1847. p.165, c6.

764 JAMES HAUGHTON *to* **REV. H. MONTGOMERY. 27 July 1847. Dublin.** Discusses Unitarians and slavery in America. 15 October 1847. p.165, c6.

765 JOSE J. DE HERRERA, IGNACIO MORA Y VILLAMIL, BERNARDO COUTO, MIGUEL ATRISTAIN *to* **MINISTER OF INTERIOR AND FOREIGN RELATIONS. 7 September 1847. Mexico.** Report on the treaty negotiations between Mexico and the United States. 15 October 1847. p.166, c1.

766 EDWARD SEARCH *to* **GARRISON. August 1847. England.** Discusses Unitarians and anti-slavery. 15 October 1847. p.166, c5.

767 JONATHAN WALKER *to* **n.n. 26 September 1847. Plymouth.** Lauds Captain Wixen's treatment of liberated slaves on a recent voyage. 15 October 1847. p.167, c3.

768 B. C. CLARK *to* **R. F. WALLCUT. 29 September 1847. Boston.** Comments on the emigration to Haiti of sixty-six free colored persons from Virginia. 22 October 1847. p.169, c4.

769 THOS. CORWIN *to* **THE EDITOR OF THE** *CINCINNATI ATLAS.* **23 September 1847. Lebanon.** Discusses the Wilmot Proviso. 22 October 1847. p.169, c6.

770 WM. GOODELL *to* **n.n. [extract] 30 July 1846. n.p.** Gives background and criticisms of Garrison, the AAS, the American and Foreign AS, and the Liberty Party. 22 October 1847. p.170, c1.

771 EDMUND QUINCY *to* **RICHARD D. WEBB. 17 October 1847. Dedham.** Answers questions concerning the "new organization" and the third party. 22 October 1847. p.170, c3.

772 THOMAS P. RODMAN *to* **THE PUBLISHERS OF THE** *LIBERATOR*. **9 October 1847. Bridgewater.** Reports on the Plymouth Colony AS. 22 October 1847. p.170, c6.

773 VALENTINE NICHOLSON *to* **EDITORS AND READERS [OF THE** *LIBERATOR*]. **25 September 1847. Harveysburgh, Oh.** Believes false theology to be the cause of all sectarian strife. 22 October 1847. p.172, c2.

774 n.n. *to* **THE EDITOR OF THE** *NEW YORK HERALD*. **24 August 1847. Florence.** Comments on the abolition of capital punishment in Tuscany, the liberalization of censorship, and the anticipation of a new constitutional government. 22 October 1847. p.172, c3.

775 A. G. BROWN *to* **WM. SMITH. 15 April 1847. Jackson, Ms.** Discusses the Wilmot Proviso. 29 October 1847. p.173, c1.

776 WM. SMITH *to* **THE GOVERNOR OF MISSISSIPPI. 10 March 1847. Richmond.** Discusses the Wilmot Proviso. 29 October 1847. p.173, c1.

777 W. S. P. *to* **MR. GARRISON. 1 October 1847. Philadelphia.** Informs Garrison that Richard Thurrow was misinformed in his comments about Rev. Gloucester. 29 October 1847. p.173, c3.

778 DONALD MacGREGOR *to* **THE CHURCH UNDER THE PASTORAL CARE OF REV. GLOUCESTER. 1 September 1847. Philadelphia.** Comments on Gloucester's denunciation of Frederick Douglass, W. L. Garrison, and others. 29 October 1847. p.173, c4.

779 HENRY C. WRIGHT *to* **THE EDITOR OF THE** *PENNSYLVANIA FREEMAN*. **19 September 1847. Philadelphia.** Discusses Rev. S. Gloucester, the "betrayer of the cause of his enslaved fellow men." 29 October 1847. p.173, c4.

780 SAM HOUSTON *to* **SIR. 18 July 1847. Huntsville, Tx.** Discusses the history of the Texas annexation. 29 October 1847. p.173, c5.

781 EDWARD SEARCH *to* **GARRISON. 17 August 1847. London.** Relates his discussions with H. C. Wright. 29 October 1847. p.174, c5.

782 HENRY C. WRIGHT *to* **ELIZABETH PEASE. 18 October 1847. Cleveland.** Discusses recent lectures by Frederick Douglass and W. L. Garrison in the West. 29 October 1847. p.174, c6.

783 RICHARD ALLEN *to* **[W. L.] GARRISON. 3 October 1847. Dublin.** Discusses Garrison's tour with Frederick Douglass; reports on anti-slavery activities in England. 5 November 1847. p.177, c3.

784 SYLVANUS JAGGER *to* **MESSRS. EDITORS. [from the** *Sandwich Observer*] **October 1847. Centerville.** Criticizes the author of an article in the *Yarmouth Register*. 5 November 1847. p.178, c1.

785 JAMES FALLS *to* **COLORED PEOPLE OF THE UNITED STATES. 10 July 1847. Santo Domingo.** Invites them to emigrate to Haiti. 5 November 1847. p.178, c4.

786 H. C. WRIGHT *to* **THE EDITOR OF THE** *LIBERATOR* **[E. QUINCY]. 22 October 1847. Buffalo.** Comments on the Massachusetts convention of the Liberty Party. 5 November 1847. p.178, c6.

787 JAMES HAUGHTON *to* **C. H. A. DALL. 29 September 1847. Dublin.** Questions whether Ireland should accept donations from slaveholders. 5 November 1847. p.179, c1.

788 C. H. A. DALL *to* **THE EDITOR OF THE** *LIBERATOR* **[E. QUINCY]. 22 October 1847. East Needham.** Comments on the education of slave children. 5 November 1847. p.179, c1.

789 WM. H. GILDER, J. P. DURLIN, I. T. COOPER, J. CASTLE *to* **METHODIST SOCIETIES OF NORTHAMPTON AND ACCOMAC. 7 April 1847. Wilmington, De.** Report on the pastoral address of the Annual Conference of the Methodist Epsicopal Church, which resolved that the church will resist any attempt to exclude slaveholders from membership. 12 November 1847. p.181, c1.

790 HENRY C. WRIGHT *to* **ELIZABETH PEASE. 31 October 1847. Boston.** Reports his return to the United States with W. L. Garrison. 12 November 1847. p.181, c3.

791 M. STOWELL *to* **MR. EDITOR [E. QUINCY]. 25 October 1847. Warren.** States that the Congregational church would not allow W. W. Brown to lecture. 12 November 1847. p.181, c4.

792 n.n. *to* **THE EDITOR OF THE** *GLASGOW CHRISTIAN NEWS*. **24 August 1847. n.p.** Warns Baptists not to be led astray by Alexander Campbell. 12 November 1847. p.181, c5.

793 THOS. DUDGEON *to* **SIR [W. L. GARRISON]. 15 October 1847. Boston.** Reports on W. L. Garrison's anti-slavery speech. 12 November 1847. p.182, c5.

794 WM. W. BROWN *to* **FRIEND QUINCY. 20 October 1847. Worcester.** Reports on a meeting of the Brookfield Association of Orthodox Ministers. 12 November 1847. p.182, c6.

795 EDWARD SEARCH *to* **n n. 17 August 1847. London.** Discusses the education and endowment questions in the forthcoming elections in England. 12 November 1847. p.183, c2.

796 H. C. WRIGHT *to* **FRIEND [E. QUINCY]. 26 October 1847. Syracuse, N. Y.** Reports on the Liberty Party meeting at Buffalo. 19 November 1847. p.185, c5.

797 PARKER PILLSBURY *to* **FRIEND QUINCY. n.d. n.p.** Relates particulars of recent anti-slavery meetings in Weymouth. 19 November 1847. p.186, c6.

798 AN OLD MEMBER *to* **MR. EDITOR [E. QUINCY]. 6 November 1847. Providence, R. I.** Criticizes satirical poem presented at the mechanics' convention which ridiculed reformers and philanthropists. 19 November 1847. p.186, c6.

799 ELKANAH NICKERSON *to* **THE EDITOR OF THE** *LIBERATOR* **[E. QUINCY]. 6 September 1847. Harwich.** States that the anti-slavery movement does not embody all aspects of Christianity. 19 November 1847. p.187, c2.

800 J. *to* **MR. EDITOR [E. QUINCY]. 6 November 1847. Abington.** Suggests that abiding by non-resistance principles may be contrary to one's conscience in some instances. 19 November 1847. p.188, c2.

801 n.n. *to* **MR. EDITOR. [from the** *Boston Whig*] **n.d. n.p.** Praises *The Narrative of William W. Brown.* 26 November 1847. p.189, c6.

802 C. *to* **FRIEND QUINCY. 10 November 1847. Upton.** Recommends W. L. Garrison as governor. 26 November 1847. p.190, c3.

803 ROBERT SMITH *to* **THE EDITOR OF THE** *LIBERATOR* **[E. QUINCY]. 1 November 1847. Islington.** Gives history of anti-slavery movement. 26 November 1847. p.190, c6.

804 JOHN BISHOP ESTLIN *to* **THE EDITOR OF THE** *LIBERATOR* **[E. QUINCY]. 3 November 1847. Bristol, England.** Discusses British Unitarians and slavery. 26 November 1847. p.191, c2.

805 C. H. A. DALL *to* **THE EDITOR OF THE** *LIBERATOR* **[E. QUINCY]. 7 November 1847. East Needham.** Comments on the education of colored children in the South. 26 November 1847. p.191, c3.

806 PETER M. DESHONG *to* **n.n. n.d. n.p.** Discusses the remarkable powers of mathematics. 26 November 1847. p.192, c4.

807 GEO. BRADBURN *to* **THE** *LIBERATOR.* **11 November 1847. Cleveland.** Corrects H. C. Wright's statement of Bradburn's position. 3 December 1847. p.195, c1.

808 S. *to* **FRIEND QUINCY. 7 November. Norton.** Reports on the removal of Negro pews in a Unitarian church. 3 December 1847. p.195, c3.

809 J. McCOMBE *to* **THE EDITOR OF THE** *LIBERATOR* **[E. QUINCY]. 20 April 1847. Georgetown.** Praises speech by former slave W. W. Brown at Georgetown. 3 December 1847. p.195, c3.

810 WILLIAM ASHBY, JR. *to* **FRIEND MAY. 23 November 1847. Newburyport.** Comments on the impact of a lecture by W. W. Brown. 3 December 1847. p.195, c3.

811 J. M. F. *to* **THE EDITOR OF THE** *LIBERATOR* **[E. QUINCY]. 29 November 1847. Brookfield.** Discusses his nomination as a candidate for senator. 10 December 1847. p.198, c4.

812 EDWARD SEARCH *to* **[W. L.] GARRISON. 2 November 1847. London.** Discusses conditions of laborers in England. 10 December 1847. p.198, c5.

813 T. P. LOCKE *to* **MR. EDITOR [E. QUINCY]. n.d. n.p. Worcester County.** Reports on the North Division AS. 10 December 1847. p.198, c5.

814 TRUMAN CASE *to* **FRIEND GARRISON. 13 November 1847. Randolph, Oh.** Praises W. L. Garrison. 10 December 1847. p.198, c6.

815 HENRY W. WILLIAMS *to* **FRIEND. 21 September 1847. Lucerne.** Describes his journey from Italy. 17 December 1847. p.201, c2.

816 C. *to* **MR. EDITOR. [from the** *Boston Whig*] **22 November 1847. Norwich, Ct.** Declares Henry Clay is not a slaveholder. 17 December 1847. p.201, c6.

817 EDMUND QUINCY *to* **REV. JOHN PIERPONT. 13 December 1847. Dedham.** Discusses controversy between Pierpont and W. L. Garrison concerning union with slaveholders. 17 December 1847. p.202, c2.

818 ALLAN AGNEW *to* **H. C. WRIGHT. 20 November 1847. Pennsbury, De.** States that the Sons of Temperance in Delaware does not admit colored people. 17 December 1847. p.203, c1.

819 JOSHUA L. FUSSELL *to* **H. C. WRIGHT. 21 November 1847. Hamorton, Pa.** States that the Sons of Temperance in Pennsylvania does not admit colored people. 17 December 1847. p.203, c1.

820 H. C. WRIGHT *to* **JAMES HAUGHTON. 25 November 1847. Dublin.** Discloses refusal of Sons of Temperance to admit a colored member. 17 December 1847. p.203, c1.

821 J. HUNTINGTON *to* **MR. EDITOR. [from the** *Hampshire Gazette***] 19 November 1847. Northampton.** Endorses Dr. Ruggles' water cure. 17 December 1847. p.204, c4.

822 JOHN G. PALFREY *to* **HON. R. C. WINTHROP. 5 December 1847. Washington.** Questions Winthrop on his quest for the speakership of the House of Representatives. 24 December 1847. p.205, c2.

823 ROBERT C. WINTHROP *to* **J. G. PALFREY. 5 December 1847. Washington.** States that he would be Speaker but he would not be obliged to anyone. 24 December 1847. p.205, c2.

824 MASSACHUSETTS AS *to* **FRIENDS OF THE ANTI-SLAVERY CAUSE. 30 November 1847. Boston.** Call for dissolution of the Union. 24 December 1847. p.207, c1.

825 E. M. McGREGOR *to* **MAJOR [JOHN B. COLTHURST]. 16 May 1837. Barbadoes.** Praises Colthurst for his conduct as special magistrate. 24 December 1847. p.207, c3.

826 EDWARD EVERETT *to* **THE COMMITTEE FOR A PUBLIC DEMONSTRATION OF SYMPATHY WITH POPE PIUS IX. 27 November 1847. Cambridge.** Expresses sympathy with the efforts of Pope Pius IX to obtain Italian independence. 24 December 1847. p.208, c5.

827 WOMEN OF SCOTLAND *to* **WOMEN OF AMERICA. n.d. n.p.** Discuss freedom and slavery. 31 December 1847. p.209, c6.

828 J. PIERPONT *to* **EDMUND QUINCY. 23 December 1847. Troy, N. Y.** Comments on N. P. Rogers and the *Herald of Freedom.* 31 December 1847. p.210, c2.

829 PARKER PILLSBURY *to* **FRIEND QUINCY. 6 December 1847. New Bedford.** Comments on Pillsbury in Bridgewater. 31 December 1847. p.210, c4.

830 H. C. WRIGHT *to* **ELIZABETH PEASE. 25 December 1847. Boston.** Reports on the National Anti-Slavery Bazaar. 31 December 1847. p.211, c1.

831 JASON WHITMAN *to* **BROTHER MAY. 11 December 1847. Lexington.** Reports on a lecture by W. W. Brown. 31 December 1847. p.211, c2.

[1848]

832 CORK AS *to* **MAJOR J. B. COLTHURST. n.d. n.p.** Expresses appreciation of Colthurst's labors during the period of transition from slavery to freedom in the British West Indies. 7 January 1848. p.2, c4.

833 RALPH VARIAN *to* **WM. LLOYD GARRISON. 11 November 1847. Cork.** Pays tribute to Major John B. Colthurst. 7 January 1848. p.2, c4.

834 J. B. COLTHURST *to* **GENTLEMEN [OF THE CORK ANTI-SLAVERY SOCIETY]. n.d. n.p.** Acknowledges the society's address of appreciation for his work in the British West Indies. 7 January 1848. p.2, c5.

835 RICHARD THURROW *to* **FRIEND [W. L. GARRISON]. 29 November 1847. Edinburgh.** Discusses Rev. Steven Gloucester's denunciation of abolitionists. 7 January 1848. p.3, c1.

836 J. C. HANCHETT *to* **WM. LLOYD GARRISON. 2 January 1848. Syracuse.** Praises W. L. Garrison for his efforts. 14 January 1848. p.5, c2.

837 J. E. G. *to* **FRIEND GARRISON. 27 December 1847. Lowell.** Declares the Prescott Street Presbyterians prevented W. W. Brown from delivering a speech. 14 January 1848. p.5, c3.

838 P. *to* **FRIEND GARRISON. 25 December 1847. Bridgewater.** Questions the wisdom of dissolving the Union. 14 January 1848. p.7, c3.

839 HENRY C. WRIGHT *to* **ANDREW PATON. 4 January 1848. Hopedale.** Laments men's subservience to institutions. 14 January 1848. p.8, c2.

840 J. H. CRANE *to* **MR. GARRISON. 12 January 1848. Warren, Ma.** Inquires whether a dissolutionist can consistently participate in the voting process. 21 January 1848. p.9, c3.

841 JOHN BAILEY *to* **FRIEND GARRISON. 2 January 1848. New Bedford.** Comments on the disappearance of a fugitive slave, Aaron Chase. 21 January 1848. p.11, c6.

842 C. K. W. *to* **MR. EDITOR [W. L. GARRISON]. 15 January 1848. Boston.** Comments on "real" sermons that can be found in "stones, trees, and brooks." 21 January 1848. p.12, c2.

843 PARKER PILLSBURY *to* **FRIEND GARRISON. n.d. n.p.** Discusses the Methodist church's expulsion of Bishop Andrew for marrying a lady who owned slaves. 28 January 1848. p.13, c2.

844 J. A. M. *to* **FRIEND GARRISON. n.d. n.p.** Protests anti-slavery lecturers whose motivations are merely mercenary. 28 January 1848. p.13, c2.

845 ISRAEL K. VAN BROKLE *to* **JOHN LEVY. 8 November 1847. St. Croix.** Comments on Danish abolition of slavery. 28 January 1848. p.13, c3.

846 TRUTH *to* **MR. EDITOR [W. L. GARRISON]. n.d. n.p.** Defends the *Christian Reflector*. 28 January 1848. p.13, c3.

847 THEODORE PARKER *to* **FELLOW CITIZENS OF AMERICA. 22 December 1847. Boston.** Opposes slavery in America. 28 January 1848. p.13, c4.

848 I. E. HOLMES *to* **THE EDITOR OF THE *CHARLESTON MERCURY*. January 1848. Washington.** Comments on Robert C. Winthrop and Southern Whigs. 28 January 1848. p.13, c5.

849 GEORGE BANCROFT *to* **COMMODORE DAVID CONNER. 13 May 1846. n.p.** Informs that the secretary of the United States Navy has issued an order allowing Gen. Santa Anna to pass freely into the Mexican ports. 28 January 1848. p.14, c2.

850 D. CONNER *to* **G. BANCROFT. 16 August 1846. Princeton, Sacrificios.** Informs the secretary of the United States Navy of Gen. Santa Anna's arrival at Vera Cruz. 28 January 1848. p.14, c2.

851 A COLORED CITIZEN *to* **MR. EDITOR [W. L. GARRISON]. n.d. n.p.** Asserts that the idea of colored citizens' forming a separate AS is ridiculous; *Liberator* editorial agrees. 28 January 1848. p.15, c2.

852 EDWARD SEARCH *to* **SIR [W. L. GARRISON]. December 1847. London.** Comments on the war with Mexico. 28 January 1848. p.15, c3.

853 HENRY C. WRIGHT *to* **ANDREW PATON. 16 January 1848. Brooklyn, Ct.** Laments men's subservience to institutions. 28 January 1848. p.16, c2.

854 EDWARD SEARCH *to* **W. L. GARRISON. 1847. London.** Comments on monopoly of the soil by the aristocracy. 4 February 1848. p.17, c2.

855 JOHN P. HALE *to* **S. LEWIS. [from the** *Cincinnati Herald***] 1 January 1848. Washington.** Accepts nomination for president of the United States. 4 February 1848. p.17, c6.

856 SAMUEL MAY, JR. *to* **MR. GARRISON. 25 January 1848. Boston.** Notes that Rev. J. L. Russell and Rev. Augustus R. Pope are friendly to the Massachusetts AS. 4 February 1848. p.19, c3.

857 HENRY C. WRIGHT *to* **ANDREW PATON. 16 January 1848. Brooklyn, Ct.** Favors institutions for men, not men for institutions. 4 February 1848. p.20, c2.

858 PRO BONO PUBLICO *to* **MR. EDITOR. [from the** *Boston Evening Herald***] n.d. n.p.** Criticizes the Massachusetts AS meeting. 11 February 1848. p.21, c1.

859 J. M. O. *to* **MESSRS. EDITORS. [from the** *Olive Branch***] 28 January 1848. Boston.** Discusses the split of the Massachusetts AS into Garrisonians and Haleites. 11 February 1848. p.21, c3.

860 W. C. NELL *to* **FRIEND GARRISON. 23 January 1848. Rochester, N.Y.** Informs Garrison that he and Frederick Douglass were barred from dinner celebrating Franklin's birthday; relates comments by Frederick Douglass about his treatment in Rochester. 11 February 1848. p.21, c3.

861 JOHN McLEAN *to* **SIR. 7 January 1848. Washington.** Comments on war with Mexico and how it must end. 11 February 1848. p.22, c1.

862 A NATIVE OF THE SOUTH *to* **SIR [W. L. GARRISON].   26 January 1848. Bucksport, Me.** States that anti-slavery agitation is helping the slaves in the South. 11 February 1848. p. 23, c1.

863 DANIEL MITCHELL *to* **FRIEND [W. L. GARRISON]. 24 January 1848. Pawtucket.** Reports on the Rhode Island AS. 11 February 1848. p.23, c1.

864 JONATHAN WALKER *to* **WM. L. GARRISON. 24 January 1848. E. Hamilton, N.Y.** Comments on anti-slavery in western New York. 11 February 1848. p.23, c2.

865 S. W. W. *to* **n.n. 5 February 1848. Providence.** Reports that an act for the protection of fugitive slaves has passed through the Rhode Island legislature. 11 February 1848. p.23, c2.

866 EDWARD SEARCH *to* **WM. LLOYD GARRISON. 1847. London.** Comments on colonial reform. 11 February 1848. p.23, c3.

867 I.S.S. *to* **WM. LLOYD GARRISON. 27 January 1848. Dorchester.** Comments on the *Anti-Slavery Call.* 11 February 1848. p.24, c2.

868 MONADNOC *to* **MESSRS. EDITORS. [from the** *New Hampshire Sentinel***] n.d. n.p.** Comments on the Garrisonians and the Sabbath. 18 February 1848. p.25, c1.

869 C. M. CLAY *to* **THE EDITORS OF THE** *CHRISTIAN REFLECTOR.* **14 January 1848. Lexington, Ky.** Discusses Clay and the Mexican War. 18 February 1848. p.25, c5.

870 ALEXANDRE DUMAS *to* **HON. J. C. C. 1 April 1847. Paris.** Fears that he will be sold as a slave if he comes to the United States. 18 February 1848. p.26, c1.

871 J. C. C. *to* **A[LEXANDRE] DUMAS. 1 August 1847. Charleston.** Agrees that his African blood would place Dumas in danger in United States. 18 February 1848. p. 26, c1.

872 MOSES SAWIN *to* **FRIEND MAY. 12 February 1848. Southboro.** Discusses disunion petitions. 18 February 1848. p.26, c2.

873 EDWARD SEARCH *to* **MR. GARRISON. 1847. London.** Discusses the general election in England. 18 February 1848. p.27, c1.

874 WENDELL PHILLIPS *to* **THE** *ANTI-SLAVERY STANDARD.* **21 September 1847. Boston.** Expresses satisfaction that the reputations of Wm. and Mary Howitt have been restored. 25 February 1848. p.30, c4.

875 M. T. JOHNSON *to* **BRETHREN [SLAVEHOLDERS]. 11 February 1848. Short Creek, Oh.** Claims that Southerners talk about consistency and freedom but their actions have nothing to do with either. 25 February 1848. p.31, c4.

876 I. S. S. *to* **WM. LLOYD GARRISON. 14 February 1848. Dorcester.** Discusses the Sabbath and the Bible. 25 February 1848. p.32, c2.

877 EDWARD SEARCH *to* **SIR [W. L. GARRISON]. n.d. n.p.** Discusses the execution of Thomas Leith. 25 February 1848. p.32, c4.

878 GEN. Z. TAYLOR *to* **GEN. R. JONES. 28 July 1839. Fort Brooke.** Discusses the procurement of bloodhounds for the army in order to find Indians in the swamps. 3 March 1848. p.33, c1.

879 JAMES HAUGHTON *to* **THE EDITOR OF** *HOWITT'S JOURNAL.* **26 December 1847. Dublin.** Discusses the "humanity" of the Co-operative League. 3 March 1848. p.33, c4.

880 M. W. CHAPMAN *to* **MR. GARRISON. 28 February 1848. Boston.** Announces a sale of goods to take place the following week, the proceeds of which will aid the anti-slavery cause. 3 March 1848. p.34, c2.

881 WILLIAM I. BOWDITCH *to* **FRIEND GARRISON. 28 February 1848. Brookline.** Defends the anti-slavery position of John P. Hale. 3 March 1848. p.35, c1.

882 SETH PAINE *to* **THE EDITOR OF THE** *LIBERATOR* **[W. L. GARRISON]. 5 February 1848. Lake Zurich.** Comments on the dissolution of the Union. 3 March 1848. p.35, c2.

883 HENRY W. WILLIAMS *to* **WENDELL PHILLIPS. [extract] n.d. n.p.** Describes his travels in Europe. 10 March 1848. p.37, c2.

884 JAMES HAUGHTON *to* **H. C. WRIGHT. 8 February 1848. Dublin.** Reports on the progress of reform in Dublin; wishes success to Frederick Douglass' paper. 10 March 1848. p.39, c1.

885 RICHARD THURROW *to* **FRIEND [W. L. GARRISON]. 16 February 1848. Edinburgh.** Reports the "Invasion Panic" in England. 10 March 1848. p.39, c2.

886 GEO. W. SAUNDERS *to* **MR. GARRISON. 26 February 1848. Canton.** Discusses the Sabbath question. 10 March 1848. p.40, c2.

887 MART NOLINGTON *to* **SIR [W. L. GARRISON]. 30 January 1848. Utica.** Criticizes W. L. Garrison for his disregard of the Sabbath. 10 March 1848. p.40, c2.

888 ALEX WAYMAN *to* **SIR [W. L. GARRISON]. 8 February 1848. Trenton.** Discusses the Sabbath question. 10 March 1848. p.40, c3.

889 JOSEPH HUTTON *to* **SAMUEL MAY, JR. 3 February 1848. King's Cross.** States that he is disturbed by abolitionist attacks on Unitarians. 17 March 1848. p.41, c2.

890 AN ENGLISH UNITARIAN WHO SIGNED THE REPLY *to* **THE EDITOR OF** *CHRISTIAN WORLD*. **January 1848. England.** Comments on abolitionists and Unitarians. 17 March 1848. p.41, c3.

891 SAMUEL MAY *to* **MR. GAY. [from the** *National Anti-Slavery Standard*] **24 February 1848. Boston.** Claims that W. G. Eliot was never a slaveowner. 17 March 1848. p.41, c4.

892 DEMOCRITUS *to* **GENTLEMEN. [from the** *Pennsylvanian*] **12 February 1848. City of Mexico.** Discusses the treaty with Mexico. 17 March 1848. p.42, c1.

893 SAMUEL MAY, JR. *to* **MR. GARRISON. 13 March 1848. Boston.** Discusses letter from Rev. Dr. Hutton on Unitarians and abolitionism. 17 March 1848. p.42, c6.

894 HENRY WATSON *to* **MR. GARRISON. 28 February 1848. Westerly.** Discusses his anti-slavery work and the narrative of his life. 17 March 1848. p.43, c1.

895 JAMES HAUGHTON *to* **WM. LLOYD GARRISON. 10 February 1848. Dublin.** Describes plight of the poor in Ireland. 17 March 1848. p.43, c1.

896 S. H. GAY *to* **[W. L.] GARRISON. n.d. n.p.** Comments on an article in the *Anti-Slavery Standard*. 17 March 1848. p.43, c1.

897 REBECCA WEAVER *to* **FRIEND DOUGLASS. 13 August 1847. Fallston.** Submits a poem on Southern slaveholders. 17 March 1848. p.44, c1.

898 I. S. S. *to* **WM. LLOYD GARRISON. 1 March 1848. Dorchester.** Discusses the Sabbath question. 17 March 1848. p.44, c2.

899 THOMAS BORTON AND ELIZABETH L. BORTON *to* **FRIENDS [ANTI-SABBATH CONVENTION]. 2 March 1848. Selma, Oh.** Comment on the Anti-Sabbath Convention. 17 March 1848, p.44, c3.

900 J. B. JETER *to* **GENTLEMEN [A LEADING POLITICAL PAPER]. n.d. n.p.** Comments on emancipation in Jamaica. 24 March 1848. p.45, c1.

901 T. *to* **n.n. [from the** *Salem* **(Ohio)** *Bugle*] **n.d. n.p.** Opposes the "fatal union" of North and South. 24 March 1848. p.45, c4.

902 EDWARD SEARCH *to* **[W. L. GARRISON]. 15 February 1848. London.** Examines mercantile, legislative, and aristocratic interests in England. 24 March 1848. p.46, c4.

903 RICHARD THURROW *to* **FRIEND [W. L. GARRISON]. 24 February 1848. Edinburgh.** Comments on the Free Church of Scotland and the Sabbath question. 24 March 1848. p.46, c5.

904 A. P. *to* **FRIEND [W. L. GARRISON]. 24 February 1848. Glasgow.** Discusses the Sabbath question in Scotland. 24 March 1848. p.46, c6.

905 MAJ. J. B. COLTHURST *to* **SIR [W. L. GARRISON]. 13 February 1848. Cork.** Discusses the clergy and abolitionism. 24 March 1848. p.46, c6.

906 NOAH SAFFORD *to* **FRIEND GARRISON. 14 March 1848. Springfield, Vt.** Describes the anti-slavery position of John P. Hale. 24 March 1848. p.47, c1.

907 A. BROOKE, VALENTINE NICHOLSON, CHAS. R. BROWN. SYBILLA L. BROWNE, W. WHIPPLE, ARTEMUS NICHERSON, ELIZABETH BROOKE, JANE NICHOLSON, MICAH BROWN, MALINDA T. JEROME, C. M. BROWNE, PHEBE WHIPPLE, ELIZABETH NICKERSON, MARGARET BROOKE, SARAH BROOKE *to* **THE ANTI-SABBATH CONVENTION IN THE CITY OF BOSTON. 10 March 1848. Oakland, Oh.** Regret they could not attend convention; support anti-sabbatarian principles. 24 March 1848. p.47, c2.

908 SAMUEL MYERS *to* **THE ANTI-SABBATH CONVENTION. 12 March 1848. New Lisbon, Oh.** Approves of the Anti-Sabbath Convention. 24 March 1848. p.47, c2.

909 J. F. SMALLEY *to* **[W. L.] GARRISON. 5 March 1848. Randolph, Oh.** Discusses the Anti-Sabbath Convention. 24 March 1848. p.47, c2.

910 DAVID LLOYD *to* **MR. GARRISON. 28 February 1848. Horsham, Pa.** Discusses the Anti-Sabbath Convention. 24 March 1848. p.48, c2.

911 SAMUEL BROOKE *to* **FRIEND [W. L. GARRISON]. 28 February 1848. Salem, Oh.** Discusses call for the Anti-Sabbath Convention. 24 March 1848. p.48, c2.

912 H. H. BRIGHAM *to* **FRIEND GARRISON. 10 March 1848. South Abington.** States that reformers' efforts seem to be bringing results. 24 March 1848. p.48, c3.

913 INQUIRER *to* **MR. EDITOR [W. L. GARRISON]. n.d. n.p.** Discusses the differences between Christian faiths. 24 March 1848. p.48, c3.

914 n.n. *to* **THE EDITOR OF THE** *LIBERATOR* **[W. L. GARRISON]. n.d. n.p.** Forwards resolutions passed by a New Hampshire Congregational church. 31 March 1848. p.49, c3.

915 HAMPDEN *to* **THE EDITORS OF THE** *ALBANY PATRIOT.* **8 March 1848. Washington.** Corrects inaccuracies in the author's previous account of Mrs. Madison and her slaves. 31 March 1848. p.49, c6.

916 HAMPDEN *to* **THE EDITORS OF THE** *ALBANY PATRIOT.* **19 February 1848. Washington City.** Discusses Mrs. Madison and her slaves. 31 March 1848. p.49, c6.

917 IRA WANZER *to* **REV. THEODORE PARKER. 29 February 1848. Brookfield.** Comments on the Anti-Sabbath Convention. 31 March 1848. p.51, c1.

918 LYMAN ALLEN *to* **FRIEND GARRISON. 26 February 1848. Northboro.** Comments on Wm. W. Brown. 31 March 1848. p.51, c3.

919 J. S. JACOBS *to* **[W. L.] GARRISON. 27 February 1848. Cato, N. Y.** Comments on Jonathan Walker and anti-slavery in western New York. 31 March 1848. p.51, c3.

920 RICHARD THURROW *to* **FRIEND [W. L. GARRISON]. 9 March 1848. Edinburgh.** Discusses the revolution in France, and the Sabbath question in Scotland. 31 March 1848. p.51, c4.

921 ELKANAH NICKERSON *to* **FRIEND GARRISON. 14 March 1848. Harwich.** Informs that God is putting new laws into the minds and hearts of men. 31 March 1848. p.52, c3.

922 MECHANIC *to* **MR. EDITOR [W. L. GARRISON]. 9 March 1848. Milford.** Favors dissolution of the Union. 7 April 1848. p.53, c3.

923 HIRAM WILSON *to* **WM. LLOYD GARRISON. 25 March 1848. Dawn Mills, Canada West.** Describes his anti-slavery efforts. 7 April 1848. p.55, c2.

924 H. C. WRIGHT *to* **JAMES HAUGHTON. 28 March 1848. Boston.** Discusses Massachusetts legislature and religion. 7 April 1848. p.56, c2.

925 HENRY M. PARKHURST *to* **MR. GARRISON. n.d. n.p.** Reports the remarks of Mr. George W. Benson, president of the Anti-Sabbath Convention, on the subject of freedom of speech. 14 April 1848. p.59, c2.

926 THOS. McCLINTOCK *to* **WM. LLOYD GARRISON. 21 March 1848. Waterloo, N.Y.** Reports on the Anti-Sabbath Convention. 14 April 1848. p.60, c2.

927 REV. SAMUEL J. MAY *to* **FRIENDS. 25 March 1848. Syracuse.** Warns readers about a forged letter of introduction for Mr. William Halyard, who is purportedly attempting to raise money to buy his mother. 21 April 1848. p.61, c2.

928 SAMUEL J. MAY *to* **FRIEND. 10 April 1848. Syracuse.** States that Mr. William Halyard is an imposter and the letter purportedly written by May is a forgery. 21 April 1848. p.61, c2.

929 JULIUS AIMES *to* **n.n. 6 April 1848. Albany [sic], N.Y.** Discusses a forged letter stating that twenty-five dollars has been raised to aid Mr. William Halyard in buying his mother out of slavery. 21 April 1848. p.61, c2.

930 EDWARD SEARCH *to* **[W. L. GARRISON]. 11 March 1848. London.** Discusses European politics. 21 April 1848. p.61, c3.

931 n.n. *to* **n.n. 17 March 1848. Washington.** Relates news of the capture of a schooner on Chesapeake Bay carrying a party of escaped slaves from Washington. 21 April 1848. p.62, c3.

932 n.n. *to* **n.n. [extract] 13 April 1848. Washington.** Describes the enthusiasm in the city of Washington aroused by the recent overthrow of Louis Philippe in France. 21 April 1848. p.62, c3.

933 n.n. *to* **n.n. 16 April 1848. Washington.** Notes the absence of sixty of the city's "finest slaves," who apparently escaped together the previous night. 21 April 1848. p. 62, c3.

934 n.n. *to* **n.n. 18 April 1848. Washington.** Reports imprisonment in Washington of captain and slaves aboard schooner captured on Chesapeake Bay. 21 April 1848. p.62, c3.

935 EDWARD SEARCH *to* **[W. L. GARRISON]. 22 March 1848. London.** Reports on the abdication of Metternich and the King of Prussia. 21 April 1848. p.62, c6.

936 AN ANTI-SABBATARIAN *to* **MR. GARRISON. 9 April 1848. Waltham.** Comments on the *Boston Trumpet* and the Anti-Sabbath Convention. 21 April 1848. p.63, c2.

937 ANTI-PRIESTCRAFT *to* **FRIEND GARRISON. n.d. n.p.** Satirizes current controversy concerning observance of the Sabbath. 21 April 1848. p.63, c2.

938 JOHN H. KEYSER *to* **MR. GARRISON. 28 March 1848. Black Water, West Florida.** Objects to the *Liberator*'s harsh criticism of the National Reform Association. 21 April 1848. p.63, c3.

939 JESSE HUTCHINSON, JR. *to* **MR. GARRISON. 5 April 1848. Philadelphia.** States that he did not vote for Caleb Cushing. 28 April 1848. p.66, c3.

940 EDWARD SEARCH *to* **[W. L. GARRISON]. March 1848. London.** Reports on political concerns in Italy, Austria, and British India. 28 April 1848. p.66, c4.

941 D. S. GRANDIN *to* **BROTHER GARRISON. n.d. n.p.** Advocates land reform in the United States. 28 April 1848. p.67, c2.

942 HENRY C. WRIGHT *to* **JAMES HAUGHTON. 14 April 1848. Wachusett Pond.** Reports on the militia in Massachusetts. 28 April 1848. p.68, c2.

943 HENRY C. WRIGHT *to* **CATHERINE PATON. 26 April 1848. Worcester.** Reports on the anti-slavery bazaar in Worcester. 5 May 1848. p.71, c1.

944 SAMUEL MAY, JR. *to* **MR. GARRISON. 30 April 1848. Boston.** Reports that the Worcester Anti-Slavery Bazaar was a success. 5 May 1848. p.71, c3.

945 GEORGE JEFFREY *to* **WM. LLOYD GARRISON. 29 March 1848. Glasgow.** Criticizes the American churches' stand on slavery. 5 May 1848. p.71, c4.

946. HENRY ALEXANDER, G. A. ARMSTRONG, FLETCHER BLAKELY, ROB'T CAMPBELL, JR., JAMES CARLEY, WM. CROZIER, W. H. DRUMMOND, WM. GLENDY, DAVID GORDON, JOHN HALL, WM. HERON, GEORGE HILL, WM. HUNTER, JOSH. HUTTON, J. C. LEDLIE, CHAS. J. M'ALESTER, DAVID MAGINNIS, FRANCIS McCAMMON, JOHN McCAW, ALEX. McCOMBE, JOSH McFADDEN, W. ORR McGOWAN, WM. B. MINNISS, H. MONTGOMERY, HUGH MOORE, SAMUEL MOORE, JAMES MULIGAN, S. C. NELSON, ALEX ORRI, JAMES ORRI, JOHN ORRI, CLASSON PORTER, J. NIXON PORTER, JOHN PORTER, J. SCOTT PORTER, THOMAS SMYTH, D. WATSON, SAMUEL WATSON, AND WM. WHITELEGGE *to* **THEIR BRETHREN IN A COMMON FAITH IN BOSTON. n.d. n.p.** Commend past efforts of Unitarians in behalf of the anti-slavery cause; exhort contemporary ministers to renew efforts for emancipation. 12 May 1848. p.74, c4.

947 HENRY C. WRIGHT *to* **JAMES HAUGHTON. 25 May 1848. Leicester.** States his belief that American republicanism is hypocritical. 12 May 1848. p.75, c1.

948 H. C. WRIGHT *to* **ELIZABETH PEASE. 1 May 1848. Hopedale.** Informs her of the death of her namesake, Elizabeth Pease Garrison. 12 May 1848. p.75, c2.

949 H. C. WRIGHT *to* **ANDREW PATON. 9 May 1848. New York.** Reports on the anniversary of the AAS; summarizes Frederick Douglass' speech. 12 May 1848. p. 75, c4.

950 HENRY C. WRIGHT *to* **RICHARD AND ANNE ALLEN. 10 May 1848. New York.**
Reports on the American Anti-Slavery Convention. 19 May 1848. p.79, c1.

951 H. C. WRIGHT *to* **FRIEND [W. L. GARRISON]. n.d. n.p.** Describes his summer plans and the beauty of Philadelphia in the spring. 19 May 1848. p.79, c2.

952 N. SOUTHARD *to* **FRIEND GARRISON. n.d. n.p.** Comments on exhibition of model of ancient Jerusalem. 19 May 1848. p.79, c3.

953 MILO A. TOWNSEND *to* **[W. L.] GARRISON. 23 April 1848. New Brighton, Pa.**
States that these are encouraging times to a "reformer." 19 May 1848. p.79, c3.

954 H. C. WRIGHT *to* **JAMES HAUGHTON. 17 April 1848. Wachusett Pond, Ma.** Contrasts English and American farmers. 26 May 1848. p.81, c2.

955 MARY B. THOMAS *to* **FRIEND. [from the** *Pennsylvania Freeman***] 19 April 1848. Downington.** Informs him of the kidnapping of a colored girl from her home by three white men. 26 May 1848. p.81, c5.

956 RICHARD ALLEN *to* **[W. L.] GARRISON. 17 April 1848. Brooklawn (near Dublin).**
Describes excitement caused by Louis Philippe's abdication. 26 May 1848. p.83, c1.

957 JONATHAN WALKER *to* **W. L. GARRISON. 14 May 1848. Plymouth.** Discusses his anti-slavery efforts. 26 May 1848. p.83, c2.

958 W. *to* **MR. GARRISON. n.d. n.p.** Appeals for funds for the New England Anti-Slavery Convention. 26 May 1848. p.83, c4.

959 HENRY GREW *to* **FRIEND GARRISON. n.d. n.p.** Discusses the Sabbath question. 26 May 1848. p.84, c2.

960 n.n. *to* **BROTHER GARRISON. 21 May 1848. Westfield, Ma.** Comments on women's rights. 2 June 1848. p.86, c5.

961 n.n. *to* **MR. GARRISON. 11 March 1848. Washington, Pa.** Praises the *Liberator*. 2 June 1848. p.86, c5.

962 STAPLETON *to* **SIR [W. L. GARRISON]. 21 May 1848. Harwich.** States that he has converted to the *Liberator*. 2 June 1848. p.86, c6.

963 C. H. S. *to* **MR. EDITOR [W. L. GARRISON]. 29 May 1848. Upton.** Informs that three men have been imprisoned for helping Washington slaves to escape. 2 June 1848. p.86, c6.

964 MARTIN STOWELL *to* **[W. L.] GARRISON. 15 May 1848. Warren.** Comments on recent lectures by William W. Brown. 2 June 1848. p.87, c1.

965 JOHN L. LORD *to* **FRIEND GARRISON. 29 May 1848. Newburyport.** Compliments recent lecture by William W. Brown. 2 June 1848. p.87, c1.

966 G. W. STACY *to* **FRIEND GARRISON. 10 April 1848. Milford.** Explains his dissent from Garrison's course regarding observance of the Sabbath. 2 June 1848. p.88, c4.

967 A FRIEND TO COLONIZATION *to* **THE** *BOSTON CHRISTIAN REFORMER*.
[extract] n.d. n.p. Maintains that colonization of blacks in Africa is the only sensible alternative to slavery. 16 June 1848. p.93, c2.

968 BENJAMIN FRANKLIN *to* **SIR [AN OLD FRIEND]. n.d. n.p.** Comments on Connecticut religion and common religion. 16 June 1848. p.96, c3.

969 W. H. BARNWELL *to* **HON. J. G. PALFREY. [extract from the** *Charleston Mercury*] **n.d. n.p.** States that the cause of abolition is dangerous to the Constitution; believes a federal law abolishing slavery could not be enforced in South Carolina; calls Palfrey a hypocrite; maintains that slavery is not unchristian. 23 June 1848. p.97, c1.

970 J. G. PALFREY *to* **THE** *NATIONAL ERA.* **8 May 1848. n.p.** Requests publication of an open letter addressed to those who have forwarded petitions to the author. 23 June 1848. p.97, c4.

971 JOHN G. PALFREY *to* **THE SIGNERS OF PETITIONS FORWARDED TO THE SUBSCRIBER FOR PRESENTATION TO THE HOUSE OF REPRESENTATIVES. 8 May 1848. n.p.** Explains circumstances in Congress which have prevented him from presenting the petitions. 23 June 1848. p.97, c4.

972 A. H. BAKER *to* **WENDELL PHILLIPS. 8 June 1848. Boston.** Discusses Phillips' Calvinism. 23 June 1848. p.98, c6.

973 A BELIEVER IN TRUTH *to* **MR. GARRISON. 13 June 1848. Fitchburg.** Discusses the ideas of Rev. Mr. Trask and Mr. Hale on the abolition of slavery in District of Columbia. 23 June 1848. p.98, c6.

974 H. C. WRIGHT *to* **JAMES HAUGHTON. 8 June 1848. New Lisbon, Oh.** Reports on Sayres, Drayton, and English, the three men who tried to help seventy-seven Washington slaves escape. 23 June 1848. p.99, c1.

975 VIATOR *to* **MR. GARRISON. 12 June 1848. New Bedford.** Condemns slavery; reports the sentencing of a woman to ten years in prison for teaching a slave to read the Bible. 23 June 1848. p.99, c2.

976 SAMUEL D. BURNS *to* **FRIEND. 29 March 1848. Dover, De.** Describes his plight as a black man who was imprisoned for trying to help other slaves escape. 30 June 1848. p.101, c2.

977 JOHN M. NILES *to* **GERARDUS BOYCE. n.d. n.p.** Urges that free territory not become slave territory. 30 June 1848. p.101, c5.

978 WM. H. SEWARD *to* **J. H. HOBART HAWES, JOSEPH R. TAYLOR, AND ROYAL H. THAYER. 13 June 1848. Auburn.** Expresses his support for Whig convention nominees. 30 June 1848. p.102, c6.

979 J. LAMBORN *to* **GARRISON. 1848. Covington, Ia.** Describes his anti-slavery sentiments. 30 June 1848. p.103, c1.

980 H. C. WRIGHT *to* **GARRISON. 14 June 1848. Steamer** *Michigan* **on Ohio River.** Denounces the nomination of Zachary Taylor. 30 June 1848. p.103, c2.

981 EDWARD SEARCH *to* **GARRISON. May 1848. London.** Describes debate on British reform. 30 June 1848. p.103, c2.

982 ROBERT C. WINTHROP *to* **THE TAYLOR RATIFICATION MEETING IN NEW YORK. 24 June 1848. Washington.** Forwards endorsement of Taylor. 7 July 1848. p.105, c2.

983 LEWIS CASS *to* **A. O. P. NICHOLSON. 24 December 1847. Washington.** Comments on Cass' opposition to the Wilmot Proviso. 7 July 1848. p.105, c2.

984 JOHN G. PALFREY *to* **CHARLES ALLEN, HENRY WILSON, AND CHARLES SUMNER. 24 June 1848. United States House of Representatives.** Declines invitation to speak at the People's Convention in Massachusetts; states that he sympathizes with the members of that convention. 7 July 1848. p.106, c2.

985 J. B. SANDERSON *to* **MR. GARRISON. 26 June 1848. New Bedford.** Mentions that Frederick Douglass was invited to the New Bedford First of August celebration. 7 July 1848. p.106, c5.

986 GEO. TRASK *to* **THE EDITOR OF THE** *LIBERATOR* **[W. L. GARRISON]. 26 June 1848. Fitchburg.** Responds to charge that he had misquoted John P. Hale. 7 July 1848. p.106, c6.

987 Z. *to* **MR. EDITOR. 2 July 1848. Cambridge.** Condemns both political parties as subservient to the South. 7 July 1848. p.106, c6.

988 HENRY C. WRIGHT *to* **GARRISON. 17 June 1848. Pittsburgh.** Discusses Zachary Taylor and land reform; recognizes no moral obligation of slave to obey his master. 7 July 1848. p.107, c1.

989 EDWARD SEARCH *to* **W. L. GARRISON. May 1848. London.** Evaluates the progress of republicanism in France; criticizes the English press. 7 July 1848. p.107, c2.

990 n.n. *to* **GENTLEMEN. [extract] 13 June 1848. Mexico.** Describes the deporting of General Worth and his division from Mexico. 7 July 1848. p.107, c2.

991 HENRY C. WRIGHT *to* **GARRISON. 19 June 1848. Ohio River.** Comments on a bathing establishment owned by blacks; criticizes Whig and Liberty parties. 14 July 1848. p.109, c2.

992 C. K. W. *to* **GEORGE. [extract] 6 July 1848. Boston.** Suggests that slaves be freed and given money "amounting to the difference between the cost of his past maintenance and the just wages of his past labor." 14 July 1848. p.109, c3.

993 HENRY HIGHLAND GARNET *to* **MR. EDITOR. [from the** *Buffalo Daily Propeller*] **20 June 1848. Buffalo.** Describes a beating he received from a railroad conductor for riding in a "white-only" car. 14 July 1848. p.110, c1.

994 PEGGY COLTHURST *to* **SIR. 22 June 1848. Dripsey Castle, Ireland.** Reports on the death of John Bowen Colthurst, who held office of special justice in the British West Indies for four years. 14 July 1848. p.110, c5.

995 PARKER PILLSBURY *to* **FRIEND GARRISON. 9 July 1848. North Bridgewater.** Reports the success of an abolitionist meeting at East Bridgewater and an incident involving an assault on Lucy Stone. 14 July 1848. p.110, c6.

996 EDWARD SEARCH *to* **GARRISON. June 1848. London.** Comments on the relationship between the poor and the land, concluding that the poor are the producers of all wealth. 14 July 1848. p.111, c1.

997 M. *to* **GARRISON. 4 July 1848. Feltonville.** States that he is encouraged by the lectures given by Adin Ballou and Dr. Hudson. 14 July 1848. p.111, c1.

998 N. P. C. PATTERSON, JEFFERSON TAYLOR, ALFRED TAYLOR, CHARLES A. DEARBORN, AND HORATIO BODGE *to* **FRIEND GARRISON. n.d. n.p.** Forward resolution in support of Rev. John Prince. 14 July 1848. p.111, c2.

999 SOUTHERNER AND SLAVEHOLDER *to* **MR. HONEYWELL, THE EDITOR OF THE** *EAGLE*. [from the *National Anti-Slavery Standard*] **n.d. Georgia.** Advocates the gallows for abolitionists. 12 July 1848. p.113, c1.

1000 JAMES HAUGHTON *to* **HENRY C. WRIGHT. 18 June 1848. Dublin.** Affirms Wright's view of the militia as enslaved victims of society and hired killers. 12 July 1848. p.113, c2.

1001 HENRY C. WRIGHT *to* **GARRISON. 22 June 1848. New Brighton, Oh.** Describes the beauty of nature in Ohio; believes that the meaning of Christianity is love. 12 July 1848. p.115, c3.

1002 HENRY C. WRIGHT *to* **GARRISON. 27 June 1848. New Lyme, Oh.** Provides description of the various abolitionist conventions. 28 July 1848. p.117, c2.

1003 MINISTER OF THE SOUTH *to* **P. [extract] n.d. n.p.** Discusses a communication received regarding views on non-voting and disunion. 28 July 1848. p.118, c6.

1004 WENDELL PHILLIPS *to* **FRIEND MAY. 24 July 1848. Lynn.** Looks forward to the picnic in Lynn, Massachusetts. 28 July 1848. p.118, c6.

1005 VIATOR *to* **MR. GARRISON. 10 July 1848. New Bedford.** Voices criticism of John Holmes in particular, and ministers in general. 28 July 1848. p.119, c1.

1006 ANSEL HARLOW *to* **FRIEND GARRISON. 17 July 1848. Plymouth.** Encloses resolutions of the Anti-Slavery Convention of 16 July in Leyden Hall. 28 July 1848. p.119, c1.

1007 YET A BELIEVER IN TRUTH *to* **MR. GARRISON. 11 July 1848. Fitchburg.** Gives a sarcastic evaluation of Trask, Hale, ministers, and the Liberty Party. 28 July 1848. p.119, c2.

1008 n.n. *to* **n.n. [extract] 7 July. St. George's, Bermuda.** Reports that Mitchell, a convict on board the *Meday*, is in very poor health. 28 July 1848. p.120, c5.

1009 ELI HAMBLETON *to* **FRIEND GARRISON. 16 July 1848. Chester County, Pa.** Relays request by Union Free Produce Society that the *Liberator* publish one of their communications. 4 August 1848. p.124, c2.

1010 n.n. *to* **n.n. [extract] 4 June. Green Horn.** Gives an account of an Apache attack. 4 August 1848. p.124, c5.

1011 M. M. NOAH *to* **SOUTHERN DELEGATES OF THE BALTIMORE DEMO-CRATIC CONVENTION. n.d. n.p.** Discusses the South's viewpoint on abolition. 11 August 1848. p.125, c1.

1012 S. W. W. *to* **BROTHER GARRISON. 31 July 1848. Providence.** Forwards news of the Milford Abolitionist Convention. 11 August 1848. p.125, c2.

1013 N. A. BORDEN AND J. B. SANDERSON *to* **MR. GARRISON. 29 June 1848. New Bedford.** Regret John Bailey's move from New Bedford to Lynn. 11 August 1848. p.125, c3.

1014 H. C. WRIGHT *to* **GARRISON. 28 June 1847. Geneva, Oh.** Opposes the Bible for its support of slavery. 11 August 1848. p.125, c3.

1015 ADIN BALLOU *to* **SAMUEL MAY, JR., GENERAL AGENT OF MASSACHU-SETTS AS. n.d. n.p.** Gives a progress report on conventions. 11 August 1848. p.125, c3.

1016 Z. TAYLOR *to* **JOHN MOREHEAD. 15 July 1848. Baton Rouge.** Accepts the Whig presidential nomination. 11 August 1848. p.126, c6.

1017 HENRY C. WRIGHT *to* **JAMES HAUGHTON. 29 June 1848. Plainesville, Oh.** Urges denunciation of the Bible if it is deemed pro-slavery; refers to atheism as the God of slaveholders. 11 August 1848. p.127, c1.

1018 JOSEPH MERRILL *to* **BROTHER GARRISON. 9 July 1848. Danvers (New Mills).** Describes a Liberty Party meeting. 11 August 1848. p.127, c2.

1019 n.n. *to* **FRIEND GARRISON. n.d. n.p.** States that he supports Hosea Ballou. 11 August 1848. p.128, c2.

1020 REV. L. OF WORCESTER COUNTY *to* **DEACON J. WHITE. [from the** *Worcester Aegis***] June 1848. n.p.** States that he was an army chaplain for approximately six years; upholds Z. Taylor's good character. 18 August 1848. p.129, c2.

1021 ADIN BALLOU *to* **SAMUEL MAY, JR. [continued from 11 August 1848] n.d. n.p.** Describes the One Hundred Conventions series in the West. 18 August 1848. p.129, c4.

1022 HENRY C. WRIGHT *to* **GARRISON. 16 July 1848. Randolph, Portage County, Oh.** Condemns those who use God as justification for war; cites Zachary Taylor and Mexico. 18 August 1848. p. 131, c1.

1023 W. *to* **MR. GARRISON. n.d. Roxbury.** Lauds the *Liberator*'s stand on the Sabbath question. 18 August 1848. p.132, c3.

1024 JAMES HAUGHTON *to* **THE EDITOR OF THE** *NERY EXAMINER AND LOUTH ADVERTISER***. 10 July 1848. 35 Eccles St.** Feels encouraged by discussion of temperance and teetotalism. 25 August 1848. p.132, c3.

1025 SAMUEL J. MAY *to* **MY DEAR COUSIN. 12 August 1848. Buffalo.** Forwards report of Buffalo convention. 25 August 1848. p.135, c1.

1026 HENRY C. WRIGHT *to* **GARRISON. 18 July 1848. Massilon.** Watches the Liberty Party in Ohio merging with Bolterism. 25 August 1848. p.135, c2.

1027 THEOBALD MATHEW *to* **n.n. 25 July 1848. Cork.** Sends thanks and appreciation. 25 August 1848. p.136, c3.

1028 W. W. BROWN *to* **FRIEND MAY. 17 AUGUST 1848. New York.** Comments on his experiences in Philadelphia; criticizes black churches in that city. 1 September 1848. p.137, c1.

1029 WM. BULL PRINGLE *to* **GEN. Z. TAYLOR. [from** *Charleston Courier***] 26 July 1848. Charleston, S. C.** Supports Taylor. 1 September 1848. p.138, c3.

1030 Z. TAYLOR *to* **WM. B. PRINGLE. 9 August 1848. Baton Rouge, La.** Expresses his appreciation of Pringle's 22 August letter of support. 1 September 1848. p.138, c3.

1031 BENJAMIN F. HATHAWAY *to* **MR. GARRISON. 28 August 1848. West Harwich.** Regrets mob violence which disrupted anti-slavery meeting in West Harwich. 1 September 1848. p.138, c4.

1032 J. B. P. *to* **MR. MAY. 21 August 1848. Salem.** Reports a successful abolitionist convention at Salem. 1 September 1848. p.138, c4.

1033 D. S. GRANDIN *to* **FRIEND Q. n.d. n.p.** Reports on a meeting of all interested in avoiding purchases of slave labor. 1 September 1848. p.139, c4.

1034 ANTI-SABBATARIAN *to* **MR. QUINCY. 16 August 1848. Waltham.** Cites hypocrisy in the changing views of prominent ministers vis-a-vis the Sabbath. 1 September 1848. p.140, c2.

1035 NATHAN APPLETON *to* **REV. J. N. DANFORTH. 9 August 1848. Pittsfield.** "Cheerfully supports" the Colonization Society and resettlement in Liberia. 8 September 1848. p.141, c1.

1036 MARTIN VAN BUREN *to* **BENJAMIN F. BUTLER, JOSEPH L. WHITE, AND SALMON P. CHASE, COMMITTEE OF BUFFALO CONVENTION. 22 August 1848. Lindenwald.** Accepts nomination as Free-Soil presidential candidate. 8 September 1848. p.141, c2.

1037 R. Y. *to* **MR. EDITOR. [from the** *Boston Daily Republican*] **27 August 1848. Harwich.** Calls mobocracy at Harwich a disgrace. 8 September 1848. p.142, c6.

1038 Z. TAYLOR *to* **GEORGE LIPPARD. 24 July 1848. Baton Rouge, La.** Declares that he is not a party candidate. 8 September 1848. p.142, c6.

1039 Z. TAYLOR *to* **n.n. [extract] n.d. Charleston.** Claims no aspirations for the presidency. 8 September 1848. p.142, c6.

1040 JOHN McLEAN *to* *CLEVELAND TRUE DEMOCRAT.* **28 July 1848. Columbus.** Refuses to allow his name to be considered for presidential nomination. 8 September 1848. p.142, c6.

1041 JOHN P. HALE *to* **MR. LEWIS. n.d. n.p.** Declines to be candidate for presidency and supports Messrs. Van Buren and Adams. 8 September 1848. p.143, c3.

1042 V. NICHOLSON *to* **FRIENDS. 18 August 1848. Harveysburgh, Oh.** Encloses account of Henry Wright and Charles C. Burleigh's visit to Harveysburgh. 8 September 1848. p.144, c2.

1043 H. HAWES *to* **BRO. GROSVENOR. 1 August 1848. Union, Me.** Accuses man, not God, of forcing man to keep the Sabbath. 8 September 1848. p.144, c3.

1044 EDWARD SEARCH *to* **GARRISON. July 1848. Old Jewry, London.** Comments on the Irish question. 15 September 1848. p.145, c2.

1045 HARRIET A. JONES *to* **THE EDITOR OF THE** *LIBERATOR* **30 August 1848. Harwich.** Criticizes the Harwich mob. 15 September 1848. p.145, c5.

1046 PARKER PILLSBURY *to* **FRIEND GAY. 2 September 1848. Barnstable.** Discusses the pro-slavery mob in Harwich. 15 September 1848. p.145, c6.

1047 [EDMUND JACKSON] *to* **THE EDITORS OF THE** *BOSTON COURIER*. **n.d. n.p.** Anonymous letter, allegedly from E. Jackson, calls African colonization "more appropriate to the latitude of Charleston than to Pittsfield." 15 September 1848. p.146, c1.

1048 PARKER PILLSBURY *to* **FRIEND QUINCY. 3 September 1848. Hyannis.** Contrasts character of two ministers at Hyannis and describes convention. 15 September 1848. p.146, c6.

1049 J. M. FISK *to* **FRIEND MAY. 3 September 1848. Saratoga Springs.** Relates his encounter with two Southerners while taking the water cure. 15 September 1848. p.147, c1.

1050 FREDERICK DOUGLASS *to* **THOMAS AULD. n.d. n.p.** Informs his former master that the quality of his life has improved and that he harbors no anti-white or anti-Southern prejudice. 22 September 1847 [1848]. p.149, c6.

1051 H. C. WRIGHT *to* **JAMES HAUGHTON. 18 August 1848. Salem, Oh.** Describes the horrors of slavery. 22 September 1847 [1848]. p.149, c2.

1052 SAMUEL BROOKE *to* **GAY. [from the** *National Anti-Slavery Standard***] n.d. n.p.** Corrects error printed in previous issue. 22 September 1847 [1848]. p.150, c3.

1053 J. C. CALHOUN *to* **THE EDITOR OF THE** *CHARLESTON MERCURY*. **[extract] 1 September 1848. Fort Hill.** Criticizes both presidential candidates. 22 September 1847 [1848]. p.150, c3.

1054 SAMUEL WILLISTON *to* **REV. R. ANDERSON. 12 September 1848. Easthampton.** Requests that no more slaveholders be allowed into American Foreign Missionary Society. 22 September 1847 [1848]. p.150, c6.

1055 EDWARD SEARCH *to* **GARRISON. 25 July 1848. London.** Reports on events in Ireland. 22 September 1847 [1848]. p.151, c1.

1056 H. C. WRIGHT *to* **GARRISON. 6 September 1848. Jefferson, Oh.** Encloses resolutions from anti-slavery meeting held at the home of Joshua R. Giddings. 22 September 1847 [1848]. p.151, c2.

1057 J. H. A. *to* **THE EDITOR OF THE** *LIBERATOR* **[W. L. GARRISON]. n.d. n.p.** Comments on Liberia and the CS. 22 September 1847 [1848]. p.151, c3.

1058 n.n. *to* **THE EDITOR OF THE** *BOSTON INVESTIGATOR*. **n.d. n.p.** Feels that politics and philosophy hinder the application of science. 22 September 1847 [1848]. p.152, c2.

1059 O. C. W. *to* **MR. BOWE. [from the** *Herkimer Freeman***] 12 August 1848. Fairfield.** Supports women's rights. 22 September 1847 [1848]. p.152, c2.

1060 H. C. WRIGHT *to* **ANDREW PATON. 22 August 1848. Columbiana, Oh.** Discusses whether the Bible is a self-evident falsehood or self-evident truth. 29 September 1847 [1848]. p.153, c2.

1061 GERRIT SMITH *to* **THE EDITOR OF THE** *MODEL WORKER*. **26 August 1848. Peterboro'.** Corrects an error in the paper which quoted him in support of Van Buren. 29 September 1847 [1848]. p.153, c5.

1062 Z. TAYLOR *to* **COL. A. M. MITCHELL. 14 July 1848. Baton Rouge, La.** Asserts that he has no land on the Rio Grande and did not send $10,000 to the District of Columbia to buy slaves. 29 September 1847 [1848]. p.154, c2.

1063 E. S. G. *to* **THE EDITOR OF THE** *CHRISTIAN REGISTER.* **5 September 1848. Boston.** Requests that a portion of the report of the Newcastle and North of England Unitarian Christian Tract and Missionary Society be printed. 29 September 1847 [1848]. p.155, c1.

1064 GEORGE HARRIS *to* **n.n. 17 August 1847. Newcastle-on-Tyne.** Expresses optimism at America's reception of resolutions passed by Newcastle and North of England Unitarian Christian Tract and Missionary Society. 29 September 1847 [1848]. p.155, c2.

1065 W. P. *to* **THE EDITOR OF THE** *CHRISTIAN REGISTER.* **29 August 1848. Raleigh, N. C.** Fails to understand why Paul did not denounce slavery. 29 September 1847 [1848]. p.155, c2.

1066 H. C. WRIGHT *to* **EDMUND [QUINCY]. 9 September 1848. New Lyme, Oh.** Supports J. R. Giddings, who he feels serves his constituents. 6 October 1848. p.157, c3.

1067 FREDERICK DOUGLASS *to* **H. G. WARNER. n.d. n.p.** Asserts that the Seward Seminary rejected his daughter because of Warner's objection to her color; lambasts Warner. 6 October 1848. p.157, c5.

1068 EDWARD SEARCH *to* **n.n. 27 July 1848. London.** Denies rumor of Irish insurrection. 6 October 1848. p.159, c1.

1069 LUCRETIA MOTT *to* **EDMUND QUINCY. 24 August 1848. Philadelphia.** Reports on her summer travels with the Indians of the Seneca Nation at Cattaraugus. 6 October 1848. p.159, c2.

1070 H. H. BRIGHAM *to* **FRIEND QUINCY. 23 September 1848. South Abington.** Regrets that some abolitionists have begun voting again. 6 October 1848. p.159, c2.

1071 ELKANAH NICKERSON *to* **FRIEND QUINCY. 20 September 1848. Harwich.** Presents his views of the Harwich mob incident, accusing abolitionists of incendiary language. 6 October 1848. p.160, c2.

1072 THOS. H. BENTON *to* **THE PEOPLE OF CALIFORNIA. 27 August 1848. Washington City.** Evaluates a state convention as the means of establishing a state government. 6 October 1848. p.160, c3.

1073 IRENAEUS *to* **n.n. [extract from the** *New York Observer***] Boston.** A pro-slavery man advocates disunion. 13 October 1848. p.161, c1.

1074 S. RHODES *to* **THE EDITOR OF THE** *BOSTON INVESTIGATOR.* **9 July 1848. Keosauqua, Ia.** Cancels his subscription to the paper because of its views against the Mexican War and slavery. 13 October 1848. p.161, c1.

1075 HENRY C. WRIGHT *to* **JAMES HAUGHTON. 31 August 1848. Ravenna, Oh.** Discusses proceedings of a Whig convention to nominate county officers and representatives to the state legislature. 13 October 1848. p.161, c2.

1076 D. L. C. *to* **GARRISON. n.d. Northampton.** Describes the military system in France. 13 October 1848. p.161, c3.

1077 EDWARD SEARCH *to* **GARRISON. August 1848. London.** Supports the Connecticut law abolishing slavery; opposes Chartists in England. 13 October 1848. p.163, c2.

1078 JOHN C. CALHOUN *to* **SIR. 9 September 1848. Fort Hill.** Sees no hope of "arresting" abolition through the presidential election. 20 October 1848. p.165, c3.

1079 PHINEAS BLINDSIGHT *to* **ALEXANDER CAMPBELL. 27 July 1848. Tarrytown.** Describes Tarrytown's handling of an escaped slave who had been baptized, explaining religious motives for their conduct. 20 October 1848. p.165, c5.

1080 PRIOR FOSTER *to* **THE EDITOR OF THE** *LIBERATOR*. **10 October 1848. Boston.** Protests charges of fraud against him; submits character references. 20 October 1868. p.166, c4.

1081 E. PRICE *to* **E. QUINCY. 10 January 1848. St. Louis.** The former master of Wm. W. Brown claims that much of what Brown wrote in his *Narrative* is untrue. 20 October 1848. p.166, c5.

1082 WM. W. BROWN *to* **EDMUND QUINCY. October 1848. Boston.** Protests E. Price's letter which claimed that much of his book was false. 20 October 1848. p.166, c5.

1083 EDWARD SEARCH *to* **GARRISON. n.d. n.p.** Foresees a general war in Europe. 20 October 1848. p.167, c2.

1084 SILVANUS JAGGAR *to* **FRIEND QUINCY. 8 October 1848. Centreville.** Attacks E. Nickerson for his defense of the Harwich mob. 20 October 1848. p.168, c2.

1085 H. *to* **MR. EDITOR. n.d. n.p.** Notes the prevalence of freemasonry in the West. 20 October 1848. p.168, c2.

1086 E. P. *to* **THE EDITOR OF THE** *TRIBUNE*. **19 July 1848. Locust Dale, Va.** Discusses the relation of the Bible to slavery. 27 October 1848. p.169, c2.

1087 HIRAM WILSON *to* **EDMUND QUINCY. 29 September 1848. Dawn Mills, Canada West.** Describes progress by blacks in Canada. 27 October 1848. p.169, c3.

1088 A. BROOKE *to* **MR. QUINCY. 12 October 1848. Oakland, Oh.** Believes that a lack of understanding of moral power is the reason for the unenthusiastic response of Ohio to abolitionism. 27 October 1848. p.170, c4.

1089 ALFRED GIBBS CAMPBELL *to* **PUBLISHERS OF THE** *LIBERATOR*. **15 October 1848. Trenton, N. J.** Complains of the difficulty of selling subscriptions to the *Liberator*, for which he blames criticisms from ministers. 27 October 1848. p.171, c1.

1090 Z. TAYLOR *to* **HEADQUARTERS, ARMY OF THE SOUTH. 28 July 1839. Fort Brooke.** Asks for bloodhounds to help track down Indians. 27 October 1848. p.171, c3.

1091 n.n. *to* **GENERAL R. JONES. n.d. n.p.** Encloses a petition from citizens to prevent the use of bloodhounds against Indians. 27 October 1848. p.171, c3.

1092 CURTIUS *to* **THE EDITOR OF THE** *PETERSBURG INTELLIGENCER*. **20 July 1848. Petersburg.** Fears that the object of the Free-Soil Party is to annihilate the South. 3 November 1848. p.173, c1.

1093 EDWARD SEARCH *to* **GARRISON. 25 August 1848. London.** Feels that Ireland is controlled by "landocracy," church, and priests; holds out little hope for freedom. 3 November 1848. p.173, c4.

1094 ALVAN WARD *to* **FRIEND. 21 October 1848. Ashburnham.** Denounces the Free-Soil Party; believes that no practicing Christian should vote. 3 November 1848. p.173, c5.

1095 LEWIS TAPPAN *to* **MARIA WARING. 14 May 1847. New York.** Explains the transfer of the editorship of the *Emancipator.* 3 November 1848. p.174, c3.

1096 PARKER PILLSBURY *to* **FRIEND GARRISON. 27 October 1848. Boston.** Feels encouraged by anti-slavery meetings in Bangor. 3 November 1848. p.175, c4.

1097 DAVID RUGGLES *to* **MR. EDITOR. [from the** *Springfield Republican***] 23 October 1848. Northampton, Ma.** Issues a warning about the devious character of William Wilcox. 3 November 1848. p.175, c6.

1098 HENRY C. WRIGHT *to* **ANDREW PATON. 15 October 1848. Richfield, Oh.** Describes the convention called by the Ohio Peace Society; relates his discussion with a Baptist minister. 10 November 1848. p.177, c2.

1099 EDWARD SEARCH *to* **W. L. GARRISON. 12 October 1848. London.** Believes that the conviction of the Chartists will not stop Chartism. 10 November 1848. p.178, c6.

1100 EDWARD WEST *to* **WILLIAM LLOYD GARRISON. 14 October 1848. Warrington, England.** Sends a copy of an article he wrote to Douglass. 10 November 1848. p.179, c1.

1101 EDWARD WEST *to* **WILLIAM LLOYD GARRISON. 14 October 1848. Warrington, England.** Contends that slavery wars against the interests of the free laboring class by lowering the wages of labor. 10 November 1848. p.179, c1.

1102 W. A. A. *to* **READERS OF** *LIBERATOR.* **24 October 1848. West Newton, Ma.** Wonders "who would vote for Jesus Christ?" 10 November 1848. p.179, c1.

1103 MILO A. TOWNSEND *to* **GARRISON. 24 October 1848. New Brighton, Pa.** Contends that war is always sinful. 10 November 1848. p.179, c2.

1104 EDWARD MORRIS *to* **MR. EDITOR. 19 October 1848. North Dennis, Ma.** Charges that P. Pillsbury was abusive at the Harwich convention. 10 November 1848. p.179, c3.

1105 D. B. M. *to* **MR. EDITOR. 29 October 1848. Malden.** Feels encouraged by progress of a new anti-slavery group. 10 November 1848. p.179, c3.

1106 W. Z. D. *to* **THE EDITOR OF THE** *PHILADELPHIA DAILY REPUBLIC.* **n.d. n.p.** Applauds the temperate behavior of colored persons of Philadelphia. 10 November 1848. p.180, c2.

1107 HENRY C. WRIGHT *to* **ANDREW PATON. 20 October 1848. Steamer** *Caroline,* **Ohio River.** Asks whether God is unjust and unchangeable, or whether Old Testament writers were wrong. 17 November 1848. p.181, c2.

1108 W. L. G. *to* **FRIEND. n.d. n.p.** Conveys his thoughts of Jesus to an invalid undergoing the water cure. 17 November 1848. p.182, c6.

1109 EDWARD SEARCH *to* **THE EDITOR OF THE** *LIBERATOR.* **19 October 1848. London.** Rejoices that abolition is a major issue in the presidential election. 17 November 1848. p.183, c1.

1110 J. C. *to* **MR. GARRISON. 12 November 1848. South Hingham.** Defends P. Pillsbury as an opponent of "spiritual tyranny." 17 November 1848. p.183, c2.

1111 J. J. FLOURNOY *to* **FREDERICK DOUGLASS. n.d. Farm nigh Athens, Ga.** Believes that colored persons should either be sent to Liberia or be held slaves in perpetuity. 24 November 1848. p.185, c1.

1112 H. C. WRIGHT *to* **ANDREW PATON. 22 October 1848. Steamer** *Dover***, Ohio River.** Believes that God is just and unchangeable. 24 November 1848. p.185, c2.

1113 SAMUEL MAY, JR. *to* **MR. GARRISON. n.d. n.p.** Reports on anti-slavery conventions. 24 November 1848. p.186, c6.

1114 EDWARD SEARCH *to* **GARRISON. 6 October 1848. London.** Recommends the water cure. 24 November 1848. p.187, c1.

1115 JOSHUA T. EVERETT *to* **FRIEND GARRISON. 2 November 1848. Everettville.** Makes suggestions concerning the National Anti-Slavery Bazaar. 24 November 1848. p.187, c1.

1116 PARKER PILLSBURY *to* **FRIEND GARRISON. n.d. n.p.** Recounts mob violence at a Harwich meeting. 24 November 1848. p.187, c2.

1117 ELKANAH NICKERSON *to* **FRIEND GARRISON. 12 November 1848. Harwich.** Criticizes the anti-slavery press. 24 November 1848. p.188, c2.

1118 SEWARD MITCHELL *to* **FRIEND GARRISON. 9 November 1848. Boston.** Declares that the Bible is "worthless." 24 November 1848. p.188, c2.

1119 CHARLES HUDSON *to* **CHARLES ALLEN. 28 May 1848. Washington.** Advises a delegate to the Philadelphia convention to support McLean for president. 1 December 1848. p.189, c2.

1120 HENRY C. WRIGHT *to* **ANDREW PATON. n.d. Fairmount, Oh.** Believes that the Bible has been construed to conform to public opinion. 1 December 1848. p.191, c1.

1121 W. M. F. *to* **FRIEND GARRISON. n.d. n.p.** Calls for a Bible convention in Boston. 1 December 1848. p.191, c4.

1122 S. MARSHALL *to* **FRIEND GARRISON. 18 November 1848. Painesville, Oh.** Responds to a charge of fraud. 1 December 1848. p.191, c4.

1123 HENRY GREW *to* **HENRY WRIGHT. n.d. n.p.** Believes that God is not 'unjust and changeable' if he commands men to put others to death. 1 December 1848. p.192, c2.

1124 FITCH WINCHESTER *to* **HENRY C. WRIGHT. 14 November 1848. Southboro'.** Voices criticisms of Wright's faith. 1 December 1848. p.192, c3.

1125 EDWARD MORRIS *to* **MR. EDITOR [W. L. GARRISON]. n.d. n.p.** Criticizes Parker Pillsbury as "neither irreproachable or immaculate." 1 December 1848. p.192, c3.

1126 J. J. FLOURNOY *to* **W. L. GARRISON. November 1848. Nigh Athens, Ga.** Affirms much of what travellers in the South report is false. 8 December 1848. p.193, c1.

1127 H. *to* **THE** *JOURNAL OF COMMERCE***. 20 November 1848. Western Reserve, Oh.** Describes the political situation in Ohio. 8 December 1848. p.193, c1.

1128 JAMES HAUGHTON *to* **H. C. WRIGHT. 3 November 1848. Dublin.** Comments on Irish farmers. 8 December 1848. p.193, c2.

1129 REV. LYMAN MAYNARD *to* **MR. EDITOR. 29 November 1848. Dennis.** Relates Pillsbury's testimony regarding a mob incident. 8 December 1848. p.193, c4.

1130 D. S. GRANDIN *to* **B. F. W. PULTENEY. 28 November 1848. Boston.** Believes that the "inalienable rights" of man make slavery essentially wrong. 8 December 1848. p.193, c5.

1131 W. G. C. *to* **MR. EDITOR. [from the** *Boston Daily Republican***] 30 November 1848. Newburyport.** Praises a sermon by Rev. Mr. Higgins on the theme, "man cannot live by bread alone." 8 December 1848. p.194, c1.

1132 F. L. CLAIBORNE *to* **A. G. BROWN, GOVERNOR OF MISSISSIPPI. 15 November 1848. Natchez.** Ascertains that Taylor's opinion is pro-slavery. 8 December 1848. p.194, c1.

1133 HENRY C. WRIGHT *to* **ANDREW PATON. 8 November 1848. Randolph, Oh.** Gives account of a debate and resolution that war is opposed to God, man, and Christianity. 8 December 1848. p.195, c1.

1134 JAMES HAUGHTON *to* **THE EDITOR OF THE** *VINDICATOR***. 27 October 1848. Dublin.** Favors education rather than coercion in order to implement teetotalism. 8 December 1848. p.196, c2.

1135 E. Y. *to* **PRESIDENT BLANCHARD. [from the** *New York Observer***] n.d. n.p.** Criticizes Dr. Blanchard's speech about slavery. 15 December 1848. p.197, c1.

1136 A. BROOKE *to* **FRIEND GARRISON. 27 November 1848. Oakland, Oh.** Congratulates Garrison on his good health; encloses letter from Henry C. Wright. 15 December 1848. p.197, c2.

1137 H. C. WRIGHT *to* **ABRAHAM BROOKE. 19 November 1848. Geneva, Oh.** Refuses to participate in voting because he feels that this endorses the right of the government to kill. 15 December 1848. p.197, c2.

1138 D. RUGGLES *to* **FRIEND GARRISON. 5 December 1848. Northampton Water Cure.** Concurs with allegation of fraud against Seth Marshal. 15 December 1848. p.197, c4.

1139 ONE OF THE COMMITTEE OF THE NATIONAL ANTI-SLAVERY BAZAAR *to* **MR. GARRISON. n.d. n.p.** Asks Garrison to publish a few words concerning the fair. 15 December 1848. p.198, c1.

1140 J. B. ESTLIN *to* **THE EDITOR OF THE** *LONDON INQUIRER***. 6 November 1848. Bristol.** Suspects that James Martineau's position is pro-slavery. 15 December 1848. p.198, c4.

1141 J. W. WALKER *to* **BROTHER GARRISON. 29 November 1848. Crawford County, Pa.** Congratulates Garrison on his good health. 15 December 1848. p.197, c5.

1142 EDWARD SEARCH *to* **THE EDITOR OF THE** *LIBERATOR* **[W. L. GARRISON]. November 1848. London.** Reports on progress of the anti-slavery movement; expects that British Guiana will soon throw off her yoke. 15 December 1848. p.199, c1.

1143 D. S. GRANDIN *to* **B. F. PULTENEY. 7 December 1848. Boston.** Fears that granting statehood to Texas and others will hasten the progress of slavery. 15 December 1848. p.199, c2.

1144 WILLIAM GOODELL *to* **HENRY C. WRIGHT. 7 December 1848. Honeoye, N. Y.** Discounts the New Testament as an authentic record of Christianity. 22 December 1848. p.201, c2.

1145 HENRY GREW *to* **HENRY C. WRIGHT. n.d. n.p.** Accuses Wright of fallibility and poor knowledge of the Bible. 22 December 1848. p.201, c4.

1146 HENRY C. WRIGHT *to* **THE READERS OF THE** *BUGLE.* **12 November 1848. Marlboro'.** Praises a children's book on slavery. 22 December 1848. p.201, c5.

1147 AN INFIDEL *to* **THE EDITOR OF THE** *BOSTON INVESTIGATOR.* **n.d. n.p.** Criticizes epithets used by abolitionists, particularly the term "infidel." p.201, c5.

1148 PRIOR FOSTER *to* **THE EDITOR [W. L. GARRISON]. 18 December 1848. Boston.** Replies to the charge that he encouraged women to change their names and go West with him. 22 December 1848. p.203, c1.

1149 J. C. HATHAWAY *to* **PRIOR FOSTER. 25 October 1848. Farmington.** Praises Foster's Woodstock Institute. 22 December 1848. p.203, c1.

1150 WM. P. RUSSELL *to* **PRIOR FOSTER. 8 November 1848. Richmond.** Relates his favorable experience with the Woodstock Institute. 22 December 1848. p.203, c1.

1151 J. C. BRIGHAM *to* **WHOM IT MAY CONCERN. 20 June 1848. Bible House, N. Y.** Provides a character reference for Prior Foster. 22 December 1848. p.203, c2.

1152 ISAAC C. KENYON *to* **FRIEND GARRISON. 14 December 1848. Richmond.** Voices criticism of Quakers. 22 December 1848. p.203, c2.

1153 MARY ANN KENYON *to* **PROVIDENCE MONTHLY MEETING OF FRIENDS. December 1848. Brooklyn.** Renounces her membership in the Society of Friends. 22 December 1848. p.203, c2.

1154 S. S. FOSTER *to* **THE GENERAL AGENT. [extract] 15 December 1848. Springfield.** Describes anti-slavery meetings. 22 December 1848. p.203, c2.

1155 JOHN BARKER *to* **n.n. 14 October 1848. n.p.** Offers a cure for cholera. 22 December 1848. p.204, c4.

1156 ROGER WILLIAMS, WASHINGTON CORRESPONDENT OF THE *CHRISTIAN WATCHMAN* **AND** *REFLECTOR to* **n.n. n.d. n.p.** Describes and condemns slavery in the District of Columbia. 29 December 1848. p.205, c3.

1157 J. H. *to* **THE EDITOR OF THE** *NONCONFORMIST.* **18 November 1848. Hamilton Place, King's Cross.** Expresses his disgust for slavery in America. 29 December 1848. p.205, c6.

1158 D. S. GRANDIN *to* **B. F. W. PULTENEY. 17 December 1848. Boston.** Attacks the Constitution and the Union for upholding slavery. 29 December 1848. p.206, c6.

1159 H. H. BRIGHAM *to* **FRIEND GARRISON. 9 December 1848. South Abington.** Supports a movement to publish the names of clergymen who voted for Taylor. 29 December 1848. p.207, c2.

1160 HENRY C. WRIGHT *to* **JAMES HAUGHTON. 14 December 1848. Saloon of Steamer** *Isaac Newton,* **Hudson River.** Observes that Taylor is well suited to be president of a pro-war, pro-slavery nation. 29 December 1848. p.208, c2.

1161 WILLIAM GOODELL *to* **WILLIAM LLOYD GARRISON. n.d. n.p.** Deems it most important to maintain old truths while searching for new ones. 29 December 1848. p.208, c3.

1162 A NORTHERN DEMOCRAT *to* **THE EDITOR OF THE** *WASHINGTON UNION.* **n.d. n.p.** Condemns Southern Whigs as the worst enemies of the South. 5 January 1849. p.1, c2.

1163 A MAN *to* **MR. EDITOR. n.d. n.p.** Doubts whether slavery in ancient times was worse than in the present. 5 January 1849. p.3, c3.

1164 HENRY WATSON *to* **THE EDITOR [W. L. GARRISON]. 1 January 1849. Boston.** Expresses thanks for pecuniary assistance. 5 January 1849. p.3, c3.

1165 W. M. F. *to* **FRIEND GARRISON. n.d. n.p.** Rejoices at the discussions of controversial subjects such as the Bible in the *Liberator*. 5 January 1849. p.4, c3.

1166 n.n. *to* **THE EDITORS OF THE** *PENNSYLVANIAN.* **n.d. n.p.** Opposes the proposition to abolish slavery in the District of Columbia. 12 January 1849. p.5, c2.

1167 COL. SCHOULER *to* **THE** *BOSTON ATLAS.* **n.d. Washington.** The editor of the *Atlas* sees selfishness motivating nine-tenths of anti- and pro-slavery movements. 12 January 1849. p.5, c2.

1168 D. S. GRANDIN *to* **B. F. W. 31 December 1848. Boston.** Sees little point in preserving the Union. 12 January 1849. p.7, c1.

1169 PARKER PILLSBURY *to* **FRIEND GARRISON. 8 January 1849. Boston.** Regrets abolitionist support of the Free-Soil Party. 12 January 1849. p.7, c2.

1170 HENRY C. WRIGHT *to* **HENRY GREW. 7 January 1849. Boston.** Argues that God's law is opposed to war and capital punishment. 12 January 1849. p.7, c3.

1171 SAMUEL MAY, JR. *to* **GARRISON. n.d. n.p.** Adds names of Garrison and John Price to the list of speakers at the Anti-Slavery Bazaar. 12 January 1849. p.7, c4.

1172 WILLIAM W. BROWN *to* **GARRISON. 4 January 1849. Pineville, Pa.** Rejoices in the heroic escape of slaves William and Ellen Craft. 12 January 1849. p.7, c4.

1173 ISAAC I. BIGELOW *to* **ANDREW PATON. 12 December 1848. Boston, Oh.** Describes his religious education which taught him that God is just and unchangeable and that man is a progressive moral being. 12 January 1849. p.8, c2.

1174 JUNIUS *to* **THE EDITOR OF THE** *CENTREVILLE* **(IN.)** *SENTINEL.* **n.d. n.p.** Discusses the right of self-defense. 12 January 1849. p.8, c4.

1175 J. J. FLOURNOY *to* **J. DICK AND FRED DOUGLASS. December, 1848. Farm nigh Athens, Ga.** Argues that blacks are inferior; advocates sending them to Liberia. 19 January 1849. p.9, c1.

1176 M. VAN BUREN *to* **JAMES CONSTADT HOLMES. 30 December 1848. Lindenwald.** Opposes extension of slavery on moral grounds; declines invitation to a soiree of the Northern Light Association. 19 January 1849. p.9, c5.

1177 JACOB S. HOWES *to* **MR. GARRISON. 8 January 1849. North Dennis.** Tells of a minister who attacked Stephen and Abby Foster. 19 January 1849. p.10, c6.

1178 H. C. WRIGHT *to* **WILLIAM GOODELL. 10 January 1849. Boston.** Asks whether God is unjust or man fallible. 19 January 1849. p.12, c2.

1179 C. STEARNS *to* **MR. GARRISON. December 1848. Boston.** Favors holding a Bible convention. 19 January 1849. p.12, c3.

1180 J. C. *to* **THE EDITOR [W. L. GARRISON]. n.d. n.p.** Forwards copy of a decree of 1705 ordering a book-burning in Boston. 19 January 1849. p.12, c3.

1181 WILLIAM SLADE *to* **EDWARD A. STANBURY. 9 December 1848. Middlebury.** Discusses John Quincy Adams' view of slavery. 26 January 1849. p.13, c5.

1182 JOHN QUINCY ADAMS *to* **WILLIAM SLADE. August 1847. Quincy, Ma.** Views anti-slavery cause as originating with Hamilcar, a Carthaginian, and Cato, a Roman. 26 January 1849. p.13, c5.

1183 C. STEARNS *to* **FRIEND GARRISON. 12 January 1849. Boston.** Favors the Free-Soil Party; fails to understand abolitionists' objections to it. 26 January 1849. p.15, c1.

1184 J. M. ALDRICH *to* **FRIEND GARRISON. n.d. n.p.** Reports on a convention in Fall River. 26 January 1849. p.15, c3.

1185 A SUBSCRIBER *to* **FRIEND GARRISON. 8 January 1849. Waltham.** Reports on the vote of the Waltham clergy in the presidential election. 26 January 1849. p.15, c3.

1186 HENRY C. WRIGHT *to* **WILLIAM GOODELL. 17 January 1849. Boston.** Argues that certain events recorded in the Old Testament portray God as unjust. 26 January 1849. p.16, c2.

1187 CLARKSON *to* **FRIEND ATKINSON. [from the** *Burlington* **(N. J.)** *Gazette*]. **30 December 1848. Philadelphia.** Objects to incendiary language used by the *Anti-Slavery Standard* in describing the escape of an eighteen-year-old. 2 February 1849. p.17, c1.

1188 ALFRED G. CAMPBELL *to* **FRIEND GARRISON. 7 January 1849. Trenton, N. J.** Decries the hypocrisy of anti-war voters who support Taylor. 2 February 1849. p.19, c5.

1189 HENRY GREW *to* **HENRY C. WRIGHT. n.d. n.p.** Argues that man's interpretation of the Bible is erroneous. 2 February 1849. p.20, c2.

1190 ANGELIQUE LE PETIT MARTIN *to* **MR. GARRISON. 15 January 1849. Braceville, Oh.** Urges reformers to work for women's rights. 2 February 1849. p.20, c3.

1191 PEGGY COLTHURST *to* **FRIENDS. 15 December 1848. Cork, Ireland.** The daughter of a West Indies official supports the abolition of slavery. 9 February 1849. p.23, c2.

1192 HENRY C. WRIGHT *to* **JAMES HAUGHTON. 2 February 1849. Boston.** Frowns upon "Gold Fever" in California. 9 February 1849. p.23, c2.

1193 T. BICKNELL *to* **MR. GARRISON. 5 February 1849. Kingston.** Comments on speeches by William and Ellen Craft at a meeting. 9 February 1849. p.23, c3.

1194 LEWIS FORD *to* **FRIEND GARRISON. 4 February 1849. Abington.** Reports on speeches by William and Ellen Craft at an AS meeting. 9 February 1849. p.23, c3.

1195 HENRY C. WRIGHT *to* **WILLIAM GOODELL. 1 February 1849. Boston.** Finds biblical punishment for crimes unjust. 9 February 1849. p.24, c1.

1196 ANGELIQUE LE PETIT MARTIN *to* **THE** *LIBERATOR*. **17 January 1849. Braceville, Oh.** Believes that America will not be free until it secures the rights of women. 9 February 1849. p.24, c3.

1197 M. R. HULL *to* **JOHNSTON. 11 January 1849. Germantown, Ky.** Attacks "evil religious bandits" who deal in slavery. 16 February 1849. p.26, c2.

1198 WENDELL PHILLIPS *to* **TO THE FRIENDS OF THE** *LIBERATOR*. **10 February 1849. Boston.** Promotes subscriptions to help meet the cost of publishing. 16 February 1849. p.26, c5.

1199 ANDREW ROBESON *to* **MR. GARRISON. n.d. New Bedford.** Reports on speeches by W. W. Brown and William and Ellen Craft at an anti-slavery meeting. 16 February 1849. p.27, c1.

1200 MARTIN STOWELL *to* **FRIEND GARRISON. 30 January 1849. Warren.** Feels proud that his wife "excommunicated" the Congregational church because its members failed to denounce slavery. 16 February 1849. p.27, c1.

1201 EDWARD WEST *to* **J. J. FLOURNOY. 25 December 1848. Warrington, Lancashire.** Disapproves of Flournoy's denunciation of Douglass. 16 February 1849. p.27, c2.

1202 EDWARD RUSHTON *to* **THOMAS PAINE. [from the** *Liberty Bell***] n.d. n.p.** Urges Paine to fight for the liberation of slaves. 23 February 1849. p.29, c2.

1203 A SUBSCRIBER *to* **FRIEND GARRISON. 15 February 1849. Waltham.** Continues discussion of the clerical vote. 23 February 1849. p.31, c1.

1204 FRANCIS JACKSON *to* **THE SECRETARY OF THE MASSACHUSETTS CHARITABLE MECHANIC ASSOCIATION. 15 December 1848. Boston.** Criticizes the association for professing a policy of temperance while investing in rum taverns. 23 February 1849. p.31, c2.

1205 JONATHAN WALKER *to* **FRIEND GARRISON. 12 February 1849. Plymouth.** Defends the rights of women. 23 February 1849. p.32, c2.

1206 J. P. *to* **W. L. GARRISON. 29 January 1849. Hanson.** Discusses conflict between carnal and spiritual aspects of man. 23 February 1849. p.32, c2.

1207 HENRY C. WRIGHT *to* **GARRISON. 14 February 1849. Boston.** Criticizes Sabbatarians. 23 February 1849. p.32, c3.

1208 HARRIET MARTINEAU *to* **MRS. CHAPMAN. [from the** *Liberty Bell***]. 9 July 1848. London.** Describes slavery in Egypt. 2 March 1849. p.33, c6.

1209 WENDELL PHILLIPS *to* **FRIENDS. 10 February 1849. Boston.** Urges friends to subscribe to the *Liberator*. 2 March 1849. p.35, c2.

1210 D. RUGGLES *to* **FRIEND GARRISON. 20 February 1849. Northampton Water Cure.** Reports subscriptions to the *Liberator*. 2 March 1849. p.35, c2.

1211 J. CUSHING *to* **MR. EDITOR. 20 February 1849. South Hingham.** Subscribes to the *Liberator*. 2 March 1849. p.35, c2.

1212 W. B. *to* **n.n. 19 February 1849. New Ipswich.** Reports a new subscription to the *Liberator*. 2 March 1849. p.35, c2.

1213 VIATOR *to* **THE EDITOR. 20 February 1849. Westboro'.** Reports that the Crafts spoke at an anti-slavery meeting. 2 March 1849. p.35, c3.

1214 LYMAN ALLEN *to* **FRIEND GARRISON. 16 February 1849. Northboro'.** Praises William and Ellen Craft for their success at anti-slavery meetings. 2 March 1849. p.35, c3.

1215 M. T. JOHNSON *to* **FRIEND GARRISON. 11 February 1849. Short Creek.** Opposes forced observance of the Sabbath. 2 March 1849. p.36, c2.

1216 E. W. TWING *to* **n.n. 31 January 1849. Springfield.** Criticizes the *Phrenological Journal* for its stand regarding criticism and reform. 2 March 1849. p.36, c2.

1217 RUFUS ANDERSON, SELAH B. TREAT, AND SWAN L. POMROY, SECRETARIES OF AMERICAN BOARD OF COMMISSIONERS FOR FOREIGN MISSIONS *to* **n.n. 20 February 1849. Missionary House, Boston.** Clarify question on the Choctaw mission and Mr. Treat's letter. 9 March 1849. p.37, c3.

1218 R. E. P. *to* **GEN. ZACHARY TAYLOR. 12 February 1849. Queen City of the West.** Criticizes Taylor's conduct in the Mexican War. 9 March 1849. p.37, c6.

1219 WILLIAM HINCKS *to* **THE EDITOR OF THE** *LONDON INQUIRER.* **n.d. n.p.** Sympathizes with Garrison on moral issues, but cannot endorse his abolitionist politics. 9 March 1849. p.38, c1.

1220 PARKER PILLSBURY *to* **FRIEND GARRISON. n.d. n.p.** Reports on a meeting in Springfield. 9 March 1849. p.39, c2.

1221 J. N. BUFFUM *to* **FRIEND GARRISON. n.d. n.p.** Feels encouraged by the Essex County AS meeting. 9 March 1849. p.39, c3.

1222 JOSEPH MERRILL *to* **BRO. GARRISON. 22 February 1849. Danvers (New Mills).** Gives account of a series of meetings held by Stephen and Abby K. Foster. 9 March 1849. p.39, c4.

1223 JOHN M. SPEAR *to* **FRIEND GARRISON. n.d. Boston.** Urges that petitions for abolition of capital punishment be sent to the legislature soon. 9 March 1849. p.39, c5.

1224 WILLIAM GOODELL *to* **HENRY C. WRIGHT. n.d. n.p.** Asks whether Henry Wright thinks himself wiser than Jesus of Nazareth. 9 March 1849. p.40, c2.

1225 AN AMERICAN CITIZEN *to* **THE EDITOR OF THE** *LONDON INQUIRER.* **n.d. n.p.** Attacks Africans for the slave trade; believes that slavery in America is not as unjust as in other countries. 16 March 1849. p.41, c1.

1226 ZETA *to* **THE EDITOR OF THE** *NEW YORK EVANGELIST.* **n.d. n.p.** Explains the presence of 215,000 free blacks in the South. 16 March 1849. p.41, c3.

1227 JAMES HAUGHTON *to* **THE EDITOR OF THE** *LONDON INQUIRER.* **8 February 1849. Dublin.** Refutes criticism of abolitionists. 16 March 1849. p.42, c2.

1228 HENRY CLAY *to* **RICHARD PINDELL. 17 February 1849. New Orleans.** Forsees and favors the gradual end of slavery in Kentucky. 16 March 1849. p.42, c3.

1229 WM. LLOYD GARRISON *to* **HENRY CLAY. n.d. n.p.** Criticizes Clay's pro-slavery attitude. 16 March 1849. p.42, c5.

1230 WILLIAM GOODELL *to* **HENRY C. WRIGHT. n.d. n.p.** Asks whether Henry Wright recognizes a creator and governor of man. 16 March 1849. p.44, c2.

1231 HENRY C. WRIGHT *to* **HENRY GREW. 25 February 1849. Boston.** Asks whether Jehu was justified in murdering seventy of Ahab's children. 16 March 1849. p.44, c3.

1232 CONCILIATOR *to* **THE EDITOR OF THE** *N. H. CONGREGATIONAL JOURNAL.* **20 February 1849. Georgia.** Supports continued religious instruction of slaves. 23 March 1849. p.45, c1.

1233 JOSHUA T. EVERETT *to* **FRIEND GARRISON. 12 March 1849. Everettville, Princeton.** Sees no guarantee of freedom for slaves; criticizes plan of Henry Clay. 23 March 1849. p.46, c5.

1234 HENRY C. WRIGHT *to* **W. L. GARRISON. 15 August 1847. Rochane Cottage, Roseneath.** Discusses his forthcoming autobiography. 23 March 1849. p.47, c2.

1235 PARKER PILLSBURY *to* **FRIEND GARRISON. 19 March 1849. Worcester.** Forwards resolutions from an anti-slavery convention at Webster. 23 March 1849. p.47, c3.

1236 PARKER PILLSBURY *to* **FRIEND GARRISON. n.d. n.p.** Asserts that presidents of county ASS must choose Sunday AS meetings over Sunday worship. 23 March 1849. p.47, c3.

1237 HENRY C. WRIGHT *to* **GARRISON. 15 March 1849. Boston.** Provides a character sketch of John Smith. 23 March 1849. p.48, c2.

1238 JOHN SMITH *to* **HENRY C. WRIGHT. 25 December 1848. Trumbull County, Oh.** Believes that God is a just and moral governor. 23 March 1849. p.48, c2.

1239 WILLIAM HINCKS *to* **THE EDITOR OF THE** *LONDON INQUIRER.* **n.d. n.p.** Rejects personal denunciation as a means of reform; cites evil of abolition. 30 March 1849. p.51, c2.

1240 H. C. WRIGHT *to* **W. L. GARRISON. 27 March 1849. Boston.** Introduces a letter from Scotland. 20 March 1849. p.52, c5.

1241 n.n. *to* **H. C. WRIGHT. 8 March 1848. Glasgow. [extract].** Reports on the Battle in Punjaub with the Seikhs. 30 March 1849. p.52, c5.

1242 HENRY C. HOWELLS *to* **FRIEND GARRISON. 6 March 1849. Bristol, Kingsdown Parade.** Criticizes vain hopes of countering slavery by establishing religious colonies in Texas; warns emigrants against settling in the South. 30 March 1849. p.52, c6.

1243 H. H. BRIGHAM *to* **MR. GARRISON. 20 March 1849. Abington.** Regrets the prevalence of anti-abolitionist feeling in the town of Abington. 30 March 1849. p.49 [53], c1.

1244 ELKANAH NICKERSON *to* **FRIEND GARRISON. 27 February 1849. Harwich.** Believes there is no greater evil than slavery. 30 March 1849. p.49 [53], c2.

1245 AMOS GILBERT *to* **FRIEND GARRISON. 19 March 1849. Oakland, Oh.** Comments on Valentine Nicholson; suggests tolerance among reformers. 6 April 1849. p.54, c4.

1246 J. T. EVERETT *to* **W. L. GARRISON. 21 March 1849. Everettville, Princeton.** Attacks the *Emancipator and Republican* for its refusal to print Clay's letter. 6 April 1849. p.54, c5.

1247 HENRY C. WRIGHT *to* **HENRY GREW. 1 April 1849. Boston.** Doubts whether crimes can be turned into virtues and duties. 6 April 1849. p.54, c6.

1248 HENRY C. WRIGHT *to* **GARRISON. 31 March 1849. Boston.** Recounts an episode in which a minister was struck down on the Sabbath while preaching Sabbatarianism. 6 April 1849. p.55, c1.

1249 LUCY STONE *to* **GARRISON. 3 April 1849. Boston.** Corrects a misinterpretation of an answer she had given to Mr. Morris. 6 April 1849. p.55, c2.

1250 SEVENTY-SIX *to* **MR. GARRISON. n.d. n.p.** Sarcastically praises the "republicanism" of slavery. 6 April 1849. p.55, c2.

1251 EZEKIEL JONES *to* **HON. DANIEL WEBSTER. 29 January 1849. Baltimore.** Favors strong discipline as an alternative to punishment in the navy. 6 April 1849. p.55, c4.

1252 HENRY GREW *to* **HENRY C. WRIGHT. n.d. n.p.** Trusts in the justness of God; believes religious truth is "unsearchable." 6 April 1849. p.56, c2.

1253 GEORGE STEARNS *to* **WM. LLOYD GARRISON. 1 April 1849. Lowell.** Supports the anti-Sabbath argument. 13 April 1849. p.59, c4.

1254 C. L. WESTON *to* **W. L. G. 28 March 1849. New Ipswich, N. H.** Expects the Sabbath question to be answered by the march of progress. 13 April 1849. p.59, c4.

1255 H. C. WRIGHT *to* **GARRISON. 7 April 1849. Boston.** Claims that Zachary Taylor was elected president because of Sabbatarianism. 13 April 1849. p.60, c2.

1256 SAMUEL N. DIXEY *to* **MESSRS. WM. HAIGH AND CO. 23 March 1849. New York.** Praises Ralston and Philips' invention, the life preserver. 13 April 1849. p.60, c3.

1257 J. A. MERRICK *to* **FRIEND GARRISON. April 1849. Princeton.** Claims that the inaction of the professed friends of reform gives the world occasion to question their sincerity and doubt their motives. 20 April 1849. p.61, c3.

1258 WILLIAM L. BRECKINRIDGE *to* **THE** *LOUISVILLE DEMOCRAT.* **n.d. n.p.** Opposes slavery because it causes a net decrease in the white population. 20 April 1849. p.61, c5.

1259 H. *to* **THE** *SYRACUSE STAR.* **20 March 1849. Alabama.** Describes a slave's environment. 20 April 1849. p.61, c6.

1260 W. TILLINGHAST *to* **THE EDITOR OF THE** *HERKIMER FREEMAN.* **20 April 1849. Devereaux.** Compares the plight of the laboring class favorably to that of the slave. 20 April 1849. p.61, c6.

1261 HENRY GREW *to* **FRIEND GARRISON. n.d. n.p.** Attacks Pillsbury's resolution on the Sabbath question as a "falsehood and absurdity." 20 April 1849. p.62, c5.

1262 N. BARNEY *to* **W. L. GARRISON. 2 April 1849. Nantucket.** Forwards contributions to the *Liberator.* 20 April 1849. p.62, c6.

1263 G. *to* **MR. GARRISON. 7 April 1849. West Cambridge.** Reports on a lecture by Lucy Stone. 20 April 1849. p.63, c1.

1264 J. M. SPEAR *to* **FRIEND GARRISON. n.d. n.p.** Encloses petitions for the abolition of capital punishment. 20 April 1849. p.63, c2.

1265 JOHN SMITH *to* **HENRY C. WRIGHT. 13 January 1849. Mecca, Oh.** Believes that Christianity must be divorced from the violence of Old Testament Judaism. 20 April 1849. p.64, c2.

1266 CHARLES K. WHIPPLE *to* **MUNICIPAL COURT OF THE CITY OF BOSTON. n.d. n.p.** Ask whether a member of the Non-Resistance Society should be a member of a jury. 20 April 1849. p.64, c3.

1267 n.n. *to* **GARRISON. n.d. n.p.** Favors reducing women's taxes since they are denied suffrage. 20 April 1849. p.64, c4.

1268 EDWARD SEARCH *to* **THE** *LIBERATOR.* **5 March 1849. London.** Details news from India. 27 April 1849. p.66, c4.

1269 PARKER PILLSBURY *to* **FRIEND GARRISON. 17 April 1849. Plymouth.** Petitions for the commutation of Washington Goode's sentence. 27 April 1849. p.67, c1.

1270 ONE OF THE AGENTS *to* **FRIEND GARRISON. 19 April 1849. n.p.** Observes that liquor eases one's conscience. 27 April 1849. p.67, c1.

1271 A. H. HARLOW *to* **FRIEND GARRISON. 15 April 1849. Plymouth.** Reports on the Plymouth AS Convention. 27 April 1849. p.67, c1.

1272 JOHN L. LORD *to* **FRIEND GARRISON. 16 April 1849. Newburyport.** Reports on speeches by W. W. Brown and the Crafts at an anti-slavery meeting. 27 April 1849. p.67, c2.

1273 HENRY GREW *to* **HENRY C. WRIGHT. 11 April 1849. Philadelphia.** Believes God is all powerful and good. 27 April 1849. p.68, c2.

1274 E. M. DAVIS *to* **W. L. GARRISON. 3 April 1849. New York.** Encloses donation for the Sabbath convention and a copy of William Logan Fisher's memorial. 27 April 1849. p.68, c3.

1275 J. R. GIDDINGS *to* **MR. GREELEY. 16 March 1849. Jefferson, Oh.** Explains a fray which took place in House of Representatives during which Mr. Meade assaulted him. 27 April 1849. p.68, c5.

1276 SOPHIA E. BONNEY *to* **W. L. G. 28 April 1849. Plympton.** Sends money to the Massachusetts AS. 4 May 1849. p.71, c1.

1277 J. M. SPEAR *to* **FRIEND GARRISON. 1 May 1849. Boston.** Encloses petitions in behalf of Washington Goode. 4 May 1849. p.71, c2.

1278 EDWARD SEARCH *to* **FRIEND GARRISON. 27 March 1847. London.** Acknowledges receipt of the Anti-Sabbath Convention proceedings. 4 May 1849. p.72, c2.

1279 C. L. WESTON *to* **FRIEND GARRISON. 14 April 1849. New Ipswich, N. H.** Urges the abolition of penal laws respecting the Sabbath. 4 May 1849. p.72, c2.

1280 JAMES HAUGHTON *to* **SIR T. F. BUXTON. 15 October 1849. Dublin.** Recognizes the value of using force to end the slave trade; discusses temperance. 4 May 1849. p.72, c4.

1281 T. FOWELL BUXTON *to* **JAMES HAUGHTON. 27 October 1840. Dublin.** Doubts the value of force in ending the slave trade. 4 May 1849. p.72, c4.

1282 JAMES HAUGHTON *to* **THE EDITOR OF THE** *SCOTTISH TEMPERANCE REVIEW*. **n.d. Dublin.** Advocates holding manufacturers and sellers accountable for the damage caused by use of intoxicants. 4 May 1849. p.72, c4.

1283 JAMES HAUGHTON *to* **THE EDITOR OF THE** *LONDON INQUIRER*. **15 March 1849. n.p.** Regrets that the column on American slavery was dropped. 11 May 1849. p.74, c1.

1284 WM. LLOYD GARRISON *to* **FRIEND. 8 May 1849. New York.** Reports on the anniversary meeting of Massachusetts AS. 11 May 1849. p.74, c3.

1285 EDWARD SEARCH *to* **GARRISON. April 1849. London.** Mocks the pope's "spiritual thunder." 11 May 1849. p.75, c1.

1286 F. W. *to* **MR. EDITOR [W. L. GARRISON]. n.d. Roxbury.** Discusses the Crafts and W. W. Brown, who recently addressed a meeting in Roxbury. 11 May 1849. p.75, c1.

1287 PARKER PILLSBURY *to* **FRIEND GARRISON. 6 May 1849. Marlborough.** Denounces Washington Goode's execution. 11 May 1849. p.75, c2.

1288 MARIA WESTON CHAPMAN *to* **MR. GARRISON. 15 April 1849. Paris.** Advocates the rights of women. 18 May 1849. p.77, c2.

1289 JOSEPH A. DUGDALE *to* **W. L. GARRISON. 9 May 1849. Selma, Clark County, Oh.** Writes on behalf of Richard Dillingham, who was jailed for aiding runaway slaves. 18 May 1849. p.79, c6.

1290 E. *to* **THE EDITORS OF THE** *BRITISH FRIEND*. **n.d. n.p.** Criticizes seizure for tithes as a "violation of Christian liberty." 18 May 1849. p.80, c3.

1291 GERRIT SMITH *to* **JOHN COCHRAN, WM. KENNEYES, ISAAC T. HOPPER, GEORGE H. EVANS, AND DANIEL C. EATON. 1 May 1849. Peterboro'.** Announces that he will give away 1,000 parcels of land. 18 May 1849. p.80, c4.

1292 RICHARD MULLINS *to* **THE EDITOR OF THE** *LEXINGTON EXAMINER*. **12 April 1849. Grassy Creek.** Refuses to accept copies of the *Lexington Examiner*. 25 May 1849. p.81, c1.

1293 OLD COLONY *to* **FRIEND GARRISON. 14 May 1849. n.p.** Laments Washington Goode's fate. 25 May 1849. p.81, c3.

1294 JOSEPH HUTTON *to* **THE EDITOR OF THE** *LONDON CHRISTIAN INQUIRER*. **n.d. n.p.** Denounces Henry Clay's pro-slavery letter to Richard Pindell. 25 May 1849. p.81, c5.

1295 REV. DR. HUTTON *to* **SAMUEL MAY, JR. [extract] 30 April 1849. King's Cross.** Criticizes Henry Clay's letter on Kentucky; approves of Frederick Douglass' answer. 25 May 1849. p.81, c5.

1296 A. BROOKE *to* **FRIEND GARRISON. 14 May 1849. Oakland, Oh.** Criticizes disregard for human rights in the United States. 25 May 1849. p.83, c1.

1297 S. MAY, JR. *to* **MR. GARRISON. n.d. n.p.** Encloses an eight-dollar donation from the Marblehead Anti-Slavery Sewing Circle to the Massachusetts AS. 25 May 1849. p.83, c1.

1298 EDWARD SEARCH *to* **THE** *LIBERATOR*. **10 May 1849. London.** Reports on the military activities of the French, Hungarians, and Italians. 1 June 1849. p.87, c1.

1299 JOSEPH BARKER *to* **WM. LLOYD GARRISON. 9 May 1849. Wortley, near Leeds.** Intends to visit the United States. 1 June 1849. p.87, c1.

1300 J. F. SMALLEY *to* **HENRY C. WRIGHT. 15 May 1849. Randolph.** Feels that the Old Testament is too violent and unchristian. 8 June 1849. p.92, c2.

1301 EDWARD SEARCH *to* **GARRISON. May 1849. London.** Reports on Bonaparte and the war in Europe; notes that the repeal of the Navigation Laws is being debated in Parliament. 15 June 1849. p.93, c2.

1302 C. H. A. DALL *to* **REV. SAMUEL MAY, JR. 4 June 1849. Lowell.** Reflects on the anniversary meetings of the New England AS. 15 June 1849. p.95, c1.

1303 EDWARD SEARCH *to* **WM. LLOYD GARRISON. May 1849. London.** Believes that abolition of slave trade in the colonies will be only a matter of time. 22 June 1849. p.97, c4.

1304 C. *to* **FRIEND GARRISON. 19 June 1849. Canton.** Encloses a fifteen-dollar contribution. 22 June 1849. p.98, c4.

1305 RICHARD D. WEBB *to* **THE** *ANTI-SLAVERY STANDARD*. **[extract] n.d. Dublin.** Praises Douglass and the *North Star.* 22 June 1849. p.98, c5.

1306 JUSTICE *to* **FRIEND GARRISON. 21 June 1849. Plymouth, Ma.** Remarks sarcastically that the *Maryland Colonization Journal* is a publication of "prudence." 22 June 1849. p.98, c5.

1307 SAMUEL GREGORY *to* **MR. EDITOR [W. L. GARRISON]. n.d. n.p.** Applauds progress made in the medical education of women after the establishment of a school in Boston. 22 June 1849. p.98, c6.

1308 OLD COLONY *to* **FRIEND GARRISON. 9 June 1849. Plymouth.** Feels encouraged by the progress of abolitionism in Plymouth. 22 June 1849. p.99, c1.

1309 N. G. *to* **FRIEND GARRISON. n.d. n.p.** Expresses interest in the Bible discussion started in the *Liberator.* 22 June 1849. p.100, c2.

1310 EDWARD SEARCH *to* **WM. LLOYD GARRISON. 1 June 1849. London.** Discusses the European war's effect on Rome, Austria, and France. 29 June 1849. p.101, c2.

1311 C. M. CLAY *to* **T. I. GODDIN. n.d. n.p.** Comments on his illness; complains that the pro-slavery press denied him an opportunity to debate Squire Turner. 13 July 1849. p.110, c2.

1312 JAS. G. GIBSON, JR. *to* **WM. LLOYD GARRISON. 2 July 1849. Philadelphia.** Criticizes Garrison's treatment of the late James K. Polk. 13 July 1849. p.111, c1.

1313 A. BROOKE *to* **WENDELL PHILLIPS. 4 July 1849. Oakland, Oh.** Declares that the "consent of the governed" is a myth; notes that even the rights of life and liberty are violated because of the nature of government. 13 July 1849. p.111, c1.

1314 OLD COLONY *to* **FRIEND GARRISON. n.d. n.p.** Corrects introduction to "Infidelity" poem by Old Colony in a previous issue; states that the poem is based on a paragraph in Douglass' speech, not the entire speech. 13 July 1849. p.111, c5.

1315 H. C. WRIGHT *to* **WENDELL PHILLIPS. 15 June 1849. Mecca, Oh.** Proposes a test question for American politics and religion: can human life be protected by killing men? 13 July 1849. p.112, c2.

1316 EDWARD *to* **FRIEND GARRISON. 1 July 1849. New Ipswich.** Reports on legislative vote in favor of the gallows in New Hampshire; calls it "barbaric." 13 July 1849. p.112, c4.

1317 A SOUTHRON *to* **THE EDITOR OF THE** *HIGHLAND MESSENGER.* **n.d. n.p.** Denounces fanatic Northern publishers and their "incendiary publications." 20 July 1849. p.113, c1.

1318 S. S. FOSTER *to* **THE EDITOR OF THE** *LONG ISLAND FARMER.* **n.d. n.p.** Criticizes mob action in Flushing which disrupted an anti-slavery meeting. 20 July 1849. p.113, c4.

1319 A. T. WOOD *to* **FRIEND HACKER. 4 June 1849. Machias Jail.** A mulatto explains particulars of his marriage to a white woman and his arrest for same. 20 July 1849. p.114, c2.

1320 J. W. S. *to* **GEN. WILSON. 14 June 1849. Boston.** Condemns the House of Punishment, known locally as the Charleston Sugar House, for its inhuman treatment of prisoners. 29 June 1849. p.101, c5.

1321 H. C. WRIGHT *to* **GARRISON. 7 June 1849. Geneva, N. Y.** Mourns the death of the abolitionist John Murray; opposes capital punishment; comments on the hanging of Washington Goode. 29 June 1849. p.102, c5.

1322 JAS. G. GIBON, JR. *to* **WM. LLOYD GARRISON. 25 June 1849. Philadelphia.** Criticizes the *Liberator*'s attacks on the late J. K. Polk; describes Polk as "virtuous, successful." 29 June 1849. p.102, c6.

1323 ALFRED WYMAN *to* **FRIEND GARRISON. 22 June 1849. Westminster.** Forwards a five-dollar donation. 29 June 1849. p.102, c6.

1324 S. GREGORY *to* **MR. EDITOR [W. L. GARRISON]. 26 June 1849. Boston.** States that the medical education of women is "natural and proper." 29 June 1849. p.103, c1.

1325 EDWARD SEARCH *to* **GARRISON. June 1849. London.** Questions the practicality of non-resistance for a continent which is at war with itself. 6 July 1849. p.105, c1.

1326 D. C. NEZAH *to* **MR. GARRISON. 1 July 1849. Groton.** Reproaches Garrison for his criticism of the late James K. Polk. 6 July 1849. p.106, c5.

1327 HENRY C. WRIGHT *to* **GARRISON. 21 June 1849. New Garden, Oh.** Gives account of a Western AS meeting held recently. 6 July 1849. p.107, c1.

1328 HENRY C. WRIGHT *to* **GARRISON. 5 June 1849. Geneva, Oh.** Rejects pantheism because it implies that God exists in evil as well as good. 6 July 1849. p.108, c2.

1329 FREDERICK DOUGLASS *to* **n.n. [extract] 30 June. Niagara, Canada.** Reports that Canadian hotels do not discriminate, unlike those in the United States. 13 July 1849. p.110, c1.

1330 HENRY C. WRIGHT *to* **W. L. G. 4 July 1849. Massillon, Stark County, Oh.** Reports on his talk at the children's picnic; regrets exclusion of colored children from schools in Massillon. 20 July 1849. p.114, c5.

1331 MONITUS *to* **EDITOR. n.d. n.p.** Claims that the Church can be the most effective vehicle against slavery. 20 July 1849. p.115, c1.

1332 JOHN LARKIN *to* **THE EDITOR [W. L. GARRISON]. 10 July 1849. South Wilbraham.** Requests donations to buy the freedom of fourteen slave children whose parents escaped. 20 July 1849. p.115, c2.

1333 S. C. WHEELER *to* **FRIEND GARRISON. 9 July 1849. Groton.** Denounces Rev. Pratt of the CS; describes him as "absurd, contradictory, wicked." 20 July 1849. p.115, c2.

1334 JOSEPH A. DUGDALE *to* **FRIEND. 5 July 1849. Salem, Columbiana County, Oh.** Notes the omission of a word from a letter by Richard Dillingham which changed the letter's meaning. 20 July 1849. p.115, c3.

1335 HENRY C. WRIGHT *to* **GARRISON. 13 July 1849. Cleveland.** Reports on an AS convention at Cleveland. 27 July 1849. p.117, c3.

1336 H. CLAY *to* **MEMBERS OF FREE-SOIL CONVENTION HELD AT CLEVELAND. 16 June 1845. Ashland.** Cautions that a celebration of the anniversary of the Ordinance of 1787 might incite further division of the country. 27 July 1849. p.118, c1.

1337 MARTIN VAN BUREN *to* **JNO. C. VAUGHAN AND THOS. BROWN. 7 July 1847. Lindenwald.** Regrets that he is unable to attend the celebration of the anniversary of the Ordinance of 1787. 27 July 1849. p.118, c1.

1338 SAMUEL MAY, JR. *to* **MR. NELL. 14 July 1849. Leicester.** Praises Garrison for providing "light and truth." 27 July 1849. p.118, c5.

1339 R. W. EMERSON *to* **WILLIAM LLOYD GARRISON. 24 July 1849. Concord.** Accepts an invitation to the Worcester anti-slavery celebration. 27 July 1849. p.119, c1.

1340 N. G. *to* **FRIEND GARRISON. n.d. South Hingham.** Reflects critically upon Ephraim Peabody's book. 27 July 1849. p.119, c3.

1341 OLD COLONY *to* **FRIEND GARRISON. 14 July 1849. Plymouth, Ma.** Asserts that he feels disrespect for James K. Polk in death as in life. 27 July 1849. p.120, c2.

1342 S. *to* **MR. EDITOR [W. L. GARRISON]. 20 July 1849. Roxbury.** Asks how Mr. Sumner's work justifies a slave insurrection. 27 July 1849. p.120, c2.

1343 H. M. ROBERTS *to* **WM. LLOYD GARRISON. 9 July 1849. Boston.** Voices harsh criticism of Garrison and H. C. Wright, censuring them as irreligious and self-serving. 3 August 1849. p.121, c1.

1344 T. BICKNELL *to* **THE EDITOR OF THE *OLD COLONY REPORTER*. 16 July 1849. Kingston.** States that newspaper attacks on anti-slavery leaders are "treasonous." 3 August 1849. p.121, c5.

1345 HORACE MANN *to* **J. C. VAUGHAN AND THOS. BROWN. 9 July 1849. West Newton.** Supports a celebration for the Ordinance of 1787. 3 August 1849. p.121, c6.

1346 JOHN G. PALFREY *to* **JNO. C. VAUGHAN AND THOS. BROWN. 4 July 1849. Cambridge, Ma.** Stresses importance of the Ordinance of 1787. 3 August 1849.p.121, c6.

1347 CHARLES FRANCIS ADAMS *to* **JNO. C. VAUGHAN AND THOS. BROWN. 24 June 1849. Quincy.** Supports a celebration for the Ordinance of 1787. 3 August 1849. p.122, c1.

1348 CHARLES SUMNER *to* **JNO. C. VAUGHAN AND THOS. BROWN. 6 July 1849. Boston.** Praises anti-slavery intent of the Ordinance of 1787. 3 August 1849. p.122, c1.

1349 C. M. CLAY *to* **JNO. C. VAUGHAN AND THOS. BROWN. 5 July 1849. Madison County, Ky.** Sympathizes with the Ordinance of 1787. 3 August 1849. p.122, c1.

1350 H. C. WRIGHT *to* **EDWARD SEARCH. 15 July 1849. Geneva, Oh.** Queries whether death is the guardian of life, noting that all governments use death to protect property, punish killers, and preserve liberty. 3 August 1849. p.122, c5.

1351 PLACIDO *to* **WM. LLOYD GARRISON. 21 July 1849. Philadelphia.** Condemns the Charleston workhouse as a "house of blood." 3 August 1849. p.123, c1.

1352 S. *to* **FRIEND GARRISON. 3 July 1849. Kingston.** Compares slavery to cholera and asks if the pro-slavery malady of the Church is contagious. 3 August 1849. p.123, c2.

1353 P. *to* **EDITOR. n.d. n.p.** Believes a slaveholder cannot be a Christian and vice versa. 10 August 1849. p.127, c2.

1354 J. H. C. *to* **FRIEND GARRISON. 6 August 1849. Pepperell.** Reports on lecture given by Miss Stone. 10 August 1849. p.127, c3.

1355 A. R. POPE *to* **FRIEND GARRISON. 14 August 1849. Kingston.** Rejects Monitor's idea of freedom. 17 August 1849. p.131, c3.

1356 ROBERT B. ROGERS *to* **FRIEND GARRISON. 13 August 1849. Boston.** Feels distressed by Father Mathew's inconsistent support of abstinence and his non-commital attitude toward slavery. 17 August 1849. p.131, c5.

1357 WENDELL PHILLIPS *to* **JAMES HAUGHTON. 20 August 1849. Boston.** Criticizes Father Mathew's silence on slavery. 24 August 1849. p.134, c6.

1358 PARKER PILLSBURY *to* **FRIEND GARRISON. 20 August 1849. Concord, N. H.** Denounces Father Mathew for not opposing slavery. 24 August 1849. p.135, c3.

1359 RICHARD D. WEBB *to* **GARRISON. 5 July 1849. Dublin.** Praises abolitionists, particularly Theodore Parker. 24 August 1849. p.135, c4.

1360 C. C. BURLEIGH *to* **BROTHER GARRISON. 19 August 1849. n.p.** Corrects typographical errors in previous issue of the *Liberator*. 24 August 1849. p.135, c4.

1361 J. H. COE *to* **MR. EDITOR [W. L. GARRISON]. 10 August 1849. Howard's Valley, Ct.** Mourns death of Caroline E. Perkins. 24 August 1849. p.135, c6.

1362 HENRY C. WRIGHT *to* **GARRISON. 22 July 1849. Jefferson, Oh.** Believes principles of Christianity will fail as long as death is a means of protection for the social order. 24 August 1849. p.136, c2.

1363 HENRY C. WRIGHT *to* **WENDELL PHILLIPS. 17 July 1849. Geneva, Oh.** Accuses man, not God, of inflicting death upon men. 24 August 1849. p.136, c2.

1364 HENRY C. WRIGHT *to* **GARRISON. 1 August 1849. Randolph, Oh.** Refutes argument that God sanctions slavery. 31 August 1849. p.137, c2.

1365 EDWARD SEARCH *to* **THE** *LIBERATOR.* **28 June 1849. London.** Predicts that the French occupation of Rome will cause problems for France. 31 August 1849. p.137, c3.

1366 J. *to* **THE EDITOR OF THE** *BOSTON REPUBLICAN.* **n.d. n.p.** Criticizes Dr. Peabody's arguments for Free-Soil as stated in his narratives of fugitive slaves. 31 August 1849. p.138, c1.

1367 J. M. BARRETT *to* **FATHER. 2 July 1849. Spartansburgh, S. C.** Explains that he is in prison for circulating abolition documents. 31 August 1849. p.138, c2.

1368 JOSHUA T. EVERETT *to* **FRIEND GARRISON. 23 August 1849. Everettville, Princeton.** Mocks Zachary Taylor's call for a national fast. 31 August 1849. p.139, c1.

1368a JOSHUA T. EVERETT *to* **THE EDITOR OF THE** *PLOUGHMAN.* **31 July 1849. Everettville, Princeton.** Denounces Zachary Taylor's call for a national fast of atonement as an unwarranted mockery in the eyes of God. 31 August 1849. p.139, c1.

1369 PLACIDO *to* **WM. LLOYD GARRISON. 21 August 1849. Philadelphia.** Prays for success of abolitionists and an end to workhouses. 31 August 1849. p.139, c2.

1370 J. M. COMBE *to* **W. L. GARRISON. 22 August 1849. Georgetown, Ma.** Expresses indignation over Father Mathew's refusal to oppose slavery. 31 August 1849. p.139, c2.

1371 A FRIEND *to* **WM. LLOYD GARRISON. 20 August 1849. Lancaster, Pa.** Issues sarcastic, moralistic warning to church-goers. 31 August 1849. p.140, c3.

1372 WM. LLOYD GARRISON *to* **THEOBALD MATHEW. 7 September 1849. Boston.** Discusses the motives behind Mathew's changed perception of slavery. 7 September 1849. p.142, c4.

1373 GRAMPUS *to* **MR. EDITOR [W. L. GARRISON]. 1 September 1849. Cape Cod.** States he is surprised by the infectiousness of slavery; discusses the change in Father Mathew. 7 September 1849. p.143, c3.

1374 HENRY C. WRIGHT *to* **JAMES HAUGHTON. 26 August 1849. Cool Spring, Oh.** Blames the Catholic church for the failure of Father Mathew. 14 September 1849. p.145, c3.

1375 ALLAN *to* **W. L. GARRISON. 30 August 1849. Plymouth.** Asserts that the criticism of Father Mathew has rendered "a great man small." 14 September 1849. p.145, c6.

1376 OLD COLONY *to* **FRIEND GARRISON. n.d. n.p.** Infers that Father Mathew is too timid to be a true abolitionist. 14 September 1849. p.146, c1.

1377 FREDERICK DOUGLASS *to* **CAPT. THOMAS AULD. 3 September 1849. Rochester.** Asserts that anti-slavery agitation does produce results. 14 September 1849. p.146, c2.

1378 WM. LLOYD GARRISON *to* **THEOBALD MATHEW. 14 September 1849. Boston.** Gives a sarcastic appraisal of Father Mathew's reputation and popularity. 14 September 1849. p.146, c5.

1379 EDWARD SEARCH *to* **GARRISON. 3 July 1849. London.** Asserts that the American government is better than the English aristocracy. 14 September 1849. p.147, c1.

1380 J. M. L. *to* **MR. EDITOR [W. L. GARRISON]. 7 September 1849. Waltham.** Expresses anger over support of school segregation by both colored and white citizens. 14 September 1849. p.147, c2.

1381 HENRY C. WRIGHT *to* **R. D. WEBB. 12 August 1849. Marlboro, Oh.** Reports on his address to an anti-slavery convention in Ohio; warns England to prepare itself to prevent a United States annexation of Canada. 21 September 1849. p.149, c6.

1382 C. PHELPS *to* **GARRISON. n.d. Cincinnati.** Sends five dollars to the *Liberator*. 21 September 1849. p.150, c3.

1383 GEO. THOMPSON *to* **GARRISON. 31 August 1849. Waterloo Place, London.** Apologizes for his lack of correspondence. 21 September 1849. p.150, c3.

1384 LUCIUS SMITH *to* **W. L. GARRISON. 18 September 1849. Randolph, Vt.** Applauds Garrison's criticism of Theobald Mathew. 21 September 1849. p.150, c3.

1385 R. THAYER *to* **FRIENDS. 16 September 1849. Bridgewater.** Describes problems of forthcoming anti-slavery meeting; hopes for its success. 21 September 1849. p.151, c3.

1386 EDWARD SEARCH *to* **W. L. G. 30 August 1849. London.** Asserts that the Peace Congress in Paris will help influence public opinion. 21 September 1849. p.152, c2.

1387 A TEMPERANCE MAN *to* **THE EDITOR OF THE *MISSISSIPPI SOUTHRON*. n.d. n.p.** Praises Father Mathew's visit to the South and his neutral attitude toward slavery. 28 September 1849. p.153, c1.

1388 A. BROOKE, MARGARET BROOKE, SARAH BROOKE, G. F. BIRDSALL, MARY HEMPSTED, ABRAHAM ALLEN, CATA W. ALLEN, MARTHA ALLEN, SARAH ALLEN, ELEANOR LEACH, SYBILLA L. BROWNE, E. M. BROWNE, JAMES C. BROWN, M.D. *to* **W. L. GARRISON. 11 September 1849. Oakland, Oh.** Thank Garrison for exposing Theobald Mathew. 28 September 1849. p.153, c2.

1389 WM. LLOYD GARRISON *to* **THEOBALD MATHEW. 28 September 1849. Boston.** Condemns Mathew's pro-slavery ideas. 28 September 1849. p.154, c4.

1390 CHARLES F. HOVEY *to* **FRIEND GARRISON. 22 September 1849. Gloucester.** Assails hypocrisy of permitting French war leaders to chair the Peace Congress in Paris. 28 September 1849. p.154, c6.

1391 EDWARD SEARCH *to* **W. L. GARRISON. 4 September 1849. London.** Argues that passports restrict personal freedom just as import-export tariffs restrict free trade. 28 September 1849. p.155, c1.

1392 MONITOR *to* **WM. L. GARRISON. n.d. n.p.** Denounces the American church for being self-serving and insensitive to human needs. 28 September 1849. p.155, c2.

1393 JOHN HUGHES *to* **THE *COURIER AND ENQUIRER*. n.d. n.p.** Asserts that Irish-Americans have the same patriotic duties as other Americans. 5 October 1849. p.157, c2.

1394 SURIMSAC *to* **THE EDITORS OF THE *BOSTON PILOT*. 19 July 1843. Norfolk, Va.** Appreciates hearing of others who feel that Daniel O'Connell's statements do not represent the sentiments of the Irish people. 5 October 1849. p.157, c4.

1395 A WHIG YET *to* **THURLOW WEED. 31 August 1849. Syracuse.** Defends Father Mathew, asserting that he opposes slavery. 5 October 1849. p.157, c5.

1396 ALLAN *to* **FRIEND GARRISON. n.d. n.p.** Informs that he will not attend an anti-slavery demonstration in Worcester; states that he is more concerned with the cause of temperance. 5 October 1849. p.157, c6.

1397 JAMES HAUGHTON *to* **H. C. WRIGHT. 9 September 1849. Dublin.** Hopes Father Mathew will have a change of heart. 5 October 1849. p.158, c1.

1398 SAMBO *to* **MASSA PUNCH. n.d. n.p.** Comments sarcastically on Father Mathew. 5 October 1849. p.158, c3.

1399 WM. LLOYD GARRISON *to* **THEOBALD MATHEW. 5 October 1849. Boston.** Accuses Mathew of being so blinded by temperance that he ignores slavery. 5 October 1849. p.158, c4.

1400 DANIEL FOSTER *to* **BROTHER GARRISON. 26 September 1849. Boston.** Describes activities of the American Union Missionary Association. 5 October 1849. p.159, c2.

1401 HENRY C. WRIGHT *to* **GARRISON. 23 September 1849. Berlin, Oh.** Feels encouraged by a convention held in the West. 5 October 1849. p.159, c3.

1402 EDWARD SEARCH *to* **GARRISON. 7 September 1849. London.** Explains the reason for sending a letter to Henry Wright. 5 October 1849. p.160, c2.

1403 EDWARD SEARCH *to* **HENRY C. WRIGHT. 7 September 1849. London.** Opposes the way force is often employed. 5 October 1849. p.160, c2.

1404 THOMAS P. SMITH *to* **MR. GARRISON. 26 September 1849. Boston.** Requests that Garrison print his letter on the school system. 5 October 1849. p.160, c3.

1405 THOMAS P. SMITH *to* **FELLOW CITIZENS. 26 September 1849. Boston.** Believes that the Smith school is vital to the education of colored children. 5 October 1849. p.160, c3.

1406 JAMES G. GIBSON, JR. *to* **WM. LLOYD GARRISON. 7 September 1849. Philadelphia.** Defends James K. Polk. 12 October 1849. p.161, c3.

1407 S. *to* **SIR. [from the *Charleston Mercury*] 16 September 1849. Pendleton.** Attacks "fanatics" who support abolitionism in Pendleton. 12 October 1849. p.161, c2.

1408 W. WELLS BROWN *to* **REV. WM. ALLEN. 2 September 1849. London.** Criticizes Allen for being a slavery apologist. 12 October 1849. p.161, c3.

1409 JUS CIVITATIS *to* **THE EDITOR OF THE *ATLAS*. 7 September 1849. n.p.** Discusses citizenship of blacks. 12 October 1849. p.161, c5.

1410 WM. LLOYD GARRISON *to* **THEOBALD MATHEW. n.d. n.p.** Criticizes Mathew for refusing to comment on slavery. 12 October 1849. p.162, c4.

1411 DANIEL RICKETSON *to* **WM. LLOYD GARRISON. 1 October 1849. Woodlee, New Bedford.** Feels that he cannot condemn the temperance work of Father Mathew. 12 October 1849. p.162, c5.

1412 JAMES C. HAUGHTON *to* **WM. LLOYD GARRISON. 10 September 1849. Dublin.** Reports favorably on W. W. Brown's speaking tour. 12 October 1849. p.162, c6.

1413 MONITOR *to* **FRIEND GARRISON. n.d. n.p.** Accuses the Church of indifference toward the "weak and wounded, sick and sore." 12 October 1849. p.163, c2.

1414 HENRY C. WRIGHT *to* **WENDELL PHILLIPS. 18 July 1849. Geneva, Oh.** Believes God's law is inviolable and that men are responsible for the deaths of other men. 12 October 1849. p.164, c2.

1415 W. H. ASHURST *to* **W. L. GARRISON. 31 August 1849. London.** Encloses a circular for the Italian Refugee Fund; urges support. 12 October 1849. p.164, c4.

1416 J. W. C. PENNINGTON *to* **THE** *NEW YORK TRIBUNE.* **24 June 1849. London.** Relates story of abuse of slaves learned from American runaway in England; calls for increased support of abolitionists. 12 October 1849. p.164, c1.

1417 HENRY C. HOWELLS *to* **FRIEND GARRISON. 24 September 1849. Worcester, England.** Denounces the pro-slavery position of Father Mathew. 19 October 1849. p.166, c5.

1418 J. BARKER *to* **FREDERICK DOUGLASS. 29 September 1849. Detroit.** Reports his travel itinerary. 19 October 1849. p.166, c5.

1419 EDWARD SEARCH *to* **THE** *LIBERATOR.* **6 September 1849. London.** Discusses the necessity of participation in government. 19 October 1849. p.168, c2.

1420 JOSEPH MAZZINI *to* **MESSIEURS DE TOCQUEVILLE AND DE FALLOUX, MINISTERS OF FRANCE. n.d. n.p.** Defends the Roman Republic. 19 October 1849. p.168, c3.

1421 W. FARMER *to* **W. L. GARRISON. 5 October 1849. London.** Celebrates the revival of English anti-slavery as a result of the controversy concerning Father Mathew. 26 October 1849. p.171, c1.

1422 H. C. WRIGHT *to* **WENDELL PHILLIPS. 20 July 1849. Geneva, Oh.** Resents those who attribute slavery, war, and oppression to God's will. 26 October 1849. p.172, c2.

1423 JOSEPH A. DUGDALE *to* **THE** *WESTERN STAR.* **29 July 1849. Selma, Oh.** Believes that reform is needed among the Quakers. 26 October 1849. p.172, c3.

1424 L. KOSSUTH *to* **LORD PALMERSTON. 20 September 1849. Widden, Turkey.** Laments the fall of Hungary. 2 November 1849. p.174, c1.

1425 JAMES HAUGHTON *to* **WENDELL PHILLIPS. 28 September 1849. Dublin.** Denounces the inexcusable pro-slavery activities of Father Mathew. 2 November 1849. p.174, c5.

1426 YOU KNOW WHO *to* **GARRISON. 8 October 1849. London.** Discusses the representative reform movement in England. 2 November 1849. p.175, c1.

1427 WM. WELLS BROWN *to* **FRIEND GARRISON. 12 October 1849. London.** Forwards an account of his visits to Dublin and Paris. 2 November 1849. p.175, c3.

1428 HENRY GREW *to* **DANIEL FOSTER. n.d. n.p.** Cites religious reasons for forbidding women to speak in church. 2 November 1849. p.176, c2.

1429 EDWARD SEARCH *to* **GARRISON. September 1849. London.** Remarks on a speech by George Thompson which mentioned Douglass as an example of the victims of American prejudice. 2 November 1849. p.176, c3.

1430 RICHARD D. WEBB *to* **GAY. [from the** *National Anti-Slavery Standard***] 21 September 1849. Dublin.** Comments on the behavior of Father Mathew. 2 November 1849. p.176, c5.

1431 X. Y. *to* **THE EDITOR OF THE** *BARRE PATRIOT***. n.d. n.p.** Refutes the assumption that only Garrisonian abolitionists are the slave's friends. 9 November 1849. p.177, c1.

1432 SAMBO *to* **MASSA PUNCH. n.d. n.p.** Satirizes teetotalism and Father Mathew. 9 November 1849. p.177, c3.

1433 JOSEPH BARKER *to* **THE** *ANTI-SLAVERY STANDARD***. 16 October 1849. New York.** Regrets having missed the abolitionist meeting held by eastern Pennsylvanians. 9 November 1849. p.177, c3.

1434 WILLIAM JAY *to* **J. W. TAYLOR. 8 October 1849. Bedford.** Criticizes the New York Democratic coalition, which includes pro-slavery elements. 9 November 1849. p.178, c5.

1435 YOU KNOW WHO *to* **GARRISON. 18 October 1849. London.** Reports on progress of movement in England for representative reform. 9 November 1849. p.178, c6.

1436 MONITUS *to* **FRIEND GARRISON. n.d. n.p.** Answers "Monitor" in support of abolitionism. 9 November 1849. p.179, c1.

1437 LORING MOODY *to* **GARRISON. 22 October 1849. Harwich.** Attributes the anti-slavery awakening of the Church to Garrison. 9 November 1849. p.179, c2.

1438 SAMUEL MAY, JR. *to* **GARRISON. 5 November 1849. Springfield.** Reports on a convention at Springfield. 9 November 1849. p.179, c3.

1439 ALFRED GIBBS CAMPBELL *to* **BROTHER GARRISON. 21 October 1849. Bridgeport, Ct.** Describes the first abolition meeting at Oxford, Connecticut. 9 November 1849. p.179, c4.

1440 DANIEL FOSTER *to* **BROTHER GARRISON. 22 October 1849. North Danvers.** Supports colored citizens in Boston who seek desegregation of schools. 9 November 1849. p.180, c3.

1441 SAMUEL MAY, JR. *to* **WALLCUT. 21 November 1849. Westfield.** Compliments speech of Charles Burleigh. 16 November 1849. p.183 [182], c6.

1442 HENRY C. WRIGHT *to* **GARRISON. 28 October 1849. n.p.** Asserts that to vote under the present Constitution implies a vote for theft, murder, and piracy. 16 November 1849. p.183, c1.

1443 LAYMAN *to* **DRS. LOWELL, HITCHCOCK, STORRS, MR. THOMPSON, MR. BRIGGS, MR. HILL, MR. LOTHROP. 8 October 1849. Plymouth.** Prefers a society based on right and justice to one based on law and duty. 16 November 1849. p.183, c2.

1444 HENRY C. WRIGHT *to* **WENDELL PHILLIPS. 21 July 1849. Geneva, Oh.** Advocates the abolition of death through medical research. 16 November 1849. p.184, c2.

1445 JOHN SMITH *to* **WILLIAM L. GARRISON. 17 October 1849. Mecca, Oh.** Forwards resolutions from the Western Peace Society. 16 November 1849. p.184, c3.

1446 THOMAS T. BOUVE *to* **MRS. ANNE GWYNN AND OTHERS, RELATIVES OF MRS. ELIZABETH GARNAUT. October 1849. Boston.** Conveys his sympathies on the death of Mrs. Garnaut. 16 November 1849. p.184, c4.

1447 n.n. *to* **THE EDITOR OF THE** *NATIONAL ERA.* **24 September 1849. St. Louis.** Gives disturbing account of the sale of three slaves. 23 November 1849. p.185, c6.

1448 TRUMAN CASE *to* **FRIEND JOHNSON. 8 October 1849. Randolph.** Condemns the inhumanity of slaveholders. 23 November 1849. p.185, c6.

1449 n.n. *to* **MR. GREELEY. 16 October 1849. Washington.** Urges the North to take action against slavery. 23 November 1849. p.186, c1.

1450 ISAAC J. RICE *to* **THE EDITOR OF THE** *LIBERATOR.* **11 November 1849. Amherstburg.** Requests financial aid for refugees in Canada. 23 November 1849. p.187, c1.

1451 LORING MOODY AND JOSHUA H. ROBBINS *to* **THE ABOLITIONISTS OF BARNSTABLE COUNTY. n.d. n.p.** Urge attendance at the coming anti-slavery convention. 23 November 1849. p.187, c2.

1452 A. BROOKE *to* **EDWARD SEARCH. 9 November 1849. Oakland, Oh.** Concludes that human rights are incompatible with human government. 23 November 1849. p.188, c2.

1453 EDWIN H. COATES *to* **FRIEND GARRISON. 4 November 1849. Chester Springs, Pa.** Denounces the double standards of Father Mathew. 23 November 1849. p.188, c3.

1454 JONATHAN WALKER *to* **W. L. GARRISON. 26 November 1849. Plymouth.** Criticizes mandatory observance of the Sabbath. 30 November 1849. p.191, c1.

1455 WM. W. BROWN *to* **WENDELL PHILLIPS. 22 November 1849. London.** Regrets that passports are denied to colored people. 30 November 1849. p.191, c1.

1456 SAMUEL J. MAY *to* **THE EDITOR OF THE** *STANDARD.* **19 November 1849. Syracuse.** Announces plans for a state convention of abolitionists. 30 November 1849. p.191, c2.

1457 AN INQUIRER *to* **THE EDITOR OF THE** *CHRISTIAN REGISTER.* **n.d. n.p.** Asserts the superiority of Christ to Mahomet. 30 November 1849. p.192, c2.

1458 SHERLOCK *to* **MR. GARRISON. n.d. n.p.** Contrasts hypocritical religion with the natural religion of Christ. 30 November 1849. p.192, c2.

1459 RHODA *to* **MR. GARRISON. n.d. n.p.** Infers that H. C. Wright thinks himself a higher authority than the Bible. 30 November 1849. p.192, c2.

1460 MONITOR *to* **MONITUS. n.d. n.p.** Attacks the American church. 7 December 1849. p.193, c2.

1461 JOS. HENRY LUMPKIN *to* **THE FRIENDS OF TEMPERANCE IN GEORGIA. 5 November 1849. Milledgeville.** Withdraws an invitation to Father Mathew to visit Georgia; claims that Mathew consorted with abolitionists. 7 December 1849. p.194, c3.

1462 EDWARD SEARCH *to* **GARRISON. November 1849. London.** Criticizes the English aristocracy as enemies of liberty. 7 December 1849. p.195, c2.

1463 RICHARD D. WEBB *to* **THE EDITOR OF** *NATIONAL ANTI-SLAVERY STANDARD.* **[extract] n.d. n.p.** Considers the Peace Congress at Paris pointless and devoid of principles. 7 December 1849. p.196, c3.

1464 GEO. THOMPSON *to* **GARRISON. 23 November 1849. Edinburgh.** Praises the *Liberator* and Garrison. 14 December 1849. p.198, c5.

1465 YOU KNOW WHO *to* **GARRISON. 20 November 1849. Edinburgh.** Fears that government patronage impedes the reform movement in England. 14 December 1849. p.198, c5.

1466 WM. WELLS BROWN *to* **CAPT. ENOCH PRICE. 23 November 1849. London.** Requests his former master to free his slaves and lead a Christian life. 14 December 1849. p.199, c1.

1467 JOHN BRAGG *to* **FRIEND GARRISON. n.d. n.p.** Notes with satisfaction the growth of abolitionist spirit. 14 December 1849. p.199, c3.

1468 n.n. *to* **WM. LLOYD GARRISON. 4 December 1849. M___, Vt.** Urges all to resist sectarian differences and unite in the cause of peace. 14 December 1849. p.200, c2.

1469 n.n. *to* **THE EDITOR OF THE** *BOSTON REPUBLICAN.* **1 December 1849. Washington.** Warns that a resurgence of the Democratic Party may provide a boost for slavery. 21 December 1849. p.201, c6.

1470 GEO. ARMSTRONG *to* **THE EDITOR OF THE** *EXAMINER.* **12 September 1849. Clifton.** Attacks the *Times* for favoring Austria in its discussion of the Hungarian question. 21 December 1849. p.104 [204], c4.

1471 HENRY C. WRIGHT *to* **RICHARD D. WEBB. 13 November 1849. Selma, Oh.** Comments on events in Europe and Father Mathew's temptation to slavery; includes geographical description of Ohio. 21 December 1849. p.104 [204], c2.

1472 Z. TAYLOR *to* **GOVERNOR UJHAZY. 20 December 1849. Washington.** Offers the protection of the United States to Hungarians who seek asylum in America. 28 December 1849. p.207, c1.

1473 HENRY C. WRIGHT *to* **RICHARD D. WEBB. 4 November 1849. Oakland.** Describes temperance and anti-slavery meetings which took place on the Lord's Day. 28 December 1849. p.208, c2.

1474 HENRY C. WRIGHT *to* **RICHARD D. WEBB. 8 November 1849. Xenia.** Discusses two murder trials taking place in Xenia. 28 December 1849. p.208, c2.

1475 HENRY C. WRIGHT *to* **RICHARD D. WEBB. 12 November 1849. Selma.** Reports on his anti-slavery lectures in Cartsville; disputes Edward Smith's claim that if the government sanctions slavery, then it is the duty of Christians to obey. 28 December 1849. p.208, c3.

[1850]

1476 ANDREW PATON *to* **WM. LLOYD GARRISON. 14 December 1849. Glasgow.** Lauds Frederick Douglass for disclosing the intention of the Evangelical Alliance to receive slaveholders as members. 4 January 1850. p.3, c1.

1477 JNO. MAWSON *to* **n.n. 14 December 1849. Newcastle-upon-Tyne.** Sympathizes with the personal sufferings of Garrison; awaits the arrival of George Thompson and W. W. Brown. 4 January 1850. p.3, c2.

1478 A. H. W. *to* **GEORGE THOMPSON. 25 December 1849. Wood's Retreat.** Asks about conditions of the workingman in the North. 4 January 1850. p.3, c3.

1479 JOHANNES SCHMIDT *to* **MR. GARRISON. 25 December 1849. Concord, Ma.** Extends an invitation to attend the anniversary celebration of the Battle of Concord. 4 January 1850. p.3, c4.

1480 HENRY GREW *to* **FRIEND GARRISON. n.d. n.p.** Advocates women's rights. 4 January 1850. p.4, c2.

1481 PARKER PILLSBURY *to* **FRIEND GARRISON. 6 January 1850. Plymouth.** Thanks him for having attended the celebration of "Forefather's Day." 11 January 1850. p.7, c3.

1482 A SLAVE *to* **HENRY CLAY. 29 December 1849. Washington, D.C.** Affirms that the essence of slavery is unchristian. 11 January 1850. p.8, c2.

1483 PTOLEMY *to* **THE EDITOR OF THE** *LIBERATOR.* **n.d. n.p.** Praises Douglass' speech in Worcester, in response to a critical article by Thomas Drew, Jr. from the *Christian Citizen.* 11 January 1850. p.8, c2.

1484 JOHN M. SPEAR *to* **FRIEND. January 1850. Boston.** Encloses a circular advocating abolition of the gallows. 18 January 1850. p.11, c3.

1485 PARKER PILLSBURY *to* **W. L. G. n.d. n.p.** Reports on the convention in Syracuse. 25 January 1850. p.14, c5.

1486 MICAJAH T. JOHNSON *to* **FRIEND GARRISON. 10 January 1850. Short Creek, Warren County.** Denounces William W. Brown for treating other Negroes with contempt. 25 January 1850. p.15, c1.

1487 ROBERT EDMONDS *to* **W. L. GARRISON. 12 January 1850. Providence.** Describes his visit with a minister in Pawtucket and the unfavorable reaction of the latter to W. L. Garrison. 25 January 1850. p.15, c1.

1488 Entry number not used.

1489 n.n. *to* **MR. GARRISON. n.d. n.p.** Describes enclosed letter of Fr. Mathew to Judge Lumpkin as "odious," "contemptible," and "pro-slavery." 25 January 1850. p.15, c2.

1490 FATHER THEOBALD MATHEW *to* **JUDGE LUMPKIN. 22 December 1849. Richmond, Va.** Replies to previous letter from Lumpkin, offering his views on temperance and pledging not to interfere with any of the institutions of the United States. 25 January 1850. p.15, c2.

1491 PARKER PILLSBURY *to* **FRIEND GARRISON. n.d. n.p.** Reports on a well attended abolitionist meeting at Foxboro'. 1 February 1850. p.19, c4.

1492 H. C. WRIGHT *to* **GARRISON. 11 January 1850. Steamer** *Genesee,* **Ohio River.** Regrets that man excuses his actions by attributing evil to God's will. 1 February 1850. p.20, c2.

1493 WM. LLOYD GARRISON *to* **SAMUEL J. MAY. 13 January 1850. Boston.** Condemns slavery as an inexcusable crime. 8 February 1850. p.23, c4.

1494 H. C. WRIGHT *to* **GARRISON. 15 February 1850. Cincinnati.** Criticizes Father Mathew's note as an example of injustice toward colored people. 7 February 1851. p.23, c4.

1495 JNO. MAWSON *to* **WM. L. GARRISON. 11 January 1850. Newcastle, England.** Describes the favorable reception given to the fugitive slave W. W. Brown in England. 8 February 1850. p.23, c4.

1496 PARKER PILLSBURY *to* **GAY. n.d. n.p.** Advocates separation of slaveholders from the remainder of the Methodist church. 8 February 1850. p.24, c3.

1497 GOV. G. M. TROUP *to* **THE** *INDEPENDENT DEMOCRAT.* **15 September 1849. Valdosta, Ga.** Argues in favor of sustaining the Union. 15 February 1850. p.25, c1.

1498 LEWIS FORD *to* **MR. GARRISON. n.d. n.p.** Corrects Brigham's account of his actions. 15 February 1850. p.26, c6.

1499 LEOPOLD *to* **J. 16 December 1849. Sacramento City.** Reports on his travels in "gold country." 15 February 1850. p.27, c1.

1500 PARKER PILLSBURY *to* **FRIEND GARRISON. n.d. n.p.** Encloses a petition to end slavery. 15 February 1850. p.27, c3.

1501 LORING MOODY *to* **FRIEND GARRISON. n.d. n.p.** Forwards resolutions from the Barnstable County AS at Brewster. 15 February 1850. p.27, c3.

1502 THOMAS PAUL SMITH *to* **MR. EDITOR. n.d. n.p.** A colored man who supports colored institutions defends the Smith School. 15 February 1850. p.27, c4.

1503 H. H. BRIGHAM *to* **FRIEND GARRISON. 1 February 1850. South Abington.** Relates incidents of religious intolerance toward himself and L. Ford. 15 February 1850. p.28, c2.

1504 A NON-JUROR *to* **FRIEND GARRISON. 5 February 1850. Providence.** Assails the Rhode Island legislature for not taking action against slavery. 15 February 1850. p.28, c3.

1505 J. W. PILLSBURY *to* **MR. GARRISON. 11 February 1850. Milford, N.H.** Would like to hear more anti-slavery lectures in New Hampshire. 22 February 1850. p.31, c4.

1506 ELIZABETH WILSON *to* **MR. GARRISON. n.d. n.p.** Discusses women's rights and duties in relation to Scripture. 22 February 1850. p.32, c2.

1507 WILLIAM JAY *to* **WILLIAM J. NELSON. 11 February 1850. New York.** Evaluates Clay's resolutions. 1 March 1850. p.33, c3.

1508 PARKER PILLSBURY *to* **FRIEND GARRISON. 19 February 1850. n.p.** Feels encouraged by an anti-slavery meeting at Bridgewater. 1 March 1850. p.35, c2.

1509 H. C. WRIGHT *to* **GARRISON. 15 February 1850. Cincinnati.** Opposes Father Mathew's consorting with slaveholders; denounces Henry Clay as a godless man. 1 March 1850. p.35, c2.

1510 A NON-JUROR *to* **FRIEND GARRISON. 18 February 1850. Providence.** Forwards proceedings of the Rhode Island legislature. 1 March 1850. p.35, c3.

1511 HIRAM WILSON *to* **FRIEND GARRISON. 12 February 1850. Dawn Mills, Canada West.** Boasts of attendance at his mission and Sabbath schools. 1 March 1850. p.36, c2.

1512 SAMUEL RHOADS *to* **WM. LLOYD GARRISON. 5 February 1850. Blackley.** Affirms Henry B. Marshall's opinions on the purchase of slave labor produce. 1 March 1850. p.36, c2.

1513 JONATHAN WALKER *to* **FRIEND GARRISON. 18 February 1850. Montpelier, Vt.** Relates his experiences as an abolitionist. 1 March 1850. p.36, c3.

1514 LUCY STONE *to* **W. L. GARRISON. 19 February 1850. Boston.** Describes a rare case of receiving aid from a clergyman, Rev. Kimball. 1 March 1850. p.36, c3.

1515 FRANCIS JACKSON *to* **ZACHARY TAYLOR. 1 September 1849. Boston.** Discusses the purpose of the Massachusetts AS. 8 March 1850. p.38, c6.

1516 THOS. GARRETT *to* **WM. LLOYD GARRISON. 1 March 1856. Wilmington, De.** Reports on anti-slavery in Delaware. 8 March 1850. p.39, c4.

1517 JOPPA *to* **FRIEND GARRISON. 24 February 1850. East Bridgewater.** Provides account of anti-slavery meetings in East Bridgewater. 8 March 1850. p.40, c2.

1518 JONATHAN WALKER *to* **FRIEND GARRISON. 24 February 1850. Ferrisburg, Vt.** Advises anti-slavery movement to support its distinguished lecturers. 8 March 1850. p.40, c2.

1519 ROBERT EDMONDS *to* **FRIEND GARRISON. 12 January 1850. Providence.** Censures those who claim that opposition to slavery is not a religious subject. 8 March 1850. p.40, c3.

1520 SAMUEL HENRY *to* **BROTHER GARRISON. March 1850. Palmer.** Condemns Daniel Webster and John Davis for supporting a constitution which encourages murder and theft. 15 March 1850. p.43, c4.

1521 ELIZABETH WILSON *to* **MR. GARRISON. 22 February 1850. Cadiz, Oh.** Refutes Mr. Grew's opinions on a woman's rights and duties. 15 March 1850. p.44, c2.

1522 EDWARD SEARCH *to* **GARRISON. February 1850. London.** Advocates free trade as an alternative to smuggling. 22 March 1850. p.48, c3.

1523 JOHN SMITH *to* **GARRISON. 27 February 1850. Mecca, Oh.** Condemns war as both a physical and moral evil. 22 March 1850. p.48, c4.

1524 PATRICK HENRY *to* **THE** *NEW YORK HERALD.* **26 February 1850. Washington.** Foresees danger for the Union from "Northern tyranny." 29 March 1850. p.49, c1.

1525 CATO *to* **DEAR DEMOCRAT. 28 February 1850. Washington.** Declares that the "mild" slavery in Washington is worse than that of the deep South. 29 March 1850. p.49, c3.

1526 WILLIAM JAY *to* **WILLIAM NELSON, M.C. 16 March 1850. Nelson, N.Y.** Discusses the compromise proposed by Clay, and Webster's response to it. 29 March 1850. p.49, c6.

1527 CHARLES FRANCIS ADAMS *to* **S. G. HOWE, WENDELL PHILLIPS, AND FRANCIS JACKSON. 23 March 1850. Boston.** Accuses Webster and the Wilmot Proviso of being pro-slavery. 29 March 1850. p.50, c4.

1528 JONATHAN WALKER *to* **FRIEND GARRISON. 3 March 1850. Springfield, Vt.** Relates his experiences in Vermont on behalf of anti-slavery. 29 March 1850. p.52, c2.

1529 PARKER PILLSBURY *to* **FRIEND GARRISON. 18 March 1850. Salem.** Reports on anti-slavery meetings in Essex County. 29 March 1850. p.52, c2.

1530 REV. CALVIN FAIRBANK *to* **CITIZENS OF BOSTON. 19 March 1850. Boston.** Details his release from prison. 5 April 1850. p.53, c5.

1531 H. C. WRIGHT *to* **ANDREW PATON. 2 March 1850. Cincinnati.** Describes Congress as a national convention on American slavery. 5 April 1850. p.56, c2.

1532 Z. *to* **THE EDITOR. 17 March 1850. Cambridge.** Declares that Douglass is "only safe in Massachusetts through the perjury of the citizens." 12 April 1850. p.58, c1.

1533 JOSEPH P. FESSENDEN *to* **DANIEL WEBSTER. 18 March 1850. South Bridgeton, Me.** Criticizes Webster for his support of Mason's Fugitive Slave Law. 12 April 1850. p.59, c3.

1534 JOHN M. SPEAR *to* **BROTHER GARRISON. n.d. n.p.** Lists the towns whose citizens petitioned the Massachusetts legislature for the abolition of capital punishment. 12 April 1850. p.60, c3.

1535 DANIEL WEBSTER *to* **THOMAS H. PERKINS, CHARLES JACKSON, MOSES STUART, DR. WOODS, WILLIAM STURGIS, PRES. SPARKS, CALEB LORING, ISAAC P. DAVIS, AND WILLIAM APPLETON. n.d. n.p.** Expresses gratitude for their support. 19 April 1850. p.62, c2.

1536 ONDINE *to* **HENRY CLAY. n.d. n.p.** Denounces Clay and Webster. 19 April 1850. p.64, c2.

1537 PARKER PILLSBURY *to* **FRIEND GARRISON. n.d. n.p.** Expresses disappointment with a poorly attended meeting at Fitchburg. 19 April 1850. p.64, c3.

1538 D. S. G. *to* **DANIEL WEBSTER. 18 April 1850. Portland.** Expresses harsh criticism of Webster. 26 April 1850. p.65, c2.

1539 SAMUEL SMITH *to* **FRIEND GARRISON. 31 March 1850. West Harwich.** Criticizes Webster and Southerners for "creating a hell." 26 April 1850. p.65, c3.

1540 ANTI-CHATTEL *to* **GARRISON. 14 April 1850. Randolph, Vt.** Criticizes Webster for his pro-slavery position. 26 April 1850. p.65, c4.

1541 MILTON Z. BULLARD *to* **SIR. 16 April 1850. North Bellingham.** Explains that he is unable to attend anti-slavery meetings due to business considerations. 26 April 1850. p.67, c3.

1542 EDWARD SEARCH *to* **SIR. 28 March 1850. London.** Comments on the Church of England Party. 26 April 1850. p.67, c4.

1543 SAMUEL MAY, JR. *to* **SAMUEL BOWLES. 14 April 1850. Bowles, Leicester.** Defends Miss Stone and Mr. Pillsbury. 3 May 1850. p.69, c4.

1544 EDWARD SEARCH *to* **GARRISON. 14 March 1850. London.** Expresses satisfaction with progress of abolitionism in the United States. 3 May 1850. p.71, c4.

1545 WM. MAUGHAN *to* **GARRISON. 14 March 1850. London.** Views the issue of slavery as world-wide, not peculiar to America. 3 May 1850. p.71, c4.

1546 LEWIS FORD *to* **FRIEND GARRISON. 29 April 1850. Abington.** Announces a forthcoming anti-slavery meeting at Abington. 3 May 1850. p.71, c5.

1547 TRUTH *to* **HON. JOSEPH T. BUCKINGHAM. n.d. n.p.** Attacks Freemasonry as an uncharitable and conspiratorial organization. 3 May 1850. p.72, c2.

1548 HENRY C. WRIGHT *to* **W. L. GARRISON. 19 April 1850. Salem, Oh.** Reports on a women's rights convention; feels that the days of inequality are numbered. 3 May 1850. p.72, c4.

1549 CALVIN FAIRBANK *to* **SAM SHY. 24 April 1850. Boston.** Protests Miss Webster's letters accusing Fairbank of pro-slavery ideas. 3 May 1850. p.72, c4.

1550 HORACE MANN *to* **JAMES RICHARDSON, I. CLEVELAND, JOHN GARD-NER, D. A. SIMMONS, JOHN J. CLARKE, FRANCIS HILLIARD, AND GEORGE R. RUSSELL. 3 May 1850. West Newton.** Favors admitting California as a free state. 10 May 1850. p.74, c1.

1551 EDWARD SEARCH *to* **GARRISON. 21 March 1850. London.** Comments on a new railway in India. 10 May 1850. p.76, c2.

1552 PARKER PILLSBURY *to* **GARRISON. 20 April 1850. West Brookfield.** Reports on the description of his speech to a meeting in Montgomery. 10 May 1850. p.76, c2.

1553 JUSTUS HARLOW *to* **DANIEL WEBSTER. 1 May 1850. Plymouth.** Criticizes Webster for hiding behind his oath in order to support a corrupt system. 10 May 1850. p.76, c3.

1554 JONATHAN WALKER *to* **FRIEND GARRISON. 28 April 1850. Plymouth.** Attacks Daniel Webster for corrupting his principles. 10 May 1850. p.76, c4.

1555 WM. LLOYD GARRISON *to* **THE EDITOR OF THE** *NEW YORK TRIBUNE.* **n.d. n.p.** Accuses the mayor and police of complicity in a pro-slavery riot. 17 May 1850. p.79, c3.

1556 A CITIZEN OF SOUTH CAROLINA AND A SLAVEHOLDER *to* **THE EDITOR OF THE** *TRIBUNE.* **n.d. n.p.** States that he was outraged by the conduct of the crowd at an abolition convention. 17 May 1850. p.79, c3.

1557 HENRY W. SMITH *to* **MR. GREELEY. 10 May 1850. New York.** Protests the constables' handling of the crowd at an abolitionist convention. 17 May 1850. p.79, c3.

1558 JOHN G. WHITTIER *to* **W. L. GARRISON. 13 May 1850. Amesbury.** Complains that Douglass' right to freedom of speech was violated at an abolitionist convention. 17 May 1850. p.79, c5.

1559 ELIZABETH CADY STANTON *to* **MARY ANNE. 7 April 1850. Seneca Falls, N.Y.** Expresses support for women's rights. 17 May 1850. p.80, c3.

1560 LUCRETIA MOTT *to* **THE WOMAN'S CONVENTION. 13 April 1850. Philadelphia.** Wishes the Woman's Rights Convention success. 17 May 1850. p.80, c4.

1561 LUCY STONE *to* **WOMAN'S RIGHTS CONVENTION. 10 April 1852. Southampton.** Praises the Woman's Rights Convention as a sign of progress. 17 May 1850. p.80, c4.

1562 WM. LLOYD GARRISON *to* **THE EDITOR OF THE** *BOSTON TRANSCRIPT.* **17 May 1850. Boston.** Refutes a charge of blasphemy. 24 May 1850. p.81, c3.

1563 W. H. BURLEIGH *to* **BALDWIN. 8 May 1850. New York.** Gives account of an anti-slavery convention in New York. 24 May 1850. p.82, c1.

1564 W. L. GARRISON *to* **THE EDITOR OF THE** *BOSTON TRANSCRIPT.* **n.d. n.p.** Refutes charges that he is blasphemous, anti-Bible, and pro-war. 31 May 1850. p.85, c5.

1565 WM. LLOYD GARRISON *to* **THE EDITOR OF THE** *BOSTON TRANSCRIPT.* **n.d. n.p.** Denies that he incited pro-slavery riots in New York; responds to the criticism of his character. 31 May 1850. p.85, c5.

1566 ISAAC T. HOPPER *to* **THE EDITOR OF THE** *TRIBUNE.* **16 May 1850. n.p.** Decries the lack of police protection at a disrupted anti-slavery meeting. 31 May 1850. p.86, c3.

1567 HENRY C. WRIGHT *to* **GARRISON. 13 May 1850. Long Island Sound.** Relates his discussions with Edmund Quincy and Wm. M. Rogers. 31 May 1850. p.86, c4.

1568 J. W. *to* **n.n. 25 May 1850. Plymouth.** Mourns the death of George Seaver. 31 May 1850. p.87, c2.

1569 CLARKSON *to* **MR. EDITOR [W. L. GARRISON]. 25 May 1850. Worcester.** Lauds the anti-slavery diorama of Henry "Box" Brown in Worcester. 31 May 1850. p.87, c3.

1570 CAROLINE W. HEALEY DALL *to* **FRIEND GARRISON. 24 May 1850. Roxbury.** Praises Douglass' oratory and his willingness to explain some of Garrison's less palatable comments to a crowd in May 1849. 31 May 1850. p.87, c3.

1571 HENRY C. WRIGHT *to* **RICHARD D. WEBB. 1 May 1850. Philadelphia.** Prefers that the Pennsylvania railway operate on the Sabbath. 31 May 1850. p.88, c2.

1572 E. R. P. *to* **MR. GARRISON. n.d. n.p.** Reports that anti-slavery in Portland was officially denounced by the city council. 31 May 1850. p.88, c2.

1573 MATTHEW FARRINGTON, WALKER FARRINGTON, AND AUGUSTUS H. VAN VOORHIS *to* **PRESIDENT OF AAS. 5 May 1850. n.p.** Criticize the government on constitutional grounds. 31 May 1850. p.88, c3.

1574 GERRIT SMITH *to* **THE EDITOR OF THE LIBERTY PARTY PAPER. 22 April 1850. Peterborough.** Reports on the Massachusetts AS. 31 May 1850. p.88, c5.

1575 CITIZENS OF NEWBURYPORT *to* **DANIEL WEBSTER. 8 April 1850. Newburyport.** Praise Webster's speech advocating the surrender of fugitive slaves. 7 June 1850. p.89, c1.

1576 DANIEL WEBSTER *to* **EDWARD S. RAND, W. B. BANISTER, REV. DR. DANA, S. W. MARSTON, AND OTHERS. 15 May 1850. Washington.** Explains his position regarding the slave; thanks them for their support. 7 June 1850. p.89, c1.

1577 AN ENQUIRER AFTER TRUTH *to* **THE EDITOR OF THE** *BOSTON INVESTIGATOR.* **19 May 1850. Boston.** Denounces the *New York Herald* for its attack on Mr. Garrison and company. 7 June 1850. p.92, c4.

1578 CAROLINE W. H. DALL *to* **FRIEND GARRISON. 2 June 1850. Roxbury.** Celebrates the anniversary week of the AS. 14 June 1850. p.95, c1.

1579 HORACE MANN *to* **THE EDITOR OF THE** *BOSTON ATLAS.* **n.d. n.p.** Refutes Daniel Webster's opposition to jury trials for runaway slaves on constitutional and historical grounds. 14 June 1850. p.95, c3.

1580 SAMUEL MAY, JR. *to* **GARRISON. 10 June 1850. Leicester.** Adds Joshua T. Everett to the list of those pledging to the AS cause. 14 June 1850. p.95, c6.

1581 SAMUEL MAY, JR. *to* **MR. GARRISON. 4 June 1850. Boston.** Sends Garrison a speech by an anonymous European. 21 June 1850. p.99, c2.

1582 J. T. EVERETT *to* **FRIEND GARRISON. 5 June 1850. Everettville.** Comments on the "efficient and powerful" New England AS Convention. 21 June 1850. p.99, c2.

1583 R. *to* **MR. EDITOR. 16 June 1850. Roxbury, Ma.** Criticizes the National Division of Sons of Temperance for refusing to admit colored men. 21 June 1850. p.99, c3.

1584 J. M. L. *to* **MR. EDITOR. 5 June 1850. Waltham, Ma.** Denounces the Sons of Temperance for not admitting persons of color. 21 June 1850. p.99, c3.

1585 J. C. *to* **FRIEND GARRISON. n.d. South Hingham.** Criticizes the Christian Anti-Slavery Organization. 21 June 1850. p.99, c3.

1586 GEORGE SUNTER, JR. *to* **WM. L. GARRISON. 25 May 1850. Derby, England.** Commends citizenry for distrusting the Church, priests, and politicians. 21 June 1850. p.100, c2.

1587 HORACE MANN *to* **THE EDITOR OF THE** *BOSTON ATLAS.* **[continued from 14 June 1850] 6 June 1850. Washington.** Affirms "due process"; lauds Webster's fugitive slave bill which calls for jury trial. 28 June 1850. p.100, c3.

1588 H. C. WRIGHT *to* **MOSES STUART. 16 June 1850. Pittsburgh.** Refutes statements about Jesus of Nazareth found in Moses Stuart's pamphlet, "Conscience and the Constitution." 28 June 1850. p.103, c3.

1589 J. W. NEWPORT *to* **HENRY C. WRIGHT. 13 June 1850. St. Clairsville, Oh.** Pleads for more moderate abolitionist language. 28 June 1850. p.103, c4.

1590 J. T. EVERETT *to* **FRIEND GARRISON. n.d. n.p.** Accuses the clergy, more than any other group, of being responsible for the continuance of slavery. 28 June 1850. p.103, c4.

1591 EDWARD SEARCH *to* **GARRISON. May 1850. London.** Promises to help right the wrongs suffered by woman. 28 June 1850. p.104, c2.

1592 JAMES HAUGHTON *to* **WM. LLOYD GARRISON. 12 June 1850. Dublin.** Reports on a discussion of free trade held with Douglass, Wright, and Thompson. 5 July 1850. p.107, c3.

1593 GERRIT SMITH *to* **FREDERICK DOUGLASS. 1 June 1850. Peterboro'.** Expresses outrage at the attack on Douglass; offers sympathy. 5 July 1850. p.108, c2.

1594 WILLIAM WELLS BROWN *to* **THE PUBLIC. 1 June 1850. London.** Relates reasons for his separation from his wife. 12 July 1850. p.111, c2.

1595 PHILIP S. WHITE *to* **THE EDITORS OF THE** *NEW ENGLANDER.* **24 June 1850. Boston.** Denies that all colored persons have been excluded from the Sons of Temperance. 12 July 1850. p.112, c3.

1596 HORATIO N. SPOONER *to* **FRIEND GARRISON. n.d. n.p.** Cautions abolitionists about the invective quality of their speeches. 19 July 1850. p.113, c2.

1597 L. MOODY *to* **FRIEND GARRISON. 23 June 1850. Joppa Village, East Bridgewater.** Describes opposition to anti-abolitionist sentiment in East Bridgewater. 19 July 1850. p.113, c2.

1598 MILLARD FILLMORE *to* **JOHN GAYLE. 31 July 1848. Albany, N.Y.** Affirms that slavery is an evil, "but one with which the National Government had nothing to do." 19 July 1850. p.114, c1.

1599 MILLARD FILLMORE *to* **SIR. 13 September 1848. Albany.** Presents constitutional arguments for states' rights regarding slavery. 19 July 1850. p.114, c1.

1600 M. STOWELL *to* **MR. GARRISON. 25 May 1850. Worcester.** Blames the government for the continuance of slavery. 19 July 1850. p.115, c2.

1601 GERRIT SMITH *to* **WM. LLOYD GARRISON. 16 June 1850. Peterboro.** Forwards twenty dollars to Robert Edmond, who was tarred and feathered for trying to teach a slave to read. 19 July 1850. p.115, c2.

1602 JACOB LEONARD *to* **FRIEND GARRISON. 14 July 1850. East Bridgewater.** Assails pro-slavery efforts in East Bridgewater. 19 July 1850. p.115, c3.

1603 JUSTIN HARLOW *to* **FRIEND GARRISON. 12 July 1850. Boston.** Decries the lack of personal liberty in California, where a freeman was arrested as a slave. 19 July 1850. p.115, c3.

1604 HENRY C. WRIGHT *to* **ANDREW PATON. 4 July 1850. Paton, Marlboro, Oh.** Declares that Independence Day and "self-evident truth" are falsehoods in light of the existence of slavery. 26 July 1850. p.117, c1.

1605 PARKER PILLSBURY *to* **FRIEND GARRISON. 22 July 1850. Boston.** Reports a poorly attended anti-slavery convention at Hingham. 26 July 1850. p.119, c4.

1606 WILLIAM JAY *to* **MOSES STUART. 25 June 1850. Bedford.** States that his father, John Jay, was an abolitionist. 26 July 1850. p.120, c2.

1607 DANIEL WEBSTER *to* **REV. MR. STUART. [extract] 30 April 1850. Boston.** Thanks Stuart for his support. 2 August 1850. p.121, c2.

1608 F. DOUGLASS *to* *NORTH STAR.* **[extract] n.d. Cincinnati.** Decries the enmity between men. 2 August 1850. p.121, c3.

1609 A. R. *to* **MR. GARRISON. 15 July 1850. Providence.** Praises Garrison's speeches delivered in Providence and Pawtucket. 2 August 1850. p.122, c4.

1610 J. L. *to* **FRIEND GARRISON. 28 July 1850. East Bridgewater.** Cites the case of Jordan and Snell, who were acquitted of leading a pro-slavery riot. 2 August 1850. p.122, c6.

1611 HENRY C. WRIGHT *to* **MOSES STUART. 14 July 1850. Salem, Oh.** Argues that the God of the Hebrews and Moses Stuart are aligned against the God of humanity. 2 August 1850. p.123, c1.

1612 n.n. *to* **W. L. GARRISON. n.d. n.p.** Notes similarity of British and American anti-slavery arguments. 2 August 1850. p.123, c2.

1613 J. W. NEWPORT *to* **H. C. WRIGHT. 20 July 1850. St. Clairsville, Oh.** Denies that Garrison wanted to "stamp Bible underfoot." 2 August 1850. p.123, c3.

1614 HIRAM WILSON *to* **GARRISON. 22 July 1850. Dawn Mills, Canada West.** Explains that he left Canada because of poor health. 2 August 1850. p.123, c3.

1615 H. N. G. *to* **THE EDITOR OF** *OHIO STATE JOURNAL.* **12 July 1850. Evergreen.** Reports on a conflict between runaway slaves and whites which he witnessed in Ohio. 9 August 1850. p.126, c2.

1616 H. C. WRIGHT *to* **MOSES STUART. 17 July 1850. New Garden, Oh.** Accuses Stuart of vindicating Daniel Webster at the expense of the Bible, God, and Jesus. 9 August 1850. p.127, c4.

1617 PRESCOT SMITH *to* **n.n. 2 June 1850. Berne, Switzerland.** Comments on slavery and emancipation. 9 August 1850. p.127, c5.

1618 S. H. L. *to* **THE EDITOR. n.d. n.p.** Considers the office of the public executioner a sad commentary on society. 9 August 1850. p.128, c2.

1619 CALVIN FAIRBANK *to* **MR. EDITOR. 24 July 1850. Warren.** Describes an anti-slavery meeting which was disrupted by a mob. 9 August 1850. p.128, c3.

1620 ROBERT EDMOND *to* **FRIEND GARRISON. 27 July 1850. Boston.** Denounces Colonel Mitchell, a Scotsman whose beliefs typify immigrant anti-Negro ideas. 9 August 1850. p.128, c4.

1621 SAMUEL J. MAY *to* **THE** *ANTI-SLAVERY STANDARD.* **n.d. n.p.** Describes an abolition meeting held to protest the kidnapping of blacks. 16 August 1850. p.131, c3.

1622 LORING MOODY *to* **FRIEND GARRISON. 9 August 1850. Fairhaven.** Comments on New Bedford anti-slavery meetings held at black churches. 16 August 1850. p.132, c2.

1623 n.n. *to* **MR. GARRISON. 16 August 1850. Portsmouth.** Describes the case of a fugitive slave in Portsmouth. 16 August 1850. p.132, c4.

1624 HOWARD *to* **CHIEF JUSTICE SHAW. n.d. n.p.** Comments on the case of Professor Webster. 16 August 1850. p.132, c2.

1625 LOUISA PERINA CLEMENS *to* **MR. GARRISON. 21 July 1850. Nelsonville, Oh.** Upholds the Sabbath as a special day. 16 August 1850. p.132, c4.

1626 MAXCY GREGG *to* **HON. H. S. FOOTE. 12 August 1850. Columbia, S. C.** Denies that he stated that South Carolina will secede upon the admission of California. 23 August 1850. p.134, c2.

1627 C. STEARNS *to* **MR. GARRISON. 18 August 1850. Boston.** Draws an analogy between General Taylor and Robespierre. 23 August 1950. p.135, c1.

1628 MILLY MORSE *to* **MR. EDITOR. 16 August 1850. Foxboro.** Appeals for financial aid for fugitives in Canada. 23 August 1850. p.135, c2.

1629 S. H. L. *to* **SHERIFF EVELETH. n.d. n.p.** Asks sheriff to justify capital punishment and his role as executioner. 23 August 1850. p.136, c2.

1630 JOHN M. SPEAR *to* **FRIEND GARRISON. n.d. n.p.** Denies that the gallows deter crimes. 23 August 1850. p.136, c3.

1631 A CITIZEN *to* **CITIZENS OF DISTRICT OF COLUMBIA. 10 August 1850. Georgetown, D.C.** Denounces abolitionists as "unscrupulous traitors." 30 August 1850. p.137, c1.

1632 G. VANTORT *to* **THE EDITOR OF THE** *BOSTON INVESTIGATOR.* **28 July 1850. Mobile, Al.** Supports the segregation policy of the Sons of Temperance. 30 August 1850. p.137, c1.

1633 ALEXANDER HUTCHISON *to* **AAS. 12 March 1850. Edinburgh.** Encloses a foreign anti-slavery bequest of forty English pounds. 30 August 1850. p.138, c5.

1634 SAMUEL MAY, JR. *to* **MR. GARRISON. 26 August 1850. Leicester.** Reports on an anti-slavery convention in Rutland. 30 August 1850. p.138, c6.

1635 H. *to* **FRIEND GARRISON. August 1850. Plymouth.** Declares that immoral oaths are not binding. 30 August 1850. p.139, c2.

1636 R. WENT *to* **THE EDITOR OF THE** *LIBERATOR.* **n.d. n.p.** Opposes capital punishment. 30 August 1850. p.139, c2.

1637 C. G. G. *to* **MR. GARRISON. n.d. n.p.** Describes three tableaux which he feels would have correctly portrayed the late President Taylor's accomplishments. 30 August 1850. p.140, c2.

1638 JOHN NOYES, JR. *to* **FRIEND GARRISON. 31 July 1850. South Abington.** Denounces eulogies lauding President Taylor. 30 August 1850. p.140, c2.

1639 LEWIS WOODSON *to* **MR. EDITOR. 27 August 1850. Pittsburgh.** Denies that he is pro-slavery. 6 September 1850. p.143, c1.

1640 H. C. WRIGHT *to* **GARRISON. August 1850. Litchfield.** Claims that Southerners attack all abolitionists as infidels and atheists. 6 September 1850. p.144, c2.

1641 ALFRED WOOD *to* **EDITORS OF THE** *PENNSYLVANIA FREEMAN.* **12 June 1850. Philadelphia.** Describes an attack upon a free man of color. 13 September 1850. p.145, c5.

1642 n.n. *to* **MR. GARRISON. n.d. n.p.** Argues that abolitionists are not guilty of blasphemy and infidelity. 13 September 1850. p.146, c3.

1643 H. C. WRIGHT *to* **R. D. WEBB. 21 August 1850. Litchfield, Oh.** Notes that a gas spring is nature's light. 13 September 1850. p.148, c2.

1644 H. N. SPOONER *to* **THE EDITOR OF THE** *LIBERATOR.* **31 August 1850. Plymouth.** Opposes capital punishment. 13 September 1850. p.148, c3.

1645 JAMES MACARA *to* **MR. GARRISON. 26 August 1850. Edinburgh.** Believes that the Bible does not justify or prevent slavery. 20 September 1850. p.150, c4.

1646 E. H. *to* **THE EDITOR OF THE** *LIBERATOR.* **29 August 1850. Brownville, Me.** Supports the *Liberator*'s anti-slavery stance; opposes its views on the Sabbath. 20 September 1850. p.150, c5.

1647 E. A. S. *to* **W. L. G. 10 September 1850. Worcester.** Announces plans for a women's rights convention. 20 September 1850. p.151, c2.

1648 M. *to* **MR. EDITOR. n.d. n.p.** Expresses outrage that pro-slavery leader Isaiah Rynders is a Democratic delegate to the state convention. 20 September 1850. p.151, c2.

1649 EDMUND QUINCY *to* **THE EDITOR OF THE** *BOSTON POST.* **9 September 1850. n.p.** Objects to the *Boston Post* editor's refusal to print his reply to slander. 20 September 1850. p.152, c4.

1650 EDMUND QUINCY *to* **THE EDITOR OF THE** *TRANSCRIPT.* **5 September 1850. Dedham.** Replies to "Sigma," accusing him of slander. 20 September 1850. p.152, c4.

1651 H. *to* **MR. EDITOR. n.d. n.p.** Comments on the debate between Quincy and "Sigma." 27 September 1850. p.155, c2.

1652 S. G. *to* **MR. EDITOR. n.d. n.p.** Corrects misapprehensions about a lecture delivered at a women's convention in Worcester. 27 September 1850. p.155, c3.

1653 G. W. F. MELLEN *to* **MR. GARRISON. n.d. n.p.** Answers Smith's charges about a remark he made against slavery. 27 September 1850. p.155, c3.

1654 HENRY C. WRIGHT *to* **JAMES HAUGHTON. 8 September 1850. Mesopotamia, Oh.** Expresses contempt for the late Zachary Taylor. 27 September 1850. p.156, c2.

1655 OLD COLONY *to* **FRIEND GARRISON. 17 September 1850. Plymouth.** Praises Professor Fowler's book on grammar. 27 September 1850. p.156, c3.

1656 HENRY C. WRIGHT *to* **GARRISON. 19 September 1850. Salem, Oh.** Condemns the Fugitive Slave Law and kidnappers of slaves. 4 October 1850. p.159, c1.

1657 GEORGE W. CARNES *to* **MESSRS. EDITORS [OF THE** *BOSTON TRAVELLER*]. **26 September 1850. Boston.** Denounces the Fugitive Slave Law. 4 October 1850. p.159, c2.

1658 T. GILBERT *to* **THE EDITOR OF THE** *BOSTON TRAVELLER.* **23 September 1850. Boston.** Opposes the Fugitive Slave Law; prefers to obey the laws of God and violate those of man. 4 October 1850. p.159, c2.

1659 R. WENT *to* **THE EDITOR OF THE** *LIBERATOR.* **n.d. n.p.** Defends his interpretation of Webster. 4 October 1850. p.160, c2.

1660 EBENEZER PRICE AND 127 OTHERS *to* **DANIEL WEBSTER. August 1850. Salisbury, N. H.** Express their appreciation for his support of the Union and the Constitution. 11 October 1850. p.161, c1.

1661 DANIEL WEBSTER *to* **REV. EBENEZER PRICE AND OTHERS. 21 September 1850. Washington.** Replies to their letter of approbation. 11 October 1850. p.161, c1.

1662 JONATHAN WALKER *to* **FRIENDS OF JUSTICE AND HUMANITY. 4 October 1850. Plymouth.** Condemns the Fugitive Slave Law as "the kidnapping bill." 11 October 1850. p.163, c1.

1663 H. C. WRIGHT *to* **GARRISON. 29 September 1850. Millbrook, Mercer County, Pa.** Rejoices at the anti-government sentiment evoked by the Fugitive Slave Law. 11 October 1850. p.163, c1.

1664 E. A. S. *to* **FRIEND GARRISON. 4 October 1850. Worcester.** Reproaches S. Gregory's lecture at Worcester as being anti-women's rights. 11 October 1850. p.163, c3.

1665 T. *to* **EDITOR. n.d. n.p.** Opposes the Fugitive Slave Law as unconstitutional. 11 October 1850. p.163, c4.

1666 ZENAS T. HAINES *to* **MR. GARRISON. n.d. n.p.** Pleads for more moderate speech from abolitionists. 11 October 1850. p.163, c4.

1667 T. W. H. *to* **MR. EDITOR. [from the *Essex County Freeman*] n.d. n.p.** Attacks supporters of the Fugitive Slave Law. 18 October 1850. p.165, c3.

1668 JOSIAH QUINCY *to* **J. INGERSOLL BOWDITCH, ESQ. 14 October 1850. Quincy.** Asserts that it is one's moral duty to aid fugitive slaves. 18 October 1850. p.166, c6.

1669 D. S. WHITNEY *to* **BRO. GARRISON. 7 October 1850. Beverly.** Reports on a meeting in Haverhill. 18 October 1850. p.167, c4.

1670 OLD COLONY *to* **FRIEND GARRISON. n.d. n.p.** Opposes the sin of capital punishment. 18 October 1850. p.168, c3.

1671 O. N. R. *to* **MR. EDITOR. n.d. n.p.** Urges "Sigma" to be silent. 18 October 1850. p.168, c3.

1672 SAMUEL J. MAY *to* **THE *NORTH STAR*. 2 October 1850. Syracuse.** Explains that his preparations for three or four fugitive slaves have kept him from other activities. 25 October 1850. p.170, c3.

1673 HIRAM WILSON *to* **FRIEND GARRISON. 22 October 1850. Boston.** Believes that the number of colored persons seeking refuge in Canada will increase. 25 October 1850. p.170, c6.

1674 RICHARD *to* **n.n. 19 October 1850. n.p.** Derides papers which affirm the "supremacy of the law until it is repealed." 25 October 1850. p.170, c6.

1675 B. T. *to* **MR. EDITOR. 15 October 1850. South Weymouth.** Favors establishing a female medical school in Boston after the battle against slavery is won. 25 October 1850. p.170, c6.

1676 HORATIO N. SPOONER *to* **FRIEND GARRISON. 21 October 1850. Plymouth.** Describes a meeting in Faneuil Hall to protest the Fugitive Slave Law. 25 October 1850. p.171, c2.

1677 S. M. *to* **FRIEND GARRISON. 20 October 1850. Boston.** Corrects a printing error in the *Liberator*. 25 October 1850. p.171, c2.

1678 HENRY C. WRIGHT *to* **JAMES HAUGHTON. 8 October 1850. Steamer *Globe*, Ohio River.** Attacks the Fugitive Slave Law; favors punishing slaveholders as felons. 25 October 1850. p.172, c2.

1679 J. W. *to* **FRIEND GARRISON. n.d. n.p.** Denounces inconsistency of temperance men. 25 October 1850. p.172, c4.

1680 D. S. GRANDIN *to* **FRIEND GARRISON. 12 October 1850. Portland.** Replies to a letter in the "Household Words" column in which Dickens lauds Taylor. 25 October 1850. p.172, c4.

1681 ZENAS T. HAINES *to* **MR. GARRISON. n.d. n.p.** Criticizes religious strictures regarding the Sabbath. 25 October 1850. p.172, c4.

1682 JNO. H. PEARSON *to* **EDMUND QUINCY, JAMES RUSSELL LOWELL. 7 September 1850. Boston.** Defends his reasons for sending a slave back to New Orleans. 1 November 1850. p.173, c1.

1683 HORACE MANN *to* **CHARLES F. ADAMS. n.d. n.p.** Opposes the Fugitive Slave Law on moral and constitutional grounds. 1 November 1850. p.173, c6.

1684 FRANCIS JACKSON *to* **J. MILLER McKIM. 10 October 1850. Boston.** Regrets he cannot attend a meeting of the Pennsylvania AS. 1 November 1850. p.174, c4.

1685 PARKER PILLSBURY *to* **FRIEND GARRISON. 18 October 1850. Norristown, Pa.** Notes large attendance at the anniversary of the Pennsylvania AS. 1 November 1850. p.176, c2.

1686 W. J. W. *to* **MR. EDITOR. 9 October 1850. Boston.** A colored man expresses his opposition to the Fugitive Slave Law. 1 November 1850. p.176, c3.

1687 DANIEL WEBSTER *to* **UNION MEETING. 28 October 1850. Franklin, N.H.** Believes that the Fugitive Slave Law should be respected since it is the law of the land. 8 November 1850. p.177, c1.

1688 W. L. G. *to* **THE EDITOR OF THE** *TIMES***. 1 November 1850. Boston.** Refutes the assertion by the *Times* that George Thompson was sent to "extinguish" the Fugitive Slave Law. 8 November 1850. p.178, c4.

1689 HENRY C. WRIGHT *to* **GARRISON. 10 October 1850. Brighton, Pa.** Declares that the Fugitive Slave Law should be resisted at all cost. 8 November 1850. p.179, c1.

1690 JOHN GRIFFIN *to* **W. L. GARRISON. 8 October 1850. New York.** Suggests that Douglass be sold South and that Garrison receive half the proceeds. 8 November 1850. p.179, c1.

1691 E. P. *to* **GARRISON. September 1850. Chester County, Pa.** Reports having seen numerous "runaway slave" posters on a trip through Central Virginia. 8 November 1850. p.179, c2.

1692 CAROLINE W. H. DALL *to* **PAULINA W. DAVIS. 2 November 1850. Boston.** Believes that women's rights can be guaranteed without infringement upon the rights of others. 8 November 1850. p.179, c3.

1693 C. C. BURLEIGH *to* **GARRISON. 21 October 1850. Leominster.** Notes a successful abolition meeting. 8 November 1850. p.180, c2.

1694 PILGRIM *to* **MR. EDITOR. 17 October 1850. Newburyport.** Assails the North's "lethargy" and "stupidity" in not opposing the Fugitive Slave Bill. 8 November 1850. p.180, c3.

1695 A. J. GROVER *to* **MR. EDITOR. 21 October 1850. Albany, Me.** Charges that Nathaniel S. Littlefield is a mob leader and supporter of the Fugitive Slave Bill. 8 November 1850. p.180, c4.

1696 ELIZABETH WILSON *to* **FRIENDS AND FELLOW LABORERS. 27 September 1850. Cadiz, Oh.** Endorses movement for women's rights. 15 November 1850. p.181, c3.

1697 O. S. FOWLER *to* **OFFICERS OF WOMAN'S CONVENTION. n.d. n.p.** Stresses women's rights and the importance of working to achieve them. 15 November 1850. p.181, c5.

1698 WM. LOVETT *to* **WILLIAM FARMER. 14 October 1850. New Road.** Regrets that he is unable to attend a soiree in honor of George Thompson. 15 November 1850. p.182, c2.

1699 CAROLINE W. H. DALL *to* **WM. L. GARRISON. 10 November 1850. Boston.** Points out a misprint in a recent issue of the *Liberator*. 15 November 1850. p.183, c5.

1700 SAMUEL MAY, JR. *to* **MR. GARRISON. n.d. n.p.** Corrects a mistake concerning the date of Pillsbury's lecture. 15 November 1850. p.183, c5.

1701 JAMES HAUGHTON *to* **HENRY C. WRIGHT. 28 October 1850. Dublin.** Discusses the magnitude of reformers' work; opposes the Fugitive Slave Law; discusses temperance in Ireland. 22 November 1850. p.185, c2.

1702 E. A. LUKENS *to* **FRIEND. October 1850. New Garden, Oh.** Asserts that the struggles for the rights of women and the abolition of slavery are linked. 22 November 1850. p.188, c2.

1703 MARGARET CHAPPELSMITH *to* **P. W. DAVIS. 20 September 1850. New Harmony, Il.** Upholds the importance of women's intellectual contributions to the struggle for liberty. 22 November 1850. p.188, c2.

1704 NANCY M. BAIRD *to* **THE WOMAN'S RIGHTS CONVENTION. n.d. n.p.** Extends her best wishes for the success of the women's rights convention. 22 November 1850. p.188, c3.

1705 JANE COWEN *to* **SISTERS. [extract] n.d. Logansport, In.** Blames the Bible for suppressing women's rights. 22 November 1850. p.188, c3.

1706 SOPHIA L. LITTLE *to* **THE WOMAN'S CONVENTION. 9 October 1850. Pawtucket.** Stresses the importance of the women's rights convention. 22 November 1850. p.188, c3.

1707 HENRY C. WRIGHT *to* **GARRISON. 2 November 1850. Centreville, In.** Reports topics discussed at the anti-slavery meeting which included women's rights and the Fugitive Slave Law. 22 November 1850. p.188, c4.

1708 FREEMAN *to* **THE EDITOR OF THE *BOSTON POST*. n.d. n.p.** Asks why the *Post* publishes writings of pro-slavery individuals. 22 November 1850. p.188, c5.

1709 EDMUND QUINCY *to* **THE EDITOR OF THE *POST*. 17 November 1850. Dedham.** Discusses whether Quincy could have prevented the disruption of George Thompson's farewell soiree. 29 November 1850. p.192, c4.

1710 W. S. DERRICK *to* **ROBERT COLLINS. 9 November 1850. Washington.** Declares that the Crafts are fugitive slaves belonging rightfully to him. 29 November 1850. p.192, c5.

1711 DANIEL WEBSTER *to* **MESSRS. WILLIAM KINNEY, BENJAMIN CRAWFORD, JAMES POINTS, L. WANDELL, WM. FRAKIER. 23 November 1850. Washington, D.C.** Regrets that he cannot attend a Union meeting. 13 December 1850. p.197, c1.

1712 DANIEL WEBSTER *to* **B. F. AYER. 16 November 1850. Boston.** Opposes disunionism and disobedience to laws. 13 December 1850. p.197, c1.

1713 DANIEL WEBSTER *to* **JOSIAH RANDALL, ISAAC HAZELHURST, ROBERT H. LEE, C. INGERSOLL, JOHN W. FORNEY, JOHN S. RIDDLE. 14 November 1850. Boston.** Regrets he is unable to attend a rally for the Constitution and Union. 13 December 1850. p.197, c2.

1714 A. L. *to* **FRIEND GARRISON. 7 December 1850. Lynn.** Praises Thompson's delivery of the Sixteenth Annual Address before the Salem Female AS. 13 December 1850. p.198, c4.

1715 JOHN T. SARGENT *to* **THE EDITOR OF THE** *EVENING TRANSCRIPT***. n.d. n.p.** Refutes the statement that George Thompson is visiting the United States in order to promote dissolution. 13 December 1850. p.198, c4.

1716 HENRY BIBB *to* **W. L. GARRISON. 20 November 1850. Sandwich, Canada West.** Feels thankful that slaves have chosen Canada as a refuge. 13 December 1850. p.198, c6.

1717 HIRAM WILSON *to* **FRIEND GARRISON. 4 December 1850. St. Catharine's.** Discusses fugitive slaves in Canada. 13 December 1850. p.198, c6.

1718 HENRY C. WRIGHT *to* **GARRISON. 19 November 1850. Portland, In.** Asserts the right of slaves to be free. 13 December 1850. p.199, c1.

1719 ONE OF THE COMMITTEE *to* **MR. GARRISON. n.d. n.p.** Announces plans for the Anti-Slavery Bazaar. 13 December 1850. p.199, c5.

1720 GRACE GREENWOOD *to* **THE** *NATIONAL ERA***. 22 November 1850. Lynn.** Reports on lectures by George Thompson in Lynn. 13 December 1850. p.200, c3.

1721 WM. J. WATKINS *to* **FRIEND GARRISON. 21 November 1850. Boston.** Praises George Thompson. 20 December 1850. p.201, c6.

1722 C. L. WESTON *to* **FRIEND GARRISON. 13 December 1850. New Ipswich.** Assails Henry Ward Beecher for implying that William Lloyd Garrison was reckless and unstable. 20 December 1850. p.203, c2.

1723 JOSEPH BARKER *to* **FRIEND GARRISON. 24 October 1850. Wortley.** Cites the Fugitive Slave Law as his reason for not moving to America. 20 December 1850. p.203, c3.

1724 J. B. SYME *to* **W. L. GARRISON. 14 December 1850. Worcester.** Calls Henry Wigham's letter an inspiration. 20 December 1850. p.203, c3.

1725 H. H. BRIGHAM *to* **FRIEND GARRISON. 17 December 1850. Abington.** Reports on a well-attended reception for George Thompson. 20 December 1850. p.203, c4.

1726 ETHAN SPIKE *to* **MESSRS. GOULD AND ELWELL. 14 October 1850. Hornby.** Opposes the Fugitive Slave Law. 20 December 1850. p.208 [204], c4.

1727 ISAAC HILL *to* **DANIEL WEBSTER. 17 April 1850. Concord, N.H.** Praises Webster's "Union" speech. 27 December 1850. p.205, c1.

1728 DANIEL WEBSTER *to* **ISAAC A. HILL. 20 April 1850. Washington.** Thanks Hills for his letter of commendation. 27 December 1850. p.205, c1.

1729 E. SPRAGUE *to* **MR. EDITOR. 3 November 1850. Abington.** Sends proceedings of the abolitionist meeting in Abington. 27 December 1850. p.207, c3.

1730 D. H. GREGORY *to* **MR. EDITOR. n.d. Princeton.** Protests the Fugitive Slave Law. 27 December 1850. p.207, c3.

1731 WILLIAM J. WATKINS *to* **FRIEND GARRISON. 17 December 1850. Boston.** Questions Southern papers which claim that slaves prefer to live in the South. 27 December 1850. p.207, c3.

1732 A DESCENDANT OF THE PILGRIMS *to* **FRIEND GARRISON. 19 November 1850. Plymouth.** Regrets that pro-slavery men prevented George Thompson from delivering a speech at Faneuil Hall. 27 December 1850. p.207, c4.

1733 HENRY C. WRIGHT *to* **GARRISON. 7 December 1850. Greensboro, In.** Criticizes Indiana for prohibiting persons of color from voting. 27 December 1850. p.208, c2.

1734 ISRAEL ROSS VAN WAKLE *to* **JOHN LEVY. 15 July 1850. St. Croix.** Provides particulars of the 1848 insurrection in St. Croix. 27 December 1850. p.208, c3.

[1851]

1735 JOHN ATWOOD *to* **COL. JOHN WHITE. 30 November 1850. New Boston.** Condemns slavery and the Fugitive Slave Law. 3 January 1851. p.1, c3.

1736 JOHN ATWOOD *to* **THE EDITORS OF THE** *NEW HAMPSHIRE PATRIOT.* **19 December 1850. New Boston.** Retracts the statements in opposition to the Fugitive Slave Law. 3 January 1851. p.1, c4.

1737 GEO. THOMPSON *to* **GARRISON. 3 October 1850. Matlock, Derbyshire, England.** Discusses motives behind his visit to the United States. 3 January 1851. p.3, c1.

1738 PARKER PILLSBURY *to* **FRIEND GARRISON. n.d. n.p.** Reports on the dedication of Union Hall at Harwich. 3 January 1851. p.3, c3.

1739 C. C. B. *to* **BROTHER GARRISON. n.d. n.p.** Encloses resolutions against the Fugitive Slave Law. 3 January 1851. p.3, c3.

1740 HENRY GREW *to* **FRIEND GARRISON. n.d. n.p.** Conveys his views of women's rights; describes the drive for equality as contrary to God's law. 3 January 1851. p.4, c2.

1741 R. WENT *to* **THE EDITOR OF THE** *LIBERATOR.* **n.d. South Boston.** Asserts that good thoughts yield good actions. 3 January 1851. p.4, c2.

1742 J. R. POINSETT *to* **FELLOW-CITIZENS. 4 December 1850. Charleston, S.C.** Supports the Union because it ensures South Carolina's prosperity. 10 January 1851. p.5, c1.

1743 SAMUEL MAY, JR. *to* **MR. GARRISON. 7 January 1851. Boston.** Forwards extracts from a letter by ''a lady of very decided orthodox views and predilections'' who opposes slavery. 10 January 1851. p.7, c1.

1744 n.n. *to* **n.n. [extract] 7 November 1850. n.p.** Admonishes the ministers of America for not being more outspoken against slavery. 10 January 1851. p.7, c1.

1745 n.n. *to* **n.n. [extract] 25 November 1850. n.p.** Applauds England's Evangelical Alliance for passing a resolution to bar slaveholders from their meeting in August. 10 January 1851. p.7, c1.

1746 n.n. *to* **n.n. [extract] 5 December 1850. n.p.** Assails the slaveholders of America. 10 January 1851. p.7, c1.

1747 n.n. *to* **SAMUEL MAY, JR. [extract] n.d. n.p.** Wishes not to be identified with the Boston Unitarians because of their views favoring slavery. 10 January 1851. p.7, c1.

1748 BENJAMIN TIRRELL *to* **FRIEND GARRISON. 3 January 1850. South Weymouth.** Gives an account of spirits "talking" at La Roy Sunderland's house. 10 January 1851. p.7, c2.

1749 H. C. WRIGHT *to* **GARRISON. 18 December 1850. Dublin, In.** Affirms the duty of the people of the North to incite and assist the slaves to escape slavery. 10 January 1851. p.8, c2.

1750 W. S. *to* **THE** *BOSTON ATLAS.* **25 December 1850. Washington.** Claims that the case of Adam Gibson is a test of the Fugitive Slave Law. 17 January 1851, p.9, c3.

1751 JOHN G. PALFREY *to* **THE FREE SOIL MEMBERS OF THE GENERAL COURT OF MASSACHUSETTS FOR THE YEAR 1851. n.d. n.p.** Denounces the political alliance between Free-Soilers and Democrats. 17 January 1851. p.9, c4.

1752 CHARLES FRANCIS ADAMS *to* **THE EDITORS OF** *BOSTON ATLAS.* **6 January 1851. Boston.** Describes activity in the Free-Soil movement. 17 January 1851. p.9, c5.

1753 HENRY C. WRIGHT *to* **GARRISON. 24 December 1850. Cambridge City, In.** Asserts that protection of the fugitive slave is a sacred duty. 17 January 1851. p.12, c3.

1754 A SLAVEHOLDER *to* **THE EDITORS OF THE** *ENQUIRER.* **10 January 1851. Washington.** Opposes the return of a slave, Henry Long, to the North. 24 January 1851. p.13, c1.

1755 P. T. BARNUM *to* **MR. RITCHIE. 14 December 1850. Baltimore.** Denies that Jenny Lind gave money to abolitionists. 24 January 1851. p.13, c2.

1756 THOMAS RITCHIE *to* **P. T. BARNUM. 12 December 1850. Washington.** Asks Barnum to refute the "insidious report" that Barnum harbored a fugitive slave. 24 January 1851. p.13, c2.

1757 P. T. BARNUM *to* **MR. RITCHIE. 12 December 1850. Washington.** Assures Ritchie that Joice Heath was a constitutionalist and a sympathizer of Southern institutions. 24 January 1851. p.13, c2.

1758 THOMAS RITCHIE *to* **P. T. BARNUM. 12 December 1850. Washington, D.C.** Asks Barnum whether his exhibit of a black man turning white is meant as a commentary on the South. 24 January 1851. p.13, c2.

1759 P. T. BARNUM *to* **THOMAS RITCHIE. 12 December 1850. Washington.** Declares that he used a Negro of spotted color in his exhibit; adds that the exhibit is not a commentary on Southern institutions. 24 January 1851. p.13, c3.

1760 THOMAS RITCHIE *to* **P. T. BARNUM. 12 December 1850.Washington.** Discusses the "secret and insidious report" that Barnum's "Fejee Mermaid" is intended to satirize the Compromise Bill, that General Foote of Mississippi is "impudently typified by monkey head," and that Webster is "personated by the codfish." 24 January 1851. p.13, c3.

1761 P. T. BARNUM *to* **THOMAS RITCHIE. 12 December 1850. Washington.** Claims that the "Fejee Mermaid" points to no moral except patriotism; explains that the mermaid represents the conjunction of the interests of two parts of country. 24 January 1851. p.13, c3.

1762 JOHN BROWN *to* **THE** *NEW YORK EVENING POST.* **27 December 1850. Jersey Ferry.** Comments on Webster's drunkenness at Jenny Lind's concert. 24 January 1851. p.13, c4.

1763 FREDRIKA BREMER *to* **MR. CRISTY. 9 December 1850. Cincinnati.** Thanks Cristy for sending his lectures on African colonization. 24 January 1851. p.14, c2.

1764 WM. WELLS BROWN *to* **W. L. G. 3 January 1851. Edinburgh.** Reports on the arrival of William and Ellen Craft in England. 24 January 1851. p.15, c2.

1765 AN ENGLISHMAN *to* **FRIENDS AND FELLOW COUNTRYMEN. 18 January 1851. Boston.** Criticizes contradictory concept of liberty held by people of the United States; notes that the North talks about abolition but takes little action. 24 January 1851. p.15, c3.

1766 JOHN N. BARBOUR *to* **MR. EDITOR [W. L. GARRISON]. 18 January 1851. Boston.** Appeals for food, clothing, and money for fugitive slaves in Canada. 24 January 1851. p.15, c4.

1767 SAMUEL WILBUR *to* **FRIEND GARRISON. n.d. North Easton, N.Y.** Supports women's rights. 24 January 1851. p.16, c4.

1768 DANIEL WEBSTER *to* **JAMES A. HAMILTON, GEORGE B. BUTLER, JOHN B. HASKIN, AND ALBERT LOCKWOOD. 27 January 1851. Washington.** Opposes disunion; believes that the controversy over disunion has abated. 7 February 1851. p.21, c3.

1769 GEORGE B. MATHEW *to* **THE GOVERNOR OF SOUTH CAROLINA, J. H. MEANS. 14 December 1850. Columbia.** Discusses trade between the West Indies and South Carolina; protests the imprisonment of British colored subjects. 7 February 1851. p.22, c2.

1770 J. H. MEANS *to* **GEORGE B. MATHEW. 16 December 1850. Columbia, S.C.** Promises that the legislature will review imprisonment of British colored subjects. 7 February 1851. p.22, c2.

1771 GEORGE B. MATHEW *to* **GOVERNOR OF SOUTH CAROLINA. 17 December 1850. Columbia.** Acknowledges receipt of letter from J. H. Means. 7 February 1851. p.22, c2.

1772 JOHN H. MEANS *to* **GEORGE B. MATHEW. 19 December 1850. Columbia.** Acknowledges receipt of letter from G. B. Mathew. 7 February 1851. p.22, c2.

1773 WILLIAM P. POWELL *to* **FRIEND GARRISON. 3 January 1851. London.** Argues that the power of capital over labor oppresses the poor in England, much as slavery oppresses Negroes in America. 7 February 1851. p.23, c3.

1774 WM. WELLS BROWN *to* **MR. GARRISON. 16 January 1851. Glasgow.** Describes an anti-slavery meeting in Glasgow. 7 February 1851. p.23, c3.

1775 H. C. WRIGHT *to* **W. L. GARRISON. 29 December 1850. Greensboro, In.** Denounces the expulsion of free colored children from public schools. 7 February 1851. p.23, c4.

1776 H. C. WRIGHT *to* **GARRISON. 29 December 1850. Greensborough, In.** Encloses a note which is indicative of the injustices suffered by colored people. 7 February 1851. p.23, c4.

1777 JOHN POLK AND PATRICK J. T. BOYLE *to* **T. S. HARPER. n.d. n.p.** Order Harper, a school trustee, to remove Negro children from school. 7 February 1851. p.23, c4.

1778 HORACE MANN *to* **THOMAS H. TALBOT. 25 January 1851. Washington.** Denounces the "manifold wickedness" of the Fugitive Slave Law. 14 February 1851. p.26, c3.

1779 ELIZA J. KENNY *to* **MR. KENNY. n.d. n.p.** Corrects a printing mistake in the *Liberator*. 14 February 1851. p.26, c6.

1780 ONE OF THE WOLVES IN SHEEPS' CLOTHING *to* **THE** *LIBERATOR*. **31 January 1851. Painesville, Oh.** Notes sarcastically that ministers could stop cannibalism in New Zealand, but not slavery in the United States. 14 February 1851. p.28, c2.

1781 JONATHAN WALKER *to* **FRIEND GARRISON. 3 February 1851. Plymouth.** Comments on his travels in Vermont. 14 February 1851. p.28, c3.

1782 E. B. KENRICK *to* **FRIEND GARRISON. 31 January 1851. Cambridgeport.** Argues that phrenology justifies slavery. 14 February 1851. p.28, c4.

1783 DANIEL WEBSTER *to* **REV. DR. SPENCER. 7 December 1850. Washington.** Defends obedience to the established government as a Christian duty. 21 February 1851. p.29, c6.

1784 SAMUEL CHURCH *to* **REV. ICHABOD S. SPENCER. 17 December 1850. Litchfield, Ct.** Describes the pleasure with which he read Spencer's "Religious Duty of Obedience to Law." 21 February 1851. p.29, c6.

1785 SAMUEL H. COX *to* **REV. DR. SPENCER. 7 December 1850. Brooklyn.** Praises Spencer's sermon. 21 February 1851. p.29, c6.

1786 J. M. VAN COTT *to* **REV. ICHABOD S. SPENCER. 9 December 1850. Brooklyn.** Praises Spencer's sermon on obedience to law. 21 February 1851. p.29, c1.

1787 FRANCIS TUKEY *to* **MAYOR JOHN P. BIGELOW. 17 February 1851. n.p.** Describes the capture of a fugitive slave. 21 February 1851. p.30, c5.

1788 G. W. P. *to* **GARRISON. 17 February 1850. Springfield, Ma.** Describes mobocracy in Springfield and the disruption of abolitionist meetings. 21 February 1851. p.31, c1.

1789 G.W.P. *to* **THE** *LIBERATOR*. **19 February 1851. Schagticoke, N.Y.** Reports on the "egging" of Mr. Thompson at Springfield. 25 February 1851. p.35, c1.

1790 FRANCIS BISHOP *to* **FRIEND GARRISON. 25 December 1850. Liverpool.** Opposes the Fugitive Slave Law; fears for the safety of William and Ellen Craft. 25 February 1851. p.35, c3.

1791 G. W. P. *to* **MR. GARRISON. n.d. n.p.** Reports on George Thompson's stay in Union Village, New York. 25 February 1851. p.35, c4.

1792 F. H. DRAKE *to* **MR. GARRISON. 19 February 1851. Leominster.** Regrets that Garrison is unable to attend the Leominster fair. 25 February 1851. p.35, c5.

1793 E. D. HUDSON *to* **n.n. 25 February 1851. Springfield.** Denounces the instigators of the Springfield riot. 25 February 1851. p.35, c5.

1794 HENRY C. WRIGHT *to* **JAMES HAUGHTON. 5 February 1851. New Garden, Oh.** Sarcastically suggests an exhibit on American slavery at the World's Fair in London; denounces Fredrika Bremer. 25 February 1851. p.36, c2.

1795 HENRY FISH *to* **BROTHER GARRISON. 17 February 1851. Hopedale, Ma.** Corrects a printing error. 25 February 1851. p.36, c4.

1796 G. E. H. *to* **MR. EDITOR. 25 January 1851. Boston.** Comments on spiritual manifestations at the Sunderland house. 25 February 1851. p.36, c4.

1797 MILLARD FILLMORE *to* **J. J. HENRY, M. TAYLOR, H. GRINEL, I. TOWNSEND, G. DOUGLASS, C. J. CARLETON, F. GRIFFIN, F. S. LATHROP, E. K. COLLINS, AND R. C. WETMORE. 17 February 1851. Washington.** Reports that he is unable to attend the celebration of Washington's birthday. 7 March 1851. p.37, c1.

1798 DANIEL WEBSTER *to* **MOSES TAYLOR, ISAAC TOWNSEND, CHAS. G. CARLETON, JOSHUA J. HENRY, FRANCIS S. LATHROP, GEORGE DOUGLASS, FRANCIS GRIFFIN, HENRY GRINNELL, AND EDWARD K. COLLINS. 20 February 1851. Washington.** Regrets that he is unable to attend the Washington's birthday celebration. 7 March 1851. p.37, c1.

1799 H. CLAY *to* **F. S. LATHROP, FRANCIS GRIFFIN, ETC. 17 February 1851. Washington.** Reports that he cannot attend the dinner celebrating Washington's birthday. 7 March 1851. p.37, c3.

1800 SIMON BEACHCROFT *to* **GEORGE THOMPSON. 25 January. New Orleans.** Invites Thompson to New Orleans, promising a warm welcome. 7 March 1851. p.37, c3.

1801 AN ABOLITIONIST *to* **THE** *LONDON PATRIOT.* **n.d. n.p.** Denounces the American Fugitive Slave Act. 7 March 1851. p.37, c6.

1802 SEVENTY-SIX *to* **BALDWIN. [from the** *Hartford Republican***] 24 February 1851. Springfield.** Assails Hunkerism and the Springfield mob. 7 March 1851. p.38, c3.

1803 n.n. *to* **WM. LLOYD GARRISON. 14 February 1851. Boston.** Clarifies an article about Josiah Henson by Eliot. 7 March 1851. p.38, c5.

1804 G. W. P. *to* **MR. GARRISON. 23 February 1851. Little Falls, N.Y.** Describes the itinerary of George Thompson in New York state. 7 March 1851. p.39, c1.

1805 GEORGE THOMPSON *to* **JOHN GRIFFIN. 22 February 1851. Little Falls, N. Y.** Describes his own attitude as pro-Ireland and pro-Catholic. 7 March 1851. p.39, c2.

1806 ELIZABETH PEASE *to* **WM. LLOYD GARRISON. 18 January 1851. Darlington, England.** Opposes the Fugitive Slave Law; urges international opposition. 7 March 1851. p.39, c3.

1807 C. M. CONRAD *to* **BREVET MAJOR GEORGE A. THOMAS. 17 February 1851. Washington.** Issues orders to enforce the Fugitive Slave Law in Boston. 7 March 1851. p.39, c6.

1808 WILL. A. GRAHAM *to* **COMMODORE JOHN DOWNES. 17 February 1851. Boston.** Commands the military to be prepared to enforce the Fugitive Slave Law. 7 March 1851. p.39, c6.

1809 EDWARD SEARCH *to* **GARRISON. January 1851. London.** Assails the papal bull creating a Catholic hierarchy in England. 7 March 1851. p.40, c2.

1810 A. H. WOOD *to* **FRIEND GARRISON. 8 February 1851. Pepperell.** Displays dismay at the refusal of some townspeople to sign abolitionist petitions. 7 March 1851. p.40, c4.

1811 HENRY GREW *to* **FRIEND GARRISON. n.d. n.p.** Supports women's rights but not equality. 7 March 1851. p.40, c5.

1812 LEWIS CASS *to* **UNION MEETING. n.d. n.p.** Cites the danger of disunion. 14 March 1851. p.41, c1.

1813 S. BOURNE *to* **MESSRS. EDITORS OF THE** *COMMONWEALTH.* **5 March 1851. n.p.** Sends a letter from Kentucky which expresses anti-abolitionist sentiments. 14 March 1851. p.41, c3.

1814 G. W. P. *to* **MR. GARRISON. 26 February 1851. Herkimer County, N.Y.** Reports on an anti-slavery convention at Peterboro' where Douglass was made an officer. 14 March 1851. p.43, c1.

1815 J. C. HANCHETT *to* **GARRISON. 5 March 1851. Syracuse, N.Y.** Praises the success of George Thompson in Syracuse. 14 March 1851. p.43, c5.

1816 ELIZABETH WILSON *to* **MR. GARRISON. 26 February 1851. Cadiz, Oh.** Assails H. Grew for his opposition to the women's rights convention in Worcester, Massachusetts. 14 March 1851. p.44, c3.

1817 SILVER GREY *to* **MR. EDITOR. n.d. n.p.** Suggests that the Holy Roman Church guide the majority's morals. 14 March 1851. p.44, c4.

1818 G. W. P. *to* **MR. GARRISON. 7 March 1851. Syracuse.** Reports on the anti-slavery convention at Syracuse; includes excerpts from George Thompson's speech. 21 March 1851. p.45, c3.

1819 FREDERICK DOUGLASS *to* **READERS. 1 March 1851. Peterboro'.** Describes George Thompson's speech. 21 March 1851. p.46, c1.

1820 EDWARD MATHEWS *to* **BRO. WALKER. 20 February 1851. Bryantsville.** Describes a beating he received at the hands of pro-slavery Kentuckians. 21 March 1851. p.46, c2.

1821 GEO. THOMPSON *to* **GARRISON. 12 March 1850. Rochester.** Reports on a visit to Rochester, where he lectured on British reform. 21 March 1851. p.47, c2.

1822 R. PLUMER *to* **FRIEND GARRISON. 14 March 1851. Newburyport.** Warns that Josephine, who masquerades as a needy runaway, is an impostor. 21 March 1851. p.47, c3.

1823 L. H. Y. *to* **FRIEND. 14 March 1851. Syracuse.** Reports on an anti-slavery convention at Syracuse. 21 March 1851. p.47, c3.

1824 RICHARD D. WEBB *to* **GARRISON. 28 February 1851. Dublin, Ireland.** Comments on Ireland, the commemoration meeting for the *Liberator*, and the Fugitive Slave Bill. 21 March 1851. p.47, c4.

1825 B. G. S. *to* **MR. GARRISON. 6 March 1851. Upton.** Lauds abolitionism in Upton. 21 March 1851. p.47, c5.

1826 CHARLES SPEAR *to* **FRIEND. January 1851. Boston.** Requests information from the British Parliament concerning the criminal laws in the United States. 21 March 1851. p.48, c5.

1827 G. W. P. *to* **MR. GARRISON. n.d. n.p.** Reviews speech by George Thompson at Rochester. 28 March 1851. p.50, c1.

1828 HENRY C. WRIGHT *to* **GARRISON. 22 February 1851. Leesburgh, Oh.** Hails the rescue of freeman Shadrach, who was mistaken for a fugitive. 28 March 1851. p.51, c2.

1829 DANIEL WEBSTER *to* **HON. JOHN P. BIGELOW. 10 March 1850. Washington.** Issues the president's acknowledgment of pro-slavery resolutions by the Boston Common Council. 28 March 1851. p.51, c5.

1830 EDWARD SEARCH *to* **GARRISON. January 1851. London.** Assails mercenary nature of popery in England. 28 March 1851. p.52, c2.

1831 G. W. P. *to* **W. L. GARRISON. 15 March 1851. Rochester.** Recounts Douglass' speech on the evils of slavery and obstacles to the anti-slavery crusade. 4 April 1851. p.53, c1.

1832 SALLIE HOLLEY *to* **W. L. GARRISON. 24 March 1851. Rochester.** Praises George Thompson's anti-slavery lectures. 4 April 1851. p.53, c6.

1833 A. C. W. *to* **FRIEND GARRISON. 24 March 1851. Rochester, N.Y.** Comments on the success of Thompson's visit to Rochester. 4 April 1851. p.60 [54], c1.

1834 GEO. THOMPSON *to* **GARRISON. 26 March 1851. Lockport, N.Y.** States that he was pleased with his Rochester visit. 4 April 1851. p.60 [54], c2.

1835 W. H. B. *to* **GARRISON. 25 March 1851. Plymouth (Old Colony).** Reports on two of Pillsbury's lectures. 4 April 1851. p.55, c2.

1836 H. C. WRIGHT *to* **GARRISON. 4 March 1851. Harrison County, Oh.** Regrets that a black child was ordered out of school. 4 April 1851. p.55, c3.

1837 A. ATWOOD *to* **WILLIAM C. WHITCOMB. 28 March 1851. Stoneham.** Assails the American church; believes it is sustained by slaveholders. 4 April 1851. p.55, c5.

1838 EDWARD MATHEWS *to* **MR. EDITOR. 17 February 1851. Whitehall.** Relates how he was again assaulted by pro-slavery Kentuckians. 11 April 1851. p.57, c3.

1839 REUBEN CARLLEY *to* **JOHN C. LAUNDERS. [from the *Independent Democrat*] n.d. Portsville, Montgomery County, Md.** Advises a slave catcher of runaways in the area. 11 April 1851. p.58, c3.

1840 AUSTIN BEARSE *to* **MR. EDITOR. n.d. n.p.** Relates his conversation with Cephas I. Ames, who claims that he discovered runaway Sims. 11 April 1851. p.59, c3.

1841 SAMUEL J. MAY *to* **GARRISON. 2 April 1851. Toronto, Upper Canada.** Reports on speeches by George Thompson in Canada. 11 April 1851. p.59, c4.

1842 S. J. MAY *to* **GARRISON. 4 April 1851. Toronto.** Describes his Toronto trip. 11 April 1851. p.59, c4.

1843 H. C. WRIGHT *to* **GARRISON. 7 March 1851. Leesburg, Oh.** Argues that slaves are protected by the Constitution no more than an outlaw is protected by the law. 11 April 1851. p.60, c2.

1844 HENRY C. WRIGHT *to* **GARRISON. 6 March 1851. Leesburg.** Condemns the nation's cry of "shoot the slave" if he escapes. 11 April 1851. p.60, c2.

1845 WILLIAM DURFEE *to* **FRIEND GARRISON. 24 March 1851. New Bedford.** Claims his conscience forbids him from aiding the government. 11 April 1851. p.60, c3.

1846 A WESTERN WOMAN *to* **MR. EDITOR. n.d. n.p.** Discusses a woman's duties to her husband and children. 11 April 1851. p.60, c3.

1847 G. W. P. *to* **MR. GARRISON. 8 April 1851. Toronto, Upper Canada.** Reports on Rev. May's anti-slavery activities in Canada. 18 April 1851. p.63, c1.

1848 SAMUEL J. MAY *to* **GARRISON. 10 April 1851. Steamboat on Lake Ontario.** Reports that he enjoyed Toronto; lauds George Thompson. 18 April 1851. p.63, c1.

1849 A YOUNG LADY *to* **FRIEND. 6 April 1851. Concord.** Cites hardships in planning the abolitionist festival at Concord. 18 April 1851. p.58 [64], c2.

1850 R. W. EMERSON *to* **FRIEND. 18 March 1851. New York.** Supports protest of the Fugitive Slave Law. 18 April 1851. p.58 [64], c3.

1851 HENRY C. WRIGHT *to* **GARRISON. 19 March 1851. Ohio.** Issues a prophetic warning to American slaveholders. 18 April 1851. p.58 [64], c3.

1852 GEORGE G. SMITH, ASA SWALLOW, HENRY CROCKER, RUFUS CHOATE, ET AL. *to* **HON. DANIEL WEBSTER. 11 April 1851. Boston.** Invite Webster to attend a meeting against disunionism. 25 April 1851. p.66, c2.

1853 DANIEL WEBSTER *to* **GEORGE C. SMITH, CALEB EDDY, ASA SWALLOW, URIEL CROCKER, ET AL. 15 April 1851. Marshfield.** Replies to invitation; reports that Faneuil Hall is closed to him. 25 April 1851. p.66, c2.

1854 EDWARD EVERETT *to* **NATHAN HALE. 16 April 1851. Cambridge.** Praises Webster's patriotism. 25 April 1851. p.66, c2.

1855 PARKER PILLSBURY *to* **FRIEND GARRISON. n.d. n.p.** Assails the lack of police cooperation at anti-slavery meetings in Saco and Biddeford, Maine. 25 April 1851. p.68, c2.

1856 HENRY C. WRIGHT *to* **GARRISON. 20 March 1851. Ohio.** Issues a warning to slaveholders. 25 April 1851. p.68, c2.

1857 JOSHUA CROWELL *to* **REV. JOSHUA CHANDLER. 14 April 1851. East Dennis.** Renounces Christianity for Judaism as a satirical criticism of the clergy. 25 April 1851. p.68, c4.

1858 A STUDENT *to* **MR. FOGG. 21 April 1851. Andover.** Encloses petitions from seminary students against slavery. 2 May 1851. p.70, c3.

1859 FRANCIS BRINLEY *to* **DANIEL WEBSTER. 18 April 1851. Marshfield, Ma.** Forwards preamble and resolutions adopted by the Common Council of Boston concerning the use of Faneuil Hall. 2 May 1851. p.70 [71], c4.

1860 DANIEL WEBSTER *to* **FRANCIS BRINLEY. 19 April 1851. Marshfield.** Expresses pleasure upon receiving communication from the Common Council of Boston. 2 May 1851. p.70 [71], c4.

1861 WM. H. SEWARD *to* **JOHN A. ANDREW. 5 April 1851. Auburn.** Opposes the Fugitive Slave Law; states that the law was designed to improve the economy of slave states. 16 May 1851. p.77, c4.

1862 LAUREN WETMORE *to* **WM. LLOYD GARRISON. 3 May 1851. New York.** Regrets that New York is not receptive to abolitionist meetings. 16 May 1851. p.78, c4.

1863 THOMAS HENNING *to* **REV. S. MAY. 5 May 1851. Toronto.** A delegate from the AS of Canada announces that he is coming to the annual meeting of the AAS. 16 May 1851. p.78, c6.

1864 D. MITCHELL *to* **FRIEND GARRISON. 25 April 1851. Pawtucket.** Warns that Samuel Ward is an impostor fugitive slave. 16 May 1851. p.79, c4.

1865 DANIEL WEBSTER *to* **THE NEW YORK COMMITTEE. 9 May 1851. Washington.** Regrets that he is unable to accept an invitation to New York. 16 May 1851. p.79, c4.

1866 C. B. SEDGWICK *to* **GEORGE THOMPSON. [from the** *Syracuse Journal***] 10 May 1851. n.p.** Apologizes for a misunderstanding which caused Thompson to feel insulted. 23 May 1851. p.82, c6.

1867 GEO. THOMPSON *to* **C. B. SEDGWICK. 10 May 1851. Syracuse, N.Y.** Accepts Sedgwick's apology. 23 May 1851. p.82, c6.

1868 HENRY C. WRIGHT *to* **W. L. G. 14 May 1851. Jericho, L.I.** Opposes reception for ''Fillmore the Kidnapper'' held in New York. 23 May 1851. p.83, c3.

1869 H. C. WRIGHT *to* **R. D. WEBB. 2 May 1851. Rochester, N.Y.** Describes his visit to the township of Northampton. 23 May 1851. p.84, c2.

1870 G. W. P. *to* **THE** *LIBERATOR***. 13 May 1851. Waterloo, N.Y.** Reports on Thompson and Garrison's meetings in central New York. 30 May 1851. p.87, c1.

1871 S. M. *to* **MR. GARRISON. 25 May 1851. Boston.** Requests that Douglass clarify his position on the Constitution. 30 May 1851. p.87, c3.

1872 M. STOWELL *to* **FRIEND GARRISON. 5 May 1851. Worcester.** Refutes the statement that a slaveholder can be an honored guest in Worcester. 30 May 1851. p.87, c3.

1873 HENRY C. WRIGHT *to* **GARRISON. 25 May 1851. Boston.** Discusses conceptions of God. 30 May 1851. p.88, c2.

1874 D. F. *to* **THE EDITOR OF THE** *LIBERATOR.* **10 May 1851. Concord, Ma.** Reports on Thomas A. Jones, a fugitive slave, who is doing well in England. 30 May 1851. p.88, c4.

1875 THOMAS H. JONES *to* **THE EDITOR OF THE** *LIBERATOR.* **6 May 1851. St. John.** Expresses thanks to all who showed him Christian hospitality. 30 May 1851. p.88, c5.

1876 THOMAS H. JONES *to* **D. F. 5 May 1851. St. John.** Views himself as an exiled patriot, not a fugitive slave. 30 May 1851. p.88, c5.

1877 HENRY C. WRIGHT *to* **GARRISON. 26 May 1851. Boston.** States that God is the inspiration of love and goodness. 6 June 1851. p.92, c2.

1878 HIRAM WILSON *to* **WM. L. GARRISON. 20 May 1851. St. Catharine's.** Discusses Canadian views on abolitionism and fugitive slaves; prefers their government and laws to those of the United States. 6 June 1851. p.92, c4.

1879 G. W. P. *to* **MR. GARRISON. 6 June 1851. Philadelphia.** Reports the itinerary of George Thompson in Pennsylvania. 13 June 1851. p.94, c5.

1880 FRANCIS S. ANDERSON *to* **MR. GARRISON. 21 April 1851. London.** A fugitive slave describes his escape. 13 June 1851. p.95, c1.

1881 SAMUEL MAY, JR. *to* **W. L. GARRISON. 7 June 1851. Leicester.** Questions Douglass' views on the Constitution and political parties. 13 June 1851. p.95, c1.

1882 JOSEPH TREAT *to* **FRIEND GARRISON. 6 June 1851. Boston.** Asserts that reform is worthless; urges radicalism. 13 June 1851. p.95, c3.

1883 GEORGE SUNTER, JR. *to* **WILLIAM LLOYD GARRISON. 7 May 1851. Regent Street, Derby.** Condemns the Fugitive Slave Law; urges anti-government agitation; assails Garrison's "priestliness." 13 June 1851. p.96, c4.

1884 JOHN HOOKER *to* **MESSRS. EDITORS. 3 June 1851. Hartford, Ct.** Provides biographical information on Rev. Dr. Pennington. 20 June 1851. p.98, c1.

1885 G. W. P. *to* **MR. GARRISON. 9 June 1851. Philadelphia.** Reports on the travels of George Thompson in Pennsylvania. 20 June 1851. p.98, c5.

1886 H. C. WRIGHT *to* **HENRY WARD BEECHER. 21 May 1851. Steamer** *Bay State*, **Long Island Sound.** Asserts that the Church is corrupted by its color prejudices. 20 June 1851. p.98, c2.

1887 J. C. H. *to* **WM. LLOYD GARRISON. 10 June 1850. Syracuse.** Expresses pleasure that Daniel Webster was given a poor reception in Syracuse. 20 June 1851. p.99, c1.

1888 AN IRISHMAN *to* **THE EDITOR OF THE** *TRIBUNE.* **12 June 1851. New York.** Praises George Thompson, noting that he is respected by Irishmen in America. 20 June 1851. p.99, c3.

1889 MILLARD FILLMORE *to* **FRANCIS BRINLEY. 9 June 1851. Washington.** Regrets that he is unable to visit Boston. 20 June 1851. p.99, c4.

1890 HENRY FISH *to* **BROTHER GARRISON. 6 June 1851. Hopedale.** Forwards an address by Mrs. A. H. Price on the conflict between Christian principles and social inequality. 20 June 1851. p.100, c2.

1891 S. C. PHILLIPS *to* **GENTLEMEN. 16 June 1851. Boston.** Regrets that he cannot attend Thompson's speech due to a prior commitment. 27 June 1851. p.101, c1.

1892 S. G. HOWE *to* **MESSRS. PHILLIPS, PARKER, AND SEWALL. 11 June 1851. South Boston.** Regrets that he cannot be present at Thompson's speech on 16 June. 27 June 1851. p.101, c1.

1893 FREDERICK DOUGLASS *to* **MESSRS. S. E. SEWALL, WENDELL PHILLIPS, AND THEODORE PARKER. 7 June 1851. Rochester.** Regrets that he cannot be present at a farewell soiree in Boston; praises Thompson. 27 June 1851. p.101, c1.

1894 PARKER PILLSBURY *to* **FRIEND GARRISON. 9 June 1851. Concord, N.H.** Laments the poor attendance of lectures in New Hampshire. 27 June 1851. p.103, c5.

1895 SAMUEL BACHE *to* **THE EDITOR OF THE** *LONDON CHRISTIAN INQUIRER.* **26 May 1851. Fairview House.** Announces anniversary of the British and Foreign Unitarian Association. 27 June 1851. p.104, c3.

1896 A UNITARIAN *to* **THE EDITOR OF THE** *DAILY ADVERTISER.* **12 June 1851. Boston.** Denounces the abolitionist and disunionist causes for promoting civil war and the destruction of the colored race. 27 June 1851. p.104, c3.

1897 W. J. W. *to* **W. L. GARRISON. 22 June 1851. Philadelphia.** An Englishman criticizes slavery. 4 July 1851. p.107, c3.

1898 HENRY C. WRIGHT *to* **JAMES HAUGHTON. 22 June 1851. Dublin, Ireland.** Assails the Irish for joining despotic, pro-slavery mobs after fleeing despotism in Ireland. 4 July 1851. p.107, c4.

1899 S. MAY, JR. *to* **MR. GARRISON. n.d. n.p.** Encloses a letter from an English lady critical of the United States' slave laws. 4 July 1851. p.108, c2.

1900 n.n. *to* **n.n. [extract] 29 May 1851. Bristol.** An English lady vehemently attacks America's Fugitive Slave Law; criticizes slavery as an act against God. 4 July 1851. p.108, c2.

1901 PARVUS JULUS *to* **MR. GARRISON. n.d. n.p.** Gives a favorable account of the treatment of slaves in the South. 4 July 1851. p.108, c3.

1902 DANIEL WEBSTER *to* **JOHN M. BOTTS. 4 June 1851. Washington.** Believes in the preservation of the Union and states' rights. 4 July 1851. p.108, c5.

1903 JOSEPH TREAT *to* **CHARLES SUMNER. 18 June 1851. Boston.** Advocates disunionism as a means to end slavery. 11 July 1851. p.109, c5.

1904 ELISHA CARD *to* **MR. BENJAMIN T. SANFORD. 23 June 1851. Portsmouth, Va.** Informs that he has signed a bond authorizing the deliverance of Thomas Scott Johnson into slavery unless he is able to certify his freedom; requests Sanford's aid in obtaining a certificate verifying Johnson's freedom. 11 July 1851. p.110, c3.

1905 PARKER PILLSBURY *to* **FRIEND GARRISON. 7 July 1851. Boston.** Encloses resolutions from a meeting at Feltonville. 11 July 1851. p.111, c5.

1906 M. A. GRIFFIN *to* **MR. GARRISON. 23 June 1851. Worcester.** Criticizes women's fashions as vain and degrading. 11 July 1851. p.112, c3.

1907 H. O. WAGONER, WM. JOHNSON, AND A. T. HALL *to* **E. C. LARNED AND GEORGE MANIERRE. 19 June 1851. Chicago.** Thank them for legal aid they provided to fugitive slaves. 11 July 1851. p.112, c5.

1908 E. C. LARNED AND GEO. MANIERRE *to* **H. O. WAGONER, WM. JOHNSON, AND A. T. HALL. n.d. n.p.** Convey their thanks for silver cups awarded them for their work on behalf of slaves. 11 July 1851. p.112, c5.

1909 E. S. DUNCAN *to* **THE EDITORS OF THE** *INQUIRER.* **2 June 1851. London.** Criticizes Horace Greeley as an enemy of the South. 18 July 1851. p.113, c2.

1910 MARIA WESTON CHAPMAN *to* **THE EDITOR OF THE** *ANTI-SLAVERY STANDARD.* **2 June 1851. London.** Reports on a meeting of French women sympathetic to abolitionism. 18 July 1851. p.113, c4.

1911 DANIEL WEBSTER *to* **MESSRS. C. C. SARGEANT, HOLLAND, STREETER AND OTHERS. 12 June 1851. Washington.** Accepts their invitation to visit Lowell. 18 July 1851. p.113, c5.

1912 DANIEL WEBSTER *to* **J. W. PRESTON, T. D. WINCHESTER, AND L. C. ALLEN. 2 July 1851. Washington.** Regrets he is unable to attend the Fourth of July celebrations in Springfield. 18 July 1851. p.113, c5.

1913 DANIEL WEBSTER *to* **GENTLEMEN. 27 June 1851. Capon Springs, Va.** Regrets he cannot attend the Fourth of July celebration at Boston. 18 July 1851. p.114, c1.

1914 J. T. BUCKINGHAM *to* **GENTLEMEN. 1 July 1851. Cambridge.** Informs them that he is unable to attend the Free-Soil Convention. 18 July 1851. p.114, c1.

1915 JOSEPH BARKER *to* **W. L. GARRISON. July 1851. Millwood, Knox County, Oh.** States that he has moved to the United States and purchased two farms. 18 July 1851. p.115, c1.

1916 SPY *to* **MR. GARRISON. n.d. n.p.** Criticizes the pro-slavery Maine Congregational Conference. 18 July 1851. p.115, c3.

1917 WM. FARMER *to* **W. L. GARRISON. 26 June 1851. London.** Reports on fugitive slaves at the World Fair. 18 July 1851. p.116, c2.

1918 J. H. PHILLEO *to* **MR. GARRISON. 25 May 1851. Rockton.** Discounts the constitutional question as grounds for opposing slavery. 18 July 1851. p.116, c4.

1919 WM. WELLS BROWN *to* **THE EDITOR OF THE** *LONDON TIMES.* **3 July 1851. Strand.** Urges other fugitive slaves to emigrate to the West Indies. 25 July 1851. p.118, c3.

1920 W. W. BROWN *to* **FREDERICK DOUGLASS. [from** *Frederick Douglass' Paper***] 27 June 1851. London.** Warns that economic conditions make England a poor place for the fugitive. 25 July 1851. p.118, c3.

1921 W. FARMER *to* **W. L. GARRISON. 8 July 1851. London.** Comments on George Thompson's arrival in England. 25 July 1851. p.118, c5.

1922 GEO. THOMPSON *to* **GARRISON. 8 July 1851. London.** Extends greetings upon arriving in England. 25 July 1851. p.118, c6.

1923 HENRY C. WRIGHT *to* **GARRISON. 28 June 1851. Albany.** Belittles the Church's views of the Sabbath. 25 July 1851. p.119, c1.

1924 E. H. N. *to* **THE EDITORS OF THE** *CLEVELAND TRUE DEMOCRAT.* **7 July 1851. Chicago.** Praises the Chicago Christian Convention and its anti-slavery position. 25 July 1851. p.119, c3.

1925 A. B. *to* **THE EDITOR OF** *LONDON MORNING ADVERTISER.* **n.d. n.p.** Congratulates American abolitionists. 1 August 1851. p.121, c5.

1926 WILLIAM P. POWELL *to* **FRIEND GARRISON. 29 July 1851. Boston.** Denounces prejudice at Plymouth, where a lodge denied admittance to blacks. 1 August 1851. p.122, c6.

1927 HORACE MANN *to* **THE EDITOR OF THE** *BOSTON COMMONWEALTH.* **23 July 1851. West Newton.** Responds to Professor Felton's criticism of him in the *Boston Courier.* 1 August 1851. p.123, c1.

1928 JOSEPH TREAT *to* **FRIEND GARRISON. 1 August 1851. Hartford.** Discusses the First of August celebration. 8 August 1851. p.126, c6.

1929 W. FARMER *to* **W. L. GARRISON. 16 July 1850. London.** Affirms that George Thompson has the support of his constituents. 8 August 1851. p.127, c2.

1930 W. FARMER *to* **GARRISON. 25 July 1851. London.** Forwards resolutions from constituents of George Thompson commending his abolition efforts. 8 August 1851. p.127, c3.

1931 REFORM *to* **MR. EDITOR. 13 June 1851. St. Louis.** Reports that fellow-abolitionists, the Hutchinsons, were denied the use of a hall in St. Louis. 8 August 1851. p.127, c5.

1932 WILLIAM MOUNTFORD *to* **THE EDITOR OF** *LONDON INQUIRER.* **16 June 1851. Gloucester, Ma.** Describes the disagreement among Unitarians over the Fugitive Slave Law. 15 August 1851. p.129, c1.

1933 n.n. *to* **EDITOR OF** *LONDON INQUIRER.* **14 July 1851. London.** Opposes efforts to divide English and American Unitarians over the slavery question. 15 August 1851. p.129, c2.

1934 JESSE McBRIDE *to* **BRO. LEE. 31 June 1851. Leesville, Oh.** Reports on a meeting held in Greensboro, North Carolina, to stop all "abolitionist agitation." 15 August 1851. p.129, c3.

1935 n.n. *to* **DANIEL WEBSTER. 20 July 1851. n.p.** Asks whether a state has the right to secede. 15 August 1851. p.129, c6.

1936 DANIEL WEBSTER *to* **n.n. n.d. n.p.** Answers that there exists no constitutional right to secession. 15 August 1851. p.129, c6.

1937 EDWARD SEARCH *to* **GARRISON. July 1851. London.** Urges resistance to the Fugitive Slave Bill. 15 August 1851. p.132, c2.

1938 BUCK-EYE STATE *to* **GENTLEMEN. 25 July 1851. Ohio.** Believes that Congress has the power to abolish slavery in the territories. 22 August 1851. p.134, c3.

1939 JOSEPH HUTTON *to* **REV. S. MAY, JR. 3 July 1851. Fairfield.** Urges American and English Unitarians to unite in opposition to the Fugitive Slave Law. 22 August 1851. p.134, c4.

1940 W. FARMER *to* **W. L. GARRISON. 31 July 1851. London.** Describes the warm reception afforded George Thompson. 22 August 1851. p.134, c5.

1941 EDWARD SEARCH *to* **GARRISON. July 1851. London.** Relates an English objection to the amount of space allocated to Americans at the World Fair. 22 August 1851. p.135, c4.

1942 W. FARMER *to* **W. L. GARRISON. n.d. n.p.** Regrets that Douglass cannot attend Thompson's farewell soiree. 29 August 1851. p.137, c4.

1943 H. C. WRIGHT *to* **GARRISON. 1 August 1851. Gradenheutten, Oh.** Discusses the Fugitive Slave Law. [partially illegible] 29 August 1851. p.137, c6.

1944 JAMES HAUGHTON *to* **HENRY C. WRIGHT. 31 July 1851. Dublin.** Comments on Irishmen and moral power. [partially illegible] 29 August 1851. p.138, c1.

1945 W. J. W. *to* **WM. LLOYD GARRISON. 29 July 1851. Boston.** Discusses Englishmen and Irishmen in America. 29 August 1851. p.138, c2.

1946 S. MAY, JR. *to* **MR. GARRISON. 27 August 1851. Boston.** Requests publication of his letter to the editors of the *Christian Register*; criticizes the *Christian Register*'s dishonest reporting of the case of Thomas Sims, a fugitive slave. 29 August 1851. p.138, c4.

1947 SAMUEL MAY, JR. *to* **EDITORS OF THE *CHRISTIAN REGISTER*. 8 July 1851. Leicester.** Replies to "personal attack." [partially illegible] 29 August 1851. p.138, c4.

1948 EDWARD MATHEWS *to* **MR. EDITOR. 8 August 1851. Oxford, England.** Corrects a mistake the paper made in quoting him. 29 August 1851. p.139, c4.

1949 AMERICAN FUGITIVE SLAVES *to* **n.n. 8 August 1851. London.** Announce a celebration of the West Indies Emancipation; welcome George Thompson. 5 September 1851. p.141, c1.

1950 PARKER PILLSBURY *to* **FRIEND GARRISON. 27 August 1851. Salem, Oh.** Reports on the anniversary of the Western AS. 5 September 1851. p.143, c4.

1951 EDWARD SEARCH *to* **GARRISON. August 1851. London.** Announces the coming session of Parliament and discussion of the papal bull. 5 September 1851. p.144, c2.

1952 JAMES LOWE *to* **MR. GARRISON. 16 August 1851. Boston.** Remarks the lack of understanding between British and Americans. 5 September 1851. p.144, c3.

1953 EDWARD SEARCH *to* **GARRISON. 1 August 1851. London.** Belittles the progress of medical science in England. 12 September 1851. p.145, c2.

1954 JAMES HAUGHTON *to* **FRIEND GARRISON. 31 July 1851. Dublin.** Speculates that abolitionism will ultimately triumph. 12 September 1851. p.145, c3.

1955 FELIX HOUSTON *to* **CITIZENS OF NEW ORLEANS. 22 August 1851. New Orleans.** Urges citizens to come to the aid of Cuba. 12 September 1851. p.145, c6.

1956 DANIEL X (HIS MARK) DAVIS *to* **THE COLORED POPULATION OF BUF-
FALO. 28 August 1851. n.p.** Declares that he would rather return to slavery in Kentucky
than live in freedom in Buffalo. 12 September 1851. p.146, c2.

1957 J. R. GIDDINGS *to* *CLEVELAND TRUE DEMOCRAT.* **29 August 1851. Jefferson.** Denies the assertion of the *True Democrat* and the *Herald* that he attempted to promote the election of General Houston to the presidency; discusses his contact with
Donaldson. 12 September 1851. p.146, c4.

1958 W. FARMER *to* **W. L. GARRISON. 21 August 1851. London.** Informs of the marriage of George Thompson's eldest daughter. 12 September 1851. p.146, c4.

1959 RICHARD D. WEBB *to* **GARRISON. n.d. n.p.** Views disunion as a Utopian dream.
12 September 1851. p.147, c1.

1960 J. F. CLARK *to* **MR. GARRISON. 8 September 1851. Sandwich.** Corrects a misprint
in the *Liberator.* 12 September 1851. p.147, c2.

1961 GEO. W. PUTNAM *to* *LIBERATOR.* **8 September 1851. Lynn.** Corrects a misprint
in the *Liberator.* 12 September 1851. p.147, c2.

1962 PARKER PILLSBURY *to* **FRIEND GARRISON. 2 September 1851. Ravenna, Oh.**
Encloses a resolution from the annual meeting of the Western AS. 12 September 1851.
p.147, c4.

1963 JONATHAN WALKER *to* **FRIEND GARRISON. 18 August 1851. Kingston, Ma.**
Relates his encounter with a clairvoyant. 12 September 1851. p.148, c3.

1964 ABBY H. PRICE *to* **GARRISON. n.d. Hopedale, Ma.** Enjoys practical new styles
for women. 12 September 1851. p.148, c4.

1965 W. FARMER *to* *LIBERATOR.* **15 August 1851. London.** Praises George Thompson's efforts. 19 September 1851. p. 149, c1.

1966 S. L. POMROY *to* **SIR CULLING E. EARDLEY. 12 April 1851. Boston.** Denounces
Thompson for meddling in American affairs. 19 September 1851. p.150, c2.

1967 W. L. G. *to* **EDITOR OF** *LONDON MORNING ADVERTISER.* **n.d. n.p.**
Responds to criticism of his policies and views on religion. 19 September 1851. p.150, c5.

1968 EDWARD SEARCH *to* **GARRISON. 29 August 1851. London.** Criticizes the British
Evangelical Alliance. 19 September 1851. p.151, c3.

1969 EDWARD MATHEWS *to* **THE EDITOR OF** *LONDON MORNING ADVER-
TISER.* **14 August 1851. Oxford.** Upholds the importance of American abolitionism. 19
September 1851. p.152, c4.

1970 W. S. DERRICK *to* **GOV. OF MARYLAND. 16 September 1851. n.p.** Comments on
the riot at Christiana. 26 September 1851. p.155, c1.

1971 PARKER PILLSBURY *to* **W. L. G. 10 September 1851. New Garden, Oh.** Reports
on abolitionism in Ohio. 26 September 1851. p.155, c4.

1972 WM. F. JOHNSTON *to* **JOHN CADWALADER, A. L. ROUMFORD, JANCE
PAGE, C. INGERSOLL, ISAAC LEECH, JR., R. SIMPSON, W. DEAL, GEO. H.
MARTIN, SAMUEL HAYS, S. R. CARNAHAN, THOMAS McGRATH, JOHN
SWIFT, AND FREDERICK McADAMS. 14 September 1851. Philadelphia.** Denies that
the riot at Christiana is the start of an insurrection. 26 September 1851. p.156, c5.

1973 n.n. *to* **MR. MAY. 25 August 1851. Medina, Oh.** Seeks further information about certain acts attributed to "infidel" Garrisonians. 3 October 1851. p.159, c2.

1974 EDWARD SEARCH *to* **GARRISON. August 1851. London.** Advocates ocean penny postage and an end to postal monopoly. 3 October 1851. p.160, c2.

1975 CANADA *to* **THE EDITORS OF THE** *EVENING TRAVELLER.* **19 September 1851. Boston.** Denounces Boston authorities for desertion of temperance principles. 3 October 1851. p.160, c3.

1976 J. ALONZO GIBSON *to* **BRO. LEE. 2 September 1851. Leicester.** Compares the Spanish invasion of Cuba with the American invasion of Mexico. 3 October 1851. p.160, c4.

1977 SAMUEL J. MAY *to* **DOUGLASS. n.d. n.p.** [from *Frederick Douglass' Paper*] Reports on the condition and prospects of fugitives in Canada. 10 October 1851. p.161, c6.

1978 T. W. HIGGINSON *to* **WM. LLOYD GARRISON. 2 October 1851. Newburyport.** Requests that Garrison print an article about Free-Soilers which had been rejected by the *Essex County Freeman.* 1 October 1851. p.163, c1.

1979 HENRY C. WRIGHT *to* **JAMES HAUGHTON. 17 September 1851. Aboit, Ia.** Charges that the American Republic is ruled by lying and hypocrisy. 10 October 1851. p.163, c2.

1980 PARKER PILLSBURY *to* **FRIEND GARRISON. 16 September 1851. Canton, Oh.** Describes trials and tribulations encountered during the abolitionist campaign in Ohio. 10 October 1851. p.163, c3.

1981 AN EYEWITNESS *to* **EDITOR OF** *SYRACUSE JOURNAL.* **n.d. n.p.** Considers the recapture of slave Jerry an indictment of America. 17 October 1851. p.166, c2.

1982 OLIVER JOHNSON *to* **GARRISON. 10 October 1851. Marlborough, Chester County, Pa.** Reports on a meeting of the Pennsylvania AS. 17 October 1851. p.166, c5.

1983 L. W. G. *to* **n.n. 28 September 1851. Burt, Pa.** Refuses to vote under a constitution which promotes slavery. 17 October 1851. p.167, c1.

1984 PARKER PILLSBURY *to* **FRIEND GARRISON. 10 October 1851. Twinsburg, Oh.** Condemns Wesleyanism of the West as pro-slavery. 17 October 1851. p.167, c2.

1985 H. C. WRIGHT *to* **W. L. GARRISON. 31 August 1851. Richmond, In.** Reports that whites fled Newport in fear of cholera, leaving their homes open to colored inhabitants. 17 October 1851. p.167, c2.

1986 EDWARD SEARCH *to* **W. L. GARRISON. 19 September 1851. London.** Describes the conflict between the government and priests in England. 17 October 1851. p.167, c3.

1987 GEO. THOMPSON *to* **S. W. WHEELER. 16 September 1851. London.** Expresses thanks for the condolences on the loss of his son. 17 October 1851. p.167, c4.

1988 E. SPRAGUE *to* **FRIEND GARRISON. n.d. n.p.** Compliments Mrs. Coe's lectures at Abington on women's rights. 17 October 1851. p.167, c4.

1989 T. W. HIGGINSON *to* **W. L. GARRISON. 15 October 1851. Newburyport.** Corrects a printing error. 17 October 1851. p.167, c5.

1990 PARKER PILLSBURY *to* **FRIEND GARRISON. 1 October 1851. Western Reserve, Oh.** Complains about his travelling accommodations. 17 October 1851. p.168, c2.

1991 HENRY C. WRIGHT *to* **GERRIT SMITH. 26 August 1851. Steamer** *Lancaster*, **Ohio River.** Assails civil government as a legitimization of murder and theft. 17 October 1851. p.168, c3.

1992 BRUTUS *to* **THE EDITOR OF THE** *PLAIN DEALER.* **12 August 1851. Washington.** Encloses letter to a Presbyterian elder asking that his slave be released to his mother. 24 October 1851. p.169, c4.

1993 WM. WELLS BROWN *to* **FREDERICK DOUGLASS. 1 September. London.** Opposes the emigration of blacks to Jamaica. 24 October 1851. p.169, c5.

1994 HENRY C. WRIGHT *to* **JAMES HAUGHTON. 18 September 1851. Aboit, Allan County, In.** Declares that Indiana, like most free states, views colored people as objects of contempt; forwards articles of the new constitution restricting immigration and employment of Negroes and mulattoes. 24 October 1851. p.171, c1.

1995 DANIEL FOSTER *to* **W. L. GARRISON. 21 October 1851. Boston.** Describes his sermons of the past few weeks and the opposition to them by supporters of slavery. 24 October 1851. p.171, c2.

1996 R. J. *to* **W. L. GARRISON. n.d. n.p.** Sends contribution to the editor for the purchase of an overcoat. 24 October 1851. p.171, c3.

1997 M. STOWELL *to* **GARRISON. [extract] 20 October 1851. Worcester.** Reports on the fugitive slave Jerry in Canada. 24 October 1851. p.171, c4.

1998 n.n. *to* **W. L. GARRISON. 12 October 1851. Portland.** Reports on the Portland AS. 24 October 1851. p.171, c4.

1999 EDWARD SEARCH *to* **W. L. GARRISON. 19 September 1851. London.** Comments on the postage system. 24 October 1851. p.172, c2.

2000 W. L. GARRISON *to* **J. MILLER McKIM. 4 October 1851. Boston.** Regrets that he cannot attend the Pennsylvania AS annual meeting; upholds the holiness of the anti-slavery cause. 1 November [31 October] 1851. p.173, c5.

2001 THEODORE PARKER *to* **W. L. GARRISON. 7 October 1851. Boston.** Believes that the United States government has taken the side of slavery. 1 November [31 October] 1851. p.174. c1.

2002 HENRY GREW *to* **PENNSYLVANIA AS. 6 October 1851. Philadelphia.** Encourages Pennsylvania AS to continue its work. 1 November [31 October] 1851. p.174, c1.

2003 HENRY C. WRIGHT *to* **JAMES HAUGHTON. 18 September 1851. Aboit, In.** Declares that Quakers, American democracy, and the Constitution hold hypocritical opinions regarding slavery. 1 November [31 October] 1851. p.175, c1.

2004 INQUIRER *to* **S. S. FOSTER. n.d. n.p.** Ponders whether or not he should vote for the Anti-Slavery Party. 1 November [31 October] 1851. p.175, c1.

2005 EDWARD SEARCH *to* **GARRISON. 12 September 1851. London.** Notes the uncertainty of European politics; reports on the conquests of the king of Prussia and the dominance of the Whig Party in England. 1 November [31 October] 1851. p.176, c2.

2006 JEANNE DEROIN AND PAULINE ROLAND *to* **CONVENTION OF WOMEN IN AMERICA. 15 June 1851. Prison of St. Lagare, Paris.** Discuss the women's rights movement. 1 November [31 October] 1851. p.176, c3.

2007 HARRIET MARTINEAU *to* **CONVENTION OF AMERICAN WOMEN. 3 August 1851. Cromer, England.** Thanks them for forwarding proceedings of the Women's Rights Convention to her; affirms her support for the cause. 1 November [31 October] 1851. p.176, c4.

2008 RICHARD B. LOMAX *to* **H. C. WRIGHT. 21 August 1851. May's Lick, Ky.** Criticizes Wright's attacks on the Union. 7 November 1851. p.177, c1.

2009 RODNEY FRENCH *to* **M. A. OUTTEN, WM. G. BRYAN, AND NEWBERN CITIZENS COUNCIL. 20 October 1851. New Bedford.** Reports on a French vessel which attempted to reclaim fugitive slaves. 7 November 1851. p.177, c2.

2010 J. B. ESTLIN *to* **n.n. 1 October 1851. Park Street.** Replies to Mr. Charleton's attack on the AAS. 7 November 1851. p.178, c2.

2011 J. J. CRITTENDEN *to* **JAMES R. LAWRENCE. 6 October 1851. Department of State, Washington.** Denounces lawless mob which "rescued a fugitive from labor" from the custody of the marshal. 7 November 1851. p.178, c4.

2012 G. W. PUTNAM *to* **MR. GARRISON. 2 November 1851. Lyman, Me.** Defends George Thompson's criticisms of the Liberty Party; denies that they were intended as a personal attack on Gerrit Smith. 7 November 1851. p.178, c5.

2013 PARKER PILLSBURY *to* **FRIEND GARRISON. 24 October 1851. New Lyme, Oh.** Discusses John Scoble's opinions on the emigration of free colored people to the West Indies. 7 November 1851. p.178, c6.

2014 EDWARD SEARCH *to* **SIR. 13 October 1851. London.** Looks forward to the arrival of Kossuth. 7 November 1851. p.179, c1.

2015 H. C. WRIGHT *to* **JAMES HAUGHTON. 26 October 1851. Selma, Oh.** Discourages the proposed visit of Kossuth to America, for fear he will be enslaved. 7 November 1851. p.179, c2.

2016 CAROLINE H. DALL *to* **MRS. P. W. DAVIS. 29 October 1851. Toronto.** Admires Mrs. Davis' involvement in the women's rights cause. 7 November 1851. p.179, c3.

2017 CALVIN FAIRBANKS *to* **GARRISON. 23 October 1851. Louisville, Ky. and Jeffersonville, In.** Comments on slavery in Kentucky and the need for laborers in Indiana. 7 November 1851. p.179, c4.

2018 GERRIT SMITH *to* **H. C. WRIGHT 23 October 1851. n.p.** Lectures on the necessity of civil government. 7 November 1851. p.179, c4.

2019 H. C. WRIGHT *to* **GARRISON. 14 October 1851. Dublin, In.** Reports on the women's rights convention in Indiana. 7 November 1851. p.180, c2.

2020 E. A. LUKENS *to* **WOMEN'S CONVENTION OF INDIANA. 2 October 1851. New Garden.** Asserts that women's rights are human rights. 7 November 1851. p.180, c2.

2021 E. C. STANTON *to* **PAULINA. 11 October 1851. Seneca Falls, N.Y.** Discusses what women must do to achieve their human rights. 7 November 1851. p.180, c3.

2022 HORACE MANN *to* **LUCY STONE. 18 September 1851. West Newton.** Declines to participate in the women's movement, although he supports its ultimate goals. 7 November 1851. p.180, c4.

2023 HENRY WARD BEECHER *to* **WOMEN'S CONVENTION. 4 October 1851. Brooklyn.** Feels that he is not qualified to speak at the women's convention; adds that he does not have time to come and listen. 7 November 1851. p.180, c4.

2024 RALPH WALDO EMERSON *to* **WOMEN'S RIGHTS CONVENTION. 7 October 1851. Concord.** Regrets that he cannot attend the women's rights convention. 7 November 1851. p.180, c5.

2025 DANIEL FOSTER *to* **BROTHER GARRISON. 10 November 1851. Concord, Ma.** Urges others to subscribe to the *Liberator*. 14 November 1851. p.181, c2.

2026 J. R. GIDDINGS *to* **EDITOR OF THE *CLEVELAND TRUE DEMOCRAT*. 28 October 1851. Jefferson.** Believes that it is the duty of the presbytery and of every church to withdraw from all union with slaveholders. 14 November 1851. p.186 [182], c3.

2027 EDWARD SEARCH *to* **GARRISON. 13 October 1851. London.** Refutes charges of infidelity against Garrison; notes the death of Lopez; condemns the Fugitive Slave Law. 14 November 1851. p.187 [183], c2.

2028 D. S. WHITNEY *to* **BROTHER GARRISON. 1 November 1851. Syracuse.** Describes an interview with Samuel May, who is accused of being the sole instigator of the liberation of Jerry. 14 November 1851. p.187 [183], c3.

2029 S. W. W. *to* **BROTHER GARRISON. 9 November 1851. Providence.** Gives an account of the Rhode Island AS meeting, which was attended by Douglass, Remond, and Burleigh. 14 November 1851. p.187 [183], c4.

2030 PARKER PILLSBURY *to* **MARIUS. 1 November 1851. Jefferson, Oh.** Reports on anti-slavery meetings in Andover. 21 November 1851. p.186, c2.

2031 GEORGE W. PUTNAM *to* **MR. GARRISON. 10 November 1851. Buxton, Me.** Reports on anti-slavery meetings in Maine. 21 November 1851. p.186, c5.

2032 DANIEL FOSTER *to* **FRIEND GARRISON. 6 November 1851. Concord, Ma.** Asserts that the Church is naive to think it can "wish" away slavery. 21 November 1851. p.186, c6.

2033 JOSEPH BARKER *to* **n.n. 20 October 1851. Millwood, Oh.** States that America cannot lead Europe in democracy until the country frees itself. 21 November 1851. p.187, c1.

2034 EDWARD SEARCH *to* **GARRISON. 12 September 1851. London.** Defends Garrison against charges of infidelity; condemns the Fugitive Slave Law. 21 November 1851. p.188, c2.

2035 H. C. WRIGHT *to* **JAMES HAUGHTON. 15 October 1851. Dublin, In.** Informs that the Fugitive Slave Law was declared unconstitutional by an Indiana court. 21 November 1851. p.188, c3.

2036 NATHANIEL BORDEN *to* **GENTLEMEN. 7 November 1851. Fall River.** Denounces the Fugitive Slave Law as "wicked." 28 November 1851. p.189, c5.

2037 J. R. GIDDINGS *to* **EDITOR OF THE** *COMMONWEALTH*. **6 November 1851. East Abington.** Informs that the Ohio Black Laws were repealed in 1848. 28 November 1851. p.190, c4.

2038 n.n. *to* **MR. MAY. 20 November 1851. Pascoag, R.I.** Discusses the conduct of the Methodist Episcopal church regarding slavery. 28 November 1851. p.191, c2.

2039 W. J. WATKINS *to* **FRIEND GARRISON. 17 November 1851. Boston.** Considers the destiny of colored people in America. 28 November 1851. p.191, c2.

2040 B. H. CLARK *to* **FRIEND GARRISON. 23 November 1851. Essex.** Reports on a meeting of the Essex AS. 28 November 1851. p.191, c3.

2041 EDWARD SEARCH *to* **GARRISON. 31 October 1851. London.** Remarks on speeches by Kossuth in England; censures European governments for limiting liberties of the people. 28 November 1851. p.192, c2.

2042 H. C. WRIGHT *to* **JAMES HAUGHTON. 25 October 1851. Selma, Oh.** States that committing treason against the United States government is fulfilling a duty to God and man; encloses resolutions from the Yearly Meeting of the Congregational Friends. 28 November 1851. p.192, c2.

2043 E. A. LUKENS *to* **GARRISON. 12 November 1851. New Garden, Oh.** Declares that the anti-slavery and women's rights movements must go hand in hand. 28 November 1851. p.192, c3.

2044 EDWARD SEARCH *to* **GARRISON. 7 November 1851. London.** Reports on the warm reception given Kossuth. 5 December 1851. p.194, c6.

2045 H. C. WRIGHT *to* **GARRISON. 15 November 1851. Hanover, Oh.** Ponders what Kossuth's position will be on American slavery. 5 December 1851. p.195, c1.

2046 PARKER PILLSBURY *to* **FRIEND GARRISON. 26 November 1851. Concord, N.H.** Refutes the slanderous story that he had baptized dogs. 5 December 1851. p.195, c2.

2047 CALEB JONES *to* **PARKER PILLSBURY. 6 August 1851. Richmond.** Cautions Pillsbury to be more temperate in his criticism of slaveholders. 5 December 1851. p.195, c2.

2048 DANIEL FOSTER *to* **GARRISON. 1 December 1851. Concord, Ma.** Informs Garrison of his desire to give anti-slavery or temperance lectures. 5 December 1851. p.195, c3.

2049 WM. J. WATKINS *to* **FRIEND GARRISON. 28 November 1851. Boston.** Reflects on the destiny of the Negro race; asserts the necessity to "show ourselves approved workmen." 5 December 1851. p.195, c4.

2050 GEORGE W. PUTNAM *to* **MR. GARRISON. 2 December 1851. Mechanics Falls, Me.** Discusses barriers to the anti-slavery cause in Maine. 12 December 1851. p.196, c2.

2051 WM J. WATKINS *to* **FRIEND GARRISON. 5 December 1851. Boston.** Reflects on the destiny of the Negro race; declares that "They who would be free, themselves must strike the blow." 12 December 1851. p.196, c3.

2052 R. D. WEBB *to* **FREDERICK DOUGLASS. [from** *Frederick Douglass's Paper*] **7 November 1851. Dublin.** Affirms his support of the Liberty Party. 12 December 1851. p.197, c3.

2053 CALVIN FAIRBANKS *to* **n.n. 13 November 1851. Louisville Jail.** Relates that he was jailed for aiding slaves. 12 December 1851. p.198, c2.

2054 EDWARD SEARCH *to* **GARRISON. 14 November 1851. London.** Praises Kossuth for his ability to "show the truth to those who are prejudiced, and wean them from error." 12 December 1851. p.198, c4.

2055 A. C. KINGSLAND AND GEO. F. FRANKLIN *to* **GOV. KOSSUTH. 24 November 1851. n.p.** The mayor and an alderman of New York welcome Kossuth. 12 December 1851. p.198, c5.

2056 RICHARD D. WEBB *to* **RICHARD ANDREWS. 17 November 1851. Dublin.** Forwards a contribution to Kossuth for Hungary. 19 December 1851. p.202, c1.

2057 LEWIS FORD *to* **FRIEND GARRISON. 8 December 1851. Norway, N.Y.** Recounts his anti-slavery peregrinations in New York. 19 December 1851. p.202, c4.

2058 SAMUEL AARON *to* **ESTEEMED** *LIBERATOR.* **30 November 1851. Norristown, Pa.** Protests Daniel Foster's views on biblical authority. 19 December 1851. p.204, c3.

2059 KOSSUTH *to* **LEWIS TAPPAN, JOSHUA LEAVITT, GEORGE WHIPPLE, WILLIAM E. WHITING, AND SAMUEL E. CORNISH. n.d. n.p.** Thanks the committee for their support of the Hungarian cause. 19 December 1851. p.204, c5.

2060 LEWIS TAPPAN, JOSHUA LEAVITT, GEORGE WHIPPLE, WILLIAM E. WHITING, AND SAMUEL E. CORNISH *to* **LOUIS KOSSUTH. 9 December 1851. New York.** Seek Kossuth's support for the American and Foreign AS. 19 December 1851. p.204, c5.

2061 LEWIS TAPPAN *to* **EDITOR OF** *COMMONWEALTH.* **20 December 1851. New York.** Corrects a "gross misinterpretation" concerning Tappan's recitation of a public letter to Kossuth. 26 December 1851. p.206, c1.

2062 EMMANUEL VITALIS SCHERB *to* **PRESIDENT OF WOMEN'S RIGHTS CONVENTION [PAULINA W. DAVIS]. 15 November 1851. Boston.** Gives his support and thoughts on the women's rights question. 26 December 1851. p.207, c1.

2063 EDWARD SEARCH *to* **GARRISON. [extract] November 1851. London.** Informs of English papers' reports about the United States. 26 December 1851. p.208, c2.

2064 H. C. WRIGHT *to* **GARRISON. 7 December 1851. Hanover, Oh.** Reports that Kossuth refuses to condem American slavery. 26 December 1851. p.208, c2.

2065 A. J. GROVER *to* **MR. GARRISON. 18 December 1851. Beverly.** Reports on his efforts in Massachusetts for the anti-slavery cause. 26 December 1851. p.208, c4.

2066 GEO. TRASK *to* **EDITOR OF THE** *ONEIDA HERALD.* **27 October 1851. Utica.** Supports the anti-tobacco cause. 26 December 1851. p.208, c5.

[1852]

2067 W. FARMER *to* **W. L. GARRISON. 1 December 1851. London.** Discusses attacks made by Frederick Douglass and John Scoble upon George Thompson. 2 January 1852. p.1, c1.

2068 WM. AND ELLEN CRAFT *to* **n.n. 20 November 1851. Surry, England.** Express gratitude for assistance in gaining admission to school. 2 January 1852. p.2, c1.

2069 W. B. REED, ATTORNEY GENERAL *to* **HON. LOUIS KOSSUTH. 23 December 1851. n.p.** Warns Kossuth against further incendiary speeches. 2 January 1852. p.3, c1.

2070 JAMES HAUGHTON *to* **H. C. WRIGHT. 9 December 1851. Dublin.** Agrees with Wright's misgivings about Kossuth's visit to America. 2 January 1852. p.3, c2.

2071 JAMES HAUGHTON *to* **AS OF GREAT BRITAIN AND IRELAND. 21 November 1851. Dublin.** Equates American hypocrisy with Austrian oppression. 2 January 1852. p.3, c3.

2072 JAMES HAUGHTON *to* **KOSSUTH. 4 November 1851. Dublin.** Entreats Kossuth not to go to America. 2 January 1852. p.3, c3.

2073 A SUBSCRIBER *to* **MR. GARRISON. 20 December 1851. Boston.** Expresses disappointment with W. L. Garrison's criticism of Kossuth. 2 January 1852. p.3, c4.

2074 GEO. W. PUTNAM *to* **MR. GARRISON. 6 December 1851. Saccarappa, Me.** Reiterates lectures given with Mr. Grover on slave power and money power. 2 January 1852. p.4, c5.

2075 LEWIS FORD *to* **FRIEND GARRISON. 19 December 1851. Brochetti Bridge, N. Y.** Reports that the Plymouth County AS was proscribed from a South Scituate hall. 2 January 1852. p.4, c5.

2076 RICHARD D. WEBB *to* **EDITOR OF THE** *LONDON MORNING ADVERTISER*. **19 November 1851. Dublin.** Wonders if Kossuth will be safe in America. 9 January 1852. p.5, c4.

2077 W. G. ALLEN *to* **FREDERICK DOUGLASS, ESQ. 30 December 1851. McGrawville, N.Y.** Comments on the address by colored people in New York to Kossuth. 9 January 1852. p.5, c5.

2078 H. P. CROZIER *to* **FREDERICK DOUGLASS. 10 December 1851. New York.** Protests the American and Foreign AS's suggestion that Kossuth remain neutral toward American slavery. 9 January 1852. p.6, c2.

2079 JUDGE WM. JAY *to* **MR. EDITOR. [from the** *National Anti-Slavery Standard***] 20 December 1851. New York.** Defends Kossuth's refusal to speak out against slavery. 9 January 1852. p.6, c2.

2080 GEORGE THOMPSON *to* **THE** *GLASGOW CHRISTIAN NEWS*. **30 November 1851. London.** Refutes Mr. Guthrie's anti-slavery speech. 9 January 1852. p.6, c3.

2081 H. C. WRIGHT *to* **GARRISON. 20 December 1851. New Lisbon, Oh.** Discusses the meaning of the terms "infidel" and "traitor." 9 January 1852. p.6, c6.

2082 EDWARD SEARCH *to* **GARRISON. 19 December 1851. London.** Praises President Fillmore's speech; discusses free trade, direct taxation, and the "all-powerful" capital. 9 January 1852. p.7, c1.

2083 LEWIS FORD *to* **FRIEND GARRISON. 26 December 1851. Rockton, N.Y.** Reports on his anti-slavery work with Parker Pillsbury in New York. 9 January 1852. p.7, c1.

2084 E. A. LUKENS *to* **FRIEND GARRISON. 12 December 1851. New Garden, Oh.** Reports on prisoners at Christiana and Syracuse. 9 January 1852. p.7, c2.

2085 WM. J. WATKINS *to* **FRIEND GARRISON. 15 December 1851. n.p.** Encourages the free colored population to unite. 9 January 1852. p.7, c3.

2086 JOHN LORD *to* **EDITOR [W. L. GARRISON]. 6 December 1851. Portland, Me.** Replies to Daniel Foster's sermon entitled, "The Bible not an Inspired Book." 9 January 1852. p.8, c2.

2087 ELLIS CLIZBE *to* **SIR [W. L. GARRISON]. 12 December 1851. Amsterdam.** Sends subscription money to the *Liberator*. 9 January 1852. p.8, c5.

2088 C. STEARNS *to* **MR. GARRISON. 20 December 1851. Boston.** Praises Dr. Noyes Wheeler's work in phrenology. 9 January 1852. p.8, c5.

2089 P. G. *to* **MR. GARRISON. 29 December 1851. Stoneham.** Lauds Lucy Stone's lectures on women's rights. 9 January 1852. p.8, c5.

2090 W. FARMER *to* **SIR [W. L. GARRISON]. 8 December 1851. London.** Refutes John Scoble's attacks on George Thompson. 16 January 1852. p.9, c1.

2091 JOSEPH TREAT *to* **MARIUS. 31 December 1851. Salem.** Commends Geo. Thompson's "electrifying" speech condemning Kossuth for his inconsistency. 16 January 1852. p.10, c2.

2092 JAMES HAUGHTON *to* **EDITOR OF THE *DUBLIN FREEMAN*. n.d. n.p.** Explains why he believes America to be the most dishonored nation in the world. 16 January 1852. p.10, c3.

2093 A. GROVER *to* **MR. GARRISON. 4 January 1852. Brunswick, Me.** Expresses his hopes for the anti-slavery cause in Maine. 16 January 1852. p.10, c6.

2094 I. FISKE *to* **FRIEND GARRISON. 7 January 1852. Fall River.** Compliments a lecture by Daniel Foster on free speech and free labor. 16 January 1852. p.10, c6.

2095 EDWARD SEARCH *to* **GARRISON. 10 December 1851. London.** Reports on another revolution in France; discusses Louis Napoleon's union with the Jesuits; stresses the moral responsibility of America to extend liberty. 16 January 1852. p.11, c1.

2096 LEWIS FORD *to* **FRIEND GARRISON. n.d. Burlington Flats, N.Y.** Suggests that abolitionists give up tobacco and donate the money thus saved to the cause. 16 January 1852. p.11, c2.

2097 BOSTON *to* **THE EDITOR OF THE *LIBERATOR* [W. L. GARRISON]. n.d. n.p.** Reports on the commencement exercises of the Philadelphia Female Medical College. 16 January 1852. p.11, c2.

2098 WILLIAM JAY *to* **REV. G. C. BECKWITH. 3 January 1852. New York.** Admires Kossuth's eloquence, talents, and patriotism, but believes that he is asking the United States to become involved in a possible war in Europe, which would be "sin and folly." 23 January 1852. p.13, c2.

2099 W. H. F. *to* **FRIEND GARRISON. 15 January 1852. Hopedale.** Rebukes Rev. Milton P. Braman for using Abby Folsom as a representative of the women's rights movement. 23 January 1852. p.14, c5.·

2100 E. W. TWING *to* **FRIEND GARRISON. 15 January 1852. Springfield.** Advises an unhappy subscriber to the *Liberator* to reply to those articles with which he disagrees. 23 January 1852. p.14, c5.

2101 LEWIS FORD *to* **FRIEND GARRISON. 13 January 1852. Cedarville, N.Y.** Reports on anti-slavery activity in central New York. 23 January 1852. p.14, c6.

2102 GEORGE W. PUTNAM *to* **MR. GARRISON. 15 January 1852. Harwick.** Reports on anti-slavery meetings. 23 January 1852. p.15, c1.

2103 H. H. BRIGHAM *to* **FRIEND GARRISON. n.d. n.p.** Informs Garrison that C. C. Burleigh was hired as an agent for the Old Colony AS. 23 January 1852. p.15, c1.

2104 M. *to* **EDITOR OF THE** *BOSTON TRAVELER.* **n.d. n.p.** Charges that the speech made by ex-slave William Jones was a hoax. 23 January 1852. p.15, c3.

2105 GIDEON LONGPROBE *to* **FRIEND GARRISON. n.d. n.p.** Expresses disappointment with Rev. Lord's reply to Daniel Foster. 23 January 1852. p.16, c2.

2106 A. H. WOOD *to* **BROTHER GARRISON. 11 January 1852. n.d. n.p.** Criticizes Rev. John Lord for his authoritarian biblical exegesis. 23 January 1852. p.16, c3.

2107 O. C., A SUBSCRIBER *to* **W. L. GARRISON. 5 January 1852. Sherwood.** Blames the slowness of the anti-slavery movement on the lack of harmony among abolitionists. 23 January 1852. p.16, c3.

2108 EDWARD SEARCH *to* **GARRISON. 25 December 1851. London.** Reports on reply by the Austrian chargé d'affaires to Mr. Webster. 23 January 1852. p.16, c4.

2109 JOSEPH TREAT *to* **MARIUS. [from the** *Anti-Slavery Bugle***] 4 January 1852. Garrettsville.** Charges that Kossuth has received too much attention. 30 January 1852. p.18, c3.

2110 H. C. WRIGHT *to* **RICHARD D. WEBB. 17 January 1852. Hazlebank, Mi.** Discusses Benjamin Lundy's views on emancipation. 30 January 1852. p.18, c5.

2111 GEO. W. PUTNAM *to* **MR. GARRISON. 23 January 1852. East Dennis.** Reports on anti-slavery meetings on the Cape. 30 January 1852. p.19, c1.

2112 A. J. G. *to* **MR. GARRISON. 21 January 1852. Augusta, Me.** Gives account of a clerical anti-slavery convention. 30 January 1852. p.19, c1.

2113 O. C. *to* **FRIEND GARRISON. 15 January 1852. Sherwood, N.Y.** Discusses tariff and free trade. 30 January 1852. p.19, c2.

2114 E. R. PLACE *to* **FRIEND GARRISON. 27 January 1852. Portland.** Reviews a lecture by Parker Pillsbury in Portland. 30 January 1852. p.19, c2.

2115 SAMUEL W. WHEELER *to* **FRIEND GARRISON. 24 January 1852. Providence.** Informs that the subject of capital punishment was brought before lawmakers in Providence. 30 January 1852. p.19, c3.

2116 CHARLES SPEAR *to* **THE EDITOR [W. L. GARRISON]. n.d. n.p.** Refutes *Transcript* article's charge that he took two servants to Europe. 30 January 1852. p.19, c3.

2117 L. KOSSUTH *to* **ADOLPH GYURMAN. 22 December 1851. New York.** Requests that the editor of the official paper, *Koezloenz,* join the cause of reform journalism. 30 January 1852. p.20, c4.

2118 A FRIEND OF HUMANITY *to* **MR. GARRISON. 1 February 1852. Salem, Ma.** Reviews speech by Parker Pillsbury. 6 February 1852. p.23, c4.

2119 D. S. WHITNEY *to* **BROTHER GARRISON. 31 January 1852. Boylston.** Reports on anti-slavery meetings in Worcester County. 6 February 1852. p.23, c4.

2120 G. W. P. *to* **MR. GARRISON. 30 January 1852. Lynn.** Corrects his last letter. 6 February 1852. p.23, c5.

2121 CONSUL MATHEWS *to* **GOV. MEANS. n.d. n.p.** Discusses treaty obligations between the United States and Great Britain; comments on the imprisonment of British seamen. 13 February 1852. p.25, c5.

2122 H. C. WRIGHT *to* **GARRISON. 21 January 1852. Hazlebank, Mi.** Eulogizes Elizabeth M. Chandler, editor of the Ladies' Department in the *Genius of Universal Emancipation.* 13 February 1852. p.27, c2.

2123 JOSHUA HUTCHINSON *to* **FRIEND GARRISON. 30 February 1851. Christiana, Pa.** Affirms that reform spirit is high in Pennsylvania. 13 February 1852. p.27, c3.

2124 A. BROOKE *to* **FRIEND GARRISON. 27 January 1852. Oakland, Oh.** Praises W. L. Garrison; reports on anti-slavery activity in Ohio. 13 February 1852. p.27, c3.

2125 M. STOWELL *to* **FRIEND GARRISON. 9 February 1852. Worcester.** A Free-Soiler gives an account of his tragic experience with slaveholders in Virginia; reports that he was forced to leave because his wife taught colored women how to read. 13 February 1852. p.27, c4.

2126 D. S. WHITNEY *to* **BROTHER GARRISON. 10 February 1852. Boylston.** Proposes a fast day in Massachusetts to commemorate the perpetual slavery of Thomas Sims. 13 February 1852. p.27, c4.

2127 A. J. GROVER *to* **MR. GARRISON. 3 February 1852. Westport.** Declares that the slavery question is primarily a question of labor. 13 February 1852. p.28, c3.

2128 GARRISON *to* **M. LOUIS KOSSUTH. n.d. n.p.** Commends Kossuth for his fight for Hungarian freedom; condemns his silence on slavery in the United States. 20 February 1852. p.29, c1.

2129 B. S. WHITING *to* **FRIEND GARRISON. 10 February 1852. South Hingham.** Praises a lecture by Lucy Stone. 20 February 1852. p.30, c6.

2130 JAMES W. BROWN *to* **FRIEND GARRISON. 10 February 1852. North Bloomfield.** Defends Kossuth and his mission. 20 February 1852. p.32, c1.

2131 G. W. SIMONDS *to* **n.n. 15 February 1852. Lexington.** Censures Kossuth for saying that he will never speak out against slavery. 20 February 1852. p.32, c1.

2132 W. H. B. *to* **FRIEND GARRISON. 12 February 1852. Plymouth.** Comments on the reform meetings held on Sunday. 20 February 1852. p.32, c2.

2133 S. W. W. *to* **FRIEND GARRISON. 15 February 1852. Providence.** Discusses the abolition of the gallows in Rhode Island. 20 February 1852. p.32, c3.

2134 PARKER PILLSBURY *to* **n.n. [from the** *Ohio Anti-Slavery Bugle***] n.d. n.p.** Claims that Kossuth has "bowed to the government" by ignoring the slave. 27 February 1852. p.33, c5.

2135 A. J. N. *to* **MR. DOUGLASS. 30 January 1852. Peterboro'.** Compares the riotous reception of Geo. Thompson with the friendly reception of Kossuth. 27 February 1852. p.33, c6.

2136 A. J. G. *to* **MR. GARRISON. 14 February 1852. North Easton.** Denies making untrue or malicious comments about the Augusta Clerical Anti-Slavery Convention. 27 February 1852. p.35, c3.

2137 J. *to* **FRIEND GARRISON. 21 February 1852. New Bedford.** Compliments lecture by Daniel Foster. 27 February 1852. p.35, c4.

2138 B. F. REMINGTON *to* **BRO. WALKER. n.d. n.p.** States his opposition to the Kossuth affair. 5 March 1852. p.37, c5.

2139 GERRIT SMITH *to* **GOVERNOR HUNT. 20 February 1852. Peterboro'.** Explains why he opposes the ACS. 5 March 1852. p.38, c1.

2140 CALVIN FAIRBANK *to* **FREDERICK DOUGLASS. 4 February 1852. Louisville Jail.** Believes that he has been deserted by anti-slavery reformers. 5 March 1852. p.38, c4.

2141 WILLIAM C. NELL *to* **FRIEND GARRISON. 19 February 1852. Rochester, N.Y.** Reports on anti-slavery lectures in Rochester by Henry Ward Beecher, Rev. John Lord, Samuel May, and Sallie Holly. 5 March 1852. p.39, c2.

2142 RICHARD D. WEBB *to* **GARRISON. 30 January 1852. Dublin.** Discusses W. R. Gregg's *Abolitionists*. 5 March 1852. p.39, c3.

2143 GEO. PUTNAM *to* **MR. GARRISON. 26 February 1852. Hyannis.** Reports on anti-slavery meetings on the Cape. 5 March 1852. p.39, c4.

2144 ELIZABETH WILSON *to* **MR. GARRISON. n.d. n.p.** Replies to Daniel Foster's controversial sermon on the Bible. 5 March 1852. p.40, c2.

2145 REV. CALVIN FAIRBANK *to* **EDITORS OF THE** *NASHVILLE CHRISTIAN ADVOCATE***. 24 December 1851. Louisville Jail.** Argues cogently on his case, the truth of the Bible, and the illegality of the Fugitive Slave Law. 12 March 1852. p.43, c1.

2146 ALONZO J. GROVER *to* **MR. GARRISON. 29 February 1852. Phenix, R.I.** Comments on freedom of the individual and anti-slavery in Rhode Island. 12 March 1852. p.43, c2.

2147 PARKER PILLSBURY *to* **FRIEND GARRISON. 4 March 1852. West Norfolk.** Reports on anti-slavery meetings in Connecticut. 12 March 1852. p.43, c3.

2148 GEO. PUTNAM *to* **MR. GARRISON. 3 March 1852. Lynn.** Reports on anti-slavery meetings on the Cape. 12 March 1852. p.43, c3.

2149 E. R. COE *to* **MR. GARRISON. n.d. n.p.** Describes anti-slavery meetings on the Cape; pleads for a "more liberal infusion of the feminine element in the public mind." 12 March 1852. p.44, c3.

2150 REV. SAMUEL H. COX *to* **A. G. PHELPS. [extract] 24 February 1852. Brooklyn.** Replies to an invitation to meet Daniel Webster; regrets that he cannot be present at the occasion. 19 March 1852. p.45, c2.

2151 JAMES HAUGHTON *to* **THE EDITOR OF THE** *BRITISH AND FOREIGN A.S. REPORTER.* **21 January 1852. Dublin.** Believes that Kossuth has injured the cause of freedom by his refusal to condemn slavery publicly. 19 March 1852. p.45, c5.

2152 LEWIS TAPPAN *to* **EDITOR [W. L. GARRISON]. n.d. n.p.** Refutes an accusation printed in the *Liberator* that he was "compromising" toward Kossuth. 19 March 1852. p.46, c6.

2153 PARKER PILLSBURY *to* **FRIEND GARRISON. n.d. n.p.** Claims there is malignant prejudice against color in Connecticut; criticizes the bigotry and brutality in a temperance lecture by John B. Gough. 19 March 1852. p.47, c1.

2154 C. F. HOVEY *to* **GARRISON. 17 March 1852. Boston.** Comments on a petition concerning Drayton and Sayres. 19 March 1852. p.47, c1.

2155 EDWARD SEARCH *to* **GARRISON. 18 February, 23 February, 27 February 1852. London.** Criticizes the English government; defends Kossuth against abolitionists' complaints. 19 March 1852. p.47, c2.

2156 GEORGE W. PUTNAM *to* **MR. GARRISON. 12 March 1852. Athol.** Reports on anti-slavery meetings. 19 March 1852. p.47, c3.

2157 H. C. WRIGHT *to* **EDWARD SEARCH. 21 February 1852. Woppokisskoo, Mi.** Censures Kossuth for fraternizing with slaveholders, slave-traders, and slave-hunters. 19 March 1852. p.48, c2.

2158 ROBERT MORRIS *to* **JOHN P. HALE. [from the** *Commonwealth***] 1 January 1852. Boston.** Presents a set of volumes of English history to Hale from the colored citizens of Boston. 19 March 1852. p.48, c3.

2159 JOHN P. HALE *to* **R. MORRIS. 18 January 1852. Washington.** Expresses gratitude for the gift. 19 March 1852. p.48, c3.

2160 ROBERT MORRIS *to* **RICHARD H. DANA, JR. 1 January 1852. Boston.** Presents Dana with a gift of historical volumes by Hallam on behalf of the colored citizens of Boston. 19 March 1852. p.48, c3.

2161 RICHARD H. DANA, JR. *to* **ROBERT MORRIS. 1 January 1852. Boston.** Expresses gratitude for the gift. 19 March 1852. p.48, c3.

2162 J. M. L. *to* **THE EDITOR. 10 March 1852. Waltham.** Wishes that the colored citizens of Boston would unite to support the Smith School. 19 March 1852. p.48, c3.

2163 n.n. *to* **n.n. [from the** *Cleveland True Democrat***] 9 March 1852. Washington City.** Relates lecture by Mr. Davis criticizing Mr. Rantoul, vindicating the coalition between the Democrats and Free-Soilers, and condemning the Fugitive Slave Law as unconstitutional. 26 March 1852. p.50, c3.

2164 H. C. WRIGHT *to* **EDWARD SEARCH. 22 February 1852. Michigan.** Condemns Kossuth and his mission for stressing patriotism instead of humanity. 26 March 1852. p.52, c2.

2165 D. M. *to* **MR. EDITOR. n.d. Boston.** Discusses his dedication to the *Liberator* and abolitionism; condemns the pro-slavery interpretation of the Constitution. 26 March 1852. p.52, c3.

2166 A. J. KNOX *to* **MR. GARRISON. 12 March 1852. Hyannis.** Defends James G. Birney against accusations that he is a colonizationist. 26 March 1852. p.52, c4.

2167 GEO. W. JONES *to* **EDITOR OF THE** *EDGEFIELD* **(S.C.)** *ADVERTISER.* **n.d. n.p.** Charges that the temperance lecturer Philip S. White, is an abolitionist. 2 April 1852. p.53, c1.

2168 P. S. WHITE *to* **JUDGE O'NEALL. 23 February 1852. Edgefield, S.C.** Denies allegation that he is an abolitionist. 2 April 1852. p.53, c1.

2169 GEO. W. JONES *to* **EDITOR OF THE** *EDGEFIELD ADVERTISER.* **n.d. n.p.** Retracts statement that P. S. White is an abolitionist. 2 April 1852. p.53, c2.

2170 WILLIAM JAY *to* **EDITORS OF** *NEW YORK EXPRESS.* **1 March 1852. New York.** Refutes claim that his father had been president of the ACS. 2 April 1852. p.53, c4.

2171 M. A. S. *to* **FRIEND. 20 March 1852. West Bridgewater.** Explains why American churches hate the Garrisonians. 2 April 1852. p.55, c1.

2172 J. E. SNODGRASS *to* **SIR [WENDELL PHILLIPS]. 1 March 1852. Baltimore.** Gives account of an address by Daniel Webster. 9 April 1852. p.57, c3.

2173 REV. ALBERT BARNES *to* **REV. S. C. AIKEN. n.d. n.p.** Rejects possible separation between churches of Ohio and the general assembly. 9 April 1852. p.57, c5.

2174 JNO. H. PEARSON *to* **WENDELL PHILLIPS. n.d. n.p.** Denounces Phillips as an agitator and a traitor. 9 April 1852. p.58, c6.

2175 A FREE SOIL ABOLITIONIST AND SON OF TEMPERANCE *to* **MR. GARRISON. 3 April 1852. n.p.** Declares that Philip S. White has spoken out against slavery. 9 April 1852. p.59, c1.

2176 A. J. GROVER *to* **MR. GARRISON. 1 April 1852. Needham.** Explains the trials and tribulations of being an anti-slavery agent. 9 April 1852. p.59, c1.

2177 PARKER PILLSBURY *to* **FRIEND GARRISON. 22 March 1852. Boston.** Reports on opposition to the anti-slavery cause in Connecticut. 9 April 1852. p.59, c2.

2178 H. W. CROSBY *to* **MR. EDITOR [W. L. GARRISON]. n.d. n.p.** Asks for an explanation of G. W. Putnam's contention that the Centerville Congregational Church is connected with slavery. 9 April 1852. p.59, c3.

2179 AMARANCY PAINE *to* **MR. GARRISON. 27 March 1852. Providence.** Acknowledges donation by an Irish person to the Rhode Island AS. 9 April 1852. p.59, c3.

2180 WILLIAM H. HADLEY *to* **REV. T. W. HIGGINSON. 10 March 1852. Portland.** Discusses the decline of poverty in Portland after the Maine temperance law was passed. 9 April 1852. p.60, c2.

2181 R. W. H. *to* **THE EDITOR OF THE** *NEW YORK EVENING POST.* **n.d. n.p.** Discusses the issue of premature burial. 9 April 1852. p.60, c4.

2182 KENTUCKIAN *to* **MR. EDITOR [W. L. GARRISON]. 24 March 1852. Dover, Ky.** Laments the cruelty of a slave hunt. 16 April 1852. p.62, c1.

2183 THEODORE WELD *to* **WENDELL PHILLIPS. 3 April 1852. Belleville, N.J.** Regrets that he cannot attend the anniversary of Thomas Sims' return to slavery under the Fugitive Slave Law of 1850. 16 April 1852. p.62, c5.

2184 C. M. CLAY *to* **WENDELL PHILLIPS. 5 April 1852. White Hall Post Office, Ky.** Regrets that he cannot speak at Thomas Sims' anniversary. 16 April 1852. p. 62, c5.

2185 JOSHUA R. GIDDINGS *to* **WENDELL PHILLIPS. 4 April 1852. Jefferson, Oh.** Reports on the anniversary of Thomas Sims' re-enslavement. 16 April 1852. p.62, c6.

2186 PARKER PILLSBURY *to* **FRIEND GARRISON. 12 April 1852. Portland.** Describes the "disappointment, vexation, and suffering" he experiences as an anti-slavery agent. 16 April 1852. p.63, c1.

2187 A. H. WOOD *to* **BRO. GARRISON. 25 March 1852. Pepperell.** Laments that Rev. Mr. Pratt of the ACS bought memberships in his society for the only two priests in Pepperell. 16 April 1852. p.63, c3.

2188 JOHN CUSHING *to* **FRIEND GARRISON. 3 April 1852. South Hingham.** Discusses a critique of the Bible. 16 April 1852. p.64, c2.

2189 n.n. *to* **EDITORS OF THE** *AMERICAN PHRENOLOGICAL JOURNAL.* **[O. S. AND L. N. FOWLER]. n.d. n.p.** States that slavery is a bulwark against human progress. 16 April 1852. p.64, c3.

2190 JOEL W. WHITE *to* **SAMUEL GREGORY. 1 April 1852. Norwich.** Supports the Female Medical Education Society. 16 April 1852. p.64, c5.

2191 DANIEL WEBSTER *to* **EDITOR OF THE** *ALEXANDRIA GAZETTE.* **10 April 1852. Washington.** Asserts that the Fugitive Slave Law is "absolutely essential to the peace of the country." 23 April 1852. p.65, c1.

2192 T. P. KNOX *to* **FRIEND GARRISON. 19 April 1852. Hyannis.** Demands to know the true position of the Episcopal, Methodist, and Baptist churches on slavery. 23 April 1852. p.65, c4.

2193 S. S. HARDING *to* **EDITORS** *OHIO TIMES.* **n.d. n.p.** Gives brief account of the trial and conviction of Rev. C. Fairbank. 23 April 1852. p.66, c1.

2194 R. M. HALL *to* **WM. REESE. 12 April 1852. Schenectady, N.Y.** Chastises Reese for hunting down Horace Preston, a fugitive slave. 23 April 1852. p.66, c2.

2195 PARKER PILLSBURY *to* **S. MAY, JR. 17 April 1852. Bath.** Comments on anti-slavery activity in Maine. 23 April 1852. p.67, c5.

2196 JOSEPH BARKER *to* **RICHARD D. WEBB. 8 April 1852. Millwood, Oh.** Reports that he is going to start lecturing on the Bible and against slavery. 23 April 1852. p.68, c2.

2197 B. F. HALLETT *to* **SIR [GEO. W. THOMPSON]. 15 March 1851. Boston.** Calls for unity within the Democratic Party. 30 April 1852. p.69, c1.

2198 G. B. STEBBINS *to* **EDITOR OF THE** *LIBERATOR.* **22 April 1852. Rochester, N.Y.** Invites all to attend the annual meeting of the AAS. 30 April 1852. p.70, c2.

2199 CONSISTENCY *to* **MR. GARRISON. n.d. n.p.** Accuses W. Phillips and T. Parker of advocating violence in regard to the Fugitive Slave Law. 30 April 1852. p.70, c2.

2200 G. B. STEBBINS *to* **FRIEND GARRISON. 24 April 1852. Rochester.** Asks Garrison to publish a letter he wrote to a clergyman. 30 April 1852. p.71, c1.

2201 G. B. STEBBINS *to* **SIR. n.d. n.p.** Criticizes a professed anti-slavery minister for maintaining fellowship with pro-slavery churches. 30 April 1852. p.71, c1.

2202 PARKER PILLSBURY *to* **FRIEND GARRISON. 27 April 1852. Concord.** Comments on the opposition to anti-slavery in Maine. 30 April 1852. p.71, c3.

2203 I. C. KENYON *to* **FRIEND GARRISON. 13 April 1852. North Providence.** Wonders why an anti-slavery office is closing in Providence. 30 April 1852. p.71, c3.

2204 C. K. W. *to* **GARRISON. n.d. n.p.** Criticizes Kossuth for ignoring the oppressed slaves. 7 May 1852. p.75, c1.

2205 WM. H. BARTLETT *to* **FRIEND GARRISON. 23 April 1852. Plymouth.** Compares the hardships of fighting for abolition with the weaknesses of the clergy. 7 May 1852. p.75, c2.

2206 A. J. *to* **FRIEND GARRISON. n.d. n.p.** Believes that the Church holds back the anti-slavery movement. 7 May 1852. p.75, c2.

2207 ERNESTINE L. ROSE *to* **MR. EDITOR. [from the** *Boston Investigator***] 18 February 1852. New York.** Reviews Horace Mann's lectures. 7 May 1852. p.76, c5.

2208 ERNESTINE L. ROSE *to* **HORACE MANN. 18 February 1852. New York.** Reviews Horace Mann's lectures. 7 May 1852. p.76, c5.

2209 HORACE MANN *to* **JOHN I. GAINES, WM. R. DAY, JOHN JACKSON, DAVID JENKINS. 21 December 1851. Washington.** Urges the Central Committee of the Ohio Convention to propose and execute a plan for the "redemption and elevation" of the colored people. 14 May 1852. p.78, c1.

2210 J. W. LOGUEN *to* **GOV. WASHINGTON HUNT. 2 December 1851. St. Catharines, Canada West.** Asks that he be granted protection if he comes to Syracuse to stand trial for the rescue of Jerry. 14 May 1852. p.78, c3.

2211 CHARLES C. BURLEIGH *to* **BROTHER GARRISON. 30 April 1852. Cincinnati.** Gives an account of an anti-slavery convention in Ohio. 14 May 1852. p.78, c6.

2212 G. C. STEARNS *to* **FRIEND GARRISON. 2 May 1852. Philadelphia.** Praises Wm. J. Mullen for his philanthropic work as president of the Philadelphia Society for the Employment and Instruction of the Poor. 15 May 1852. p.79, c2.

2213 GRUNBEIN *to* **BRO. STEVENS. [from the** *Herald and Journal***] 30 December 1851. n.p.** Gives an account of slave-trading in western Virginia. 21 May 1852. p.81, c1.

2214 H. M. N. *to* **BRO. STEVENS. [from the** *Herald and Journal***] 21 January 1852. Williamsburg.** Laments the continuation of slavery in the Methodist Episcopal church. 21 May 1852. p.81, c2.

2215 ISAAC HOPPER *to* **THE EXECUTIVE COMMITTEE OF THE PRISON ASSOCIATION. 15 April 1852. New York.** Thanks the committee for resolutions commending his course while serving as an agent for discharged convicts. 21 May 1852. p.82, c2.

2216 GERRIT SMITH *to* **WILLIAM LLOYD GARRISON. 6 May 1852. Peterboro'.** Declares that the AAS and the Liberty Party misunderstand one another; feels that their only differences concern the issue of voting. 21 May 1852. p.82, c4.

2217 G. T. D. [MR. DOWNING, A COLORED CITIZEN FROM NEW YORK] *to* **THE EDITORS OF THE** *NEW YORK EVENING POST.* **n.d. n.p.** Corrects misconception about a meeting held at St. Philip's Church; asserts that the meeting was not called to resist the Fugitive Slave Law. 12 May 1852. p.83, c1.

2218 EDWARD SEARCH *to* **n.n. 1 May 1852. London.** Discusses differences between despotism, constitutional monarchy, and democracy. 21 May 1852. p.83, c2.

2219 DANIEL FOSTER *to* **FRIEND GARRISON. 15 May 1852. Concord, Ma.** Describes the abuse he received while lecturing on slavery in Newburyport. 21 May 1852. p.83, c3.

2220 M. R. DELANY *to* **MR. GARRISON. 14 May 1852. Philadelphia.** Thanks Garrison for the notice he took of Delany's book. 21 May 1852. p.83, c4.

2221 W. H. B. *to* **FRIEND GARRISON. 15 May 1852. Plymouth.** Gives an account of Kossuth's visit and address at Old Plymouth. 21 May 1852. p.83, c4.

2222 M. R. DELANY *to* **EDITOR OF THE** *PENNSYLVANIA FREEMAN.* **30 April 1852. Philadelphia.** Refutes the editor's criticism of his book. 28 May 1852. p.85, c5.

2223 J. R. GIDDINGS *to* **EDITOR OF THE** *PENNSYLVANIA FREEMAN.* **4 May 1852. n.p.** Proposes a monument to the memory of William Smith. 28 May 1852. p.86, c2.

2224 J. H. *to* **FRIEND GARRISON. 17 May 1852. Plymouth.** Encloses extracts from an address by Daniel Webster at Plymouth; discusses its relevance to the Fugitive Slave Law. 28 May 1852. p.86, c6.

2225 A. H. W. *to* **REV. SAMUEL MAY, JR. 20 May 1852. Pepperell.** Reports on the abolition lectures given by Rev. Foster at Pepperell. 28 May 1852. p.87, c1.

2226 DANIEL FOSTER *to* **FRIEND GARRISON. 22 May 1852. Concord.** Reports on his anti-slavery lectures in Fall River. 28 May 1852. p.87, c1.

2227 A. J. G. *to* **MR. GARRISON. n.d. n.p.** Comments on the degeneracy and growing corruption of the Church. 28 May 1852. p.88, c2.

2228 D. S. S. *to* **EDITOR OF** *ROCHESTER DEMOCRAT.* **n.d. n.p.** Recommends that Northerners consider slavery from a Southerner's viewpoint. 4 June 1852. p.89, c1.

2229 SPARTA *to* **EDITOR OF THE** *SAN FRANCISCO HERALD.* **n.d. n.p.** Argues in favor of slavery for California. 4 June 1852. p.89, c2.

2230 A. MAHAN *to* **REV. WM. SCOTT. [from the** *Glasgow Examiner***] December 1851. Cleveland, Oh.** Assails the AAS as an infidel, anti-human-government movement. 4 June 1852. p.89, c3.

2231 R. WRIGHT *to* **n.n. n.d. n.p.** Comments on the "amiable, Christian nature" of Mr. Mahan's letter denouncing the AAS. 4 June 1852. p.89, c4.

2232 C. M. CLAY *to* **ANTI-SLAVERY CONVENTION IN CINCINNATI. 15 June 1852. White Hall, Ky.** Regrets he cannot attend the anti-slavery convention. 4 June 1852. p.89, c5.

2233 EDWARD SEARCH *to* **n.n. 10 May 1852. London.** Compares India with America. 4 June 1852. p.92, c5.

2234 WASHINGTON HUNT *to* **SIR [EDWIN D. MORGAN, SENATOR]. 22 May 1852. Albany.** Discusses the pardon of James P. Snowdon, a colored convict. 11 June 1852. p.93, c5.

2235 n.n. *to* **MR. GARRISON. 30 May 1852. Charlestown.** Sends a contribution for the anti-slavery cause. 11 June 1852. p.95, c1.

2236 SHERMAN S. GRISWOLD *to* **MR. GARRISON. 9 April 1852. Greenmanville.** Declares that freedom of speech is the foundation of universal liberty. 11 June 1852. p.95, c2.

2237 DANIEL FOSTER *to* **FRIEND GARRISON. 30 May 1852. Concord.** Reports on anti-slavery activity in Acton. 11 June 1852. p.95, c2.

2238 E. A. LUKENS *to* **MR. GARRISON. 29 May 1852. New Garden, Oh.** Reports on the women's convention in Ohio. 11 June 1852. p.95, c3.

2239 WM. R. KING *to* **C. H. DONALDSON, ESQ. 26 July 1851. Tuscaloosa, Al.** Comments on the split within the Democratic Party. 18 June 1852. p.97, c1.

2240 GEN. FRANKLIN PIERCE *to* **C. G. ATHERSON. [from the** *New York Journal of Commerce*] **12 January 1852. Concord.** Acknowledges his nomination for the presidency by the Democratic State Convention. 18 June 1852. p.97, c1.

2241 WILLIAM R. KING *to* **ROBERT G. SCOTT. 20 May 1852. Senate Chamber.** A candidate for the presidency states his support of the Fugitive Slave Law. 18 June 1852. p.97, c2.

2242 GERRIT SMITH *to* **FREDERICK DOUGLASS. 25 May 1852. Peterboro'.** States that Kossuth is a patriot, not a philanthropist; praises Kossuth as a man of "extraordinary judgement, skill, tact." 18 June 1852. p.97, c3.

2243 AN OLD SUNDAY SCHOOL TEACHER *to* **THE EDITOR OF THE** *LONDON MORNING ADVERTISER.* **n.d. n.p.** Thanks the editor for condemning the Committee of the Sunday School Union, which invited Dr. Dyer, an advocate of slavery, to speak. 18 June 1852. p.97, c6.

2244 LIBERTY *to* **THE EDITOR OF THE** *LONDON MORNING ADVERTISER.* **n.d. n.p.** Thanks the editor for condemning the Committee of the Sunday School Union for inviting an advocate of slavery, Dr. Dyer, to speak. 18 June 1852. p.97, c6.

2245 WILLIAM GROSER *to* **THE EDITOR OF THE** *LONDON MORNING ADVERTISER* **n.d. n.p.** Secretary of the Sunday School Union denies that Dr. Dyer is a pro-slavery man. 18 June 1852. p.97, c6.

2246 JAMES S. HEATHER *to* **THE EDITOR OF THE** *BRITISH BANNER.* **7 May 1852. n.p.** Inquires whether Dr. Dyer from Philadelphia is a slaveholder or advocate of slavery. 18 June 1852. p.98, c1.

2247 ROBERT GAMMAN *to* **THE EDITOR OF THE** *BRITISH BANNER.* **n.d. n.p.** Wishes to know Rev. Dr. Dyer's views of slavery. 18 June 1852. p.98, c1.

2248 T. S. MARKS *to* **THE EDITOR OF THE** *BRITISH BANNER*. **7 May 1852. n.p.** Believes that the Sunday School Union has annulled its anti-slavery stand by inviting Dr. Dyer to speak. 18 June 1852. p.98, c2.

2249 F. W. BIRD *to* **SIR. 14 June 1852. East Walpole.** States that he is not the editor of *Commonwealth*. 18 June 1852. p.98, c4.

2250 ISAAC POST *to* **FRIEND. 31 May 1852. Rochester.** Discusses Quaker practices regarding dating. 18 June 1852. p.98, c5.

2251 DANIEL FOSTER *to* **FRIEND GARRISON. 11 June 1852. Concord, Ma.** Reports on anti-slavery lectures in Essex and Stoneham. 18 June 1852. p.98, c6.

2252 HENRY C. WRIGHT *to* **GARRISON. 27 May 1852. New Garden, Oh.** Discusses the Church, the clergy, and Paine's *Age of Reason*. 18 June 1852. p.100, c2.

2253 DAVID HARROWER *to* **THE EDITOR OF THE** *LIBERATOR* **[W. L. GARRISON]. 9 June 1852. Troy, N.Y.** Forwards letter from Rev. A. Browning of Scotland; provides a brief biographical sketch. 18 June 1852. p.100, c3.

2254 REV. ARCHIBALD BROWNING *to* **n.n. [extract] n.d. Tillicoultry, Scotland.** Places W. L. Garrison and H. C. Wright above Kossuth, whom he believes is "one with slaveholders and the enemy of the poor slaves." 18 June 1852. p.100, c3.

2255 GEN. FRANK PIERCE *to* **COL. LALLEY. [extract] 27 May 1852. Tremont House, Boston.** Believes in the necessity of constitutional compromise in resolving differences between the North and the South. 25 June 1852. p.101, c1.

2256 LUCY STONE *to* **FRIEND GARRISON. 22 June 1852. West Brookfield.** Forwards a letter from Prof. Fairchild. 25 June 1852. p.102, c6.

2257 J. H. FAIRCHILD *to* **MISS STONE. 15 June 1852. Oberlin.** Denies the accusation that his wife owns slaves. 25 June 1852. p.102, c6.

2258 HENRY C. WRIGHT *to* **HENRY VINCENT. 16 June 1852. Toledo, Oh.** Encloses a newspaper advertisement which fills him with disgust toward America. 25 June 1852. p.103, c1.

2259 JOSEPH MERRILL *to* **BROTHER GARRISON. 20 June 1852. Danversport.** Anticipates the annual meeting of the Essex County AS. 25 June 1852. p.103, c2.

2260 W. STICKNEY *to* **MR. GARRISON. 11 June 1852. Canastota.** Praises the Garrisonian view of the Constitution. 25 June 1852. p.104, c2.

2261 J. H. SWETT *to* **FRIEND GARRISON. 23 February 1852. Milford, N.H.** Wonders when the "foul demon of slavery" will be overcome. 25 June 1852. p.104, c2.

2262 WM. H. BARTLETT *to* **FRIEND GARRISON. 13 June 1852. Plymouth.** Hopes that the presidency will never belong to Daniel Webster. 25 June 1852. p.104, c3.

2263 JAMES FREEMAN CLARKE *to* **THE EDITOR. [from the** *National Era***] May 1852. Meadville, Western Pa.** Forwards proposals for the formation of a new anti-slavery association. 2 July 1852. p.105, c3.

2264 n.n. *to* **EDITORS OF THE** *TRUE DEMOCRAT*. **4 June 1852. Washington City.** Derides the "base subserviency to slave power" displayed at the Baltimore convention. 2 July 1852. p.105, c5.

2265 FRANKLIN PIERCE *to* **GENTLEMEN. 17 June 1852. Concord, N.H.** Accepts nomination as the Democratic candidate for president of the United States. 2 July 1852. p.106, c1.

2266 WM. R. KING *to* **J. S. BARBOUR, J. THOMPSON, ALPHEUS FELCH, AND P. SOULE. 22 June 1852. Senate Chamber.** Acknowledges his nomination for vice-president. 2 July 1852. p.106, c1.

2267 WINFIELD SCOTT *to* **J. G. CHAPMAN. 21 June 1852. Washington.** Accepts the nomination for president. 2 July 1852. p.106, c1.

2268 SILONA *to* **BELOVED SISTER. 9 June 1852. Hartford, Ct.** Describes a metaphorical "Book of Life" composed of the mind and body. 2 July 1852. p.107, c1.

2269 L. S. *to* **JOSEPH BARKER. n.d. n.p.** Supports Barker's view of the Bible as a fallible creation of man. 2 July 1852. p.107, c2.

2270 DANIEL FOSTER *to* **FRIEND GARRISON. 22 June 1852. Woonsocket.** Reports on anti-slavery activity in Worcester and Woonsocket. 2 July 1852. p.108, c2.

2271 REV. JOSHUA LEAVITT *to* **MR. EDITOR. [from the** *New York Evening Post***] n.d. n.p.** Feels anxious about rumors that Franklin Pierce is a drunkard. 2 July 1852. p.108, c4.

2272 SAMUEL W. WHEELER *to* **FRIEND GARRISON. 3 July 1852. Providence.** Criticizes the press and the public of Providence for upholding slavery. 9 July 1852. p.110, c5.

2273 S. W. WHEELER *to* **FRIEND GARRISON. 7 July 1852. Providence.** Describes mob persecution of reformers in Providence. 9 July 1852. p.110, c6.

2274 CHARLES STEARNS *to* **FRIEND GARRISON. 30 June 1852. Kennett Square, Pa.** Gives sketch of his travels among the Quakers. 9 July 1852. p.111, c1.

2275 HENRY C. WRIGHT *to* **GARRISON. 25 June 1852. Lenaware, Mn.** Critiques certain objectionable characteristics of *Uncle Tom's Cabin.* 9 July 1852. p.111, c3.

2276 LUCY STONE *to* **FRIEND GARRISON. 6 June 1852. West Brookfield.** Reports on North Brookfield anti-slavery meetings. 9 July 1852. p.111, c4.

2277 GEORGE ARMSTRONG *to* **HIS EXCELLENCY LOUIS KOSSUTH. 9 October 1851. Bristol.** Welcomes Kossuth and warns him of the difficulties he may encounter in the United States. 9 July 1852. p.112, c2.

2278 n.n. *to* **n.n. [extract] n.d. England.** A gentleman of great respectability and influence declares that Kossuth, whom he had idolized, is no longer worthy of the interest he excites. 9 July 1852. p.112, c2.

2279 DANIEL FOSTER *to* **FRIEND GARRISON. 9 July 1852. Reading, Ma.** Reports on anti-slavery activity in Reading. 9 July 1852. p.112, c3.

2280 THOMAS GALBREATH *to* **WILLIAM L. GARRISON. 29 May 1852. New Garden, Oh.** Criticizes the *Liberator*'s treatment of the Church and the Bible. 9 July 1852. p.112, c3.

2281 A. W. *to* **FRIEND GARRISON. 25 June 1852. Mystic, Ct.** Praises the *Liberator*; discusses S. S. Griswold's search for freedom. 9 July 1852. p.112, c4.

2282 S. S. GRISWOLD *to* **FRIEND GARRISON. n.d. n.p.** Disagrees with Joseph Barker's view of the Bible. 9 July 1852. p.112, c4.

2283 M. VAN BUREN *to* **GENTLEMEN. 9 July 1852. Lindenwald.** Expresses gratitude for an invitation to meet the Tammany Society. 16 July 1852. p.113, c2.

2284 JAMES PHILLIPS *to* **WIFE. 20 June 1852. Richmond.** Relates the story of a slave who was taken from a family in Pennsylvania and resold. 16 July 1852. p.113, c4.

2285 CHARLES SUMNER *to* **E. L KEYES. 3 July 1852. Washington.** Discusses anti-slavery meeting to be held at Worcester; laments the Baltimore convention's servility to slavery. 16 July 1852. p.113, c5.

2286 J. R. GIDDINGS *to* **E. L. KEYES, ESQ. 3 July 1852. Washington City.** Accepts invitation to the Worcester convention. 16 July 1852. p.113, c5.

2287 GEORGE SUNTER, JR. *to* **W. L. GARRISON. 17 June 1852. England.** Praises W. L. Garrison's writing and work. 16 July 1852. p.114, c4.

2288 J. C. H. *to* **WILLIAM L. GARRISON. 8 July 1852. Syracuse.** Expresses delight that the Great Northern Apostate, Daniel Webster, did not win the presidential nomination. 16 July 1852. p.114, c5.

2289 HENRY C. WRIGHT *to* **GARRISON. 29 June 1852. Lenawee, Mi.** Reports that he is attending a water cure establishment. 16 July 1852. p.114, c6.

2290 L. C. MATLACK *to* **DANIEL FOSTER. [from the** *True Wesleyan***] 24 June 1852. n.p.** Returns Foster's letter on the pro-slavery nature of the Wesleyan church. 16 July 1852. p.115, c1.

2291 DANIEL FOSTER *to* **LUCIUS C. MATLACK. [from the** *True Wesleyan***] 24 June 1852. Concord, Ma.** Explains why the Wesleyan Methodist church is not anti-slavery. 16 July 1852. p.115, c1.

2292 DR. D. S. GRANDIN *to* **MR. GARRISON. 5 July 1852. Portland.** Declares that chloroform is not dangerous if used correctly. 16 July 1852. p.115, c3.

2293 C. STEARNS *to* **FRIEND GARRISON. 3 July 1852. Christiana, Pa.** Discusses Quakerism in Pennsylvania. 16 July 1852. p.115, c3.

2294 SILONA *to* **MY DEAR SISTER. 15 June 1852. Hartford, Ct.** Comments on God's laws and her religious sentiments. 16 July 1852. p.110 [116], c2.

2295 CHARLES F. HOVEY *to* **GARRISON. 4 July 1852. Gloucester.** Discusses an extract from Godwin's *Political Justice* concerning truth, morals, religion, and government. 16 July 1852. p.110 [116], c3.

2296 MOSES B. CHURCH *to* **MR. EDITOR. [from the** *Boston Investigator***] n.d. n.p.** Relates an experience which led him to believe in spiritualism. 16 July 1852. p.110 [116], c5.

2297 A. *to* **MR. EDITOR. [from the** *Zion's Herald***] 22 June 1852. Plattsburgh.** Forwards letter from a friend in California. 23 July 1852. p.117, c6.

2298 A MINISTER *to* **A. [extract from the** *Zion's Herald***] n.d. California.** Laments the introduction of slavery in California; declares he is likely to turn into a "terrible abolitionist." 23 July 1852. p.117, c6.

2299 J. McBRIDE *to* **MR. EDITOR. [from the** *True Wesleyan*] **11 June 1852. Meredith County, Oh.** Reports that a man in Virginia was whipped because of his anti-slavery convictions. 23 July 1852. p.118, c1.

2300 CASSIUS M. CLAY *to* **THE EDITOR OF THE** *NATIONAL ERA*. **5 July 1852. Madison, Ky.** Declines candidacy for vice-president on the Free Democratic ticket. 23 July 1852. p.118, c1.

2301 DAVID BONNER *to* **W. L. G. 29 June 1852. Greenfield, Oh.** Requests that all parties unite under the banner of liberty. 23 July 1852. p.118, c4.

2302 GEORGE DOUGHTY *to* **SIR [W. L. GARRISON]. 18 July 1852. Long Island.** Encloses donation to the *Liberator*. 23 July 1852. p.118, c4.

2303 REV. JEHIEL CLAFLIN *to* **FRIEND GARRISON. 12 July 1852. Northfield, Vt.** Declares that he is a Garrisonian abolitionist. 23 July 1852. p.118, c5.

2304 n.n. *to* **GARRISON. 13 July 1852. Penn Yan.** Inquires into the whereabouts of Henry Bradley. 23 July 1852. p.118, c5.

2305 DANIEL FOSTER *to* **FRIEND GARRISON. 16 July 1852. New Bedford.** Reports on anti-slavery in New Bedford and Fair Haven. 23 July 1852. p.119, c1.

2306 J. LEONARD *to* **FRIEND GARRISON. 18 July 1852. East Bridgewater.** Believes that the Bible should not be discussed in the *Liberator*. 23 July 1852. p.119, c2.

2307 A FRIEND OF PROGRESS *to* **FRIEND GARRISON. 18 July 1852. Newburyport.** Asserts that it is arrogant to condemn the Bible. 23 July 1852. p.119, c2.

2308 MICAJAH T. JOHNSON *to* **FRIEND GARRISON. 16 July 1852. South Creek, Oh.** Advocates pure Christian non-resistance. 23 July 1852. p.119, c2.

2309 SILONA *to* **H. 21 June 1852. Hartford, Ct.** Prays for the coming of God's kingdom. 23 July 1852. p.120, c2.

2310 S. S. GRISWOLD *to* **MR. GARRISON. n.d. n.p.** Refutes A. W.'s contention that fighting for church ceremonies impedes humanitarian efforts. 23 July 1852. p.120, c3.

2311 SAMUEL MAY, JR. *to* **MR. GARRISON. 28 July 1852. Leicester.** Describes the site chosen for First of August celebration. 30 July 1852. p.122, c2.

2312 DANIEL FOSTER *to* **FRIEND GARRISON. 24 July 1852. Concord, Ma.** Reports on anti-slavery in Nantucket. 30 July 1852. p.121 [123], c1.

2313 REV. J. G. FORMAN *to* **WILLIAM LLOYD GARRISON. 24 July 1852. Nantucket.** Praises Daniel Foster's lectures. 30 July 1852. p.121 [123], c2.

2314 T. BICKNELL *to* **FRIEND GARRISON. 26 July 1852. Kingston.** Denounces Daniel Webster as the "personification of all that is evil." 30 July 1852. p.121 [123], c2.

2315 HIRAM WILSON *to* **FRIEND GARRISON. 20 July 1852. Canada West.** Describes the condition of colored people in Canada. 30 July 1852. p.121 [123], c3.

2316 JOSEPH TREAT *to* **FRIEND GARRISON. 27 July 1852. Hartford.** Denies having said that Henry Clay was freed from blame in the spirit world. 30 July 1852. p.121 [123], c3.

2317 SILONA *to* **SISTER. 1 July 1852. Hartford.** Believes that "love is life" and "God is all and all." 30 July 1852. p.124, c2.

2318 EDWARD SEARCH *to* **GARRISON. 6 July 1852. London.** Believes that to plead against intervention is a mistake. 6 August 1852. p.127, c1.

2319 BUCKEYE *to* **THE *LIBERATOR*. 23 July 1852. Warren, Oh.** Describes the capture of a fugitive slave from Kentucky. 6 August 1852. p.127, c3.

2320 JOSEPH BARKER *to* **FRIEND. 22 July 1852. Millwood, Oh.** Expresses his views on the Bible. 6 August 1852. p.128, c3.

2321 NIHIL NOVUM *to* **GARRISON. n.d. n.p.** Solicits Garrison's views on the Bible. 6 August 1852. p.128, c4.

2322 P. S. M. *to* **FRIEND EVANS. 17 July 1852. Baltimore.** Reports on the kidnapping of Rachel Parker. 6 August 1852. p.128, c5.

2323 GERRIT SMITH *to* **WM. R. SMITH. 16 June 1852. Peterboro'.** Regrets that he paid $10,000 for Mr. Chaplin's bail in Maryland. 13 August 1852. p.130, c2.

2324 HENRY C. WRIGHT *to* **R. D. WEBB. 26 July 1852. Michigan.** Discusses the compromise of 1776. 13 August 1852. p.130, c5.

2325 JOSEPH BARKER *to* **THE *LIBERATOR*. 28 July 1852. Millwood, Oh.** Gives his views on the authority of the Bible. 13 August 1852. p.131, c1.

2326 W. H. B. *to* **FRIEND GARRISON. 1 August 1852. Plymouth.** Hopes that the abolition cause will succeed despite the current antipathy between anti-slavery, politics, and the Church. 13 August 1852. p.131, c2.

2327 JOSEPH TREAT *to* **FRIEND GARRISON. 2 August 1852. Hartford.** Prefers to draw a distinction between a man and his sins. 13 August 1852. p.131, c3.

2328 DANIEL FOSTER *to* **GARRISON. 31 July 1852. Concord, Ma.** Forwards letter from Thomas Jones, a fugitive slave. 13 August 1852. p.132, c2.

2329 REV. THOMAS H. JONES *to* **REV. DANIEL FOSTER. 15 July 1852. Liverpool.** A fugitive slave and Methodist minister informs Foster of his asylum in England; reports that he is trying to raise money to buy his son from a lady in North Carolina. 13 August 1852. p.132, c2.

2330 A. P. BOWMAN *to* **W. L. GARRISON. n.d. n.p.** Discusses a man's relationship to the rest of humanity. 13 August 1852. p.132, c2.

2331 H — N *to* **GARRISON. n.d. n.p.** Wonders why abolitionists argue with the Bible. 13 August 1852. p.132, c3.

2332 JOHN CADWALLADER *to* **JOSEPH BARKER. 30 July 1852. Ripley, Oh.** Supports Barker's view of the Bible. 13 August 1852. p.132, c3.

2333 H. B. *to* **S. S. GRISWOLD. n.d. n.p.** Disagrees with Griswold's belief that the Bible should be regarded as divine authority. 13 August 1852. p.132, c3.

2334 JAMES CLEMENT *to* **FRIEND GARRISON. 1 August 1852. Middlefield, Oh.** Praises the *Liberator* for its policy of free discussion; sends a donation. 13 August 1852. p.132, c4.

2335 S. D. *to* **FRIEND GARRISON. 25 July 1852. South Abington.** Condemns the clergy of the Methodist church for their "criminal indifference" to slavery. 13 August 1852. p.132, c4.

2336 PARKER PILLSBURY *to* **FRIEND GARRISON. 8 August 1852. Hudson, Oh.** Reports on anti-slavery meetings in Ohio. 20 August 1852. p.134, c5.

2337 C. H. A. DALL *to* **BROTHER. 3 August 1852. Toronto, Canada West.** Reports on a West Indies Emancipation celebration by the colored community in Toronto. 20 August 1852. p.134, c6.

2338 ANGELINA J. KNOX *to* **MR. GARRISON. 14 August 1852. Hyannis.** Asserts that the Church is wrong to withhold support from the anti-slavery cause. 20 August 1852. p.135, c2.

2339 S. W. *to* **GARRISON. 10 August 1852. North Easton, N.Y.** Relates the experiences of a slaveholder's wife with slavery in the South. 20 August 1852. p.135, c3.

2340 B. *to* **FRIEND GARRISON. 11 August 1852. New Ipswich, N.H.** Reports on anti-slavery lectures in New Hampshire. 20 August 1852. p.135, c4.

2341 S. M. SEAVER *to* **BRO. GARRISON. 1 August 1852. Williamstown, Vt.** Criticizes Brother Claflin for asking whether participants at the Baltimore convention prayed. 20 August 1852. p.135, c4.

2342 DANIEL FOSTER *to* **FRIEND GARRISON. n.d. n.p.** Reports on an anti-slavery meeting in Old Barnstable; encloses resolutions. 20 August 1852. p.136, c2.

2343 H. C. WRIGHT *to* **GARRISON. n.d. n.p.** Deplores the arrogance of those who believe the Bible to be infallible. 20 August 1852. p.136, c3.

2344 SARAH D. FISH *to* **WILLIAM LLOYD GARRISON. 8 August 1852. Rochester.** Advocates the restoration of rights to women; criticizes the treatment of domestics. 20 August 1852. p.136, c4.

2345 E. OAKES SMITH *to* **THE EDITOR OF THE** *NEW YORK TRIBUNE.* **n.d. n.p.** Affirms her belief that women should be allowed to do good in the world as well as in the home. 20 August 1852. p.136, c5.

2346 FRANK PIERCE *to* **EDWIN DE LEON. 23 July 1852. Concord, N.H.** Asserts that his opinions regarding the constitutional rights of the South have been consistent. 27 August 1852. p.137, c2.

2347 GERRIT SMITH *to* **THE LIBERTY PARTY OF MADISON COUNTY. 13 August 1852. Pittsburgh.** Declares the Pittsburgh convention a failure. 27 August 1852. p.137, c3.

2348 PARKER PILLSBURY *to* **FRIEND GARRISON. 20 August 1852. Salem, Oh.** Reports on politics in northern Ohio; concludes that the political leaders are all that hold the people back. 27 August 1852. p.138, c6.

2349 JOSEPH BARKER *to* **THE EDITOR OF THE** *LONDON LEADER.* **7 August 1852. Millwood, Oh.** Questions the *Leader*'s praise of Henry Clay; censures Clay for his role in passing the Fugitive Slave Law. 27 August 1852. p.139, c1.

2350 HENRY C. WRIGHT *to* **REV. WM. SCOTT. 28 July 1852. Michigan.** Refutes Rev. Asa Mahan's belief that the AAS is an "infidel" organization. 27 August 1852. p.139, c2.

2351 E. A. LUKENS *to* **FRIEND. 8 August 1852. New Garden, Oh.** Praises letters from Silona. 27 August 1852. p.139, c3.

2352 J. J. LOCKE *to* **GARRISON. 17 August 1852. Boston.** Reports on anti-slavery meetings in New Hampshire. 27 August 1852. p.139, c4.

2353 CHARLES BABBIDGE *to* **MR. HUTSON. n.d. n.p.** Explains that he is not at liberty to cancel afternoon services, despite the fact that Garrison will be speaking. 27 August 1852. p.140, c2.

2354 DANIEL FOSTER *to* **FRIEND GARRISON. 16 August 1852. Harwich.** Reports on anti-slavery work in Harwich and Brewster. 27 August 1852. p.140, c3.

2355 J. S. GREEN *to* **GERRIT SMITH. [from** *Frederick Douglass' Paper*] **26 April 1852. Sandwich Islands.** Laments the persistence of slavery in the Sandwich Islands. 3 September 1852. p.141, c4.

2356 LEANDER *to* **THE** *ANTI-SLAVERY STANDARD.* **6 August 1852. London.** Reports on the West Indies Emancipation celebration in London; gives an account of speeches by Wm. Douglass, Francis Kellogg, Wm. W. Brown, and W. and E. Craft. 3 September 1852. p.143, c1.

2357 WILLIAM H. BARTLETT *to* **FRIEND GARRISON. 27 August 1852. Plymouth.** Reports on the Old Colony AS. 3 September 1852. p.143, c4.

2358 DANIEL FOSTER *to* **FRIEND GARRISON. 27 August 1852. Concord.** Reports on anti-slavery lectures on the Cape. 3 September 1852. p.143, c4.

2359 H. R. H. *to* **MRS. MARY H. EASTMAN. n.d. n.p.** An abolitionist reports that he has been converted to pro-slavery after reading Eastman's book, *Aunt Phillis' Cabin.* 3 September 1852. p.144, c2.

2360 A SOUTHERNER *to* **GARRISON. 21 August 1852. Boston.** Answers arguments from *Aunt Phillis' Cabin*; declares that all slavery of the mind is wrong. 3 September 1852. p.144, c3.

2361 HENRY C. WRIGHT *to* **GARRISON. 25 July 1852. Michigan.** Argues that children have a sacred right to health. 3 September 1852. p.144, c4.

2362 PARKER PILLSBURY *to* **FRIEND GARRISON. 30 August 1852. Salem, Oh.** Reports on speeches by Oliver Johnson, Jane Jones, James Walker, and Frederick Douglass at the anniversary of the Western AS. 10 September 1852. p.147, c1.

2363 ALONZO J. GROVER *to* **GARRISON. 31 August 1852. Smithville Seminary, R.I.** Reports on anti-slavery sentiment in Rhode Island. 10 September 1852. p.147, c1.

2364 GEO. J. PETERSON *to* **FRIEND GARRISON. 1 September 1852. Duxbury.** Describes anti-slavery meetings in Duxbury. 10 September 1852. p.147, c3.

2365 I. S. *to* **THE EDITOR [W. L. GARRISON]. n.d. n.p.** Corrects mistakes in his article published 20 August. 10 September 1852. p.147, c4.

2366 ELIZABETH WILSON *to* **MR. GARRISON. 20 August 1852. Cadiz, Oh.** Comments on the Bible; criticizes Joseph Barker's belief that "all believers in the Bible are in favor of the Fugitive Slave Law." 10 September 1852. p.148, c2.

2367 H. C. WRIGHT *to* **GARRISON. 11 August 1852. Lake Erie.** Argues that it is absurd to regard the Bible as infallible. 10 September 1852. p.148, c4.

2368 EDWARD SEARCH *to* **n.n. August 1852. London.** States that he feels less strongly about slavery than does H. C. Wright. 10 September 1852. p.148, c5.

2369 HORACE MANN *to* **FELLOW CITIZENS. 10 September 1852. West Newton.** Refuses to run again as representative to Congress; urges fellow citizens to form an anti-slavery coalition. 17 September 1852. p.150, c5.

2370 JOHN P. HALE *to* **HENRY WILSON. 6 September 1852. Dover, N.H.** Accepts nomination from the Free Democratic National Convention despite protest from his wife and children. 17 September 1852. p.151, c1.

2371 J. CUSHING *to* **FRIEND GARRISON. 31 August 1852. South Hingham.** Questions inconsistencies in Rev. Parker's speeches. 17 September 1852. p.151, c2.

2372 THEO. PARKER *to* **GARRISON. 13 September 1852. West Newton.** Denies having referred to the publisher who refused his book as "Mr. Gagspeech." 17 September 1852. p.151, c2.

2373 SAMUEL J. MAY *to* **GARRISON. 11 September 1852. Syracuse.** Gives account of a women's rights convention, at which Lucretia Mott presided. 17 September 1852. p.151, c3.

2374 HENRY C. WRIGHT *to* **GARRISON. 29 August 1852. Leesburgh, Oh.** Reports on the anniversary of the Western AS. 17 August 1852. p.151, c4.

2375 ALONZO J. GROVER *to* **MR. GARRISON. 8 September 1852. East Abington.** Reports on anti-slavery in Rhode Island. 17 September 1852. p.151, c4.

2376 S. MITCHELL *to* **GARRISON. 26 August 1852. Cornwall, Me.** Reports on anti-slavery in Maine. 17 September 1852. p.151, c5.

2377 FAIR PLAY *to* **FRIEND GARRISON. 20 August 1852. Springfield.** Expresses surprise that H. C. Wright could "find it in his heart" to deride *Uncle Tom's Cabin,* a book that has done so much for the anti-slavery cause. 17 September 1852. p.152, c3.

2378 H. C. WRIGHT *to* **GARRISON. 10 August 1852. Adrian, Mi.** Replies to Nihil Novum's criticism of his discourse on Paine's *Age of Reason.* 17 September 1852. p.152, c5.

2379 A. J. G. *to* **MR. GARRISON. n.d. East Abington.** Admires Miss Holley's manner of speaking in public. 17 September 1852. p.152, c5.

2380 LUCY STONE *to* **FRIEND GARRISON. 21 September 1852. West Brookfield.** Attempts to explain the "living spirit" of the women's rights convention at Syracuse. 24 September 1852. p.154, c6.

2381 DANIEL DRAYTON *to* **THE EDITOR OF THE *LIBERATOR* [W. L. GARRISON]. 18 September 1852. Boston.** Expresses gratitude to those who helped him. 24 September 1852. p.154, c6.

2382 DANIEL FOSTER *to* **FRIEND GARRISON. 16 September 1852. Cambridge, Ma.** Reports on anti-slavery meetings in Leominster. 24 September 1852. p.155, c1.

2383 G. B. STEBBINS *to* **WM. LLOYD GARRISON. 15 September 1852. Belfast, N.Y.** Comments on anti-slavery sentiment in New York. 24 September 1852. p.155, c2.

2384 H. W. B. *to* **MR. GARRISON. 19 September 1852. Port Norfolk.** Describes an anti-slavery meeting at which Sallie Holley spoke. 24 September 1852. p.155, c2.

2385 H. R. H. *to* **MR. EDITOR [W. L. GARRISON]. n.d. n.p.** Asserts that he is both an abolitionist and an infidel. 24 September 1852. p.155, c3.

2386 EDWARD SEARCH *to* **GARRISON. 1 August 1852. London.** Encourages persistence in the anti-slavery cause. 24 September 1852. p.156, c2.

2387 GEO. ARMSTRONG *to* **THE EDITOR OF THE** *LONDON INQUIRER.* **2 September 1852. Clifton.** Comments on corrupted morals and politics in America and Europe. 1 October 1852. p.158, c1.

2388 MRS. FRANCES D. GAGE *to* *PENNSYLVANIA FREEMAN.* **[extract] n.d. Cleveland, Oh.** Discusses an anti-slavery speech by Mr. Hale, a women's rights meeting, and her hopes for future agitation in Ohio. 1 October 1852. p.158, c1.

2389 JAMES HAUGHTON *to* **THE EDITOR OF THE** *DUBLIN ADVOCATE.* **24 July 1852. n.p.** Censures Henry Clay as "an unrelenting enemy of the colored brethren." 1 October 1852. p.158, c2.

2390 EDWARD SEARCH *to* **GARRISON. September 1852. London.** Declares that no war will arise from the fishery question. 1 October 1852. p.158, c4.

2391 JOSEPH BARKER *to* **FRIEND GARRISON. 16 August 1852. Near Millwood, Oh.** Invites W. L. Garrison to come to Ohio in order to rest. 1 October 1852. p.158, c5.

2392 S. D. SHORT *to* **FRIEND GARRISON. 22 September 1852. Bloomfield, Me.** Asks why Garrisonians do not vote. 1 October 1852. p.158, c6.

2393 H. H. BRIGHAM *to* **FRIEND GARRISON. 4 September 1852. South Abington.** Declares that Rev. Nathaniel Colver "is not what he should be" with respect to the anti-slavery cause, yet considers him to be far in advance of his church. 1 October 1852. p.159, c1.

2394 W. H. B. *to* **FRIEND GARRISON. 24 September 1852. Plymouth.** Expresses approval of the resolutions of the Free Democratic State Convention. 1 October 1852. p.159, c2.

2395 R. A. UPTON *to* **EDITOR OF THE** *NEW ORLEANS BEE.* **8 August 1852. Iberville.** Denies rumor that Gen. Scott favors the Free-Soil Party. 8 October 1852. p.161, c1.

2396 EDMUND KELL *to* **THE EDITOR OF THE** *LONDON INQUIRER.* **17 August 1852. Newport.** Recommends sending contributions to the Anti-Slavery Bazaar in Boston; praises *Uncle Tom's Cabin.* 8 October 1852. p.162, c3.

2397 EDWARD SEARCH *to* **n.n. August 1852. London.** Lectures on the weakness of England and the potential strength of America. 8 October 1852. p.163, c1.

2398 DANIEL FOSTER *to* **FRIEND GARRISON. 1 October 1852. Fitchburg.** Reports on anti-slavery lectures in Manchester and Gloucester. 8 October 1852. p.163, c3.

2399 CARLISLE *to* **MR. BARNES. [from the** *Leeds Mercury***] 6 September 1852. Naworth Castle.** Praises *Uncle Tom's Cabin* for its "fairness, fidelity, and truth." 15 October 1852. p.165, c3.

2400 GEORGE THOMPSON *to* **GARRISON. 24 September 1852. London.** Laments his defeat in the recent election. 15 October 1852. p.166, c4.

2401 S. P. CHASE *to* **SIR [R. R. RAYMOND]. 27 September 1852. Cincinnati.** Regrets that he cannot attend the Jerry Rescue celebration; states that the Fugitive Slave Law is a "usurpation of power not delegated to the Constitution." 15 October 1852. p.166, c5.

2402 SAMUEL LEWIS *to* **REV. SAMUEL J. MAY. 29 September 1852. Cincinnati.** Regrets that he is unable to attend the Jerry Rescue celebration. 15 October 1852. p.166, c5.

2403 CHARLES FRANCIS ADAMS *to* **REV. SAMUEL J. MAY. 30 September 1852. Quincy.** Regrets that he is unable to attend the Jerry Rescue celebration. 15 October 1852. p.166, c5.

2404 R. HILDRETH *to* **n.n. 28 September 1852. Boston.** Regrets that he is unable to attend the Jerry Rescue celebration. 15 October 1852. p.166, c5.

2405 JOHN G. WHITTIER *to* **FRIEND. 29 September 1852. Amesbury.** Regrets that he is unable to attend the Jerry Rescue celebration. 15 October 1852. p.166, c5.

2406 ELIZUR WRIGHT *to* **WM. L. CRANDALL AND OTHERS. 27 September 1852. Boston.** Comments on the Jerry Rescue celebration. 15 October 1852. p.166, c6.

2407 REV. GEO. W. PERKINS *to* **n.n. 28 September 1852. Meriden.** Regrets that he is unable to attend the Jerry Rescue celebration. 15 October 1852. p.166, c6.

2408 SAMUEL J. MAY, JR. *to* **REV. SAMUEL MAY. 29 September 1852. Leicester.** Regrets that he is unable to attend the Jerry Rescue celebration. 15 October 1852. p.166, c6.

2409 S. E. SEWALL *to* **REV. S. J. MAY. 25 September 1852. Boston.** Regrets that he cannot attend the Jerry Rescue celebration. 15 October 1852. p.167, c1.

2410 CAROLINE HEALEY DALL *to* **MRS. PAULINA W. DAVIS. 27 September 1852. Toronto, Canada.** Comments on the purpose of the women's rights convention. 15 October 1852. p.167, c1.

2411 J. M. ALDRICH *to* **FRIEND GARRISON. 5 October 1852. Fall River.** Praises a lecture by Sallie Holley. 15 October 1852. p.167, c3.

2412 H. C. WRIGHT *to* **GARRISON. 5 September 1852. Litchfield, Oh.** Forwards a funeral discourse he delivered upon the death of a female friend of the anti-slavery cause. 15 October 1852. p.168, c2.

2413 PASTOR *to* **GENTLEMEN OF THE** *CHRISTIAN PRESS***. 23 September 1852. Connecticut.** Questions whether slavery can be legalized. 22 October 1852. p.169, c2.

2414 JAMES L. HILL *to* **EDITOR OF THE** *NEW YORK EVANGELIST***. 17 September 1852. Springfield, Il.** Affirms the validity of *Uncle Tom's Cabin* by relating his own experience with slavery. 22 October 1852. p.169, c4.

2415 A CONSTANT READER *to* **THE EDITOR OF THE** *LONDON TIMES.* **n.d. n.p.** Argues that *Uncle Tom's Cabin* hurts the anti-slavery cause. 22 October 1852. p.170, c2.

2416 DANIEL FOSTER *to* **FRIEND GARRISON. 16 October 1852. Cambridge.** Reports on anti-slavery in Westminster and Gardner. 22 October 1852. p.170, c4.

2417 E. R. JOHNSON *to* **HORACE MANN. n.d. New Bedford.** Forwards extract of earlier letter from Mann; solicits Mann's current views on the subject of the letter. 22 October 1852. p.170, c4.

2418 HORACE MANN *to* **E. R. JOHNSON. [extract] 5 October 1852. West Newton.** Reaffirms his belief that each race prospers in its own portion of the globe. 22 October 1852. p.170, c5.

2419 REV. THEODORE PARKER *to* **SAMUEL J. MAY. 25 September 1852. West Newton.** Discusses the legal nuances of the Jerry Rescue case. 22 October 1852. p.171, c1.

2420 J. E. SNODGRASS *to* **R. R. RAYMOND. 27 September 1852. Raymond, Baltimore.** Regrets he is unable to attend the Jerry Rescue celebration; condemns the Fugitive Slave Law. 22 October 1852. p.171, c2.

2421 L. A. HINE *to* **BRO. JOHONNOT. 28 September 1852. Cincinnati.** Declares he will be present in spirit at the Jerry Rescue celebration; declares that the Fugitive Slave Law is moribund. 22 October 1852. p.171, c3.

2422 SARAH CLAY *to* **WM. LLOYD GARRISON. 17 October 1852. Lowell.** Compliments the eloquence of Sallie Holley. 22 October 1852. p.171, c3.

2423 SAMUEL LEWIS *to* **J. F. MORSE. 13 September 1852. Cincinnati.** Regrets he is unable to attend the Giddings Festival. 29 October 1852. p.173, c2.

2424 GEO. W. JULIAN *to* **J. F. MORSE AND OTHERS. 11 September 1852. Centreville, In.** Hails Giddings as "that glorious old patriarch of freedom" but regrets he cannot attend his testimonial. 29 October 1852. p.173, c3.

2425 AMASA WALKER *to* **J. F. MORSE AND OTHERS. 12 September 1852. North Brookfield, Ma.** Declares that no greater "friend of human freedom" than Giddings exists, but regrets he cannot attend the testimonial. 29 October 1852. p.173, c3.

2426 LUCIUS V. BIERCE *to* **GENTLEMEN. 13 September 1852. Akron.** Regrets that business will not allow him time to attend the Giddings testimonial. 29 October 1852. p.173, c3.

2427 C. M. CLAY *to* **J. F. MORSE AND OTHERS. 11 September 1852. White Hall Post Office, Ky.** Praises Giddings as the true supporter of principles of 1776; regrets that he cannot attend his testimonial. 29 October 1852. p.173, c4.

2428 JOHN W. HOWE *to* **J. F. MORSE AND OTHERS. 14 September 1852. Franklin, Pa.** Eulogizes Giddings as a "Son of Thunder" and a "well-tried friend of Human Freedom"; regrets that he cannot attend his testimonial. 29 October 1852. p.173, c4.

2429 JOSEPH CABLE *to* **J. F. MORSE AND OTHERS. 4 September 1852. Carrollton, Oh.** Describes Giddings as "pre-eminently great"; regrets he cannot attend his testimonial. 29 October 1852. p.173, c4.

2430 DANIEL RICKETSON *to* **NEW BEDFORD COLORED CITIZENS. n.d. n.p.** Refutes Horace Mann's theory of the inferiority of the African race. 29 October 1852. p.174, c1.

2431 J. McBRIDE *to* **EDITOR OF THE** *TRUE WESLEYAN.* **4 October 1852. n.p.** Relates the story of a fugitive slave's escape on the railroad. 29 October 1852. p.174, c2.

2432 J. E. SNODGRASS *to* **FRIENDS. n.d. n.p.** Addresses Quakers and asks them to vote for Hale and Julian, the Free Democratic candidates for president and vice-president. 29 October 1852. p.174, c5.

2433 H. C. WRIGHT *to* **GARRISON. 9 October 1852. New Garden, Oh.** Reports on Horace Greeley's speech in Ohio. 29 October 1852. p.174, c6.

2434 P. W. DAVIS *to* **MRS. C. H. DALL. 16 October 1852. Providence.** Responds to Mrs. Dall's interest in the women's rights convention. 29 October 1852. p.175, c1.

2435 DANIEL FOSTER *to* **FRIEND GARRISON. 1 November 1852. Cambridge.** Reports on anti-slavery meetings at Feltonville, Acton, Bolton, Concord, Danvers, and Marlboro. 5 November 1852. p.179, c5.

2436 ISABELLA SCOTT *to* **WM. LLOYD GARRISON. 1 October 1852. Edinburgh.** States her opinions on the biblical argument between Joseph Barker and Elizabeth Wilson. 5 November 1852. p.180, c2.

2437 L. KOSSUTH *to* **THE CONGRESS OF THE AMERICAN** *REZOLUTIONS-BUND* **FOR EUROPE. [from the** *New York Tribune***] 31 August 1852. London.** Discloses that the Hungarians are prepared to rise en masse against oppression. 5 November 1852. p.180, c3.

2438 PARKER PILLSBURY *to* **FRIEND GARRISON. 21 October 1852. Adrian, Mi.** Reports on the Michigan state anti-slavery convention; encloses preamble and resolutions. 12 November 1852. p.821[182], c6.

2439 THOS. GARRETT *to* **FRIEND. 4 November 1852. Wilmington, De.** Gives an account of Sallie Holley's lecture; relates the principal facts surrounding the prosecution of John Hunn and himself by Judge Taney for helping slaves to escape. 12 November 1852. p.183, c2.

2440 MARY E. BIBB *to* **MR. GARRISON. 27 October 1852. Windsor, Canada.** Opposes a resolution passed at the Windsor meeting on "discrimination in favor of begging for gospel purposes." 12 November 1852. p.183, c3.

2441 H. O. S. *to* **HENRY C. WRIGHT. 25 October 1852. Framingham, Ma.** Claims that Wright looks at disease and death from an exclusively idealistic point of view. 12 November 1852. p.184, c2.

2442 GERRIT SMITH *to* **THE VOTERS OF THE COUNTIES OF OSWEGO AND MADISON. 2 November 1852. Peterboro'.** Explains his political creed. 19 November 1852. p.186, c1.

2443 C. STEARNS *to* **MR. EDITOR [W. L. GARRISON]. 1 November 1852. Boston.** Argues that Daniel Webster lacked skill, devotion, and true greatness. 19 November 1852. p.187, c2.

2444 JOHN S. BROWN *to* **MR. EDITOR [W. L. GARRISON]. 8 November 1852. Fitzwilliam, N.H.** Praises lectures of Daniel Foster. 19 November 1852. p.187, c3.

2445 JAMES BALLANTINE *to* **THE EDITOR OF THE** *SCOTTISH PRESS.* **n.d. n.p.** Discusses fund-raising in behalf of fugitive slaves. 26 November 1852. p.189, c3.

2446 WILLIAM G. ALLEN *to* **FREDERICK DOUGLASS, ESQ.** [from *Frederick Douglass' Paper*] **25 October 1852. McGrawville.** Defends Horace Mann's letter to the black convention in Cincinnati. 26 November 1852. p.190, c1.

2447 HENRY C. WRIGHT *to* **GARRISON. 14 November 1852. New Garden, Oh.** Addresses the question of whether the Bible sanctions slavery. 26 November 1852. p.191, c1.

2448 D. S. G. *to* **GARRISON. 17 November 1852. Portland.** Expresses disapproval of the commemoration of Daniel Webster. 26 November 1852. p.191, c2.

2449 JOSEPH BARKER *to* **GARRISON. n.d. n.p.** Relates a religious dialogue between E. Wilson and himself. 26 November 1852. p.192, c2.

2450 DANIEL FOSTER *to* **FRIEND GARRISON. 22 November 1852. Cambridge.** Reports on his lecture tour through New Hampshire. 3 December 1852. p.195, c1.

2451 G. B. STEBBINS *to* **WM. LLOYD GARRISON. 15 November 1852. Hazlebank, Mi.** Pays tribute to Elizabeth M. Chandler. 3 December 1852. p.195, c2.

2452 SARAH D. FISH *to* **CHARLES SPEAR. 18 November 1852. Rochester.** Comments on Daniel Webster's misuse of influence and intellect. 3 December 1852. p.195, c3.

2453 CHARLES SUMNER *to* **GENTLEMEN.** [from the *Nantucket Mirror*] **5 November 1852. Boston.** Gives reasons for not travelling to Nantucket to speak. 3 December 1852. p.195, c4.

2454 M. *to* **n.n.** [from the *New York Evening Post*] **1 December 1852. Boston.** Describes the funeral of Daniel Webster. 10 December 1852. p.198, c1.

2455 VIGILANCE *to* **MR. EDITOR.** [from the *Portland Transcript*] **n.d. n.p.** Remarks on the decision of Judge Paine in the New York slave case. 10 December 1852. p.198, c3.

2456 WM. C. NELL *to* **FRIEND GARRISON. December 1852. Boston.** Gives account of public meetings held by colored Free-Soilers; discusses the position of colored citizens of Boston. 10 December 1852. p.199, c1.

2457 OFFICERS OF THE WINSOR MEETING *to* **THE EDITOR OF THE** *LIBERATOR* **[W. L. GARRISON]. 23 November 1852. Winsor, Canada West.** Challenge Garrison's impression that the Windsor meeting did not reflect the feelings of the majority of fugitive slaves. 10 December 1852. p.199, c3.

2458 DANIEL FOSTER *to* **FRIEND GARRISON. 2 December 1852. Cambridge.** Reports on his anti-slavery work in Marlboro'. 10 December 1852. p.199, c4.

2459 R. H. *to* **MESSRS. EDITORS.** [from the *Commonwealth*] **n.d. n.p.** Reviews Lysander Spooner's book, *Essay on the Trial by Jury*. 17 December 1852. p.201, c2.

2460 WILLIAM CRAFT *to* **MR. MAY. 10 November 1852. Ockham School.** Informs that his wife gave birth; states he cannot mourn the death of Daniel Webster; reports that *Uncle Tom's Cabin* and *The White Slave* are arousing the English against American slavery. 17 December 1852. p.203, c1.

2461 ELLEN CRAFT *to* **SIR. 10 November 1852. Ockham School, near Surrey.** Denies rumor that she is returning to bondage. 17 December 1852. p.203, c1.

2462 G. W. BUNGAY *to* **EDITOR [W. L. GARRISON]. n.d. n.p.** Gives brief biographical sketch of John C. Cluen, a temperance lecturer. 17 December 1852. p.203, c1.

2463 P. G. *to* **BROTHER GARRISON. 7 December 1852. Stoneham.** Discusses Milton P. Braman and his views on women. 17 December 1852. p.203, c2.

2464 D. C. O'DANIELS *to* **MR. EDITOR [W. L. GARRISON]. 5 December 1852. Meadville.** Gives a sketch of Meadville. 17 December 1852. p.203, c3.

2465 DANIEL FOSTER *to* **FRIEND GARRISON. 12 December 1852. Cambridge.** Reports on anti-slavery meetings. 17 December 1852. p.203, c3.

2466 ONE *to* **MR. EDITOR [W. L. GARRISON]. 12 December 1852. Salem.** Praises a lecture by Wm. C. Nell. 17 December 1852. p.203, c4.

2467 DANIEL FOSTER *to* **A. H. WOOD. 10 October 1852. Hubbardston.** Reports that Cutler denied having made slanderous remarks about him. 17 December 1852. p.204, c2.

2468 J. H. CRANE *to* **FRIEND WOOD. 10 October 1852. Worcester.** Reports that Cutler considers Foster's views "dangerous to the community." 17 December 1852. p.204, c2.

2469 A. H. WOOD *to* **BROTHER GARRISON. 24 October 1852. n.p.** Forwards evidence to support his claim that Cutler is guilty of dissimulation. 17 December 1852. p.204, c2.

2470 H. C. WRIGHT *to* **GARRISON. 28 November 1852. Salem.** Reports on a Bible convention in Ohio; forwards resolutions. 17 December 1852. p.204, c3.

2471 MARENDA B. RANDALL *to* **MR. GARRISON. 6 December 1852. Woodstock, Vt.** Forwards what she claims is a "spirit communication" to W. L. Garrison from N. P. Rogers. 17 December 1852. p.204, c4.

2472 N. P. ROGERS *to* **WILLIAM LLOYD GARRISON. n.d. Second Sphere.** Through a medium, the spirit of the late N. P. Rodgers declares that he no longer supports immediate emancipation, and bemoans the use of force. 17 December 1852. p.204, c4.

2473 W. L. JUDD *to* **MESSRS. EDITORS. [from the** *Boston Traveller***] 28 October 1852. Boston.** Relates his experience as a missionary of the American Free Mission Society in Haiti. 24 December 1852. p.205, c4.

2474 PARKER PILLSBURY *to* **MARIUS. [from the** *Ohio Anti-Slavery Bugle***] 16 November 1852. Boston.** Gives an account of the stage production of *Uncle Tom's Cabin*. 24 December 1852. p.205, c5.

2475 DANIEL FOSTER *to* **FRIEND GARRISON. 27 December 1852. Cambridge.** Reports on anti-slavery lectures in Millbury and Grafton. 24 December 1852. p.207, c1.

2476 C. C. FOOTE *to* **MR. GARRISON. 14 December 1852. Philadelphia.** Examines an article in the *Liberator* on sending aid for fugitive slaves to Canada. 24 December 1852. p.207, c2.

2477 EQUITY *to* **THE EDITORS OF THE** *JOURNAL OF COMMERCE***. 19 November 1852. New York.** Encloses thirty dollars for the Lemmon Indemnity Fund. 31 December 1852. p.210. c1.

2478 STEWART, GREER & CO. *to* **MESSRS. HALLOCK, BUTLER, AND HALE. 20 November 1852. New York.** Encloses fifty dollars for the Lemmon Indemnity Fund. 31 December 1852. p.210, c1.

2479 H. LE ROY NEWBOLD *to* **MESSRS. HENRYS, SMITH, AND TOWNSEND. 20 November 1852. Westchester.** Enclose twenty-five dollars for the Lemmon Indemnity Fund. 31 December 1852. p.210, c1.

2480 ULYSSES McALLISTER *to* **JOHN P. JEWETT AND CO. 22 November 1852. Aberdeen, Mi.** Advertises that he will pay seventy-five dollars for a runaway mulatto woman. 31 December 1852. p.210, c6.

2481 LEWIS FORD *to* **FRIEND GARRISON. 5 December 1852. Abington.** Reports on Rev. Trask's anti-tobacco lectures. 31 December 1852. p.211, c2.

[1853]

2482 GOV. JOSEPH JOHNSON *to* **THE GENERAL ASSEMBLY OF VIRGINIA. 17 December 1852. n.p.** Submits record of trial concerning the slaves of Jonathan Lemmon, who were discharged by Justice Paine of New York. 7 January 1853. p.1, c1.

2483 HENRY D. LAPAUGH *to* **GOV. JOSEPH JOHNSON. 4 December 1852. Johnson, N.Y.** Forwards record of trial concerning Lemmon's slaves. 7 January 1853. p.1, c1.

2484 n.n. *to* **CHARLES SUMNER. [from the** *Banner of the Cross***]** 1852. **Livingston, Al.** A pro-slavery minister opposes the repeal of the Fugitive Slave Law. 7 January 1853. p.1, c2.

2485 GENERAL FRANK PIERCE *to* **COL. LALLY. [extract] 27 May 1852. Boston.** Urges the Baltimore convention to maintain the compromise measure. 7 January 1853. p.1, c3.

2486 JOHN JOLLIFFE *to* **ROBERT F. WALLCUT. 10 October 1852. Cincinnati, Oh.** Cancels subscription to the *Liberator.* 7 January 1853. p.2, c4.

2487 R. E. DUNGAN *to* **WM. LLOYD GARRISON. 13 December 1852. Colerain.** Renews subscription to the *Liberator.* 7 January 1853. p.2, c4.

2488 H. W. BEECHER *to* **W. L. GARRISON. 20 October 1852. Brooklyn.** Requests subscription to the *Liberator.* 7 January 1853. p.2, c4.

2489 DANIEL FOSTER *to* **FRIEND GARRISON. 20 December 1852. Cambridge.** Describes his Lyceum anti-slavery lectures. 7 January 1853. p.3, c1.

2490 J. S. BROWN *to* **A. A. BENT. 17 December 1852. Fitzwilliam.** Regrets that he is unable to attend the anti-slavery convention. 7 January 1853. p.3, c3.

2491 GERRIT SMITH *to* **WM. LLOYD GARRISON. 1 January 1853. Peterboro'.** Pays for his subscription. 7 January 1853. p.3, c4.

2492 HENRY C. WRIGHT *to* **GARRISON. 21 December 1852. Millwood, Oh.** Describes his religious discussions with the Barker family and his experiences with spiritualism. 7 January 1853. p.4, c3.

2493 ELIZUR WRIGHT *to* **MESSRS. EDITORS. [from the** *Commonwealth***] 28 December 1852. Boston.** Announces the birth of twin sons; ridicules the Fugitive Slave Law. 7 January 1853. p.4, c5.

2494 THE EARL OF SHAFTESBURY *to* **JOSEPH STURGE AND G. W. ALEX-ANDER. n.d. n.p.** Approves their address urging immediate abolition; admits his own preference for gradual abolition over a period of three years. 14 January 1853. p.5, c6.

2495 DANIEL FOSTER *to* **FRIEND GARRISON. 12 January 1853. Cambridge.** Contrasts pro-slavery Providence and anti-slavery Coventry. 14 January 1853. p.6, c6.

2496 WM. FARMER *to* **n.n. 8 December 1852. London.** Describes the equal status and education of colored refugees in England. 14 January 1853. p.7, c1.

2497 PARKER PILLSBURY *to* **MR. EDITOR. [from the** *New Hampshire Independent Democrat***] 11 January 1853. Concord.** Announces that he and Stephen S. Foster will promote the anti-slavery cause in New Hampshire for several weeks. 14 January 1853. p.7, c5.

2498 P. G. *to* **R. F. WALLCUT. 9 January 1853. Springfield.** Requests subscription to the *Liberator.* 21 January 1853. p.10, c6.

2499 PARKER PILLSBURY *to* **FRIEND GARRISON. 17 January 1853. Concord, N.H.** Describes his and Stephen S. Foster's anti-slavery activities in New Hampshire. 21 January 1853. p.10, c6.

2500 DANIEL FOSTER *to* **FRIEND GARRISON. [continued from 14 January 1853] 12 January 1853. Cambridge.** Describes his successful lecture tour in Mystic valley; informs Garrison that he has procured four new subscribers to the *Liberator.* 21 January 1853. p.11, c1.

2501 H. O. S. *to* **W. L. GARRRISON. 9 January 1853. Framingham.** Criticizes the Ameican Board of Foreign Missions for ignoring American slavery. 21 January 1853. p.11, c2.

2502 HENRY C. WRIGHT *to* **GARRISON. 25 December 1852. Millwood, Oh.** On Christmas Day, he reflects on the hypocrisy of Christians who support or even tolerate slavery. 21 January 1853. p.11, c3.

2503 I. FISKE *to* **FRIEND GARRISON. 13 January 1853. Fall River.** Praises Sallie Holley's anti-slavery lecture in Fall River. 21 January 1853. p.11, c4.

2504 S. K. LOTHROP, ELLIS GRAY LORING, EPHRAIM PEABODY, WILLIAM I. BOWDITCH, J. INGERSOLL BOWDITCH, JOHN P. ROBINSON, AND THOS. STARR KING *to* **n.n. 3 January 1853. Boston.** Enclose certification that Peter Still is a free man and solicit money to buy his family's freedom. 21 January 1853. p.11, c5.

2505 GEORGE SUNTER, JR. *to* **FRIEND. 6 December 1852. Derby, England.** Argues that the spirit, not the letter, of the law must guide Americans toward abolishing slavery. 21 January 1853. p.12, c2.

2506 E. A. L. *to* **FRIEND. 4 January 1853. Marlboro'.** Requests that the enclosed letter by Joseph Barker be printed. 21 January 1853. p.12, c3.

2507 JOSPEH BARKER *to* **FRIEND. 16 December 1852. Millwood, Oh.** Describes communications with spirits via a young medium. 21 January 1853. p.12, c3.

2508 n.n. *to* **n.n. [extract] n.d. n.p.** Praises Lucy Stone's anti-slavery speech at West Chester, Pennsylvania. 28 January 1853. p.14, c2.

2509 n.n. *to* **CHILD. 30 October 1852. Edinburgh.** Informs her of the death of a little girl. 28 January 1853. p.15, c2.

2510 N. TOURGUENEFF *to* **MADAME. 30 October 1852. Paris.** Expresses horror upon reading defenses of slavery; compares Russian serfdom with American slavery. 28 January 1853. p.15, c5.

2511 W. DIXON *to* **FRIEND GARRISON. 16 December 1852. Upland.** Defends Quaker dress. 28 January 1853. p.16, c2.

2512 HIRAM WILSON *to* **BROTHER BIBB. 1 January 1853. St. Catharines, Canada.** Rejoices at the successful escape of fugitives into Canada. 4 February 1853. p.17, c6.

2513 SAMUEL JOHNSON *to* **REV. S. MAY, JR. 22 January 1853. Brooklyn, N.Y.** Reports that he is unable to attend the anti-slavery convention; believes that private inspiration is the strength of the abolition movement. 4 February 1853. p.18, c3.

2514 SHERMAN GRISWOLD *to* **THE MASSACHUSETTS AS, CONVENED IN ITS ANNUAL MEETING. 24 January 1853. Germanville.** Sends support in absentia. 4 February 1853. p.19, c4.

2515 LORING MOODY *to* **FRIEND GARRISON. 18 January 1853. Cincinnati.** Describes the escape of fugitives across the Ohio River. 4 February 1853. p.19, c5.

2516 DANIEL FOSTER *to* **FRIEND GARRISON. 24 January 1853. Woodstock.** Lists anti-slavery activities in New London and Windham counties. 4 February 1853. p.20, c2.

2517 LIBERTY *to* **SALLIE HOLLEY. n.d. n.p.** Asks five questions about the anti-slavery movement. 4 February 1853. p.20, c3.

2518 S. W. W. *to* **FRIEND GARRISON. 24 January 1853. Providence.** Praises Sallie Holley. 4 February 1853. p.20, c3.

2519 ELIZABETH B. CHASE *to* **GARRISON. 25 January 1853. Valley Falls, R.I.** Praises Sallie Holley. 4 February 1853. p.20, c3.

2520 LORING MOODY *to* **FRIEND GARRISON. 15 January 1853. Cincinnati, Oh.** Reports on the state temperance convention. 4 February 1853. p.20, c4.

2521 REV. SAMUEL WOLCOTT *to* **MR. GARRISON. 5 February 1853. Belchertown.** Submits notes on his speech published in the *Liberator*. 11 February 1853. p.22, c6.

2522 SALLIE HOLLEY *to* **A FRIEND. [extract] 6 February 1853. Brookfield.** Explains why she lectures with Garrisonian abolitionists. 11 February 1853. p.22, c6.

2523 L. S. R. *to* **BROTHER GARRRISON. 24 January 1853. Easthampton.** Describes Edward Everett's speech on the thirty-sixth anniversary of the ACS. 11 February 1853. p.23, c1.

2524 SAXON *to* **FRIEND GARRISON. 4 February 1853. Taunton.** Urges abolitionists to insist that they be allowed to speak in public. 11 February 1853. p.23, c2.

2525 D. M. *to* **FRIEND GARRISON. 26 January 1853. Pawtucket.** Praises Sallie Holley's anti-slavery lectures at Pawtucket. 11 February 1853. p.23, c2.

2526 A SUBSCRIBER *to* **MR. GARRISON. 7 February 1853. Boston.** Requests the publication of Burleigh's speech. 11 February 1853. p.23, c3.

2527 J. PRINCE *to* **FRIEND GARRISON. n.d. n.p.** Lauds Parker Pillsbury's lecture on the French Revolution. 18 February 1853. p.27, c4.

2528 A DANVERS MAN *to* **EDITOR. [from the** *Essex County Freeman***] 27 January 1853. Danvers.** Praises Parker Pillsbury's lecture on the French Revolution. 18 February 1853. p.27, c4.

2529 PARKER PILLSBURY *to* **FRIEND GARRISON. 15 February 1853. New Market, N.H.** Reports on Pillsbury and Foster's anti-slavery efforts in New Hampshire. 18 February 1853. p.27, c4.

2530 SAXON *to* **FRIEND GARRISON. 8 February 1853. Cambridge.** Discusses anti-slavery activities in Attleboro'. 18 February 1853. p.27, c4.

2531 T. W. HIGGINSON *to* **SIR. 9 February 1853. Brattleboro', Vt.** Praises Lucy Stone's anti-slavery lecture in Brattleboro'. 18 February 1853. p.27, c5.

2532 GEORGE TRASK *to* **FATHERS AND BRETHREN. 5 February 1853. Fitchburg.** Alerts the clergy to the dangers of tobacco. 18 February 1853. p.28, c2.

2533 F. W. CHESSON *to* **THE EDITOR OF THE** *MORNING ADVERTISER***. n.d. n.p.** Defends the AAS and William Lloyd Garrison. 25 February 1853. p.30, c4.

2534 SAXON *to* **FRIEND GARRISON. 21 February 1853. Cambridge.** Reports on his anti-slavery efforts in Wrentham, Foxboro', Canton, Stoughton, Norton, and Warwick. 25 February 1853. p.31, c2.

2535 G. F. CLARK *to* **FRIEND GARRISON. 12 February 1853. Norton, Ma.** Disputes Parker Pillsbury's opinion of Charles Sumner's speech to the Senate. 25 February 1853. p.31, c3.

2536 DOW JOHNSON *to* **ELLIS GRAY LORING. 10 February 1853. Boston.** Describes the process of purchasing his wife from a slaveholder. 25 February 1853. p.31, c4.

2537 A. R. *to* **MR. EDITOR. n.d. n.p.** Reports that Mrs. Johnson, a freed slave, is searching for her father, George Frost. 25 February 1853. p.31, c5.

2538 PARKER PILLSBURY *to* **FRIEND GARRISON. 21 February 1853. Dover, N.H.** Reports on anti-slavery meetings in New Hampshire. 25 February 1853. p.31, c5.

2539 S. MITCHELL *to* **FRIEND GARRISON. 20 February 1853. Boston.** Requests that Pillsbury deliver his lecture on the French Revolution in Boston. 25 February 1853. p.31, c5.

2540 H. B. STOWE *to* **DR. WARDLAW. 4 December 1852. n.p.** Expresses gratitude for Scotland's praise of her book. 4 March 1853. p.33, c5.

2541 n.n. *to* **MR. EDITOR. [from the** *Independent Democrat***] 8 February 1853. Washington.** Describes a slave auction. 4 March 1853. p.34, c1.

2542 HORACE MANN *to* **WM. L. GARRISON, ESQ. 21 February 1853. Washington.** Accuses Wendell Phillips of slandering him in a speech published in the *Liberator*. 4 March 1853. p.34, c3.

2543 WENDELL PHILLIPS *to* **n.n. 1 March 1853. Boston.** Answers accusations by Horace Mann. 4 March 1853. p.34, c4.

2544 SAXON *to* **FRIEND GARRISON. 25 February 1853. Cambridge.** Reports on anti-slavery activities in Acton. 4 March 1853. p.35, c1.

2545 G. B. STEBBINS *to* **WM. LLOYD GARRISON. 12 February 1853. Rochester, N.Y.** Reports that Methodist ministers at the East Genesee District Ministers' Conference failed to defend the exclusion of slaveholders from church fellowship. 4 March 1853. p.35, c1.

2546 MRS. C. I. H. NICHOLS *to* **MR. GARRISON. 27 February 1853. Brattleboro', Vt.** Assures Garrison that the women's rights movement has supporters in Brattleboro'. 4 March 1853. p.35, c2.

2547 GEO. W. STACY *to* **FRIEND GARRISON. 25 February 1853. Milford.** Praises anti-slavery lecture by Miss Sallie Holley in Milford. 4 March 1853. p.35, c3.

2548 TIOT *to* **MESSRS. EDITORS. [from the** *Commonwealth***] 21 February 1853. n.p.** Describes Edmund Quincy's lecture at Dedham. 4 March 1853. p.35, c4.

2549 MARY A. SHADD *to* **MR. GARRISON. 12 January 1853. Windsor, Canada West.** Reports that colored fugitives oppose the Refugees' Home Society. 4 March 1853. p.36, c2.

2550 J. THEODORE HOLLY *to* **MR. EDITOR [W. L. GARRISON]. 15 January 1853. Windsor, Canada West.** Defends the Refugees' Home Society. 4 March 1853. p.36, c3.

2551 n.n. *to* **MR. EDITOR. [from the** *Hampshire* **(Northampton)** *Gazette***] n.d. n.p.** Describes a local choir concert and Wendell Phillips' address. 4 March 1853. p.36, c5.

2552 DORVELAS DORVAL *to* **FRIENDS OF TRUTH IN AMERICA. 10 December 1852. Gonaives, Hayti.** Recommends *The History of Hayti* by Thomas Madiou, Jr. 11 March 1853. p.37, c6.

2553 R. *to* **FRIEND GARRISON. 28 February 1853. New Bedford.** Reports on lectures by Lucy Stone in New Bedford. 11 March 1853. p.37, c6.

2554 ENQUIRER *to* **MR. GARRISON. n.d. n.p.** Defends Horace Mann's stance on slavery; advocates amending the Constitution. 11 March 1853. p.38, c3.

2555 W. *to* **SIR. 7 March 1853. Fairhaven.** A Free-Soiler regrets that Horace Mann and Wendell Phillips publicly disagree with each other. 11 March 1853. p.38, c4.

2556 D. C. SIMONDS *to* **MR. GARRISON. 1 March 1853. LeRoy.** Criticizes the eulogy of Antoinette Brown in the *Whig*. 11 March 1853. p.38, c4.

2557 WENDELL PHILLIPS *to* **n.n. 4 March 1853. Boston.** Defends his statement that Dr. Beecher has failed publicly to support the anti-slavery cause; encloses extracts from a letter by his daughter, Mrs. Stowe. 11 March 1853. p.39, c1.

2558 MRS. STOWE *to* **WENDELL PHILLIPS. [extract] n.d. n.p.** Asserts that her father, Mr. Beecher, conducted himself properly with regard to the slavery issue at Lane Seminary. 11 March 1853. p.39, c1.

2559 WILLIAM C. NELL *to* **n.n. February 1853. Boston.** Describes anti-slavery activities; lists the officers of the Garrison Association. 11 March 1853. p.39, c2.

2560 PARKER PILLSBURY *to* **FRIEND GARRISON. 28 February 1853. Portsmouth, N.H.** Reports on disturbances at anti-slavery meetings in Portsmouth. 11 March 1853. p.39, c2.

2561 SAXON *to* **FRIEND GARRISON. 5 March 1853. Cambridge.** Describes a week of anti-slavery meetings. 11 March 1853. p.39, c3.

2562 N. GILMAN *to* **BROTHER WILLIAMS. 3 March 1853. Boston.** Explains the medical uses of alcohol. 11 March 1853. p.40, c2.

2563 HORACE MANN *to* **WM. L. GARRISON, ESQ. 14 March 1853. West Newton.** Replies to "further injurious strictures" by Wendell Phillips. 18 March 1853. p.42, c4.

2564 WM. P. MERRILL *to* **n.n. 7 March 1853. Amesbury, Ma.** Accuses J. J. Locke of misrepresenting Merrill's behavior and his attitude toward slavery. 18 March 1853. p.43, c3.

2565 J. J. LOCKE *to* **THE EDITOR OF THE** *LIBERATOR* **[W. L. GARRISON]. n.d. n.p.** Objects to Rev. Wm. P. Merrill's letter; sustains his previous complaints against Merrill's recent behavior. 18 March 1853. p.43, c3.

2566 ELIZABETH WILSON *to* **MR. GARRISON. 24 January 1853. Cadiz, Oh.** Defends biblical authority, in contradiction to an argument presented by Joseph Barker. 18 March 1853. p.44, c2.

2567 EDWARD MATHEWS *to* **n.n. [from the** *American Baptist***] 7 January 1853. Bristol, England.** Reports high expectations for Mr. L. A. Chamerovzow's performance as new secretary of the New Broad Street administration. 25 March 1853. p.45, c3.

2568 A YOUNG NEW YORKER *to* **THE** *NEW YORK TRIBUNE***. 3 March 1853. Richmond, Va.** Describes a slave auction in Virginia. 25 March 1853. p.45, c5.

2569 WENDELL PHILLIPS *to* **WM. L. GARRISON. 21 March 1853. Boston.** Replies to Horace Mann, defending his criticisms of Mann. 25 March 1853. p.46, c1.

2570 SAMUEL MAY, JR. *to* **MR. GARRISON. 12 March 1853. Leicester.** Reports on Mr. Foss' lecture in Leicester. 25 March 1853. p.47, c1.

2571 SAXON *to* **FRIEND GARRISON. n.d. n.p.** Describes his lecturing tour in Rhode Island. 25 March 1853. p.47, c2.

2572 W. P. A. *to* **MR. GARRISON. n.d. n.p.** Responds to questions asked by Wendell Phillips of Horace Mann. 25 March 1853. p.47, c3.

2573 ELIZABETH WILSON *to* **MR. GARRISON. [continued from 18 March 1853] n.d. n.p.** Defends biblical authority, in contradiction to an argument by Joseph Barker. 25 March 1853. p.48, c2.

2574 EDWARD SEARCH *to* **W. L. GARRISON. February 1853. London.** Supports Joseph Barker's position on the Scriptures. 25 March 1853. p.48, c5.

2575 n.n. *to* **THE** *NEW YORK EVENING POST***. [extract] n.d. Missouri.** Charges that Illinois became a slave state when the new slave law was passed. 1 April 1853. p.49, c4.

2576 REV. T. W. HIGGINSON *to* **MESSRS. EDITORS. [from the** *Commonwealth***] n.d. n.p.** Gently criticizes Mr. Robinson for his stand on the Phillips-Mann controversy. 1 April 1853. p.50, c3.

2577 ENQUIRER *to* **MR. GARRISON. n.d. n.p.** Defends Horace Mann's allegiance to the Constitution. 1 April 1853. p.50, c4.

2578 IRA HOAR *to* **FRIEND GARRISON. 25 March 1853. Wachusett Village.** Corrects the *Liberator*'s quotations from a book on the Bible written by his son, a professed medium. 1 April 1853. p.50, c4.

2579 C. C. GOSS *to* **MR. EDITOR [W. L. GARRISON]. 15 March 1853. Clifton Springs.** Corrects G. B. Stebbin's account of the East Genesee Conference. 1 April 1853. p.50, c5.

2580 E. HARWOOD *to* **DR. SPENCER H. CONE. 15 February 1853. Cincinnati.** Asks whether the *Liberator*'s account of a Baptist society meeting is correct. 1 April 1853. p.50, c5.

2581 E. HARWOOD *to* **FRIEND GARRISON. 7 March 1853. Cincinnati.** Encloses a letter from Dr. Spencer H. Cone's secretary. 1 April 1853. p.50, c5.

2582 WM. H. WYCKOFF *to* **E. HARWOOD. 26 February 1853. New York.** Claims that the American and Foreign Bible Society never voted on the question of distributing Bibles to all American families. 1 April 1853. p.50, c5.

2583 O. P. DRURY *to* **GARRISON. 18 March 1853. Dowagiac, Mi.** Renews his subscription. 1 April 1853. p.50, c5.

2584 S. M., JR. *to* **MR. GARRISON. n.d. n.p.** Reports on the success of Lewis Hayden's clothing store. 1 April 1853. p.50, c6.

2585 ENGLISH FRIEND *to* **n.n. n.d. England.** Relays the news of Ellen Craft's first freeborn child; suspects that Rev. Edmund Kelly of New Bedford, Massachusetts, is a fraud. 1 April 1853. p.50, c6.

2586 ELIHU BURRIT *to* **MR. EDITOR [W. L. GARRISON]. 18 November 1853. London.** Advocates adoption of the ocean penny postage reform. 1 April 1853. p.50, c6.

2587 n.n. *to* **n.n. 4 March 1853. West Brookfield.** Reports that Sallie Holley's lecture in West Brookfield received little publicity or cooperation from church officials. 1 April 1853. p.51, c1.

2588 F. H. D. *to* **MR. GARRISON. 22 March 1853. Leominster.** Praises Sallie Holley's work at Leominster. 1 April 1853. p.51, c2.

2589 GEO. TRASK *to* **MOSES GRANT, ESQ. 11 March 1853. Fitchburg.** Promotes the anti-tobacco movement. 1 April 1853. p.51, c3.

2590 J. J. WHEELER *to* **MR. EDITOR [W. L. GARRISON]. 7 February 1853. Winfield, N.Y.** Encloses the first editon of the *Journal of Man*. 1 April 1853. p.51, c3.

2591 HENRY C. WRIGHT *to* **GARRISON. 23 January 1853. New Garden, Oh.** Lauds Garrison for providing a forum for open discussion of the Bible question. 1 April 1853. p52, c2.

2592 HENRY C. HOWELLS *to* **FRIEND GARRISON. 3 March 1853. Rose Dale, Pa.** Praises the free discussion of moral questions in the *Liberator*. 1 April 1853. p.52, c3.

2593 MATTHEW FARRINGTON *to* **MR. GARRISON. 14 February 1853. Nautrille, Ia.** Advocates continued free discussion of the Bible question. 1 April 1853. p.52, c4.

2594 J.R. GIDDINGS *to* **THE PEOPLE OF CUYOHOGA, LAKE, AND GEAUGA COUNTIES. [from the** *Anti-Slavery Bugle*] **8 March 1853. Jefferson, Oh.** Informs the citizens that he no longer represents them in Congress; encourages anti-slavery efforts. 8 April 1853. p.53, c1.

2595 N. R. JOHNSTON *to* **WILLIAM STILL. [extract from the** *Pennsylvania Freeman*] **n.d. Topsham, Vt.** Expresses sympathy for Peter Still and for fugitive slaves; abhors *"political* anti-slavery." 8 April 1853. p.53, c5.

2596 HORACE MANN *to* **W. L. GARRISON. 14 April 1853. West Newton.** Replies to Wendell Phillips, defending his position on slavery and the Constitution. 8 April 1853. p.54, c3.

2597 C. STEARNS *to* **MR. GARRISON. 23 February 1853. Boston.** Questions whether spiritual manifestations originate from spirits. 8 April 1853. p.56, c2.

2598 MICAJAH T. JOHNSON *to* **FRIEND GARRISON. 1 January 1853. Short Creek, Oh.** Opposes the Maine liquor laws. 8 April 1853. p.56, c3.

2599 JOHN W. FOSTER *to* **WM. L. GARRISON. 12 February 1853. Hopkinton, R.I.** Criticizes Garrison's anti-religious stance; cancels his subscription. 8 April 1853. p.56, c3.

2600 J. T. EVERETT *to* **n.n. n.d. n.p.** Praises the *Liberator* for encouraging free discussion; defends the authority of the Bible against arguments by Joseph Barker and Henry C. Wright. 8 April 1853. p.56, c4.

2601 PACIFICA *to* **THE FRIENDS OF FREE DISCUSSION. February 1853. Ireland.** Praises the *Liberator*'s policy of free discussion. 8 April 1853. p.56, c4.

2602 A SCOTCHMAN *to* **MR. GARRISON. 14 March 1852. Edinburgh, Scotland.** Praises the *Liberator*, especially for its courage in maintaining free discussion. 8 April 1852. p.56, c5.

2603 S. W. SEAVER *to* **FRIEND GARRISON. 1 February 1853. Williamstown.** Encloses money for a new subscription to replace a coward's cancelled one. 8 April 1853. p.56, c5.

2604 WENDELL PHILLIPS *to* **W. L. GARRISON. 17 April 1853. Boston.** Continues his argument criticizing Mann's position on slavery and the Constitution. 15 April 1853. p.58, c3.

2605 HORACE MANN *to* **WM. L. GARRISON. 18 April 1853. West Newton.** Identifies misprints in the *Liberator*. 15 April 1853. p.59, c3.

2606 LUCY STONE *to* **GARRISON. 12 April 1853. Boston.** Denies that she wrote the women's rights circular and petition; attributes them to Wendell Phillips. 15 April 1853. p.59, c3.

2607 J. CUSHING *to* **FRIEND GARRISON. 20 March 1853. South Hingham.** Supports the Refugees' Home Society. 15 April 1852. p.59, c4.

2608 CAROLINE H. W. DALL *to* **WM. GARRISON, ESQ. 27 March 1852. Toronto.** Thanks the ladies of Framingham for their contribution of five dollars to aid fugitives. 15 April 1853. p.59, c4.

2609 C. STEARNS *to* **MR. GARRISON. 23 March 1853. Boston.** Objects to belief in spiritual manifestations. 15 April 1853. p.60, c3.

2610 A LADY IN NEW HAMPSHIRE *to* **FRANKLIN PIERCE. [extract] n.d. New Hampshire.** Argues that the death of Pierce's son should motivate Pierce to abolish the Fugitive Slave Law and to work against slavery in his new political office. 15 April 1853. p.60, c4.

2611 H. F. GARDNER, M.D. *to* **n.n. [from the** *Springfield Republican* **via the** *Salem Observer*] **28 February 1853. Springfield.** Documents a case of spiritual manifestation. 15 April 1853. p.60, c5.

2612 A. T. FOSS *to* **FRIEND GARRISON. 14 April 1853. Blackstone.** Corrects Wm. H. Wykoff's report of an incident at a meeting of the American and Foreign Bible Society. 22 April 1853. p.61, c4.

2613 MRS. C. S. BROWN *to* **BROTHER GARRISON. 7 April 1852. Hubbardston.** Supports Foss' statement about the American and Foreign Bible Society. 22 April 1853. p.61, c5.

2614 A. J. SIMMONS *to* **FRIEND GARRISON. 9 April 1853. Walworth.** Affirms that Methodist Episcopal ministers at the East Genesee Conference invoked the Bible in defense of slavery. 22 April 1853. p.61, c5.

2615 A FEW UNITARIANS *to* **MR. GARRISON. n.d. n.p.** Defend the actions of the Unitarian church during Sallie Holley's stay at Leominster. 22 April 1853. p.62, c1.

2616 J. NOYES, JR. *to* **FRIEND GARRISON. 18 April 1853. Abington.** Describes spiritualism and anti-slavery meetings at Abington; believes the Constitution to be a pro-slavery document. 22 April 1853. p.62, c2.

2617 WM. H. FISH *to* **FRIEND GARRISON. n.d. n.p.** Describes Fast Day at Upton. 22 April 1853. p.62, c2.

2618 SAXON *to* **FRIEND GARRISON. 14 April 1853. Cambridge.** Reports on an anti-slavery convention at Lowell. 22 April 1853. p.63, c1.

2619 L. P. COURTAULD CLEMENS *to* **WM. LLOYD GARRISON. n.d. Nelsonville, Oh.** Praises the *Liberator*. 22 April 1853. p.63, c2.

2620 JONATHAN WALKER *to* **n.n. [extract from the** *Ohio Bugle*] **n.d. Fond du lac, Wi.** Finds little true anti-slavery sentiment in Wisconsin; plans to increase his efforts. 22 April 1853. p.63, c2.

2621 JOSEPH BARKER *to* **FRIEND GARRISON. 31 March 1853. Millwood, Oh.** Replies to Elizabeth Wilson concerning the Bible question. 22 April 1853. p.64, c2.

2622 HENRY C. WRIGHT *to* **JAMES HAUGHTON. 7 April 1853. Springfield.** Describes a "Spiritual Convention" in Springfield. 22 April 1853. p.64, c5.

2623 EDMUND SQUIRE *to* **THE EDITOR OF THE** *LONDON INQUIRER*. **1 February 1853. n.p.** Defends his conduct during Rev. Francis Bishop's anti-slavery speech at a Unitarian convention. 29 April 1853. p.65, c2.

2624 FRANCIS BISHOP *to* **SIR. 9 March 1853. Liverpool.** Responds to Edmund Squire's report on Bishop's speech. 29 April 1853. p.65, c2.

2625 F. W. CHESSON *to* **THE EDITOR OF THE** *BRITISH BANNER*. **n.d. n.p.** Condemns pro-slavery American churches. 29 April 1853. p.65, c6.

2626 C. M. CLAY *to* **THE EDITORS OF THE** *ENQUIRER.* **8 April 1853. Cincinnati, Oh.** Accuses Thomas Corwin of being a "mercenary renegade." 29 April 1853. p.66, c1.

2627 n.n. *to* **n.n. [from the** *Traveller***] n.d. London.** Describes public reaction to the appearance in London of *A Key to Uncle Tom's Cabin* by Harriet Beecher Stowe. 29 April 1853. p.66, c1.

2628 J. GIRDWOOD *to* **THE EDITOR OF THE** *LIBERATOR* **[W. L. GARRISON]. 4 April 1853. New Bedford, Ma.** Defends Rev. Edmund Kelly's good character. 29 April 1853. p.66, c4.

2529 HORACE MANN *to* **W. L. GARRISON. 19 April 1853. West Newton.** Replies to Phillips, defending his views on slavery and the Constitution. 29 April 1853. p.66, c5.

2630 ADELPHOS *to* **MR. EDITOR. 13 April 1853. Cummington.** Praises Rev. E. A. Stockman. 29 April 1853. p.67, c4.

2631 DAVID BROWN *to* **RESPECTED FRIEND. 8 March 1853. Four Mile Creek.** A fugitive slave requests money. 29 April 1853. p.68, c2.

2632 H. C. WRIGHT *to* **GERRIT SMITH. 15 April 1853. Boston.** Discusses the contradiction in Smith's position as both legislator and abolitionist. 29 April 1853. p.68, c2.

2633 PATRICK HENRY *to* **n.n. [extract] 18 January 1773. Hanover.** Regrets that he owns slaves; hopes for the future abolition of slavery. 6 May 1853. p.69, c6.

2634 REV. JOHN G. FEE *to* **CHRISTIAN DONALDSON AND OTHER FRIENDS OF UNIVERSAL LIBERTY. n.d. Glenville, Ky.** Reports that he cannot attend the Cincinnati convention of abolitionists. 6 May 1853. p.70, c3.

2635 ROBERT B. DOBBINS *to* **BRETHREN. 8 April 1853. Ipavia.** Regrets that he is too old and poor to attend the convention. 6 May 1853. p.70, c3.

2636 C. M. CLAY *to* **C. DONALDSON, ETC., COMMITTEE. 25 March 1853. White Hall Post Office, Ky.** Hopes to attend the anti-slavery convention. 6 May 1853. p.70, c3.

2637 WENDELL PHILLIPS *to* **THE EDITOR OF THE** *LIBERATOR* **[W. L. GARRISON]. 29 April 1853. Northampton.** Replies to Horace Mann in defense of his accusations concerning caste schools. 6 May 1853. p.70, c6.

2638 EDMUND JACKSON *to* **MR. GARRISON. 2 May 1853. Boston.** Charges that Horace Mann never publicly opposed caste schools. 6 May 1853. p.71, c3.

2639 JUSTICE *to* **W. L. GARRISON. 3 May 1853. Boston.** Supports Wendell Phillips. 6 May 1853, p.71, c4.

2640 N. *to* **MR. GARRISON. 1 May 1853. Portsmouth.** Praises the labors of Sallie Holley in Portsmouth. 6 May 1853. p.71, c4.

2641 HENRY C. WRIGHT *to* **GARRISON. 16 April 1853. Boston.** Suggests how to treat sinners. 6 May 1853. p.72, c2.

2642 PARKER PILLSBURY *to* **FRIEND GARRISON. 16 March 1853. Concord, N.H.** Regrets that the creeds of theological seminaries retard progressiveness in the Church. 6 May 1853. p.72, c2.

2643 HENRY WARD BEECHER *to* **THE EDITOR OF THE** *NEW YORK TRIBUNE.* **n.d. n.p.** Denounces the controversy over Theodore Parker. 6 May 1853. p.72, c3.

2644 HORACE MANN *to* **W. L. GARRISON. 9 May 1853. West Newton.** Replies to accusations made by Wendell Phillips. 13 May 1853. p.74, c5.

2645 HENRY C. WRIGHT *to* **GARRISON. 7 May 1853. Boston.** Expresses disappointment that W. L. Garrison failed to appear at Adrian, Michigan. 13 May 1853. p.75, c3.

2646 WOODLAND OWEN *to* **HENRY C. WRIGHT. 2 May 1853. Adrian, Mi.** Expresses his sorrow that W. L. Garrison was unable to speak in Adrian because of illness. 13 May 1853. p.75, c3.

2647 C. STEARNS *to* **MR. GARRISON. 15 April 1853. Boston.** Justifies his disbelief in spiritual manifestations. 13 May 1853. p.76, c2.

2648 G. B. STEBBINS *to* **MR. GARRISON. 14 April 1853. Boston.** Replies to Rev. C. C. Goss concerning the East Genesee Methodist Episcopal Conference. 13 May 1853. p.76, c3.

2649 C. F. *to* **MR. EDITOR [W. L. GARRISON]. n.d. n.p.** Praises Sallie Holley's work in Portland. 13 May 1853. p.76, c4.

2650 THOMAS GATES *to* **FRIEND GARRISON. 22 April 1853. Williams College.** Praises Wendell Phillips and Dr. Hopkins, the college president; relates an experience with spiritualism. 13 May 1853. p.76, c4.

2651 TRUTH *to* **MR. GARRISON. n.d. n.p.** Recommends Nelson's *Cause and Cure of Infidelity* for the proposed discussion of Jewish and Christian Scriptures. 13 May 1853. p.76, c4.

2652 W. J. WATKINS *to* **MR. EDITOR. [from the** *Boston Herald***] 22 April 1853. n.p.** Criticizes the Committee on the Militia for violating the rights of blacks. 13 May 1853. p.76, c5.

2653 SALMON P. CHASE *to* **SIR. 8 May 1853. Cincinnati.** Reports that he is unable to attend the anti-slavery meeting. 20 May 1853. p.89 [79], c1.

2654 WILLIAM JAY *to* **SIR. 9 May 1853. Bedford.** Responds that he is unable to attend the anti-slavery meeting. 20 May 1853. p.89 [79], c1.

2655 SAMUEL J. MAY *to* **FRIEND. 4 May 1853. Syracuse.** Responds that he is unable to attend the anti-slavery meeting. 20 May 1853. p.89 [79], c1.

2656 DAVID A. WASSON *to* **WENDELL PHILLIPS, ESQ. 12 May 1853. Groveland.** Feels that Phillips was "needlessly harsh" in his debate with Horace Mann. 20 May 1853. p.89 [79], c2.

2657 J. W. PILLSBURY *to* **MR. GARRISON. 16 May 1853. Milford, N.H.** Praises Sallie Holley's lectures in Milford. 20 May 1853. p.89 [79], c2.

2658 LUCY STONE *to* **MR. GARRISON. 17 May 1853. Boston.** Describes the controversy over the exclusion of women from the World's Temperance Convention. 20 May 1853. p.89 [79], c3.

2659 EDWARD SEARCH *to* **THE** *LIBERATOR.* **22 April 1853. London.** Discusses spiritualism, postage reform, and abolition. 20 May 1853. p.80, c2.

2660 RICHARD ALLEN *to* **FRIEND. 29 March 1853. Dublin.** Supports the ocean penny postage reform. 20 May 1853. p.80, c3.

2661 L. P. C. C. *to* **MR. GARRISON. n.d. n.p.** Discusses the Bible and spiritual manifestations. 20 May 1853. p.80, c4.

2662 J. P. B. *to* **MR. EDITOR. n.d. n.p.** Argues with D. Y. about the Constitution's stand on slavery. 20 May 1853. p.80, c5.

2663 A SUBSCRIBER *to* **n.n. n.d. n.p.** Questions the accuracy of intelligence Henry C. Wright received from the "spirits" concerning his brother's death. 27 May 1853. p.93 [83], c5.

2664 N. H. WHITING *to* **FRIEND MAY. 23 May 1853. Marshfield.** Reports that he is unable to attend the New England anti-slavery meeting; forwards five dollars. 3 June 1853. p.97 [87], c2.

2665 WM. WELLS BROWN *to* **MR. GARRISON. 17 May 1853. London.** Reports on an anti-slavery meeting at Exeter Hall. 3 June 1853. p.97 [87], c3.

2666 P. REASONER *to* **WM. LLOYD GARRISON. 1 May 1853. Adrian, Mi.** Expresses sorrow that Garrison could not appear at Adrian. 3 June 1853. p.97 [87], c4.

2667 HORACE MANN *to* **WM. L. GARRISON, ESQ. 20 May 1853. West Newton.** Justifies voting and holding government office while slavery still exists. 3 June 1853. p.98 [88], c2.

2668 PARKER PILLSBURY *to* **MARIUS. [from the** *Ohio Anti-Slavery Bugle***] 18 May 1853. Concord, N.H.** Supports Wendell Phillips in his debate with Horace Mann. 10 June 1853. p.90, c5.

2669 J. G. *to* **MR. GARRISON. n.d. n.p.** Identifies inconsistencies in Horace Mann's arguments against Wendell Phillips. 10 June 1853. p.92, c2.

2670 W. *to* **FRIEND. 25 May 1853. Ravenna.** Reports on the women's rights convention in Ohio. 10 June 1853. p.92, c2.

2671 HORACE MANN *to* **WM. L. GARRISON, ESQ. 11 June 1853. West Newton.** Defines his position on the Constitution and slavery. 17 June 1853. p.94, c1.

2672 HENRY C. WRIGHT *to* **GARRISON. 7 June 1853. Hartford.** Reports on the controversial Bible convention in Hartford, Connecticut. 17 June 1853. p.95, c3.

2673 S. W. W. *to* **FRIEND GARRISON. 20 June 1853. Providence.** Reports on the annual meeting of the Rhode Island Congregational clergymen in Barrington, Rhode Island. 24 June 1853. p.99, c3.

2674 N. H. WHITING *to* **FRIEND MAY. [extract] 17 June 1853. Marshfield.** Calls for an anti-slavery campaign in the West. 24 June 1853. p.99, c3.

2675 n.n. *to* **GARRISON. 1 June 1853. London.** Encloses a copy of the address from English Democrats to the Democrats of the United States. 24 June 1853. p.99, c3.

2676 GEORGE W. SIMONDS *to* **n.n. n.d. n.p.** Asks Professor Stowe to present statistics to support his statement that cotton, rice, and sugar are of little importance to the American consumer. 24 June 1853. p.99, c3.

2677 E. B. C. *to* **FRIEND GARRISON. 18 May 1853. Valley Falls.** Praises Parker Pillsbury's lecture on the French Revolution. 24 June 1853. p.99, c4.

2678 DAVID BROWN *to* **FRIEND. 3 June 1853. Four Mile Creek, Canada.** Thanks his Boston friends for their financial support. 24 June 1853. p.99, c4.

2679 EDWARD SEARCH *to* **GARRISON. 20 May 1853. London.** Reports on the reception of Professor Stowe and Harriet Beecher Stowe in London. 24 June 1853. p.100, c4.

2680 GEORGE SUNTER, JR. *to* **THE EDITOR OF THE** *LIBERATOR* **[W. L. GARRISON]. 9 May 1853. Derby, England.** Protests against the Maine Law. 24 June 1853. p.100, c5.

2681 D. S. GRANDIN *to* **W. GARRISON. 4 June 1853. Portland.** Opposes Horace Mann's letter printed in the 3 June *Liberator*. 1 July 1853. p.101, c1.

2682 W. S. F. *to* **THE EDITOR OF THE** *LIBERATOR* **[W. L. GARRISON]. n.d. n.p.** Argues with J. P. B.; believes that the Constitution is pro-slavery. 1 July 1853. p.102, c5.

2683 J. P. B. *to* **FRIEND GARRISON. n.d. n.p.** Argues with Garrison on the character of the Constitution. 1 July 1853. p.102, c6.

2684 A. GUEPIN *to* **WILLIAM LLOYD GARRISON. 25 March 1853. Paris.** Conveys the support of French believers in the religion of science for Garrison's work. 1 July 1853. p.104, c2.

2685 CONSOLATION *to* **THE EDITOR OF THE** *NEW YORK TRIBUNE.* **9 June 1853. Newark.** Argues with J. P. B.'s analysis of the Hartford Bible convention; condemns Protestantism. 1 July 1853. p.104, c2.

2686 THEODORE PARKER *to* **JOSEPH A. DUGDALE. 2 May 1853. Boston.** Expresses admiration for the Progressive Friends. 1 July 1853. p.104, c3.

2687 SAMUEL J. MAY *to* **FRIENDS. 17 May 1853. Syracuse.** Appreciates the Old Kennett meeting of Progressive Friends as a step toward unifying Christians. 1 July 1853. p.104, c3.

2688 WM. LLOYD GARRISON *to* **JOSEPH A. DUGDALE. 19 May 1853. Boston.** Reports that he is unable to attend the meeting of Progressive Friends at Old Kennett; submits suggestions for their consideration. 1 July 1853. p.104, c4.

2689 THOMAS WENTWORTH HIGGINSON *to* **J. A. DUGDALE. 20 May 1853. Worcester.** Discusses the improvement of church organization. 1 July 1853. p.104, c4.

2690 GERRIT SMITH *to* **JOSEPH A. DUGDALE. 9 April 1853. Peterboro', N.Y.** Reports that he is unable to attend the Progressive Friends' meeting; condemns sectarianism. 1 July 1853. p.104, c5.

2691 CHARLES C. BURLEIGH *to* **n.n. [extract from the** *Pennsylvania Freeman***] n.d. n.p.** Describes speeches by Lucy Stone and Wendell Phillips proposing that women be permitted to vote on the adoption of amendments to the Massachusetts constitution. 1 July 1853. p.104, c5.

2692 F. W. CHESSON *to* **THE EDITOR OF THE** *MORNING ADVERTISER*. **n.d. n.p.** Refutes Rev. Dr. Long's statement that Garrison and the abolitionists are responsible for the increasingly pro-slavery stance of Virginia. 8 July 1853. p.105, c6.

2693 n.n. *to* **FRIEND FOGG. [from the** *New Hampshire Independent Democrat*] **25 June 1853. Plymouth.** Praises Sallie Holly. 8 July 1853. p.106, c2.

2694 ARCHBISHOP RICHARD WHATELY *to* **W. L. GARRISON, ESQ. 16 June 1853. Dublin.** Denies that he wrote the review of *Uncle Tom's Cabin* in the *North British*. 8 July 1853. p.106, c5.

2695 C. E. STOWE *to* **MR. G. W. SIMONDS. 30 June 1853. Andover.** Explains his earlier remarks on the British consumption of slave-grown cotton. 8 July 1853. p.106, c5.

2696 CHARLES HAZELTINE *to* **FRIEND GARRISON. 4 July 1853. Littleton, N.H.** Reports on Miss Sallie Holley's reception in New Hampshire. 8 July 1853. p.106, c5.

2697 LEVI J. HICKS *to* **n.n. 6 June 1853. Walworth, N.Y.** Reports on a vote to exclude slaveholders from the Methodist Episcopal church. 8 July 1853. p.106, c6.

2698 A. THAYER *to* **MR. GARRISON. 23 June 1853. Blackstone.** Reports on the warm reception of Andrew T. Foss' anti-slavery lectures. 8 July 1853. p.106, c6.

2699 LEONARD GIBBS *to* **MR. GARRISON. 28 June 1853. Greenwich.** Praises the *Liberator*; reports the death of Angelina Mowry. 8 July 1853. p.106, c6.

2700 J. *to* **MR. EDITOR [W. L. GARRISON]. 3 July 1853. East Bridgewater.** Opposes building a monument to Daniel Webster. 8 July 1853. p.107, c2.

2701 n.n. *to* **n.n. 25 June 1853. Washington.** Announces that the United States would declare war rather than allow the abolition of slavery in Cuba. 8 July 1853. p.107, c2.

2702 EDWARD SEARCH *to* **THE EDITOR OF THE** *LIBERATOR* **[W. L. GARRISON]. 10 June 1853. London.** Discusses women's rights, slavery, and theology. 8 July 1853. p.108, c2.

2703 W.C.N. *to* **ESTEEMED FRIEND GARRISON. n.d. Boston.** Forwards letter from John T. Hilton, a veteran soldier. 8 July 1853. p.108, c3.

2704 JOHN T. HILTON *to* **W. C. NELL. 25 May 1853. n.p.** A colored war veteran reports on abolitionists and the New England AS Convention. 8 July 1853. p.108, c3.

2705 S. W. W. *to* **FRIEND GARRISON. 27 June 1853. Providence.** Reports on Andrew T. Foss' anti-slavery lectures in Providence. 8 July 1853. p.108, c4.

2706 n.n. *to* **WM. LLOYD GARRISON. 6 June 1853. New York.** Denounces the Bible convention at Hartford; calls Garrison satanic. 8 July 1853. p.108, c4.

2707 A GENTLEMAN IN ALABAMA *to* **THE EDITORS OF THE** *NEW YORK EVENING POST*. **8 May 1853. Alabama.** A slaveholder praises *Uncle Tom's Cabin*. 8 July 1853. p.108, c5.

2708 R. POTTER *to* **MR. EDITOR. [from the** *Pawtucket Gazette and Chronicle*] **15 June 1853. Pawtucket, R.I.** Attacks Horace Mann's views on the Constitution. 15 July 1853. p.109, c1.

2709 EDWARD MATHEWS *to* **n.n. 3 June 1853. Oxford, England.** Discusses Prof. Stowe's anti-slavery speech. 15 July 1853. p.109, c3.

2710 F. W. CHESSON *to* **REV. THOMAS JONES. n.d. n.p.** Summarizes the history of the American Free Baptist Missionary Society. 15 July 1853. p.109, c6.

2711 T. W. HIGGINSON *to* **SIR [W. L. GARRISON]. 9 July 1853. Worcester.** Corrects several printing errors in his letter to the Progressive Friends. 15 July 1853. p.111, c4.

2712 J. P. B. *to* **THE EDITOR OF THE** *LIBERATOR* **[W. L. GARRISON]. n.d. n.p.** Replies to questions by W. S. F. concerning the Constitution. 15 July 1853. p.112, c3.

2713 AUGUSTUS O. MOORE *to* **SIR. [from the** *New York Tribune***] 6 June 1853. Hartford.** Details the order of events at the Hartford Bible convention. 15 July 1853. p.112, c4.

2714 MARY WELSH AND ELIZA ANDERSON *to* **HARRIET BEECHER STOWE. 14 April 1853. Glasgow.** Praise H. B. Stowe on behalf of the Glasgow Female AS. 22 July 1853. p.113, c3.

2715 HARRIET BEECHER STOWE *to* **MARY WALSH AND ELIZA ANDERSON. 17 April 1853. Glasgow.** Thanks the Glasgow Female AS for their letter. 22 July 1853. p.113, c4.

2716 EDWARD SEARCH *to* **THE** *LIBERATOR***. 22 June 1853. London.** Supports increased cooperation between England and the United States; admires women's rights leaders; discusses the production of cotton in India and the treatment of slavery by the press. 22 July 1853. p.115, c1.

2717 J. W. PILLSBURY *to* **MR. GARRISON. 8 July 1853. Milford, N.H.** Describes the Fourth of July at Milford. 22 July 1853. p.115, c2.

2718 ADELPHOS *to* **MR. GARRISON. 5 July 1853. Cummington, Ma.** Describes the anti-slavery celebration of the Fourth of July at Cummington, Massachusetts. 22 July 1853. p.115, c3.

2719 SHARPSTICK *to* **MR. GARRISON. n.d. n.p.** Assails the Texas slave code, the *New York Observer,* and the *Boston Courier.* 22 July 1853. p.115, c3.

2720 A. T. FOSS *to* **FRIEND GARRISON. 13 July 1853. Marshfield.** Corrects misprints in the *Liberator* account of his speech at Abington. 22 July 1853. p.115, c3.

2721 PROF. WM. G. ALLEN *to* **WM. LLOYD GARRISON, ESQ. 20 June 1853. London.** Praises George Thompson; reports an absence of prejudice against Negroes in England; offers news about abolitionists; praises Frederick Douglass' speech in New York. 22 July 1853. p.116, c2.

2722 J. *to* **THE EDITOR OF THE** *LIBERATOR* **[W. L. GARRISON]. n.d. n.p.** Wishes to read Thomas Paine on slavery. 22 July 1853. p.116, c3.

2723 E. P. GOFF *to* **W. L. GARRISON. 1 July 1853. Ridgway, Pa.** Requests information concerning speeches by Garrison and Phillips. 22 July 1853. p.116, c3.

2724 L. P. C. *to* **n.n. n.d. n.p.** Reports on a meeting of the Worcester County North Division AS in East Princeton; criticizes H. C. Wright. 22 July 1853. p.116, c3.

2725 WILLIAM GOODELL *to* **SAMUEL MAY, JR. 16 July 1853. New York.** Challenges May to substantiate charges of falsification in Goodell's book. 29 July 1853. p.118, c3.

2726 SAMUEL MAY, JR. *to* **WILLIAM GOODELL. 26 July 1853. Boston.** Explains that he must present Goodell's letter to the managers of the Massachusetts AS. 29 July 1853. p.118, c3.

2727 REV. DANIEL FOSTER *to* **[S.] MAY, [JR.] AND GARRISON. 18 July 1853. Cambridge.** Opposes the "non-voting theory" and "Disunion"; advocates circulation of William Goodell's *History of the Anti-Slavery Enterprise.* 29 July 1853. p.118, c4.

2728 SAMUEL MAY, JR. *to* **MR. GARRISON. 26 July 1853. Boston.** Takes issue with Daniel Foster's letter and with his views on voting and on William Goodell's book. 29 July 1853. p.118, c5.

2729 SETH PAINE *to* **EDITOR** *LIBERATOR* **[W. L. GARRISON]. n.d. n.p.** Discusses Frederick Douglass' reversal of opinion concerning the Constitution; calls for the abolition of the Constitution. 29 July 1853. p.119, c1.

2730 A SUBSCRIBER FOR THE *LIBERATOR to* **THE EDITOR OF THE** *LIBERATOR* **[W. L. GARRISON]. 6 July 1853. New York.** Believes in the plenary inspiration of the Bible. 29 July 1853. p.120, c2.

2731 HENRY C. WRIGHT *to* **W. L. GARRISON. 19 July 1853. Plympton.** Examines the implications of spiritualism for practical reform. 29 July 1853. p.120, c3.

2732 J. F. C. *to* **MR. GARRISON. 20 July 1853. Sandwich.** Describes the Fourth of July in North Dennis. 29 July 1853. p.120, c4.

2733 SETH PAINE *to* **EDITOR** *COMMERCIAL ADVERTISER.* **12 July 1853. Chicago.** Expresses outrage that a local businessman, Ira B. Eddy, was unjustly kidnapped and placed in an asylum in Connecticut. 29 July 1853. p.120, c5.

2734 HENRY T. TUCKERMAN *to* **THE EDITORS OF THE** *HOME JOURNAL.* **n.d. n.p.** Eulogizes the late Pierre Toussaint, a highly respected New York Negro. 5 August 1853. p.121, c6.

2735 ABBY K. FOSTER *to* **FRIEND GARRISON. 31 July 1853. Worcester.** Exposes a female fugitive slave impostor. 5 August 1853. p.122, c6.

2736 PARKER PILLSBURY *to* **FRIEND GARRISON. 23 July 1853. New Ipswich, N.H.** Recommends a quiet water cure retreat in New Ipswich. 5 August 1853. p.123, c1.

2737 S. W. W. *to* **FRIEND GARRISON. 12 July 1853. Providence.** Denounces the *Providence Daily Post,* and *Daily Journal,* as well as *New York Express,* for sympathizing with slaveholders. 12 August 1853. p.125, c3.

2738 E. *to* **MR. GARRISON. n.d. n.p.** Discusses the responsibilities of voters; does not oppose voting. 12 August 1853. p.125, c3.

2739 REV. MR. THAYER *to* **n.n. [extract] n.d. Austria.** An American clergyman explains the vigorous watch Austrian police maintain over visitors. 19 August 1853. p.128, c5.

2740 HENRY ATKINSON *to* **MR. GOWDY. n.d. Windsor, Canada.** A fugitive slave informs his master of his successful escape. 19 August 1853. p.129, c4.

2741 REV. WILLIAM P. TILDEN *to* **n.n. n.d. n.p.** Regrets that he cannot attend the commemoration of West Indies Emancipation in Fitzwilliam, New Hampshire; discusses the significance of the emancipation. 19 August 1853. p.130, c2.

2742 ISAAC STEARNS *to* **MR. GARRISON. 6 May 1853. Mansfield.** Discusses resolutions he introduced into the House of Representatives concerning Negroes in Illinois. 19 August 1853. p.130, c6.

2743 HENRY C. WRIGHT *to* **WILLIAM WHITING. 16 July 1853. Plymouth.** Asserts his belief in the existence of God. 19 August 1853. p.132, c6.

2744 A SUBSCRIBER *to* **P. DONAHOE, ESQ. 14 July 1853. Richibucto.** Asks whether a Catholic can be a slaveholder and still receive the sacraments. 26 August 1853. p.133, c3.

2745 WILLIAM MEADE *to* **THE EDITOR OF THE** *COLONIZATIONIST.* **23 July 1853, n.p.** Believes that colonization in Liberia is preferable to freedom in America. 26 August 1853. p.133, c4.

2746 A YOUNG MAN RESIDING AT THE SOUTH *to* **n.n. [extract from the** *Concord* **(N.H.)** *Independent Democrat***] n.d. n.p.** Ridicules and rebukes a cruel slaveholder who considers himself a Christian. 26 August 1853. p.133, c5.

2747 n.n. *to* **n.n. [extract] n.d. n.p.** Describes a Kentucky Presbyterian elder's use of an iron collar on his ten-year-old slave. 26 August 1853. p.133, c6.

2748 MAZZINI *to* **AN ENGLISH FRIEND OF GARRISON. [extract] n.d. Italy.** The leader of the Italian patriots praises American anti-slavery efforts; declares that abolitionists' goals are shared by the Italian patriots. 26 August 1853. p.134, c6.

2749 L. N. FOWLER *to* **EDITOR** *LIBERATOR* **[W. L. GARRISON]. 9 August 1853. New York.** Submits his phrenological analysis of the character of Wm. Henry Ashurst. 26 August 1853. p.136, c2.

2750 S. S. GRISWOLD *to* **FRIEND GARRISON. 15 August 1853. Haunsfield.** Fears the dissolution of the Union. 26 August 1853. p.136, c3.

2751 VERA CATHOLICA *to* **MR. GARRISON. n.d. n.p.** Examines the inspiration and authority of the Bible. 26 August 1853. p.136, c3.

2752 HENRY C. WRIGHT *to* **GARRISON. 15 August 1853. Brattleboro, Vt.** Describes a lecture by Lucy Stone; discusses the fate of the Church; describes a water cure. 26 August 1853. p.136, c4.

2753 PARKER PILLSBURY *to* **FRIEND GARRISON. 20 August 1853. Conneautville, Pa.** Describes lodgings and travel in the West. 2 September 1853. p.137, c1.

2754 NELSON BROWN *to* **MR. GARRISON. n.d. n.p.** Reports on an anti-slavery convention at Cummington. 2 September 1853. p.137, c2.

2755 S. M., JR. *to* **MR. GARRISON. 22 August 1853. Leicester.** Praises the anti-slavery meeting at Cummington. 2 September 1853. p.137, c2.

2756 REV. THOMAS H. JONES *to* **MR. GARRISON. 22 August 1853. Cummington.** Reports on his reception in Cummington. 2 September 1853. p.137, c3.

2757 HENRY C. WRIGHT *to* **GARRISON. 21 August 1853. Saratoga Springs.** Reports on an anti-slavery lecture by Lucy Stone; relates a conversation he had on slavery while in Brattleboro'; reports on a Saratoga Springs anti-slavery meeting; advocates women's rights. 2 September 1853. p.137, c3.

2758 H. C. *to* **n.n. 22 August 1853. Randolph, Vt.** Reports on Lucy Stone's lectures in Vermont. 2 September 1853. p.137, c4.

2759 A POOR LABORING MAN IN HAMPDEN COUNTY *to* **JOHN M. FISK. n.d. n.p.** Believes that the history of Egypt should be a warning to us; encloses seven dollars for Sallie Holley. 2 September 1853. p.137, c5.

2760 J. MERCER LANGSTON *to* **WILLIAM C. NELL. [extract] 19 August 1853. Oberlin, Oh.** Hopes to make Ohio the "anti-slavery state of the Union." 2 September 1853. p.137, c6.

2761 A REGULAR THEATREGOER *to* **WM. LLOYD GARRISON. n.d. n.p.** Queries why colored people are allowed only in the gallery of the Howard Athenaeum of Boston. 2 September 1853. p.137, c6.

2762 WILLIAM C. NELL *to* **MR. FREDERICK DOUGLASS. 13 August 1853. Boston.** Reports on proceedings of the anti-slavery meeting at Boston. 2 September 1853. p.138, c5.

2763 W. C. N. *to* **FRIEND DOUGLASS. 19 August 1853. Boston.** Complains that Frederick Douglass would not publish W.C.N.'s speeches or letters. 2 September 1853. p.138, c5.

2764 JEHIEL CLAFLIN *to* **GARRISON. 25 August 1853. West Brookfield, Vt.** Reports on lectures by Lucy Stone in Vermont. 2 September 1853. p.139, c3.

2765 J. W. EDMONDS *to* **THE PUBLIC. [from the** *Spiritual Telegraph***] 1 August 1853. New York.** Defends his religious beliefs. 2 September 1853. p.140, c2.

2766 G. B. STEBBINS *to* **FRIEND GARRISON. 31 August 1853. Marlboro', N.H.** Reports on anti-slavery activity in New Hampshire; states that he does not support the Free-Soil movement. 9 September 1853. p.143, c1.

2767 MARTHA O. BARRETT *to* **MR. GARRISON. 5 September 1853. Danvers.** Announces the death of Lucy A. Colby. 9 September 1853. p.143, c2.

2768 HENRY C. WRIGHT *to* **GARRISON. 26 August 1853. Niagara Falls.** Describes the natural beauty of Niagara Falls. 9 September 1853. p.144, c2.

2769 MUTTON *to* **MR. EDITOR. [from the** *Southern Mississippi Journal***] n.d. n.p.** Describes a barbecue for slaves at the S. A. Douglas plantation. 16 September 1853. p.145, c2.

2770 A SLAVE-OWNER *to* **MESSRS. EDITORS. [from the** *Southern Reveille***] n.d. n.p.** Endeavors to stop the purchase of more slaves. 16 September 1853. p.145, c3.

2771 W. L. CRANDAL, T. WHITE, J. FULLER, E. FILKINS, L. SAVAGE, J. SAVAGE, AND J. LOGUEN *to* **GERRIT SMITH. 3 September 1853. Syracuse.** Request that Smith preside at the Jerry Rescue celebration. 16 September 1853. p.145, c4.

2772 GERRIT SMITH *to* **FELLOW CITIZENS. 5 September 1853. Peterboro'.** Accepts the honor of presiding at the Jerry Rescue celebration. 16 September 1853. p.145, c4.

2773 WENDELL PHILLIPS *to* **HON. NEAL DOW. n.d. n.p.** Comments on Antoinette Brown. 16 September 1853. p.147, c2.

2774 HENRY C. WRIGHT *to* **GARRISON. 5 September 1853. Crystal Palace, N.Y.** Offers his opinion on the purpose of the World's Fair. 16 September 1853. p.147, c3.

2775 GEORGE W. PUTNAM *to* **FRIEND GARRISON. 4 September 1853. Lynn.** Objects to W. C. Nell's charge that he is dissatisfied with the Massachusetts AS. 16 September 1853. p.147, c4.

2776 ROBERT PURVIS *to* **MR. GARRISON. 22 August 1853. Byberry, Philadelphia County.** Criticizes Douglass' remarks about him in the 12 August issue of *Frederick Douglass' Paper.* 16 September 1853. p.147, c4.

2777 JOHN A. DIX *to* **I. P. GARVIN. 31 August 1853. New York.** States that he is not an abolitionist. 23 September 1853. p.149, c2.

2778 WENDELL PHILLIPS *to* **NEAL DOW. [from the** *New York Tribune***] 12 September 1853. n.p.** Criticizes the World's Temperance Convention. 23 September 1853. p.149, c5.

2779 PARKER PILLSBURY *to* **FRIEND GARRISON. 12 September 1853. Granville, Oh.** States that the greatest enemy of anti-slavery is infidelity; claims the Bible is pro-slavery; doubts the Bible's divine authority; condemns the Free-Soil Party. 23 September 1853. p.151, c1.

2780 AMY POST *to* **W. C. N. [extract] September 1853. n.p.** Informs that she has just aided twelve fugitive slaves in their escape to Canada. 23 September 1853. p.151, c2.

2781 JUSTUS HARLOW *to* **MR. ROGERS. 27 August 1853. Plymouth.** Asks whether Rogers purchased two slaves and freed them. 23 September 1853. p.151, c2.

2782 B. R. P. *to* **LIBERATOR. 9 September 1853. Philadelphia.** Reports the staging of *Uncle Tom's Cabin* at the Philadelphia Theater. 23 September 1853. p.152, c3.

2783 W. E. HERENDON, P.M. *to* **JOHN LAWRENCE. n.d. Greenville, Va.** Informs that the *Religious Telegraph* cannot be distributed in Virginia. 30 September 1853. p.153, c2.

2784 C. M. CLAY *to* **THE PEOPLE OF KENTUCKY. 2 September 1853. Whitehall Post Office.** Responds to criticisms by Rockcastle citizens. 30 September 1853. p.153, c4.

2785 W. J. LINTON *to* **SIR. 23 August 1853. Coniston, Lancashire, England.** States that George Jacob Holyoake's sentiments on slavery are not representative of the general sentiment in England. 30 September 1853. p.154, c4.

2786 J. P. B. *to* **MR. EDITOR. n.d. n.p.** Describes the tenets of free democracy. 30 September 1853. p.154, c4.

2787 SALLIE HOLLEY *to* **FRANCIS JACKSON. [extract] 17 September 1853. Jonesville, Mi.** Reports on anti-slavery activities in the West. 30 September 1853. p.154, c6.

2788 JOHN CALKINS *to* **ROBERT F. WALLCUT. 19 September 1853. South Wilbraham.** Renews subscription to the *Liberator.* 30 September 1853. p.154, c6.

2789 LEWIS TAPPAN *to* **THE EDITOR OF THE** *NATIONAL ERA***. 12 September 1853. Brooklyn, N.Y.** Reports that someone has been writing letters under his name. 30 September 1853. p.155, c1.

2790 JOHN O. WATTLES *to* **n.n. 12 September 1853. Newark, N.J.** Reports on lectures by Lucy Stone at Newark. 30 September 1853. p.156, c5.

2791 LOOKER-ON IN BALTIMORE *to* **THE EDITOR OF THE** *COMMONWEALTH.* **18 September 1853. Baltimore.** Comments on the death of Hope H. Slatter. 7 October 1853. p.157, c2.

2792 W. L. CRANDAL *to* **JOHN P. HALE. 1 September 1853. Syracuse.** Debates the constitutionality of slavery. 7 October 1853. p.157, c4.

2793 J. R. GIDDINGS *to* **JAMES FULLER. 22 September 1853. Jefferson, Oh.** Discusses the Fugitive Slave Law. 7 October 1853. p.157, c5.

2794 H. B. STOWE *to* **MAYOR OF LIVERPOOL. n.d. n.p.** Thanks the mayor for his hospitality during her stay. 7 October 1853. p.158, c3.

2795 H. B. STOWE *to* **MR. BURNARD. n.d. n.p.** Thanks Burnard for a bust of herself. 7 October 1853. p.158, c4.

2796 PARKER PILLSBURY *to* **FRIEND GARRISON. 25 September 1853. Richmond, In.** Reports on the Woman's State Temperance Convention; criticizes General Cary's views on woman's temperance. 7 October 1853. p.158, c6.

2797 ISAAC G. MOTT *to* **FRIEND. 12 September 1853. Hopary Grove.** Asks whether the Methodist Episcopal Church of the North, the New School Presbyterian Church, or the Baptist Church accepts the testimony of colored persons. 7 October 1853. p.159, c2.

2798 GERRIT SMITH *to* **THE PEOPLE OF THE COUNTY OF ONTARIO. 19 September 1853. Peterboro'.** Condemns the Fugitive Slave Law. 7 October 1853. p.159, c3.

2799 N. H. WHITING *to* **GARRISON. 25 September 1853. Marshfield.** Requests that letters on infidelity be published. 7 October 1853. p.160, c1.

2800 n.n. *to* **NATHANIEL WHITING. n.d. n.p.** Discusses the infidel versus the Christian as an issue in the French Revolution. 7 October 1853. p.160, c1.

2801 N. H. WHITING *to* **n.n. 31 August 1853. Marshfield.** Defends his "infidelity." 7 October 1853. p.160, c3.

2802 JOSEPH CARPENTER *to* **WM. LLOYD GARRISON. 13 September 1853. New Rochelle.** Inquires about the sentiments of George Fox. 7 October 1853. p.160, c6.

2803 J. H. ALLEN *to* **THE EDITOR. [from the** *London Inquirer***] 13 July 1853. Bangor, Me.** Refutes J. B. Estlin's remark that he supported the Fugitive Slave Law. 14 October 1853. p.161, c3.

2804 J. B. ESTLIN *to* **THE EDITOR. 25 August 1853. Bristol.** Discusses American Unitarian ministers' views on slavery. 14 October 1853. p.161, c3.

2805 THOMAS GARRETT *to* **ROBERT F. WALLCUT. 6 October 1853. Wilmington.** Renews subscription to the *Liberator*; praises the *Liberator* and W. L. Garrison. 14 October 1853. p.162, c5.

2806 EDWARD SEARCH *to* **FRIEND GARRISON. n.d. n.p.** Laments the death of John Childs; reports on a Bible convention at Salem. 14 October 1853. p.162, c6.

2807 E. A. STOCKMAN *to* **MR. MAY. 30 September 1853. Cummington.** Reports on anti-slavery meetings. 14 October 1853. p.163, c2.

2808 JOHN R. NEILL *to* **FRIEND. 16 September 1853. Belfast, Ireland.** Praises the anti-slavery speeches of J. Miller McKim in Belfast. 14 October 1853. p.163, c3.

2809 EDWARD F. UNDERHILL *to* **EDITOR** *LIBERATOR* **[W. L. GARRISON]. 21 September 1853. New York.** Comments on an article by Seth Paine entitled "Constitutions and Governments." 14 October 1853. p.164, c2.

2810 n.n. *to* **n.n. [extract] 30 September 1853. Brandon, Vt.** Encloses a poem by Rev. Byron Sanderlin. 21 October 1853. p.165, c2.

2811 WILLIAM GOODELL *to* **SAMUEL MAY, JR., FRANCIS JACKSON, R. F. WALLCUT, AND THE MANAGERS OF THE MASSACHUSETTS AS. 3 October 1853. New York.** Discusses his book on the history of the anti-slavery movement. 21 October 1853. p.166, c6.

2812 n.n. *to* **W. L. GARRISON. n.d. n.p.** Announces that a German abolitionist newspaper, *Zeitung*, is being published in Boston. 21 October 1853. p.167, c1.

2813 PARKER PILLSBURY *to* **FRIEND QUINCY. 11 October 1853. Richmond, In.** Reports on anti-slavery activities in southern Indiana. 21 October 1853. p.167, c2.

2814 HENRY C. WRIGHT *to* **GARRISON. 13 September 1853. Columbus, Oh.** Pities the prisoners of the penitentiary and the lunatic asylum in Ohio. 21 October 1853. p.168, c2.

2815 VERA CATHOLICA *to* **MR. GARRISON. n.d. n.p.** Comments on Garrison's speech "the Plenary Inspiration of the Sacred Scriptures." 21 October 1853. p.168, c3.

2816 S. W. W. *to* **MR. EDITOR. [from the** *Rhode Island Freeman***] 3 October 1853. Providence.** Discusses women's rights and temperance. 21 October 1853. p.168, c4.

2817 T. W. HIGGINSON *to* **REV. S. WOLCOTT. 9 September 1853. Worcester.** States that he respects Wolcott's views on women's rights. 21 October 1853. p.168, c4.

2818 SAMUEL WOLCOTT *to* **REV. T. W. HIGGINSON. 12 September 1853. Providence.** Criticizes female delegates at the temperance convention. 21 October 1853. p.168, c4.

2819 SAMUEL WOLCOTT *to* **REV. T. W. HIGGINSON. 1 October 1853. Providence.** Examines the rights of delegates to the temperance conventions. 21 October 1853. p.168, c5.

2820 JOHN CHAMBERS *to* **MR. BIRNEY. [from the** *Philadelphia Register***] n.d. n.p.** Responds to an attack by Wm. H. Channing. 28 October 1853. p.169, c3.

2821 FRED W. CHESSON *to* **THE EDITOR OF THE** *ANTI-SLAVERY ADVOCATE.* **12 September 1853. Manchester.** Discusses the problems encountered by English abolitionists. 28 October 1853. p.169, c4.

2822 n.n. *to* **MESSRS. EDITORS. [from the** *Greylock Sentinel***] 30 September 1853. Cheshire.** Reports on a lecture by Rev. E. A. Stockman. 28 October 1853. p.170, c3.

2823 PARKER PILLSBURY *to* **FRIEND QUINCY. 20 October 1853. Winchester, In.** Reports on government, education, and religion in Indiana. 28 October 1853. p.171, c2.

2824 WM. H. FISH *to* **n.n. [extract] n.d. n.p.** Describes an anti-slavery meeting at Franklin. 28 October 1853. p.171, c3.

2825 n.n. *to* **MR. GARRISON. n.d. n.p.** Discusses a forthcoming lecture on spiritualism. 28 October 1853. p.171, c3.

2826 n.n. *to* **MR. EDITOR. n.d. n.p.** Announces the beginning of the term at the New England Female Medical College. 28 October 1853. p.171, c3.

2827 HENRY C. WRIGHT *to* **R. D. WEBB. 19 September 1853. Muskingum River, Oh.** Describes gas-spring salt works in Ohio. 28 October 1853. p.172, c3.

2828 JAMES HAUGHTON *to* **MY COUNTRYMEN. [from the** *Drogheda Argus***] 19 September 1853. 35 Eccles Street, Dublin.** Gives an account of James McKim's anti-slavery lectures in Ireland; reports his attempts to rouse anti-slavery sentiments. 4 November 1853. p.173, c2.

2829 PARKER PILLSBURY *to* **FRIEND QUINCY. 24 October 1853. Bellefontaine, Oh.** Announces the triumph of the Democrats in Ohio in the last election; deplores the making of whiskey; informs that kidnapping flourishes in Ohio. 4 November 1853. p.175, c1.

2830 W. WELLS BROWN *to* **REV. S. MAY, JR. 8 October 1853. London.** Informs that his daughters are in training school; states that he is publishing a new work entitled *Clotel; or, The President's Daughter.* 4 November 1853. p.175, c2.

2831 A. T. FOSS *to* **FRIEND MAY. [extract] 24 October 1853. Millville.** Reports on anti-slavery meetings he has attended. 4 November 1853. p.175, c2.

2832 HENRY C. WRIGHT *to* **GARRISON. 5 October 1853. Mansfield.** Describes western railroads; criticizes the United States for allowing slavery to exist. 4 November 1853. p.176, c3.

2833 ONE OF THE BOYS *to* **FRIEND GARRISON. 17 October 1853. Spring Arbor, Mi.** Comments on female speakers; favors women's rights. 4 November 1853. p.176, c4.

2834 WM. HENRY CHANNING *to* **THE EDITOR OF THE** *DAILY REGISTER***. 18 October 1853. Rochester.** Defends himself against charges by Rev. John Chambers that he is vindictive. 4 November 1853. p.176, c4.

2835 JAMES M'CUNE SMITH *to* **THE EDITOR OF THE** *NEW YORK TRIBUNE***. 8 September 1853. New York.** Discusses the rejection of his credentials for admittance to a temperance convention. 4 November 1853. p.176, c5.

2836 C. CUSHING *to* **HON. R. FROTHINGHAM, JR. [from the** *New York Tribune***] 29 October 1853. Washington.** Discusses the coalition between Democrats and Free-Soilers. 11 November 1853. p.178, c2.

2837 MATTHEW S. CLAPP *to* **H. M. ADDISON. 21 September 1853. Mentor.** Endorses the anti-slavery convention planned for January. 11 November 1853. p.178, c3.

2838 EDWIN H. NEVIN *to* **THE EDITOR OF THE** *NEW YORK TRIBUNE***. 14 October 1853. Cleveland.** Objects to the charge that he castigated Garrison; agrees that he answered the charges which Joseph Barker made against the Church. 11 November 1853. p.178, c5.

2839 S. S. HUNTING *to* **FRIEND GARRISON. 17 October 1853. Brookfield.** Reports the conversion of a Boston mechanic to abolitionism. 11 November 1853. p.179, c3.

2840 HENRY C. WRIGHT *to* **GARRISON. 10 October 1853. Pittsburgh.** Describes Pittsburgh; declares that nature is the word of God. 11 November 1853. p.180, c2.

2841 W. *to* **GARRISON. n.d. n.p.** Praises the *Liberator*; requests that Garrison lecture in Vermont. 11 November 1853. p.180, c2.

2842 ANTOINETTE L. BROWN *to* **THE READERS OF THE** *UNA*. **16 September 1853. South Butler.** Describes the proceedings of the World's Temperance Convention. 11 November 1853. p.180, c5.

2843 T. W. H. *to* **MESSRS. EDITORS. [from the** *Massachusetts Spy*] **n.d. n.p.** Corrects a misstatement in the reporting of the Cleveland Women's Rights Convention. 11 November 1853. p.180, c6.

2844 WILLIAM E. LUKINS *to* **n.n. [extract] 9 August 1844. Cadiz, Oh.** Contradicts Mr. Nevin's account of his being "most favorably welcomed" at an anti-slavery meeting. 18 November 1853. p.182, c3.

2845 H. B. S. *to* **MR. EDITOR. n.d. n.p.** Comments on the justice of God. 18 November 1853. p.184, c2.

2846 J. T. C. *to* **MR. GARRISON. 26 October 1853. Chicago.** Gives a complimentary evaluation of Douglass' lecture in Chicago. 18 November 1853. p.184, c3.

2847 PARKER PILLSBURY *to* **FRIEND GARRISON. 12 November 1853. Medina, Oh.** Condemns American politicians as pro-slavery. 25 November 1853. p.185, c2.

2848 G. B. STEBBINS *to* **FRIEND GARRISON. 14 November 1853. Providence, R.I.** Reports on anti-slavery meetings in the East. 25 November 1853. p.185, c3.

2849 C. F. WILLISTON *to* **FRIEND GILLET. 29 October 1853. Syracuse.** Protests inaccuracies found in the obituary of Jerry. 25 November 1853. p.185, c6.

2850 HARRIET MARTINEAU *to* **THE EDITOR OF THE** *LIBERATOR* **[W. L. GARRISON]. 1 November 1853. London.** Decries the attack on G. T. Holyoake's character. 25 November 1853. p.186, c6.

2851 RICHARD ALLEN *to* **GARRISON. 3 November 1853. Dublin.** Considers the possibilities of a European war; reports on the anti-slavery campaign in Dublin. 25 November 1853. p.186, c6.

2852 E. A. STOCKMAN *to* **MR. MAY. 7 November 1853. Cummington.** Reports on antislavery meetings; encourages support. 25 November 1853. p.187, c1.

2853 S---S *to* **MR. EDITOR. n.d. n.p.** Requests that an article which the *Republican Standard* refused be published in the *Liberator*. 25 November 1853. p.188, c2.

2854 S---S *to* **MR. EDITOR. n.d. n.p.** Criticizes the editor for blaming the disturbance at a temperance convention on the women who attended. 25 November 1853. p.188, c2.

2855 DR. HARRIOT K. HUNT *to* **THE AUTHORITIES OF THE CITY OF BOSTON, MASSACHUSETTS, AND CITIZENS, GENERALLY. 5 November 1853. Boston.** Protests taxation of women without representation. 25 November 1853. p.188, c3.

2856 F. W. CHESSON *to* **THE** *WESLEYAN*. **17 October 1853. Edinburgh, Scotland.** Reports on the Peace Congress; lists and discusses speakers. 25 November 1853. p.188, c4.

2857 C. CUSHING *to* **THE PRESIDENT. 14 November 1853. Attorney General's Office.** Discusses the case of John Freeman, an alleged fugitive slave. 2 December 1853. p.189, c1.

2858 PARKER PILLSBURY *to* **FRIEND GARRISON. 21 November 1853. Concord, N.H.** Gives an account of his tour of Indiana, Ohio, and western Pennsylvania; discusses morality in the churches. 2 December 1853. p.190, c6.

2859 MARY M. GUILD *to* **R. F. WALLCUT. 16 November 1853. Cincinnati.** Encloses a donation to the *Liberator*. 2 December 1853. p.190, c6.

2860 G. J. HOLYOAKE *to* **WILLIAM LLOYD GARRISON. 29 October 1853. London.** Replies to W. J. Linton that "superstition and slavery are defended by the same people the world over." 2 December 1853. p.191, c1.

2861 W. J. LINTON *to* **THE EDITOR OF THE** *LIBERATOR* **[W. L. GARRISON]. 5 November 1853. Brantwood, Coniston, Windermere.** Replies to Martineau's defense of Holyoake. 2 December 1853. p.191, c3.

2862 ANNA DOUGLASS *to* **W. L. GARRISON. 21 November 1853. Rochester.** Dismisses the charge that "a certain person in the office" of Frederick Douglass causes unhappiness in her family. 2 December 1853. p.191, c4.

2863 H. E. B. *to* **C. K. W. n.d. n.p.** Presents his view of God as a "sympathizing, suffering, self-denying Redeemer." 2 December 1853. p.192, c2.

2864 GEORGE SUNTER, JR. *to* **THE EDITOR OF THE** *LIBERATOR* **[W. L. GARRISON]. 26 November 1853. Boston.** Requests publication of a letter and an essay in the *Liberator*. 9 December 1853. p.193, c2.

2865 GEORGE SUNTER, JR. *to* **SIR. 4 November 1852. Derby.** Advocates proper observance of the Sabbath. 9 December 1853. p.193, c2.

2866 GEORGE SUNTER, JR. *to* **THE EDITOR OF THE** *LEADER*. **March 1853. Derby.** Discusses Franklin Pierce and his subservience to slavery. 9 December 1853. p.193, c3.

2867 GEO. W. JULIAN *to* **WM. LLOYD GARRISON. 20 November 1853. Centreville, In.** Reports that he is unable to attend the twentieth anniversary of the AAS. 9 December 1853. p.193[195], c2.

2868 HENRY C. HOWELLS *to* **n.n. 28 November 1853. Rose Dale, Pa.** Declares the Church devoid of compassion; regrets that he is unable to attend the twentieth anniversary of the AAS. 9 December 1853. p.193[195], c2.

2869 C. M. CLAY *to* **WM. LLOYD GARRISON, W. PHILLIPS, E. QUINCY, AND S. H. GAY. 21 November 1853. Cincinnati, Oh.** Reports that he is unable to attend the twentieth anniversary of the AAS. 9 December 1853. p.193[195], c3.

2870 T. W. HIGGINSON *to* **WENDELL PHILLIPS, EDMUND QUINCY, AND S. H. GAY. 2 December 1853. Worcester, Ma.** Regrets that he is unable to attend the twentieth anniversary of the AAS. 9 December 1853. p.193[195], c3.

2871 WM. G. W. LEWIS *to* **WENDELL PHILLIPS, EDMUND QUINCY, AND S. H. GAY. 29 November 1853. Cincinnati.** Reports that Samuel Lewis is unable to attend the twentieth anniversary of the AAS. 9 December 1853. p.193[195], c4.

2872 GERRIT SMITH *to* **MESSRS. GARRISON, QUINCY, PHILLIPS, AND GAY. n.d. n.p.** Regrets that he is unable to attend the twentieth anniversary of the AAS. 9 December 1853. p.193[195], c4.

2873 E. H. CHAPIN *to* **WM. LLOYD GARRISON, W. PHILLIPS, E. QUINCY, AND S. H. GAY. 24 November 1853. New York.** Reports that he is unable to attend the twentieth anniversary of the AAS. 9 December 1853. p.193[195], c4.

2874 SARAH E. YOUNG *to* **AUTHORITIES OF THE CITY OF LOWELL, MASSA-CHUSETTS, AND CITIZENS. 22 November 1853. Lowell, Ma.** Protests taxation without representation. 9 December 1853. p.193[195], c4.

2875 C. K. W. *to* **H. B. S. n.d. n.p.** Believes that the role of God in human affairs ensures that evil is not eternal. 9 December 1853. p.196, c2.

2876 FREDERICK WM. CHESSON *to* **SIR. [from the** *British Banner***] 29 September 1853. Manchester.** Praises American abolitionists. 16 December 1853. p.195[197], c2.

2877 WILLIAM C. NELL *to* **MR. EDITOR. [from the** *Commonwealth***] November 1853. n.p.** Describes Monsieur Jullien's concerts. 16 December 1853. p.195[197], c4.

2878 ROBERT PURVIS *to* **FRIEND BURLEIGH. [from the** *Pennsylvania Freeman***] 5 November 1853. Byberry, Pa.** Encloses a copy of a letter he wrote to the collector of taxes. 16 December 1853. p.195[197], c5.

2879 ROBERT PURVIS *to* **JOS. J. BUTCHER. [from the** *Pennsylvania Freeman***] 4 November 1853. Byberry, Pa.** A colored citizen refuses to pay the school tax because his children have been excluded from the public schools. 16 December 1853. p.195[197], c5.

2880 ANNA DOUGLASS *to* **W. L. GARRISON. 21 November 1853. Rochester.** Claims that the presence of a certain person in the office of Frederick Douglass does not cause the family unhappiness. 16 December 1853. p.196[198], c5.

2881 WM. C. NELL *to* **n.n. 12 December 1853. Boston.** Refutes editorial comments made about him. 16 December 1853. p.196[198], c5.

2882 H. B. S. *to* **C. K. W. n.d. n.p.** Discusses his belief in the benevolence of God. 16 December 1853. p.198[200], c2.

2883 JAMES HAUGHTON *to* **THOMAS FRANCIS MEAGHER. 15 November 1853. Dublin.** Comments that violence effectively overthrows tyranny. 23 December 1853. p.201, c2.

2884 LORD HOWDEN *to* **F. CORBIN. 14 November 1853. Paris.** Questions rumors of British designs on Cuba. 23 December 1853. p.201, c6.

2885 WILLIAM LLOYD GARRISON *to* **n.n. 30 November 1853. Boston.** Praises the *Liberator*'s free discussion; comments on the Bible. 23 December 1853. p.202, c4.

2886 PARKER PILLSBURY *to* **FRIEND GARRISON. 20 December 1853. Boston.** Dismisses Douglass' claim that Pillsbury did not attend AAS meeting because of his radical views. 23 December 1853. p.203, c1.

2887 HENRY C. WRIGHT *to* **GARRISON. 18 December 1853. Boston.** Dismisses Douglass' charge that Wright declined to attend the AAS meetings at the request of the AAS committee. 23 December 1853. p.203, c1.

2888 W. S. GEORGE *to* **MR. GARRISON. 18 December 1853. Charlestown, Ma.** Discusses diet reforms of hydropathists and vegetarians. 23 December 1853. p.203, c2.

2889 HENRY C. WRIGHT *to* **n.n. 16 December 1853. Boston.** Replies to Douglass' claim that the executive committee of the AAS asked Wright not to attend meetings. 23 December 1853. p.204, c2.

2890 HENRY GREW *to* **FRIEND GARRISON. n.d. n.p.** Affirms the divine authority of the Bible. 23 December 1853. p.204, c2.

2891 S. W. W. *to* **FRIEND GARRISON. n.d. n.p.** Reports on lectures of Antoinette L. Brown and Neale. 23 December 1853. p.204, c4.

2892 J. H. ALLEN *to* **THE EDITOR OF THE** *LIBERATOR.* **14 December 1853. Bangor.** Requests that the *Liberator* publish his letter to the *London Inquirer.* 30 December 1853. p.205, c2.

2893 J. H. ALLEN *to* **THE EDITOR OF THE** *LONDON INQUIRER.* **2 October 1853. Bangor, Me.** Criticizes Mr. Estlin's attack on him; discusses slavery in America. 30 December 1853. p.205, c2.

2894 JOSEPH BARKER *to* **FRIEND. 15 December 1853. Salem, Oh.** Requests donations for Daniel Kauffman. 30 December 1853. p.206, c5.

2895 G. S. F. *to* **FRIEND GARRISON. n.d. n.p.** Reports on anti-slavery activities in Rutland. 30 December 1853. p.206, c5.

2896 P. *to* **FRIEND GARRISON. 7 December 1853. Newburyport.** Reports on Parker Pillsbury's lectures in Newburyport. 30 December 1853. p.207, c6.

2897 HENRY C. WRIGHT *to* **n.n. 16 December 1853. Boston.** Answers to charges that he is an infidel. 30 December 1853. p.208, c2.

[1854]

2898 JAMES HAUGHTON *to* **THE EDITOR OF THE** *NATION.* **3 December 1853. Dublin.** Comments on Thomas Francis Meagher and James O'Callaghan. 6 January 1854. p.1, c4.

2899 MRS. H. B. STOWE *to* **THE COMMITTEE OF THE LADIES NEW AS IN GLASGOW. 18 November 1853. Andover.** Mentions that an account of Miss Miner's school will appear in *Frederick Douglass' Paper*; intends to request that Douglass send an account of the colored convention to the committee. 6 January 1854. p.2, c5.

2900 JAMES BARR AND ROBERT GILLAN *to* **OWNERS AND CONDUCTORS OF THE STEAMBOAT CALLED THE** *EMPEROR.* **11 August 1853. n.p.** Urge owners not to run steamboats on Sundays. 6 January 1854. p.4, c2.

2901 ANDREW PATON *to* **GLASGOW PRESBYTERY, ESTABLISHED CHURCH OF SCOTLAND. 26 August 1853. Glasgow.** States that he will continue to run the steamboat *Emperor* on Sundays. 6 January 1854. p.4, c2.

2902 DAVID *to* **BRO. WALKER. [from the** *American Baptist***] n.d. n.p.** Discusses Northern Baptists' fellowship with Southern slaveholders. 13 January 1854. p.5, c6.

2903 HENRY C. WRIGHT *to* **GARRISON. 8 January 1854. Boston.** Declares that to admit Nebraska as a state would nullify the Missouri Compromise. 13 January 1854. p.7, c2.

2904 N. H. WHITING *to* **FRANCIS JACKSON. 3 January 1854. Marshfield.** Encloses a contribution to the Daniel Drayton Fund. 13 January 1854. p.7, c4.

2905 W. STICKNEY *to* **MR. GARRISON. n.d. n.p.** Believes that reform journals carry on God's work. 13 January 1854. p.8, c2.

2906 LA ROY SUNDERLAND *to* **MR. EDITOR [W. L. GARRISON]. 7 January 1854. n.p.** Denies charge by "Q" that he has seceded from the anti-slavery cause. 20 January 1854. p.9, c3.

2907 JOSEPH BARKER *to* **FRIEND. 27 December 1853. Salem, Oh.** Reports on the formation of an association of liberal people for mutual improvement and social enjoyment; describes lectures and meetings. 20 January 1854. p.9, c4.

2908 GEORGE THOMPSON *to* **THE *BRITISH ANTI-SLAVERY ADVOCATE*. 29 November 1853. Manchester.** Presents his itinerary. 27 January 1854. p.13, c1.

2909 JOSEPH BARKER *to* **MY DEAR FRIEND. [from the *Pennsylvania Freeman*] n.d. n.p.** Relates his disappointment that John Mitchel, the Irish Republican of 1848, turned out to be a despot and a slaveholder. 27 January 1854. p.14, c2.

2910 SAMUEL MAY, JR. *to* **THE EDITOR OF THE *COMMONWEALTH*. 19 January 1854. Franklin Place.** Condemns the slaveholding creed of John Mitchel; denies that Mr. Haughton is a "bore." 27 January 1854. p.14, c2.

2911 SAMUEL J. MAY *to* **GARRISON. 13 January 1854. Syracuse.** Explains his position on political action. 27 January 1854. p.14, c6.

2912 W. C. N. *to* **FRIEND GARRISON. January 1854. Boston.** Reports on a meeting of the Massachusetts State Council of Colored Americans. 27 January 1854. p.15, c2.

2913 ABNER BELCHER *to* **BROTHER GARRISON. 23 January 1854. Wrentham.** Forwards a forty-dollar contribution to the *Liberator*. 27 January 1854. p.15, c3.

2914 JOSEPH BARKER *to* **FRIEND. 25 January 1854. Boston.** Increases his contribution to the Stephen Weakley Fund. 27 January 1854. p.15, c3.

2915 JOHN MITCHEL *to* **REV. HENRY WARD BEECHER. 23 January 1854. Beecher, N.Y.** Refutes comments on Egyptian slavery. 3 February 1854. p.17, c1.

2916 ALEXANDRE HOLINSKI *to* **JOHN MITCHEL. [from the *Evening Post*] n.d. n.p.** States that Mitchel's position on slavery is unchristian. 3 February 1854. p.17, c3.

2917 E. QUINCY *to* **MR. EDITOR [W. L. GARRISON]. n.d. n.p.** Defends his criticism of La Roy Sunderland, which appeared in an article on Goodell's book. 3 February 1854. p.19, c2.

2918 HENRY C. WRIGHT *to* **GARRISON. 23 January 1854. Boston.** States that "it is well" that John Mitchel has revealed his desire to breed and trade slaves. 3 February 1854. p.19, c3.

2919 HENRY WARD BEECHER *to* **JOHN MITCHEL. [from the *New York Independent*] n.d. n.p.** Responds to Mitchel's defense of slavery. 10 February 1854. p.22, c1.

2920 PARKER PILLSBURY *to* **FRIEND GARRISON. 18 January 1854, Liverpool.** Describes the ocean voyage to England and relates his conversations with Canadians on the subject of American slavery. 10 February 1854. p.22, c4.

2921 J. D. McNEELY *to* **MR. GARRISON. 1 February 1854. Hopedale, Oh.** Relates public discussion between Mr. Barker and Mr. Hartzell on the authority of the Bible. 10 February 1854. p.22, c5.

2922 JOSEPH BARKER *to* **THE** *LIBERATOR*. **7 February 1854. Boston.** Replies to letter of Mrs. McNeely and calls Jonas Hartzell "mean, contemptible, selfish, unjust." 10 February 1854. p.22, c5.

2923 HIRAM WILSON *to* **FRIEND GARRISON. 13 January 1854. St. Catharine's, Canada West.** Reports on refugees in Canada. 10 February 1854. p.22, c6.

2924 D. S. GRANDIN *to* **GARRISON. 23 January 1854. Portland.** Comments on the death of Rev. Mr. Pitman. 10 February 1854. p.23, c1.

2925 JOHN MITCHEL *to* **REV. HENRY WARD BEECHER. 7 February 1854. New York.** Believes that slaveholding is not a crime. 17 February 1854. p.25, c1.

2926 C. K. W. *to* **GARRISON. n.d. n.p.** Reports on Henry Ward Beecher's lecture at the Park Street Church. 17 February 1854. p.26, c2.

2927 PARKER PILLSBURY *to* **FRIEND GARRISON. 3 February 1854. Dublin.** Reports on his stay in Dublin and the retirement of James Haughton. 24 February 1854. p.31, c3.

2928 JOSEPH BARKER *to* **FRIEND W. L. GARRISON. 19 February 1854. Boston.** Forwards letter from Mr. Spooner; informs that Spooner opposes both the Free-Soilers and the Nebraska Bill. 24 February 1854. p.31, c3.

2929 LYSANDER SPOONER *to* **THE EDITOR OF THE** *COMMONWEALTH*. **13 February 1854. Boston.** Declares that he is not a member of the Free-Soil Party, as the paper inferred. 24 February 1854. p.31, c3.

2930 JOSEPH BARKER *to* **FRIEND W. L. GARRISON. n.d. n.p.** Reports on lectures by Andrew Jackson Davis. 24 February 1854. p.31, c4.

2931 G. B. STEBBINS *to* **FRIEND GARRISON. 17 February 1854. Rochester, N.Y.** Reports on the aims of the Women's Rights Convention at Albany. 24 February 1854. p.31, c5.

2932 MRS. C. I. H. NICHOLS *to* **n.n. [extract] 20 February 1854. Brattleboro'.** Praises Mrs. Stanton's address at the women's rights convention at Albany. 24 February 1854. p.31, c5.

2933 T. W. HIGGINSON *to* **WILLIAM LLOYD GARRISON. 18 February 1854. n.p.** Corrects a printing error in the section of his sermon referring to Douglass' speech. 24 February 1854. p.31, c5.

2934 LA ROY SUNDERLAND *to* **MR. EDITOR [W. L. GARRISON]. 8 February 1854. Boston.** Criticizes Edmund Quincy's invasion of his privacy. 24 February 1854. p.32, c5.

2935 HENRY C. WRIGHT *to* **GARRISON. 26 February 1854. Boston.** Reports on lectures by Andrew Jackson Davis. 3 March 1854. p.35, c2.

2936 GEORGE S. RAWSON *to* **THE EDITOR OF THE** *LIBERATOR* **[W. L. GARRISON]. n.d. n.p.** Protests the repeal of the Missouri Compromise. 3 March 1854. p.35, c2.

2937 DANIEL MANN *to* **MR. GARRISON. n.d. n.p.** Sympathizes with Mr. Barker in his dispute with Dr. Berg over the Bible. 3 March 1854. p.36, c5.

2938 HENRY C. WRIGHT *to* **GARRISON. 2 March 1854. Boston.** Reports on a lecture by Rev. Edward Beecher at the Tremont Temple. 10 March 1854. p.38, c6.

2939 AN OLD WOMAN *to* **MR. W. L. GARRISON. n.d. n.p.** Discusses the need for abolitionists to take political action. 10 March 1854. p.39, c1.

2940 JANE D. McNEELY *to* **W. L. G. 20 February 1854. Hopedale, Oh.** Comments on debate between Mr. Hartzel and Joseph Barker. 10 March 1854. p.39, c3.

2941 JOHN GORDON *to* **FRIEND GARRISON. 22 February 1854. Salem, Oh.** Defends Joseph Barker against criticism by Jane D. McNeely. 10 March 1854. p.39, c3.

2942 L. O. LEFAVRE *to* **WM. C. WHITCOMB. n.d. n.p.** Asks why, in view of the evils of slavery, Whitcomb feels that one anti-slavery sermon every two or three years is sufficient. 10 March 1854. p.39, c4.

2943 H. KELLY *to* **MR. EDITOR [W. L. GARRISON]. 9 February 1854. New Bedford.** Feels that free discussion is causing a loss of subscribers. 10 March 1854. p.39, c4.

2944 JAMES HAUGHTON *to* **THE EDITOR OF THE** *NATION.* **6 February 1854. 35 Eccles Street.** Denounces the claim of John Mitchel that it is lawful to hold men and women as slaves. 17 March 1854. p.41, c4.

2945 JAMES McMASTER, J. THOMPSON, J. PORTER, S. McELROY, T. MITCH- ELL, J. McCONNELL, R. AIKIN, J. REID, J. MATEER, W. BOSTON, A. WALKER, R. PALMER, J. TAGGART, J. McCLELLAND, J. ROBB, J. SANDERSEN, J. McGILL, T. MATEER, G. BARR, W. CLENDINING, D. GRIER, GEORGE LEECH, R. FLEMMING, J. ROBB, W. C. McMASTER, J. LOWRY, R. CROWTHERS, J. McMASTER, J. ALLEN, H. McGEARY, J. HENON, J. MARSHALL, J. CASSIDY, W. MARSHALL, T. DAVISON, J. THOMPSEN, T. DICKSON, AND W. DICKSON *to* **JOHN MITCHEL. [from the** *New York Tribune***] n.d. n.p.** Criticize Mitchel's pro-slavery views. 17 March 1854. p.43 [42], c1.

2946 SIGNED BY 103 LADIES *to* **STEPHEN A. DOUGLAS. [from the** *Ohio Anti- Slavery Bugle***] 1 March 1854. Alliance.** Send Douglas thirty pieces of silver with the suggestion that he do as Judas did and hang himself. 17 March 1854. p.43 [42], c2.

2947 S. W. W. *to* **BRO. GARRISON. n.d. n.p.** Reports on a Nebraska Bill meeting in Rhode Island. 17 March 1854. p.44 [43], c2.

2948 GEORGE JACOB HOLYOAKE *to* **WM. LLOYD GARRISON. 17 February 1854. London.** Discusses the validity of an anti-slavery address from English Democrats. 17 March 1854. p.44 [43], c2.

2949 W. J. LINTON *to* **THE EDITOR OF THE** *LIBERATOR* **[W. L. GARRISON]. 22 February 1854. Brantwood, Windermere.** Replies to G. J. Holyoake's letter in the *Reasoner* of 19 February. 17 March 1854. p.44 [43], c3.

2950 S. MAY, JR. *to* **MR. GARRISON. n.d. n.p.** Encloses letters sent to May which included donations in aid of Stephen F. Weakly of Pennsylvania. 17 March 1854. p.44 [43], c4.

2951 A FRIEND *to* **SAMUEL MAY, JR. [extract] n.d. New Bedford.** Encloses donation for Stephen F. Weakly. 17 March 1854. p.44 [43], c4.

2952 G. R. RUSSELL *to* **S. MAY, JR. 22 February 1854. Jamaica Plain.** Sends donation for Stephen F. Weakly. 17 March 1854. p.44 [43], c4.

2953 WARREN DELANO *to* **SAMUEL MAY, JR. 27 February 1854. Fair Haven.** Sends donation for Stephen F. Weakly. 17 March 1854. p.44 [43], c4.

2954 N. H. WHITING *to* **FRIEND MAY. 5 March 1854. Marshfield.** Sends donation for Stephen F. Weakly. 17 March 1854. p.44 [43], c4.

2955 J. P. BLANCHARD *to* **REV. SAMUEL MAY. 6 March 1854. Boston.** Sends donation for Stephen F. Weakly. 17 March 1854. p.44 [43], c4.

2956 M. *to* **W. L. GARRISON. n.d. n.p.** Reports that Mr. Chesson withdrew from the Manchester Anti-Slavery Union because Rev. F. Hemming was elected as its agent. 17 March 1854. p.44 [43], c4.

2957 VERA CATHOLICA *to* **MR. EDITOR [W. L. GARRISON]. n.d. n.p.** Refutes Lucy Stone's opinion that the Bible may contain things abhorrent to God and the truth. 17 March 1854. p.44, c2.

2958 M. HIGGINS *to* **MR. GARRISON. n.d. n.p.** Reports on the fraudulent medical practices of La Roy Sunderland. 17 March 1854. p.44, c2.

2959 E. SPRAGUE *to* **FRIEND GARRISON. 3 March 1854. Abington.** Reports on the death and funeral of Abraham Randall. 17 March 1854. p.44, c3.

2960 M. *to* **THE EDITOR OF THE *LIBERATOR* [W. L. GARRISON]. n.d. n.p.** Believes that Bible should be left out of anti-slavery debates. 17 March 1854. p.44, c3.

2961 N. H. WHITING *to* **FRIEND. 12 March 1854. Marshfield.** Predicts that the Nebraska Bill will be passed. 24 March 1854. p.47, c1.

2962 S. W. W. *to* **BRO. GARRISON. n.d. n.p.** Reports on a Nebraska Bill meeting in Providence, R. I. 24 March 1854. p.47, c1.

2963 PENTUCKET *to* **MR. GARRISON. 13 March 1854. Haverhill.** Reports on C. C. Burleigh's speech. 24 March 1854. p.47, c2.

2964 REV. E. A. STOCKMAN *to* **MR. MAY. [extract] 10 February 1854. Cummington.** Concludes that there is no hope for the slave under the present Constitution. 24 March 1854. p.47, c2.

2965 T. W. H. *to* **MR. GARRISON. 22 March 1854. Worcester.** Recommends Mrs. Emma R. Coe's lectures. 24 March 1854. p.47, c3.

2966 ONE OF THE NEW ENGLAND CLERGY *to* **THE EDITORS OF THE *BOSTON POST*. n.d. n.p.** Explains his refusal to protest against the Nebraska Bill. 31 March 1854. p.49, c2.

2967 W. S. F. *to* **THE EDITOR OF THE *LIBERATOR* [W. L. GARRISON]. n.d. n.p.** Blames problems related to recent compromises on the fact that the Constitution itself is a compromise. 31 March 1854. p.49, c2.

2968 L. HOLMES *to* **MR. GARRISON. 27 March 1854. n.p.** Questions the authorship of the article entitled, "Climax of Insolence." 31 March 1854. p.50, c4.

2969 A. J. GROVER *to* **MR. GARRISON. 3 March 1854. Earlville, Il.** Reports on slavery in Illinois. 31 March 1854. p.50, c5.

2970 LA ROY SUNDERLAND *to* **FRIEND GARRISON. n.d. Boston.** Refutes Mr. Higgins' charge of fraud. 31 March 1854. p.51, c2.

2971 GERRIT SMITH *to* **FREDERICK DOUGLASS. 6 March 1854. Washington.** Explains that he voted against the Homestead Bill because it applied only to white people. 31 March 1854. p.52, c6.

2972 A CLERGYMAN *to* **THE EDITORS OF THE** *JOURNAL OF COMMERCE.* **n.d. n.p.** Discusses the Nebraska Bill. 7 April 1854. p.53, c1.

2973 HIRAM CORLISS *to* **FRIEND GARRISON. 17 March 1854. Union Village.** Reports that Douglass lectured in Union Village, Galeville, Lakeville, Shushan, Cambridge, and Easton. 7 April 1854. p.55, c2.

2974 JOHN L. LORD *to* **FRIEND GARRISON. 16 March 1854. Newburyport.** Reports on A. T. Foss' lectures. 7 April 1854. p.55, c3.

2975 D. MANN *to* **MR. GARRISON. n.d. n.p.** Corrects a translation of St. Paul's injunction, "If thou be able to become free, take advantage of it." 7 April 1854. p.55, c3.

2976 JOHN G. WHITTIER *to* **FRIEND GARRISON. 12 April 1854. Amesbury.** Encloses money for Stephen Weakly. 7 April 1854. p.55, c4.

2977 SARAH ERNST, ANDREW ERNST, JULIA HARWOOD, EDWARD HARWOOD, CHRISTIAN DONALDSON, ELIZABETH COLEMAN, MARY MANN, MARY DEGRAW, JOHN JOLIFFE, H. P. BLACKWELL, MARY GUILD, AND N. M. GUILD *to* **THE FRIENDS OF IMPARTIAL FREEDOM. n.d. n.p.** Announce an antislavery convention to be held in Cincinnati, Ohio. 7 April 1854. p.55, c5.

2978 JAMES McCUNE SMITH *to* **MR. EDITOR. [from** *Frederick Douglass' Paper***] 3 April 1854. New York.** Reports that the Mechanic's Institute in New York does not teach mechanical trades. 14 April 1854. p.58, c2.

2979 n.n. *to* **MR. EDITOR [W. L. GARRISON]. 27 March 1854. Windsor, Vt.** Explains the unfavorable reaction in Vermont to the Nebraska Bill. 14 April 1854. p.59, c1.

2980 SUSAN B. ANTHONY *to* **MR. GARRISON. April 1854. Baltimore.** Observes little interest in reform in Maryland. 14 April 1854. p.59, c3.

2981 ANGELINA J. KNOX *to* **SENATOR DOUGLAS. 31 March 1854. Boston.** Calls Douglas a traitor; responds to his desire to become president with the declaration that "pigmies are pigmies still though perched on Alps." 14 April 1854. p.60, c2.

2982 REV. E. A. STOCKMAN *to* **n.n. [extract] 11 March 1854. Cummington.** Affirms his loyalty to the Massachusetts AS, despite disagreements with the society. 14 April 1854. p.60, c3.

2983 REV. EDMUND KELL *to* **n.n. [extract] 19 January 1854. Southampton, England.** Writes to a friend in America on his sermon condemning American slavery. 14 April 1854. p.60, c3.

2984 JOSE GREGORIO MONAGAS *to* **GENTLEMEN OF THE HOUSE OF REPRESENTATIVES. n.d. n.p.** Discusses abolition of slavery in Venezuela. 21 April 1854. p.62, c2.

2985 MONTAGUE BRATTELL *to* **MARIUS. 14 April 1854. New Lyme.** Reports the death of James W. Walker. 21 April 1854. p.63, c2.

2986 E. HALE *to* **FRIEND GARRISON. 12 April 1854. Madison, Oh.** Preaches practical Christianity; criticizes Henry Ward Beecher for predicting that the names of reformers will be glorified in the after life, instead of the present. 21 April 1854. p.64, c2.

2987 HENRY C. WRIGHT *to* **GARRISON. 9 April 1854. Newburgh, Oh.** Gives an account of Shaker worship; laments the death of James. W. Walker. 21 April 1854. p.64, c4.

2988 R. P. *to* **FRIEND GARRISON. 9 April 1854. Newburyport.** Relates George Colby's order for the free use of city hall. 21 April 1854. p.64, c4.

2989 M. RYAN, J. G. DE RUSSEY, F. H. HATCH. GEO. McWHORTER, AND D. CORCORAN *to* **MR. JOHN MITCHEL, EDITOR OF THE** *CITIZEN.* **30 March 1854. Baton Rouge, La.** Invite him to visit Louisiana on behalf of its citizens. 28 April 1854. p.65, c1.

2990 JOHN MITCHEL *to* **JOINT COMMITTEE OF THE SENATE AND HOUSE OF REPRESENTATIVES OF LOUISIANA. 17 April 1854. New York.** Accepts their invitation to visit Louisiana. 28 April 1854. p.65, c1.

2991 N. P. TALLMADGE *to* **MESSRS. GALES AND SEATON. [from the** *National Intelligencer***] 18 April 1854. Washington.** Supports a scientific investigation of spiritual manifestations. 28 April 1854. p.66, c1.

2992 G. M. BESWICK, I. H. JAMISON, S. DYER, AND T. A. MILLS *to* **MINISTERS AND CHURCHES OF INDIANA AND GEORGIA. 9 January 1854. Indianapolis.** Advocate freedom for John Freeman. 28 April 1854. p.66, c3.

2993 PARKER PILLSBURY *to* **PHILLIPS. 4 April 1854. Bristol, England.** Reports on his ill health, his dismal reception in London, and his warm reception in Dublin. 28 April 1854. p.66, c6.

2994 HENRY C. WRIGHT *to* **GARRISON. 8 April 1854. Cleveland, Oh.** Contrasts religion of ''facts'' with religion of ''form.'' 28 April 1854. p.67, c1.

2995 M. *to* **THE EDITOR OF THE** *LIBERATOR* **[W. L. GARRISON]. n.d. n.p.** Believes the Bible is merely a cultural instrument; denies that it is anti-slavery. 28 April 1854. p.67, c2.

2996 T. W. H. *to* **MR. EDITOR. [from the** *Commonwealth***] 12 April 1854. Worcester.** Discusses the African school as an option for colored students. 28 April 1854. p.67, c3.

2997 J. W. LOGUEN *to* **FRIEND. 28 April 1854. Syracuse.** A fugitive slave praises the *Liberator.* 5 May 1854. p.71, c3.

2998 FEMALE PETITIONER *to* **HOUSE COMMITTEE OF THE NEW JERSEY LEGISLATURE. n.d. n.p.** Declares that laws discriminating against women are unjust and should be repealed. 5 May 1854. p.72, c4.

2999 EDWARD SEARCH *to* **GARRISON. 21 April 1854. London.** Derides the politics of John Mitchel; reveals the desire of the aristocracy for war. 12 May 1854. p.75, c1.

3000 JOSEPH BARKER *to* **FRIEND. n.d. n.p.** Delivers a farewell epistle. 12 May 1854. p.75, c2.

3001 D. M. *to* **MR. GARRISON. n.d. n.p.** Corrects correspondent M.'s interpretation of Scripture. 12 May 1854. p.75, c3.

3002 GERRIT SMITH *to* **S. M. BOOTH. [from the** *Free Democrat***] 23 March 1854. Washington.** Requests that Booth choose jail over bail for his participation in the Glover rescue. 12 May 1854. p.76, c5.

3003 S. P. CHASE *to* **SIR. [from the** *Free Democrat***] 31 March 1854. Washington.** Asserts that the Fugitive Slave Act is as intolerable as the Alien and Sedition Acts or Stamp Act. 12 May 1854. p.76, c5.

3004 B. S. J. *to* **n.n. [from the** *Pennsylvania Freeman***] n.d. n.p.** Gives brief biographical sketch of James W. Walker. 19 May 1854. p.77, c3.

3005 WORCESTER *to* **MR. GARRISON. n.d. n.p.** Cautions that Charles Devens, Jr., a slave-catcher, has just opened a law office in Worcester. 19 May 1854. p.79, c6.

3006 HIRAM WILSON *to* **WM. LLOYD GARRISON. 5 May 1854. St. Catharines, Canada West.** Encourages fugitive slaves to come to Canada. 19 May 1854. p.80, c5.

3007 A. K. FOSTER *to* **FRIEND. 25 April 1854. Wolcott's Mills, In.** Comments on the death of James W. Walker. 26 May 1854. p.82, c2.

3008 JOSEPHINE BROWN *to* **MR. MAY. 27 April 1854. East Plumstead School, Plumstead, Woolwich.** Reports a lack of color consciousness in Europe. 26 May 1854. p.82, c6.

3009 HENRY C. WRIGHT *to* **GARRISON. 3 May 1854. Cleveland, Oh.** Discusses the refusal of the Ohio legislature to discuss the Nebraska Bill. 26 May 1854. p.83, c1.

3010 EDWARD SEARCH *to* **GARRISON. 28 April 1854. London.** Discusses the English aristocracy and their desire for war with Russia. 26 May 1854. p.83, c2.

3011 DORVELAS DORVAL *to* **SIR AND FRIEND. 25 August 1853. Gonaives, Hayti.** Reports on hostility between Haitians and Dominicans. 26 May 1854. p.83, c3.

3012 D. A. W. *to* **MR. GARRISON. 20 May 1854. Groveland.** Comments on Professor Agassiz and his book on slavery. 26 May 1854. p.83, c3.

3013 THE PEOPLE *to* **FELLOW "BLOOD HOUNDS." 28 April 1854. n.p.** Protest murder of W. H. G. Butler by Matt. F. Ward; announce meeting to vindicate verdict of the Hardin County jury. 26 May 1854. p.84, c4.

3014 NOBLE BUTLER *to* **THE PEOPLE OF LOUISVILLE. 29 April 1854. n.p.** Appeals to the people of Louisville to stop the violence. 26 May 1854. p.84, c4.

3015 SAMUEL MAY, JR. *to* **MR. GARRISON. n.d. n.p.** Contradicts the report of the New York anti-slavery meeting. 2 June 1854. p.87, c5.

3016 D. A. W. *to* **MR. EDITOR [W. L. GARRISON]. 19 May 1854. Groveland.** Reviews *Types of Mankind* by J. C. Nott and George R. Gliddon. 2 June 1854. p.88, c4.

3017 DORVELAS DORVAL *to* **WM. LLOYD GARRISON. 20 April 1854. Gonaives, Hayti.** Discusses the precarious state of the government in Haiti. 2 June 1854. p.88, c5.

3018 A RETIRED OFFICER OF H. B. M. INF'TRY SERVICE *to* **THE EDITOR OF THE** *LIBERATOR* **[W. L. GARRISON]. 18 May 1854. Boston.** Objects to Americans discussing British affairs. 2 June 1854. p.88, c5.

3019 n.n. *to* **JAMES GORDON BENNETT. [from Bennett's** *Herald***] 11 May 1854. New York.** Protests against lease of Mr. Chapin's church to "such an outrageous rabble." 9 June 1854. p.89, c1.

3020 G. *to* **MESSRS. EDITORS. [from the** *Journal of Commerce***] n.d. n.p.** Protests the power of Protestant popes. 9 June 1854. p.89, c1.

3021 H. W. ALLEN *to* **THE EDITORS OF THE** *BOSTON POST***. 2 June 1854. Boston.** Comments on the trial of Anthony Burns, fugitive slave. 9 June 1854. p.89, c6.

3022 JOSEPH K. HAYES *to* **THE MAYOR OF BOSTON. 2 June 1854. Boston.** Resigns his office because he refuses to enforce the Fugitive Slave Law. 9 June 1854. p.90, c6.

3023 WATSON FREEMAN *to* **THE PRESIDENT OF THE UNITED STATES. 27 May 1854. Boston.** A United States marshal recounts an attack made upon the courthouse in an attempt to rescue a fugitive slave. 9 June 1854. p.91, c5.

3024 FRANKLIN PIERCE *to* **WATSON FREEMAN. 27 May 1854. Washington.** Approves of Freeman's conduct in enforcing the Fugitive Slave Law. 9 June 1854. p.91, c5.

3025 SIDNEY WEBSTER *to* **B. F. HALLETT. 30 May 1854. Washington.** Inquires about the status of the Burns case. 9 June 1854. p.91, c5.

3026 B. F. HALLETT *to* **SIDNEY WEBSTER. 30 May 1854. Boston.** Discusses the necessity of using arms during the course of the Burns trial. 9 June 1854. p.91, c5.

3027 FRANKLIN PIERCE *to* **B. F. HALLETT. 31 May 1854. Washington.** Urges the use of any military force necessary to execute the law. 9 June 1854. p.91, c5.

3028 B. F. HALLETT *to* **SIDNEY WEBSTER. 31 May 1854. Boston.** States that the mayor will preserve the peace during the Burns case. 9 June 1854. p.91, c5.

3029 B. F. HALLETT *to* **SIDNEY WEBSTER. 2 June 1854. Boston.** Reports that "law reigns" and that the fugitive in the Burns case is being extradicted to the federal authorities. 9 June 1854. p.91, c5.

3030 JOHN G. WHITTIER *to* **WM. LLOYD GARRISON. 3 June 1854. Amesbury.** Renews subscription to the *Liberator*. 9 June 1854. p.91, c6.

3031 M. T. E. *to* **GARRISON. 27 May 1854. Indianapolis.** Reports on a convention of the "Old line Democratic Robinsonians." 9 June 1854. p.92, c3.

3032 THOMAS SWENEY *to* **THE EDITOR OF THE** *HERALD***. 29 May 1854. Boston.** The publisher of the *American Celt* asserts that Irish adopted citizens will not oppose Fugitive Slave Law. 16 June 1854. p.93, c3.

3033 AN ARTILLERIST *to* **THE EDITOR OF THE** *HERALD***. 1 June 1854. Boston.** Refutes statement that "U.S. troops will run away on the appearance of a few thousand abolitionists." 16 June 1854. p.93, c3.

3034 EDMUND QUINCY *to* **SIR. 3 June 1854. Dedham.** Discusses the resolution of the New England AS Convention concerning Anthony Burns. 16 June 1854. p.94, c5.

3035 RICHARD H. DANA, JR. *to* **EDMUND QUINCY. 5 June 1854. Boston.** Replies to the New England AS Convention resolutions concerning Anthony Burns. 16 June 1854. p.94, c5.

3036 C. M. ELLIS *to* **n.n. 5 June 1854. Boston.** Replies to the New England AS Convention resolutions concerning Anthony Burns. 16 June 1854. p.94, c5.

3037 N. H. WHITING *to* **EMORY WASHBURN, GOVERNOR OF MASSA-CHUSETTS. 4 June 1854. Marshfield.** Resigns his commission as justice of the peace in protest of the Burns case. 16 June 1854. p.94, c6.

3038 LORING MOODY *to* **THE FRIENDS OF FREEDOM. n.d. n.p.** Proposes to become an anti-slavery lecturer. 16 June 1854. p.95, c5.

3039 BENJAMIN PRATT *to* **THE EDITOR OF THE** *LIBERATOR* **[W. L. GARRISON]. 4 June 1854. Northampton, Ma.** Argues support of non political action. 16 June 1854. p.96, c4.

3040 GEORGE T. CURTIS *to* **THE EDITOR OF THE** *NEW BEDFORD MERCURY***. 7 June 1854. Boston.** Replies to those who criticized him for upholding Fugitive Slave Law. 23 June 1854. p.97, c2.

3041 WENDELL PHILLIPS *to* **R. H. DANA, JR. 14 June 1854. n.p.** Offers thanks on behalf of the Vigilance Committee of Boston for Dana's defense of Burns. 23 June 1854. p.98, c3.

3042 RICHARD H. DANA, JR. *to* **WENDELL PHILLIPS, ESQ. 15 June 1854. n.p.** Replies to letter of commendation from the Vigilance Committee of Boston. 23 June 1854. p.98, c3.

3043 C. M. ELLIS *to* **MR. PHILLIPS. 15 June 1854. n.p.** Replies to letter of commendation from the Vigilance Committee of Boston. 23 June 1854. p.98, c3.

3044 MR. PILLSBURY *to* **MR. MAY. [extract] 2 June 1854. Liverpool.** Describes the anniversary of the British and Foreign AS; and a fugitive slave. 23 June 1854. p.99, c1.

3045 WATCHMAN *to* **FRIEND GARRISON. 17 June 1854. New Bedford.** Reports on a meeting to discuss the Nebraska Bill; encloses resolution. 23 June 1854. p.99, c2.

3046 A. T. FOSS *to* **FRIEND GARRISON. 13 June 1854. Manchester.** Relates discussion of slavery at the Congregational Conference of Ministers. 23 June 1854. p.99, c3.

3047 A. K. FOSTER *to* **FRIEND. 5 June 1854. Worcester.** Encloses letter from C. F. Putnam on activities of Sallie Holley. 23 June 1854. p.99, c3.

3048 C. F. PUTNAM *to* **MRS. FOSTER. 29 May 1854. Farmersville, N.Y.** Reports on the ten-day speaking tour of Miss Holley. 23 June 1854. p.99, c3.

3049 JAMES NOWELL *to* **BROTHER GARRISON. 2 June 1854. Portsmouth.** Forwards donation of one hundred dollars to the Massachusetts AS. 23 June 1854. p.99, c3.

3050 JOSEPH BARKER *to* **FRIEND. 25 May 1854. Betley, England.** Describes his travels. 23 June 1854. p.100, c4.

3051 GEORGE T. CURTIS *to* **THE EDITOR OF THE** *NEW BEDFORD MERCURY***. 14 June 1854. Boston.** Believes that one must execute the law, even the Fugitive Slave Law. 30 June 1854. p.101, c2.

3052 R. L. CURTIS, E. D. CHENEY, S. H. WILLARD, AND JULIE TAFT *to* **JOSEPH K. HAYES. 11 June 1854. Boston.** Send money as a token of their respect. 30 June 1854. p.103 [102], c5.

3053 H. B. STOWE *to* **MR. HAYES. 6 June 1854. Boston.** Presents Hayes with a copy of *Uncle Tom's Cabin*. 30 June 1854. p.103 [102], c5.

3054 CHAS. G. DAVIS *to* **JOSEPH K. HAYES. 17 June 1854. Plymouth.** Praises Hayes' refusal to execute the Fugitive Slave Law. 30 June 1854. p.103 [102], c5.

3055 PARKER PILLSBURY *to* **FRIEND GARRISON. June 1854. Ambleside.** Laments the callousness of the North toward anti-slavery. 30 June 1854. p.103, c1.

3056 HENRY C. WRIGHT *to* **GARRISON. 21 June 1854. Norristown, Pa.** Advocates resistance to the Fugitive Slave Law. 30 June 1854. p.103, c2.

3057 W. STICKNEY *to* **GARRISON. 14 June 1854. Canastota, N. Y.** Likens the "crucifixion" of Anthony Burns to that of Christ. 30 June 1854. p.103, c3.

3058 VERA CATHOLICA *to* **SIR. n.d. n.p.** Grieves at statement by H. C. Wright that children should not be told that God made them. 30 June 1854. p.104, c5.

3059 G. M. *to* **MR. EDITOR [W. L. GARRISON]. 21 June 1854. Concord, N.H.** Reports on the formation of the State Teachers Association. 30 June 1854. p.104. c5.

3060 M. *to* **W. L. GARRISON. 21 June 1854. Manchester, N. H.** Gives account of Mrs. Coe's lecture on reform. 30 June 1854. p.104, c5.

3061 GERRIT SMITH *to* **CONSTITUENTS. 27 June 1854. Washington.** Relates his decision to resign from Congress. 7 July 1854. p.106, c1.

3062 AN ABOLITIONIST *to* **GARRISON. 5 July 1854. Boston.** An abolitionist contributes fifty dollars to the widow of James W. Walker. 7 July 1854. p.107, c1.

3063 AMICUS *to* **MR. EDITOR [W. L. GARRISON]. n.d. n.p.** Condemns pro-slavery newspapers for rejoicing that the Fugitive Slave Law was enforced in Boston. 7 July 1854. p.107, c3.

3064 JOSEPH BARKER *to* **FRIEND. 9 July 1854. Betley, England.** Describes the English view of war with Russia as a struggle for civilization. 7 July 1854. p.108, c2.

3065 E. W. TWING *to* **FRIEND GARRISON. June 1854. Springfield.** Requests publication of article rejected by the *Portland Pleasure Boat*. 7 July 1854. p.108, c4.

3066 G. W. P. *to* **MR. GARRISON. 25 June 1854. Lynn.** Praises the colored people of Boston for their support of Burns. 7 July 1854. p.108, c5.

3067 L. BURNHAM *to* **THE EDITOR OF THE** *LIBERATOR***. 26 June 1854. Holden.** Compliments Anne E. Ruggles' lecture on temperance. 7 July 1854. p.108, c5.

3068 '76 *to* **FRIEND GARRISON. 28 May 1854. Stoughton.** Asks by what authority the President keeps troops in the streets of Boston. 7 July 1854. p.108, c5.

3069 COL. CHAS. F. SUTTLE *to* **THE EDITOR OF THE** *ALEXANDRIA GAZETTE***. 3 July 1854. Alexandria.** Criticizes Mayor Smith of Boston. 14 July 1854. p.110, c5.

3070 PARKER PILLSBURY *to* **FRIEND GARRISON. 21 June 1854. Liverpool.** Relates that Britain is at war with Russia; discusses his illness. 14 July 1854. p.111, c2.

3071 WM. ENDICOTT *to* **MR. EDITOR [W. L. GARRISON]. 18 June 1854. Danvers.** Discusses the specious abolitionism of the Third Congregational Society. 14 July 1854. p.111, c2.

3072 JOHN G. WHITTIER *to* **SAMUEL E. SEWALL. 2 July 1854. Amesbury.** Encloses donation to the Boston Vigilance Committee. 14 July 1854. p.111, c2.

3073 ALL WILBRAHAM *to* **MR. EDITOR [W. L. GARRISON]. 15 June. North Wilbraham.** Reports that Ben Hallet was hanged in effigy. 14 July 1854. p.111, c3.

3074 WARREN BURTON *to* **MR. GARRISON. 6 July 1854. Cambridgeport.** Corrects a misinterpretation of his statement on women and educational reform. 14 July 1854. p.111, c3.

3075 JOSEPH BARKER *to* **FRIEND. June 1854. Betley, England.** Describes the countryside of England. 14 July 1854. p.112, c2.

3076 L. KOSSUTH *to* **G. N. SANDERS. 3 June 1854. London.** Censures foreign interference in the domestic affairs of any nation. 21 July 1854. p.113, c3.

3077 THE GERMAN RADICALS *to* **MR. EDITOR. [from the** *Commonwealth***] n.d. n.p.** Denounce Kossuth for his stance on slavery. 21 July 1854. p.113, c3.

3078 F. W. CHESSON *to* **THE EDITOR OF THE** *ANTI-SLAVERY ADVOCATE.* **17 May 1854. Manchester.** Forwards letter from Mazzini to Dr. Beard. 21 July 1854. p.113, c3.

3079 JOSEPH MAZZINI *to* **REV. DR. BEARD. n.d. n.p.** Regrets he is unable to attend a North of England AA meeting. 21 July 1854. p.113, c4.

3080 JAMES HAUGHTON *to* **THE EDITOR OF THE** *DUBLIN NATION.* **8 May 1854. 35 Eccles Street.** Criticizes Messrs. Mitchel and Meagher for retarding the cause of liberty in Ireland. 21 July 1854. p.113, c6.

3081 S. ALFRED STEINTHAL *to* **REV. SAMUEL MAY, JR. 28 June 1854. Bridgewater, England.** Regrets the sad outcome of the Burns case. 21 July 1854. p.114, c6.

3082 S. B. *to* **FRIEND GARRISON. 1 July 1854. Nashua.** Relates facts concerning the closing of the city hall to Mrs. Coe's lectures. 21 July 1854. p.115, c4.

3083 EDWARD BAINES *to* **THE EDITORS OF NEWSPAPERS IN BOSTON. 1 July 1854. Massachusetts.** Claims that all of Britain detests American slavery; comments on Anthony Burns. 28 July 1854. p.117, c3.

3084 SEN. S. P. CHASE *to* **KOSSUTH. 26 July 1854. Washington.** Regrets Sanders' charge that Kossuth is indifferent to slavery. 28 July 1854. p.118, c3.

3085 PARKER PILLSBURY *to* **FRIEND GARRISON. 8 July 1854. Dublin.** Contrasts American government and British government; states that the British detest slavery. 28 July 1854. p.119, c1.

3086 RICHARD D. WEBB *to* **GARRISON. 7 July 1854. Dublin.** Comments on Pillsbury's health. 28 July 1854. p.119, c2.

3087 FREDERICK HAZELTINE *to* **FRIEND GARRISON. 18 July 1854. Littleton, N.H.** Eulogizes Ivah P. Bullard, a female abolitionist. 28 July 1854. p.119, c6.

3088 JOHN BALL, JR. *to* **WILLIAM LLOYD GARRISON. 20 July 1854. Iowa.** Forwards letters written while travelling through the South. 4 August 1854. p.123, c2.

3089 J. B. *to* **PARENTS AND FRIENDS. 30 March 1854. Richmond, Va.** Describes his journey to Charleston and a slave auction he witnessed there. 4 August 1854. p.123, c2.

3090 L. F. WALDO *to* **SAMUEL MAY, JR. 26 June 1854. North Brookfield.** Encloses resolutions adopted at the Brookfield Conference of Churches. 4 August 1854. p.123, c3.

3091 n.n. *to* **FRIEND GARRISON. 15 July 1854. Marlboro, N. H.** Corrects errors in the report of proceedings of the New Hampshire legislature. 4 August 1854. p.123, c4.

3092 GERRIT SMITH *to* **GARRISON. 28 July 1854. House of Representatives.** States that Congress is not becoming any more sympathetic to Garrison. 4 August 1854. p.123, c4.

3093 SAMUEL HENRY *to* **BROTHER GARRISON. 18 July 1854. Thorndike.** Expresses sympathy for abolitionists. 4 August 1854. p.123, c4.

3094 WM. H. FISH *to* **MR. GARRISON. 17 July 1854. Hopedale.** Reports on anti-slavery meetings in Worcester County. 4 August 1854. p.124, c2.

3095 A. H. W. *to* **FRIEND GARRISON. 12 July 1854. Pepperell, Ma.** Reports on Henry C. Wright's speech in Pepperell. 4 August 1854. p.124, c3.

3096 L. L. R. *to* **FRIEND GARRISON. 23 July 1854. Weymouth, Oh.** Declares that Americans worship a "cotton God." 4 August 1854. p.124, c4.

3097 D. S. GRANDIN *to* **GARRISON. 22 July 1854. Portland.** States that the Irish enjoy freedom in their own person and the privilege of oppressing others. 4 August 1854. p.124, c4.

3098 FRED W. CHESSON *to* **THE EDITOR OF THE *LONDON DAILY NEWS*. 2 July 1854. Manchester.** Discusses correspondence between G. N. Sanders and Mazzini. 11 August 1854. p.125, c6.

3099 H. W. BEECHER *to* **n.n. 13 July 1854. Brooklyn.** Regrets he is unable to attend the First of August celebration. 11 August 1854. p.127, c1.

3100 O. B. FROTHINGHAM *to* **FRANCIS JACKSON, WM. LLOYD GARRISON, AND SAMUEL MAY, JR. 15 July 1854. Salem.** Regrets he may not be able to attend the First of August celebration. 11 August 1854. p.127, c1.

3101 SAMUEL JOHNSON *to* **n.n. 15 July 1854. Salem.** Regrets he is unable to attend the First of August celebration. 11 August 1854. p.127, c1.

3102 HENRY C. WRIGHT *to* **GARRISON. 1 August 1854. Hopedale.** Describes the First of August celebration in Hopedale. 11 August 1854. p.127, c2.

3103 JOHN BALL, JR. *to* **WILLIAM LLOYD GARRISON. 1 April 1854. Wilmington, N.C.** Reports that colored citizens of Virginia hold little esteem for the North. 11 August 1854. p.128, c2.

3104 DANIEL WRIGHT *to* **n.n. 28 July 1854. Auburn, N.Y.** Reports on a settlement in Kansas; encloses five dollars. 11 August 1854. p.128, c4.

3105 n.n. *to* **THE EDITORS OF THE *JOURNAL OF COMMERCE*. 20 July 1854. Edgefield, S.C.** Describes the injurious effects of abolitionism. 18 August 1854. p.129, c1.

3106 SALLIE HOLLEY *to* **FRANCIS JACKSON. 29 July 1854. Wellsville, N.Y.** Relates an argument between an anti-slavery lawyer and Mr. Smith, the pro-slavery author of *Uncle Tom's Cabin As It Is*; describes her anti-slavery tour. 18 August 1854. p.129, c2.

3107 AN ABOLITIONIST *to* **MR. EDITOR [W. L. GARRISON]. 15 July 1854. Lynn.** Believes that purchasing slave produce is not immoral. 18 August 1854. p.129, c3.

3108 SIGNED BY SEVENTY-ONE LADIES *to* **JOSEPH K. HAYES. 10 June 1854. Herron.** Express admiration for his conduct concerning Anthony Burns. 18 August 1854. p.129, c5.

3109 JOSEPH K. HAYES *to* **E. BEARCE FOR SEVENTY OTHERS. 20 June 1854. Boston.** Thanks the ladies for their expression of admiration. 18 August 1854. p.129, c5.

3110 O. *to* **MR. HARRIS. [from the *Rhode Island Freeman*] 1854. Eastport, Me.** Censures Southern insolence and Northern cowardice during the search for a fugitive slave. 18 August 1854. p.130, c2.

3111 JONATHAN WALKER *to* **FRIEND GARRISON. 6 July 1854. Winouski, Wi.** Praises C. C. Burleigh's lectures. 18 August 1854. p.131, c4.

3112 DANIEL FOSTER *to* **MR. GARRISON. 8 August 1854. East Princeton.** Testifies to the integrity of Rev. Thomas H. Jones, a fugitive slave. 18 August 1854. p.131, c4.

3113 JOSEPH BARKER *to* **n.n. June 1854. Betley, England.** Describes Club Day, an English festival at Audlem. 18 August 1854. p.132, c2.

3114 C. M. STRAUB *to* **THE EDITORS OF THE *WASHINGTON SENTINEL*. 31 July 1854. Washington.** Reports that he voted against the repeal of the Fugitive Slave Law. 25 August 1854. p.133, c1.

3115 W. FARMER *to* **n.n. 3 August 1854. Manchester, England.** Reports on the West Indies Emancipation celebration in Manchester. 25 August 1854. p.135, c1.

3116 S. OXON *to* **MR. CHESSEN. 3 August 1854. Near Llandoff.** The Lord Bishop of Oxford answers inquiries about the West India Colonies, trade in slave-grown sugar, and his opinion of the abolitionists in America. 18 August 1854. p.135, c2.

3117 JOSEPH BARKER *to* **FRIEND. June 1854. Betley, England.** Reports on anti-slavery lectures in England. 25 August 1854. p.136, c2.

3118 WM. C. WHITCOMB *to* **n.n. 10 August 1854. Stoneham.** Corrects a printing error. 25 August 1854. p.136, c3.

3119 J. NOYES *to* **FRIEND GARRISON. 6 August 1854. Abington.** Censures the editor of the *Plymouth Rock* as an "ambitious politician." 25 August 1854. p.136, c4.

3120 REES E. PRICE *to* **FRIEND GARRISON. 5 August 1854. Mount Zion, Oh.** Praises Gerrit Smith's lecture on the federal Constitution. 25 August 1854. p.136, c4.

3121 W. FARMER *to* **SIR. [continued from 25 August 1854] 5 August 1854. Manchester, England.** Reports on the Manchester conference and anti-slavery meeting. 1 September 1854. p.138, c6.

3122 SAMUEL JOHNSON *to* **WM. L. GARRISON. 24 August 1854. Salem.** Explains a section of a letter he sent to the anti-slavery meeting of Abington. 1 September 1854. p.139, c3.

3123 HENRY C. WRIGHT *to* **FRIEND GARRISON. 19 August 1854. Salem, Oh.** Praises J. R. Giddings' compromise with the Whigs; condemns the Fugitive Slave Law. 1 September 1854. p.139, c4.

3124 JOHN BALL, JR. *to* **n.n. 14 April 1854. Charleston Hotel, S.C.** Relates conversations with slaves near Richmond and Wilmington. 1 September 1854. p.140, c2.

3125 MR. WENTWORTH *to* **n.n. [from the** *Chicago Democrat***] 10 August 1854. Washington.** Reports that the Homestead Bill was defeated in the Senate. 8 September 1854. p.141, c3.

3126 S. A. DOUGLAS *to* **DEMOCRATIC STATE CENTRAL COMMITTEE OF INDIANA. 8 August 1854. Washington.** Replies to a letter of the committee inviting him to Indiana. 8 September 1854. p.141, c4.

3127 W. FARMER *to* **W. L. GARRISON. 10 August 1854. Manchester, England.** Gives concluding account of the anti-slavery conference at Manchester; encloses resolutions. 8 September 1854. p.142, c1.

3128 REV. S. A. STEINTHAL *to* **SAMUEL MAY, JR. [extract] 17 August 1854. Bridgewater, England.** Relates that Joseph Barker was not permitted to speak at the Manchester anti-slavery conference. 8 September 1854. p.143, c1.

3129 HENRY C. WRIGHT *to* **GARRISON. 27 August 1854. Salem, Oh.** Reports on the anti-slavery tent from Ohio at the Western AS anniversary. 8 September 1854. p.143, c3.

3130 L. V. LEFAIRE *to* **MR. GARRISON. 4 September 1854. Stoneham.** Praises Mr. Whitcomb and his church for helping fugitives. 8 September 1854. p.143, c5.

3131 JOHN BALL, JR. *to* **FELLOW GENTILES. 10 April 1854. Charleston Hotel, S.C.** Gives observations during his travels through South Carolina. 8 September 1854. p.144, c2.

3132 JOSEPH BARKER *to* **n.n. [from the** *London Reasoner***] 4 August 1854. n.p.** States that he is lecturing in England and thinking about publishing a "small book on the Bible." 8 September 1854. p.144, c5.

3133 C. STETSON *to* **THE** *LIBERATOR***. 30 August 1854. South Scituate.** Reports that Sojourner Truth spoke in South Scituate. 15 September 1854. p.146, c4.

3134 ONE OF YOUR SUBSCRIBERS EVER SINCE 1835 *to* **FRIEND GARRISON. 31 August 1854. Danversport.** Attacks Pillsbury for failing to denounce the aristocracy in England. 15 September 1854. p.146, c5.

3135 D. S. GRANDIN *to* **PARKER PILLSBURY. 10 September 1854. Portland.** Reports that every state has repudiated the Kansas and Nebraska fraud; derides the conduct of Samuel R. Ward in seconding a resolution on behalf of the American Board of Commissioners for Foreign Missions. 15 September 1854. p.147, c1.

3136 HENRY C. WRIGHT *to* **GARRISON. 7 September 1854. Geneva, Oh.** Reports on a dry spell in Ohio, the rescue of a fugitive slave, and the Fusionist Convention. 15 September 1854. p.148, c2.

3137 WM. S. FLANDERS *to* **W. L. G. 14 August 1854. Cornville.** Disagrees with Wendell Phillips' speech at Abington advocating political action. 15 September 1854. p.148, c3.

3138 AARON M. POWELL *to* **FRANCIS JACKSON. [extract] 23 August 1854. Ghent, N.Y.** Declares that the time is favorable for anti-slavery labor; censures Rev. Charles Lester's "foul-mouthed slander" of Abby Foster and W. L. Garrison. 15 September 1854. p.148, c4.

3139 JACOB WALTON, JR. *to* **FRIEND GARRISON. 13 August 1854. Adrian, Mi.** Reports on the Yearly Meeting of Progressive Friends in Michigan. 15 September 1854. p.148, c5.

3140 J. R. GIDDINGS *to* **ISAAC PIERCE. [from the** *Ohio Anti-Slavery Bugle*] **16 August 1854. Jefferson, Oh.** Asserts his opposition to the Fugitive Slave Law. 22 September 1854. p.149, c4.

3141 N. ADAMS *to* **H. A. WISE. 15 August 1854. Boston.** Describes his visit to Georgia, South Carolina, and Virginia; solicits Wise's opinion on the future of slaves. 22 September 1854. p.150, c1.

3142 HENRY A. WISE *to* **REV. N. ADAMS. 22 August 1854. Only, Va.** Believes that slaves are private property and that slavery Christianized heathen Africans. 22 September 1854. p.150, c1.

3143 WM. WELLS BROWN *to* **MR. GARRISON. 29 August 1854. London.** Reports that he will return to the United States after having been absent five years. 22 September 1854. p.151, c2.

3144 A. T. FOSS *to* **FRIEND GARRISON. n.d. n.p.** Reports meager attendance at an anti-slavery meeting in Manchester; praises C. L. Remond's speech. 22 September 1854. p.151, c3.

3145 JAMES HAUGHTON *to* **THE PEOPLE OF IRELAND. [from the** *Dublin Freeman's Journal*] **August 1854. Dublin.** Criticizes Irishmen and their attitude toward slavery. 29 September 1854. p.153, c3.

3146 PARKER PILLSBURY *to* **WILLIAM LLOYD GARRISON. 7 September 1854. Glasgow.** Discusses the character of abolitionists who come to England. 29 September 1854. p.154, c5.

3147 INQUIRER *to* **FRIEND GARRISON. 12 September 1854. New Bedford.** Asks why God has not answered the prayers of the slave. 29 September 1854. p.155, c2.

3148 N. ADAMS *to* **H. A. WISE. 26 September 1854. Boston.** Complains about the publication of his correspondence with Wise. 29 September 1854. p.155, c3.

3149 GEORGE H. WASHINGTON *to* **n.n. 28 August 1854. Wilbraham.** Retracts his groundless criticisms of Thomas H. Jones. 29 September 1854. p.155, c3.

3150 PAULINA W. DAVIS *to* **n.n. n.d. n.p.** Announces a convention on women's rights to be held in Philadelphia. 29 September 1854. p.155, c5.

3151 SETH HUNT *to* **n.n. 26 September 1854. Northampton, Ma.** Believes that the Bible is not the "only rule of faith and practice." 29 September 1854. p.156, c4.

3152 STEPHEN J. W. TABOR *to* **SIR. 18 September 1854. Shelburne Falls, Ma.** Commends the *Liberator*. 29 September 1854. p.156, c4.

3153 W. S. MOORE *to* **REV. C. C. FOOTE. 23 May 1854. Longview, Ky.** Informs of the escape of his slave, Sina. 6 October 1854. p.157, c1.

3154 n.n. *to* **THE EDITORS OF THE** *NATIONAL ANTI-SLAVERY STANDARD.* **n.d. n.p.** Returns paper and longs for opportunity to "be gratified by the administering of a good cowhide on the backs of you unprincipled scoundrels." 6 October 1854. p.157, c1.

3155 W. L. JUDD *to* **BROTHER HARRIS. [from the** *Michigan Christian Herald***] 9 September 1854. Detroit.** Condemns United States policy toward Haiti. 6 October 1854. p.157, c6.

3156 CHARLES SUMNER *to* **SIR. 28 September 1854. Boston.** Regrets that he cannot attend the meeting about the Fugitive Slave Bill in Syracuse. 6 October 1854. p.158, c3.

3157 HENRY WILSON *to* **NOMINATING COMMITTEE. 18 September 1854. Natick.** Accepts the Republican nomination for governor of Massachusetts. 6 October 1854. p.159, c1.

3158 JOSEPH MERRILL *to* **BROTHER GARRISON. 25 September 1854. Danvers Port.** Praises the anti-slavery lectures of Sojourner Truth. 6 October 1854. p.159, c1.

3159 FRANCIS BURRY *to* **WM. S. FLANDERS. n.d. Berlin Heights, Oh.** Agrees that the Constitution is anti-slavery. 6 October 1854. p.159, c1.

3160 CLERICUS *to* **MR. EDITOR [W. L. GARRISON]. n.d. n.p.** Reviews anti-slavery books. 6 October 1854. p.159, c2.

3161 DUMAS J. VAN DEREN *to* **MESSRS. EDITORS. [from the** *Charleston Courier***] 16 September 1854. Charleston, Il.** Proposes the introduction of slavery into Illinois. 13 October 1854. p.161, c1.

3162 H. W. BEECHER *to* **SIR. 23 September 1854. Brooklyn.** Regrets that he is unable to attend the Jerry Rescue celebration at Syracuse. 13 October 1854. p.161, c4.

3163 E. B. OLDS *to* **n.n. [extract] 4 March 1854. Washington.** Admits that the Nebraska Bill is an unfortunate affair for the democracy of the North. 13 October 1854. p.162, c2.

3164 E. B. OLDS *to* **n.n. 27 May 1854. Washington.** Explains that it is certain that the Nebraska Bill will be passed. 13 October 1854. p.162, c2.

3165 SAMUEL MAY, JR. *to* **n.n. 16 July 1854. Boston.** Praises the labors of the abolitionists; sends encouragement for future work. 13 October 1854. p.162, c3.

3166 ANGELINA J. KNOX *to* **MR. GARRISON. 5 October 1854. Rochester.** Gives an account of meeting a fugitive slave. 13 October 1854. p.162, c5.

3167 W. S. G. *to* **MR. GARRISON. n.d. n.p.** Comments that Democratic Tories view Anglo-Saxons as superior to Irish and blacks. 13 October 1854. p.162, c5.

3168 JOHN T. SARGENT *to* **MR. EDITOR [W. L. GARRISON]. 8 October 1854. Boston.** States the object of the organization, the Guardian of Friendless Girls. 13 October 1854. p.162, c6.

3169 D. S. GRANDIN *to* **FRIEND GARRISON. 9 October 1854. Portland.** Comments on T. W. Higginson's discourse entitled "Scripture Idolatry." 13 October 1854. p.163, c1.

3170 S. P. BANKHEAD *to* **n.n. [from the** *Memphis Whig***] 16 September 1854. Memphis.** Forwards proceedings of a public meeting discussing the treatment of J. J. Robinson by abolitionists in Ohio. 20 October 1854. p.165, c2.

3171 REV. THEODORE CLAPP *to* **THE** *PICAYUNE.* **9 September 1854. Bridgewater.** Believes that slavery is the "best operation on the face of the earth." 20 October 1854. p.165, c2.

3172 RICHARD D. WEBB *to* **GARRISON. 21 August 1854. Dublin.** Explains why the impoverished Irish feel no compassion for the slave. 20 October 1854. p.167, c1.

3173 GEO. W. STACY *to* **FRIEND GARRISON. 12 October 1854. Montreal.** Reports on the Unitarian autumnal convention. 20 October 1854. p.167, c1.

3174 T. W. HIGGINSON *to* **THE** *LIBERATOR.* **16 September 1854. Worcester.** Discusses criticism of his "Scripture Idolatry." 20 October 1854. p.167, c3.

3175 THEO. PARKER *to* **JOSEPH A. DUGDALE. 19 May 1854. Boston.** Discusses the commercial, philosophical, and religious progress attributed to the long peace in Europe. 20 October 1854. p.168, c2.

3176 C. M. CLAY *to* **FRIEND. 12 May 1854. White Hall Post Office, Ky.** Regrets that he is unable to attend the annual meeting of the Progressive Friends. 20 October 1854. p.168, c2.

3177 THOS. WENTWORTH HIGGINSON *to* **n.n. 20 May 1854. Worcester, Ma.** Regrets that he is unable to attend the Yearly Meeting of the Progressive Friends. 20 October 1854. p.168, c2.

3178 n.n. *to* **THE** *LIBERATOR.* **n.d. n.p.** Urges the abolition of the death penalty. 20 October 1854. p.168, c2.

3179 NORMAL *to* **THE EDITOR OF THE** *REPUBLICAN.* **[extract] 3 October 1854. Middletown.** Concludes from speeches of the colored convention that Douglass is capable of equalling but not surpassing the oratorical powers of A. G. Beman. 27 October 1854. p.169, c3.

3180 PARTICULAR *to* **n.n. 6 October 1854. Washington, D.C.** Describes the pursuit and capture of a fugitive slave. 27 October 1854. p.170, c2.

3181 TWELVE OF US *to* **YOUNG BEMAN. 5 October 1833. Middletown.** Threaten to resort to forcible means to prevent colored students from speaking at Wesleyan University. 27 October 1854. p.170, c2.

3182 S. P. DOLE *to* **n.n. n.d. n.p.** Reiterates a professor's remarks about the threat made by twelve students to a colored student at Wesleyan University. 27 October 1854. p.170, c2.

3183 S. ALFRED STEINTHAL *to* **REV. S. MAY, JR. 29 September 1854. Bridgwater, England.** Comments on American misconceptions concerning English institutions. 27 October 1854. p.170, c5.

3184 W. S. G. *to* **MR. GARRISON. n.d. n.p.** Remarks that there are no colored speakers scheduled to lecture on slavery. 27 October 1854. p.171, c3.

3185 WM. S. FLANDERS *to* **THE EDITOR OF THE** *LIBERATOR* **[W. L. GARRISON]. 12 October 1854. Coonville, Me.** Maintains that the United States Constitution is pro-slavery. 27 October 1854. p.171, c3.

3186 E. B. PRATT *to* **FRIEND GARRISON. 8 October 1854. Oramel.** Describes antislavery activity in New York. 27 October 1854. p.171, c4.

3187 JOHN BALDWIN AND FRIENDS *to* **DR. ROBINSON. 6 October 1854. Kansas Territory.** Missourians threaten to move a Yankee's tent off land which they claim to own. 27 October 1854. p.171, c5.

3188 C. ROBINSON AND FRIENDS *to* **JOHN BALDWIN AND FRIENDS. 6 October 1854. Kansas Territory.** Yankees reply to threats from Missourians. 27 October 1854. p.171, c5.

3189 J. A. DUGDALE AND S. PIERCE *to* **THE SENATE AND HOUSE OF REPRESENTATIVES OF THE STATE OF PENNSYLVANIA. May 1854. Old Kennett, Chester County.** Condemn capital punishment. 27 October 1854. p.172, c4.

3190 H. *to* **FRIEND GARRISON. 31 October 1854. Worcester.** Corrects statements about A. O. Butman, "the notorious arrester and kidnapper of Thomas Sims and Anthony Burns." 3 November 1854. p.175, c4.

3191 CHARLES SUMNER *to* **THE EDITORS OF THE** *NATIONAL INTELLI-GENCER.* **22 October 1854. Boston.** Discusses whether slavery is a national or sectional institution. 10 November 1854. p.177, c2.

3192 D. S. GRANDIN *to* **GARRISON. 23 October 1854. Portland.** Declares that the Irish are not pro-slavery. 17 November 1854. p.181, c2.

3193 N. C. NASH *to* **MR. GARRISON. 2 November 1854. Boston.** Forwards an article from the *New York Journal of Commerce*; asks who the Boston correspondent is. 17 November 1854. p.181, c2.

3194 WILLIAM GUEST *to* **THE EDITOR OF THE** *SCOTTISH PRESS.* **25 September 1854. Leeds.** Opposes holding anti-slavery meetings on the Sabbath. 17 November 1854. p.182, c1.

3195 PARKER PILLSBURY *to* **THE EDITOR OF THE** *SCOTTISH PRESS.* **30 September 1854. Glasgow.** Comments on anti-slavery meetings held on the Sabbath. 17 November 1854. p.182, c1.

3196 JOHN H. PEARSON *to* **HON. CHARLES ALLEN. [from the** *Boston Courier***] 11 November 1854. Boston.** Responds to a Free-Soiler's criticism; denies that he is a notorious slave-catcher. 17 November 1854. p.182, c2.

3197 AARON M. POWELL *to* **MR. GARRISON. 8 November 1854. Olean, N.Y.** Reports on anti-slavery meetings in western New York. 17 November 1854. p.182, c6.

3198 A. T. FOSS *to* **FRIEND GARRISON. 1 November 1854. Orland, In.** Describes his travels in Indiana and an anti-slavery meeting he attended. 17 November 1854. p.182, c6.

3199 HIGH PRIVATE *to* **THE EDITOR OF THE** *BOSTON BEE.* **n.d. n.p.** Queries why the military is not paid. 17 November 1854. p.183, c3.

3200 GEO. TRASK *to* **DOERS OF GOOD OF EVERY NAME AND PLACE. November 1854. Fitchburg.** Favors abstinence from tobacco. 17 November 1854. p.183, c3.

3201 GERRIT SMITH *to* **FRANCIS JACKSON. 12 November 1854. Peterboro'.** Contributes thirty dollars for new series of tracts by the AAS. 17 November 1854. p.183, c4.

3202 D. M. ALLEN *to* **MR. EDITOR [W. L. GARRISON]. 29 October 1854. Westminster.** Criticizes the editor of the *Barre Patriot*, the handling of the report of the anti-slavery meeting, and misrepresentations of facts. 17 November 1854. p.184, c3.

3203 FIRST PRINCIPLES *to* **BRETHREN AND SISTERS BELOVED IN THE LORD.**
n.d. n.p. Gives advice regarding elections. 17 November 1854. p.184, c4.

3204 JOSEPH CARPENTER *to* **FRIEND GARRISON. 20 October 1854. New Rochelle.**
Notes the inconsistency of some speeches at the Jerry Rescue Celebration. 17 November
1854. p.184, c4.

3205 H. J. *to* **THE EDITOR OF THE** *NEW YORK TRIBUNE.* **16 October 1854. New**
York. Discusses various sermons on the Arctic disaster. 17 November 1854. p.184, c4.

3206 THOMAS FOSTER *to* **GENTLEMEN. [from the** *New York Tribune***] 24 October**
1854. New Orleans. Reports on a slave auction. 24 November 1854. p.185, c2.

3207 JOSEPH BARKER *to* **THE EDITOR OF THE** *LEADER.* **n.d. n.p.** Takes issue with
G. N. Sanders' letter to Kossuth; argues that Europeans should speak and write about
American slavery. 24 November 1854. p.185, c3.

3208 S. A. WORCESTER *to* **THE EDITORS OF THE** *NEW YORK OBSERVER.* **9 Oc-**
tober 1854. Park Hill, Cherokee Nation. Believes that no true minister can support slavery.
24 November 1854. p.185, c4.

3209 E. *to* **H. 12 November 1854. Philadelphia.** Comments on the death of Edward S.
Ingraham, a slave-hunter. 24 November 1854. p.186, c1.

3210 FRANCIS JACKSON *to* **JOHN H. PEARSON. 20 November 1854. Boston.** Gives
evidence that Pearson was a slave-catcher. 24 November 1854. p.186. c4.

3211 GEORGE W. PUTNAM *to* **MR. GARRISON. 17 November 1854. Lynn.** Comments
on crime and oppression in Britain; condemns capitalist monopoly of the soil. 24
November 1854. p.186, c3.

3212 D. Y. KILGORE *to* **SAMUEL MAY, JR. 14 November 1854. Madison, Wi.**
Discusses new anti-slavery tracts. 24 November 1854. p.186, c6.

3213 JOSEPH P. FESSENDEN *to* **FRANCIS JACKSON. 13 November 1854. South**
Bridgton. Contributes five dollars to the AAS. 24 November 1854. p.186, c6.

3214 THOS. G. BANVARD *to* **n.n. 12 November 1854. Norway, Me.** States that his faith
in political anti-slavery grows weak. 24 November 1854. p.186, c6.

3215 SAMUEL MAY, JR. *to* **MR. GARRISON. 20 November 1854. Boston.** Discusses
Wm. Guest's views of the Sabbath question. 24 November 1854. p.187, c1.

3216 GERRIT SMITH *to* **GARRISON. 19 November 1854. Peterboro', N.Y.** Criticizes the
limited support of women's rights by Henry Ward Beecher. 24 November 1854.
p.187, c1.

3217 PHILLIPS, SAMPSON AND COMPANY *to* **THE EDITORS OF THE** *NEW*
YORK EVENING POST. **15 November 1854. Boston.** State that Mrs. Stowe did not write
the book *Ida May.* 24 November 1854. p.187, c2.

3218 HIRAM WILSON *to* **FRANCIS JACKSON. 25 October 1854. St. Catharines,**
Canada West. Notes an increasing number of fugitives in Canada. 24 November 1854.
p.188, c3.

3219 FRANCIS BARRY *to* **n.n. n.d. Berlin Heights, Oh.** Denies that the Constitution is
the supreme law and that God exists. 24 November 1854. p.188, c3.

3220 HARRIOT K. HUNT *to* **FREDERICK U. TRACY. 15 November 1854. Boston.** Protests taxation of women without representation. 24 November 1854. p.188, c4.

3221 LEGATION *to* **THE EDITOR OF THE** *FRANKFORT* **(KY.)** *YEOMAN.* **18 November. n.p.** Gives an account of the kidnapping of free Negroes in Kentucky. 1 December 1854. p.190, c1.

3222 JOSEPH JENNINGS *to* **n.n. n.d. n.p.** Informs his friends that he has purchased the dark bay horse Star, and the mulatto girl Sarah. 1 December 1854. p.190, c5.

3223 PARKER PILLSBURY *to* **THE EDITOR OF THE** *MANCHESTER WEEKLY ADVERTISER.* **October 1854. Belfast.** Believes that American slavery is far worse than Russian serfdom. 1 December 1854. p.190, c5.

3224 FRED W. CHESSON *to* **EDITOR OF THE** *MANCHESTER WEEKLY ADVERTISER.* **26 October 1854. Manchester.** Comments on the lack of Christianity among some American abolitionists. 1 December 1854. p.190, c5.

3225 ONE WHO HEARD HIM *to* **MR. EDITOR [W. L. GARRISON]. 24 November 1854. Lynn.** Assails Dr. Dewey's willingness to "send his mother into slavery to save the Union." 1 December 1854. p.190, c6.

3226 HENRY C. WRIGHT *to* **GARRISON. 20 November 1854. Greenfield.** Reports on anti-slavery meetings; claims that lectures on "no union with slaveholders" are popular. 1 December 1854. p.191, c1.

3227 W. H. FISH *to* **FRIEND GARRISON. n.d. n.p.** Reports on an anti-slavery party held in Blackstone. 1 December 1854. p.191, c2.

3228 n.n. *to* **MESSRS. EDITORS OF THE** *ALTA-CALIFORNIA.* **20 October 1854. Monterey.** Reports that an entire family was murdered by a band of Mexican and American robbers. 1 December 1854. p.191, c3.

3229 S. MITCHELL *to* **FRIEND GARRISON. 20 November 1854. Cornville, Me.** Cites arguments against all forms of government. 1 December 1854. p.192. c2.

3230 DR. Q. R. P. D., P. B. M. D. *to* **THE EDITOR OF THE** *DETROIT DAILY ADVERTISER.* **n.d. n.p.** Claims he has made his fortune through the patent medicine business. 1 December 1854. p.192, c4.

3231 SKY HY *to* **DOCTOR. 31 June 1854. Sall Harbor.** Sarcastically praises the doctor's balsam. 1 December 1854. p.192, c4.

3232 CHOCTAW *to* **n.n. 10 October 1854. n.p.** Discusses the effects on the Choctaw Missions of the American Board's action concerning teachers leaving the Choctaw Nation. 8 December 1854. p.193, c1.

3233 GEORGE ARMSTRONG *to* **THE EDITOR OF THE** *LONDON INQUIRER.* **n.d. n.p.** Criticizes the elasticity of moral standards. 8 December 1854. p.193, c3.

3234 EDWARD MATHEWS *to* **THE EDITOR OF THE** *LONDON MORNING ADVERTISER.* **n.d. n.p.** Comments on religious alliances with slaveholders. 8 December 1854. p.193, c4.

3235 W. FARMER *to* **W. L. GARRISON. 17 November 1854. London.** Discusses George Thompson's assumption of the editorship of the *Empire.* 8 December 1854. p.194, c5.

3236 CLARISSA G. OLDS *to* **FRANCIS JACKSON. 12 November 1854. Winslow, Me.** Sends two dollars to support the distribution of anti-slavery tracts. 8 December 1854. p.195, c1.

3237 SAMUEL BARRY *to* **BROTHER GARRISON. 30 November 1854. Philadelphia.** Comments on the death of Esther Moore. 8 December 1854. p.195, c2.

3238 REBECCA THOMAS *to* **n.n. n.d. n.p.** Relates an interview she once had with Esther Moore. 8 December 1854. p.195, c2.

3239 n.n. *to* **n.n. [extract] n.d. n.p.** Commends the *Liberator*; believes abolition must come by violence; praises Mrs. Stowe. 8 December 1854. p.196, c2.

3240 JOHN BALL, JR. *to* **WILLIAM LLOYD GARRISON. 25 November 1854. Liberty Lodge, Far South.** Discusses the conduct of abolitionists in the South. 8 December 1854. p.196, c2.

3241 ONE OF THE PROSCRIBED CLASS *to* **FRIEND GARRISON. 1 December 1854. Boston.** Encloses extracts from the letter of a colored citizen now in Australia. 8 December 1854. p.196, c2.

3242 n.n. *to* **n.n. [extract] n.d. n.p.** Praises the *Liberator* and W. L. Garrison for furthering the anti-slavery cause; believes slavery in the United States will soon be eradicated; predicts abolition will come through violence. 8 December 1854. p.196, c2.

3243 LEWIS STARK *to* **MR. GARRISON. 29 October 1854. Placerville, Ca.** Discusses prejudice in the Methodist Episcopal church. 8 December 1854. p.196, c3.

3244 W. H. B. *to* **THE EDITOR OF THE *LIBERATOR* [W. L. GARRISON]. 1 December 1854. New York.** Reports on the annual meeting of the New York City Bible Society; states his opposition to the Bible. 8 December 1854. p.196, c3.

3245 n.n. *to* **n.n. 25 November. Burlington, Vt.** Encloses an act passed by the Vermont legislature concerning the defense of liberty and the punishment of kidnappers. 15 December 1854. p.198, c1.

3246 HENRY C. WRIGHT *to* **GARRISON. 5 December 1854. Springfield.** Reports the election of Nash [Trask], an anti-slavery man, as mayor of Springfield. 15 December 1854. p.199, c1.

3247 WM. S. FLANDERS *to* **THE EDITOR OF THE *LIBERATOR* [W. L. GARRISON]. 1 December 1854. Cornville, Me.** Believes that war and slavery are products of the Constitution. 15 December 1854. p.199, c3.

3248 FRANCIS BARRY *to* **n.n. n.d. Berlin Heights, Oh.** Corrects a printing error in the *Liberator*. 15 December 1854. p.199, c3.

3249 ANTOINETTE L. BROWN *to* **n.n. 20 November 1854. Henrietta.** Discusses the right of a woman to hold the position of minister. 15 December 1854. p.200, c2.

3250 n.n. *to* **n.n. 18 November 1854. Douglas City, Kansas Territory.** Believes that Kansas will be a slave state. 22 December 1854. p.201, c1.

3251 JOSEPH BARKER *to* **THE EDITOR OF THE *LONDON ANTI-SLAVERY AD-VOCATE*. n.d. n.p.** Encloses a declaration against American slavery. 22 December 1854. p.201, c3.

3252 F. H. *to* **n.n. [from the** *New York Evening Post***] 6 December 1854. Boston.** Discusses the indictment and arrest of Theodore Parker for sedition. 22 December 1854. p.201, c6.

3253 S. F. T. *to* **THE EDITORS OF THE** *BOSTON ATLAS.* **30 November 1854. Lawrence, Kansas Territory.** Notes that citizens of neighboring states may vote in Kansas. 22 December 1854. p.202, c2.

3254 A. F. *to* **FRIEND GARRISON. 15 December 1854. Providence.** Praises Mrs. E. L. Rose's lecture, "Independent Course." 22 December 1854. p.202, c5.

3255 PARKER PILLSBURY *to* **W. L. G. 25 November 1854. Liverpool.** Reports on the London Anti-Slavery Conference; states that Unitarian ministers are more anti-slavery than evangelical. 22 December 1854. p.202, c6.

3256 GEORGE W. PUTNAM *to* **MR. GARRISON. 14 December 1854. Lynn.** Praises the poem by Rev. Wm. S. Studley on the "follies of the times." 22 December 1854. p.203, c2.

3257 E. W. TWING *to* **FRIEND GARRISON. 17 December 1854. Springfield.** Corrects a misprint in the *Liberator* which substituted "Nash" for the name of Eliphalet Trask. 22 December 1854. p.203, c2.

3258 H. W. B. *to* **THE EDITOR OF THE** *CHRISTIAN REGISTER.* **n.d. n.p.** Praises Dr. Solger's lectures on the present state of Europe. 22 December 1854. p.203, c3.

3259 FRANCIS BARRY *to* **GERRIT SMITH. 1 December 1854. Berlin Heights, Erie County, Oh.** Opposes women's rights on biblical grounds. 22 December 1854. p.204, c2.

3260 LAURA S. HAVILAND *to* **FRIEND FREDERICK. 30 November 1854. Refugee Home School.** Describes the mistreatment of prisoner Calvin Fairbanks. 29 December 1854. p.205, c4.

[1855]

3261 A LOVER OF TRUTH *to* **n.n. [from the** *New York Journal of Commerce***] 1 December 1854. Richmond, Va.** Believes that free Negroes have no morals. 5 January 1855. p.1, c1.

3262 ROCHESTER *to* **GENTLEMEN. [from the** *Salem Observer***] 14 December 1854. Chicago, Il.** Informs that Chicago citizens are aiding seventeen fugitive slaves. 5 January 1855. p.1, c2.

3263 JOSIAH QUINCY *to* **SIR. 16 October 1854. Quincy.** Believes that the South fears disunion. 5 January 1855. p.1, c3.

3264 C. F. H. *to* **MESSRS. EDITORS. [from the** *New York Evening Post***] 4 December 1854. Boston, Ma.** States that abolitionists favor free trade. 5 January 1855. p.1, c5.

3265 WASHINGTON CORRESPONDENT OF THE *NEW YORK TRIBUNE to* **n.n. [extract] n.d. n.p.** Beseeches Anthony Burns' friends to buy him out of slavery. 5 January 1855. p.2, c2.

3266 H. C. WRIGHT *to* **PARKER PILLSBURY. 29 December 1854. Boston.** Reflects on the state of American slavery and Christianity after living abroad for a year; notes that the son of W. E. Channing caused J. S. Rogers to be expelled from the Know-Nothing Party. 5 January 1855. p.2, c5.

3267 JOSEPH BARKER *to* **FRIEND. 15 December 1854. Betley, Staffordshire, England.** Reports on his anti-slavery lectures; answers Mr. Steinthal's questions about American slavery and British bondage. 5 January 1855. p.3, c1.

3268 RICHARD D. WEBB *to* **FRIEND GARRISON. 11 December 1854. Dublin.** Discusses progress in Britain against land monopoly; believes that social conditions in Britain are more tolerable than those in America. 5 January 1855. p.3, c3.

3269 n.n. *to* **n.n. n.d. n.p.** A slaveholder informs the husband of one of his slaves that he has increased the price of his wife to $600, as there has been an extraordinary demand for slaves since the original price of $450 was agreed upon. 5 January 1855. p.4, c2.

3270 S. W. W. *to* **FRIEND GARRISON. n.d. n.p.** Praises a lecture by J. W. C. Pennington. 5 January 1855. p.4, c3.

3271 n.n. *to* **MR. WHEELER. 21 December 1854. Providence.** Discusses a "mild and temperate" lecture by J. W. C. Pennington. 5 January 1855, p.4, c3.

3272 ALEXANDER McARTHUR *to* **MR. EDITOR [W. L. GARRISON]. 11 December 1854. Pictou, N.S.** Refutes arguments supporting atheism. 5 January 1855. p.4, c4.

3273 E. R. JOHNSON *to* **CAPT. DANIEL DRAYTON. 18 December 1854. New Bedford.** States that he saw no abject poverty during his visit to Canada. 5 January 1855. p.4, c5.

3274 H. O. S. *to* **FRIEND GARRISON. n.d. n.p.** Comments on Know-Nothingism in the Unitarian church. 5 January 1855. p.4, c5.

3275 A. J. SIMMONS *to* **FRIEND GARRISON. 17 December 1854. Walworth, N. Y.** Believes that a revival of anti-slavery activity is needed in western New York. 5 January 1855. p.4, c5.

3276 WM. F. CHANNING *to* **THE EDITOR OF THE *LIBERATOR*. 8 January 1855. Boston.** Contradicts Henry Wright's statement that Channing is a member of the Know-Nothing Party. 12 January 1855. p.10 [6], c5.

3277 JOHN S. ROGERS *to* **W. L. GARRISON. 8 January 1855. Boston.** Claims that the son of John Pierpont precipitated his expulsion from the Know-Nothing Party. 12 January 1855. p.10 [6], c5.

3278 HENRY C. WRIGHT *to* **W. L. GARRISON. 9 January 1855. Boston.** Acknowledges his mistake in reporting that it was the son of W. E. Channing who caused J. S. Rogers' expulsion from the Know-Nothings. 12 January 1855. p.10 [6], c5.

3279 C. STEARNS *to* **MR. GARRISON. 24 December 1854. Lawrence, Kansas Territory.** Believes that there is no possibility of Kansas' becoming a slave state because abolitionists in Kansas "don't want niggers here." 12 January 1855. p.10 [6], c6.

3280 HENRY C. WRIGHT *to* **GARRISON. 8 January 1855. Stoneham.** Questions the value of American Christianity; reports on a lecture by Wendell Phillips. 12 January 1855. p.11 [7], c1.

3281 LEONARD GIBBS *to* **MR. GARRISON. 21 December 1854. Greenwich, N.Y.** Criticizes the sectional slavery plan of Sumner, Chase, Hale, and others. 12 January 1855. p.11 [7], c2.

3282 F. *to* **FRIEND GARRISON. 4 January 1855. Providence.** Reports on a lecture by Antoinette L. Brown. 12 January 1855. p.11 [7], c3.

3283 W. H. B. *to* **THE EDITOR OF THE** *LIBERATOR* **[W. L. GARRISON]. 7 January 1855. New York.** Discusses Douglass' change of heart about Christianity. 12 January 1855. p.11 [7], c3.

3284 J. Q. ADAMS *to* **CHARLES B. SEDGWICK. 30 December 1835. Washington.** Remarks that all United States presidents have been Christians. 12 January 1855. p.8, c6.

3285 A CITIZEN OF BOSTON *to* **THE EDITOR OF THE** *NEW YORK TRIBUNE.* **2 January 1855. Boston.** Discusses the indictment of Theodore Parker and Wendell Phillips. 19 January 1855. p.9, c4.

3286 ISRAEL WASHBURN *to* **FRIEND GARRISON. 22 December 1854. Fair Haven, Ma.** Announces the death of Capt. John Bunker. 12 January 1855. p.10, c4.

3287 GEO. T. DAY *to* **S. W. WHEELER, ESQ. 9 January 1855. Olneyville, R. I.** Regrets that he is unable to attend the anti-slavery convention to be held in Providence. 19 January 1855. p.10. c5.

3288 GEO. W. PUTNAM *to* **MR. GARRISON. 11 January 1855 .Lynn.** Replies to Richard Webb, asserting that England limits the freedom of peers. 19 January 1855. p.11, c1.

3289 HIRAM WILSON *to* **FRIEND GARRISON. 10 January 1855. St. Catharines, Canada West.** Expresses satisfaction that he is able to offer aid in Canada to escaped slaves. 19 January 1855. p.11, c3.

3290 A. *to* **MR. EDITOR [W. L. GARRISON]. 12 January 1855. Andover.** Reports on a lecture by Antoinette L. Brown in Andover. 19 January 1855. p.12, c2.

3291 SAMUEL MAY, JR. *to* **MRS. LOUISA LORING. 27 December 1854. Boston.** Sends thanks for the gift of a silver cup and saucer. 26 January 1855. p.14, c1.

3292 JOHN H. POPE *to* **THE CHIEF OF POLICE, MONTREAL, CANADA. 1 January 1855. Frederick, Md.** Requests that he cooperate with the Fugitive Slave Law. 26 January 1855. p.14, c4.

3293 C. A. WALL *to* **FRIEND GARRISON. 22 January 1855. Worcester.** Approves of Henry Wilson, the anti-slavery candidate for senator. 26 January 1855. p.15, c1.

3294 C. K. W. *to* **THE EDITOR OF THE** *EVENING TELEGRAPH.* **n.d. n.p.** Accuses the Curtis brothers of kidnapping and of working against the anti-slavery movement. 26 January 1855. p.15, c2.

3295 ONE OF THE NAME *to* **THE EDITOR OF THE** *NEW YORK TRIBUNE.* **13 January 1855. Boston.** States that the Curtis family are defenders of law and order. 26 January 1855. p.15, c2.

3296 MECHANIC *to* **MR. EDITOR. 17 January 1855. Andover.** Criticizes James Gordon Bennett for his ineffective advocacy of "the rights of the people." 26 January 1855. p.15, c2.

3297 SHAWSHEEN *to* **MR. EDITOR [W. L. GARRISON]. 13 January 1855. Andover.** Discusses the indictment against Theodore Parker. 26 January 1855. p.15, c2.

3298 A. *to* **MR. EDITOR [W. L. GARRISON]. 17 January 1855. Andover.** Comments on Rev. L. Whiting's refusal to deliver a lecture at the Lyceum because Miss A. L. Brown had been allowed to speak. 26 January 1855. p.15, c3.

3299 A. B. C. *to* **THE EDITOR OF THE** *TRAVELLER.* **n.d. n.p.** Criticizes a lecture by F. Douglass which slandered the Church. 2 February 1855. p.17, c1.

3300 SAMUEL MAY, JR. *to* **THE EDITOR OF THE** *UNION.* **13 January 1855. Boston.** Requests printing of the enclosed "Friendly Remonstrance on the Subject of Slavery." 2 February 1855. p.19, c4.

3301 FRANCIS BARRY *to* **BRO. McARTHUR. 14 January 1855. Berlin Heights, Oh.** Believes that God existed for an eternity "doing nothing" before creating the universe; comments on God's ability to abolish slavery. 2 February 1855. p.20, c2.

3302 E. W. TWING *to* **W. L. GARRISON. 21 January 1855. Springfield.** Claims that the Bible sanctions slavery. 2 February 1855. p.20, c3.

3303 S. G. HOWE *to* **MR. EDITOR. [from the** *Boston Daily Advertiser***] 2 February 1855. South Boston.** Discusses indictments against Wendell Phillips and Theodore Parker. 9 February 1855. p.22, c2.

3304 S. ALFRED STEINTHAL *to* **MR. GARRISON. 2 January 1855. Bridgwater, England.** Defends himself against charges made by George W. Putnam; deplores the English factory system. 9 February 1855. p.23, c1.

3305 SARAH OTIS ERNST *to* **THE ANTI-SLAVERY SEWING CIRCLE. 17 January 1855. Cincinnati.** Gives a retrospective view of the anti-slavery sewing circle's labor and position; lists reasons for resigning as an officer. 9 February 1855. p.23, c3.

3306 R. T. *to* **MR. GARRISON. 2 February 1855. Philadelphia.** Summarizes Douglass' speech on anti-slavery in Philadelphia. 9 February 1855. p.23, c4.

3307 DEFOE *to* **LORD SHAFTSBURY. [from the** *London Empire***] n.d. n.p.** Accuses Lord Shaftsbury of being a hypocrite. 16 February 1855. p.25, c3.

3308 THOMAS B. CURTIS *to* **THE EDITORS. [from the** *Boston Daily Advertiser***] n.d. n.p.** Defends himself against the charge of kidnapping Anthony Burns. 16 February 1855. p.25, c6.

3309 EDWARD G. LORING *to* **THE SENATE AND HOUSE OF REPRESEN-TATIVES. 9 February 1855. Boston.** Replies to the request that he be removed from office. 16 February 1855. p.26, c1.

3310 GEORGE THOMPSON *to* **MEMBERS OF THE MANCHESTER ANTI-SLAVERY CONFERENCE AND OF THE COMMITTEE OF THE GLASGOW EMAN-CIPATION SOCIETY. 15 January 1855. London.** Forwards a report of the proceedings of the anti-slavery conference which was published in the *Anti-Slavery Advocate.* 16 February 1855. p.26, c4.

3311 D. M. *to* **THE EDITOR OF THE** *CHRISTIAN REGISTER.* **n.d. n.p.** Praises Samuel Osgood's lecture on Ambrose. 16 February 1855. p.26, c6.

3312 GEO. J. PETERSON *to* **n.n. 26 January 1855. Duxbury.** States that he is unable to attend the annual meeting of the Massachusetts AS. 16 February 1855. p.26, c6.

3313 RICHARD PLUMER *to* **GENERAL AGENT. [extract] 4 February 1855. Newbury-port.** Reports on an anti-slavery meeting at which Mr. Foster spoke. 16 February 1855. p.26, c6.

3314 CLARISSA G. OLDS *to* **MR. GARRISON. 28 January 1855. Winslow, Ma.** Recommends the book *Ida May*. 16 February 1855. p.26, c6.

3315 C. STEARNS *to* **MR. GARRISON. 20 January 1855. Lawrence, Kansas Territory.** States that men are taking sides on the slavery issue in Kansas Territory. 16 February 1855. p.28, c2.

3316 H. B. STOWE *to* **THE** *NATIONAL ERA***. 2 February 1855. Boston.** Praises Wendell Phillips as an outstanding orator. 23 February 1855. p.29, c2.

3317 WILLIAM JAY *to* **SHERMAN M. BOOTH. 2 February 1855. New York.** Sends money to Booth, who was jailed for opposing the Fugitive Slave Law. 23 February 1855. p.30, c2.

3318 S. P. CHASE *to* **SHERMAN M. BOOTH. 7 February 1855. Washington.** Believes that the Fugitive Slave Law is unconstitutional. 23 February 1855. p.30, c2.

3319 EDWARD G. LORING *to* **JOINT STANDING COMMITTEE ON FEDERAL RELATIONS. 19 February 1855. Boston.** Refuses to heed the petition for his removal from office. 23 February 1855. p.30, c3.

3320 GEO. W. MEEKER *to* **JUDGES OF THE CIRCUIT DISTRICT COURT, U.S. DISTRICT, ILLINOIS. 29 January 1855. Chicago.** Resigns as United States commissioner. 23 February 1855. p.30, c4.

3321 S. ALFRED STEINTHAL *to* **THE** *LIBERATOR***. 1 February 1855. Bridgwater, England.** Explains his views to Joseph Barker; expresses interest in the effect India reform will have on slaveholders; praises lectures of Dr. Lee. 23 February 1855. p.30, c6.

3322 S. ALFRED STEINTHAL *to* **MR. MAY. [extract] 23 January 1855. Bridgwater, England.** Points out the inconsistencies in Mr. Dalton's article on the effects of emancipation in British Guiana. 23 February 1855. p.30, c6.

3323 WM. CRAFT *to* **MR. GARRISON. 4 September 1854. Gunnersbury Place, London.** Expresses interest in the anti-slavery movement in England. 23 February 1855. p.31, c1.

3324 BOSTON *to* **n.n. [from the** *Boston Journal***] 9 February 1855. New Orleans.** Reports on another Cuba expedition about to take place. 23 February 1855. p.31, c3.

3325 J. C. FARGO *to* **n.n. 15 February 1855. Randolph, Vt.** Laments the death of Howard Griswold. 23 February 1855. p.31, c5.

3326 HENRY C. WRIGHT *to* **CHARLES F. HOVEY. 9 February 1855. Boston.** Comments on Adams' *South Side View of Slavery*. 23 February 1855. p.32, c2.

3327 X. Y. Z. *to* **W. L. GARRISON. 2 February 1855. Stoneham.** States that there are no differences between slaveholders, slave hunters, and Rev. Nehemiah Adams. 23 February 1855. p.32, c3.

3328 LOUIS KOSSUTH *to* **SOCIETY OF FRIENDS IN GREAT BRITAIN. [from the** *London Times***] 15 January 1855. London.** Refutes the "Christian Appeal" for peace; gives a justification for war. 23 February 1855. p.32, c3.

3329 n.n. *to* **SIR. 30 October 1854. Wayland.** Believes that Judge Loring did not willfully corrupt the law, but that he was easily influenced. 2 March 1855. p.35, c4.

3330 B. *to* **n.n. [from the** *New York Evening Post***] 15 February 1855. Boston.** Reports on a meeting of the House of Representatives at which slavery was discussed. 2 March 1855. p.36, c5.

3331 VESPASIAN ELLIS *to* **HON. HENRY WILSON. [from the** *American Organ***] 17 February 1855. Washington.** Addresses questions to him about states' rights and the power of Congress to interfere with slavery. 9 March 1855. p.37, c6.

3332 HENRY WILSON *to* **VESPASIAN ELLIS. n.d. n.p.** Responds to questions about states' rights and the powerlessness of Congress to interfere with slavery. 9 March 1855. p. 37, c6.

3333 A. T. FOSS *to* **W. L. GARRISON. 24 February 1855. Rome, In.** Reports on the anti-slavery meetings held at the Baptist church. 9 March 1855. p.39, c1.

3334 SALLIE HOLLEY *to* **W. L. GARRISON. 26 February 1855. Dover, N.H.** Reports on Indiana anti-slavery meetings. 9 March 1855. p.40, c2.

3335 ALFRED GIBBS CAMPBELL *to* **GARRISON. 25 February 1855. Paterson, N.J.** Believes that popular religion is a fraud. 9 March 1855. p.40, c3.

3336 GERRIT SMITH *to* **WENDELL PHILLIPS. 20 February 1855. Peterboro.** Compares republican and monarchical institutions; discusses Cuban slavery; believes that American Christianity is not biblical. 16 March 1855. p.41, c1.

3337 C. STEARNS *to* **W. L. GARRISON. 8 February 1855. Lawrence, Kansas Territory.** Declares Kansas is a free state; discusses the Emigrant Aid Company. 16 March 1855. p.43, c3.

3338 JAS. H. SWETT *to* **W. L. GARRISON. 5 March 1855. Milford, N.H.** Describes a lecture by the Fosters and a political aid party. 16 March 1855. p.43, c4.

3339 ALEX McARTHUR *to* **W. L. GARRISON. 19 February 1855. Pictou, Nova Scotia.** Wishes to end the Francis Barry controversy. 16 March 1855. p.43, c5.

3340 W. G. B. *to* **THE PRESIDENT. 1855. n.p.** Questions the constitutionality of slavery. 16 March 1855. p.43, c5.

3341 J. MILLER McKIM *to* **THE** *NATIONAL ANTI-SLAVERY STANDARD.* **12 March. Philadelphia.** Notifies of Cyrus Burleigh's death. 23 March 1855. p.46, c2.

3342 R. *to* **n.n. n.d. n.p.** Comments on the removal of Judge Loring from office. 23 March 1855. p.47, c3.

3343 J. H. PHILLEO *to* **FRIEND GARRISON. 10 March 1855. Rushford, N.Y.** Informs of the death of Edward B. Pratt. 23 March 1855. p.47, c5.

3344 HENRY C. WRIGHT *to* **W. L. GARRISON. 20 March 1855. Boston.** Details the experiences of Solomon Northrup. 23 March 1855. p.47, c6.

3345 S. E. W. *to* **W. L. GARRISON. 4 March 1855. Worcester.** Comments on women's political rights; discusses the poll tax. 23 March 1855. p.48, c2.

3346 ROBERT JOHNSTON *to* **LOUIS KOSSUTH. 27 February 1855. New York.** Questions Kossuth's position on war. 23 March 1855. p.48, c3.

3347 GERRIT SMITH *to* **WILLIAM H. SEWARD. 13 March 1855. Peterboro'.** Questions Seward's speech on the Fugitive Slave Act. 30 March 1855. p.49, c2.

3348 CHARLES SUMNER *to* **DOCTOR. 19 February. Washington.** Informs of a slave child who has been freed. 30 March 1855. p.50, c1.

3349 LUCIUS HOLMES *to* **FRIEND GARRISON. n.d. New York.** Eulogizes Juliette Reed. 30 March 1855. p.51, c1.

3350 ANDREW JACKSON DAVIS *to* **BELOVED GARRISON. 21 March 1855. Brooklyn, N.Y.** Praises the Western Progressive Friends and the Garrisonian schools. 30 March 1855. p.51, c1.

3351 LUCY STONE *to* **W. L. GARRISON. 17 March 1855. Syracuse.** Requests correction of a printing error regarding Margaret Hyatt's death. 30 March 1855. p.51, c1.

3352 A. LILLIE AND E. WIGHAM *to* **SIR. 22 December 1854. n.p.** Secretaries of the Edinburgh Ladies' Emancipation Committee criticize the attitude toward abolition of the American Board of Commissioners for Foreign Missions. 6 April 1855. p.53, c5.

3353 S. B. TREAT *to* **THE EDITOR OF THE** *CHRISTIAN OBSERVER.* **7 October 1854. Missionary House, Boston.** Denies that he tried to exclude slaveholders from the commission. 6 April 1855. p.53, c6.

3354 S. R. WARD *to* **EDINBURGH LADIES' EMANCIPATION COMMITTEE. n.d. n.p.** Presents his reason for supporting Turkish missionary activity. 6 April 1855. p.54, c1.

3355 LEWIS TAPPAN *to* **THE EDITOR OF THE** *NONCONFORMIST.* **23 November 1854. New York.** Comments on the American Board of Commissioners for Foreign Missions and its fellowship with slaveholders. 6 April 1855. p.54, c2.

3356 SECRETARY OF THE BRISTOL AND CLIFTON AS *to* **GENERAL AGENT OF THE MASSACHUSETTS AS. 8 March 1855. Bristol, England.** Wishes to know whether or not H. B. Stowe and Rev. H. Ward Beecher support the American Board of Foreign Missions. 6 April 1855. p.54, c3.

3357 JOHN G. WHITTIER *to* **FRIEND [W. L. GARRISON]. 26 March 1855. Amesbury.** Sends a contribution to the Vigilance Committee to help resist the Fugitive Slave Law. 6 April 1855. p.54, c4.

3358 E. B. CHAPMAN LAUGEL *to* **W. L. GARRISON, FRANCIS JACKSON, AND WENDELL PHILLIPS. 8 March 1855. Paris.** Forwards letters regarding Thomas Sturge's contribution. 6 April 1855. p.54, c5.

3359 ESTHER STURGE *to* **H. G. CHAPMAN. 26 February 1855. Northfleet, near London.** Comments on Thomas Sturge's one hundred-pound donation to the AAS. 6 April 1855. p.54, c5.

3360 E. B. CHAPMAN LAUGEL *to* **THOMAS STURGE, ESQ. 2 March 1855. Paris.** Thanks Sturge for making her the medium of his contribution to the AAS. 6 April 1855. p.54, c5.

3361 BENJAMIN S. JONES *to* **n.n. [extract from the** *Anti-Slavery Bugle***] n.d. n.p.** Eulogizes Cyrus Burleigh. 6 April 1855. p.55, c1.

3362 B. RUSH PLUMLEY *to* **M. [from the** *Ohio Anti-Slavery Bugle***] 10 March 1855. Philadelphia.** Sends eulogy of Cyrus M. Burleigh; describes his life and death. 6 April 1855. p.55, c1.

3363 MARY GREW *to* **W. L. GARRISON. [extract] n.d. Philadelphia.** Eulogizes C. M. Burleigh. 6 April 1855. p.55, c1.

3364 ALEXANDER *to* **n.n. [extract from the** *Chronicle and Sentinel***] 5 February 1855. Cumming, Ga.** Explains that he supports lowered tariffs on imported fabric; hopes this will "cripple and break down the North!" 13 April 1855. p.57, c4.

3365 GEORGE W. PUTNAM *to* **MR. GARRISON. 2 April 1855. Lynn, Ma.** Describes the lecture by Charles Sumner at Lynn. 13 April 1855. p.59, c1.

3366 G. NEEDHAM *to* **FRIEND GARRISON. 29 March 1855. Providence, R.I.** Forwards his letter denouncing Rhode Island's miscegenation law. 13 April 1855. p.60, c5.

3367 G. NEEDHAM *to* **THE EDITOR OF THE** *PROVIDENCE DAILY TRIBUNE***. n.d. n.p.** Denounces Rhode Island's law forbidding interracial marriages. 13 April 1855. p.60, c5.

3368 CLARISSA G. OLDS *to* **MR. MAY. [extract] 18 March 1855. Windham, Me.** Discusses anti-slavery tracts, non-fellowship with slaveholders, and colonization. 13 April 1855. p.60, c5.

3369 S. S. GRISWOLD *to* **FRIEND GARRISON. 5 April 1855. Greenmanville.** Discusses the lack of principle displayed by political parties and politicians. 20 April 1855. p.61, c3.

3370 CHARLES LOWELL *to* **THE EDITOR OF THE** *BOSTON EVENING TELE-GRAPH***. 10 April 1855. Cambridge, Ma.** Comments on the Epistle to Philemon and Dr. Adams' pro-slavery book. 20 April 1855. p.62, c5.

3371 COSMOPOLITE *to* **THE** *LIBERATOR***. 26 March 1855. Manatee, Fl.** Discusses his anti-slavery conversion, slave power in Cuba, and the mistreatment of Indians. 20 April 1855. p.62, c6.

3372 S. E. W. *to* **W. L. GARRISON. 2 April 1855. Worcester.** Examines women's rights and the rights of wives. 20 April 1855. p.62, c6.

3373 C. LOWELL *to* **GENTLEMEN. [from the** *New York Evening Post***] n.d. n.p.** Expresses gratitude for the circulation of his notice on the Epistle to Philemon; comments on pro-slavery excerpt from the Bible. 27 April 1855. p.66, c6.

3374 CHARLES STEARNS *to* **MR. GARRISON. 7 April 1855. Lawrence, Kansas Territory.** Describes preparations necessary for emigration to Kansas; discusses Kansas' first fugitive slave case, involving the return of a female fugitive to her former master. 27 April 1855. p.67, c2.

3375 HENRY C. HOWELLS *to* **WM. LLOYD GARRISON. 8 April 1855. Perth Amboy.** Comments on the true purpose of the American Board of Foreign Missions. 27 April 1855. p.67, c3.

3376 H. C. WRIGHT *to* **REV. LYMAN BEECHER. February 1855. Boston.** Discusses capital punishment in reference to John W. Webster, the murderer, and Joseph Eveleth, the hangman; examines the difference between them. 27 April 1855. p.68, c2.

3377 GEORGE ARMSTRONG *to* **SIR. [from the** *Bristol Mercury*] **27 March 1855. Redland.** Discusses the British churches and American slavery. 4 May 1855. p.69, c3.

3378 CHARLES H. PAYNE *to* **MR. EDITOR. [from** *Zion's Herald*] **9 April 1855. Savannah, Ga.** A Northerner travelling South condemns slavery and relates conversations with urban and plantation slaves concerning their treatment. 4 May 1855. p.69, c4.

3379 n.n. *to* **MR. EDITOR. [from the** *Platte Argus, Extra*] **14 April 1855. Parkville, Mo.** Describes how mob stormed into office of *Luminary Press*, and threatened to tar and feather owners, G. S. Park and J. W. Patterson, for aiding in cause of abolition. 4 May 1855. p.69, c6.

3380 H. C. WRIGHT *to* **PARKER PILLSBURY. 27 April 1855. Senate Chamber, Boston.** Rejoices at the removal of Judge Loring by the Massachusetts legislature. 4 May 1855. p.70, c6.

3381 SAMUEL KEESE *to* **ESTEEMED FRIEND. 4 April 1855. Peru, N.Y.** Discusses the lectures by A. M. Powell and why he was accused of being an infidel by ministers in northern New York. 4 May 1855. p.72, c3.

3382 E. H. LONGSHORE *to* **S. MAY, JR. 31 January 1855. Cerro Gordo, In.** States that they are hungry for some anti-slavery food. 4 May 1855. p.72, c3.

3383 REV. FRANCIS BISHOP *to* **PARKER PILLSBURY. [extract] n.d. Liverpool, England.** Discusses English poverty and philanthropy. 4 May 1855. p.72, c4.

3384 FRANCIS BARRY *to* **ALEXANDER McARTHUR. 2 April 1855. Berlin Heights, Oh.** Examines the implications of God's failure to abolish slavery. 4 May 1855. p.72, c4.

3385 W. G. B. *to* **FRIEND GARRISON. n.d. n.p.** Believes that a tract describing the "true church" is needed. 11 May 1855. p.76, c3.

3386 VICTOR HUGO *to* **LOUIS BONAPARTE. 8 April 1855. n.p.** Entreats Bonaparte not to come to London; advises him to leave exiles alone. 11 May 1855. p.76, c3.

3387 BLACKSTONE *to* **MR. EDITOR. [from the** *Boston Herald*] **16 May 1855. New York.** Discusses candidacy of Sumner and Wilson, two Massachusetts senators who support a platform of disunion; foresees anarchy and chaos if they are victorious. 25 May 1855. p.81, c4.

3388 WILLIAM JAY *to* **THE EDITOR OF THE** *EVENING POST.* **15 May 1855. New York.** Corrects printed distortions of John Jay's view of slavery. 25 May 1855. p.82, c1.

3389 W. S. G. *to* **FRIEND GARRISON. 20 May 1855. Wilmington, De.** Describes a Hutchinson family concert, Theodore Parker's lecture, and a Progressive Friends meeting. 25 May 1855. p.83, c4.

3390 HENRY C. WRIGHT *to* **PARKER PILLSBURY. 11 May 1855. New York.** Reports on the anniversary meetings of the various ASS in New York City. 25 May 1855. p.84, c2.

3391 JOSEPH BARKER *to* **FRIEND [W. L. GARRISON]. 3 May 1855. Salem. Oh.** Regrets missing the anniversary meeting; advocates a war of extermination against slavery. 25 May 1855. p.84, c3.

3392 HENRY W. BELLOWS *to* **OLIVER JOHNSON, ESQ. 17 April 1855. New York.** Declines an invitation to speak at an AAS meeting because of the blasphemous language which will be used there. 25 May 1855. p.84, c4.

3393 E. OAKES SMITH *to* **THE EDITOR OF THE** *NEW YORK TRIBUNE.* **n.d. n.p.** Denounces P. T. Barnum's sexism. 25 May 1855. p.84, c5.

3394 GEO. S. PARK *to* **THE PUBLIC. 23 April 1855. Parkville, Mo.** Bids the public farewell; predicts civil war; declares that he is leaving after the destruction of his press. 1 June 1855. p.85, c6.

3395 REES E. PRICE *to* **FRIEND GARRISON. 19 May 1855. Mount Zion.** Denounces democracy because the vile and ignorant outnumber the virtuous and wise. 1 June 1855. p.87, c4.

3396 THOMAS M'CLINTOCK *to* **W. L. GARRISON. n.d. n.p.** Submits for publication a letter to Abram Pryne about the Progressive Friends. 1 June 1855. p.88, c2.

3397 THOMAS M'CLINTOCK *to* **ABRAM PRYNE. 10 July 1855. Waterloo, N.Y.** Refutes Pryne's remarks that the spirit of the Yearly Meeting of Congregational Friends was "negative," that it "denies the past" and "hardly comprehends and adapts itself to the present"; questions Pryne about his religious beliefs. 1 June 1855. p.88, c2.

3398 n.n. *to* **n.n. n.d. n.p.** Entitled "Reply to Thomas M'Clintock," column supports charges previously made against the Progressive Friends. 1 June 1855. p.88, c2.

3399 THOMAS M'CLINTOCK *to* **ABRAM PRYNE. 7 August 1854. Waterloo, N.Y.** Criticizes justification offered for earlier charges against the Progressive Friends. 1 June 1855. p.88, c3.

3400 REV. MR. HASSALL *to* **BROTHER GARRISON. 14 May 1855. Hanley, Staffordshire, England.** Describes incidents aboard a steamer bound for England and a Southerner's reaction to anti-slavery literature. 8 June 1855. p.91, c4.

3401 W. G. CAMBRIDGE *to* **MR. EDITOR. n.d. n.p.** Corrects a report concerning the barring of Sojourner Truth from a church where she was invited to lecture. 8 June 1855. p.91, c5.

3402 CATHARINE E. BEECHER *to* **THE EDITOR OF THE** *NEW YORK TRIBUNE.* **n.d. n.p.** Denies having been insulted by the students at the University of Virginia while visiting a professor there. 8 June 1855. p.92, c4.

3403 T. BAILEY MYERS *to* **MAYOR FERNANDO WOOD, MAYOR OF NEW YORK. 25 May 1855. Office of the Sixth Avenue Railroad Company.** Discusses Pennington's sermon urging colored people to assert their right to sit wherever they choose; comments on his attempt to practice what he preached, and the railroad's justification for segregation. 8 June 1855. p.92, c4.

3404 P. T. BARNUM *to* **SIR. [from the** *Cleveland Leader***] n.d. n.p.** Demands fifty to one hundred dollars for lecturing on the "Philosophy of Humbug" and on temperance. 15 June 1855. p.96, c5.

3405 D. A. WASSON *to* **MR. GARRISON. 18 June 1855. Groveland.** Encloses his speech and explains his views on helping fugitive slaves; discusses slave insurrections. 22 June 1855. p.98, c5.

3406 REV. D. H. PLUMB *to* **FRIEND GARRISON. 15 June 1855. Warren, Ma.** Explains his anti-slavery convictions. 22 June 1855. p.99, c1.

3407 S. W. W. *to* **FRIEND GARRISON. 14 June 1855. Providence, R.I.** Reports on the meeting of Rhode Island Congregationalists which resolved not to associate with slaveholders or join those who do so. 22 June 1855. p.99, c2.

3408 n.n. *to* **GRANDMOTHER. 3 June 1855. Worcester.** Describes the birthday party for Stephen S. Foster's father. 22 June 1855. p.99, c2.

3409 JOSEPH BARKER *to* **FRIEND [W. L. GARRISON]. 12 June 1855. Salem. Oh.** Describes his anti-slavery labors in the West. 22 June 1855. p.100, c2.

3410 W. S. NORMAN, S. M. VARNADOE, A. WINN, W. S. BAKER, J. B. BARNARD *to* **THE CHURCH AND SOCIETY OF DORCHESTER, MASSACHUSETTS. [from the** *Savannah* **(Ga.)** *Republican***] 4 June 1855. Riceboro, Liberty County, Ga.** Rejoice that abolitionists have not obliterated all kindly feeling in the North for Southerners. 29 June 1855. p.101, c3.

3411 n.n. *to* **SIR. [from the** *Boston Courier***] n.d. n.p.** A member of the Society of Friends in Philadelphia compliments article entitled "What is Unitarianism?"; views abolitionists as fanatical and short-sighted, not "*genuine* and really enlarged philanthropists." 29 June 1855. p.101, c3.

3412 GEORGE SUNTER, JR. *to* **FRIEND [W. L. GARRISON]. 17 June 1855. Paris, Canada West.** Asserts that the United States Constitution is pro-slavery. 29 June 1855. p.103, c1.

3413 SAMUEL KEESE *to* **FRIEND GARRISON. 22 May 1855. Peru, N.Y.** Criticizes Francis Barry's position of rejecting God while embracing reform as absurd. 29 June 1855. p.104, c2.

3414 D. HITCHINGS *to* **FRANCIS BARRY. 26 May 1855. Richfield, N.Y.** Argues for belief in God. 29 June 1855. p.104, c2.

3415 A GARRISONIAN ABOLITIONIST *to* **THE EDITORS OF THE [***LONDON***]** *EM-PIRE***. n.d. n.p.** Denies the *British Banner*'s charge that Garrison is an infidel. 6 July 1855. p.106, c2.

3416 GEO. W. PUTMAN *to* **REV. DR. GANNETT. n.d. n.p.** Explains why he disagreed with Theodore Parker's praise of Gannett for defending a commissioner of the Fugitive Slave Law. 6 July 1855. p.106, c6.

3417 CASTIGATION *to* **MR. EDITOR. n.d. n.p.** Declares that the *Liberator*'s criticism of H. W. Beecher's "Star Papers" was apt. 6 July 1855. p.107, c1.

3418 AMOS GILBERT *to* **FRIEND GARRISON. n.d. n.p.** Praises John Prost, a humble anti-slavery worker. 6 July 1855. p.108, c2.

3419 W. G. CAMBRIDGE *to* **FRIEND GARRISON. 28 June 1855. Weymouth.** Denies that he claimed the Warren Society barred Sojourner Truth from the meetinghouse. 6 July 1855. p.108, c2.

3420 FRANCIS A. WALKER *to* **SIR. 25 June 1855. Lancaster, Ma.** Wonders why no effective pro-slavery novel has been written; believes *The Planter's Northern Bride* comes closest to being adequate, but contains many absurdities. 6 July 1855. p.108, c3.

3421 HENRY WILSON *to* **WENDELL PHILLIPS, ESQ. 30 June 1855. Natick, Ma.** Explains that he cannot attend a Fourth of July anti-slavery celebration at Framingham. 13 July 1855. p.110, c5.

3422 E. M. BALLARD *to* **MR. EDITOR. 21 May 1855. Grand Rapids, Mi.** Reports that men in Michigan are collecting arms for the defense of Northern men and their rights. 20 July 1855. p.113, c3.

3423 J. B. ESTLIN *to* **THE EDITOR OF THE** *ANTI-SLAVERY ADVOCATE.* **7 June 1855. Bristol.** Forwards a letter he wrote to the British Foreign AS withdrawing his subscription. 20 July 1855. p.113, c4.

3424 J. B. ESTLIN *to* **L. A. CHAMEROVZOW, SECRETARY OF THE BRITISH AND FOREIGN AS. 21 May 1855. Bristol, England.** Gives reasons for withdrawing from British and Foreign AS. 20 July 1855. p.113, c4.

3425 WM. COATES *to* **FRIEND WALLCUT. 9 July 1855. Boonton, Morris County, N.J.** Asks whether John H. Marshall, a professed ex-slave who is collecting money to purchase his family's freedom, is to be trusted. 20 July 1855. p.114, c5.

3426 REV. JOSEPH P. FESSENDEN *to* **THE EDITORS OF THE** *CONGREGA-TIONALIST.* **15 June 1855. South Bridgton.** Charges that the *Congregationalist*, like all other religious journals, tolerates slavery and its supporters; cancels his subscription. 20 July 1855. p.114, c6.

3427 SOUTH DANVERS *to* **FRIEND GARRISON. n.d. n.p.** Ridicules the *Boston Trumpet*, a sectarian paper, for not condemning slavery. 20 July 1855. p.115, c6.

3428 GNOSTIC *to* **FRIEND GARRISON. 11 July 1855. Stonington.** Declares that the Seventh-Day Baptists are among the few denominations which meet the high standards of true abolitionism. 20 July 1855. p.115, c1.

3429 JOSEPH BARKER *to* **FRIEND [W. L. GARRISON]. 30 June 1855. Salem, Oh.** Lists the subjects on which he is prepared to lecture when he returns East. 20 July 1855. p.115, c1.

3430 G. B. STEBBINS *to* **W. L. GARRISON. 4 July 1855. Aurora, Il.** Presents sketches of Illinois. 20 July 1855. p.116, c2.

3431 J. C. *to* **FRIEND GARRISON. 8 June 1855. South Hingham.** Encloses an article about a Southerner who claims that no connection exists between spiritualism and slavery. 20 July 1855. p.116, c3.

3432 n.n. *to* **MR. GARRISON. 8 July 1855. East Bridgewater.** Describes the Fourth of July celebration in East Bridgewater. 20 July 1855. p.116. c4.

3433 W. G. B. *to* **GARRISON. 4 July 1855. n.p.** A pacifist advocates abstaining from fellowship with a pro-slavery government. 20 July 1855. p.116, c5.

3434 F. H. PRICE, WESLEY SHROPSHIRE, R. M. YOUNG, B. F. CHASTAIN, AND WM. A. FORT *to* **HON. JOHN H. LUMPKIN. [from the** *Rome* **(Ga.)** *Southerner***] 13 June 1855. Calhoun, Ga.** Inform Judge Lumpkin of his nomination as Democratic candidate for Congress. 27 July 1855. p.117, c1.

3435 JOHN H. LUMPKIN *to* **F. H. PRICE, WESLEY SHROPSHIRE, R. M. YOUNG, B. F. CHASTAIN, AND WM. A. FORT. 27 June 1855. Rome, Ga.** Accepts nomination as Democratic candidate for Congress; promises to maintain the Fourth Resolution of the People of Georgia, adopted in 1850. 27 July 1855. p.117, c1.

3436 WM. H. FISH *to* **FRIEND GARRISON. 25 July 1855. Hopedale.** Reports that plans are underway to hold a celebration of emancipation in the West Indies in Hopedale. 27 July 1855. p.118, c2.

3437 PARKER PILLSBURY *to* **FRIEND MAY. 7 July 1855. Bristol, England.** Praises J. B. Estlin. 27 July 1855. p.118, c3.

3438 HENRY C. WRIGHT *to* **W. L. GARRISON. 16 July 1855. Randolph, Oh.** Reports on the persisting pro-slavery sentiment in Ohio. 27 July 1855. p.118, c5.

3439 AARON M. POWELL *to* **GENERAL AGENT. [extract] 21 July 1855. Ghent, N.Y.** Discusses the pro-slavery attitude of a minister in Ghent. 27 July 1855. p.118, c6.

3440 JOHN JOLIFFE *to* **MESSRS. EDITORS. [from the** *Cincinnati Gazette*] **16 July 1855. Cincinnati, Oh.** Reports that he was badly treated in Barnwell, South Carolina while on business there. 27 July 1855. p.119, c4.

3441 C. STEARNS *to* **W. L. GARRISON. 4 July1855. Lawrence, Ks.** Analyzes the state of affairs in Kansas; foresees either dissolution of the Union or submission of the South. 27 July 1855. p.120, c2.

3442 JOHN M. SPEAR *to* **BROTHER GARRISON. 5 July 1855. Boston.** Sends a report on spiritualism. 27 July 1855. p.120, c4.

3443 F. HINKLY *to* **MR. GARRISON. 17 July 1855. Hyannis.** Describes Rev. Wilder's lecture attacking abolitionists and defending the churches. 27 July 1855. p.120, c5.

3444 HENRY CHAPIN *to* **GOV. HENRY J. GARDINER. 20 July 1855. Worcester.** Accepts the office of commissioner under the Massachusetts Personal Liberty Bill. 3 August 1855. p.123, c1.

3445 REV. A. T. FOSS *to* **FRIEND GARRISON. n.d. n.p.** Describes his anti-slavery lecture tour. 3 August 1855. p.123. c2.

3446 E. R. B. *to* **W. L. GARRISON. 27 July 1855. Cheshire, Ma.** Reports on A. T. Foss' lectures in Cheshire. 3 August 1855. p.123, c2.

3447 GERRIT SMITH *to* **THE** *NEW YORK TRIBUNE.* **17 July 1855. Peterboro', N.Y.** Declares his satisfaction that the *New York Tribune* finally reported his vote against the Nebraska Bill; discusses his position with regard to the bill. 3 August 1855. p.124, c2.

3448 K. *to* **MR. EDITOR. [from the** *Dedham Gazette*] **n.d. n.p.** Criticizes Gov. Gardner; confesses that the governor's popularity is a mystery to him. 10 August 1855. p.125, c6.

3449 W. STILL *to* **THE EDITOR OF THE** *NEW YORK TRIBUNE.* **30 July 1855. Philadelphia.** Details the Philadelphia slave case involving the agency of Mr. Passmore Williamson. 10 August 1855. p.126, c1.

3450 JOHN A. ANDREW *to* **REV. SAMUEL MAY, JR. 31 July 1855. Boston.** Explains that legal business prevents him from attending the West Indies Emancipation celebration in Abington. 10 August 1855. p.127, c1.

3451 JOHN ADAMS, M. J. MILLER, J. HOPLIN, AND R. G. WILLIAMS *to* **COL. C. M. CLAY. 12 July 1855. Mt. Vernon, Ky.** Committee warns that abolitionist speakers will no longer be able to give lectures in their county; sends resolutions. 17 August 1855. p.129, c5.

3452 C. M. CLAY *to* **MESSRS. J. ADAMS, &C. 16 July 1855. Berea, Ky.** Defends himself against accusation that he is "revolutionary"; defies resolutions made by John Adams' committee. 17 August 1855. p.129, c6.

3453 CHAS. STEARNS *to* **W. L. GARRISON. 28 July 1855. Lawrence, Ks.** Reports on threats of violence against abolitionists in Kansas. 17 August 1855. p.130, c5.

3454 COLPORTEUR *to* **REV. WM. WARREN. n.d. n.p.** Assails Warren's defense of the American Tract Society. 17 August 1855. p.130, c5.

3455 WM. COATES *to* **W. L. GARRISON. 29 July 1855. Boonton, Morris County, N.J.** Reports on John H. Marshall's speech defending himself from the *Liberator*'s accusations and attacking the abolitionists; adds that Marshall asked his audience to consider how the abolitionists had abused and persecuted Frederick Douglass. 17 August 1855. p.130, c6.

3456 FRANCIS BARRY *to* **D. HITCHINGS. 26 July 1855. Berlin Heights, Oh.** Argues against the existence of God. 17 August 1855. p.132, c2.

3457 FRANCIS BARRY *to* **SAMUEL KEESE. 31 July 1855. Berlin Heights, Oh.** Asserts that God does not exist and that, if he does, he is mean and lazy. 17 August 1855. p.132, c2.

3458 WM. WELLS BROWN *to* **MR. GARRISON. 6 August 1855. n.p.** Reports from the anti-slavery lecture field in Maine; notes having met a "cunning-looking colored man," John Randolph, who claimed to be the son of John Randolph of Roanoke and absconded with funds collected from AS meeting. 17 August 1855. p.132, c3.

3459 J. B. SYME *to* **ELIHU BURRITT. 25 August 1847. Edinburgh.** Presents his autobiography. 17 August 1855. p.132, c4.

3460 T. W. HIGGINSON *to* **MR. GARRISON. 19 August 1855. Worcester, Ma.** Discusses the meaning of the attempted rescue of Burns. 24 August 1855. p.134, c4.

3461 TOURIST *to* **MR. GARRISON. n.d. n.p.** Discusses the size of the colored population in Chatham, Canada West. 24 August 1855. p.134, c4.

3462 JOSEPH TREAT *to* **MR. GARRISON. 21 August 1855. Boston.** Disavows belief in God and immortality. 24 August 1855. p.134, c5.

3463 L. W. *to* **MR. GARRISON. 20 August 1855. Manchester, Ma.** Describes Manchester anti-slavery meetings featuring Wm. Wells Brown. 24 August 1855. p.134, c5.

3464 W. H. WILLEY *to* **MR. EDITOR. [from the** *Missouri Democrat***] 8 August 1855. St. Louis, Mo.** Reports that a Southerner was warned to leave the state because he was suspected of being a Northern abolitionist. 31 August 1855. p.137, c4.

3465 HON. DANIELS S. DICKINSON *to* **n.n. [extract from the** *Tallahasee Floridian and Journal***] June 1855. n.p.** Denounces the Personal Liberty Bill as a monstrosity and "treason of the deepest dye." 31 August 1855. p.138, c3.

3466 A. H. WOOD *to* **W. L. GARRISON. 15 August 1855. Pepperell.** Reports on J. J. Locke's lecture condemning the American church. 31 August 1855. p.139, c1.

3467 L. M. PERHAM *to* **W. L. GARRISON. 23 August 1855. Mendon.** Reports on S. S. Foster's lecture on "manstealing." 31 August 1855. p.139, c1.

3468 SEN. CHARLES SUMNER *to* **PASSMORE WILLIAMSON. 11 August 1855. On steamer, the** *North Star*, **in Lake Superior.** Congratulates Williams, a jailed abolitionist, for attempting to free a slave brought North by his master. 31 August 1855. p.139, c2.

3469 PARKER PILLSBURY *to* **THE EDITOR OF THE** *LONDON INQUIRER*. **4 August 1855. Manchester, England.** Explains why American abolition must be accomplished by moral means; gives examples of how not to be an abolitionist. 7 September 1855. p.141, c2.

3470 DEA. HIRAM BROWN *to* **n.n. [extract] 22 August 1855. Cummington, Ma.** Discusses anti-slavery lectures by Messrs. Foss and Burleigh. 7 September 1855. p.142, c4.

3471 HENRY C. WRIGHT *to* **W. L. GARRISON. 29 August 1855. New Lisbon, Oh.** Criticizes the platform of Ohio Republicans under the leadership of S. P. Chase. 7 September 1855. p.142, c5.

3472 J. *to* **FRIEND GARRISON. n.d. n.p.** Discusses the rescue of Burns. 7 September 1855. p.142, c6.

3473 ALMIGHTY DOLLAR *to* **W. L. GARRISON. n.d. n.p.** Reports on a Southern slave-trading vessel which has just left Boston Harbor. 7 September 1855. p.142, c6.

3474 S. MITCHELL *to* **FRIEND GARRISON. 28 August 1855. Cornville, Me.** Declares that political abolitionists in Maine cannot be looked to for guidance; argues against union with slaveholders. 7 September 1855. p.143, c1.

3475 HENRY C. WRIGHT *to* **PARKER PILLSBURY. 27 August 1855. Alliance, Oh.** Describes the anti-slavery meeting in Ohio; lists resolutions. 14 September 1855. p.145, c3.

3476 C. STEARNS *to* **W. L. GARRISON. 21 August 1855. Lawrence, Ks.** Fears there will be a "Black Law" in Kansas. 14 September 1855. p.145, c4.

3477 LUCY STONE *to* **MR. GARRISON. 9 September 1855. West Brookfield.** Announces women's rights conventions to be held in Cincinnati and Boston. 14 September 1855. p.146, c3.

3478 ROBERT MORRIS *to* **THE EDITOR OF THE** *BOSTON EVENING TELEGRAPH*. **n.d. Boston.** Reports on the Boston colored militia and the Massachusetts governor's refusal to provide it with state arms. 14 September 1855. p.148, c4.

3479 JOHN H. CLIFFORD *to* **GOV. HENRY J. GARDINER. 17 August 1855. New Bedford, Ma.** Explains why Gardiner should refuse to issue state arms to the Boston colored militia. 14 September 1855. p.148, c4.

3480 S. *to* **THE EDITOR OF THE** *NEW YORK CHRISTIAN INQUIRER*. **10 August 1855. Brooklyn.** Defends Theodore Parker's view that God is in everything. 14 September 1855. p.148, c5.

3481 JOHN ORVIS *to* **SIR [W. L. GARRISON]. 17 September 1855. Boston.** Defends the newly-formed Association of Philanthropic Commercialists. 21 September 1855. p.150, c5.

3482 AGRICOLA *to* **THE EDITOR OF THE** *LIBERATOR* **[W. L. GARRISON]. 16 September 1855. Manchester, N.H.** Reports on the New Hampshire State Agricultural Fair. 21 September 1855. p.150, c5.

3483 H. C. WRIGHT *to* **W. L. GARRISON. 9 September 1855. Mesopotamia, Oh.** Rebukes the slaveholding church and advocates a free Northern confederacy. 21 September 1855. p.150, c6.

3484 CORRESPONDENT OF *NEW YORK TRIBUNE* *to* **n.n. 18 September 1855. Philadelphia.** Relates his visit to Passmore Williamson; adds that "his body is confined within the walls of his narrow cell . . . but his soul is free." 21 September 1855. p.151, c1.

3485 A CORRESPONDENT *to* **n.n. 12 September 1855. Norfolk.** Reports a total of 1700 deaths from the fever. 21 September 1855. p.151, c2.

3486 WM. S. FLANDERS *to* **FRANCIS BARRY. 12 September 1855. Cornville, Me.** Argues for the existence of God. 21 September 1855. p.152, c2.

3487 D. HITCHINGS *to* **FRANCIS BARRY. 1 September 1855. Richfield, N.Y.** Argues that God exists. 21 September 1855. p.152, c3.

3488 JOHN ORVIS *to* **SIR [W. L. GARRISON]. n.d. n.p.** Proposes a new system of equitable commerce based on humanitarian values. 28 September 1855. p.154, c6.

3489 GEO. W. STACY *to* **W. L. GARRISON. 15 September 1855. Milford.** Reports on his lecture in Marlboro, Massachusetts. 21 September 1855. p.154, c6.

3490 n.n. *to* **FRIEND IN BOSTON. [extract] 3 July 1855. Canton.** Gives bloody details of mass execution of rebels in Canton, China. 28 September 1855. p.156, c5.

3491 S. G. HOWE, SAMUEL MAY, THOMAS RUSSELL, NATHANIEL B. SHURTLEFF, JOHN M. CLARK, JOSEPH STORY, PHILO SANFORD, AND JAMES STONE *to* **SENATOR STEPHEN DOUGLAS. 2 August 1855. Boston.** Invite him to lecture on slavery in Boston. 5 October 1855. p.157, c6.

3492 SEN. S. A. DOUGLAS *to* **DR. J. W. STONE AND OTHERS, COMMITTEE. 11 August 1855. Chicago.** Declines invitation to lecture on slavery in Boston. 5 October 1855. p.157, c6.

3493 SEN. A. P. BUTLER *to* **JAMES W. STONE. [extract] n.d. n.p.** Declares that he would probably give a pro-slavery speech if he accepted an invitation to lecture in Boston. 5 October 1855. p.157, c6.

3494 JAMES W. STONE *to* **A. P. BUTLER. 4 August 1855. Boston.** Replies that Boston would be receptive to hearing a Southerner's view of slavery. 5 October 1855. p.157, c6.

3495 GEORGE A. JOHNSON *to* **JOHN W. FOSTER. 6 August 1855. North Chelmsford, Ma.** The secretary of a Know-Nothing council writes to the president of the state council informing him that they do not recognize him as such. 5 October 1855. p.158, c1.

3496 J. W. FOSTER *to* **GEO. A. JOHNSON. 11 August 1855. Monson.** Sends his regrets but refuses to support the slaveholders' platform. 5 October 1855. p.158, c1.

3497 C. STEARNS *to* **FRIEND [W. L. GARRISON]. 10 September 1855. Lawrence, Ks.** Declares that his next letter will probably be dated from prison. 5 October 1855. p.160, c2.

3498 H. C. WRIGHT *to* **W. L. GARRISON. 23 September 1855. Akron, Oh.** Describes his stay in Akron, where he is advocating disunion. 5 October 1855. p.160, c2.

3499 H. W. B. *to* **W. L. GARRISON. 23 September 1855. Port Norfolk.** Suggests celebrating the twentieth anniversary of the mobbing of George Thompson. 5 October 1855. p.160, c3.

3500 S. W. W. *to* **FRIEND GARRISON. 6 October 1855. Providence.** Reports on Rev. N. Adams' sermon in Providence. 12 October 1855. p.163, c1.

3501 JOSEPH BARKER *to* **THE EDITOR OF THE** *ANTI-SLAVERY BUGLE.* **n.d. n.p.** Discusses the debate with S. S. Foster about political abolitionism and the Republican Party. 12 October 1855. p.163, c1.

3502 PASSMORE WILLIAMSON *to* **SIR. 29 September 1855. Philadelphia County Prison.** Acknowledges efforts to free him. 12 October 1855. p.163, c3.

3503 KANSAS *to* **THE EDITORS OF THE** *MORNING LEADER.* **20 October 1855. Leavenworth, Ks.** Reports murder and lawlessness in Kansas. 19 October 1855. p.165, c4.

3504 GERRIT SMITH *to* **MR. GARRISON. 14 October 1855. Peterboro', N.Y.** Answers his criticisms of the Jerry Rescue celebration; defends the Liberty Party. 19 October 1855. p.166, c3.

3505 WM. GOODELL *to* **FRIEND GARRISON. 13 October 1855. New York.** Denies that he opposes women's suffrage. 19 October 1855. p.166, c4.

3506 H. C. WRIGHT *to* **W. L. GARRISON. 7 October 1855. Battle Creek, Mi.** Reports on the resolutions and debate of an anti-slavery convention. 19 October 1855. p.166, c6.

3507 HENRY A. WISE *to* **S. G. HOWE, J. M. CLARK, S. MAY, P. SANFORD, N. B. SHURTLEFF, J. STORY, T. RUSSELL, AND J. W. STONE. 5 October 1855. Onancock, Va.** Declines an invitation to lecture on slavery in Virginia. 19 October 1855. p.167, c1.

3508 OHIO YEARLY MEETING OF FRIENDS OF HUMAN PROGRESS *to* **JUDGE KANE. n.d. Salem, Oh.** Pleads with Judge Kane to reverse his decision on Passmore Williamson. 19 October 1855. p.168, c2.

3509 REV. WALTER SCOTT *to* **F. W. CHESSON. n.d. Lancaster, Scotland.** Comments on the infidelity of abolitionists. 26 October 1855. p.169, c3.

3510 EMELINE M. RANDALL *to* **FRIEND GARRISON. n.d. n.p.** Reports on the Abington Anti-Slavery Fair. 26 October 1855. p.171, c3.

3511 G. Q. C. *to* **MR. EDITOR [W. L. GARRISON]. 17 October 1855. Salem.** Asks for a matching sum of $750 to purchase two slaves in the South. 26 October 1855. p.171, c4.

3512 LOUDON S. LONGLEY *to* **W. L. GARRISON. 10 October 1855. Huntington, Vt.** Argues that slavery can be abolished constitutionally. 26 October 1855. p.172, c3.

3513 AMOS GILBERT *to* **W. L. GARRISON. 12 October 1855. Salem, Oh.** Questions why the *Liberator* and other anti-slavery newspapers have not printed the notice of publication of "A Memoir of Frances Wright." 26 October 1855. p.172, c3.

3514 FRANCIS BARRY *to* **H. C. WRIGHT. 17 October 1855. Berlin Heights. Oh.** An anarchist chides Wright for settling for the establishment of a Northern republic. 2 November 1855. p.176, c2.

3515 ANDREW J. DAVIS *to* **S. B. BRITTAN. 16 October 1855. Brooklyn.** Comments on the discussion between himself and Brittan on the recent publication denying the spiritual origin of "Modern Mysteries" by Pres. Mahan. 2 November 1855. p.176, c3.

3516 W. S. G. *to* **W. L. GARRISON. n.d. n.p.** Declares that Southerners are more concerned about their own than they are about the American Union; believes that the South dominates the North politically. 9 November 1855. p.178, c6.

3517 A UNITARIAN GARRISONIAN ABOLITIONIST *to* **THE EDITOR OF THE** *LIBERATOR* **[W. L. GARRISON]. n.d. n.p.** Defends early Unitarians from W. Phillips' strictures. 9 November 1855. p.179, c3.

3518 GEO. W. STACY *to* **FRIEND GARRISON. 30 October 1855. Milford.** Sends money to help publish the proceedings of a meeting held on the anniversary of the Boston mob of 1835, which brutally mistreated the anti-slavery advocates. 9 November 1855. p.179, c3.

3519 M. A. *to* **W. L. GARRISON. 19 October 1855. Peacham, Vt.** Discusses the anti-slavery lectures of Wm. W. Brown and Oliver Johnson. 9 November 1855. p.179, c3.

3520 G. *to* **THE** *NEW ORLEANS DELTA***. 17 October 1855. Baton Rouge.** Relates rumor of possible uprising of Negroes in Baton Rouge, the mobilization of the citizens in anticipation of the rebellion, and the arrest of a Negro barber named Joe Craig, president of a local Negro association, who was reportedly driven from Montgomery, Alabama, for tampering with slaves. 9 November 1855. p.180, c5.

3521 J. M. MASON *to* **MR. SAMUEL G. HOWE AND OTHERS. 9 October 1855. Salma, Va.** Declines invitation to speak; believes that Northerners should not question the Southerners' right to enslave the African race. 16 November 1855. p.181, c3.

3522 D. B. ATCHISON *to* **MESSRS. W. B. WILSON, JNO. L. MILLER, AND S. M. MELTON. n.d. n.p.** Informs that he cannot attend the celebration of the Battle of King's Mountain; declares "the prosperity or the ruin of the whole South depends on the Kansas struggle." 16 November 1855. p.181, c3.

3523 W. L. GARRISON *to* **DR. SAMUEL G. HOWE, AND OTHERS. n.d. n.p.** Gives his reasons for declining their invitation to lecture on slavery. 16 November 1855. p.182, c3.

3524 GEO. B. WOOD *to* **FRIEND GARRISON. 28 October 1855. Marlboro.** Comments on Sallie Holley's lectures in Marlboro and Northboro. 16 November 1855. p.183, c2.

3525 G. W. S. *to* **FRIEND GARRISON. n.d. Milford.** Reports on a fugitive slave's escape to Canada. 16 November 1855. p.183, c2.

3526 CHARLES SUMNER *to* **THE EDITORS OF THE** *BOSTON POST***. 16 November 1855. Hancock Street.** Discusses his tour of the South. 23 November 1855. p.186, c2.

3527 W. C. NELL *to* **REV. SAMUEL MAY, JR. 21 October 1855. En route from Philadelphia to Boston.** Recalls the Boston mob incident in 1835; relates the reminiscences of other Boston colored people. 23 November 1855. p.186, c4.

3528 D. S. W. *to* **MR. EDITOR. n.d. n.p.** Reports on anti-slavery work in Massachusetts. 23 November 1855. p.186, c5.

3529 n.n. *to* **W. L. GARRISON. 29 October 1855. Topeka, Ks.** States that the majority regard slavery as a question of dollars and cents. 23 November 1855. p.186, c5.

3530 F. S. C. *to* **W. L. GARRISON. 17 November 1855. New York.** Commends Garrison's decision to decline the invitation to speak on slavery. 23 November 1855. p.187, c4.

3531 H. C. WRIGHT *to* **W. L. GARRISON. 8 November 1855. n.p.** Discusses the decline of Boston morality since 1765, the year of the Stamp Act. 23 November 1855. p.188, c2.

3532 D. S. W. *to* **MR. EDITOR [W. L. GARRISON]. n.d. n.p.** Argues that the infrequency of insanity among colored people disproves their detractors' assumptions that they are shiftless and that there is a relation between poverty and lunacy. 23 November 1855. p.188, c3.

3533 REV. ROBT. H. BRECKENRIDGE *to* **W. H. SEWARD. [extract] n.d. n.p.** Discusses the postures of the North and South regarding slavery. 30 November 1855. p.189, c1.

3534 HENRY A. WISE *to* **CHARLES G. CHASE AND OTHERS. 11 November 1855. Onancock, Va.** Regrets that he cannot lecture for the Mercantile Library Association of Boston. 30 November 1855. p.189, c2.

3535 A CORRESPONDENT *to* **THE** *BOSTON TELEGRAPH.* **[extract] n.d. Topeka, Ks.** Declares that a clear majority in the convention advocate the exclusion of Negroes from the Kansas territory. 30 November 1855. p.189, c2.

3536 PARKER PILLSBURY *to* **n.n. [extract] 7 November 1855. Edinburgh, Scotland.** Declares that every friend of the Union, even a Free-Soiler, is a foe of freedom. 30 November 1855. p.190, c4.

3537 GEO. B. WOOD *to* **W. L. GARRISON. 18 November 1855. Pepperell, Ma.** Reminds W. L. Garrison that the *Boston Daily Reformer* denounced the Boston mob of 1835. 30 November 1855. p.191, c1.

3538 ABIGAIL MOSES *to* **MRS. BALDWIN. [from the** *New York Evening Post*] **n.d. n.p.** Explains how she found out what her "Innard Natur" required. 30 November 1855. p.190[192], c3.

3539 n.n. *to* **MR. EDITOR [W. L. GARRISON]. n.d. n.p.** Requests that the *Liberator* print a letter illustrating "how these Christians love one another." 30 November 1855. p.190[192], c4.

3540 J. L. BENNETT, A. F. SPALDING, AND C. McCURDY *to* **REV. F. W. HOLLAND. n.d. n.p.** Inform him of their desire to return to former relations between their respective denominations and sever their acquaintance with him. 30 November 1855. p.190[192], c4.

3541 S. *to* **THE EDITOR OF THE** *LIBERATOR* **[W. L. GARRISON]. n.d. n.p.** Discusses the Passmore Williamson case. 7 December 1855. p.194, c5.

3542 BENJAMIN FISH *to* **W. L. GARRISON. 22 October 1855. Rochester, N.Y.** Sends fruit trees for the Boston Anti-Slavery Bazaar. 7 December 1855. p.194, c6.

3543 H. C. WRIGHT *to* **W. L. GARRISON. 27 November 1855. Florence, Ma.** Commends Garrison for refusing to join slaveholders on the lecture platform. 7 December 1855. p.196, c2.

3544 A. W. BENTON *to* **MESSRS. PARTRIDGE AND BRITTAN. 28 September 1855. Fulton, Il.** Examines a question of biblical history. 7 December 1855. p.196, c4.

3545 MARY F. DAVIS *to* **A. W. BENTON. November 1855. Brooklyn.** Discusses the question of biblical authority. 7 December 1855. p.196, c4.

3546 B. F. STRINGFELLOW *to* **n.n. [from the** *Montgomery Advertiser***] 6 October 1855. Weston.** States that abolitionists have abandoned the contest in Kansas, and intend to resume it in Congress. 14 December 1855. p.197, c1.

3547 B. C. L. *to* **THE EDITORS OF THE** *DEMOCRATIC PRESS.* **9 November 1855. Parkville, Mo.** Reports on a confrontation between supporters of George S. Park and mobocratic disunionists who hope to expel Park from Parkville for the second time. 14 December 1855. p.197, c4.

3548 DELIA WEBSTER *to* **REV. DR. CHEEVER. 19 October 1855. Worcester.** Reports on the persecution in Kentucky of a Yankee school teacher, allegedly an abolitionist. 14 December 1855. p.197, c4.

3549 DR. S. G. HOWE *to* **W. L. GARRISON. 5 December 1855. Boston.** Replies to Garrison's attack on the committee sponsoring a series of lectures on slavery in Boston. 14 December 1855. p.198, c3.

3550 W. C. NELL *to* **SAMUEL MAY, JR. 10 December 1855. Boston.** Discusses a biography of W. L. Garrison; includes quotes and sonnet written by Garrison. 14 December 1855. p.198, c6.

3551 S. HOLLEY *to* **n.n. [extract] n.d. Worcester.** Reports on Rev. Wasson's sermon. 14 December 1855. p.198, c6.

3552 PARKER PILLSBURY *to* **SAMUEL MAY, JR. [extract] n.d. Newcastle, England.** Comments on the Boston mob of 1835 and the anniversary celebration. 14 December 1855. p.199, c3.

3553 VIATOR *to* **MESSRS. MORRIS AND WILLIS. [from** *Morris and Willis's Home Journal***] n.d. n.p.** Relates a sentimental story about a Southern slaveholder mourning the death of his "good old friend" and slave, John. 14 December 1855. p.200, c4.

3554 F. P. BLAIR *to* **MESSRS. DANIEL R. GOODLOE AND LEWIS CLEPHANE. 1 December 1855. Silver Springs, Md.** Declines invitation to join the Republican Association of Washington City, but concurs with its aims. 21 December 1855. p.201, c1.

3555 P. WILLIAMSON *to* **M. [from the** *Anti-Slavery Standard***] 6 December 1855. n.p.** Reports on his lawyer's attempt to free him from prison. 21 December 1855. p.202, c1.

3556 GEO. SUNTER, JR. *to* **THE EDITOR OF THE** *LIBERATOR* **[W. L. GARRISON]. 6 December 1855. Paris, Canada West.** Denounces political abolitionism. 21 December 1855. p.203, c1.

3557 C. STEARNS *to* **W. L. GARRISON. 3 December 1855. Lawrence, Ks.** Reports that the border ruffians have burnt Lawrence. 21 December 1855. p.203, c2.

3558 SETH HUNT *to* **FRIEND GARRISON. 9 December 1855. Northampton.** Encloses a testimonial in favor of H. C. Wright's lectures. 21 December 1855. p.203, c3.

3559 THEODORE PARKER *to* **W. C. NELL. 18 December 1855. Boston.** Regrets his inability to attend Nell's testimonial meeting. 28 December 1855. p.207, c5.

[1856]

3560 D. Y. *to* **THE** *ANTI-SLAVERY STANDARD.* **24 December 1855. Boston.** Reports on an anti-slavery celebration in Plymouth. 4 January 1856. p.2, c2.

3561 H. C. WRIGHT *to* **W. L. GARRISON. 28 December 1855. Boston.** Discusses lecture by Samuel May, Jr. on the rise and progress of anti-slavery. 4 January 1856. p.2, c3.

3562 C. STEARNS *to* **W. L. GARRISON. 7 December 1856. Lawrence, Ks.** Reports on the civil war in Kansas; declares that his non-resistance has yielded. 4 January 1856. p.2, c5.

3563 E. L. C. *to* **FRIEND GARRISON. 24 December 1855. Worcester.** Praises Jane Elizabeth Jones's lecture in Worcester. 4 January 1856. p.3, c3.

3564 WILSON SHANNON *to* **CHAS. ROBINSON AND J. H. LANE. 9 December 1855. Lawrenceville, Ks.** Reports that the governor of Kansas has authorized them to take measures for the protection of Lawrence. 4 January 1856. p.3, c3.

3565 H. O. S. *to* **PARKER PILLSBURY. 23 December 1855. Framingham, Ma.** Reports on the indifference to slavery in three Framingham churches. 4 January 1856. p.4, c2.

3566 CHARLES E. MICKLEY *to* **W. L. GARRISON. 13 December 1855. Fairfield, Mi.** Describes anti-slavery activities in Fairfield. 4 January 1856. p.4, c3.

3567 E. W. TWING *to* **W. L. GARRISON. 23 December 1855. Springfield.** Reports on H. C. Wright's lectures to the friends of spiritualism on "the ante-natal history and the rights of children." 4 January 1856. p.4, c4.

3568 A. BATTLES *to* **THE EDITOR OF THE** *WHIG & COURIER.* **17 December 1855. Bangor.** Announces that Rev. G. B. Little's conduct forces him to make public their controversy. 4 January 1856. p.4, c4.

3569 A. BATTLES *to* **REV. G. B. LITTLE. 10 December 1855. Bangor.** Defends the right of Mrs. E. L. Rose, an agnostic abolitionist, to lecture in Bangor. 4 January 1856. p.4, c4.

3570 FRANCES D. GAGE *to* **FREDERICK DOUGLASS. [from** *Frederick Douglass' Paper*] **24 December 1855. Rochester.** Criticizes letter from G. Smith to E. C. Stanton, which charged that the women's rights movement suffered from poor leadership. 4 January 1856. p.4, c5.

3571 S. H. WOODSON *to* **GEN. SHIELDS. 3 December 1855. Independence, Mo.** The former acting governor of Kansas sends troops into battle. 11 January 1856. p.5, c3.

3572 S. H. WOODSON *to* **W. MUSGROVE. 4 December 1855. Independence, Mo.** States that he would not attack Lawrence, Kansas, until reinforcements arrive. 11 January 1856. p.5, c4.

3573 S. H. WOODSON *to* **GEN. SHIELDS. 6 December 1855. Independence, Mo.** Tells volunteers to join the attack on Lawrence, Kansas. 11 January 1856. p.5, c4.

3574 HARRIOT K. HUNT *to* **FREDERICK U. TRACY. 1 December 1855. Boston.** Protests to the Boston treasurer against taxation of women without representation. 11 January 1856. p.7, c1.

3575 JOHN STEPHENSON *to* **n.n. 3 January 1856. Boston.** Comments on the anti-slavery lectures of Francis E. Watkins, a young lady of color. 11 January 1856. p.7, c2.

3576 ROBERT JOHNSTON *to* **MR. EDITOR. 15 December 1855. New York.** Reports on a deputation of Irish Methodists raising funds for the conversion of Ireland to Methodism; doubts the anti-slavery sentiments of the deputation. 11 January 1856. p.7, c3.

3577 REV. HIRAM WILSON *to* **W. L. GARRISON. 1 January 1855. St. Catharines, Canada West.** Comments on further arrivals of fugitive slaves to St. Catharines during 1855. 11 January 1856. p.7, c4.

3578 H. C. WRIGHT *to* **W. L. GARRISON. 27 December 1855. Boston.** Defines his life work and ideals; sends an outline of a series of lectures on the ante-natal history of the child, its rights, and the responsibilities of parenthood. 11 January 1856. p.8, c2.

3579 JONATHAN WALKER *to* **W. L. GARRISON. 18 December 1855. Winouski, Wi.** Encloses a letter to S. M. B. 11 January 1856. p.8, c3.

3580 JONATHAN WALKER *to* **S. M. B. n.d. n.p.** Details the advantages of western emigration. 11 January 1856. p.8, c3.

3581 MATILDA ASHURST BIGGS *to* **SIR. 27 December 1855. Borden Park, Kent, England.** Informs of the death of her father, Wm. Ashurst. 18 January 1856. p.10, c3.

3582 PARKER PILLSBURY *to* **GENERAL AGENT OF THE MASSACHUSETTS AS. [extract] 21 December 1855. Manchester, England.** Commends Garrison's refusal to join slaveholders on the lecture platform. 18 January 1856. p.10, c6.

3583 REV. S. A. STEINTHAL *to* **S. MAY, JR. 4 December 1855. Bridgwater, England.** Discusses abolitionism in England, J. B. Estlin, Unitarians, and Garrison's refusal to debate with slaveholders. 18 January 1856. p.11, c1.

3584 A. H. WOOD *to* **W. L. GARRISON. 10 January 1856. Pepperell.** Describes an anti-slavery New Year's Eve party. 18 January 1856. p.11, c2.

3585 G. B. W. *to* **FRIENDS. n.d. n.p.** Encloses poems and comments on events of the preceding year. 18 January 1856. p.11, c2.

3586 W. L. GARRISON *to* **GEO. THOMPSON. [extract] n.d. n.p.** Chastises Thompson, editor of the *London Empire*, for printing the falsehood that "American slavery leaves the mind unfettered." 18 January 1856. p.11, c3.

3587 J. F. *to* **W. L. GARRISON. 7 January 1856. New Lisbon, Oh.** Eulogizes George Garretson, an abolitionist. 18 January 1856. p.11, c5.

3588 MARY STORY *to* **MISS WESTON. n.d. Lymington.** Thanks her for an account of the Boston bazaar; states that she is a distant relative of Judge Joseph Story. 25 January 1856. p.13, c3.

3589 A. J. W. *to* **ANNE W. WESTON. n.d. n.p.** Offers her congratulations on the anti-slavery bazaar. 25 January 1856. p.13, c3.

3590 M. *to* **THE *DOVER MORNING STAR*. 31 December 1855. New York.** Recounts celebration of the landing of the Pilgrims, which included speakers Oliver W. Holmes and Mr. Pierpont. 25 January 1856. p.14, c2.

3591 HENRY CLAY *to* **REV. CALVIN COLTON. 2 September 1843. Ashland.** Suggests Colton write a tract condemning the abolitionists. 25 January 1856. p.14, c5.

3592 H. O. S. *to* **W. L. GARRISON. n.d. n.p.** Comments on a new book, *Buds for the Bridal Wreath.* 25 January 1856. p.14, c6.

3593 SALLIE HOLLEY *to* **GRACE. [extract] 14 January 1856. Brooklyn, Ct.** Admonishes Rev. Ireneus Prime, a pro-slavery writer. 25 January 1856. p.14, c6.

3594 AARON M. POWELL *to* **SAMUEL MAY, JR. [extract] n.d. n.p.** Claims that the Republican Party and the spiritualists in Michigan are hurting the anti-slavery cause. 25 January 1856. p.14, c6.

3595 JOSEPH BARKER *to* **FRIEND [W. L. GARRISON]. 2 January 1856. Muscatine, Ia.** Reaffirms his abolitionism; questions the wisdom of bringing together political abolitionists and pro-slavery politicians. 25 January 1856. p.15, c1.

3596 GEORGE W. CARNES *to* **MR. EDITOR [W. L. GARRISON]. 21 January 1856. Boston.** Advocates the formation of "Freedom Leagues" in the event that the state personal liberty bill is defeated. 25 January 1856. p.15, c1.

3597 H. C. WRIGHT *to* **W. L. GARRISON. 20 January 1856. Harwich, Cape Cod.** Reports on his lectures. 25 January 1856. p.15, c2.

3598 PETER FUNKS *to* **SIR [W. L. GARRISON]. 7 January 1856. Lawrence, Ks.** Reports that a Negro desperado and his gang of ruffians threatened destruction of Lawrence and murdered Thomas Barber. 25 January 1856. p.15, c2.

3599 JEREMIAH B. SANDERSON *to* **W. C. NELL. [extract] n.d. California.** Describes the recent convention of colored men in Sacramento and the colored community in general. 25 January 1856. p.15, c2.

3600 JOHN H. PEARSON *to* **J. B. BROWN OF KEY WEST. 2 January 1856. Boston.** Declines to help Brown recover two fugitive slaves. 25 January 1856. p.15, c4.

3601 n.n. *to* **SIR. 19 November 1855. n.p.** A young lady of nineteen years writes to inform marriageable males of her desirability and availability. 25 January 1856. p.16, c5.

3602 RUTH PARTINGTON *to* **FRIENDS. 25 December 1855. Boston.** Regrets that she cannot be with them for Christmas. 25 January 1856. p.16, c5.

3603 CORNELIUS BRAMHALL *to* **FRANCIS JACKSON. 18 January 1856. New York.** Resigns from the board of managers of the Massachusetts AS. 1 February 1856. p.18, c6.

3604 T. C. *to* **MR. EDITOR [W. L. GARRISON]. 8 December 1855. Caledonia.** A freethinker submits an article on infidelity. 1 February 1856. p.20, c2.

3605 PARKERITE *to* **W. L. GARRISON. n.d. Sherburne, Ma.** Laments the neglect of Christian precepts. 1 February 1856. p.20, c2.

3606 EZRA KELLEY *to* **W. L. GARRISON. 23 January 1856. New Bedford.** Reports on Richard Johnson, a colored merchant who has sought diligently after intelligence, position, and wealth. 1 February 1856. p.20, c3.

3607 J. CUSHING *to* **W. L. GARRISON. n.d. South Hingham, Ma.** Ridicules Bible instruction as offered in Sabbath schools. 1 February 1856. p.20, c3.

3608 X. *to* **W. L. GARRISON. 1 February 1856. Worcester.** Questions the validity of the appeal for money by Delia Webster, who claims to have been persecuted for abolitionism in Kentucky. 8 February 1856. p.22, c4.

3609 GEO. W. STACY *to* **W. L. GARRISON. 27 January 1856. Milford.** Describes the farewell sermon of Rev. Hassall. 8 February 1856. p.22, c5.

3610 FRED W. CHESSON *to* **W. L. GARRISON. 16 January 1856. London, England.** Informs Garrison that Geo. Thompson has gone to India for an indefinite period. 8 February 1856. p.22, c6.

3611 S. S. G. *to* **n.n. 8 January 1856. Greenmanville.** Challenges the assertion made in the *Independent* that converts to spiritualism were once infidels. 8 February 1856. p.22, c6.

3612 J. R. JOHNSON *to* **W. L. GARRISON. 22 January 1856. Putnam, Ct.** Describes the lectures of Miss Putnam and S. Holley in Putnam. 8 February 1856. p.22, c6.

3613 J. B. ESTLIN *to* **n.n. 7 June 1855. Bristol, England.** Charges that Frederick Douglass is a selfish man seeking to aggrandize his own interests, and that he left the only pure AS in America; declares that *Frederick Douglass' Paper* is not a pure anti-slavery sheet because of its political nature. 15 February 1856. p.27, c1.

3614 MARY A. ESTLIN *to* **W. L. GARRISON. 10 January 1856. Bristol, England.** Thanks Garrison for the testimonial to her late father, J. B. Estlin; sends one hundred pounds. 15 February 1856. p.27, c1.

3615 EDWARD DAVIS *to* **MR. EDITOR [W. L. GARRISON]. 29 January 1856. Scarborough, Me.** Defends the Methodist Episcopal church from the charge of a lack of faithfulness to the cause of the slave. 15 February 1856. p.27, c1.

3616 A. H. WOOD *to* **S. MAY, JR. 31 January 1856. Pepperell.** Comments on A. T. Foss' lecture on the hypocrisy of the American government and church. 15 February 1856. p.27, c2.

3617 C. STEARNS *to* **W. L. GARRISON. 23 January 1856. Lawrence, K.T.** Declares that non-resistance is as dear to him as ever, but that such a philosophy cannot apply to life among the "Missouri wild beasts." 15 February 1856. p.27, c3.

3618 GERRIT SMITH *to* **D. JENKINS, L. D. TAYLOR, J. WATSON, J. MARVIN, W. P. SCOTT, J. BOOKER, W. H. DAY. 27 December 1855. Peterboro'.** Regrets that he cannot attend the convention of colored people in Columbus, Ohio, on 16 January 1856. 15 February 1856. p.29, c5.

3619 J. R. GIDDINGS *to* **D. JENKINS, L. D. TAYLOR, J. WATSON, J. MARVIN, W. A. SCOTT, J. BOOKER, AND W. H. DAY. 26 December 1855. House of Representatives.** Regrets that he cannot attend the convention of colored people in Columbus, Ohio, on 16 January 1856. 15 February 1856. p.29, c5.

3620 W. G. B. *to* **W. L. GARRISON. 5 February 1856. n.p.** Argues against any compromise with slavery. 15 February 1856. p.29, c5.

3621 ISAAC TRESCOTT AND BENJ. JONES OF THE WESTERN AS *to* **SPEAKER OF THE HOUSE OF REPRESENTATIVES OF OHIO. 5 February 1856. Salem, Oh.** Advocate dissolution of the Union. 22 February 1856. p.31, c3.

3622 J. H. LANE, C. ROBINSON, J. R. GOODIN, GEO. DEITZER *to* **FRANKLIN PIERCE. 21 January 1856. Lawrence, Ks.** Appeal for United States troops. 22 February 1856. p.31, c6.

3623 J. H. LANE AND C. ROBINSON *to* **THE PRESIDENT OF THE UNITED STATES. 23 January 1856. Lawrence, Ks.** Appeal for United States troops. 22 February 1856. p.31, c6.

3624 A. BOWEN *to* **THE EDITOR OF THE** *NEW YORK TRIBUNE.* **[extract] n.d. Ulster County, N.Y.** Reports that most free state men in Kansas wish to exclude blacks from the territory. 22 February 1856. p.32, c1.

3625 n.n. *to* **S. MAY. n.d. n.p.** A Southern abolitionist requests anti-slavery tracts. 22 February 1856. p.32, c2.

3626 WALTER SCOTT *to* **WILSON ARMISTEAD. 14 January 1856. Airedale College, Manchester, England.** Deplores the conduct of American churches and the Board of Missions. 22 February 1856. p.32, c2.

3627 VERITAS *to* **W. L. GARRISON. n.d. Cambridge, Ma.** Forwards a refutation by M. Victor, a cousin of Dr. Lord; asserts that slaveholding is morally correct. 22 February 1856. p.32, c2.

3628 ANNA E. D. *to* **W. L. GARRISON. 22 January 1856. Philadelphia.** Describes Southern outrages toward slaves. 22 February 1856. p.32, c2.

3629 PARKER PILLSBURY *to* **SAMUEL MAY. [extract] 18 January 1856. Fentonfield, England.** Discusses his lectures; criticizes Congress. 22 February 1856. p.32, c3.

3630 A CONSTANT READER *to* **W. L. GARRISON. 26 January 1856. New York.** Believes slaveholders are corrupting the Methodist Episcopal church. 22 February 1856. p.32, c3.

3631 JOHN W. HUTCHINSON *to* **FRIEND. 24 January 1856. Indianapolis.** Reports on anti-slavery in the West. 22 February 1856. p.32, c3.

3632 JOHN McQUEEN, M. C. *to* **LEWIS TAPPAN. 5 February 1856. Washington.** Advises him to reform the abuses in the North before meddling with slavery. 29 February 1856. p.33, c1.

3633 SAMUEL D. MOORE *to* **MARIUS. [from the** *Ohio Anti-Slavery Bugle***] 12 January 1856. Ypsilanti, Mi.** Refuses to pay state and national taxes in order to express his opposition to support of slavery by Michigan's state government. 29 February 1856. p.33, c5.

3634 CUTHBERT G. YOUNG, SECRETARY OF THE TURKISH MISSIONS AID SOCIETY *to* **THE EDITOR OF THE** *ANTI-SLAVERY REPORTER.* **18 January 1856. Adelphi.** Believes that Parker Pillsbury's attack on the American Board of Missions was unmerited. 29 February 1856. p.33, c5.

3635 L. A. CHAMEROVZOW *to* **REV. C. G. YOUNG. 19 January 1856. London.** Believes with Pillsbury that the American Board of Missions is pro-slavery. 29 February 1856. p.33, c5.

3636 CHARLES K. WHIPPLE *to* **PRESIDENT AND DIRECTORS OF THE AMERICAN TRACT SOCIETY. 25 February 1856. Boston.** Desires that his life membership dues be applied to the publication of two anti-slavery tracts. 29 February 1856. p.34, c1.

3637 CHARLES SUMNER *to* **CHARLES G. CHASE. 19 February 1856. Washington.** Suggests that George Washington's name be invoked for the suppression of the slave power. 29 February 1856. p.34, c2.

3638 H. C. WRIGHT *to* **W. L. GARRISON. 15 February 1856. Cleveland, Oh.** Comments on Governor Chase's message respecting Kansas; reports on Margaret Garner, a mother who killed her child rather than permit it to be sold into slavery; discusses Anthony Burns' excommunication. 29 February 1856. p.35, c2.

3639 JOSHUA T. EVERETT *to* **BROTHER GARRISON. 17 February 1856. Everettville.** Lauds Garrison's refusal to join slaveholders on the lecture platform, but objects to the pro-slavery material in the "Refuge of Oppression" section of the paper. 29 February 1856. p.35, c3.

3640 R. GLAZIER, JR. *to* **W. L. GARRISON. 25 February 1856. Romeo, Mi.** Reports on his anti-slavery agitation in the West. 29 February 1856. p.35, c3.

3641 A. D. TASKER *to* **S. MAY, JR. [extract] 16 February 1856. West Milan, N.H.** Expresses his anti-slavery convictions. 29 February 1856. p.35, c4.

3642 PARKER PILLSBURY *to* **n.n. [extract] 31 January 1856. Nottingham, England.** Reports on his anti-slavery lectures and sources of abolitionism in England. 29 February 1856. p.35, c4.

3643 REV. ELNATHAN DAVIS *to* **GENERAL AGENT OF THE MASSACHUSETTS AS. [extract] 19 February 1856. n.p.** Proclaims his faithfulness to the slave. 29 February 1856. p.35, c4.

3644 GEO. SUNTER *to* **THE EDITOR OF THE** *LIBERATOR* **[W. L. GARRISON]. 13 February 1856. Toronto, Canada West.** Discusses the relationship of sectarianism to anti-slavery, and the sectarianism of the AAS. 29 February 1856. p.36, c2.

3645 REV. CYRUS KINGSBURY *to* **n.n. [extract] n.d. Choctaw Nation.** Praises the new book, *South Side View of Slavery*. 7 March 1856. p.37, c1.

3646 REV. E. J. PIERCE *to* **n.n. [extract] n.d. Gaboon Mission.** Declares that he would rather be a slave in the South than a heathen in Africa. 7 March 1856. p.37, c1.

3647 C. CUMINGS *to* **W. L. GARRISON. 21 February 1856. Worcester.** Insists that Delia Webster's suffering is genuine. 7 March 1856. p.37, c2.

3648 R. M. JOHNSTON *to* **W. L. GARRISON. 21 February 1856. New York.** Criticizes the Methodist Episcopal church in the United States for tolerating slavery. 7 March 1856. p.37, c3.

3649 J. R. GIDDINGS *to* **TWENTIETH CONGRESSIONAL DISTRICT OF OHIO. 8 February 1856. Washington.** Rejoices at the election of Banks as Speaker of the House. 7 March 1856. p.37, c6.

3650 JOHN STEVENS *to* **MR. COBB, EDITOR OF THE** *CHRISTIAN FREEMAN.* **11 February 1856. Wentworth, N.H.** Cancels his subscription because of the paper's abolitionism. 7 March 1856. p.38, c1.

3651 ALF'D BURNET *to* **THE EDITORS OF THE** *CINCINNATI COMMERCIAL.* **n.d. n.p.** Reports that he was driven out of Kentucky by a slaveholding mob. 7 March 1856. p.38, c1.

3652 H. C. WRIGHT *to* **PARKER PILLSBURY. 25 February 1856. Linesville, Pa.** Praises Pillsbury's work in England; ascribes the success of Republicans to the agitation of Garrisonians. 7 March 1856. p.39, c1.

3653 GEORGE SUNTER, JR. *to* **FRIEND [W. L. GARRISON]. 18 February 1856. Toronto, Canada West.** Derides political abolitionism. 7 March 1856. p.39, c2.

3654 A. HOGEBOOM *to* **W. L. GARRISON. 12 February 1856. Shad's Corners, N.Y.** Describes the worship of "border ruffianism" in a church in Shads Corners. 7 March 1856. p.39, c2.

3655 D. HITCHINGS *to* **W. L. GARRISON. 22 February 1856. Utica.** Opposes celebrating the birthday of the slaveholder and soldier, George Washington. 7 March 1856. p.39, c3.

3656 HENRY J. GARDNER *to* **THE SPEAKER OF THE HOUSE OF REPRESENTATIVES. [from the *Boston Journal*] n.d. n.p.** Sends letter written to Gardner concerning affairs in Kansas. 7 March 1856. p.39, c4.

3657 CORRESPONDENT *to* **THE *NEW YORK TRIBUNE*. n.d. Washington.** Reports that the government has received word that affairs in Kansas are at a standstill: no military force will be employed unless the civil process is resisted. 7 March 1856. p.39, c4.

3658 RICHARD FULLER *to* **n.n. n.d. n.p.** A Southern slaveholder desires abolition but fears its consequences. 14 March 1856. p.41, c2.

3659 WILSON LUMPKIN *to* **n.n. [extract] 12 February 1856. Athens, Ga.** A previous governor of Georgia endorses Pierce's policy; asks for loyalty to the Constitution and rights of the South. 14 March 1856. p.41, c3.

3660 CASSIUS M. CLAY *to* **LOUIS CLEPHANE AND E. M. JOSLIN. n.d. n.p.** Approves of the Republican Party; affirms the superiority of a free over a slave civilization and urges that the slave power be stopped. 14 March 1856. p.41, c5.

3661 WM. J. IVERSON, H. C. LIVINGSTON, J. WHITEHEAD, M. DAVISON, P. METANA, F. BOYNTON *to* **WHOM IT MAY CONCERN. 18 August 1856. Liverpool, England.** Explorers in southern, western, and northern Africa attest to Leo Lloyd's good character. 14 March 1856. p.42, c6.

3662 PRINCE LEO L. LLOYD *to* **THE *LIBERATOR*. 12 March 1856. Cambridgeport.** The Prince of Nubia denies that he is an impostor lining his own pockets. 14 March 1856. p.42, c6.

3663 R. GLAZIER, JR. *to* **W. L. GARRISON. 5 March 1856. Ann Arbor, Mi.** Reports on anti-slavery lectures with Mr. Powell. 14 March 1856. p.43, c1.

3664 n.n. *to* **W. L. GARRISON. 6 February 1856. Augusta, Ga.** An abolitionist condemns the slaveholding spirit. 14 March 1856. p.43, c2.

3665 SALLIE HOLLEY *to* **n.n. 4 March 1856. n.p.** Discusses her anti-slavery friends in Rhode Island and Connecticut. 14 March 1856. p.43, c2.

3666 S. MITCHELL *to* **BROTHER GARRISON. 2 March 1856. Cornville, Me.** Argues that if political action is wrong, we should not advise others to do certain political acts. 14 March 1856. p.43, c3.

3667 HENRY JOHNSON *to* **BOARD OF TRUSTEES OF THE AFRICAN M.E.B. CHURCH. 18 December 1855. New Bedford, Ma.** Reports that the New Bedford Vigilant Aid Society would like to use the church for one of its meetings. 14 March 1856. p.43, c4.

3668 JOHN WARFIELD *to* **HENRY JOHNSON. 18 December 1855. New Bedford, Ma.** Refuses to allow the Vigilant Aid Society to hold a meeting in the African M.E.B. Church. 14 March 1856. p.43, c4.

3669 P. S. BASSETT *to* **n.n. [from the** *American Baptist***] 12 February 1856. Fairmount Theological Seminary, Cincinnati.** Relates interview held with a slave woman jailed for killing her baby in order to save it from enslavement. 14 March 1856. p.43, c5.

3670 REV. WALTER AYRAULT *to* **W. R. G. MELLEN. 19 November 1852. Auburn, N.Y.** Declines an invitation to speak because of Mellen's Universalist affiliations. 14 March 1856. p.44, c2.

3671 W. R. G. MELLEN *to* **REV. WALTER AYRAULT. 17 November 1852. Auburn, N.Y.** Rebukes Ayrault for lacking Christian charity and tolerance. 14 March 1856. p.44, c2.

3672 T. BICKNELL *to* **W. L. GARRISON. 3 March 1856. Kingston.** Urges abolitionists to read Dr. Parson's *A Tour Among The Planters.* 14 March 1856. p.44, c2.

3673 GERRIT SMITH *to* **GEORGE. n.d. n.p.** Urges a young boy to give up tobacco. 14 March 1856. p.44, c3.

3674 JACOB LEONARD *to* **FRIEND GARRISON. 2 March 1856. East Bridgewater.** Endorses articles in the "Refuge of Oppression" column. 14 March 1856. p.44, c3.

3675 J. *to* **W. L. GARRISON. 1 March 1856. Glen Haven.** Announces a convention to consider reforms in woman's dress. 14 March 1856. p.44, c3.

3676 JOHN S. C. ABBOTT *to* **EMPEROR NAPOLEON III. 28 August 1855. Brunswick, Me.** Sends copies of his books on Napoleon I. 14 March 1856. p.44, c5.

3677 GERRIT SMITH *to* **GOV. S. P. CHASE. [extract] n.d. n.p.** Fears that the Republican Party will seriously weaken the anti-slavery sentiment of the country. 21 March 1856. p.45, c5.

3678 W. L. GARRISON *to* **THE EDITOR OF THE** *LONDON ANTI-SLAVERY ADVOCATE.* **18 March 1856. Boston.** Answers charges of infidelity. 21 March 1856. p.46, c3.

3679 J. A. F. *to* **W. L. GARRISON. 14 March 1856. Utica.** Charges that Prince Leo L. Lloyd is an impostor. 21 March 1856. p.46, c6.

3680 PROF. J. P. NICHOL *to* **MR. EDITOR [W. L. GARRISON]. 27 February 1856. Observatory, Glasgow.** Corrects a misleading report concerning Nichol's lecture about the moon. 21 March 1856. p.47, c1.

3681 W. R. G. *to* **THE EDITOR OF THE** *LIBERATOR* **[W. L. GARRISON]. 14 March 1856. Gloucester.** Expresses annoyance that the *Liberator* published his correspondence without permission. 21 March 1856. p.47, c1.

3682 W. B. T. *to* **W. L. GARRISON. 20 March 1856. Boston.** Reports that the Boston correspondent of the *Journal of Commerce* is Luther Farnum, not Hubbard Winslow. 21 March 1856. p.47, c1.

3683 n.n. *to* **THE** *RICHMOND DISPATCH.* **n.d. Weldon, N.C.** Relates terrible train accident that occurred when trestlework gave out; foul play suspected. 21 March 1856. p.47, c3.

3684 GEORGE SUNTER, JR. *to* **W. L. GARRISON. 8 March 1856. Toronto, Canada West.** Comments on the sectarianism of the AAS. 21 March 1856. p.48, c2.

3685 PELEG CLARKE *to* **FRIEND GARRISON. 11 February 1856. Coventry, R.I.** Describes S. Holley's lectures in Coventry. 21 March 1856. p.48, c2.

3686 A. J. GLOVER *to* **S. MAY, JR. [extract] 29 February 1856. Earlville, Il.** Announces the need for anti-slavery lecturers in Earlville. 21 March 1856. p.48, c2.

3687 JOHN BALL, JR. *to* **THE EDITORS OF THE** *ANTI-SLAVERY STANDARD.* **n.d. Newport, Ky.** Solicits money for an abolitionist editor, Mr. Bailey, of the *Newport News.* 28 March 1856. p.50, c2.

3688 PARKER PILLSBURY *to* **n.n. [extract]. 28 February 1856. Manchester, England.** Criticizes the Republicans and political abolitionists in general. 28 March 1856. p.51, c1.

3689 D. M. *to* **H. W. BEECHER. 12 February 1856. Boston.** Regrets that Garrison was criticized in the *Independent.* 28 March 1856. p.51, c2.

3690 H. W. BEECHER *to* **SIR. 1 March 1856. Brooklyn.** Disclaims responsibility for an article in the *Independent* which criticized W. L. Garrison. 28 March 1856. p.51, c2.

3691 D. M. *to* **H. W. BEECHER. 8 March 1856. Boston.** Inquires again whether Beecher endorses the statement that Garrison is a "degraded" infidel. 28 March 1856. p.51, c2.

3692 n.n. *to* **S. MAY, JR. [extract] n.d. Cincinnati.** Thanks him for anti-slavery tracts. 28 March 1856. p.51, c3.

3693 X. *to* **W. L. GARRISON. 18 March 1856. Worcester.** Asserts that Delia Webster is an untruthful abolitionist and undeserving of donations. 28 March 1856. p.52, c2.

3694 HENRY C. HOWELLS *to* **W. L. GARRISON. 16 March 1856. Eagleswood, Perth Amboy.** Compares "infidel" abolitionists with "pro-war" ministers. 28 March 1856. p.52, c3.

3695 T. N. *to* **MR. EDITOR [W. L. GARRISON]. 16 March 1856. New York.** Presents religious testimony against war. 28 March 1856. p.52, c3.

3696 E. A. W. *to* **S. MAY, JR. 26 March 1856. Keene, N.H.** Reports on Foss and Howland's anti-slavery lectures in Keene. 4 April 1856. p.53, c3.

3697 SALMON RECKARD *to* **THE EDITOR OF THE** *IRONTON REGISTER.* **17 March 1856. Quaker Bottom, Oh.** Reports that a Virginia mob disrupted a Kansas meeting in Quaker Bottom. 4 April 1856. p.53, c6.

3698 DR. O. W. HOLMES *to* **THE** *EXETER NEWS LETTER.* **[extract] n.d. n.p.** States that he believes in freedom, but accuses abolitionists of breaking a contract and thereby committing treason. 4 April 1856. p.54, c2.

3699 THOMAS H. BENTON *to* **SIR. [from the** *Missouri Democrat***] 12 March 1856. Washington.** Describes his life in retirement: reports that he has no regrets about leaving politics; writes from morning to midnight. 4 April 1856. p.55, c2.

3700 N. H. WHITING *to* **FRIEND GARRISON. 30 March 1856. Marshfield.** Comments on pro-slavery feeling in the churches and the damage done by revivalism. 4 April 1856. p.55, c3.

3701 T. C. *to* **MR. EDITOR** [*W. L. GARRISON*]. **10 March 1856. Caledonia.** Discusses the plenary inspiration of the Bible. 4 April 1856. p.56, c2.

3702 REV. H. W. BEECHER *to* **C. B. LINES. 28 March 1856. Brooklyn.** Sends Bibles and rifles to a Connecticut group heading for Kansas. 11 April 1856. p.58, c3.

3703 H. C. WRIGHT *to* **W. L. GARRISON. 28 March 1856. Cleveland.** Comments on Margaret Garner, the slave who sacrificed her baby; discusses the Republicans of Ohio and agents of Rev. Nehemiah Adams. 11 April 1856. p.59, c2.

3704 PARKER PILLSBURY *to* **n.n. [extract] 13 and 14 March 1856. Liverpool, England.** Relates the story of a stowaway slave on a boat from New Orleans. 11 April 1856. p.59, c3.

3705 S. S. GRISWOLD *to* **FRIEND GARRISON. 4 April 1856. Greenmanville, Ct.** Describes the anti-slavery sentiment in the Mystic Valley. 11 April 1856. p.59, c4.

3706 CARNOT *to* **n.n. [from the** *Liberty Bell*] **1855. Paris.** Deplores the existence of slavery in America. 11 April 1856. p.60, c2.

3707 EMILE DE GIRARDIN *to* **n.n. [from the** *Liberty Bell*] **1855. Paris.** Deplores American slavery. 11 April 1856. p.60, c2.

3708 ALEXIS DE TOCQUEVILLE *to* **n.n. [from the** *Liberty Bell*] **1855. France.** Laments that American slavery exists. 11 April 1856. p.60, c2.

3709 H. PASSEY *to* **n.n. [from the** *Liberty Bell*] **28 January 1855. Nice.** Deplores slavery. 11 April 1856. p.60, c2.

3710 N. TOURGUENEFF *to* **MRS. HENRY G. CHAPMAN. [from the** *Liberty Bell*] **29 September 1855. Paris.** Praises Garrison for his efforts against slavery. 11 April 1856. p.60, c3.

3711 n.n. *to* **n.n. [extract from the** *Columbia* **(S.C.)** *Banner*] **15 February 1856. Leavenworth City.** Condemns the activities of the abolitionists in the South. 18 April 1856. p.61, c1.

3712 STERLING G. CATO *to* **W. G. M. DAVIS. [extract from the** *Talahassee Floridian* **via the** *Savannah Morning News*] **n.d. n.p.** States that border ruffians in Kansas are peaceful and law-abiding. 18 April 1856. p.61, c2.

3713 CASSIUS M. CLAY *to* **G. W. BROWN. [from the** *Kansas Herald of Freedom*] **12 February 1856. Whitehall, Ky.** Sympathizes with Brown and other Kansas settlers who are troubled by the border ruffians. 18 April 1856. p.61, c4.

3714 DR. A. BROOKE *to* **FRIEND AND BROTHER. 10 April 1856. Marlboro', Oh.** A non-resistant criticizes abolitionists who advocate force in Kansas as a means of self-defense. 18 April 1856. p.63, c2.

3715 COL. J. C. FREMONT *to* **GOV. CHAS. ROBINSON. [from the** *Boston Atlas*] **17 March 1856. New York.** Expresses views on the Free State Party in Kansas. 18 April 1856. p.63, c2.

3716 AN INHABITANT OF WORCESTER *to* **W. L. GARRISON. 8 April 1856. n.p.** Upholds Garrison's non-resistance position with regard to Kansas. 18 April 1856. p.64, c2.

3717 JEHIEL CLAFLIN *to* **FRIEND GARRISON. 6 April 1856. East Westmoreland, N.H.** Supports Garrison's non-resistance policy with regard to Kansas. 18 April 1856. p.64, c2.

3718 REV. SAMUEL HENRY *to* **BROTHER GARRISON. 5 April 1856. Throndike.** Favors Garrison's non-resistance policy with regard to Kansas. 18 April 1856. p. 64, c3.

3719 H. H. BRIGHAM *to* **FRIEND GARRISON. 6 April 1856. South Abington.** Defends Garrison's non-resistance policy with regard to Kansas. 18 April 1856. p.64, c3.

3720 G. *to* **FRIEND GARRISON. 10 April 1856. Philadelphia.** Praises Garrison's non-resistance policy with regard to Kansas. 18 April 1856. p.64, c4.

3721 L. FL—N *to* **THE EDITOR OF THE** *THE BOSTON COURIER.* **n.d. Cambridge.** Takes issue with Rev. Mr. Garnet's estimation of the benefits of West Indies emancipation. 25 April 1856. p.65, c2.

3722 BENJ. J. PRESCOTT *to* **W. L. GARRISON. 16 April 1856. Sylvania, Ga.** Defends the South from abolitionist slanders. 25 April 1856. p.67, c1.

3723 PARKER PILLSBURY *to* **n.n. [extract] n.d. Dublin, Ireland.** Comments on his visit to an Irish "model farm." 25 April 1856. p.67, c1.

3724 GEORGE J. PETERSON *to* **FRIEND GARRISON. 13 April 1856. Duxbury, Ma.** Suggests that an abolitionist picture be distributed at the coming New England convention. 25 April 1856. p.67, c2.

3725 E. W. TWING *to* **FRIEND GARRISON. 20 April 1856. Springfield.** Upholds Garrison's peace principles as applied to Kansas. 25 April 1856. p.67, c2.

3726 ONE OF THE SQUATTERS *to* **THE EDITOR OF THE** *MISSOURI DEMOCRAT.* **7 April 1856. Leavenworth, Ks.** Presents update of border ruffians in Kansas. 25 April 1856. p.67, c4.

3727 D. HITCHINGS *to* **GERRIT SMITH. April 1856. Richfield.** Asks Smith to define his concept of a "Righteous Civil Government," especially with regard to peace principles. 25 April 1856. p.68, c2.

3728 A. D. TASKER *to* **FRIEND S. MAY, JR. 16 March 1856. West Milan, N.H.** Comments on the anti-slavery cause in New Hampshire. 25 April 1856. p.68, c2.

3729 BENJ. SILLIMAN *to* **HON. J. P. HALE. 16 April 1856. New Haven, Ct.** Defends the character of New England settlers in Kansas and the practice of emigrating in armed colonies. 2 May 1856. p.69, c2.

3730 WM. H. HERNDON *to* **THE EDITORS OF THE** *ILLINOIS JOURNAL.* **[extract] n.d. n.p.** Advises that the North resist slavery encroachment in Kansas and the territories. 2 May 1856. p.70, c1.

3731 J. A. HARKREADER *to* **n.n. [extract] 21 July 1855. Salt Lake City, Ut.** Discusses slavery and polygamy in Utah. 2 May 1856. p.70, c1.

3732 A CONSTANT READER *to* **BROTHER GARRISON. 20 April. n.p.** Corrects Rev. Henry's misquotation of Scripture. 2 May 1856. p.71, c3.

3733 n.n. *to* **n.n. n.d. New York.** Reports receiving very poor treatment from people in Rochester, New York. 2 May 1856. p.71, c4.

3734 JAMES HAUGHTON *to* **THE EDITOR OF THE** *DUBLIN FREEMAN.* **n.d. n.p.** Describes the Irish immigrant in America and the racism that is directed against him. 9 May 1856. p.73, c3.

3735 AN ON-LOOKER *to* **THE EDITOR OF THE** *SCOTTISH PRESS.* **14 April 1856. n.p.** Presents the female anti-slavery proceedings in Edinburgh, Scotland; criticizes the Rochester Ladies' AS and J. Griffiths for the inconsistency between their liberal professions and sectarian practices. 9 May 1856. p.73, c4.

3736 ANTHONY BURNS *to* **REV. JOHN CLARK. n.d. n.p.** Defends his escape from slavery. 9 May 1856. p.73, c6.

3737 WM. H. FISH *to* **S. MAY, JR. 27 April 1856. Hopedale.** Describes anti-slavery activities in central New York. 9 May 1856. p.74, c4.

3738 SPECTATOR *to* **THE EDITOR OF THE** *TELEGRAPH.* **2 May 1856. Charlestown.** Discusses the exclusion of two colored girls from the Charlestown High School. 9 May 1856. p.74, c5.

3739 O. C. EVERETT *to* **THE EDITOR OF THE** *TELEGRAPH.* **26 April 1856. Charlestown.** A school board committeeman defends the committee against charges of racism. 9 May 1856. p.74, c5.

3740 T. W. HIGGINSON *to* **n.n. [extract] 19 March 1856. Fayal, Azores.** Pines for the moral atmosphere of New England. 9 May 1856. p.74, c6.

3741 JONATHAN WALKER *to* **FRIEND GARRISON. 14 April 1856. Winooski, Wi.** Suggests publishing, in pamphlet form, Garrison's comments on the statements by Beecher and Parker regarding the use of force in Kansas. 9 May 1856. p.74, c6.

3742 SARAH CLAY *to* **WM. LLOYD GARRISON. 1 May 1856. Lowell.** Informs that Delia Webster is again in Massachusetts, and is seeking money. 9 May 1856. p.75, c1.

3743 YOUNG MAN *to* **HIS MOTHER. [extract] 28 November 1855. Swotow, China.** Writes of the horrible atrocities the coolies are experiencing on board the ship *Winged Racer.* 9 May 1856. p.75, c1.

3744 CORRESPONDENT OF THE *ST. LOUIS DEMOCRAT to* **n.n. 20 and 22 April. n.p.** Describes the renewal of troubles in Kansas. 9 May 1856. p.75, c2.

3745 EUGENE HUTCHINSON *to* **FRIEND GARRISON. 27 April 1856. Milford, N.H.** Upholds non-resistance as a means to combat border ruffianism in Kansas. 9 May 1856. p.76, c2.

3746 A. H. WOOD, C. A. HUTSON, AND JOSIAH A. BABCOM *to* **THOS. STEVENS. 26 April 1856. Pepperell, Ma.** State reasons for their withdrawal from a church in Pepperell; report the existence of parish bigotry. 9 May 1856. p.76, c3.

3747 JOHN OF MORLEY *to* **THE** *LIBERATOR.* **n.d. n.p.** Comments on religious creeds. 16 May 1856. p.80, c2.

3748 SAMUEL HENRY *to* **BROTHER GARRISON. May 1856. Throndike.** Thanks a *Liberator* correspondent for correcting his Scripture misquotation. 16 May 1856. p.80, c2.

3749 PARDEE BUTLER *to* **n.n. 7 May 1856. Lawrence, Ks.** Describes outrages upon him by border ruffians. 23 May 1856. p.82, c1.

3750 CHARLES STEARNS *to* **FRIEND GARRISON. 27 April 1856. Lawrence, Ks.** Ponders the issues of non-resistance and general affairs in Kansas. 23 May 1856. p.82, c5.

3751 H. H. BRIGHAM *to* **FRIEND GARRISON. 18 May 1856. South Abington.** Reports on Marius R. Robinson's anti-slavery lecture in South Abington. 23 May 1856. p.83, c1.

3752 F. W. CHESSON *to* **W. L. GARRISON. 29 April 1856. London, England.** Describes George Thompson's arrival in India. 23 May 1856. p.83, c1.

3753 SETH HUNT *to* **FRIEND GARRISON. 19 May 1856. Northampton.** Reports on S. Holley's anti-slavery address in Northampton. 23 May 1856. p.83, c1.

3754 H. C. WRIGHT *to* **FRIEND. 8 May 1856. Chicago.** Describes Chicago as a "Monument of Human Power." 23 May 1856. p.84, c4.

3755 L. L. R. *to* **FRIEND GARRISON. n.d. n.p.** Asks A. J. Davis to clarify his attitude toward Garrison. 23 May 1856. p.84, c4.

3756 E. W. TWING *to* **FRIEND GARRISON. 15 May 1856. Springfield.** Encloses a scurrilous news report of S. Holley's lecture in Springfield. 23 May 1856. p.84, c5.

3757 n.n. *to* **THE** *BOSTON DAILY ADVERTISER.* **28 May. Washington.** Informs of deteriorating physical condition of Mr. Sumner. 30 May 1856. p.87, c5.

3758 WATSON FREEMAN *to* **THE PRESIDENT OF THE UNITED STATES, FRANKLIN PIERCE. 27 May 1854. Boston.** Reports that two companies of troops are stationed in the court house since attempt was made to rescue fugitive slaves. 30 May 1856. p.88, c3.

3759 CHAS. F. HOVEY *to* **W. L. GARRISON. n.d. n.p.** Encloses a brief speech which he had planned to deliver at the convention. 6 June 1856. p.91, c1.

3760 JOSIAH QUINCY *to* **E. R. HOAR. 27 May 1856. Quincy.** Expresses outrage at the actions of the slave power. 6 June 1856. p.91, c1.

3761 WM. H. FISH *to* **FRIEND GARRISON. 28 May 1856. Boston.** Praises the qualifications of Wm. S. and Abbie S. Haywood, teachers at the Hopedale School. 6 June 1856. p.91, c5.

3762 PALMETTO *to* **MESSRS. EDITORS OF THE** *CHARLESTON MERCURY.* **24 May 1856. Washington.** Confirms news that Col. Brooks "punished" Mr. Sumner, who "richly deserved it." 13 June 1856. p.93, c4.

3763 C. F. HOVEY *to* **W. L. GARRISON. 6 June 1856. Boston.** Asks Garrison to correct Hovey's statement which was misprinted. 13 June 1856. p.95, c1.

3764 D. A. W. *to* **W. L. GARRISON. 5 June 1856. Groveland.** Describes W. W. Brown's reading in Groveland. 13 June 1856. p.95, c1.

3765 TRUTH *to* **FRIEND. 27 May 1856. Lawrence, Ks.** Sees no chance of averting a civil war. 13 June 1856. p.95, c3.

3766 P. S. BROOKS *to* **H. WILSON. 27 May 1856. Fint' Hotel.** Insinuates that he wants a duel because of Wilson's remarks about his character. 13 June 1856. p.95, c5.

3767 HENRY WILSON *to* **P. S. BROOKS. 29 May 1856. Washington.** Reasserts his opinion of Brook's character; denounces duelling. 13 June 1856. p.95, c5.

3768 R. S. KELLEY *to* **PROUTS AND GUNDIFF. 30 April 1856. Atchison, Ks.** Reports the tarring and feathering of Pardee Butler, an abolitionist. 20 June 1856. p.97, c2.

3769 W. L. GARRISON *to* **THE EDITOR OF THE** *EVENING TELEGRAPH.* **17 June 1856. n.p.** Takes exception to the editor's interpretation of the anti-slavery petition for disunion as a ploy of the border ruffian party. 20 June 1856. p.98, c3.

3770 T. C. S. *to* **W. L. GARRISON. 4 June 1856. Roxbury.** Approves Garrison and Phillips' course at the late AAS anniversary. 20 June 1856. p.98, c6.

3771 E. *to* **W. L. GARRISON. 11 June 1856. Chesnut Ridge, Oh.** Stresses the brutality of the slave power. 20 June 1856. p.99, c1.

3772 H. C. WRIGHT *to* **W. L. GARRISON. 10 June 1856. Chicago.** Gives proposals of the Women's Liberty Convention in Chicago. 20 June 1856. p.99, c1.

3773 WM. P. POWELL *to* **THE EDITOR OF THE** *ANTI-SLAVERY ADVOCATE.* **15 May 1856. Liverpool.** Praises Parker Pillsbury. 20 June 1856. p.99, c2.

3774 CORRESPONDENT IN KANSAS *to* **THE** *NEW YORK TRIBUNE.* **3 June 1856. Lawrence, Ks.** Asserts that he is being hunted by pro-slavery people. 20 June 1856. p.99, c3.

3775 C. H. BARLOW *to* **THE EDITOR OF THE** *CHICAGO TRIBUNE.* **11 June 1856. Chicago.** Informs him of abuses inflicted on free state men in Kansas by border ruffians. 20 June 1856. p.99, c3.

3776 LOUISA J. WHITING *to* **W. L. GARRISON. n.d. Concord, Ma.** Denounces Preston Brooks and calls for disunion. 20 June 1856. p.100, c2.

3777 JOHN OF MORLEY *to* **THE** *LIBERATOR.* **n.d. n.p.** Denounces the ineffectual anti-slavery views held by members of the New School Presbyterian General Assembly. 20 June 1856. p.100, c2.

3778 H. C. WRIGHT *to* **W. L. GARRISON. 22 May 1856. Waukesha, Wi.** Discusses Wisconsin's defiance of the Fugitive Slave Law. 20 June 1856. p.100, c3.

3779 J. *to* **W. L. GARRISON. 8 June 1856. Worcester.** Objects to the *Liberator's* praise of David A. Wasson. 20 June 1856. p.100, c4.

3780 ROBT. C. WINTHROP *to* **S. G. HOWE. 2 June 1856. Boston.** Deplores the course of affairs in Kansas. 27 June 1856. p.101, c2.

3781 JAMES D. MOORE *to* **THE EDITORS OF THE** *NEW YORK INDEPENDENT.* **6 June 1856. Clinton, Ct.** Encloses for publication a letter to Sumner. 27 June 1856. p.101, c3.

3782 JAMES KILBOURN, EDGAR J. DOOLITTLE, JAMES D. MOORE, S. D. JEWETT, NATHANIEL MINER, E. B. HILLARD, S. A. LOPER, HIRAM BELL, D. S. BRAINERD, S. McCALL, G. W. CORMITT, JAMES A. GALLOP AND JAMES D. MOORE *to* **CHARLES SUMNER. 4 June 1856. Hadlyme, Ct.** Connecticut Congregationalists wish Charles Sumner a speedy recovery. 27 June 1856. p.101, c3.

3783 JOHN McLEAN *to* **JNO. C. HORNBLOWER. [extract from the** *Newark Daily Advertiser***] n.d. n.p.** Presents observations on the presidency. 27 June 1856. p.101, c5.

3784 MARGARET W. L. WOOD *to* **n.n. 26 May 1856. Lawrence.** Comments on the outrages in Kansas. 27 June 1856. p.102, c2.

3785 E. R. FALLEY *to* **n.n. [from the** *New Hampshire Gilead Sentinel***] 28 May. Lawrence.** Relates experience of being a prisoner at a South Carolina camp. 27 June 1856. p.102, c3.

3786 GOV. C. ROBINSON *to* **J. C. FREMONT. [from the** *Tribune***] 3 June 1856. Lecompton.** Describes the crisis in Kansas. 27 June 1856. p.102, c3.

3787 S. MAY, JR. *to* **W. L. GARRISON. 23 June 1856. Leicester.** Informs Garrison of arrangements made for the anti-slavery Fourth of July celebration in Framingham. 27 June 1856. p.102, c4.

3788 X. *to* **THE** *LIBERATOR***. 26 May 1856. Worcester.** Denounces Delia Webster as a fraud. 27 June 1856. p.102, c6.

3789 NO COMPROMISE *to* **n.n. 15 June 1856. Providence.** Chronicles the annual meeting of the Rhode Island Consociation (Orthodox Congregationalists). 27 June 1856. p.104, c2.

3790 ELIZABETH M. POWELL *to* **FRIEND GARRISON. 16 June 1856. Ghent, N.Y.** Declares that ministers of popular religion in the United States are one of the greatest hindrances to the cause of freedom. 27 June 1856. p.104, c3.

3791 H. C. WRIGHT *to* **W. L. GARRISON. 26 May 1856. Milwaukee, Wi.** Advocates a Northern confederacy. 27 June 1856. p.104, c3.

3792 JOHN OF MORLEY *to* **THE EDITOR OF THE** *LIBERATOR* **[W. L. GARRISON]. May 1856. Wellsboro', Pa.** Rebukes the editor of *Harper's Magazine* for his attack on the "Higher Law" advocates. 27 June 1856. p.104, c5.

3793 S. S. FARRAR AND OTHERS *to* **PRESTON S. BROOKS. 28 May 1856. Charleston, S.C.** His constituents present Brooks with a cane in support of his chastisement of Sumner. 4 July 1856. p.105, c2.

3794 P. S. BROOKS *to* **S. S. FARRAR. 12 June 1856. Washington, D.C.** Thanks Farrar for the gift of a cane. 4 July 1856. p.105, c2.

3795 A. A. LAWRENCE *to* **D. R. ATCHISON. 31 March 1855. Boston.** Calls for honesty and openness for the free state settlers in Kansas. 4 July 1856. p.105, c6.

3796 D. R. ATCHISON *to* **A. A. LAWRENCE. 15 April 1855. Platte City, Mo.** Vindicates the slaveholders' right to live in Kansas. 4 July 1856. p.105, c6.

3797 CHARLES SUMNER *to* **SETH WEBB, JR. 21 June 1856. Silver Spring, Md.** Endorses the nomination of J. C. Fremont and Dayton for president and vice-president. 4 July 1856. p.106, c1.

3798 H. *to* **FRIEND GARRISON. 26 June 1856. Worcester.** Acknowledges that Wm. M. Evarts may have made anti-slavery progress, but claims that he still supports the Fugitive Slave Law. 4 July 1856. p.106, c5.

3799 EX-MAYOR SMITH *to* **THE** *GAZETTE.* **[extract] 21 June 1856. Fort Leavenworth.** Details the political circumstances and social conditions of the pioneer settlers in Kansas. 4 July 1856. p.107, c1.

3800 W. G. BABCOCK *to* **W. L. GARRISON. 24 June 1856. Harvard.** Commends Garrison's adherence to the principles of liberty. 4 July 1856. p.108, c2.

3801 SARAH M. GRIMKE *to* **FRIEND GARRISON. 15 May 1856. Eagleswood.** Forwards her interpretation of a French article on women's rights written by R. Michelet. 4 July 1856. p.108, c2.

3802 L. MARIA CHILD *to* **PENNSYLVANIA YEARLY MEETING OF PROGRESSIVE FRIENDS. 14 April 1856. Wayland, Ma.** Condemns religious sectarianism. 4 July 1856. p.108, c5.

3803 n.n. *to* **n.n. [from the** *Carolina Times***] 25 May 1856. Camp Carolina, Ks.** Describes the condition of the deserted town and the men in his troop. 11 July 1856. p.109, c1.

3804 CLARENCE COOK *to* **n.n. [from the** *National Anti-Slavery Standard***] 28 May 1856. Newburgh-on-the-Hudson.** Addresses the people of the North, advising them of their jeopardy, and suggests they calmly consider the question of disunion. 11 July 1856. p.109, c2.

3805 ADIN BALLOU *to* **SIR AND BROTHER. 28 June 1856. Hopedale.** Responds that he will not speak at the Fourth of July celebration. 11 July 1856. p.111, c5.

3806 G. B. STEBBINS *to* **W. L. GARRISON. June 1856. Michigan.** Relates his travelling and speaking experiences in Michigan. 11 July 1856. p.112, c2.

3807 WILLIAM GREEN, JR. *to* **THE EDITOR OF THE** *TELEGRAPH.* **18 June 1856. Brooklyn, Long Island.** Refutes the libelous statement that spiritualist A. J. Davis is an adulterer. 11 July 1856. p.112, c5.

3808 n.n. *to* **THE EDITOR OF THE** *TIMES.* **4 July 1856. Cambridge.** Expresses strong pro-slavery sentiments. 18 July 1856. p.113, c1.

3809 T. W. HIGGINSON *to* **THE** *WORCESTER SPY.* **n.d. n.p.** Reports on his recent visit to Missouri; describes the Kansas emigrants from Worcester. 18 July 1856. p.113, c4.

3810 n.n. *to* **THE EDITOR OF THE** *TRAVELLER.* **8 July 1856. Washington.** Encloses extract of a sermon given by Rev. M. D. Conway, pastor of the First Unitarian Society in Washington. 18 July 1856. p.114, c1.

3811 A. FAIRBANKS *to* **FRIEND GARRISON. 15 July 1856. Providence, R.I.** Praises the no-compromise spirit of the anti-slavery Fourth of July celebration at Framingham; denounces the slave power. 18 July 1856. p.114, c5.

3812 D. M. ALLEN *to* **REV. AMES. 7 July. Westminster.** Rebukes Ames for consorting with border ruffians, failing to post a notice of a recent anti-slavery meeting, and ignoring the AAS. 18 July 1856. p.114, c5.

3813 H. *to* **W. L. GARRISON. 6 July 1856. Worcester, Ma.** Questions J. C. Fremont's abolitionism. 18 July 1856. p.114, c6.

3814 n.n. *to* **SIR. [from the** *Boston Daily Bee***] 1 July 1856. Lawrence, Ks.** Relays conditions in Kansas from his own personal observations. 18 July 1856. p.115, c1.

3815 n.n. *to* **THE EDITOR OF THE** *MISSOURI DEMOCRAT.* **28 June 1856. Lawrence, Ks.** Describes inhumane treatment of prisoners. 18 July 1856. p.115, c2.

3816 BAXTER C. DENNIS *to* **n.n. [extract from the** *Western Christian Democrat***]** **13 June 1856. Lawrence, Ks.** Reports on the condition of affairs in Kansas. 25 July 1856. p.117, c6.

3817 J. F. CUMMINGS *to* **SIR. n.d. n.p.** Presents the case of a Northern printer who was tarred and feathered in Missouri. 25 July 1856. p.117, c6.

3818 GOV. JOHN A. WINSTON *to* **GOV. HENRY J. GARDNER. 19 June 1856. Montgomery, Al.** Returns the resolutions of the Massachusetts legislature regarding Kansas; eschews future communication with Massachusetts. 25 July 1856. p.118, c1.

3819 GOV. H. J. GARDNER *to* **GOV. J. A. WINSTON. 5 July 1856. Boston.** Defends Massachusetts and the state legislature's Kansas resolutions from the insults of the Alabama government. 25 July 1856. p.118, c1.

3820 HENRY C. WRIGHT *to* **W. L. GARRISON. 9 June 1856. Waukegan, Il.** Discusses the right and duty of the North to dissolve the Union and create a Northern confederacy. 25 July 1856. p.118, c6.

3821 SYLVESTER *to* **FRIEND GARRISON. 21 July 1856. Randolph, Vt.** Believes that the Republican Party is a slaveholding party; advocates the formation of a Northern republic. 25 July 1856. p.118, c6.

3822 GEO. FITZHUGH *to* **W. L. GARRISON. 18 July 1856. Port Royal, Va.** Solicits Garrison's opinion on Fitzhugh's labeling of abolitionists as communists. 25 July 1856. p.119, c1.

3823 H. *to* **W. L. GARRISON. 18 July 1856. Worcester.** Requests that a correction be made in his letter of the previous week. 25 July 1856. p.119, c1.

3824 JOHN M. SPEAR *to* **W. L. GARRISON. 18 July. n.p.** Relates a communication he had with the spirit world. 25 July 1856. p.120, c2.

3825 H. C. WRIGHT *to* **W. L. GARRISON. 16 June 1856. Shelboygan Falls.** Comments on the relationship between spiritualism and reform. 25 July 1856. p.120, c3.

3826 A. HOGEBOOM *to* **n.n. 30 June 1856. Shed's Corners.** Ridicules the attempt to maintain a union between slavery and freedom. 25 July 1856. p.120, c3.

3827 DAVID HITCHINGS *to* **FRIEND GARRISON. 1 June 1856. Richfield, N.Y.** Denounces *Godey's Lady's Book* for encouraging women to wear fashions which are licentious and injurious to the health. 25 July 1856. p.120, c3.

3828 T. B. DREW *to* **W. L. GARRISON. 14 July 1856. Kingston.** Forwards a pre-revolutionary newspaper clipping relevant to the present state of affairs. 25 July 1856. p.120, c4.

3829 C. ROBINSON *to* **COL. E. V. SUMNER. 7 July 1856. Lecompton, Ks.** Presents complaint of free state men in Kansas against President Pierce. 1 August 1856. p.122, c1.

3830 B. *to* **MR. EDITOR. n.d. n.p.** Relates a discussion of whether abolitionists are supporting a pro-slavery government by voting in elections; questions whether slavery or war is the greater evil. 1 August 1856. p.122, c4.

3831 MR. A. BURLINGAME *to* **n.n. [extract] 28 July 1856. Washington.** States facts relating to the contemplated duel between Mr. Brooks and himself. 1 August 1856. p.123, c1.

3832 L. L. R. *to* **FRIEND GARRISON. 11 July 1856. Bath, Mi.** Tells of occurrences at a Sabbath school celebration. 1 August 1856. p.124, c2.

3833 WM. LLOYD GARRISON *to* **S. MAY, JR. 1 August 1856. Boston.** Regrets that he cannot attend the West Indies Emancipation celebration in Abington. 8 August 1856. p.126, c3.

3834 SARAH M. GRIMKE *to* **JEANNE DEROIN. 21 May 1856. Eagleswood School.** Questions how females who are enchained to fashions may be alerted to the cause of women's rights. 8 August 1856. p.128, c3.

3835 GERRIT SMITH *to* **L. B. KERN. 20 June 1856. Peterboro'.** Verifies that Col. and Mrs. Fremont both oppose slavery. 8 August 1856. p.128, c6.

3836 WM. WHITNEY *to* **MR. STUART. n.d. n.p.** Forwards a letter from Isaac K. Fay. 15 August 1856. p.129, c3.

3837 ISAAC K. FAY *to* **WM. WHITNEY. 7 July 1856. Elgin, Il.** Concludes that the Free-Soilers are being driven out of Missouri. 15 August 1856. p.129, c3.

3838 J. C. UNDERWOOD *to* **SIR. [from the** *New York Evening Post*] **7 July 1856. Washington, D.C.** Describes himself, Clark County, Virginia, and the circumstances surrounding his banishment from the state. 15 August 1856. p.129, c6.

3839 SAM F. TAPPAN *to* **SETH WEBB, JR. 28 July 1856. Boston.** Sends a chain which was fastened on the ankles of a free state man in Kansas; describes the incident. 15 August 1856. p.130, c1.

3840 F. H. DRAKE *to* **MR. GARRISON. 7 August 1856. Leominster.** Comments on Parker Pillsbury's address in Leominster. 15 August 1856. p.130, c6.

3841 ELIZUR WRIGHT *to* **MR. EDITOR. n.d. n.p.** Defends the propriety and wisdom of electing a Republican governor in Kansas. 15 August 1856. p.131, c1.

3842 W. C. NELL *to* **FRIEND GARRISON. 4 August 1856. Oberlin, Oh.** Describes the West Indies Emancipation celebration in Salem. 15 August 1856. p.131, c2.

3843 NELSON BROWN *to* **n.n. n.d. n.p.** Describes the First of August celebration at Cummington. 15 August 1856. p.131, c2.

3844 AMELIA R. M. ROBINSON *to* **THE EDITOR OF THE** *CLEVELAND LEADER.* **1 August 1858. Cleveland.** Challenges P. S. Brooks to a duel. 15 August 1856. p.131, c3.

3845 A. G. BROWN *to* **S. R. ADAMS. 18 June 1856. Washington City.** Gives account of his interview with Mr. J. Buchanan; endorses the Cincinnati platform. 22 August 1856. p.137, c2.

3846 L. C. TODD *to* **MR. EDITOR. 27 July 1856. Parkman.** Presents recommendations for the gentlemen of the township committee of Kansas. 22 August 1856. p.138, c3.

3847 S. MAY, JR. *to* **FRIEND WALLCUT. 15 August 1856. Westgrove, Pa.** Describes his endeavors to overthrow slavery. 22 August 1856. p.138, c6.

3848 HENRY C. WRIGHT *to* **W. L. GARRISON. 1 August 1856. Salem, Oh.** Describes the West Indies Emancipation celebration; reiterates arguments for a Northern republic. 22 August 1856. p.139, c1.

3849 JOHN OF MORLEY *to* **THE EDITOR OF THE** *LIBERATOR* **[W. L. GARRISON]. 2 August 1856. n.p.** Describes censorship in the South. 22 August 1856. p.139, c1.

3850 GEO. SUNTER, JR. *to* **THE EDITOR OF THE** *LIBERATOR* **[W. L. GARRISON]. 13 August 1856. Windsor, Canada West.** Desires clarification of W. Phillips' "Higher Law" theory. 22 August 1856. p.139, c2.

3851 A. M. P. *to* **MR. GARRISON. 8 August 1856. Troy, N.Y.** Describes state teachers' convention; discusses the progress of women's rights within the state teachers' organization. 22 August 1856. p.140, c2.

3852 A. J. GROVER *to* **MR. GARRISON. 1 August 1856. Earlville, Il.** Encloses a petition which is in circulation to impeach Franklin Pierce. 22 August 1856. p.140, c2.

3853 A. HOGEBOOM *to* **FRIEND GARRISON. 6 August 1856. Shed's Corners, N.Y.** Confesses that his belief that the Church might favor abolition is wavering. 22 August 1856. p.140, c3.

3854 EMELINE HOGEBOOM *to* **BROTHER HOGEBOOM. 3 August 1856. Ghent.** Reports that a pro-slavery clergyman lives in Ghent. 22 August 1856. p.140, c3.

3855 FRANCIS BARRY *to* **BROTHER WRIGHT. 31 July 1856. Berlin Heights, Oh.** Defends free love from the aspersions of spiritualists. 22 August 1856. p.140, c3.

3856 PARKER PILLSBURY *to* **FRIEND WALLCUT. 25 August 1856. Springfield.** Describes his anti-slavery work in Springfield; reports on the Republican Party's encroachment on the anti-slavery domain. 29 August 1856. p.141, c2.

3857 JOHN HENRY WILLAN *to* **SIR. n.d. n.p.** Reports that slaveholders are sending insane slaves to Canada. 29 August 1856. p.141, c2.

3858 JAMES BARNABY *to* **FRIEND GARRISON. 30 July 1856. Salem, Oh.** Criticizes the writings of the spiritualist A. J. Davis. 29 August 1856. p.142, c2.

3859 L. M. PERHAM *to* **FRIEND GARRISON. [extract] 12 August 1856. Viroqua, Wi.** Reports on anti-slavery sentiment in Viroqua. 29 August 1856. p.142, c3.

3860 DR. F. A. ROSS *to* **REV. A. BLACKBURN. [from the** *Knoxville Presbyterian Witness***] 14 July 1856. Huntsville, Al.** Concludes that the sectional crisis will confirm the slaveholding interpretation of the Bible. 5 September 1856. p.143, c1.

3861 F. SCHEFFER *to* **THE EDITOR OF THE** *NEW YORK TIMES.* **6 August 1856. Richmond.** Reports that his fugitive slave has not returned. 5 September 1856. p.143, c5.

3862 WM. SELLERS *to* **BRO. CONKLIN. 1 August. Anamesa, Ia.** Tells of his tar and feathering in Rochester, Missouri. 5 September 1856. p.146, c1.

3863 MRS. LYDIA HOLLAND *to* **n.n. [extract from the** *Central Christian Advocate***] n.d. n.p.** Relates the murder of her husband, Benjamin Holland. 5 September 1856. p.146, c2.

3864 ADAM ROMIG *to* **W. L. GARRISON. 23 August 1856. Middlebury, In.** Asks if Garrison supports J. C. Fremont. 5 September 1856. p.146, c5.

3865 F. H. BEMIS *to* **WM. LLOYD GARRISON. 14 August 1856. Meadville, Pa.** Inquires about Garrison's position regarding the Republican Party and J. C. Fremont. 5 September 1856. p.146, c5.

3866 GEORGE SUNTER, JR. *to* **THE EDITOR OF THE** *LIBERATOR* **[W. L. GARRISON]. 26 August 1856. Windsor, Canada West.** Reports on racism and intolerance in Canada West. 5 September 1856. p.147, c1.

3867 SAMUEL JOHNSON *to* **SIR. 27 August 1856. Salem, Ma.** Reports on Lucretia Mott's speech in Lynn, Massachusetts. 5 September 1856. p.147, c2.

3868 J. A. HUTCHINSON *to* **n.n. [from the** *Richmond Whig***] 19 August 1856. Kansas City, Mo.** Informs that the border ruffians plan to make Kansas a slave state. 5 September 1856. p.147, c3.

3869 REV. MR. NUTE *to* **REV. MR. TIFFANY. 22 August 1856. Lawrence, Ks.** Decries attacks perpetrated on abolitionists in Leavenworth by the border ruffians. 5 September 1856. p.147, c3.

3870 MR. LINES *to* **n.n. 22 August. Lawrence.** Relates horrible torture of a woman in Lawrence. 5 September 1856. p.147, c3.

3871 HORACE GREELEY *to* **THE EDITORS OF THE** *JOURNAL OF COMMERCE.* **n.d. n.p.** Disavows a disunionist statement attributed to him in the *Journal of Commerce.* 5 September 1856. p.147, c4.

3872 MR. HENRY W. TITUS *to* **n.n. [extract] n.d. n.p.** Describes sailboat disaster at Bellport, Long Island. 5 September 1856. p.147, c5.

3873 W. HOPKINS *to* **W. L. GARRISON. 11 August 1856. Fremont, In.** Desires a clarification of Garrison's concept of divine government. 5 September 1856. p.148, c2.

3874 HENRY C. WRIGHT *to* **FRIEND FRANCIS BARRY. 25 August 1856. Farmington, Mi.** Debates spiritualism and free love. 5 September 1856. p.148, c2.

3875 B. W. DYER *to* **W. L. GARRISON. 25 August 1856. Randolph, Vt.** Encloses resolutions rejected by the Republican Party in Chelsea, Vermont. 5 September 1856. p.148, c2.

3876 W. C. BABCOCK *to* **THE** *LIBERATOR.* **26 August. Harvard, Ma.** Advocates uncompromising morality, which outrages some Fremonters. 5 September 1856. p.148, c3.

3877 D. A. WASSON *to* **W. L. GARRISON. 29 August 1856. Gloucester.** Explains his disagreement with Wendell Phillips' reform philosophy. 5 September 1856. p.148, c3.

3878 HENRY C. WRIGHT *to* **W. L. GARRISON. 2 September 1856. Detroit, Mi.** Advocates a Northern republic. 19 September 1856. p.155, c1.

3879 HENRY C. WRIGHT *to* **W. L. GARRISON. 3 September 1856. Northville, Mi.** Reports on a Republican mass meeting in Northville. 19 September 1856. p.155, c1.

3880 HENRY C. WRIGHT *to* **W. L. GARRISON. 7 September 1856. Fowlersville, Mi.** Describes a spiritualist convention in Fowlersville. 19 September 1856. p.155, c1.

3881 PRO-SLAVERY LODGE *to* **n.n. [from the** *Newport* **(Ky.)** *News***] 27 August 1856. Jessamine County.** Declares desire that non-slaveholders should be silenced. 26 September 1856. p.157, c2.

3882 n.n. *to* **n.n. [extract from the** *Missouri Republican***] 25 August 1856. n.p.** Catholic missionaries in the Osage Nation tell of finding three colored bodies and one red body. 26 September 1856. p.157, c3.

3883 GENTLEMAN IN THE CHEROKEE NATION *to* **A CITIZEN. 20 August 1856. Tahlequah.** Describes fighting between Negroes and Indians. 26 September 1856. p.157, c3.

3884 GOV. HENRY A. WISE *to* **THE PUBLIC. 6 September 1856. Richmond, Va.** Concludes that the election of Fremont to the presidency will bring about the dissolution of the American Confederacy of States. 26 September 1856. p.157, c3.

3885 P. *to* **THE EDITOR OF THE** *NEWBURYPORT HERALD***. 2 September 1856. Fort Leavenworth, Ks.** Relates eyewitness account of outrages occurring in Kansas. 26 September 1856. p.157, c6.

3886 REV. F. WAYLAND *to* **n.n. [extract] n.d.** Comments on the issue of slavery in the 1856 election. 26 September 1856. p.158, c2.

3887 SAMUEL MAY, JR. *to* *NATIONAL ANTI-SLAVERY STANDARD***. [extract] n.d. n.p.** Discusses Benjamin Franklin's abolitionism. 26 September 1856. p.158, c2.

3888 E. NUTE, JR. *to* **REV. DR. MILES. 11 September 1856. Lawrence, Ks.** Describes the outrages committed upon free state men in Lawrence and the need for relief. 26 September 1856. p.158, c6.

3889 J. T. BROWN *to* **MAJ. W. H. TRIMMIER. [extract from the** *Spartanburg* **(S.C.)** *Spartan***] 17 August 1856. Leavenworth.** Informs that a South Carolina man in Kansas vows to exterminate the abolitionists. 26 September 1856. p.159, c1.

3890 ANDREW JACKSON *to* **n.n. 28 February 1845. Hermitage.** Expresses opinion that James Buchanan lacks moral courage. 26 September 1856. p.159, c2.

3891 J. T. C. *to* **W. L. GARRISON. 11 September 1856. Oshkosh, Wi.** Debates the right and duty of abolitionists to vote. 26 September 1856. p.150*, c2.

3892 Y. Y. *to* **THE EDITOR OF THE** *LIBERATOR* **[W. L. GARRISON]. 20 September 1856. Boston.** Argues that non-voting abolitionists should not vote for the ineffectual abolitionism embraced by the Republican Party. 26 September 1856. p.150*, c3.

3893 R. L. ALEXANDER *to* **THE EDITOR OF THE** *LIBERATOR* **[W. L. GARRISON]. 14 September 1856. Livonia, Mi.** Defends the writings of A. J. Davis, a spiritualist, against James Barnaby's criticisms. 26 September 1856. p.150*, c4.

3894 AMOS GILBERT *to* **VALUED FRIEND GARRISON. 15 September 1856. Salem, Oh.** Comments on spiritualism and the originality of A. J. Davis' ideas. 26 September 1856. p.150*, c4.

3895 FRANCIS BARRY *to* **H. C. WRIGHT. n.d. n.p.** Advocates free love. 26 September 1856. p.150*, c5.

3896 JOHN H. ROBSON, H. A. TATUM, AND J. H. HICKS *to* **THE EDITORS OF THE** *GALVESTON NEWS***. 9 September 1856. Columbus, Colorado County, Tx.** Relate the discovery of plans for a slave insurrection in Columbus. 3 October 1856. p.151*, c4.

3897 FLORILLA B. ADAIR *to* **n.n. 1 September 1856. n.p.** Chronicles the border ruffian outrages in Kansas. 3 October 1856. p.151*, c5.

3898 DR. R. M. S. JACKSON *to* **n.n. 8 September 1856. Cresson, Allegheney Mt.** Charles Sumner's physician reports on Sumner's condition. 3 October 1856. p.159*, c1.

3899 PARKER PILLSBURY *to* **FRIEND GARRISON. 26 September 1856. Jefferson, Oh.** States the reasons for a poor agricultural season; discusses the encroachment by Republicans on abolitionist strength in Ohio. 3 October 1856. p.159*, c3.

3900 HENRY C. WRIGHT *to* **W. L. GARRISON. 24 September 1856. Cold Water, Mi.** Describes a Republican meeting in Cold Water; reiterates the call for a Northern republic. 3 October 1856. p.159*, c4.

3901 n.n. *to* **MR. EDWARD BUFFUM. n.d. n.p.** Informs of death of Buffum's son. 3 October 1856. p.159*, c1.

3902 n.n. *to* **n.n. [extract] 17 September 1856. n.p.** Reports the suffocation of a fugitive slave; laments the calamity. 3 October 1856. p.159*, c2.

3903 JOHN STEPHENSON *to* **THE EDITOR OF THE** *TELEGRAPH.* **n.d. n.p.** Colored member of the Boston Mercantile Library Procession protests his treatment by officers of the association at a ceremony unveiling the Benjamin Franklin statue. 3 October 1856. p.159*, c4.

3904 GOVERNOR JOHN A. WINSTON *to* **GOV. H. GARDINER. 30 August 1856. Montgomery, Al.** Defends slavery and the South from Massachusetts' vituperations. 10 October 1856. p.161, c2.

3905 GEN. J. H. LANE *to* **A. W. DONIPHAN AND A. G. BOON. 22 September 1856. Fremont County, Ia.** Justifies his conduct in Kansas; challenges one hundred slaveholders to battle with one hundred free state Kansas men before twelve United States congressmen to settle the Kansas issue. 10 October 1856. p.162, c1.

3906 n.n. *to* **THE EDITOR OF THE** *BOSTON LIBERATOR* **[W. L. GARRISON]. 22 September 1856. Wyoming, Pa.** Requests a copy of the *Liberator* in order to determine whom Garrison supports in the presidential election. 10 October 1856. p.162, c5.

3907 n.n. *to* **WM. LLOYD GARRISON. 29 September 1856. Bloomington, Il.** Questions Garrison regarding his presidential preference. 10 October 1856. p.162, c5.

3908 n.n. *to* **W. L. GARRISON. 30 September 1856. Chicago.** Requests a copy of the *Liberator* so he may ascertain whether or not Garrison has expressed himself in favor of Fremont in the forthcoming presidential election. 10 October 1856. p.162, c5.

3909 n.n. *to* **WM. LLOYD GARRISON. 8 October 1856. Morristown, N.J.** Questions Garrison regarding his presidential preference. 10 October 1856. p.162, c5.

3910 JUSTICE *to* **FRIEND. 31 August 1856. Lawrence, Ks.** Reports on anti-slavery army in Kansas; requests contributions. 10 October 1856. p.163, c1.

3911 JUSTICE *to* **n.n. 21 September 1856. n.p.** Reports on skirmishes with ruffians at the Kansas border. 10 October 1856. p.163, c2.

3912 HENRY C. WRIGHT *to* **S. J. MAY. 28 September 1856. Angola, In.** Presents the hazards of voting for Fremont. 10 October 1856. p.163, c2.

3913 WM. H. FISH *to* **FRIEND MAY. 25 September 1856. McLean, N.Y.** Warns against descending to Republican principles. 10 October 1856. p.163, c3.

3914 GEO. FITZHUGH *to* **W. L. GARRISON. 29 September 1856. Port Royal, Va.** Accepts A. Hogeboom's challenge to debate slavery; asks abolitionists to ascertain the success of a free society before asking the South to try the experiment. 10 October 1856. p.163, c4.

3915 EMELINE M. RANDALL *to* **FRIEND GARRISON. n.d. n.p.** Describes the Abington Anti-Slavery Fair. 10 October 1856. p.163, c4.

3916 RICHARD YEADON *to* **THEODORE PARKER. 14 September 1856. Boston.** The editor of the *Charleston Courier* rebukes Parker for his abolitionism; defends slavery, using the Scriptures. 17 October 1856. p.165, c1.

3917 A. HOGEBOOM *to* **FRIEND GARRISON. 7 October 1856. Shed's Corner, Madison County, N.Y.** Discovers Republican inconsistencies. 17 October 1856. p.167, c2.

3918 T. LEONARD *to* **FRIEND GARRISON. 3 October 1856. Grafton.** Wishes J. T. C. to explain how the three-fifths representative clause of the Constitution can be interpreted in behalf of freedom. 17 October 1856. p.167, c2.

3919 HENRY C. WRIGHT *to* **W. L. GARRISON. 7 October 1856. Battle Creek, Mi.** Comments on the Yearly Meeting of the Friends of Progress in Battle Creek. 17 October 1856. p.167, c3.

3920 n.n. *to* **THE EDITOR OF THE *POST*. 7 October 1856. Smithfield.** Informs Garrison of Henry C. Wright's loyalty to Queen Victoria. 17 October 1856. p.167, c4.

3921 C. F. P. *to* **W. L. GARRISON. September. Cattaraugus County, N.Y.** Comments on S. Holley's lectures in Cattaraugus County. 17 October 1856. p.168, c2.

3922 W. G. BABCOCK *to* **W. L. G. n.d. n.p.** Comments on N. P. Banks' speech in New York. 17 October 1856. p.168, c2.

3923 MRS. STOWE *to* **THE EARL OF HARRINGTON. [extract] n.d. n.p.** Declines his invitation to speak; upholds temperance. 24 October 1856. p.169, c6.

3924 S. J. MAY *to* **THE EDITORS OF THE *NATIONAL ANTI-SLAVERY STANDARD*. 20 August 1856. Syracuse.** Explains his reasons for supporting Fremont and Dayton. 24 October 1856. p.170, c1.

3925 S. J. MAY *to* **H. C. WRIGHT. 14 October 1856. Syracuse.** Stresses the importance of voting for Fremont. 24 October 1856. p.171, c2.

3926 JOSEPH BARKER *to* **FRIEND. 7 October 1856. Omaha City, Ne.** Complains of extravagant statements by lecturers of the Western AS, such as the charge that H. W. Beecher is as fatal an enemy to the anti-slavery movement as are pro-slavery Northern newspapers; considers Frederick Douglass' recent political course wise and manly, and surmises that Douglass has also been unjustly abused by these same lecturers. 24 October 1856. p.171, c3.

3927 HENRY C. WRIGHT *to* **W. L. GARRISON. 6 October 1856. Livonia, Mi.** Describes convention of the Michigan AS in Livonia; calls for a Northern republic. 24 October 1856. p.172, c2.

3928 JEFFERSON DAVIS *to* **ARTHUR SIMPKINS, JAMES GILLAM, AND OTHERS. 22 September 1856. Washington.** Esteems P. S. Brooks. 31 October 1856. p.173, c1.

3929 SEN. J. M. MASON *to* **GENTLEMEN. 29 September 1856. Selma, Va.** Praises P. S. Brooks; describes the issues confronting the South. 31 October 1856. p.173, c1.

3930 HORACE GREELEY *to* **W. L. GARRISON. 29 October 1856. New York.** Requests a clarification of Garrison's attitude toward Fremont. 31 October 1856. p.174, c2.

3931 S. J. MAY *to* **HENRY C. WRIGHT. 21 October 1856. Syracuse.** Defends his decision to vote for Fremont. 31 October 1856. p.174, c4.

3932 JACOB LEONARD *to* **FRIEND GARRISON. 25 October 1856. East Bridgewater.** Recommends that Garrisonians resist descending to the Republican platform; argues that it would be inconsistent with their views on the Constitution. 31 October 1856. p.174, c6.

3933 C. E. C. *to* **FRIEND GARRISON. 21 October 1856. Detroit.** Gives a brief account of a new organization, the Friends of Human Progress. 7 November 1856. p.177, c2.

3934 MERCY B. JACKSON *to* **THE CITIZENS OF MASSACHUSETTS. 15 October 1856. Plymouth, Ma.** Condemns the oppression of women. 7 November 1856. p.177, c3.

3935 S. MITCHELL *to* **FRIEND GARRISON. 29 October 1856. Cornville, Me.** Affirms the principles of non-resistance. 7 November 1856. p.178, c5.

3936 J. WEBSTER PILLSBURY *to* **W. L. GARRISON. 27 October 1856. Milford.** Pleads for charity towards abolitionists who do not agree with him. 7 November 1856. p.178, c6.

3937 S. S. GRISWOLD *to* **FRIEND GARRISON. 28 October 1856. Greenmanville.** Reports on anti-slavery and Republican Party activities in the Mystic Valley. 7 November 1856. p.178, c6.

3938 THOMAS H. GLADSTONE *to* **THE EDITOR OF THE** *LONDON TIMES.* **9 October. Surrey, England.** Presents observations made while travelling to Kansas. 7 November 1856. p.180, c3.

3939-3943 Entry numbers not used.

3944 R. R. M. *to* **THE EDITOR OF THE** *NEW YORK TRIBUNE.* **10 October 1856. Georgia.** A Southerner reports that his mail is monitored by suspicious neighbors. 14 November 1856. p.181, c6.

3945 J. T. C. *to* **W. L. GARRISON. 27 October 1856. Oshkosh, Wi.** Defends the right of abolitionists to vote. 14 November 1856. p.182, c3.

3946 W. C. N. *to* **FRIEND GARRISON. 10 November 1856. Boston.** Discusses his recent visit to Ohio and the progress of rights of colored people there. 14 November 1856. p.183, c1.

3947 A. T. FOSS *to* **W. L. GARRISON. 4 November 1856. St. Mary's Lake, Pennfield, Mi.** Describes political excitement in the West; reports on the Harmonial School. 14 November 1856. p.183, c2.

3948 CALVIN STOWE *to* **THE EDITOR OF THE** *BOSTON TELEGRAPH.* **10 November 1856. Andover, Ma.** Forwards a letter from Lord Byron's widow, A. T. Noel Byron. 14 November 1856. p.183, c3.

3949 A. T. NOEL BYRON *to* **MRS. STOWE. 18 October 1856. n.p.** Sends contribution towards the relief of the sufferers in Kansas. 14 November 1856. p.183, c3.

3950 WILLIAM STONE *to* **H. WILSON. 11 September 1856. Eagle Pass, Tx.** Denounces Wilson's speeches. 14 November 1856. p.183, c4.

3951 JOSEPH BARKER *to* **n.n. 22 October 1856. Omaha City, Ne.** Reports on interviews with slaveholders. 14 November 1856. p.184, c2.

3952 R. BARNWELL RHETT *to* **GOV. JAS H. ADAMS. n.d. n.p.** Discusses the state of public affairs. 21 November 1856. p.185, c1.

3953 H. C. WRIGHT *to* **S. J. MAY. 4 November 1856. Sheboygan Falls, Wi.** Criticizes May for voting for Fremont; calls for a Northern republic. 21 November 1856. p.186, c6.

3954 G. *to* **n.n. 10 November 1856. St. Louis.** Speculates on what President Buchanan will accomplish. 21 November 1856. p.187, c1.

3955 D. R. ATCHISON *to* **R. M. FULLER. [from the** *Edgefield* **(S.C.)** *Advertiser***] 9 October 1856. Platte City.** Declares that Southern men have carried the Kansas election and that Kansas will be a slave state in twelve months. 21 November 1856. p.187, c2.

3956 H. *to* **FRIEND GARRISON. 11 November 1856. Boston.** Advocates forming freedom clubs throughout New England. 21 November 1856. p.188, c2.

3957 LUCY N. COLMAN *to* **FRIEND GARRISON. 4 November 1856. Ypsilanti, Mi.** Reports on anti-slavery and women's rights activities in Ypsilanti. 21 November 1856. p.188, c2.

3958 W. C. NELL *to* **FRIEND GARRISON. November 1856. Boston.** Decribes his recent tour in Ohio and the colored community there. 21 November 1856. p.188, c2.

3959 CLERGYMAN *to* **CLERGYMAN. 8 November 1856. Philadelphia.** Describes James Buchanan as a man of high religious and moral character. 28 November 1856. p.189, c1.

3960 WM. P. HALL *to* **MESSRS. GREELEY AND McELRATH. 26 September 1856. Shinnston, Va.** Reveals that he will be threatened with Grand Jury action if he persists in efforts to form a *New York Tribune* club. 28 November 1856. p.189, c5.

3961 IRA HART *to* **THE EDITOR OF THE** *NEW YORK TRIBUNE.* 2 October 1856. Clarksburgh, Va. Reports being indicted for circulating the *New York Tribune.* 28 November 1856, p.189, c5.

3962 WM. P. HALL *to* **MESSRS. GREELEY AND McELRATH. 20 October 1856. Shinnston, Va.** Requests that Greeley and McElrath discontinue the club for the *New York Tribune* 28 November 1856. p.189, c5.

3963 PROF. HEDRICK *to* **A SOUTHERN REPUBLICAN FRIEND IN NEW YORK. [extract] 27 October 1856. n.p.** Reports his dismissal from the staff of the University of North Carolina. 28 November 1856. p.189, c6.

3964 CHARLES SUMNER *to* **JOSEPH STORY. 24 November 1856. Boston.** Expresses esteem for Anson Burlingame. 28 November 1856. p.190, c2.

3965 TIMOTHY STANNARD *to* **THE EDITORS OF THE** *NEW HAVEN PALLADIUM.* **17 November 1856. Fair Haven.** Informs that a Northern resident was driven out of Norfolk, Virginia, for voting the Fremont ticket. 28 November 1856. p.190, c2.

3966 W. E. EPPES *to* **COL. PRYOR. [from the** *Memphis Enquirer***] 2 November 1856. Lafayette Depot, Tn.** Informs of slave conspiracy in Tennessee. 28 November 1856. p.190, c3.

3967 HENRY C. WRIGHT *to* **W. L. GARRISON. 18 November 1856. Waukegan.** Comments on anti-slavery people in Waukegan and Theodore Parker's lecture; stresses the need for a Northern republic. 28 November 1856. p.190, c5.

3968 A SOUTHERNER *to* **WM. LLOYD GARRISON. 18 November 1856. Virginia.** Defends slave civilization. 28 November 1856. p.190, c6.

3969 WM. G. BABCOCK *to* **W. L. GARRISON. 18 November 1856. Harvard.** Praises the *Liberator* for remaining calm during the elections. 28 November 1856. p.192, c2.

3970 REV. JEHIEL CLAFLIN *to* **BROTHER GARRISON. 19 November 1856. East Westmoreland, N.H.** Expresses his ambivalence towards the Republican Party; discusses abolition among the ministry and the lack of public morality. 28 November 1856. p.192, c2.

3971 ALEXANDER McARTHUR *to* **W. L. GARRISON. 11 November 1856. Pictou, Nova Scotia.** Hopes the Republicans will learn from Buchanan's election that they should not compromise. 28 November 1856. p.192, c3.

3972 J. A. THOMAS, ASSISTANT SECRETARY OF STATE *to* **H. H. RICE. 4 November 1856. Washington.** Refuses to issue passports to free colored persons on the grounds that they are not United States citizens. 28 November 1856. p.192, c3.

3973 CIVIS *to* **SECRETARY OF STATE WM. L. MARCY. 14 November 1856. New York.** Contends that colored Americans are United States citizens. 28 November 1856. p.192, c3.

3974 H. H. RICE *to* **SECRETARY OF STATE WM. L. MARCY. 11 November 1856. New York.** Asks what proof is necessary to show that eleven blacks sailing for Europe are free born and entitled to passports. 28 November 1856. p.192, c4.

3975 WM. G. SIMMS *to* **SIR. 21 November 1856. New York.** Regrets he must abandon his Northern lecture tour because of the personal abuse to which he has been subjected. 5 December 1856. p.194, c2.

3976 HENRY C. WRIGHT *to* **S. J. MAY. 16 November 1856. Rockford, Il.** Reproaches May for voting for Fremont, which he declares is the same as voting to perpetuate slavery. 5 December 1856. p.195, c2.

3977 R. G. *to* **FRIEND GARRISON. 26 November 1856. New Ipswich.** Asserts that the Republican Party is not worth an abolitionist's time; recommends not voting. 5 December 1856. p.195, c2.

3978 A READER *to* **MR. EDITOR [W. L. GARRISON]. 25 October 1856. Conneea County, Al.** Declares that there are frauds in the land office in Conneea County. 5 December 1856. p.195, c2.

3979 AARON M. POWELL *to* **n.n. [extract] 26 November 1856. Easton, N.Y.** Believes that Republican politics have left people demoralized and have injured the abolitionist cause. 5 December 1856. p.195, c3.

3980 DAN'L WEBSTER *to* **REV. FURNESS. 15 February 1850. Washington.** Discusses ways to curb slavery. 12 December 1856. p.197, c4.

3981 SAM *to* **A GENTLEMAN IN NEW YORK. [extract] n.d. Boston.** Details Col. Benton's speech. 12 December 1856. p.198, c2.

3982 JANE ASHBY *to* **n.n. [extract] England.** Fears that the United States must be bathed in blood before slavery is ended. 12 December 1856. p.198, c3.

3983 DORVELAS DORVAL *to* **FRIEND GARRISON. 4 October 1856. Gonaives, Hayti.** Justifies suppression of uprisings in Haiti, but deplores the recent war with the Dominicans. 12 December 1856. p.198, c6.

3984 R. H. OBER *to* **FRIEND GARRISON. 18 November 1856. Weare Centre, N.H.** Relates the activities of Garrisonians in Weare Centre. 12 December 1856. p.198, c6.

3985 C. F. P. *to* **W. L. GARRISON. 30 November 1856. Dryden, N.Y.** Discusses S. Holley's lectures in Dryden. 12 December 1856. p.198, c6.

3986 AMOS GILBERT *to* **FRIEND W. L. G. n.d. n.p.** Clarifies non-resistance principles. 12 December 1856. p.199, c1.

3987 JEHIEL CLAFLIN *to* **FRIEND OF UNIVERSAL PEACE. 20 November 1856. East Westmoreland, N.H.** Praises the peace principles. 12 December 1856. p.199, c1.

3988 DANIEL HITCHINGS *to* **FRIEND GARRISON. 3 December 1856. Knoxville, Il.** Asserts that A. P. Butler of South Carolina is a ''concerted simpleton.'' 12 December 1856. p.199, c2.

3989 SOME OF YOUR FORMER FRIENDS *to* **ORVILLE DEWEY. 29 October 1856. Charleston, S.C.** Declare that slaveholders in Charleston were upset by Dewey's recent anti-South oration. 19 December 1856. p.201, c1.

3990 A SOUTH CAROLINIAN *to* **THE EDITORS OF THE** *EVENING POST.* **9 December 1856. Washington.** Explains what constitutes a Southern man, according to his definition. 19 December 1856. p.202, c1.

3991 WM. HENRY HURLBUT *to* **THE EDITOR OF THE** *NEW YORK EVENING POST.* **20 December 1856. New York.** Claims to be a South Carolinian, though neither a slavery extensionist nor a disunionist. 19 December 1856. p.202, c1.

3992 RICHARD YEADON *to* **W. L. GARRISON. 16 November 1856. Charleston.** Desires Garrison to forward copies of the *Liberator* to him in South Carolina, since Garrison has chosen to report and comment on his conversation in New York City with T. Parker. 19 December 1856. p.202, c3.

3993 A SOUTHERNER *to* **W. L. GARRISON. 10 December 1856. Virginia.** Discusses the despotism of capital. 19 December 1856. p.202, c5.

3994 A. HOGEBOOM *to* **W. L. GARRISON. 3 December 1856. Shed's Corners, Madison County, N.Y.** Informs of an important geological discovery. 19 December 1856. p.202, c6.

3995 LIZZIE A. ELWELL *to* **S. MAY. 6 December 1856. Manchester, Ma.** Sends contribution to the anti-slavery tract fund. 19 December 1856. p.202. c6.

3996 TURNER ASHBY *to* **J. C. UNDERWOOD. 24 November 1856. Marham Station, Va.** Advises Underwood that he may return, but only to pack his bags for a permanent departure. 19 December 1856. p.203, c4.

3997 M. D. HAYNES *to* **ANDREW PATTERSON. 31 October 1856. Yazoo City.** Reports that he authorized a postmaster not to deliver Patterson's *Cincinnati Gazette*. 19 December 1856. p.203, c4.

3998 n.n. *to* **THE EDITOR OF THE** *TRIBUNE.* **[extract] n.d. West Point, Ga.** Bemoans murder and suicide of Negroes in Alabama. 19 December 1856. p.204, c5.

3999 A NEW YORKER *to* **WM. LLOYD GARRISON. 21 December 1856. New York.** Replies to a Southerner's defense of slavery. 26 December 1856. p.204, c5.

4000 F. C. ADAMS *to* **THE EDITORS OF THE** *NEW YORK EVENING POST.* **n.d. n.p.** Decribes the slave pens in Charleston and the instruments of torture used to maintain discipline. 26 December 1856. p.205, c2.

4001 O. M. MARCH *to* **SIR. 13 November. Lecompton, Ks.** A free state man relates why he is imprisoned in Lecompton. 26 December 1856. p.205, c4.

4002 A. HOGEBOOM *to* **G. 9 December. Shed's Corners, N.Y.** Declares that any true anti-slavery party must be sectional, not national. 26 December 1856. p.206, c6.

4003 JOSEPH CARPENTER *to* **WM. LLOYD GARRISON. 12 December 1856. New Rochelle.** States that the apostle Paul opposed non-resistance. 26 December 1856. p.206, c6.

4004 E. A. LUKENS *to* **FRIEND. 14 December 1856. New Garden, Oh.** Describes the Minnesota territory and its settlers. 26 December 1856. p.207, c1.

4005 n.n. *to* **THE EDITOR OF THE** *LIBERATOR* **[W. L. GARRISON]. 21 December 1856. Manchester, N.H.** Informs of anti-slavery meetings in Manchester. 26 December 1856. p.207, c2.

4006 AARON M. POWELL *to* **n.n. [extract] n.d. Ogdensburg, N.Y.** Informs that a hotel in Ogdensburg refused to accommodate C. L. and Mrs. Remond. 26 December 1856. p.207, c2.

[1857]

4007 C. E. C. *to* **FRIEND GARRISON. 28 December 1856. Detroit, Mi.** Comments on W. Phillips' lecture in Detroit. 2 January 1857. p.3, c1.

4008 THEODORE PARKER *to* **W. L. GARRISON. 2 January 1857. Boston.** Describes the state of the anti-slavery movement and its prospects. 9 January 1857. p.5, c3.

4009 REV. H. FURNESS *to* **W. L. GARRISON. 29 December 1856. Philadelphia.** Praises the Massachusetts AS. 9 January 1857. p.5, c3.

4010 CHARLES LOWELL *to* **W. L. GARRISON, SAMUEL MAY, JR. AND FRANCIS JACKSON. 30 December 1856. Cambridge.** Sends his regards and hopes for success. 9 January 1857. p.5, c3.

4011 REV. O. B. FROTHINGHAM *to* **MESSRS. GARRISON, JACKSON AND MAY. 28 December 1856. Jersey City.** Sends his regards to the Massachusetts AS. 9 January 1857. p.5, c3.

4012 SAMUEL J. MAY *to* **FRIEND. 1 January 1857. Springfield.** Regrets he is unable to attend the anniversary celebration of Massachusetts AS. 9 January 1857. p.5, c4.

4013 REV. HENRY GREW *to* **MESSRS. GARRISON, JACKSON AND MAY, JR. 30 December 1856. Philadelphia.** Reaffirms anti-slavery principles and sends regards. 9 January 1857. p.5, c4.

4014 PROF. CONVERS FRANCIS *to* **MESSRS. GARRISON, JACKSON AND MAY, JR. 30 December 1856. Cambridge.** Sends regards to Massachusetts AS. 9 January 1857. p.5, c5.

4015 THEODORE D. WELD *to* **FRIEND GARRISON. 31 December 1856. Eagleswood, Perth Amboy.** Reaffirms anti-slavery principles. 9 January 1857. p.5, c5.

4016 ARNOLD BUFFUM *to* **W. L. GARRISON, FRANCIS JACKSON AND SAMUEL MAY, JR. 29 December 1856. Eagleswood, Perth Amboy.** Sends regards and reaffirms anti-slavery principles. 9 January 1857. p.5, c5.

4017 ABBY K. FOSTER *to* **W. L. GARRISON. 2 January 1857. Worcester.** Affirms that her spirit is with the celebration of the founding of the Massachusetts AS. 9 January 1857. p.5, c6.

4018 JOSHUA COFFIN *to* **SIR. 1 January 1857. Newbury.** Reaffirms principles and gives information on the original signers of the constitution of the New England AS. 9 January 1857. p.5, c6.

4019 WM. W. BROWN *to* **W. L. GARRISON. 1 January 1857. Boston.** Sends regards to the anniversary celebration of the Massachusetts AS. 9 January 1857. p.6, c1.

4020 JOHN T. HILTON *to* **W. L. GARRISON, FRANCIS JACKSON AND SAMUEL MAY, JR. 1 January 1857. Brighton.** Sends regards to the anniversary celebration of the Massachusetts AS. 9 January 1857. p.6, c1.

4021 SALLIE HOLLEY *to* **n.n. [extract] 27 December 1856. Sherwood, Cayuga County, N.Y.** Comments on the anti-slavery movement in Sherwood. 9 January 1857. p.6, c4.

4022 REV. MOSES THACHER *to* **W. L. GARRISON, FRANCIS JACKSON, SAMUEL MAY, JR. 6 January 1857. Pitcher, Chenango County, N.Y.** Reaffirms anti-slavery principles and sends regards to anniversary celebration of the New England AS. 16 January 1857. p.10, c1.

4023 WILLIAM JAY *to* **W. L. GARRISON. 10 January 1857. New York.** Expresses admiration for the zeal of the Massachusetts AS. 16 January 1857. p.10, c2.

4024 HENRY C. WRIGHT *to* **W. L. GARRISON. 20 December 1856. Toledo.** Discusses anti-slavery conventions in Michigan and Indiana; comments on the need to create a Northern republic. 16 January 1857. p.11, c1.

4025 AARON M. POWELL *to* **W. L. GARRISON. 10 January 1857. Rome, Oneida County, N.Y.** Discusses anti-slavery convention in Oswego. 16 January 1857. p.11, c2.

4026 C. F. PUTNAM *to* **W. L. GARRISON. 29 December 1856. Union Springs, N.Y.** Comments on abolitionist friends and fugitive slaves in Union Springs. 16 January 1857. p.11, c3.

4027 REV. W. G. BABCOCK *to* **THE *LIBERATOR*. 6 January 1857. Harvard.** Discusses W. Phillips and J. B. Willard's talk at Harvard. 16 January 1857. p.11, c3.

4028 B. CHASE *to* **FRIEND GARRISON. n.d. Auburn, N.H.** Desires clarification from Dr. Lord regarding the "duty" of whites to enslave Africans. 16 January 1857. p.11, c3.

4029 JOHN KINGSLEY *to* **THE EDITORS OF THE *NASS*. 7 January 1857. Portsmouth, Oh.** Relates how a slave was whipped and burned to death in Kentucky. 23 January 1857. p.13, c4.

4030 AMASA WALKER *to* **T. W. HIGGINSON. 10 January 1857. North Brookfield.** Reports that he is a Union man, but is glad the question of disunion is to be discussed at the Disunion Convention. 23 January 1857. p.14, c1.

4031 HENRY WILSON *to* **T. W. HIGGINSON. 10 January 1857. Washington, D.C.** Defends the Union and hopes the delegates at the Disunion Convention change their minds. 23 January 1857. p.14, c2.

4032 THEODORE PARKER *to* **T. W. HIGGINSON. 18 January 1857. Railroad cars from New Haven to Boston.** Expresses satisfaction that Higginson called the Disunion Convention; describes the possible boundaries of a Northern republic. 23 January 1857. p.14, c2.

4033 J. R. GIDDINGS *to* **T. W. HIGGINSON. 7 January 1857. Washington, D.C.** States that he has no respect for this slaveholding Union, which the slave power has dominated through the federal government; gives reasons, however, for remaining in the Union. 23 January 1857. p.14, c3.

4034 FRANCIS JACKSON *to* **T. W. HIGGINSON. 14 January 1857. Boston.** Advocates disunion. 23 January 1857. p.14, c5.

4035 H. C. WRIGHT *to* **W. L. GARRISON. 8 January 1857. New Garden, Oh.** Comments on the right of slaves to resist their masters by such means as they deem right and expedient. 23 January 1857. p.16, c2.

4036 ROBERT JOHNSTON *to* **MR. EDITOR. [from the** *Christian Advocate and Journal***] 11 January 1857. New York.** Discusses the fallibility of the Bible. 23 January 1857. p.16, c3.

4037 B. *to* **THE EDITOR OF THE** *TORONTO GLOBE.* **18 December 1856. Toronto.** Stresses the need for revising the law repecting the rights of married women. 23 January 1857. p.16, c5.

4038 M. PERCIVAL *to* **MRS. HERBERT THOMAS. n.d. n.p.** Sends gifts made by children for the National Anti-Slavery Bazaar. 30 January 1857. p.17, c4.

4039 MARA STORY *to* **MRS. CHAPMAN. 10 September 1856. Lymington Hants.** Encloses letter to be forwarded to Charles Sumner. 30 January 1857. p.17, c5.

4040 LOUIS BRIDEL *to* **M. W. CHAPMAN. [extract] n.d. Lausanne, Switzerland.** Sends contribution to National Anti-Slavery Bazaar. 30 January 1857. p.17, c5.

4041 JAMES WILLIAM MASSIE *to* **MRS. CHAPMAN. 14 November 1856. London.** Encloses contribution for the Boston Anti-Slavery Bazaar; notes that his wife is not well. 30 January 1857. p.17, c5.

4042 A. G. PHILLIPS, C. F. HOVEY, L. LORING, M. MAY, M. CHAPMAN, E. QUINCY, S. MAY, JR., H. SARGENT, ROBBINS, S. RUSSELL, F. JACKSON, E. JACKSON, S. CABOT, C. WILD, A. MAY, F. KINGSBURY, WM. GARRISON, H. GARRISON, T. EARLE *to* **MRS. CHAPMAN. 1 January 1857. n.p.** Send tapestry made by Harriet Martineau. [partially illegible] 30 January 1857. p.17, c6.

4043 GEORGE R. RUSSELL *to* **T. W. HIGGINSON. 12 January 1857. Jamaica Plain.** Declares that the North is justified in dicussing disunion, though he questions whether or not this is the time for separation. 30 January 1857. p.19, c1.

4044 WM. H. FISH *to* **n.n. [extract] n.d. Cortland, N.Y.** Comments on the Anti-Slavery Convention in Cortland. 30 January 1857. p.19, c3.

4045 CHARLES FRANCIS ADAMS *to* **T. W. HIGGINSON. 10 January 1857. Boston.** Informs that he cannot support disunion; gives reasons. 30 January 1857. p.20, c3.

4046 EDWARD WADE *to* **T. W. HIGGINSON. 14 January 1857. Washington.** Gives reasons for not supporting disunion. 30 January 1857. p.20, c4.

4047 C. E. STOWE *to* **T. W. HIGGINSON. 12 January 1857. Andover, Ma.** Advocates non-union with slaveholders. 30 January 1857. p.20, c5.

4048 SEN. HENRY M. DEXTER *to* **T. W. HIGGINSON. 14 January 1857. Boston.** Does not believe the time for disunion has arrived; declares he will welcome disunion when it comes. 30 January 1857. p.20, c5.

4049 O. W. ALBEE *to* **T. W. HIGGINSON. 12 January 1857. Boston.** States that he does not believe the "triumph of freedom" requires disunion. 30 January 1857. p.20, c5.

4050 REV. HENRY W. BELLOWS *to* **T. W. HIGGINSON. 6 January 1857. New York.** Gives reasons for opposing disunion. 6 February 1857. p.21, c1.

4051 JOSEPH BARKER *to* **H. C. WRIGHT. 8 January 1857. Omaha City, Ne.** Defends voting; states that abolitionism is strong in the West. 6 February 1857. p.23, c3.

4052 C. W. WALLACE, H. H. HARTWELL, R. O. BARTLETT, J. M. COBURN, J. G. HUBBARD, C. W. H. CLARK *to* **DIRECTORS OF THE MANCHESTER LYCEUM. 25 December 1856. Manchester, N.H.** Report that clergymen in Manchester object to inviting T. Parker to lecture. 6 February 1857. p.24, c5.

4053 JOHN L. KELLEY *to* **THE DIRECTORS OF THE MANCHESTER (N.H.) LYCEUM. n.d. n.p.** Criticizes the sectarian bigotry demonstrated by denying T. Parker the right to lecture in Manchester. 6 February 1857. p.24, c6.

4054 DANIEL FOSTER *to* **THE EDITOR OF THE** *TELEGRAPH,* **AND OTHER PAPERS. 27 January 1857. Boston.** Appeals for aid for Wm. Bailey, editor of the *Newport* (Ky.) *News*, an abolitionist paper. 13 February 1857. p.26, c1.

4055 W. B. REED *to* **MR. EDITOR. 11 January 1857. Nininger City, Mn.** Describes the inducements offered to immigrants by Minnesota. 13 February 1857. p.28, c4.

4056 C. E. C. *to* **FRIEND GARRISON. 31 January 1857. Detroit.** Praises C. C. Burleigh and other abolitionists. 13 February 1857. p.28, c5.

4057 G. W. S. *to* **W. L. GARRISON. 22 January 1857. Milford.** Rejoices in anti-slavery progress. 13 February 1857. p.28, c5.

4058 G. *to* **THE EDITOR OF THE** *NEW YORK TRIBUNE.* **30 January 1857. Port Jervis, N.Y.** Discusses Anthony Adams, a New York colored man condemned to slavery. 20 February 1857. p.29, c6.

4059 C. R. H. *to* **JAMES BENNET. 21 July 1856. New York.** Requests help for Anthony Adams, a New York Negro now in jail in Edenton, North Carolina, on suspicion of being a fugitive. 20 February 1857. p.29, c6.

4060 WM. R. SKINNER *to* **JAMES BENNET. 17 November 1856. Edenton, N.C.** Informs of Anthony Adams, a New York Negro in jail on suspicion of being a runaway slave. 20 February 1857. p.30, c1.

4061 GEO. E. BAKER *to* **JAMES BENNET. 6 December 1856. Albany, N.Y.** Explains the steps which must be taken by New York in order to send an agent to North Carolina to free Anthony Adams. 20 February 1857. p.30, c1.

4062 FRED L. ROBERTS *to* **WM. H. SEWARD. 14 December 1856. Edenton, N.C.** Informs Seward of Anthony Adams' imprisonment in Edenton. 20 February 1857. p.30, c1.

4063 WM. H. SEWARD *to* **FRED L. ROBERTS. 17 December 1856. Washington.** Thanks Roberts for the information regarding A. Adams' imprisonment; desires details of Adams' jail expenses. 20 February 1857. p.30, c1.

4064 GEO. E. BAKER *to* **JAMES BENNET. 26 December 1856. Albany.** The governor of New York expresses his desire to aid Bennet in securing Anthony Adams' release, but states that he lacks the power. 20 February 1857. p.30, c1.

4065 J. P. *to* **THE EDITOR OF THE** *TELEGRAPH AND CHRONICLE.* **n.d. n.p.** Comments on P. Pillsbury's lecture concerning foreign travel. 20 February 1857. p.30, c3.

4066 M. W. CHAPMAN *to* **W. L. GARRISON. 17 February 1857. Weymouth.** Commends the *Anti-Slavery Bugle.* 20 February 1857. p.30, c6.

4067 JOHN BALL, JR. *to* **THE** *LIBERATOR.* **1 February 1857. St. Louis, Mo.** Describes the abolition movement and politics in St. Louis. 20 February 1857. p.31, c2.

4068 SETH HUNT *to* **FRIEND GARRISON. 2 February 1857. Northampton.** Defines his position regarding disunion, which he endorses. 20 February 1857. p.31, c4.

4069 COLPORTEUR *to* **FRIEND MAY. 23 January 1857. Lowell.** Comments on the anti-slavery movement in Lowell. 20 February 1857. p.31, c4.

4070 A. T. FOSS *to* **FRIEND MAY. [extract] 5 February 1857. Sterling, Whitesale County, Il.** Comments on anti-slavery work in Sterling. 20 February 1857. p.31, c5.

4071 JOHN W. LYON *to* **W. L. GARRISON. 5 February 1857. Cleveland, Oswego County, N.Y.** Comments on the anti-slavery convention in Cleveland. 20 February 1857. p.31, c5.

4072 n.n. *to* **n.n. 20 February 1857. Syracuse, N.Y.** Disparages Garrisonians. 27 February 1857. p.33, c1.

4073 HENRY GREW *to* **HENRY WILSON. 3 February 1857. Philadelphia.** Commends Wilson's righteousness, but feels that it falls short of embracing true doctrines of liberty. 27 February 1857. p.33, c5.

4074 JNO. B. *to* **THE EDITOR OF THE** *LONDON ANTI-SLAVERY ADVOCATE.* **1 January 1857. n.p.** Declares that religious beliefs should not prevent others from cooperating with Garrison in abolition work; adds that if Garrison is an infidel, he should not use the *Liberator* to propagate his views. 27 February 1857. p.34, c1.

4075 GILES B. STEBBINS *to* **THE PRESIDENT OF THE ANTI-SLAVERY CONVENTION IN ROCHESTER. 6 February 1857. Mendota.** Discusses anti-slavery progress and the long road yet to travel. 27 February 1857. p.35, c3.

4076 COLPORTEUR *to* **FRIEND MAY. 28 January 1857. Nashua, N.H.** Comments on the difficulty of procuring a meeting place in Nashua because churches are closed to abolitionists. 27 February 1857. p.35, c4.

4077 OBSERVER *to* **MR. EDITOR. 15 February 1857. New York.** Criticizes Joseph Barker's defense of political abolitionism. 27 February 1857. p.35, c5.

4078 WM. HOWE *to* **GEORGE T. DOWNING. 10 February 1857. Boston.** Expresses satisfaction with the progress of school integration in Boston. 27 February 1857. p.35, c5.

4079 JAMES H. BATTIS *to* **THE EDITOR OF THE** *NEWPORT* **(KY.)** *NEWS.* **February 1857. Salem, Ma.** Reproaches Henry Wilson for comparing Garrisonian disunionists with Southern disunionists. 6 March 1857. p.37, c5.

4080 J. R. GIDDINGS *to* **THOMAS H. BENTON. [from the** *New York Tribune***] 17 February 1857. Jefferson.** Refutes Benton's argument that the Constitution recognizes man as property. 6 March 1857. p.38, c1.

4081 W. G. MYERS, N. W. MILLER, AND E. HARLESTON *to* **WM. LLOYD GARRISON. 20 February 1857. Troy, N.Y.** Three Southerners propose to share profits with Garrison which could be earned from exhibiting Garrison throughout the South in an iron cage. 6 March 1857. p.38, c3.

4082 C. F. P. *to* **THE** *LIBERATOR.* **23 February 1857. Groton, Tompkins County, N.Y.** Discusses S. Holley's lectures in Groton. 6 March 1857. p.39, c1.

4083 LUCY N. COLMAN *to* **FRIEND GARRISON. 4 February 1857. Sterling, Whiteside County, Il.** Relates anti-slavery agitation in Sterling. 6 March 1857. p.39, c2.

4084 A. T. FOSS *to* **FRIEND MAY. [extract] 20 February 1857. Sterling, Whiteside County, Il.** Comments on his anti-slavery meetings in Sterling. 6 March 1857. p.39, c3.

4085 A. HOGEBOOM *to* **GEORGE FITZHUGH. 22 February 1857. Shed's Corner, Madison County, N.Y.** States that their debate on slavery versus free society is available in pamphlet form; wants Fitzhugh to circulate one-half of them in his section of the country. 6 March 1857. p.39, c3.

4086 JUSTICE *to* **W. L. GARRISON. 25 February 1857. Boston.** Explains the origin of the Industrial School at Lancaster. 6 March 1857. p.39, c3.

4087 n.n. *to* **n.n. [extract] 12 February 1857. Rhode Island.** Praises H. C. Wright's speech. 6 March 1857. p.39, c4.

4088 BENJAMIN S. JONES *to* **n.n. [extract] 27 February 1857. Etna, N.Y.** Expresses pleasure upon visiting Tompkins County. 6 March 1857. p.39, c4.

4089 J. A. H. *to* **FRIEND GARRISON. n.d. n.p.** Hopes that abolitionists who voted for Fremont will note that S. J. May remarked in Rochester that he regretted voting Republican. 6 March 1857. p.39, c4.

4090 BENJAMIN S. JONES *to* **n.n. [extract] 27 February 1857. Etna, Tompkins County, N.Y.** Comments on anti-slavery meetings in Etna. 6 March 1857. p.39, c4.

4091 SAMUEL J. MAY *to* **THE ALBANY (N.Y.) ANTI-SLAVERY CONVENTION. 20 February 1857. Syracuse.** Gives reasons for advocating disunion; expresses disappointment at the colorphobia of the Republican Party. 6 March 1857. p.40, c2.

4092 SARAH E. WALL *to* **MASSACHUSETTS SENATE AND HOUSE OF REPRESENTATIVES. 1857. Worcester, Ma.** Appeals for equal rights and the elective franchise for women. 6 March 1857. p.40, c3.

4093 L. G. CALKINS *to* **THE EDITOR OF THE** *LIBERATOR* **[W. L. GARRISON]. n.d. Central College, N.Y.** Describes New York Central College and the claims which it has upon the reform public. 6 March 1857. p.40, c5.

4094 THEODORE PARKER *to* **PRES. L. G. CALKINS. 26 November 1856. Boston.** Praises New York Central College. 6 March 1857. p.40, c5.

4095 GERRIT SMITH *to* **PRES. L. G. CALKINS. 21 October 1856. Peterboro'.** Praises New York Central College. 6 March 1857. p.40, c5.

4096 AZARIAH SMITH *to* **READER. February 1857. McGrawville, Cortland County, N.Y.** New York Central College's librarian appeals for aid. 6 March 1857. p.40, c5.

4097 A. J. GROVER *to* **W. L. GARRISON. 24 February 1857. Earlville, LaSalle County, Il.** Fails to understand why non-resistants refuse to support and encourage slave insurrections; gives reasons for his support. 13 March 1857. p.41, c3.

4098 A. T. FOSS *to* **FRIEND GARRISON. 2 March 1857. Lyons, Ia.** Discusses anti-slavery work in Lyons. 13 March 1857. p.43, c2.

4099 COLPORTEUR *to* **FRIEND MAY. 18 February 1857. Pepperell.** Comments on Colporteur's anti-slavery lectures in New Hampshire. 13 March 1857. p.44, c2.

4100 WELCOME O. SPENCER *to* **W. L. GARRISON. 21 February 1857. Lakeport, N.Y.** Feels no love for the Union, but fears that separation would further entrench slavery and isolate the South from the North's reformatory influence. 13 March 1857. p.44, c2.

4101 WILLIAM G. BABCOCK *to* **THE** *LIBERATOR.* **3 March 1857. Harvard.** Advocates disunion. 13 March 1857. p.44, c3.

4102 WM. H. BARTLETT *to* **W. L. GARRISON. 2 March 1857. Plymouth.** Expresses pleasure with Rev. R. Tomlinson's anti-slavery sermon in Plymouth. 13 March 1857. p.44, c4.

4103 C. M. CLAY *to* **W. L. GARRISON, F. JACKSON, AND S. MAY, JR. 5 March 1857. n.p.** Defends his political abolitionism and that of the Republican Party. 20 March 1857. p.46, c6.

4104 OBSERVER *to* **MR. EDITOR. 24 February 1857. New York.** Takes issue with Rev. F. I. Jobson's defense of the American Methodists to English audiences. 20 March 1857. p.47, c1.

4105 RICHARD THURROW *to* **W. L. GARRISON. 20 January 1857. England.** Comments on the Scottish Free church's pro-slavery connection; discusses the growing suicide rate in England. 20 March 1857. p.47, c2.

4106 E. R. B. *to* **W. L. GARRISON. 8 March 1857. Elmwood, Peoria County, Il.** Desires anti-slavery action in Elmwood and hopes A. T. Foss will visit; suggests that Negro lecturers might dispel some of the racism in the West, which is anti-slavery's greatest obstacle. 20 March 1857. p.47, c2.

4107 H. *to* **FRIEND GARRISON. n.d. n.p.** Informs that a portrait of anti-slavery pioneers is being processed. 20 March 1857. p.47, c3.

4108 CHARLES SUMNER *to* **JAMES REDPATH. 7 March 1857. On Steamship** *Fulton.* Endorses the free state movement in Kansas. 20 March 1857. p.47, c3.

4109 A. H. WILLIS *to* **REV. HALL. 2 March 1857. Ipava, Il.** Gives reasons for becoming an infidel. 20 March 1857. p.48, c2.

4110 HENRY C. WRIGHT *to* **W. L. GARRISON. 9 March 1857. Milford, N.H.** Criticizes *Merry's Museum,* a publication intended to show children positive aspects of slavery; forwards letters from a young girl to Mr. Merry. 20 March 1857. p.48, c3.

4111 A YOUNG GIRL *to* **MR. MERRY. n.d. n.p.** Replies to question posed by Mr. Merry; states that she did not know that slavery had a bright side. 20 March 1857. p.48, c3.

4112 A YOUNG GIRL *to* **MR. MERRY. n.d. n.p.** Asks why Mr. Merry deleted part of her letter in *Merry's Museum.* 20 March 1857. p.48, c3.

4113 BROTHER OF THE YOUNG GIRL *to* **MR. MERRY. 4 February 1857. n.p.** Recommends that Mr. Merry present all aspects of slavery, not only the pro-slavery point of view. 20 March 1857. p.48, c4.

4114 E. J. ALDEN *to* **FRIEND GARRISON. 9 March 1857. Lowell.** Comments on the origins of the Industrial School for Girls. 20 March 1857. p.48, c5.

4115 S. M. SEAVER *to* **W. L. GARRISON. 10 March 1857. Williamstown, Vt.** Advocates disunion; denounces Henry Wilson. 27 March 1857. p.51, c2.

4116 CHARLES BRIGHAM *to* **FRIEND GARRISON. 20 March 1856. Feltonville.** Encloses notice of Benjamin Prentice's death. 27 March 1857. p.51, c2.

4117 J. W. PILLSBURY *to* **W. L. GARRISON. 16 March 1857. Milford.** Discusses H. C. Wright's lectures in New Hampshire. 27 March 1857. p.51, c3.

4118 C. W. WILLARD *to* **CHARLES SUMNER. 9 February 1857. Montpelier, Vt.** Vermont's secretary of state forwards commendatory resolutions from the state house of representatives. 27 March 1857. p.51, c3.

4119 CHARLES SUMNER *to* **GOV. RYLAND FLETCHER. 7 March 1857. New York.** Thanks Vermont for its resolutions approving his Senate speech. 27 March 1857. p.51, c3.

4120 J. P. BLANCHARD *to* **GERRIT SMITH. 16 March 1857. Boston.** Defends his work with the Republican Party; does not believe that the Constitution authorizes the federal government to abolish slavery in the states; advises disunion, which would lead to emancipation and avoid civil war. 27 March 1857. p.52, c2.

4121 H. C. WRIGHT *to* **W. L. GARRISON. 16 March 1857. Fall River.** Describes antislavery meetings in Fall River; supports the need for a Northern republic. 27 March 1857. p.52, c3.

4122 GERRIT SMITH *to* **D. C. LITTLEJOHN. 18 March 1857. Peterboro'.** Suggests that the Dred Scott decision is a logical extension of the Republican Party doctrine that slavery is legal in some states. 3 April 1857. p.53, c4.

4123 J. R. GIDDINGS *to* **JUDGE R. TANEY. [from the** *Cleveland Leader***] n.d. n.p.** Comments on the Dred Scott decision. 3 April 1857. p.53, c5.

4124 GEORGE T. DOWNING *to* **n.n. [extract] n.d. n.p.** Comments on colored citizenship. 3 April 1857. p.54, c4.

4125 AARON M. POWELL *to* **n.n. [extract] n.d. n.p.** Reports on the anti-slavery convention in New York. 3 April 1857. p.54, c4.

4126 BENJAMIN S. JONES *to* **n.n. [extract] 25 March 1857. Carbondale, Pa.** Comments on anti-slavery sentiment in New York and Pennsylvania. 3 April 1857. p.54. c4.

4127 n.n. *to* **W. L. GARRISON. n.d. n.p.** Encloses article by William Penn. 3 April 1857. p.54, c5.

4128 L. N. PERHAM *to* **FRIEND GARRISON. 1857. Viroqua, Wi.** Believes that the Republican party is not anti-slavery. 3 April 1857. p.55, c1.

4129 C. S. BROWN *to* **FRIEND GARRISON. 23 March 1857. Boston.** Discusses the Industrial School for Girls. 3 April 1857. p.55, c2.

4130 EMPEROR OF CHINA *to* **DR. J. C. AYER. n.d. n.p.** Acknowledges the medicine sent by Dr. Ayer. 3 April 1857. p.55, c5.

4131 CORRESPONDENT *to* **THE** *PAULDING* **(MS.)** *CLARION.* **[extract] n.d. n.p.** Details confrontation between a Negro and his superintendent. 3 April 1857. p.56, c2.

4132 n.n. *to* **THE** *ELBA DEMOCRAT.* **[extract] n.d. Dadeville, Al.** Describes wounding and subsequent death of A. B. McCarthy. 3 April 1857. p.56, c3.

4133 LUDVIGH *to* **H. 22 February 1857. New Orleans.** Informs of the arrest of a Baltimore German language newspaper editor. 10 April 1857. p.57, c5.

4134 ROBERT TOMPKINS *to* **MR. EDITOR OF THE** *ONEIDA SACHEM.* **n.d. n.p.** Informs that the Dred Scott decision converted "this former doughface" into a Garrisonian disunionist. 10 April 1857. p.57, c6.

4135 SPECTATOR *to* **THE** *LIBERATOR.* **26 March 1857. Painesville, Oh.** Criticizes E. Burritt's scheme of compensated emancipation. 10 April 1857. p.59, c1.

4136 H. C. WRIGHT *to* **W. L. GARRISON. 28 March 1857. Providence.** Comments on the slave power's ruling strategy and the price that the North pays to preserve the Union. 10 April 1857. p.60, c2.

4137 ANNIE *to* **W. L. GARRISON. 25 March 1857. Boston.** Communicates with N. P. Rogers' ghostly spirit on anti-slavery and women's rights. 10 April 1857. p.60, c3.

4138 A. FAIRBANKS *to* **FRIEND. 30 March 1857. Providence.** Describes H. C. Wright's lectures in Providence on the rights of children. 10 April 1857. p.60, c3.

4139 S. G. *to* **THE EDITOR OF THE** *ATLAS.* **n.d. n.p.** Discusses Gov. Gardner and the clergy. 10 April 1857. p.60, c6.

4140 EDWARD MATHEWS *to* **n.n. 13 March 1857. Bristol, England.** Questions how slaveholders can deny slaves "the right to the bible." 17 April 1857. p.61, c4.

4141 EDWARD HARRIS *to* **WENDELL PHILLIPS. 5 April 1857. Woonsocket.** Reminisces about early anti-slavery struggles. 17 April 1857. p.62, c6.

4142 B. G. WRIGHT *to* **MR. EDITOR. n.d. Camden Mills, Rock Island County, Il.** Invites Garrisonians to lecture in Camden Mills. 17 April 1857. p.63, c1.

4143 THOS. H. BENTON *to* **n.n. n.d. n.p.** Condemns the abolition movement in the assembly. 17 April 1857. p.63, c1.

4144 n.n. *to* **THE** *CHICAGO PRESS* **[extract] 25 March. Lecompton.** Assails the illegal and unjust census-taking occurring in Kansas. 17 April 1857. p.63, c3.

4145 S. S. GRISWOLD *to* **FRIEND GARRISON. n.d. n.p.** Forwards an abusive letter from a West Virginian. 17 April 1857. p.64, c2.

4146 ALEXANDER M. HOLDEN, JR. *to* **S. S. GRISWOLD. 8 February 1857. Clarksburg, Va.** Condemns Griswold for an anti-slavery article he wrote. 17 April 1857. p.64, c2.

4147 LUCY N. COLMAN *to* **FRIEND GARRISON. 31 March 1857. Waukegan.** Comments on anti-slavery agitation in Waukegan. 17 April 1857. p.64, c2.

4148 AZARIAH SMITH *to* **THE EDITOR OF THE** *LIBERATOR* **[W. L. GARRISON]. 31 March 1857. New York Central College.** Forwards two letters for publication. 17 April 1857. p.64, c3.

4149 DAVID MERRITT *to* **AZARIAH SMITH. 9 March 1857. Salem, Ma.** Approves of New York Central College's principles. 17 April 1857. p.64, c3.

4150 ALEX. MONTGOMERY *to* **AZARIAH SMITH. 10 March 1857. New York.** Sends five dollars for New York Central College Library. 17 April 1857. p.64, c3.

4151 CHARLES W. SLACK *to* **n.n. [extract] 9 February 1857. Boston.** Comments on equal school rights reform in Boston. 17 April 1857. p.64, c4.

4152 JOHN D. PHILBRICK *to* **GEO. T. DOWNING. 27 February 1857. Boston.** Boston school superintendent expresses disappointment with the results of integration in Boston. 17 April 1857. p.64, c4.

4153 ERNESTINE L. ROSE *to* **THE EDITOR OF THE** *BOSTON INVESTIGATOR.* **27 March 1857. New York.** Comments on the late John Finch of Liverpool, England. 17 April 1857. p.64, c5.

4154 HON. ELI THAYER *to* **n.n. [from the** *New York Herald***] 12 March. Worcester, Ma.** Discusses the future of the North American Homestead Company. 24 April 1857. p.66, c2.

4155 GEORGE W. STACY *to* **WORCESTER AS CONVENTION. 18 April 1857. Milford.** Regrets that he is unable to be with them; denounces the slave power. 24 April 1857. p.67, c1.

4156 WM. J. S. C. ADAMS *to* **W. L. GARRISON. n.d. Charlestown, Ma.** Denounces obscene literature. 24 April 1857. p.68, c3.

4157 A. FAIRBANKS *to* **FRIEND GARRISON. 14 April 1857. Providence.** Informs of racism in the school committee of Providence. 24 April 1857. p.68, c3.

4158 CHARLES WESLEY WOLFE *to* **THE SUMTER TOWN COUNCIL. [from the** *Sumter Watchman***] n.d. Sumter, S.C.** Comments on a suspicious Ohio woman, Mrs. Emerson, who is lecturing in the area. 1 May 1857. p.71, c2.

4159 WM. HENRY BRISBANE *to* **FRIEND BOOTH. 9 April 1857. Arena, Wi.** Regrets that Wisconsin sacrificed Booth to the slave-catchers. 1 May 1857. p.71, c5.

4160 H. C. WRIGHT *to* **W. L. GARRISON. 20 April 1857. Buffalo.** Reports that the *Commercial Advertiser* of Buffalo condemned Wright as a water-cure doctor, abolitionist, heretic, and writer of pestilent books. 1 May 1857. p.72, c4.

4161 A LOOKER-ON *to* **FRIEND GARRISON. 26 April 1857. Newburyport.** Describes Caleb Cushing's indifferent reception in Newburyport. 1 May 1857. p.73, c1.

4162 S. CLAY *to* **W. L. GARRISON. 20 April 1857. Lowell.** Informs of the Fast Day celebration in Lowell. 1 May 1857. p.73, c1.

4163 S. MAY, J. FULLER, WM. ABBOTT, S. SALSBURY *to* **THE EDITOR OF THE** *NORTHERN INDEPENDENT.* **n.d. Syracuse, N.Y.** Report on the African Aid Society in Syracuse. 1 May 1857. p.73, c3.

4164 ONE OF THEM *to* **W. L. GARRISON. 16 April 1857. Hampton, N.H.** Predicts that only through bloodshed can slavery be ended. 1 May 1857. p.74, c2.

4165 D. N. BROWN *to* **W. L. GARRISON. 20 April 1857. Kingsboro', N.Y.** States that all true spiritualists are abolitionists. 1 May 1857. p.74, c2.

4166 LEWIS FORD *to* **MR. EDITOR [W. L. GARRISON]. 16 April 1857. Faribault, Rice County, Minnesota Territory.** Comments on Indian troubles in the Minnesota Territory. 8 May 1857. p.76, c3.

4167 LEWIS FORD *to* **MR. EDITOR [W. L. GARRISON]. 19 April 1857. Prescott, Wi.** Comments on Indian troubles in Prescott. 8 May 1857. p.76, c3.

4168 LEWIS FORD *to* **MR. EDITOR [W. L. GARRISON]. 26 April 1857. Hastings, Wi.** Comments on Indian troubles in Hastings. 8 May 1857. p.76, c3.

4169 A SOUTHERNER *to* **n.n. [from the** *Charleston Mercury***] 6 April 1857. Yale, Ct.** Comments on the Rev. John Dutton's church. 15 May 1857. p.77, c1.

4170 CHARITY *to* **MR. EDITOR OF THE** *SOUTHBRIDGE PRESS.* **14 April 1857. Lowell.** Reports on the New England Methodist Conference. 15 May 1857. p.77, c4.

4171 G. W. W. *to* **n.n. [from the** *Zion's Herald***] 24 April 1857. Danbury, Ct.** Reports on the New York East Conference. 15 May 1857. p.77, c5.

4172 JOHN JAY *to* **THE HON. ELIAS BOUDINOT. [from the** *Philadelphia Times***] 17 November 1819. Bedford, N.Y.** Expresses his views on slavery. 15 May 1857. p.77, c6.

4173 HOWARD CROSBY *to* **CHAS. SELDEN. 18 April 1857. n.p.** Resigns membership in the New York YMCA. 15 May 1857. p.78, c6.

4174 GARDINER SPRING, GEORGE POTTS, WM. ADAMS, J. N. KNOX AND NINE OTHER MINISTERS *to* **CHAS. SELDEN. 22 April 1857. n.p.** Withdraw from the New York YMCA. 15 May 1857. p.78, c6.

4175 J. G. W. *to* **THE EDITOR OF THE** *NEWBURYPORT HERALD.* **May 1857. Amesbury.** Relays news of Joshua Coffin's illness. 15 May 1857. p.79, c1.

4176 n.n. *to* **n.n. [extract] 23 April 1857. Kingston, Jamaica.** Describes the capture of an American slaver off the coast of Cuba. 15 May 1857. p.79, c1.

4177 DANIEL FOSTER *to* **SIR. 1 May 1857. Boston.** Appeals for aid for Wm. Bailey, abolitionist editor of the *Newport* (Ky.) *News.* 15 May 1857. p.80, c3.

4178 RUMINA A. PARKER *to* **THE EDITOR OF THE** *NEW YORK TRIBUNE.* **n.d. n.p.** Comments on female vanity and extravagance. 22 May 1857. p.84, c2.

4179 BYLES *to* **n.n. [from the** *New York Tribune***] 30 April 1857. Boston.** Offers his opinion on the existence of spirits. 22 May 1857. p.84, c3.

4180 J. MUNROE, B. WAINWRIGHT, E. COWDIN, S. HOLMES, A. MONTANT, T. DALE, G. REED, J. TUCKER, G. RICHARDS, A. COOPER, G. MILNE, C. SHARPS-TEEN, H. WOODS, W. ENDICOTT, JR., J. MARTIN, W. LEWIS, G. TODD, D. LANE, V. MOORE, J. DEMING, J. CURTIS, AND A. STRANGE *to* **CHARLES SUMNER. 28 April 1857. Paris.** American merchants invite Sumner to attend a public dinner. 29 May 1857. p.86, c5.

4181 C. SUMNER *to* **JOHN MUNROE, B. G. WAINWRIGHT, ELLIOT C. COWDIN, ESQUIRES AND OTHERS. 30 April 1857. Paris, France.** Reports that health considerations compel him to decline invitation to attend public dinner. 29 May 1857. p.86, c5.

4182 F. W. CHESSON *to* **n.n. [extract] 22 April 1857. London, England.** Comments on Geo. Thompson's illness in India. 29 May 1857. p.86, c6.

4183 H. W. B. *to* **MR. WHIPPLE. 18 May 1857. Port Norfolk.** Observes that abolitionists in Port Norfolk are protesting the pro-slavery behavior of the American Tract Society. 29 May 1857. p.87, c2.

4184 C. F. P. *to* **n.n. May 1857. Michigan.** Gives account of Miss Holley's lectures. 29 May 1857. p.87, c3.

4185 A. S. CARTER *to* **MR. EDITOR [W. L. GARRISON]. 24 May 1857. Leominster.** Encloses death notice of Hannah C. Field from the *Granite State Register*. 29 May 1857. p.87, c4.

4186 C. C. F. *to* **THE EDITOR OF THE** *BOSTON DAILY TRANSCRIPT.* **9 May 1857. Cambridge.** Gives a brief biographical sketch of Joshua Coffin. 29 May 1857. p.87, c5.

4187 PURITAN *to* **W. L. GARRISON. 11 May 1857. On the Missouri River.** Discusses emigration to Kansas. 29 May 1857. p.88, c3.

4188 M. D. CONWAY *to* **n.n. [extract] 17 May 1857. Alton, Il.** Regrets missing the New England AS Convention; reports on his visit to the site of Lovejoy's martyrdom. 5 June 1857. p.89, c3.

4189 FRANCIS JACKSON *to* **THE EDITOR OF THE** *TRAVELLER.* **29 May 1857. Boston.** Rebukes editor for the *Traveller*'s unfavorable reports on the New England AS Convention. 5 June 1857. p.90, c5.

4190 B. *to* **FRIEND GARRISON. 31 May 1857. South Abington.** Denounces the *Boston Traveller* for its contemptuous treatment of the New England AS Convention. 5 June 1857. p.90, c6.

4191 GEORGE ODIORNE *to* **FREDERICK BRINSLEY. 6 March 1830. Boston.** A committee member of the Park Street Church warns Brinsley to use the Negro pews henceforth. 5 June 1857. p.91, c1.

4192 REV. MOSES THACHER *to* **THE EDITOR OF THE** *LIBERATOR* **[W. L. GARRISON]. 25 May 1857. Pitcher, N.Y.** Realizes that the vast majority of churches in the country have become thoroughly abolitionist. 12 June 1857. p.95, c2.

4193 MATTHEW R. HALL *to* **W. L. GARRISON. 5 June 1857. Worcester.** Comments on being an abolitionist martyr. 12 June 1857. p.95, c2.

4194 G. W. S. *to* **FRIEND GARRISON. 9 June 1857. Milford.** Denounces slanderers of the AAS. 12 June 1857. p.95, c3.

4195 P. L. *to* **FRIEND GARRISON. 7 June 1857. East Bridgewater.** Expresses indignation at the *Traveller*'s coverage of the New England AS Convention. 12 June 1857. p.95, c3.

4196 G. W. S. *to* **FRIEND GARRISON. 2 June 1857. Milford.** Explains the Universalist convention's resolution to oppose slavery. 12 June 1857. p.96, c3.

4197 PURITAN *to* **W. L. GARRISON. 20 May 1857. Mapleton, Ks.** Comments on a group of emigrants from Vermont who are settling in southern Kansas. 12 June 1857. p.96, c3.

4198 n.n. *to* **THE EDITOR OF THE** *ADRIAN WATCHTOWER.* **n.d. n.p.** Discusses Miss Holley's lecture at the Odd Fellows' Hall. 12 June 1857. p.96, c5.

4199 HENRY C. WRIGHT *to* **W. L. GARRISON. 31 May 1857. New Garden, Oh.** Advocates a Northern republic; denounces state's rights. 19 June 1857. p.99, c2.

4200 PROGRESS *to* **W. L. GARRISON. 10 June 1857. Waterloo, N.Y.** Discusses meeting of the Friends of Human Progress in Waterloo. 19 June 1857. p.99, c3.

4201 T. W. HIGGINSON *to* **W. L. GARRISON. 15 June. Worcester.** Corrects misprints of his statement appearing in the *Liberator*. 19 June 1857. p.99, c3.

4202 J. R. GIDDINGS *to* **THE EDITOR OF THE** *CHRISTIAN OBSERVER.* **15 April 1857. Jefferson, Oh.** Describes the God he worships. 26 June 1857. p.101, c3.

4203 S. J. MAY *to* **FRIEND. 19 June 1857. Syracuse.** Reports on the National Dress Reform Convention in Syracuse. 26 June 1857. p.102, c6.

4204 AN ABOLITIONIST *to* **MESSRS. EDITORS. n.d. n.p.** Disputes charge made against the abolitionists. 26 June 1857. p.103, c4.

4205 R. D. WEBB *to* **n.n. [extract from the** *National Anti-Slavery Standard***] 15 May 1857. Dublin, Ireland.** An Englishman sends donation to the *Liberator*. 3 July 1857. p.105, c5.

4206 N. P. BANKS *to* **GEO. W. MESSINGER. 17 June 1857. Waltham.** Accepts the American Party's nomination for governor. 3 July 1857. p.106, c1.

4207 N. P. BANKS *to* **JOS. WHITE AND THOS. J. MARSH. 29 June 1857. Waltham.** Accepts Republican nomination for governor. 3 July 1857. p.106, c2.

4208 J. P. B. *to* **THE EDITOR OF THE** *LIBERATOR* **[W. L. GARRISON]. n.d. n.p.** Requests clarification concerning the authority of the judiciary. 3 July 1857. p.106, c4.

4209 J. A. H. *to* **FRIEND GARRISON. 29 June 1857. Worcester.** Discusses the Massachusetts Republican Convention. 3 July 1857. p.106, c5.

4210 INO. *to* **FRIEND GARRISON. 24 June 1857. Worcester.** Details the Massachusetts Republican Convention. 3 July 1857. p.106, c6.

4211 SINCERITY *to* **W. L. GARRISON. 27 June 1857. Boston.** Defends Republican Party against Garrisonian criticism. 3 July 1857. p.106, c6.

4212 PARKER PILLSBURY *to* **S. J. MAY. 27 June 1857. Framingham.** Reports on his meeting with John B. Gough of Framingham. 3 July 1857. p.107, c3.

4213 D. M. ALLEN *to* **FRIEND GARRISON. 27 June 1857. Westminister.** Issues a plea for the Indians. 3 July 1857. p.107, c3.

4214 J. S. *to* **THE EDITOR OF THE** *LIBERATOR* **[W. L. GARRISON]. 30 May 1856. Boston.** Encloses article for the *Liberator*. 3 July 1857. p.107, c3.

4215 HENRY C. WRIGHT *to* **W. L. GARRISON. 15 June 1857. Lake Erie.** Relates an incident involving a fugitive slave in Cincinnati. 3 July 1857. p.108, c2.

4216 LYMAN ALLEN *to* **MR. EDITOR. 10 June 1857. Union Grove, Mn.** Pleads for justice for the Indians. 3 July 1857. p.108, c3.

4217 W. C. N. *to* **FRIEND GARRISON. June 1857. Boston.** Details the struggle of California colored people for justice. 3 July 1857. p.108, c4.

4218 JOHN B. GOUGH *to* **REV. S. J. MAY, JR. 1 July 1857. Hillside, Boylston.** Regrets that he is unable to attend the anti-slavery Fourth of July meeting. 10 July 1857. p.111, c5.

4219 JOHN BOYDEN *to* **S. J. MAY, JR. 20 June 1857. Woonsocket.** Regrets that he will not be able to speak at the anti-slavery Fourth of July celebration. 10 July 1857. p.111, c5.

4220 WM. S. FLANDERS *to* **THE EDITOR OF THE** *LIBERATOR* **[W. L. GARRISON]. 22 June 1857. Cornville, Me.** Asserts that if it were self-evident that all men are created equal, slavery would not exist, and support for the AAS would be stronger. 10 July 1857. p.112, c2.

4221 n.n. *to* **C. K. WHIPPLE. 11 May 1857. Oregon City, Or.** Discusses anti-slavery strategy in Oregon City. 10 July 1857. p.112, c3.

4222 BASIL MANLY *to* **REV. JAS. H. DE VOTIE. 3 June 1857. Charleston, S.C.** Urges that the American Tract Society retain its policy of avoiding the subject of slavery. 17 July 1857. p.113, c1.

4223 WM. A. HALLOCK AND O. EASTMAN *to* **EVANGELICAL CHRISTIANS. 15 June 1857. New York.** Corresponding secretaries of the American Tract Society declare that the society will not abandon its catholic policies. 17 July 1857. p.113, c1.

4224 JOS. P. THOMPSON *to* **THE EXECUTIVE COMMITTEE OF THE AMERICAN TRACT SOCIETY. 27 March 1857. New York.** Sends award-winning tract on "Slavery and the Family" for publication. 17 July 1857. p.113, c2.

4225 WM. A. HALLOCK *to* **BROTHER THOMPSON. 13 April 1857. New York.** Informs that the American Tract Society rejected the tract on "Slavery and the Family." 17 July 1857. p.113, c2.

4226 YOUR OBEDIENT SERVANT *to* **REV. JOSEPH P. THOMPSON. 5 June 1857. Glasgow.** Discusses the American Tract Society's rejection of Thompson's tract on slavery. 17 July 1857. p.113, c2.

4227 JOS. P. THOMPSON *to* **THE EDITORS OF THE** *NEW YORK INDEPENDENT.* **18 June 1857. New York.** Comments on his tract's rejection by the American Tract Society. 17 July 1857. p.113, c2.

4228 F. W. BIRD *to* **THE EDITOR OF THE *LIBERATOR* [W. L. GARRISON]. 5 July 1857. East Walpole.** Reconciles his presidency of the recent Disunion Convention in Worcester with his attendance as a delegate at the Republican convention in Philadelphia. 17 July 1857. p.114, c5.

4229 J. A. H. *to* **FRIEND GARRISON. n.d. n.p.** Acknowledges that he did not mean to misrepresent F. W. Bird. 17 July 1857. p.114, c6.

4230 S. J. MAY *to* **W. L. GARRISON. n.d. n.p.** Comments on the Dress Reform Convention. 17 July 1857. p.114, c6.

4231 WM. S. BAILEY *to* **FRANCIS JACKSON. 29 June 1857. Newport, Ky.** Comments on effects of slavery and how it is to be overthrown. 17 July 1857. p.115, c1.

4232 JOSHUA COFFIN *to* **MR. EDITOR. n.d. n.p.** Sends an eighteenth century petition from a New England slave begging to be married. 17 July 1857. p.115, c2.

4233 L. H. Y. *to* **W. L. GARRISON. n.d. n.p.** Comments on the commencement at New York Central College. 17 July 1857. p.115, c2.

4234 H. C. WRIGHT *to* **W. L. GARRISON. 25 June 1857. St. Mary's Lake, Mi.** Sends sketches from St. Mary's Lake; delivers animadversions against slavery. 17 July 1857. p.116, c2.

4235 J. L. *to* **THE EDITORS OF THE *NEW YORK OBSERVER*. n.d. n.p.** Calls attention to an A. W. Beecher sermon. 24 July 1857. p.119, c1.

4236 JOSEPH A. DUGDALE *to* **LITTLE GIRLS AND BOYS. 2 July 1857. Near Longwood, Pa.** Comments on a children's convention to celebrate West Indies Emancipation. 24 July 1857. p.119, c2.

4237 R. L. A. *to* **THE *LIBERATOR*. 4 July 1857. Livonia, Mi.** Defines the meaning of Independence Day. 24 July 1857. p.119, c2.

4238 BUMP *to* **MR. EDITOR. n.d. n.p.** Comments on the futility of abolitionists' efforts. 24 July 1857. p.119, c2.

4239 LEWIS SPAULDING *to* **W. L. GARRISON. 10 July 1857. Borodino, N.Y.** States the aims of New York Central College. 24 July 1857. p.120, c2.

4240 n.n. *to* **C. K. WHIPPLE. 8 June 1857. Oregon City.** Discusses the prospect of Oregon's becoming a free state. 24 July 1857. p.120, c2.

4241 n.n. *to* **n.n. [extract] n.d. n.p.** Discusses colorphobia. 24 July 1857. p.120, c3.

4242 D. F. G. *to* **THE *LIBERATOR*. 1 July 1857. Chelsea.** Calls for a new Catholicism. 24 July 1857. p.120, c3.

4243 S. C. PHILLIPS *to* **C. K. WHIPPLE. 30 July 1845. Salem.** Regrets he will not be able to attend the West Indies Emancipation celebration. 31 July 1857. p.122, c3.

4244 SALLIE HOLLEY *to* **S. J. MAY, JR. [extract] 1 July. Farmersville, N.Y.** Discusses conservation in the New School General Assembly. 31 July 1857. p.122, c6.

4245 n.n. *to* **W. L. GARRISON. 21 July 1857. Cincinnati, Oh.** Comments on a liberal medical college in Cincinnati. 31 July 1857. p.122, c6.

4246 T. V. *to* **MR. EDITOR. n.d. n.p.** Comments on "flunkeyism" among the Boston press. 31 July 1857. p.123, c1.

4247 A. D. MAYO *to* **PROGRESSIVE FRIENDS. 6 May 1857. Albany.** Comments on the struggle between religious creeds in America. 31 July 1857. p.121 [124], c2.

4248 PHILO *to* **BRO. HANSON. 15 June 1857. North Hartland, Vt.** Describes a visit to Boston and T. Parker. 31 July 1857. p.121 [124], c3.

4249 JOHN PRINCE *to* **THE EDITOR OF THE** *COLONIST.* **26 June 1857. Toronto.** A member of the Canadian mounted police makes racial slurs against the Canadian colored people. 7 August 1857. p.122 [125], c2.

4250 A. T. AUGUSTA *to* **THE EDITOR OF THE** *BRITISH COLONIST.* **9 July 1857. Toronto.** Defends colored people against John Prince's aspersions. 7 August 1857. p.122 [125], c3.

4251 W. B. JARVIS *to* **A. T. AUGUSTA. 3 July 1857. Toronto.** Describes the gallantry of Canadian colored soldiers in the rebellion of 1837-38. 7 August 1857. p.122 [125], c4.

4252 WILLIAM R. ALGER *to* **W. L. GARRISON. 30 July 1857. Swampscot.** Regrets that he cannot attend the West Indies Emancipation celebration. 7 August 1857. p.127, c2.

4253 AARON M. POWELL *to* **n.n. [extract] 28 July 1857. Ghent, N.Y.** Comments on Wm. Marcy's funeral. 7 August 1857. p.128, c4.

4254 REV. JOHN G. FEE *to* **n.n. 21 July 1857. Berea, Ky.** Describes how he was assaulted. 14 August 1857. p.129, c6.

4255 J. M. McLAIN *to* **MR. EDITOR OF THE** *FREE PRESBYTERIAN.* **n.d. n.p.** Describes the pro-slavery mobbing of John G. Fee in Kentucky. 14 August 1857. p.130, c1.

4256 F. M. D. *to* **THE EDITORS OF THE** *NEW YORK EVANGELIST.* **25 July 1857. Urbana, Oh.** Discusses the hunting of fugitive slaves in Ohio by the United States marshal. 14 August 1857. p. 130, c1.

4257 S. MAY, JR. *to* **THE EDITOR OF THE** *BOSTON TRANSCRIPT.* **8 August 1857. Leicester.** Denies that P. Pillsbury once baptized three dogs in the name of the Father, Son, and Holy Ghost. 14 August 1857. p.130, c2.

4258 W. A. H. AND O. E. *to* **EVANGELICAL CHRISTIANS. 23 July 1857. New York.** Relate their efforts to prevent disaffected Southern members from leaving the American Tract Society. 14 August 1857. p.131, c3.

4259 LEONARD G. CALKINS *to* **W. L. GARRISON. 29 July 1857. New York Central College.** Denies T. Spauldings' charges against New York Central College. 14 August 1857. p.131, c4.

4260 H. C. WRIGHT *to* **W. L. GARRISON. 24 July 1857. New Garden.** Prays for the creation of a Northern republic. 14 August 1857. p.132, c2.

4261 A. F. RAYMOND *to* **W. L. GARRISON. 3 August 1857. Springfield, Ma.** Describes the West Indies Emancipation celebration in Springfield. 14 August 1857. p.132, c4.

4262 O. C. *to* **THE EDITOR OF THE** *BOSTON COURIER.* **July 1857. Richmond, Va.** States a Southern view of Northern abolitionism and its results. 21 August 1857. p.133, c1.

4263 PETER GULICK *to* **BROTHER WRIGHT. June 1837. Honolulu.** A missionary advocates immediate abolition. 21 August 1857. p.134, c1.

4264 H. R. HITCHCOCK *to* **THE EDITOR OF THE** *EMANCIPATOR.* **18 November 1837. Kaluaaha.** Favors immediate emancipation. 21 August 1857. p.134, c1.

4265 W. L. GARRISON *to* **THE EDITOR OF THE** *BOSTON TRANSCRIPT.* **13 August 1857. Boston.** Denounces the *Transcript's* correspondent *Sigma* for accusing P. Pillsbury of baptizing three dogs. 21 August 1857. p.134, c4.

4266 PARKER PILLSBURY *to* **FRIEND GARRISON. 16 August 1857. Lynn.** Assails the *Boston Transcript*'s libel of Pillsbury. 21 August 1857. p.134, c5.

4267 PARKER PILLSBURY *to* **THE EDITOR OF THE** *BOSTON TRANSCRIPT.* **14 August 1857. Concord, N.H.** Comments on the alleged baptism of three dogs. 21 August 1857. p.134, c5.

4268 S. MAY, JR. *to* **W. L. GARRISON. 15 August 1857. Leicester.** Encloses letter he sent to the *Transcript* and then withdrew. 21 August 1857. p.134, c6.

4269 S. MAY, JR. *to* **THE EDITOR OF THE** *BOSTON TRANSCRIPT.* **14 August 1857. Leicester.** Comments on Pillsbury's alleged baptism of three dogs. 21 August 1857. p.134, c6.

4270 DOG-DAYS *to* **MR. EDITOR. n.d. n.p.** Describes *Sigma,* correspondent of the *Transcript,* as an insolent puppy. 21 August 1857. p.134, c6.

4271 B. *to* **W. L. GARRISON. 8 August 1857. New York.** Discusses the exclusion of colored people and women from the New York State Teachers' Convention in Binghamton, New York. 21 August 1857. p.136, c2.

4272 PARKER PILLSBURY *to* **MARIUS ROBINSON. 10 August 1857. Lynn, Ma.** Describes how slavery has corrupted all our institutions. 28 August 1857. p.138, c4.

4273 E. R. B. *to* **n.n. 18 August 1857. Elmwood, Il.** Comments on affairs in Elmwood. 28 August 1857. p.138, c5.

4274 REBECCA BAILEY *to* **S. MAY, JR. [extract] 12 August 1857. Newport, Ky.** Details the abuse received by her father, Wm. Bailey. 28 August 1857. p.138, c6.

4275 JAMES FREEMAN CLARKE *to* **THE EDITOR OF THE** *BOSTON COURIER.* **n.d. n.p.** Charges that his speech in Abington was misrepresented. 28 August 1857. p.140, c4.

4276 GENTLEMAN FROM BOSTON *to* **n.n. [extract from the** *Boston Puritan Recorder***] n.d. n.p.** Relates horror of a Negro slave auction. 4 September 1857. p.142, c1.

4277 S. P. C. *to* **MESSRS. EDITORS. n.d. n.p.** Criticizes the plan of compensated emancipation. 4 September 1857. p.142, c2.

4278 ELIZABETH COATES *to* **SIR. 27 August 1857. Woodlawn, Pa.** States that the Clarkson AS supports the idea of a national disunion convention. 4 September 1857. p.142, c3.

4279 L. A. SWIFT *to* **THE LECTURERS AND AGENTS OF THE AAS. 20 August 1857. Hart's Village, Dutchess County, N.Y.** Discusses anti-Christianity and lack of charity for enemies displayed by Garrisonians; states that these are two reasons she has not joined them. 4 September 1857. p.142, c3.

4280 H. C. WRIGHT *to* **W. L. GARRISON. 22 August 1857. Cherry Valley, Oh.** Denounces the Union and its supporters. 4 September 1857. p.144, c2.

4281 H. C. WRIGHT *to* **W. L. GARRISON. 23 August 1857. Andover, Oh.** Denounces the Union and its supporters. 4 September 1857. p.144, c2.

4282 R. S. *to* **FRIEND GARRISON. 24 August 1857. Upton.** Details the decline of anti-slavery zeal in Upton. 4 September 1857. p.144, c3.

4283 n.n. *to* **THE EDITOR OF THE** *LIBERATOR* **[W. L. GARRISON]. 21 August 1857. Manchester, N.H.** Sends resolutions on religious exercises which the American Institute for Instruction refused to consider. 4 September 1857. p.144, c4.

4284 LEWIS SPAULDING *to* **FRIEND GARRISON. 22 August 1857. McGrawville, N.Y.** Replies to L. Calkins' charges against him. 4 September 1857. p.144, c4.

4285 PRES. JAMES BUCHANAN *to* **B. SILLIMAN AND FORTY-TWO OTHERS. 15 August 1857. Washington.** Defends the Kansas policy. 11 September 1857. p.145, c2.

4286 B. G. WRIGHT *to* **JOS. A. HOWLAND. 20 August 1857. Rock Island County, Il.** Supports the Disunion Convention, even though he opposes disunion. 11 September 1857. p.146, c4.

4287 W. L. GARRISON *to* **THE EDITOR OF THE** *BOSTON TRANSCRIPT.* **8 September 1857. Boston.** Denounces Symes' slanderous and false story of Pillsbury's dog baptism. 11 September 1857. p.146, c5.

4288 ELI F. BURNHAM AND JAMES N. BUFFUM *to* **THE EDITOR OF THE** *TRANSCRIPT.* **8 September 1857. Danvers.** Denounce the Pillsbury dog baptism story. 11 September 1857. p.146, c6.

4289 W. W. B. *to* **W. L. GARRISON. n.d. n.p.** Details the anti-slavery meetings in western New York. 11 September 1857. p.146, c6.

4290 A. BIGWOOD *to* **n.n. 24 August 1857. Ottawa, Wi.** Sends five dollars for the support of Mr. Foster's army. 11 September 1857. p.146, c6.

4291 H. C. WRIGHT *to* **W. L. GARRISON. 25 August 1857. Cleveland.** Denounces the scheme of compensated emancipation; comments on the convention in Cleveland to debate the question. 11 September 1857. p.148, c2.

4292 MICHAEL J. SHEEHY *to* **PATRICK J. O'BRIEN. 1 September 1857. Boston.** An Irishman appeals for abolition. 11 September 1857. p.148, c3.

4293 H. J. P. *to* **THE EDITORS OF THE** *NATIONAL ANTI-SLAVERY STANDARD.* **22 August 1857. Boston.** Comments on Pillsbury's alleged dog baptism. 11 September 1857. p.148, c4.

4294 H. W. B. *to* **W. L. GARRISON. 13 September 1857. Port Norfolk.** Comments on a church in Dorchester which shuts its doors to Garrisonians. 18 September 1857. p.150, c6.

4295 THOS. B. RICHARDSON *to* **n.n. 5 September 1857. Dorchester.** Reports that the Second Methodist Episcopal Church of Dorchester grants provisional use of the church. 18 September 1857. p.150, c6.

4296 SAMUEL H. ALLEN *to* **W. L. GARRISON. 7 September 1857. Windsor Locks, Ct.** Comments on Geo. Thompson, a fugitive slave in the area. 18 September 1857. p.150, c6.

4297 LA ROY SUNDERLAND *to* **YERRINTON. 14 September 1857. Boston.** An old friend encloses a letter from Garrison written twenty-five years ago. 18 September 1857. p.151, c1.

4298 W. L. GARRISON *to* **LA ROY SUNDERLAND. 18 September 1831. Boston.** Thanks Sunderland for warning about threat to his personal safety. 18 September 1857. p.151, c1.

4299 n.n. *to* **THE EDITOR OF THE** *LIBERATOR* **[W. L. GARRISON]. 9 September 1857. Kentucky.** Details a slave law in Kentucky. 18 September 1857. p.151, c1.

4300 GENTLEMAN IN MISSOURI *to* **n.n. [extract] n.d. n.p.** Speculates on the demise of slavery. 18 September 1857. p.151, c1.

4301 AARON M. POWELL *to* **W. L. GARRISON. 10 September 1857. Elmira Water Cure, N.Y.** Informs of anti-slavery meetings in upstate New York. 18 September 1857. p.151, c2.

4302 C. L. REMOND *to* **FRIEND GARRISON. 9 September 1857. Marlboro, Stark County, Oh.** Discusses the anti-slavery meetings near Marlboro. 18 September 1857. p.151, c2.

4303 PARKER PILLSBURY *to* **FRIEND MAY. 9 September 1857. Salem, Oh.** Details a meeting of the Western AS. 18 September 1857. p.151, c2.

4304 J. N. *to* **W. L. GARRISON. 14 September 1857. Portsmouth, N.H.** Comments on an error in the *Tribune.* 18 September 1857. p.151, c2.

4305 JOHN TYLER *to* **THE EDITORS OF THE** *RICHMOND ENQUIRER.* **31 August 1857. n.p.** Defends his policy of suppressing African slave trade. 18 September 1857. p.151, c3.

4306 n.n. *to* **n.n. [extract] 6 September. Washington.** Details the escape of seventeen slaves and the subsequent recapture of nine of them. 18 September 1857. p.151, c4.

4307 W. W. B. *to* **W. L. GARRISON. n.d. n.p.** Details the anti-slavery meetings in western New York. 18 September 1857. p.152, c2.

4308 JOHN G. FEE *to* **n.n. [extract] 14 August 1857. Boone, Madison County, Ky.** Discusses the anti-abolitionist mobs in Kentucky. 18 September 1857. p.152, c5.

4309 WM. G. BROWNLOW *to* **THE EDITORS OF THE** *NEW YORK TIMES.* **12 September 1857. Knoxville, Tn.** Defends the lynching of a slave accused of murder. 25 September 1857. p.154, c3.

4310 W. W. B. *to* **W. L. GARRISON. n.d. n.p.** Reports on anti-slavery meetings in western New York. 25 September 1857. p.155, c1.

4311 H. C. WRIGHT *to* **W. L. GARRISON. 9 September 1857. Hartwick, N.Y.** Proudly sends a list of his relatives and family in Hartwick who signed a call for disunion. 25 September 1857. p.156, c2.

4312 n.n. *to* **n.n. [extract from the** *London Times***]** **13 June. Benares.** Anticipates a year of famine, plague, and pestilence. 25 September 1857. p.156, c4.

4313 OFFICER *to* **n.n. 23 June. Allahabad.** Agonizes over the spread of cholera. 25 September 1857. p.156, c4.

4314 WIFE OF AN INDIAN OFFICER *to* **n.n. [extract from the** *Inverness Courier***]** **22 June. Simla.** Anxiously awaits arrival of Sir Patrick Grant to take command of the army. 25 September 1857. p.156, c4.

4315 M. W. BALL [POSTMASTER] *to* **THE EDITOR OF THE** *SABBATH RECORDER***. n.d. Janelew, Ky.** Declares he will not circulate the *Sabbath Recorder.* 25 September 1857. p.156, c5.

4316 N. TAYLOR, T. WOOLSEY, H. DUTTON, C. ENGLISH, J. BROCKWAY, E. BLAKE, B. SILLIMAN, JR., T. THACHER, J. DAVENPORT, W. HOOKER, P. BLAKE, A. TOWNSEND, J. BREWSTER, E. IVES, S. HUBBARD, J. BLAKE, W. RUSSELL, A. SKINNER, C. ROBINSON, J. HAWES, G. CALHOUN, L. BACON, H. KINGSLEY, S. SILLIMAN, SR., C. IVES, J. GIBBS, J. BABCOCK, A. WALKER, H. OLMSTED *to* **PRES. JAMES BUCHANAN. [from the** *New Haven Palladium***]** **n.d. New Haven, Ct.** Criticize Buchanan's Kansas policy. 2 October 1857. p.157, c2.

4317 C. K. W. *to* **THE** *NEWBURYPORT HERALD***. n.d. n.p.** Criticizes Burritt's scheme of compensated emancipation. 2 October 1857. p.157, c6.

4318 P. WOOD *to* **W. L. GARRISON. 25 September 1857. Port Norfolk.** Defends his church from the charge of proscribing abolitionists. 2 October 1857. p.158, c6.

4319 B. G. WRIGHT *to* **W. L. GARRISON. 16 September 1857. Rock Island County, Il.** Discusses whether Northern disunion would be treason, as defined by the United States Constitution. 2 October 1857. p.158, c6.

4320 A. T. FOSS *to* **FRIEND GARRISON. 23 September 1857. Connotton.** Details anti-slavery meetings near Connotton. 2 October 1857. p.159, c1.

4321 SETH HUNT *to* **FRIEND GARRISON. 22 September 1857. Northampton.** Questions the whereabouts of the disunion petitions sent to Congress last year. 2 October 1857. p.159, c2.

4322 B. G. WRIGHT *to* **W. L. GARRISON. 24 September 1857. Rock Island County, Il.** Denounces the anti-Democratic nature of the federal government. 9 October 1857. p.163, c1.

4323 JAMES HAUGHTON *to* **FRIEND GARRISON. 15 September 1857. Dublin.** Applauds the AAS movement; denounces John Mitchel's defense of slavery. 9 October 1857. p.163, c2.

4324 FRANCIS MULLIGAN *to* **JAS. HAUGHTON. 5 September 1857. Dublin.** Condemns John Mitchel's defense of slavery. 9 October 1857. p.163, c3.

4325 PARKER PILLSBURY *to* **FRIEND GARRISON. 2 October 1857. Cleveland, Oh.** Discusses anti-slavery lectures in Cleveland. 9 October 1857. p.163, c4.

4326 S. MITCHELL *to* **FRIEND GARRISON. 13 September 1857. Cornville, Me.** Denounces the scheme of compensated emancipation. 9 October 1857. p.163, c4.

4327 WILLIAM JAY *to* **MESSRS. HIGGINSON, PHILLIPS, MANN, AND GARRISON. 24 September 1857. Bedford, N.Y.** Welcomes the exposure of the evils of the present Union, but doubts that the disunion movement will succeed. 9 October 1857. p.163, c4.

4328 HENRY C. WRIGHT *to* **W. L. GARRISON. 27 September 1857. Smyrna, Chanango County, N.Y.** Discusses W. E. Channings's view of the Union; stresses the need for disunion. 9 October 1857. p.163, c6.

4329 JOS. A. HOWLAND *to* **FRIEND GARRISON. n.d. n.p.** Encloses letters from correspondents throughout the North who favor the National Disunion Convention. 9 October 1857. p.164, c4.

4330 CHAUNCEY RICHARDSON *to* **n.n. [extract] n.d. Woodstock, Vt.** Supports the Northern Convention. 9 October 1857. p.164, c4.

4331 N. H. WHITING *to* **n.n. [extract] Marshfield, Ma.** Upholds the Northern Convention. 9 October 1857. p.164, c4.

4332 S. LASAR *to* **n.n. [extract] n.d. New York City.** Approves the Northern Convention which calls for a discussion of disunion. 9 October 1857. p.164, c4.

4333 JOHN TILLINGHAST *to* **n.n. [extract] n.d. Factoryville, Pa.** Would rather see the Union dissolved than a single human being enslaved. 9 October 1857. p.164, c4.

4334 W. W. WALKER *to* **n.n. n.d. Pulaski, Pa.** Wishes success to the Northern Convention. 9 October 1857. p.164, c4.

4335 R. W. MELENDY *to* **n.n. n.d. California, Mi.** Favors disunion. 9 October 1857. p.164, c4.

4336 BENJ. B. BALL *to* **n.n. n.d. Wasiogo, Mn.** Supports the Northern Convention. 9 October 1857. p.164, c5.

4337 MRS. C. L. MORGAN *to* **n.n. n.d. Sylvester, Wi.** Pleads for someone who will preach the "whole truth." 9 October 1857. p.164, c5.

4338 W. W. WALKER *to* **n.n. n.d. Pulaski, Pa.** Relates success in petitioning people who are in favor of the Northern Convention or disunion; states that the majority are registered to vote. 9 October 1857. p.164, c5.

4339 P. PILLSBURY *to* **THE EDITOR OF THE** *ANTI-SLAVERY BUGLE.* **n.d. n.p.** Urges Northerners to resist the aggressions of the slaveholding South. 16 October 1857. p.165, c6.

4340 S. MAY, JR. *to* **A FRIEND IN ENGLAND. [from the** *London Anti-Slavery Reporter*] **8 September 1857. Leicester, Ma.** Discusses the Northern disunion movement. 16 October 1857. p.166, c1.

4341 B. G. WRIGHT *to* **W. L. GARRISON. 24 September 1857. Rock Island County, Il.** Questions whether disunion will lead to the abolition of slavery; admits that disunion will weaken the institution of slavery. 16 October 1857. p.167, c1.

4342 WM. W. BROWN *to* **W. L. GARRISON. n.d. n.p.** Discusses the Yearly Meeting of Progressive Friends at North Collins, New York. 16 October 1857. p.168, c3.

4343 WM. W. BROWN *to* **W. L. GARRISON. n.d. n.p.** Discusses anti-slavery convention in Collins Center, New York. 16 October 1857. p.168, c3.

4344 H. W. B. *to* **W. L. GARRISON. 5 October 1857. Port Norfolk.** Comments on the alleged proscription of abolitionists by a church in Port Norfolk. 16 October 1857. p.168, c3.

4345 W. L. GARRISON *to* **THE ANNUAL MEETING OF THE PENNSYLVANIA AS. 20 October 1857. Boston.** Speculates on the state of the country. 23 October 1857. p.170, c4.

4346 REV. N. R. JOHNSTON *to* **n.n. [extract] n.d. Vermont.** States that a meeting of presbyteries will prevent the Vermont delegation to the Disunion Convention from becoming larger. 23 October 1857. p.171, c2.

4347 PARKER PILLSBURY *to* **FRIEND GARRISON. 13 October 1857. Battle Creek, Mi.** Comments on the progress of disunionism in Battle Creek. 23 October 1857. p.171, c2.

4348 B. G. WRIGHT *to* **W. L. GARRISON. 24 September 1857. Rock Island County, Il.** Discusses the meaning of the Declaration of Independence in relation to secession. 23 October 1857. p.171, c3.

4349 LUCY N. COLMAN *to* **S. J. MAY, JR. 10 October 1857. Fairmont, Oh.** Discusses anti-slavery meetings in Fairmont. 23 October 1857. p.171, c4.

4350 ARNOLD BUFFUM *to* **AMERICAN BRETHREN. 12 October 1857. Perth Amboy, N.J.** Denounces the American Tract Society. 23 October 1857. p.171, c4.

4351 J. W. LOGUEN *to* **THE FRIENDS OF HUMANITY. 17 September 1857. Syracuse.** Intends to devote himself to the care of fugitives who stop in Syracuse for assistance. 23 October 1857. p.171, c6.

4352 REV. JEHIEL CLAFLIN *to* **THE EDITOR OF THE** *MONTPELIER CHRISTIAN REPOSITORY.* **12 October 1857. East Westmoreland, N.H.** Believes that disunion is a moral duty. 30 October 1857. p.174, c1.

4353 WM. W. BROWN *to* **W. L. GARRISON. 20 October 1857. Linesville.** Describes the anti-slavery meetings in the West. 30 October 1857. p.175, c1.

4354 JOSEPH TREET *to* **FRIEND GARRISON. October 1857. Elyria, Oh.** Believes that slavery prevented the Disunion Convention in Cleveland from being held. 30 October 1857. p.175, c1.

4355 WM. S. BAILEY *to* **THE EDITOR OF THE** *BOSTON BEE.* **20 October 1857. Boston.** Acknowledges a contribution of 200 dollars. 30 October 1857. p.175, c2.

4356 HIRAM FOOTE *to* **WM. S. BAILEY. 6 October 1857. Janesville, Wi.** Donates 200 dollars. 30 October 1857. p.175, c2.

4357 A. HOGEBOOM *to* **FRIEND GARRISON. 16 October 1857. Shed's Corners, N.Y.** Criticizes scheme of compensated emancipation. 30 October 1857. p.170 [176], c2.

4358 W. *to* **THE EDITOR OF THE** *LIBERATOR* **[W. L. GARRISON]. n.d. n.p.** Argues that slavery can be abolished within the Union. 30 October 1857. p.170 [176], c2.

4359 MICHAEL BROWN *to* **H. R. HELPER. 28 September 1857. Salisbury, N.C.** Denies the story that he and Helper were once partners in a book business from which Helper embezzled money. 6 November 1857. p.180 [178], c2.

4360 PARKER PILLSBURY *to* **FRIEND GARRISON. 26 October 1857. Adrian, Mi.** Expresses an interest in the National Disunion Convention; feels disappointed by its postponement. 6 November 1857. p.180 [178], c5.

4361 H. *to* **THE EDITOR OF THE** *LIBERATOR* **[W. L. GARRISON]. 2 November 1857. n.p.** Argues for compensated emancipation. 6 November 1857. p.179, c1.

4362 WM. W. BROWN *to* **W. L. GARRISON. n.d. n.p.** Details anti-slavery convention in the West. 6 November 1857. p.179, c3.

4363 H. C. WRIGHT *to* **W. L. GARRISON. 6 October 1857. Norwich, N.Y.** Reminisces about childhood; proclaims man the measure of all things; calls for a Northern republic. 6 November 1857. p.180, c2.

4364 JAMES HAUGHTON *to* **THE EDITOR OF THE** *CARLOW POST.* **5 October 1857. Dublin.** Denounces English vindictiveness toward India. 6 November 1857. p.180, c3.

4365 JAMES HEATON *to* **THOMAS JEFFERSON. 20 April 1826. Middletown, Oh.** Requests that Jefferson write a treatise on the emancipation of slaves. 13 November 1857. p.182, c2.

4366 THOMAS JEFFERSON *to* **JAMES HEATON. 20 May 1826. Monticello.** Believes in the emancipation of slaves, but feels that the time is not right to declare his feelings publicly. 13 November 1857. p.182, c2.

4367 PARKER PILLSBURY *to* **FRIEND GARRISON. 8 November 1857. Concord, N.H.** Comments on the Cleveland Disunion Convention. 13 November 1857. p.182, c3.

4368 B. G. WRIGHT *to* **W. L. GARRISON. 25 October 1857. Rock Island County, Il.** Clarifies his position on the Fugitive Slave Law; discusses politics. 13 November 1857. p.182, c6.

4369 n.n. *to* **W. L. GARRISON. n.d. n.p.** Discusses F. E. Watkins' lecture in Salem. 13 November 1857. p.182, c6.

4370 C. STETSON *to* **MR. EDITOR. 30 October 1856. South Scituate.** Comments on D. Foster's lectures on Kansas. 13 November 1857. p.183, c3.

4371 J. WARD CHRISTIAN *to* **n.n. [extract from the** *Los Angeles Star***] 4 October 1857. San Bernardino.** Reports on the massacre of emigrants travelling by train from Missouri and Arkansas to California; suggests that Indians, probably ill-treated by emigrants, were the murderers. 13 November 1857. p.183, c3.

4372 HENRY C. WRIGHT *to* **W. L. GARRISON. 11 October 1857. Lackawana Valley, Pa.** Describes the Lackawana Valley; calls for a Northern confederacy. 13 November 1857. p.184, c2.

4373 HENRY C. WRIGHT *to* **W. L. GARRISON. 18 October 1857. Wyoming Valley, Pa.** Reports that Pennsylvania bows to the dictates of slavery. 13 November 1857. p.184, c2.

4374 G. B. STEBBINS *to* **W. L. GARRISON. 28 October 1857. Rochester, N.Y.** Describes the Collins Yearly Meeting of Friends. 13 November 1857. p.184, c3.

4375 F. WAYLAND *to* **REV. J. HAWES AND REV. R. PALMER. 19 October 1857. Providence.** Sends a copy of a paper he sent to the Investigating Committee of the American Tract Society. 20 November 1857. p.185, c2.

4376 F. WAYLAND *to* **THE INVESTIGATING COMMITTEE OF THE AMERICAN TRACT SOCIETY. n.d. n.p.** Questions recent actions by the American Tract Society. 20 November 1857. p.185, c2.

4377 W. C. HORT *to* **THE EDITOR OF THE** *NEW YORK CHRISTIAN ADVOCATE AND JOURNAL.* **n.d. Middletown, Ct.** States John Wesley's views on slavery. 20 November 1857. p.185, c5.

4378 A. HOGEBOOM *to* **FRIEND GARRISON. 9 November 1857. Shed's Corners, N.Y.** Asks whether the Constitution sanctions white slavery, as it has already been interpreted as supporting Negro slavery. 20 November 1857. p.186, c6.

4379 LUCY N. COLMAN *to* **W. L. GARRISON. 10 November 1857. New Lyme, Oh.** Discusses anti-slavery agent and lecturer's difficulty in overcoming the libel which pro-slavery malignancy has heaped on him. 20 November 1857. p.187, c1.

4380 WM. W. BROWN *to* **W. L. GARRISON. 12 November 1857. Green, Oh.** Describes anti-slavery conventions in his area of Ohio. 20 November 1857. p.187, c1.

4381 J. R. GIDDINGS *to* **n.n. n.d. n.p.** Rebukes an immigrant for voting Democratic and for being racist. 20 November 1857. p.187, c2.

4382 GEO. SUNTER *to* **THE EDITOR OF THE** *LIBERATOR* **[W. L. GARRISON]. 5 November 1857. Brantwood, Canada West.** Criticizes lyceums for customarily inhibiting free speech in order to promote harmony. 20 November 1857. p.188, c2.

4383 PARKER PILLSBURY *to* **THE LYCEUM COMMITTEE. [extract] n.d. n.p.** Explains his "terms" as a lyceum lecturer. 20 November 1857. p.188, c2.

4384 JUSTICE *to* **W. L. GARRISON. 10 November 1857. Battle Creek, Mi.** Describes the anti-slavery movement in Michigan. 20 November 1857. p.188, c3.

4385 IRISH *to* **THE EDITOR OF THE** *LIBERATOR* **[W. L. GARRISON]. 3 November 1857. Boston.** Criticizes Irish pro-slavery sentiment. 20 November 1857. p.188, c3.

4386 n.n. *to* **THE** *SENTINEL.* **12 November 1857. Boston.** Relates the tale of Betty, a slave who prefers to face the future with friends in the South rather than confront the unknown in the North. 27 November 1857. p.189, c2.

4387 M. D. CONWAY *to* **MESSRS. EDITORS OF THE** *CINCINNATI GAZETTE.* **4 November 1857. Cincinnati.** Comments on a fugitive slave case in Cincinnati. 27 November 1857. p.189, c3.

4388 M. W. BALL *to* **THE EDITOR OF THE** *SABBATH RECORDER.* **n.d. Janelew, Ky.** Orders the *Sabbath Recorder* to discontinue subscriptions in the town of Janelew. 27 November 1857. p.189, c6.

4389 n.n. *to* **n.n. [extract] 8 November 1857. Kansas.** Explains the intentions of the Free State Party. 27 November 1857. p.190, c2.

4390 L. C. LOCKWOOD *to* **THE NORTHERN CONVENTION. 23 October 1857. Meriden, Ct.** Favors disunion. 27 November 1857. p.190, c4.

4391 C. PEIRCE *to* **W. L. GARRISON. 23 November 1857. West Newton.** Thanks Garrison for his praise. 27 November 1857. p.190, c6.

4392 MRS. FRANCIS H. DRAKE *to* **n.n. [extract] 1 November 1857. Leominster.** Reports that there is support in Leominster for the AAS. 27 November 1857. p.190, c6.

4393 A. BROOKE *to* **FRIEND GARRISON. 18 November 1857. Marlboro', Oh.** Details the proceedings of the Cleveland Disunion Convention. 27 November 1857. p.191, c1.

4394 COL. E. B. ALEXANDER *to* **GOV. BRIGHAM YOUNG. 2 October 1857. Camp Winfield on Hams Fork.** Reports that United States troops are in Utah by order of the president and receive orders only from competent military authority. 27 November 1857. p.192, c5.

4395 A SPECTATOR *to* **SIR. 21 November 1857. Newburyport.** Comments on the schools in Newburyport. 4 December 1857. p.194, c2.

4396 THOS. H. BENTON *to* **GEO. ROBERTSON. 1 November 1857. Washington.** Regrets the Supreme Court's decision on the Missouri Compromise. 4 December 1857. p.195, c1.

4397 F. H. DRAKE *to* **MAY. 28 November 1857. Leominster.** Describes Pillsbury's meetings in Leominster. 4 December 1857. p.196, c2.

4398 n.n. *to* **n.n. [extract] n.d. Parish of Calcasieu.** Reports on a murder in Calcasieu. 4 December 1857. p.196, c2.

4399 n.n. *to* **n.n. 21 November. Vicksburg, Ms.** Gives account of a duel between W. D. Roy of the *Vicksburg Sun* and R. H. Purdon of the *Port Gibson Herald.* 4 December 1857. p.196, c5.

4400 HENRY C. WRIGHT *to* **W. L. GARRISON. 29 November 1857. New Garden, Oh.** Argues that disunion would facilitate abolition. 11 December 1857. p.199, c1.

4401 S. S. FOSTER *to* **W. L. GARRISON. 29 November 1857. West Boscawen, N.H.** Comments on the postponement of the National Disunion Convention. 11 December 1857. p.199, c2.

4402 DAVID DEAN *to* **W. L. GARRISON. 26 November 1857. Hannibal, Mo.** A slaveholder urges the North to remember that Southerners are moral, dislike slavery, treat their slaves well, and fear that emancipation would harm slaves. 11 December 1857. p.199, c3.

4403 A. B. *to* **W. L. GARRISON. 27 November 1857. Fowler's Mills, Geauga County, Oh.** Comments on anti-slavery activities near Fowler's Mills. 11 December 1857. p.199, c3.

4404 A. HOGEBOOM *to* **FRIEND GARRISON. 27 November 1857. Shed's Corners, N.Y.** Discusses his dispute with a "supercilious" minister in Shed's Corners. 11 December 1857. p.200, c2.

4405 A. HOGEBOOM *to* **REV. HINMAN. 5 August 1857. Shed's Corners, N.Y.** Berates Rev. Hinman for saying that a woman who was penitent on her deathbed went to hell. 11 December 1857. p.200, c2.

4406 A. HOGEBOOM *to* **REV. HINMAN. 23 August 1857. Shed's Corners, N.Y.** Debates the nature of God. 11 December 1857. p.200, c2.

4407 LUCY STONE *to* **W. L. GARRISON. 27 November 1857. Orange, N.J.** Announces the availability of the *Woman's Rights Almanac*. 11 December 1857. p.200, c2.

4408 n.n. *to* **n.n. [extract] n.d. Washington.** Advises wives to accompany their husbands to Washington. 11 December 1857. p.200, c5.

4409 R. HASSALL *to* **BROTHER MAY. 8 December 1857. Haverhill.** Informs of Hassall's expulsion from his Unitarian pastorship. 18 December 1857. p.203, c4.

4410 AARON M. POWELL *to* **W. L. GARRISON. 14 December 1857. New York.** Reacts to the death of William H. Topp. 18 December 1857. p.203, c5.

4411 AARON M. POWELL *to* **W. L. GARRISON. 5 December 1857. New York.** Appraises the anti-slavery cause in New Jersey. 18 December 1857. p.204, c2.

4412 RICHARD GLAZIER *to* **W. L. GARRISON. 6 December 1857. Ann Arbor, Mi.** Defends Pillsbury and S. S. Foster against the criticisms of "Justice." 18 December 1857. p.204, c2.

4413 J. W. *to* **FRIEND GARRISON. 5 December 1857. Adrian, Mi.** Disputes "Justice" 's assertion that Pillsbury and S. S. Foster hurt the anti-slavery cause in Michigan when they visited in 1855. 18 December 1857. p.204, c3.

4414 SAMUEL D. MOORE *to* **W. L. GARRISON. 4 December 1857. Ypsilanti, Mi.** Defends Pillsbury and S. S. Foster against charges made by "Justice"; argues that spiritualism is an obstacle to anti-slavery in Ypsilanti. 18 December 1857. p.204, c4.

4415 J. A. H. *to* **W. L. GARRISON. 5 December. Cherry Valley, Ashtabula County, Oh.** Proclaims that spiritualism is undercutting abolitionism. 18 December 1857. p.204, c5.

4416 J. H. P. *to* **SIR. 14 December 1857. Salem.** Returns a petition calling for Judge Loring's removal. 25 December 1857. p.206, c3.

4417 CAROLINE H. DALL *to* **W. L. GARRISON. 20 December 1857. Boston.** Reminds friends about the coming woman's rights convention. 25 December 1857. p.206, c3.

4418 PLATO *to* **THE EDITOR OF THE *BOSTON JOURNAL*. n.d. n.p.** Comments on the American Tract Society. 25 December 1857. p.206, c4.

4419 C. K. W. *to* **THE EDITOR OF THE *BOSTON JOURNAL*. n.d. n.p.** Denounces the American Tract Society. 25 December 1857. p.206, c4.

4420 C. C. *to* **W. L. GARRISON. 17 December 1857. Wellsville, N.Y.** Comments on Sallie Holley's lectures in Wellsville. 25 December 1857. p.206, c6.

4421 A. HOGEBOOM *to* **FRIEND GARRISON. 14 December 1857. Shed's Corners, N.Y.** Corrects an error in his last letter. 25 December 1857. p.206, c6.

4422 R. A. A. *to* **W. L. GARRISON. 6 December 1857. Washington, N.Y.** Informs of the death of Lydia Swift, an earnest and zealous advocate of the cause of freedom. 25 December 1857. p.206, c6.

4423 SAMUEL KEESE *to* **FRIEND GARRISON. 14 December 1857. Peru, Clinton County, N.Y.** Denounces the concept of original sin. 25 December 1857. p.208, c2.

[1858]

4424 J. P. THOMPSON, S. H. TYNG, A. D. SMITH, T. E. VERMILYE, R. S. STORRS, JR., A. D. GILLETTE, AND J. KENNADAY *to* **AMERICAN CHRISTIANS.** [from the *New York Independent*] **3 December 1857. New York.** Request that the *New York Independent* print the address of the synod in Switzerland. 1 January 1858. p.1, c3.

4425 LS. BURNIER, TROVON, LS. BRICHEL, P. LERESCHE, AND A. RAYMOND *to* **CHRISTIANS OF THE UNITED STATES. 14 May 1857. Vevey, Switzerland.** State that the Synod of the Free Church of the Canton Vaud supports emancipation. 1 January 1858. p.1, c3.

4426 THOMAS H. BENTON *to* **n.n. [extract] n.d. n.p.** States that he expects to finish writing another volume of the *Thirty Years' View* by summer. 1 January 1858. p.1, c4.

4427 I. A. BAIR *to* **n.n. [extract from the *Northern Independent*] n.d. n.p.** Questions the appropriateness of a Christian melody. 1 January 1858. p.1, c6.

4428 J. R. GIDDINGS *to* **THE EDITOR OF THE** *ASHTABULA SENTINEL.* **15 December. Washington.** Reminisces about early anti-slavery struggles in the United States House of Representatives. 1 January 1858. p.2, c2.

4429 COMMODORE PAULDING *to* **THE SECRETARY OF THE NAVY. 15 December 1857. Off Aspinwall.** Details circumstances under which General Walker was arrested. 1 January 1858. p.3, c4.

4430 S. J. MAY *to* **FRIEND. 17 December 1857. Glen Haven.** Requests publication of a paragraph he enjoyed reading in the book, *Memoir of Cyrus Pierce.* 1 January 1858. p.4, c2.

4431 E. W. TWING *to* **FRIEND GARRISON. 21 December 1857. Springfield.** Defends spiritualism, which he believes is able to convert even slaveholders to abolitionism. 1 January 1858. p.4, c2.

4432 H. *to* **FRIEND GARRISON. 12 December 1857. Upton.** Comments on clerical bigotry in Upton. 1 January 1858. p.4, c3.

4433 ABNER BELCHER *to* **W. L. GARRISON. 31 December 1857. Wrentham.** Discusses an abolitionist impostor in the area of Wrentham. 8 January 1858. p.6, c6.

4434 SAMUEL FLINT *to* **W. L. GARRISON. 28 December 1857. Lyme, N.H.** Reports on a Negro impostor. 8 January 1858. p.6, c6.

4435 WARREN CHASE *to* **MR. EDITOR. 28 December 1857. Tecumseh, Mi.** A spiritualist denies that spiritualism has dampened anti-slavery ardor. 8 January 1858. p.7, c2.

4436 L. O. LE FAVRE *to* **W. L. GARRISON. 2 January 1858. Stoneham.** Reports on Pillsbury and Remond's lectures in Stoneham. 8 January 1858. p.7, c3.

4437 H. C. WRIGHT *to* **W. L. GARRISON. 16 December 1857. Collamer, Oh.** Advocates Northern disunion. 8 January 1858. p.8, c2.

4438 W. H. F. *to* **FRIEND GARRISON. 29 December 1857. Cortland, N.Y.** Relates anti-slavery agitation in a Presbyterian church in Cortland. 8 January 1858. p.8, c3.

4439 G. W. P. *to* **FRIEND GARRISON. n.d. Milford, Ma.** Encloses petition urging the removal of Judge E. G. Loring. 15 January 1858. p.10, c4.

4440 STEPHEN J. W. TABOR *to* **ROBERT F. WALLCUT. 5 January 1858. Independence, Ia.** Praises the *Liberator*. 15 January 1858. p.10, c5.

4441 S. D. C. *to* **FRIEND GARRISON. 1 January 1858. Nashua, N.H.** Criticizes the noncommital anti-slavery position held by Republicans. 15 January 1858. p.10, c5.

4442 n.n. *to* **REV. CRAWFORD OF NANTUCKET. 20 December 1857. New Bedford.** Sympathizes with Rev. Crawford, a colored preacher, who tried to ransom his slave niece. 15 January 1858. p.10, c5.

4443 A. D. R. *to* **THE EDITOR OF THE** *BOSTON JOURNAL.* **31 December 1857. Leavenworth, Ks.** Comments on free state politics in Leavenworth. 15 January 1858. p.11, c2.

4444 H. C. WRIGHT *to* **W. L. GARRISON. 25 December 1857. Coneaut, Pa.** Articulates the difference between the Christ of Calvary and the Christ of Christendom. 15 January 1858. p.12, c2.

4445 C. K. W. *to* **THE EDITORS OF THE** *CONGREGATIONALIST.* **n.d. n.p.** Discusses the duties of dancing masters. 15 January 1858. p.12, c4.

4446 WM. S. FLANDERS *to* **THE EDITOR OF THE** *LIBERATOR* **[W. L. GARRISON]. 29 December 1857. Cornville, Me.** Discusses the relationship of slavery to the United States Constitution. 22 January 1858. p.15, c1.

4447 H. C. WRIGHT *to* **W. L. GARRISON. 15 January 1858. Newark, N.J.** Declares that the condition of women in the slave states provides an argument for disunion. 29 January 1858. p.17, c3.

4448 JUSTICE *to* **W. L. GARRISON. n.d. Battle Creek, Mi.** Defends his earlier criticisms of sectarian abolitionists; denies that spiritualism weakens abolitionism. 29 January 1858. p.17, c4.

4449 n.n. *to* **THE EDITORS OF THE** *SALEM OBSERVER.* **n.d. n.p.** Discusses lecture by Susan B. Anthony, delivered at the Beverly Lyceum. 29 January 1858. p.19, c1.

4450 S. D. C. *to* **FRIEND GARRISON. 22 January 1858. Nashua, N.H.** Reports on anti-slavery meetings in Nashua. 29 January 1858. p.19, c2.

4451 LUCY STONE *to* **MR. MANDEVILLE. 18 December 1857. Orange, N.J.** Refuses to pay taxes in order to protest taxation of women without representation. 29 January 1858. p.19, c5.

4452 PARKER PILLSBURY *to* **THE** *OHIO ANTI-SLAVERY BUGLE.* **[extract] n.d. n.p.** Comments on his current political activities. 5 February 1858. p.21, c3.

4453 JUSTUS HARLOW *to* **FRIEND GARRISON. 22 January 1858. Plymouth.** Proposes formation of an "Anti-Devil Society." 5 February 1858. p.24, c2.

4454 COMMODORE H. PAULDING *to* **WALKER. December 1857. U.S.S.** *Wabash.* Informs Walker that he is violating United States laws by his acts of violence in Punta Arenas. 5 February 1858. p.24, c3.

4455 BERIAH GREEN *to* **n.n. October 1857. Whitesboro'.** States his reasons for declining to be a candidate for office in the Radical Abolition Party. 5 February 1858. p.24, c3.

4456 GEORGE B. CHEEVER *to* **THE NEW YORK YMCA. n.d. n.p.** Discusses the YMCA's duty in regard to slavery. 5 February 1858. p.24, c4.

4457 JOSEPH HOWLAND *to* **n.n. [extract from the** *Anti-Slavery Bugle***]** **n.d. n.p.** Reports on the colored community in Deer Creek, Ohio. 5 February 1858. p.24, c5.

4458 J. Q. ADAMS *to* **E. QUINCY. 28 July 1838. Quincy.** Praises abolitionists. 12 February 1858. p.25, c2.

4459 FRANCES A. V. LONDONDERRY *to* **MRS. CHAPMAN. n.d. Seaham.** Thanks Mrs. Chapman for sending her copies of the *Liberty Bell.* 12 February 1858. p.25, c5.

4460 MARGARET BRACHEN *to* **MRS. CHAPMAN. 13 October 1857. Halifax.** Compliments Mrs. Chapman on the success of the National Anti-Slavery Bazaar. 12 February 1858. p.25, c5.

4461 H. B. STOWE *to* **MRS. CHAPMAN. 29 January 1858. Brooklyn.** Praises the contributors to the Boston Bazaar. 12 February 1858. p.26, c1.

4462 CALEB CUSHING *to* **JOHN G. WHITTIER. 8 November 1838. Salem.** Favors abolition of slavery in the District of Columbia. 12 February 1858. p.26, c5.

4463 CALEB CUSHING *to* **ANDREW ROBESON AND JOHN BURRAGE. 5 September 1837. Washington.** Opposes annexation of Texas. 12 February 1858. p.26, c5.

4464 PARKER PILLSBURY *to* **FRIEND GARRISON. 5 February 1858. Boston.** Comments on the Vermont Anti-Slavery Convention. 12 February 1858. p.27, c1.

4465 G. W. S. *to* **BRO. GARRISON. 8 February 1858. Milford.** Reports on Parker Pillsbury's lecture in Milford. 12 February 1858. p.27, c2.

4466 WM. S. BAILEY *to* **n.n. [extract] 28 January 1858. Newport, Ky.** Reports on anti-abolitionist mobs in Newport. 19 February 1858. p.30, c6.

4467 S. S. FOSTER *to* **W. L. GARRISON. 11 February 1858. Worcester.** Informs that the stenographer's account of his speech at the recent Massachusetts AS meeting is garbled and misleading. 19 February 1858. p.31, c3.

4468 SAMUEL MAY, JR. *to* **W. L. GARRISON. n.d. n.p.** Claims he took special pains to record Foster's speech faithfully at the Massachusetts AS meeting. 19 February 1858. p.31, c3.

4469 S. M., JR. *to* **W. L. GARRISON. n.d. n.p.** Calls attention to a printing error in a letter from Parker Pillsbury. 19 February 1858. p.31, c3.

4470 AMERICAN TRAVELLER *to* **HIS BROTHER IN NEW YORK. 12 December 1857. Barbadoes.** Discusses emancipation in the West Indies. 26 February 1858. p.33, c3.

4471 ABNER BELCHER *to* **n.n. 19 February 1858. Wrentham.** Informs of the death of Edward Lane. 26 February 1858. p.34, c6.

4472 REV. N. R. JOHNSTON *to* **DR. MANN, EDITOR OF THE** *BRADFORD* **(VT.)** *TELEGRAPH.* **n.d. n.p.** Defends the abolitionist platform of disunion. 5 March 1858. p.37, c2.

4473 S. S. FOSTER *to* **W. L. GARRISON. n.d. n.p.** Affirms that the record of his speech at the Massachusetts AS meeting was garbled. 5 March 1858. p.39, c3.

4474 W. H. F. *to* **W. L. GARRISON. n.d. n.p.** Reports on the speeches of W. Phillips, C. C. Burleigh, and W. W. Brown in Cortland, New York. 5 March 1858. p.39, c4.

4475 C. E. *to* **THE EDITOR OF THE** *CORTLAND COUNTY* **(N.Y.)** *REPUBLICAN.* **n.d. n.p.** Discusses W. Phillips' lecture in Cortland, New York. 12 March 1858. p.41, c2.

4476 EDWARD G. LORING *to* **JOINT SPECIAL COMMITTEE OF THE MASSA-CHUSETTS LEGISLATURE. 2 March 1858. Boston.** Defends his legal conduct. 12 March 1858. p.41, c4.

4477 T. W. HIGGINSON *to* **W. C. NELL. 5 March 1858. Worcester.** Praises the colored heroes which Massachusetts has produced. 12 March 1858. p.43, c2.

4478 THOMAS RUSSELL *to* **W. C. NELL. 5 March 1858. Boston.** Regrets that he is unable to attend the Boston Massacre celebration. 12 March 1858. p.43, c5.

4479 J. G. WHITTIER *to* **W. C. NELL. 29 January 1858. Amesbury.** Praises black soldiers. 12 March 1858. p.43, c5.

4480 P. PILLSBURY *to* **W. L. GARRISON. 6 March 1858. Boston.** Defines his position regarding the Kansas Free State Party. 12 March 1858. p.43, c6.

4481 J. A. H. *to* **FRIEND GARRISON. n.d. n.p.** Discusses the Topeka constitution. 12 March 1858. p.43, c6.

4482 CHARLES K. WHIPPLE *to* **A CHRISTIAN CHURCH RECENTLY ESTAB-LISHED IN THE WEST. n.d. n.p.** Discusses the duty of the church. 12 March 1858. p.44, c2.

4483 NOGGS *to* **THE EDITORS OF THE** *TRAVELLER.* **2 March 1858. Haverhill.** Comments on Rev. Hassall's closing sermon. 12 March 1858. p.44, c3.

4484 W. L. GARRISON *to* **REV. N. R. JOHNSTON. 25 January 1858. Boston.** Discusses the goals of the Vermont Anti-Slavery Convention. 19 March 1858. p.46, c5.

4485 S. J. MAY *to* **FRIEND GARRISON. 11 March 1858. New York.** Reports on the anti-slavery convention in Albany. 19 March 1858. p. 46,c6.

4486 A. T. FOSS *to* **FRIEND GARRISON. 23 February 1858. Linesville, Crawford County, Pa.** Reports on anti-slavery sentiment and scheming politicians in Linesville. 19 March 1858. p.47, c4.

4487 T. W. H. *to* **W. L. GARRISON. 15 March 1858. Worcester.** Discusses the Topeka constitution. 19 March 1858. p.47, c5.

4488 S. E. W. *to* **W. L. GARRISON. 7 March 1858. Worcester.** Discusses the rights of women. 19 March 1858. p.48, c2.

4489 SALLIE HOLLEY *to* **FRANCIS JACKSON. 16 February 1858. Riceville, Crawford County, Pa.** Reports on anti-slavery meetings and friends in Riceville. 19 March 1858. p.48, c3.

4490 H. A. *to* **W. L. GARRISON. 23 February 1858. Marlboro'.** Praises an anti-slavery poem he has heard. 19 March 1858. p.48, c3.

4491 GEO. SUNTER *to* **THE EDITOR OF THE** *LIBERATOR* **[W. L. GARRISON]. 1 March 1858. Brantford, Canada West.** Questions the usefulness of religious sects. 19 March 1858. p.48, c3.

4492 J. W. SPAULDING *to* **BROTHER GARRISON. 24 February 1858. Pepperell.** Comments on H. C. Wright's lectures in Pepperell. 19 March 1858. p.48, c4.

4493 L. *to* **THE EDITOR OF THE** *LIBERATOR* **[W. L. GARRISON]. n.d. n.p.** Explains the Old School Covenanter Church's views on the anti-slavery movement. 19 March 1858. p.48, c4.

4494 R. J. WALKER *to* **INDIANA STATE DEMOCRATIC CONVENTION. n.d. n.p.** Gives details of the Kansas-Nebraska Act. 19 March 1858. p.48, c5.

4495 W. L. GARRISON *to* **S. J. MAY. 6 March 1858. Boston.** Regrets that he is unable to attend the anti-slavery convention at Albany, New York. 26 March 1858. p.51, c3.

4496 N. R. JOHNSTON *to* **MR. McINDOE OF THE** *AURORA OF THE VALLEY* **(VT.). n.d. n.p.** Defends Garrisonian abolitionists. 26 March 1858. p.52, c2.

4497 LUCY N. COLMAN *to* **W. L. GARRISON. 3 February 1858. Rochester, N.Y.** Reports on anti-slavery labors in the West. 26 March 1858. p.52, c3.

4498 HELEN NORTON *to* **W. L. GARRISON. n.d. Erieville, N. Y.** Supports women's rights. 26 March 1858. p.52, c4.

4499 R. *to* **THE EDITOR OF THE** *LIBERATOR* **[W. L. GARRISON]. n.d. n.p.** Condemns Old School Covenanter Church in New York City for refusing to allow a female abolitionist to speak in their church. 2 April 1858. p.55, c3.

4500 EDWARD G. LORING *to* **THE INHABITANTS OF THE COUNTY OF SUFFOLK. n.d. n.p.** Defends himself after being removed from the probate court by the governor. 2 April 1858. p.55, c4.

4501 JOHN T. TILLEY *to* **n.n. 21 December 1857. Newport.** Informs that he is being denied the opportunity to renew his pew in church. 2 April 1858. p.56, c2.

4502 E. H. H. *to* **W. L. GARRISON. 22 March 1858. Providence.** Describes the hostility of Rhode Island Republicans toward true abolitionism and anti-discrimination reforms in the schools. 2 April 1858. p.56, c2.

4503 J. A. H. *to* **FRIEND GARRISON. 16 March 1858. Marlboro', Stark County, Oh.** Reports on the colored community in Deer Creek, Ohio. 2 April 1858. p.56, c3.

4504 EDWARD PALMER *to* **FRIENDS OF UNIVERSAL EMANCIPATION. 20 March 1858. Perth Amboy, N. J.** Advocates a "root and branch" reform of the present commercial system. 2 April 1858. p.56. c4.

4505 J. A. H. *to* **W. L. GARRISON. 22 March 1858. Salem, Oh.** Discusses the Topeka constitution. 2 April 1858. p.56, c4.

4506 T. R. DAVIS *to* **THE EDITOR OF THE** *LIBERATOR* **[W. L. GARRISON]. 11 March 1858. Castalia, Erie County, Oh.** Questions why the *Liberator* has failed to publish the reports on anti-slavery meetings in Erie County. 2 April 1858. p.56, c4.

4507 H. B. *to* **W. L. GARRISON. n.d. Marlboro', N.H.** Ridicules religious revival in Marlboro'. 2 April 1858. p.56, c5.

4508 A COLORED MAN *to* **THE EDITOR OF THE** *NEW YORK TRIBUNE.* **25 March 1858. New York.** Describes an incident of Jim Crowism in a church in New York. 2 April 1858. p.56, c5.

4509 JOHN MITCHEL *to* **J. J. HOOPER, EDITOR OF THE** *MONTGOMERY* **(AL.)** *MAIL.* **13 February 1858. Knoxville, Tn.** An Irish patriot denounces abolitionism. 9 April 1858. p.57, c2.

4510 n.n. *to* **MR. EDITOR OF THE** *NEW BEDFORD STANDARD.* **30 March 1858. Cape Cod.** Discusses the feelings of people in Cape Cod regarding the dismissal of Judge Loring. 9 April 1858. p.58, c2.

4511 E. FOLLEN, W. PHILLIPS, S. MAY, JR., E. QUINCY, C. HODGES, A. FOS-TER, M. MAY, C. HOVEY, S. MAY, C. REMOND, WM. GARRISON, AND F. JACKSON *to* **SARAH H. EARLE. 25 December 1857. Boston.** Send gift in gratitude for her faithful service. 9 April 1858. p.59, c1.

4512 H. W. G. *to* **THE** *ANTI-SLAVERY BUGLE.* **n.d. Schuylkill, Chester County, Pa.** Praises S. H. Gay. 9 April 1858. p.59, c1.

4513 G. W. MADOX *to* **FRIEND GARRISON. 1 April 1858. Ellsworth, Me.** Comments on H. C. Wright's lectures in Ellsworth. 9 April 1858. p.59, c1.

4514 H. C. WRIGHT *to* **W. L. GARRISON. 31 March 1858. Ellsworth, Me.** Asserts that after Judge Loring's removal, Massachusetts must ensure that no man need ever stand trial to determine whether he is the property of another. 9 April 1858. p.59, c2.

4515 G. B. STEBBINS *to* **FRIEND GARRISON. 26 March. Battle Creek, Mi.** Adopts a tolerant and hopeful view of spiritualists. 16 April 1858. p.61, c3.

4516 LEWIS CASS *to* **HENRY WILSON. 2 April 1858. Department of State, Washington, D.C.** States that since passports are certificates of citizenship, they have never been issued to persons of color. 16 April 1858. p.62, c2.

4517 H. C. WRIGHT *to* **W. L. GARRISON. 6 April 1858. Ellsworth, Me.** Discusses revivals and false religions in Ellsworth. 16 April 1858. p.63, c2.

4518 EMMA V. BROWNE *to* **W. L. GARRISON. 1 April 1858. Miss Miner's School, Washington.** Praises the *Liberator.* 16 April 1858. p.63, c3.

4519 VITELLO *to* **MR. EDITOR. 29 March 1858. Harwich Port.** Reports on a religious revival in Harwich Port. 16 April 1858. p.63, c3.

4520 SOUTHERNER *to* **THE EDITOR OF THE** *RICHMOND SOUTH.* **30 March 1858. Savannah.** Ponders past and present events in New England. 23 April 1858. p,65, c1.

4521 J. A. H. *to* **FRIEND GARRISON. 14 April 1858. Worcester.** Discusses the annual meeting of the New England Methodist Conference. 23 April 1858. p.65, c3.

4522 C. C. B. *to* **FRIEND GARRISON. n.d. n.p.** Sends an extract from an essay by Coleridge. 23 April 1858. p.65, c5.

4523 L. *to* **THE EDITOR OF THE** *LIBERATOR* **[W. L. GARRISON]. 7 April 1858. St. Louis, Mo.** Discusses the election in St. Louis of an "emancipationist" mayor who is also a slaveholder. 23 April 1858. p.65, c5.

4524 W. *to* **FRIEND GARRISON. n.d. n.p.** Uses "foul anchor" as a metaphor to express the need for properly mooring the ship of state. 23 April 1858. p.65. c6.

4525 A. B. H. *to* **W. L. GARRISON. 13 April 1858. Lancaster.** Encloses a eulogy of the late Sarah H. Earle. 23 April 1858. p.65, c6.

4526 FRANCIS E. WATKINS *to* **A FRIEND. [extract] n.d. n.p.** States that she misses New England; describes racism in Pennsylvania. 23 April 1858. p.67, c2.

4527 JEFFERSON *to* **FRIEND GARRISON. n.d. n.p.** Asks abolitionist disunionists to explain how they plan to sever the Union. 23 April 1858. p.67, c3.

4528 ETHER SHEPLEY *to* **REV. SETH BLISS. 30 March 1858. Portland, Me.** Upholds the American Tract Society. 30 April 1858. p.69, c2.

4529 ROBERT C. WINTHROP *to* **SIR. 5 April 1858. Boston.** Supports the American Tract Society. 30 April 1858. p.69, c3.

4530 RUFUS CHOATE *to* **SIR. n.d. n.p.** Praises the American Tract Society. 30 April 1858. p.69, c3.

4531 REV. THOMAS SHEPARD *to* **SIR. 5 April 1858. Bristol, R.I.** Supports the American Tract Society's decision not to print abolitionist literature. 30 April 1858. p.69, c3.

4532 N. LORD *to* **SIR. 29 March 1858. Hanover, N.H.** Supports the American Tract Society. 30 April 1858. p.69, c3.

4533 JOHN RICHARDS *to* **SIR. 5 April 1858. Hanover, N.H.** Admires letters to members of the Tract Society. 30 April 1858. p.69, c3.

4534 R. T. HAINES *to* **SIR. 1 April 1858. Elizabeth, N.J.** Praises the American Tract Society. 30 April 1858. p.69, c3.

4535 F. W. CHESSON *to* **THE EDITOR OF THE** *CARLISLE* **(ENGLAND)** *EXAMINER.* **March 1858. London.** Gives an extensive extract from an editorial in the *Northern Daily Express* praising Julia Griffith's mission to raise funds for *Frederick Douglass' Paper*; objects vigorously to the *Express'* claim that Frederick Douglass has had to contend against the bigotry of certain abolitionists; defends the AAS against the charge of infidelity. 30 April 1858. p.69, c4.

4536 LUCY N. COLMAN *to* **W. L. GARRISON. 20 April 1858. Rochester.** Comments on anti-slavery and women's rights lectures in western New York. 30 April 1858. p.70, c6.

4537 CHARLES K. WHIPPLE *to* **SETH BLISS. 20 April 1858. Boston.** Criticizes the pamphlet in defense of the American Tract Society. 30 April 1858. p.71, c1.

4538 WM. A. HALLOCK *to* **MR. WHIPPLE. n.d. n.p.** States that *The Slaveholder* is unadaptable for use as a tract. 30 April 1858. p.71, c1.

4539 MR. BLISS *to* **THE EXECUTIVE COMMITTEE OF THE AMERICAN TRACT SOCIETY. March 1856. n.p.** States the objectives of the Tract Society publication; hopes the committee will publish tracts opposing slaveholding. 30 April 1858. p.71, c1.

4540 WILLIAM A. HALLOCK *to* **CHARLES K. WHIPPLE. 16 February 1858. New York.** States that no action has been taken on the "Duties of Dancing-Masters" manuscript. 30 April 1858. p.71, c2.

4541 C. F. P. *to* **W. L. GARRISON. 4 March 1858. Jamestown, Chautauga County, N. Y.** Describes the revival contagion and moral apathy in Jamestown. 7 May 1858. p.73, c2.

4542 SUSAN B. ANTHONY *to* **W. L. GARRISON. 16 April 1858. Rochester.** Comments on the Old School Covenanter Church's proscription of women speakers. 7 May 1858. p.73, c2.

4543 HAVERHILL *to* **ROBT. F. WALCUTT. n.d. n.p.** Discusses T. Parker and W. L. Garrison's lectures in Groveland. 7 May 1858. p.73, c4.

4544 C. K. W. *to* **BRETHREN. n.d. n.p.** Believes that the publishing committee of the American Tract Society should be removed. 7 May 1858. p.74, c1.

4545 W. L. GARRISON *to* **JOHN W. LE BARNES. 29 April 1858. Boston.** Gives tribute to Orsini, who was beheaded for attempting Louis Napoleon's assassination. 7 May 1858. p.74, c6.

4546 CHAS. C. BURLEIGH *to* **S. MAY, JR. 24 April 1858. Cummington, Ma.** Comments on revivals in Cummington and the American Tract Society. 7 May 1858. p.75, c3.

4547 G. F. C. *to* **W. L. GARRISON. 2 May 1858. Leominster.** Forwards a resolution which he omitted in his report on the Worcester County North AS meeting. 7 May 1858. p.75, c3.

4548 LOUIS SWEET *to* **JAS. G. BENNETT. 22 April 1858. Nashville, Tn.** Denies the rumor that his slave, Betty, has escaped to Cincinnati. 7 May 1858. p.75, c4.

4549 JOSEPH MAZZINI *to* **THE EDITOR OF THE** *LONDON DAILY NEWS.* **8 April. n.p.** Describes persecutions in Louis Napoleon's France. 7 May 1858. p.76, c6.

4550 GOV. ROBT. C. WICKLIFFE *to* **GOVERNOR OF MAINE. 17 April. Baton Rouge, La.** Returns the "revolutionary, insulting and aggressive" resolutions adopted by the Maine legislature expressing its views on slavery. 14 May 1858. p.77, c4.

4551 n.n. *to* **n.n. [extract] 21 March. St. Petersburg.** Discusses the emancipation of the serfs in Russia. 14 May 1858. p.78, c2.

4552 BYLES *to* **THE** *NEW YORK TRIBUNE.* **[extract] n.d. n.p.** Details the visit of Mrs. Everett to Charleston. 14 May 1858. p.79, c2.

4553 J. J. LOCKE *to* **FRIEND GARRISON. 4 May 1858. Greenwood, South Reading, Ma.** Comments on a church in South Reading that refused to admit Garrisonian "infidels." 14 May 1858. p.79, c2.

4554 J. R. GIDDINGS *to* **W. L. GARRISON. 7 May 1858. Washington.** Conveys greetings to the AAS; examines congressional and world-wide progress, and suggests the formation of an international organization of philanthropists. 21 May 1858. p.80, c5.

4555 EDWARD EVERETT *to* **SIR. 31 October. Medford, Ma.** Regrets having signed an inflammatory statement about the Sumner assault. 28 May 1858. p.85, c1.

4556 J. H. D. *to* **WM. S. BAILEY. [from the** *Kentucky News*] **n.d. Kentucky.** An outraged slaveholder reports that he sold his slaves in order to put them beyond the reach of a local abolitionist paper. 28 May 1858. p.85, c3.

4557 CHARLES SUMNER *to* **THE PEOPLE OF MASSACHUSETTS. 22 May 1858. New York Harbor.** Bids farewell to the people of Massachusetts; reports that he suffers medical complications. 4 June 1858. p.90, c1.

4558 T. W. HIGGINSON *to* **W. L. GARRISON. 31 May 1858. Worcester.** Promotes Frances D. Gage's lecture on "Woman as Mother." 4 June 1858. p.91, c4.

4559 S. S. FOSTER *to* **W. L. GARRISON. 6 June 1858. Worcester.** Praises F. D. Gage's lecture in Worcester. 11 June 1858. p.95, c4.

4560 JOHN P. HALE *to* **REV. S. H. TYNG. 24 May 1858. Washington.** Inquires about Dudley Tyng's attitude toward his anti-slavery actions. 11 June 1858. p.96, c3.

4561 STEPHEN H. TYNG *to* **J. P. HALE. 26 May 1858. New York.** Replies to Hale's inquiries; states that Dudley Tyng never regretted his protests against slavery. 11 June 1858. p.96, c3.

4562 DUDLEY TYNG *to* **DR. CASPER MORRIS. 8 December 1856. Philadelphia.** Sends a copy of his anti-slavery sermon. 11 June 1858. p.96, c3.

4563 AL. HUMBOLDT *to* **JULIUS FROEBEL. 11 January 1858. Berlin, Germany.** Denounces American slavery. 11 June 1858. p.96, c5.

4564 G. WASHINGTON *to* **GEN. R. PUTNAM. 2 February 1783. Headquarters.** Orders court of inquiry to investigate the claim that a Negro man in the army is the property of Mr. Hobby. 11 June 1858. p.96, c5.

4565 HOWELL COBB *to* **WM. F. COLCOCK. n.d. Washington, D. C.** The United States secretary of the treasury informs the collector of customs at Charleston, South Carolina, that an attempt to import "African emigrants" is a ruse to reopen the African slave trade. 18 June 1858. p.98, c1.

4566 HARRIET MARTINEAU *to* **E. G. LORING. [extract] n.d. n.p.** Comments on Abner Kneeland, editor of the *Boston Investigator*. 18 June 1858. p.100, c4.

4567 E. G. LORING *to* **H. MARTINEAU. 6 June 1839. Boston.** Discusses Abner Kneeland, editor of the *Boston Investigator*. 18 June 1858. p.100, c4.

4568 KNOX *to* **REVEILLE. 18 May 1858. Nashville.** Reports on the Methodist General Conference in Nashville and a debate on a slavery resolution. 25 June 1858. p.101, c1.

4569 JOHN Y. MASON *to* **L. CASS. [extract] 19 February 1858. Paris.** States that France and England are beginning to regret the emancipation of slaves in their colonies. 25 June 1858. p.101, c4.

4570 S. S. FOSTER *to* **W. L. GARRISON. n.d. n.p.** Defends the use of violence and politics on behalf of emancipation; calls for a platform on which all abolitionists can stand. 25 June 1858. p.103, c1.

4571 JUSTITIA *to* **W. L. GARRISON. 17 June 1858. Boston.** Sends poem, "The American Tract Society, and its Southern Masters." 25 June 1858. p.104, c1.

4572 S. E. W. *to* **W. L. GARRISON. 23 May 1858. Worcester.** Supports the right of women's suffrage. 25 June 1858. p.104, c2.

4573 CAROLINE H. DALL *to* **W. L. GARRISON. 11 June 1858. West Whately, Ma.** Supports a petition for women's suffrage. 25 June 1858. p.104, c3.

4574 F. P. BLAIR *to* **ELIHU BURRITT. [from the** *Connecticut South and North*] **10 May 1858. Silver Spring, Md.** Endorses compensated emancipation, but argues that, to be effective, it must be coupled with Negro colonization, preferably in Central America. 2 July 1858. p.105, c1.

4575 JOHN W. ADAMS *to* **WM. S. BAILEY. [from the** *Newport Kentucky News***] 2 June 1858. Rye, N.H.** Supports emancipation, but regrets that the *Newport Kentucky News* chooses to reprint "infidel" articles from the *Liberator*. 2 July 1858. p.105, c3.

4576 MIFFLIN W. GIBBS *to* **THE EDITOR OF THE** *SAN FRANCISCO BULLETIN***. n.d. n.p.** A black man from San Francisco defends the abilities of blacks and denounces the Republicans for resorting to racism in order to disprove charges of abolitionism from the Democratic press. 2 July 1858. p.105, c5.

4577 N. TOURGUENEFF *to* **MADAM HENRY G. CHAPMAN. [from the** *National Anti-Slavery Standard***] 1 April 1858. Paris, France.** Discusses the Russian emancipation. 2 July 1858. p.105, c6.

4578 PARKER PILLSBURY *to* **FRIEND GARRISON. 30 June 1858. Boston.** Reports on the Reform Convention in Rutland, Vermont. 2 July 1858. p.106, c5.

4579 LUCY N. COLMAN *to* **FRIEND GARRISON. 21 June 1858. Hancock, N.H.** Reports on anti-slavery meetings in Hancock and its surroundings. 2 July 1858. p.106, c6.

4580 D. J. MANDELL, AND OTHERS *to* **THE THIRTY-FIFTH UNITED STATES CONGRESS. December 1857. Athol (Depot), Ma.** Petition Congress to eliminate slavery so that "history may have no blot to record against the name or vote of any of you." 2 July 1858. p.107, c1.

4581 D. B. S. *to* **MR. EDITOR. 20 June 1858. Northampton.** Rejoices at hearing an abolitionist sermon delivered by an orthodox minister. 2 July 1858. p.107, c2.

4582 CHARLES SUMNER *to* **SIR. 13 June 1856. Boston.** Dismisses efforts to honor him for his "Crime against Kansas" speech. 2 July 1858. p.107, c5.

4583 E. H. H. *to* **W. L. GARRISON. 18 June 1858. Providence.** Defends reform and rebukes conservatism in Rhode Island. 2 July 1858. p.108, c1.

4584 LORD DENMAN *to* **MR. MURRAY. 22 May 1858. Middleton.** States that he is sending an unbroken colt. 2 July 1858. p.108, c4.

4585 A SCOTCH PRESBYTERIAN *to* **THE EDITOR OF THE** *BRITISH STANDARD***. 5 June 1858. Edinburgh.** Expresses his views on an article in the *British Standard* which discusses the American religious revival and its relation to American slavery. 9 July 1858. p.109, c3.

4586 JEHIEL CLAFLIN *to* **BROTHER GARRISON. 29 June 1858. West Brookfield, Vt.** Discusses Sallie Holley's anti-slavery work in West Brookfield. 9 July 1858. p.111, c3.

4587 GEO. SENNOTT *to* **THE EDITOR OF THE** *BOSTON COURIER***. n.d. n.p.** Defends the Rutland, Vermont Reform Convention. 9 July 1858. p.111, c3.

4588 GENTLEMAN IN PARIS *to* **A FRIEND OF SENATOR SUMNER. [extract from the** *Boston Advertiser***] 17 June 1858. Paris.** Explains the medical procedure used in Charles Sumner's treatment. 9 July 1858. p.111, c5.

4589 S. URBINO *to* **W. L. GARRISON. n.d. n.p.** Forwards article vindicating Orsini's character. 9 July 1858. p.112, c2.

4590 JAMES CATLIN, M. D. *to* **W. L. GARRISON. 26 June 1858. Sugar Grove, Pa.** Praises the *Liberator* and Sallie Holley. 9 July 1858. p.112, c2.

4591 A. D. R. *to* **THE** *BOSTON JOURNAL*. **[extract] n.d. n.p.** Relates his experiences while touring Kansas Territory. 9 July 1858. p.112, c5.

4592 JOHN MITCHEL *to* **THE** *SOUTHERN CITIZEN*. **[extract] n.d. n.p.** Relates his impressions of the South and Southern society. 16 July 1858. p.113, c4.

4593 JUSTITIA *to* **FRIEND GARRISON. 2 July 1858. Boston.** Reports witnessing the execution of McGee. 16 July 1858. p.116, c2.

4594 SUBSCRIBER *to* **THE** *ATLANTIC MONTHLY* *to* **MESSRS. PHILLIPS, SAMPSON AND CO. n.d. n.p.** Satirically suggests replacing Negro field workers with steam engines. 23 July 1858. p.117, c1.

4595 CHAS. BODMAN *to* **H. WILLIS. 11 June 1858. Cincinnati.** Rebukes Willis for meddling in his affairs. 23 July 1858. p.117, c2.

4596 JOSIAH QUINCY *to* **MESSRS. FOLLETT, FOSTER AND CO. 3 July 1858. Quincy.** Comments on J. R. Giddings' *Exiles of Florida*. 23 July 1858. p.118, c3.

4597 JUSTITIA *to* **W. L. GARRISON. 16 July 1858. Boston.** Comments on the execution of McGee. 23 July 1858. p.119, c1.

4598 E. R. PLACE *to* **W. L. GARRISON. n.d. n.p.** Discusses spiritualism and anti-slavery. 23 July 1858. p.119, c2.

4599 VERULUM *to* **W. L. GARRISON. n.d. n.p.** Proclaims that a consistent spiritualist must be an abolitionist. 23 July 1858. p.119, c3.

4600 n.n. *to* **n.n. [extract] n.d. South Newmarket, N.H.** Discusses a recent meeting of the friends of the anti-slavery cause in Newmarket. 23 July 1858. p.119, c4.

4601 CHARLES K. WHIPPLE *to* **THE PASTOR AND MEMBERS OF THE CROMBIE STREET CHURCH, SALEM. 22 July 1839. Boston.** States his reasons for withdrawing from the church. 23 July 1858. p.120, c2.

4602 CHARLES TAPPAN *to* **THE EDITOR OF THE** *NEW YORK TRIBUNE*. **n.d. Boston, Ma.** Discusses the results of emancipation in the West Indies. 30 July 1858. p.121, c1.

4603 S. B. BLACK *to* **CHARLES TAPPAN. 24 May 1858. At sea.** Details the practical results of emancipation in Jamaica. 30 July 1858. p.121, c1.

4604 FIDELITAS *to* **THE EDITOR OF THE** *NEW YORK TRIBUNE*. **n.d. n.p.** Reassures the editor that plantations are more prosperous under British emancipation than under slavery. 30 July 1858. p.122, c2.

4605 W. H. F. *to* **FRIEND GARRISON. n.d. Cortland, N.Y.** Reports on the National Dress Reform Convention in Cortland. 30 July 1858. p.122, c6.

4606 LUCY N. COLMAN *to* **FRIEND GARRISON. 12 July 1858. Springfield.** Reports on anti-slavery meetings in New Hampshire. 30 July 1858. p.123, c1.

4607 G. W. MADOX *to* **FRIEND GARRISON. 8 July 1858. Ellsworth, Me.** Suggests that someone collect and publish W. Phillips' speeches. 30 July 1858. p.123, c2.

4608 PARIS CORRESPONDENT *to* **THE** *NEW YORK JOURNAL OF COMMERCE.* **[extract] n.d. n.p.** Believes that Mr. Mason is wrong to believe that a denunciation of American slavery will be moderated in France. 30 July 1858. p.123, c3.

4609 D. B. L. *to* **W. L. GARRISON. n.d. n.p.** Defends capital punishment. 30 July 1858. p.124, c2.

4610 H. C. WRIGHT *to* **FRIEND. 18 July 1858. Waukegan, Il.** Reports on the Reform Convention in Vermont and the Lincoln-Douglas senatorial campaign. 30 July 1858. p.124, c3.

4611 JOHN LANDON *to* **THE EDITOR OF THE** *NEW YORK TRIBUNE.* **n.d. n.p.** Defends the character of the recent Reform Convention in Rutland, Vermont. 30 July 1858. p.124, c4.

4612 JOHN LANDON *to* **THE EDITOR OF THE** *RUTLAND* **(VT.)** *HERALD.* **20 July 1858. n.p.** Sends resolution on marriage passed by the recent Reform Convention in Rutland. 30 July 1858. p.124, c5.

4613 E. R. PLACE *to* **W. L. GARRISON. n.d. n.p.** Criticizes the *Banner of Light* for refusing to publish an article by Theodore Parker. 6 August 1858. p.125, c2.

4614 GILES B. STEBBINS *to* **W. L. GARRISON. 26 July 1858. Wellsboro', Tioga County, Pa.** Criticizes Rochester University for its failure to encourage reform sentiments among its students. 6 August 1858. p.125, c3.

4615 F. W. CHESSON *to* **W. L. GARRISON. 23 July 1858. London.** Reports on George Thompson's illness. 6 August 1858. p.127, c6.

4616 JUSTITIA *to* **MR. EDITOR [W. L. GARRISON]. 28 July 1858. Boston.** Argues against capital punishment. 6 August 1858. p.128, c2.

4617 JUSTITIA *to* **MR. EDITOR [W. L. GARRISON]. 30 July 1858. Boston.** Encloses a South Carolinian's eulogy of P. Brooks, including poems entitled "Preston S. Brooks" and "Charles Sumner." 6 August 1858. p.128, c4.

4618 n.n. *to* **THE EDITOR OF THE** *BOSTON COURIER.* **n.d. n.p.** Reports on Mr. Parker's society picnic at Waverly Grove, attended by Senator Hale and Mr. Burlingame. 13 August 1858. p.129, c1.

4619 ANTHONY BURNS *to* **MR. EDITOR. August 1858. n.p.** The famous fugitive slave denies that he was in a Massachusetts penitentiary; gives an account of his recent history. 13 August 1858. p.130, c4.

4620 W. E. *to* **MR. EDITOR. 9 August 1858. Danversport.** Comments on lectures by Messrs. Pillsbury and Foss in Danversport. 13 August 1858. p. 131, c2.

4621 C. H. E. *to* **W. L. GARRISON. 28 July 1858. Rutland, Ma.** Reports on E. H. Heywood's anti-slavery lecture in Rutland. 13 August 1858. p.131, c2.

4622 N. H. WHITING *to* **n.n. [extract] n.d. Marshfield.** Praises E. H. Heywood. 13 August 1858. p. 131, c2.

4623 A LADY *to* **n.n. 26 July 1858. Valley Falls, R. I.** Expresses optimism that slavery will end; discusses Mr. Foss' speech. 13 August 1858. p.131, c2.

4624 FRANCIS HINCKS *to* **CHAS. TAPPAN. 9 January 1858. Barbadoes.** The governor of Barbadoes refutes the claim that slave labor is less costly than free labor. 20 August 1858. p.133, c2.

4625 A. F. RAYMOND *to* **W. L. GARRISON. 4 August 1858. Springfield, Ma.** Comments on the West Indies Emancipation celebration in Springfield. 20 August 1858. p.135, c1.

4626 W. W. B. *to* **W. L. GARRISON. 10 August 1858. Philadelphia.** Comments on the West Indies Emancipation celebration at Christiana. 20 August 1858. p.135, c1.

4627 SALLIE HOLLEY *to* **S. H. MAY, JR.** [extract] **7 August 1858. St. Johnsbury, Vt.** Reports on anti-slavery activities in St. Johnsbury. 20 August 1858. p.135, c2.

4628 W. C. M. *to* **THE EDITOR OF THE** *LIBERATOR.* **17 August 1858. Worcester.** Reports on commencement exercises at Amherst. 20 August 1858. p.135, c3.

4629 E. W. TWING *to* **FRIEND GARRISON. 11 July 1858. Springfield.** Expresses surprise that the *Springfield Republican* appears to be a convert to Garrisonianism. 20 August 1858. p.135, c3.

4630 D. B. L. *to* **MR. GARRISON. 9 August 1859 [1858]. n.p.** Defends capital punishment. 20 August 1858. p.136, c2.

4631 JUSTITIA *to* **MR. EDITOR. 12 August 1858. Boston.** Argues against capital punishment. 20 August 1858. p.136, c3.

4632 W. ROBSON *to* **W. L. GARRISON. 25 July 1858. Cincinnati.** The postmaster at Warrington, England states that he is depressed by slavery's blighting effects. 20 August 1858. p.136, c4.

4633 AN INDIAN OFFICIAL *to* **THE** *NEW YORK TRIBUNE.* **20 May 1858. Mussoorie.** Decries English ignorance of India. 20 August 1858. p.136, c5.

4634 H. C. WRIGHT *to* **GARRISON. n.d. n.p.** Calls on Massachusetts to affirm every man's self-evident right to citizenship. 27 August 1858. p.183 [138], c4.

4635 JUSTITIA *to* **MR. EDITOR. 12 August 1858. Boston.** Relates conversation with an officer of the Southern Aid Society. 27 August 1858. p.183 [138], c4.

4636 C. H. E. *to* **MR. GARRISON. n.d. n.p.** Reports on Pillsbury's lectures at Rutland, Massachusetts. 27 August 1858. p.183 [138], c5.

4637 H. C. WRIGHT *to* **GARRISON. 13 August 1858. Mountain House.** Reports from the Catskills; contends that use of tobacco is inconsistent with true spirituality. 27 August 1858. p.140, c4.

4638 ERNESTINE L. ROSE *to* **THE EDITOR OF THE** *NEW YORK TIMES.* **29 June 1858. New York.** Denies that she advocates free love. 27 August 1858. p.140, c5.

4639 R. PLUMER *to* **FRIEND GARRISON. 25 August 1858. Newburyport.** Reports on Parker Pillsbury's radical remarks at the Essex County AS meeting. 3 September 1858. p.143, c2.

4640 H. G. GARCELON *to* **W. L. GARRISON. 28 August 1858. Lewiston, Me.** Dispels rumor that Anthony Burns is in prison; reports on Burns' travels in New England with an exhibition showing the realities of slavery. 3 September 1858. p.143, c2.

4641 T. W. H. *to* **W. L. GARRISON. 27 August 1858. Worcester.** Praises the Rutland Convention for its vigor and moral dignity. 3 September 1858. p.143, c3.

4642 JUSTITIA *to* **MR. EDITOR [W. L. GARRISON]. 12 August 1858. Boston.** Replies to *Liberator* correspondent D. B. L.'s criticism of his opinion on the execution of McGee. 3 September 1858. p.144, c3.

4643 EDWARD PALMER *to* **GERRIT SMITH. n.d. Perth Amboy, N. J.** Thanks Smith for his sermon on unjust economic disparity between rich and poor. 3 September 1858. p.144, c5.

4644 H. G. *to* **MESSRS. EDITORS OF THE *NATICK OBSERVER*. n.d. n.p.** Charges that Parker Pillsbury's mode of reform is quackery because it is not based on Christian principle. 10 September 1858. p.145, c1.

4645 EDWARD MATHEWS *to* **THE EDITOR OF THE *LONDON STATESMAN*. 9 August 1858. Oxford.** Gives an account of Rev. John Newton's discussion of the slave trade. 10 September 1858. p.145, c5.

4646 SALLIE HOLLEY *to* **MRS. FOSTER. 3 September 1858. Orleans County.** Describes hospitality encountered during a three-month lecture tour in Vermont. 10 September 1858. p.147, c2.

4647 F. S. BLISS *to* **FRIEND GARRISON. 6 September 1858. Barre, Vt.** Forwards resolution of the testimony of the Universalists. 10 September 1858. p.147, c2.

4648 W. ROBSON *to* **SIR. 29 August 1858. Boston.** Expresses his thoughts as a foreigner on the church in the United States. 10 September 1858. p.148, c2.

4649 HENRY C. WRIGHT *to* **GARRISON. n.d. n.p.** Compares social and moral conditions in slave states with those in non-slave states. 10 September 1858. p.148, c3.

4650 GEO. T. EVE *to* **THE EDITOR. [from the *New Bedford Mercury*] 24 August 1858. New Bedford.** Explains how he manumitted a woman and her three children in spite of his wealthy father's disapproval. 10 September 1858. p.148, c4.

4651 HENRY C. WRIGHT *to* **W. L. GARRISON. 20 August 1858. Quebec, Lower Canada.** Promotes Canada as an asylum for the slave; describes scenery. 17 September 1858. p.149, c4.

4652 J. A. H. *to* **THE EDITOR OF THE *ANTI-SLAVERY BUGLE*. n.d. n.p.** Describes his visit to the tomb of George Washington. 17 September 1858. p.150, c2.

4653 CHARLES SUMNER *to* **MORSE. 17 August 1858. Paris.** Regrets that he is unable to attend the banquet in honor of Morse's great discovery. 17 September 1858. p.150, c5.

4654 PARKER PILLSBURY *to* **W. L. GARRISON. 13 September. Utica, N.Y.** Reports on spiritualism at the Utica Philanthropic Convention; encloses resolutions. 17 September 1858. p.150, c6.

4655 WILLIAM C. NELL *to* **FRIEND GARRISON. 6 September 1858. Southfield, Mi.** Expresses indignation of the Colored Methodist Conference over the kidnapping of two colored men in Cincinnati. 17 September 1858. p.151, c1.

4656 H. *to* **THE EDITOR [W. L. GARRISON]. n.d. n.p.** Claims that the Democratic Party is pro-slavery. 17 September 1858. p.151, c2.

4657 B. *to* **THE EDITOR [W. L. GARRISON]. 30 August 1858. Kingston.** Discusses the paradox of capital punishment. 17 September 1858. p.151, c2.

4658 SHAHMAH *to* **BROTHER HASSAN. [extract from** *Shahmah in Pursuit of Freedom***] 20 February. At sea.** A fictional character gives a graphic delineation of slavery in the South. 24 September 1858. p.153, c2.

4659 ROBERT MORRIS *to* **MR. MASON. 6 September 1858. Chelsea.** Explains how he was forced to abandon his intention to purchase a mansion because of color prejudice. 24 September 1858. p.153, c6.

4660 W. ROBSON *to* **SIR. 16 September 1858. Boston.** Explains that he has not visited the South because the heinousness of slavery is already evident to him. 24 September 1858. p.154, c3.

4661 M. *to* **W. L. GARRISON. 19 September 1858. Newton Corner.** Feels that the Republican Party has made no progress. 24 September 1858. p.154, c5.

4662 L. S. *to* **FRIEND GARRISON. n.d. Richfield, N.Y.** Gives an account of dialogue between Rev. Mr. E. and a Methodist sister on the American Tract Society. 24 September 1858. p.154, c6.

4663 C. K. W. *to* **SIR. 2 September 1858. Boston.** Thanks a Trinitarian for his letter of remonstrance and attempts to define the limitations of their disagreement. 24 September 1858. p.156, c2.

4664 HENRY C. WRIGHT *to* **GARRISON. 8 September 1858. Rochester Court House.** Questions Gerrit Smith on his views of government and his qualifications for the office of governor. 24 September 1858. p.156, c5.

4665 W. ROBSON *to* **THE EDITOR OF THE** *NEW YORK TRIBUNE.* **28 August 1858. n.p.** An Englishman gives his impressions of the postal service and education in America. 1 October 1858. p.158, c4.

4666 PARKER PILLSBURY *to* **FRIEND GARRISON. 25 September 1858. Boston.** Reports on disappointing turnout at the Utica Philanthropic Convention. 1 October 1858. p.158, c4.

4667 A. HOGEBOOM *to* **CHARLES L. REMOND. 24 September 1858. Shed's Corners, N.Y.** Criticizes Remond's positions at Convention of Colored Citizens on the anniversary of the West Indies Emancipation; charges that they alienate and exclude whites from the anti-slavery cause. 1 October 1858. p.158, c5.

4668 EQUAL RIGHTS *to* **THE EDITOR. [from the** *Chelsea Telegraph***] 10 September 1858. Chelsea.** Expresses anger upon learning that because of his dark complexion, Robert Morris was prevented from purchasing a house in Chelsea. 1 October 1858. p.159, c1.

4669 A. PRYNE *to* **THE EDITOR. [from the** *New York Tribune***] 18 September 1858. New York.** Reports that Parson Brownlow returned to Tennessee after declining to debate the slavery question in the Northern states. 1 October 1858. p.159, c1.

4670 WILLIE LIGHTHEART *to* **n.n. [extract from the** *Spartanburg Spartan***] n.d. n.p.** Laments the fate of poor Negroes shipped back to Africa and "left upon its desolate coast to perish." 8 October 1858. p.161, c2.

4671 AMATEUR *to* **THE EDITOR. [from the** *Vermont Watchman***] n.d. n.p.** Criticizes Garrison for devoting himself to a single idea. 8 October 1858. p.162, c1.

4672 A. *to* **THE EDITOR. [from the** *Vermont Watchman*] **n.d. n.p.** Derides Amateur for his "assumptions, sneers, and black-guardism"; supports the efforts of W. L. Garrison. 8 October 1858. p.162, c1.

4673 J. A. H. *to* **FRIEND GARRISON. 23 September 1858. Springfield.** Tells of the Springfield muster which was staged to promote the military. 8 October 1858. p.163, c1.

4674 HENRY C. WRIGHT *to* **W. L. GARRISON. 29 September 1858. Utica.** Relates his excitement upon hearing William Wells Brown recite from his own drama about the effects of labor on the family relations of masters and slaves. 8 October 1858. p.163, c2.

4675 H. *to* **EDITOR. 27 September 1858. Boston.** States that the Republican Party is the only progressive political party. 8 October 1858. p.163, c2.

4676 DANIEL S. WHITNEY *to* **n.n. [extract] 20 September 1858. Delhi, Ia.** States that Democrats take an anti-slavery stand while Republicans are noncommital. 8 October 1858. p.163, c3.

4677 J. A. H. *to* **FRIEND GARRISON. 3 October 1858. Worcester.** Censures the American Missionary Association for its hypocritical piety and indecisive stance toward slavery. 15 October 1858. p.165, c2.

4678 WILLIAM HAYWARD *to* **FRIEND W. L. GARRISON. 1 October 1858. Silver Lake, Kosciusko County, In.** Gives an account of the lectures by Sojourner Truth in Indiana. 15 October 1858. p.165, c3.

4679 A. *to* **THE EDITOR. [from the** *Vermont Watchman*] **6 September 1858. n.p.** Defends Garrison against criticism from Amateur, a Vermont correspondent. 15 October 1858. p.165, c4.

4680 CHARLES TAPPAN *to* **n.n. [from the** *National Era*] **1 January 1858. Barbadoes, West Indies.** Poses questions concerning emancipation in the British West Indies. 15 October 1858. p.165, c5.

4681 REV. J. Y. EDGHILL *to* **SIR. 27 January 1858. Moravian Missionary.** Acknowledges emancipation as a blessing. 15 October 1858. p.165, c5.

4682 SAMUEL WOLCOTT *to* **REV. DR. HALLOCK. 14 June 1858. Providence.** Requests the secretary of the American Tract Society to publish a tract against oppression. 15 October 1858. p.166, c2.

4683 WM. A. HALLOCK *to* **SAMUEL WOLCOTT. 14 September 1858. New York.** Refuses to publish an anti-slavery biblical tract because it does not "promise usefulness." 15 October 1858. p.166, c3.

4684 J. P. HARRIMAN *to* **n.n. [extract] 3 October 1858. Davies County, Il.** Reports on the large number of abolitionists in Davies County, Illinois. 15 October 1858. p.167, c1.

4685 D. S. GRANDIN *to* **FRIEND GARRISON. 30 September 1858. Bethel, Me.** Observes that there are few dedicated abolitionists in Maine. 15 October 1858. p.167, c2.

4686 AARON M. POWELL *to* **FRIEND WALLCUT. 8 October 1858. Rochester, N.Y.** Reports on shameful riot in Rochester where F. Douglass organized a protest against capital punishment. 15 October 1858. p.167, c2.

4687 H. ABRAM *to* **THE EDITOR OF THE** *EVENING POST.* **19 September 1858. Richmond, Va.** Reaffirms his intention to run as anti-slavery candidate for governor of Virginia. 15 October 1858. p.167, c3.

4688 LUCY N. COLMAN *to* **MR. GARRISON. 9 October 1858. Rochester.** Gives account of a riot in Rochester at a meeting to protest capital punishment. 22 October 1858. p. 169, c3.

4689 A METHODIST *to* **THE EDITOR OF THE** *NEW YORK TRIBUNE.* **n.d. n.p.** Forwards article from the *Philadelphia Evening Bulletin* on a colored preacher put into a Maryland penitentiary for owning a copy of *Uncle Tom's Cabin.* 22 October 1858. p.169, c6.

4690 W. P. *to* **FRIEND. n.d. n.p.** Explains various abolitionist views on the nature of the Constitution regarding slavery. 22 October 1858. p.170, c1.

4691 W. L. GARRISON *to* **READERS. 15 October 1858. Salem, Oh.** Describes his tour through Ohio and Pennsylvania. 22 October 1858. p.170, c2.

4692 H. C. WRIGHT *to* **GARRISON. 10 October 1858. Laona, N.Y.** Discusses a possible convention on issues of practical reform. 22 October 1858. p.172, c2.

4693 J. R. GIDDINGS *to* **GOV. THOMAS CORWIN. 13 October 1858. Jefferson, Oh.** Cautions Corwin on the danger of admitting Cuba as a slave state. 29 October 1858. p.173, c5.

4694 W. L. G[ARRISON] *to* **READERS. 25 October 1858. Syracuse.** Reports on the hopeful spirit of the Western AS meeting. 29 October 1858. p.174, c5.

4695 SALLIE HOLLEY *to* **MR. GARRISON. 6 October 1858. Greensboro, Vt.** Describes hospitality received in Barton, Albany, Troy, and Charleston. 29 October 1858. p.175, c2.

4696 SARAH CLAY *to* **MR. GARRISON. 27 October 1858. Lowell.** Praises Sarah P. Remond for her public speaking skills. 5 November 1858. p.177, c2.

4697 ANDREW T. FOSS *to* **SAMUEL MAY. 19 October 1858. Lyons, Mi.** Encloses summary of his itinerary; foresees dismal future for abolitionism in Michigan. 5 November 1858. p.177, c2.

4698 J. E. E. *to* **MR. GARRISON. 23 October 1858. Rutland, Ma.** Gives an account of the anti-slavery lecture by E. H. Heywood. 5 November 1858. p.177, c2.

4699 D. S. GRANDIN *to* **W. L. GARRISON. 25 October 1858. Bethel, Me.** Reports his suspicion that John Randolph, "a light mulatto about thirty years old," has stolen money from anti-slavery contributions. 5 November 1858. p.177, c2.

4700 F. W. CHESSON *to* **W. L. GARRISON. 14 October 1858. London.** Comments on George Thompson's improved health. 5 November 1858. p.178, c5.

4701 A. F. R. *to* **GARRISON. 11 October 1858. Springfield.** Criticizes Col. Foot for his role in the Springfield muster. 5 November 1858. p.178, c5.

4702 DR. A. BROOKE *to* **W. L. GARRISON. 24 October 1858. Marlboro, Oh.** Laments present internecine quarrels between abolitionists and the Republican Party. 5 November 1858. p.179, c1.

4703 A. T. FOSS *to* **FRIEND GARRISON. 25 October 1858. Waukegan, Il.** Reports on anti-Catholic lectures delivered at Pontiac and Lyons, Iowa. 5 November 1858. p.179, c2.

4704 C. K. W. *to* **MESSRS. EDITORS. [extract from the** *Puritan***] n.d. n.p.** Discusses Calvin's belief that the Sabbath was a Jewish institution. 5 November 1858. p.180, c2.

4705 HON. R. C. WINTHROP *to* **COL. I. H. WRIGHT AND OTHERS. [extract] 30 October 1858. n.p.** Believes that anti-slavery agitation is the major source of trouble in the United States. 12 November 1858. p.181, c1.

4706 B. F. HALLETT *to* **GENTLEMEN. 6 August 1858. Boston, Ma.** Praises James L. Orr for consistently advocating cooperation between Southern and Northern Democrats. 12 November 1858. p.181, c1.

4707 REPUBLICAN *to* **MR. EARLE. n.d. n.p.** Denies that Garrison started the Republican Party. 12 November 1858. p.181, c2.

4708 JAMES HAUGHTON *to* **THE EDITOR. [from the** *Dublin Nation***] 12 October 1858. n.p.** Reproaches his fellow Irishmen in America for sustaining the shameful system of slavery. 12 November 1858. p.181, c4.

4709 P. BEVERLY RANDOLPH *to* **W. L. GARRISON. 8 November 1858. Brooklyn, N.Y.** Defends himself against D. Grandin's accusation of thievery; resents slanders "being heaped on my devoted head by newspaperdom, headed by the *Liberator*." 12 November 1858. p.183, c1.

4710 F. H. D. *to* **MR. GARRISON. 6 November 1858. Leominster.** Discusses Parker Pillsbury's lecture on the French Revolution. 12 November 1858. p.183, c1.

4711 PARKER PILLSBURY *to* **W. L. GARRISON. 8 November 1858. Dover, N.H.** Reports on speeches by Charles and Sarah Remond at a successful anti-slavery meeting in Dover. 12 November 1858. p.183, c2.

4712 HENRY C. WRIGHT *to* **GARRISON. 28 October 1858. West Winfield, N.Y.** Describes the split between Democrats and Republicans in New York; condemns Gerrit Smith's leadership as autocratic. 12 November 1858. p.184, c2.

4713 WILLIAM C. NELL *to* **FRIEND GARRISON. 24 September 1858. Detroit.** Reports on the conclusion of an anti-slavery tour given in the West with Miss Frances Ellen Watkins. 12 November 1858. p.184, c3.

4714 H. MATTISON *to* **THE EDITOR OF THE** *NEW YORK TRIBUNE***. n.d. n.p.** Corrects "A Methodist" on facts relating to the imprisoned colored minister, Samuel Green. 19 November 1858. p.185, c5.

4715 JAMES L. BOWERS *to* **THE EDITORS OF THE** *NORTH AMERICAN***. 20 October 1858. Philadelphia.** Describes his experience of being tarred and feathered in Maryland. 19 November 1858. p.185, c6.

4716 SARAH PARKER REMOND *to* **FRIEND. [from the** *London Anti-Slavery Advocate***] 18 September 1858. Salem, Ma.** Affirms her intention to be in London before the winter. 19 November 1858. p.186, c1.

4717 BRETHREN IN JESUS CHRIST *to* **BRETHREN. n.d. n.p.** Confirms belief that Christians should be anti-slavery. 19 November 1858. p.186, c1.

4718 WM. H. PULLEN *to* **THE EDITOR OF THE** *ANTI-SLAVERY ADVOCATE***. 9 October 1858. Elmwood, Leeds.** Forwards copy of "Christian Remonstrance" from the Leeds Young Men's AS and encloses resolutions adopted at their meeting. 19 November 1858. p.186, c1.

4719 J. H., JR. *to* **S. MAY, JR. n.d. n.p.** Reports on the success of a petition to prohibit the return of a fugitive slave from Vermont. 19 November 1858. p.187, c1.

4720 D. S. GRANDIN *to* **W. L. GARRISON. 15 November 1858. Bethel, Me.** States that P. Beverly Randolph's defense was self-incriminating; gives account of his meeting with Wm. Wells Brown. 19 November 1858. p.187, c1.

4721 A MEMBER OF SYNOD *to* **MESSRS. EDITORS. [from the** *New York Independent***] n.d. n.p.** Traces history of an unjust resolution sustaining the action of the secretaries of the Tract Society. 26 November 1858. p.190, c2.

4722 J. B. *to* **FRIEND GARRISON. 15 November 1858. Ilion, Herkimer County, N.Y.** Praises the *Liberator* and Henry C. Wright for doing battle against the combined powers of bigotry and oppression. 26 November 1858. p.190, c6.

4723 READER *to* **MR. EDITOR. [from the** *New York Life Illustrated***] n.d. n.p.** Warns of the danger of educating women; expresses fear that "as woman becomes better educated, she is so much the more fascinating." 26 November 1858. p.192, c5.

4724 GEORGE B. CHEEVER *to* **THE EDITORS OF THE** *EVANGELIST.* **n.d. n.p.** Defends himself against charge of misrepresentation made by a correspondent of the *Evangelist.* 3 December 1858. p.193, c4.

4725 N. R. JOHNSTON *to* **n.n. 25 November 1858. Topsham, Vt.** Declares that the Fugitive Slave Law shall never be repealed in Vermont. 3 December 1858. p.194, c6.

4726 PARKER PILLSBURY *to* **n.n. 29 November 1858. Salem.** Reports on the success of meetings at Hingham and East Abington. 3 December 1858. p.195, c1.

4727 D. S. GRANDIN *to* **MR. GARRISON. 28 November 1858. New Gloucester.** States that P. Beverly Randolph was arrested because he was thought to be someone else. 3 December 1858. p.195, c1.

4728 STEPHEN BREWER *to* **W. L. GARRISON. 19 November 1858. Cortland, N.Y.** Defends the position of American Board of Commissioners for Foreign Missions regarding slavery. 3 December 1858. p.196, c2.

4729 LUCY N. COLMAN *to* **W. L. GARRISON. 29 October 1858. Rochester, N.Y.** Denounces the execution of Ira Stout. 3 December 1858. p.196, c3.

4730 PUBLICOLA *to* **THE EDITOR OF THE** *LONDON DISPATCH.* **17 October. n.p.** Refutes an article published in the *National Review* which denies women the right to follow a traditionally masculine career. 3 December 1858. p.196, c4.

4731 J. McM. SIMPSON *to* **FRIEND BAILEY. [from the** *Free South***] 3 November 1858. Zanesville, Oh.** Condemns arrival of slave catchers in the free state of Ohio. 10 December 1858. p.197, c4.

4732 M. W. C. *to* **W. L. GARRISON. n.d. n.p.** Announces date and place of the Financial Anti-Slavery Festival. 10 December 1858. p.198, c2.

4733 J. H., JR. *to* **GARRISON. 5 December 1858. West Randolph, Vt.** Quotes text of a law forbidding slave-hunting in Vermont. 10 December 1858. p.199, c2.

4734 D. S. GRANDIN *to* **W. L. GARRISON. 3 December 1858. Bethel, Me.** Clears P. Beverly Randolph of suspicion of being dishonest. 10 December 1858. p.199, c2.

4735 A. H. WILLIS *to* **JOHN DOBBIN. 1 November 1858. Ipava, Il.** Denounces the Church and the Constitution for "standing on the side of the oppressor." 10 December 1858. p.200, c2.

4736 FRANCIS JACKSON *to* **REVEREND SIR. 17 December 1857. Boston.** Calls for an end to slave-hunting in the Old Bay State. 17 December 1858. p.202, c3.

4737 M. W. C. *to* **THE EDITOR OF THE** *LIBERATOR* **[W. L. GARRISON]. n.d. n.p.** Announces date and place of the Financial Anti-Slavery Festival. 17 December 1858. p.202, c3.

4738 A. T. FOSS *to* **SAMUEL MAY, JR. 30 November 1858. Sterling, Whiteside County, Il.** Complains of difficulties encountered while lecturing in the West. 17 December 1858. p.203, c2.

4739 n.n. *to* **n.n. 13 December 1858. Washington.** Reports on the purchase of the yacht *Wanderer* and the re-opening of the slave trade in South Carolina. 24 December 1858. p.205, c4.

4740 C. B. *to* **MR. GARRISON. 16 December 1858. Montague.** Gives an account of Sallie Holley's lectures in Montague. 24 December 1858. p.206, c6.

4741 H. STEVENS *to* **MR. GARRISON. 15 December 1858. Greenfield.** Praises Sallie Holley as "a noble woman engaged in a noble cause." 24 December 1858. p.206, c6.

4742 D. S. WHITNEY *to* **SAMUEL MAY. 12 November 1858. Edinburg, Oh.** Reports on anti-slavery meetings at Quasqueton, Iowa; Delhi, Delaware County; Galena; and Beloit. 24 December 1858. p.206, c6.

4743 W. E. *to* **THE EDITOR [W. L. GARRISON]. 20 December 1858. Danversport.** Praises D. S. Whitney's poem. 24 December 1858. p.206, c6.

4744 WILLIAM C. NELL *to* **W. L. GARRISON. n.d. n.p.** Gives account of his travels in Canada West. 24 December 1858. p.207, c1.

4745 HARRIOT K. HUNT *to* **n.n. 6 December 1858. Boston.** Condemns taxation of women without representation. 24 December 1858. p.207, c4.

4746 FRANCIS JACKSON *to* **C. LENOX REMOND. 15 December 1858. Boston.** Declares that "hunting of fugitive slaves must cease." 31 December 1858. p.211, c1.

4747 GERRIT SMITH *to* **P. B. RANDOLPH. 29 August 1858. Peterboro.** Praises Randolph's discourses on intemperance. 31 December 1858. p.211, c1.

4748 M. W. C. *to* **W. L. GARRISON. n.d. n.p.** Answers queries about the Financial Anti-Slavery Festival. 31 December 1858. p.211, c5.

4749 ELIZABETH B. CHASE *to* **ABBY WHEATON CHASE. 26 November 1858. Valley Falls.** Declines invitation to manage the Mount Vernon Association. 31 December 1858. p.212, c2.

4750 ELIZABETH CADY STANTON *to* **MARY MORRIS HAMILTON. 27 August 1858. Seneca Falls.** Feels that the money used to purchase Mount Vernon should have been used to educate daughters of the Republic. 31 December 1858. p.212, c2.

4751 L. L. RUGGLES *to* **PASTOR AND MEMBERS OF THE FIRST CONGREGA-TIONAL OR ORTHODOX CHURCH, UPTON, MASS. 22 December 1858. Toledo, Oh.** Explains reasons for his withdrawal from their "pro-slavery" church. 31 December 1858. p.212, c3.

[1859]

4752 PARKER PILLSBURY *to* **THE EDITOR [W. L. GARRISON]. 2 January 1859. Manchester, Ma.** Feels that P. Beverly Randolph is a colored man who "nearly proves the often heard assertion that the colored race is fit only for slavery." 7 January 1859. p.3, c1.

4753 SAMUEL J. MAY. *to* **THE EDITOR [W. L. GARRISON]. 10 December 1858. Syracuse, N.Y.** Forwards circular declaring Wm. Brown to be an impostor; states that Professor Brown is doing the underground railroad much harm. 7 January 1859. p.3, c2.

4754 J. M. H. *to* **THE EDITOR [W. L. GARRISON]. 21 December 1858. Manchester, N.H.** Comments on grog-selling mayor of Manchester; notes the absence of temperance and presence of colorphobia; praises anti-slavery lectures of Mr. Foss. 7 January 1859. p.4, c2.

4755 J. S. LINCOLN *to* **FRIEND GARRISON. 28 December 1858. Rowe.** Compliments speeches of C. C. Burleigh and Sallie Holley. 7 January 1859. p.4, c2.

4756 A. HOGEBOOM *to* **FRIEND GARRISON. 23 December 1858. Shed's Corners, Madison County, N.Y.** Demands that Henry C. Wright either retract or prove his assertion about Gerrit Smith. 7 January 1859. p.4, c2.

4757 COL. JOHN H. SAVAGE *to* **HON. JAMES P. HAMBLETON. [extract] n.d. n.p.** Claims that "a Negro is never so free as when he is the servant of a white man." 14 January 1859. p.5, c2.

4758 n.n. *to* **THE EDITOR OF THE** *NEW YORK TRIBUNE.* **n.d. n.p.** Lists the names of various eminent people connected with slavery. 14 January 1859. p.5, c3.

4759 GEO. TRASK *to* **SIR. 1859. Fitchburg, Ma.** Discusses the "history and poetry" of tobacco. 14 January 1859. p.6, c5.

4760 E. H. H. *to* **W. L. GARRISON. 5 January 1859. Hubbardston.** Reports on his abolition lectures in New Jersey. 14 January 1859. p.6, c6.

4761 H. C. WRIGHT *to* **A. HOGEBOOM. 7 January 1959. Boston.** Defends his criticism of Gerrit Smith. 14 January 1859. p.7, c2.

4762 M. W. C. *to* **THE EDITOR [W. L. GARRISON]. n.d n.p.** Answers queries concerning the Financial Anti-Slavery Festival. 14 January 1859. p.7, c5.

4763 n.n. *to* **SIR. n.d. n.p.** Believes that anyone who steals or sells a man should be put to death. 14 January 1859. p.8, c2.

4764 n.n. *to* **n.n. n.d. n.p.** Proclaims that the slaveholder is God's rival. 14 January 1859. p.8, c2.

4765 n.n. *to* **THE EDITOR [W. L. GARRISON]. January 1859. Vermont.** Stresses the benefits of contact with a wise and aged man; encloses extracts from several other letters. 14 January 1859. p.8, c2.

4766 n.n. *to* **n.n. n.d. n.p.** Declares that God is the slave's avenger. 14 January 1859. p.8, c2.

4767 n.n. *to* **n.n. n.d. n.p.** Describes the duties of Christian ministers. 14 January 1859. p.8, c2.

4768 n.n. *to* **THE EDITOR OF THE** *NEW YORK TRIBUNE.* **n.d. n.p.** Comments on the plethora of Doctors of Divinity. 14 January 1859. p.8, c4.

4769 WILLIAM GOODELL *to* **THE EDITOR OF THE** *NEW YORK TIMES.* **19 November 1858. New York.** Remarks on the low crime rate of the black population. 21 January 1859. p.9, c5.

4770 A. F. R. *to* **W. L. GARRISON. 15 January 1859. Springfield, Ma.** Gives an account of George D. Prentice's lecture. 21 January 1859. p.11, c3.

4771 HENRY C. WRIGHT *to* **W. L. GARRISON. 9 January 1859. West Duxbury.** Queries whether Massachusetts will allow fugitive slaves to be kidnapped. 21 January 1859. p.12, c2.

4772 AMOS GILBERT *to* **W. L. GARRISON. 3 January 1859. Eden, Lancaster County, Pa.** Supports Essex County AS resolutions; compliments letters of Elizabeth B. Chase and Elizabeth Cady Stanton. 21 January 1859. p.12, c2.

4773 SPECTATOR *to* **THE EDITOR OF THE** *NEW YORK TRIBUNE.* **11 January 1859. New York.** Defends Dr. Cheever and the Church of the Puritans. 21 January 1859. p.12, c5.

4774 J. H. HAMMOND *to* **PETER HARVEY. 22 December 1858. Washington.** Regrets that he is unable to attend dinner in honor of Webster's birthday. 28 January 1859. p.13, c2.

4775 JEFFERSON DAVIS *to* **PETER HARVEY. 2 January 1859. Washington, D.C.** Regrets he is unable to attend dinner in celebration of Webster's birthday. 28 January 1859. p.13, c2.

4776 BENJ. S. JONES *to* **F. M. WRIGHT. 15 January 1859. Salem, Oh.** States that he was taxed last spring for property he does not own. 28 January 1859. p.13, c5.

4777 JOSHUA HUDSON *to* **MR. FRANCIS JACKSON. n.d. n.p.** Prays that success may crown Jackson's efforts on behalf of justice and freedom. 28 January 1859. p.14, c5.

4778 PHILIP SCARBOROUGH *to* **FRIEND W. L. GARRISON. 23 January 1859. Brooklyn, Ct.** Expresses his support of the anti-slavery cause. 28 January 1859. p.14, c5.

4779 C. C. BURLEIGH *to* **W. L. GARRISON. n.d. n.p.** Mourns the death of William D. Cochran. 28 January 1859. p.14, c6.

4780 J. A. H. *to* **W. L. GARRISON. n.d. n.p.** Expresses concern for Mrs. Scranton's health. 28 January 1859. p.15, c1.

4781 R. PLUMER *to* **W. L. GARRISON. 24 January 1859. Newburyport.** Reports favorably on the lectures of Henry C. Wright. 28 January 1859. p.15, c1.

4782 n.n. *to* **W. L. GARRISON. 10 January 1859. St. Louis, Mo.** Asserts that considerable abolitionist sentiment exists in Missouri. 28 January 1859. p.15, c1.

4783 ANDREW T. FOSS *to* **SAMUEL MAY. 12 January 1859. Nora, Joe Davis County, Il.** Gives account of successful abolitionist meetings in Palmyra, New Genesee, and Unionville. 28 January 1859. p.15, c2.

4784 H. E. PECK *to* **THE EDITOR OF THE** *STATE JOURNAL.* **18 January 1859. Oberlin.** Recounts story of a slave rescue in Ohio. 28 January 1859. p.15, c3.

4785 S. B. SLACK *to* **THE EDITOR OF THE** *NEW YORK TRIBUNE.* **12 January 1859. New York.** Refutes allegation that women in Jamaica are forced to fetch coal for American steamers. 28 January 1859. p.15, c4.

4786 G. W. S. *to* **W. L. GARRISON. 17 January 1859. Milford.** Gives account of a lecture by Adin Ballou on the inspiration of the Bible. 28 January 1859. p.16, c2.

4787 E. W. TWING *to* **W. L. GARRISON. 17 January 1859. Springfield.** Condemns a spiritual paper for its refusal to "say anything about slavery." 28 January 1859. p.16, c3.

4788 S. MITCHELL *to* **THE EDITOR OF THE** *LIBERATOR* **[W. L. GARRISON]. 19 January 1859. Cornville, Me.** States that although he subscribes to the spiritual papers, he does not intend to uphold any wrong. 28 January 1859. p.16, c3.

4789 JOSIAH BREWER *to* **ROBERT F. WALLCUT. 28 January 1859. Stockbridge, Ma.** Discusses problems of collecting signatures for an anti-slavery petition. 4 February 1859. p.19, c5.

4790 B. PETTINGILL *to* **SON. 21 January 1859. Salisbury, N.H.** Asks whether the United States shall be governed by slave power. 4 February 1859. p.20, c2.

4791 J. *to* **MR. EDITOR [W. L. GARRISON]. n.d. n.p.** Favors the non-extension of slavery. 4 February 1859. p.20, c2.

4792 F. W. CHESSON *to* **THE EDITOR OF THE** *ANTI-SLAVERY REPORTER.* **15 December 1858. London.** Describes American intrigues in St. Domingo. 4 February 1859. p.20, c3.

4793 W. ROBSON *to* **SIR. 11 January 1850. Warrington, England.** Announces the safe arrival in England of Rev. S. J. May and Sarah P. Remond. 11 February 1859. p.22, c6.

4794 J.M. ALDRICH *to* **W. L. GARRISON. 5 February 1859. Fall River.** Reports on C. C. Burleigh's speech in Fall River. 11 February 1859. p.23, c1.

4795 THEODORE PARKER *to* **MUCH VALUED FRIENDS. 27 January 1859. Exeter Place.** Thanks friends for listening to him and bids them farewell upon his departure to the West Indies. 11 February 1859. p.23, c4.

4796 M. D. CONWAY *to* **n.n. 21 January. Cincinnati.** Beseeches friends of freedom to keep their "golden wedding" with the cause of abolitionism. 18 February 1859. p.26, c4.

4797 WILLIAM P. POWELL *to* **THE PRESIDENT OF THE NATIONAL ANTI-SLAVERY SUBSCRIPTION ANNIVERSARY, BOSTON, MASSACHUSETTS. 10 December 1858. Liverpool.** Encourages fellow abolitionists to continue fighting. 18 February 1859. p.26, c4.

4798 S. J. MAY *to* **MRS. CHAPMAN. 29 December 1858. Boston.** Regrets he is unable to attend the Financial Anti-Slavery Festival. 18 February 1859. p.26, c5.

4799 CHARLES W. ELLIOTT *to* **MRS. FOLLEN. 21 January 1859. New York.** Asserts that God is stronger than the devil. 18 February 1859. p.26, c5.

4800 H. R. HELPER *to* **n.n. 24 January 1859. New York.** Acknowledges receipt of contributions to the Massachusetts AS. 18 February 1859. p.26, c5.

4801 STEPHEN BARKER *to* **MADAM. 26 January 1859. Leominister.** Forwards contribution of twenty dollars to the Massachusetts AS. 18 February 1859. p.26, c5.

4802 MARY ANN B. BLAIR *to* **MRS. CHAPMAN. n.d. n.p.** Forwards contribution of twelve dollars to the Massachusetts AS. 18 February 1859. p.26, c5.

4803 JOHN S. ROCK *to* **FRIEND GARRISON. 10 February 1859. 34 Garden Street, Boston.** Discusses his health after treatment in Paris. 18 February 1859. p.27, c2.

4804 A. T. FOSS *to* **SAMUEL MAY. n.d. Nora, Joe Davis County, Il.** Gives an account of abolitionist meetings in the West. 18 February 1859. p.27, c3.

4805 F. *to* **W. L. GARRISON. 15 February 1859. Worcester.** Describes Miss Holley's lecture in Worcester and its effect. 18 February 1859. p.27, c3.

4806 LUCIUS HOLMES *to* **W. L. GARRISON. 18 February 1859. Charlton, Ma.** Compliments Miss Holley's excellent lecture. 18 February 1859. p.27, c4.

4807 AARON M. POWELL *to* **MR. GARRISON. 10 February 1859. Ghent, N.Y.** Mourns the death of Lucia Marriott. 18 February 1859. p.27, c5.

4808 JUSTITIA FIAT *to* **MR. EDITOR [W. L. GARRISON]. n.d. n.p.** Hopes the statue of Webster will not be placed on the statehouse grounds. 25 February 1859. p.30, c2.

4809 SUSAN B. ANTHONY *to* **READERS OF THE** *LIBERATOR.* **22 February 1859. Albany.** Requests signatures for a petition concerning protection of fugitive slaves. 25 February 1859. p.30, c2.

4810 FIDELITER *to* **MR. GARRISON. 6 February. Boston.** Criticizes inconsistency of the Republican Party; believes in "no union with slaveholders or their supporters." 25 February 1859. p.32, c2.

4811 FRANKLIN *to* **GARRISON. 14 February 1859. Westerly, R.I.** Gives account of three lectures by Henry C. Wright. 25 February 1859. p.32, c2.

4812 G. B. STEBBINS *to* **W. L. GARRISON. 5 February 1859. Ann Arbor, Mi.** Reports on anti-slavery meetings and speeches he attended while traveling through Indiana. 25 February 1859. p.32, c3.

4813 F. W. CHESSON *to* **THE EDITOR OF THE** *ANTI-SLAVERY REPORTER.* **14 December 1858. London.** Discusses American intrigues in St. Domingo. 4 March 1859. p.33, c1.

4814 GEORGE THOMPSON *to* **GARRISON. 31 January 1859. London.** Recounts his joyful visit with Samuel May; describes his journey to India. 4 March 1859. p.35, c3.

4815 n.n. *to* **THE EDITOR OF THE** *LIBERATOR* **[W. L. GARRISON]. n.d. n.p.** Corrects Wendell Phillips on his misinterpretation of Thomas Paine. 4 March 1859. p.36, c3.

4816 IRA STEWARD *to* *LIBERATOR.* **24 February 1859. Hopedale.** Protests a statement by Wendell Phillips regarding Thomas Paine. 4 March 1859. p.36, c4.

4817 A. HOGEBOOM *to* **HENRY C. WRIGHT. 8 February 1859. Shed's Corners, N.Y.** Defends Gerrit Smith from charges of religious intolerance. 4 March 1859. p.36, c4.

4818 GEO. TRASK *to* **BROTHER. 1859. Fitchburg.** Warns against the evils of tobacco. 4 March 1859. p.36, c4.

4819 J. C. *to* **MESSRS. EDITORS. [from the** *Hingham Gazette***] 13 February 1859. South Hingham.** Praises Mrs. Dall's lecture in South Hingham. 4 March 1859. p.36, c5.

4820 S.G.W.B. *to* **THE EDITORS OF THE** *INDEPENDENT***. 15 January 1858. Brookfield.** Informs that "Uncle Tom" appeared as a weekly serial in a Greek newspaper. 11 March 1859. p.38, c1.

4821 JOSEPH A. HORNER *to* **PARKER PILLSBURY. 9 February 1859. Wakefield, Yorkshire, England.** Asks whether or not the American Board of Commissioners for Foreign Missions is anti-slavery. 11 March 1859. p.38, c2.

4822 W. *to* **W. L. GARRISON. 24 February 1859. North Abington.** Criticizes the method of gathering names for petitions against the Fugitive Slave Law. 11 March 1859. p.39, c3.

4823 SUSAN B. ANTHONY *to* **W. L. GARRISON. 8 March 1859. Albany, N.Y.** Asks people to petition against the Anti-Fugitive Slave Law; comments on Dr. Cheever in Albany. 11 March 1859. p.39, c3.

4824 J. H., JR. *to* **SIR. 6 March 1859. West Randolph, Vt.** Reports on progress made by abolitionists in Vermont. 11 March 1859. p.39, c4.

4825 H. C. CUTLER *to* **MR. GARRISON. 8 March 1859. Putnam, Ct.** Mourns the death of Asa Cutler, an abolitionist. 11 March 1859. p.39, c5.

4826 GEO. W. STACY *to* **FRIEND GARRISON. n.d. n.p.** Discusses an arrogant lecture by Mr. George of Natick. 11 March 1859. p.40, c2.

4827 DOCTOR DOY AND CHARLES DOY *to* **n.n. 7 February 1859. Platte City Prison.** Narrate the true story of their kidnapping and imprisonment. 18 March 1859. p.42, c1.

4828 T. *to* **SIR. 11 March 1859. Natick.** Describes lectures by Mr. Pillsbury in Natick and their effect. 18 March 1859. p.43, c4.

4829 F. D. GAGE *to* **GARRISON. 27 February 1859. New Orleans.** Describes her tour through the South; affirms that emancipation has begun in Missouri. 18 March 1859. p.44, c2.

4830 J. A. H. *to* **FRIEND GARRISON. n.d. n.p.** Praises C. C. Burleigh's speech; advocates free speech and free press. 18 March 1859. p.44, c3.

4831 S. M. SEAVER *to* **GARRISON. 15 February 1859. Williamstown, Vt.** Lauds passage of the Personal Liberty Bill in Vermont. 18 March 1859. p.44, c3.

4832 n.n. *to* **GARRISON. 9 March 1859. Worcester.** Criticizes clergymen at the Evangelical Anti-Slavery Convention for refusing to censure slaveholders. 18 March 1859. p.44, c4.

4833 ANDREW H. REED *to* **W. L. GARRISON. 13 January 1859. Mendon.** Demands that the African Aid Society be put in a better light before the public. 18 March 1859. p.44, c4.

4834 NATHANIEL T. SHEPARD *to* **W. L. GARRISON. 3 February 1859. Foxboro'.** Refutes criticism of the African Aid Society. 18 March 1859. p.44, c4.

4835 L. *to* **n.n. 13 March 1859. St. Louis.** Praises the piety, sagacity and unselfish benevolence of the Missouri legislature. 25 March 1859. p.46, c5.

4836 S. M., JR. *to* **MR. GARRISON. n.d. n.p.** Eulogizes Asa Cutler, one of the first abolitionists of New England. 25 March 1859. p.46, c5.

4837 E. R. BROWN *to* **SAMUEL MAY. 23 February 1859. Elmwood, Il.** Commends interesting lectures by A. T. Foss in Illinois. 25 March 1859. p.47, c1.

4838 J. A. HOWLAND *to* **SAMUEL MAY. 7 March 1859. Wrightstown, Belmont County, Oh.** Reports on the abolition campaign in Ohio. 25 March 1859. p.48, c2.

4839 A. T. FOSS *to* **SAMUEL MAY. 7 March 1859. Fremont, Il.** Reports on his abolitionist meetings in Iowa. 25 March 1859. p.48, c3.

4840 X. *to* **n.n. 13 March 1859. St. Louis.** Forwards the closing arguments made in the case of *Charlotte* v. *Chouteau*, which had been in court for sixteen years. 25 March 1859. p.48, c4.

4841 WM. H. ANTHON *to* **SIR. 9 March 1859. New York.** Promotes Hinton Rowan Helper's *Impending Crisis of the South*. 1 April 1859. p.60 [50], c1.

4842 C. *to* **THE EDITOR OF THE** *LIBERATOR* **[W. L. GARRISON]. n.d. n.p.** Claims that James Freeman Clarke underestimated the value of colored people's property in Philadelphia. 1 April 1859. p.61 [51], c3.

4843 R. HEINZEN *to* **W. L. GARRISON. 22 March 1859. Boston.** Advocates equal political rights for colored men. 8 April 1859. p.54, c3.

4844 ANN ROBSON *to* **SIR. 18 March 1859. Warrington, England.** Contributes $100 to the AAS. 8 April 1859. p.54, c6.

4845 ROBERT GASKELL *to* **W. L. GARRISON. 18 March 1859. Warrington, England.** Sends donation from the Warrington AS; praises Miss Remond and protests against the Immigration Bill. 8 April 1859. p.54, c6.

4846 ARNOLD BUFFUM *to* **THE** *ANTI-SLAVERY STANDARD*. **[extract] 18 January 1859. Eagleswood.** Declares his support of all those fighting for the anti-slavery cause. 8 April 1859. p.55, c3.

4847 JAMES M. DE GARMO *to* **FRIEND GARRISON. 27 March 1859. Poughkeepsie, N.Y.** Believes that the anti-slavery cause in New York is starting to awaken more individuals. 8 April 1859. p.56, c2.

4848 W. H. F. *to* **W. L. GARRISON. n.d. n.p.** Discusses the theological dispute between H. W. Beecher and Theodore Parker. 8 April 1859. p.56, c3.

4849 T. S. McFARLAND *to* **THE EDITORS OF THE** *GAZETTE*. **14 March 1859. Urbana, Oh.** Gives a brief biographical sketch of Richard Stanhope, one of Washington's servants; lauds Stanhope as an "honest man and a good citizen." 8 April 1859. p.56, c5.

4850 GEORGE THOMPSON *to* **GARRISON. 24 March 1859. London.** Describes his health problems; reports on the Reform Bill before the House of Commons. 15 April 1859. p.58, c5.

4851 L. *to* **THE EDITOR OF THE** *LIBERATOR* **[W. L. GARRISON]. 5 April 1859. St. Louis.** Reports on the Republican victory in St. Louis. 15 April 1859. p.58, c6.

4852 A. T. FOSS *to* **FRIEND MAY. 1 April 1859. Troy, Oh.** Gives account of abolitionist meetings in Orland, Ann Arbor, and Livonia. 15 April 1859. p.59, c1.

4853 W. S. A. *to* **THE EDITOR OF THE** *BOSTON POST*. **9 April 1859. n.p.** Equates the returning of slaves to masters and the returning of ships to pirates. 15 April 1859. p.59, c2.

4854 JOSEPH A. DUGDALE *to* **W. L. GARRISON. 23 March 1859. Longwood, Pa.** Reports on meetings of the Indian Aid Association. 15 April 1859. p.60, c5.

4855 LEONARD ANET *to* **CHRISTIANS OF THE UNITED STATES WHO SUPPORT SLAVERY. 1 February 1859. Brussels.** Expresses his hope to "banish from the United States a vice which brings scandal on Christianity, " slavery. 22 April 1859. p.62, c2.

4856 JOSEPH MAZZINI *to* **n.n. 21 March 1859. London.** Acknowledges receipt of money for their Italian school; supports anti-slavery cause. 22 April 1859. p.62, c2.

4857 H. T. C. *to* **W. L. GARRISON. n.d. n.p.** Finds the report on the Church AS "lamentably incorrect and deficient"; makes corrections. 22 April 1859. p.62, c5.

4858 BYRAN MORSE *to* **W. L. GARRISON. 14 April 1859. Groveland.** Discusses the Liberty Bill and opposition from the editor of the *Boston Journal* to its passage. 22 April 1859. p.63, c3.

4859 AARON M. POWELL *to* **SAMUEL MAY. 13 April 1859. Grent, N.Y.** Expresses hope for passage of the Personal Liberty Law in New York and other states. 22 April 1859. p.63, c4.

4860 YOUNG AFRICA *to* **THE EDITOR OF THE** *LIVERPOOL NORTHERN TIMES.* **26 March 1859. Liverpool.** Asserts that England is not responsible for slavery in America. 29 April 1859. p.65, c5.

4861 THEODORE PARKER *to* **FRANCIS JACKSON. 21 March 1859. West End Santa Cruz.** Describes the environs. 29 April 1859. p.66, c5.

4862 C. B. CAMPBELL *to* **W. L. GARRISON. February 1859. Clinton, Ia.** Summarizes the itinerary of A. T. Foss in the West. 29 April 1859. p.67, c2.

4863 AMOS GILBERT *to* **FRIEND PARTRIDGE. nd. Eden, Pa.** Declares that "spiritualism is paramount among reforms." 29 April 1859. p.67, c3.

4864 THOMAS B. DREW *to* **W. L. GARRISON. 5 April 1859. Plymouth.** Requests the publication of a letter by Son of Africa. 29 April 1859. p.67, c4.

4865 A SON OF AFRICA *to* **n.n. n.d. n.p.** Believes that slavery is a sin and a contradiction of British law. 29 April 1859. p.67, c4.

4866 HENRY WILSON *to* **FRANCIS GILLETTE. 20 April 1859. Natick, Ma.** Opposes the Two Years Amendment in Massachusetts. 6 May 1859. p.69, c3.

4867 JOSEPH A. HORNER *to* **CHAS. K. WHIPPLE. 13 April 1859. Wakefield, England.** On the treachery of Dr. Pomroy; criticizes the American church as the "bulwark of American slavery." 6 May 1859. p.71, c2.

4868 X. *to* **W. L. GARRISON. n.d. n.p.** Encloses copies of the *Providence Journal* and the *Providence Post*; reports on the Rhode Island Convention. 6 May 1859. p.71, c5.

4869 H. T. C. *to* **THE EDITOR OF THE** *LIBERATOR.* **23 April 1859. Jewett City, Ct.** Refutes the charge of clerical calumny made against the AAS and the Church AS. 6 May 1859. p.72, c2.

4870 RICHARD D. WEBB *to* **n.n. [extract from the** *Anti-Slavery Standard***] n.d. n.p.** Describes the arrival of the Neapolitan exiles at Cork, Ireland. 13 May 1859. p.73, c3.

4871 V. C. *to* **THE EDITORS OF THE** *NEW YORK EVENING POST.* **28 April 1859. Philadelphia.** Narrates Cordelia Loney's escape. 13 May 1859. p.73, c5.

4872 H. L. C. *to* **GARRISON. 3 May 1859. Ellsworth, Me.** Praises Henry C. Wright's lectures; compares the slave's suffering to that of Christ. 13 May 1859. p.75, c2.

4873 G. W. MADOX *to* **W. L. GARRISON. 2 May 1859. Ellsworth.** On Henry C. Wright's lectures in Maine; recommends that Maine be made a free state. 13 May 1859. p.75, c2.

4874 A. HOGEBOOM *to* **W. L. GARRISON. 22 April 1859. n.p.** A spiritualist apologizes for an article published in the *Spiritual Telegraph* which glorifies the Democratic Party and C. E. Lester. 13 May 1859. p.75, c3.

4875 FRANCES D. GAGE *to* **FRIEND GARRISON. 1 April 1859. St. Thomas.** Relates conversations with ex-slaves in the West Indies. 13 May 1859. p.76, c2.

4876 SIMEON SIMPLE *to* **THE EDITOR [W. L. GARRISON]. n.d. n.p.** Hopes to see the reading of the Bible in schools abolished. 13 May 1859. p.76, c3.

4877 AARON M. POWELL *to* **THE EDITOR OF THE** *LIBERATOR* **[W. L. GARRISON]. n.d. n.p.** Discusses the death penalty in Michigan; encloses letter from E. A. Thompson. 13 May 1859. p.76, c3.

4878 E. A. THOMPSON, DEPUTY SECRETARY OF STATE *to* **A. M. POWELL. 19 March 1859. Lansing, Mi.** Informs him that the death penalty has not been restored in Michigan, nor is it being seriously contemplated, as statistics indicate a decrease in murder convictions since its abolition. 13 May 1859. p.76, c3.

4879 E. HAWLEY *to* **THE EDITOR OF THE** *LEADER.* **28 April 1859. Alliance, Oh.** Forwards anti-slavery resolutions adopted by Ohio citizens. 20 May 1859. p.77, c5.

4880 JUSTICE *to* **MR. GARRISON. n.d. n.p.** Accuses the marshal of the District of Boston of kidnapping a slave. 20 May 1859. p.79, c5.

4881 HENRY F. CHEEVER *to* **THE EDITOR OF THE** *LIBERATOR* **[W. L. GARRISON]. 16 May 1859. Jewett City, Ct.** Responds to remarks by C. K. W. which criticized the Christian character of the Church AS [editorial response from C. K. W. printed below]. 27 May 1859. p.84, c2.

4882 HON. J. R. GIDDINGS *to* **RALPH PLUMB. 4 May 1859. Jefferson.** Discusses actions of the Oberlin citizens imprisoned for violating the Fugitive Slave Law. 27 May 1859. p.84, c4.

4883 REV. HENRY BLEBY *to* **W. L. GARRISON. 20 April 1859. Barbados.** Responds to anti-slavery news from the *Liberator* and the *Standard*; reports on education and low crime rate in Barbados. 3 June 1859. p.87, c5.

4884 ROBERT C. WINTHROP *to* **REV. T. W. ALFORD. 18 May 1859. Boston.** Resigns from Boston Tract Society. 10 June 1859, p.89. c1.

4885 GEO. SUNTER *to* **THE EDITOR OF THE** *EXPOSITOR.* **15 May 1859. Brantford.** Discusses Negroes in Canada and the Canadians' response to them. 10 June 1859. p.89, c5.

4886 SALLIE HOLLEY *to* **THE LEGISLATIVE COMMITTEE ON CASTE SCHOOLS IN RHODE ISLAND. n.d. n.p.** Criticizes the closing of school doors to colored students in Rhode Island. 10 June 1859. p.91, c3.

4887 C. M. CLAY *to* **MESSRS. S. O. GRISWOLD, ETC. n.d. n.p.** Condemns the Fugitive Slave Law and slavery in general. 17 June 1859. p.93, c4.

4888 CHARLES SUMNER *to* **SIR. 12 May 1859. Rome, Italy.** Discusses the election of a Wisconsin judge. 17 June 1859. p.94, c2.

4889 J. CUSHING *to* **FRIEND GARRISON n.d. n.p.** Encloses an extract from a valedictory discourse delivered by Reverend W. T. Clarke. 17 June 1859. p.94, c5.

4890 HENRY C. WRIGHT *to* **W. L. GARRISON. 5 June 1859. Chagrin Falls, Oh.** Comments on destruction of crops by the frost; condemns the Fugitive Slave Law and demise of liberty in Ohio; reports the death of Lima S. H. Ober. 17 June 1859. p.95, c1.

4891 JUSTITIA *to* **FRIEND GARRISON. 13 June 1859. Boston.** Compares anti-slavery and colonization. 17 June 1859. p.95, c2.

4892 HENRY C. WRIGHT *to* **GARRISON. n.d. n.p.** Mourns the death of Charles F. Hovey. 24 June 1859. p.98, c6.

4893 HENRY C. WRIGHT *to* **GARRISON. 11 June 1859. New Garden, Oh.** Compares the blight on crops to the blight on the moral nature of Ohio. 24 June 1859. p.98, c6.

4894 JUSTITIA *to* **W. L. GARRISON. 21 June 1859. Boston.** Opposes the execution planned for Plumer. 24 June 1859. p.99, c1.

4895 JOSEPH A. DUGDALE, ELIZABETH JACKSON AND OLIVER JOHNSON *to* **THEODORE PARKER. n.d. n.p.** Send greetings from Progressive Friends. 24 June 1859. p.99, c1.

4896 AMOS GILBERT *to* **W. L. GARRISON. n.d. Eden, Lancaster County, Pa.** Recommends a book he has read to "those who have thoughtlessly admitted that War, Slavery and Speculation are compatible with the precepts or the principles of Jesus Christ." 24 June 1859. p.100, c2.

4897 DELTA *to* **W. L. GARRISON. 4 June 1859. Framingham.** Defends his opinions of the late Charles F. Hovey. 24 June 1859. p.100, c3.

4898 n.n. *to* **GARRISON. n.d. n.p.** Praises the kindness of the late Charles F. Hovey. 24 June 1859. p.100, c3.

4899 A. J. GROVER *to* **MR. MAY. n.d. Earlville, La Salle County, Il.** Pledges money to the AAS; regrets he cannot attend anti-slavery conventions. 1 July 1859. p.102, c6.

4900 J. A. H. *to* **FRIEND GARRISON. 24 June 1859. Worcester.** Reports on the anti-slavery resolutions adopted by the Salem Street church. 1 July 1859. p.103, c2.

4901 Z. T. W. *to* **FRIEND GARRISON. 19 June 1859. Rochester, N.Y.** Announces the success of the Waterloo Yearly Meeting of Friends of Human Rights. 1 July 1859. p.104, c2.

4902 M. W. BOYCE [*sic***]** *to* **MR. C. P. P. [from the** *Columbia Guardian*] **11 May 1859. Sabine Farm.** Gives opinions of territorial legislature and slavery. 8 July 1859. p.105, c1.

4903 HARRIET MARTINEAU *to* **THE EDITOR OF THE** *NATIONAL ANTI-SLAVERY STANDARD.* **6 June 1859. London.** Describes cruelties inflicted by a captain upon American seamen. 8 July 1859. p.105, c4.

4904 ROBT. C. WINTHROP *to* **HIRAM KETCHUM. 20 May 1859. Boston.** Approves a resolution suggesting that discussion of slavery be discontinued. 15 July 1859. p.109, c2.

4905 G. B. STEBBINS *to* **FRIEND GARRISON. 30 June 1859. Ann Arbor, Mi.** Gives account of commencement at Michigan State University. 15 July 1859. p.111, c1.

4906 W. TAPPAN *to* **FRIEND GARRISON. 6 July 1859. Bradford, N.H.** Suggests alterations in the laws of District of Columbia. 15 July 1859. p.111, c2.

4907 H. C. ATWATER *to* **MR. EDITOR. [from the** *Zion's Herald***] October 1857. Boston.** Corrects an editorial previously printed in the *Zion's Herald*. 15 July 1859. p.112, c3.

4908 JUNIUS [REV. J. S. LANE] *to* **MR. EDITOR. [from the** *Zion's Herald***] 23 December 1857. n.p.** Describes food, clothing, and shelter provided by Methodist slaveholders for Methodist slaves. 15 July 1859. p.112, c5.

4909 n.n. *to* **THE EDITOR OF THE** *CLEVELAND LEADER***. 7 July 1859. Oberlin.** Gives account of the enthusiastic reception for Oberlin rescuers. 22 July 1859. p.113, c6.

4910 A. D. JENNINGS, J. K. LOWE, SAMUEL DAVIS, R. P. MITCHELL *to* **GEO. W. BELDEN. 5 July 1859. Cleveland, Oh.** Request a *nolle prosequi* ruling in regard to indictments against them. 22 July 1859. p.114, c2.

4911 R. H. STANTON, ROBT. A. COCHRAN, JOHN C. BACONTO *to* **HON. G. W. BELDEN. 5 July 1859. Cleveland.** Request *nolle prosequi* ruling in cases pending against Plumb, Peck, and others. 22 July 1859. p.114, c2.

4912 R. H. STANTON AND D. K. CARTER *to* **n.n. 6 July 1859. Cleveland, Oh.** Deny responsibility for settlement of the case involving Jennings and others. 22 July 1859. p.114, c3.

4913 HENRY C. WRIGHT *to* **GARRISON. 8 July 1850. Ravenna, Oh.** Informs of the release of Ohio rescuers. 22 July 1859. p.115, c3.

4914 C. STEARNS *to* **GARRISON. 30 June 1859. Lawrence, Ky.** Discusses the trial of Dr. Doy. 22 July 1859. p.115, c3.

4915 THEODORE PARKER *to* **THE GOOD PEOPLE OF THE TWENTY-EIGHTH CONGREGATIONAL SOCIETY. 25 June 1859. Montreux, Switzerland.** Describes Italy and Italians; discusses the Italian war, the Pope, and Christianity. 22 July 1859. p.116, c2.

4916 H. J. *to* **THE EDITOR OF THE** *LIBERATOR* **[W. L. GARRISON]. 3 July. Newport, R.I.** Explains the spiritual laws of health. 22 July 1859. p.116, c3.

4917 J. A. H. *to* **FRIEND GARRISON. 15 July 1859. Worcester.** Encloses essay on military training and the future of the youth of America. 22 July 1859. p.116, c4.

4918 JOHN BEESON *to* **THE EDITOR [W. L. GARRISON]. n.d. n.p.** Asserts his belief that helping the Indian is the quickest way to free the black. 22 July 1859. p.116, c4.

4919 W. S. A. *to* **MR. GARRISON. n.d. n.p.** Upholds the rights of fugitive slaves. 29 July 1859. p.118, c4.

4920 R. S. *to* **FRIEND GARRISON. 16 July 1859. Toledo.** Questions the discrepancy between T. W. Higginson's speeches and his actions. 29 July 1859. p.118, c5.

4921 JUSTITIA *to* **FRIEND GARRISON. 25 July 1859. Boston.** Comments on the death of Rufus Choate. 29 July 1859. p.118, c6.

4922 W. C. M. *to* **MR. EDITOR [W. L. GARRISON]. n.d. n.p.** Eulogizes Rufus Choate. 29 July 1859. p.118, c6.

4923 JAMES BUCHANAN *to* **JOHN CLARK. 18 July 1859. Washington.** Mourns the death of Rufus Choate. 29 July 1859. p.119, c1.

4924 HENRY C. WRIGHT *to* **GARRISON. 1859. Quincy, Il.** Criticizes Hindu doctrines. 29 July 1859. p.120, c2.

4925 J. H. *to* **MR. GARRISON. 8 June 1859. Plymouth.** Reminds that the love of money is the root of all evil. 29 July 1859. p.120, c3.

4926 WM. HENRY ANTHON *to* **THE EDITOR OF THE** *NEW YORK TRIBUNE.* **15 July 1859. New York.** Affirms John C. Underwood's appointment to the Helper fund. 29 July 1859. p.120, c5.

4927 n.n. *to* **HARPER & BROTHERS OF NEW YORK. 26 November 1858. Georgia.** Requests that his name be removed from the subscription list if magazines and books will not be published on a regular basis. 27 July 1859. p.120, c5.

4928 J. C. C. *to* **THE EDITORS OF THE** *JOURNAL OF COMMERCE.* **16 July 1859. Alabama.** Upholds constitutional rights of the South. 5 August 1859. p.121, c1.

4929 S. OXON *to* **LORD BROUGHAM. [from the** *London Morning Star***] 12 July 1859. n.p.** Regrets that he will not be able to attend a meeting on the following day. 5 August 1859. p.121, c4.

4930 GEORGE W. STACY *to* **FRIEND GARRISON. n.d. n.p.** Informs of a successful anti-slavery meeting held on 1 August at Milford. 5 August 1859. p.123, c4.

4931 LYDIA MARIA CHILD *to* **THE PROGRESSIVE FRIENDS. 2 May 1859. Wayland.** Stresses the need for moral courage. 5 August 1859. p.124, c2.

4932 WILLIAM C. NELL *to* **FRIEND GARRISON. 26 July 1859. Boston.** Calls for justice for Crispus Attucks. 5 August 1859. p.124, c3.

4933 GEO. TRASK *to* **REV. GARDINER SPRING. 1959. Fitchburg, Ma.** Lectures on the evils of tobacco. 5 August 1859. p.124, c4.

4934 A. T. FOSS *to* **THE EDITORS OF THE** *INDEPENDENT DEMOCRAT.* **16 July 1859. Manchester.** Reports on progress of the Personal Liberty Bill. 12 August 1859. p.125, c2.

4935 WENDELL PHILLIPS *to* **LEMUEL SHAW AND JAMES WALKER. 1 August 1859. n.p.** Lectures on intoxicating drinks. 12 August 1859. p.126, c2.

4936 C. C. BURLEIGH *to* **GARRISON. 5 August 1859. Florence.** Reports on the First of August celebration at Florence, Massachusetts. 12 August 1859. p.127, c2.

4937 THOMAS WENTWORTH HIGGINSON *to* **W. L. GARRISON. n.d. n.p.** Discusses spiritualist papers and slavery. 12 August 1859. p.127, c3.

4938 HENRY C. WRIGHT *to* **GARRISON. 2 August 1859. Plymouth.** Criticizes Gov. Banks, who "ignored the living slave, and eulogized the dead Pilgrims," in his speech in honor of a monument to the Pilgrims. 12 August 1859. p.127, c4.

4939 DANEUIL *to* **MR. GARRISON. n.d. n.p.** Discusses the forthcoming inauguration of the Webster statue. 12 August 1859. p.127, c4.

4940 GEO. THOMPSON *to* **WENDELL PHILLIPS. [extract] 15 July 1859. South Lambeth, London.** Thanks Phillips for remittances. 12 August 1859. p.127, c5.

4941 JUSTITIA *to* **FRIEND GARRISON. 1 August 1859. Boston.** Criticizes the address given by Dr. Adams at the funeral of Rufus Choate. 12 August 1859. p.128, c2.

4942 HENRY C. WRIGHT *to* **GARRISON. 27 July 1859. East River, N.Y.** Charges that the Church and clergy ignore the obligations of men to the living present and speak only of the dead past. 12 August 1859. p.128, c2.

4943 A HEARER *to* **THE** *LIBERATOR.* **1 August 1859. Haverhill.** Reports on a sermon by Rev. Mr. Clark, pastor of the Unitarian Society, commemorating emancipation in the West Indies. 12 August 1859. p.128, c3.

4944 SAMUEL JOHNSON *to* **GARRISON. 1 August 1859. London.** Describes the twenty-fifth anniversary celebration of the abolition of slavery in the West Indies. 12 August 1859. p.128, c3.

4945 REV. SAMUEL JOHNSON *to* **THE YEARLY MEETING OF PROGRESSIVE FRIENDS. 23 May 1859. Salem, Ma.** Emphasizes the importance of love of Truth. 12 August 1859. p.128, c3.

4946 J. M. DEGARMO *to* **FRIEND GARRISON. 7 August 1859. Poughkeepsie, N.Y.** Describes the colored people's commemoration of Emancipation Day in Poughkeepsie. 12 August 1859. p.128, c5.

4947 JOSEPH A. DUGDALE *to* **LITTLE GIRLS AND BOYS. [from the** *Anti-Slavery Standard*] **3 September 1859. n.p.** Discusses the children's enthusiasm for the children's convention. 12 August 1859. p.128, c5.

4948 D. M. FROST *to* **THE EDITOR OF THE** *CHICAGO TIMES.* **3 August 1859. St. Louis.** A Southerner whose escaped slaves returned to him voluntarily testifies that they preferred a kind master in a slave state to starvation or penitentiary in a free state. 19 August 1859. p.129, c1.

4949 H. C. WRIGHT *to* **n.n. 1 August 1859. St. Louis.** Comments on the celebration of the First of August in St. Louis. 19 August 1859. p.131, c3.

4950 [illegible] *to* **FRIEND GARRISON. 7 August. Worcester.** Reports that the Salem Street Church has failed to live up to the anti-slavery stand of its resolutions. 19 August 1859. p.131, c3.

4951 REV. JAMES C. WILSON *to* **THE EDITOR OF THE** *TEXAS CHRISTIAN AD-VOCATE.* **2 July 1859. Gonzales.** Criticizes the unchristian conduct displayed by Northern Methodists toward their Southern brethren because of the latter's connection with slavery. 26 August 1859. p.133, c1.

4952 INQUIRER *to* **MR. EDITOR. [from the** *Newburyport Herald***] n.d. n.p.** Points out that the American Tract Society has not published a word against slavery. 26 August 1859. p.133, c2.

4953 L. *to* **n.n. August 1859. St. Louis.** Approves the imprisonment of Dr. Doy for abolitionism; informs of a threat to tar and feather Philip Carpenter if he gives his anti-slavery speech as planned; notes Edward Wyman's role in assuring that the speech was not given. 26 August 1859. p.134, c6.

4954 JUSTITIA *to* **n.n. 20 August 1859. Boston.** Gives account of Dr. Adams' address at the funeral of Rufus Choate. 26 August 1859. p.135, c1.

4955 G. W. M. *to* **W. L. GARRISON. 14 August 1859. Ellsworth.** Gives account of criticism levied at abolitionists by a priest. 26 August 1859. p.135, c2.

4956 LUCY N. COLMAN *to* **MR. GARRISON. 2 August 1859. Honeoye.** Describes the beauty of western New York; discusses female suffrage. 26 August 1859. p.135, c2.

4957 A. P. B. *to* **W. L. GARRISON. 21 August 1859. Worcester.** Discusses pro-slavery sentiments of Rev. Adams. 26 August 1859. p.135, c3.

4958 D. Y. *to* **n.n. 15 August 1859. Boston.** Praises Rufus Choate. 2 September 1859. p.137, c4.

4959 JACKSON WHITNEY *to* **WM. REILEY. 19 March 1859. Sandwich, C.W.** A fugitive slave writes to his former master. 2 September 1859. p.138, c1.

4960 SAMUEL MAY *to* **W. L. GARRISON. 29 August 1859. Leicester.** Reports that Miss Holley is dying. 2 September 1859. p.138, c4.

4961 n.n. *to* **SAMUEL MAY, JR. 11 August 1859. Maine.** Explains that illness prevents her sister, Sallie Holley, from delivering a lecture. 2 September 1859. p.138, c4.

4962 R. H. OBER *to* **FRIEND GARRISON. 28 August 1859. Manchester, N.H.** Reports on anti-slavery activity in Manchester. 2 September 1859. p.138, c4.

4963 G. W. S. *to* **GARRISON. 25 August 1859. Milford.** Denounces hypocrisy on the part of many abolitionists. 2 September 1859. p.138, c5.

4964 PETER LIBBY *to* **BROTHER GARRISON. 23 August 1859. Buxton.** Praises Sallie Holley's lectures in Maine. 2 September 1859. p.138, c5.

4965 C. F. PUTNAM *to* **MR. GARRISON. 22 August 1859. South Bridgton, Me.** Reports revival of the foreign slave trade and the anchoring of the "pirate ships" in Northern harbors. 2 September 1859. p.138, c6.

4966 C. C. BURLEIGH *to* **FRIEND GARRISON. n.d. n.p.** Points out incorrect numeration of issues of the *Liberator*. 2 September 1859. p.138, c6.

4967 HENRY C. WRIGHT *to* **GARRISON. 25 August 1859. Ohio.** Informs that the *Liberator* printed an incorrect version of the Declaration of Sentiments adopted at the Plymouth Convention. 2 September 1859. p.139, c1.

4968 JUSTITIA *to* **FRIEND GARRISON. 21 August 1859. Boston.** Relates Charles F. Hovey's advice to young men. 2 September 1859. p.140, c3.

4969 W. H. LOWDERBACK *to* **W. S. BAILEY, THE EDITOR OF THE** *FREE SOUTH.* **16 August 1859. Gruntz, Owen County, Ky.** Criticizes *Free South.* 9 September 1859. p.141, c3.

4970 S. E. W. *to* **W. L. GARRISON. n.d. n.p.** Discusses Rev. Nehemiah Adams' lecture. 9 September 1859. p.142, c6.

4971 S. E. W. *to* **MR. EDITOR [W. L. GARRISON]. n.d. n.p.** Comments on the failure of citizens to mention the plight of slaves during a Fourth of July celebration. 9 September 1859. p.143, c1.

4972 F. HINKLY *to* **MR. GARRISON. 4 September 1859. Hyannis.** Recounts the kidnapping of Columbus Jones. 9 September 1859. p.143, c2.

4973 HANCOCK *to* **MR. GARRISON. n.d. n.p.** Considers the concern of the Massachusetts legislature for the Webster statue an insult to the people of Massachusetts. 9 September 1859. p.143, c2.

4974 HOMER B. SPRAGUE *to* **THE SALEM STREET CONGREGATIONAL CHURCH, WORCESTER, MASS. n.d. n.p.** Believes fellowship with slaveholders is incompatible with Christian principles. 9 September 1859. p.144, c2.

4975 GERRIT SMITH *to* **JOHN THOMAS. 27 August 1859. Peterboro'.** Announces the anniversary of the Rescue of Jerry. 16 September 1859. p.146, c1.

4976 FRANKLIN PIERCE *to* **GENTLEMEN. 10 September 1859. Andover, Ma.** Expresses appreciation for invitation to attend the inauguration of the Webster statue; promises to attend. 16 September 1859. p.146, c3.

4977 n.n. *to* **MR. GARRISON. n.d. n.p.** Discloses that Daniel Webster died leaving a $20,000 debt to his children. 16 September 1859. p.146, c4.

4978 THEODORE PARKER *to* **FRANCIS JACKSON. 23 August 1859. Combe Varin Brot-Dessus, Neuchatel, Suisse.** Describes his stay at Professor Desor's house; comments on gloomy state of United States politics. 16 September 1859. p.146, c5.

4979 S. P. CHASE *to* **FREDERICK W. LINCOLN. 10 September 1859. Columbus.** Regrets he is unable to attend inauguration ceremonies for the Webster statue. 16 September 1859. p.146, c5.

4980 F. S. BLISS *to* **FRIENDS OF THE ENSLAVED. 30 August 1857. Barre, Vt.** Considers the cause of the oppressed "the highest, the truest, the most living expression of Christianity." 16 September 1859. p.146, c6.

4981 S. E. W. *to* **MR. GARRISON. n.d. n.p.** Speculates why his articles were not published in the *Spy.* 16 September 1859. p.147, c3.

4982 HERBERT GLEASON *to* **W. L. GARRISON. 5 September 1859. Malden.** Wonders whether the Mayflower Pilgrims enslaved Indians. 16 September 1859. p.147, c4.

4983 W. G. BABCOCK *to* **BROTHER GARRISON. n.d. n.p.** Criticizes the self-righteous tone of abolitionist speeches. 16 September 1859. p.147, c4.

4984 CEPHAS H. KENT *to* **MESSRS. EDITORS. [from the** *Vermont Chronicle***] n.d. n.p.** Forwards review of a circular of the New York American Tract Society. 23 September 1859. p.149, c5.

4985 SAMUEL MAY, JR. *to* **W. L. GARRISON. 2 September 1859. n.p.** Mourns the death of Effingham L. Capron. 23 September 1859. p.150, c3.

4986 HENRY C. WRIGHT *to* **GARRISON. 4 September 1859. Alliance, Oh.** Forwards account of the anniversary meeting of the Western AS. 23 September 1859. p.150, c5.

4987 GEO. W. STACY *to* **FRIEND GARRISON. 19 September 1859. Milford.** Comments on Adin Ballou's criticism of abolitionists. 23 September 1859. p.150, c6.

4988 WM. WELLS BROWN *to* **MR. GARRISON. 10 September 1859. Albany, N.Y.** Forwards account of the Wilberforce Centennial celebration. 23 September 1859. p.151, c3.

4989 G. W. M. *to* **FRIEND GARRISON. n.d. Ellsworth, Me.** Describes Miss Holley's lectures in Maine. 23 September 1859. p.151, c3.

4990 C. C. BURLEIGH *to* **FRIEND GARRISON. 15 September 1859. Florence.** Reports on a man impersonating a fugitive slave. 23 September 1859. p.151, c4.

4991 S. P. CHASE *to* **SIR. 10 September 1859. Columbus.** Declares he must deny himself the "gratification" of being present at the inauguration of the Webster statue. 30 September 1859. p.154, c3.

4992 A. B. *to* **MR. GARRISON. 19 September 1859. Bangor.** Describes Harriot K. Hunt's visit to Maine. 30 September 1859. p.155, c1.

4993 JEHIEL CLAFLIN *to* **BROTHER GARRISON. 20 September 1859. West Brookfield, Vt.** Describes the stormy West Randolph Anti-Slavery Convention. 30 September 1859. p.155, c2.

4994 ELIZABETH B. CHASE *to* **FRIEND GARRISON. 26 September 1859. Valley Falls.** Commends the philanthropy of the late Effingham L. Capron. 30 September 1859. p.155, c3.

4995 H. O. STONE *to* **MR. GARRISON. 25 September 1859. Framingham.** Declares that John Johnson is an imposter. 30 September 1859. p.155, c3.

4996 M. H. S. *to* **THE EDITOR OF THE *LIBERATOR* [W. L. GARRISON]. 8 September 1859. Foxboro.** Reports that Wendell Phillips' letter of denunciation to Judge Shaw and President Walker was read at a temperance meeting in Union Grove. 30 September 1859. p.155, c4.

4997 G. W. ALLEN *to* **THE EDITOR [W. L. GARRISON]. 23 September 1859. Worcester.** Discusses inconsistent attitude of the Church regarding slavery. 30 September 1859. p.156, c2.

4998 A. H. *to* **MR. GARRISON. n.d. n.p.** Reports on the West Randolph Anti-Slavery Convention. 30 September 1859. p.156, c3.

4999 A MEMBER OF THE CONVENTION *to* **W. L. GARRISON. n.d. n.p.** Forwards the proceedings of the West Randolph Abolition Convention. 30 September 1859. p.156, c4.

5000 ETHAN ALLEN *to* **FRIEND GARRISON. n.d. n.p.** Discusses liberal Christianity in Vermont. 30 September 1859. p.156, c4.

5001 P. *to* **MR. GARRISON. n.d. n.p.** Describes the Religious Reform convention at Ellenville, New York. 30 September 1859. p.156, c5.

5002 JOSEPH A. HORNER *to* **THE EDITORS OF THE** *WAKEFIELD FREEMAN*. **23 July 1859. n.p.** Refers to Rev. Baron Stow's exclusion of Negroes from his church as a base act. 7 October 1859. p.157, c6.

5003 J. A. H. *to* **THE EDITOR OF THE** *LIBERATOR* **[W. L. GARRISON]. 3 October 1859. Worcester.** Reports that the matter of the collection for the American Board of Commissioners for Foreign Missions at the Salem Street Church is yet unresolved. 7 October 1859. p.159, c2.

5004 SALLIE HOLLEY *to* **MR. MAY. 26 September 1859. Eastport, Me.** Discusses her anti-slavery junkets. 7 October 1859. p.159, c3.

5005 J. ATKINS *to* **THE EDITOR OF THE** *NEW YORK DAILY NEWS*. **23 September 1859. New York.** Believes that Virginia slaves are better off than English laborers; describes English enthusiasm at the prospect of an anti-slavery American president. 14 October 1859. p.161, c1.

5006 A WEBSTER WHIG—NO DEMOCRAT *to* **THE EDITORS OF THE** *TRAVELLER*. **n.d. n.p.** Remarks that Webster's statue has "not so much of a likeness to him as is usually found in a caricature." 14 October 1859. p.162, c2.

5007 S. *to* **MR. GARRISON. 27 September 1859. Bangor.** Criticizes the Church AS for its hypocritical action regarding slavery. 14 October 1859. p.162, c5.

5008 SIMEON SIMPLE *to* **MR. EDITOR [W. L. GARRISON]. n.d. n.p.** Protests the actions of the legislature in "allowing the Capitol grounds to be desecrated" by the statue of Webster. 14 October 1859. p.162, c6.

5009 J. A. H. *to* **THE EDITOR OF THE** *LIBERATOR* **[W. L. GARRISON]. 8 October 1859. Worcester.** Criticizes the Salem Street Church for boasting of its financial well-being. 14 October 1859. p.163, c1.

5010 AGITATOR *to* **W. L. GARRISON. 4 October 1859. Topsham.** Reports on opposition to anti-slavery petitions circulated in Topsham. 14 October 1859. p.163, c1.

5011 W. C. N. *to* **FRIEND GARRISON. 12 October 1859. Boston.** Discusses the meetings concerning the Buxton settlement in Canada West. 14 October 1859. p.163, c1.

5012 A. J. GROVER *to* **W. L. GARRISON. 24 September 1859. Earlville, Il.** Discusses the anti-slavery convention in Illinois. 14 October 1859. p.164, c5.

5013 THEODORE PARKER *to* **n.n. [extract] 13 September. Montreux, Switzerland.** Praises the goodness of Horace Mann. 21 October 1859. p.165, c4.

5014 H. MATTISON *to* **THE EDITORS OF THE** *NEW YORK TRIBUNE*. **n.d. n.p.** Expresses thanks on the behalf of all Methodists for the *Tribune*'s truthful portrayal of their position regarding slavery. 21 October 1859. p.165, c5.

5015 S. A. DOUGLAS *to* **MRS. LUCY STONE. [from the** *Sentinel*] **14 July 1859. Washington.** Regrest he is unable to attend a convention of the ladies of the Northwest. 21 October 1859. p.166, c2.

5016 LUCY STONE *to* **W. L. GARRISON. 12 October 1859. Boston.** Reveals Stephen A. Douglas' letter of 14 July 1859 as a fraud. 21 October 1859. p.166, c2.

5017 CAROLINE F. PUTNAM *to* **n.n. 17 September 1859. Machias, Me.** Praises George F. Talbot and George S. Hillard. 21 October 1859. p.166, c3.

5018 A. P. B. *to* **FRIEND GARRISON. n.d. n.p.** Believes that the editor of *American Messenger* is becoming heretical; advocates moral courage and reform. 21 October 1859. p.166, c6.

5019 WILLIAM C. NELL *to* **HENRY L. DAWES. 26 September 1859. North Adams, Ma.** Encloses resolutions adopted by the Convention of Colored Citizens of New England. [partially illegible] 21 October 1859. p.168, c5.

5020 HON. JOSHUA R. GIDDINGS *to* **n.n. 24 October 1859. Philadelphia.** Claims that John Brown never consulted him regarding the Virginia expedition. 28 October 1859. p.170, c3.

5021 SAMUEL J. MAY *to* **W. L. GARRISON. 5 October 1859. London.** Relates that he is soon to return to the United States; discusses his cousin, Samuel May, Jr.; gives account of travels in Britain, Ireland, Switzerland, Rome. 28 October 1859. p.170, c6.

5022 C. L. H. *to* **W. L. GARRISON. 19 October 1859. West Gouldsboro'.** Praises the earnest labors of Sallie Holley in Maine. 28 October 1859. p.170, c6.

5023 GERRIT SMITH *to* **CAPT. JOHN BROWN. 4 June 1859. Peterboro'.** Sends $200 to Brown. 28 October 1859. p.171, c3.

5024 L. MARIA CHILD *to* **FRIENDS OF HUMAN PROGRESS. 26 August 1859. Wayland.** Congratulates and encourages all those who are honest in their efforts for human progress; discusses religion and morals. 28 October 1859. p.172, c2.

5025 THEODORE PARKER *to* **MEMBERS OF THE TWENTY-EIGHTH CONGRE-GATIONAL SOCIETY IN BOSTON. 12 September 1859. Montreux, Switzerland.** Resigns as minister because of his poor health. 28 October 1859. p.172, c4.

5026 REPUBLICAN *to* **THE EDITOR OF THE** *NEW YORK TIMES.* **n.d. n.p.** Stresses that the crimes at Harpers Ferry must be punished; believes W. Phillips should accept blame. 4 November 1859. p.173, c2.

5027 FREDERICK DOUGLASS *to* **THE EDITOR OF THE** *ROCHESTER DEMOCRAT AND AMERICAN.* **31 October 1859. Canada West.** Replies to Cook's charge of cowardice. 11 November 1859. p.177, c5.

5028 L. MARIA CHILD *to* **GOV. WISE. 26 October 1859. Wayland, Ma.** Sympathizes with the ''brave and suffering'' John Brown. 11 November 1859. p.179, c2.

5029 L. MARIA CHILD *to* **CAPT. BROWN. 26 October 1859. Wayland, Ma.** Conveys her admiration of Brown's intentions. 11 November 1859. p.179, c2.

5030 HENRY A. WISE *to* **L. MARIA CHILD. 29 October 1859. Richmond, Va.** Promises to forward her letter to John Brown. 11 November 1859. p.179, c2.

5031 JOHN BROWN *to* **E. B. OF RHODE ISLAND. 1 November 1859. Charlestown, Va.** Requests that comforting letters be sent to his relatives. 11 November 1859. p.179, c2.

5032 E. B. *to* **JOHN BROWN. 27 October 1859. Newport, R.I.** Sends words of consolation. 11 November 1859. p.179, c2.

5033 JUSTITIA *to* **MR. EDITOR [W. L. GARRISON]. 31 October 1859. Boston.** Laments the tragedy at Harpers Ferry. 11 November 1859. p.180, c2.

5034 SARAH E. WALL *to* **n.n. 30 October 1859. Worcester.** Criticizes the inconsistency of Stephen S. Foster regarding non-resistance. 11 November 1859. p.180, c3.

5035 X. Y. [GOV. WISE] *to* **THE** *BOSTON TRANSCRIPT.* **n.d. n.p.** Refers to Mrs. Child as the "Florence Nightingale of Wayland." 18 November 1859. p.182, c5.

5036 L. MARIA CHILD *to* **THE EDITOR OF THE** *NEW YORK TRIBUNE.* **10 November 1859. Boston.** Gives reasons for her failure to visit John Brown. 18 November 1859. p.182, c5.

5037 JOHN BROWN *to* **L. MARIA CHILD. n.d. n.p.** Suggests that she not visit him. 18 November 1859. p.182, c5.

5038 S. G. HOWE *to* **n.n. 14 November 1859. Boston.** Asserts that he had nothing to do with Harpers Ferry. 18 November 1859. p.182, c5.

5039 A. M. POWELL *to* **FRIEND [W. L. GARRISON]. 1 November 1859. Albany, N.Y.** Appeals to the people of New York State to sign a petition for the Personal Liberty Law. 18 November 1859. p.184, c4.

5040 AARON M. POWELL *to* **THE EDITOR OF THE** *LIBERATOR* **[W. L. GARRISON]. 2 November 1859. New York.** Requests money from the *Liberator* in support of the Personal Liberty Law. 18 November 1859. p.184, c5.

5041 GEO. H. HOYT *to* **n.n. [from the** *New York Tribune***] 16 November 1859. National House, Washington.** Criticizes the explusion of Jewett and himself from Charleston. 25 November 1859. p.186, c1.

5042 THADDEUS HYATT *to* **THE EDITOR OF THE** *NEW YORK TRIBUNE.* **15 November 1859. New York.** Reports on the success of the John Brown Fund. 25 November 1859. p.186, c3.

5043 THADDEUS HYATT *to* **n.n. 14 November 1859. New York.** Praises John Brown's courage; requests aid for Brown's family. 25 November 1859. p.186, c3.

5044 GEORGE H. HEPWORTH *to* **SIR. 19 November. Boston.** Opposes the movement in support of John Brown's family and declines to attend meeting concerning the issue. 25 November 1859. p.186, c4.

5045 OBSERVER *to* **W. L. GARRISON. 15 November 1859. New York.** Gives an account of his trip to Kansas. 25 November 1859. p.188, c3.

5046 ACCOMACK *to* **THE EDITOR OF THE** *NEW YORK HERALD.* **5 November 1859. Norfolk.** Warns of the threat of secession. 2 December 1859. p.189, c2.

5047 n.n. *to* **GOV. FLOYD. 20 August 1859. Cincinnati.** Relates his discovery of a society dedicated to liberation of slaves by general insurrection. 2 December 1859. p.189, c5.

5048 L. W. BACON *to* **THE EDITORS OF THE** *NEW YORK INDEPENDENT.* **21 November 1859. Litchfield, Ct.** Informs editors that Rev. H. L. Vaile, John Brown's former teacher, sent a letter to Brown. 2 December 1859. p.189, c6.

5049 JOHN BROWN *to* **REV. H. L. VAILE. 15 November 1859. Charleston, Va.** Thanks Vaile for his letter; gives his evaluation of the Harpers Ferry incident. 2 December 1859. p.189, c6.

5050 JOHN BROWN *to* **n.n. 15 November 1859. Charleston, Va.** Expresses his thoughts on God and the abolitionist cause. 2 December 1859. p.188, c1.

5051 THEODORE PARKER *to* **MR. GARRISON. 20 September 1859. Montreux, Switzerland.** Discusses liberation of serfs and the African slave trade. 2 December 1859. p.190, c5.

5052 LUCY N. COLMAN *to* **MR. GARRISON. 9 November 1859. Rochester, N.Y.** Reports on various anti-slavery meetings held in Rochester and speeches by Dr. Cheever and A. D. Mayo; announces future meetings. 2 December 1859. p.190, c6.

5053 J. M. H. *to* **THE EDITOR OF THE** *LIBERATOR* **[W. L. GARRISON]. 28 November 1859. Manchester, N.H.** Reviews Parker Pillsbury's lecture on John Brown. 2 December 1859. p.190, c6.

5054 SAMUEL CHILTON *to* **HENRY A. WISE. n.d. n.p.** Submits evidence that many members of John Brown's family were insane; prays for postponement of Brown's execution on grounds that he is insane. 2 December 1859. p.191, c3.

5055 n.n. *to* **THE EDITOR OF THE** *RICHMOND WHIG.* **23 November 1859. University of Virginia.** Reports on a meeting of students of the University of Richmond concerning their support of Governor Wise. 2 December 1859. p.191, c3.

5056 J. J. *to* **THE EDITOR [W. L. GARRISON]. 20 November 1859. Philadelphia.** Praises anti-slavery efforts of Mrs. Sarah M. Douglass. 2 December 1859. p.192, c5.

5057 AMOS GILBERT *to* **W. L. GARRISON. 11 November 1859. Eden, Pa.** Forwards anti-slavery poem praising John Brown. 9 December 1859. p.196, c3.

5058 HENRY C. WRIGHT *to* **W. L. GARRISON. 21 November 1859. Grantville.** Forwards resolution adopted at Natick; discusses slaves' right to resist their masters. 9 December 1859. p.196, c4.

5059 F. W. CHESSON *to* **n.n. 25 November 1859. New York.** Reports that the London Emancipation Committee supports the aims of the African Civilization Society. 9 December 1859. p.196, c4.

5060 SANGAREE *to* **THE EDITOR OF THE** *LOUISVILLE JOURNAL.* **1 November 1859. Glennary.** A Southerner criticizes John Brown and abolitionists. 9 December 1859. p.196, c4.

5061 MATILDA DOYLE *to* **JOHN BROWN. 20 November 1859. Chattanooga, Tn.** A woman whose husband and sons were murdered by Brown hopes he will receive his "just reward." 16 December 1859. p.197, c4.

5062 R. J. HINTON *to* **THE** *BOSTON TRAVELLER.* **3 December 1859. n.p.** Refutes allegations made in *Traveller* article against John Brown. 16 December 1859. p.197, c4.

5063 JOHN BROWN *to* **WIFE. 16 November 1859. Charlestown, Va.** Sends a tender letter of farewell to her. 16 December 1859. p.197, c5.

5064 HENRY M. DEXTER *to* **SAMUEL E. SEWALL. 2 December 1859. Boston.** Praises motives which prompted John Brown's actions. 16 December 1859. p.198, c4.

5065 REPUBLICAN FROM THE START *to* **HENRY WILSON. n.d. n.p.** Defends John Brown's action. 16 December 1859. p.198, c4.

5066 G. W. S. *to* **GARRISON. n.d. n.p.** Describes meeting held in Milford on the eve of John Brown's execution. 16 December 1859. p.198, c6.

5067 J. R. TUCKER *to* **SIR. 26 November 1859. Richmond, Va.** States that he agrees with the law allowing postmasters to tamper with the mail. 23 December 1859. p.201, c5.

5068 SAMUEL JACKSON *to* **L. MARIA CHILD. n.d. n.p.** Requests pictures of Lydia M. Child and John Brown. 23 December 1859. p.202, c6.

5069 JOHN E. COOK AND EDWIN COPPIC *to* **n.n. 16 December 1859. Charleston.** Describe their attempted escape from jail; declare that they were not aided by the guards. 23 December 1859. p.203, c3.

5070 A. M. GREEN, J. P. CAMPBELL, AND JEREMIAH ASHER *to* **H. A. WISE. 3 December 1859. Philadelphia.** Request the bodies of Shields Green and John Copeland for burial, in the event of their execution. 23 December 1859. p.203, c3.

5071 C. C. FOUKE *to* **THE EDITOR OF THE** *ST. LOUIS REPUBLICAN.* **27 November 1859. Harpers Ferry.** Explains that she shielded Thompson from being shot in a hotel in order that he could be brought to justice under the law. 23 December 1859. p.203, c4.

5072 JOHN BROWN *to* **SON OF THOMAS MUSGRAVE. 17 November 1859. Charlestown, Va.** Thanks him for his sympathy. 23 December 1859. p.140 [204], c4.

5073 HENRY A. WISE *to* **SAMUEL R. GLEN, AND OTHERS, COMMITTEE OF JACKSON CLUB, BOSTON. 10 December 1859. Richmond, Va.** Accepts resolution of the Jackson Democratic Club of Boston. 30 December 1859. p.205, c1.

5074 MILLARD FILLMORE *to* **MESSRS. SAMUEL L. M. BARLOW, WILSON G. HUNT, AND JAMES BROOKS. 16 December 1859. Buffalo.** Pleads for the preservation of the Union. 30 December 1859. p.205, c3.

5075 J. W. VANSANT, J. B. GLASSFORD, AND J. L. COLLINS *to* **THE PUBLIC. 2 December 1859. Baltimore.** Plead innocent to the charge of antagonism toward the state of Ohio. 30 December 1859. p.206, c2.

5076 HENRY A. WISE *to* **GOV. CHASE OF OHIO. 25 November 1859. Richmond, Va.** Requests cooperation in enforcing federal laws. 30 December 1859. p.207, c3.

5077 S. P. CHASE *to* **HENRY A. WISE. 1 December 1859. Columbus.** Promises to uphold laws concerning escaped slaves but forbids invasion of Ohio territory by Virginia authorities. 30 December 1859. p.207, c3.

5078 M. J. C. MASON *to* **L. MARIA CHILD. 11 November 1859. Alto, King George's County, Va.** Condemns L. Maria Child and John Brown as hypocrites and murderers. 31 December 1859. p.209, c1.

5079 L. MARIA CHILD *to* **M. J. C. MASON. 17 December 1859. Wayland, Ma.** Replies to M. J. C. Mason's letter, attempting to brush "the veil of prejudice" from her eyes. 31 December 1859. p.209, c1.

5080 THEODORE PARKER *to* **SIR. 24 November 1859. Rome.** Discusses John Brown and the issue of the slave's freedom. 31 December 1859. p.209, c4.

5081 HORACE GREELEY *to* **POSTMASTER. n.d. Lynchburg, Va.** Defies his order to stop sending the *Tribune* to Lynchburg because of its "incendiary nature." 31 December 1859. p.210, c4.

5082 VICTOR HUGO *to* **THE EDITOR OF THE** *LONDON NEWS.* **2 December 1859. Hauteville House.** Hopes for a stay of John Brown's execution; believes his murder would "penetrate the Union with a secret fissure which would in the end tear it asunder." 31 December 1859. p.210, c5.

5083 A. J. GROVER *to* **MR. GARRISON. 3 December 1859. Earlville, LaSalle County, Il.** Gives account of Parker Pillsbury's activities in Earlville. 31 December 1859. p.211, c1.

5084 G. W. P. *to* **MR. GARRISON. 11 December 1859. Peterboro', N.Y.** Attempts to stir anti-slavery men to action; finds that the patient approach is no longer useful. 31 December 1859. p.211, c2.

5085 HARRIOT K. HUNT *to* **FREDERICK U. TRACY. 22 December 1859. Boston.** Condemns taxation of women without representation. 31 December 1859. p.211, c2.

5086 DRUMGOOL *to* **GARRISON. n.d. n.p.** Compares the execution of John Brown to that of Christ. 31 December 1859. p.211, c3.

5087 J. C. H. S. *to* **THE EDITORS OF THE** *MISSOURI DEMOCRAT.* **15 December 1859. Osawatomie, Ks.** Reports on an unsuccessful attempt to retrieve a fugitive slave. 31 December 1859. p.211, c5.

5088 VICTOR HUGO *to* **MARIA WESTON CHAPMAN. 6 July 1859. Paris.** Exhorts her to pursue her holy work. 31 December 1859. p.211, c6.

[1860]

5089 D. WORTH *to* **n.n. 26 December 1859. Greensboro Jail.** Explains that he was jailed for selling incendiary books. 6 January 1860. p.2, c2.

5090 F. SNOW *to* **n.n. 28 December 1859. Glastenbury, Ct.** Discusses the charges of treason brought against Mr. Alberton. 6 January 1860. p.2, c3.

5091 C. K. W. *to* **MR. GARRISON. n.d. n.p.** Discusses the Boston clergy's mistreatment of colored people. 6 January 1860. p.2, c5.

5092 CHARLES K. WHIPPLE *to* **THE EDITOR OF THE** *CONGREGATIONALIST.* **6 December 1859. Boston.** Refutes statements made by the *Congregationalist* concerning the *Atlantic Monthly*; discloses the Rowe Street Baptist Church's practice of reserving pews for whites. 6 January 1860. p.2, c5.

5093 F. W. CHESSON *to* **n.n. 16 December 1859. London.** Comments on the American embassy's disgraceful refusal to grant passports to blacks. 6 January 1860. p.2, c6.

5094 C. B. CAMPBELL *to* **SAMUEL MAY, JR. 11 December 1859. Clinton, Ia.** Gives account of a meeting commemorating John Brown in Iowa. 6 January 1860. p.3, c1.

5095 GEO. H. HOYT *to* **E. A. BRACKETT. 21 December 1859. Boston.** Admires Brackett's bust of John Brown. 6 January 1860. p.3, c3.

5096 JOHN BROWN *to* **REV. McFARLAND. 23 November 1859. Charleston.** Expresses his ardent belief in Christianity. 13 January 1860. p.5, c5.

5097 JOHN A. COPELAND *to* **BROTHER. 10 December 1859. Charleston, Va.** Compares his actions at Harpers Ferry to those of fighters of the American Revolution. 13 January 1860. p.6, c2.

5098 JOHN A. COPELAND *to* **FATHER, MOTHER, BROTHERS HENRY, WILLIAM, AND FREDDY AND SISTERS SARAH AND MARY. n.d. n.p.** Requests that they not mourn his death. 13 January 1860. p.6, c2.

5099 HENRY WILSON *to* **HENRY C. WRIGHT. 17 December 1859. Natick, Ma.** Accuses Wright of misrepresenting his views on slave resistance. 13 January 1860. p.7, c3.

5100 ABBY HUTCHINSON *to* **MR. GARRISON. n.d. n.p.** Gives account of a meeting held in commemoration of John Brown at West Brookfield, Vermont. 13 January 1860. p.8, c2.

5101 THOS. REID *to* **FRIEND GARRISON. 11 December 1859. Waukegan.** Gives account of a meeting commemorating the death of John Brown. 13 January 1860. p.8, c3.

5102 JANE ASHBY *to* **n.n. 1 December 1859. Tenterden, England.** Condemns the cruel treatment of John Brown. 13 January 1860. p.8, c5.

5103 J. P. BLANCHARD *to* **W. L. GARRISON. n.d. n.p.** Reports on the arrest of four colored seamen in the District of Columbia. 13 January 1860. p.8, c5.

5104 SARAH P. REMOND *to* **n.n. 4 December 1859. London.** Discusses the prohibition of first-class accommodations to colored Americans on board the Cunard steamers. 20 January 1860. p.9, c2.

5105 N. H. WHITING *to* **THE EDITOR OF THE** *ABINGTON STANDARD.* **22 December 1859. North Abington.** Warns abolitionists of the danger of informers in the North. 20 January 1860. p.9, c2.

5106 SUBSCRIBER *to* **THE EDITOR OF THE** *TRANSCRIPT.* **n.d. n.p.** Discusses the evils of slavery in St. Domingo. 20 January 1860. p.9, c6.

5107 WM. S. DEMOTT *to* **B. R. SULGROVE. 20 December 1859. Cove Spring, Mercer County.** An Indianian abolitionist describes his hostile reception in Kentucky. 20 January 1860. p.10, c2.

5108 L. *to* **n.n. 19 December 1859. St. Louis.** Proposes arguments in favor of slavery. 20 January 1860. p.10, c6.

5109 JAMES REDPATH *to* **W. L. GARRISON. 13 January 1860. Boston.** Speculates on how Brown would have supported himself, had the insurrection been successful. 20 January 1860. p.11, c2.

5110 D. SAUNDERS, JR. *to* **HON. NATHAN APPLETON. 13 January 1860. Lawrence.** Requests aid for those devastated by fire. 20 January 1860. p.11, c3.

5111 M. B. BIRD *to* **W. L. GARRISON. 2 December 1859. St. Heliers, Jersey, England.** Describes the Fourth of July celebration at Framingham Grove; informs Garrison he is writing a book on Haiti. 20 January 1860. p.12, c3.

5112 E. A. L. *to* **MR. GARRISON. n.d. n.p.** Praises John Brown's efforts. 20 January 1860. p.12, c4.

5113 WM. SHREVE BAILEY *to* **FELLOW CITIZENS OF KENTUCKY AND FRIENDS OF THE LIBERTY OF THE PRESS. n.d. n.p.** Reports a burglary of his office. 27 January 1860. p.13, c2.

5114 CASSIUS M. CLAY *to* **n.n. [from the** *National Era***] n.d. n.p.** Criticizes attempts by Republican leaders at Washington to dictate a choice of candidates to their party. 27 January 1860. p.13, c4.

5115 M. R. ROBINSON *to* *LIBERATOR***. n.d. n.p.** Discusses the success of the anti-slavery convention at Auburn. 27 January 1860. p.14, c6.

5116 HIRAM WILSON *to* **W. L. GARRISON. 19 January 1860. St. Catharines, Canada West.** Observes that fugitives from "the land of slavery" arouse Canadians' sympathy for those left behind. 27 January 1860. p.15, c2.

5117 JUSTITIA *to* **MR. EDITOR [W. L. GARRISON]. 17 January 1860. Boston.** Asserts that Garrisonian abolitionism is the only viable form of anti-slavery agitation. 27 January 1860. p.15, c3.

5118 JOHN GRODON *to* **n.n. 31 December 1859. Salem, Oh.** Gives an account of the funeral of Coppock. 27 January 1860. p.15, c3.

5119 C. K. W. *to* **MR. GARRISON. n.d. n.p.** Evaluates the newspaper, the *Congregationalist*. 27 January 1860. p.16, c2.

5120 CHARLES K. WHIPPLE *to* **THE EDITOR OF THE** *CONGREGATIONALIST***. 6 December 1859. Boston.** Accuses the *Congregationalist* of printing erroneous information about the American Board and its Indian missions. 27 January 1860. p.16, c2.

5121 C. K. W. *to* **MR. GARRISON. n.d. n.p.** Criticizes the *Congregationalist* for its failure to print information regarding the Sabbath. 27 January 1860. p.16, c3.

5122 C. K. WHIPPLE *to* **THE EDITOR OF THE** *CONGREGATIONALIST***. n.d. n.p.** Discusses biblical tenets regarding the Sabbath. 27 January 1860. p.16, c3.

5123 J. G. WHITTIER *to* **FRIEND GARRISON. 15 January 1860. Amesbury.** Denounces war and slavery. 27 January 1860. p.16, c3.

5124 AARON M. POWELL *to* **MAY. 15 January 1860. Rochester, N.Y.** Gives an account of the Auburn convention; discusses Garrison's article on Whittier. 27 January 1860. p.16, c4.

5125 C. ROBINSON *to* **THE EDITOR OF THE** *LIBERATOR* **[W. L. GARRISON]. 2 December 1859. Holley, N.Y.** Believes that the Constitution is an anti-slavery document. 27 January 1860. p.16, c4.

5126 THEODORE PARKER *to* **n.n. [extract] 24 December 1859. Rome.** Declares John Brown a saint; expresses compassion for fugitive slaves. 3 February 1860. p.20, c2.

5127 PRESIDENT LORD, DARTMOUTH COLLEGE *to* **J. M. CONRAD, ESQ. 1 December 1859. n.p.** Discusses the public opinion of the North regarding Harpers Ferry. 10 February 1860. p.21, c1.

5128 C. J. INGERSOLL *to* **GENTLEMEN. 5 January 1860. Philadelphia.** Likens American abolitionists to the Jacobins and other "miscreants of misrule." 10 February 1860. p.21, c3.

5129 CAROLINE FREEMAN, MARY HILL, CHARLOTTE JAMES, LOUISA GILBERT, AND ESTHER WASHINGTON *to* **WENDELL PHILLIPS. 1 December 1859. Elmira, N.Y.** Enclose contribution for the family of John Brown. 10 February 1860. p.23, c1.

5130 J. B. SMITH *to* **WENDELL PHILLIPS. 29 December 1859. Boston.** Forwards donation from colored friends in Boston for John Brown's family. 10 February 1860. p.23, c1.

5131 JAMES POINDEXTER *to* **WENDELL PHILLIPS. 31 December 1859. Columbus, Oh.** Forwards contribution from colored people of Columbus for John Brown's family. 10 February 1860. p.23, c1.

5132 WM. B. WARNER *to* **MR. EDITOR [W. L. GARRISON]. n.d. Boston.** Declares that John Brown was not responsible for the murders of Wilkinson, Sherman, and the Doyles at Pottawatomie. 10 February 1860. p.23, c1.

5133 GEO. A. SHERIDAN *to* **MR. EDITOR [W. L. GARRISON]. 28 January 1860. Worcester.** Asserts that the Constitution does not invest Congress with the authority to abolish slavery. 10 February 1860. p.23, c1.

5134 JOHN MAWSON *to* **n.n. 1 January 1860. Bensham, Gateshead, England.** Encourages him in his "mission of love"; laments deaths of George Harris and John Brown. 10 February 1860. p.23, c2.

5135 AARON M. POWELL *to* **MR. MAY. 3 February 1860. Albany, N.Y.** Feels gratified by the results of the Albany Anti-Slavery Convention. 10 February 1860. p.23, c3.

5136 M. JOHNSON *to* **JOHN BROWN, JR. 24 January 1860. Jefferson.** Summons Brown to appear before the Select Committee of the Senate. 10 February 1860. p.23, c4.

5137 JOHN BROWN, JR. *to* **M. JOHNSON. 25 January 1860. Dorset, Oh.** Refuses to appear before the Select Committee of the Senate. 10 February 1860. p.23, c4.

5138 MARIUS R. ROBINSON *to* **GARRISON. 26 January 1860. Hudson, N.Y.** Reports on seven conventions and hopes for the Union's dissolution. 10 February 1860. p.24, c5.

5139 RICHARD REALF *to* **THE EDITOR OF THE *NEW YORK TRIBUNE*. 30 January 1860. Washington, D.C.** Argues that John Brown's actions were not influenced by Republican Party teachings. 17 February 1860. p.25, c1.

5140 MARY ANN BROWN *to* **THE EDITOR OF *NEW YORK TRIBUNE*. 17 January 1860. North Elba.** Claims that Brown is innocent of the murder of several individuals. 17 February 1860. p.25, c2.

5141 SALMON BROWN *to* **SIR. 27 December 1859. North Elba.** States that John Brown was not a participant in the Pottawatomie murders. 17 February 1860. p.25, c2.

5142 C. H. SPURGEON *to* **THE *CHRISTIAN WATCHMAN AND REFLECTOR*. January 1860. Clapham, London.** Denies charge that he omitted anti-slavery works in his American edition of sermons. 17 February 1860. p.25, c5.

5143 SARAH P. REMOND *to* **MR. DALLAS. 12 December 1859. Brunswick Square, W.C.** Relates difficulties in obtaining a passport because of her color. 17 February 1860. p.25, c5.

5144 BENJAMIN MORAN *to* **SARAH P. REMOND. 14 December 1859. London.** Replies to Sarah Remond's letter explaining that she was denied a passport because she is not a citizen. 17 February 1860. p.25, c5.

5145 SARAH P. REMOND *to* **BENJAMIN MORAN. n.d. n.p.** Criticizes Moran for denying her a passport because of her color. 17 February 1860. p.25, c6.

5146 N. PAGE, JR. *to* **FRIEND GARRISON. 6 February 1860. Danversport.** Reports on an anti-slavery meeting of South Danvers. 17 February 1860. p.27, c2.

5147 C. K. W. *to* **THE EDITOR OF THE** *CONGREGATIONALIST.* **n.d. n.p.** Refutes pro-slavery argument put forth by their correspondent J. S. R. 17 February 1860. p.28, c2.

5148 A. D. R. *to* **THE EDITOR OF THE** *BOSTON JOURNAL.* **8 February 1860. Medway, Ma.** Discusses whether or not John Brown was at Pottawatomie. 24 February 1860. p.30, c1.

5149 ANN ROBSON AND HENRIETTA BOLTON *to* **SIR. 4 February 1860. Warrington, England.** Send donation to the AAS. 24 February 1860. p.30, c3.

5150 N. PAGE, JR. *to* **FRIEND GARRISON. n.d. n.p.** Corrects a misprint in the *Liberator.* 24 February 1860. p.30, c5.

5151 JAMES HAUGHTON *to* **COUNTRYMEN. n.d. Dublin.** Requests the Irish in America to support slaves in America. 24 February 1860. p.30, c6.

5152 HENRY C. WRIGHT *to* **GARRISON. 13 February 1860. Georgetown, Oh.** Forwards resolutions of a meeting affirming the right and duty of invasion and insurrection to free slaves. 24 February 1860. p.30, c6.

5153 O. S. MURRAY *to* **BROTHER GARRISON. 10 February 1860. Foster's Crossings, Oh.** Ridicules Southerners' response to John Brown. 24 February 1860. p.31, c1.

5154 T. R. DAVIS *to* **n.n. 9 February 1860. Margaretta, Oh.** Praises lectures by Frances Ellen Watkins. 24 February 1860. p.31, c2.

5155 MARIUS R. ROBINSON *to* **MR. MAY. [extract] 9 February 1860. Salem, Oh.** Praises the anti-slavery work of Mrs. Griffing. 24 February 1860. p.31, c2.

5156 B. *to* **MR. EDITOR. [from the** *New York Journal of Commerce***] n.d. n.p.** Appeals to the humanity of the legislature of Virginia in determining the fate of Hazlett and Stevens. 24 February 1860. p.31, c3.

5157 WILLIAM WHITING *to* **REV. GEORGE BETHUNE. 2 January 1860. Pembroke, Ma.** Attacks Reverend Bethune's speech. 24 February 1860. p.32, c2.

5158 C. C. FOOTE *to* **THE EDITOR OF THE** *NEW YORK HERALD.* **n.d. n.p.** Discusses the state of colored refugees in Canada. 2 March 1860. p.33, c3.

5159 F. B. SANBORN *to* **J. M. MASON. 1 February 1860. n.p.** Declines to appear before the Senate committee to testify on the Harpers Ferry incident. 2 March 1860. p.33, c6.

5160 D. F. MURPHY *to* **THADDEUS HYATT. 14 February 1860. Washington, D.C.** Issues summons to appear before the Select Committee. 2 March 1860. p.34, c1.

5161 THADDEUS HYATT *to* **J. M. MASON. 17 February 1860. Washington, D.C.** Requests an extension of the date of his appearance before the Select Committee. 2 March 1860. p.34, c1.

5162 D. F. MURPHY *to* **THADDEUS HYATT. 17 February 1860. Washington, D.C.** Denies an extension of the date of Murphy's appearance before the Select Committee. 2 March 1860. p.34, c1.

5163 THADDEUS HYATT *to* **J. M. MASON. 20 February 1860. Washington, D.C.** Requests an additional ten days before appearance before Select Committee. 2 March 1860. p.34, c1.

5164 J. M. MASON *to* **THADDEUS HYATT. 20 February 1860. Washington, D.C.** Insists upon Hyatt's appearance before Select Committee without delay. 2 March 1860. p.34, c2.

5165 THADDEUS HYATT *to* **J. M. MASON. 21 February 1860. Washington, D.C.** Informs Mason that the constitutionality of the Select Committee's insistent request is to be tested, thus creating a delay in Hyatt's appearance. 2 March 1860. p.34, c2.

5166 THADDEUS HYATT *to* **D. R. McNAIR. 24 February 1860. Boston.** Informs the sergeant at arms of his whereabouts on 7 March. 2 March 1860. p.34, c2.

5167 THADDEUS HYATT *to* **J. M. MASON. 24 February 1860. Boston.** Informs Mason that he has hired Samuel E. Sewall as his attorney. 2 March 1860. p.34, c2.

5168 CHARLES SUMNER *to* **SIR. 21 February 1860. Washington, D.C.** Regrets he is unable to attend a Washington celebration. 2 March 1860. p.34, c2.

5169 THOMAS GARRETT *to* **FRIEND GARRISON. 24 January 1860. Wilmington, De.** Congratulates himself on his rescue of over 2000 slaves. 2 March 1860. p.34, c4.

5170 LIZZIE DE GARMO *to* **MR. GARRISON. 1 February 1860. Poughkeepsie.** Forwards resolutions of the convention at Poughkeepsie. 2 March 1860. p.34, c5.

5171 H. W. CARTER *to* **JAMES WHITTEMORE. 5 February 1860. Athol.** Praises the heroic deeds of John Brown. 2 March 1860. p.35, c2.

5172 JACOB LEONARD *to* **n.n. 19 February 1860. East Bridgewater.** Condemns slavery; upholds the work of Garrison and the abolitionists. 2 March 1860. p.35, c4.

5173 J. J. ORMOND *to* **SUSAN B. ANTHONY. 26 December 1859. Tuscaloosa.** Informs of the rejection of a women's rights petition by the Alabama legislature. 2 March 1860. p.36, c3.

5174 J. H. F. *to* **W. L. GARRISON. 25 February 1860. Boston.** Denounces the imprisonment of Manuel Moran for obeying the laws of God and nature. 2 March 1860. p.36, c5.

5175 ANN L. RALEY *to* **GOV. LETCHER. 2 February 1860. Springdale. Ia.** Criticizes the treatment of John Brown and his men after their capture. 9 March 1860. p.37, c5.

5176 JOHN MAWSON *to* **FRIEND. 14 February 1860. Newcastle, Bensham, England.** Reports on the lectures of George Thompson. 9 March 1860. p.38, c5.

5177 DANIEL WORTH *to* **REV. WM. C. WHITCOMB. 16 February 1860. Greensboro' Prison, N.C.** Expresses pleasure at receiving his letter of encouragement. 9 March 1860. p.38, c5.

5178 M. HESLEY, M. H. SIGNOR, J. BEHEL, AND HENRY E. McKINNEY *to* **SIR. n.d. Earlville, Il.** Describe Parker Pillsbury's lectures in Earlville. 9 March 1860. p.38, c6.

5179 HENRY C. WRIGHT *to* **GARRISON. 4 February 1860. Ohio.** Urges that there be no truce made with slaveholders; laments the death of Edwin Coppoch. 9 March 1860. p.39, c1.

5180 S. S. FOSTER *to* **EMMETT DENSMORE. 4 March 1860. Worcester.** Defines his differences with radical abolitionists; discusses the Constitution. 9 March 1860. p.39, c2.

5181 CHAS D. MILLER *to* **WATTS SHERMAN. 13 February 1860. Peterboro.** Claims that Gerrit Smith was not connected with the Central Association. 9 March 1860. p.38, c3.

5182 ROYAL PHELPS *to* **C. D. MILLER. 18 February 1860. New York.** Denies that he signed the New York Vigilante Association's publication slandering Gerrit Smith. 9 March 1860. p.39, c3.

5183 MRS. S. L. M. BARLOW *to* **n.n. [extract] n.d. n.p.** Insists that Gerrit Smith had no connection with the Central Association. 9 March 1860. p.39, c3.

5184 CHARLES IRWIN *to* **SIR. n.d. n.p.** Gives an account of a tribute to the memory of John Brown. 9 March 1860. p.39, c4.

5185 VICTOR HUGO *to* **HAITIANS. n.d. n.p.** Sends thanks; discusses John Brown at Harpers Ferry. 9 March 1860. p.39, c4.

5186 C. ROBINSON *to* **HENRY WILSON. 10 February 1860. Holley, N.Y.** Criticizes the weak stand of Republicans on the issue of slavery. 9 March 1860. p.40, c2.

5187 JACOB WALTON *to* **W. L. GARRISON. 10 November 1859. Adrian.** Forwards an account of an anti-slavery convention in Adrian. 9 March 1860. p.40, c4.

5188 JOSIAH PERHAM *to* **JOHN LETCHER, GOV. OF VIRGINIA. 1 February 1860. Boston, Ma.** Extends invitation to members of the Virginia legislature to visit the Massachusetts legislature while it is in session. 9 March 1860. p.40, c5.

5189 JAMES HAUGHTON *to* **THE EDITOR OF THE** *SLIGO CHAMPION.* **November 1859. 35 Eccles Street.** Urges the Irish to take a stronger stand on American slavery. 16 March 1860. p.41, c2.

5190 GEO. T. DOWNING *to* **W. C. NELL, ESQ. 3 March 1860. Newport.** Regrets he is unable to attend the Attucks celebration at Boston. 16 March 1860. p.43, c1.

5191 n.n. *to* **WM. C. NELL. 20 February 1860. New London.** Gives a favorable review of Wendell Phillips' lecture on the "Lost Arts." 16 March 1860. p.43, c2.

5192 DANIEL MANN *to* **MR. GARRISON. n.d. Plainesville, Oh.** Opposes the non-resistance principle. 16 March 1860. p.44, c3.

5193 R. J. HINTON *to* **THE EDITOR OF THE** *TRAVELLER.* **16 March 1860. Boston.** Discusses the lives of the late Aaron C. Stephens and Albert Hazlett. 23 March 1860. p.48 [46], c1.

5194 A. D. STEVENS *to* **FRIENDS. 17 December 1859. Charleston, Va.** Reflects upon his impending execution. 23 March 1860. p.48 [46], c4.

5195 A. D. STEVENS *to* **FRIENDS. 17 February 1860. n.p.** Expresses his thoughts about death. 23 March 1860. p.48 [46], c5.

5196 WILLIAM S. BAILEY *to* **FRIEND GARRISON. 13 March 1860. Newport, Ky.** Requests pecuniary aid. 23 March 1860. p.47, c1.

5197 SAMUEL MAY, JR. *to* **MR. GARRISON. n.d. n.p.** Requests that a letter from Andrew T. Foss be printed in *Liberator*. 23 March 1860. p.47, cl.

5198 A. T FOSS *to* **MAY. 5 March 1860. Harwich.** Gives an account of anti-slavery meetings; describes the anti-slavery work of Mr. Munsell and Joshua H. Robbins. 23 March 1860. p.47, c2.

5199 A. FETTIERRE *to* **OUR FELLOW-CITIZENS AND FRIENDS. n.d. n.p.** Beseeches friends to give to the support of John Brown's widow. 23 March 1860. p.47, c4.

5200 n.n. *to* **THE EDITOR OF THE** *BOSTON TRAVELLER.* **16 March 1860. Washington.** Discusses the circumstances of Hyatt's imprisonment. 23 March 1860. p.47, c4.

5201 REUBEN H. OBER *to* **FRIEND GARRISON. n.d. n.p.** Informs Garrison that he is sending the *Liberator* to the family of John Brown. 23 March 1860. p.47, c5.

5202 A. G. S. *to* **THE** *LIBERATOR.* **n.d. n.p.** Admits his inconsistency in being a John Brown sympathizer and believing in non-resistance. 23 March 1860. p.48, c2.

5203 AN ABOLITIONIST *to* **THE EDITOR OF THE** *DAILY CHRONICLE.* **3 March 1860. Newcastle, England.** Points out inconsistencies in Douglass' view of the Constitution. 30 March 1860. p.49, c6.

5204 A. D. STEVENS *to* **FRIEND. [extract from the** *Cleveland Agitator*] **28 February 1860. Charleston jail, Va.** States his belief in spiritual theory. 30 March 1860. p.50, c2.

5205 JUSTITIA *to* **FRIEND GARRISON. 27 March 1860. Boston.** Tells of the presentation of Charles F. Hovey's protrait to his friends. 30 March 1860. p.51, c2.

5206 GEORGE THOMPSON *to* **W. L. GARRISON. 9 March 1860. Glasgow.** Forwards a copy of the anti-slavery resolution adopted by the people of Port Glasgow. 30 March 1860. p.51, c3.

5207 WM. BIRKMYRE *to* **THE EDITOR OF THE** *LIBERATOR* **[W. L. GARRISON]. 6 March 1860. Port Glasgow.** Forwards the resolution adopted at a public meeting for publication in the *Liberator*. 30 March 1860. p.51, c3.

5208 ANDREW GLENDINNING *to* **THE EDITOR OF THE** *LIBERATOR* **[W. L. GARRISON]. 7 March 1860. Greenock.** Encloses copy of the resolution opposing slavery in the United States. 30 March 1860. p.51, c3.

5209 FOWLER AND WELLS *to* **THE EDITOR OF THE** *LIBERATOR* **[W. L. GARRISON]. 26 March 1860. New York.** Reply to criticism of Rev. W. W. Cazlet's *Human Voice*. 30 March 1860. p.51, c3.

5210 n.n. *to* **MR. GARRISON. n.d. n.p.** Inquires whether he has heard of John Madison, a professed anti-slavery lecturer. 30 March 1860. p.51, c3.

5211 A. J. GROVER *to* **FRIEND GARRISON. 16 March 1860. Earlville, Il.** Defends Parker Pillsbury, stating that he is not a falsifier. 30 March 1860. p.52, c3.

5212 A. P. B. *to* **FRIEND GARRISON. 20 March 1860. Worcester.** Wishes that the Boston Tract Society had an "abolition notion" in it. 30 March 1860. p.52, c4.

5213 E. W. T. *to* **FRIEND H. 18 March 1860. Springfield.** Praises a touching speech by William H. Seward. 30 March 1860. p.52, c4.

5214 THEODORE PARKER *to* **FRIEND. 25 February 1860. Rome.** Criticizes Italy for its emphasis on art rather than labor. 6 April 1860. p.54, c5.

5215 R. *to* **MR. EDITOR [W. L. GARRISON]. 1 April 1860. Philadelphia.** Remarks on the indifference of the public to the case of Moses Harper, a fugitive slave. 6 April 1860. p.54, c6.

5216 E. R. PLACE *to* **MR. GARRISON. n.d. n.p.** Discusses Thomas Jefferson's opposition to the Sedition Law. 6 April 1860. p.55, c3.

5217 THOMAS GUTHRIE *to* **THE EDITOR OF THE *PRESBYTERIAN*. 27 February 1860. Edinburgh.** Criticizes the American church for its silence on slavery. 13 April 1860. p.57, c6.

5218 A. F. B. *to* **FRIEND P. [from the *New York Journal*] n.d. n.p.** Criticizes Edward Everett for his small donation to the *New York Ledger*. 13 April 1860. p.58, c6.

5219 F. B. SANBORN *to* **THE CITIZENS OF MASSACHUSETTS. 13 April 1860. Concord, Ma.** Claims his arrest was a cowardly assault. 13 April 1860. p.59, c1.

5220 CASSIUS M. CLAY *to* **B. n.d. n.p.** Describes the current "war" between the Republicans and the Democrats following the overthrow of William Bailey's press. 13 April 1860. p.59, c4.

5221 J. H. C. *to* **SAMUEL MAY, JR. [extract] n.d. n.p.** A Republican deplores the timid and compromising policy of his party. 20 April 1860. p.63, c3.

5222 A. HOGEBOOM *to* **STEPHEN S. FOSTER. 10 April 1860. Shed's Corners, N.Y.** Warns of political action in defense of the slave. 20 April 1860. p.63, c4.

5223 C. ROBINSON *to* **WILLIAM H. SEWARD. 16 March 1860. Holley, N.Y.** A common laborer expresses his views of the Union. 20 April 1860. p.64, c4.

5224 S. HOXIE RICHARDSON *to* **THE *LIBERATOR*. 22 March 1860. Earlville, Il.** Praises Parker Pillsbury's lectures. 20 April 1860. p.64, c6.

5225 W. C. N. *to* **W. L. GARRISON. n.d. n.p.** Forwards letter of support to Garrison for publication. 20 April 1860. p.64, c6.

5226 n.n. *to* **n.n. [extract] n.d. n.p.** Believes that slavery can never be abolished peacefully; concurs with Garrison's views on the subject. 20 April 1860. p.64, c6.

5227 ALPHA *to* **THE EDITOR OF THE *BOSTON TRAVELLER*. 10 April 1860. Washington.** Informs that Alexander Scarborough is a suspected fugitive slave. 27 April 1860. p.65, c4.

5228 SARAH LOGUE *to* **REV. J. W. LOGUEN. [from the** *New York Standard***] 20 February 1860. Maury County, Tn.** A former mistress threatens to have him hunted down unless he forwards $1000 to her. 27 April 1860. p.65, c5.

5229 J. W. LOGUEN *to* **MRS. SARAH LOGUE. 28 March 1860. Syracuse, N.Y.** Refuses to comply with her demands. 27 April 1860. p.65, c5.

5230 F. S. BLISS *to* **MR. EDITOR [W. L. GARRISON]. n.d. n.p.** Discusses the influence of slavery on Northern young men. 27 April 1860. p.66, c6.

5231 MARY CARPENTER *to* **MRS. CHAPMAN. 9 March 1860. Red Ridge House, Bristol, England.** Pays tribute to Mrs. Follen. 27 April 1860. p.67, c1.

5232 n.n. *to* **n.n. [extract] n.d. n.p.** Criticizes an anti-slavery speech by the Rev. Dr. Guthrie. 4 May 1860. p.69, c2.

5233 R. FULLER *to* **BROTHER. n.d. n.p.** Condemns Mr. Spurgeon as a "reckless fanatic" and murderer. 4 May 1860. p.69, c5.

5234 THADDEUS HYATT *to* **THE FRIENDS OF CONSTITUTIONAL LIBERTY OF ALL PARTIES. 16 April 1860. Washington Jail.** Criticizes the Senate's handling of his case. 4 May 1860. p.70, c4.

5235 JOHN JAY *to* **THADDEUS HYATT. 12 April 1860. Katonah, N.Y.** Supports him in his conflict with the Senate. 4 May 1860. p.70, c4.

5236 WM. M. EVARTS *to* **THADDEUS HYATT. 12 April 1860. New York.** Regrets he is unable to participate in a public discussion concerning Hyatt's case. 4 May 1860. p.70, c4.

5237 JOHN PIERPONT *to* **THADDEUS HYATT. 19 March 1860. West Medford, Ma.** Expresses his admiration for Hyatt. 4 May 1860. p.70, c4.

5238 GEORGE B. CHEEVER *to* **THADDEUS HYATT. 4 April 1860. n.p.** Thanks Hyatt for his example of integrity. 4 May 1860. p.70, c4.

5239 WENDELL PHILLIPS *to* **THADDEUS HYATT. 3 April. n.p.** Suggests that he try other means of rousing public sentiment, rather than die in vain. 4 May 1860. p.70, c5.

5240 ALEX M. GOW *to* **THADDEUS HYATT. 1 April 1860. Dixon, Lee County, Il.** Expresses sympathy for Hyatt in his persecution. 4 May 1860. p.70, c5.

5241 J. H. FOWLER *to* **HON. OWEN LOVEJOY. 28 April 1860. Cambridge.** States his views on the Constitution and its relation to slavery. 4 May 1860. p.70, c5.

5242 PARKER PILLSBURY *to* **THE EDITORS OF THE** *ROCHESTER AMERICAN***. 15 April 1860. Concord, N.H.** Criticizes the article entitled "Garrisonian Ultras." 4 May 1860. p.71, c1.

5243 JAMES M. WEST *to* **THE EDITOR OF THE** *GOLCONDA WEEKLY HERALD***. 12 April 1860. Broad Oaks, Pope County, Il.** Criticizes paper for printing falsehoods about him in order to injure his reputation. 11 May 1860. p.73, c2.

5244 A REPUBLICAN *to* **n.n. 11 April 1860. Lewis, De.** Reports that postmasters were ordered not to deliver the *New York Tribune* or the *Delaware Republican*. 11 May 1860. p.73, c5.

5245 JOHN G. FEE *to* **THE EDITORS OF THE** *CINCINNATI GAZETTE*. **9 April 1860. Cincinnati.** Rebukes C. M. Clay's erroneous criticism of Fee and the "Kentucky radicals." 11 May 1860. p.73, c5.

5246 S. M. BOOTH *to* **THE EDITORS OF THE** *FREE DEMOCRAT*. **18 April 1860. Milwaukee.** Protests his imprisonment. 11 May 1860. p.74, c1.

5247 S. M. BOOTH *to* **n.n. 5 April 1860. United States Custom House, Milwaukee.** Relates the story of the rescue of Joshua Glover and Booth's subsequent imprisonment. 11 May 1860. p.74, c2.

5248 WENDELL PHILLIPS *to* **THE** *INDEPENDENT*. **20 April 1860. Boston.** Defends W. L. Garrison, who he insists is not an infidel. 11 May 1860. p.74, c4.

5249 n.n. *to* **n.n. [extract] 6 May 1860. At sea.** Tells of the discovery of a fugitive slave. 11 May 1860. p.75, c2.

5250 ANDREW JACKSON *to* **FREE COLORED INHABITANTS OF LOUISIANA. 21 September 1814. Mobile.** Asks for volunteers to fight against the British. 18 May 1860. p.78, c2.

5251 M. D. CONWAY *to* **MR. MAY. 11 March 1860. Cincinnati.** States that he may not be able to attend the AAS meeting. 18 May 1860. p.79, c3.

5252 JOSHUA YOUNG *to* **SAMUEL MAY, JR. 18 March 1860. Burlington, Vt.** Regrets he is unable to attend the AAS meeting. 18 May 1860. p.79, c4.

5253 T. T. O. *to* **FRIEND GARRISON. 14 May 1860. Brooklyn.** Reports on the anniversary meetings of the AS in New York, which criticized Mrs. Stanton for bringing up the issue of women's rights during the meetings. 18 May 1860. p.79, c4.

5254 C. M. CLAY *to* **THE EDITOR OF THE** *NEW YORK TRIBUNE*. **30 April 1860. White Hall.** Requests donations for William S. Bailey, editor of the *Free South*. 18 May 1860. p.79, c5.

5255 W. H. FURNESS *to* **FRIEND. n.d. n.p.** Regrets he is unable to attend the AAS convention. 25 May 1860. p.83, c2.

5256 GEO. M. SIMONDS *to* **MR. GARRISON. 30 May 1860. Boston.** Reports on a Methodist convention honoring Millard Fillmore. 1 June 1860. p.87, c1.

5257 E. C. S. *to* **MR. EDITOR [W. L. GARRISON]. n.d. n.p.** Objects to the legal disadvantages women face in marriage and divorce. 1 June 1860. p.88, c2.

5258 CHARLES HOWARD MALCOM *to* **SAMUEL MAY, JR. 21 May 1860. Newport, R.I.** Reports he will attend the New England AS convention. 8 June 1860. p.90, c4.

5259 GERRIT SMITH *to* **WILLIAM GOODELL. 1 May 1860. Peterboro.** Discusses his faith and his recent mental collapse. 8 June 1860. p.92, c2.

5260 WILLIAM S. BAILEY *to* **THE EDITOR OF THE** *NEW YORK TRIBUNE*. **21 May 1860. Newport, Ky.** Discusses his argument with Mr. Clay; states that he did not abandon the Kentucky Free State platform. 15 June 1860. p.94, c1.

5261 JEHIEL CLAFLIN *to* **MAY. 26 May 1860. West Brookfield, Vt.** Prefers that Republicans come into power. 15 June 1860. p.95, c1.

5262 W. C. N. *to* **MR. GARRISON. June 1860. Boston.** Forwards an abstract of the proceedings of a 30 April meeting of the colored citizens of Boston. 15 June 1860. p.95, c1.

5263 JAS. REDPATH *to* **C. H. BRAINARD. 1 June 1860. Malden.** Expresses appreciation for a portrait of a young child bearing the heading, "Light of Our Home." 15 June 1860. p.95, c1.

5264 PERLEY *to* **THE EDITOR OF THE** *BOSTON JOURNAL.* **1 June 1860. Washington.** Notes that even the "Hotspurs of the South" listened to the lecture by Charles Francis Adams. 15 June 1860. p.96, c2.

5265 JOSIAH QUINCY *to* **SUMNER. 5 June 1860. Boston.** Compliments Sumner on his speech. 22 June 1860. p.99, c4.

5266 DANIEL MANN *to* **W. L. GARRISON. 8 May 1860. Painesville, Oh.** Criticizes nonresistance. 22 June 1860. p.100, c2.

5267 L. MARIA CHILD *to* **THE** *NEW YORK BEE.* **25 May 1860. Wayland.** Asserts that she never had a son or daughter, in response to an article published in the paper. 29 June 1860. p.101, c4.

5268 ELIAS BOWEN *to* **n.n. [extract from the** *Northern Independent***] n.d. n.p.** Claims he is embarrassed by slaveholding Methodists. 29 June 1860. p.101, c4.

5269 W. P. N. *to* **n.n. n.d. n.p.** Conveys his observations on Haiti. 29 June 1860. p.101, c5.

5270 MRS. CHILD *to* **n.n. n.d. n.p.** Encloses reply of a friend to a letter of remonstrance. 29 June 1860. p.102, c3.

5271 n.n. *to* **n.n. [extract] n.d. n.p.** Defends her "Parkerism." 29 June 1860. p.102, c3.

5272 A. J. FOSS *to* **W. L. GARRISON. 19 June 1860. Clinton.** Gives an account of the successful convention at DeWitt; describes compassion demonstrated during a tornado; refutes a Southern slaveholder's argument. 29 June 1860. p.102, c5.

5273 A REPUBLICAN *to* **MR. EDITOR [W. L. GARRISON]. 14 June 1860. Northern Egyptian Line, Il.** Corrects W. Phillips' statements on Lincoln and the "irrepressible conflict." 29 June 1860. p.102, c6.

5274 A. HOGEBOOM *to* **n.n. 22 June 1860. Shed's Corners, N.Y.** Gives favorable review of Mr. Sumner's speech. 29 June 1860. p.103, c3.

5275 R. J. HINTON AND JAMES REDPATH *to* **THE EDITOR OF THE** *LIBERATOR.* **1 June 1860. Boston, Ma.** Discuss the lives of John Brown's men. 29 June 1860. p.104, c2.

5276 E. W. T. *to* **n.n. n.d. Springfield, Ma.** Gives an account of abolition activity in Springfield. 29 June 1860. p.104, c5.

5277 JAS. B. TAYLOR *to* **n.n. [from the** *Watchman and Reflector***] 8 March 1860. Richmond, Va.** Reports on the Southern view of the irrepressible conflict. 6 July 1860. p.105, c1.

5278 E. H. HEYWOOD *to* **GARRISON. 21 June 1860. Boston.** Corrects misstatements made about the Princeton centennial celebration. 6 July 1860. p.106, c3.

5279 E. R. P. *to* **MR. GARRISON. n.d. n.p.** Warns of the possible extension of the power of slaveholders. 6 July 1860. p.106, c5.

5280 A. B. *to* **MR. MAY. 12 June 1860. West Randolph, Vt.** Gives a favorable review of Sumner's speech. 6 July 1860. p.106, c6.

5281 D. A. WASSON *to* **n.n. n.d. n.p.** Commemorates Theodore Parker. 6 July 1860. p.107, c2.

5282 GOV. W. DENISON *to* **GOV. ISHAM G. HARRIS. 2 June 1860. Columbus.** Refuses to issue extradition papers for "Negro-stealers." 6 July 1860. p.107, c3.

5283 GOV. ISHAM G. HARRIS *to* **GOV. W. DENISON. 26 May 1860. Nashville, Tn.** Condemns the governor's refusal to arrest Negro-stealers. 6 July 1860. p.107, c3.

5284 THOMAS P. KNOX *to* **GARRISON. n.d. n.p.** Gives an account of lectures by Parker Pillsbury in Hyannis. 6 July 1860. p.107, c4.

5285 SAMUEL MAY, JR. *to* **MR. GARRISON. 2 July 1860. Leicester.** Regrets he is unable to attend the Fourth of July anti-slavery meeting. 13 July 1860. p.109, c3.

5286 HENRY C. WRIGHT *to* **W. L. GARRISON. 8 July 1860. Milford, Ma.** Advocates resistance to slaveholders and obedience to God. 13 July 1860. p.111, c3.

5287 LUCRETIA MOTT *to* **HARRIOT K. HUNT. 21 June 1860. Roadside, near Philadelphia.** Regrets she is unable to attend her silver wedding celebration. 13 July 1860. p.112, c5.

5288 JAMES HAUGHTON *to* **THE EDITOR OF THE** *DUBLIN NEWS.* **19 June 1860. Dublin.** Criticizes the *London Times'* handling of moral issues, especially in its criticism of a recent speech by Charles Sumner. 20 July 1860. p.114, c6.

5289 F. D. GAGE *to* **FRIEND GARRISON. n.d. Carbondale, Il.** Praises the late Theodore Parker. 20 July 1860. p.115, c2.

5290 S. *to* **MR. EDITOR [W. L. GARRISON]. n.d. n.p.** Comments on the movement in Massachusetts for physical education. 20 July 1860. p.115, c3.

5291 C. M. S. *to* **MR. GARRISON. n.d. n.p.** Corrects misprinted line of a poem. 20 July 1860. p.115, c3.

5292 DANIEL MANN *to* **W. L. GARRISON. n.d. n.p.** Corrects errors in the printing of his letter; compares Mr. Whipple's views of non-resistance with his own. 20 July 1860. p.116, c3.

5293 ONE *to* **MR. GARRISON. 2 July 1860. Johnstown.** Envisions the culmination of the women's rights movement in the Apocalypse. 20 July 1860. p.116, c3.

5294 J. E. KINGMAN *to* **n.n. 4 July 1860. Clifton, Il.** Reports on the abduction of three colored men. 20 July 1860. p.116, c5.

5295 CHARLES SUMNER *to* **HON. F. W. LINCOLN. 1 July 1860. Washington.** Regrets he is unable to attend a festival in Boston. 20 July 1860. p.116, c5.

5296 FRANCIS JACKSON, SAMUEL MAY, JR., E. H. HEYWOOD, W. L. GAR-RISON, EDMUND QUINCY, AND SAMUEL T. MAY *to* **THE EDITOR OF THE** *LONDON ANTI-SLAVERY ADVOCATE.* **11 June 1860. Leicester.** Refute Miss Bird's defamation of Wendell Phillips. 27 July 1860. p.117, c3.

5297 THOS. WENTWORTH HIGGINSON *to* **MRS. BROWN. 29 June 1860. Worcester, Ma.** Regrets he is unable to attend the Fourth of July celebration. 27 July 1860. p.117, c6.

5298 H. FORD DOUGLASS *to* **MESSRS. HINTON AND REDPATH. 29 June 1860. Boston.** Regrets he is unable to attend the Fourth of July celebration. 27 July 1860. p.117, c6.

5299 J. STELLA MARTIN *to* **GENTLEMEN. 30 June 1860. Boston.** Regrets he is unable to attend the Fourth of July celebration. 27 July 1860. p.117, c6.

5300 JAMES REDPATH *to* **JOHN BROWN, JR. 2 July 1860. Malden, Ma.** Regrets he is unable to attend the Fourth of July celebration. 27 July 1860. p.117, c6.

5301 F. B. SANBORN *to* **FRIEND. 1 July 1860. Concord.** Regrets he is unable to attend the Fourth of July celebration. 27 July 1860. p.118, c1.

5302 C. H. BRAINARD *to* **JAMES REDPATH. 1 July 1860. Boston.** Regrets he is unable to attend the Fourth of July celebration. 27 July 1860. p.118, c1.

5303 FREDERICK DOUGLASS *to* **JAMES REDPATH. 29 June 1860. Rochester.** Regrets he is unable to attend the Fourth of July celebration; praises John Brown; feels little hope for peaceful emancipation of slave. 27 July 1860. p.118, c1.

5304 THEODORE PARKER *to* **PROGRESSIVE FRIENDS IN PENNSYLVANIA. 25 September 1859. Montreux, Switzerland.** States that his poor health will prohibit him from continuing to preach. 27 July 1860. p.118, c5.

5305 WENDELL PHILLIPS *to* **MR. EDITOR [W. L. GARRISON]. n.d. n.p.** Denounces the *Tribune* and a bill proposed by Mr. Lincoln. 27 July 1860. p.119, c2.

5306 B. G. KNIGHT *to* **GARRISON. n.d. Rural, Rock Island County, Il.** Praises the Cambridge Reform Convention. 27 July 1860, p.119, c2.

5307 D. M. A. *to* **W. L. GARRISON. 9 July 1860. East Lempster, N.H.** Reports on an anti-slavery lecture in New Hampshire. 27 July 1860. p.119, c3.

5308 D. M. ALLEN *to* **REV. MR. FANKS. 15 July 1860. Newbury, Geauga County, Oh.** Asserts that the Methodist Episcopal church is pro-slavery. 27 July 1860. p.119, c3.

5309 A VERMONTER *to* **MR. GARRISON. 8 July 1860. Williamstown, Vt.** Gives reasons for renewing his subscription to the *Liberator*. 27 July 1860. p.119, c4.

5310 JOHN C. UNDERWOOD *to* **CORNELIA BARBOUR. [from the** *New York Tribune***]** 9 July 1860. New York. Rejoices in her decision to free her slaves. 27 July 1860. p.119, c4.

5311 S. M. BOOTH *to* **THE EDITORS OF THE** *FREE DEMOCRAT.* **28 June 1860. United States Custom House.** Clarifies the circumstances of his imprisonment for violating the Fugitive Slave Law. 3 August 1860. p.121, c2.

5312 CHAS. R. PAYOR *to* **CAPT. DE LISLE. 15 July 1860. Dallas.** Warns of a plot to burn northern Texas. 3 August 1860. p.123, c1.

5313 W. L. GARRISON *to* **n.n. [extract] 24 July. Northumberland.** Reports on his arrival at Northumberland. 3 August 1860. p.123, c2.

5314 n.n. *to* **n.n. [extract] n.d. Illinois.** Reports that many Republicans in northern Illinois find it hard to support Lincoln because of his anti-slavery principles. 3 August 1860. p.123, c3.

5315 VINDEX *to* **n.n. 1 July 1860. New Braunfels, Tx.** Sends copy of new laws regarding slaves. 3 August 1860. p.123, c4.

5316 S. HARBAUGH *to* **THE EDITOR OF THE** *MISSOURI DEMOCRAT.* **8 July 1860. King's Hotel.** Describes his being driven out of Lexington, Missouri. 3 August 1860. p.123, c4.

5317 A. C. H. *to* **THE EDITOR OF THE** *CHRISTIAN INQUIRER.* **16 July. Jersey City.** Praises the late Theodore Parker. 3 August 1860. p.124, c5.

5318 HENRY BLEBY *to* **OLIVER JOHNSON. 8 July 1860. Barbados.** Praises Mr. Jordan's anti-slavery sentiments and activities. 10 August 1860. p.125, c1.

5319 CHARLES SUMNER *to* **W. L. GARRISON. 30 July 1860. Boston.** States that the condition of the Negroes in the West Indies has improved since emancipation. 10 August 1860. p.125, c3.

5320 CHARLES FRANCIS ADAMS *to* **W. L. GARRISON. 21 July 1860. Quincy.** Pronounces emancipation in the West Indies a "grave failure." 10 August 1860. p.125, c4.

5321 JOHN A. ANDREW *to* **W. L. GARRISON. 31 July 1860. Boston.** Asserts that the question of emancipation is not sectional but universal. 10 August 1860. p.125, c4.

5322 W. L. GARRISON *to* **E. H. HEYWOOD. 30 July 1860. Northumberland, N.H.** Describes the success of emancipation in the West Indies. 10 August 1860. p.125, c5.

5323 CHARLES K. WHIPPLE *to* **THE EDITOR OF THE** *CHRISTIAN WATCHMAN AND REFLECTOR.* **June 1860. n.p.** Refutes the paper's charge that Theodore Parker rejected Christianity. 10 August 1860. p.128, c2.

5324 CHARLES K. WHIPPLE *to* **THE EDITOR OF THE** *CHRISTIAN WATCHMAN AND REFLECTOR.* **29 July 1860. Boston.** Writes in defense of Theodore Parker's beliefs. 10 August 1860. p.128, c2.

5325 W. L. GARRISON *to* **GEORGE W. STACY. 31 July 1860. Northumberland.** Describes the success of emancipation in the West Indies. 17 August 1860. p.130, c5.

5326 ANDREW WELLINGTON *to* **FRIEND GARRISON. 31 July 1860. East Lexington.** Gives an account of the Middlesex County AS meeting. 17 August 1860. p.131, c2.

5327 C. B. CAMPBELL *to* **FRIEND PILLSBURY. July 1860. Clinton, Ia.** Reports on the conventions in Illinois and Iowa. 17 August 1860. p.132, c2.

5328 n.n. *to* **THE EDITOR OF THE** *TELEGRAPH.* **21 July 1860. Dallas, Tx.** Gives an account of the burning of Dallas. 24 August 1860. p.133, c1.

5329 JOHN BROWN, JR. *to* **GENERAL FABRE GEFFRARD, PRESIDENT OF THE REPUBLIC OF HAYTI. 16 April 1860. Jefferson, Oh.** Thanks Haitians for their sympathy. 24 August 1860. p.133, c4.

5330 J. R. GIDDINGS *to* **WENDELL PHILLIPS. 30 July 1860. Jefferson.** Discusses actions of Mr. Lincoln regarding slavery. 24 August 1860. p.133, c5.

5331 R. *to* **MR. EDITOR [W. L. GARRISON]. 29 July 1860. Philadelphia.** Reports on the arrest of a fugitive slave, Ben Herd. 24 August 1860. p.135, c3.

5332 H. W. CARTER *to* **REV. JOHN PIERPONT. 8 August 1860. Athol.** Pays tribute to Theodore Parker. 24 August 1860. p.136, c2.

5333 HENRY C. WRIGHT *to* **W. L. GARRISON. 2 August 1860. Pratt's Hall, Providence, R.I.** Discusses the convention of spiritualists and a speech by Abby K. Foster. 24 August 1860. p.136, c4.

5334 A. F. R. *to* **GARRISON. 18 August 1860. Springfield.** Requests that a reply to the *Springfield Republican* article, "What Shall be Done With the Darkies" be published. 31 August 1860. p.137, c2.

5335 R. *to* **THE EDITOR OF THE *SPRINGFIELD REPUBLICAN*. n.d. n.p.** Addresses the question "what is to be done with the darkies?" 31 August 1860. p. 137, c2.

5336 A. H. *to* **n.n. [from the *Montpelier Watchman*] 29 July 1860. West Randolph.** Reports on William Wells Brown's endeavors to create deeper anti-slavery sentiments. 31 August 1860. p.137, c3.

5337 S. HARBAUGH *to* **THE EDITORS OF THE *MISSOURI DEMOCRAT*. 8 July 1860. King's Hotel.** Reports mobbing of the *Citizen's Public Advertiser* for supporting Lincoln and Hamlin. 31 August 1860. p.137, c5.

5338 n.n. *to* **THE EDITOR OF THE *REPUBLICAN*. 4 August 1860. Wyandot, Kansas Territory.** Reports on kidnapping in the Kansas Territory. 31 August 1860. p.138, c1.

5339 FRANCES D. GAGE *to* **MR. GARRISON. 15 August 1860. Carbondale, Il.** Discusses the beneficial results of emancipation in the West Indies. 31 August 1860. p.138, c5.

5340 S. E. W. *to* **MR. GARRISON. n.d. n.p.** Believes that behind every reform there is a "moral agency" acting independently of politics; feels that Mr. Foster overlooks this in his zeal to hasten the abolition of slavery. 31 August 1860. p.138, c6.

5341 G. W. S. *to* **W. L. GARRISON. n.d. n.p.** Reports on some new and zealous converts to Republicanism. 31 August 1860. p.138, c6.

5342 JOSEPHINE S. GRIFFING *to* **PARKER PILLSBURY. 22 August 1860. Franklin Mills, Oh.** Reports on past and future anti-slavery conventions in the West. 31 August 1860. p.139, c1.

5343 n.n. *to* **THE EDITOR OF THE *LIBERATOR* [W. L. GARRISON]. n.d. n.p.** Discusses defects of the educational system. 31 August 1860. p.140, c2.

5344 H. C. WRIGHT *to* **GARRISON. 14 August 1860. North Elba, N.Y.** Praises the martyrs William Wallace and John Brown. 31 August 1860. p.140, c3.

5345 n.n. *to* **THE EDITOR OF THE** *BOSTON JOURNAL.* **7 August 1860. Buffalo.** Remarks that a female, Lydia A. Jenkins, has been preaching. 31 August 1860. p.140, c6.

5346 S. M. BOOTH *to* **n.n. 6 August 1860. Ripon.** Gives an account of the first time someone attempted to arrest him. 7 September. 1860. p.142, c2.

5347 GEORGE THOMPSON *to* **GARRISON. 17 August 1860. London.** Reports on the First of August celebration and Dr. Cheever's speech. 7 September 1860. p.142, c6.

5348 JOSHUA COFFIN *to* **MR. EDITOR [W. L. GARRISON]. n.d. New York.** Forwards an indenture from 1772 for printing. 7 September 1860. p.143, c2.

5349 HENRY WARD BEECHER *to* **BOARD OF TRUSTEES, AMHERST COLLEGE. n.d. n.p.** Rejects the title of Doctor of Divinity. 7 September 1860. p.143, c4.

5350 HENRY C. WRIGHT *to* **W. L. GARRISON. 3 August 1860. Rocky Point, R.I.** Reports on discussion and resolutions of an unofficial anti-slavery meeting held at a clambake. 7 September 1860. p.134 [144], c2.

5351 A YANKEE READER *to* **THE EDITOR OF THE** *LONDON AMERICAN.* **n.d. n.p.** Criticizes Dr. Cheever and Garrisonianism. 14 September 1860. p.145, c1.

5352 GEORGE THOMPSON *to* **THE EDITOR OF THE** *LONDON AMERICAN.* **n.d. n.p.** Criticizes the article entitled "A Yankee Reader." 14 September 1860. p.145, c1.

5353 PUBLICOLA *to* **SAMUEL CUNARD. [from the** *London Weekly Dispatch***] n.d. n.p.** Criticizes of the treatment of colored passengers aboard one of his steamers. 14 September 1860. p.145, c4.

5354 H. *to* **MR. EDITOR [W. L. GARRISON]. 10 September 1860. Boston.** Urges voters to support John A. Andrew, the Republican anti-slavery candidate for governor. 14 September 1860. p.146, c6.

5355 T. W. HIGGINSON *to* **MR. GARRISON. 7 September 1860. Worcester.** Criticizes Henry C. Wright's resolutions concerning moral obligations, presented at a recent convention in Rhode Island. 14 September 1860. p.146, c6.

5356 C. ROBINSON *to* **HON. WASHINGTON HUNT. August 1860. Holley, N.Y.** Declares slavery a permanent threat to the Union, and union under present conditions "a sham." 14 September 1860. p.147, c1.

5357 THADDEUS HYATT *to* **S. J. T. [from the** *Lawrence* **(Ks.)** *Republican***] 26 August 1860. Hyatt, Ks.** Believes that flying machines can be perfected by man. 14 September 1860. p.148, c5.

5358 DESOR *to* **FRIEND. 10 June 1860. Neufchatel.** Praises the work of Theodore Parker. 21 September 1860. p.150, c4.

5359 LUCY N. COLMAN *to* **FRIEND GARRISON. 10 September 1860. Ellenville, N.Y.** Gives an account of the convention at Ellenville. 21 September 1860. p.150, c6.

5360 WM. WELLS BROWN *to* **GARRISON. 13 September 1860. Ashburnham, Ma.** Reports on anti-slavery activity in Vermont. 21 September 1860. p.151, c1.

5361 JOHNATHAN WATSON *to* **MRS. JANE WIGHAM. [from the** *London Anti-Slavery Advocate***] 14 August 1860. Edinburgh.** States that no "slave upholder" will be heard at commemoration meetings. 21 September 1860. p.151, c2.

5362 ST. JOHN B. L. SKINNER *to* **A. S. EVANS. 15 August 1860. n.p.** Reports on the procedure regarding incendiary mail. 21 September 1860. p.151, c2.

5363 H. *to* **THE EDITORS. [from the** *New York Journal of Commerce***] n.d. n.p.** Declares that Negro slavery is neither the only nor the worst form of slavery; warns abolitionists that "false notions of liberty threaten the destruction of all liberty." 28 September 1860. p.153, c1.

5364 A. T. JONES *to* **R. T. PENNEFATHER. 24 August 1860. London, Canada West.** A gentleman of color requests an audience with the Prince of Wales. 28 September 1860. p.153, c4.

5365 GERRIT SMITH *to* **THE PRESIDENT OF THE LIBERTY PARTY CONVENTION. 27 August 1860. Peterboro'.** Discusses the duties of civil government and the Church. 28 September 1860. p.153, c5.

5366 R. T. PENNEFATHER *to* **A. T. JONES. 1 September 1860. Ottawa.** Denies Jones an audience with Prince of Wales. 28 September 1860. p.153, c5.

5367 ERNEST NOEL *to* **THE EDITOR OF THE** *LEEDS MERCURY.* **16 November 1860. n.p.** Discusses free labor in the West Indies. 28 September 1860. p.154, c1.

5368 WM. S. BAILEY *to* **THE EDITOR OF** *THE NEW YORK TRIBUNE.* **n.d. n.p.** Discusses the rift between Cassius M. Clay and himself. 28 September 1860. p.154, c2.

5369 J. Q. A. FOSTER *to* **n.n. [from the** *Cincinnati Commercial***] 29 July 1860. Newport, Ky.** Accuses H. D. Helm of political fraud. 28 September 1860. p.154, c4.

5370 SHERIFF HELM *to* **THE EDITOR OF THE** *COMMERCIAL.* **[extract] 30 July. Newport, Ky.** Claims that J. Q. A. Foster's charges are false. 28 September 1860. p.154, c4.

5371 J. A. H. *to* **W. L. GARRISON. 22 September 1860. Worcester.** Reports on a political anti-slavery convention at Worcester where Frederick Douglass spoke. 28 September 1860. p.155, c3.

5372 ERNEST NOEL *to* **THE EDITOR OF THE** *LEEDS MERCURY.* **27 November 1859. Jamaica.** Discusses the success of emancipation in Jamaica. 5 October 1860. p.157, c3.

5373 T. M. EDDY *to* **JAMES BUCHANAN. 7 September 1860. Chicago.** Clarifies the sentiments of the Methodist Episcopal church in regard to slavery. 5 October 1860. p.157, c4.

5374 WM. S. BAILEY *to* **THE EDITOR OF THE** *CLEVELAND HERALD.* **[from the** *Free South***] 10 June 1860. Newport, Ky.** Explains dispute between Mr. Clay and himself concerning the Free State platform. 5 October 1860. p.158, c1.

5375 DANIEL E. SOMES *to* **GERRIT SMITH. 27 August 1860. Biddeford, Me.** Urges that people vote for Abraham Lincoln. 5 October 1860. p.159, c1.

5376 HENRY C. WRIGHT *to* **GARRISON. 15 September 1860. West Goldsboro', Me.** Reports on the Democratic State Convention held in Portland. 5 October 1860. p.159, c2.

5377 C. K. W. *to* **W. L. GARRISON. n.d. n.p.** Discusses pamphlet entitled "Self-Contradictions of the Bible." 5 October 1860. p.160, c2.

5378 JAMES REDPATH *to* **SARAH BURTON. [extract from the** *Boston Traveller***] 18 August 1860. Port-au-Prince.** Discusses his interview with the Haitian president and the presentation of a bust of John Brown; praises the stately Madame Geffrard. 5 October 1860. p.160, c5.

5379 INQUIRER *to* **MR. EDITOR [W. L. GARRISON]. n.d. n.p.** Asks Garrison's response to questions concerning the duty of Northern churches toward their slaveholding counterparts. 12 October 1860. p.161, c1.

5380 ERNEST NOEL *to* **THE EDITOR OF THE** *LEEDS MERCURY***. 17 December 1859. n.p.** Discusses means of restoring prosperity in Jamaica. 12 October 1860. p.161, c2.

5381 ERNEST NOEL *to* **n.n. 12 March 1860. Warley House.** Defends himself against accusations made by the *Jamaican Press*. 12 October 1860. p.161, c3.

5382 THOS P. KNOX *to* **W. L. GARRISON. 9 October 1860. Boston.** Condemns the proslavery principles of the American Board of Commissioners for Foreign Missions. 12 October 1860. p.162, c5.

5383 C. F. P. *to* **W. L. GARRISON. 29 September 1860. Provincetown.** Reports on his anti-slavery labors near the Cape in Massachusetts. 12 October 1860. p.162, c6.

5384 THE COMPILER *to* **W. L. GARRISON. 6 October 1860. New York.** Discusses his points of disagreement with the article entitled "Self-Contradictions of the Bible." 12 October 1860. p.162, c6.

5385 PARKER PILLSBURY *to* **THE EDITOR [W. L. GARRISON]. 3 October 1860. Adrian, Mi.** Gives an account of the Cummington convention and other anti-slavery meetings. 12 October 1860. p.163, c1.

5386 J. S. G. *to* **THE** *LIBERATOR***. 23 September 1860. Salem, Oh.** Reports on Pillsbury's lectures in Ohio. 12 October 1860. p.163, c1.

5387 J. A. H. *to* **W. L. GARRISON. 1 October 1860. Worcester.** Comments on a mistake in reporting T. W. Higginson's remarks at the Foster Convention. 12 October 1860. p.163, c2.

5388 C. L. H. *to* **W. L. GARRISON. 25 September 1860. West Gouldsboro'.** Gives an account of lectures by Henry C. Wright in Easton, Maine. 12 October 1860. p.163, c2.

5389 H. W. BLANCHARD *to* **REV. ANGIER. 1 September 1860. Port Norfolk.** Questions his belief that the preaching of the Gospel will eventually abolish slavery. 12 October 1860. p.164, c2.

5390 GEORGE SUNTER, JR. *to* **W. L. GARRISON. 28 September 1860. Branford, Canada West.** Disputes letter from T. W. Higginson; defends resolution presented by H. C. Wright at a Rhode Island meeting. 12 October 1860. p.164, c4.

5391 DR. SMITH *to* **n.n. [from the** *Springfield Republican***] 3 August 1860. Steamship** *Arabia***.** Gives a graphic account of the steamship *Arabia*'s narrow escape from shipwreck on Fasnet Rock, Cape Clear. 12 October 1860. p.164, c5.

5392 JOHN HOSSACK *to* **CITIZENS OF COOK COUNTY. 3 October 1860. Chicago jail.** Gives an account of his violation of the Fugitive Slave Law. 19 October 1860. p.165, c5.

5393 J. G. MOTT *to* **FRIEND GARRISON. 10 October 1860. Chicago.** Condemns the jailing of John Hossack and Joseph Stout. 19 October 1860. p.166, c3.

5394 OLIVER JOHNSON *to* **MR. GARRISON. 15 October 1860. New York.** Corrects report of his day in court; relates that the judge found him to be a conscientious man and insisted he sit on the jury. 19 October 1860. p.166, c5.

5395 PARKER PILLSBURY *to* **THE EDITOR OF THE** *ASHTUBULA SENTINEL.* **16 September 1860. Jefferson.** Gives various interpretations of the Declaration of Independence. 19 October 1860. p.166, c6.

5396 J. R. GIDDINGS *to* **THE EDITOR OF THE** *ASHTABULA SENTINEL.* **n.d. n.p.** Asserts the right of the Negro to vote. 19 October 1860. p.166, c6.

5397 WM. A. WILSON *to* **MR. GARRISON. 11 October 1860. Worcester.** Requests publication of letters. 19 October 1860. p.167, c1.

5398 CHARLES SUMNER *to* **A. P. BROWN. 9 September 1860. Boston.** Believes that the Constitution has no power to affect slavery. 19 October 1860. p.167, c1.

5399 HENRY T. CHEEVER *to* **STEPHEN S. FOSTER. 15 September 1860. Jewett City, Ct.** Supports the organization of a political party based on an anti-slavery interpretation of Constitution. 19 October 1860. p.167, c1.

5400 ELNATHAN DAVIS *to* **A. P. BROWN. 17 September 1860. Fitchburg.** Declares that slavery is unconstitutional. 19 October 1860. p.167, c1.

5401 HOMER B. SPRAGUE *to* **SIR. 17 September 1860. New Haven.** Endorses a political anti-slavery party. 19 October 1860. p.167, c2.

5402 G. W. MADOX *to* **n.n. 5 October 1860. Ellsworth.** Gives an account of lectures by Henry Wright in Ellsworth, Maine. 19 October 1860. p.167, c2.

5403 FREDERICK AMTHOR *to* **n.n. 18 September 1860. Le Roy, Il.** Gives an account of his being attacked by a mob in Texas. 19 October 1860. p.167, c3.

5404 CHARLES SUMNER *to* **WM. J. BREWSTER. 20 October 1856. Boston.** Rejoices that friends of freedom in Middleboro are about to organize. 19 October 1860. p.167, c4.

5405 CHARLES INGLEBY AND WM. S. McCOY *to* **COL. RATHER. 13 September 1860. Charleston, S.C.** Declare their hatred for Garrisonian abolitionists. 19 October 1860. p.167, c4.

5406 MARY *to* **MR. GARRISON. n.d. Worcester, Ma.** Comments on the work to be done to combat slavery. 19 October 1860. p.168, c2.

5407 CHARLES SUMNER *to* **REV. S. J. MAY. 9 September 1860. Boston.** Regrets that he is unable to attend the Jerry Rescue celebration. 19 October 1860. p.168, c4.

5408 A UNION DEMOCRAT *to* **THE EDITORS OF THE** *NEW YORK JOURNAL OF COMMERCE.* **9 October 1860. Talbotton, Ca.** Fears for the perpetuity and safety of the Union. 26 October 1860. p.169, c2.

5409 GEORGE THOMPSON *to* **MR. GARRISON. [extract] 22 October 1835. Marblehead.** Gives an account of a mob in Boston which tried to suppress free speech. 26 October 1860. p.170, c5.

5410 PARKER PILLSBURY *to* **THE EDITOR [W. L. GARRISON]. October 1860. Earlville, Il.** Remarks on the growing importance of the West. 26 October 1860. p.171, c2.

5411 M. B. BIRD *to* **W. L. GARRISON. 20 October 1860. New York.** States that his sentiments toward slavery have been sharpened by his time spent in Haiti, a "land of the free." 26 October 1860. p.171, c3.

5412 FREDERICK DOUGLASS *to* **MR. GARRISON. 15 October 1860. Rochester.** Replies to J. A. H.'s estimation of his role at the Political Abolition Convention in Worcester. 26 October 1860. p.172, c4.

5413 HENRY C. WRIGHT *to* **W. L. GARRISON. 18 September 1860. Steuben, Me.** Believes it is his duty to defend humanity. 26 October 1860. p.172, c5.

5414 LEVERETT SALTONSTALL *to* **B. B. McCRAW. 3 October 1860. Boston.** Questions sending his children to school with blacks. 2 November 1860. p.173, c5.

5415 SARAH CLAY *to* **J. L. JENKINS. 29 April 1859. Lowell.** Discusses the pro-slavery tendencies of her church. 2 November 1860. p.174, c5.

5416 n.n. *to* **MR. GARRISON. 27 October 1860. Lowell.** Asserts the anti-slavery character of New England Congregational churches. 2 November 1860. p.174, c5.

5417 J. L. JENKINS *to* **SARAH CLAY. 22 April 1859. Lowell.** Warns that the Standing Committee of the First Congregational Church shall remove Clay's name from the list of members due to her inattendance. 2 November 1860. p.174, c5.

5418 GERRIT SMITH *to* **D. E. SOMES. 16 October 1860. Peterboro.** Claims he cannot vote for Lincoln and the Republican Party. 2 November 1860. p.174, c6.

5419 J. A. H. *to* **W. L. GARRISON. 28 October 1860. Worcester.** Discusses Douglass' charges against the AAS, which he later qualified. 2 November 1860. p.174, c6.

5420 J. COLLAMER *to* **N. R. JOHNSTON. 5 October 1860. Woodstock, Vt.** Discusses moral and religious means to bring about abolition of slavery. 2 November 1860. p.175, c2.

5421 W. L. GARRISON *to* **REV. N. R. JOHNSTON. 15 October 1860. Boston.** States that the reason for his silence at the Bradford convention was a bronchial difficulty. 2 November 1860. p.175, c2.

5422 A. HOGEBOOM *to* **HON. D. E. SOMES. 21 November 1860. Shed's Corners, N.Y.** Disputes Somes' letter which criticized Gerrit Smith. 2 November 1860. p.176, c3.

5423 RALPH FARNHAM *to* **THE EDITOR OF THE** *BOSTON JOURNAL.* **20 October 1860. Boston.** Expresses gratitude to those who have contributed money for his benefit. 2 November 1860. p.176, c5.

5424 RALPH FARNHAM *to* **THE EDITORS OF THE** *BOSTON TRAVELLER.* **23 October 1860. Acton, Me.** Gives account of receptions arranged in his behalf. 2 November 1860. p.176, c6.

5425 n.n. *to* **THE EDITOR OF THE** *NEW YORK HERALD.* **8 October 1860. Charleston.** Forwards a South Carolina petition condemning Northern "white slavery"—hard labor with long hours and low wages—to be presented to Congress in the event of Lincoln's election. 9 November 1860. p.177, c1.

5426 CHARLES HAPP *to* **F. DOUGLASS. 15 October 1860. Auburn.** A white man offers to marry Douglass' daughter for $15,000 or $20,000. 9 November 1860. p.178, c1.

5427 FREDERICK DOUGLASS *to* **CHARLES HAPP. n.d. Auburn, N.Y.** Rejects Happ's offer to wed his daughter. 9 November 1860. p.178, c1.

5428 W. L. GARRISON *to* **J. MILLER McKIM. 11 October 1860. Boston.** Regrets he is unable to attend the Pennsylvania Anti-Slavery Convention. 9 November 1860. p.178, c3.

5429 ELIZUR BUTLER *to* **S. A. WORCESTER. [extract] n.d. n.p.** Claims that they cannot forbid admission of slaveholders to their church. 9 November 1860. p.178, c4.

5430 PARKER PILLSBURY *to* **THE EDITOR [W. L. GARRISON]. 2 November 1860. Spring Dale, Ia.** Reports on anti-slavery in the West. 9 November 1860. p.178, c6.

5431 S. C. POMEROY *to* **n.n. 31 October 1860. Atchison, R.I.** Expresses concern for the refugees from Arkansas and Texas. 9 November 1860. p.178, c6.

5432 D. H. *to* **FRIEND GARRISON. 28 September 1860. Washington, D.C.** Describes the District of Columbia. 9 November 1860. p.180, c3.

5433 WILLIAM J. BREWSTER *to* **THE *NEW YORK TRIBUNE*. 17 October 1860. Boston.** Gives an account of his experience with mob law in northern Alabama. 16 November 1860. p.181, c5.

5434 n.n. *to* **GENTLEMEN. 24 October 1860. New York.** Reports that his firm will be unable to fill orders by Southerners now that Lincoln's election is "hardly doubtful." 16 November 1860. p.182, c2.

5435 N. R. JOHNSTON *to* **W. L. GARRISON. 5 November 1860. New York.** Relates resolutions passed by New York Presbytery of the Reformed Presbyterian church. 16 November 1860. p.182, c4.

5436 PARKER PILLSBURY *to* **THE EDITOR [W. L. GARRISON]. 10 November 1860. Mendota, Il.** Laments the degraded condition of women. 16 November 1860. p.182, c5.

5437 P. B. D. *to* **MESSRS. HARNEY, HUGHES, AND CO. September 1860. Lamar County, Tx.** Dispells rumors of arson epidemic in Texas. 23 November 1860. p.185, c4.

5438 WM. C. WOOD *to* **THE EDITORS OF THE *BOSTON JOURNAL*. 15 November 1860. West Roxbury.** Gives an account of his expulsion from South Carolina. 23 November 1860. p.185, c5.

5439 MANY CITIZENS *to* **MR. EDDY. 8 November 1860. Augusta, Ga.** Order him to leave Augusta immediately because he expressed abolitionist sentiments. 23 November 1860. p.185, c6.

5440 A. *to* **THE EDITOR [W. L. GARRISON]. 18 November 1860. Boston.** Recommends a book entitled *Harrington*. 23 November 1860. p.186, c5.

5441 PARKER PILLSBURY *to* **MR. EDITOR [W. L. GARRISON]. 13 November 1860. Chicago, Il.** Describes the anti-slavery convention in Mendota. 23 November 1860. p.186, c6.

5442 J. H. C. *to* **n.n. 19 November 1860. New York.** Asks "What will the South do?" 23 November 1860. p.187, c1.

5443 A. H. *to* **MR. GARRISON. n.d. n.p.** Describes an anti-slavery meeting in Vermont; forwards resolutions. 23 November 1860. p.187, c1.

5444 A MAN *to* **MESSRS. EDITORS.** [from the *Traveller*] **n.d. n.p.** Offers facts and statistics regarding colored emigration from South Carolina. 23 November 1860. p.187, c5.

5445 HENRY T. CHEEVER *to* **REV. LEONARD BACON. 8 November 1860. Jewett City, Ct.** Criticizes the American Board's actions regarding its African missions. 23 November 1860. p.188, c1.

5446 GEORGE N. REYNOLDS, HENRY S. FARLEY, JNO. Y. WOFFORD, T. S. WEATHERBY, JNO. R. BLOCKER, J. B. BOATWRIGHT, AND JAS H. HAMILTON *to* **THE** *COLUMBIA SOUTH CAROLINIAN.* **9 November 1860. West Point.** Declare their support for South Carolina if she secedes. 30 November 1860. p.189, c1.

5447 A BAPTIST CLERGYMAN *to* **n.n.** [from the *Charleston Mercury*] **14 November 1860. Columbia, S.C.** Advocates immediate secession of South Carolina. 30 November 1860. p.189, c1.

5448 A CAROLINA MOTHER *to* **THE EDITOR OF THE** *CHARLESTON MERCURY.* **n.d. n.p.** Points out the patriotism of South Carolina women. 30 November 1860. p.189, c2.

5449 40° N. LATITUDE *to* **JAMES R. CHESTNUT.** [from the *New York Tribune*] **n.d. n.p.** Asks why South Carolina wishes to secede. 30 November 1860. p.189, c5.

5450 ORONO *to* **THE EDITOR OF THE** *BOSTON JOURNAL.* **20 November 1860. Boston.** Warns of the danger of lynching to Northerners travelling South. 30 November 1860. p.190, c2.

5451 F. R. THAYER *to* **THE** *NEW YORK TRIBUNE.* **16 November 1860. Worcester, Ma.** Gives account of circumstances surrounding his expulsion from Georgia. 30 November 1860. p.190, c2.

5452 PARKER PILLSBURY *to* **THE EDITOR [W. L. GARRISON]. 25 November 1860. Concord, N.H.** Corrects a printing error in an earlier edition of *Liberator.* 30 November 1860. p.191, c1.

5453 B. *to* **THE** *TUSKEGEE* **(AL.)** *REPUBLICAN.* **n.d. n.p.** Warns of dangerous abolition books used in Sabbath schools. 7 December 1860. p.193, c1.

5454 A. B. MOORE *to* **REV. I. T. TICHENOR. 16 November 1860. n.p.** Acknowledges the receipt of declarations adopted by the Baptist State Convention of Alabama. 7 December 1860. p.193, c2.

5455 W. L. GARRISON *to* **JAMES REDPATH. 1 December 1860. Boston.** Declares that slavery should be recognized as eternally unjust, that its supporters should be exposed, and that it should be immediately and unconditionally abolished. 7 December 1860. p.194, c4.

5456 D. A. WASSON *to* **MR. GARRISON. 1 December 1860. Boston.** Comments on Mrs. Howe's trip to Cuba. 7 December 1860. p.194, c5.

5457 C. K. W. *to* **n.n. n.d. n.p.** Comments on Baron Stow's views regarding slavery. 7 December 1860. p.194, c5.

5458 WM. BARKER *to* **REV. BARON STOW. 29 February 1860. London, England.** Disputes validity of Stow's claim of being an anti-slavery man. 7 December 1860. p.194, c6.

5459 PARKER PILLSBURY *to* **THE EDITOR [W. L. GARRISON]. 2 December 1860. Concord, N.H.** Reports on the celebration of the John Brown anniversary. 7 December 1860. p.194, c6.

5460 E. R. BROWN *to* **n.n. 15 November 1860. Elmwood, Il.** Gives an account of the convention at Mendota. 7 December 1860. p.195, c1.

5461 GEORGE PORTER PAINE *to* **n.n. 4 November 1860. Neasho Falls, Ks.** Reports on a meeting for the prevention of famine in Kansas. 7 December 1860. p.196, c2.

5462 CAROLINE HINCKLEY *to* **MR. GARRISON. n.d. Kiantone, N.H.** States her beliefs concerning marriage and divorce. 7 December 1860. p.196, c3.

5463 WM. S. BAILEY *to* **W. L. GARRISON. 6 December 1860. Newport, Ky.** Describes his being indicted by the Grand Jury. 14 December 1860. p.198, c3.

5464 GEO. THOMPSON *to* **W. L. GARRISON. 23 November 1860. London.** Rejoices at Lincoln's election; praises Wendell Phillips. 14 December 1860. p.198, c3.

5465 HENRY WILSON *to* **JAMES REDPATH AND OTHERS OF THE COMMITTEE. 27 November 1860. Natick.** Reports he will be unable to attend the John Brown celebration because of his belief in non-violence. 14 December 1860. p.199, c2.

5466 A. *to* **MR. EDITOR [W. L. GARRISON]. 10 December 1860. Boston.** Suggests that the author of *Harrington* be invited to speak at the Twenty-eighth Congregational Society. 14 December 1860. p.199, c3.

5467 MOSES KIMBALL *to* **THE EDITOR OF THE *BOSTON JOURNAL*. 10 December 1860. n.p.** Requests publication of enclosed letter. 14 December 1860. p.199, c4.

5468 JOHN A. ANDREW *to* **MOSES KIMBALL. 4 December 1860. Boston.** Reports on the city Republican convention. 14 December 1860. p.199, c4.

5469 FREE SPEECH *to* **n.n. 5 December 1860. Boston.** Criticizes the riotous crowd at a Tremont Temple meeting. 21 December 1860. p.201, c3.

5470 ETHAN SPIKE *to* **n.n. [from the *Portland* (Me.) *Transcript*] 19 November 1860. Hornby.** Declares that the town of Hornby is seceding from the Union. 21 December 1860. p.204, c5.

5471 H. G. ROLLINS *to* **MR. EDITOR [W. L. GARRISON]. 19 December 1860. Groveland, Ma.** Gives an account of actions of a pro-slavery mob in Boston. 28 December 1860. p.206, c6.

5472 D. S. GRANDIN *to* **MR. GARRISON. n.d. n.p.** Supports Mr. Dow's action with the Portland mob. 28 December 1860. p.206, c6.

5473 A. T. FOSS *to* **W. L. GARRISON. 14 December 1860. Valley Falls, R.I.** Gives an account of his anti-slavery labors in New Hampshire during October. 28 December 1860. p.207, c4.

5474 HARRIOT K. HUNT *to* **FREDERICK U. TRACY. 6 November 1860. Boston.** Protests the taxation of women without representation. 28 December 1860. p.208, c3.

5475 FRANCES D. GAGE *to* **FRIEND GARRISON. 1 December 1860. Mendota, Il.** Compares the condition of women to that of slaves. 28 December 1860. p.208, c4.

5476 n.n. *to* **UNCLE. [extract] 1 December 1860. South Carolina.** Fears that secession is near. 28 December 1860. p.208, c6.

5477 REV. S. C. BARTLETT *to* **THE** *NEW YORK INDEPENDENT*. **23 November 1860. Chicago.** Encloses letters concerning the burning of a slave. 31 December 1860. p.209, c1.

5478 S. B. TREAT, SECRETARY OF THE AMERICAN BOARD OF COMMISSIONERS FOR FOREIGN MISSIONS *to* **REV. S. C. BARTLETT. 27 October 1860. Mission House, Boston.** Claims that the American Board knows nothing of the burning of a slave woman. 31 December 1860. p.209, c1.

5479 REV. SAMUEL C. BARTLETT *to* **S. B. TREAT, SECRETARY OF THE AMERICAN BOARD OF COMMISSIONERS FOR FOREIGN MISSIONS. 22 October 1860. Chicago.** Questions the burning of a slave woman at a public meeting. 31 December 1860. p.209, c1.

5480 WALTER LOWRIE *to* **REV. SAMUEL C. BARTLETT. 30 October 1860. Mission House, N.Y.** Claims that the Mission is not responsible for the burning of a slave. 31 December 1860. p.209, c1.

5481 ALEXANDER HENRY *to* **JAMES W. WHITE. 11 December 1860. Philadelphia.** Suggests that George W. Curtis be forbidden to speak. 31 December 1860. p.209, c3.

5482 JOHN McQUEEN, M. L. BONHAM, W. A. BOYCE, J. D. ASHMORE *to* **THE HOUSE OF REPRESENTATIVES. n.d. n.p.** Dissolve their connection with the House of Representatives. 31 December 1860. p.210, c2.

5483 ANDREW JACKSON *to* **REV. ANDREW J. CRAWFORD. 1 May 1833. Washington.** Despises secessionists. 31 December 1860. p.210, c2.

5484 DAVID A. WASSON *to* **MR. GARRISON. 13 December 1860. Worcester.** Believes that it is important to judge Negroes as equal men on equal ground. 31 December 1860. p.210, c4.

5485 HENRY C. WRIGHT *to* **GARRISON. 2 December 1860. Willimantic.** Relates Gov. Gist's statement that whites are the ruling race. 31 December 1860. p.210, c5.

5486 C. F. PUTNAM *to* **W. L. GARRISON. 25 December 1860. Fall River.** Praises Dr. Ide and Mr. Hunt's anti-slavery sentiments. 31 December 1860. p.210, c6.

5487 K. *to* **W. L. GARRISON. n.d. n.p.** Asks Garrison to explain his inconsistency concerning his view of the Constitution and his charge that secession by South Carolina would be treason. 31 December 1860. p.210, c6.

5488 M. L. WHITTEN *to* **W. L. GARRISON. 20 December 1860. Brocksport.** Reports an attempt to suppress free speech by a mob in Boston. 31 December 1860. p.212, c2.

5489 C. C. KNOWLES *to* **W. L. GARRISON. 25 November 1860. East Greenwich, R.I.** Describes anti-slavery sentiment in Rhode Island. 31 December 1860. p.212, c3.

5490 E. W. T. *to* **FRIEND GARRISON. 9 December 1860. Springfield.** Denounces Dr. Holland's book, *Miss Gilbert's Career,* as anti-women's rights. 31 December 1860. p.212, c3.

5491 B. D. S. *to* **FRIEND BURT. 14 December 1860. Omaha, Ne.** Describes the selling of a Negro into slavery. 31 December 1860. p.212, c4.

[1861]

5492 WM. WHITING *to* **FRIEND. 16 December 1860. Concord.** Informs that he took up a collection for famine victims. 4 January 1861. p.4 [2], c4.

5493 A. BROOKE *to* **FRIEND. 14 December 1860. Marlboro, Oh.** Criticizes the *Liberator*'s lenient evaluation of a Boston mob. 4 January 1861. p.4 [2], c4.

5494 N. R. JOHNSTON *to* **MR. GARRISON. 6 December 1860. Topsham, Vt.** Discusses Vermont's refusal to repeal the Personal Liberty Law; forwards resolutions of an anti-slavery meeting held in honor of the John Brown celebration. 4 January 1861. p.3, c2.

5495 RICHARD J. HINTON *to* **W. L. GARRISON. 20 December 1860. Atchison, Ks.** Describes troubles in southern Kansas; tells of capture of kidnappers. 4 January 1861. p.3, c3.

5496 RICHARD J. HINTON *to* **W. L. GARRISON. 20 December 1860. Atchison, Ks.** Reports on the famine in Kansas. 4 January 1861. p.4, c2.

5497 W. G. B. *to* **FRIEND GARRISON. 3 December 1860. North Scituate.** Criticizes the tardiness of Unitarian clergymen in joining anti-slavery agitation. 4 January 1861. p.4, c3.

5498 GEO. TRASK *to* **SIR. n.d. n.p.** Condemns the use of tobacco. 4 January 1861. p.4, c5.

5499 C. K. W. *to* **MR. GARRISON. n.d. n.p.** Discusses church action on slavery. 11 January 1861. p.7, c1.

5500 MARIUS R. ROBISON *to* **BROTHER GARRISON. 25 December 1860. Salem, Oh.** Praises Parker Pillsbury's speeches. 11 January 1861. p.8, c3.

5501 PARKER PILLSBURY *to* **THE EDITOR [W. L. GARRISON]. 30 December 1860. Sterling, Il.** Describes the weather and terrain in Illinois. 11 January 1861. p.8, c3.

5502 S. P. C. *to* **MR. EDITOR [W. L. GARRISON]. 2 January 1861. Georgetown.** Forwards resolutions recently adopted by a church in Georgetown. 11 January 1861. p.8, c4.

5503 n.n. *to* **CHARLES FRANCIS ADAMS. n.d. n.p.** Protests admission of New Mexico as slave state. 18 January 1861. p.9, c5.

5504 M. D. CONWAY *to* **THE *LIBERATOR*. 9 January 1861. Cincinnati, Oh.** States that the magazine, *Dial,* will not be discontinued. 18 January 1861. p.11, c5.

5505 HENRY C. WRIGHT *to* **W. L. GARRISON. 4 January 1861. West Randolph, Vt.** Describes the excitement in the Green Mountain area due to the downfall of the Republic. 18 January 1861. p.12, c3.

5506 H. L. S. *to* **MR. GARRISON. 3 January 1860. Lawrence.** Gives an account of the quarterly meeting of the Essex County AS. 18 January 1861. p.12, c3.

5507 E. C. S. *to* **THE EDITOR OF THE** *NATIONAL ANTI-SLAVERY STANDARD.* **5 January 1861. Buffalo.** Denounces mob rule and threats to free speech in Buffalo. 18 January 1861. p.12, c5.

5508 GARDNER SPRING, W. W. PHILLIPS, GEORGE POTTS, J. McELROY, JOHN M. KREBS, C. P. McILVAINE, G. T. BEDELL, AND F. L. HAWKES *to* **CHURCH AND LAITY OF CHRISTIAN CHURCHES IN THE SOUTHERN STATES OF THE UNION. 1 January 1861. New York.** Plead for clear-headedness in matters of the Union. 25 January 1861. p.13, c3.

5509 A. M. P. *to* **W. L. GARRISON. 19 January 1861. Syracuse, N.Y.** Gives an account of anti-slavery conventions in central and western New York. 25 January 1861. p.15, c3.

5510 WM. C. NELL *to* **MR. GARRISON. 21 January 1861. Boston.** Recommends *Linda,* a book about a slave girl. 25 January 1861. p.15, c3.

5511 PARKER PILLSBURY *to* **MR. EDITOR [W. L. GARRISON]. January 1861. Dixon, Il.** Describes anti-slavery activity in the West. 25 January 1861. p.15, c4.

5512 JOSEPH M. WIGHTMAN *to* **JOSEPH K. HAYES. January 1861. Boston.** Discusses the feasibility of holding a fair in Tremont Temple. 25 January 1861. p.15, c4.

5513 J. K. HAYES AND EZRA H. HEYWOOD *to* **n.n. 17 January 1861. Boston.** Inquire whether the mayor would assure protection from mobs, if an anti-slavery convention were held. 25 January 1861. p.15, c4.

5514 W. L. GARRISON *to* **EDMUND QUINCY [COADJUTOR]. 25 January 1861. Boston.** Regrets he is unable to attend the Massachusetts AS Convention. 1 February 1861. p.17, c1.

5515 WM. H. JAMESON, GEO. W. CHIPMAN, GEO. S. DEXTER, JOSEPH STORY, T. GILBERT *to* **HON. J. M. WIGHTMAN. n.d. n.p.** Notify him that thirty riotous people are engaged in disrupting an anti-slavery meeting at Tremont Temple. 1 February 1861. p.18, c5.

5516 JOSEPH M. WIGHTMAN *to* **DANIEL J. COBURN. 24 January 1861. Boston.** Issues an order to clear Tremont Temple. 1 February 1861. p.18, c6.

5517 JOSEPH WIGHTMAN *to* **W. H. JAMESON, GEORGE W. CHIPMAN, AND TRUSTEES OF THE TREMONT TEMPLE. 24 January 1861. Boston.** Assumes responsibility for closing Tremont Temple to the anti-slavery meeting. 1 February 1861. p.18, c6.

5518 EDMUND QUINCY *to* **TRUSTEES OF TREMONT TEMPLE. 25 January 1861. Boston.** Refuses to use Tremont Temple after having been shut out by the mayor. 1 February 1861. p.19, c3.

5519 W. ROBSON *to* **n.n. 5 January 1861. Warrington, England.** Discusses the progress of abolitionism. 1 February 1861. p.20, c3.

5520 W. R. *to* **n.n. 8 January 1861. Warrington, England.** Rejoices at the secession of Southern states; hopes there will be no bloodshed. 1 February 1861. p.20, c4.

5521 MRS. J. S. GRIFFING *to* **THE EDITOR [W. L. GARRISON]. 16 December 1861. Salem, In.** Gives an account of anti-slavery in Lagrange, Noble, and Steuben counties in northern Indiana. 1 February 1861. p.20, c4.

5522 A MASSACHUSETTS WOMAN *to* **W. L. GARRISON. 23 January 1861. Lowell.** Pays tribute to Wendell Phillips. 1 February 1861. p.20, c4.

5523 LUCIUS SLADE *to* **n.n. [from the *Literary and Temperance Crusader*] n.d. n.p.** Expresses sympathy for the South; hopes the Union will be saved. 8 February 1861. p.21, c1.

5524 PARKER PILLSBURY *to* **n.n. [extract] 30 January 1861. Ann Arbor, Mi.** Describes a pro-slavery mob at Ann Arbor. 8 February 1861. p.23, c4.

5525 STEPHEN ELLIOT *to* **CLERGY IN THE PROTESTANT EPISCOPAL CHURCH IN THE DIOCESE OF GEORGIA. 14 January 1861. Atlanta, Ga.** Declares that if Georgia secedes, the clergy will introduce the new prayer, "A Prayer in Time of War and Tumult." 8 February 1861. p.23, c4.

5526 SUSAN B. ANTHONY *to* **n.n. [extract] 18 January. Rome, N.Y.** Reports on mob disruption of anti-slavery meetings at Rome. 8 February 1861. p.23, c5.

5527 N. R. JOHNSTON *to* **MR. GARRISON. 15 January 1861. Topsham, Vt.** Claims that many in Topsham did not keep the president's fast; forwards resolutions of an anti-slavery meeting; believes the Episcopal church is pro-slavery. 8 February 1861. p.24, c2.

5528 A. WESTCOTT *to* **SAMUEL J. MAY. 26 January 1861. Syracuse, N.Y.** Requests that the anti-slavery convention be postponed. 15 February 1861. p.25, c1.

5529 THOS. T. DAVIS, JOHN WILKINSON, WM. E. ABBOTT, E. W. LEVEN-WORTH, HIRAM PUTNAM, O. T. BURT, E. B. WICKS, AND D. P. PHELPS *to* **REV. SAMUEL J. MAY. n.d. n.p.** Request that the anti-slavery convention be delayed. 15 February 1861. p.25, c1.

5530 S. J. MAY *to* **GENTLEMEN. 28 January 1861. Syracuse.** Claims he has no authority to postpone the anti-slavery convention. 15 February 1861. p.25, c2.

5531 PARKER PILLSBURY *to* **FRIEND GARRISON. 5 February 1861. Livonia, Mi.** Describes the anti-slavery convention at Livonia. 15 February 1861. p.27, c2.

5532 SARAH BAKER *to* **FRIEND GARRISON. 26 January 1861. Dorchester.** Criticizes a mob's actions at an anti-slavery meeting. 15 February 1861. p.27, c4.

5533 JOSEPHINE S. GRIFFING *to* **THE EDITOR [W. L. GARRISON]. 6 February 1861. Plymouth, Mi.** Reports on abolition activity in the West. 15 February 1861. p.27, c5.

5534 SAMUEL GALE *to* **L. MARIA CHILD. 23 January 1861. Montreal.** Criticizes the slaveholders for the perpetuation of slavery. 15 February 1861. p.28, c3.

5535 THADDEUS HYATT *to* **MARIA WESTON CHAPMAN. 23 January 1861. Washington, D.C.** Regrets he is unable to attend the National Anti-Slavery Subscription Anniversary Meeting. 15 February 1861. p.28, c3.

5536 NATHAN WINSLOW *to* **MARIA W. CHAPMAN AND ASSOCIATES. 21 January 1861. Portland, Me.** Regrets he is unable to attend the National Anti-Slavery Subscription Anniversary Meeting. 15 February 1861. p.28, c4.

5537 CATHARINE A. F. STEBBINS *to* **MRS. GARRISON. 21 January 1861. Ann Arbor, Mi.** Supports the National Anti-Slavery Subscription Anniversary Meeting. 15 February 1861. p.28, c4.

5538 BENJAMIN CHASE *to* **MARIA W. CHAPMAN. 20 January 1861. Auburn, N.H.** Encloses a contribution to the Massachusetts AS. 15 February 1861. p.28, c4.

5539 W. T. POTTER *to* **MARIA W. CHAPMAN. 23 January 1861. New Bedford.** Regrets he is unable to attend the National Anti-Slavery Subscription Anniversary Meeting. 15 February 1861. p.28, c4.

5540 EDWARD HARRIS *to* **MARIA WESTON CHAPMAN AND OTHER LADIES. 23 January 1861. Woonsocket, R.I.** Regrets he is unable to attend the National Anti-Slavery Subscription Anniversary Meeting. 15 February 1861. p.28, c4.

5541 LORD BROUGHAM *to* **JAMES REDPATH. 20 November. n.p.** Hopes for a lawful end to slavery. 22 February 1861. p.29, c1.

5542 JAMES REDPATH *to* **HENRY, LORD BROUGHAM. 28 January 1861. Boston.** Criticizes Brougham's definition of a lawful end to slavery. 22 February 1861. p.29, c1.

5543 NORTHUMBRIAN *to* **THE EDITOR OF THE** *REYNOLD'S NEWSPAPER.* **n.d. n.p.** Evaluates Lord Brougham's views of slavery and abolitionists. 22 February 1861. p.29, c1.

5544 n.n. *to* **THE EDITOR. [from the** *Yarmouth Port Register***] 30 January 1860. Boston.** Criticizes the mob attack against free speech. 22 February 1861. p.29, c5.

5545 W. C. N. *to* **MR. GARRISON. n.d. n.p.** Submits a record of the colored citizens' reactions to the proposed Crittenden Compromises. 22 February 1861. p.31, c3.

5546 R. H. OBER *to* **FRIEND GARRISON. 28 January 1861. Newbury, Oh.** Reports on progress of the anti-slavery movement. 22 February 1861. p.31, c4.

5547 JAMES HAUGHTON *to* **THE EDITOR OF THE** *DUBLIN NEWS.* **26 January 1861. Dublin.** Discusses differences between the North and South. 1 March 1861. p.33, c4.

5548 H. B. VINCENT *to* **BROTHER DAVIS. 20 September 1860. Chagrin Falls, Oh.** Makes predictions concerning the future of America. 1 March 1861. p.33, c6.

5549 REV. A. BATTLES *to* **SIR. 4 February 1861. Bangor, Me.** Condemns Mayor Wightman for prohibiting an AS meeting. 1 March 1861. p.34, c5.

5550 H. O. STONE *to* **E. H. HEYWOOD. 6 February 1861. Framingham.** Compliments the work of the Massachusetts AS. 1 March 1861. p.34, c5.

5551 A. K. SOUTHWICK *to* **SIR. 13 February 1861. Grantville.** Inquires how the aid for Kansas has been distributed. 1 March 1861. p.34, c6.

5552 C. C. BURLEIGH *to* **FRIEND GARRISON. 25 February 1861. Florence.** Corrects errors in the printed report of his speech. 1 March 1861. p.34, c6.

5553 n.n. *to* **MR. GARRISON. n.d. n.p.** Gives an account of James Freeman Clarke's speech. 1 March 1861. p.34, c6.

5554 G. W. S. *to* **FRIEND GARRISON. 24 February 1861. Milford, Ma.** Praises the speech by Miss Holley. 1 March 1861. p.35, c1.

5555 C. A. F. S. *to* **THE EDITOR OF THE** *LIBERATOR* **[W. L. GARRISON]. 8 February 1861. Ann Arbor, Mi.** Describes attempt by a pro-slavery mob in Ann Arbor to break up an anti-slavery meeting. 1 March 1861. p.35, c2.

5556 CHARLES K. WHIPPLE *to* **THE EDITOR OF THE** *RECORDER.* **15 December 1859. Boston.** Accuses religious papers of refusing to retract falsehoods. 1 March 1861. p.36, c3.

5557 GILBERT HAVEN *to* **W. L. GARRISON. 29 January 1861. Cambridge.** Discusses evangelical religion. 1 March 1861. p.36, c3.

5558 WILLIAM DEHON *to* **REV. DR. VINTON. [from the** *Boston Journal***] 25 January 1861. Charleston.** Reports on Southern reception of the sermon, "The Christian Idea of Civil Government." 8 March 1861. p.37, c1.

5559 FRANCIS VINTON *to* **REV. WILLIAM DEHON. 29 January 1861. New York.** Discusses the North's view of the South. 8 March 1861. p.37, c1.

5560 JNO. GOSHORN AND WM. S. GOSHORN *to* **THE EDITORS OF THE** *CLEVELAND HERALD.* **24 January 1861. Wheeling, Va.** Relate a story of a Negro waiter's refusal to serve them, and his consequent dismissal. 8 March 1861. p.37, c5.

5561 C. ROBINSON *to* **GOV. MORGAN. 1861. Holley, N.Y.** Discusses the conflict between freedom and slavery. 8 March 1861. p.39, c1.

5562 H. W. C. *to* **n.n. 23 February 1861. Athol.** Praises the wisdom of William H. Seward. 8 March 1861. p.39, c2.

5563 WENDELL PHILLIPS *to* **KARL HEINZEN. 24 February 1861. Boston.** Congratulates the *Pionier* for its fidelity to truth and freedom. 8 March 1861. p.39, c5.

5564 KARL HEINZEN *to* **WENDELL PHILLIPS. 25 February 1861. Boston.** Sends his sincere thanks on behalf of the *Pionier*. 8 March 1861. p.39, c5.

5565 PETER STEVENS *to* **ROBERT F. WALLCUT. 21 February 1861. Neosho Falls, Ks.** Expresses gratitude for donation to famine victims in Kansas. 8 March 1861. p.39, c6.

5566 A NORTHERN LABORER *to* **FRIEND GARRISON. 26 February 1861. Haverhill, Ma.** Reports on a mob in Boston. 8 March 1861. p.40, c4.

5567 A. T. SWEENY *to* **MATTHEW JOHNSON. 15 February 1861. Wheeling.** Praises Johnson's actions regarding the fugitive slave Lucy; forwards resolutions from the City Council of Wheeling. 15 March 1861. p.41, c1.

5568 A. T. SWEENY *to* **W. C. CLELAND. 15 February 1861. Wheeling.** Praises Cleland's actions regarding the fugitive slave Lucy; forwards resolutions from the City Council of Wheeling. 15 March 1861. p.41, c1.

5569 G. GARDNER *to* **THE EDITOR OF THE** *NEW YORK TRIBUNE.* **13 February 1861. Wilmington, N.C.** States that he is suspected of advocating anti-slavery. 15 March 1861. p.41, c6.

5570 H. W. BEACH *to* **FATHER AND MOTHER. [extract] 13 February 1861. Nebraska City.** States that he has been accused of being an abolitionist. 15 March 1861. p.42, c1.

5571 SARAH CLAY *to* **MR. GARRISON. 4 March 1861. Lowell.** Praises the anti-slavery speech by Mr. Foss in Lowell. 15 March 1861. p.43, c2.

5572 A LADY *to* **n.n. [extract] n.d. n.p.** Describes a sermon by a Boston clergyman who claimed it was an "inestimable blessing" to be born an American citizen instead of a European. 15 March 1861. p.44, c4.

5573 THOS. F. DAVIS *to* **CLERGY OF PROTESTANT EPISCOPAL CHURCH IN DIOCESE OF SOUTH CAROLINA. 19 February 1861. Charleston.** States that prayers have been altered to suit the new political status of South Carolina. 15 March 1861. p.44, c6.

5574 D. T. BALDWIN *to* **THE EDITOR OF THE** *HERALD OF PROGRESS.* **February 1861. Houston, Tx.** Gives critique of abolitionists. 22 March 1861. p.45, c2.

5575 W. L. GARRISON *to* **JOHN S. RAREY. 20 March 1861. Boston.** Discusses humane treatment of animals. 22 March 1861. p.46, c3.

5576 RICHARD D. WEBB *to* **GARRISON. 19 February 1861. Dublin.** Remarks that Gerrit Smith's views on the Anderson case coincide with those of the English press; criticizes the South for cruelty and murder of Northern citizens. 22 March 1861. p.46, c5.

5577 C. ROBINSON *to* **WENDELL PHILLIPS. n.d. Holley, N.Y.** Advises abolitionists to address the problem of the poor degraded whites as well as the blacks. 22 March 1861. p.47, c1.

5578 SALLIE HOLLEY *to* **n.n. n.d. n.p.** Attempts to convince friend of the merits of abolitionism. 22 March 1861. p.47, c2.

5579 YALENSIS *to* **THE EDITOR [W. L. GARRISON]. 15 March 1861. Yale College.** Reports on a lecture by Wendell Phillips in New Haven. 22 March 1861. p.47, c2.

5580 ERNESTINE L. ROSE *to* **MR. EDITOR. [from the** *Boston Investigator***] 21 February 1861. New York.** Gives an account of a mob attempt to crush free speech. 22 March 1861. p.48, c4.

5581 GEORGE H. THACHER *to* **D. V. KING. 1 February 1861. Albany.** Reports on mobs in Albany. 22 March 1861. p.48, c4.

5582 JOEL H. BUTTON *to* **N. B. BLANTON. n.d. Honey Grove, Fannin County, Tx.** Advises abolitionists to "commence the work at home." 29 March 1861. p.49, c1.

5583 M. *to* **THE EDITORS OF THE** *CLEVELAND LEADER.* **n.d. n.p.** Proclaims that Republicans will be "wiped out." 29 March 1861. p.49, c4.

5584 PARKER PILLSBURY *to* **FRIEND GARRISON. 27 March 1861. Albany, N.Y.** Regrets seeing the *Herald of Progress* mentioned in the "Refuge of Oppression" column. 29 March 1861. p.51, c3.

5585 HENRY C. WRIGHT *to* **W. L. GARRISON. 18 March 1861. Boston.** Hopes for peaceful dissolution of Union. 29 March 1861. p.51, c4.

5586 J. J. CRITTENDEN *to* **JOSEPH M. WIGHTMAN. 13 March 1861. Washington.** States that his visit to Boston will be somewhat delayed. 29 March 1861. p.51, c5.

5587 GILBERT HAVEN *to* **W. L. GARRISON. 18 March 1861. Cambridge.** Discusses W. L. Garrison's humility and principles. 29 March 1861. p.52, c2.

5588 FERNANDO WOOD *to* **MRS. BOTTSFORD. 23 October. New York.** Reports that Bottsford has been jailed for uttering "dangerous and seditious sentiments," and that the mayor is unable to help. 5 April 1861. p.53, c4.

5589 B. G. WRIGHT *to* **W. L. GARRISON. 18 March 1861. Rural, Il.** Believes that secession is not treason. 5 April 1861. p.54, c5.

5590 WALTER D. MADDOCKS *to* **THE EDITORS OF THE** *NEW YORK TRIBUNE.* **16 March 1861. New York.** Reports on the arrival of the ship *Indian Queen*. 12 April 1861, p.58, c1.

5591 JAMES REDPATH *to* **THE EDITOR OF THE** *TRIBUNE.* **1 April 1861. Boston.** Gives a history of the island of Haiti. 12 April 1861. p.58, c6.

5592 JOSEPHINE S. GRIFFING *to* **THE EDITOR [W. L. GARRISON]. 27 March 1861. Bourbon, In.** Discusses her tour of the West. 12 April 1861. p.59, c2.

5593 BERIAH GREEN *to* **GARRISON. 28 March 1861. Whitesboro'.** Praises William Goodell, Amos A. Phelps, and Charles B. Storrs. 12 April 1861. p.60, c4.

5594 BERIAH GREEN *to* **W. L. GARRISON. n.d. Whitesboro, N.Y.** Offers a definition of treason. 19 April 1861. p.63, c1.

5595 A. LINCOLN *to* **MESSRS. PRESTON, STAUT, AND RANDOLPH. n.d. n.p.** States that he intends to pursue the course marked out at his inaugural address. 19 April 1861. p.63, c4.

5596 A. G. MEACHAM *to* **THE EDITOR OF THE** *LIBERATOR* **[W. L. GARRISON]. n.d. Mont Meacham, Il.** Refuses to consider compromise in his anti-slavery beliefs. 19 April 1861. p.64. c2.

5597 G. W. S. *to* **W. L. GARRISON. n.d. Milford, Ma.** Praises the speech of Mrs. Ernestine L. Rose. 19 April 1861. p.64, c2.

5598 GEORGE T. DOWNING *to* **W. L. GARRISON. April 1861. Boston.** Suggests that the *Anglo-African* be re-named the *Anglo-Saxon* under its new editor. 19 April 1861. p.64, c3.

5599 ALEXANDER *to* **GRAND DUKE CONSTANTINE NICHOLAIEVITCH. [from the** *Journal de Saint Petersbourg***] 19 February. St. Petersburg.** Discusses the serfs in Russia. 19 April 1861. p.64, c5.

5600 B. G. WRIGHT *to* **W. L. GARRISON. 14 April 1861. Rural, Il.** Discusses his letter concerning rights of secession; attacks abolitionists who once advocated disunion, but now call it a "treasonable" offense. 26 April 1861. p.66, c1.

5601 A. J. GROVER *to* **MR. GARRISON. 16 April 1861. LaSalle County, Il.** Heartily endorses opposition to Southern secession, which he calls "indefensible." 26 April 1861. p.67, c1.

5602 GERRIT SMITH *to* **WM. LLOYD GARRISON. 17 April 1861. Peterboro, N.Y.** Accepts invitation to address the AAS. 26 April 1861. p.67, c2.

5603 YOUR BROTHER *to* **BROTHER. 20 April 1861. Baltimore.** Rejects offer to come North; plans to procure weapons to fight against Lincoln and his "hordes." 3 May 1861. p.69, c1.

5604 n.n. *to* **THE EDITORS OF THE** *BOSTON TRAVELLER.* **19 April 1861.** **Charleston, S.C.** Extends a "cordial invitation" to Massachusetts militia to come South; declares that South Carolina is "anxious for a fight." 3 May 1861. p.69, c6.

5605 E. A. L. *to* **THE EDITOR OF THE** *LIBERATOR.* **26 April 1861. Salem, Oh.** Describes the preparations of Ohio militia for war. 3 May 1861, p.70, c6.

5606 ABOLITIONIST *to* **MR. GARRISON. n.d. n.p.** Proposes that the Fourth of July be celebrated by re-affirming the Declaration of Independence. 3 May 1861. p.71, c1.

5607 SALLIE HOLLEY *to* **FRIEND. 20 April 1861. Oswego, N.Y.** Recollects her visit to Gerrit Smith. 3 May 1861. p.72, c2.

5608 J. R. *to* **THE EDITOR OF THE** *BOSTON JOURNAL.* **n.d. n.p.** Encourages slaves to run away from their masters in order to make the South aware that their way of life is imperiled by war. 10 May 1861. p.74, c1.

5609 A. H. L. *to* **WM. LLOYD GARRISON. 4 April 1861. Philadelphia.** Rejoices that Garrison still upholds principles of peace and non-resistance. 10 May 1861. p.74, c4.

5610 YALE STUDENT *to* **MR. EDITOR [W. L. GARRISON]. 6 May 1861. Yale College.** Decries the hypocrisy of abolitionists who, after having advocated disunion for thirty years, now advocate war to save the Union. 10 May 1861. p.74, c5.

5611 AN OLD LINE ABOLITIONIST *to* **FRIEND GARRISON. 27 April 1861. Newton.** Denounces Wendell Phillips' defense of Mr. Lincoln and renunciation of "No Union with Slaveholders." 10 May 1861. p.74, c6.

5612 W. G. *to* **MR. EDITOR [W. L. GARRISON]. 29 April 1861. Dedham.** Defends atheism; attacks the Church as pro-slavery. 10 May 1861. p.74, c6.

5613 J. M. HAWKS *to* **THE EDITOR OF THE** *LIBERATOR* **[W. L. GARRISON]. 2 April 1861. Saint Marc, Hayti.** Cites immorality as Haiti's greatest problem. 10 May 1861. p.76, c3.

5614 JOSEPH PEASE *to* **FRIENDS AND FELLOW CHRISTIANS. 29 April 1861. Johnstown, Oh.** Believes that history will vindicate abolitionists. 10 May 1861. p.76, c4.

5615 C. G. O. *to* **MR. GARRISON. 29 April. Johnstown, Oh.** Holds the anti-slavery cause to be "the stone of stumbling and rock of offence" of the present day, as was the Gospel in the time of Christ. 10 May 1861. p.76, c4.

5616 D. *to* **EDITORS OF THE** *DAILY ATLAS AND BEE.* **19 April 1861. Boston.** Applauds colored people as patriotic; believes he will fight as a patriot. 10 May 1861. p.76, c6.

5617 n.n. *to* **BROTHER. 25 April 1861. Baltimore, Md.** Provides an account of attacks on Union sympathizers; beseeches his brother not to join the Union cause. 17 May 1861. p.77, c5.

5618 FRANCIS JACKSON *to* **EXECUTIVE COMMITTEE OF THE AAS. 1 May 1861. Boston.** Reports that ill health forces his resignation as treasurer of the AAS. 17 May 1861. p.78, c4.

5619 WM. LLOYD GARRISON *to* **GEORGE T. DOWNING, JOHN V. DE GRASSE AND ROBERT MORRIS. 13 May 1861. Boston.** Opposes Haitian emigration as a solution to the "colored problem." 17 May 1861. p.78, c4.

5620 WM. LLOYD GARRISON AND WENDELL PHILLIPS *to* **FRANCIS JACKSON. 1 May 1861. Boston.** Regret Jackson's resignation as treasurer of the AAS. 17 May 1861. p.78, c4.

5621 ISAAC STEARNS *to* **THE** *DAILY ATLAS AND BEE.* **4 May 1861. Mansfield.** Asks why the paper did not print an address by Wendell Phillips. 17 May 1861. p.79, c1.

5622 n.n. *to* **MR. GARRISON. n.d. n.p.** Encloses resolution passed unanimously to raise two military companies in Wayland. 17 May 1861. p.79, c4.

5623 BENJ. F. BUTLER *to* **GOV. JOHN A. ANDREW. 9 May 1861. Annapolis.** Cites moral, military, and political reasons for using Massachusetts militia to suppress Maryland insurgents. 17 May 1861. p.79, c5.

5624 JOHN A. ANDREW *to* **BRIG. GEN. BUTLER. 25 April 1861. Boston.** Opposes the use of Massachusetts militia to suppress civil uprising in Maryland. 17 May 1861. p.79, c5.

5625 REV. SAMUEL JOHNSON *to* **n.n. [extract] 8 April 1861. Florence, Italy.** Describes Italians as staunchly Catholic despite opposition to the Pope. 17 May 1861. p.80, c2.

5626 B. G. WRIGHT *to* **SIR. 5 May 1861. Rural, Il.** Observes that some slaveholders favor Union as a means of perpetuating slavery. 24 May 1861. p.83, c1.

5627 FRANCIS BARRY *to* **GARRISON. 7 April 1861. Berlin Heights, Oh.** Defends spiritualism in contradiction to remarks made by Wendell Phillips. 24 May 1861. p.84, c5.

5628 CAPT. J. MYRICK *to* **THE** *BOSTON JOURNAL.* **4 May 1861. West Dennis.** Reports that his ship was vandalized and his men attacked by secessionists in Norfolk, Virginia. 24 May 1861. p.84, c6.

5629 LA ROY SUNDERLAND *to* **THE** *BOSTON INVESTIGATOR.* **3 May 1861. Boston.** Defends Wendell Phillips' remarks on atheists. 24 May 1861. p.84, c6.

5630 AMERICAN TRAVELLER *to* **THE** *JAMAICAN GUARDIAN.* **16 January 1861. n.p.** Prefers free labor in Jamaica to slave labor in the South. 31 May 1861. p.86, c1.

5631 S. E. W. *to* **GARRISON. 16 May 1861. Worcester.** Discusses the fate of non-resistance and the coming war. 31 May 1861. p.86, c5.

5632 J. T. EVERETT *to* **GARRISON. 19 May 1861. East Princeton.** Believes that no abolitionist should fight unless the war will guarantee an end to slavery. 31 May 1861. p.87, c2.

5633 D. F. G. *to* **MR. GARRISON. 2 May 1861. Weymouth, Ma.** Reports on talks by Henry C. Wright in Weymouth. 31 May 1861. p.87, c2.

5634 GEORGE W. SIMONDS *to* **THE EDITOR OF THE** *LIBERATOR* **[W. L. GARRISON]. n.d. n.p.** Expresses dismay that Massachusetts militia has been returning runaways to their masters. 31 May 1861. p.87, c3.

5635 ORSON S. MURRAY *to* **BROTHER GARRISON. 15 May 1861. Foster's Crossings, Warren County, Oh.** Opposes the war; denounces priests and politicians. 31 May 1861. p.88, c2.

5636 CHARLES STEWART *to* **GEO. W. CHILDS. 4 May 1861. Bordentown.** Relates a conversation he held in 1812 with John C. Calhoun concerning sectionalism. 31 May 1861. p.88, c6.

5637 THOMAS T. GANTT *to* **GEN. WM. S. HARNEY. 14 May 1841. St. Louis.** Believes that the government of the United States will not interfere with slavery in Missouri; requests Harney's opinion on the matter. 7 June 1861. p.89, c3.

5638 GEN. WILLIAM S. HARNEY *to* **THOMAS T. GANTT. 14 May 1841. n.p.** Agrees with Gantt that federal troops should not interfere with slaves or other property. 7 June 1861. p.89, c3.

5639 R. J. *to* **THE EDITOR OF THE** *NEW YORK TRIBUNE.* **n.d. n.p.** Describes the return of runaway slaves by Union troops as "inhuman and cruel." 7 June 1861. p.89, c5.

5640 ALFRED H. LOVE *to* **WILLIAM LLOYD GARRISON. 27 May 1861. Philadelphia.** Urges abolitionists to reject war as a means of obtaining their goals. 7 June 1861. p.90, c6.

5641 GEN. BUTLER *to* **GEN. SCOTT. n.d. n.p.** Inquires whether he may refuse to return runaway slaves if they have been used for military purposes, and whether taking the father away from the mother and children is inhuman. 7 June 1861. p.91, c4.

5642 CASSIUS M. CLAY *to* **THE** *LONDON TIMES.* **17 May 1861. London.** Replies to a list of misstatements made by the *Times* about America. 14 June 1861. p.94, c1.

5643 EDWARD EVERETT *to* **n.n. 15 May 1861. Boston.** Believes conflict between South and North was created by "ambitious politicians." 14 June 1861. p.94, c2.

5644 J. G. F. *to* **GARRISON. 4 June 1861. Alton, Il.** Detests pro-slavery elements in Illinois. 14 June 1861. p.95, c2.

5645 G. W. S. *to* **GARRISON. 10 June 1861. Milford.** Stresses that anti-slavery work must not be suspended because current allies in the cause are unreliable. 14 June 1861. p.95, c3.

5646 BENJAMIN CHASE *to* **BROTHER GARRISON. 2 June 1861. Greenland, N.H.** Favors non-resistance but understands the position of those who support "the party nearest right." 14 June 1861. p.95, c3.

5647 J. B. LYON *to* **GARRISON. n.d. Cleveland, Oh.** Opposes the principle of peace at any price; views war as necessary to human growth. 14 June 1861. p.96, c4.

5648 IRON POINT *to* **THE EDITOR OF THE** *UNION.* **n.d. n.p.** Contends that the war will end only when the question of slavery is resolved. 21 June 1861. p.97, c6.

5649 JUSTIN PERKINS *to* **EARL OF SHAFTESBURY. 24 May. London.** Views the crisis in America as moral, not political. 21 June 1861. p.98, c1.

5650 DANIEL FOSTER *to* **FRIEND GARRISON. 12 May 1861. Centralia, Ks.** Describes conditions in Kansas. 21 June 1861. p.99, c1.

5651 CHARLES STEARNS *to* **GARRISON. 25 April 1861. Central City, Colorado Territory.** Credits the increasing influence of the abolitionist movement with hastening the fight for freedom. 21 June 1861. p.99, c1.

5652 JAMES HAUGHTON *to* **WM. LLOYD GARRISON. 29 May 1861. Dublin.** Praises recent events and changes in United States. 21 June 1861. p.100, c2.

5653 DORLAND *to* **FRIEND GARRISON. 4 June 1861. Newark, N.J.** Encloses resolutions from the annual meeting of the Friends of Human Progress. 21 June 1861. p.100, c2.

5654 EMMA HARDINGE *to* **THE** *BOSTON JOURNAL.* **1 June 1861. Boston.** Stresses need for support if she is to continue her work with "outcast females" of Boston. 21 June 1861. p.100, c4.

5655 MRS. A. J. DONELSON *to* **GEN. SCOTT. [from the** *Memphis Bulletin*] **29 April 1861. Memphis.** Claims that Scott can stop the war; urges him to denounce Northern force against Southern states. 28 June 1861. p.101, c3.

5656 GEO. THOMPSON *to* **GARRISON. 7 June 1861. Northumberland, England.** Expresses confidence that slavery in the United States is doomed. 28 June 1861. p.102, c4.

5657 HENRY T. CHEEVER *to* **THE EDITOR OF THE** *LIBERATOR* **[W. L. GARRISON]. 11 June 1861. Jewett City, Ia.** Criticizes the *Independent,* which refused to print his attack on the Church. 28 June 1861. p.102, c6.

5658 A BUSINESS MAN *to* **W. L. GARRISON. 19 June 1861. Boston.** Urges examination of the "Crittenden" compromise, which permits slaveholding in the border states. 28 June 1861. p.103, c2.

5659 JOSEPHINE S. GRIFFING *to* **FRIEND. 20 June 1861. Angola, In.** Describes conditions and race relations in Indiana. 28 June 1861. p.103, c2.

5660 WM. C. NELL *to* **GARRISON. 26 June 1861. Boston.** Reports that a hall used for early anti-slavery meetings was recently torn down. 28 June 1861. p.103, c3.

5661 R. K. HOWELL, W. C. RAYMOND, H. T. BARTLETT *to* **THE YOUNG MEN'S CHRISTIAN ASSOCIATION OF NORTH AMERICA. 22 May 1861. New Orleans.** Beg Christian brothers of North and South to unite in an effort to end the war. 5 July 1861. p.105, c1.

5662 HARRIET BEECHER STOWE *to* **THE** *NEW YORK INDEPENDENT.* **n.d. n.p.** Finds her patience tried by England and its support of the South in the war. 5 July 1861. p.105, c2.

5663 B. G. WRIGHT *to* **n.n. 26 May 1861. Rural, Il.** Laments that the charge of treason against Southern secessionists inhibits Northern disunionism. 5 July 1861. p.107, c1.

5664 J. P. HARRIMAN *to* **FRIEND GARRISON. 9 June 1861. Nora.** Opposes Illinois black laws. 5 July 1861. p.107, c4.

5665 B. G. WRIGHT *to* **n.n. n.d. n.p.** A radical abolitionist favors the right of secession. 5 July 1861. p.108, c2.

5666 BENJAMIN FISH *to* **GARRISON. 16 June 1861. Rochester, N.Y.** Stresses the need to maintain peace principles. 5 July 1861. p.108, c3.

5667 SEWARD MITCHELL *to* **THE EDITOR OF THE** *LIBERATOR* **[W. L. GARRISON]. 20 June 1861. Cornville, Me.** Describes the present as a time for "true friends of peace" to surface. 5 July 1861. p.108, c3.

5668 JAMES REDPATH *to* **WM. LLOYD GARRISON. 2 July 1861. Boston.** Criticizes the *Liberator's* unfavorable review of Redpath's *Guide to Hayti.* 12 July 1861. p.112, c2.

5669 S. C. D. *to* **THE** *JOURNAL OF COMMERCE.* **20 June 1861. Alabama.** Cites contented slaves and plentiful produce as reasons why the South will never re-enter the Union. 19 July 1861. p.113, c1.

5670 G. W. S. *to* **FRIEND GARRISON. n.d. n.p.** Chronicles a "moving sermon" he gave against slavery which prompted some parishioners to walk out. 19 July 1861. p.114, c4.

5671 E. J. W. *to* **GARRISON. 12 July 1861. Boston.** Believes the role and duty of abolitionists in the war is to free the slaves. 19 July 1861. p.114, c5.

5672 D. L. CHILD *to* **GARRISON. 12 July 1861. Wayland.** Decries inconsistency of applying war doctrine of contraband. 19 July 1861. p.114, c6.

5673 LIBERTY *to* **FRIEND. 14 July 1861. Newburyport.** Reports on seizure of ship by Confederates. 19 July 1861. p.114, c6.

5674 E. W. TWING *to* **FRIEND GARRISON. July 1861. Springfield.** Admires speeches by E. H. Heywood and W. Phillips on the war. 19 July 1861. p.116, c2.

5675 D. S. GRANDIN *to* **FRIEND GARRISON. 3 July 1861. Mechanic Falls, Me.** Pleased by progress of anti-slavery forces. 19 July 1861. p.116, c5.

5676 PHILOXOGUS *to* **THE EDITOR [W. L. GARRISON]. n.d. n.p.** Questions the overemphasis on the study of Latin. 19 July 1861. p.116, c5.

5677 JAMES F. HARVEY *to* **n.n. 11 June 1861. Paris.** Comments on widespread support of abolition in England, Scotland, and Ireland. 19 July 1861. p.116, c6.

5678 PETER SINCLAIR *to* **n.n. [from the** *Manchester Examiner***] 29 July 1861. n.p.** A British traveller gives his observations on events in the United States. 26 July 1861. p.117, c2.

5679 J. R. GIDDINGS *to* **THE** *NEW YORK TRIBUNE.* **6 June 1861. Montreal.** States that his examination of the history of governmental treatment of fugitive slaves leads him to urge slaves to escape; hopes that this will hurt the South's war effort. 26 July 1861. p.117, c4.

5680 J. S. GRIFFING *to* **FRIEND. 16 July 1861. Battle Creek, Mi.** Forwards petitions urging Congress to abolish slavery. 26 July 1861. p.119, c2.

5681 RICHARD D. WEBB *to* **MR. GARRISON. 18 June 1861. Dublin.** Questions the United States' anger at British declaration of neutrality. 26 July 1861. p.120, c2.

5682 H. C. WRIGHT *to* **GARRISON. 14 July 1861. Rockland, Me.** Reports on his lectures. 26 July 1861. p.120, c3.

5683 GERRIT SMITH *to* **OWEN LOVEJOY. 12 July 1861. Peterboro'.** Advocates that the president liberate slaves. 2 August 1861. p.121, c6.

5684 J. W. *to* **THE EDITOR OF THE** *LIBERATOR* **[W. L. GARRISON]. 21 July. New York.** Cites profits that the North has made from slavery; believes emancipation will bring about greater evils. 2 August 1861. p.122, c2.

5685 J. C. *to* **MR. EDITOR [W. L. GARRISON]. n.d. n.p.** Defends the Union and the need for continued agitation by abolitionists. 2 August 1861. p.122, c4.

5686 HENRY C. WRIGHT *to* **GARRISON. 16 July 1861. Rockland, Me.** Opposes the use of Federal troops to return fugitive slaves. 2 August 1861. p.122, c6.

5687 E. T. C. *to* **GARRISON. 23 July 1861. Worcester.** Encloses reprints of a speech asking for freedom and liberty for all. 2 August 1861. p.122, c6.

5688 BENJ. CHASE *to* **GARRISON. n.d. Auburn, N.H.** Stresses need for vigilance and no compromise on the slave issue. 2 August 1861. p.123, c1.

5689 Z. *to* **MR. GARRISON. 26 July 1861. Harwich.** States that he is impressed by A. T. Foss' anti-slavery speech. 2 August 1861. p.123, c1.

5690 JOSEPH A. DUGDALE *to* **CHILDREN. 17 August 1861. Chester County, Pa.** Encloses annual letter to the Children's Convention from Uncle Joseph. 2 August 1861. p.123, c5.

5691 J. E. *to* **THE EDITOR OF THE** *INDEPENDENT.* **5 July 1861. England.** Grieves not that the American government is suppressing rebellion, but that lives are being lost. 9 August 1861. p.126, c2.

5692 N. H. WHITING *to* **W. L. GARRISON. 31 July 1861. Boston.** Regrets he cannot attend the AS convention. 9 August 1861. p.126, c3.

5693 GEN. BUTLER *to* **HON. SIMON CAMERON, SECRETARY OF WAR. 30 July 1861. Headquarters Dept. of Virginia.** Inquires how slaves' status will be affected by the state of rebellion; awaits clarification. 9 August 1861. p.127, c5.

5694 GERRIT SMITH *to* **SENATOR BRECKENRIDGE. 23 July 1861. Peterboro.** Criticizes speech by Breckenridge which accused Lincoln of starting the war. 9 August 1861. p.128, c4.

5695 DOUGLAS *to* **THE EDITOR OF THE** *HERALD.* **29 July 1861. Newburyport.** Urges "crushing" abolitionism and an end to "this infernal nigger business." 16 August 1861. p.129, c2.

5696 DEMOCRACY OF WALPOLE *to* **THE EDITOR OF THE** *HERALD.* **29 July 1861. Walpole, N.H.** Applauds the *Herald*'s "bold" stand against blacks. 16 August 1861. p.129, c3.

5697 J. S. *to* **THE** *VERMONT CHRONICLE.* **10 June 1861. Springfield, Vt.** Advocates "War before Tyranny!" and "Death before Slavery!" 16 August 1861. p.129, c4.

5698 P. F. CONWAY *to* **n.n. 14 July. Failfax Courthouse [*sic*].** One who claims to be a soldier in the South sends a sarcastic, poorly-written letter. 16 August 1861. p.130, c2.

5699 SIMON CAMERON *to* **GENERAL BUTLER. August 1861. Washington.** Orders Butler not to interfere with slaves owned by peaceable citizens nor to encourage slaves to leave their masters. 16 August 1861. p.131, c5.

5700 D. X. *to* **THE EDITORS OF THE** *JOURNAL OF COMMERCE.* **n.d. n.p.** Cites statistics indicating that Jamaican Negroes were more productive before emancipation than at present. 23 August 1861. p.133, c1.

5701 GERRIT SMITH *to* **NEW YORK STATE DEMOCRATIC COMMITTEE. 13 August 1861. Peterboro'.** Affirms the needs of Democrats to put aside partisanship for the war efforts. 23 August 1861. p.134, c1.

5702 J. W. *to* **THE EDITOR [W. L. GARRISON]. 12 August 1861. New York.** Discusses Southern secession, the possibility of neutrality, and the means to end slavery. 23 August 1861. p.134, c6.

5703 CAMBRIDGE *to* **THE** *LIBERATOR.* **n.d. n.p.** Stresses the need for emancipation. 23 August 1861. p.135, c3.

5704 N. P., JR. *to* **FRIEND GARRISON. 8 August 1861. Davenport.** Believes anti-slavery people should hold fewer meetings and take more action. 23 August 1861. p.135, c3.

5705 G. W. S. *to* **FRIEND GARRISON. 19 August 1861. Milford, Ma.** Feels the hour of trial for abolitionists is at hand. 23 August 1861. p.135, c4.

5706 J. B. LYON *to* **WILLIAM LLOYD GARRISON. n.d. n.p.** Urges freeing the slaves in order to end the war. 23 August 1861. p.135, c4.

5707 H. C. WRIGHT *to* **JAMES HAUGHTON. 20 July 1861. Dublin.** Feels that the antagonistic ideas of liberty and slavery were the cause of the war. 23 August 1861. p.136, c2.

5708 STEPHEN A. DOUGLAS *to* **VIRGIL HICKOX. 10 May 1861. Chicago.** Describes his role in trying to avoid war by compromise. 30 August 1861. p.137, c5.

5709 W. J. POTTER *to* **WM. LLOYD GARRISON. 27 August 1861. New Bedford.** Corrects misquote in letter by correspondent J. W. 30 August 1861. p.139, c3.

5710 ORSON S. MURRAY *to* **BROTHER GARRISON. 7 July 1861. Foster's Crossings, Oh.** Cites economic reasons, including capitalist need for labor, as causes of the war. 30 August 1861. p.140, c1.

5711 T. PERRONET THOMPSON *to* **WM. LLOYD GARRISON. 20 July 1861. Blackheath, London.** Expresses pride that he stopped the slave trade while he was governor in Sierra Leone. 6 September 1861. p.142, c4.

5712 A WESTERN WOMAN *to* **n.n. n.d. n.p.** Declares her pride in America and its free institutions which are not found on the "other side." 6 September 1861. p.143, c4.

5713 EDWARD BATES *to* **J. L. McDOWELL, UNITED STATES MARSHAL. 23 July 1861. Attorney General's Office.** Affirms responsibility of the United States marshal to enforce all laws, including the Fugitive Slave Law. 13 September 1861. p.145, c1.

5714 GERRIT SMITH *to* **PRESIDENT LINCOLN. 31 August 1861. Peterboro.** Rejoices that General Fremont has freed Missouri slaves; hopes similar actions will follow. 13 September 1861. p.146, c1.

5715 A RADICAL REPUBLICAN *to* **THE EDITOR OF THE *LIBERATOR* [W. L. GARRISON]. n.d. n.p.** Explains why the war must be a war for liberty. 13 September 1861. p.147, c2.

5716 R. PLUMER *to* **FRIEND GARRISON. 4 September 1861. Newburyport.** Denounces the impounding of cargo vessels by the Northern navy. 13 September 1861. p.147, c3.

5717 A. HOGEBOOM *to* **J. P. B. n.d. Shed's Corners, N.Y.** Opposes any compromise with Southern "barbarism." 13 September 1861. p.148, c5.

5718 T. PERRONET THOMPSON *to* **THE *BRADFORD ADVERTISER*. 29 August 1861. Eliot Vale, Blackheath, London, England.** Describes mixed response in England to the United States war and slavery. 20 September 1861. p.149, c2.

5719 RICHARD D. WEBB *to* **THE *NATIONAL ANTI-SLAVERY STANDARD*. 24 August 1861. Dublin.** Feels report of the First of August celebration in Abington treated Southerners lightly. 20 September 1861. p.150, c1.

5720 F. W. CHESSON *to* **W. L. GARRISON. 27 August 1861. London.** Sends letter introducing General T. Perronet Thompson. 20 September 1861. p.150, c5.

5721 HENRY C. WRIGHT *to* **WM. LLOYD GARRISON. 5 September 1861. Livonia, Mi.** Expects that the war will procure liberty for the slaves. 20 September 1861. p.150, c6.

5722 R. L. ALEXANDER *to* **THE** *LIBERATOR.* **5 September 1861. Livonia, Mi.** Discusses recent visit by H. C. Wright. 20 September 1861. p.151, c1.

5723 A. LINCOLN *to* **MAJOR GENERAL FREMONT. 11 September 1861. Washington, D.C.** Requests that Fremont modify order freeing Missouri slaves. 20 September 1861. p.151, c3.

5724 A. LINCOLN *to* **B. MAGOFFIN, GOVERNOR OF KENTUCKY. 24 August 1861. Washington, D.C.** Claims that a limited military force consisting of Kentuckians is active in Kentucky. 20 September 1861. p.151, c4.

5725 CHARLES K. WHIPPLE *to* **REV. JUSTIN PERKINS. 8 September 1861. Boston.** Restates his censure of Perkins for his silence on slavery. 20 September 1861. p.152, c2.

5726 D. S. GRANDIN *to* **FRIEND GARRISON. 30 August 1861. Mechanic Falls, Me.** Advocates that all slaves be freed and recruited as colored soldiers. 20 September 1861. p.152, c4.

5727 BENJ. F. BUTLER *to* **F. A. HILDRETH. 27 August 1861. Off Cape Hatteras.** Declines nomination for governor of Massachusetts. 20 September 1861. p.152, c6.

5728 THOS. FRANCIS MEAGHER *to* **B. S. TREANOR. 11 September 1861. Headquarters, Irish Brigade.** Promises that the brigade will assist the "good great cause" of the Union. 20 September 1861. p.152, c6.

5729 J. HOLT *to* **A. LINCOLN. 12 September 1861. Washington.** Denounces Fremont's proclamation freeing slaves in Missouri. 27 September 1861. p.153, c1.

5730 A. LINCOLN *to* **JOSEPH HOLT. 12 September 1861. Executive Mansion.** Forwards [unprinted] copy of letter sent to Fremont concerning the Missouri proclamation. 27 September 1861. p.153, c1.

5731 R. J. HINTON *to* **THE EDITOR OF THE** *LIBERATOR* **[W. L. GARRISON]. 17 September 1861. Washington, D.C.** Mourns the death of Barclay Coppic, a veteran of the John Brown raid. 27 September 1861. p.154, c6.

5732 HENRY PARKER *to* **SIR. 8 August 1861. Birmingham, England.** Asserts that the hearts and minds of England are with the North. 27 September 1861. p.155, c2.

5733 D. S. GRANDIN *to* **MR. GARRISON. n.d. n.p.** Requests evidence to support David Lee Child's report of the betrayal of troops by "the black traitor Twiggs" and other scandals. 27 September 1861. p.155, c3.

5734 H. C. WRIGHT *to* **WM. LLOYD GARRISON. 15 September 1861. St. Mary's Lake, Battle Creek, Mi.** Implores Garrison to take the water cure. 27 September 1861. p.156, c2.

5735 JOHN C. FREMONT *to* **SIR. 26 September. St. Louis.** Describes ability of the enemy to conduct guerilla war while the Union defends fixed positions. 4 October 1861. p.158, c2.

5736 JAMES HAUGHTON *to* **H. C. WRIGHT. 8 September 1861. Dublin.** Describes Southerners as "rebels without a just cause." 4 October 1861. p.159, c1.

5737 DANIEL RICKETSON *to* **WM. C. NELL. 18 September 1861. New Bedford.** Advocates recruitment of colored soldiers. 4 October 1861. p.159, c3.

5738 A. HOGEBOOM *to* **J. P. B. n.d. n.p.** Believes that the only chance for peace lies in the destruction of slavery. 4 October 1861. p.159, c3.

5739 HENRY WILLIS *to* **MR. GARRISON. 16 September 1861. St. Mary's Lake, Mi.** Reports on meeting and speech by H. C. Wright at St. Mary's Lake. 4 October 1861. p.160, c3.

5740 MRS. CHILD *to* **JESSIE FREMONT. n.d. n.p.** Respects women like Jessie Fremont, who are supportive of their husbands' efforts. 11 October 1861. p.162, c5.

5741 H. C. WRIGHT *to* **GARRISON. n.d. n.p.** Calls slaveholders and their apologists spies and traitors. 11 October 1861. p.163, c3.

5742 A. H. *to* **MR. GARRISON. 1 October 1861. West Randolph, Vt.** Reports that A. T. Foss is lecturing in Vermont. 11 October 1861. p.163, c4.

5743 JAMES BUCHANAN *to* **CHAIRMAN OF THE GREAT UNION MEETING. n.d. n.p.** Believes that this is a time for swift action, not peace proposals. 11 October 1861. p.163, c5.

5744 A. T. *to* **THE EDITOR OF THE** *LIBERATOR* **[W. L. GARRISON]. n.d. n.p.** "Blesses" Fremont for his anti-slavery proclamation. 11 October 1861. p.163, c7.

5745 D. L. C. *to* **GARRISON. n.d. n.p.** Cites numerous instances of voter fraud in Pennsylvania. 11 October 1861. p.164, c2.

5746 H. C. WRIGHT *to* **GARRISON. 22 September 1861. Elkhart, In.** Urges placing limits on presidential powers. 11 October 1861. p.164, c4.

5747 DANIEL MANN *to* **MR. GARRISON. n.d. n.p.** Laments that little progress has been made in obtaining rights for women in Ohio. 11 October 1861. p.164, c4.

5748 A. WELLINGTON *to* **GARRISON. 18 October 1861. Winchester, Middlesex.** Reports on Middlesex AS meeting. 18 October 1861. p.167, c3.

5749 GERRIT SMITH *to* **W. W. CHAPMAN. 8 October 1861. Peterboro'.** Refuses to assist in the coming elections. 18 October 1861. p.167, c3.

5750 JOHN BROWN, JR. *to* **THE** *LEADER.* **12 October 1861. Cleveland, Oh.** Refutes rumor that his military company is to disband because of lack of numbers. 18 October 1861. p.167, c4.

5751 B. R. DOWNES *to* **MR. GARRISON. 21 October 1861. Bradford.** Regrets that the abolitionist position is so misunderstood. 25 October 1861. p.171, c1.

5752 THOMAS HUGHES *to* **MR. EDITOR [W. L. GARRISON]. 12 August 1861. Cromer.** Believes that the British support the Union despite military setbacks. 1 November 1861. p.174, c2.

5753 D. D. V. *to* **THE EDITOR OF THE** *NEW YORK TRIBUNE.* **n.d. Morrisania, N.Y.** Cites opposition to slavery by St. Patrick in the fifth century. 1 November 1861. p.176, c5.

5754 HIRAM WILSON *to* **FRIEND GARRISON. 30 October 1861. St. Catharines, Canada.** Believes there is no need for American aid to fugitive slaves in Canada since they are well off. 8 November 1861. p.178, c6.

5755 G. *to* **THE EDITOR OF THE** *LIBERATOR.* **n.d. n.p.** Fears that the war will result in a military rule over North and South. 8 November 1861. p.179, c1.

5756 G. W. S. *to* **GARRISON. n.d. Milford, Ma.** Reports on commendable speech by Sen. Sumner on the origins of the rebellion. 8 November 1861. p.179, c2.

5757 HENRY C. WRIGHT *to* **GARRISON. 3 November 1861. West Winfield, N.Y.** Believes the Union would not be worth saving at the expense of preserving slavery. 8 November 1861. p.179, c2.

5758 G. GARIBALDI *to* **MR. QUIGGLE, UNITED STATES CONSUL AT ANTWERP. 10 September 1861. Caprera.** Believes that the North will win quickly; adds that if the war lingers on, he will come to its defense. 8 November 1861. p.179, c3.

5759 THOMAS CURTIS *to* **THE EDITOR OF THE** *LIBERATOR* **[W. L. GARRISON]. 30 October 1861. Philadelphia.** Criticizes speech made by Garrison attacking orthodoxy. 8 November 1861. p.180, c2.

5760 C. E. C. *to* **GARRISON. 30 October 1861. Detroit.** Praises lectures by H. C. Wright on the origins of the war. 8 November 1861. p.180, c2.

5761 T. PERRONET THOMPSON *to* **THE** *BRADFORD ADVERTISER.* **24 October 1861. Eliot Vale, England.** Describes opposition to anti-slavery in England as divided and theoretical. 8 November 1861. p.180, c5.

5762 H. C. WRIGHT *to* **GARRISON. 5 November 1861. Forest Lake, Pa.** Believes a compromise to end the war must be avoided. 15 November 1861. p.183, c1.

5763 H. C. WRIGHT *to* **GARRISON. 6 November 1861. Forest Lake, Pa.** Feels that Southern secession destroys the abolition campaign for disunion. 15 November 1861. p.183, c1.

5764 n.n. *to* **n.n. 3 November 1861. n.p.** Calls for honesty in the legislature. 15 November 1861. p.183, c2.

5765 GEORGE K. RADCLIFFE *to* **THE** *LIBERATOR.* **5 November 1861. Haverhill, Ma.** Thanks paper for printing speech of Chas. Sumner. 15 November 1861. p.183, c3.

5766 J. S. *to* **THE EDITOR OF THE** *LIBERATOR* **[W. L. GARRISON]. 30 October 1861. Springfield, Ct.** Regrets the absence of anti-slavery in Vermont. 15 November 1861. p.184, c3.

5767 THEODORE PARKER *to* **HORACE A. KEACH. 3 September 1861. Brookline, Ma.** Gives advice on how to speak well. 15 November 1861. p.184, c4.

5768 C. W. *to* **THE** *CHICAGO TRIBUNE.* **9 November 1861. Cairo, Il.** Reports on the bravery of a mulatto servant in the Battle of Belmont. 22 November 1861. p.186, c2.

5769 W. H. F. *to* **FRIEND GARRISON. n.d. n.p.** Praises the Union army for its growing opposition to slavery. 22 November 1861. p.187, c4.

5770 W. C. N. *to* **FRIEND GARRISON. 12 November 1861. Boston.** Encloses petitions advocating equal rights for all people. 22 November 1861. p.188, c5.

5771 MARY A. SHADD CARY *to* **W. L. LLOYD GARRISON. n.d. n.p.** Expresses appreciation on behalf of slaves who have escaped to the North. 29 November 1861. p.191, c3.

5772 GERRIT SMITH *to* **EDWIN CROSWELL. 27 November 1861. Peterboro'.** Agrees with the need to "avail ourselves of the black man's help" in the war. 6 December 1861. p.195, c1.

5773 A. T. FOSS *to* **FRIEND GARRISON. n.d. n.p.** Comments on his recent lecture in Vermont. 6 December 1861. p.195, c3.

5774 n.n. *to* **THE EDITOR OF THE** *LIBERATOR* **[W. L. GARRISON]. [extract] 13 November. n.p.** Fears that the North is morally incapable of destroying slavery. 6 December 1861. p.196, c3.

5775 GENERAL OBSERVER *to* **THE EDITOR OF THE** *LIBERATOR* **[W. L. GARRISON]. n.d. n.p.** Urges use of any means to crush rebellion. 13 December 1861. p.199, c1.

5776 G. A. B. *to* **MR. EDITOR. 2 December 1861. Boston.** Observes public confusion concerning the cause of the war. 13 December 1861. p.199, c2.

5777 M. L. WHITTEN *to* **MR. EDITOR [W. L. GARRISON]. 17 November 1861. Erna, Me.** Rejoices at the news of an attack on Ft. Sumter. 13 December 1861. p.199, c2.

5778 WILLIAM H. SEWARD *to* **GEN. GEORGE B. McCLELLAN. 4 December 1861. Washington, D.C.** Orders McClellan to provide protection for fugitive slaves. 13 December 1861. p.199, c4.

5779 CARLETON *to* **THE** *BOSTON JOURNAL.* **2 December 1861. Washington, D.C.** Cites cases of Virginia runaways in the District of Columbia jail. 13 December 1861. p.200, c5.

5780 G. K. RADCLIFFE *to* **G. 14 December 1861. Haverhill.** Lists new officers of the Emancipation League. 27 December 1861. p.206, c2.

5781 THOMAS McCLINTOCK *to* **W. L. GARRISON. 30 October 1861. Philadelphia.** Encloses a prophesy from the spirit world concerning the Civil War. 27 December 1861. p.206, c2.

[1862]

5782 GERRIT SMITH *to* **HON. J. A. GURLEY. 16 December 1861. Peterboro'.** Speaks out against racist legislation pertaining to slaves, which was introduced by Gurley. 3 January 1862. p.1, c5.

5783 T. PERRONET THOMPSON *to* **THE** *BRADFORD ADVERTISER.* **12 December 1861. England.** Attacks slavery zealots in England. 3 January 1862. p.2, c1.

5784 JOHN GORDON *to* **FRIEND GARRISON. 26 December 1861. Salem, Oh.** Censures those who put his brother in prison. 3 January 1862. p.2, c6.

5785 RINGBOLT *to* **THE EDITOR OF THE** *BOSTON COURIER.* **n.d. n.p.** Accuses Seward of fostering bad relations between the United States and England. 10 January 1862. p.5, c5.

5786 F. W. B. *to* **THE** *LIBERATOR*. **n.d. n.p.** Cautions abolitionists not to join "demagogues and traitors" in the anti-England campaign. 10 January 1862. p.6, c6.

5787 PARKER PILLSBURY *to* **FRIEND GARRISON. 7 January 1862. Leominster.** Discusses his activities of the past few years. 10 January 1862. p.7, c2.

5788 T. PERRONET THOMPSON *to LONDON MORNING ADVERTISER*. **27 December 1861. Eliot Vale, London.** Stresses the need for England to support the Union. 17 January 1862. p.9, c4.

5789 BENJAMIN CHASE *to* **REV. LINUS H. SHAW. n.d. Auburn, N.H.** Responds to Shaw's Thanksgiving sermon. 17 January 1862. p.12, c4.

5790 L. MARIA CHILD *to* **MAY. 15 January 1862. Wayland.** Thanks May for the copy of *Life and Letters of John Brown*. 24 January 1862. p.15, c3.

5791 S. E. W. *to* **GARRISON. 19 January 1862. Worcester.** Reports on Wendell Phillips' stay in Worcester. 31 January 1862. p.20, c2.

5792 G. A. B. *to* **MR. EDITOR. 20 January 1861. Boston.** Debates British policy toward the United States war. 31 January 1862. p.20, c3.

5793 n.n. *to* **THE EDITOR OF THE** *BOSTON COURIER*. **n.d. Suffolk.** Expresses disgust at popular support for the "heartless and cold-blooded traitor," Wendell Phillips; attacks the *Boston Journal* for its intentionally inadequate coverage of abolitionist activities. 7 February 1862. p.21, c1.

5794 RICHARD D. WEBB *to* **MR. GARRISON. 10 January 1862. Dublin.** Defends England's behavior in the Trent affair. 7 February 1862. p.23, c1.

5795 DANIEL RICKETSON *to* **RESPECTED FRIENDS. 22 January 1862. New Bedford, Ma.** Regrets that he is unable to attend a meeting of the Massachusetts AS. 7 February 1862. p.23, c4.

5796 SARAH CLAY *to* **MR. GARRISON. 3 February 1862. Lowell.** Describes meeting of the Middlesex County AS. 7 February 1862. p.23, c4.

5797 A. HOGEBOOM *to* **FRIEND GARRISON. 18 January 1862. Shed's Corners, N.Y.** Writes an obituary for his son, William A. Hogeboom. 7 February 1862. p.23, c5.

5798 H. W. B. *to* **FRIEND GARRISON. January 1862. Port Norfolk.** Presents a biographical sketch and obituary of Richard Clap, an active member of the Dorchester AS. 7 February 1862. p.23, c5.

5799 T. PERRONET THOMPSON *to* **THE EDITOR OF THE** *BRADFORD* **(ENGLAND)** *ADVERTISER*. **26 December 1861. Eliot Vale, Blackheath.** Resents the response of the English AS to American abolitionist efforts; objects to the unfair censure of abolitionists for their inability to convince the South to emancipate slaves without recourse to war. 7 February 1862. p.24, c2.

5800 COL. CROCKER *to* **THE SECRETARY OF STATE. 6 January 1862. Headquarters, Jefferson City, Mo.** Urges war between the states; claims that no slaveholders who are loyal to the Union remain. 7 February 1862. p.24, c6.

5801 GERRIT SMITH *to* **GEORGE THOMPSON. 25 January 1862. Peterboro'.** Discusses the Trent affair; hopes Thompson and others can improve relations between Britain and the Northern states. 14 February 1862. p.25, c1.

5802 J. M. H. *to* **EDITOR** *LIBERATOR* **[W. L. GARRISON]. 1 February 1862. Washington, D.C.** Describes an address by Ralph Waldo Emerson. 14 February 1862. p.27, c2.

5803 COMMODORE A. H. FOOTE *to* **THE SECRETARY OF THE NAVY. 6 February 1862. Off Fort Henry, Tennessee River.** Dispatch from the United States flag ship *Cincinnati* announces the capture of Fort Henry; reports casualties. 14 February 1862. p.27, c4.

5804 n.n. *to* **n.n. 10 February 1862. Norfolk, Va.** Dispatch to Richmond announces the burning of Elizabeth City by residents; reports that all but one gunboat were captured by the enemy; awaits the arrival of General Wise. 14 February 1862. p.27, c5.

5805 LIEUTENANT PHILLIPS *to* **FLAT OFFICER FOOTE. 10 February 1862. Railroad Crossing, Gunboat** *Conestoga.* Reports a successful expedition to Florence near Muscle Shoals, Alabama; adds that rebel boats were burned or captured with military supplies on board. 14 February 1862. p.27, c5.

5806 n.n. *to* **THE** *CINCINNATI GAZETTE.* **n.d. Nelson's division in Kentucky.** Reports that a Southern Unionist advises the North to attack the South immediately and forcefully rather than prolong the suffering. 14 February 1862. p.27, c5.

5807 SAMUEL J. MAY *to* **THE** *LIBERATOR.* **[extract] 18 January 1862. Syracuse, N.Y.** Feels that abolitionists will be needed, even after slaves are freed, to guide, protect, and encourage them to realize their potential. 14 February 1862. p.28, c2.

5808 EDWIN CHAPMAN *to* **MRS. L. M. CHILD. [extract] 27 November 1861. Bristol, England.** Sends money for the AS. 14 February 1862. p.28, c3.

5809 SAMUEL GALE *to* **MRS. L. MARIA CHILD. 17 January 1862. Montreal, Canada.** Sends money for the AS. 14 February 1862. p.28, c3.

5810 n.n. *to* **RESPECTED LADIES. 20 January 1862. n.p.** Regrets that he cannot attend the subscription anniversary meeting; suggests that they accept the mission to teach slaves once they are all freed. 14 February 1862. p.28, c3.

5811 EDWARD HARRIS *to* **LADIES. 15 January 1862. Woonsocket, R.I.** Regrets that he cannot attend the subscription anniversary. 14 February 1862. p.28, c3.

5812 A LADY IN NEW HAMPSHIRE *to* **THE** *LIBERATOR.* **[extract] n.d. New Hampshire.** Encourages the anti-slavery movement to persist in its efforts to bring equality to slaves, even if the government fails to emancipate them. 14 February 1862. p.28, c3.

5813 WM. LLOYD GARRISON *to* **GEORGE THOMPSON. n.d. n.p.** Counters England's arguments against the Union stand. 21 February 1862. p.30, c3.

5814 AARON M. POWELL *to* **MR. GARRISON. 13 February 1862. Ghent, N.Y.** Encloses a petition to the New York senate and assembly in support of the abolition of slavery under the war power. 21 February 1862. p.30, c5.

5815 BENJAMIN CHASE *to* **FRIEND GARRISON. 29 January 1862. Auburn, N.H.** Approves of Garrison's recent New York speech. 21 February 1862. p.30, c5.

5816 L. M. C. *to* **THE EDITOR OF THE** *LIBERATOR* **[W. L. GARRISON]. n.d. n.p.** Recommends that Garrison read the late Major Theodore Whiting's *John Brent.* 21 February 1862. p.30, c5.

5817 PARKER PILLSBURY *to* **FRIEND GARRISON. 12 February 1862. Albany.** Sends an extract of a letter from Edwin R. Brown discussing anti-slavery activities in Illinois. 21 February 1862. p.31, c3.

5818 EDWIN R. BROWN *to* **n.n. [extract] n.d. Illinois.** Describes difficulties encountered while delivering anti-slavery lectures in Illinois; expresses disdain for schemes involving compulsory colonization and expatriation of freed slaves. 21 February 1862. p.31, c3.

5819 n.n. *to* **THE *TIMES*. 16 February 1862. Fort Donelson.** Details the surrender of Fort Donelson to Union troops; reports casualties. 21 February 1862. p.31, c4.

5820 H. W. HALLECK, MAJOR GENERAL *to* **MAJOR GENERAL McCLELLAN. 18 February 1862. Headquarters.** Announces the southwest army's successful invasion of Arkansas under General Curtis, after driving Price from Missouri. 21 February 1862. p.31, c4.

5821 H. W. HALLECK, MAJOR GENERAL *to* **MAJOR GENERAL McCLELLAN. 19 February 1862. St. Louis.** Dispatch announces the capture of General Price and his staff. 21 February 1862. p.31, c4.

5822 WARD H. LAMON *to* **JAILER AND GUARDS OF THE PUBLIC JAIL IN THE DISTRICT OF COLUMBIA. 9 February 1862. Washington, D.C.** United States marshal orders jailers to release all prisoners held for thirty days or more who are not charged with any crime. 21 February 1862. p.31, c5.

5823 REV. DR. STRICKLAND *to* **n.n. n.d. Port Royal.** Describes accommodations in Port Royal for the slaves; presumes that slaves will be housed there for safekeeping. 21 February 1862. p.31, c5.

5824 n.n. *to* **n.n. [from the *New York Herald*] 12 February. Louisville.** Announces the evacuation of Bowling Green by Southerners, the evacuation of Weldon, and the burning of homes because of the rumored arrival of Union troops. 21 February 1862. p.31, c6.

5825 ENGLISH ABOLITIONIST *to* **n.n. 7 December 1861. England.** Discusses the English view of the North's waging war to liberate the slaves; feels that the war is a violation of the South's right to self-government. 21 February 1862. p.32, c2.

5826 ENGLISH ABOLITIONIST *to* **n.n. 5 December 1861. Scotland.** Explains British sentiments on the Civil War; doubts that the war is anti-slavery; encourages the small undercurrent of true anti-slavery feeling to be more active. 21 February 1862. p.32, c3.

5827 P. A. T. *to* **n.n. 16 January 1862. London.** An English abolitionist reassures Americans that the English still oppose slavery; cites reasons for their disbelief that the war is being fought to free the slave; urges America to declare country for emancipation. 21 February 1862. p.32, c3.

5828 F. W. B. *to* **MR. GARRISON. n.d. n.p.** States that Europeans do not sympathize with the Unionists because they are not convinced that the war is being fought for the emancipation of slaves; supports his argument with extracts from military instructions. 21 February 1862. p.32, c4.

5829 MR. LOCKWOOD *to* **n.n. [extract] n.d. Fortress Monroe.** Missionary quotes part of a prayer by Carey, a colored contraband, for liberation and the victory of the Union cause. 21 February 1862. p.32, c6.

5830 WM. LLOYD GARRISON *to* **GEORGE THOMPSON. [continued from 21 February 1862] n.d. n.p.** Justifies the right of the North to suppress Southern rebellion. 28 February 1862. p.34, c3.

5831 n.n. *to* **n.n. n.d. St. Louis, Mo.** Provides evidence of a changing trend in St. Louis popular opinion toward opposition to slavery. 28 February 1862. p.34, c4.

5832 n.n. *to* **THE** *CHICAGO TRIBUNE.* **25 February 1862. Cairo.** Dispatch announces the occupation of Nashville by 20,000 troops under General Buell's command. 28 February 1862. p.34, c4.

5833 HUMANITY *to* **MR. EDITOR. [from the** *Greenfield* **(Ma.)** *Gazette and Courier]* **n.d. n.p.** Criticizes the Greenfield Democrats' attacks on lectures by W. L. Garrison, Rt. Rev. Bishop Clark, and B. Taylor. 28 February 1862. p.34, c6.

5834 ORSON S. MURRAY *to* **THE EDITOR OF THE** *LIBERATOR* **[W. L. GARRISON]. 10 February 1862. Foster's Crossings, Warren County, Oh.** Encloses an article criticizing Lincoln's administration for holding a lavish ball with funds needed for the war effort. 28 February 1862. p.35, c1.

5835 MARY A. SHADD CARY *to* **WM. LLOYD GARRISON. n.d. n.p.** Reports on the mission school affair in Chatham, Canada. 28 February 1862. p.35, c2.

5836 M. *to* **FRIEND GARRISON. 22 February 1862. Newton Corner.** Relates the pleasant surprise of hearing an anti-slavery speech delivered by the Newtonville high school principal, T. D. Adams. 28 February 1862. p.35, c3.

5837 J. H., JR. *to* **EDITOR** *LIBERATOR* **[W. L. GARRISON]. 6 February 1862. Washington, D.C.** Regrets that the nation's capital is located in Washington, the site of continual conflict between pro- and anti-slavery factions. 28 February 1862. p.36, c3.

5838 J. M. HAWKS *to* **EDITOR** *LIBERATOR* **[W. L. GARRISON]. 16 February 1862. Fortress Monroe, Va.** Describes the condition of the fugitive slaves. 28 February 1862. p.36, c4.

5839 WM. LLOYD GARRISON *to* **GEORGE THOMPSON. [continued from 28 February 1862] n.d. n.p.** Desires that British abolitionists recognize the progress of American abolitionists. 7 March 1862. p.38, c3.

5840 C. *to* **BROTHER GARRISON. 3 March 1862. West Cambridge.** Praises a speech by E. H. Heyward titled "The Cause and Cure of the War." 7 March 1862. p.38, c4.

5841 WM. LLOYD GARRISON *to* **COL. JAMES McKAYE. 4 March 1862. Boston.** Reports that he is unable to attend the meeting, but sympathizes with the committee's work. 7 March 1862. p.38, c5.

5842 HENRY C. WRIGHT *to* **GARRISON. 25 February 1862. Boston.** Believes the question of the war to be whether Congress can re-enslave freed slaves. 7 March 1862. p.38, c6.

5843 n.n. *to* **n.n. [from the** *New York Times]* **10 January. General Hooker's division.** Relates an account of a freed Negro, Jack Scroggin, who was returned by an army officer to his master, Samuel Cox, and then dragged behind a horse and whipped to death. 7 March 1862. p.38, c6.

5844 SECRETARY S. P. CHASE *to* **MR. EDWARD L. PIERCE. [extract] n.d. n.p.**
The secretary of the treasury authorizes Pierce, agent in charge of Port Royal contrabands, to maintain and cultivate abandoned plantations in that area. 7 March 1862. p.39, c4.

5845 GEN. H. W. HALLECK *to* **MAJOR GEN. McCLELLAN. n.d. n.p.** Reports that the enemy has evacuated Columbus and surrendered; adds that much artillery was captured. 7 March 1862. p.39, c5.

5846 n.n. *to* **n.n. 4 March 1862. Columbus.** Dispatch announces the complete evacuation and widespread destruction of Columbus. 7 March 1862. p.39, c5.

5847 PRESTON KING *to* **JAMES McKAYE. 5 March 1862. Washington, D.C.** Regrets that he cannot accept the invitation to attend the New York meeting for a free Republic. 14 March 1862. p.41, c6.

5848 CHARLES SUMNER *to* **JAMES McKAYE. 5 March 1862. Senate Chamber.** Regrets that he cannot attend the meeting at Cooper Institute in New York due to concurrent Senate sessions; declares slavery "dead" in the Southern states because the states themselves "died" when they failed to abide by the United States Constitution. 14 March 1862. p.41, c6.

5849 HENRY WILSON *to* **JAMES McKAYE. 4 March 1862. Washington, D.C.** Regrets that he cannot attend the meeting at Cooper Institute in New York; recommends that slavery, the cause of the war, be exterminated; advocates abolition of slavery in the District of Columbia, repeal of the black code, and federal support of Northern efforts toward emancipation. 14 March 1862. p.42, c1.

5850 DAVID WILMOT *to* **JAMES McKAYE. 5 March 1862. Washington, D.C.** Replies that he cannot attend the meeting at Cooper Institute in New York; asserts that the nation has the right to eradicate slavery, the sole cause of the war; recommends compensating loyal slaveholders for their loss. 14 March 1862. p.42, c1.

5851 GEORGE W. JULIAN *to* **JAMES McKAYE. 4 March 1862. Washington, D.C.** Reports that he cannot attend the meeting at Cooper Institute in New York; insists that slavery is the sole cause of the war, and its eradication the only cure. 14 March 1862. p.42, c1.

5852 REV. JOHN PIERPONT *to* **JAMES McKAYE. 3 March 1862. Washington, D.C.** Informs that he cannot attend the meeting at Cooper Institute in New York; encloses a short poem advocating an end to slavery. 14 March 1862. p.42, c2.

5853 MRS. FRANCES D. GAGE *to* **FRIEND GARRISON. 4 March 1862. Columbus, Oh.** States that most of the population of Columbus strongly oppose the Lincoln administration's failure to act against slavery. 14 March 1862. p.42, c6.

5854 JOSEPH CARPENTER *to* **GARRISON. 7 February 1862. New Rochelle, N.Y.** Describes anti-slavery meetings held in West Chester County by Aaron M. Powell; reports that few people or churches oppose slavery. 14 March 1862. p.42, c6.

5855 SENATOR CHARLES SUMNER *to* **WM. M. WERMERSKIRCH. 25 February 1862. Senate Chamber.** Thanks the German Republican Central Committee of New York for their support of Sumner's presentation to the Senate on the status of rebel states. 14 March 1862. p.44 [43], c2.

5856 COMMODORE DUPONT *to* **n.n. 4 March 1862. Flat Ship** *Mohican,* **Harbor Fernandina, Fl.** Reports the capture of Cumberland Island, the Sound of Fernandina, Amelia Island, and St. Mary's. 14 March 1862. p.44, c3.

5857 n.n. *to* **n.n. [from the** *New York Herald*] **11 March 1862. Washington, D.C.** Dispatch announces the evacuation of Manassas and retreat of rebel forces toward Richmond, Virginia. 14 March 1862. p.44, c3.

5858 H. W. HALLECK, MAJOR GENERAL *to* **MAJOR GENERAL McCLELLAN. n.d. n.p.** Dispatch announces Union victory, under General Curtis, over forces of Van Dorn, McCulloch, Price, and McIntosh; adds that rebels are fleeing. 14 March 1862. p.44, c3.

5859 MR. WEBB *to* **n.n. [extract from the** *Anti-Slavery Standard*] **n.d. n.p.** Presents statistics to support the argument that American emancipation would be at least as safe as was British emancipation. 14 March 1862. p.44, c3.

5860 A PRIVATE IN THE SECOND OHIO CAVALRY *to* **HIS MOTHER. [from the** *Cleveland Leader*] **17 February. Platte City, Mo.** Tells of a fugitive slave's return to his master by order of a commanding officer and of his subsequent escape with the help of Union soldiers. 14 March 1862. p.44, c5.

5861 MONTGOMERY BLAIR *to* **THE COMMITTEE OF INVITATION, ETC. 2 March 1862. Washington, D.C.** Informs that he cannot attend the meeting at Cooper Institute in New York; believes antagonism of race to be the source of current conflicts between the states; recommends removing blacks from "the temperate regions of America" once they have been freed. 21 March 1862. p.45, c1.

5862 LUCIUS HOLMES *to* **MR. GARRISON. 18 March 1862. Charlton, Ma.** Defends a speech by President Lincoln. 21 March 1862. p.46, c3.

5863 C. K. W. *to* **MR. GARRISON. n.d. n.p.** Argues against correspondent "C" 's suggestion that the slave system of the South be replaced by the old Metayer system of farming. 21 March 1862. p.46, c5.

5864 G. B. STEBBINS *to* **W. L. GARRISON. 10 March 1862. Rochester, Mi.** Discusses Stebbins' speaking tour. 21 March 1862. p.47, c2.

5865 GEN. GEO. B. McCLELLAN *to* **SOLDIERS OF THE ARMY OF THE POTOMAC. 14 March 1862. Headquarters Army of the Potomac, Fairfax Court House, Va.** Announces that the period of inaction and preparation for battle is over; expresses confidence in the army's ability to win. 21 March 1862. p.47, c5.

5866 REV. STARR KING *to* **THE EDITOR OF THE** *BOSTON TRANSCRIPT.* **20 January 1862. San Francisco.** Details the disastrous effects of a flood in California. 21 March 1862. p.48, c4.

5867 WM. S. PIERCE, GEORGE H. EARLE, GEO. A. COFFEE, B. RUSH PLUMLY, J. STEWART DEPUY, MARMADUKE MOORE, T. B. PUGH, WM. B. THOMAS, ALFRED H. LOVE, OWEN JONES, WM. WAINWRIGHT, AND D. CROWELL *to* **MISS ANNA E. DICKINSON. 4 March 1862. Philadelphia.** Request that Dickinson deliver her lecture, "The Present War," at Concert Hall. 28 March 1862. p.50, c4.

5868 ANNA E. DICKINSON *to* **MESSRS. PIERCE, EARLE, COFFEE, ET CETERA. 5 March 1862. Philadelphia.** Accepts the invitation to deliver "The National Crisis" on 11 March 1862. 28 March 1862. p.50, c4.

5869 K. W. M. *to* **EDITORS. [from the** *Rochester Express***] n.d. Byron.** Praises the oratorical talent of Wm. Carlos Martyn, a New Haven resident, and the singing of George W. Clark. 28 March 1862. p.50, c5.

5870 WM. CARLOS MARTYN *to* **WM. LLOYD GARRISON. 10 March 1862. Norwich, Ct.** Gives an account of his speaking tour. 28 March 1862. p.50, c5.

5871 ANDREW PATON *to* **WM. I. BOWDITCH. 28 February 1862. Glasgow, Scotland.** Sends money; reports that business is bad in Scotland. 28 March 1862. p.50, c6.

5872 A. G. *to* **FRIEND GARRISON. 22 March 1862. Harwich Port.** Describes anti-slavery meetings on Cape Cod; praises Parker Pillsbury's ability to convince audiences that peace and slavery are mutually exclusive. 28 March 1862. p.50, c6.

5873 LUCIUS HOLMES *to* **MR. GARRISON. n.d. Charlton.** Praises Garrison's analysis of Lincoln's recent proclamation; expresses dismay at the nation's reluctance to do what is right. 28 March 1862. p.50, c6.

5874 A REPUBLICAN *to* **HON. W. H. SEWARD. 15 March 1862. Boston.** Accuses Seward of failing to adhere to his anti-slavery campaign pledges; blames him for prolonging the current conflict between the states. 28 March 1862. p.51, c1.

5875 L. G. B. *to* **THE EDITOR OF THE** *LIBERATOR* **[W. L. GARRISON]. 16 March 1862. Burlington, Vt.** Criticizes the Ninety-sixth Regiment New York Volunteers for rejecting John Brown's son, Salmon Brown. 28 March 1862. p.51, c2.

5876 W. G. SPENCER *to* **WM. LLOYD GARRISON. 8 February 1862. Derby, England.** Asks that Wendell Phillips clarify statements concerning England in his recent speech. 28 March 1862. p.51, c3.

5877 THOMAS J. MOORE *to* **WM. LLOYD GARRISON. 17 March 1862. Starfield, Il.** Criticizes Lincoln's grand ball. 28 March 1862. p.51, c3.

5878 AN OFFICER OF THE TWENTY-SECOND MASSACHUSETTS REGIMENT *to* **n.n. [extract] 18 March 1862. Alexandria, Va.** Describes the headless corpses of Zouaves found at Bull Run and Centreville. 28 March 1862. p.51, c4.

5879 n.n. *to* **n.n. [extract] 15 March 1862. Gunboat off Newbern, N.C.** Notes that poisoned rum and whiskey were left for Union soldiers by fleeing citizens of Newbern. 28 March 1862. p.51, c5.

5880 ORSON S. MURRAY *to* **THE EDITOR OF THE** *LIBERATOR* **[W. L. GARRISON]. 12 March 1862. Foster's Crossings, Warren County, Oh.** Abhors Lincoln's failure to act against slavery. 28 March 1862. p.52, c2.

5881 J. R. UNDERWOOD *to* **THE EDITORS OF THE** *LOUISVILLE JOURNAL.* **17 March 1862. Louisville, Ky.** Encloses a letter from Gen. Buell for publication; endorses Buell's opinion that abolishing slavery in the South would be unconstitutional. 4 April 1862. p.53, c1.

5882 GEN. D. C. BUELL *to* **HON. J. R. UNDERWOOD. 6 March 1862. Headquarters, Department of the Ohio, Nashville.** States that he and his army obey the law by returning fugitive slaves to their masters. 4 April 1862. p.53, c1.

5883 EX. *to* **THE EDITOR OF THE** *NEW YORK TRIBUNE.* **22 March 1862. New York.** Relates untold facts about the death of "Negro Jack" from a whipping administered by Cox. 4 April 1862. p.54, c1.

5884 n.n. *to* **MR. GARRISON. 29 March 1862. Yale College.** Accuses Wm. Carlos Martyn of dishonesty. 4 April 1862. p.54, c6.

5885 R. THAYER *to* **FRIEND GARRISON. 1 April 1862. Boston.** Submits for publication a poem, "Spurn Not The Guilty," by Caroline M. Sawyer. 4 April 1862. p.56, c1.

5886 REPUBLICAN *to* **A UNITED STATES SENATOR. [extract] 11 March 1862. n.p.** Submits objections to Lincoln's recent "Resolutions and Message of the President." 4 April 1862. p.56, c2.

5887 TYRO *to* **MR. GARRISON. 25 March 1862. East Somerville.** Concludes that Lincoln intends to abolish slavery only if it is necessary in order to end the rebellion. 4 April 1862. p.56, c3.

5888 A. GIBBS CAMPBELL *to* **MR. GARRISON. 22 March 1862. Paterson, N.J.** Expresses dismay at the timidity of the message from Abraham Lincoln. 4 April 1862. p.56, c3.

5889 HARRIET MARTINEAU *to* **THE EDITOR OF THE** *NATIONAL ANTI-SLAVERY STANDARD.* **7 February 1862. n.p.** Disagrees with the paper's treatment of the Trent affair. 4 April 1862. p.56, c5.

5890 JOHN W. MENARD *to* **THE EDITOR OF THE** *LIBERATOR* **[W. L. GARRISON]. 26 March 1862. Chatham, Canada.** Defends the mission school at Chatham. 11 April 1862. p.58, c4.

5891 Z. H. HOWE *to* **FRIEND GARRISON. 1 April 1862. Madison, Wi.** Praises Wendell Phillips' speech in Madison; describes his good effect on the audience. 11 April 1862. p.58, c5.

5892 MR. PHILLIPS *to* **A FRIEND IN BOSTON. n.d. Milwaukee.** Describes a mob attack which occurred during his speech in Cincinnati. 11 April 1862. p.58, c5.

5893 DANIEL FOSTER *to* **GARRISON. 25 March 1862. Seneca, Ks.** Abolitionist minister and educator defends himself while in jail. 11 April 1862. p.59, c1.

5894 WM. HENRY BURR *to* **THE EDITOR OF THE** *NEW YORK TRIBUNE.* **2 April 1862. New York.** Encloses an extract from a friend's letter as evidence that wooden log imitations, "Quaker Cannon," were used at Centreville. 11 April 1862. p.59, c2.

5895 n.n. *to* **WM. HENRY BURR. [extract from the** *New York Tribune***] n.d. n.p.** Describes the fifty to sixty fake cannon found at Centreville. 11 April 1862. p.59, c2.

5896 WM. CARLOS MARTYN *to* **MR. GARRISON. 12 April 1862. New York.** Replies to attack on him recently printed in the *Liberator.* 18 April 1862. p.63, c1.

5897 C. B. P. *to* **FRIEND** *LIBERATOR.* **13 April 1862. Newport. R.I.** Praises Anna E. Dickinson's powerful lecture on the national crisis. 18 April 1862. p.63, c2.

5898 JOHN E. WOOL, MAJOR GENERAL *to* **THE HON. E. M. STANTON, SECRETARY OF WAR. 11 April 1862. Fortress Monroe.** States that the *Merrimac, Jamestown, Yorktown,* and several other boats were sighted nearby; adds that two small Union boats were captured. 18 April 1862. p.63, c4.

5899 IRWIN McDOWELL, MAJ. GEN. *to* **HON. EDWIN M. STANTON, SECRETARY OF WAR. 13 April 1862. Cattlet's Station.** Relays information learned from two Negroes that rebel forces left Fredericksburg for Richmond and Yorktown. 18 April 1862. p.63, c4.

5900 SERGEANT GERRIT S. HAMBLETON *to* **HIS MOTHER. [extract] 4 September. n.p.** Requests his mother's consent to fight for the Union; later writes a farewell on his deathbed. 18 April 1862. p.63, c5.

5901 SERGEANT GERRIT S. HAMBLETON *to* **HIS PARENTS. 8 December. Fortress Monroe.** Confirms his commitment to the Union cause just before leaving for Port Royal. 18 April 1862. p.63, c5.

5902 GERRIT SMITH *to* **MONTGOMERY BLAIR. 5 April 1862. Peterboro.** Advocates emancipation; opposes colonization of freed slaves. 18 April 1862. p.64, c2.

5903 SARAH D. FISH *to* **WILLIAM LLOYD GARRISON. 2 April 1862. Rochester, N.Y.** Pities those who uphold slavery. 18 April 1862. p.64, c5.

5904 REVERDY JOHNSON *to* **n.n. [from the** *Baltimore American*] **n.d. n.p.** Supports President Lincoln's policy of gradual emancipation with compensation to slaveholders and separation of the races. 25 April 1862. p.65, c6.

5905 A. FAIRBANKS *to* **FRIEND GARRISON. 20 April 1862. Providence.** Lauds the anti-slavery lectures of Anna E. Dickinson. 25 April 1862. p.67, c2.

5906 BENJAMIN CHASE *to* **FRIEND GARRISON. n.d. Auburn, N.H.** Fears the prospect of a compromise with slavery when the war ends. 25 April 1862. p.68, c2.

5907 G. A. S. *to* **FRIEND. 30 March 1862. Washington, D.C.** Gives an account of her discovery that rebel soldiers exhumed many bodies, keeping bones and skulls as trophies. 25 April 1862. p.68, c3.

5908 CHAPLAIN A. H. QUINT *to* **THE** *CONGREGATIONALIST.* **n.d. Winchester, Va.** Illustrates Southern brutality: reports sale of Northern skulls for ten dollars apiece after the Bull Run battle. 25 April 1862. p.68, c4.

5909 AN OFFICER OF THE ARMY OF THE POTOMAC *to* **FRIEND. [extract] 22 March 1862. Centreville.** Confirms the existence of wooden imitation cannon in the fort at Centreville; states that Manassas was not impregnable. 25 April 1862. p.68, c5.

5910 G. WALTER ALLEN *to* **MR. GARRISON. 25 April 1862. Worcester.** Replies to latest letter by Wm. Carlos Martyn. 2 May 1862. p.70, c4.

5911 D. HENRY CHAMBERLAIN *to* **MR. GARRISON. 22 April 1862. West Brookfield, Ma.** Replies to the latest letter by Wm. Carlos Martyn. 2 May 1862. p.70, c4.

5912 JUNIUS *to* **MR. EDITOR [W. L. GARRISON]. 19 April 1862. Springfield.** Confirms Garrison's belief that Prof. Clarence Butler is a dangerous hypocrite. 2 May 1862. p.70, c6.

5913 D. W. *to* **SIR. n.d. Auburn, N.Y.** Sends money; hopes that the Union cause will result in emancipation. 2 May 1862. p.70, c6.

5914 A FREEDOM-LOVING SOLDIER *to* **FRIEND GARRISON. n.d. Camp of—Regt., Massachusetts Volunteers, near Newbern, N.C.** Distributes copies of the *Liberator* to freed slaves. 2 May 1862. p.70, c6.

5915 A. T. FOSS *to* **FRIEND MAY. [extract] 15 April 1862. West Williamsburg, Oh.** Describes anti-slavery meetings and sentiments in his neighborhood. 2 May 1862. p.71, c1.

5916 VINCENT COLLIER *to* **n.n. [extract] 2 April 1862. Newbern, N.C.** An agent of the New York Y.M.C.A. describes his role as "Superintendent of the Poor"; attempts to find employment for one thousand colored persons and sixty white families. 2 May 1862. p.71, c2.

5917 COL. C. R. JENNISON *to* **THE** *LIBERATOR.* **[extract] n.d. Weston, Mo.** Declares his ignorance of the charges against him; suspects that he was arrested because he favors freedom. 2 May 1862. p.71, c3.

5918 COL. C. R. JENNISON *to* **FRIEND STEARNS. 21 April 1862. Military Prison, St. Louis, Mo.** Complains of ill treatment in prison; affirms his commitment to abolition. 2 May 1862. p.71, c3.

5919 REBEL SOLDIER CAPTURED AT BOWLING GREEN *to* **SIS. n.d. n.p.** Sends his sister a ring he made from the bullet that killed Colonel Slocum of the Seventy-first New York Regiment. 2 May 1862. p.71, c4.

5920 JOHN W. WOOL, MAJOR GENERAL *to* **HON. E. M. STANTON, SECRETARY OF WAR. 29 April. Fortress Monroe.** Reports that New Orleans is held by Federal forces. 2 May 1862. p.71, c5.

5921 AN EMINENT AMERICAN, FORMERLY A DEMOCRAT *to* **THE** *TRIBUNE.* **n.d. Europe.** Declares that to preserve the status of slavery would be crazy. 2 May 1862. p.71, c5.

5922 n.n. *to* **n.n. [extract from the** *New York Post***] 25 April 1862. Yorktown.** Reports on rebel casualties. 2 May 1862. p.71, c5.

5923 E. W. H. *to* **n.n. n.d. n.p.** A teacher chronicles the experiences of those who teach Negroes at Beaufort; requests contributions of cheap cloth and salt. 2 May 1862. p.72, c5.

5924 K. *to* **EDITORS OF THE** *NEW YORK JOURNAL OF COMMERCE.* **28 April 1862. New York.** Challenges the paper's contention that "fanatical plans" are in action at Port Royal. 9 May 1862. p.73, c1.

5925 A MASSACHUSETTS SOLDIER *to* **THE** *NEWBURYPORT* **(MA.)** *HERALD.* **n.d. n.p.** Threatens military violence against the *Herald,* the *New York Tribune,* and Greeley; desires that the military select the next president. 9 May 1862. p.73, c5.

5926 MR. A. E. COCHRAN *to* **THOMAS BUTLER KING. [extract from the** *National Intelligencer***] 5 March 1861. Macon, Ga.** States that most Georgians interpret Lincoln's inaugural speech as a " 'no fight' measure." 9 May 1862. p.74, c1.

5927 J. COWLES *to* **THOMAS BUTLER KING. [extract from the** *National Intelligencer***] 10 April 1861. New York.** Predicts the sequence of events leading to secession. 9 May 1862. p.74, c1.

5928 BEVERLY TUCKER *to* **THOMAS BUTLER KING. [extract from the** *National Intelligencer***] June 1861. n.p.** Gloats over three rebel victories and "the rotten Government at Washington." 9 May 1862. p.74, c1.

5929 MARYLAND *to* **THOMAS BUTLER KING. [extract from the** *National Intelligencer***] n.d. n.p.** Expresses confidence that British officials will recognize the Southern Confederacy. 9 May 1862. p.74, c1.

5930 CH. HAUSSOLLIER *to* **THOMAS BUTLER KING. [extract from the** *National Intelligencer***] n.d. France.** Mentions a "gratifying" interview between King and the minister. 9 May 1862. p.74, c1.

5931 THOMAS BUTLER KING *to* **EARL RUSSELL. [extract from the** *National Intelligencer***] 6 December 1861. n.p.** Declares his satisfaction with Mr. Crawford, the British consul at Havana. 9 May 1862. p.74, c1.

5932 ROBERT HUTCHINSON *to* **MR. YANCEY. [extract from the** *National Intelligencer***] n.d. n.p.** Requests Thomas Butler King's address in order that he might arrest him for debt. 9 May 1862. p.74, c1.

5933 GERRIT SMITH *to* **WM. LLOYD GARRISON. 16 April 1862. Peterboro.** Offers moral support and money to the AAS. 9 May 1862. p.74, c3.

5934 J. M. McKIM *to* **THE EXECUTIVE COMMITTEE OF THE PENNSYLVANIA AS. 22 January 1862. Anti-Slavery Office.** Submits his resignation as corresponding secretary. 9 May 1862. p.75, c2.

5935 REUBEN TOMLINSON, RECORDING SECRETARY *to* **MR. McKIM. 23 January 1862. n.p.** Submits portion of minutes from the Executive Committee of the Pennsylvania AS asking McKim to reconsider his resignation. 9 May 1862. p.75, c2.

5936 J. M. McKIM *to* **REUBEN TOMLINSON. 24 January 1862. Anti-Slavery Office.** Maintains his desire to resign post as corresponding secretary of the Pennsylvania AS. 9 May 1862. p.75, c2.

5937 JAMES MOTT, LUCRETIA MOTT, ROBERT PURVIS, ABBY KIMBER, MARY GREW, BENJAMIN C. BACON, SARAH PUGH, MARGARET J. BURLEIGH, AND REUBEN TOMLINSON *to* **J. M. McKIM. 9 February 1862. Philadelphia.** Reluctantly accept McKim's resignation as corresponding secretary of the Pennsylvania AS. 9 May 1862. p.75, c3.

5938 J. M. McKIM *to* **n.n. [extract] n.d. n.p.** Believes that the iconoclastic role of the anti-slavery movement should now be replaced by a constructive role. 9 May 1862. p.75, c3.

5939 n.n. *to* **n.n. [extract from the** *Anglo-African***] 28 April. Washington.** Denies reports that Negroes in the District of Columbia petitioned for colonization in Central America. 9 May 1862. p.75, c4.

5940 O. P. Q. *to* **MR. EDITOR [W. L. GARRISON] n.d. n.p.** Forwards M. R. Miller's speech replying to Mr. F. Pickles' pro-slavery speech given at a debate on slavery in Cincinnati. 9 May 1862. p.76, c3.

5941 WILLIAM DRIVER *to* **BROTHER GEORGE. [from the** *Salem Register***] 1 May 1862. Nashville, Tn.** Loyalist lauds Northern anti-slavery cause. 23 May 1862. p.81, c4.

5942 H. J. RAYMOND, EDITOR OF THE *NEW YORK TIMES to* **n.n. 8 May 1862. Yorktown.** Reports that Brig. Gen. Rains supervises the planting of torpedoes in evacuated areas to kill invading Union troops. 23 May 1862. p.81, c5.

5943 ARMY SURGEON *to* **n.n. [extract from the** *Detroit Free Press***] 17 April. Paducah, Ky.** Details treatment of wounded at Paducah. 23 May 1862. p.81, c5.

5944 C. K. W. *to* **MR. GARRISON. n.d. n.p.** Encloses two letters concerning distribution of anti-slavery tracts; recommends Mrs. Child's pamphlet, "The Right Way the Safe Way." 23 May 1862. p.82, c5.

5945 PRUDENCE CRANDALL PHILLEO *to* **C. K. W. [extract] 10 May 1862. Mendota, La Salle Co., Il.** Describes method of distributing anti-slavery tracts; encloses note received from Charles Higgins. 23 May 1862. p.82, c5.

5946 CHAS. M. HIGGINS *to* **MRS. PRUDENCE CRANDALL PHILLEO. 8 May 1862. Mendota.** Thanks Mrs. Philleo for "The Right Way the Safe Way," which convinced Higgins that British emancipation in the West Indies was successful. 23 May 1862. p.82, c5.

5947 J. L. DOUTHIT *to* **SAMUEL MAY, JR. 9 May 1862. Shelbyville, Il.** Requests anti-slavery tracts for distribution in Shelbyville; declares himself "an uncompromising abolitionist." 23 May 1862. p.82, c6.

5948 W. FOSTER, JR. *to* **SIR. 5 May 1862. Providence.** Contests statements made in the *Liberator* concerning Professor Clarence Butler. 23 May 1862. p.82, c6.

5949 D. D. CONE *to* **WM. LLOYD GARRISON. 8 May 1862. Washington, D.C.** Exposes a plot by slaveholders in response to abolition in the District of Columbia; discloses that runaways who attempt to return home as freemen are apprehended in Baltimore and sold for their former master's profit. 23 May 1862. p.82, c6.

5950 H. M. TRACY CUTLER *to* **THE *LIBERATOR*. May 1862. Pontiac, Il.** Reports upsurge in mid-western abolitionist enthusiasm. 23 May 1862. p.83, c1.

5951 A. T. FOSS *to* **MR. GARRISON. 28 April 1862. Ashtabula, Oh.** Recommends that abolitionists publicly recognize "the second great event of the century," the abolition of slavery in Washington, D.C. 23 May 1862. p.83, c1.

5952 G. W. S. *to* **FRIEND GARRISON. n.d. n.p.** Praises quarterly meeting of the Middlesex County AS; mentions speeches by Parker Pillsbury and Brother May. 23 May 1862. p.83, c2.

5953 DAVID CAMPBELL, COLONEL, FIFTH CAVALRY *to* **HON. EDWIN M. STANTON, SECRETARY OF WAR. 11 May 1862. Williamsburg.** Reports repulsion of five gunboats from Fort Daring and the explosion of a gun on the *Naugatuck*. 23 May 1862. p.83, c4.

5954 n.n. *to* **n.n. [extract from the *Bulletin*] 19 May 1862. Fortress Monroe.** Relays bad news about conditions on the *Naugatuck, Galena,* and *Monitor*; notes that Col. Brown of the Twentieth Indiana Regiment is reported missing or dead. 23 May 1862. p.83, c4.

5955 GEO. B. McCLELLAN, MAJOR GENERAL *to* **n.n. 17 May 1862. White House, Headquarters of the Army of the Potomac.** Announces destruction of Confederate steamers and schooners. 23 May 1862. p.83, c4.

5956 K. *to* **THE EDITOR OF THE *NEW YORK TRIBUNE*. 7 May 1862. n.p.** Encloses extract of a letter illustrating desire of Negroes to learn. 23 May 1862. p.83, c5.

5957 A YOUNG SCHOLAR AND SOLDIER OF MASSACHUSETTS *to* **K. [extract] 7 May 1862. Port Royal.** Recounts incidents illustrating eagerness of Negroes to learn. 23 May 1862. p.83, c5.

5958 n.n. *to* **GEORGE C. RICHARDSON. 4 May 1862. Missouri.** Laments prevalence of private assassinations of Unionists; calls for strong immediate action to end slavery. 23 May 1862. p.84, c3.

5959 n.n. *to* **CHARLES SUMNER. n.d. Camp of General Hooker.** Encloses orders of General Hooker concerning the new ruling that Union officers may not surrender Negroes to their alleged masters; exposes violations of the legislation; requests better enforcement. 30 May 1862. p.85, c3.

5960 E. P. HALSTED, ASSISTANT ADJUTANT GENERAL *to* **LT. COL. JOHN D. SHAUL, COMMANDING SEVENTY-SIXTH REGIMENT NEW YORK VOLUNTEERS. 6 April 1862. Headquarters, Military Defenses, North of the Potomac, Washington.** Imforms Shaul of the new article of war prohibiting officers from surrendering Negroes to those claiming to be their masters. 30 May 1862. p.85, c3.

5961 SOLDIER *to* **PARENTS. [extract] 8 March 1862. Camp Andy Johnson, near Nashville, Tn.** Regrets the surrender of Henry, a Negro working in their camp, to his secessionist master by two sentries who earned fifteen dollars each for the deed. 30 May 1862. p.85, c4.

5962 IRWIN McDOWELL, MAJOR GENERAL *to* **HON. EDWIN M. STANTON, SECRETARY OF WAR. 13 April. Catlettsville Station, Va., Fifteen Miles South of Manassas Junction.** Reports that two Negroes informed him that Confederate troops were moving toward Richmond and Yorktown. 30 May 1862. p.85, c5.

5963 GOV. JOHN A. ANDREW *to* **HON. E. M. STANTON, SECRETARY OF WAR. 19 May 1862. Boston.** Replies to enclosed telegram; requests more infantry regiments from Massachusetts; estimates that forty days will be required to raise three regiments; hopes the president will accept black volunteers. 30 May 1862. p.86, c3.

5964 L. THOMAS, ADJUTANT GENERAL *to* **JOHN A. ANDREW. 19 May 1862. n.p.** Asks how soon three or four new infantry regiments could be raised. 30 May 1862. p.86, c3.

5965 A. J. GROVER *to* **MR. GARRISON. 15 May 1862. Earlville, Il.** Discusses the proposed constitution for Illinois. 30 May 1862. p.86, c5.

5966 MRS. H. M. TRACY CUTLER *to* **THE *LIBERATOR*. 20 May 1862. El Paso, Il.** Presents reactions to her tour of Illinois. 30 May 1862. p.86, c6.

5967 J. W. SPAULDING *to* **FRIEND GARRISON. 24 May 1862. East Pepperell.** Praises a lecture by Wm. Wells Brown. 30 May 1862. p.87, c1.

5968 G. B. STEBBINS *to* **W. L. GARRISON. 20 May 1862. Rochester, N.Y.** Reminds abolitionists that they still have work to do. 30 May 1862. p.87, c1.

5969 JUSTITIA *to* **MR. EDITOR [W. L. GARRISON]. 24 May 1862. Boston.** Illustrates metaphorically that the government cannot abolish and condemn slavery as long as it maintains any connection with it. 30 May 1862. p.87, c1.

5970 CHARLES K. WHIPPLE *to* **MR. GARRISON. n.d. n.p.** Sends anti-slavery letter written by A. H. Quint, for publication in the *Liberator*. 30 May 1862. p.87, c2.

5971 A. H. QUINT *to* **CHARLES K. WHIPPLE. 4 May 1862. Harrisonburg, Va.** Amends a statement in the writer's earlier letter, which had seemed tolerant of slaveholders; warns of the danger inherent in compromise. 30 May 1862. p.87, c2.

5972 N. P. BANKS, MAJ. GEN. COMMANDING *to* **HON. E. M. STANTON. 25 May 1862. Headquarters, Martinsburg.** Sends official report of battle between 15,000 rebels and Union force of only 4,000. 30 May 1862. p.87, c3.

5973 N. P. BANKS, MAJ. GEN. COMMANDING *to* **HON. E. M. STANTON. 25 May 1862. Headquarters, beyond Martinsburg.** Relays news learned from a rebel prisoner; reports that he and his troops safely passed the Potomac and will begin long march. 30 May 1862. p.87, c3.

5974 N. P. BANKS, MAJOR GENERAL COMMANDING *to* **THE PRESIDENT. 26 May 1862. Williamsport.** Reports gains and losses incurred since the march from Strasburg on 24 May. 30 May 1862. p.87, c4.

5975 n.n. *to* **GOVERNOR CURTIN. 26 May 1862. Chambersburg.** Reports having received testimony that sick and imprisoned Northerners are treated brutally by rebels. 30 May 1862. p.87, c4.

5976 n.n. *to* **n.n. [extract] 11 May 1862. Nashville, Tn.** Accuses the Confederacy of destroying its own Tennessee countryside and pushing the state toward financial ruin. 30 May 1862. p.87, c4.

5977 S. F. DUPONT, FLAG OFFICER, COMMANDING, ETC. *to* **SIR [AT THE NAVY DEPARTMENT]. [extract] n.d. n.p.** Forwards dispatch from Commander Parrott; provides further information about the captured steamer *Planter*; recommends that Robert Small, a Negro pilot, be recognized for his role in the capture. 30 May 1862. p.87, c5.

5978 COMMANDER PARROTT *to* **S. F. DUPONT. 13 May 1862. U. S. Steamship** *Augusta,* **off Charleston.** Dispatch informs Dupont of the capture of *Planter,* an armed rebel steamer, and if its transference to Port Royal. 30 May 1862. p.87, c5.

5979 WM. CARLOS MARTYN *to* **MR. GARRISON. 12 May 1862. New Haven, Ct.** Continues debate with Messrs. Allen and Chamberlin, denying charges that he falsely claimed to be a Yale student. 30 May 1862. p.88, c5.

5980 JAMES M. FULLER *to* **WM. LLOYD GARRISON. 5 May 1862. Buffalo, N.Y.** Supports Wm. Carlos Martyn in his dispute with Mr. Chamberlain. 30 May 1862. p.88, c6.

5981 J. P. A. *to* **MESSRS. EDITORS. [from the** *Rochester Democrat***] 7 November 1861. LeRoy.** Praises Wm. Carlos Martyn's speech at war meeting in LeRoy. 30 May 1862. p.88, c6.

5982 AMOS KENDALL *to* **EDITORS OF THE** *NATIONAL INTELLIGENCER.* **19 May 1862. Washington.** Denies support of General Hunter's order that all slaves in his military district be freed. 6 June 1862. p.89, c2.

5983 n.n. *to* **n.n. [extract from the** *Philadelphia Press***] n.d. Washington.** Credits Amos Kendall with proposing the order, given by General Hunter, to free all slaves in his military district. 6 June 1862. p.89, c2.

5984 F. D. GAGE *to* **FRIEND GARRISON. 28 May 1862. Cleveland, Oh.** Reports that public opinion in Ohio supports a governmental declaration of emancipation; repeats a popular joke about public response to Wendell Phillips. 6 June 1862. p.91, c2.

5985 REV. JEHIEL CLAFLIN *to* **GARRISON. 24 May 1862. West Brookfield, Vt.** Informs that he cannot attend the New England convention. 6 June 1862. p.91, c2.

5986 H. W. HALLECK, MAJOR GENERAL *to* **HON. E. M. STANTON, SECRETARY OF WAR. n.d. Camp near Corinth.** Reports flight of General Beauregard's army from a strong position in front of Corinth; General Pope estimates 2,000 rebels captured. 6 June 1862. p.91, c3.

5987 GEORGE B. McCLELLAN, MAJOR GENERAL COMMANDING *to* **WAR DEPARTMENT. 1 June 1862. Field of Battle, near Richmond.** Describes "desperate battle" with large numbers of rebel troops near Richmond. 6 June 1862. p.91, c3.

5988 EDWIN M. STANTON, SECRETARY OF WAR *to* **HON. EDWARD STANLY, MILITARY GOVERNOR OF NORTH CAROLINA. 2 May 1862. War Department, Washington, D.C.** Instructs Stanly about his duties, the most important being to reestablish the federal government's authority in North Carolina. 13 June 1862. p.94, c1.

5989 JESSE STEDMAN *to* **JACOB COLLAMER. 8 May 1862. Springfield, Vt.** Disagrees with Collamer's reports concerning the Confiscation Bill. 13 June 1862. p.94, c6.

5990 H. M. T. CUTLER *to* **THE** *LIBERATOR.* **26 May 1862. Elmwood, Il.** Describes her lecture tour in Illinois. 13 June 1862. p.95, c1.

5991 H. M. T. CUTLER *to* **THE** *LIBERATOR.* **2 June 1862. Canton, Il.** Continues the account of her lecture tour. 13 June 1862. p.95, c1.

5992 G. B. McCLELLAN, MAJOR GENERAL COMMANDING *to* **HON. EDWIN M. STANTON, SECRETARY OF WAR. n.d. n.p.** Lists the numbers wounded, killed, and missing in the Battle of Fair Oaks. 13 June 1862. p.95, c3.

5993 CHARLES ELLETT, JR., COLONEL COMMANDING RAM FLOTILLA *to* **HON. E. M. STANTON. 5 June 1862 via Cairo, 8 June 1862. Opposite Randolph, below Fort Pillow.** Dispatch announces the evacuation of Forts Pillow and Randolph. 13 June 1862. p.95, c3.

5994 C. H. DAVIS, FLAG OFFICER COMMANDING PRO TEM. *to* **HON. GIDEON WELLES, SECRETARY OF THE NAVY. 6 June 1862. United States Steamer** *Benton* **off Memphis.** Describes a naval battle off Memphis which resulted in the capture or destruction of seven rebel ships and the surrender of Memphis. 13 June 1862. p.95, c3.

5996 CHARLES ELLETT, COLONEL COMMANDING THE RAM FLEET *to* **HON. EDWIN M. STANTON, SECRETARY OF WAR. 6 June 1862 via Cairo, 8 June 1862. Opposite Memphis.** Describes the capture of a rebel fleet off Memphis; reports his leg wound. 13 June 1862. p.95, c4.

5997 C. H. DAVIS, FLAG OFFICER *to* **MAYOR OF THE CITY OF MEMPHIS. 6 June 1862. U.S. Steamer** *Benton,* **Off Memphis.** Requests the surrender of Memphis to the United States. 13 June 1862. p.95, c4.

5998 MAYOR OF MEMPHIS *to* **C. H. DAVIS, FLAG OFFICER. [extract] n.d. Memphis, Tn.** Surrenders Memphis to the United States. 13 June 1862. p.95, c4.

5999 J. C. FREMONT, MAJOR GENERAL *to* **E. M. STANTON. 7 June 1862. Headquarters, Army in the Field, Harrisonburg.** Describes attack on rebel forces and their subsequent retreat; reports death of General Ashby. 13 June 1862. p.95, c5.

6000 J. C. FREMONT, MAJOR GENERAL *to* **E. M. STANTON, SECRETARY OF WAR. 8 June 1862. Headquarters, Army in the Field, Camp near Fort Republic.** Describes battle near Harrisonburg against Jackson's entire troop; reports heavy casualties, especially among officers. 13 June 1862. p.95, c5.

6001 H. [R.] HELPER *to* **GOVERNOR STANLY. 30 May 1862. Newbern, N.C.** Offers to help convince North Carolinians to comply with Lincoln's new policy encouraging gradual emancipation; expresses concern that Stanly's decision to close schools for Negroes indicates a pro-slavery slant. 13 June 1862. p.96, c6.

6002 DAN MESSENGER, PROVOST-MARSHAL *to* **H. [R.] HELPER, ESQ. 31 May 1862. Office of the Provost-Marshal, Newbern, N. C.** Orders Helper, on behalf of Governor Stanly, to leave North Carolina on the first northbound vessel. 13 June 1862. p.96, c6.

6003 EDWARD ATKINSON, CHAIRMAN FINANCE COMMITTEE *to* **THE EDITORS OF THE** *BOSTON DAILY ADVERTISER.* **9 June 1862. Boston.** Presents evidence to support his assertion that the Boston Educational Commission has been successful; encloses a letter by J. M. Forbes on the same subject. 20 June 1862. p.99, c2.

6004 J. M. FORBES *to* **MR. EDWARD ATKINSON. 23 May 1862. Boston.** Details the positive results achieved by the Boston Educational Commission. 20 June 1862. p.99, c2.

6005 S. E. W. *to* **MR. GARRISON. 14 June 1862. Worcester.** Analyzes President Lincoln's policy concerning emancipation. 20 June 1862. p.99, c3.

6006 DR. J. M. HAWKS *to* **EDITOR OF THE** *LIBERATOR* **[W. L. GARRISON]. 7 June 1862. On board steamer** *Potomac,* **making her voyage from Edisto to Hilton Head, S.C.** Describes the island of Edisto, now Union territory, and the process of educating Negroes who fled to Edisto from surrounding rebel territory; discusses problems with the current status of Edisto Negroes; expresses confidence that Lincoln will call for emancipation. 20 June 1862. p.99, c4.

6007 SENATOR CHARLES SUMNER *to* **SIR. [from the** *Boston Journal***] 5 June 1862. Senate Chamber.** Declares that Lincoln does not condone Stanly's closing of Negro schools or reenslavement of fugitives who enter Union territory; assures his impatient friend that Lincoln opposes slavery. 20 June 1862. p.99, c5.

6008 G. B. STEBBINS *to* **W. L. GARRISON. 5 June 1862. Rochester, N.Y.** Describes the proceedings of the Fourteenth Yearly Meeting at Waterloo of the Friends of Human Progress; reports the adoption of a memorial to Congress urging the abolition of slavery. 20 June 1862. p.100, c4.

6009 JOSEPH M. WIGHTMAN, MAYOR *to* **HIS EXCELLENCY ABRAHAM LINCOLN, PRESIDENT OF THE UNITED STATES, WASHINGTON, D.C. [from the** *Philadelphia Inquirer***] 23 May 1862. Mayor's Office, City Hall, Boston.** Contradicts Governor Andrew, stating that Massachusetts citizens do not link anti-slavery efforts with the war to reunite the states; declares the readiness of citizens to volunteer for military service. 27 June 1862. p.101, c1.

6010 COL. GIBSON, OF THE FORTY-NINTH OHIO REGIMENT *to* **n.n. [extract] n.d. Tennessee.** Describes slaves as happy, well cared for, and frightened of emancipation; calls for suppression of the rebellion without emancipation. 27 June 1862. p.101, c2.

6011 WM. C. TENNEY *to* **ABRAHAM LINCOLN. 23 June 1862. Marlboro', Ma.** Contradicts Mayor Wightman's analysis of the feelings of people of Massachusetts; calls for emancipation of slaves. 27 June 1862. p.102, c6.

6012 DAN. MESSENGER, PROVOST MARSHAL *to* **H. [R.] HELPER. n.d. n.p.** Relays instructions from Governor Stanly of North Carolina to leave the area on the first northbound ship. 27 June 1862. p.103, c5.

6013 GIDEON WELLES *to* **CAPTAIN J. G. ROWAN, COMMANDING NAVAL FORCES, NORTH CAROLINA SOUNDS. 8 June 1862. Navy Department, Washington.** Reminds Rowan that enlisted men, including fugitive slaves, cannot be discharged without departmental permission or given to anyone against their will. 27 June 1862. p.103, c5.

6014 GENERAL McCLELLAN *to* **n.n. [extract] 25 June 1862. n.p.** Reports on the progress of the advance on Richmond against heavy rebel resistance. 27 June 1862. p.103, c6.

6015 SCOUT *to* **THE EDITOR OF THE** *BOSTON JOURNAL.* **13 June 1862. Newbern, N.C.** Details the incident concerning Mr. and Mrs. Bray's young female slave, and her escape with the aid of unidentified soldiers; denies that Massachusetts soldiers were involved. 27 June 1862. p.104, c5.

6016 MARRIANNE *to* **JOHN, A PRISONER AT CAMP MORTON, INDIANA. n.d. Nashville, Tn.** Declares her desire to kill "Lincoln devils." 27 June 1862. p.104, c6.

6017 MEMBER OF BATTERY A, NEW YORK ARTILLERY, IN CASEY'S DIVISION *to* **A RELATIVE IN NEW YORK. [extract] n.d. n.p.** Describes his first day of front line battle against the rebel army outside Richmond. 27 June 1862. p.104, c6.

6018 n.n. *to* **n.n. [extract] n.d. n.p.** Describes a bloody battle scene. 27 June 1862. p.104, c6.

6019 TRUTH *to* **THE EDITORS OF THE** *NEW YORK EXPRESS.* **n.d. n.p.** Quotes Daniel Webster's prediction that abolitionists and "fanatics" would cause a bloody conflict in the United States and violate the Constitution; believes that the prediction was realized. 4 July 1862. p.105, c2.

6020 SHEVA *to* **FRIEND SWIFT. [from the** *Yarmouth Register***] 22 May 1862. Chatham.** Characterizes symptoms and causes of the "Negro-equality-phobia" afflicting those who oppose recognition of Haiti and Liberia as independent states. 4 July 1862. p.105, c5.

6021 ABRAHAM LINCOLN *to* **GOVERNORS OF THE LOYAL STATES. 1 July 1862. Executive Mansion, Washington.** Responds, to their request, that he plans to call an additional 300,000 soldiers into service. 4 July 1862. p.106, c3.

6022 VINCENT COLYER, SUPERINTENDENT OF THE POOR *to* **THE EDITOR OF THE** *NEW YORK TRIBUNE.* **21 June 1862. Newbern, N.C.** Explains, at the request of Governor Stanly, that he misunderstood Stanly's intentions; states that the governor will not close schools for colored people nor return fugitive slaves to their masters. 4 July 1862. p.106, c3.

6023 NON-COMMISSIONED OFFICER IN MASSACHUSETTS VOLUNTEERS *to* **N. H. WHITING. [extract] 17 June 1862. Camp at Fair Oaks near Richmond, Va.** Describes the battle at Fair Oaks and the multitude of the wounded; expresses his conviction that the present army would never fight to free Negroes, but only to restore the Union. 4 July 1862. p.106, c5.

6024 N. H. WHITING *to* **FRIEND GARRISON. 28 June 1862. Boston.** Forwards correspondence between himself and a friend concerning the possibility of ending slavery with the war. 4 July 1862. p.106, c5.

6025 N. H. WHITING *to* **NON-COMMISSIONED OFFICER IN MASSACHUSETTS VOLUNTEERS. 24 June 1862. Boston.** Points out the absurdity of two armies fighting as enemies, one for the preservation of slavery and the other for the preservation of both slavery and the Union; argues that the army would have to obey the government if emancipation were proclaimed. 4 July 1862. p.106, c6.

6026 HENRY C. WRIGHT *to* **GARRISON. 23 June 1862. Harwich, Ma.** Reports increased enthusiasm for the cause of abolition in the Orthodox church. 4 July 1862. p.107, c1.

6027 E. R. BROWN *to* **THE** *LIBERATOR.* **23 June 1862. Lewistown, Il.** Calls for more anti-slavery lecturers in the West. 4 July 1862. p.107, c2.

6028 R. H. OBER *to* **FRIEND GARRISON. 23 June 1862. Nashua, N.H.** Praises lectures by Parker Pillsbury. 4 July 1862. p.107, c2.

6029 A. J. GROVER *to* **MR. GARRISON. 26 June 1862. Earlville, Il.** Reports the defeat of the proposed state constitution in Illinois. 4 July 1862. p.107, c3.

6030 GEN. BENJ. F. BUTLER *to* **PRESIDENT LINCOLN. [extract] n.d. n.p.** Forwards report by General Phelps requesting governmental permission to override Butler's order prohibiting 150 Negro fugitives from receiving food and shelter in Phelps' camp. 4 July 1862. p.107, c4.

6031 H. M. T. CUTLER *to* **THE** *LIBERATOR.* **10 June 1862. Jacksonville, Il.** Relates his discovery of prejudice against Negroes and women while lecturing in Jacksonville. 4 July 1862. p.108, c4.

6032 n.n. *to* **n.n. [extract] n.d. Clarksburg, Va.** Describes Jenny Green, a charismatic young rebel who continued to demonstrate her violent hatred of Yankees even when she was sent to Wheeling prison. 4 July 1862. p.108, c6.

6033 RINGBOLT *to* **THE EDITOR OF THE** *BOSTON COURIER.* **2 July. New York.** Reports that the consensus at the recent Union meeting in Cooper Institute favored restoration of the Union without abolition of slavery; threatens Sumner. 11 July 1862. p.109, c2.

6034 A MINISTER *to* **THE** *BOSTON COURIER.* **n.d. n.p.** States that Congregational ministers in New England are moderate and quiet about political matters; praises the *Courier's* editorial stand on the war. 11 July 1862. p.109, c2.

6035 AN OFFICER *to* **THE EDITOR OF THE** *NEW YORK TRIBUNE.* **3 June 1862. Newbern, N.C.** Testifies to the trustworthiness and helpfulness of "contrabands." 11 July 1862. p.109, c4.

6036 D. HUNTER, MAJOR GENERAL COMMANDING *to* **HON. E. M. STANTON, SECRETARY OF WAR. 28 June 1862. Port Royal.** Responds to questions from the Adjutant General of the Army: states that a regiment of fugitive slaves has not been formed, but that a regiment has been formed of persons "whose late masters are fugitive rebels." 11 July 1862. p.109, c4.

6037 RICHARD BUSTEED *to* **THE EDITOR OF THE** *NEW YORK TRIBUNE.* **3 July 1862. New York.** A prominent New York lawyer denies any affiliation with the "anti-abolition, anti-secession" meeting led by Fernando Wood at Cooper Institute. 11 July 1862. p.110, c1.

6038 CHARLES SUMNER *to* **SIR. 2 July 1862. Senate Chamber.** Reports that he cannot attend Fourth of July celebration in Boston; encourages anti-slavery efforts. 11 July 1862. p.111, c1.

6039 REV. DANIEL FOSTER *to* **FRIEND GARRISON. 4 July 1862. Boston.** Responds to Dr. Hidden's accusations; warns of the danger of "malignant spite, sectarian bigotry, and pro-slavery wrath." 11 July 1862. p.111, c3.

6040 PARKER PILLSBURY *to* **G. W. S. [extract] n.d. n.p.** Accuses the government of "deliberately murdering its young men in behalf of slavery." 11 July 1862. p.111, c4.

6041 AN OFFICER ON GENERAL McCLELLAN'S STAFF *to* **n.n. [extract] 17 June 1862. n.p.** Announces his conversion to abolitionism; declares Southern chivalry a fraud. 11 July 1862. p.111, c4.

6042 GEN. GEO. B. McCLELLAN *to* **SOLDIERS OF THE ARMY OF THE POTOMAC. 4 July 1862. Headquarters of the Potomac, Camp near Harrison's Landing.** Praises his soldiers' performance; urges commitment to reestablishing the Union. 11 July 1862. p.111, c5.

6043 H. W. HALLECK, MAJOR GENERAL *to* **THE SECRETARY OF WAR [E. M. STANTON]. 6 July 1862. Corinth, Ms.** Commends Colonel Sheridan for his conduct in the 1 July 1862 battle at Booneville, Mississippi. 11 July 1862. p.111, c5.

6044 A SOUTHERN BUSINESSMAN *to* **n.n. [extract] n.d. n.p.** Advocates rapid abolition of slavery in order to end the war, even though he has supported slavery for thirty years. 11 July 1862. p.112, c6.

6045 THURLOW WEED *to* **THE EDITORS OF THE** *COMMERCIAL ADVERTISER.* **n.d. n.p.** Supports Gen. Butler's recommendations that ''contrabands'' be given unarmed assignments by the Union army and that loyal masters be compensated; hopes to weaken the South in this manner. 18 July 1862. p.114, c2.

6046 JOHN POPE, MAJ. GEN. COMMANDING *to* **THE OFFICERS AND SOLDIERS OF THE ARMY OF VIRGINIA. 14 July 1862. Washington.** Announces that he has assumed command of the Army of Virginia; urges an offensive, rather than defensive, attitude. 18 July 1862. p.115, c4.

6047 BENJ. F. BUTLER, MAJOR GENERAL COMMANDING *to* **A GENTLEMAN OF BOSTON. 2 July 1862. Headquarters Department of the Gulf, New Orleans.** Describes the ill conduct which provoked his order that ''women who insult my soldiers are to be regarded and treated as common women plying their vocation''; acknowledges that the appropriate response would have been to ignore such women. 18 July 1862. p.115, c5.

6048 JEFFERSON DAVIS *to* **THE ARMY IN EASTERN VIRGINIA. [from the** *Richmond Dispatch*] **5 July 1862. Richmond, Va.** Congratulates the army for withstanding a series of bloody battles in Richmond. 18 July 1862. p.115, c5.

6049 N. P. BANKS, MAJ. GEN. COMMANDING *to* **HON. D. W. GOOCH. 19 June 1862. Winchester.** Denies truth of a rumor that blacks used government transportation during the retreat from Strasburg while whites were forced to walk; relates incident in which an eight-year-old girl of uncertain color rode after a twenty-seven mile march. 18 July 1862. p.115, c5.

6050 CHARLES SUMNER *to* **CHARLES GOULD, ESQ., SECRETARY OF SELECT COMMITTEE. 14 July 1862. Washington.** Regrets that he cannot attend war meeting in New York because of a concurrent Senate session; calls for a unified effort to end the rebellion. 25 July 1862. p.118, c1.

6051 n.n. *to* **THE** *LIBERATOR.* **11 July 1862. Newbern, N.C.** Denounces Governor Stanly for actions which demonstrate sympathy for the rebel cause. 25 July 1862. p.118, c3.

6052 DAVID GRAY *to* **MAYOR JOSEPH M. WIGHTMAN OF BOSTON. 28 June 1862. Andover, Ma.** Opposes Mayor Wightman in his debate with Governor Andrew about slavery and the people of Massachusetts. 25 July 1862. p.118, c6.

6053 C. C. BURLEIGH *to* **GARRISON. 22 July 1862. Florence.** Corrects several of his own remarks as quoted by Yerrinton. 25 July 1862. p.119, c5.

6054 AN ENGLISH TRAVELLER *to* **THE** *LONDON SPECTATOR*. **n.d. Boston.** Praises Wendell Phillips' courageous anti-slavery efforts. 25 July 1862. p.119, c6.

6055 G. B. McCLELLAN, MAJOR GENERAL COMMANDING *to* **HON. EDWIN M. STANTON, SECRETARY OF WAR. 5 May. Bivouac in front of Williamsburg.** Reports military status of the attempt to reach Richmond; believes the rebel force to be much larger than his own. 1 August 1862. p.121, c5.

6056 JUSTITIA *to* **EDITOR [W. L. GARRISON]. 23 July 1862. Boston.** Demonstrates the importance of finding and removing the cause of the war. 1 August 1862. p.122, c5.

6057 G. W. S. *to* **GARRISON. 14 July 1862. Milford, Ma.** Praises a speech by Parker Pillsbury. 1 August 1862. p.122, c6.

6058 JOSEPH A. HOWLAND *to* **MR. GARRISON. 27 July 1862. Worcester.** Expresses dismay upon hearing that Samuel May encourages enlistment; favors ending the rebellion by abolishing slavery. 1 August 1862. p.122, c6.

6059 GEORGE W. JULIAN *to* **DR. ROCK. 1 July 1862. House of Representatives, Washington City.** Summarizes conversation he held with Mr. Johnson about compulsory colonization. 1 August 1862. p.123, c1.

6060 W. *to* **THE EDITOR OF THE** *LIBERATOR* **[W. L. GARRISON]. 29 July 1862. Boston.** Advocates a proclamation of universal emancipation, allowing perhaps some compensation to loyal slaveholders. 1 August 1862. p.123, c1.

6061 MISSIONARY *to* **n.n. [extract] n.d. Port Royal, S.C.** Reports that the Negro population of Edisto Island was evacuated on overcrowded boats. 1 August 1862. p.123, c4.

6062 M. HONZEAU *to* **n.n. [from** *L'Independence* **via the** *New York Evening Post*] **27 April 1862. Matamoras, Mexico.** Catalogues atrocities committed by secessionists upon Negroes and white loyalists. 8 August 1862. p.125, c6.

6063 M. HONZEAU *to* **n.n. [from** *L'Independence* **via the** *New York Evening Post*] **13 May 1862. Matamoras, Mexico.** Expresses relief that he is now safe after having lost all his property in Texas; describes mass burning of slaves to prevent their emancipation; states that the revolution exemplifies social monomania. 8 August 1862. p.126, c1.

6064 GENERAL D. HUNTER *to* **REV. STEPHEN H. TYNG, PRESIDENT OF THE NATIONAL FREEDMAN'S RELIEF ASSOCIATION. 17 July 1862. Headquarters, Department of the South, Hilton Head, Port Royal, S.C.** Fears that the government will not act to abolish slavery until many more have been killed; favors arming the Negroes; believes free Negroes will remain concentrated in the South. 8 August 1862. p.126, c2.

6065 SAMUEL MAY, JR. *to* **MR. GARRISON. 4 August 1862. Leicester.** Replies to a critical letter about himself previously submitted to the *Liberator* by Mr. Joseph A. Howland. 8 August 1862. p.127, c4.

6066 ABIJAH WELLS, SETH B. HOUGH, OTIS A. OSBORNE, ROBERT MORSE, ROBERT BRONAUGH, ADAM B. BRUNER, LANGDON MORSE, ABRAM HUMER, EMMA ENSIGN, P. A. MORSE, MARY J. OSBORNE, P. I. WELLS, ELIZA J. McCUTCHEON, MINA I. HAMILTON, MARY C. HAMILTON, SAMANTHA R. CLINE, MYRA ENSIGN, AND ADA BARNES *to* **MR. GARRISON. 30 July 1862. Centralia, Ks.** Defend Rev. Daniel Foster and their school against criticisms levelled by Dr. Hidden and others. 8 August 1862. p.127, c5.

6067 J. M. McKIM *to* **STEPHEN COLWELL, ESQ., CHAIRMAN OF THE PORT ROYAL RELIEF COMMITTEE. 24 July 1862. Philadelphia.** Provides extensive analysis of conditions in South Carolina; recommends that General Hunter and Commodore Dupont be recognized for their assistance to freed blacks. 8 August 1862. p.128, c2.

6068 A SUPERINTENDENT *to* **J. M McKIM. n.d. n.p.** Illustrates the courage of blacks. 8 August 1862. p.128, c2.

6069 DR. JAMES P. GREVES, SURGEON AND SUPERINTENDENT *to* **J. M. McKIM. n.d. Port Royal, S.C.** Credits "Aunt Hannah," an old colored nurse, with having taught him to treat smallpox. 8 August 1862. p.128, c4.

6070 MR. PHILBRICK, THE SUPERINTENDENT FROM BOSTON *to* **J. M. McKIM. n.d. Port Royal.** Describes the industrious and forgiving attitude of freed blacks in Port Royal. 8 August 1862. p.128, c4.

6071 MR. RICHARD SOULE, JR. OF MASSACHUSETTS *to* **J. M. McKIM. n.d. Port Royal.** Concludes from his experiences with freed Negroes in Port Royal that Negroes work as well in freedom as in slavery, that they will not emigrate North, and that they need the official status of freedmen in addition to day wages and education. 8 August 1862. p.128, c4.

6072 DR. JAMES P. GREVES, SUPERINTENDENT AND PHYSICIAN *to* **J. M. McKIM. n.d. Edgely Plantation, Port Royal.** Pleads for help in providing decent clothing and shelter for freed Negroes. 8 August 1862. p.128, c5.

6073 SENATOR HENRY WILSON *to* **JAMES GORDON BENNETT, ESQ. [from the *New York Herald*] 6 August 1862. Natick, Ma.** Protests an article that charges him with responsibility for a dearth of men in the army; defends his past actions and statements. 15 August 1862. p.130, c1.

6074 JOHN S. ROCK *to* **WM. H. PAGE, M.D. 11 August 1862. Boston.** Asks whether captured colored servants of Union officers are sold into slavery. 15 August 1862. p.131, c4.

6075 WM. H. PAGE *to* **JOHN S. ROCK, ESQ. 11 August 1862. Boston.** Responds affirmatively to Rock's question on whether captured colored servants of Union officers are sold into slavery; adds that those captured with weapons are shot. 15 August 1862. p.131, c4.

6076 W. H. OSBORN, PRESIDENT; J. M. DOUGLAS, RESIDENT DIRECTOR; W. R. ARTHUR, GENERAL SUPERINTENDENT *to* **n.n. 12 August 1862. Chicago.** Deny any acquaintance with Wendell Phillips. 15 August 1862. p.131, c5.

6077 F. J. REEVE *to* **THE EDITOR OF THE *ASHTABULA SENTINEL*. 8 July 1862. Rome.** Encloses a letter from a soldier fighting under a general who returns fugitive slaves; protests the persistence of the practice, which Congress had banned. 15 August 1862. p.132, c6.

6078 ONE OF JOHN BROWN'S MEN *to* **F. J. REEVE. [extract] 12 June 1862. Tennessee.** Describes the conflict between Jennison's Jayhawkers and General Mitchell over returning slaves to their masters. 15 August 1862. p.132, c6.

6079 BENJAMIN F. BUTLER, MAJ. GEN. COMMANDING *to* **HON. EDWIN M. STANTON, SECRETARY OF WAR. 2 August 1862. Headquarters, Department of the Gulf, New Orleans.** Sends copies of orders and correspondence concerning General Phelps' five companies of Negroes and his requisition for supplies, Butler's order to employ the Negroes elsewhere, and Phelps' subsequent resignation. 22 August 1862. p.133, c5.

6080 J. W. PHELPS, BRIGADIER GENERAL *to* **CAPT. R. S. DAVIS, A.A.A. GENERAL. 30 July 1862. Headquarters, Department of the Gulf, New Orleans, La.** Submits requisitions for arms and other military supplies for three regiments of "Africans"; justifies his decision to accept "Africans" into the army. 22 August 1862. p.133, c5.

6081 MAJOR GENERAL BUTLER *to* **R. S. DAVIS, CAPTAIN AND A.A.A.G. 31 July 1862. Headquarters, Department of the Gulf, New Orleans.** Orders Davis to employ the contrabands in cutting wood. 22 August 1862. p.133, c5.

6082 J. W. PHELPS, BRIGADIER GENERAL *to* **CAPT. R. S. DAVIS, ACTING ASSISTANT ADJUTANT GENERAL. 31 July 1862. Headquarters, Department of the Gulf, New Orleans.** Resigns his commission rather than employ the contrabands in cutting down trees; suggests that a large force guard the contrabands at their work. 22 August 1862. p.133, c5.

6083 BENJ. F. BUTLER, MAJ. GEN. COMMANDING *to* **BRIG. GEN. PHELPS, COMMANDING FORCES AT CAMP PARAPET. 2 August 1862. Headquarters, Department of the Gulf, New Orleans.** Agrees to forward Phelps' application to Lincoln, but warns Phelps that he has no right to arm blacks until so ordered by Lincoln. 22 August 1862. p.133, c5.

6084 BENJAMIN F. BUTLER, MAJOR GENERAL COMMANDING *to* **GENERAL PHELPS. 2 August 1862. Headquarters, Department of the Gulf, New Orleans.** Refuses Phelps' resignation and request for immediate leave of absence; insists that his order to use the Africans to remove the wood between the camp and Lake Ponchartrain be carried out. 22 August 1862. p.133, c6.

6085 n.n. *to* **THE EDITOR OF THE** *INDEPENDENT.* **8 August 1862. Fortress Monroe.** Reveals the persecution of colored people in the Fortress Monroe military district by subordinate officers in violation of General Dix's orders. 22 August 1862. p.134, c2.

6086 WENDELL PHILLIPS *to* **S. C. CLARKE. 14 August 1862. Boston.** Informs Clarke that he never claimed to know or to quote the three directors of the Illinois Central Company. 22 August 1862. p.134, c6.

6087 A RADICAL ABOLITIONIST *to* **THE EDITOR OF THE** *LIBERATOR* **[W. L. GARRISON]. 15 August 1862. Springfield, Vt.** Laments the decline of anti-slavery sentiments when military successes occur. 22 August 1862. p.135, c1.

6088 HENRY C. WRIGHT *to* **WM. LLOYD GARRISON. 17 August 1862. Gloucester, Ma.** Shares his memories of the late Hannah Webb. 22 August 1862. p.135, c2.

6089 DANIEL FOSTER *to* **FRIEND GARRISON. 17 August 1862. Washington, D.C.** Comments on slavery as the cause of war; lists the activities of the Thirty-third Massachusetts Regiment. 22 August 1862. p.135, c3.

6090 PHILO. *to* **THE EDITOR OF THE** *NEW YORK TRIBUNE.* **n.d. n.p.** Forwards record of Wendell Phillips' speech at Abington to disprove reports that Phillips "discourages enlistments in the Union armies." 22 August 1862. p.135, c3.

6091 T. B. *to* **THE EDITOR OF THE** *NEW YORK TRIBUNE.* **5 August 1862. New York.** Warns of the potential danger of unchecked rioting; blames secessionists and the press for disruptions. 22 August 1862. p.135, c3.

6092 JOSEPH A. HOWLAND *to* **MR. GARRISON. 10 August 1862. Worcester.** Continues debate with Samuel May over enlistment. 22 August 1862. p.136, c2.

6093 SEWARD MITCHELL *to* **FRIEND GARRISON. n.d. n.p.** Thinks of the current bloodshed as righteous retribution for the sin of slavery. 22 August 1862. p.136, c3.

6094 REV. HIRAM WILSON *to* **REV. MR. GRIMES. 28 July 1862. St. Catharines, Canada West.** Announces the death of Anthony Burns. 22 August 1862. p.136, c4.

6095 WENDELL PHILLIPS *to* **THE EDITOR OF THE** *NEW YORK TRIBUNE.* **16 August 1862. n.p.** Denies that he discourages enlistments in the Union armies; criticizes the *Tribune* and Lincoln's administration. 29 August 1862. p.137, c5.

6096 n.n. *to* **THE EDITORS OF THE** *NEW YORK EVENING POST.* **August 1862. Staten Island.** Suggests methods of utilizing the new army of 600,000 soldiers; recommends making South Carolina a Negro colony. 29 August 1862. p.137, c6.

6097 A. LINCOLN *to* **HON. HORACE GREELEY. 22 August 1862. Executive Mansion, Washington.** Declares that his first priority is to preserve the Union, not to destroy or maintain slavery. 29 August 1862. p.139, c1.

6098 L. MARIA CHILD *to* **PRESIDENT LINCOLN. n.d. n.p.** Urges Lincoln to abolish slavery. 29 August 1862. p.139, c2.

6099 RICHARD HINCHCLIFFE *to* **MR. GARRISON. 25 August 1862. Andover.** Forwards a preamble and resolution passed at a town meeting in Andover asking Lincoln to abolish slavery immediately. 29 August 1862. p.139, c3.

6100 ENQUIRER *to* **MR. EDITOR [W. L. GARRISON]. n.d. n.p.** Challenges Lincoln's statement to a committee of colored men that the presence of their race caused the war; substitutes the enslavement of their race as the cause. 29 August 1862. p.139, c4.

6101 S. E. W. *to* **MR. GARRISON. 18 August 1862. Worcester.** Criticizes Lincoln's stand on slavery and colonization. 29 August 1862. p.139, c4.

6102 ANDREW T. FOSS *to* **MR. MAY. 23 August 1862. Hyannis, Cape Cod.** Describes his lecture tour on the Cape. 29 August 1862. p.139, c4.

6103 SENEX *to* **MR. EDITOR [W. L. GARRISON]. n.d. n.p.** Protests the policy of universal conscription. 29 August 1862. p.139, c5.

6104 SAMUEL MAY, JR. *to* **MR. GARRISON. n.d. n.p.** Refers readers to his letter in the previous issue of the *Liberator* as a response to Joseph A. Howland's second letter; blames the North for Lincoln's hesitance to free the slaves. 29 August 1862. p.139, c5.

6105 I. S. *to* **MR. GARRISON, n.d. n.p.** Observes some anti-slavery progress in the New Church. 29 August 1862. p.140, c2.

6106 A. M. J. M. PAGE *to* **FRIEND GARRISON. 18 August 1862. Deerfield Centre, N.H.** Submits for publication his criticism of the abolitionists' position on the war. 29 August 1862. p.140, c3.

6107 FRANCIS W. HUGHES *to* **HON. WILLIAM H. SEWARD, SECRETARY OF STATE. 11 August 1862. Headquarters of the Democratic State Central Committee of Philadelphia, Pa.** Recommends that Seward read the enclosed documents opposing abolitionism. 29 August 1862. p.140, c4.

6108 WILLIAM H. SEWARD *to* **F. W. HUGHES, ESQ. 19 August 1862. Department of State, Washington.** Implies that the united effort of all Union men to suppress the rebellion is more important than the desire of Hughes' committee to suppress abolitionism. 29 August 1862. p.140, c5.

6109 A. P. SMITH *to* **PRESIDENT LINCOLN. n.d. Saddle River, N.J.** A colored man responds critically to Lincoln's colonization plan. 5 September 1862. p.141, c1.

6110 HENRY C. WRIGHT *to* **WM. LLOYD GARRISON. 24 August 1862. Gloucester.** Describes his conversation with Jessie and John C. Fremont and staff about abolishing slavery in order to win the war. 5 September 1862. p.142, c5.

6111 J. S. *to* **EDITOR** *LIBERATOR* **[W. L. GARRISON]. 1 September 1862. Springfield,Vt.** Expresses dismay upon reading Lincoln's letter to Horace Greeley. 5 September 1862. p.142, c6.

6112 G. W. S. *to* **FRIEND GARRISON. 29 August 1862. Milford.** Describes his recent anti-slavery vacation tour in Rhode Island. 5 September 1862. p.142, c6.

6113 LINDA *to* **MR. GARRISON. n.d. n.p.** Describes life among the contrabands. 5 September 1862. p.144, c2.

6114 JUSTICE *to* **THE EDITOR OF THE** *LIBERATOR* **[W. L. GARRISON]. 23 August 1862. Boston.** Denies that the rights of white laborers should take precedence over those of freed blacks. 5 September 1862. p.144, c4.

6115 MILO A. TOWNSEND *to* **PRESIDENT LINCOLN. n.d. New Brighton, Pa.** Argues that the end of slavery would be a significant boost to end the fighting. 5 September 1862. p.144, c5.

6116 JUDGE HENRY DUTTON *to* **MR. EDITOR. [from the** *New Haven Palladium***] 27 August 1862. New Haven.** Sides with Lincoln in his argument with Greeley over slavery and the war. 12 September 1862. p.145, c2.

6117 ROBERT PURVIS *to* **HON. S. C. POMEROY, GOVERNMENT COLONIZATION AGENT. 28 August 1862. Byberry, Philadelphia.** Argues against colonization. 12 September 1862. p.146, c6.

6118 ISAAC STEARNS *to* **HON. CHARLES SUMNER. 8 September 1862. Mansfield, Ma.** Fears that the North may lose the war because Lincoln will not abolish slavery. 12 September 1862. p.147, c2.

6119 DANIEL FOSTER *to* **THE** *LIBERATOR***. 3 September 1862. Alexandria, Va.** The chaplain of the Thirty-third Massachusetts Regiment offers his observations on the war and the need to free the slaves. 12 September 1862. p.147, c2.

6120 A. T. FOSS *to* **W. L. GARRISON. 1 September 1862. Yarmouth.** Describes his anti-slavery lecture tour on Cape Cod. 12 September 1862. p.147, c3.

6121 A. T. FOSS *to* **MR. GARRISON. 4 September 1862. Manchester, N.H.** Recommends the blind lecturer Rev. Wm. Hoisinton to his audiences in the West. 12 September 1862. p.147, c3.

6122 HENRY C. WRIGHT *to* **WM. LLOYD GARRISON. 7 September 1862. Lockport, N.Y.** Reports on abolitionist resolutions discussed at a meeting in Lockport. 19 September 1862. p.150, c6.

6123 LEWIS FORD *to* **FRIEND MAY. 7 September 1862. Minneapolis Mn.** Gives an account of Indian problems in Minnesota. 19 September 1862. p.151, c3.

6124 ORPHEUS C. KERR [ROBERT HENRY NEWELL] *to* **n.n. [extract] n.d. n.p.** Fictional political satire of the desire for the "Union as it was." 19 September 1862. p.152, c5.

6125 JOHN OLIVER *to* **MR. EDITOR [W. L. GARRISON]. 21 May 1862. Fortress Monroe, Va.** Describes the occupation of the Fortress Monroe area by Federals. 26 September 1862. p.155, c1.

6126 JOHN OLIVER *to* **MR. EDITOR [W. L. GARRISON]. 6 August 1862. Newport News, Va.** A Negro from Boston comments on the ill treatment of Negroes by the Union army. 26 September 1862. p.155, c1.

6127 GERRIT SMITH *to* **WM. LLOYD GARRISON. 21 September 1862. Peterboro', N.Y.** Praises Garrison's "Drafting—the Hour of Trial." 26 September 1862. p.155, c2.

6128 M. L. WHITTEN *to* **MR. EDITOR [W. L. GARRISON]. 13 September 1862. Fort De Kalb, Va.** Reports on conditions at the battle front. 26 September 1862. p.156, c3.

6129 AN ARMY CHAPLAIN *to* **n.n. [extract] 22 August 1862. Camp near Russelville, Al.** Believes that the Confiscation Act has severely weakened the South's resistance. 3 October 1862. p.157, c6.

6130 RICHARD BUSTEED, GENERAL *to* **THE** *NEW YORK TRIBUNE.* **23 September 1862. New York.** Praises Lincoln's proclamation of emancipation. 3 October 1862. p.158, c2.

6131 HANNAH D. WESTWOOD *to* **ANTHONY PRYOR. n.d. n.p.** Requests that Anthony, her former slave, send food and money to help support herself and her children. 3 October 1862. p.158, c4.

6132 HENRY C. WRIGHT *to* **GARRISON. 26 September 1862. Hume, N.Y.** Describes the last twenty-one days of his lecture tour. 3 October 1862. p.158, c6.

6133 C. ROBINSON *to* **n.n. 22 September 1862. Holley, N.Y.** Gives a favorable account of Henry Wright's lecture in Holley. 3 October 1862. p.158, c6.

6134 REV. DANIEL FOSTER *to* **GARRISON. 21 September 1862. Alexandria, Va.** Praises anti-slavery newspapers; describes life as an army chaplain. 3 October 1862. p.159, c1.

6135 A VERMONT ABOLITIONIST *to* **MR. EDITOR [W. L. GARRISON]. 24 September 1862. Windsor, Vt.** Evaluates the success of the anti-slavery movement and press in Vermont. 3 October 1862. p.159, c1.

6136 ALLEN *to* **MR. EDITOR [W. L. GARRISON]. n.d. n.p.** Discusses Boston conservatism and the need to elect Sumner. 3 October 1862. p.160, c2.

6137 W. *to* **MR. GARRISON. 23 September 1862. Bristol, Pa.** Criticizes the *Liberator* editorial on drafting. 3 October 1862. p.160, c4.

6138 L. *to* **THE EDITOR OF THE** *BOSTON COURIER.* **n.d. n.p.** Interprets the president's Emancipation Proclamation as an unconstitutional document. 10 October 1862. p.161, c1.

6139 n.n. *to* **WILLIAM LLOYD GARRISON. n.d. n.p.** Reviews the late Colonel William Whiting's life and his contribution to abolitionism. 10 October 1862. p.163, c1.

6140 A. T. FOSS *to* **MR. MAY. 2 October 1862. Barre, Vt.** Describes his abolitionist tour in Vermont and his stay with Alexander Gilchrist. 10 October 1862. p.163, c1.

6141 n.n. *to* **FRIEND. 20 August 1862. Atlantic Squadron.** Describes skirmishes with rebels and the response of contrabands to his assistance. 10 October 1862. p.163, c3.

6142 GEN. CURTIS *to* **n.n. [extract] n.d. n.p.** Offers advice about winning the war. 10 October 1862. p.163, c4.

6143 WM. H. JOHNSON *to* **FRIEND GARRISON. 24 September 1862. New Bedford.** Praises lectures by Wm. A. Jackson, a former coachman to Jefferson Davis. 10 October 1862. p.164, c4.

6144 NIHIL NOVI *to* **MR. GARRISON. 5 October 1862. Camp near Alexandria, Va.** Reports on the Thirty-third Massachusetts Volunteers, "the Anti-Slavery Regiment." 17 October 1862. p.167, c2.

6145 DANIEL FOSTER *to* **THE** *LIBERATOR.* **7 October 1862. Camp Slough, Alexandria, Va.** Discusses the implications of the Emancipation Proclamation. 17 October 1862. p.167. c3.

6146 HENRY C. WRIGHT *to* **GARRISON. 29 September 1862. Portage, N.Y.** Reports on his abolitionist lecture tour. 17 October 1862. p.167, c3.

6147 AARON M. POWELL *to* **n.n. [extract] 13 October 1862. Ghent, N.Y.** Analyzes the significance of the Emancipation Proclamation. 17 October 1862. p.167, c5.

6148 E. S. C. *to* **WM. LLOYD GARRISON. 4 October 1862. Salem, Ma.** Forwards a letter he wrote to the *Boston Journal* pointing out the inconsistencies of its handling of Sumner's anti-slavery stand. 17 October 1862. p.168, c2.

6149 GENERAL EMANCIPATION [E. S. C.] *to* **THE EDITOR OF THE** *BOSTON JOUR-NAL.* **n.d. n.p.** Points out inconsistencies in the *Journal's* editorial stance on Sumner. 17 October 1862. p.168, c2.

6150 J. S. *to* **THE EDITOR OF THE** *LIBERATOR* **[W. L. GARRISON]. 7 October 1862. Springfield, Vt.** Opposes colonization. 17 October 1862, p.168, c4.

6151 C. S. B. SPEAR *to* **FRIEND GARRISON. 26 August 1862. Washington.** Relates encounter with a young wounded ex-slave. 17 October 1862. p.168, c5.

6152 DUDLEY WILLITS *to* **MR. EDITOR [W. L. GARRISON]. 28 September 1862. New Boston, Mercer County, Il.** Believes in the innate humanity of God's children; does not fear war with Europe. 17 October 1862. p.168, c5.

6153 GENERAL KEARNY *to* **MR. O. S. HALSTEAD, JR. 4 August 1862. Harrison's Landing.** Criticizes several Union generals. 24 October 1862. p.169, c4.

6154 W. C. GRIER *to* **L. W. HALL. 8 October 1862. Cincinnati, Oh.** Reports on the persecution of Union men in Kentucky. 24 October 1862. p.169, c5.

6155 D. *to* **EDITORS OF THE** *CHICAGO TRIBUNE.* **22 September 1862. Valparaiso, In.** Inquires about hiring fifteen or sixteen contrabands. 24 October 1862. p.169, c6.

6156 G. W. S. *to* **GARRISON. n.d. n.p.** Describes a Unitarian meeting in Brooklyn. 24 October 1862. p.170, c6.

6157 REV. DANIEL FOSTER *to* **GARRISON. 17 October 1862. Fairfax Courthouse, Va.** Explains why slavery must be ended. 24 October 1862. p.171, c1.

6158 A. H. BULLOCK *to* **JOHN A. ANDREW. 12 September 1862. Worcester.** Announces Andrew's renomination as governor of Massachusetts. 24 October 1862. p.171, c2.

6159 JOHN A. ANDREW *to* **A. H. BULLOCK, PRESIDENT OF THE REPUBLICAN STATE CONVENTION. 18 October 1862. Boston.** Accepts renomination as governor of Massachusetts. 24 October 1862. p.171, c2.

6160 ERASTUS ROCKWOOD *to* **THE EDITOR OF THE** *BOSTON JOURNAL.* **16 October 1862. Franklin, Norfolk County.** Denies any affiliation with the People's Convention. 24 October 1862. p.171, c3.

6161 GEN. RUFUS SAXTON *to* **THE PORT ROYAL RELIEF COMMITTEE. n.d. n.p.** Praises Lincoln's Emancipation Proclamation. 24 October 1862. p.171, c4.

6162 WEBB WILDER, EDITOR OF THE *LEAVENWORTH* **(KS.)** *CONSERVATIVE to* **n.n. [extract] n.d. Washington.** Accuses West Point of producing traitors; satirizes George G. McClellan's egotism. 24 October 1862. p.171, c4.

6163 A. H. HARLOW *to* **FRIEND GARRISON. 11 October 1862. Hopedale.** Urges working class people to support the war against oppression. 24 October 1862. p.172, c3.

6164 HENRY C. WRIGHT *to* **W. L. GARRISON. 14 October 1862. Cortland, N.Y.** Describes his lecture tour and discusses the Emancipation Proclamation. 24 October 1862. p.172, c4.

6165 GAULT AND KETCHUM, KENTUCKY SLAVE-DEALERS *to* **J. SELLA MARTIN. n.d. n.p.** Inform Martin that they have bought the slave Caroline and her two children with the intention to sell them to him for a reasonable price. 24 October 1862. p.172, c4.

6166 J. SELLA MARTIN *to* **JOHN CURWEN. 6 September 1862. Boston.** Describes his reunion with his sister Caroline and her two children. 24 October 1862. p.172, c4.

6167 E. W. FARNHAM *to* **THE EDITOR OF THE** *HERALD OF PROGRESS.* **24 September 1862. New York.** Relates story of a medium who warned him not to sail on the ill-fated *Golden Gate*. 24 October 1862. p.172, c5.

6168 REVEREND DORSON *to* **J. SELLA MARTIN. 5 June. Columbus, Ga.** Reminds Martin that he owes a debt to his old master because he ran away; claims to fear for the soul of his freed slave, Caroline, who is in Boston. 24 October 1862. p.172, c5.

6169 ANSEL H. HARLOW, POSTMASTER AT HOPEDALE *to* **HON. MONTGOMERY BLAIR, POSTMASTER GENERAL OF THE UNITED STATES. 22 September 1862. Hopedale, Ma.** Resigns as postmaster at Hopedale in protest of Blair's opposition to the abolition of slavery under the war power. 24 October 1862. p.172, c6.

6170 ONE OF THE SONS OF HAM *to* **THE EDITOR OF THE** *TORONTO GLOBE.* **2 October 1862. Toronto, Canada.** Analyzes the significance of Emancipation in the United States. 31 October 1862. p.173, c3.

6171 ANDAX *to* **THE EDITORS OF THE** *BOSTON DAILY ADVERTISER.* **n.d. n.p.** Warns the people of Massachusetts to beware of George Fitzhugh and the "No Party" movement. 31 October 1862. p.173, c5.

6172 GEN. WINFIELD SCOTT *to* **WILLIAM H. SEWARD. 3 March 1861. Washington.** Lists four possible methods of handling the disintegration of the Union. 31 October 1862. p.173, c5.

6173 THEOPHILUS PARSONS *to* **THE EDITORS OF THE** *BOSTON DAILY ADVERTISER.* **n.d. Cambridge.** Examines Lincoln's executive powers. 31 October 1862. p.175, c4.

6174 GEORGE BANCROFT *to* **THE UNION COMMITTEE. [extract] 18 October 1862. n.p.** Denies any affiliation between the Democratic Party and Southern secessionists; supports President Lincoln and his "vigorous prosecution of the war." 31 October 1862. p.175, c5.

6175 ROBERT DALE OWEN *to* **THE PRESIDENT ABRAHAM LINCOLN. [extract] 17 September 1862. n.p.** Argues that Lincoln has a constitutional right to emancipate the slave since slavery endangers the nation. 31 October 1862. p.175, c5.

6176 ISAAC STEARNS *to* **CHARLES SUMNER. 21 September 1862. Mansfield, Ma.** Attacks Sumner's statement that Stearns fully concurs with the president's handling of the slavery question. 31 October 1862. p.176, c2.

6177 HENRY C. WRIGHT *to* **WM. LLOYD GARRISON. 20 October 1862. Hamilton, N.Y.** Refuses to sympathize with non-resisters; examines the current status of the war against slavery. 31 October 1862. p.176, c3.

6178 HENRY C. WRIGHT *to* **GARRISON. 9 October 1862. Raspberry and Rattlesnake Mt., Pa.** Describes his anti-slavery lecture tour and encounters with pro-slavery sympathizers. 31 October 1862. p.176, c3.

6179 BISHOP-GENERAL LEONIDAS POLK *to* **HON. GARRET DAVIS. 28 January 1862. Columbus, Ky.** Viciously attacks Davis' speech concerning Mr. Bright's letter; defends the right of the South to secede from the Union. 7 November 1862. p.177, c5.

6180 A SLAVEHOLDER *to* **THE** *MISSOURI DEMOCRAT.* **n.d. n.p.** Urges states to proclaim emancipation and receive the benefits of Lincoln's offer. 7 November 1862. p.177, c4.

6181 GEORGE WILKES, EDITOR OF THE *NEW YORK SPIRIT OF THE TIMES to* **THE** *NEW YORK SPIRIT OF THE TIMES.* **n.d. Washington.** Relates an alleged conversation between President Lincoln and General McClellan in which Lincoln criticized McClellan. 7 November 1862. p.178, c2.

6182 HENRY C. WRIGHT *to* **GARRISON. 27 October 1862. Bainbridge, N.Y.** Examines the origins of the rebellion and British and European sympathies. 7 November 1862. p.178, c6.

6183 JESSE STEDMAN *to* **EDITOR [W. L. GARRISON]. 3 November 1862. Springfield, Vt.** Admonishes the Church for its refusal to promote the anti-slavery cause. 7 November 1862. p.179, c1.

6184 B. *to* **THE EDITOR OF THE** *LIBERATOR* **[W. L. GARRISON]. 27 October 1862. Wilton, Ia.** Encloses the vote of Iowa soldiers currently in the fields; reports that most vote Republican. 7 November 1862. p.179, c2.

6185 G. K. R. *to* **FRIEND GARRISON. 27 October 1862. Haverhill.** Praises William Wells Brown and his recent speech in Town Hall. 7 November 1862. p.179, c2.

6186 n.n. *to* **THE** *PHILADELPHIA LEDGER.* **n.d. n.p.** A recent visitor to General Mc-Clellan's camp describes the severe shortage of clothing and shelter there. 7 November 1862. p.179, c5.

6187 PLEB. *to* **EDITOR OF THE** *WORCESTER SPY.* **n.d. n.p.** Encloses "The Hunker's Last Appeal," a verse from *Rejected Addresses.* 7 November 1862. p.180, c5.

6188 G. K. R. *to* **FRIEND GARRISON. 9 November 1862. Haverhill.** Praises lectures by Wm. Wells Brown. 14 November 1862. p.183, c1.

6189 G. B. STEBBINS *to* **W. L. GARRISON. 30 October 1862. Barre, N.Y.** Describes the departure of New York volunteers for Virginia; lauds the Emancipation Proclamation. 14 November 1862. p.183, c1.

6190 H. W. HALLECK, GENERAL IN CHIEF *to* **HON. E. M. STANTON, SECRETARY OF WAR. 28 October 1862. Headquarters of the Army, Washington.** Details a justification for his distribution of supplies to General McClellan's army; forwards a telegraph from General McClellan to General Meigs. 14 November 1862. p.183, c2.

6191 G. B. McCLELLAN, MAJOR GENERAL *to* **BRIGADIER GENERAL MEIGS. 22 October 1862. General McClellan's Headquarters.** Explains that he intended to emphasize the urgent need for clothing among some of his command, and not to imply any negligence on Meigs's part. 14 November 1862. p.183, c3.

6192 GOV. WM. SPRAGUE *to* **GENERAL BURNSIDE, COMMANDER-IN-CHIEF OF THE ARMY OF THE POTOMAC. 10 November 1862. State of Rhode Island, Executive Department, Providence.** Congratulates Burnside on his appointment to the command of the Army of the Potomac. 14 November 1862. p.183, c3.

6193 A. E. BURNSIDE, MAJOR GENERAL *to* **GOV. WM. SPRAGUE. 10 November 1862. Headquarters Army.** Thanks Sprague for his expression of confidence. 14 November 1862. p.183, c3.

6194 F. W. B. *to* **EDITOR,** *TRANSCRIPT.* **n.d. n.p.** Submits for publication extracts from a letter warning that the migration of Negroes to the North may have detrimental consequences. 14 November 1862. p.183, c4.

6195 n.n. *to* **F. W. B. [extract] 1 November 1862. Fortress Monroe.** Advocates universal emancipation; believes that Negroes will naturally concentrate in the South and contribute to its economic prosperity. 14 Novenber 1862. p.183, c4.

6196 n.n. *to* **A BOSTON BUSINESS FIRM. n.d. New Orleans.** Supports the Emancipation Proclamation; reveals that the secessionists hope that an opposition party will divide Northern strength. 14 November 1862. p.183, c5.

6197 O. M. MITCHELL, MAJOR-GENERAL *to* **SECRETARY S. P. CHASE. 13 October 1862. Headquarters Department of the South, Hilton Head, Port Royal, S.C.** Details his plans for the Negroes at Port Royal. 14 November 1862. p.184, c5.

6198 AN AMERICAN GENTLEMAN *to* **n.n. n.d. London.** Declares that British sentiment now favors the North and blames the South for the war. 14 November 1862. p.184, c6.

6199 GOVERNOR ANDREW *to* **MAJOR BOLLES. n.d. n.p.** Argues against Bolles' plan to transport Fort Monroe contrabands to Massachusetts. 21 November 1862. p.185, c5.

6200 JOSIAH QUINCY *to* **REV. R. C. WATERSTON. 9 August 1862. Quincy.** Encourages Mr. Livermore's intention to research slavery and Negro soldiers in the Revolutionary War period. 21 November 1862. p.186, c3.

6201 RICHARD J. HINTON, ADJUTANT FIRST REGIMENT KANSAS COLORED VOLUNTEERS *to* **n.n. 7 November 1862. Leavenworth, Ks.** Requests recognition of Negro volunteers who have trained and fought; demands that Negro volunteers be mustered and paid or else disbanded. 21 November 1862. p.186, c5.

6202 J. H. FOWLER, CHAPLAIN FIRST REGIMENT SOUTH CAROLINA VOLUNTEERS *to* **MR. GARRISON. 1 November 1862. Beaufort, S.C.** Begs Northerners to use their influence to prevent General Brannan's promotion to major general of the South Carolina department; predicts escalation of racial tension if Brannan is appointed. 21 November 1862. p.186, c6.

6203 HENRY C. WRIGHT *to* **WM. L. GARRISON. 13 November 1862. Wyalusing, Pa.** Compares a minister's prayer with that of an escaped slave. 21 November 1862. p.186, c6.

6204 AARON M. POWELL *to* **n.n. [extract] 10 November 1862. Ghent, N.Y.** Regrets to report the election of Horatio Seymour as governor of New York; ascribes this victory to the failure of anti-slavery groups to educate the public. 21 November 1862. p.187, c1.

6205 MR. W. C. GANNET *to* **n.n. [extract from the** *Transcript***] 30 October 1862. St. Helena.** Reports that rebel attacks were twice repulsed by Negroes with guns. 21 November 1862. p.187, c3.

6206 N. B. *to* **GARRISON. 7 November. Nantucket.** Encloses a tribute to Gov. Andrew for his devotion to his country and humanity. 21 November 1862. p.188, c2.

6207 D. M. *to* **MR. EDITOR. n.d. n.p.** Mocks article in the *Ledger* on "reduced prices to sewing women" sewing pants at the United States Arsenal; suggests that the money saved can compensate "conquered rebels." 21 November 1862. p.188, c2.

6208 CARBON *to* **WM. LLOYD GARRISON. n.d. n.p.** Warns Americans of the presence of Louis Napoleon's spies. 21 November 1862. p.188, c2.

6209 WM. A. JACKSON *to* **MR. EDITOR [W. L. GARRISON]. 6 November 1862. London.** Ex-coachman to Jefferson Davis reports on his English tour. 28 November 1862. p.190, c4.

6210 GEORGE THOMPSON *to* **GARRISON. 7 November 1862. London.** Relates a conversation with Wm. A. Jackson, former coachman to Jefferson Davis. 28 November 1862. p.190, c4.

6211 A. T. FOSS *to* **MR. MAY. 15 November 1862. n.p.** Reports on his tour in Vermont. 28 November 1862. p.190, c6.

6212 ORPHEUS C. KERR *to* **THE** *NEW YORK SUNDAY MERCURY.* **n.d. Washington, D.C.** Satirizes Lincoln's tendency to produce an appropriate story for every occasion. 28 November 1862. p.192, c5.

6213 CARBON *to* **WM. LLOYD GARRISON. n.d. n.p.** Claims that the English distrust Lincoln and doubt his commitment to abolition. 5 December 1862. p.195, c1.

6214 J. P. B. *to* **FRIEND GARRISON. n.d. n.p.** Praises Garrison for maintaining the motto of "no union with slaveholders." 5 December 1862. p.195, c2.

6215 DANIEL FOSTER *to* **GARRISON. 25 November 1862. Fairfax Courthouse, Va.** Denounces "Copperhead" victories and traitors in Washington who have plagued the war effort. 5 December 1862. p.195, c2.

6216 A. T. FOSS *to* **FRIEND MAY. 25 November 1862. Manchester, N.H.** Describes his speaking tour in New Hampshire. 5 December 1862. p.195, c3.

6217 GEN. L. A. SWAIN *to* **COL. UTLEY. [from the** *Racine Advocate***] n.d. n.p.** Issues orders to return four contrabands. 5 December 1862. p.195, c4.

6218 COL. WM. UTLEY *to* **GENERAL GILMORE. n.d. Headquarters, Twenty-second Regiment, Wisconsin Volunteers.** Declares he had nothing to do with the escape of fugitive slaves to his camp and will have nothing to do with sending them out; recognizes the president as the sole authority on the subject. 5 December 1862. p.195, c4.

6219 A. M. P. *to* **MR. GARRISON. 29 November 1862. Rochester, N.Y.** Mourns the death of Daniel Anthony, a leader in anti-slavery and reform causes. 5 December 1862. p.195, c5.

6220 GOV. JOHNSON *to* **PRESIDENT LINCOLN. [extract] n.d. n.p.** Asserts that General Buell, who is in command of the army of the West, is "very popular with the rebels" and favors a Southern confederacy. 5 December 1862. p.195, c5.

6221 GEO. B. McCLELLAN *to* **MAJOR-GENERAL FITZ JOHN PORTER. 1 September. War Department.** Urges Porter to assist the military operations of General Pope. 12 December 1862. p.198, c2.

6222 BRITISH AND FOREIGN AS *to* **PRESIDENT LINCOLN. 17 November 1862. London.** Forwards copy of an anti-slavery address, and conveys respects and encouragement. 12 December 1862. p.199, c1.

6223 HENRY C. WRIGHT *to* **GARRISON. 25 November 1862. Hartwich, N.Y.** Describes favorable reaction in the army to the Emancipation Proclamation, which provides a rallying point for the Union. 12 December 1862. p.199, c1.

6224 C. F. *to* **FRIEND. 20 November 1862. Beaufort, S.C.** Describes her move to Beaufort, South Carolina, held by Union soldiers, where she will teach freed Negroes. 12 December 1862. p.199, c2.

6225 A PRIVATE, FORTY-FOURTH MASSACHUSETTS REGIMENT *to* **MOTHER. 15 November 1862. Newbern, N.C.** Forwards his impression of fugitive slaves in North Carolina; notes that they are "less dull than I expected, some surprisingly intelligent." 12 December 1862. p.199, c3.

6226 PARKER PILLSBURY *to* **FRIEND GARRISON. 1 December 1862. Concord, N.H.** Assails the North for not fighting the war to end slavery. 12 December 1862. p.200, c2.

6227 WILLIAM BUDD *to* **REV. M. FRENCH. 7 November 1862. Sapelo River, Ga.** Testifies to the admirable conduct of Negro troops under fire. 12 December 1862. p.200, c5.

6228 n.n. *to* **SAMUEL WILKINSON. [from the** *New York Tribune***] n.d. The Peninsula.** Relates threatening conversation with "Sam," an intelligent slave who told him that slaves were organizing to offer their military services to the North or South in exchange for freedom. 19 December 1862. p.201, c5.

6229 C. L. F. *to* **MR. GARRISON 27 November 1862. Beaufort, S.C.** Expresses pleasure upon reading the *Liberator*; describes Thanksgiving Day celebration on St. Helena's Island. 19 December 1862. p.203, c1.

6230 HENRY C. WRIGHT *to* **GARRISON. 27 November 1862. South Hartwich, N.Y.** Describes his tour; assails pro-slavery Democrats. 19 December 1862. p.203, c3.

6231 ORSON S. MURRAY *to* **THE EDITOR OF THE** *LIBERATOR* **[W. L. GARRISON].** **n.d. n.p.** Encloses articles on Parson Brownlow and his leadership of an anti-abolitionist riot. 19 December 1862. p.203, c3.

6232 T. *to* *NEW YORK JOURNAL OF COMMERCE.* **11 December 1862. Hartford, Ct.** Decries the pro-Republican politicization of the clergy at Cooper Institute. 26 December 1862. p.205, c1.

6233 MILTON *to* **THE EDITORS OF THE** *JOURNAL OF COMMERCE.* **n.d. n.p.** Opposes official church involvement in purely political matters. 26 December 1862. p.205, c2.

6234 GEORGE THOMPSON *to* **GARRISON. 5 December 1862. London.** Discusses his lectures on the "American Question" in England. 26 December 1862. p.206, c5.

6235 C. C. B. *to* **FRIEND GARRISON. n.d. n.p.** Mourns the death of Darius P. Lawton, an activist. 26 December 1862. p.207, c5.

6236 JOHN OLIVER *to* **THE** *NEW YORK ANGLO-AFRICAN.* **27 November 1862. Newport News, Va.** Describes the harsh treatment of fugitive slaves living in makeshift camps. 26 December 1862. p.208, c2.

6237 XYZ *to* **MR. GARRISON. n.d. n.p.** Expresses pride that the manhood of the Negro is proven in battle. 26 December 1862. p.208, c3.

6238 A. J. GROVER *to* **MR. GARRISON. 15 December 1862. Washington, D.C.** Reports on an anti-slavery meeting held at the House of Representatives. 26 December 1862. p.208, c3.

[1863]

6239 JOSEPH MERRILL *to* **FRIEND GARRISON. 24 December 1862. Danvers Post.** Regrets that the *Liberator* might cease publication for lack of money. 2 January 1863. p2, c3.

6240 DANIEL RICKETSON *to* **WM. LLOYD GARRISON. 24 December 1862. New Bedford, Ma.** Expresses concern at the news that the *Liberator* might be discontinued because of lack of money; encloses three dollars. 2 January 1863. p2, c3.

6241 BENJAMIN CHASE *to* **FRIEND GARRISON. 21 December 1862. Auburn, N.H.** Encloses money for a subscription and a donation after learning that the *Liberator* could be discontinued because of lack of money. 2 January 1863. p.2, c3.

6242 ISAAC BUCKLEN *to* **WM. LLOYD GARRISON. 29 December 1862. Ekhart, In.** Encloses eight dollars in response to the news that the *Liberator* desperately needs money. 2 January 1863. p.2, c3.

6243 SEWARD MITCHELL *to* **MR. GARRISON. 20 December 1862. Cornville, Me.** Responds to the news about *Liberator*'s financial difficulties. 2 January 1863. p.2, c4.

6244 JEHIEL CLAFLIN *to* **BROTHER GARRISON. 27 December 1862. W. Brookfield, Vt.** Exhorts abolitionists to help the *Liberator* survive financially. 2 January 1863. p.2, c4.

6245 E. W. REYNOLDS *to* **WM. LLOYD GARRISON. 29 December 1862. Watertown, N.Y.** Responds to the *Liberator*'s need for money with a request for a new subscription. 2 January 1863. p.2, c4.

6246 JESSE STEDMAN *to* **MR. EDITOR [W. L. GARRISON]. 30 December 1862. Springfield, Vt.** Encloses five dollars in response to the *Liberator*'s near bankruptcy. 2 January 1863. p.2, c4.

6247 C. A. STACKPOLE *to* **MR. GARRISON. 8 December 1862. Gorham, Me.** Renews subscription in response to the news that the *Liberator* might go bankrupt. 2 January 1863. p.2, c4.

6248 GEORGE THOMPSON *to* **GARRISON. 12 December 1862. London.** Comments on his anti-slavery activities in England. 2 January 1863. p.3, c1.

6249 WM. EVANS, CHAIRMAN OF THE LONDON EMANCIPATION SOCIETY *to* **MINISTERS. 9 December 1862. London.** Issues copies of the Emancipation Proclamation. 2 January 1863. p.3, c1.

6250 HENRY C. WRIGHT *to* **GARRISON. 4 December 1862. Cooperstown, N.Y.** Contrasts the support for the Emancipation Proclamation with the lack of preparation to assist freed slaves. 2 January 1863. p.3, c3.

6251 n.n. *to* **THE EDITOR OF THE** *BOSTON COURIER.* **n.d. n.p.** Denounces abolitionists and preachers who feel that they have the final word on biblical authority. 9 January 1863. p.5, c1.

6252 GEORGE THOMPSON *to* **GARRISON. 19 December 1862. London.** Reports on abolitionist activities in England. 9 January 1863. p.7, c3.

6253 J. P. B. *to* **THE EDITOR OF THE** *LIBERATOR* **[W. L. GARRISON]. n.d. n.p.** Disputes George Thompson's arguments against the right of secession. 9 January 1863. p.8, c2.

6254 PERLEY *to* **THE EDITOR OF THE** *BOSTON JOURNAL.* **1 January 1863. Washington.** Declares that Lincoln's proclamation gives him renewed joy and hope. 16 January 1863. p.9, c5.

6255 C. G. OLDS *to* **MR. GARRISON. 8 January 1863. Hampton, N.H.** Feels cheered by the *Liberator;* encloses three dollars. 16 January 1863. p.10, c5.

6256 HENRIETTA HYDE *to* **MR. GARRISON. 10 January 1863. Bangor, Me.** Thanks Garrison for his abolitionist efforts. 16 January 1863. p.10, c5.

6257 CHARLOTTE L. HILL *to* **MR. GARRISON. 5 January 1863. Ellsworth, Me.** Urges Garrison to continue publishing the *Liberator*. 16 January 1863. p.10, c5.

6258 GEO. SUNTER *to* **FRIEND GARRISON. 9 January 1863. Brantford, Canada West.** Supports the motives of the *Liberator;* criticizes the lack of abolitionist enthusiasm among Lincoln and his colleagues. 16 January 1863. p.10, c5.

6259 SAMUEL GALE *to* **WM. LLOYD GARRISON. 12 January 1863. Montreal.** Forwards a Bank of Montreal note for twenty dollars to help the *Liberator*. 16 January 1863. p.10, c5.

6260 THOS. GARRETT *to* **FRIEND GARRISON. 5 January 1863. Wilmington, De.** Urges subscribers to sustain the *Liberator*. 16 January 1863. p.10, c5.

6261 GEORGE THOMPSON *to* **GARRISON. 25 December 1862. London.** Disputes H. W. Beecher's remark that England is becoming increasingly pro-slavery. 16 January 1863. p.11, c1.

6262 A. T. FOSS *to* **MR. MAY. 5 January 1863. Ellsworth, Me.** Feels encouraged by the response to his lectures against slavery. 16 January 1863. p.11, c2.

6263 JESSE STEADMAN *to* **HON. JUSTIN S. MORRILL. 25 December 1862. Springfield, Vt.** Denounces President Lincoln's offer of gradual emancipation in exchange for peace. 16 January 1863. p.11, c3.

6264 G. W. S. *to* **GARRISON. 12 January 1863. Milford, Ma.** Praises a recent lecture in Boston by Mr. W. 16 January 1863. p.11, c3.

6265 GOV. JOHN A. ANDREW *to* **WM. C. NELL. 1 January 1863. Boston.** Regrets his inability to attend an anti-slavery jubilee. 16 January 1863. p.12, c4.

6266 CHARLES SUMNER *to* **WM. C. NELL. 1 January 1863. Washington.** Regrets his inability to attend the anti-slavery meeting. 16 January 1863. p.12, c5.

6267 FELIX *to* **MR. GARRISON. 20 January 1863. Boston.** Reports on a memorable abolitionist meeting. 23 January 1863. p.14, c5.

6268 DANIEL FOSTER *to* **GARRISON. 16 January 1863. Fredericksburg, Va.** Relates his experiences with the Thirty-third Massachusetts Regiment at the Battle of Fredericksburg. 23 January 1863. p.15, c3.

6269 A LADY IN NEW YORK *to* **n.n. [extract] n.d. n.p.** Expresses the desire to teach colored people; eagerly awaits their emancipation. 23 January 1863. p.15, c3.

6270 L. A. SAWYER *to* **MR. EDITOR. n.d. n.p.** Refutes criticism of his book on biblical theories. 23 January 1863. p.16, c2.

6271 JOSEPH A. DUGDALE *to* **W. L. GARRISON. 3 January 1863. Mt. Pleasant, Ia.** Reports on anti-slavery activities in Iowa. 23 January 1863. p.16, c3.

6272 SIGMA *to* **MR. HASKELL. [from the** *Boston Transcript***] n.d. n.p.** Advocates education for the Negro race; discounts the inferiority of Negroes. 23 January 1863. p.16, c5.

6273 A. J. GROVER *to* **MR. GARRISON. 20 January 1863. Washington, D.C.** Declares that the ACS is an organization which "should have died years ago." 30 January 1863. p.19, c3.

6274 F. W. CHESSON *to* **GARRISON. 9 January 1863. London.** Claims that the mass rallies in England prove that the country is anti-slavery. 30 January 1863. p.19, c4.

6275 GERRIT SMITH *to* **HORATIO SEYMOUR. 12 January 1863. n.p.** Criticizes a recent speech by Seymour for assailing Lincoln but not the rebels. 30 January 1863. p.20, c2.

6276 L. A. SAWYER *to* **MR. EDITOR. n.d. n.p.** Assails the *Boston Review* for its attack on his book about biblical authority. 30 January 1863. p.20, c4.

6277 A. J. GROVER *to* **GARRISON. 15 January 1863. Washington.** Congratulates abolitionists for converting General Butler. 30 January 1863. p.20, c6.

6278 GEN. O. O. HOWARD *to* **THE EDITOR OF THE** *NEW YORK TIMES.* **1 January 1863. Near Falmouth, Va.** Urges the elimination of apathy which might prove fatal to Union morale and the war effort. 6 February 1863. p.21, c6.

6279 T. W. HIGGINSON *to* **GOV. ANDREW. 19 January 1863. Port Royal, S.C.** Reports on the conditions and high recruitment rates of the First South Carolina Regiment at Port Royal. 6 February 1863. p.23, c2.

6280 GEO. W. STACY *to* **WM. CLAFLIN. n.d. Milford, Ma.** Discusses political support for Claflin, who is known as an honest man. 6 February 1863. p.23, c3.

6281 L. A. SAWYER *to* **MR. EDITOR OF THE** *LIBERATOR.* **n.d. n.p.** Defends his scholarship in response to the *Boston Review* article on his book about biblical construction. 6 February 1863. p.24, c2.

6282 GERRIT SMITH *to* **HORATIO SEYMOUR. 12 January 1863. Peterboro'.** Criticizes a recent speech by Seymour for being selfish and unpatriotic. 6 February 1863. p.24, c4.

6283 J. H. F. *to* **MR. GARRISON. 21 January 1863. Camp Saxton, Port Royal Island.** Commends Colonel Higginson as a soldier who is trusted and respected by all. 6 February 1863. p.24, c5.

6284 R. D. WHATELY, ARCHBISHOP OF DUBLIN *to* **MRS. H. B. STOWE. 6 January 1863. Dublin.** Reports that Irish views on slavery, secession, and the war are either divided or neutral. 13 February 1863. p.25, c3.

6285 R. K. T. *to* **CITY OF NEW ORLEANS. n.d. n.p.** Reports on changing attitudes in Louisiana, where free people of color are arrested and conscripted into the rebel army. 13 February 1863. p.25, c6.

6286 PARKER PILLSBURY *to* **GARRISON. 9 February 1863. Woonsocket, R.I.** Identifies the need for a bureau of government to aid Negroes who are freed by the Emancipation Proclamation. 13 February 1863. p.27, c3.

6287 F. HINCKLY *to* **MR. GARRISON. 9 February 1863. Hyannis.** Praises the work of Henry C. Wright. 13 February 1863. p.27, c3.

6288 S. *to* **W. L. GARRISON. 23 January 1863. Augusta, Me.** Describes A. T. Foss' tour of Maine. 13 February 1863. p.27, c3.

6289 G. W. S. *to* **GARRISON. n.d. n.p.** Declares his satisfaction with the annual meeting at Music Hall. 13 February 1863. p.27, c4.

6290 n.n. *to* **MR. GARRISON. n.d. n.p.** Contrasts Jonas H. French and George W. Smalley, pro- and anti-slavery leaders in Boston. 13 February 1863. p.27, c4.

6291 L. A. SAWYER *to* **MR. EDITOR. n.d. n.p.** Asserts that the Bible has meaning and purpose in each passage and that one must study it thoroughly in order to understand it. 13 February 1863. p.28, c5.

6292 FRANCIS BISHOP *to* **THE** *INQUIRER.* **14 January 1863. Chesterfield.** Praises the firmness of Lincoln's proclamation; denounces threats by Davis. 20 February 1863. p.29, c4.

6293 A. F. STODDARD *to* **THE** *GLASGOW HERALD.* **20 January 1863. n.p.** Forwards an anti-slavery address by Mrs. H. B. Stowe. 20 February 1863. p.29, c4.

6294 SAMUEL J. MAY *to* **FRIEND. 19 January 1863. Syracuse, N.Y.** Believes that abolitionists should not feel responsible for the condition of the nation or for the war. 20 February 1863. p.30, c4.

6295 THOMAS WORCESTER *to* **MRS. CHILD. n.d. n.p.** Renounces his former belief that slavery was beneficial to Negroes; thanks abolitionists for his conversion. 20 February 1863. p.30, c4.

6296 ELIZABETH CADY STANTON *to* **MRS. CHILD. 26 January 1863. Brooklyn, N.Y.** Encloses five dollars to help Boston anti-slavery efforts. 20 February 1863. p.30, c5.

6297 J. SCOTT *to* **MRS. CHILD. 22 January 1863. Sudbury.** Encloses a contribution for the anti-slavery cause. 20 February 1863. p.30, c5.

6297a R. W. L. *to* **n.n. 27 January 1863. Tarrytown.** Elderly widow sends one dollar to support the *National Anti-Slavery Standard.* 20 February 1863. p.30, c5.

6298 A. M. P. *to* **n.n. 27 January 1863. Ghent, N.Y.** Contributes to the *Liberator* on the occasion of its anniversary. 20 February 1863. p.30, c6.

6299 EDGAR KETCHUM *to* **MRS. CHILD. 10 January 1863. Harlem, N.Y.** Encloses a check for twenty dollars. 20 February 1863. p.30, c6.

6300 JOHN P. JEWETT *to* **MR. GARRISON. 30 January 1863. London.** Forwards an account of an anti-slavery meeting in London. 20 February 1863. p.31, c3.

6301 C. HENRY ADAMS *to* **MR. GARRISON. 3 February 1863. Boston.** Suggests publishing the names of the patriotic stores which did not close in respect to McClellan; adds that he kept his store open out of respect to himself as well as loyalty to the government. 20 February 1863. p.31, c4.

6302 THOMAS WHITTET *to* **W. L. GARRISON. 20 January 1863. Perth, North Britain.** Asserts that the image of the United States government in Europe is one of incompetence and vacillation. 20 February 1863. p.32, c3.

6303 E. B. CHASE *to* **FRIEND GARRISON. 1863. Valley Falls, R.I.** Commends the *Liberator* for printing letters from subscribers. 20 February 1863. p.32, c4.

6304 LEA W. GAUSE *to* **MR. GARRISON. n.d. n.p.** Hopes that Garrison lives long enough to see his labors "crowned with success." 20 February 1863. p.32, c4.

6305 S. M. SEAVER *to* **W. L. GARRISON. 22 January 1863. Williamstown, Vt.** Reflects on the importance of the *Liberator*; encloses a contribution. 20 February 1863. p.32, c4.

6306 FRED N. DOW *to* **WM. LLOYD GARRISON. 26 January 1863. Portland, Me.** Wants to be a permanent subscriber to the *Liberator.* 20 February 1863. p.32, c4.

6307 THOS. WALLACE *to* **EDITOR OF THE *LIBERATOR* [W. L. GARRISON]. 3 February 1863. Birmingham, Ct.** Encloses subscriptions for three copies of the *Liberator.* 20 February 1863. p.32, c4.

6308 C. B. LEBARON *to* **WM. LLOYD GARRISON. 27 January 1863. New York.** Encloses five dollars to sustain the *Liberator.* 20 February 1863. p.32, c4.

6309 GEN. SAXTON *to* **E. M. STANTON, SECRETARY OF WAR. 25 January 1863. Beaufort, S.C.** Reports on successful efforts to organize colored volunteer troops. 20 February 1863. p.32, c6.

6310 W. S. ROSECRANS *to* **GENERAL ASSEMBLY OF OHIO. 3 February. Murfrees-boro, Tn.** Appreciates the resolution of support from Ohio. 27 February 1863. p.34, c1.

6311 GEORGE THOMPSON *to* **GARRISON. 5 February 1863. London.** Reports on anti-slavery activities in England. 27 February 1863. p.34, c5.

6312 REV. DANIEL FOSTER *to* **GARRISON. n.d. Stafford Courthouse, Va.** Praises General Hooker's leadership. 27 February 1863. p.35, c4.

6313 W. H. G. *to* **GEN. N. P. BANKS. 10 January 1863. New Orleans.** Requests that General Banks release all fugitive slaves currently jailed by Union troops. 6 March 1863. p.36, c2.

6314 W. H. G. *to* **DR. HARRIS COWDRY. 9 February 1863. At sea.** Reports that General Banks is returning New Orleans slaves to their masters, despite the Emancipation Proclamation; condemns his actions. 6 March 1863. p.39, c1.

6315 JOHN WADDINGTON *to* **THE** *LONDON MORNING STAR.* **12 February. Surrey-Square.** Protests against England's recognition of the Confederacy. 6 March 1863. p.39, c4.

6316 A WORKING MAN *to* **THE** *LONDON MORNING STAR.* **n.d. n.p.** Angrily acknowledges the pro-slavery sentiments of the upper class, but asserts that the working class will never embrace slavery. 6 March 1863. p.39, c4.

6317 ABRAHAM LINCOLN *to* **ABEL HEYWOOD. 19 January 1863. Washington.** Admits to the "workingmen of Manchester" that the Civil War has impaired the English as well as the American economy; hopes for a speedy end to the war. 6 March 1863. p.40, c5.

6318 FREDERICK DOUGLASS *to* **n.n. 2 March 1863. Rochester.** Calls for the Negroes to arm themselves and earn the nation's respect. 13 March 1863. p.42, c1.

6319 JOHN P. JEWETT *to* **GARRISON. 26 February 1863. London.** Describes emancipation celebrations in England. 13 March 1863. p.43, c1.

6320 WM. P. POWELL *to* **GARRISON. 26 February 1863. Colored Sailors' Home, N.Y.** Expresses pride in the *Liberator* for its role in the abolitionist cause. 13 March 1863. p.43, c3.

6321 SEWARD MITCHELL *to* **FRIEND GARRISON. 22 February 1863. Cornville, Me.** Thanks Garrison for involving him in the abolitionist movement; supports the war. 13 March 1863. p.44, c4.

6322 GEORGE LAWRENCE, JR. *to* **THE** *NEW YORK SUNDAY MERCURY.* **2 March 1863. New York.** Corrects article which mistakenly identified Haiti as a kingdom, not a republic. 13 March 1863. p.44, c6.

6323 GEORGE THOMPSON *to* **GARRISON. 27 February 1863. London.** Describes the multitude of anti-slavery activities and emancipation meetings in England. 20 March 1863. p.46, c3.

6324 JOHN P. JEWETT *to* **GARRISON. 26 February 1863. London.** Reports on a meeting held in honor of George Thompson. 20 March 1863. p.46, c5.

6325 MRS. FRANCES D. GAGE *to* **GARRISON. 8 March 1863. Paris Island, S.C.** Comments on conditions in South Carolina and the general state of the country. 20 March 1863. p.46, c6.

6326 A. J. GROVER *to* **MR. GARRISON. 6 March 1863. Washington.** Expresses admiration for "Tribe of ASA," an abolitionist singing group in the District of Columbia. 20 March 1863. p.47, c2.

6327 THOMAS RUSSELL *to* **WM. C. NELL. 5 March 1861. Boston.** Regrets he is unable to attend Crispus Attucks' celebration. 20 March 1863. p.47, c2.

6328 M. D. CONWAY *to* **WM. C. NELL. n.d. n.p.** Regrets he is unable to attend Crispus Attucks' celebration. 20 March 1863. p.47, c2.

6329 DANIEL FOSTER *to* **GARRISON. n.d. Camp of Thirty-third Massachusetts Volunteers.** States that he is encouraged by the response of soldiers to the *Liberator* and other anti-slavery papers; claims that the *Liberator* boosts morale. 20 March 1863. p.47, c3.

6330 ONE OF THE CATEGORY *to* **SIR. 6 March 1863. Washington, D.C.** Urges the termination of Southern barbarism. 20 March 1863. p.47, c3.

6331 J. S. MILL *to* **SIR. 11 February. Blackheath Park.** Expresses hope for the "future welfare and greatness of the American Republic" in this its "darkest hour." 20 March 1863. p.47, c3.

6332 C. STEARNS *to* **FRIEND. 21 January 1863. Central City.** Argues that the work of abolitionists is not completed with the Emancipation Proclamation. 20 March 1863. p.48, c4.

6333 S. S. H. *to* **THE** *CHRISTIAN INQUIRER.* **9 March 1863. Detroit.** Expresses disgust with pro-slavery mob which rioted in Detroit. 20 March 1863. p.48, c5.

6334 C. F. B. *to* **THE** *BOSTON JOURNAL.* **n.d. n.p.** Reveals the existence of anti-slavery volumes at the Boston Atheneum which were bound by the founding fathers. 27 March 1863. p.49, c5.

6335 FREDERICK WILLIAMS *to* **FRIEND GARRISON. 14 March 1863. Port Royal, S.C.** Asserts that colored people in South Carolina are capable of freedom; notes that the government is helping them. 27 March 1863. p.51, c1.

6336 J. T. PAINE *to* **GARRISON. 28 February 1863. Fort St. Leon, La.** Declares that he refuses to silence his abolition sentiments. 27 March 1863. p.51, c2.

6337 ABRAHAM LINCOLN *to* **WORKINGMEN OF LONDON. 2 February 1863. Washington.** Expresses appreciation for the petition they sent in support of freedom and the Union. 27 March 1863. p.51, c3.

6338 HENRY C. WRIGHT *to* **GARRISON. 1 March 1863. Raspberry Mt., Pa.** Asserts that the South is responsible for the war; comments on speech by Alexander Stephens, vice-president of the Confederacy. 27 March 1863. p.52, c3.

6339 A. J. GROVER *to* **MR. GARRISON. 20 March 1863. Washington, D.C.** Encloses the proceedings of the Methodist Conference held in the District of Columbia. 3 April 1863. p.53, c2.

6340 WM. FLANDERS *to* **MR. GARRISON. 23 March 1863. Cornville, Me.** Views war as conflict between states' rights and the rights of the individual. 3 April 1863. p.53, c3.

6341 J. W. PECKHAM *to* **W. L. GARRISON. 2 March 1863. Easton, N.Y.** Praises the *Liberator* and encloses a contribution. 3 April 1863. p.53, c4.

6342 J. W. PECKHAM *to* **WM. L. GARRISON. 2 March 1863. Easton, N.Y.** Asserts that it is the duty of the few to support the anti-slavery newspapers. 3 April 1863. p.53, c4.

6343 A MASSACHUSETTS ARMY CAPTAIN *to* **n.n. [extract] 22 March 1863. Newbern, N.C.** Discerns a great deal of anti-Negro sentiment in the Union army. 3 April 1863. p.54, c5.

6344 EDWARD M. MacGRAW *to* **MR. GARRISON. 23 March 1863. Pontiac, Mi.** Criticizes newspaper accounts which blame Negroes for recent anti-Negro rioting in Detroit. 3 April 1863. p.55, c2.

6345 GEORGE SUNTER *to* **MR. GARRISON. 11 March 1863. Branford, Canada West.** Refutes speech by George Thompson on tariffs; argues that the South favors free trade. 3 April 1863. p.55, c3.

6346 EARL RUSSELL *to* **LORD LYONS. 17 January 1863. n.p.** Declares that the Emancipation Proclamation is too limited in scope for abolitionists. 3 April 1863. p.55, c4.

6347 J. K. HERBERT *to* **THE** *BOSTON TRAVELLER.* **23 March 1863. Boston.** Discusses instances where Union soldiers were ordered to return slaves to their masters. 3 April 1863. p.55, c4.

6348 HENRY WILSON *to* **FERNANDO WOOD. 30 March 1863. Natick, Ma.** Defends the Conscription Act as beneficial to the poor who can be hired as "substitutes" for wealthier draftees. 10 April 1863. p.57, c2.

6349 CARLETON *to* **THE** *BOSTON JOURNAL.* **24 March 1863. Hilton Head.** States that he is bemused by Southern indignation at being attacked by freed slaves. 10 April 1863. p.57, c6.

6350 J. M. H. *to* **GARRISON. 23 March 1863. Beaufort, S.C.** Discusses the need for more colored soldiers to fight the war. 10 April 1863. p.59, c4.

6351 DANIEL FOSTER *to* **GARRISON. 3 March 1863. Aquia Creek, Va.** Denounces Copperhead activities in army; urges abolitionists to oppose them. 10 April 1863. p.59, c4.

6352 L. A. SAWYER *to* **THE EDITOR [W. L. GARRISON]. n.d. n.p.** Asserts that love and good deeds constitute the true basis of Christianity. 10 April 1863. p.60, c4.

6353 HARRIET JACOBS *to* **n.n. 18 March 1863. Alexandria, Va.** An ex-slave reports on deplorable conditions of freedmen. 10 April 1863. p.60, c5.

6354 JEFFERSON DAVIS *to* **FERNANDO WOOD. 1 February 1863. Richmond.** States his belief that the Southern states will win because they are war-like and agrarian; feels no hope for reunion. 17 April 1863. p.61, c4.

6355 T. PERRONET THOMPSON *to* **THE** *BRAXFORD ADVERTISER.* **n.d. Eliotvale, Blackheath, England.** Blames all world problems on color prejudice. 17 April 1863. p.61, c6.

6356 SARAH AND BENJAMIN FISH *to* **FRIENDS. n.d. Rochester, N.Y.** Express thanks to George Thompson, English abolitionists, and friends for their assistance. 17 April 1863. p.62, c6.

6357 THOMAS BAYLEY POTTER *to* **PARLIAMENT. 23 March 1863. Manchester, England.** Petitions Parliament to stop British firms from building ships for the Confederacy. 17 April 1863. p.63, c3.

6358 CHARLES WILSON *to* **PARLIAMENT. n.d. n.p.** Urges ban on British ship-building for the Confederacy, as well as on Confederate use of British ports. 17 April 1863. p.63, c3.

6359 REV. GEORGE HEPWORTH *to* **GEN. N. P. BANKS. 24 March 1863. New Orleans.** Lauds Banks' plan to return fugitive slaves to their plantations and to arrange for them to be hired as free laborers and treated accordingly. 17 April 1863. p.63, c4.

6360 n.n. *to* **n.n. n.d. n.p.** Urges North to "trust in God and do Right." 17 April 1863. p.64, c5.

6361 GEO. THOMPSON *to* **GARRISON. 2 February 1863. London.** Describes abolitionist work in England. 24 April 1863. p.66, c5.

6362 GRANDPIERRE PASTEUR, G. MONOD, L. ROGNON, L. PULSFORD, FRED MONOD, AND EVE BERSIER *to* **MINISTERS AND PASTORS OF ALL EVANGELICAL DENOMINATIONS IN GREAT BRITAIN. 12 February 1863. Paris.** Issue a pro-Union anti-slavery statement. 24 April 1863. p.66, c6.

6363 n.n. *to* **MR. EDITOR [W. L. GARRISON]. 19 April 1863. Concord, Ma.** States that he is saddened by literary men who use the slave for poetry or picturesque settings, instead of aiding in his liberation. 24 April 1863. p.67, c1.

6364 GURDON JUDSON *to* **THE AMERICAN REFORM TRACT AND BOOK SOCIE-TY. n.d. n.p.** Enclosed $200 to help purchase suitable reading material for the troops. 24 April 1863. p.67, c3.

6365 JOHN BRIGHT *to* **SIR. 9 March 1863. Rochdale.** Supports the Union cause. 24 April 1863. p.67, c3.

6366 J. H. G. *to* **MR. EDITOR [W. L. GARRISON]. n.d. n.p.** Denounces the *Boston Pilot* for opposing the Emancipation Proclamation. 24 April 1863. p.68, c3.

6367 HENRY C. WRIGHT *to* **GARRISON. 12 March 1863. Raspberry Mt., Pa.** Assails Copperheads for their capitalism. 24 April 1863. p.68, c4.

6368 L. A. SAWYER *to* **MR. EDITOR [W. L. GARRISON]. n.d. n.p.** Expands his biblical theories. 24 April 1863. p.68, c5.

6369 REV. LORD *to* **BOSTON COURIER. n.d. n.p.** Refutes the abolitionist position that the war will destroy either the government or slavery. 1 May 1863. p.69, c1.

6370 S. P. CHASE *to* **GEORGE OPDYKE, GEORGE GRISWOLD, AND OTHERS. 9 April 1863. Washington.** Recommends use of colored troops to defend the Republic; notes Jackson's use of colored troops to fight the British as an historical precedent. 1 May 1863. p.70, c1.

6371 n.n. *to* **W. L. GARRISON. n.d. Lawrence, Ks.** Remarks on changing attitudes in Kansas where fugitive slaves are now welcomed. 1 May 1863. p.71, c2.

6372 J. B. LYON *to* **W. L. GARRISON. n.d. Cleveland, Oh.** Believes that the best way to end the war is to arm Negroes and to promise them land confiscated from the Southern aristocracy. 1 May 1863. p.71, c2.

6373 CATHARINE A. F. STEBBINS *to* **THE *LIBERATOR*. 21 April 1863. Rochester, N.Y.** Urges loyal women of the nation to provide "moral enthusiasm" for the Republic. 1 May 1863. p.72, c4.

6374 REV. LORD *to* **THE** *BOSTON COURIER.* **[continued from 1 May 1863] n.d. n.p.** Criticizes positions taken by both abolitionists and secessionists in the conflict over slavery. 8 May 1863. p.73, c1.

6375 ANNA E. DICKINSON *to* **HENRY C. CAREY, WM. D. KELLEY, AND CO. 25 April 1863. Philadelphia.** Accepts invitation to address Philadelphians. 8 May 1863. p.73, c6.

6376 HENRY C. CAREY, WM. D. KELLEY, AND CO. *to* **MISS ANNA E. DICKINSON. 24 April 1863. Philadelphia.** Extend invitation for her to lecture at the Philadelphia Hall of Music. 8 May 1863. p.73, c6.

6377 GENTLEMAN *to* **THE LOYAL NATIONAL LEAGUE. 14 April 1863. Hartford, Ct.** Praises the abilities of Anna Dickinson. 8 May 1863. p.74, c1.

6378 J. W. BATTERSON *to* **A GENTLEMAN IN NEW YORK. 15 April 1863. Hartford, Ct.** Urges attendance at lecture by Anna E. Dickinson, who has been aiding the Republican cause in Connecticut. 8 May 1863. p.74, c1.

6379 GEN. JOHN T. SPRAGUE *to* **GOV. HORATIO SEYMOUR. 20 April 1863. Albany.** Issues report on success of Pinner's Ambulance Kitchen, a locomotive cooking apparatus. 8 May 1863. p.74, c6.

6380 HENRY C. WRIGHT *to* **GARRISON. 28 April 1863. Norwich, N.Y.** Comments that the public will now support the use of Union black troops in order to save the Union. 8 May 1863. p.74, c6.

6381 JESSE STEDMAN *to* **MR. EDITOR. 1 May 1863. Springfield, Vt.** Denounces the hypocrisy of a national fast for peace. 8 May 1863. p.74, c6.

6382 REV. G. H. HEPWORTH *to* **THE** *TRANSCRIPT.* **[extract] 10 April. New Orleans.** Observes how all slaves hate their masters but love the Union soldiers. 15 May 1863. p.77, c6.

6383 ABIJAH GILBERT *to* **SIR. 13 April 1863. Jackson County, Ky.** Feels despondent over rebel atrocities in Kentucky. 15 May 1863. p.78, c1.

6384 W. G. B. *to* **FRIEND GARRISON. 10 March 1863. North Scituate, Ma.** Favors withholding the elective franchise from drunkards and those who make them drunk. 15 May 1863. p.78, c6.

6385 L. A. SAWYER *to* **MR. EDITOR [W. L. GARRISON]. n.d. n.p.** Declares that freeing the slaves will be the greatest act of Christianity in history. 15 May 1863. p.79, c1.

6386 S. B. TRUE *to* **FRIEND GARRISON. 14 April 1863. Amesbury.** Argues that the administration should "allow the South to go" and take slavery with it. 15 May 1863. p.79, c2.

6387 JANE WIGHAM *to* **MRS. CHILD. [extract] n.d. Edinburgh.** Reports on anti-slavery in Scotland. 15 May 1863. p.79, c4.

6388 EDWARD S. BUNKER *to* **MR. GARRISON. 26 April 1863. Brooklyn, N.Y.** Rejoices in news that local Presbyterians elected a colored man as their minister. 15 May 1863. p.79, c4.

6389 T. S. H. *to* **FRIEND. n.d. Rodney, Ms.** Wife of a minister reacts with fear to Harpers Ferry attack by John Brown. 22 May 1863. p.81, c2.

6390 D. S. DICKINSON *to* **MESSRS. DUKEHART, RICH, AND BRUCE. 14 April 1863. Albany, N.Y.** Rejoices at formation of Union League. 22 May 1863. p.81, c4.

6391 DANIEL FOSTER *to* **GARRISON. 10 May 1863. Aquia Creek Camp, Va.** Reports from battle with the Thirty-third Massachusetts Regiment. 22 May 1863. p.83, c2.

6392 SAMUEL J. MAY *to* **WM. LLOYD GARRISON. 11 May 1863. Syracuse.** Regrets his inability to attend AAS meeting. 29 May 1863. p.85, c2.

6393 A. T. AUGUSTA *to* **THE** *REPUBLICAN.* **18 May 1863. Washington.** A Negro army surgeon reports on being assaulted in Baltimore. 29 May 1863. p.85, c3.

6393a WM. G. WEBSTER *to* **THE EDITOR OF THE** *BOSTON JOURNAL.* **n.d. 22 Beacon St.** Refutes a *Journal* article which charged General Lee with mistreating his slaves; asserts that "before he became a traitor, he was a gentleman and a Christian." 29 May 1863. p.86, c4.

6394 SAMUEL P. PUTNAM *to* *BOSTON JOURNAL.* **17 May 1863. Fort Albany.** Asserts that General Lee whipped his slaves. 29 May 1863. p.86, c5.

6395 E. M. DAVIS *to* **J. M. McKIM. 11 May 1863. Philadelphia.** Accepts Emancipation Proclamation as "the dawning," but not the "fulfillment," of the anti-slavery mission. 29 May 1863. p.87, c1.

6396 CATHARINE A. F. STEBBINS *to* **MR. GARRISON. 16 May 1863. New York.** Reports on attending the National Convention of Women. 29 May 1863. p.87, c5.

6397 GEN. ROSECRANS *to* **THE** *CATHOLIC TELEGRAPH.* **[extract] 27 April 1863. Murfreesboro.** Favors an end to slavery; asserts that the Emancipation Proclamation will do much to hasten the end of the war. 5 June 1863. p.89, c6.

6398 F. J. W. *to* **FRIEND GARRISON. 11 May 1863. Port Royal, S.C.** Cites difficulties in organizing colored men of Port Royal into an army. 5 June 1863. p.91, c4.

6399 ALFRED H. LOVE *to* **WM. LLOYD GARRISON. 27 April 1863. Philadelphia.** Defends non-resistance as essential to the perfection of the soul and the prosperity of humanity. 5 June 1863. p.92, c4.

6400 PAUL FRY *to* *BOSTON COURIER.* **n.d. n.p.** Denounces Union League meeting as "ridiculous" and filled with "anti-nigger" sentiment; assails those who would promote slavery to preserve the Union. 12 June 1863. p.93, c1.

6401 M. F. CONWAY *to* *NEW YORK TRIBUNE.* **29 May 1863. Washington.** Denounces reunion with slavery; fears that Gerrit Smith and others have abandoned the anti-slavery cause. 12 June 1863. p.93, c4.

6402 L. JUDD PARDEE *to* **THE** *LIBERATOR.* **1863. Boston.** Advocates Negro emancipation and the establishment of a Negro nation in the future. 12 June 1863. p.94, c6.

6403 JESSE STEDMAN *to* **MR. EDITOR [W. L. GARRISON]. n.d. Springfield, Vt.** Expresses apprehension that war will end in compromise and not victory for the anti-slavery forces. 12 June 1863. p.95, c1.

6404 CORRESPONDENT *to* **FRIEND GARRISON. n.d. n.p.** Advocates "weeding out" pro-slavery soldiers in the Union army. 12 June 1863. p.95, c3.

6405 THUD *to* **THE** *LIBERATOR.* **31 May 1863. Newbern, N.C.** Commends colored troops in North Carolina. 12 June 1863. p.95, c3.

6406 SALLIE HOLLEY *to* **MR. GARRISON. 1 June 1863. Farmersville, N.Y.** Mourns the death of Charlotte Hill, an active participant in the New England AS. 12 June 1863. p.95, c5.

6407 L. A. SAWYER *to* **MR. EDITOR [W. L. GARRISON]. n.d. n.p.** Reports of attacks made on his biblical theories. 12 June 1863. p.96, c3.

6408 GEN. D. HUNTER *to* **GOVERNOR OF MASSACHUSETTS. [extract] 4 May 1863. Port Royal, S.C.** Reports that prejudice toward colored soldiers is lessening at Port Royal. 19 June 1863. p.97, c5.

6409 PRESIDENT LINCOLN *to* **HON. ERASTUS CORNING. 12 June 1863. Washington.** Asserts that the president has the constituional power to order military arrests. 19 June 1863. p.98, c1.

6410 THUD *to* **THE** *LIBERATOR.* **7 June 1863. 1st, S.C.** Reports increase in black enlistments in the Union army. 19 June 1863. p.98, c5.

6411 M. L. WHITTEN *to* **MR. EDITOR [W. L. GARRISON]. 10 June 1863. Frederick, Md.** Warns that copperheads are capable of hurting the administration's war effort. 19 June 1863. p.98, c5.

6412 G. B. STEBBINS *to* **GARRISON. 9 June 1863. Rochester, N.Y.** Encloses resolutions of a Waterloo yearly meeting of the Friends of Human Progress. 19 June 1863. p.98, c6.

6413 J. THEODORE HOLLY *to* **MRS. SARAH DOUGLASS. 13 November 1862. N.Y.** Reports on Haiti and increased emigration. 19 June 1863. p.99, c1.

6414 DANIEL FOSTER *to* **GARRISON. 4 June 1863. Aquia Creek, Va.** Expresses satisfaction with Montgomery's and Higginson's colored regiments in South Carolina. 19 June 1863. p.99, c3.

6415 GEN. DANIEL ULLMAN *to* **THE** *ERA.* **25 May 1863. New Orleans.** Urges clarification of government policy regarding colored soldiers; cites instance when colored soldiers were disarmed and returned to the plantation. 19 June 1863. p.99, c4.

6416 GERRIT SMITH *to* **REV. HENRY WARD BEECHER. 20 May 1863. Peterboro, N.Y.** Respects the late Stonewall Jackson, but denies that he was a Christian. 19 June 1863. p.100, c5.

6417 GEN. JOHN FREMONT *to* **GOV. GILMORE. 16 June 1863. New York.** Regrets his inability to attend the Union Convention; stresses that "victory and safety" do not come from half-way measures or compromise. 26 June 1863. p.103, c4.

6418 AMOS GILBERT *to* **W. L. G. 15 June 1863. Bart, Lancaster County, Pa.** Reports on Longwood annual meeting of Progressive Friends. 26 June 1863. p.104, c6.

6419 C. K. W. *to* **MR. GARRISON. n.d. n.p.** Criticizes Mr. Lincoln but asserts that he harbors greater hostility toward the secessionists. 3 July 1863. p.106, c4.

6420 HENRY C. WRIGHT *to* **GARRISON. 22 June 1863. Detroit.** Reports on attending meetings in support of the Union. 3 July 1863. p.106, c6.

6421 J. M. MASON *to* **SIR. [from the** *London Times***] 17 June 1863. Portman Square.** Submits a series of correspondence between Moncure D. Conway and himself. 10 July 1863. p.111 [110], c1.

6422 MONCURE D. CONWAY *to* **J. M. MASON. [from the** *London Times***] 10 June 1863. Notting Hill, London.** Proposes that if the Confederate states emancipate Negro slaves at once, the Northern states will oppose the prosecution of the war. 10 July 1863. p.111 [110], c1.

6423 J. M. MASON *to* **MONCURE D. CONWAY. [from the** *London Times***] 11 June 1863. Portman Square.** Requests to know who will be responsible for supervising the emancipation of slaves under Conway's plan to end the Civil War. 10 July 1863. p.111 [110], c1.

6424 MONCURE D. CONWAY *to* **J. M. MASON. [from the** *London Times***] 16 June 1863. Notting Hill, London.** Informs he will present in writing evidence of his authority to propose a plan to end the Civil War. 10 July 1863. p.111 [110], c1.

6425 J. M. MASON *to* **MONCURE D. CONWAY. [from the** *London Times***] 17 June 1863. Portman Square.** Expresses his satisfaction with Conway's pending address to the English Parliament about his plan. 10 July 1863. p.111 [110], c1.

6426 MONCURE D. CONWAY *to* **THE** *LONDON TIMES.* **22 June. Notting Hill.** Reasserts his proposal that the South emancipate all slaves in exchange for the cessation of Northern hostilities. 10 July 1863. p.111 [110], c1.

6427 HENRY WILSON *to* **SIR. 1 July 1863. Washington.** Denounces Conway's proposition made in England regarding ending the Civil War; asserts that Conway should represent himself and not speak for other abolitionists. 10 July 1863. p.111*, c1.

6428 FRANCES GAGE *to* **FRIEND GARRISON. 5 July 1863. West Newton, Ma.** Advocates a liberal education for freedmen because she feels it will make them more civic-minded. 10 July 1863. p.111*, c5.

6429 M. PINNER *to* **GARRISON. 6 July 1863. Washington, D.C.** Lauds the leadership of the *Liberator.* 10 July 1863. p.111*, c5.

6430 J. P. BLANCHARD *to* **SAMUEL J. MAY. 2 June 1863. Roxbury.** Reports on the AAS meeting. 10 July 1863. p.112, c6.

6431 J. T. PAINE *to* **MR. GARRISON. 9 June 1863. Port Hudson, La.** Expresses pride at the fighting ability of the colored troops. 17 July 1863. p.114, c6.

6432 D. M. *to* **MR. MAY. [extract] 14 June 1863. Newbern, N.C.** Admires the performance of the colored troops. 17 July 1863. p.115, c1.

6433 DANIEL FOSTER *to* **GARRISON. 5 July 1863. Gettysburg, Pa.** Reports on the Battle of Gettysburg. 17 July 1863. p.115, c2.

6434 HENRY C. WRIGHT *to* **GARRISON. 29 June 1863. Detroit.** Encloses pro-war resolutions from meeting of Friends of Progress at Farmington. 17 July 1863. p.115, c2.

6435 COL. E. E. CROSS *to* **n.n. [extract] 4 June 1863. Hancock's Division.** Reports that he was nearly killed at the Battle of Fredericksburg. 24 July 1863. p.117, c6.

6436 WM. P. POWELL *to* **GARRISON. 18 July 1863. New Bedford.** Laments that his Colored Sailors' Home was attacked during the New York riots. 24 July 1863. p.118, c4.

6437 NOYES WHEELER *to* **FRIEND GARRISON. 20 July 1863. New York.** Protests the New York riots against Negroes. 24 July 1863. p.118, c4.

6438 G. B. STEBBINS *to* **MR. GARRISON. 10 July 1863. Rochester.** Reports on the yearly meeting of Friends of Human Progress. 24 July 1863. p.118, c6.

6439 W. O. DUVALL *to* **BRO. GARRISON. 30 June 1863. Hayti.** Assails the *Liberator* for supporting American politicans Lincoln and Blair. 24 July 1863. p.118, c6.

6440 G. B. STEBBINS *to* **GARRISON. 11 July 1863. Rochester.** Criticizes Theodore Parker for denying existence of "spirits." 24 July 1863. p.120, c5.

6441 A WOMAN *to* **MR. EDITOR [W. L. GARRISON]. n.d. n.p.** Defends Mrs. Hatch, a medium who claims that Theodore Parker is speaking through her. 24 July 1863. p.120, c5.

6442 WENDELL PHILLIPS *to* **SIR. 21 July 1863. n.p.** Defends changing from a dis-unionist to a proponent of the Union because he believes the Union means peace and liberty, and protection for the slave. 31 July 1863. p.122, c5.

6443 SUSAN B. ANTHONY *to* **GARRISON. 25 July 1863. New York.** Discusses the Women's Loyal League Association. 31 July 1863. p.122, c6.

6444 ORSON S. MURRAY *to* **THE *LIBERATOR*. 10 July 1863. Fostor's Crossings, Oh.** Denounces Lincoln's fast for peace as pointless; urges an end to slavery and no compromise. 31 July 1863. p.123, c1.

6445 WILLIAM WHITING *to* **EDWARD GILBERT. 10 July 1863. Washington, D.C.** Regrets that he is unable to address a convention of colored citizens; urges them to fight for freedom, justice, and humanity. 31 July 1863. p.123, c2.

6446 H. W. LITTLEFIELD *to* **THE *BOSTON JOURNAL*. 23 July 1863. Beaufort, S.C.** Respects colored troops who have proved themselves under fire. 31 July 1863. p.123, c3.

6447 S. E. W. *to* **MR. GARRISON. 20 July 1863. Worcester.** Reacts favorably to a speech supporting non-resistance by Mr. Heywood. 31 July 1863. p.124, c2.

6448 H. H. BRIGHAM *to* **FRIEND GARRISON. 18 July 1863. South Abington.** Applauds Heywood's discourse published by the *Liberator*. 31 July 1863. p.124, c3.

6449 GEO. W. STACY *to* **FRIEND. 20 July 1863. Milford.** Informs of his attendance at the Heywood lecture. 31 July 1863. p.124, c3.

6450 A FIELD OFFICER *to* **LONDON *MORNING STAR*. 25 June. n.p.** Asserts that British Negro troops in Barbados, Grenada, and Trinidad are soldierly, sober, and well-disciplined. 31 July 1863. p.124, c4.

6451 L. H. *to* **FRIEND GARRISON. 1 August 1863. Orange.** Denounces the *Boston Journal* as a dishonest and abusive publication. 7 August 1863. p.127, c2.

6452 ROBERT HAMILTON *to* **THE *LIBERATOR*. n.d. New York.** Appeals for subscribers to the *Afro-American*, which encountered financial difficulties during the New York riots. 7 August 1863. p.127, c2.

6453 CHARLES SUMNER *to* **EDWARD GILBERT. 13 July 1863. Boston.** Argues that the motivation of colored troops is high because they are fighting enemies of their race. 7 August 1863. p.127, c2.

6454 L. L. RUGGLES *to* **GARRISON. n.d. Toledo, Oh.** Defends medium who claimed that spirit of Theodore Parker spoke through her. 7 August 1863. p.128, c3.

6455 M. BRETTELL *to* **THE** *LIBERATOR.* **n.d. n.p.** Mourns death of Captain James Reeves, an anti-slavery farmer who volunteered to fight for the abolition cause. 7 August 1863. p.128, c4.

6456 WM. WHITING *to* **UNION LEAGUE OF PHILADELPHIA. n.d. n.p.** Argues that the Constitution of the conquered states must include adequate safeguards for the freedom of all. 14 August 1863. p.131, c2.

6457 BION BRADBURY *to* **GEN. S. J. ANDERSON. 3 August 1863. Eastport.** Regrets that he is unable to attend the Democratic (Copperhead) Convention; urges support for the Constitution and Union "as it was." 21 August 1863. p.134, c1.

6458 C. F. HUDSON *to* **WM. L. GARRISON. 11 August 1863. Boston.** Provides account of the murder of Dr. Hudson, a well-known anti-slavery lecturer. 21 August 1863. p.135, c1.

6459 DANIEL FOSTER *to* **GARRISON. 7 August 1863. Catlett's Station, Va.** Reports on events in the field with the Thirty-third Massachusetts Regiment. 21 August 1863. p.135, c1.

6460 W. P. G. *to* **SIR. 10 July 1863. Boston.** Objects to war and the taxes that support it, but states that he is willing to compromise by paying a substitute $300 to serve in his place. 21 August 1863. p.135, c5.

6461 CAROLINE F. PUTNAM *to* **MR. GARRISON. 3 August 1863. Farmsville, N.Y.** Appeals to spiritualists to promote temperance in western New York. 21 August 1863. p.135, c6.

6462 ALFRED H. LOVE *to* **FRIEND GARRISON. 8 August 1863. Philadelphia.** Announces that he has received a draft notice; declares that he cannot serve both God and country, so he will not fight. 21 August 1863. p.136, c2.

6463 n.n. *to* *BOSTON DAILY ADVERTISER.* **n.d. n.p.** Declares it a "mockery" that colored soldiers are fighting bravely for Union and freedom while their families are hounded by brutal mobs. 21 August 1863. p.136, c6.

6464 DANIEL O'CONNELL *to* **D. T. DISNEY, W. H. HUNTER, AND CO. 11 October 1843. Dublin.** Urges Irish-Americans to oppose slavery. 28 August 1863. p.137, c2.

6465 CHARLES K. WHIPPLE *to* **THE** *HERALD OF PEACE.* **26 March 1863. Boston.** Argues that genuine men of peace must oppose all war. 28 August 1863. p.140, c1.

6466 HENRY RICHARD *to* **CHARLES K. WHIPPLE. 30 June 1863. London.** Regrets that Whipple's defense of the war cannot be reconciled with the principles Whipple formerly held. 28 August 1863. p.140, c5.

6467 GOV. REYNOLDS *to* **HON. JEFFERSON DAVIS AND EX-GOV. SMITH. 28 December 1860. Belleville, Il.** Urges slave states to unite and either separate from Union or force a constitutional amendment to protect slavery. 4 September 1863. p.141, c1.

6468 PROF. CHARLES HACKLEY *to* **JEFFERSON DAVIS. 26 December 1860. Columbia College, N.Y.** Sympathizes with South but urges restraint on expansion of slavery into territories; stresses necessity of preserving the Union. 4 September 1863. p.141, c1.

6469 PRICE WILLIAMS *to* **JEFFERSON DAVIS. 14 December 1860. Mobile.** Foresees little hope or desire for compromise on slave question; supports a Southern Confederacy. 4 September 1863. p.141, c1.

6470 JOHN D. McPHERSON *to* **JEFFERSON DAVIS. 19 November 1860. Washington, D.C.** Urges the South to unite and demand veto power over acts of Congress as well as the right to exclude any candidate from the presidency. 4 September 1863. p.141, c1.

6471 WM. ANDERSON *to* **HON. JEFFERSON DAVIS. 11 January 1861. Ann Arbor, Mi.** Advises that measures be taken to prevent runaway slaves from fleeing to the North. 4 September 1863. p.141, c2.

6472 JOHN COWDON *to* **COL. JEFFERSON DAVIS. 17 December 1860. Hazelhurst.** Advocates that Buchanan turn forts at Charleston over to South Carolina in order to prevent bloodshed and preserve the Union. 4 September 1863. p.141, c2.

6473 JOHN BRODHEAD *to* **JEFFERSON DAVIS. 7 March 1860. Philadelphia.** Declares that he is tired of being a "white slave" in the North, and longs for life in the South. 4 September 1863. p.141, c2.

6474 H. E. *to* **BRO. GARRISON. n.d. n.p.** Gives account of how a minister who denounced "American sins" was removed from his position by wealthy pro-slavery elements in his town. 4 September 1863. p.143, c2.

6475 AARON M. POWELL *to* **n.n. [extract] 31 August. Kingston.** Reports on his "excellent meeting" with several *Liberator* readers. 4 September 1863. p.143, c2.

6476 DANIEL FOSTER *to* **GARRISON. 3 September 1863. Bristow, Va.** Approves conduct of the war; cites conditions on the battlefield. 11 September 1863. p.146, c5.

6477 HENRY C. WRIGHT *to* **GARRISON. 1 September 1863. Camp Ann.** Urges "law of the land" recognition be accorded to the Emancipation Proclamation. 11 September 1863. p.146, c6.

6478 L. HOLMES *to* **MR. WALCUT. 4 September 1863. Orange, Ma.** Requests that the *Liberator* print a previously published article on Rev. George Trask's anti-tobacco crusade. 11 September 1863. p.147, c1.

6479 WM. H. SEWARD *to* **THOMAS BAYLEY POTTER, ESQ. 25 July 1863. Washington.** Thanks Potter on behalf of Lincoln for his anti-slavery efforts in England; stresses the importance of preventing the establishment of a state founded on slavery. 11 September 1863. p.147, c2.

6480 ROBERT DALE OWEN *to* **HON. WM. H SEWARD. n.d. n.p.** Argues that since the South waged war, it no longer has equal rights; believes the South should be treated as a defeated enemy after the war is over, not as an equal partner in the Union. 18 September 1863. p.149, c5.

6481 WM. FISH *to* **n.n. 1 September 1863. Vernon, N.Y.** Assails those who hold that abolitionism was responsible for the New York riot. 18 September 1863. p.150, c5.

6482 AARON M. POWELL *to* **MR. GARRISON. 15 September 1863. Boston.** Reports on a lecture which he delivered on the Cape. 18 September 1863. p.150, c6.

6483 J. SELLA MARTIN *to* **THE *LIBERATOR*. 24 July 1863. Bromley, London.** States that Mr. Conway, who offered a compromise to end the war, was neither a British nor an American anti-slavery agent. 18 September 1863. p.150, c6.

6484 n.n. *to* **MR. EDITOR [W. L. GARRISON]. [extract] 1 September 1863. Folly Island, near Charleston.** Credits colored regiments for the military prowess they displayed while under fire. 18 September 1863. p.151, c1.

6485 GEN. R. TOOMBS *to* **DR. A. BEES. [from the** *Sumter Republican***] 17 August 1863. Washington, Ga.** Refutes report that he favors reconstructing the Union; declares that he opposes it under any circumstances, preferring death. 18 September 1863. p.151, c3.

6486 LUCY N. COLMAN *to* **MR. EDITOR [W. L. GARRISON]. 5 September 1863. Rochester.** Forwards anti-slavery resolutions from a meeting of Friends of Progress. 18 September 1863. p.152, c3.

6487 TRUTH *to* **FRIEND GARRISON. n.d. n.p.** Claims that a medium, Mrs. Hatch, spoke to the spirit of Theodore Parker. 18 September 1863. p.152, c4.

6488 ROBERT DALE OWEN *to* **HON. WM. H. SEWARD. [continued from 18 September 1863] n.d. n.p.** Opposes any compromise with Southern states since he believes that the South is responsible for the present conflict. 25 September 1863. p.153, c4.

6489 GEO. E. TYLER *to* **THE** *BOSTON LIBERATOR***. 10 September 1863. New Orleans.** Encloses a sample of the first cotton ever produced in New Orleans by free labor. 25 September 1863. p.154, c5.

6490 HARRISON REED *to* **SAMUEL J. MAY. 1 September 1863. Fernandina, Fl.** Praises the patriotism and desire to learn demonstrated by freedmen. 25 September 1863. p.154, c5.

6491 GEO. TRASK *to* **CHRISTIAN MINISTERS. n.d. n.p.** Believes that the temperance cause failed because it relied too much on government, laws, and paid lecturers; adds that ministers have not done enough work for temperance. 25 September 1863. p.154, c6.

6492 CHARLES WHEELER DENISON *to* **THE EDITOR [W. L. GARRISON]. 21 September 1863. Hyde Park, Ma.** Defends himself against charges made by Rev. J. Sella Martin that he misrepresented himself in England. 25 September 1863. p.155, c1.

6493 A SON OF THE KEYSTONE STATE *to* **THE** *EVENING POST***. n.d. n.p.** Claims that George W. Woodward, a candidate for governor, led the mob which disrupted an abolitionist gathering twenty-five years ago. 25 September 1863. p.155, c2.

6494 EDW. M. MacGRAW *to* **MR. GARRISON. 13 September 1863. Pontiac, Mi.** Encloses letter from a freedman who joined the Union army. 25 September 1863. p.156, c2.

6495 WM. C. BARROWS *to* **MR. E. M. MacGRAW. n.d. n.p.** Describes how he volunteered to fight for the Union. 25 September 1863. p.156, c2.

6496 LUCY CHASE *to* **GARRISON. 16 September 1863. Norfolk, Va.** Reports the organization of a committee to respond to the needs of Negroes working for the government. 25 September 1863. p.156, c3.

6497 L. HOLMES *to* **n.n. 14 September 1863. Orange.** Expresses pleasure with Sumner's speech and the favorable response to it by the *Springfield Republican*. 25 September 1863. p.156, c3.

6498 DAVID WILLIAMS *to* **n.n. n.d.** Believes that the use of Negro troops is essential to winning the war. 2 October 1863. p.157, c4.

6499 WILLIAM H. GIBBS *to* **THE EDITORS OF THE** *DEMOCRAT.* **29 August 1863. Natchez, Ms.** Inquires whether the captured correspondence of Jefferson Davis includes any letters between Davis and Franklin Pierce. 2 October 1863. p.158, c1.

6500 FRANKLIN PIERCE *to* **HON. JEFFERSON DAVIS. 6 January 1860. Clarendon Hotel.** Assails the "madness" of Northern abolitionists as a stimulus to war; comments on his campaign efforts in Connecticut and New Hampshire in support of anti-abolitionist candidates. 2 October 1863. p.158, c2.

6501 E. CADY STANTON *to* **SOLDIERS OF OUR SECOND REVOLUTION. n.d. n.p.** Gives support to soldiers on behalf of loyal women of the nation. 2 October 1863. p.158, c3.

6502 EZRA H. HEYWOOD *to* **MR. GARRISON. 28 September 1863. Princeton, Ma.** Believes that the spirit of Theodore Parker spoke through the medium Mrs. Hatch. 2 October 1863. p.158, c6.

6503 AARON M. POWELL *to* **MR. GARRISON. 20 September 1863. Valley Falls, R.I.** Reports on his lecture tour in Rhode Island. 2 October 1863. p.159, c2.

6504 LIEUT. MAURY *to* **THE** *LONDON TIMES.* **[extract] n.d. n.p.** Believes that the South is winning the war and that the North has lost the will to fight. 9 October 1863. p.161, c1.

6505 C. L. VALLANDIGHAM *to* **PRESIDENT OF THE DEMOCRATIC MASS MEETING AT CARTHAGE, OHIO. 17 September 1863. Windsor.** Accuses Lincoln of being a "Military Dictator"; censures his suspension of the writ of habeas corpus and his policy of conscription; urges Ohio voters to oppose him. 9 October 1863. p.161, c2.

6506 PETER COOPER *to* **GOV. HORATIO SEYMOUR. 22 September 1863. New York.** Urges Democrats to support a "vigorous prosecution of the war." 9 October 1863. p.161, c6.

6507 QUILIBET *to* **THE EDITOR OF THE** *LIBERATOR.* **5 October 1863. Boston.** Feels encouraged by a change in public attitude toward arming blacks; asserts that the chief obstacle now is not prejudice but a lack of officers. 9 October 1863. p.162, c4.

6508 C. L. VALLANDIGHAM *to* **REV. SAVIN HOUGH. 26 April 1861. Dayton, Oh.** Encloses copy of a speech which asserts the necessity of a peaceful dissolution of the Union. 9 October 1863. p.163, c1.

6509 CAPT. S. TYLER REED *to* **GOV. JOHN A. ANDREW. 28 August 1863. New Orleans, La.** Presents Andrew with an iron yoke which he removed from the neck of a slave girl in New Orleans. 9 October 1863. p.163, c2.

6510 JOHN A. ANDREW *to* **MESSRS. WILLIAMS AND EVERETT. 10 September 1863. Boston.** Requests that the iron yoke from the neck of a New Orleans slave girl be placed in their Boston exhibit. 9 October 1863. p.163, c2.

6511 FRANCIS GEORGE SHAW *to* **BRIG. GEN. GILMORE. 24 August 1863. New York.** Rejects efforts to recover the body of his son who was killed in battle; asserts that the appropriate burial place for a soldier is on the battlefield. 9 October 1863. p.163, c2.

6512 GEN. Q. A. GILMORE *to* **F. G. SHAW. 5 September 1863. Morris Island, S.C.** Expresses sympathy on the death of Colonel Shaw. 9 October 1863. p.163, c2.

6513 HELEN GIBBS *to* **MISS ANTHONY. 18 September 1863. Rome.** Conveys her late father's fond regard for Miss Anthony. 9 October 1863. p.163, c5.

6514 JOHN P. JEWETT *to* **GARRISON. 25 September 1863. London.** Describes events in London where there is a positive reaction to the war and the Union cause. 16 October 1863. p.166, c4.

6515 JOSIAH QUINCY *to* **A. LINCOLN. [from the** *New York Evening Post***] 7 September 1863. Quincy, Ma.** Asserts that Union victory and the end of slavery are inevitable. 16 October 1863. p.167, c1.

6516 CHARLES FRANCIS ADAMS *to* **JOHN BRIGHT, M.D. n.d. London.** States his belief that the trade union's declaration against slavery represents the sentiment of the British people. 16 October 1863. p.167, c2.

6517 JESSE STEDMAN *to* **THE** *LIBERATOR.* **n.d. Springfield, Vt.** Attacks Horace Greeley's article printed in the *Independent*, which claims that Garrison and Phillips had little to do with the emergence of slavery as the major issue in the Civil War. 16 October 1863. p.168, c3.

6518 MRS. GAGE *to* **THE** *NEW YORK TRIBUNE.* **29 August 1863. Paris Island, S.C.** Cites the many virtues of the emancipated Negro and blames slavery for his vices. 16 October 1863. p.168, c4.

6519 J. Q. ADAMS *to* **REV. WM. E. CHANNING. 11 August 1837. Quincy.** Describes political machinations designed to bring Cuba into the North American Union as a slave state. 24 [23] October 1863. p.169, c4.

6520 KEYSTONE STATE *to* **THE** *EXETER NEWS-LETTER.* **6 October 1863. Philadelphia.** Describes changing attitudes toward abolitionists, who used to be jailed, but are now applauded; believes that total reform will come eventually. 24[23] October 1863. p.169, c6.

6521 HENRY C. WRIGHT *to* **GARRISON. 9 October 1863. Freeport, In.** Urges no compromise with the South; asserts that either the Republic ("the Christ of Liberty") or the Confederacy ("the Barabas of Slavery") must die in the struggle. 23 October 1863. p.171, c1.

6522 STANDISH *to* **FRIEND GARRISON. n.d. n.p.** Questions the inactivity of the Old Colony AS. 23 October 1863. p.171, c1.

6523 G. W. S. *to* **GARRISON. n.d. n.p.** Reports on an AS meeting held at Worcester, Massachusetts. 23 October 1863. p.171, c2.

6524 J. M. MASON *to* **COL. JEFFERSON DAVIS. 30 September 1856. Selma, near Winchester, Va.** Advocates a meeting between Virginia, North and South Carolina, and Louisiana to discuss disbursement of weapons. 23 October 1863. p.171, c3.

6525 GEORGE THOMPSON *to* **GARRISON. 3 October 1863. London.** Foresees imminent defeat for Confederates and Copperheads. 23 [30] October 1863. p.176 [174], c4.

6526 SAMUEL MAY, JR. *to* **SECRETARY OF WORCESTER COUNTY AS. 11 October 1863. Leicester.** Regrets that he is unable to attend the annual meeting; discusses antislavery work which needs to be done. 23 [30] October 1863. p.171 [175], c2.

6527 DANIEL FOSTER *to* **GARRISON. October 1863. Stevenson, Al.** Reports on military events with the Thirty-third Massachusetts in the field; lauds Lincoln's attack on slavery. 23 [30] October 1863. p.171 [175], c3.

6528 B. G. BROWN, FRED MOENCH, H. T. BLOW, J. W. McCLURG, EMIL PRETORIUS, S. H. BOYD, BEN. LOAN, C. E. MOSS, SAM KNOX, JAMES LINDSAY *to* **FRIENDS OF FREEDOM IN THE UNITED STATES. n.d. n.p.** Express desire to hold a convention in Kentucky to discuss the assimilation of slave states into the Union. 23 [30] October 1863. p.171 [175], c3.

6529 JESSE STEDMAN *to* **MR. EDITOR [W. L. GARRISON]. 25 October 1863. Springfield, Vt.** Denounces clerical Copperheads. 23[30] October 1863. p.171 [175], c4.

6530 WM. THIRDS *to* **MR. GARRISON. 8 October 1863. Natchez, Ms.** Asks for clothing and shoes to aid the colored population of Mississippi. 23 [30] October 1863. p.171 [175], c4.

6531 GERRIT SMITH *to* **WILLIAM LLOYD GARRISON. 25 October 1863. Peterboro', N.Y.** Encloses a draft for $200 to aid the AAS in hiring more lecturers. 23 [30] October 1863. p.171 [175], c5.

6532 EZRA H. HEYWOOD *to* **MR. GARRISON. 29 October 1863. Princeton.** Claims that the "general emancipation" of all slaves would be more effective than any military general in ending the war. 6 November 1863. p.179, c2.

6533 G. W. S. *to* **GARRISON. n.d. n.p.** Believes that America's salvation can only be gained through the work of radical abolitionists. 6 November 1863. p.179, c2.

6534 COL. M. S. LITTLEFIELD *to* **COL. A. G. BROWN, JR. 15 October 1863. Morris Island, S.C.** States that he is proud of a colored soldier who was praised by troops for keeping the flag from touching the ground during battle with the rebels. 6 November 1863. p.180, c4.

6535 WILLIAM H. CARNEY *to* **COL. M. S. LITTLEFIELD. 13 October 1863. Morris Island, S.C.** Declares that his decision to join the colored troops came from a desire to serve God and country. 6 November 1863. p.180, c5.

6536 SENEX *to* **HON. JEFFERSON DAVIS. 18 November 1856. Memphis, Tn.** Urges that Southerners be appointed as secretaries of state, war, treasury, navy, and attorney general in order to prevent Republican domination of the country in 1860. 13 November 1863. p.181, c1.

6537 ORION *to* **n.n. 1 November 1863. Washington, D.C.** Expresses pride at the progress of the anti-slavery cause. 13 November 1863. p.182, c5.

6538 HENRY C. WRIGHT *to* **GARRISON. 30 October 1863. Battle Creek, Mi.** Expresses pleasure at the growth of the Union League of America whose slogan is "Slavery is the cause and Abolition is the cure." 13 November 1863. p.183, c1.

6539 HENRY C. WRIGHT *to* **GARRISON. 28 October 1863. Battle Creek, Mi.** Mourns the death of Joseph Merritt, anti-slavery leader. 13 November 1863. p.183, c2.

6540 LAWRENCE *to* **JOHN J. DOLAND. n.d. n.p.** Criticizes Doland for becoming a Democratic politician. 13 November 1863. p.183, c3.

6541 E. D. AND ANNA T. DRAPER *to* **EXECUTIVE COMMITTEE OF AAS. 7 November 1863. Hopedale.** Pledge $100 per month for five months in support of anti-slavery lectures. 13 November 1863. p.183, c3.

6542 A. LINCOLN *to* **LADIES OF THE NORTHWESTERN FAIR FOR THE SANITARY COMMISSION, CHICAGO, ILLINOIS. 26 October 1863. Washington.** Forwards the original copy of the Emancipation Proclamation to be sold at a fair to benefit the soldiers. 13 November 1863. p.183, c4.

6543 A. P. BUTLER *to* **COL. JEFFERSON DAVIS. 16 June 1851. Near Edgefield.** Fears that the secession of South Carolina would be a "vain sacrifice" if other Southern states did not do likewise. 20 November 1863. p.185, c2.

6544 AUGUSTUS CAMPBELL *to* **ROBERT TRIMBLE. 10 October 1863. Chilwell.** The rector of Liverpool criticizes H. W. Beecher for advocating an abolition policy destined to produce more bloodshed and slave insurrections. 20 November 1863. p.185, c2.

6545 A TRAVELLER *to* **THE** *INDEPENDENT***. 21 October 1863. London.** Reports that the speech given by H. W. Beecher at Exeter Hall was well received. 20 November 1863. p.186, c1.

6546 A. T. FOSS *to* **THE AAS. 12 November. Milton, N.H.** Reports on a well-attended AAS meeting in Strafford, which proceeded despite attempts by "hunkers" to disrupt it. 20 November 1863. p.186, c4.

6547 DANIEL FOSTER *to* **GARRISON. 1 November 1863. Chattanooga, Tn.** Reports on his unit's "baptism of blood" at the Battle of Lookout Mountain. 20 November 1863. p.187, c1.

6548 L. HOLMES *to* **THE** *LIBERATOR***. 5 November 1863. Orange, Ma.** Urges military reforms such as better food, better pay, and respect for the individual. 20 November 1863. p.188, c6.

6549 JOHN H. HOPKINS *to* **REV. ALONZO POTTER. 5 October 1863. Burlington, Vt.** Argues that slavery is not sinful; claims that the way a slave is treated constitutes the sin. 27 November 1863. p.189, c1.

6550 S. W. C. *to* **THE** *PORTLAND PRESS***. 26 October 1863. Bowdoenham, Me.** Discusses the published works of Wendell Phillips. 27 November 1863. p.190, c2.

6551 D. M. *to* **FRIEND. [extract] 5 October 1863. Norfolk, Va.** Describes poverty and despair in the South; notes the growing dependency on Union troops for sustenance. 27 November 1863. p.190, c5.

6552 HENRY W. BELLOWS *to* **THE** *NEW YORK TRIBUNE***. n.d. n.p.** Encloses a musical piece for churches entitled "President Hymn." 27 November 1863. p.191, c2.

6553 WILLIAM WHITING *to* **A GENTLEMAN IN BOSTON. 20 November 1863. Washington City.** Maintains that the exchange of prisoners of war has been hampered by the rebels' refusal to release colored Union soldiers and the South's policy of sending released rebels back into combat. 27 November 1863. p.191, c3.

6554 REV. DR. ELIOT *to* **THE** *DAILY ADVERTISER***. 30 October 1863. St. Louis.** Decries a system of conscription which drafts white boys but exempts colored slaves; feels embittered because loyal citizens are treated worse than slaveholders. 11 December 1863. p.197, c5.

6555 JOHN M. THAYER *to* **THE** *MISSOURI DEMOCRAT.* **14 November 1863. Little Rock, Ak.** Encloses extracts from a speech by Gen. E. W. Gantt, a rebel general who surrendered and now advocates a Union without slavery. 11 December 1863. p.198, c2.

6556 CHARLES SUMNER *to* **GARRISON. 24 November 1863. Boston.** Forwards a letter on emancipation in the West Indies. 11 December 1863. p.198, c6.

6557 ELLIS GRAY LORING *to* **SIR. 1847. Boston.** Analyzes emancipation and hopes that it will some day become a reality. 11 December 1863. p.198, c6.

6558 G. B. STEBBINS *to* **THE** *LIBERATOR.* **25 November 1863. Lyons, Mi.** Requests donations of clothing and shoes for colored troops; advocates holding a fair to benefit those troops. 11 December 1863. p.199, c1.

6559 DANIEL FOSTER *to* **GARRISON. 29 November 1863. Norfolk, Va.** Reports on colored troops and their unceasing enthusiasm in North Carolina. 11 December 1863. p.200, c4.

6560 LA ROY SUNDERLAND *to* **GARRISON. 24 November 1863. Boston.** States that he anxiously awaits the visit of George Thompson. 11 December 1863. p.200, c4.

6561 J. C. VAUGHAN *to* **JUDGE M. F. CONWAY. 23 November 1863. Leavenworth, Ks.** Expresses dissatisfaction with a speech by Conway advocating disunion. 18 December 1863. p.201, c4.

6562 M. F. CONWAY *to* **J. C. VAUGHAN. 27 November 1863. Lawrence, Ks.** Replies to Vaughan's criticism; asserts that he was opposed to war previously because he felt that preserving the Union meant preserving slavery. 18 December 1863. p.201, c4.

6563 ARTHUR TAPPAN *to* **GARRISON. 17 November 1863. New Haven.** Regrets that his ill health prevents him from attending the annual meeting of the AAS. 18 December 1863. p.202, c4.

6564 JOHN G. WHITTIER *to* **GARRISON. 24 November 1863. Amesbury.** Regrets that ill health prevents him from attending the annual meeting of the AAS. 18 December 1863. p.202, c4.

6565 JOSHUA R. GIDDINGS *to* **GARRISON. 30 November 1863. Jefferson.** Accepts an invitation to attend the annual meeting of the AAS. 18 December 1863. p.202, c4.

6566 JOHN RANKIN *to* **GARRISON. 19 November 1863. Ohio.** Regrets that he will be unable to attend the annual meeting of the AAS. 18 December 1863. p.202, c4.

6567 O. W. ALBEE *to* **MR. GARRISON. 12 November 1863. Marlboro.** Accepts an invitation to attend the annual meeting of the AAS. 18 December 1863. p.202, c4.

6568 SAMUEL FESSENDEN *to* **FRIEND GARRISON. n.d. n.p.** Regrets that he is unable to attend the annual meeting of the AAS. 18 December 1863. p.202, c4.

6569 JAMES FREEMAN CLARKE *to* **W. L. GARRISON. 26 November 1863. Jamaica Plain.** Regrets that he is unable to attend the annual meeting of the AAS. 18 December 1863. p.202, c5.

6570 THEODORE WELD *to* **FRIENDS. 1 December 1863. West Newton.** Regrets that he is unable to attend the annual meeting of the AAS. 18 December 1863. p.202, c5.

6571 ANGELINA WELD *to* **FRIENDS. 1 December 1863. West Newton.** Regrets that she is unable to attend the annual meeting of the AAS. 18 December 1863. p.202, c5.

6572 SARAH GRIMKE *to* **FRIENDS. 1 December 1863. West Newton.** Forwards an anti-slavery proxy to the annual meeting of the AAS. 18 December 1863. p.202, c5.

6573 O. B. FROTHINGHAM *to* **FRIEND GARRISON. 23 November 1863. New York.** Fears that his church activities will prevent his attending the annual meeting of the AAS. 18 December 1863. p.202, c5.

6574 OWEN LOVEJOY *to* **W. L. GARRISON. 22 November 1863. Princeton.** Responds to the invitation stating that he is unable to attend the annual meeting of the AAS. 18 December 1863. p.202, c5.

6575 B. GRATZ BROWN *to* **W. L. GARRISON. 21 November 1863. St. Louis.** Applauds the AAS for arousing the moral sense of the nation. 18 December 1863. p.203, c3.

6576 CHARLES SUMNER *to* **WM. LLOYD GARRISON. 1 December 1863. Boston.** Blesses the good work of the AAS. 18 December 1863. p.203, c3.

6577 ORSON S. MURRAY *to* **THE** *LIBERATOR.* **5 December 1863. Philadelphia.** Responds favorably to the annual meeting of the AAS; lauds the growth of the anti-slavery movement. 18 December 1863. p.204, c5.

6578 JOHN BROWN *to* **REV. LUTHER HUMPHREY. 19 November 1859. Charleston, Va.** Forwards biographical data while awaiting death. 18 December 1863. p.204, c6.

6579 GRAYBEARD *to* **THE** *INDEPENDENT.* **5 December.Philadelphia.** Thanks God for the change he sees in the American people; rejoices that abolitionist meetings are well attended and no longer disrupted by mobs. 25 December 1863. p.205, c2.

6580 N. H. WHITING *to* **FRIEND GARRISON. 28 November 1863. Boston.** Explains that duties at home prevent him from attending the meeting of the AAS. 25 December 1863. p.205, c2.

6581 M. F. CONWAY *to* **W. L. GARRISON. 20 November 1863. Lawrence, Ks.** Regrets that duties in Kansas prohibit his attending the annual meeting of the AAS. 25 December 1863. p.205, c4.

6582 GEORGE W. JULIAN *to* **GENTLEMEN. 27 November 1863. Centreville, In.** Expresses regret that he cannot attend the AAS meeting. 25 December 1863. p.205, c5.

6583 REV. A. BATTLES *to* **MR. GARRISON. 27 November 1863. Bangor, Me.** Forgoes an invitation to attend the meeting of the AAS. 25 December 1863. p,205, c6.

[1864]

6584 DAVID THURSTON *to* **WM. LLOYD GARRISON. 20 November 1863. Litchfield Corner, Me.** Asserts that he is the oldest living member of the AAS and has never deviated from its principles. 1 January 1864. p.1, c1.

6585 CHARLES G. AMES *to* **MR. GARRISON. 1 December 1863. Albany, N.Y.** Regrets that he is unable to attend the AAS meeting. 1 January 1864. p.1, c5.

6586 GEO. E. BAKER *to* **GENTLEMEN. 2 December 1863. Washington, D.C.** Regrets that circumstances prevent his attending the AAS meeting; urges the "rapid extinction" of slavery. 1 January 1864. p.1, c6.

6587 GEO. THOMPSON *to* **GARRISON. 8 December 1863. London.** Assesses the Union war effort and military situation; foresees war resulting in total abolition and Negro suffrage. 1 January 1864. p.3, c4.

6588 MRS. E. C. STANTON *to* **GARRISON. 13 December 1863. New York.** Comments on the constitutional amendment voted on at the AAS meeting; favors a petition drive for universal emancipation. 1 January 1864. p.4, c4.

6589 AGENOR DE GASPARIN, AUGUSTIN COCHIN, EDOUARD LABOULAYE, AND HENRI MARTIN *to* **LOYAL NATIONAL LEAGUE OF NEW YORK. 31 October 1863. Paris.** Apologize for Europe's misgivings over the Union cause and for support given to the Confederacy; hope that the end of the war is near and that slavery will be abolished. 8 January 1864. p.6, c1.

6590 SARAH CLAY *to* **MR. GARRISON. 28 December 1863. Lowell.** Encloses a resolution in favor of freeing and arming slaves, which was passed at a meeting of the Middlesex County AS. 8 January 1864. p.7, c3.

6591 DANIEL FOSTER *to* **GARRISON. 29 December 1863. Norfolk, Va.** Recapitulates the events of the year; discusses the great advantage now enjoyed by the Union. 8 January 1864. p.8, c4.

6592 REV. THOMAS CALAHAN *to* **CAPT. JAMES A. EHIN. 10 November. Goodrich's Landing, La.** Expresses amazement at the freed slaves' enthusiasm for learning; praises their fighting ability. 8 January 1864. p.8, c6.

6593 JOHN JAY *to* **COMMITTEE OF AAS. n.d. n.p.** Commemorates the thirtieth anniversary of the AAS. 15 January 1864. p.9, c1.

6594 JESSE STEDMAN *to* **SIR. n.d. n.p.** Acknowledges receipt of an invitation to attend the thirtieth anniversary of the AAS; urges abolitionists to continue the cause. 15 January 1864. p.9, c4.

6595 REV. JEHIEL CLAFLIN *to* **GARRISON. 28 November 1863. E. Westmoreland, N.H.** Regrets that he will be unable to attend the thirtieth anniversary of the AAS. 15 January 1864. p.9, c5.

6596 SARAH M. GRIMKE *to* **BROTHER GARRISON. 30 November 1863. W. Newton.** Wishes to accept the invitation to attend the thirtieth anniversary of the AAS. 15 January 1864. p.9, c5.

6597 ARCHIBALD A. McINTYRE *to* **J. M. McKIM. 1 December 1863. Philadelphia.** Declines the invitation to attend the thirtieth anniversary of the AAS. 15 January 1864. p.9, c5.

6598 JOSHUA COFFIN *to* **GARRISON. 30 November 1863. Newbury.** Regrets that he will be unable to attend the thirtieth anniversary of the AAS; comments on the anti-slavery progress. 15 January 1864. p.9, c5.

6599 JOHN M. LANGSTON *to* **W. L. GARRISON. 3 December 1863. Oberlin.** Regrets that ill health prevents him from attending the thirtieth anniversary of the AAS. 15 January 1864. p.9, c6.

6600 GEORGE WM. CURTIS *to* **SIR. November 1863. Staten Island, N.Y.** Regrets that he is unable to attend the thirtieth anniversary of the AAS. 15 January 1864. p.9, c6.

6601 ELIZA WIGHAM *to* **THE** *SCOTSMAN.* **11 November 1863. n.p.** Accuses those who did not listen to the abolitionists of forcing the nation into war. 15 January 1864. p.9, c6.

6602 SAMUEL G. HOWE *to* **T. D. ELLIOT. n.d. n.p.** Urges justice and nothing less than complete equality for the freedmen. 15 January 1864. p.10, c1.

6603 WILLIAM THIRDS *to* **GARRISON. 12 December 1863. Natchez, Ms.** Expresses amusement at the prospect of tracking down rebel "bandits" with colored freedmen in Mississippi. 15 January 1864. p.12, c3.

6604 GEORGE W. STACY *to* **GARRISON. n.d. n.p.** Commends Mr. Wm. Denton's lectures on geology. 15 January 1864. p.12, c4.

6605 A. W. THAYER *to* **W. L. GARRISON. 8 December 1863. Northampton.** Recounts Garrison's former imprisonment; notes that J. G. Whittier received money from Henry Clay to pay the fine to release Garrison. 15 January 1864. p.12, c4.

6606 GEO. SUNTER *to* **MR. GARRISON. 4 January 1864. Brantford, Canada West.** Relates reminiscences prompted by an AAS meeting; urges maintaining the "spirit" of abolition after slavery is abolished. 22 January 1864. p.14, c3.

6607 GEO. THOMPSON *to* **GARRISON. 1 January 1864. London.** Regrets that he is unable to attend the AAS meeting. 22 January 1864. p.14, c4.

6608 J. G. WHITTIER *to* **GARRISON. 17 January 1864. Amesbury.** Upholds Thayer's letter of 15 January regarding Henry Clay's offer to help release Garrison from jail. 22 January 1864. p.14, c4.

6609 DANIEL FOSTER *to* **GARRISON. 4 January 1864. Norfolk, Va.** Reports that he and colored troops are helping slaves to escape. 22 January 1864. p.14, c5.

6610 ANDREW PATON *to* **WM. I. BOWDITCH. 26 December 1863. Glasgow.** Sends money to help support the AAS; discusses how Lincoln has increased British support for the war. 22 January 1864. p.14, c6.

6611 C. V. S. *to* **MR. EDITOR. 6 January 1864. Washington.** Assails Mayor Wallach of the District of Columbia for opposing the use of Negro troops. 22 January 1864. p.14, c6.

6612 G. *to* *LONDON DAILY NEWS.* **n.d. n.p.** Suggests that the North raise a monument to Colonel Shaw, who died gallantly at the head of his troops. 22 January 1864. p.15, c3.

6613 JEFFERSON DAVIS *to* **POPE PIUS IX. [from** *La France***] 23 September 1863. Richmond.** Thanks the pontiff for his efforts on behalf of peace; claims that the South is also praying for an end to the devastation of the country. 29 January 1864. p.17, c1.

6614 PIUS IX *to* **JEFFERSON DAVIS. [from** *La France***] 3 December 1863. Rome.** States that he was pleased to learn that the South also prays for peace. 29 January 1864. p.17, c1.

6615 NEW ENGLANDER *to* *JOURNAL OF COMMERCE.* **8 January 1864. New York.** Thanks the *Journal of Commerce* for exposing the misrepresentation of the early Puritans which is prevalent in western states. 29 January 1864. p.17, c1.

6616 J. L. P. *to* *DOVER MORNING STAR.* **6 January 1864. New York.** Reports on a gathering of Negroes at Cooper Institute; states that they sang patriotic songs and urged Negroes to volunteer to fight for the Union. 29 January 1864. p.18, c1.

6617 S. J. R. *to* **THE** *LIBERATOR.* **18 January 1864. Folly Island, S.C.** Argues that colored troops should be led by colored officers. 29 January 1864. p.18, c4.

6618 JESSE STEDMAN *to* **JUSTIN S. MORRILL. 19 January 1864. Washington.** Favors providing each slave with a book, a rifle, land, and the right to vote in order to end slavery permanently. 29 January 1864. p.18, c5.

6619 HENRY C. WRIGHT *to* **FRIEND GARRISON. 1 January 1864. West Randolph.** Demands that Lincoln insure freedom to slaves in his Reconstruction plans. 29 January 1864. p.18, c5.

6620 J. T. EVERETT *to* **BROTHER GARRISON. 10 January 1864. Everettville.** Credits Garrison's moral vision for aiding the progress of abolition. 29 January 1864. p.18, c6.

6621 LUCY CHASE *to* **MR. GARRISON. December 1863. Norfolk, Va.** Reports that General Butler has improved conditions for the Negroes in Norfolk. 29 January 1864. p.19, c1.

6622 JOHN S. BROWN *to* **WM. LLOYD GARRISON. 6 January 1864. Lawrence, Ks.** Regrets that Negroes in Kansas suffer because of Quantrell. 29 January 1864. p.19, c2.

6623 n.n. *to* **WM. LLOYD GARRISON. 22 January 1864. Portland.** Wishes Garrison could see the enthusiastic crowd which greeted Frederick Douglass' address in Portland. 29 January 1864. p.19, c2.

6624 DANIEL FOSTER *to* **GARRISON. 22 January 1864. Norfolk, Va.** Regrets the death of John Cutler, who led a Christian life and worked in the abolitionist cause. 29 January 1864. p.19, c2.

6625 ALFRED H. LOVE *to* **WM. LLOYD GARRISON. 7 January 1864. Philadelphia.** Opposes drafting conscientious objectors. 29 January 1864. p.20, c3.

6626 ANGELINA J. KNOX *to* **MR. GARRISON. 15 January 1864. Boston.** Forwards a letter from her husband; comments on the sorrow which slavery has caused her family. 29 January 1864. p.20, c5.

6627 THOMAS P. KNOX *to* **GARRISON. 5 December 1863. Beaufort, S.C.** Notes with irony that a bell which used to call slaves to the field was used to announce a meeting in Coosaw Island on the anniversary of Brown's martyrdom. 29 January 1864. p.20, c5.

6628 n.n. *to* **THE** *MORNING STAR.* **20 January 1864. New York.** Applauds the speech by Frederick Douglass at Cooper Institute. 5 February 1864. p.21, c4.

6629 GEO. THOMPSON *to* **GARRISON. 9 January 1864. London.** Expresses gratitude for the articles written about him. 5 February 1864. p.22, c1.

6630 A. W. THAYER *to* **W. L. GARRISON. 27 January 1864.** Argues that had Henry Clay lived, he would have urged peace through compromise, not through emancipation. 5 February 1864. p.22, c6.

6631 REV. SAMUEL MAY *to* **n.n. [extract] Syracuse, N.Y.** Insists that newly freed people of color should have housing priority in the South as compensation for their years of suffering. 5 February 1864. p.22, c6.

6632 F. J. W. *to* **FRIEND GARRISON. 1 January 1864. Port Royal, S.C.** Expresses anxiety because he is unsure how best to guide the freedmen. 5 February 1864. p.24, c5.

6633 W. FARMER *to* **THE** *LIBERATOR*. **15 January 1864. London.** Asserts that public opinion in England overwhelmingly supports abolition. 12 February 1864. p.25, c1.

6634 JOHN BRIGHT *to* **F. W. CHESSON. 14 January. Rochdale.** Commends Geo. Thompson on his departure from London; cites him as "the real liberator" of slaves in England. 12 February 1864. p.25, c5.

6635 P. A. TAYLOR *to* **SIR. 12 January. Aldermanbury.** Regrets that he is unable to be present for Geo. Thompson's departure. 12 February 1864. p.25, c5.

6636 GOLDWIN SMITH *to* **SIR. 4 January. Oxford.** Expresses appreciation for Thompson's efforts. 12 February 1864. p.25, c5.

6637 J. E. CAIRNES *to* **SIR. 13 January. Dublin.** Regrets that he cannot attend Geo.Thompson's departure. 12 February 1864. p.25, c5.

6638 N. W. GOVE *to* **GARRISON. 23 January 1864. New Orleans.** Points to an abolitionist address as a sign of growing free speech in New Orleans. 12 February 1864. p.26, c5.

6639 A. H. LOVE *to* **WM. LLOYD GARRISON. 2 February 1864. Philadelphia.** Urges a policy of genuine non-resistance for conscientious objectors. 12 February1864. p.26, c6.

6640 JOHN WEST *to* **GARRISON. 7 February 1864. Philadelphia.** Asserts that the right to life is paramount and that conscription conflicts with that right. 12 February 1864. p.27, c1.

6641 DAVID WELLMAN *to* **W. L. GARRISON. 1864. Woodbury, Ct.** Praises the *Liberator*; believes that the war could have ended sooner if Lincoln had committed troops in 1861. 12 February 1864. p.28, c4.

6642 SEWARD MITCHELL *to* **BROTHER GARRISON. 31 January 1864. Cornville, Me.** Describes non-resistance as outdated; asserts that tyrants only understand war. 12 February 1864. p.28, c5.

6643 WILLIAM FARMER *to* **THE** *LIBERATOR*. **n.d. n.p.** Announces his biography of George Thompson. 19 February 1864. p.29, c2.

6644 SARAH JANE CLEMESHA *to* **GEORGE THOMPSON. 18 January 1864. Preston.** Reports that the Preston AS praises Thompson on his return to the United States and urges him to continue his abolitionist work. 19 February 1864. p.30, c1.

6645 JOHN A. ANDREW AND CITIZENS *to* **GEORGE THOMPSON. 11 February 1864. Boston.** Offer to hold a public reception for Thompson to honor his defense of the Union and his efforts to change British sentiment on slavery. 19 February 1864. p.30, c3.

6646 GEORGE THOMPSON *to* **JOHN A. ANDREW, J. E. FIELD, A. H. BULLOCK, JAMES L. LITTLE, SAMUEL G. WARD, AND OTHERS. 12 February 1864. Boston.** Accepts the offer of a reception to honor his work in England; adds that 23 February would be convenient. 19 February 1864. p.30, c3.

6647 SAMUEL MAY, JR. *to* **MRS. MARY MAY, LOUISA LORING, AND OTHERS. 26 January 1864. Syracuse, N.Y.** Regrets that he cannot attend the subscription anniversary; forwards a contribution. 19 February 1864. p.30, c5.

6648 EDGAR KETCHUM *to* **FRIENDS. 20 January 1864. New York.** Encloses an "offering and benediction" to honor the thirtieth anniversary of the AAS. 19 February 1864. p.30, c5.

6649 SAMUEL GALE *to* **MRS. L. MARIA CHILD. [extract] n.d. Montreal.** Urges the AAS not to relax its efforts; encloses $500 for its anniversary. 19 February 1864. p.30, c5.

6650 TYLER BIGELOW *to* **MISS ABBY FRANCIS. 19 January 1864. Watertown.** Declares that he is gratified by the invitation to the AAS anniversary; encloses a contribution. 19 February 1864. p.30, c5.

6651 BENJ. F. BUTLER, MAJ. GEN. *to* **MRS. MARY MAY, AND OTHERS. 22 January 1864. Fortress Monroe.** Reports that military duties will prevent his attending the AAS meeting. 19 February 1864. p.30, c5.

6652 J. M. HAWKS *to* **FRIEND GARRISON. 12 January 1864. Hilton Head, S.C.** Claims that "even the silvery tones of Wendell Phillips are not more eloquent than the glistening bayonets of black men. . ." 19 February 1864. p.30, c5.

6653 NATHANIEL HALL *to* **MR. MAY. 27 January 1864. Dorchester.** Regrets that illness prevents his attendance at the AAS anniversary. 19 February 1864. p.30, c6.

6654 FREDERICK FROTHINGHAM *to* **FRIENDS. 29 January 1864. n.p.** Encloses thirty dollars for the AAS. 19 February 1864. p.30, c6.

6655 JOHN T. HILTON *to* **MRS. MARY MAY. 26 January 1864. Brighton.** Forwards "God's blessing" and one dollar for the AAS anniversary. 19 February 1864. p.30, c6.

6656 DANIEL B. STEDMAN *to* **MISS CAROLINE THAYER. [extract] n.d. Boston.** Encloses twenty dollars for the AAS. 19 February 1864. p.30, c6.

6657 L. MARIA CHILD *to* **FRIEND. n.d. n.p.** Reports on the success of the AAS. 19 February 1864. p.31, c3.

6658 M. DU PAYS *to* **THE *LIBERATOR*. 11 February 1864. New York.** Assails Lincoln for interpreting freedom as the simple absence of slavery; warns of Republican "Copperheads." 19 February 1864. p.31, c4.

6659 JAMES REDPATH *to* **WM. LLOYD GARRISON. 12 February 1864. Boston.** Announces that a fund for the families of veterans of the John Brown raid has been established by the people of Haiti. 19 February 1864. p.31, c6.

6660 JOHN GORDON *to* **FRIEND GARRISON. 11 February 1864. Salem, Oh.** Claims that the thirtieth anniversary of the AAS foretells the ultimate triumph of the anti-slavery cause. 26 February 1864. p.35, c1.

6661 H. F. M. *to* **THE *LIBERATOR*. 15 February 1864. New York.** Urges that the petition drive to demand total emancipation be continued. 26 February 1864. p.35, c1.

6662 WILLIAM FARMER *to* **THE *LIBERATOR*. n.d. England.** Traces the abolitionist career of Geo. Thompson from 1832 to the present. 26 February 1864. p.36, c1.

6663 G. T. RUBY *to* **THE *LIBERATOR*. 4 February 1864. New Orleans.** Expresses pleasure at the growth of the free colored population in New Orleans; extends an invitation to Frederick Douglass to visit and lecture. 26 February 1864. p.36, c6.

6664 M. DU PAYS *to* **THE** *LIBERATOR.* **25 February 1864. New York.** Expresses concern about the efficacy of Lincoln's Reconstruction policy. 4 March 1864. p.39, c3.

6665 L. MARIA CHILD *to* **THE** *NATIONAL ANTI-SLAVERY STANDARD.* **n.d. n.p.** Reminiscences about George Thompson's first visit to the United States. 4 March 1864. p.39, c5.

6666 WILLIAM FARMER *to* **THE** *LIBERATOR.* **n.d. n.p.** Provides biographical data on George Thompson; discusses Thompson's involvement with the Anti-Corn Law League and abolition. 11 March 1864. p.41, c2.

6667 JAMES McKAYE *to* **THE** *EVENING POST.* **1 March 1864. New York.** Gives statistics on the high literacy rate and relative wealth of free colored people in Louisiana before the war. 11 March 1864. p.42, c1.

6668 JNO. PIERPONT, LEWIS CLEPHANE, W. A. CROFFAT, C. STORRS, JOHN R. FRENCH, N. B. DEVEREUX, CHAS. ROESER, AND Z. RICHARDS *to* **GEO. THOMPSON. 27 February 1864. Washington, D.C.** Invite Thompson to lecture in Washington. 11 March 1864. p.42, c2.

6669 JESSE STEDMAN *to* **J. H. LANE. 29 February 1864. Springfield, Vt.** Criticizes a lecture by Lane advocating a compromise with slavery in Kansas. 11 March 1864. p.42, c6.

6670 M. L. WHITTEN *to* **MR. EDITOR [W. L. GARRISON]. 22 February 1864. Mitchell's Station, Va.** Asserts that the North has the right to impose a Reconstruction plan forbidding slavery. 11 March 1864. p.42, c6.

6671 D. B. H. *to* **THE** *LIBERATOR.* **n.d. Providence, R.I.** Censures separate schools for colored children in Providence. 11 March 1864. p.43, c1.

6672 SUSAN B. ANTHONY *to* **FRIEND. 7 March 1864. New York.** Forwards a sample petition urging Congress constitutionally to outlaw slavery. 11 March 1864. p.43, c2.

6673 W. FARMER *to* **THE** *LIBERATOR.* **5 February 1864. London.** Describes the indifferent and divided reactions in England to American affairs. 11 March 1864. p.44, c1.

6674 A. BROOKE *to* **MR. GARRISON. 20 February 1864. Marlboro, Oh.** Urges the nation to adhere to "divine principles" and avoid so-called "necessary evils" such as conscription and prisons. 11 March 1864. p.44, c4.

6675 WILLIAM FARMER *to* **THE** *LIBERATOR.* **n.d. n.p.** Describes the involvement of George Thompson in the affairs of the East India Company. 18 March 1864. p.46, c2.

6676 MONCURE D. CONWAY *to* **n.n. 20 February. London.** Fears that abolitionist criticisms of Lincoln are being overshadowed by pro-slavery censure; doubts that Lincoln is committed to the anti-slavery cause. 18 March 1864. p.46, c4.

6677 M. DU PAYS *to* **THE** *LIBERATOR.* **10 March 1864. New York.** Discusses Union politics and Lincoln's re-election plans. 18 March 1864. p.46, c4.

6678 FIGLIO *to* **THE** *LIBERATOR.* **12 March 1864. Brooklyn, N.Y.** Reports on George Thompson's lectures in the Plymouth churches. 18 March 1864. p.46, c5.

6679 JOHN G. FEE *to* **WENDELL PHILLIPS. n.d. n.p.** Assails the amnesty proclamation for rebels as unnecessary and harmful to the Union. 18 March 1864. p.47, c1.

6680 WILLIAM FARMER *to* **THE** *LIBERATOR*. **1864. London.** Traces George Thompson's anti-slavery career, focusing on his election to Parliament in 1847. 25 March 1864. p.49, c2.

6681 O. R. SINGLETON *to* **J. B. HANCOCK. 1864. Richmond.** A rebel assesses conditions in the South as "gloomy." 25 March 1864. p.50, c1.

6682 ALEX A. BULLOCK, J. M. EARLE, AND T. W. HARMOND *to* **GEORGE THOMPSON. n.d. Worcester.** Invite Thompson to speak in Worcester. 25 March 1864. p.50, c2.

6683 GEO. THOMPSON *to* **GENTLEMEN. 19 March 1864. Boston.** Accepts the invitation to speak in Worcester. 25 March 1864. p.50, c2.

6684 GERRIT SMITH *to* **WILLIAM BARNES. 12 March 1864. Peterboro'.** Expresses surprise at winning the Emancipation Proclamation as a lottery prize; requests that it be sold to raise funds for the Union cause. 25 March 1864. p.50, c6.

6685 n.n. *to* **THE** *BOSTON JOURNAL*. **19 March 1864. Fortress Monroe.** Describes Negro troops as orderly, capable, and disciplined; states that respect for General Butler runs high among freed colored people. 25 March 1864. p.51, c2.

6686 n.n. *to* **THE** *LIBERATOR*. **n.d. n.p.** Favorably reviews a pamphlet written by Charles Babcock advocating colored emigration to Honduras and claiming that it has many advantages over Haiti. 25 March 1864. p.52, c2.

6687 OWEN LOVEJOY *to* **FRIEND GARRISON. 22 February 1864. Washington.** Supports Garrison's statement that Lincoln is not "the best conceivable President, but he is the best possible." 1 April 1864. p.54, c2.

6688 M. DU PAYS *to* **THE** *LIBERATOR*. **24 March 1864. New York.** Reports on anti-slavery election victories in Arkansas and Tennessee; states that the rebellion is lost, provided that the Copperheads are defeated at the polls in November. 1 April 1864. p.54, c6.

6689 B. F. R. *to* **MR. EDITOR [W. L. GARRISON]. 22 March 1864. Boston.** Reports on the success enjoyed by "Uncle Tom" Father Henson, a fugitive slave who is a leading farmer in Canada. 1 April 1864. p.55, c3.

6690 BENJ. F. COOK, MAJOR *to* **EDWIN M. STANTON, SEC. OF WAR. 14 December 1863. Camp near Kelly's Fort.** Reports that John Wesley Pratt refuses to obey orders and incites the troops with "treasonable language." 1 April 1864. p.56, c2.

6691 J. WESLEY PRATT *to* **CAPT. J. W. D. HALL. 2 October 1863. Quincy.** Asserts that he will not evade or obstruct the government, but adds that his first duty is to humanity; declares that he will not fight in the army. 1 April 1864. p.56, c2.

6692 J. WESLEY PRATT *to* **FRIEND GARRISON. 16 March 1864. Quincy, Ma.** Forwards correspondence outlining his belief in non-resistance. 1 April 1864. p.56, c2.

6693 L. J. BARROWS *to* **F. G. SHAW. 20 March 1864. Long Island Sound.** Refutes the slanderous claim that white teachers at Port Royal, South Carolina, were having mulatto babies; defends the teachers' character and morals. 8 April 1864. p.57, c4.

6694 GERRIT SMITH *to* **WM. LLOYD GARRISON. 17 March 1864. Peterboro'.** Contributes to the fund for George Thompson. 8 April 1864. p.58, c3.

6695 PRO BONO PUBLICO *to* **FRIEND GARRISON. n.d. Boston.** Praises Turkish and Roman baths for their therapeutic values. 8 April 1864. p.60, c3.

6696 WM. S. FLANDERS *to* **GARRISON. 16 March 1864. Cornville, Me.** Accepts the concept of non-resistance, but asserts that an attack on equal rights is an attack on the Republic which must be repulsed. 8 April 1864. p.60, c3.

6697 JESSE STEDMAN *to* **MR. EDITOR [W. L. GARRISON]. n.d. Springfield, Vt.** Denounces Lincoln's proposal to allow pro-slavery forces back into the Union. 8 April 1864. p.60, c4.

6698 D. S. WHITNEY *to* **MR. GARRISON. 27 March 1864. Southboro'.** Supports Garrison's position that Lincoln is "the man of the hour" despite his faults. 8 April 1864. p.60, c4.

6699 n.n. *to* **n.n. [extract] 4 March. Jamaica.** Reports on the progress of black people in Jamaica; states that he would put them on a par with any other nation in the world. 8 April 1864. p.60, c4.

6700 JOHN W. FORNEY *to* **J. MILLER McKIM. 2 April 1864. Washington.** Describes his defection from the pro-slavery Democratic Party. 15 April 1864. p.61, c5.

6701 GEORGE THOMPSON *to* **JAMES R. MORRIS. 5 April 1864. Washington.** Questions the validity of the resolution which rescinded the invitation for him to speak to Congress because of his alleged support for disunion in 1834; denies ever having supported disunion. 15 April 1864. p.62, c4.

6702 J. R. MORRIS *to* **GEORGE THOMPSON. 6 April. Washington.** Uses Thompson's letter to Congress advocating disunion in 1834 to defend the resolution rescinding the invitation for Thompson to address Congress. 15 April 1864. p.62, c5.

6703 n.n. *to* **THE** *LIBERATOR*. **6 April 1864. Washington.** Expresses pleasure with an address delivered by George Thompson in Washington during which he urged no compromise with slavery. 15 April 1864. p.63, c2.

6704 M. DU PAYS *to* **THE** *LIBERATOR*. **7 April 1864. New York.** Forwards the results of the Louisiana election. 15 April 1864. p.63, c3.

6705 A. M. POWELL *to* **n.n. [extract] 13 April. Ghent, N.Y.** Expresses gratification at the Senate passage of an anti-slavery amendment to the Constitution. 22 April 1864. p.66, c4.

6706 ALFRED H. LOVE *to* **GARRISON. 18 April 1864. Philadelphia.** Reports on George Thompson's reception in Philadelphia. 22 April 1864. p.66, c6.

6707 DANIEL MANN *to* **MR. MAY. 1864. Folly Island, S.C.** Describes anti-slavery struggle in the South as a military and philanthropic effort. 22 April 1864. p.66, c6.

6708 HENRY C. WRIGHT *to* **GARRISON. 10 April 1864. Easton, N.Y.** Announces his lecture themes of "Abolition and Prohibition." 22 April 1864. p.67, c1.

6709 GEORGE TRASK *to* **GARRISON. n.d. Fitchburg, Ma.** Assails the use of alcohol in the army. 22 April 1864. p.68, c3.

6710 THOMAS H. BARKER *to* **GOV. ANDREW. 31 March 1864. Manchester.** Encloses a resolution praising the abolitionist work of George Thompson in England. 29 April 1864. p.70, c4.

6711 THOMAS EVANS *to* **W. L. GARRISON. 25 March 1864. Lawrence, Ma.** A working man voices his opposition to slavery. 29 April 1864. p.70, c6.

6712 FRANCES D. GAGE *to* **THE** *LIBERATOR.* **12 April 1864. St. Louis, Mo.** Appeals for clothes and money to assist freedmen in Mississippi. 29 April 1864. p.71, c2.

6713 E. H. K. *to* **MR. GARRISON. 25 April 1864. Princeton.** Mourns the death of George S. Flint, a former Worcester AS president. 29 April 1864. p.71, c5.

6714 M. DU PAYS *to* **THE** *LIBERATOR.* **21 April 1864. New York.** Praises the Senate vote to accept an anti-slavery constitutional amendment. 29 April 1864. p.72, c4.

6715 A CITIZEN *to* *BOSTON JOURNAL.* **n.d. n.p.** Assails the barbarism of the rebel army at Columbus, Kentucky, which murdered all captured Negro troops; censures the *Courier*'s pitiful apology for the rebels. 29 April 1864. p.72, c6.

6716 A. LINCOLN *to* **MR. A. G. HODGES. 4 April 1864. Washington.** Declares that the use of colored troops is a gain for the Union cause. 6 May 1864. p.73, c5.

6717 E. A. STUDWELL *to* **THE** *NATIONAL ANTI-SLAVERY STANDARD.* **25 April 1864. Rochester, N.Y.** Praises the welcome given George Thompson in Rochester. 6 May 1864. p.74, c4.

6718 GEORGE THOMPSON *to* **GARRISON. 30 April 1864. Syracuse, N.Y.** Describes his tour of America. 6 May 1864. p.74, c4.

6719 CAROLINE H. DALL *to* **THE WOMEN OF THE LOYAL LEAGUE. 1 May 1864. Boston.** Criticizes women of the Loyal League for opposing Lincoln. 6 May 1864. p.74, c6.

6720 ONE OF THE VOTERS *to* **THE** *LIBERATOR.* **n.d. n.p.** Desires that the president be a man whom the majority of loyal people will "delight to honor." 6 May 1864. p.75, c4.

6721 FRANCES D. GAGE *to* **SAMUEL MAY, JR. 19 April 1864. St. Louis.** Acknowledges receipt of contributions to assist escaped slaves. 6 May 1864. p.75, c4.

6722 E. H. H. *to* **MR. GARRISON. 25 April 1864. Princeton, Ma.** Argues that the government has no more right to conscript than to enslave. 6 May 1864. p.76, c3.

6723 L. P. F. *to* **SIR. 25 April 1864. Vicksburg.** Reports on rebel atrocities near Vicksburg. 6 May 1864. p.76, c4.

6724 TOM ANCHORITE *to* **THE** *HOUSTON DAILY TELEGRAPH.* **30 April 1864. n.p.** Relates tale of rebel soldiers using Yankee bones and skulls for a game of ten-pin; regrets that he was unable to participate. 6 May 1864. p.76, c6.

6725 EDWARD BATES, ATTORNEY GENERAL *to* **PRESIDENT LINCOLN. 23 April. Washington. D.C.** States his opinion that Samuel Harrison, a colored chaplain in the army, is entitled to full wages, not the wages paid those of "African descent" as prescribed by law. 13 May 1864. p.77, c2.

6726 JAMES WALLACE, J. B. H. FERIS, S. G. WRIGHT, H. A. McKELVBY, J. B. WEEKS, J. G. THORN, AND WM. G. THOMPSON, M.D. *to* **GEN. TUTTLE. 1 April 1864. Natchez, Ms.** Request that Tuttle rescind his order requiring that all freed colored citizens be removed from Natchez to prevent the spread of communicable diseases; argue that the order is demoralizing to colored troops fighting for the Union. 13 May 1864. p.77, c5.

6727 M. DU PAYS *to* **THE** *LIBERATOR.* **6 May 1864. New York.** Discusses anti-slavery legislatures in Arkansas and Virginia. 13 May 1864. p.78, c6.

6728 WENDELL PHILLIPS *to* **JUDGE STALLO. n.d. n.p.** Supports total victory over the South, the confiscation of rebel lands, and the extension of universal suffrage; believes that the current Lincoln administration must be defeated in order to achieve these ends. 13 May 1864. p.79, c1.

6729 DAVID D. PORTER *to* **HON. GIDEON WELLES. 7 April 1864. Off Grand Ecore, La.** Mourns the death of Lt. Joseph P. Couthouy, commander of the U.S.S. *Chilicothe.* 13 May 1864. p.79, c5.

6730 J. G. DODGE *to* **GARRISON. 19 April 1864. Jacksonville, Fl.** Reports on conditions of freedmen in Florida; notes that they are industrious and desirous of education. 13 May 1864. p.80, c1.

6731 CARLETON *to* **THE** *BOSTON JOURNAL.* **25 April 1864. Washington.** Assails rebel massacres as savage; urges government retaliation against those who are "outside the pale of civilization." 13 May 1864. p.80, c5.

6732 Q. A. GILLMORE *to* **MAJ. GEN. H. W. HALLECK. 14 December 1863. Folly Island, S.C.** Advocates military reforms, including equal pay for colored and white soldiers, land for families of colored soldiers, and colored officers for colored regiments. 20 May 1864. p.84, c2.

6733 A RAIDER *to* **THE** *BALTIMORE AMERICAN.* **n.d. n.p.** Relates atrocities inflicted by rebels on Union soldiers held captive by Colonel Dahlgren. 20 May 1864. p.84, c3.

6734 M. DU PAYS *to* **THE** *LIBERATOR.* **19 May 1864. New York.** Lauds General Grant for maintaining high morale in the Union army. 27 May 1864. p.87, c3.

6735 EDWARD BATES *to* **PRESIDENT LINCOLN. 18 May 1864. Boston.** Discusses the case of Rev. Harrison, a colored chaplain who demanded the same wages as white soldiers; urges that Lincoln prevent this from happening in the future. 27 May 1864. p.87, c5.

6736 E. CADY STANTON *to* **MRS. DALL. 7 May 1864. New York.** Asserts that politics as well as morals belong to a woman's proper spheres of action. 3 June 1864. p.89, c1.

6737 A FRIEND TO THE CAUSE *to* **MR. GARRISON. 16 April 1864. n.p.** Urges perseverance in the anti-slavery cause and opposition to slavery on moral, not political grounds. 3 June 1864. p.89, c2.

6738 B. CHASE *to* **THE** *LIBERATOR.* **n.d. Auburn, N.H.** Stresses the responsibility of abolitionists to guarantee equality to freedmen. 3 June 1864. p.90, c4.

6739 D. B. WILSON *to* **THE** *LIBERATOR.* **31 May 1864. Boston.** Forwards resolutions from the spiritual convention opposing slavery. 3 June 1864. p.90, c5.

6740 WM. S. FLANDERS *to* **MR. GARRISON. 11 May 1864. Cornville, Me.** Refutes Gerrit Smith's statement that some of John Brown's judgments were "unsound and visionary"; asserts that, in light of history, they were "sound and practical." 3 June 1864. p.90, c6.

6741 WENDELL PHILLIPS *to* **EDWARD GILBERT. 27 May 1864. Boston.** Criticizes Lincoln's plan for Reconstruction as upholding the status quo. 3 June 1864. p.91, c1.

6742 EDWIN STANTON *to* **MAJOR GENERAL DIX. 31 May. Washington.** Reports that Union troops repulsed a rebel attack on the east side of the Appomatox. 3 June 1864. p.91, c5.

6743 R. P. BUCKLAND *to* **D. L. JUNE. 8 May 1864. Memphis.** Refutes accusations in newspaper articles which claimed that he callously moved slave children away from the contraband camp; asserts that he did it for the children's welfare. 3 June 1864. p.92, c2.

6744 DON MARINO VAQUE AND DON PAUL ARMENGOL *to* **LADY DONNA CAROLINA CORONADO DE PERRY. October 1863. Barcelona.** Praise a prophetic letter written to Lincoln in 1861 by the wife of the secretary of the United States legation at Madrid; explain that the letter predicts the outbreak and liberation of the slave. 3 June 1864. p.92, c3.

6745 CAROLINA CORONADO *to* **DON MARINO VAQUE, DON PAUL ARMENGOL. 14 January 1864. Madrid.** States that she is surprised and pleased that the Catalan Liberals remember her letter to Lincoln; urges them not to fear for the slaves because the victorious North will set them free. 3 June 1864. p.92, c3.

6746 M. DU PAYS *to* **THE** *LIBERATOR.* **2 June 1864. New York.** Decries the cost and waste of war; supports Lincoln because he feels that the nation has less to fear from a civilian than from a military hero. 10 June 1864. p.95, c5.

6747 J. C. FREMONT *to* **MESSRS. W. G. SNETHEN, EDWARD GILBERT, CASPAR BUTZ, CHARLES E. MOSS, N. P. SAWYER. 4 June 1864. New York.** States his belief that the re-election of Lincoln will mean the end of constitutional liberty in America; accepts the nomination for the presidency on the basis of patriotism. 10 June 1864. p.95, c6.

6748 A PRINTER *to* **FRIEND GARRISON. n.d. n.p.** Encloses an anti-slavery article which the *New York Observer* and *Times* would not print; describes these newspapers as "an insult to Christianity and Republicanism." 10 June 1864. p.96, c2.

6749 GERRIT SMITH *to* **E. CADY STANTON. 6 June 1864. Peterboro'.** Warns against allowing politics to divide those who want to end slavery. 17 June 1864. p.97, c3.

6750 GEORGE THOMPSON *to* **THE** *LIBERATOR.* **13 June 1864. Boston.** Forwards resolutions from churches opposing slavery. 17 June 1864. p.99, c3.

6751 JOHN G. FEE *to* **THE** *LIBERATOR.* **n.d. n.p.** Opposes Lincoln's renomination, claiming that Lincoln is not totally in favor of equality. 17 June 1864. p.100, c2.

6752 FRANCIS HINCKLY *to* **FRIEND. 23 May 1864. St. Helena Island, S.C.** Cites advances of freedmen in South Carolina. 17 June 1864. p.100, c2.

6753 M. DU PAYS *to* **THE** *LIBERATOR.* **16 June 1864. New York.** Opposes Lincoln's nomination, but realizes that the choice now lies between Abraham Lincoln and Jefferson Davis. 24 June 1864. p.102, c6.

6754 W. *to* **THE** *LIBERATOR.* **18 June 1864. Springfield, Vt.** Advocates enforcement of the Monroe doctrine regarding the French intrusion into Mexico. 24 June 1864. p.102 [103], c1.

6755 HENRY C. WRIGHT *to* **GARRISON. 13 June 1864. Granville, N.Y.** Rejoices that slavery is doomed. 24 June 1864. p.102, [103], c1.

6756 PEACE DEMOCRAT *to* **THE** *NEW YORK DAILY NEWS.* **13 June 1864. New York.** Urges support for General Fremont because he can defeat Lincoln and insure an end to the war. 24 June 1864. p.102 [103], c3.

6757 HON. MONTGOMERY BLAIR *to* **WM. LLOYD GARRISON. 21 June 1864. Washington.** States that he is gratified that Garrison agrees with him on the common goal of emancipation; doubts, however, that freedom for the black and white masses is possible in the same community. 1 July 1864. p.106, c3.

6758 FRANCIS W. NEWMAN *to* **W. L. GARRISON. 7 June 1864. London.** States his opinion that Lincoln exhibited hypocrisy in issuing the Emancipation Proclamation because he refused to free all the slaves. 1 July 1864. p.106, c4.

6759 SAMUEL MAY, JR. *to* **GARRISON. 25 June 1864. Leicester.** Admits that, in Garrison's absence, he wrote an anti-Fremont article which provoked an attack from the *New Nation.* 1 July 1864. p.106, c5.

6760 HENRY C. WRIGHT *to* **GARRISON. 20 June 1864. Saratoga, N.Y.** Sees little difference between Copperhead and Radical Democrats; notes that both are "down with Lincoln" but not "down with slavery." 1 July 1864. p.106, c6.

6761 HENRY C. WRIGHT *to* **GARRISON. 21 June 1864. Saratoga, N.Y.** Urges support of Lincoln; reports on the Baltimore convention. 1 July 1864. p.106, c6.

6762 MARY H. COFFIN *to* **MR. GARRISON. 28 June 1864. Newbury.** Encloses the last letter her late father wrote. 1 July 1864. p.107, c1.

6763 JOSHUA COFFIN *to* **GARRISON. 20 June 1864. Newbury.** Discusses the first antislavery tract ever published in Massachusetts, claiming that it was authored in 1710 by Judge Samuel Sewall. 1 July 1864. p.107, c1.

6764 NATHAN *to* **MR. EDITOR [W. L. GARRISON]. n.d. Boston.** Reports on a YMCA convention where resolutions against "dancing, card-playing, theater-going and intemperance" were endorsed. 1 July 1864. p.108, c2.

6765 JESSE STEDMAN *to* **MR. EDITOR [W. L. GARRISON]. 14 May 1864. Springfield, Vt.** Assails Lincoln's amnesty proclamation, claiming that the South can take advantage of the three-fifths compromise. 1 July 1864. p.108, c3.

6766 HENRY C. WRIGHT *to* **GARRISON. 12 June 1864. Middle Granville, N.Y.** Forwards numerous resolutions from the Friends of Progress convention. 1 July 1864. p.108, c5.

6767 A. LINCOLN *to* **HON. JOHN H. BRYANT. 30 May 1864. Washington.** Declines to attend a meeting to discuss the erection of a monument to Hon. Owen Lovejoy. 1 July 1864. p.108, c6.

6768 WILLIAM DENNISON *to* **HON. ABRAHAM LINCOLN. 14 June 1864. New York.** Informs Lincoln of his unanimous nomination for president, expresses the earnest hope that Lincoln will accept the nomination of the convention. 8 July 1864. p.109, c3.

6769 ABRAHAM LINCOLN *to* **HON. WILLIAM DENNISON. 27 June 1864. Washington.** Accepts the nomination for president and endorses the platform of the convention. 8 July 1864. p.109, c3.

6770 WENDELL PHILLIPS *to* **THE** *NEW YORK INDEPENDENT.* **June 1864. n.p.** Endorses the anti-Lincoln campaign of Fremont; asserts that Republicans cannot be trusted. 8 July 1864. p.109, c6.

6771 AARON M. POWELL *to* **THE EDITOR [W. L. GARRISON]. n.d. n.p.** Regrets that he has misplaced the resolutions of the New England AS. 8 July 1864. p.110, c5.

6772 M. DU PAYS *to* **THE** *LIBERATOR.* **30 June 1864. New York.** Notes loss of territory by rebels; advocates voting for Lincoln in order to end slavery. 8 July 1864. p.110, c5.

6773 HENRY C. WRIGHT *to* **GARRISON. 28 June 1864. Florence, Ma.** Attacks the Radical Democrats as a divisive, pro-slavery party. 8 July 1864. p.110, c6.

6774 HENRY C. WRIGHT *to* **GARRISON. 20 June 1864. Troy, N.Y.** Cites the progress made in bringing freedom to colored people during the Lincoln administration. 8 July 1864. p.110, c6.

6775 S. W. ELY *to* **THE** *BOSTON TRAVELLER.* **25 June 1864. St. Louis.** Refutes the claim that a donation from a colored regiment to a charitable organization was refused; notes that the gift was gratefully accepted. 8 July 1864. p.111, c4.

6776 RICHARD T. BLACK *to* **THE** *LIBERATOR.* **24 June 1864. Worcester, Ma.** Informs that he is not renewing his subscription because of the *Liberator's* stand in support of Lincoln's re-election. 8 July 1864. p.112, c1.

6777 WENDELL PHILLIPS *to* **THE** *NEW YORK INDEPENDENT.* **n.d. n.p.** Kindly concludes that the *Independent's* criticism of his earlier letter, which denounced the expulsion of Negro delegates from the Union convention, was written without having read the letter. 15 July 1864. p.113, c2.

6778 W. L. GARRISON *to* **PROFESSOR NEWMAN. n.d. n.p.** Replies to Newman in defense of Lincoln. 15 July 1864. p.114, c3.

6779 B. S. *to* **MR. GARRISON. n.d. n.p.** Expresses amazement at the remark by Dr. Stebbins that "ministers as a class foresaw and announced" the evil that would befall the nation because of its treatment of the African race; concludes that he must have been sleeping through such pronouncements. 15 July 1864. p.114, c6.

6780 DR. DANIEL MANN *to* **n.n. [extract] n.d. Folly Island, S.C.** Suggests levying a substantial tax on whiskey to finance the expenses of war and reduce consumption. 15 July 1864. p.114, c6.

6781 A COLORED PRIVATE *to* **W. L. GARRISON. 26 June 1864. Morris Island, S.C.** Reports that the troops who fired one-hundred-pound guns on Charleston were abolitionists and subscribers to the *Liberator.* 15 July 1864. p.114, c6.

6782 S. DYER *to* **MR. WALLCUT. 10 July 1864. South Abington.** Encloses an additional subscription to the *Liberator* to compensate for a termination of subscription by Mr. Buck. 15 July 1864. p.114, c6.

6783 MRS. R. H. WILSON *to* **MR. GARRISON. 6 June 1864. Carrolton, La.** Encloses a copy of the newspaper edited by colored soldiers at Camp Parapet. 15 July 1864. p.115, c1.

6784 D. S. WHITNEY *to* **MR. GARRISON. 5 July 1864. Southboro.** Describes drinking in moderation as a precursor to intemperance. 15 July 1864. p.115, c1.

6785 CARLETON *to* **THE** *BOSTON JOURNAL*. **30 June 1864. Petersburg, Va.** Reports on the humanity demonstrated by colored troops in their assistance of wounded rebels. 15 July 1864. p.115, c2.

6786 SARAH CLAY *to* **MR. GARRISON. 11 July 1864. Lowell.** Mourns the death of George Sumner Allen, who was killed in battle. 15 July 1864. p.115, c6.

6787 HON. SCHUYLER COLFAX *to* **MARK L. McCLELLAND. n.d. Washington.** Supports Lincoln and Johnson because they are anti-slavery and anti-treason. 22 July 1864. p.117, c3.

6788 W. L. GARRISON *to* **PROFESSOR NEWMAN. n.d. Boston.** Discusses the differences between their views on Lincoln. 22 July 1864. p.118, c2.

6789 C. K. W. *to* **MR. GARRISON. n.d. n.p.** Asserts that testimony of ministers against slavery has been limited in the past thirty years. 22 July 1864. p.118, c4.

6790 WM. P. POWELL *to* **MR. EDITOR [W. L. GARRISON]. 14 July 1864. Washington, D.C.** Reports on philanthropic work done by the Soldiers Relief Association. 22 July 1864. p.118, c4.

6791 M. DU PAYS *to* **THE** *LIBERATOR*. **14 July 1864. New York.** Discusses the debate within Lincoln's administration on the enfranchisement of Negroes. 22 July 1864. p.118, c5.

6792 GEORGE THOMPSON *to* **GARRISON. 16 July 1864. Northampton, Ma.** Cites names of various persons who were particularly helpful during the war. 22 July 1864. p.118, c6.

6793 AMASA WALKER *to* **GARRISON. n.d. n.p.** Reports on a speech by George Thompson at Amherst; rejoices that Thompson has conquered his enemies without having to change. 22 July 1864. p.118, c6.

6794 SELLA MARTIN *to* **MR. GARRISON. 13 June 1864. New York.** Responds to a letter from Mr. Buck who dropped his subscription to the *Liberator* because of its support of Lincoln. 22 July 1864. p.119, c1.

6795 GEO. W. SIMONDS *to* **MR. EDITOR [W. L. GARRISON]. 17 July 1864. Roxbury, Ma.** Terminates his subscription to the *Liberator* because it supports Lincoln. 22 July 1864. p.119, c1.

6796 G. B. STEBBINS *to* **GARRISON. 15 July 1864. Rochester, N.Y.** Criticizes the Cleveland convention; notes lack of support for Fremont. 22 July 1864. p.119, c1.

6797 D. S. GRANDIN *to* **MR. EDITOR [W. L. GARRISON]. 15 July 1864. Brunswick, Me.** Refutes criticism of the YMCA's support of prohibition. 22 July 1864. p.119, c3.

6798 A. G. *to* **FRIEND GARRISON. 7 July 1864. Newbern, N.C.** Praises the freed slaves' desire for education and their willingness to join the army. 22 July 1864. p.120, c2.

6799 n.n. *to* **THE** *PRESS*. **[extract] 11 July 1864. Philadelphia.** States that officers view the Negro soldier as "a man, a soldier, a hero" who instills fear in the rebels. 22 July 1864. p.120, c4.

6800 A SOLDIER *to* **n.n. [extract] 18 June 1864. Near Richmond.** Reports that Union troops are welcomed in Virginia as liberators; relates his discovery of white slaves on a plantation. 22 July 1864. p.120, c5.

6801 FRANCES D. GAGE *to* **THE** *LIBERATOR.* **5 July 1864. Soldiers Home, Vicksburg.** Reports on a Fourth of July celebration held on Jefferson Davis' former plantation. 29 July 1864. p.121, c6.

6802 A. BROOKE *to* **THE EDITOR OF THE** *NATIONAL ANTI-SLAVERY STANDARD.* **12 July 1864. Marlboro, Oh.** Criticizes the New England AS. 29 July 1864. p.122, c1.

6803 CHARLES W. ELLIOTT *to* **THE** *NEW YORK TRIBUNE.* **n.d. n.p.** Argues that General Banks' "Labor System" pays the freedmen a decent wage and provides them with shelter and security; denies that this system benefits the planter. 29 July 1864. p.122, c2.

6804 E. W. CHESSON *to* **WILLIAM LLOYD GARRISON. 5 July 1864. London.** Mourns the death of Washington Wilks, supporter of the abolitionist cause; lists members of the committee in charge of aid for his family. 29 July 1864. p.122, c6.

6805 BENJAMIN EMERSON *to* **MR. EDITOR [W. L. GARRISON]. 22 July 1864. Haverhill, Ma.** Criticizes the *Liberator* for supporting Lincoln's re-election. 29 July 1864. p.123, c3.

6806 INCENTIVE *to* **RICHARD T. BUCK. n.d. n.p.** Refutes Buck's claim that the *Liberator* is comforting to Jefferson Davis and Copperheads. 29 July 1864. p.123, c3.

6807 J. D. *to* **FATHER. 9 July 1864. Near City Point, Va.** Praises the change in national spirit which made it possible to progress from merely suppressing rebellion to liberating the slaves. 29 July 1864. p.123, c4.

6808 MARY F. THOMAS *to* **THE** *NATIONAL ANTI-SLAVERY STANDARD.* **6 July 1864. Nashville, Tn.** Encloses a letter from Colonel Mussey responding to the invitation to attend a Fourth of July celebration. 29 July 1864. p.124, c5.

6809 COL. R. D. MUSSEY *to* **W. S. CHEATHAM. 3 July 1864. Nashville.** Declines to attend a Fourth of July celebration because his colored troops were not invited; asserts that the axiom of the Fourth of July is that "all men are created equal." 29 July 1864. p.124, c6.

6810 CARLETON *to* **THE** *BOSTON JOURNAL.* **14 July 1864. Washington, D.C.** Informs of the president's call for troops; notes that Copperheads will advocate use of Negro troops. 5 August 1864. p.125, c5.

6811 ANDREW JOHNSON *to* **THE** *NASHVILLE UNION.* **[extract] n.d. n.p.** Accepts the Baltimore convention nomination for vice-president of the United States; assails slavery for causing the rebellion and asserts that both slavery and the rebellion must end together. 5 August 1864. p.125, c6.

6812 M. DU PAYS *to* **THE** *LIBERATOR.* **28 July 1864. New York.** Comments on the heat wave in New York. 5 August 1864. p.126, c2.

6813 WM. BASSETT *to* **W. L. GARRISON. 28 July 1864. Lynn, Ma.** Claims that the recent cancellations of the *Liberator* reminded him to renew his subscription. 5 August 1864. p.126, c4.

6814 L. C. PAINE FREER *to* **WM. L. GARRISON. 26 July 1864. Chicago.** Criticizes Garrison for supporting Lincoln. 5 August 1864. p.128, c3.

6815 H. *to* **WILLIAM LLOYD GARRISON. 25 July 1864. Charlestown, Ma.** Believes that people are beginning to hold Lincoln accountable for "imbecile fogies" like Seward and Blair. 5 August 1864. p.128, c3.

6816 n.n. *to* **THE** *PHILADELPHIA CHRISTIAN RECORDER.* **n.d. n.p.** Expresses indignation at a Delaware law which allowed for the arrest and punishment by fine of a free colored person from Canada who entered the state. 5 August 1864. p.128, c5.

6817 GERRIT SMITH *to* **FRIEND GARRISON. 1 August 1864. Peterboro', N.Y.** Laments the possible discontinuation of the *Liberator* for financial reasons. 12 August 1864. p.130, c4.

6818 JEHIEL CLAFLIN *to* **GARRISON. 4 August 1864. East Westmoreland, N.H.** Expresses concern over the possible discontinuation of the *Liberator*; regrets that old friends are cancelling subscriptions. 12 August 1864. p.130, c4.

6819 F. D. GAGE *to* **MR. GARRISON. 3 August 1864. St. Johnsbury, Vt.** States that she supports the *Liberator*; gives a sarcastic critique of Garrison's "lunacy" and support of freedom and truth. 12 August 1864. p.130, c4.

6820 SEWARD MITCHELL *to* **FRIEND GARRISON. 31 July 1864. Cornville, Me.** Encloses a contribution in support of the *Liberator*. 12 August 1864. p.130, c5.

6821 ISAAC FISKE *to* **GARRISON. 2 August 1864. Fall River.** An abolitionist states that he supports Lincoln and the *Liberator*; encloses a subscription. 12 August 1864. p.130, c5.

6822 F. W. CHESSON *to* **THE** *LIBERATOR.* **20 July 1864. London.** Encloses a letter from Judge Winter of Georgia, whom he describes as a "true patriot." 12 August 1864. p.130, c5.

6823 JOHN G. WINTER *to* **F. W. CHESSON. 15 July 1864. Chester, England.** Eulogizes the late Washington Wilks for his support of the Union cause. 12 August 1864. p.130, c5.

6824 L. C. LOCKWOOD *to* **MR. EDITOR [W. L. GARRISON]. n.d. n.p.** Discusses the success of the Delaware Improvement Association, an agricultural collective. 12 August 1864. p.130, c6.

6825 WM. ALSTON *to* **THE CHRISTIAN PUBLIC OF PHILADELPHIA. 19 July 1864. Philadelphia.** Relates an incident concerning his sick child who was refused admittance to a Philadelphia street car because he was colored; denounces this action as "barbaric," particularly since colored citizens pay taxes and serve in the army. 12 August 1864. p.131, c2.

6826 S. B. S. *to* **THE** *NEW YORK TRIBUNE.* **25 July 1864. Washington.** Requests donations of blackberries to be used to combat a diarrhea epidemic in the army; forwards a recipe for blackberry brandy. 12 August 1864. p.132, c4.

6827 E. C. E. *to* **THE** *PHILADELPHIA PRESS.* **21 July 1864. Philadelphia.** Assails the degraded state of society in the South where wives and daughters are not shocked that their husbands and fathers have sired mulatto children. 12 August 1864. p.132, c5.

6828 SELLA MARTIN *to* **THE** *EVENING POST.* **n.d. New York.** Gives a brief biographical sketch of Judge Winter of Georgia, a benevolent slaveholder and Unionist. 19 August 1864. p.134, c3.

6829 EDGAR KETCHUM *to* **GARRISON. 15 August 1864. New York.** Supports Garrison and expresses his desire for the *Liberator* to continue. 19 August 1864. p.134, c4.

6830 ALFRED H. LOVE *to* **GARRISON. 12 August 1864. Philadelphia.** Supports Garrison and encourages the continuation of the *Liberator*. 19 August 1864. p.134, c4.

6831 E. W. TWING *to* **GARRISON. 13 August 1864. Springfield.** Supports Garrison and assails those who question his commitment to anti-slavery. 19 August 1864. p.134, c4.

6832 E. F. PENNYPACKER *to* **GARRISON. 8 August 1864. Phoenixville, Pa.** Supports Garrison and his endorsement of Lincoln. 19 August 1864. p.134, c4.

6833 HELEN P. BRIGHT *to* **GARRISON. 2 August 1864. Rochdale, England.** Urges Garrison to visit England soon. 19 August 1864. p.134, c5.

6834 GERRIT SMITH *to* **B. F. WADE AND H. W. DAVIS. 8 August 1864. Peterboro', N.Y.** Rebukes Wade and Davis for making divisive comments about Lincoln. 19 August 1864. p.134, c5.

6835 M. DU PAYS *to* **THE** *LIBERATOR.* **11 August 1864. New York.** Comments on the inevitable conflict between Lincoln and Congress over Reconstruction. 19 August 1864. p.135, c1.

6836 HENRY C. WRIGHT *to* **FRIEND GARRISON. 5 August 1864. Straits of Mackinaw.** Identifies Lincoln as the only man so closely associated with freedom and free labor; urges Lincoln's re-election. 19 August 1864. p.135, c2.

6837 LA ROY SUNDERLAND *to* **GARRISON. 15 August 1864. Boston.** Gives an account of colored troops who fought better than white officers. 19 August 1864. p.135, c3.

6838 L. A. GRIMES *to* **MR. GARRISON. 16 August 1864. Boston.** Cautions against giving aid to a Mrs. Julia Lewis, who has collected large sums of money under the pretense of bringing freed women North. 19 August 1864. p.135, c4.

6839 N. W. GOVE *to* **THE** *LIBERATOR.* **4 August 1864. Concord, N.H.** Comments on the hypocrisy of previously silent clergy who now oppose slavery. 10 August 1864. p.136, c3.

6840 GEN. T. W. SHERMAN *to* **JOHN A. SPOONER. 30 July 1864. Near Atlanta.** Discusses Spooner's appointment as provost marshal under a new law designed to recruit volunteers in Georgia, Alabama, and Mississippi; fears that the new law will bring an inferior recruit into the army and create a nuisance. 19 August 1864. p.135, c5.

6841 M. *to* **THE** *BOSTON TRAVELLER.* **n.d. n.p.** Asserts that the letter from Sherman to Spooner was discourteous; claims that Sherman's arguments for a universal draft are biased against the poor. 26 August 1864. p.138, c1.

6842 BENJAMIN EMERSON *to* **MR. EDITOR [W. L. GARRISON]. August 1864. Haverhill, Ma.** Denounces the *Liberator* for its defense of Lincoln. 26 August 1864. p.138, c4.

6843 HARVEY CHASE *to* **GARRISON. 20 August 1864. Valley Falls.** Supports the *Liberator*; encloses a contribution. 26 August 1864. p.138, c5.

6844 ARTHUR TAPPAN *to* **W. L. GARRISON. 17 November 1863. New Haven.** Regrets his growing estrangement from Garrison. 26 August 1864. p.138, c5.

6845 ALFRED H. LOVE *to* **WM. LLOYD GARRISON. 20 August 1864. Philadelphia.** Gives support to the *Liberator* to compensate for those who have withdrawn support. 26 August 1864. p.138, c5.

6846 HENRY MILES *to* **WM. LLOYD GARRISON. 20 August 1864. Monkton, Vt.** Supports the *Liberator*, regretting that old subscribers should now abandon Garrison. 26 August 1864. p.138, c5.

6847 JOHN GORDON *to* **ROBERT WALLCUT. 12 August 1864. Salem, Oh.** Supports the *Liberator*; denounces its opponents as friends of Jefferson Davis. 26 August 1864. p.138, c6.

6848 WM. THIRDS *to* **MR. GARRISON. 27 July 1864. Natchez.** Opposes Fremont; urges support of the Union with Lincoln. 26 August 1864. p.138, c5.

6849 R. HASSALL *to* **FRIEND GARRISON. 15 August 1864. Keokuk, Ia.** Reports on festivities in Keokuk for West Indies Emancipation Day. 26 August 1864. p.139, c1.

6850 J. S. G. *to* **MR. GARRISON. 19 August 1864. Washington.** Urges legislation to improve the condition of freedmen. 26 August 1864. p.139, c1.

6851 M. D. CONWAY *to* **THE *LIBERATOR*. 6 August 1864. London.** Refutes a charge made by Sella Martin that abolitionists are prejudiced. 26 August 1864. p.139, c2.

6852 HENRY C. WRIGHT *to* **FRIEND GARRISON. 11 August 1864. Chicago.** Suspects that the spiritualists' convention may adopt pro-slavery, pro-rebellion resolutions. 26 August 1864. p.140, c2.

6853 HENRY C. WRIGHT *to* **GARRISON. 14 August 1864. Chicago.** Praises a convention of spiritualists for opposing slavery; denounces a convention of Copperheads which cried "peace" but not "down with slavery." 26 August 1864. p.140, c2.

6854 J. G. M. *to* **THE *PHILADELPHIA PRESS*. n.d. n.p.** Justifies Lincoln's decision to veto the Wade-Davis bill on Reconstruction; protests that the bill was presented only one hour before adjournment *sine die*. 2 September 1864. p.141, c4.

6855 GEORGE STERNS, S. R. UBINO, JAMES STONE, ELIZUR WRIGHT, EDWARD HABSCH, SAM'L G. HOWE *to* **GENERAL FREMONT. 20 August 1864. Boston.** Request that both Lincoln and Fremont withdraw from the presidential race and unite behind a third candidate. 2 September 1864. p.142, c2.

6856 J. C. FREMONT *to* **GENTLEMEN. 25 August 1864. Nahant.** Rejects the suggestion that he withdraw his presidential bid; claims that he was nominated by a significant segment of the population and feels obligated to them; states that the restoration of the Union is his main concern. 2 September 1864. p.142, c2.

6857 J. G. WHITTIER *to* **FRIEND. 29 August 1864. Amesbury.** Expresses displeasure at the *Liberator*'s criticism of Fremont. 2 September 1864. p.142, c5.

6858 D. S. WHITNEY *to* **MR. GARRISON. 26 August 1864. Southboro'.** A former defender of Fremont supports the *Liberator*'s endorsement of Lincoln. 2 September 1864. p.142, c5.

6859 J. T. EVERETT *to* **GARRISON. 28 August 1864. Everettville.** Supports the *Liberator* for its honesty and candor; states that he is surprised by those who attack it. 2 September 1864. p.142, c5.

6860 E. H. HEYWOOD *to* **MR. GARRISON. 30 August 1864. Princeton.** Supports the *Liberator* with a contribution. 2 September 1864. p.142, c6.

6861 L. MARIA CHILD *to* **GARRISON. 20 August 1864. Wayland.** States that the *Liberator* is more important than politics or war. 2 September 1864. p.142, c6.

6862 M. DU PAYS *to* **MR. EDITOR [W. L. GARRISON]. 25 August 1864. New York.** Reports from inside the Confederacy. 2 September 1864. p.142, c6.

6863 JONATHAN WALKER *to* **GARRISON. n.d. n.p.** Describes his experiences in eastern Virginia aiding a freedmen's industrial project. 2 September 1864. p.143, c1.

6864 SELLA MARTIN *to* **MR. GARRISON. 26 August 1864. New York.** Replies to M. D. Conway, who once declared that Lincoln was the most popular man in England but who now calls him a Negro-hater. 2 September 1864. p.143, c2.

6865 HENRY C. WRIGHT *to* **W. L. GARRISON. 20 August 1864. Lockport, Il.** Denounces the "Peace Democrat" convention as a pro-slavery gathering designed to divide the Union. 2 September 1864. p.144, c1.

6866 GEORGE LYNN *to* **FRIEND GARRISON. 22 August 1864. Lockport, Il.** Urges abolitionist unity in order to end slavery. 2 September 1864. p.144, c4.

6867 ENOCH F. JACKMAN *to* **THE** *INDEPENDENT DEMOCRAT.* **8 August 1864. Near Point of Rocks.** Refutes the story that colored troops fled under fire. 2 September 1864. p.144, c4.

6868 U. S. GRANT *to* **GEN. R. E. LEE. 8 August 1864. City Point, Va.** Requests that the two armies exchange prisoners. 9 September 1864. p.145, c5.

6869 JAMES F. JAQUES, JAMES R. GILMORE *to* **J. P. BENJAMIN. 17 July 1864. Richmond, Va.** Request meeting with Jefferson Davis in order to open official negotiations to end the war. 9 September 1864. p.145, c6.

6870 MISS SALLIE HOLLEY *to* **MR. GARRISON. 29 August 1864. Rochester, N.Y.** Reports on a talk by Sojourner Truth in Rochester. 9 September 1864. p.147, c1.

6871 HENRY C. WRIGHT *to* **GARRISON. 30 August 1864. Chicago.** Assails the "Peace Democrat" convention in Chicago whose slogan is down with Lincoln "by ballots or bullets." 9 September 1864. p.147, c2.

6872 H. W. C. *to* **MR. GARRISON. 29 August 1864. Dorchester.** Criticizes the *Liberator* for typographical errors found in his previous letter. 9 September 1864. p.147, c3.

6873 ANNA E. DICKINSON *to* **FRIEND. [from the** *New York Independent***] 3 September 1864. Philadelphia.** Urges support for the party of abolition represented by Lincoln. 16 September 1864. p.150, c1.

6874 M. DU PAYS *to* **THE** *LIBERATOR.* **8 September 1864. New York.** Believes that Lincoln's victory is inevitable in election of 1864. 16 September 1864. p.151, c1.

6875 GEORGE L. STEARNS *to* **THE** *LIBERATOR.* **12 September 1864. Boston.** Asserts that few Republicans support Lincoln; believes that Lincoln is unfit for office. 16 September 1864. p.151, c2.

6876 C. STETSON *to* **MR. GARRISON. 5 September 1864. Lexington.** Supports the *Liberator* with an additional subscription. 16 September 1864. p.151, c2.

6877 WM. STILL *to* **W. L. GARRISON. 6 September 1864. Philadelphia.** Supports the *Liberator*'s stand in favor of Lincoln; encloses two new subscriptions. 16 September 1864. p.151, c2.

6878 D. ROBINSON, JR. *to* **WM. LLOYD GARRISON. 2 September 1864. Boston.** Approves of the *Liberator*'s viewpoint on national affairs; encloses a contribution. 12 September 1864. p.151, c2.

6879 CHARLES FRANCIS ADAMS *to* **JOHN H. ESCOURT. 19 August 1864. London.** Reports that Lincoln was pleased to receive pro-Union, anti-slavery resolutions from the Manchester Emancipation Society. 16 September 1864. p.151, c2.

6880 GEO. B. McCLELLAN *to* **HORATIO SEYMOUR. 8 September 1864. Orange, N.Y.** Accepts the nomination of the Democratic National Convention; promises to restore full liberty to states that return to the Union; also hopes to restore a sound financial system to the country. 16 September 1864. p.151, c5.

6881 U. S. GRANT *to* **E. B. WASHBURN. [extract] 8 September 1864. Washington.** Urges the North to persevere and win the war; argues that the rebels are desperate since they are using young boys and old men to defend the South. 16 September 1864. p.151, c5.

6882 SAMUEL KEESE *to* **FRIEND GARRISON. 5 September 1864. Peru, N.Y.** Denounces the Peace Party as "war-like." 16 September 1864. p.152, c4.

6883 MR. MacKAY *to* **THE** *LONDON TIMES.* **[extract] n.d. n.p.** States that the "insane desire" of Lincoln for re-election motivated his military Reconstruction plan; discusses the possibility of a "peace" candidate defeating Lincoln. 23 September 1864. p.153, c4.

6884 GEN. BUTLER *to* **REBEL COMMISSIONERS OF EXCHANGE. August 1864. In the Field.** Requests that rebels exchange prisoners, including colored soldiers, with the North; notes that the South has repeatedly refused to do this, with the claim that colored soldiers are "property"; accuses Southerners of placing more value on their "property" than on their soldiers. 23 September 1864. p.153, c6.

6885 THOMAS H. BARKER *to* **W. L. GARRISON. 27 August 1864. Manchester, England.** Discusses English support of the American Union and freedom. 23 September 1864. p.154, c5.

6886 HENRY C. WRIGHT *to* **GARRISON. 11 September 1864. Lake St. Mary, Mi.** Reports on his lecture tour in Michigan. 23 September 1864. p.155, c3.

6887 B. RUSH PLUMLY *to* **GARRISON. 6 September 1864. New Orleans.** Reports on the reform of the educational system in Louisiana to aid freedmen. 23 September 1864. p.155, c4.

6888 FREDERICK DOUGLASS *to* **GARRISON. 17 September 1864. Rochester, N.Y.** Replies to a news story about himself in the *Liberator*; announces his support of Lincoln. 23 September 1864. p.155, c4.

6889 JOHN D. STEVENSON *to* **HON. E. M. STANTON. 20 September. Harper's Ferry, Va.** Forwards a report from Sheridan on a major victory for Union army in Virginia. 23 September 1864. p.155, c5.

6890 ELIZABETH P. NICHOL *to* **FRIEND. 1 September 1864. Huntly Lodge, Edinburgh.** Supports the *Liberator*; grieves that some oppose Garrison's right to free speech. 23 September 1864. p.155, c5.

6891 UNION AND EMANCIPATION SOCIETY *to* **PEOPLE OF BRITAIN AND IRELAND. 6 September 1864. Manchester.** Declares that the defeat of slavery is essential to the establishment of an era of peace and freedom. 30 September 1864. p.157, c2.

6892 G. L. STEARNS, S. R. URBINO, JAMES STOWE, F. W. BIRD, SAMUEL G. HOWE, ELIZUR WRIGHT *to* **MAJ. GEN. JOHN C. FREMONT. 9 September 1864. Boston.** Describe the Chicago convention as "cowardly and treasonable"; invite Fremont to speak in Boston. 30 September 1864. p.157, c5.

6893 J. C. FREMONT *to* **MESSRS. GEORGE L. STEARNS AND OTHERS. 17 September 1864. Nahant, Ma.** Withdraws his candidacy for president; recommends a united Republican Party without Lincoln's leadership. 30 September 1864. p.157, c5.

6894 JOHN COCHRANE *to* **WAR DEMOCRATS OF THE UNITED STATES. 21 September 1864. New York.** Regards "peace and division" or "war and the Union" as the only alternatives in 1864; withdraws his candidacy for vice-president. 30 September 1864. p.157, c6.

6895 F. W. NEWMAN *to* **THE** *ENGLISH LEADER.* **1 September 1864. n.p.** Assails the pro-slavery character of Lincoln; disagrees with Garrison's support for Lincoln. 30 September 1864. p.158, c2.

6896 THOS. HUGHES *to* **WM. LLOYD GARRISON. 9 September 1864. London.** Describes the debate between Garrison and Newman as divisive to abolitionist cause. 30 September 1864. p.158, c4.

6897 M. DU PAYS *to* **THE** *LIBERATOR.* **22 September 1864. New York.** Assails McClellan as either a knave or a fool. 30 September 1864. p.158, c6.

6898 HENRY C. WRIGHT *to* **FRIEND GARRISON. 17 September 1864. Livonia, Mi.** Claims that aliens will be imported to aid the Democrats in defeating Lincoln and electing McClellan. 30 September 1864. p.158, c6.

6899 E. Y. CHENEY *to* **THE** *LIBERATOR.* **27 September 1864. Lebanon, N.H.** Reports on the successful speaking engagement of William Andrew Jackson, former coachman for Jefferson Davis. 30 September 1864. p.159, c1.

6900 WM. P. POWELL *to* **GARRISON. 24 September 1864. n.p.** Traces the progress of the anti-slavery movement, crediting the *Liberator* with its success. 30 September 1864. p.159, c1.

6901 W. T. SHERMAN *to* **GEN. J. R. HOOD. 21 September 1864. Washington.** Responds to Hood's protest against Sherman's burning of Atlanta; reminds Hood that rebels plunged the nation into war; asks him to fight it out like a man and not to commit sacrilege by asking God's mercy. 30 September 1864. p.159, c2.

6902 SAMUEL AARON, S. G. WRIGHT, JOSEPH HEMMATT, A. J. HINKS, S. C. DARR, MILLER JONES *to* **THE** *NEW YORK TRIBUNE.* **n.d. n.p.** Enclose resolutions passed by the New Jersey Baptists' Association urging total victory over the rebels. 30 September 1864. p.159, c3.

6903 A. LINCOLN *to* **LT. GEN. GRANT. 30 April 1864. Washington, D.C.** Encourages Grant's efforts in the field; expresses full confidence in him. 30 September 1864. p.159, c3.

6904 GEN. U. S. GRANT *to* **PRESIDENT LINCOLN. 1 May 1864. Culpepper, Va.** Thanks Lincoln for expressing confidence in his ability. 30 September 1864. p.159, c3.

6905 GEORGE B. McCLELLAN *to* **SIR. 29 August 1861. Washington.** Issues a first proposal for universal conscription, arguing that men will not volunteer. 7 October 1864. p.161, c2.

6906 GEORGE THOMPSON *to* **GARRISON. n.d. n.p.** Encloses a letter received from Mr. Greening. 7 October 1864. p.162, c6.

6907 E. O. GREENING *to* **GEORGE THOMPSON. 14 September 1864. Manchester, England.** States that the English upper class is pro-rebel, while the working class supports Union. 7 October 1864. p.162, c6.

6908 JOHN T. SARGENT *to* **GARRISON. 1 October 1864. Boston.** Encloses an extract of a letter written to his wife. 7 October 1864. p.163, c2.

6909 JOHN T. SARGENT *to* **MRS. JOHN T. SARGENT. [extract] n.d. New York.** Relates a tale of meeting a crippled soldier whom he assisted in getting a job. 7 October 1864. p.163, c2.

6910 W. C. N. *to* **FRIEND GARRISON. 30 September 1864. Boston.** Encloses extracts of letters praising the heroism and patriotism of colored soldiers. 7 October 1864. p.163, c3.

6911 AN OFFICER OF FIFTY-FIFTH MASSACHUSETTS *to* **W. C. N. [extract] n.d. Charleston Jail.** Reports on the humane treatment of prisoners held by the Confederate cavalry. 7 October 1864. p.163, c3.

6912 A SERGEANT IN THE FIFTY-FOURTH MASSACHUSETTS *to* **W. C. N. [extract] 26 August 1864. Morris Island.** Desires black officers to lead black troops in order to instill confidence in the soldiers. 7 October 1864. p.163, c3.

6913 GEORGE DRAPER *to* **GARRISON. 4 October 1864. Hopedale.** Hopes that the *Liberator* and Lincoln will maintain unity in the Union cause. 7 October 1864. p.163, c4.

6914 HENRY C. WRIGHT *to* **GARRISON. 18 September 1864. Farmington, Mi.** Interprets the war as a rebellion of the Democratic Party against majority rule. 7 October 1864. p.164, c2.

6915 B. *to* **MR. EDITOR. n.d. n.p.** Describes a scuffle between Irish and Negroes in Boston; voices doubt that the Irish can be assimilated into society, owing to their violent nature. 7 October 1864. p.164, c2.

6916 GEN. B. F. BUTLER *to* **HON. SIMON CAMERON. n.d. n.p.** Discusses the conscription of all white residents between seventeen and fifty years old into the rebel army; doubts that the Democrats who are adamant about "Lincoln's tyranny" will protest the conscription. 14 October 1864. p.165, c6.

6917 ELIZ. PEASE NICHOL *to* **FRIEND GARRISON. 23 September 1864. Edinburgh.** Forwards a donation to the *Liberator*. 14 October 1864. p.166, c5.

6918 ALBERT DICEY AND JOHN NICHOL *to* **W. L. GARRISON n.d. n.p.** State that the English support Lincoln because they view no viable alternative. 14 October 1864. p.166, c5.

6919 EDWARD EVERETT *to* **A. W. CAMPBELL. [from the *Wheeling Intelligencer*] 28 September 1864. Boston.** Expresses warm regards on behalf of the North toward the loyal inhabitants of West Virginia. 14 October 1864. p.167, c3.

6920 A. LINCOLN *to* **HON. HENRY HOFFMAN. 10 October. Washington.** Hopes that the people of Maryland will ratify the new constitution with a proviso outlawing slavery. 14 October 1864. p.167, c3.

6921 ABRAHAM LINCOLN *to* **HON MONTGOMERY BLAIR. 23 September 1864. Washington.** Accepts Blair's resignation as postmaster general. 14 October 1864. p.167, c3.

6922 M. BLAIR *to* **PRESIDENT LINCOLN. 23 September 1864. Post Office Department.** Tenders his formal resignation as postmaster. 14 October 1864. p.167, c3.

6923 M. BLAIR *to* **S. P. HANSCOM. [from the** *National Republican***] n.d. n.p.** Refutes the claim that he resigned because of resolutions passed at a Baltimore convention criticizing cabinet members. 14 October 1864. p.167, c3.

6924 U. S. GRANT *to* **HON. E. M. STANTON. 10 October. City Point, Va.** Reports to the secretary of war that he inflicted heavy casualties on the rebel army in Virginia. 14 October 1864. p.167, c5.

6925 GEN. SHERIDAN *to* **GEN. GRANT. 9 October. Strasburg, Va.** Relates Custer's successful capture of rebel artillery in Shenandoah valley. 14 October 1864. p.167, c5.

6926 GEN. B. F. BUTLER *to* **GEN. U. S. GRANT. 7 October . n.p.** Reports that rebel General Gregg was killed in battle. 14 October 1864. p.167, c5.

6927 J. B. M. *to* **THE** *LIBERATOR.* **5 October 1864. Washington, D.C.** Refutes a newspaper article which claims that Negro equality is recognized in the public transportation of the District of Columbia; cites numerous examples of discrimination. 14 October 1864. p.168, c2.

6928 EMILE BOURLIER *to* *NATIONAL UNION CLUB.* **14 September 1864. Philadelphia.** Doubts the loyalty of many McClellan supporters. 14 October 1864. p.168, c4.

6929 HON. D. S. CODDINGTON *to* **W. A. DARLING AND COMMITTEE. 27 September 1864. New York.** Discusses the election choice between Jefferson Davis and Abraham Lincoln. 21 October 1864. p.169, c6.

6930 M. DU PAYS *to* **THE** *LIBERATOR.* **6 October 1864. New York.** Declares that victory in the election of 1864 is the last hope for the South. 21 October 1864. p.170, c4.

6931 GERRIT SMITH *to* *AMERICAN BAPTIST.* **8 September 1864. Peterboro.** Corrects a misconception about his position on slavery and rebellion; asserts that rebellion is not always a crime, but that slavery is the greatest of crimes. 21 October 1864. p.170, c6.

6932 GEN. BANKS *to* **BUREAU OF FREE LABOR. 9 September 1864. New Orleans.** Praises the Bureau of Free Labor for assisting freedmen in New Orleans. 21 October 1864. p.172, c4.

6933 J. HOLT, JUDGE ADVOCATE *to* **HON. E. M. STANTON. 8 October 1864. Washington, D.C.** Forwards a lengthy report on the treasonous conspiracy known as the "Knights of the Golden Circle," whose purpose is to foster anti-draft agitation, give aid to rebels, and establish a new confederacy in the West. 28 October 1864. p.173, c1.

6934 M. DU PAYS *to* **THE** *LIBERATOR.* **20 October 1864. New York.** Asserts that those who vote for McClellan deserve to be hanged. 28 October 1864. p.175, c5.

6935 GERRIT SMITH *to* **MASSES OF THE DEMOCRATIC PARTY. 20 October 1864. Peterboro'.** Asks rank and file Democrats to "disappoint" their leaders by voting for patriotism. 4 November 1864. p.177, c1.

6936 EDWARD LABOULAYE *to* **n.n. n.d. n.p.** Claims that a vote for Lincoln is a vote for the Union and for liberty. 4 November 1864. p.177, c4.

6937 A JEFFERSONIAN DEMOCRAT *to* **THE** *BOSTON JOURNAL.* **n.d. n.p.** Indicts the South on account of slavery and the war. 4 November 1864. p.177, c5.

6938 F. W. NEWMAN *to* **GARRISON. 14 October 1864. London.** States that he has changed his position against Lincoln and now agrees with Garrison. 4 November 1864. p.178, c3.

6939 JAMES SINCLAIR *to* **GARRISON. 15 October 1864. Glasgow.** Forwards statement of support from Scotland. 4 November 1864. p.178, c6.

6940 A. H. *to* **MR. GARRISON. 23 October 1864. Braintree, Vt.** Reports on well-received address given by George Thompson at the Vermont capitol. 4 November 1864. p.179, c2.

6941 THOS. H. BARKER *to* **MR. GARRISON. 4 October 1864. Manchester, England.** Describes English view of Lincoln based on his military and political victories in the United States. 4 November 1864. p.180, c2.

6942 J. G. FISH *to* **MR. EDITOR [W. L. GARRISON]. 20 October 1864. Ganges, Mi.** Replies to H. C. Wright's letter attacking spiritualists. 4 November 1864. p.180, c3.

6943 B. RUSH PLUMLY *to* **GARRISON. 20 October 1864. New Orleans.** Reports on the progress of free colored people in New Orleans. 11 November 1864. p.182, c5.

6944 ALFRED H. LOVE *to* **GARRISON. 2 November 1864. Philadelphia.** Reports on attending an emancipation celebration with colored people in Maryland. 11 November 1864. p.182, c6.

6945 S. ALFRED STEINTHAL *to* **GARRISON. 15 October 1864. Manchester, England.** Lauds the conversion of the entire North to the abolition cause. 11 November 1864. p.182, c6.

6946 WM. E. MATTHEWS *to* **GARRISON. 6 November 1864. Baltimore.** Announces that the ratification of a new constitution makes Maryland a free state. 11 November 1864. p.182, c6.

6947 M. D. CONWAY *to* **EDWARD BEALES. 13 October 1864. London.** Asks Beales to settle debate between Conway and J. Sella Martin. 11 November 1864. p.183, c1.

6948 M. D. CONWAY *to* **THE** *LIBERATOR.* **22 October 1864. London.** Continues debate with J. Sella Martin; encloses correspondence. 11 November 1864. p.183, c1.

6949 E. BEALES *to* **M. D. CONWAY. 21 October 1864. Boulogne.** Settles continuing debate between Conway and Martin affirming that Martin accused abolitionists like Garrison of having anti-Negro sentiments. 11 November 1864. p.183, c1.

6950 M. DU PAYS *to* **THE** *LIBERATOR.* **3 November 1864. New York.** Praises adoption of Maryland's new constitution as major victory for abolition. 11 November 1864. p.183, c2.

6951 SARAH P. REMOND *to* **MR. GARRISON. 22 October 1864. London.** Encloses five dollars for the *Liberator*. 11 November 1864. p.183, c2.

6952 GEN. U. S. GRANT *to* **GEN. R. E. LEE. 28 October 1864. n.p.** Promises Lee that he will retaliate for any harm done to colored prisoners held by rebels. 11 November 1864. p.183, c5.

6953 E. H. H. *to* **MR. GARRISON. 17 October 1864. Princeton.** Criticizes Lincoln's war plan. 11 November 1864. p.184, c2.

6954 G. P. JONSON *to* **THE** *LIBERATOR.* **14 October 1864. Folly Island, S.C.** Forwards resolution thanking Garrison for his support of equal pay for the colored soldiers of the Fifty-fifth Massachusetts Regiment. 11 November 1864. p.184, c4.

6955 A UNION MAN *to* **THE** *BOSTON DAILY ADVERTISER.* **4 November 1864. n.p.** Encloses article by Henri Martin from *La Siècle* of Paris offering Lincoln the moral support of Europeans who will "vote with their heart." 18 November 1864. p.185, c4.

6956 MRS. L. M. CHILD *to* **THE** *NATIONAL ANTI-SLAVERY STANDARD.* **n.d. n.p.** Announces fair for widows and orphans of colored soldiers in Boston. 18 November 1864. p.185, c6.

6957 GOLDWIN SMITH *to* **THE** *LONDON DAILY NEWS.* **18 October 1864. Toronto.** Refutes Southern propaganda that the North is tired of war. 18 November 1864. p.186, c1.

6958 JAMES RODGERS *to* **THE** *LIBERATOR.* **n.d. n.p.** Praises United Presbyterian church for publishing Theo. Weld's *The Bible Against Slavery.* 18 November 1864. p.186, c5.

6959 W. H. F. *to* **MR. GARRISON. n.d. n.p.** Predicts that the election of 1864 will be a victory for Lincoln and ensure the unity of the abolitionists. 18 November 1864. p.186, c6.

6960 LEICESTER A. SAWYER *to* **MR. EDITOR [W. L. GARRISON]. n.d. n.p.** Describes the precepts of rationalism as anti-spiritualistic. 18 November 1864. p.188, c2.

6961 n.n. *to* **THE** *PHILADELPHIA INQUIRER.* **17 October 1864. Gen. Butler's Head-quarters.** Recounts rebel atrocities inflicted on wounded colored soldiers; notes that rebel hospital attendants interceded to prevent further atrocities. 18 November 1864. p.188, c4.

6962 M. DU PAYS *to* **THE** *LIBERATOR.* **17 November 1864. New York.** Denounces the attempt to tamper with the Democratic ballot during recent election. 25 November 1864. p.190, c4.

6963 SISTER *to* **ANNIE BROWN. [extract] 9 October 1864. Red Bluff, Ca.** A member of John Brown's family describes their migration to California. 25 November 1864. p.190, c5.

6964 LEICESTER A. SAWYER *to* **MR. EDITOR [W. L. GARRISON]. n.d. n.p.** Discusses rationalism in the pulpit. 25 November 1864. p.192, c2.

6965 C. H. B. *to* **GEO. WILLIAMS. 4 October 1864. San Francisco, Ca.** Suggests that freedmen emigrate to Mexico. 25 November 1864. p.192, c2.

6966 JNO. PIERPONT *to* **W. L. GARRISON. 11 November 1864. Washington, D.C.** Praises court decision by Judge Underwood of the United States District Court of Virginia to allow colored men to testify in court. 25 November 1864. p.192, c3.

6967 CORN BREAD *to* **THE** *ADVERTISER AND REGISTER*. **19 October 1864. Biloxi, Ms.** Discusses ramifications of proposal that Confederacy draft slaves to fight; urges slaveholders to persuade their slaves to volunteer in exchange for "home and freedom" in the South. 25 November 1864. p.192, c5.

6968 GEN. BENJ. BUTLER *to* **HON. WM. CLAFLIN. 30 October 1864. Virginia.** Declines invitation to speak in Massachusetts because he is convinced that voters there will not "abandon the doctrine of our fathers"; doubts that Massachusetts questions Lincoln's ability or patriotism. 2 December 1864. p.193, c2.

6969 W. G. BROWNLOW *to* **GEORGE D. PRENTICE. 5 November 1864. n.p.** Denounces the Prentice family and charges that Prentice's paper, the *Knoxville Whig*, is pro-rebel. 2 December 1864. p.193, c6.

6970 M. D. CONWAY *to* **THE** *NATIONAL ANTI-SLAVERY STANDARD*. **n.d. London.** Argues that he was sent by abolitionists to negotiate a peace in England. 2 December 1864. p.194, c4.

6971 JOHN W. ESTCOURT *to* **GARRISON. 9 November 1864. Manchester, England.** Supports the *Liberator*'s stand in the election; wants a constitutional amendment abolishing slavery. 2 December 1864. p.194, c5.

6972 SENATOR D. H. HILL *to* **THE PEOPLE OF GEORGIA. [from the** *Chronicle***] 18 November 1864. Richmond, Va.** Urges every "citizen with a gun" and "every Negro with his spade and ax" to fight the Yankees. 2 December 1864. p.195, c4.

6973 ADM. DAVID PORTER *to* **GIDEON WELLES. n.d. n.p.** Reports on the sinking of the steamer *Florida*. 2 December 1864. p.195, c5.

6974 J. F. W. HERSCHEL *to* **CAPEL H. BERGER. 6 September 1864. Collingwood.** Refuses to sign a declaration which states that there is no contradiction between Scripture and science. 2 December 1864. p.196, c6.

6975 JOHN BOWRING *to* **PROFESSOR STENHOUSE. 27 August 1864. Claremont, London, England.** Recommends testing the Bible by the laws of nature and science. 2 December 1864. p.196, c6.

6976 GEORGE NEWCOMB *to* **THE** *LIBERATOR*. **9 November 1864. Beaufort, S.C.** Reports on the election and the new school and bank in Beaufort. 9 December 1864. p.197, c4.

6977 G. JULIAN HARNEY *to* **THE** *LIBERATOR*. **6 December 1864. Boston.** Believes that an important question about the use of war to end slavery was raised by the "Conway Controversy." 9 December 1864. p.198, c2.

6978 W. L. GARRISON *to* **J. R. W. LEONARD. 25 November 1864. Boston.** Regrets that he is unable to attend the Maryland emancipation celebration. 9 December 1864. p.198, c5.

6979 GEO. B. CHEEVER *to* **SIR. 28 November 1864. New York.** Regrets his absence from the celebration of freedom in Maryland held at Cooper Institute. 9 December 1864. p.198, c5.

6980 M. DU PAYS *to* **THE EDITOR OF THE** *LIBERATOR* **[W. L. GARRISON]. 1 December 1864. New York.** Discusses the political climate in New York during the recent election. 9 December 1864. p.198, c6.

6981 HUMANITAS *to* **n.n. 28 November 1864. Camp Nelson, Ky.** Describes the cruel treatment of the families of colored soldiers. 9 December 1864. p.199, c3.

6982 ALEX FULTON *to* **n.n. 1 December 1864. Baltimore.** Reveals information he received regarding the recent attempt to burn New York City. 9 December 1864. p.199, c4.

6983 A. LINCOLN *to* **JOHN PHILLIPS. 21 November 1864. Washington.** Thanks Phillips for his devotion to civic duties. 9 December 1864. p.199, c5.

6984 LEICESTER A. SAWYER *to* **MR. EDITOR OF THE** *LIBERATOR.* **n.d. n.p.** Discusses rationalism in the Church. 9 December 1864. p.200, c2.

6985 B. GRATZ BROWN *to* **THE EDITOR OF THE** *COSMOS.* **15 November 1864. St. Louis.** Comments on Negro suffrage. 16 December 1864. p.201, c2.

6986 GOLDWIN SMITH *to* **THE EDITOR OF THE** *PHILADELPHIA PRESS.* **n.d. n.p.** Describes British aid to Confederates. 16 December 1864. p.202, c1.

6987 G. *to* **THE EDITOR OF THE** *PHILADELPHIA PRESS.* **5 December 1864. Philadelphia.** States his views on the "American ship incident" to which Mr. Goldwin Smith referred. 16 December 1864. p.202, c1.

6988 S. P. CHASE *to* **GEORGE R. HAYNES. 24 November 1864. Cincinatti.** Regrets that he cannot attend the banquet for General Ashley. 16 December 1864. p.202, c3.

6989 CHARLES SUMNER *to* **n.n. 8 November 1864. Boston.** Regrets that he is unable to attend the banquet honoring General James Ashley. 16 December 1864. p.202, c3.

6990 D. S. WHITNEY *to* **W. L. GARRISON. 21 November 1864. City Point, Va.** Comments on the hospital for colored troops. 16 December 1864. p.203, c2.

6991 GERRIT SMITH *to* **GEN. BANKS. 21 November 1864. Peterboro'.** Thanks General Banks for the informative speech he delivered in Boston. 16 December 1864. p.203, c4.

6992 LEICESTER A. SAWYER *to* **MR. EDITOR OF THE** *LIBERATOR.* **n.d. n.p.** Comments on the rationalist theory of the Bible as the rule of faith. 16 December 1864. p.204, c2.

6993 PETROLEUM V. NASBY *to* **n.n. 10 November 1864. n.p.** Fictional political satire. 16 December 1864. p.204, c6.

6994 F. W. NEWMAN *to* **n.n. 25 November 1864. London.** Comments on American political events. 23 December 1864. p.206, c4.

6995 M. DU PAYS *to* **THE EDITOR OF THE** *LIBERATOR* **[W. L. GARRISON]. 15 December 1864. New York.** Describes the Pennsylvania Freedmen's Relief Association. 23 December 1864. p.206, c5.

6996 ROLAND JOHNSON *to* **n.n. 10 December 1864. Orange, N.Y.** Encloses a recent letter from Sojourner Truth. 23 December 1864. p.206, c6.

6997 SOJOURNER TRUTH *to* **FRIEND. 17 November 1864. Freedman's Village, Va.** Comments on an interview with Lincoln. 23 December 1864. p.206, c6.

6998 JOHN M. LANGSTON *to* **THE COLORED PEOPLE OF THE UNITED STATES. 24 November 1864. Philadelphia.** Discusses the National Equal Rights League. 23 December 1864. p.207, c1.

6999 GOLDWIN SMITH *to* **HENRY T. TUCKERMAN. 8 December 1864. New York.** Thanks Tuckerman for his hospitality during Smith's trip to America. 23 December 1864. p.207, c3.

7000 L. A. SAWYER *to* **THE** *LIBERATOR***. 12 December 1864. Boston.** Informs of two misprints in Sawyer's article in the *Liberator*. 23 December 1864. p.208, c5.

7001 HARRIOT K. HUNT *to* **FREDERICK U. TRACY. 7 December 1864. Boston.** Opposes the taxation of Negroes since they are not permitted to vote. 23 December 1864. p.208, c5.

7002 TH. P. TURNER *to* **THE EDITOR OF THE** *DISPATCH***. 2 December 1864. Richmond, Va.** Disputes an article in *Dispatch* regarding military prisons in Richmond. 23 December 1864. p.208, c6.

7003 J. MILLER McKIM *to* **W. L. GARRISON. 19 December 1864. Philadelphia.** Encloses payment for his subscription to the *Liberator*; discusses the need to educate blacks. 30 December 1864. p.210, c6.

7004 HENRY C. WRIGHT *to* **GARRISON. 23 December 1864. Barnstable.** Expects passage of a constitutional amendment abolishing slavery. 30 December 1864. p.211, c2.

7005 A. TURNSTELL WELCH *to* **J. B. NOYES. 29 November 1864. Washington.** Proclaims that there is no distinction made regarding color when issuing passports. 30 December 1864. p.211, c2.

7006 W. T. SHERMAN *to* **PRES. LINCOLN. 22 December 1864. Savannah, Ga.** Presents the city of Savannah to Lincoln as a Christmas gift. 30 December 1864. p.211, c3.

7007 J. G. FOSTER *to* **LT. GEN. GRANT AND MAJ. GEN. HALLECK. 22 December. Savannah River.** Relates details of the occupation of Savannah. 30 December 1864. p.211, c3.

7008 WILLIAM A. BOARDMAN *to* **ALL PERSONS SYMPATHETIC TO MRS. PACKARD. 3 December 1864. Waukegan, Il.** Upholds Mrs. Packard's character. 30 December 1864. p.212, c2.

7009 S. S. JONES *to* **SYMPATHIZERS OF MRS. PACKARD. 2 December 1864. St. Charles, Il.** Certifies that Mrs. Packard is sane; argues that she is a victim of cruel conspiracy. 30 December 1864. p.212, c2.

7010 MANDEVILLE PINTO LINAGE *to* **THE EDITORS OF THE** *LONDON DAILY STAR***. n.d. n.p.** Satirizes the style of writing preferred by the American people. 30 December 1864. p.212, c5.

[1865]

7011 TWEED *to* **n.n. 10 December. Nashville.** Cites examples of Southern cities and states where slaves were mistreated but now receive retribution; declares that the Lord helps those in distress. 6 January 1865. p.1, c1.

7012 W. F. B. *to* **THE** *BOSTON JOURNAL***. n.d. n.p.** Presents his observations on the war after visiting Charleston. 6 January 1865. p.2, c1.

7013 R. D. WEBB *to* **FRIEND GARRISON. 7 December 1864. Dublin.** Comments on Lord Morpeth's death; supports the *Liberator*. 6 January 1865, p.2, c3.

7014 KARL BLIND *to* **F. W. CHESSON, ESQ. 15 December. London.** Regrets that he is unable to participate in the Emancipation Society presentation; affirms that he sympathizes with the emancipation cause. 6 January 1865. p.2, c6.

7015 JOSEPH A. DUGDALE *to* **FRIEND WM. L. GARRISON. 24 December 1864. Baltimore, Md.** Gives an account of his experiences in Maryland when the proclamation of freedom was made. 6 January 1865. p.3, c1.

7016 M. DU PAYS *to* **THE EDITOR OF THE *LIBERATOR* [W. L. GARRISON]. 29 December 1864. New York.** Discusses Congress' response to United States foreign policy, Reconstruction, and the Civil War. 6 January 1865. p.3, c2.

7017 J. H. FOWLER *to* **FRIEND GARRISON. 24 December 1864. Hilton Head, S.C.** Describes Sherman's successful expedition. 6 January 1865. p.3, c3.

7018 LEICESTER A. SAWYER *to* **MR. EDITOR OF THE *LIBERATOR*. 26 December 1864. Boston.** Encloses a notice from the *New York Observer* regarding Sawyer's views on rationalism. 6 January 1865. p.4, c2.

7019 W. F. MITCHELL *to* **J. MILLER McKIM. 7 December 1864. Nashville, Tn.** Discusses the condition of Tennessee freedmen. 6 January 1865. p.4, c5.

7020 THEODORE PARKER *to* **n.n. [extract] November 1859. Rome.** Laments that slavery cannot be abolished without bloodshed. 13 January 1865. p.5, c6.

7021 ANDREW JACKSON *to* **COL. J. A. HAMILTON. 2 November 1832. Washington.** Acknowledges receipt of Hamilton's letter; declares that the Union will be preserved. 13 January 1865. p.6, c1.

7022 ANDREW JACKSON *to* **COL. J. A. HAMILTON. 6 December 1832. Washington.** Declares that citizens of South Carolina must adhere to the Constitution which they have sworn to support. 13 January 1865. p.6, c1.

7023 HENRY C. WRIGHT *to* **WM. LLOYD GARRISON. n.d. n.p.** Details the *Liberator*'s history of opposition to slavery and support of Lincoln. 13 January 1865. p.6, c6.

7024 JAMES DENSMORE *to* **THE EDITOR OF THE *LIBERATOR* [W. L. GARRISON]. n.d. Miller Farm, Oil Creek, Pa.** Praises the *Liberator* for its generally impartial political views, but opposes its support of Lincoln. 13 January 1865. p.8, c2.

7025 JEHIEL CLAFLIN *to* **FRIEND GARRISON. 7 January 1865. East Westmoreland, N.H.** Praises the *Liberator* for its unceasing criticism of slavery; accepts the *Liberator*'s support of Lincoln. 13 January 1865. p.8, c2.

7026 J. LAMBORN *to* **FRIEND GARRISON. 25 December 1864. Mount Gilbore, In.** Recalls when Garrison was jailed in his youth for being an abolitionist; prays that Garrison will live to see slavery abolished. 13 January 1865. p.8, c2.

7027 JOHN BAILEY *to* **FRIEND GARRISON. 5 January 1865. Lynn.** Discontinues his subscription because he is unable to pay; urges the *Liberator* to continue its opposition to slavery. 13 January 1865. p.8, c2.

7028 D. H. BLAKE *to* **THE** *NEW YORK TRIBUNE*. **n.d. n.p.** Decries the deplorable condition of prisoners in the Andersonville stockade. 13 January 1865. p.8, c3.

7029 THEODORE TILTON *to* **THE** *MISSOURI DEMOCRAT*. **5 January. Chicago.** Raises the issue of "giving voting privileges to those who can read" to members of the Missouri Constitutional Convention. 20 January 1865. p.10, c2.

7030 M. D. CONWAY *to* *COMMONWEALTH*. **17 December 1864. London.** Refutes Garrison's comments on Conway. 20 January 1865. p.10, c3.

7031 M. DU PAYS *to* **THE EDITOR OF THE** *LIBERATOR* **[W. L. GARRISON]. 12 January 1865. New York.** Remarks on the war and the presence of slavery in the border states. 20 January 1865. p.11, c1.

7032 WM. H. SEWARD *to* **n.n. 15 January 1865. Washington.** Informs that the president requests that Edward Everett's death be announced. 20 January 1865. p.11, c2.

7033 GOV. JOHN A. ANDREW *to* **HON. CHARLES SUMNER AND HON. HENRY WILSON. 15 January 1865. Boston.** Proclaims that the state of Massachusetts mourns the death of Edward Everett. 20 January 1865. p.11, c2.

7034 CHARLES SUMNER *to* **MR. WHITE. 26 December 1864. Senate Chamber.** Regrets that he is unable to attend the second anniversary celebration of the Emancipation Proclamation; adds that he will celebrate in his heart. 20 January 1865. p.11, c2.

7035 FREDERICK DOUGLASS *to* **n.n. [extract] n.d. n.p.** States that he is unable to attend the Emancipation Proclamation celebration at National Hall. 20 January 1865. p.11, c2.

7036 F. C. FLETCHER *to* **GOV. A. G. CURTIN. 11 January 1865. Jefferson City, Mo.** Announces that the state of Missouri, which has abandoned slavery, greets her oldest sister, the state of Pennsylvania. 20 January 1865. p.11, c3.

7037 A. G. CURTIN *to* **F. C. FLETCHER. n.d. n.p.** Replies that the state of Pennsylvania welcomes the state of Missouri because it has abolished slavery. 20 January 1865. p.11, c3.

7038 SAMUEL CONY, GOVERNOR OF MAINE *to* **GOV. FLETCHER. 13 January 1865. Augusta, Me.** Announces that the state of Maine welcomes Missouri into the family of non-slaveholding states. 20 January 1865. p.11, c3.

7039 F. C. FLETCHER *to* **GOVERNOR OF NEW YORK. 11 January 1865. Jefferson City, Mo.** Announces that free Missouri greets the state of New York. 20 January 1865. p.11, c3.

7040 R. E. FENTON *to* **GOVERNOR FLETCHER. 12 January 1865. Albany, N.Y.** Blesses Missouri because it is now a non-slaveholding state. 20 January 1865. p.11, c3.

7041 GOV. JOHN A. ANDREW *to* **GOV. F. C. FLETCHER. 13 January 1865. Boston.** Announces that Massachusetts salutes Missouri as a commonwealth of freedmen. 20 January 1865. p.11, c3.

7042 JOHN PARKMAN, F. J. CHILD, AND WM. ENDICOTT, JR., EXECUTIVE COMMITTEE OF THE NEW ENGLAND FREEDMEN'S AID SOCIETY *to* **THE EDITOR OF THE** *BOSTON JOURNAL*. **n.d. n.p.** Enclose an appeal from General Saxton; ask for contributions to benefit liberated Georgia Negroes. 20 January 1865. p.11, c4.

7043 GEN. RUFUS SAXTON *to* **NEW ENGLAND FREEDMEN'S AID SOCIETY. 6 January 1865. Beaufort, S.C.** Appeals for contributions to aid thousands of suffering Negroes whom General Sherman liberated. 20 January 1865. p.11, c4.

7044 ALFRED H. TERRY *to* **BRIG. GEN. JOHN A. RAWLINGS. 15 January. North Carolina.** Announces with gratification that Washington has been notified of the fall of Fort Fisher. 20 January 1865. p.11, c4.

7045 JOHN A. ANDREW *to* **LEWIS HAYDEN. 21 December 1864. Boston.** Sends a gavel, made from the whipping post at Hampton, Virginia, for presentation to the Prince Hall Grand Lodge. 20 January 1865. p.11, c5.

7046 W. J. POND *to* **W. L. GARRISON, ESQ. 6 January 1865. Washington, D.C.** Declares that Negroes were excluded from the reception for the president; adds that the majority of whites approved this action. 20 January 1865. p.12, c2.

7047 GEO. TRASK *to* **MR. EDITOR [W. L. GARRISON]. January 1865. Fitchburg Temperance Depository, Ma.** Warns that more effort is needed to curb intemperance; adds that temperance tracts must be distributed. 20 January 1865. p.12, c3.

7048 MALLAH *to* **n.n. [from the *Watchman and Reflector*] 28 December 1864. Norfolk, Va.** Pleads for a serious effort to aid blacks in slave states. 20 January 1865. p.12, c4.

7049 J. F. MURRAY *to* **MR. GARRISON. 15 January 1865. Bangor.** Encloses money for a year's subscription to the *Liberator*; praises Garrison. 27 January 1865. p.14, c6.

7050 S. S. FOSTER *to* **THE EDITOR OF THE *LIBERATOR* [W. L. GARRISON]. 16 January 1865. Worcester.** Urges the Worcester County AS not to give financial support to the *Liberator* because it approves the appointment of McClellan as commander-in-chief of the army. 27 January 1865. p.14, c6.

7051 S. J. MAY, JR. *to* **MR. GARRISON. 24 January 1865. Boston.** Disagrees with Mr. Foster's charge that the anti-slavery cause has been betrayed by W. L. Garrison. 27 January 1865. p.14, c6.

7052 J. M. McKIM *to* **FRIEND. 17 January 1865. Philadelphia.** Stresses that the Negro's right to vote must be on the same terms as that of the white man. 27 January 1865. p.15, c1.

7053 AMASA WALKER *to* **GARRISON. 10 January 1865. North Brookfield.** Describes an eloquent lecture given by their mutual friend, George Thompson. 27 January 1865. p.15, c1.

7054 MARTHA B. GOODRICH *to* **MR. GARRISON. Christmas 1864. Boston.** Thanks the *Liberator* for its contribution to her education; encloses fifty dollars. 27 January 1865. p.15, c1.

7055 BERWICK *to* **THE EDITOR OF THE *BOSTON JOURNAL*. 15 January 1865. Nashville.** Describes a convention in Tennessee concerning the abolition of slavery in that state. 27 January 1865. p.15, c2.

7056 EDWARD EVERETT *to* **MR. GRAY. 12 January 1865. Summer Street.** Informs Gray of his ill health and continued activity. 27 January 1865. p.15, c3.

7057 W. H. SEWARD *to* **GOV. ANDREW OF BOSTON. 18 January. Washington.** Informs that it is impossible for Lincoln and his cabinet to attend Edward Everett's funeral. 27 January 1865. p.15, c3.

7058 ALFRED H. LOVE *to* **WM. LLOYD GARRISON. 17 January 1865. Philadelphia.** Praises an eloquent lecture by George Thompson at the Concert Hall in Philadelphia. 27 January 1865. p.16, c2.

7059 WILLIAM E. MATTHEWS *to* **MR. GARRISON. 14 January 1865. Baltimore.** Chronicles events in Maryland since emancipation. 27 January 1865. p.16, c2.

7060 PRES. ABRAHAM LINCOLN *to* **ELIZA P. GURNEY. n.d. n.p.** Feels indebted to Mrs. Gurney and other good Christians for their prayers; declares that God knows best and that some good will come from the trials of oppression. 27 January 1865. p.16, c5.

7061 n.n. *to* **THE EDITOR OF THE** *BOSTON JOURNAL.* **15 January. Washington.** Contrasts Henry S. Foote's current anti-slavery views with his pro-slavery convictions of twenty years ago. 3 February 1865. p.17, c4.

7062 GEO. NEWCOMB *to* **MR. EDITOR. 6 January 1865. Beaufort, S.C.** Reports on the liberty celebration by blacks in Beaufort. 3 February 1865. p.17, c5.

7063 NATH. HALL *to* **MR. GARRISON. 27 January 1865. Dorchester.** Encloses ten dollars; thanks Garrison for helping him and for working to abolish slavery. 3 February 1865. p.18, c2.

7064 J. M. McKIM *to* **MR. THOMPSON. 25 January 1865. Philadelphia.** Implores Mr. Thompson to continue working in behalf of the abolitionist cause; believes that slaves have been liberated but not freed. 3 February 1865. p.19, c3.

7065 M. DU PAYS *to* **THE EDITOR [W. L. GARRISON]. January 1865. New York.** Reports on new state legislation concerning blacks. 3 February 1865. p.19, c4.

7066 A. H. LOVE *to* **WM. LLOYD GARRISON. 21 January 1865. Philadelphia.** Praises George Thompson's lecture at the Spring Garden Institute. 3 February 1865. p.19, c5.

7067 C. A. F. S. *to* **THE EDITOR OF THE** *LIBERATOR* **[W. L. GARRISON]. 16 January 1865. Rochester.** Criticizes a lecture given by Dr. Holland, editor of the *Springfield Republican*; reports that Holland ridiculed emancipation. 3 February 1865. p.20, c2.

7068 A. G. GOODWIN *to* **H. D. CUSHING, ESQ. 18 February 1864. Boston.** States that the Boston Provident Association has aided 34,126 families over the past eleven years. 3 February 1865. p.20, c6.

7069 JOHN W. WARREN *to* **H. D. CUSHING, ESQ. 26 February 1864. Boston.** States that over the past seven years the city of Boston has helped approximately 284,000 people. 3 February 1865. p.20, c6.

7070 R. G. *to* **FRIEND GARRISON. 16 January 1865. Boston.** Encloses money, asking that the *Liberator* be sent to his elderly friend, John Bailey of Lynn. 17 February 1865. p.27, c1.

7071 ABRAHAM LINCOLN *to* **MR. GARRISON. 7 February 1865. Washington.** Apologizes for not sooner acknowledging receipt of the painting "Waiting for the Hour," sent by William Garrison. 17 February 1865. p.27, c1.

7072 H. W. BEECHER *to* **MR. GARRISON. 4 February 1865. Brooklyn.** Donates twenty-five dollars to the *Liberator* in appreciation for having received it free in the past; declares that slavery is evil. 17 February 1865. p.27, c1.

7073 M. DU PAYS *to* **THE EDITOR [W. L. GARRISON]. 9 February 1865. New York.** Expresses concern that freedmen will not be treated as equals, despite emancipation. 17 February 1865. p.27, c2.

7074 GEO. TRASK *to* **MR. GARRISON. 9 February 1865. Fitchburg.** Reports his receipt of $300 from friends of religious societies who bade him continue his temperance mission. 17 February 1865. p.27, c3.

7075 ALEXANDER H. STEPHENS, R. M. T. HUNTER, AND J. A. CAMPBELL *to* **THE PRESIDENT OF THE CONFEDERATE STATES. n.d. n.p.** Describe an informal conference they had with President Lincoln and Secretary of State Seward regarding the president's plans for peace. 17 February 1865. p.27, c4.

7076 EBENEZER D. BASSETT AND WILLIAM J. ALSTON *to* **THE EDITOR OF THE** *PHILADELPHIA PRESS.* **12 January 1865. Philadelphia.** Report on discrimination in Philadelphia's passenger cars. 17 February 1865. p.28, c6.

7077 GERRIT SMITH *to* **J. M. ASHLEY. 6 February 1865. Peterboro.** Details the antislavery measures proposed in the United States Congress. 24 February 1865. p.29, c3.

7078 N. P. BANKS *to* **WM. LLOYD GARRISON. 30 January 1865. Washington, D.C.** Details the proposed course of action regarding freedmen in Louisiana. 24 February 1865. p.30, c2.

7079 JAMES BOWEN *to* **W. L. GARRISON. 11 February 1865. New York.** Praises the efforts of General Banks to help colored people in Louisiana. 24 February 1865. p.30, c6.

7080 RICHARD B. IRWIN *to* **MAJOR GENERAL N. P. BANKS. 3 January 1865. New York.** Replies to Banks that the Negro troops at Port Hudson were not refused permission to use Port Hudson on their standards. 24 February 1865. p.30, c6.

7081 JNO. M. B. BARCLAY *to* **N. P. BANKS. 30 December 1864. House of Representatives, United States.** Informs Banks of Senate activity concerning amendment of the charter of the city of Washington. 24 February 1865. p.30, c6.

7082 G. PILLSBURY *to* **MR. GARRISON. 18 February 1865. Hilton Head, S.C.** Responds to charges made by Dr. T. P. Knox against General Saxton regarding the condition of freedmen in South Carolina; explains that conditions are deplorable despite sincere efforts to improve them. 24 February 1865. p.31, c1.

7083 n.n. *to* **MR. GARRISON. 17 February 1865. Point Lookout, Md.** Praises the fidelity and high military and personal merit of Colonel Henry S. Russell; encloses a letter from the officers of Colonel Russell's regiment. 24 February 1865. p.31, c2.

7084 n.n. *to* **COL. HENRY S. RUSSELL. 5 February 1865. Point Lookout, Md.** States that all thirty-seven officers present with the regiment regret that Colonel Russell is leaving the service. 24 February 1865. p.31, c2.

7085 WM. S. FLANDERS *to* **n.n. 11 February 1865. Cornville, Me.** Contrasts the plight of the Negro with that of Joan of Arc. 24 February 1865. p.31, c2.

7086 SARAH B. SHAW *to* **MR. GARRISON. 14 February 1865. Staten Island.** Encloses fifty dollars for a year's subscription to the *Liberator.* 24 February 1865. p.31, c3.

7087 W. T. ALLAN *to* **BROTHER GARRISON. 9 February 1865. Geneseo, Il.** Praises the *Liberator.* 24 February 1865. p.31, c3.

7088 WM. H. CHANNING *to* **W. L. GARRISON. 3 February 1865. Washington.** States that suffering among Negroes in Washington is intense; questions the *Liberator*'s support of Lincoln. 24 February 1865. p.31, c3.

7089 Q. A. GILMORE *to* **MAJOR-GENERAL HALLECK. 18 February 1862. Charleston, S.C.** Announces that Charleston has been completely occupied. 24 February 1865. p.31, c4.

7090 DANIEL W. BAKER *to* **MR. GARRISON. 1 February 1865. Boston.** Encloses an article for insertion in the *Liberator*. 24 February 1865. p.32, c2.

7091 HENRY C. WRIGHT *to* **W. L. GARRISON. 1 February 1865. Cape Ann.** Rejoices that slavery is forever prohibited in the United States. 24 February 1865. p.32, c3.

7092 CAROLINE H. DALL *to* **THE EDITOR OF THE** *COMMONWEALTH.* **11 February. Boston.** Criticizes a letter in the *Commonwealth* for stating that Australia was the first place to recognize the right of women's suffrage; details the history of women's suffrage. 24 February 1865. p.32, c5.

7093 EDWARD HARRIS *to* **LYDIA MARIA CHILD, MARY MAY, AND LOUISA LORING. n.d. n.p.** Encloses a contribution to assist their cause; states that "Females govern the world." 3 March 1865. p.33, c2.

7094 SAMUEL J. MAY *to* **LYDIA CHILD, MARY MAY, LOUISA LORING, AND OTHERS. 20 January 1865. Syracuse.** Speaks warmly of his association with W. L. Garrison and the AS; extends best wishes for the success of the National Anti-Slavery Subscription Anniversary. 3 March 1865. p.33, c3.

7095 THEODORE TILTON *to* **MRS. L. M. CHILD. 22 January 1865. New York.** Urges that every person who can read, regardless of color, be given the opportunity to vote. 3 March 1865. p.33, c3.

7096 EDGAR KETCHUM *to* **n.n. 12 January 1865. New York.** Encloses a check for the ladies' committee of the National Anti-Slavery Subscription Anniversary; rejoices at the announcement of freedom for Missouri. 3 March 1865. p.33, c3.

7097 SOPHIA L. LITTLE *to* **LADIES OF AS. 22 January 1865. Newport.** Sends moral support and money for the AS festival. 3 March 1865. p.33, c3.

7098 MARTHA SMITH *to* **FRIENDS. 23 January 1865. Plainfield, Ct.** Sends money to Friends of Slaves in order to further their cause. 3 March 1865. p.33, c3.

7099 M. E. WHITCOMB *to* **MRS. MAY. [extract] 12 January 1865. Brooklyn, N.Y.** Encloses money for the cause of freedom. 3 March 1865. p.33, c3.

7100 S. LASAR *to* **WILLIAM I. BOWDITCH. 23 January 1865. New York.** Sends money to help rid the country of slavery. 3 March 1865. p.33, c4.

7101 NATHANIEL BARNEY *to* **L. M. CHILD. 23 January 1865. Yonkers, N.Y.** Encloses money for the national anti-slavery treasury; ponders the early sacrifices which L. M. Child made on behalf of the AS. 3 March 1865. p.33, c4.

7102 THOMAS WORCESTER *to* **MRS. CHILD. 25 January 1865. n.p.** Thanks Mrs. Child for helping him to see the evil of slavery; realizes that war is necessary for the country's welfare. 3 March 1865. p.33, c5.

7103 E. W. TWING *to* **THE MANAGERS OF THE ANTI-SLAVERY SUBSCRIPTION ANNIVERSARY. 22 January 1865. Springfield.** Praises their work in behalf of the AAS; encloses a check. 3 March 1865. p.33, c5.

7104 MARY P. PAYSON *to* **LADIES. 22 January 1865. Peterboro, N.H.** Encloses a check but declines to visit them in Boston because of poor health. 3 March 1865. p.33, c5.

7105 DANIEL MANN *to* **n.n. 8 January 1865. City Point, Va.** Feels confident that freedom will triumph. 3 March 1865. p.33, c5.

7106 AN OLD ABOLITIONIST *to* **WILLIAM LLOYD GARRISON, n.d. n.p.** Suggests that the AS be replaced by a society to promote the personal welfare of Indians after emancipation is completed. 3 March 1865. p.34, c1.

7107 E. M. WHEELOCK *to* **MR. GARRISON. 8 February 1865. New Orleans.** Supports Banks' labor system in Louisiana. 3 March 1865. p.34, c4.

7108 M. DU PAYS *to* **THE EDITOR OF THE** *LIBERATOR* **[W. L. GARRISON]. 23 February 1865. New York.** Reports on celebrations in New York over the "taking of Charleston." 3 March 1865. p.34, c6.

7109 PARKER PILLSBURY *to* **FRIEND GARRISON. 26 February 1865. Concord, N.H.** Regrets that his remarks at the anti-slavery meeting were misinterpreted, thus doing General Saxton a grave injustice. 3 March 1865. p.35, c1.

7110 JOHN BAILEY *to* **FRIEND GARRISON. 27 February 1865. Lynn, Ma.** Thanks those who paid for his subscription to the *Liberator*. 3 March 1865. p.35, c2.

7111 HENRY WARD BEECHER *to* **n.n. 13 February 1865. Brooklyn.** Discusses the success of emancipation in Maryland; expresses hope for black education; claims that J. Davis wanted to defeat the amendment act. 10 March 1865. p.37, c1.

7112 JOHN G. WHITTIER *to* **ROBERT C. WATERSTON. 27 January 1865. Amesbury.** Pays tribute to Edward Everett. 10 March 1865. p.37, c5.

7113 CARLETON *to* **THE** *BOSTON JOURNAL.* **13 February 1865. Savannah.** Describes the effect of the war on the South. 10 March 1865. p.37, c6.

7114 CARLETON *to* **THE** *BOSTON JOURNAL.* **23 February 1865. Charleston.** Reports on conditions in Charleston. 10 March 1865. p.38, c1.

7115 GEORGE SUNTER *to* **MR. GARRISON. 28 February 1865. Bradford, Canada West.** Discusses "white" provisions in the new state constitutions of Nevada and Louisiana. 10 March 1865. p.39, c1.

7116 THOMAS P. KNOX *to* **THE EDITOR OF THE** *LIBERATOR* **[W. L. GARRISON]. 2 March 1865. Boston.** Explains his expulsion from South Carolina by General Saxton. 10 March 1865. p.39, c2.

7117 CHAPLAIN J. H. FOWLER *to* **FRIEND GARRISON. 27 February 1865. Beaufort, S.C.** Criticizes Thomas Knox's character. 10 March 1865. p.39, c2.

7118 SAMUEL MAY, JR. *to* **MR. GARRISON. 6 March 1865. Leicester.** States that Pillsbury's remarks about General Saxton were reported accurately. 10 March 1865. p.39, c3.

7119 E. M. STANTON *to* **MAJOR GENERAL DIX. 5 March. Washington.** States that notification of the defeat and capture of General Early and the capture of Charlottesville has been received; discusses General Sheridan at Staunton. 10 March 1865. p.39, c4.

7120 U. S. GRANT *to* **HON. E. M. STANTON, SECRETARY OF WAR. 5 March, 11 a.m. City Point, Va.** Informs that deserters report that Sheridan routed General Early and captured Charlottesville. 10 March 1865. p.39, c4.

7121 U. S. GRANT *to* **E. M. STANTON. 5 March, 2 p.m. City Point, Va.** States that many deserters confirm that Charlottesville was captured by General Sheridan. 10 March 1865. p.39, c4.

7122 U. S. GRANT *to* **E. M. STANTON. 5 March, 4 p.m. City Point, Va.** Reports that refugees confirm the capture of General Early and most of his force. 10 March 1865. p.39, c4.

7123 GERRIT SMITH *to* **WILLIAM LLOYD GARRISON. 22 February 1865. Peterboro.** Believes that theology is a hindrance to justice and reform. 10 March 1865. p.40, c2.

7124 DAVID S. CODDINGTON *to* **ABRAHAM LINCOLN. 4 March 1865. New York.** Congratulates Lincoln upon his second inauguration as president of behalf of the Workingmen's Association of New York. 17 March 1865. p.41, c2.

7125 R. E. LEE *to* **HON. E. BARKSDALE. 18 February. Richmond, Va.** Agrees that Negroes should be employed as soldiers; concludes that, under proper circumstances, Negroes will make efficient soldiers. 17 March 1865. p.41, c5.

7126 J. C. FLETCHER *to* **EDITOR OF THE** *BOSTON JOURNAL.* **11 March 1865. Boston.** Requests that anti-slavery sermons and pamphlets be forwarded to J. M. Whittemore and Company in Boston. 17 March 1865. p.42, c2.

7127 JOHN G. WHITTIER *to* **C. C. COFFIN. 9 March 1865. Amesbury.** Rejoices in Coffin's arrival in Boston with the slavery relics. 17 March 1865. p.42, c2.

7128 JOHN HUTCHINS *to* **WILLIAM LLOYD GARRISON. 22 February 1865. Washington.** Defends General Banks' plans in Louisiana regarding the welfare of freedmen. 17 March 1865. p.42, c3.

7129 AMANDA H. GEST *to* **WILLIAM LLOYD GARRISON. 22 February 1865. New Orleans.** Defends Banks' plans for improving conditions of freedmen. 17 March 1865. p.42, c5.

7130 THOMAS P. KNOX *to* **THE EDITOR OF THE** *LIBERATOR* **[W. L. GARRISON]. 13 March 1865. Boston.** Criticizes Chaplain Fowler for writing a degrading letter about him; states that no charge by General Saxton was ever levelled against Knox. 17 March 1865. p.43, c1.

7131 M. DU PAYS *to* **THE EDITOR OF THE** *LIBERATOR* **[W. L. GARRISON]. 9 March 1865. New York.** Discusses the Fugitive Slave Law and the Compromise of 1850. 17 March 1865. p.43, c2.

7132 J. H. FOWLER *to* **FRIEND GARRISON. 24 February 1865. Beaufort, S.C.** Declares that Negroes deserve respect and should be given land. 17 March 1865. p.44, c4.

7133 L. MARIA CHILD *to* **THE** *INDEPENDENT.* **7 March 1865. Wayland.** States that the slaves' living conditions are improving slowly. 24 March 1865. p.45, c2.

7134 A SUBSCRIBER *to* **THE** *BOSTON DAILY ADVERTISER.* **n.d. n.p.** Encloses an extract of a speech at Ashton-under-Lyne by Hon. T. Milner Gibson, an English friend. 24 March 1865. p.45, c6.

7135 A CONSTANT READER *to* **MR. GARRISON. n.d. n.p.** Encloses an article from the *Boston Traveller* on Garrison's anti-slavery work; questions whether the *Liberator* will be discontinued at the end of the volume. 24 March 1865. p.46, c2.

7136 L. MARIA CHILD *to* **FRIEND GARRISON. 15 March 1865. Wayland.** Urges Garrison to continue to protect Negroes; disagrees with Garrison regarding General Banks' labor system in Louisiana. 24 March 1865. p.46, c3.

7137 F. W. CHESSON *to* **MR. GARRISON. 18 February 1865. London.** Discusses politics in the United States and England; comments on the progress of Haiti under President Geffrard. 24 March 1865. p.46, c5

7138 HENRY C. WRIGHT *to* **WM. LLOYD GARRISON. 19 March 1865. West Gloucester.** Details a Confederate discussion about arming blacks. 24 March 1865. p.46, c5.

7139 L. MARIA CHILD *to* **EDITOR OF THE** *TRANSCRIPT.* **n.d. n.p.** Encloses a letter she received from Rev. William H. Channing. 24 March 1865. p.46, c6.

7140 WM. H. CHANNING *to* **L. M. CHILD. 8 March 1865. Washington.** Comments on the progress of black liberation; discusses Lincoln's inauguration. 24 March 1865. p.46, c6.

7141 WM. HOWARD DAY *to* **WM. C. NELL. 3 March 1865. New York City.** Implores that the truth about Negroes be broadcast so that they will be treated justly. 24 March 1865. p.47, c2.

7142 R. FOSTER *to* **THE** *LIBERATOR.* **n.d. n.p.** Seeks aid for the family of the late Daniel Foster. 24 March 1865. p.48, c3.

7143 MILES R. ROBINSON, JAMES WALLACE, AND R. C. MARSHALL *to* **THE** *PHILADELPHIA PRESS.* **n.d. n.p.** Describe the experience of not being allowed to ride Philadelphia streetcars. 24 March 1865. p.48, c5.

7144 A. BATTLES *to* **MR. GARRISON. 22 March 1865. Bangor.** Sends financial and moral support for the *Liberator.* 31 March 1865. p.50, c4.

7145 SAMUEL H. VIRGIN *to* **n.n. 20 March 1865. Leominster.** Recommends Mrs. Frances E.W. Harper as a lecturer. 31 March 1865. p.50, c4.

7146 DANIEL MANN *to* **FRIEND. 27 March 1865. Washington, D.C.** Praises the late Daniel Foster. 31 March 1865. p.50, c4.

7147 M. DU PAYS *to* **THE EDITOR [W. L. GARRISON]. 23 March 1865. New York.** Describes the condition of freedmen in various locations throughout the South. 31 March 1865. p.50, c5.

7148 THOMAS H. BARKER *to* **MR. GARRISON. 4 March 1865. Manchester, England.** States that the Emancipation Society criticizes the United States because the slaves are gaining their rights too slowly. 31 March 1865. p.50, c6.

7149 B. RUSH PLUMLY *to* **THE EDITOR [W. L. GARRISON]. 6 March 1865. New Orleans, La.** Defends Banks' programs in Louisiana, especially those concerning education. 31 March 1865. p.51, c3.

7150 GEORGE NEWCOMB *to* **n.n. 9 March. Charleston, S.C.** Discusses changes occurring in Charleston now that the rebels have left the city. 31 March 1865. p.51, c4.

7151 T. J. DURANT *to* **CUTHBERT BULLITT. 15 July 1862. New Orleans.** Comments on the political manipulations in Louisiana during the Reconstruction. 7 April 1865. p.54, c5.

7152 ABRAHAM LINCOLN *to* **CUTHBERT BULLITT. 28 July 1862. Washington, D.C.** Questions why Durant chooses to criticize the government rather than to contribute to its improvement. 7 April 1865. p.55, c1.

7153 JOHN A. ANDREW *to* **EDWIN M. STANTON. 3 April 1865. Boston.** Sends a congratulatory dispatch regarding the downfall of Petersburg and Richmond; reports that businesses are closing and people are celebrating. 7 April 1865. p.55, c5.

7154 EDWIN M. STANTON *to* **MAJOR GEN. DIX. 3 April. City Point, Va.** States that Richmond was captured at 8:15 a.m. on 3 April. 7 April 1865. p.55, c6.

7155 ABRAHAM LINCOLN *to* **E. M. STANTON. 2 April, 4 p.m., City Point, Va.** Reports that General Grant telegraphed troops about enveloping Petersburg. 7 April 1865. p.55, c6.

7156 ABRAHAM LINCOLN *to* **E. M. STANTON. 2 April, 4 p.m. City Point, Va.** Reports that Petersburg is being captured. 7 April 1835. p.55, c6.

7157 JAMES PEDDIE *to* **COL. BENEDICT. 1 January 1863. La Premiere Plantation.** Seeks aid in controlling his contrabands. 7 April 1835. p.56, c2.

7158 T. K. HERBERT *to* **WM. LLOYD GARRISON. 6 March 1865. Washington.** Defends himself against General Banks' accusation that he gave a false report of a flogging. 7 April 1865. p.56, c2.

7159 M. TREVINO *to* **HIS EXCELLENCY M. ROMERO. 22 February 1864. Brownsville.** Informs that he has no knowledge of an offer by Captain Herbert to deliver several persons to Mexican authorities. 7 April 1865. p.56, c5.

7160 F. J. HERRON *to* **JOSEPH HOLT. 21 February 1864. Brownsville, Tx.** Confirms the gentlemanly conduct of Captain Herbert. 7 April 1865. p.56, c5.

7161 n.n. *to* **MR. MAY. 15 March 1865. Dublin.** A young Irishman writes of his elation upon hearing that Congress passed the anti-slavery amendment. 14 April 1865. p.58, c5.

7162 M. DU PAYS *to* **THE EDITOR [W. L. GARRISON]. 6 April 1865. New York.** Discusses the end of the war; agrees that the *Liberator* has achieved its goals and should end publication. 14 April 1865. p.58, c5.

7163 GEORGE THOMPSON *to* **MR. WALLCUT. 8 April 1865. New York.** Reports that he is preparing to embark on a voyage to historic Charleston with Garrison, Theodore Tilton, and Senator Wilson. 14 April 1865. p.58, c6.

7164 EDWIN M. STANTON *to* **MAJOR GEN. DIX. 9 April 1865. Washington.** States that the War Department received the official report of surrender by General Lee to Lieutenant General Grant on 9 April. 14 April 1865. p.59, c1.

7165 U. S. GRANT *to* **E. M. STANTON. 9 April. Headquarters Armies of United States.** Proclaims that General Lee surrendered the Army of Northern Virginia. 14 April 1865. p.59, c1.

7166 R. E. LEE *to* **GEN. GRANT. 9 April 1865. n.p.** Requests an interview to discuss the proposition of 8 April. 14 April 1865. p.59, c1.

7167 U. S. GRANT *to* **R. E. LEE. 9 April 1865. n.p.** Acknowledges receipt of Lee's note; agrees to push forward in order to meet him. 14 April 1865. p.59, c1.

7168 U. S. GRANT *to* **GEN. R.E. LEE. 9 April 1865. Appomattox Court House.** Proposes to receive the surrender of the Army of Northern Virginia; includes the terms of surrender. 14 April 1865. p.59, c1.

7169 U. S. GRANT *to* **EDWIN M. STANTON. 9 April 1865. Clifton House, Va.** Encloses correspondence between Lee and himself. 14 April 1865. p.59, c1.

7170 U. S. GRANT *to* **GEN. R. E. LEE. 8 April 1865. n.p.** Lists the conditions necessary to accept surrender. 14 April 1865. p.59, c1.

7171 R. E. LEE *to* **GENERAL GRANT. 8 April 1865. n.p.** Explains that he intended to ask for Grant's terms of peace, but not the surrender of the Army of Northern Virginia. 14 April 1865. p.59, c1.

7172 U. S. GRANT *to* **GEN. LEE. 9 April 1865. n.p.** Acknowledges receipt of the note of 8 April; explains that he has no authority to "treat" on the subject of peace, but that he is as anxious for peace as is Lee. 14 April 1865. p.59, c1.

7173 EDWIN M. STANTON *to* **GEN. GRANT. 9 April 1865. Washington, D.C.** Thanks God for their great victory. 14 April, 1865. p.59, c1.

7174 P. H. SHERIDAN *to* **LIEUT. GEN. GRANT. 6 April. n.p.** Reports an enemy attack on the Burks Station Road. 14 April 1865. p.59, c3.

7175 D. W. B. *to* **MR. EDITOR. n.d. n.p.** Discusses his recent visit to Washington. 14 April 1865. p.60, c2.

7176 MR. HACKETT *to* **n.n. 6 March 1865. New York.** Gives a character sketch of Andrew Johnson. 14 April 1865. p.60, c6.

7177 HENRY C. WRIGHT *to* **WM. LLOYD GARRISON. 3 April 1865. West Newbury.** Discusses the question of suffrage. 21 April 1865. p.62, c5.

7178 L. MARIA CHILD *to* **FRIEND GARRISON. 4 April 1865. Wayland.** Notes the success of F. E. W. Harper's lecture. 21 April 1865. p.62, c6.

7179 EDWIN M. STANTON *to* **MAJOR GEN. DIX. 16 April. Washington.** Discusses the shooting of President Lincoln at Ford's Theatre; reports that the President is not expected to live. 21 April 1865. p.63, c1.

7180 E. M. STANTON *to* **MAJOR GENERAL DIX. 15 April. Washington.** Announces the death of Abraham Lincoln. 21 April 1865. p.63, c1.

7181 THOMAS HASKELL *to* **FRIEND GARRISON. 2 April 1864. West Gloucester, Ma.** Criticizes article by E. H. H. in the *Liberator* because it condemns the North and approves the South. 21 April 1865. p.64, c2.

7182 C. STEARNS *to* **GARRISON. 27 March 1865. Central City, Colorado Territory.** Believes that abolitionists will continue their efforts if they emanate from a love of man rather than a hatred of slavery. 21 April 1865. p.64, c2.

7183 CARLETON *to* **THE EDITOR OF THE** *BOSTON JOURNAL.* **5 April 1865. Richmond.** Comments on conditions in Richmond. 21 April 1865. p.64, c3.

7184 E. M. STANTON *to* **LIEUT. GEN. GRANT. 3 March 1865. Washington.** States that the president directs Stanton not to confer with Lee or discuss political questions; states that it is the president alone who discusses such questions. 28 April 1865. p.66, c2.

7185 M. DU PAYS *to* **THE EDITOR OF THE** *LIBERATOR* **[W. L. GARRISON]. 20 April 1865. New York.** Comments on the end of the war and the death of Lincoln. 28 April 1865. p.67, c3.

7186 HENRY C. WRIGHT *to* **W. L. GARRISON. 15 April 1865. Gloucester.** Believes that slaveholders are responsible for the death of Lincoln; declares Lincoln a martyr to free labor. 28 April 1865. p.67, c3.

7187 WENDELL PHILLIPS *to* **THE MEMBERS OF THE AAS. 10 April 1865. Boston.** States that the disbanding of the AAS is not possible until its work is accomplished. 28 April 1865. p.67, c4.

7188 EDWIN M. STANTON *to* **n.n. 24 April 1865. Washington.** States belief that the president's murder was organized in Canada. 28 April 1865. p.67, c6.

7189 DONALD G. MITCHELL *to* **JOHN PIERPONT. [from the** *Washington Chronicle***] 25 March 1865. Edgewood.** Sends greetings to Pierpont on his eightieth birthday. 28 April 1865. p.68, c4.

7190 RICHARD H. DANA, JR. *to* **REV. JOHN PIERPONT, D.D. [from the** *Washington Chronicle***] 6 April 1865. n.p.** Extends birthday wishes; thanks Pierpont for writing the book, *American First Class.* 28 April 1865. p.68, c5.

7191 L. MARIA CHILD *to* **HONORED FRIEND PIERPONT. [from the** *Washington Chronicle***] 6 April 1865. Wayland.** Extends eightieth birthday wishes; declares Pierpont is blessed to live to see the abolition of slavery in America. 28 April 1865. p.68, c5.

7192 HENRY W. LONGFELLOW *to* **CHARLES H. MORSE. [from the** *Washington Chronicle***] 30 March 1865. Cambridge.** Sends cordial salutations in honor of poet and prophet Pierpont. 28 April 1865. p.68, c5.

7193 CHARLES SUMNER *to* **JOHN PIERPONT. [from the** *Washington Chronicle***] 2 April 1865. Washington.** Extends birthday wishes. 28 April 1865. p.68, c5.

7194 E. P. WHIPPLE *to* **REV. JOHN PIERPONT. [from the** *Washington Chronicle***] 4 April 1865. Boston.** Sends to Pierpont congratulations on his birthday. 28 April 1865. p.68, c6.

7195 WILLIAM LLOYD GARRISON *to* **JOHN PIERPONT. [from the** *Washington Chronicle***] 4 April 1865. Boston.** Praises Pierpont for his distinguished career; sends congratulations on his eightieth birthday. 28 April 1865. p.68, c6.

7196 J. G. DODGE *to* **FRIEND GARRISON. 22 April 1865. Hilton Head, S.C.** Sends resolutions from the Council of Administration held at Mitchellville. 5 May 1865. p.71, c1.

7197 SALLIE HOLLEY *to* **MR. GARRISON. 20 April 1865. Detroit, Mi.** Reports that upon arriving in Detroit, she was informed of William Buffum's death. 5 May 1865. p.71, c2.

7198 n.n. *to* **THE** *LONDON TIMES.* **[extract] 4 March. Richmond.** States his belief that General Sherman's sympathies are not with the slave. 5 May 1865. p.71, c5.

7199 EDWIN M. STANTON *to* **MAJOR GEN. DIX. 25 April. Washington.** Forwards dispatch received in Washington. 5 May 1865. p.71, c5.

7200 GENERAL GRANT *to* **WAR DEPARTMENT IN WASHINGTON. 24 April Raleigh.** Delivers report to General Sherman on his negotiations with Johnston; reports that Johnston has received instructions to terminate truce. 5 May 1865. p.71, c5.

7201 n.n. *to* **MAJOR GENERAL DIX. 13 April 1865. Washington.** Discusses directives regarding drafting and recruiting. 5 May 1865. p.71, c5.

7202 F. M. *to* **THE EDITORS OF THE** *EVENING POST.* **n.d. n.p.** Suggests burying Booth under pavement of Ford Theatre since Booth wanted to immortalize his own name. 5 May 1865. p.71, c5.

7203 SELLA MARTIN *to* **THE EDITORS OF THE** *EVENING POST.* **24 April 1865. New York.** Laments the injustice of excluding colored people from Lincoln's funeral. 5 May 1865. p.72, c6.

7204 M. DU PAYS *to* **THE EDITOR OF THE** *LIBERATOR* **[W. L. GARRISON]. 4 May 1865. New York.** Contrasts the attitudes of North and South on the end of the war, Lincoln's death, and the future of the black man. 12 May 1865. p.74, c5.

7205 LADIES OF PARISH *to* **REV. SAMUEL J. MAY. n.d. n.p.** Express thanks for his faithful guidance during the past twenty years; enclose gift. 12 May 1865. p.76, c2.

7206 F.W.B. *to* **THE** *NEW YORK COMMERCIAL ADVERTISER.* **13 April. Hilton Head, S.C.** Reports on meeting of freedmen in village of Mitchellville; states that Mitchellville is the first self-governing settlement of freedmen in the United States. 12 May 1865. p.76, c3.

7207 ABRAHAM LINCOLN *to* **GEN. VAN ALEN. 14 April 1865. n.p.** Thanks Van Alen for assurance of support from conservatives. 19 May 1865. p.77, c2.

7208 THOMAS H. BARKER *to* **MR. GARRISON. 29 April 1865. Manchester, England.** Mourns death of Lincoln. 19 May 1865. p.79, c2.

7209 F. W. NEWMAN *to* **T. H. BARKER. 29 April 1865. London.** States that he is appalled by the assassination of Lincoln. 19 May 1865. p.79, c2.

7210 GEORGE SUNTER *to* **MR. GARRISON. 11 May 1865. Brantford, Canada West.** Praises the *Liberator* for its past success. 19 May 1865. p.79, c2.

7211 RICHARD D. WEBB *to* **MR. GARRISON. 28 April 1865. Dublin.** Expresses horror upon learning of the death of Lincoln. 19 May 1865. p.79, c3.

7212 CAROLINE H. DALL *to* **MR. GARRISON. 16 May 1865. Boston.** Encloses letters from Englishmen pertaining to the death of Lincoln. 19 May 1865. p.79, c4.

7213 EDWARD PEACOCK *to* **FRIEND DALL. 27 April 1865. Brigg, England.** Expresses sympathy upon learning of the death of Lincoln. 19 May 1865. p.79, c4.

7214 JAMES SINCLAIR *to* **THE EDITOR OF THE** *LIBERATOR* **[W. L. GARRISON]. 29 April 1865. Glasgow.** Encloses address from the Union and Emancipation Society of Glasgow to President Andrew Johnson. 19 May 1865. p.79, c4.

7215 LUCY PEACOCK *to* **MRS. DALL. 27 April 1865. England.** Expresses deep sorrow upon learning of the death of President Lincoln. 19 May 1865. p.79, c4.

7216 THOMAS BAYLEY POTTER, FRANCIS TAYLOR, AND SAMUEL WATTS *to* **MRS. LINCOLN. 27 April 1865. Manchester.** Extend sympathy to Mrs. Lincoln and the United States on the loss of President Lincoln. 19 May 1865. p.79, c5.

7217 E.M. STANTON *to* **MAJOR GENERAL DIX. 13 May. Washington.** Encloses dispatch from General Wilson. 19 May 1865. p.79, c6.

7218 J. H. WILSON *to* **LIEUT. GEN. GRANT AND THE SECRETARY OF WAR. 12 May. Macon, Ga.** Reports on the capture of Jefferson Davis and his staff. 19 May 1865. p.79, c6.

7219 EDWIN M. STANTON *to* **MAJOR GEN. DIX. 14 May. n.p.** Encloses details of the capture of Jefferson Davis. 19 May 1865. p.79, c6.

7220 D. B. PRITCHARD *to* **CAPT. T. W. SCOTT. 11 May 1865. Cumberlandville, Ga.** States that he surprised and captured Jefferson Davis and his family. 19 May 1865. p.79, c6.

7221 J. H. WILSON *to* **E. M. STANTON. 13 May. Macon, Ga.** Details the capture of Jefferson Davis. 19 May 1865. p.79, c6.

7222 CATHARINE A. F. STEBBINS *to* **DR. DIO LEWIS. 1 May 1865. Rochester, N.Y.** Asks Dr. Lewis to comment on the disadvantages of women wearing tight garments. 19 May 1865. p.80, c4.

7223 WM. H. CHANNING *to* **SAMUEL MAY, JR. 29 April 1865. Washington.** Clarifies a speech given by Andrew Johnson many years ago; believes that "Johnson is for freedom." 19 May 1865. p.80, c5.

7224 L. MARIA CHILD *to* **FRIEND TILTON. 6 May 1865. Wayland, Ma.** Observes that spring brings hope of a better life. 26 May 1865. p.84, c4.

7225 EDWIN M. STANTON *to* **MAJOR GEN. DIX. 27 May 1865. Washington, D.C.** Reports that arrangements for the surrender of rebel forces in the trans-Mississippi department are concluded. 2 June 1865. p.87, c5.

7226 ROBERT TOOMBS *to* **DUDLEY. 24 March 1865. Washington, Ga.** Describes conditions in the Confederacy; discusses possibility of using slaves as soldiers. 9 June 1865. p.89, c4.

7227 n.n. *to* **n.n. [extract] n.d. n.p.** Notes that he contributed money at an anti-slavery meeting; declares that the anti-slavery cause must continue. 9 June 1865. p.90, c3.

7228 CATHARINE A. F. STEBBINS *to* **MR. GARRISON. 2 June 1865. Boston.** Discusses recent meeting of the Boston AS. 9 June 1865. p.90, c4.

7229 WM. LLOYD GARRISON *to* **REV. GEORGE TRASK. 27 May 1865. Boston.** Sympathizes with the American Anti-Tobacco Society. 9 June 1865. p.90, c5.

7230 COLORED OFFICER *to* **n.n. [extract] 30 May. Orangeburg, S.C.** Notes that military men are inducing freedmen to stay on plantations; adds that hostile feelings exist. 9 June 1865. p.90, c5.

7231 M. DU PAYS *to* **THE EDITOR OF THE *LIBERATOR* [W. L. GARRISON]. 1 June 1865. New York.** Considers whether allowing Southern states to use their former state laws will further Johnson's efforts toward Reconstruction. 9 June 1865. p.90, c6.

7232 CAROLINE H. DALL *to* **MR. GARRISON. 2 June 1865. Boston.** Discusses women's suffrage in Calcutta. 9 June 1865. p.91, c1.

7233 MARGARET E. KNIGHT *to* **MRS. DALL. 6 April 1865. Calcutta, India.** Comments on women's suffrage. 9 June 1865. p.91, c1.

7234 ELIZA WIGHAM *to* **FRIEND. 28 April 1865. Edinburgh.** Laments the death of Lincoln. 9 June 1865. p.91, c2.

7235 D. S. GRANDIN *to* **FRIEND GARRISON. 8 May 1865, Brunswick, Me.** Expresses support for Garrison. 9 June 1865. p.91, c2.

7236 JOEL McMILLAN, JOHN GORDON, AND M. R. ROBINSON *to* **THE WESTERN AS. 22 May 1865. Salem, Oh.** Report on the dissolution of the Western AS. 9 June 1865. p.91, c3.

7237 AUSTIN KENT *to* **FRIEND GARRISON. n.d. East Stockholm, N.Y.** Mourns the death of Lincoln. 9 June 1865. p.91, c4.

7238 SAMUEL WEBB *to* **FRIEND GARRISON. 9 May 1865. New Hartford, N.Y.** Comments on Garrison's trip to Charleston. 9 June 1865. p.91, c4.

7239 T. E. HALL *to* **WM. LLOYD GARRISON. 16 May 1865. Camp Nelson, Ky.** Requests aid for colored people in his contraband camp. 9 June 1865. p.91, c4.

7240 VICTOR HUGO *to* **AMERICAN MINISTER AT LONDON. n.d. n.p.** Agrees that "If liberty should fall in America, there would be a shipwreck in humanity." 9 June 1865. p.91, c5.

7241 O. B. *to* **JOHN. 15 April 1865. Washington.** Presents a letter in code which refers presumably to Lincoln, Johnson, and Grant. 9 June 1865. p.91, c5.

7242 IRA STEWARD *to* **MR. GARRISON. 31 May 1865. Boston.** Pleads on behalf of the Boston laborers for a shorter working day. 9 June 1865. p.92, c4.

7243 N. H. ANDERSON, RICHARD CARTER, ROBERT W. JOHNSON, MADISON CARTER, SPENCER SMITHEN, AND MANY OTHERS *to* **THE EDITOR OF THE *NEW YORK TRIBUNE*. 7 June 1865. Richmond, Va.** Detail the humilities freedmen must endure in Richmond; plead for a decent government. 16 June 1865. p.94, c3.

7244 THEODORE TILTON *to* **MR. SARGENT. 31 May. Boston.** Regrets that he is unable to attend the New England AS Convention; demands immediate passage of a constitutional amendment granting universal male suffrage; notes that South Carolina is unfair to Negroes. 16 June 1865. p.94, c6.

7245 GEO. THOMPSON *to* **n.n. 13 June. Boston.** Details proceedings of the Yearly Meeting of the Progressive Friends in Longwood, Pennsylvania. 16 June 1865. p.95, c1.

7246 DEBIT AND CREDIT *to* **MR. GARRISON. 9 June 1865. New York.** Describes the presentation of money to Oliver Johnson, editor of the *National Anti-Slavery Standard*, at an anti-slavery meeting in New York. 16 June 1865. p.95, c2.

7247 AUGUSTIN L. TAVEAU *to* **THE EDITOR OF THE** *NEW YORK TRIBUNE.* **24 April 1865. Charleston, S.C.** A South Carolinian gives his views on the nation and the war. 23 June 1865. p.97, c1.

7248 EDMUND QUINCY AND OLIVER JOHNSON *to* **THE EDITOR OF THE** *LIBERATOR* **[W. L. GARRISON]. 17 June 1865. n.p.** Enclose resolution from the AAS which expresses appreciation for their service as editors of the *National Anti-Slavery Standard.* 23 June 1865. p.98, c4.

7249 EDMUND QUINCY *to* **C. K. WHIPPLE. 27 May 1865. Dedham.** Refuses to accept resolution from the AAS praising him as editor of the *National Anti-Slavery Standard* because he feels that the AAS is no longer necessary. 23 June 1865. p.98, c4.

7250 OLIVER JOHNSON *to* **CHARLES K. WHIPPLE. 29 May 1865. New York.** An editor of the *National Anti-Slavery Standard* refuses to accept praise from the AAS because it sanctioned Mr. Phillips' false statements. 23 June 1865. p.98, c4.

7251 WENDELL PHILLIPS *to* **THE EDITORS OF THE** *NEW YORK EVENING POST.* **14 June 1865. Boston.** Submits a record of his statements on repudiating the national debt. 23 June 1865. p.98, c5.

7252 ALFRED H. LOVE *to* **WM. LLOYD GARRISON. 12 June 1865. Philadelphia.** Stresses the need to oppose Johnson's Reconstruction policy and aid Southern colored people. 23 June 1865. p.99, c2.

7253 J. W. FOWLER *to* **FRIEND GARRISON. 9 June 1865. Savannah, Ga.** Comments on his work in Georgia, where he is circulating petitions for the right to vote. 23 June 1865. p.99, c3.

7254 MARSHAL LAMON *to* **PRESIDENT A. LINCOLN. 10 December 1864. Washington City.** Warns the president about plots against his life. 23 June 1865. p.99, c3.

7255 LLEWELLYN *to* **THE EDITOR OF THE** *NEW YORK TRIBUNE.* **n.d. n.p.** Suggests that the Quakers rescind their resolution disowning the late Isaac T. Hopper; states that Hopper's only "offense" was being opposed to slavery. 23 June 1865. p.100, c5.

7256 HENRY MILES *to* **WM. LLOYD GARRISON. 9 June 1865. Monkton, Vt.** Praises Garrison and the *Liberator.* 23 June 1865. p.100, c5.

7257 JOHN STUART MILL *to* **SIR. 13 May 1865. Avignon.** Urges total usurpation of the slaveholders' power in order to insure emancipation. 30 June 1865. p.101, c2.

7258 CHARLES G. LORING *to* **n.n. [extract] n.d. n.p.** Proposes different methods of dealing with the rights of former slave states. 30 June 1865. p.102, c1.

7259 JOHN ANDREW *to* **SIR. 19 June 1865. Boston.** Regrets that he cannot attend the meeting in Boston on the reorganization of the rebel states. 30 June 1865. p.102, c1.

7260 A. H. BULLOCK *to* **GENTLEMEN. 19 June 1865. Worcester.** Regrets that he is unable to attend the meeting on the reorganization of the rebel states. 30 June 1865. p.102, c1.

7261 W.G. BLANCHARD *to* **n.n. 10 June. Boston.** Charges that editors are unfair to Mr. Wendell Phillips. 30 June 1865. p.102, c4.

7262 n.n. *to* **W. L. GARRISON. 19 June 1865. Granville, N.Y.** Encloses resolutions from the Friends of Progress Convention in Middle Granville, New York. 30 June 1865. p.102, c6.

7263 HENRY C. WRIGHT *to* **CITIZENS OF THE UNITED STATES. n.d. n.p.** Stresses the power of the ballot. 30 June 1865. p.102, c6.

7264 G. B. STEBBINS *to* **W. L. GARRISON. 20 June 1865. Portsmouth, Oh.** Gives observations on his trip to Cincinnati. 30 June 1865. p.103, c2.

7265 N. S. *to* **FRIEND GARRISON. n.d. n.p.** Perceives that the wall between colonizationists and abolitionists has broken down; affirms that freedmen must be given equal rights. 30 June 1865. p.103, c2.

7266 EDWIN THOMPSON *to* **MR. EDITOR OF THE** *LYNN BULLETIN.* **n.d. n.p.** Reminisces about the bravery of the late Erastus Ware, who hid George Thompson from a mob. 30 June 1865. p.103, c3.

7267 JEFFERSON DAVIS *to* **THE SECRETARY OF THE UNITED STATES TREASURY. 14 March 1849. Senate Chamber.** Comments on a letter of recommendation for Dr. Blackburn. 30 June 1865. p.103, c4.

7268 G. GARIBALDI *to* **MR. MARSH. 27 March 1865. Caprera.** States that he regards Lincoln as a Christ figure; adds that he is proud to perpetuate the name of Lincoln in his family. 30 June 1865. p.103, c4.

7269 GEN. SAXTON *to* **GEN. HOWARD. [extract] n.d. n.p.** Decries treatment of freedmen in the area near Summerville, South Carolina; notes that conditions are worse than during slavery. 30 June 1865. p.103, c5.

7270 ROBERT DALE OWEN *to* **THE PRESIDENT [ANDREW JOHNSON]. 21 June 1865. New York.** Comments on Negro suffrage and representation of the population. 7 July 1865. p.105, c3.

7271 S. P. CHASE *to* **J. D. ROUDANEZ, L. GOLIS, AND L. BANKS. 6 June 1863. New Orleans.** Regrets that he cannot attend the meeting of colored Americans of New Orleans; explains his support of their rights as citizens. 7 July 1865. p.106, c2.

7272 JOSEPH MAZZINI *to* **MR. FISHER. 21 May 1865. n.p.** Urges the continuance of anti-slavery work in the United States. 7 July 1865. p.106, c2.

7273 M. DU PAYS *to* **THE EDITOR OF THE** *LIBERATOR* **[W. L. GARRISON]. 29 June 1865. New York.** Compares rebels in Virginia with those in North Carolina. 7 July 1865. p.106, c5.

7274 E. C. W. *to* **MR. GARRISON. 30 June 1865. Newburyport.** Notes that Garrison's presence was missed at the recent Laurel Party meeting. 7 July 1865. p.107. c1.

7275 J. LEONARD *to* **FRIEND GARRISON. 3 July 1865. Dorchester.** Questions why there is so much discussion about what Mr. Phillips said at the New England AS Convention on the subject of repudiation. 7 July 1865. p.107, c1.

7276 ABRAHAM LINCOLN *to* **DR. JOHN MacLEAN. 27 December 1864. Washington.** Thanks trustees of College of New Jersey for conferring upon him the degree of Doctor of Laws. 7 July 1865. p.107, c2.

7277 LOUIS KOSSUTH *to* **THE EDITOR OF THE** *TRIBUNE.* **[extract] 28 May. n.p.** States his retrospective observations on the war. 7 July 1865. p.107, c3.

7278 MAJOR GEN. A. H. TERRY *to* **n.n. 23 June 1865. Richmond, Va.** Defines the rights and privileges of freedmen in Virginia. 7 July 1865. p.107, c3.

7279 MAJOR GEN. HARTSUFF *to* **n.n. 22 June 1865. Petersburg, Va.** Discusses an order he received on the regulation of Negro labor. 7 July 1865. p.107, c3.

7280 HON. ISAAC W. ARNOLD *to* **B. B. SHERMAN. n.d. n.p.** An old friend of Lincoln questions the progress of fund raising for his family; notes that they are left in circumstances of comparative poverty. 7 July 1865. p.107, c3.

7281 G. T. BEAUREGARD *to* **HON. WM. P. MILES. 13 October 1862. Charleston, S.C.** Questions whether bill for the execution of abolition prisoners has been passed. 7 July 1865. p.107, c4.

7282 G. S. *to* **THE EDITORS OF THE** *TRAVELLER.* **25 June 1865. Cambridgeport.** Relates his horrendous experience as a Union soldier in a rebel prison. 14 July 1865. p.109, c3.

7283 LOUIS PHILLIPPE D'ORLEANS *to* **CHARLES SUMNER. [from the** *Boston Transcript*] **5 May 1865. Twickenham.** Grieves upon learning of the death of Lincoln. 14 July 1865. p.109, c4.

7284 HENRY C. WRIGHT *to* **WM. LLOYD GARRISON. 4 July 1865. Vineland, N.J.** Relays his reflections after a Fourth of July celebration. 14 July 1865. p.111, c1.

7285 JOHN A. ANDREW *to* **F. W. LINCOLN. 30 June 1865. Boston.** Discusses the anniversary of the American Independence celebration in Boston which he will be unable to attend this year. 14 July 1865. p.111, c5.

7286 GEN. B. F. BUTLER *to* **n.n. [extract] n.d. n.p.** Presents suggestions on the reorganization of the rebel states. 21 July 1865. p.113, c4.

7287 F. G. ENSIGN *to* **JOHN COVODE. [from the** *New York Tribune*] **15 June 1865. Memphis, Tn.** Suggests ways to alleviate problems of freedmen in Tennessee. 21 July 1865. p.113, c4.

7288 JAMES TRIMBLE *to* **MR. EDITOR. [from the** *Boston Traveller*] **n.d. n.p.** Supports Negro suffrage; states that he comes from one of the first families of Tennessee, but now is anti-aristocratic. 21 July 1865. p.113, c5.

7289 M. DU PAYS *to* **THE EDITOR OF THE** *LIBERATOR* **[W. L. GARRISON]. 13 July 1865. New York.** Reports on the reoccupation of Norfolk after a withdrawal of just one month. 21 July 1865. p.114, c5.

7290 JAMES REDPATH *to* **WM. LLOYD GARRISON. n.d. n.p.** Discusses General Knox's verbal attack on General Saxton; praises Gilbert Pillsbury and Reuben Tomlinson. 21 July 1865. p.115, c1.

7291 D. M. *to* **REV. JOHN WARE. n.d. n.p.** Questions significance of sermon preached by Ware. 21 July 1865. p.115, c2.

7292 L. MARIA CHILD *to* **THE EDITOR OF THE** *BOSTON TRANSCRIPT.* **5 July 1865. Wayland.** Describes life in the country; discusses the evil influence of slavery, and comments on a copperhead celebration. 21 July 1865. p.115, c3.

7293 JOS. JACKSON, GEO. DOLLY, BENJ. ROBERTS, PETER DUNCAN, AND JOS. TISON *to* **HON. CHARLES SUMNER. 15 June 1865. Savannah.** Submit petition for Sumner to present to President Johnson requesting the right of suffrage. 28 July 1865. p.119, c1.

7294 CHARLES SUMNER *to* **JOS. JACKSON, GEO. DOLLY, BENJ. ROBERTS, PETER DUNCAN, AND JOS. TISON. 8 July 1865. Boston.** States that he has forwarded petition from recipients of this letter to President Johnson; assures them that suffrage will be granted. 28 July 1865. p.119, c1.

7295 J. S. S. *to* **THE EDITOR OF THE** *NEW YORK TRIBUNE.* **n.d. n.p.** Rebukes United States military officers aboard the steamship *Continental* for refusing to permit Rev. George W. Levere, a chaplain and colored officer, to eat with them. 28 July 1865. p.119, c1.

7296 n.n. *to* **n.n. n.d. Rio Janeiro.** Observes the growth of the anti-slavery movement in Brazil. 28 July 1865. p.119, c1.

7297 n.n. *to* **n.n. [extract] 22 July. Fortress Monroe.** Reports that the steamer *Quinnebaug* was wrecked on the bar off Morehead City. 28 July 1865. p.119, c3.

7298 n.n. *to* **n.n. [extract] 28 June. Alexandria.** Reports on the heavy incidence of cholera in Alexandria; notes that deaths are rising to 250 per day; describes mass exodus from city. 28 July 1865. p.119, c4.

7299 CHARLES A. FOSTER *to* **THE** *ST. LOUIS DEMOCRAT.* **[extract] n.d. n.p.** Asserts that John Brown, who is accused of leading the Pottawatomie massacre, knew nothing of the massacre until it had occurred. 28 July 1865. p.119, c4.

7300 n.n. *to* **n.n. [extract] 9 July 1865. Fort Mott, S.C.** Charges that the mistreatment of freedmen is rampant; asserts that Negroes must be given land and the ballot. 28 July 1865. p.120, c4.

7301 PETROLEUM V. NASBY *to* **n.n. 12 June 1865. New Jersey.** A fictional political satire offers a plan to unite the country for the forthcoming election. 28 July 1865. p.120, c5.

7302 REV. G. DE FELICE *to* **n.n. 7 May 1865. n.p.** Expresses grief and horror felt by the people of France upon learning of the death of Abraham Lincoln. 4 August 1865. p.121, c6.

7303 M. DU PAYS *to* **THE EDITOR OF THE** *LIBERATOR* **[W. L. GARRISON]. 27 July 1865. New York.** Discusses universal male suffrage; encloses address of the Hon. B.F. Perry. 4 August 1865. p.122, c4.

7304 W. P. G. *to* **THE EDITOR OF THE** *LIBERATOR* **[W. L. GARRISON]. 31 July 1865. New York.** Encloses copy of a letter from Major General Wilson. 4 August 1865. p.122, c6.

7305 MAJ. GEN. JAS. H. WILSON *to* **SIR. 19 July 1865. Macon, Ga.** Informs that Maria Smith, the mother of Mrs. Craft, is living with colored friends near his headquarters. 4 August 1865. p.122, c6.

7306 C. K. W. *to* **n.n. [extract] 26 July 1865. Boston.** Writes to a Northern soldier in the South about his belief that voting is a right of citizenship; desires the United States to encourage acquisition of knowledge by granting citizenship one year earlier to those who fulfill certain requirements. 4 August 1865. p.124, c2.

7307 L. MARIA CHILD *to* **MR. TILTON. 23 July 1865. Wayland.** Expresses her feelings about the war. 11 August 1865. p.125, c5.

7308 L. N. FOWLER *to* **WM. LLOYD GARRISON. 24 April 1865. London.** Describes feelings of jubilation prompted by anti-slavery events in the United States. 11 August 1865. p.126, c6.

7309 N. H. WHITING *to* **C. K. WHIPPLE. 30 July 1865. Marshfield.** Asks for assistance in the South to elevate Negroes. 11 August 1865. p.127, c1.

7310 n.n. *to* **n.n. [extract] n.d. n.p.** Thanks Mr. Sumner for convincing him that to grant immediate representation to the rebel states would be a breach of honor to freedmen. 11 August 1865. p.127, c2.

7311 J. M. PALMER *to* **PRESIDENT ANDREW JOHNSON. 27 July 1865. Louisville, Ky.** Answers charges regarding practice of issuing "free papers" to colored people. 11 August 1865. p.127, c4.

7312 EX-SENATOR FOOTE *to* **MR. A. O. P. NICHOLSON. n.d. n.p.** Discusses the state of the South and Negro suffrage. 11 August 1865. p.127, c4.

7313 ROBERT TYLER *to* **THE EDITOR OF THE *RICHMOND REPUBLIC*. 2 August 1865. Richmond, Va.** Advises that no person who has held a commission in civil or military service of the Confederate government should be a candidate for the legislature. 11 August 1865. p.127, c5.

7314 JUDGE KELLEY *to* **THE *PHILADELPHIA INQUIRER*. n.d. n.p.** Informs that Southern leaders plan to accomplish through politics what they failed to accomplish through war. 18 August 1865. p.129, c4.

7315 M. DU PAYS *to* **THE EDITOR OF THE *LIBERATOR* [W. L. GARRISON]. 10 August 1865. New York.** Informs of proposal to punish South Carolina for its leadership role in the war by dividing her land among blacks. 18 August 1865. p.130, c5.

7316 WM. H. MILLER *to* **WM. LLOYD GARRISON. 9 August 1865. Lexington, Ky.** Requests Garrison's help in writing an almanac. 18 August 1865. p.131, c1.

7317 ABRAHAM LINCOLN *to* **COUNT A. DE GASPARIN. 14 August 1862. Washington.** Answers Gasparin's questions pertaining to the war. 18 August 1865. p.131, c3.

7318 PETROLEUM V. NASBY *to* **n.n. 12 July 1865. New Jersey.** A fictional political satire describes a meeting with "General Marion Gusher." 18 August 1865. p.132, c6.

7319 GLOVER *to* **THE EDITOR OF THE *PHILADELPHIA PRESS*. n.d. n.p.** Declares that Southern states are plotting to keep former slaves in ignorance and degradation. 25 August 1865. p.133, c4.

7320 JACOB D. COX *to* **n.n. [extract from the *New York Independent*] n.d. n.p.** Answers questions posed by citizens of Oberlin, Ohio, regarding granting suffrage to Negro males; expresses his anti-Negro feelings. 25 August 1865. p.134, c1.

7321 NATH'L THAYER, J. M. FORBES, PELEG CHANDLER, S. FROTHINGHAM, JR. AND 210 OTHERS *to* **PRES. JOHNSON. n.d. n.p.** Discuss the necessity of justice during the Reconstruction. 25 August 1865. p.134, c4.

7322 W. C. N. *to* **FRIEND GARRISON. 11 October 1865. Boston.** Encloses extract of a letter from Sgt. Charles W. Lenox. 25 August 1865. p.135, c1.

7323 CHARLES W. LENOX *to* **n.n. [extract] 20 July 1865. Charleston, S.C.** Announces that in deference to the feelings of the rebels in Richmond, the colored troops are to be removed. 25 August 1865. p.135, c1.

7324 X *to* **FREEDMEN'S AID ASSOCIATION OF NEW ORLEANS. 1 August 1865. Iberville Parish, La.** Notes his complete success with freedmen working the farm and sharing the profits. 25 August 1865. p.135, c2.

7325 n.n. *to* **THE EDITORS OF THE** *NEW ORLEANS TRIBUNE.* **31 July 1865. Mobile.** Decries the physical tortures currently experienced by the colored people in Alabama. 25 August 1865. p.135, c3.

7326 n.n. *to* **n.n. [from the** *Chicago Tribune***] n.d. n.p.** Cites instances of brutality suffered by Negroes in Mobile; notes that many Negroes have been found murdered. 25 August 1865. p.135, c3.

7327 MR. GREELEY *to* **n.n. n.d. n.p.** Replies negatively to inquiry about whether he is going to leave the *Tribune.* 25 August 1865. p.135, c4.

7328 n.n. *to* **THE** *BALTIMORE AMERICAN.* **[extract] n.d. Richmond.** Defends General Lee's application for pardon. 25 August 1865. p.135, c4.

7329 P. T. BARNUM *to* **THE EDITOR OF THE** *NATION.* **29 July 1865. Bridgeport, Ct.** Admonishes the *Nation*'s criticism of his museum. 25 August 1865. p.136, c3.

7330 N. TOURGUENEFF *to* **THE EDITOR OF THE** *NATION.* **14 July 1865. n.p.** Chronicles emancipation in Russia. 1 September 1865. p.137, c1.

7331 EDWARD M. RICHARDS *to* **n.n. August 1865. Mound City, Ks.** Advises those interested in humanitarian topics to read "Needle and Garden" in the *Atlantic Monthly,* an article concerning the oppression of seamstresses. 1 September 1865. p.138, c4.

7332 M. DU PAYS *to* **THE EDITOR OF THE** *LIBERATOR* **[W. L. GARRISON]. 24 August 1865. New York.** Comments on political questions which remain to be solved. 1 September 1865. p.138, c5.

7333 X *to* **GARRISON. 26 August 1865. New York.** Decribes the impressive return of the colored troops of the Thirty-second Regiment. 1 September 1865. p.139, c1.

7334 J. E. JOHNSTON *to* **n.n. [from the** *Fredericksburg* **(Va.)** *Ledger***] 17 August 1865. Mecklenberg County, Va.** Recognizes that Virginia is once again one of the United States. 1 September 1865. p.139, c3.

7335 GEORGE ANDERSON *to* **P. H. ANDERSON. 7 August 1865. Dayton, Oh.** Declines offer of a "good chance" if he returns to his former master in Big Spring, Tennessee. 1 September 1865. p.140, c5.

7336 J. A. SAXTON *to* **PROF. F. J. CHILD. [extract] n.d. n.p.** Addresses the topic of the freedmen in the South. 8 September 1865. p.142, c3.

7337 HENRY C. WRIGHT *to* **n.n. 27 August 1865. Ludlow, Vt.** Comments on the convention of spiritualists and Friends of Progress in Vermont. 8 September 1865. p.142, c5.

7338 L. W. ELLIOTT *to* **SIR. 6 June 1865. Red Bluff, Ca.** Praises the great work done by Garrison. 8 September 1865. p.142, c6.

7339 W. W. TATE *to* **SIR. 12 August 1865. Santa Fe, N.M.** Praises the *Liberator*. 8 September 1865. p.142, c6.

7340 L. HOLMES *to* **FRIEND GARRISON. 15 August 1865. Orange, Ma.** Commends the great work of the *Liberator*. 8 September 1865. p.142, c6.

7341 GOV. W. G. BROWNLOW *to* **GEORGE T. CURTIS. 18 August 1865. Nashville, Tn.** Justifies the treatment of W. C. Kain, a prisoner jailed for murder. 8 September 1865. p.143, c2.

7342 RICHARD COBDEN *to* **n.n. [from the** *New York Citizen*] **May 1864. n.p.** Predicts that the North will conquer the South through persistence; discusses the Mexican situation. 8 September 1865. p.143, c2.

7343 GEN. CARL SCHURZ *to* **THE** *BOSTON DAILY ADVERTISER*. **[extract] 31 July. Savannah.** Relates his observations upon touring the South. 8 September 1865. p.144, c5.

7344 PETROLEUM V. NASBY *to* **n.n. 31 July 1865. New Jersey.** Satirizes Southern democracy. 8 September 1865. p.144, c6.

7345 GEN. SHERMAN *to* **n.n. [extract from the** *Huntsville Advocate*] **10 August 1865. Near Alabama.** Describes the beginnings of secession. 15 September 1865. p.145, c3.

7346 BISHOP ELLIOTT *to* **n.n. [from the** *Boston Universalist*] **n.d. n.p.** Outlines conditions under which the Episcopal Church South will fraternize with the Episcopal Church North. 15 September 1865. p.145, c4.

7347 HENRY VINCENT *to* **FRIEND GARRISON. 25 November 1864. London.** Sends his autograph to W. L. Garrison. 15 September 1865. p.146, c2.

7348 M. DU PAYS *to* **THE EDITOR OF THE** *LIBERATOR* **[W. L. GARRISON]. 7 September 1865. New York.** Inquires whether the United States is at war or at peace. 15 September 1865. p.146, c4.

7349 SALLIE HOLLEY *to* **THE EDITOR OF THE** *NATIONAL ANTI-SLAVERY STANDARD*. **28 August 1865. Oberlin, Oh.** Reports on a graduation speech by Theodore Weld at Oberlin. 15 September 1865. p.146, c5.

7350 GEN. STONEMAN *to* **MR. KING. 16 August 1865. Tennessee.** Affirms that Mr. King's parish will continue to be used to educate Negroes. 15 September 1865. p.147, c1.

7351 PETROLEUM V. NASBY *to* **n.n. 11 August 1865. New Jersey.** Satirizes biblical history and the "Dimekrats," whose purpose he sees as "Keepin the nigger down." 15 September 1865. p.148, c6.

7352 GERRIT SMITH *to* **WM. LLOYD GARRISON AND WENDELL PHILLIPS. 12 September 1865. Peterboro'.** Discusses the consequences of participating in the abolitionist movement for a long time. 22 September 1865. p.150, c6.

7353 HENRY C. WRIGHT *to* **WM. LLOYD GARRISON. 12 September 1865. Unity, N.H.** States that Congress will decide who will be allowed to vote. 22 September 1865. p.152, c2.

7354 M. DU PAYS *to* **THE EDITOR OF THE** *LIBERATOR* **[W. L. GARRISON]. 21 September 1865. New York.** Describes General Slocum's assignment in Mississippi; notes that the war is over, but not the fighting. 29 September 1865. p.154, c5.

7355 L. G. J. *to* **THE EDITOR OF THE** *LIBERATOR* **[W. L. GARRISON]. 19 September 1865. Providence, R.I.** Comments on the progress toward equal rights for all men. 29 September 1865. p.156, c2.

7356 W. P. P. *to* **FRIEND GARRISON n.d. n.p.** Notes encouraging signs in Washington regarding equal rights for blacks. 29 September 1865. p.156, c2.

7357 FREDERICK DOUGLASS *to* **W. J. WILSON. 8 August 1865. Rochester, N.Y.** Explains why he will not allow his name to be used as an officer of the Educational Monument Association. 29 September 1865. p.156, c2.

7358 W. M. DICKSON *to* **THE EDITORS. 19 September 1865. Cincinnati.** Encloses a letter from John S. Mill. 6 October 1865. p.157, c1.

7359 JOHN S. MILL *to* **HON. JUDGE DICKSON. 1 September 1865. Blackheath Park, England.** Comments on the relative progress made by American Negroes. 6 October 1865. p.157, c1.

7360 C. W. HOWARD *to* **THE EDITOR OF THE** *INTELLIGENCER.* **20 August 1865. Spring Bank.** Speculates on the future course of the South. 6 October 1865. p.157, c4.

7361 HENRY C. WRIGHT *to* **WM. LLOYD GARRISON. 20 September 1865. Charlestown, N.H.** Explains why actions of the Democratic Party make Negro suffrage a necessity. 6 October 1865. p.158, c4.

7362 J. H. FOWLER *to* **GARRISON. 20 September 1865. Charleston, S.C.** Fears that a conflict between the races is inevitable. 6 October 1865. p.158, c6.

7363 ABRAHAM LINCOLN *to* **GEN. WADSWORTH. [extract from the** *Southern Advocate***] n.d. n.p.** States his desire to extend the right to vote to blacks and to grant universal amnesty. 6 October 1865. p.159, c1.

7364 PETROLEUM V. NASBY *to* **n.n. 20 August 1865. New Jersey.** Fictional satire examines democracy. 6 October 1865. p.160, c5.

7365 CHARLES SUMNER *to* **THE EDITORS OF THE** *EVENING POST.* **28 September 1865. Boston.** Discusses the ratification of the constitutional amendment abolishing slavery. 13 October 1865. p.161, c1.

7366 D. A. PAYNE *to* **GENTLEMEN. 20 September 1865. Baltimore.** Regrets that he cannot attend the opening of the Douglass Institute. 13 October 1865. p.162, c5.

7367 CHARLES SUMNER *to* **GENTLEMEN. 28 September 1865. Boston.** Regrets that he cannot attend the opening of the Douglass Institute. 13 October 1865. p.162, c5.

7368 W. S. HANCOCK *to* **MR. WOOD. 26 September 1865. Baltimore.** Regrets that he cannot attend the opening of the Douglass Institute. 13 October 1865. p.162, c5.

7369 M. DU PAYS *to* **THE EDITOR [W. L. GARRISON]. 5 October 1865. New York.** Comments on the end of slavery and the importance of suffrage. 13 October 1865. p.163, c4.

7370 JOHN NOBLE, JR. *to* **GEORGE THOMPSON. [extract] 21 September 1865. London.** Hopes that Thompson is pleased to witness the death of slavery. 13 October 1865. p.163, c3.

7371 PETROLEUM V. NASBY *to* **n.n. n.d. n.p.** Satirizes the leadership of the Democratic Party. 13 October 1865. p.164, c3.

7372 W. L. SHARKEY *to* **WM. H. SEWARD. 28 August. Jackson, Ms.** Presents Seward with copy of the constitution of Mississippi. 20 October 1865. p.166, c2.

7373 W. H. SEWARD *to* **W. L. SHARKEY. n.d. n.p.** Acknowledges receipt of Sharkey's letter and a copy of the constitution of Mississippi. 20 October 1865. p.166, c2.

7374 W. H. SEWARD *to* **JOHN A. ANDREW. 4 September. Washington.** Forwards a copy of the constitution of Mississippi, asking whether it would be satisfactory to the citizens of the state of Massachusetts. 20 October 1865. p.166, c2.

7375 JOHN A. ANDREW *to* **WM. L. GARRISON. 6 September . Boston, Ma.** Requests that Garrison, the prophet of the anti-slavery movement, reject or ratify the constitution of Mississippi. 20 October 1865. p.166, c2.

7376 WILLIAM L. GARRISON *to* **GOV. JOHN A. ANDREW. 7 September. Boston.** Consents to ratify the constitution of Mississippi. 20 October 1865. p.166, c2.

7377 SAMUEL MAY, JR. *to* **MR. GARRISON. n.d. n.p.** Encloses a letter from Peter Randolph, a former slave. 20 October 1865. p.166, c4.

7378 PETER RANDOLPH *to* **SAMUEL MAY, JR. 12 October 1865. Richmond, Va.** Describes the persecution of poor colored people in Richmond. 20 October 1865. p.166, c5.

7379 SALEM *to* **THE EDITORS OF THE** *BOSTON DAILY ADVERTISER***. n.d. n.p.** Identifies a mounted officer as Capt. Wirz. 20 October 1865. p.167, c2.

7380 WM. W. COLEMAN *to* **THE SECRETARY OF THE FREEDMEN'S CONVENTION. 27 September 1865. Concord, N.C.** Discusses the convention and demands for equality before the law. 27 October 1865. p.169, c3.

7381 GEN. W. T. SHERMAN *to* **GOV. TOD. [extract] March 1863. n.p.** Declares that the people of the North must either conquer or be conquered. 27 October 1865. p.169, c5.

7382 GEN. O. O. HOWARD *to* **JAMES E. RHOADES. 9 October 1865. Washington.** Believes that education will eliminate hostility and prejudice against the blacks. 27 October 1865. p.170, c5.

7383 GEORGE H. STUART *to* **THE AMERICAN FREEDMEN'S AID COMMISSION. n.d. n.p.** Approves of the aims of the association. 27 October 1865. p.170, c5.

7384 M. DU PAYS *to* **THE EDITOR OF THE** *LIBERATOR* **[W. L. GARRISON]. 19 October 1865. New York.** Compares Lincoln with Johnson. 27 October 1865. p.171, c1.

7385 GEORGE L. STEARNS *to* **PRESIDENT JOHNSON. 8 October 1865. Medford, Ma.** Discusses their earlier meeting concerning Reconstruction of the rebel states. 27 October 1865. p.171, c2.

7386 HENRY C. WRIGHT *to* **FRIEND GARRISON. 6 October 1865. South Hanover, N.H.** Reports on the temperance convention in Essex County. 27 October 1865. p.171, c3.

7387 J. M. BROADHEAD *to* **n.n. 18 October 1865. Washington.** Informs of the decision to treat colored soldiers entering the military as freemen. 27 October 1865. p.171, c5.

7388 WM. W. WILSON *to* **FREDERICK DOUGLASS. 6 September 1865. Washington, D.C.** States that he was surprised at a recent letter from Douglass. 27 October 1865. p.172, c4.

7389 VIATOR *to* **THE EDITOR OF THE** *NATION.* **25 September 1865. Rome, Italy.** Expresses his views on United States politics and politicians. 3 November 1865. p.173, c1.

7390 JOHN M. PALMER *to* **HON. E. M. STANTON. 2 October 1865. Washington, D.C.** Comments on his removal from command in Kentucky. 3 November 1865. p.173, c5.

7391 JOHN M. PALMER *to* **HON. E. M. STANTON. 15 October 1865. Louisville, Ky.** Inquires what course he should take regarding ferrymen who refuse to carry Negroes across the Ohio River. 3 November 1865. p.174, c1.

7392 JOHN M. PALMER *to* **E. M. STANTON. 16 October 1865. Louisville, Ky.** Orders the post commandant to compel the ferry boat drivers to carry the Negroes across the Ohio River. 3 November 1865. p.174, c1.

7393 E. M. STANTON *to* **MAJ. GEN. PALMER. 20 October 1865. Washington.** Praises Palmer for his good judgment regarding the use of the ferry boats on the Ohio River by the Negroes. 3 November 1865. p.174, c1.

7394 E. D. TOWNSEND *to* **MAJ. GEN. PALMER. 20 October 1865. Washington.** Reports that President Johnson, with the support of Major General Thomas, approves of Palmer's retaining command in Kentucky. 3 November 1865. p.174, c1.

7395 S. E. D. *to* **n.n. 27 October. Portland, Me.** Reports on Garrison and McKim's work in Maine on behalf of the American Freedmen's Aid Commission. 3 November 1865. p.174, c4.

7396 HENRY C. WRIGHT *to* **WM. LLOYD GARRISON. 25 October 1865. Harwich.** Declares that it is the responsibility of Congress to act on behalf of the freedmen. 3 November 1865. p.174, c5.

7397 CHARLES DEVENS, JR. *to* **MRS. CHILD. n.d. Worcester, Ma.** Offers to contribute the sum needed to redeem Thomas Sims from slavery. 10 November 1865. p.177, c3.

7398 L. MARIA CHILD *to* **FRIEND TILTON. [from the** *New York Independent***]. n.d. n.p.** Declares that "Andy Johnson . . . will be more deeply cursed by History than is Benedict Arnold" if he betrays the people's trust in him; describes the hard work of an emancipated slave and the demoralizing effects of slavery. 10 November 1865. p.177, c3.

7399 WILLIAM H. SEWARD *to* **JAMES J. JOHNSON. 26 October 1865. Washington.** Announces that President Johnson refuses to recognize people of any state who promote war or rebellion. 10 November 1865. p.178, c1.

7400 CHARLES SUMNER *to* **THE EDITOR OF THE** *INDEPENDENT.* **29 October 1865. Boston.** Praises the *Independent* for its support of equal rights. 10 November 1865. p.178, c3.

7401 M. DU PAYS *to* **THE EDITOR OF THE** *LIBERATOR* **[W. L. GARRISON]. 2 October 1865. New York.** Describes the activities of the provisional state governments in the South. 10 November 1865. p.179, c1.

7402 GEO. W. PUTNAM *to* **MR. GARRISON. 26 October 1865. Peterboro', N.Y.** Describes activities of an anti-slavery friend, George Thompson. 10 November 1865. p.179, c3.

7403 P. B. RANDOLPH *to* **MR. GARRISON. 14 October 1865. New Orleans.** Informs that a grammar school has been named after Garrison; requests assistance from the city of Boston for classroom materials. 10 November 1865. p.179, c3.

7404 ANDREW JOHNSON *to* **JAMES JOHNSON. 28 October 1865. Washington, D.C.** Declares that no debt incurred for the purposes of the Union may be paid by taxes levied on the people. 10 November 1865. p.179, c4.

7405 JAS. S. BRISBIN *to* **THE MAJOR OF LEXINGTON, KY. [from the** *Missouri Democrat***] 20 October 1865. Lexington, Ky.** Relays message from General Palmer, stating that the major will cease to discriminate against freedmen. 10 November 1865. p.179, c4.

7406 ANDREW JOHNSON *to* **GOV. MURPHY. 30 October 1865. Washington, D.C.** Approves of Gov. Murphy's organization of state government. 10 November 1865. p.179, c5.

7407 n.n. *to* **n.n. [from the** *Cincinnati Commercial***] 11 November. Griffin, Ga.** Reports on cruel torture of a Negro woman in Georgia. 10 November 1865. p.180, c3.

7408 A PRO-SLAVERY MAN *to* **THE PEOPLE OF THE SLAVEHOLDING STATES. [from the** *Charleston Courier***] n.d. Boston.** Advises that if Fremont is elected president, no cotton, rice, or tobacco be sent North; hopes that the North will suffer and become pro-slavery. 17 November 1865. p.181, c2.

7409 P. A. TAYLOR *to* **M. D. CONWAY. n.d. n.p.** A member of the British Parliament expresses views on American affairs. 17 November 1865. p.181, c3.

7410 J. T. TROWBRIDGE *to* **THE** *WATCHMAN AND REFLECTOR***. [extract] n.d. Harpers Ferry.** Relates a conversation with a gentleman at Harpers Ferry; believes that people are beginning to realize that slavery is wrong. 17 November 1865. p.181, c6.

7410a SALLIE HOLLEY *to* **MR. GARRISON. n.d. n.p.** Speaks enthusiastically about the Elmira water cure. 17 November 1865. p.182 [183], c2.

7410b n.n. *to* **n.n. [extract from the** *Cincinnati Gazette***] n.d. Milledgeville, Ga.** Expresses ambivalence toward the advances that have been made by the Negro. 17 November 1865. p.182 [183], c4.

7410c n.n. *to* **THE** *CINCINNATI GAZETTE***. [extract] n.d. Texas.** Expresses the feelings experienced by the Germans in Texas during the war. 17 November 1865. p.182 [183], c5.

7410d CHARLES ADAMS *to* **EARL RUSSELL. [extract] n.d. n.p.** Explains his views on the indemnity question. 17 November 1865. p.182 [183], c5.

7410e W. H. SEWARD *to* **B. F. PERRY. n.d. n.p.** Acknowledges receipt of letter; relays message that President Johnson wishes Perry to continue to exercise his duties as provisional governor of South Carolina. 17 November 1865. p.182 [183], c5.

7411 H. H. BRIGHAM *to* **H. D. WALKER. n.d. n.p.** Discusses a biblical dispute over a letter written by Walker in 1864. 17 November 1865. p.184, c2.

7412 JAMES AYTOUN *to* **THE EDITOR OF THE** *LONDON MORNING ADVER-TISER.* **21 October 1865. St. Anne's Hill, Cork.** Comments on the United States' relations with Britain; disagrees with arguments of Earl Russell. 24 November 1865. p.185, c1.

7413 F. H. B. *to* **THE** *INDEPENDENT.* **[extract] n.d. n.p.** Describes the life of a freedman in North Carolina. 24 November 1865. p.185, c3.

7414 JOSEPH HOLT *to* **HON. HENRY WILSON. n.d. n.p.** Praises Wilson's political textbook. 24 November 1865. p.185, c6.

7415 GEORGE MEADE *to* **GENTLEMEN OF THE COMMITTEE. 12 November 1865. Philadelphia.** Regrets that he is unable to attend the reception for colored soldiers. 24 November 1865. p.186, c1.

7416 BENJAMIN F. BUTLER *to* **GENTLEMEN OF THE COMMITTEE. 3 November. Lowell, Ma.** Hopes to attend the reception for colored troops. 24 November 1865. p.186, c1.

7417 GEORGE L. STEARNS *to* **GENTLEMEN OF THE COMMITTEE. n.d. n.p.** Believes that history will vindicate the patriotism of colored citizens of the free states. 24 November 1865. p.186, c1.

7418 M. DU PAYS *to* **THE EDITOR OF THE** *LIBERATOR* **[W. L. GARRISON]. 16 November 1865. New York.** Discusses politics in New Jersey. 24 November 1865. p.186, c6.

7419 SAMUEL J. MAY *to* **THE EDITOR OF THE** *LIBERATOR* **[W. L. GARRISON]. 14 November 1865. Syracuse.** Describes his visit with George Thompson. 24 November 1865. p.187, c1.

7420 JOSEPH MAZZINI *to* **M. D. CONWAY. [from the** *Commonwealth***] 30 October 1865. n.p.** Addresses the issue of suffrage for colored men. 24 November 1865. p.187, c1.

7421 n.n. *to* **THE** *CHICAGO TRIBUNE.* **[extract] 6 November. Montgomery, Al.** Reports the denial of a pardon to Colonel Gayle of Cahawba, who offered one million dollars for the assassination of President Lincoln. 24 November 1865. p.187, c5.

7422 J. JOHNSON *to* **PRES. ANDREW JOHNSON. n.d. n.p.** Reports that the convention repudiated the war debt by a vote of 133 to 117. 24 November 1865. p.187, c5.

7423 A WEST COUNTRY MINISTER *to* **THE EDITOR OF THE** *GLASGOW HERALD.* **n.d. n.p.** Clarifies the Sabbath controversy. 24 November 1865. p.188, c2.

7424 PETROLEUM V. NASBY *to* **n.n. 12 July 1865. New Jersey.** Satirizes the political climate of the South. 24 November 1865. p.188, c5.

7425 COL. FORNEY *to* **THE** *PHILADELPHIA PRESS.* **[extract] n.d. n.p.** Criticizes the South Carolina legislature's reluctance to adopt the constitutional amendment abolishing slavery. 1 December 1865. p.189, c2.

7426 W. G. BROWNLOW *to* **THE EDITORS OF THE** *CINCINNATI GAZETTE.* **13 November 1865. Nashville.** Informs that rebels hope to split the government. 1 December 1865. p.189, c3.

7427 ABRAHAM LINCOLN *to* **DR. THEODORE CANISIUS. 17 May 1859. Springfield.** Answers questions posed by German citizens prior to Lincoln's nomination for the presidency. 1 December 1865. p.189, c5.

7428 L. S. HART *to* **WM. LLOYD GARRISON. 15 November 1865. Nashville, Tn.** Announces the establishment of the Kansas Homestead Colonization Association. 1 December 1865. p.185 [191], c1.

7429 MARY CARPENTER *to* **WILLIAM LLOYD GARRISON. 26 October 1865. Bristol, England.** Praises Garrison. 1 December 1865. p.185 [191], c3.

7430 GEO. WHIPPLE *to* **CHARLES TAPPAN. 24 November 1865. New York.** Praises the work of the American Missionary Association; comments on the conditions of freedmen in the South. 1 December 1865. p.185 [191], c4.

7431 ANDREW JOHNSON *to* **B. G. HUMPHREYS. [from the** *National Republican***] n.d. n.p.** Announces that troops will be withdrawn from Mississippi only when peace and order can be maintained without them. 1 December 1865. p.185 [191], c5.

7432 n.n. *to* **THE** *CHICAGO TRIBUNE. [extract]* **n.d. St. Louis.** Learns from an army officer that Southern rebels assume responsibility for the support of wounded rebel soldiers. 1 December 1865. p.186 [192], c5.

7433 ROBERT DALE OWEN *to* **THE EDITORS OF THE** *NEW YORK EVENING POST.* **22 November 1865. New York.** Emphasizes the need for a constitutional guarantee of fundamental rights for Negroes. 8 December 1865. p.193, c2.

7434 EDWIN M. STANTON *to* **GOV. HUMPHREYS. 3 November 1865. Washington.** Acknowledges President Johnson's receipt of Humphreys' telegram; informs that Sheriff Redus is to be released from prison; requests that Colonel Gilson be relieved of command. 8 December 1865. p.193, c6.

7435 PROF. FRANCIS W. NEWMAN *to* **THE** *TRANSCRIPT.* **8 November 1865. London.** Worries about the future of America after the Civil War. 8 December 1865. p.194, c1.

7436 OWEN LOVEJOY *to* **EX-GOVERNOR HAHN. [extract from the** *Washington Republican***] March 1864. n.p.** Suggests that initially only colored soldiers and literate blacks be allowed to vote. 8 December 1865. p.194, c2.

7437 HARRIET MARTINEAU *to* **HER AMERICAN PUBLISHERS. 8 November 1865. The Knoll, Ambleside.** Thanks the company for her final payment; informs that she is ill and is terminating her literary career. 8 December 1865. p.194, c4.

7438 M. DU PAYS *to* **THE EDITOR OF THE** *LIBERATOR* **[W. L. GARRISON]. 30 November 1865. New York.** Discusses the course of Reconstruction. 8 December 1865. p.194, c6.

7439 C. G. MORGAN *to* **THE EDITOR OF THE** *LIBERATOR* **[W. L. GARRISON]. n.d. Albany, Greene County, Wi.** Presents scriptural and historical evidence that oppression has not yet ended. 8 December 1865. p.196, c3.

7440 HENRY C. WRIGHT *to* **FRANCIS AND LOUISA HINCKLEY. 1 November 1865. Yarmouth Port, S.C.** Praises his friends who continue the anti-slavery effort as teachers of freedom; warns that the spirit and effects of chattel slavery linger. 15 December 1865. p.199, c2.

7441 JAMES F. HINCKLEY *to* **HENRY C. WRIGHT. 15 November 1865. Coffin's Point, S.C.** Criticizes freedmen's attempts to expose the horrors of slavery. 15 December 1865. p.199, c2.

7442 ANDREW JOHNSON *to* **HON. W. W. HOLDEN. 27 November 1865. Washington.** Commends Holden for his efficient management as provisional governor of North Carolina; speculates on the future of North Carolina. 15 December 1865. p.199, c4.

7443 HENRY C. WRIGHT *to* **WM. LLOYD GARRISON. 2 December 1865. Taunton.** Considers suffrage a conventional right, not a natural right. 15 December 1865. p.200, c4.

7444 CHIEF JUSTICE S. P. CHASE *to* **LYMAN ABBOTT. 20 November 1865. Washington, D.C.** Regrets that he is unable to attend a meeting to aid freedmen; promises to try to relieve suffering in the South. 22 December 1865. p.201, c5.

7445 GOLDWIN SMITH *to* **THE EDITORS OF THE** *BOSTON DAILY ADVERTISER.* **2 December 1865. Oxford.** Relates details of the insurrection in Jamaica. 22 December 1865. p.202, c1.

7446 SARAH P. REMOND *to* **THE EDITOR OF THE** *LONDON DAILY NEWS.* **n.d. n.p.** Defends the character of Negroes and their descendents. 22 December 1865. p.202, c2.

7447 SAMUEL MAY, JR. *to* **THE** *LIBERATOR* **n.d. n.p.** Commends the *Liberator* for its crusade against slavery. 22 December 1865. p.203, c1.

7448 REV. JEHIEL CLAFLIN *to* **FRIEND GARRISON. 12 December 1865. East Westmoreland, N.H.** Regrets the discontinuation of the *Liberator*. 22 December 1865. p.203, c2.

7449 S. M. SEAVER *to* **MR. GARRISON. 7 December 1865. Williamstown.** Concurs with Mr. Whipple's opinion that the right to vote is a natural right. 22 December 1865. p.203, c2.

7450 MALADIE DU PAYS *to* **THE EDITOR OF THE** *LIBERATOR* **[W. L. GARRISON]. 14 December 1865. New York.** Praises the Thirty-ninth Congress; bids farewell to the *Liberator*. 22 December 1865. p.203, c3.

7451 H. W. BLANCHARD *to* **MR. GARRISON. 18 December 1865. Neponset.** Bids farewell to the *Liberator*; remarks that he has subscribed for thirty years. 22 December 1865. p.203, c3.

7452 JAMES REDPATH *to* **MR. MAY. 18 December 1865. Malden.** Informs that General Saxton befriended the Negroes of the Sea Islands. 22 December 1865. p.203, c3.

7453 CHARLES SUMNER *to* **MRS. COBDEN. 5 October 1865. Boston.** The president of the Republicans of Massachusetts conveys his sympathy to Mrs. Cobden for the loss of her husband. 22 December 1865. p.203, c4.

7454 WILLIAM H. SEWARD *to* **LEVI E. PARSONS. 18 December 1864. Washington.** Informs him, by order of President Johnson, that he will be relieved of his duties as provisional governor of Alabama as soon as the governor is ready to resume command; praises Parsons' fidelity and loyalty. 22 December 1865. p.203, c5.

7455 L. MARIA CHILD *to* **THE EDITOR OF THE** *INDEPENDENT.* **n.d. n.p.** Reminisces about the early anti-slavery movement. 29 December 1865. p.205, c1.

7456 S. E. SEWALL *to* **WM. LLOYD GARRISON. 24 December 1865. Melrose.** Congratulates Garrison as the end of the *Liberator*'s career is nearing; cautions that the consequences of slavery will not be easily eradicated. 29 December 1865. p.206, c4.

7457 SAMUEL J. MAY *to* **WILLIAM LLOYD GARRISON. 17 December 1865. Syracuse.** Expresses a deep sense of obligation to Garrison as the *Liberator* ceases publication. 29 December 1865. p.206, c4.

7458 HENRY C. WRIGHT *to* **W. L. GARRISON. 18 December 1865. Oak Hill, Cape Ann.** Declares that the *Liberator*'s spirit will never die. 29 December 1865. p.206, c5.

7459 OLIVER JOHNSON *to* **W. L. GARRISON. 26 December 1865. New York.** Bids farewell to the *Liberator*. 29 December 1865. p.206, c6.

7460 THEODORE TILTON *to* **THE** *LIBERATOR*. **26 December 1865. New York.** Bids farewell to the *Liberator*. 29 December 1865. p.206, c6.

7461 M. R. ROBINSON *to* **MR. GARRISON. 19 December 1865. Salem, Oh.** Thanks the *Liberator* for its untiring efforts against slavery. 29 December 1865. p.206, c6.

7462 JOSEPH A. DUGDALE *to* **FRIEND WM. LLOYD GARRISON. 15 December 1865. Mt. Pleasant, Ia.** Bids farewell to the *Liberator*. 29 December 1865. p.206, c6.

7463 RUTH DUGDALE *to* **FRIEND WM. L. GARRISON. n.d. n.p.** Bids farewell to the *Liberator*. 29 December 1865. p.206, c6.

7464 NATHANIEL BARNEY *to* **FRIEND W. L. GARRISON. 1865. Yonkers, N.Y.** Pays tribute to the *Liberator*. 29 December 1865. p.206, c6.

7465 ROBERT F. WALLCUT *to* **MR. GARRISON. 27 December 1865. Boston.** Bids farewell to the *Liberator*. 29 December 1865. p.207, c1.

7466 ALFRED H. LOVE *to* **WM. LLOYD GARRISON. 24 December 1865. Philadelphia.** Bids farewell to the *Liberator*. 29 December 1865. p.207, c1.

7467 DANIEL RICKETSON *to* **n.n. 20 December 1865. New Bedford.** Bids farewell to the *Liberator*. 29 December 1865. p.207, c1.

7468 B. *to* **MR. EDITOR [W. L. GARRISON]. n.d. n.p.** Praises the *Liberator* for its many contributions and hopes it will have a suitable successor. 29 December 1865. p.207, c2.

7469 DAVID THOMAS *to* **THE EDITOR OF THE** *LIBERATOR* **[W. L. GARRISON]. 26 December 1865. Boston.** Conveys an Englishman's reactions to America. 29 December 1865. p.207, c4.

7470 E. CADY STANTON *to* **MR. GARRISON. n.d. New York.** Requests that the last *Liberator* speak for women's suffrage. 29 December 1865. p.207, c5.

7471 MILO A. TOWNSEND *to* **WM. LLOYD GARRISON. 12 December 1865. New Brighton, Pa.** Praises a lecture by George Thompson. 22 December 1865. p.208, c3,

7472 WM. C. NELL *to* **FRIEND GARRISON. 21 October 1865. Boston.** Expresses gratitude to Garrison for his efforts in the anti-slavery cause; bids farewell to the *Liberator*. 29 December 1865. p.208, c4.

7473 G. W. GORDON *to* **BELOVED WIFE. n.d. n.p.** Informs his wife that he is to be executed immediately for his connection with the slaughter of blacks in Jamaica. 29 December 1865. p.208, c5.

New York *Anti-Slavery Record*

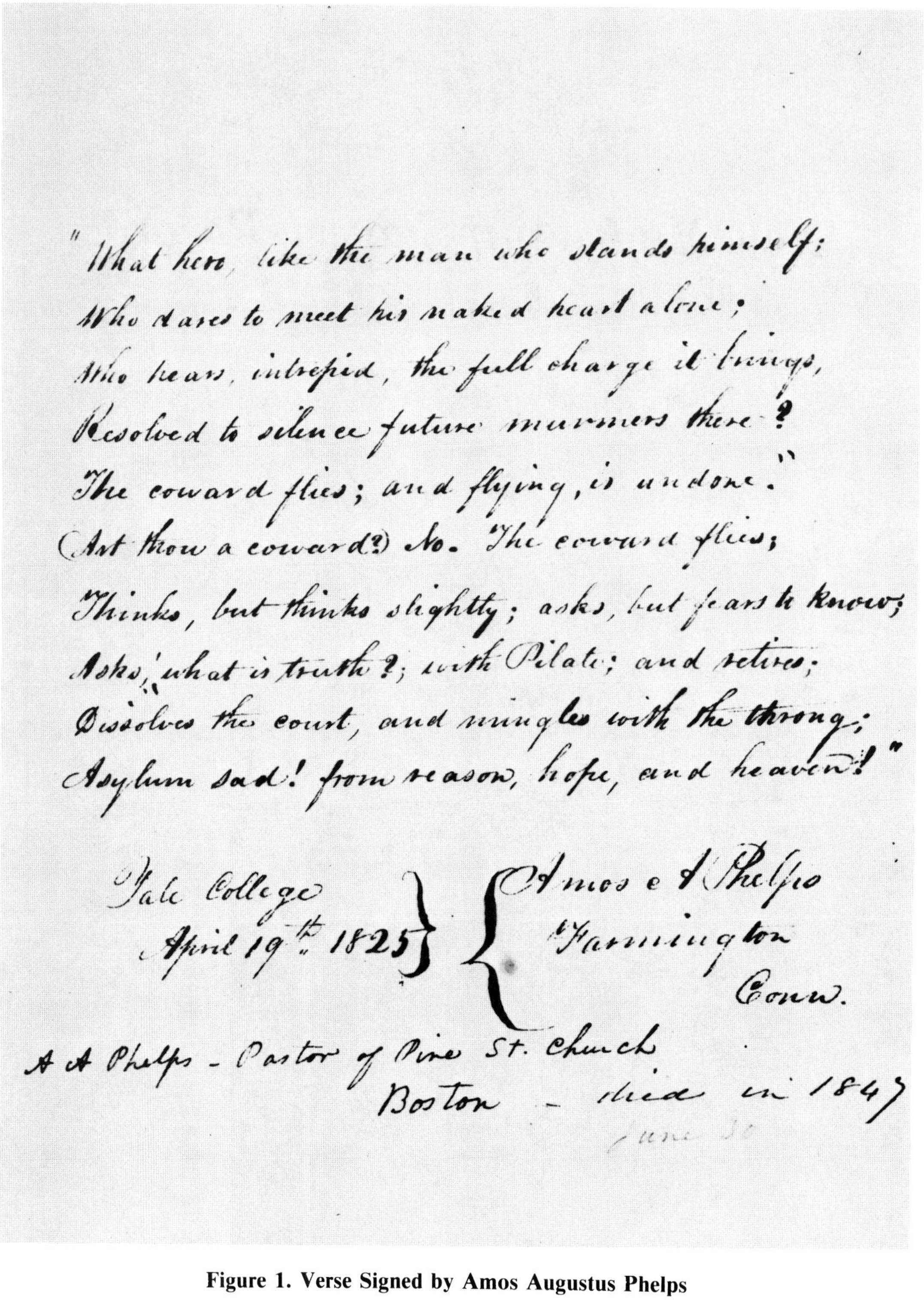

"What hero, like the man who stands himself;
Who dares to meet his naked heart alone;
Who hears, intrepid, the full charge it brings,
Resolved to silence future murmurs there?
The coward flies; and flying, is undone."
(Art thou a coward?) No. "The coward flies;
Thinks, but thinks slightly; asks, but fears to know;
Asks, "what is truth?; with Pilate; and retires;
Dissolves the court, and mingles with the throng;
Asylum sad! from reason, hope, and heaven!"

Yale College   Amos A Phelps
April 19th 1825 }{ Farmington
                                Conn.

A A Phelps - Pastor of Pine St. Church,
            Boston - died in 1847
                    June 30

Figure 1. Verse Signed by Amos Augustus Phelps

Amos A. Phelps

[Editor, *Anti-Slavery Record*]

Mr. Phelps was born of pious but humble parents, at Farmington, Connecticut, the 11th November, 1804. He graduated at Yale college in 1826. He subsequently spent two years at Andover, and one year at New Haven. His collegiate and theological education being complete, he became the pastor of a Congregational Church at Hopkinton, Massachusetts at the age of twenty-seven. He subsequently became the pastor of the church, at Pine-street, Boston. It was during the time he was associated with that Christian community, in the early part of 1833, that his attention was first drawn to the anti-slavery cause; a careful investigation of the subject led him to repudiate the scheme of colonization as delusive; and to embrace the doctrine of immediate emancipation. From this time he gave himself heartily and unreservedly to the cause of the slave, and has been one of its most diligent, disinterested, and useful advocates.

Mr. Phelps was a member of the Convention, at Philadelphia, in December, 1833, which organized the American Anti-slavery Society. Early, we believe, in the next year, he resigned the pastoral charge of the Pine-street church, that he might devote his whole energies to the great cause, which, with two or three intermissions, occupied the remainder of his active and useful life. In 1834, Mr. P[helps] being then the most prominent agent of the Society, accompanied Mr. George Thompson, in his anti-slavery tour through the greater part of New England, and portions of New York; and rendered the anti-slavery cause the greatest service.

After Mr. Thompson was driven from the country, Mr. Phelps continued to labour in various capacities in the anti-slavery enterprize. As an agent of the American Society, and as the general agent and secretary of the Massachusetts Society, and as the editor of the *Emancipator,* he spent the five or six years which followed 1835 performing an incredible amount of labour, exhibiting his usual wisdom and skill, addressing public audiences, conventions, ecclesiastical and legislative bodies, writing reports, counselling in committees, issuing addresses, publishing pamphlets, and contributing to newspapers, confronting mobs, enduring persecution, combatting prejudices, refuting sophistries, reasoning down objections, urging the churches and ministry to duty, restraining wayward fanaticism, and rebuking slumbering inactivity, and always calm, firm, cautious, zealous, hopeful, modest, yielding everything to conciliation but principle; ah, the cause of solid, staid, enduring abolition in New England knows not how much it is indebted to him, for the hold it now has on the common sense and conscience of the people!

Mr. Phelps was an invaluable man in the more private departments of anti-slavery labour—the places where the measures were to be devised and adopted by which the public mind was to be aroused and moulded to the great enterprize. Those who were accustomed to act with him on committees in New York and Boston, will bear witness to his great merits as a counsellor in trying emergencies. As fertile in expedients as he was calm in judgment, as cautious to devise as he was prompt to execute, there was no crisis which he was not able to face with a clear eye and an unperturbed spirit, and overmaster the difficulties which beset the cause by his well-balanced mind, practical sagacity, and unflinching courage; thus often patiently working through obstacles and leading his brethren through paths where they alone were ready to stumble and fall.

Mr. Phelps was a man of the most unblemished morals, of the sternest adherence to his convictions of duty, and though far removed from sectarian bigotry, he possessed firmly settled theological opinions, and was devotedly pious. He was a warm friend, cherishing all the domestic affections, and loved the cause of the slave not merely as a principle of duty, but from the impulses of the heart. All who corresponded with him will remember his almost invariable mode of closing his letters, *"Your's for the slave."*

Among the first to discover that policy as well as duty pointed to the use of the suffrage for the overthrow of slavery, Mr. P[helps] became the warm advocate of political action. He regarded human government not as a thing of man's device, but as a divinely appointed institution; and politics, not as a mere chessboard for the display of the arts, or the trickeries, or the ambition of wily and aspiring men, but as one of God's agencies for the establishment of His kingdom on earth. Of course, then, he carried his religion into his politics; and his abolition being the result of religious conviction, he was among the first to advocate the erection of an anti-slavery standard of political action. He early discovered the controlling influence of the slave power upon the two leading parties of the country, and was in the front rank of the wise and determined few who declared for an independent political party. To no other man is the Liberty party of Massachusetts so much indebted for its organization and establishment, as to him. His efforts to this end during the first year of its existence were among the most untiring and able of the great services which he rendered the cause of humanity. His doctrines on this subject are embodied in the motto at the head of many Liberty newspapers, and which he originated—"LIBERTY THE RIGHT OF ALL—LAW ITS DEFENCE."

In 1844, he attended the second World's Convention in London, and was among the most active and influential of its members. He ever took a warm interest and leading part in the work of purifying the churches, and the ecclesiastical organizations and benevolent societies of our country, from the stain of slavery. After his return from England, he vainly endeavoured to bring the American Board of Missions, to adopt a line of anti-slavery action; and, failing in this, was among the most zealous in promoting the cause of free missions to the heathen. Though he early espoused and always advocated the politics of the Liberty party, his chief efforts during the last five or six years of his life, were devoted to the work of correcting the religious sentiment of the country, on the subject of slavery. He was for some time the editor of the *Anti-slavery Reporter,* at New York, and was at his death one of the corresponding editors of the *National Era,* at Washington. Before he entered into this engagement, his great labours in the cause of emancipation, had impaired his physical powers, and uniting with constitutional tendencies towards pulmonary consumption, hastened him to his decline. While he stood by the prostrated form of Torrey, whose bosom friend he was, in the prison-house at Baltimore, he promised to write a sketch of the martyr's life. But waning health compelled him to relinquish that task to other and kindred hands. On the approach of the last winter, he fled to Jamaica, hoping there, while he refreshed his spirit by witnessing with his own eyes, the glorious triumphs of the common cause, to invigorate his wasting frame by breathing its genial atmosphere. But he was too late. He returned to the bosom of his native land to die a martyr to cheerful but exhausting labours for the emancipation of the helpless and broken-hearted slave. . . .

Mr. Phelps sailed for Haiti, in quest of health, October 20th, 1846. He passed a short time in that island, and thence proceeded to Jamaica. In a letter dated February the 10th, referring to the state of his health, he wrote, "I think I have done being anxious about the result, and am quite resigned to the Divine will, be it what it may." In April, this year, he embarked for New Orleans, where he arrived on the 18th of that month, and reached New York on the 5th of June, a mere skeleton, able to speak only in a whisper, his throat very sore, and with every symptom of rapid consumption.

During his absence he had been re-elected corresponding secretary to the American and Foreign Anti-slavery Society, but of course was obliged to decline it. . . .

Mr. Phelps took with him to the West Indies several unfinished manuscripts, in the hope of being able to complete them, but he was scarcely able to look at them during his absence. He was particularly desirous of writing out his views of the Bible respecting slavery, and to vindicate it from affording any countenance to chattel slavery, either under the old or new dispensation, feeling satisfied that he could demonstrate that the assertion that the Bible sanctions the iniquitous system is wholly unfounded.

On one occasion he was asked if he felt disappointed that he was prevented by the Providence of God from prosecuting his labours. He replied: "It will be ordered right in any event. I cannot say I prefer to live, or shall be disappointed not to live. I have been very desirous of completing several things that I have undertaken or planned in my mind, especially my Bible views on the subject of slavery. But perhaps God means that the Bible shall vindicate itself. The churches have fallen into dis-esteem, and it may be that God will permit the Bible to do so for a time."

Calling upon him one morning during his short stay in this city [New York], he said, smiling, and with an animated countenance, "I held an argument for an hour, last evening, on the Bible question, with a Virginian." He was asked, "How could you do so in your feeble state of health?" "Why," said he, "he was conversing with a gentleman present, and said some foolish things respecting Jamaica. Having just been there, I could not refrain from correcting him, and thus I was led into the conversation." He had exhausted himself by that conversation, and was only able to converse in the morning with a pencil and paper.

In speaking of the unhappy division of the American Anti-slavery Society in 1840, in which he took a prominent part, he said, "I have never regretted it."

He said he had a desire to write a short article on the Evangelical Alliance, to bring out what American ministers had said and written when in England and at home. He spoke particularly of Rev. Robert Baird's objectionable remarks in the *New York Evangelist,* and said they ought to be held up for reprobation. He rejoiced that the Committee had protested against the doings of the Alliance with reference to American slavery, and that its separation of Christian morals from Christian doctrine had been made to stand out clearly.

After stopping eleven days in New York, he proceeded to Boston and Castine, Maine, where his family resided, with their relatives. There his health rapidly failed, as the weather was cold and stormy, and the place wholly unsuited to a person in his situation. Still, July 8th, the weather becoming milder, he revived, and prepared for re-publication his able letters, which were originally published in the *Boston Recorder,* on "Organic Sins," in reply to the positions of Professor Stowe, Rev. Edward Beecher, and the American Board of Commissioners for Foreign Missions. He also intended to prepare for re-publication the other discussions concerning the American Board of Commissioners for Foreign Missions, that had so greatly engrossed his attention for a year or two. He thought they ought to be published, "not so much with a view of present sale, as for a permanent document for future reference and occasional use." He said, he would try to arrange them, and add something to them. His declining health forbade, and the work is left for another hand.

The weather becoming unfavourable, his bad symptoms became aggravated, and new ones were developed. He made preparations for leaving Castine, and on the 21st of July he left that place for Boston, where he arrived on the 23rd. His friend and brother-in-law, Rev. E. D. Moore, invited him to his house in Roxbury, where he was comfortably situated, frequently expressing his regret that he had not enjoyed the quietness and salubrity the place afforded previously. On the 25th, the writer spent two hours with him. He could converse but little, but whispered that his letters to Stowe were ready for the press, and added: "The letters to Bacon may be added. I see no objection to it." He was told that Orange Scott (who has been an able anti-slavery lecturer and editor) was lying in a similar condition, drawing near the end of his mortal career; that he was in a happy state of mind, &c., he smiled. He conversed about his family. He had received assurances from friends that his wife and children (now three in number) would be befriended after his decease, and he spoke of it with great sensibility. He seemed perfectly conscious of his approaching decease. Perceiving that he conversed with much pain, I took his hand, saying, I have been thinking of the precious words of the Saviour—"Let not your heart be troubled; ye believe in God, believe also in me." He was much affected, pressed my hand, and, with an expressive look, bade me adieu.

Throughout his protracted illness faith alone sustained him. He could lift up his heart and say—"I know that my Redeemer liveth." When informed that he could not survive till morning, he exclaimed, "I am glad to hear that—I am ready—I am ready!" [He died at Roxbury, in the forty-third year of his age, of pulmonary consumption.]

British and Foreign Anti-Slavery Reporter,
n.s. II (September, 1847), 134-36.

ANTI-SLAVERY RECORD.

| VOL. I. | FEBRUARY, 1835. | NO. 2. |

HOW SLAVERY HONORS OUR COUNTRY'S FLAG.

[From Rankin's Letters.]

" In the summer of 1822, as I returned with my family from a visit to the Barrens of Kentucky, I witnessed a scene such as I never witnessed before, and such as I hope never to witness again. Having passed through Paris in Bourbon county, Ky. the sound of music (beyond a little rising ground) attracted my attention, I looked forward, and saw the flag of my country waving. Supposing that I was about to meet a military parade, I drove hastily to the side of the road; and having gained the top of the ascent, I discovered (I suppose) about forty black men all chained together after the following manner; each of them was handcuffed, and they were arranged in rank and file. A chain perhaps 40 feet long, the size of a fifth-horse chain, was stretched between the two ranks, to which

Vol. I.   2

Figure 2

Journal Data

TITLE: The *Anti-Slavery Record*

MOTTO: "And tears and toil have been my lot, / Since I the white man's thrall became; / And sorer griefs I wish forgot— / Harsh blows and burning shame!" —Pringle

INCLUSIVE DATES OF PUBLICATION: Jan. 1835 - Dec. 1837.

PLACE OF PUBLICATION: New York, N. Y.

FREQUENCY OF PUBLICATION: Monthly

AVERAGE NUMBER OF PAGES PER ISSUE: 12

SIZE: 4 3/4 x 7 1/2 (bound)

NUMBER OF COLUMNS PER PAGE: 1

EDITOR(s): William Goodell (1835); Amos Augustus Phelps (?-1837); Rev. Joshua Leavitt (1836)

PUBLISHER: AAS; publishing agent, R. G. Williams

SPECIAL FEATURE: Illustrations; Annual Indexes

PERSPECTIVE: Abolitionist

MISCELLANEOUS DATA: The *Anti-Slavery Record* was one of four alternating journals published by the AAS as its official organ. It was issued the second week of each month. During the first, third, and fourth weeks, the AAS published *Human Rights,* the *Emancipator,* and *Slave's Friend.*

REPOSITORY: The Beinecke Rare Book and Manuscript Library, Yale University. Jan. 1835–Dec. 1837.

Goals

This is plain. Public opinion is now wrong. It holds that slavery is right *under present circumstances,* and *for the present* must be *continued.* This must be set right by presenting facts and arguments,—a *moral influence.* The reformation has commenced, both at the North and the South. The more the subject is discussed, by the pulpit, by the press, at the bar, in the legislative hall and in private conversation, the faster will the change proceed. When any individual slave holder is brought to believe that slavery is sinful, he will immediately emancipate his own slaves. When a majority of the nation are brought to believe in *immediate emancipation,* Congress will, of course, pass a law abolishing slavery in the District of Columbia. When the people of the several slave states are brought upon the same ground, they will severally abolish slavery within their respective limits.

The Anti-Slavery Record,
New York, N. Y. Jan. 1835,
(vol. I, no. [Title supplied.]

7474 TOUSSAINT L'OUVERTURE *to* **NAPOLEON BONAPARTE. [extract] n.d. n.p.** Responds to a letter of 27 Brumaire, stating that he cannot owe any obligation to the enemy [the French]; responds to Napoleon's offer of consideration, honors and fortune, declaring that his consideration is placed in the respect of his countrymen, his honors in their attachment, and his fortune in their disinterested fidelity; declares that he will resign only at the request of his people. April 1835 (vol. I, no. 4) p.38.

7475 n.n. *to* **n.n. [extract] n.d. Ohio.** Insists upon the necessity of rallying the free states in the North and West to the support of emancipation before success can be achieved; argues that the indifference of the free states lulls the conscience of the slaveholders. April 1835 (vol. I, no. 4) p.46.

7476 n.n. *to* **THE EDITOR. [extract] n.d. n.p.** Recounts the discovery of a man near death at the home of a Tennessee slaveholder; the dying man was found in a bloodstained room where the master was known to whip his slaves. May 1835 (vol. I, no.5) p.52.

7477 n.n. *to* *DUMFRIES COURIER* **[SCOTLAND]. [extract] n.d. Richmond, Va.** Describes a Richmond slave auction in which the auctioneer had some difficulty bartering off "Ponto," an outspoken field hand. May 1835 (vol. I, no. 5) p.57.

7478 C. STUART *to* **EDITOR OF THE** *ANTI-SLAVERY RECORD.* **24 March 1835. Rome, N.Y.** Relates a conversation with a fellow traveler which started by comparing women's complexions, and ended in argument over the inferiority or equality of those of a different color. May 1835 (vol. I, no. 5) p.59.

7479 D. HOYT *to* **n.n. [extract from the** *Millennial Trumpeter***] n.d. n.p.** Reports the death from exposure of a female slave sent to chop wood in freezing weather; recounts the cruel separation of a slave family through sales to different owners. June 1835 (vol. I, no. 6) p.64.

7480 n.n. *to* **MR. OVERTON. [extract from a report on the Free Colored Population of Ohio] n.d. n.p.** Informs his slave that he owes $150 plus ten percent interest to his master toward the purchase of his legal freedom. July 1835 (vol. I, no. 7) p.78.

7481 S. A. *to* **SIR. n.d. n.p.** Briefly introduces the attached translation from "Travels of Arfwedson," originally published in the French periodical, *L'Ami De La Jeunesse.* September 1835 (vol. I, no. 9) p.102.

7482 n.n. *to* **R. G. WILLIAMS, PUBLISHER OF THE** *EMANCIPATOR.* **6 August 1835. Georgetown, District of Columbia.** Returns a copy of the *Emancipator* and warns the authors and distributors that their covert actions may lead to "an ignominious death." September 1835 (vol. I, no. 9) p. 105.

7483 R. *to* **MR. EDITOR. n.d. n.p.** Ridicules a recent meeting in Tammany Hall of eighteen Southerners proposing a "frank and dispassionate discussion" of slavery; includes an editorial extracted from the *Columbia* (South Carolina) *Telescope,* which concludes that slavery "must remain for ever." September 1835 (vol. I, no. 9) p.106.

7484 B. *to* **MR. EDITOR. n.d. n.p.** Introduces letter from a Virginia slave woman to her husband. October 1835 (vol. I, no. 10) p.117.

7485 L. *to* **n.n. 5 June 1835. n.p.** A Virginia slave woman writes to her husband, who has been working two years in New York toward the ransom of his wife and their two children. October 1835 (vol. I, no. 10) p.118.

7486 A MINISTER IN MASSACHUSETTS *to* **THE** *RECORD.* **[extract] 4 September 1835. Ware, Ma.** Advocates "vigorous and bold action" in the cause of immediate emancipation. October 1835 (vol. I, no. 10) p.118.

7487 GEORGE WASHINGTON *to* **PHILLIS WHEATLEY. 28 February 1776. Cambridge.** Apologizes for such a tardy reply to her "favor of 26th October"; praises her "poetical talents" and states that he shall be happy to see her at Cambridge. 1835 (vol. I, appendix) p. 170.

[1836]

7488 DR. ROBERT MOORE *to* **MRS. TILGHMAN. n.d. n.p.** Informs that her grandson, Tench Tilghman, has captured and re-enslaved the escaped children and grandchild of her former seamstress and nurse, the manumitted Harriet Coward; implores her to free the successive generations before her death. February 1836 (vol. II, no. 14) p.15.

7489 H. M. TILGHMAN *to* **DR. ROBERT MOORE. 17 April 1835. Hope, near Easton.** The owner of a fugitive slave named Betty states that she is willing to sell her to the new owner of James Mathis, Betty's husband; pledges that Betty will not be separated from her family again if she wishes to rejoin them. February 1836 (vol. II, no. 14) p.16.

7490 ROBERT W. WILLIAMS *to* **JAMES MOTT. 30 June 1835. Baltimore, Md.** The owner of James Mathis offers to buy fugitive slave Betty, James' wife, in order "to oblige James," whom he describes as "perfectly happy and satisfied with his situation, except the absence of his wife." February 1836 (vol. II, no. 14) p.18.

7491 EDWARD HOPPER *to* **ROBERT W. WILLIAMS. 3 July 1835. Philadelphia.** Responds to Williams' offer to purchase fugitive slave Betty, stating that he does not know where she is and does not recommend that she go to Williams; suggests to Williams that he manumit her husband. February 1836 (vol. II, no. 14) p.19.

7492 J. T. *to* **MRS. S. E. n.d. n.p.** A church clerk informs Mrs. E. that members of her family have been excommunicated from their congregation "for being so long time absent" from service, although they had been denied access to a pew because of alleged deceit in its purchase. May 1836 (vol. II, no. 17) p.53.

7493 MRS. E. *to* **THE CHURCH IN S_____.n.d. n.p.** Replies to note of J. T., a church clerk, that she is "dissatisfied" with the church's excommunication of her family, and that she cannot remain in a church which makes "a distinction on account of complexion." May 1836 (vol. II, no. 17) p.54.

7494 JAMES G. BIRNEY *to* **SIR. 30 April 1836. Columbus, Oh.** Regrets his projected absence at a May assembly; reports he was recently assaulted by an anti-abolitionist mob at Granville; predicts future violence and pledges "faithfulness unto death." June 1836 (vol. II, no. 18) p.67.

7495 S. J. M. *to* **n.n. n.d. n.p.** A New England clergyman recounts an 1821 visit to Virginia, where he was first exposed to slavery; relates narrative of a "gentleman" whose "people" had independently managed his plantation for three years while he practiced law in Fredericksburgh; under the new arrangement, the plantation became "more profitable to him than ever." December 1836 (vol. II, no. 24) p.161.

7496 ATTORNEY-GENERAL OF BARBADOS *to* **LORD SEAFORTH, GOVERNOR OF THE ISLAND. [extract] n.d. n.p.** Describes a recent case, in which he served as counsel, involving the murder of "an African lad" belonging to an unnamed plantation manager; reports that the accused, Messrs. C. and H., "did not . . . come to a hearing, but paid the penalties . . ." December 1836 (vol. II, no. 24) p.167.

7497 E. S. ABDY, ESQ. *to* **n.n. [extract] n.d. n.p.** Notes conversation with the Turkish *chargé d'affaires,* who denies prejudice against colored people in his country or in Mahometan religion. December 1836 (vol. II, no. 24) p.170.

[1837]

7498 IGNATIUS SANCHO *to* **MR. LAURENCE STERNE. 1766. n.p.** Commends Sterne for his literary works and sermons "in favor of my miserable colored brethren." December 1837 (vol. III, no. 36) p.137.

7499 LAURENCE STERNE *to* **IGNATIUS SANCHO. 27 July 1766. Coxwould.** Assures Sancho that he is "at the service of the afflicted." December 1837 (vol. III, no. 36) p.137.

7500 BENJAMIN FRANKLIN *to* **THE SENATE AND HOUSE OF REPRESENT-ATIVES OF THE UNITED STATES. 3 February 1790. Philadelphia.** Recommends legislation for the abolition of slavery in a letter first printed in the *Federal Gazette,* 1790. December 1837 (vol. III, no. 36) p.171.

7501 THOMAS JEFFERSON *to* **M. WARVILLE. [extract] February 1788. Paris.** Acknowledges abolitionist philosophy, but declines an invitation to join a French anti-slave trade society. December 1837 (vol. III, no. 36) p.173.

7502 THOMAS JEFFERSON *to* **EDWARD COLE. 25 August 1814. n.p.** Responds to his letter of 31 July; regrets having pleaded the cause of the slaves in vain. December 1837 (vol. III, no. 36) p.173.

New York *Human Rights*

Figure 3. Joshua Leavitt

Joshua Leavitt

[Editor, *Human Rights*]

Rev. Joshua Leavitt, D. D., an American journalist and author, born in Heath, Franklin County, Mass., September, 1784; died in New York City, January 16, 1873. He received his early education in Franklin County, and graduated from Yale College in 1814. He then taught awhile, after which he studied law in Northampton, Mass., and opened an office in Putney, Vt. Soon afterward he went to New Haven and entered the Theological Seminary. Finishing his course, he settled in Stratford, Conn., where he remained in a very successful ministry for four years. In 1819, while a student of law in Heath, Mr. Leavitt organized one of the first Sabbath-schools in Western Massachusetts, embracing not only the children, but the entire congregation, all of whom were arranged in classes for religious study. An earnest revival resulted, and the school grew into one of the strongest churches in the region.

He early became interested in the improvement of the public schools. Before he entered the Theological Seminary, he prepared a new reading-book, called "Easy Lessons in Reading," which met with an extensive sale. To this, he subsequently added other books, to furnish a complete course of readers; but these, though possessing much merit, encountered more competition than the "Easy Lessons," and were not as popular. Mr. Leavitt, through his writings in the press and in other ways, aided materially to elevate the character of the schools of the town and State. He was among the first to perceive the evils of intemperance, and exerted all his influence against it, and when the American Temperance Society was formed he became its first secretary, and was one of its traveling agents, spent several months in lecturing in New Haven, Northampton, in many places delivering the first temperance lecture the people there had ever heard.

In 1828 he came to New York City as secretary of the American Seamen's Friend Society and editor of the *Sailor's Magazine*, and had ever since been engaged in editorial work. The society, under his management, became popular and useful. He established chapels in Canton, the Sandwich Islands, Havre, New Orleans, and other domestic and foreign ports. At this time, too, he aided in starting the first city temperance society, and became its first secretary. Perceiving early the advantage of having a combined hymn and tune book for use in revival and social meetings, nothing of the kind then existing, he, in company with an excellent young musician, prepared one, which was published under the name of "The Christian Lyre." This has always been considered one of the best of its kind.

He became, in 1831, editor and proprietor of the *Evangelist*, which had been started a year before, during which time he had frequently assisted in its editorial work. Under his energetic management his paper soon became one of the most powerful in the land; it was the organ of the more liberal religious movements, and was outspoken on the subjects of temperance and slavery. It early became noted for doctrinal discussions, in which Mr. Leavitt was completely at home, possessing a keen argumentative mind, and a perfect mastery of the contested points in theology.

Mr. Leavitt bore a conspicuous part in the early antislavery conflict, his services going back to his Stratford pastorate, where he wrote ably on the subject in the *Christian Spec-*

tator, and other periodicals. His denunciation of slavery during the time of the excitement attending the formation of the first abolition societies and the robbery of the mails at Charleston cost his paper its circulation in the South and a large portion in the North, and wellnigh compelled its suspension. To bring up its circulation again he undertook the difficult feat of reporting in full Finney's revival lectures, which, though not a short-hand reporter, he accomplished so successfully that his subscribers came back by hundreds, till his list reached 12,000. These reports were afterward published in book-form, and sold largely here, and to the extent of 100,000 copies in Great Britain. The financial crash of 1837 compelled him, while erecting a new building, to sell out the *Evangelist*.

In 1833 he devoted his whole time to the cause, as editor of the *New York Emancipator*, which John C. Calhoun said was more dangerous to Southern interests than any thing else in the country. [He also edited the monthly publications *Human Rights* and the *Anti-Slavery Record*]. At this time troubles arose in the society, and, the old committee and officers having been turned out, the *Emancipator* was transferred to the Young Men's Antislavery Society, by which it was conducted for a year, then transferred again to Mr. Leavitt, who moved it to Boston.

Mr. Leavitt early argued that the antislavery movement must become a political power, though in this he was strongly opposed by many leading abolitionists. In the convention which met in Albany in 1840, and organized the Liberal [Liberty] party, Mr. Leavitt took a prominent part, and afterward earnestly supported its measures in the *Emancipator*. He was also chairman of the National Committee from 1844 to 1847. In the latter year, perceiving the necessity of nominating a strong man for the presidency, he secured the adhesion of John P. Hale to the party, and aided in placing him at the head of the ticket.

In 1848 Mr. Leavitt became office-editor of the *Independent*, which had just been started by three Congregational merchants, and was connected editorially with it until his death. On reaching the age of seventy, however, he relinquished the active duties of managing editor, and took a post of less labor, and during the last few years his waning health had prevented his performing much work. Dr. Leavitt had also been engaged for some time in preparing a history of the anti-slavery conflict, for which he was peculiarly fitted. This work his death leaves in a very unfinished state, and it is doubtful if any one else can complete it.

Mr. Leavitt was also a most earnest and powerful speaker, and to his speeches in the antislavery cause, of which he made many, are attributed largely the growth of the movement. In 1855 Wabash College conferred on him the honorary degree of D.D. Dr. Leavitt's correspondence with Cobden, and his "Memoir on Wheat," setting forth the unlimited capacity of our Western territory for the growth and exportation of wheat, were very instrumental in procuring the repeal of the English corn laws. During his visit to Europe he also became much interested in Sir Rowland Hill's system of cheap postage, which he advocated for adoption in this country, both through the newspapers and before the Congress committee. In 1847 he founded the Cheap Postage Society of Boston, and in 1848-'49 he labored in Washington in its behalf, for the establishment of a two-cent system. During several years past, Dr. Leavitt had devoted much time to the study of the subject of free trade, of which he was an earnest advocate. In 1869 he received a gold medal from the Cobden Society of England for an essay on our commercial relations with Great Britain, in which he took an advanced position in favor of free trade.

Tall and commanding in figure, and striking in countenance, Dr. Leavitt's appearance was most imposing. In manner he was kind and gentle, and in thought and expression most pure and chaste.

American Annual Cyclopaedia . . . 1873
(New York, 1874), XIII, 408-409.
[Some paragraph indentations added.]

HUMAN RIGHTS.

OUR OBJECT IS LIBERTY FOR ALL; GAINED BY MORAL POWER, AND REGULATED BY IMPARTIAL LAWS.

VOL. I.] NEW-YORK, MAY, 1836. [NO. 11.

PLEASE READ & CIRCULATE.

PUBLISHED MONTHLY FOR THE AM. A. S. SOCIETY
BY R. G. WILLIAMS.
Office, corner of Nassau and Spruce streets, opposite the City Hall. Entrance, No. 2 Spruce st.

TERMS

Single copy, 25 cents per annum.
20 copies *to one address*, $3 50 or 17½ cts. per ann.
40 " do. 5 00 or 12½ " do.
100 " do. 10 00 or 10 " do.

Payment in all cases in ADVANCE, FREE OF POSTAGE. On all letters enclosing money, double postage should be paid. Otherwise, the addition (as is right) is made at this Post Office, and must be paid out of the money enclosed.

HUMAN RIGHTS.

LETTER FROM KENTUCKY.

The following *instructive* letter from a citizen of Kentucky will be read with great interest and benefit. We copy it from the Philanthropist, which copied it from the Cincinnati Journal and Luminary. We preserve the prefatory remarks of the two papers.

ED. HUM. RIGHTS.

We re-publish Mr. Green's letter to the Journal and Luminary, with great pleasure,—not because we concur in all the opinions and reasonings advanced in it—but, because it contains the candid opinion of an honest and intelligent man, who is really acting up to his professions in reference to slave-emancipation, so far as he is concerned. We cherish the hope that Mr. Green will be found practising the complete righteousness of instant emancipation,—and that he will yet be seen acting the high part for which God, by his gifts, has well qualified him—and which, from the situation in which he has placed him, he demands at his hands.

We will not abandon our expectations of seeing the blaze of holy action, in reference to slavery break out in the college and in the whole church at Danville.—*Phil.*

THE SLAVERY QUESTION IN KENTUCKY.

Anxious to do our duty in these times of excessive excitement, and believing that our southern brethren are the best judges of what is proper to be done, we wrote several letters to gentlemen of the first respectability in the Presbyterian church of Kentucky, soliciting their views on the subject of slavery. By the courtesy of John Green, Esq. of Danville, we are enabled to spread the following letter before the public. It contradicts some impressions which we had imbibed and expressed in our paper. Our intercourse with Kentuckians had led us to adopt opinions different from those of Mr. Green, as to the disposition of our sister state to rid herself of a great evil. But from the better opportunity of Mr. Green to obtain information, we fear he is right and we were wrong.—*J. & L.*

LINCOLN, Ky. March 1, 1836.

My dear Sir:—Your favor of the 2d Feb. was received in due time, and should have been attended to at an earlier day; but the combined influences of several causes, (among which was an evil spirit of procrastination,) united to prevent.

It is generally thought in Kentucky, that 'Abolition' has done much injury to the cause of gradual emancipation; and it is certain, that at present, the efforts of the friends of gradualism are greatly paralyzed. Little is doing for the negro, either in the way of African colonization, or voluntary emancipation, or of religious instruction; and a general apathy on the subject prevails, not only in the world, but in the church. Many attribute all this to the rampant zeal of the abolitionists, in attempting to force public opinion; and, with apparent self complacency, justify themselves in doing nothing, because they were required to do too much. It cannot be denied that there does exist at present a greater apparent opposition to emancipation in any form, than has appeared at any previous period within my recollection. But I am not sure that abolition has been the *cause*. I would rather say that it has been the *occasion of manifesting* that opposition which previously existed, but laid dormant for want of an exciting cause. I feel well assured that our slaveholders do not fear that the abolitionists will incite our slaves to revolt. Our white population is too strong, compared to the blacks, to permit a hope of success by insurrection to be entertained by the most ignorant fanatic. We know that very few of our negroes can read the abolition publications; and if they could, they would find in them nothing but what they thought and felt before they ever heard of abolition—the injustice of slavery. And as to the pictorial representations, which appeal so strongly to the sympathies of our northern brethren, the slave has once and again seen most of the scenes which most of those pictures are intended to represent, acted out in real life. They of course give him no new idea, and furnish no stimulus to insurrection. But the abolitionists have, some of them, indulged in all the uncharitableness towards us, and called us all manner of hard names, and we have returned the compliment with interest; and while you of the free states have engaged in the laudable work of mobbing your own citizens, to prove your attachment to the union, and please us, we have barely thanked you for the spirit of accommodation you manifested. For myself, I think with Mr. Jefferson, that 'error of opinion should be freely tolerated, while reason is left free to combat it;' and having no peculiar dread of the abolitionists, feel inclined to see them treated like all other *errorists in opinion*—put down by strong arguments. If the better reasons lie on the side of their opponents, they certainly may be made manifest; and must be perceived and appreciated by the world, when fairly exhibited. May it not be that abolition has rendered a service to the cause of truth, in the evidence it has drawn forth, tending to prove that the difficulties in the way of emancipation are much greater than have been apprehended by us? It certainly is important that those who would grapple with the monster should know the true dimensions of all the obstacles that lay in the way of success. Among these obstacles, the prejudices of the slaveholders are the greatest; and I know not how else the sentiments and feelings of the south could have been made to explode upon the world, than by those incendiary attacks upon their supposed rights. In the conflict of opinion, feeling and interest which is going on, facts will be collected and made public, and truth elicited, and all parties will understand the subject, and each other much better, than if the contest had not taken place. I have not, therefore, felt disposed to take exceptions to your occasional insertion of articles in favor of abolition in your journal. Dr. Nelson's letter to his old congregation at Danville, is one of the strongest I have noticed; and, although he probably made few converts, it was kindly received. As an evidence of the correctness of this opinion, I mention the fact that since the appearance of the letter, the ladies of the congregation have paid him the compliment of making him a member of the American Tract Society.

In regard to what ought to be your future course, I feel very incompetent to advise; but will, as you request it, suggest a few considerations which may be entitled to more or less weight in coming to right conclusions on the subject.

This is your position. You are the editor of a Christian newspaper. A violent controversy on the (for the present) all absorbing subject of slavery, pervades the whole community. The public press, the legislative hall, the primary assemblies of the social circles, the domestic board, the ecclesiastical court, and the court of conscience within, are more or less agitating and being agitated by this universal theme. You believe that the system of slavery, as it exists among us, is a moral evil, and that it ought to be terminated, but you are alike opposed to the *ultraism* of the abolitionists and the pro-slavery advocates. It seems to me that the great object of your vocation as an editor, should be to teach the gospel, to make your readers acquainted with the whole body of moral truth as revealed in the Scriptures, that they may be brought to submit to its requirements. In this respect, your aim is that of every honest minister; and although your labors differ in form, they are, or ought to be, in substance, much alike. And as the Christian minister should be careful to avoid every occasion of offence, and to render his ministrations as attractive as possible, in due subordination to other and higher considerations, so with the Christian editor; he should esteem his periodicals the chief field of his usefulness, and should labor with all diligence, to make that field a garden beautiful and attractive to the eye of taste, as well as abundant in the production of good fruits. The editor who fails to throw upon his sheet, a due degree of interest, or gives unnecessary offence; will soon cease to have readers—subscribers—or bread. But still duty must be performed, and we would *trust* that the difficulties which obstruct the path, are not insurmountable: nor are the dangers all lions in the way which will certainly devour us.—'*First* pure, *then* peaceable,' is the order of our duties; and as with the minister so with the editor. The whole truth should be advocated and insisted on, in due order and proportion, and nothing should be kept back which time and circumstances require to be brought forward. Is intemperance a growing vice in a congregation—the faithful pastor will not fail to denounce it, although his whiskey-making elder will denounce him in consequence. The readers of your journal are your congregation, and you are bound to warn them against any obliquity of principle or practice which you find prevalent among them. Is the system of slavery opposed by the moral law? Is it sinful? You answer in the affirmative. Have you then any choice? Are you not then bound, on your allegiance, to denounce it, not once or twice merely, but so often and so long as time and opportunity may permit you to do it in a manner calculated to do good. With the political bearings you have little to do. The moral aspects of the system should principally engage your attention and labors. 'Masters render to your servants that which is just and equal,' is the great text from which you should preach; from that I derive the doctrine I am endeavoring to practice.

A late number of your journal contains the expressions of some opinions respecting slavery in Kentucky, which I think incorrect. It is but natural that a stranger in passing through our country should take up such impressions, from the liberal tone in which our politicians and other intelligent men speak on the subject, so long as they are permitted to deal in generals, and to qualify their remarks by the important word *if*. But when you call upon them to propose some plan, and to commence action, they will *almost universally* draw back. I think I know something of the temper of the public men, and I tell you they are for doing *nothing*. They have no idea of cutting loose from the south on the subject of slavery, but on the contrary, the south is every day acquiring influence among us. I once hoped that Kentucky was on the verge of adopting a system of emancipation, on the *post nati principle*; but I now believe I was mistaken; and were we even to call a convention, I would have little hope of any thing being done to better the condition of the colored race. It is true that we are not lynching or mobbing our citizens for the free expression of honest opinions; nor are we passing any of those oppressive laws which withhold from the slave the exercise of benevolence on the part of the master. But our forbearance is to [illegible] attributed in a great degree to the fact [illegible] planters perform the part of a great colonization society, taking off every year as many as we can well spare from our farms and manufactories; and among the number, most of our refractory characters. It follows as a consequence, that those who remain are more easily managed, and cruel punishments are less necessary. So long as the present state of things continues, the system will continue more tolerable than it is in the south. And I am inclined to the opinion, that as the causes which usually result in the abolition of slavery, exist to a greater extent in the south than with us, and as those causes are acquiring maturity in the south more rapidly than with us, so the probabilities are, that emancipation will begin in the south, and ours will be among the last of our states which will grant liberty to their slaves.

With sincere regard,
Your friend,
JOHN GREEN.

ARKANSAS.

Arkansas asks to be taken into the Union—a Union which is said to be already in danger of splitting by the slightest agitation of the slavery question—and yet we find in one of her newspapers, published "BY AUTHORITY," the following law, by which it appears that persons may be arrested and sold as runaways for the benefit of the county, when no *owners* appear to claim them—of course that *free-men* may be sold into perpetual slavery, if they cannot prove their freedom. Alas! we have too much of this horrible stuff in the republic. Guilt is heavy, and a little more will sink us.

AN ACT, supplementary to the law concerning Runaway Slaves.

SECTION 1. *Be it enacted by the General Assembly of the Territory of Arkansas*, That if the owner or owners of any slave or slaves, sold as runaways under the law to which this is a supplement, shall fail to appear within three years after such sale has been made, and establish their ownership and right to such slave or slaves, the surplus of the proceeds of such sale, if there be any after deducting the costs and charges, shall become a part of the revenue of the county in which said slave or slaves have been sold, and to be accounted for by the treasurer, in the same manner that other monies are.

SEC. 2. *Be it further enacted*, That any monies that may now be in the treasury of any county in this Territory, deposited as the proceeds of any runaway slave or slaves, which has or may remain in said treasury for the term of three years, the ownership of which has not been established within that time, shall be, and it is hereby made a part of the revenue of said county, and be appropriated as other monies are, to county purposes.

SEC. 3. *And be it fu[illegible]nacted*, That this act shall take effect and be [illegible] force from and after its passage.

ABSALOM FOWLER, Speaker of the House of Rep. pro tem.
CHARLES CALDWELL, President of the Legislative Council.
Approved November 2, 1835.
WM. S. FULTON.

COMMUNICATIONS.

For the Human Rights.

Mr. Editor—It is truly painful to advert to the frequent occurrences of persecution of respectable and unoffending American citizens, by this cruel and wicked prejudice against color, which has taken such deep root in the minds of many, professing to be the disciples of him who declared, that unless we love God above all, and our neighbor as ourselves, it is impossible to enter the kingdom of heaven. And yet, perhaps, the cause of religion and humanity will be advanced by an an exposure of them to public view.

A few days since three respectable, well dressed colored persons, two men and and a young woman, wished to take a passage in the stage from a village about 23 miles distant, to this city. They had taken their seats, when a gentleman, differing a little in complexion from themselves, objected to it in such a furious and blustering manner, that the driver had to sacrifice his freedom and independence, to satisfy the demands of this dictatorial passenger, and ordered them to get out. The colored persons made no reply to the indignities and insults that were heaped upon them by this would be gentleman, but quietly left the stage. Fortunately, however, there was another [illegible], which belonged to the same proprietor, where they made application and were permitted to take seats. This also gave offence to the few whites who had been previously seated, amongst whom was a female half intoxicated, who all left the stage to join their companions in the one from whence the colored persons had been driven—the female alluded to seating herself beside this extremely sensitive gentleman. The stage drove off, and all parties seemed perfectly happy and contented with their respectable society. In the course of the passage, however, the lady had been so liberally filled with gin, as to become unable to sit up, and she would frequently find a resting place for her head upon this gentleman who had expressed so much repugnance to a dark skin

Now, Mr. Editor, let us take a glance at the consistency of this gentleman. He felt such a punctilious regard for his reputation, that he was unwilling to have these respectable colored persons in the stage, though seated at a distance—complaining that there would be an unpleasant effluvium—when at the same time he could sit for four or five hours together, cheek by jowl, with this daughter of Bacchus, inhaling the noisome and pestiferous effluvia of her lungs, without complaining or manifesting the least uneasiness for his reputation, by being seated beside a white female, debased by all the concomitant vices of drunkenness. Oh, no—it was hale fellow well met.

Indeed, Mr. Editor, the part which the people of this country are taking in relation to slavery, and the oppression of our free colored citizens, is becoming a complete moral test. Their characters may be estimated with much accuracy from the side they take in this great question. So it was during the arduous struggle for the abolition of the trade in Great Britain. It had become so conspicuous, that in many of the important divisions of the House on the question, the spectator was forcibly reminded of the parable of the sheep and the goats. None who voted on the negative were known to possess a pure and unsullied moral character.

True it is, Mr. Editor, we are a boasting people; there is no nation under heaven so loud in its own praise, and perhaps it is well for us that we have something to test the integrity of our virtue, for by it we must know we have retrograded not only from moral rectitude, but from the spirit of Republicanism, and are daily "living down the foundation principle of our glorious and happy constitution," and that unless there is some redeeming influence speedily to be exerted upon us, the days of our national prosperity are numbered.

E.

Figure 4

Journal Data

TITLE: *Human Rights*

MOTTO: Our Object is Liberty for All; Gained by Moral Power, and Regulated by Impartial Laws

INCLUSIVE DATES OF PUBLICATION: July 1835–Feb. 1839

PLACE OF PUBLICATION: New York, N.Y.

FREQUENCY OF PUBLICATION: Monthly

AVERAGE NUMBER OF PAGES PER ISSUE: 4

NUMBER OF COLUMNS PER PAGE: 4

EDITOR(s): William Goodell (1835); Amos Augustus Phelps (?–1837); Rev. Joshua Leavitt (1837–1838)

PUBLISHER(s): AAS; publishing agents, R. G. Williams (July 1835–Feb. 1838); George Russell (Apr. 1838–May 1838); S. W. Benedict (June 1838)

SPECIAL FEATURES: Advertisements; Illustrations

PRICE: Annual Subscription $ .25

AVERAGE CIRCULATION FIGURES (per issue): 7,000

PERSPECTIVE: Abolitionist

MISCELLANEOUS   *Human Rights* was one of four alternating journals published by the AAS as its official organ. It was issued the first week of each month. During the remaining weeks, the AAS published the *Anti-Slavery Record*, the *Emancipator*, and *Slave's Friend*.

REPOSITORY: Lewis Tappan's Anti-slavery Library, Carnegie Library, Howard University. July 1835–June 1838.

Prospectus

This newspaper is not started as a means of pecuniary profit. It is not sent out by any one man. Thousands of our fellow citizens have a[s]sociated in different parts of our country to obtain the fr[e]edom of the SLAVES,---yes, of *two and a quarter millions* of Americans, who, shame to tell it, are in this Republic, SLAVES. Already there are numbered more than TWO HUNDRED Anti-Slavery Societies acting through a central Society called the American Anti-Slavery Society.'' These citizens who have thus taken the part of the slave, ask a hearing. Their opinions and measures are often spoken against and denounced as fanaticism and treason, sometimes out of malice and hatred to the slave, but much oftener from ignorance. But those Anti-Slavery opinions, nevertheless, are gaining ground daily, especially among the great body of the people who support themselves in the good old-fashioned republican way of honest and honorable industry. The design of this paper is, therefore, to make known, plainly and honestly, to the great body of the American people, what the "Immediate Abolitionists" *think*, and what they are trying to *do*. Will you read it? We shall speak out without reserve. We have no thoughts, nor feelings, nor plans towards the free colored people, or the slaves, or the slave masters, which will be concealed or kept back. It will hurt no man, woman or child to take a little pains to know what abolitionists really *mean*, and here it may be found in a short space, in plain language, and fair type.

Human Rights, New York, N.Y.
July 1835, (vol. I, no. 1)
[Title supplied.]

[1835]

7503 DANIEL O'CONNELL *to* **THE EDITOR OF THE** *MORNING CHRONICLE.* **16 May 1835. n.p.** Criticizes the *Chronicle*'s report that he had called Americans "the vilest of mankind" while in London; explains that he was referring only to slaveholding Americans, whom he charges with violating the honor of the Declaration of Independence by denying equality and the pursuit of happiness to all. July 1835 (vol. I, no. 1) p.2, c4.

7504 J. W. CLARK *to* **n.n. 20 June 1835. Columbia, S.C.** Offers a $1000 reward for the arrest of a white man who gave Clark's servant his freedom papers and took him out of the state. July 1835 (vol. I, no.1) p.3, c4.

7505 n.n. *to* **THE EDITOR OF THE** *LIBERIA HERALD.* **31 January 1835. n.p.** Complains that merchants are forced to purchase rum so that tobacco shipments will continue. August 1835 (vol. I, no. 2) p.6, c1.

7506 A POSTMASTER IN VIRGINIA *to* **n.n. 15 August 1835. n.p.** Reports that he has received *Human Rights* and the *Emancipator*; believes that the struggles for reason, truth, justice, and anti-slavery are one. September 1835 (vol. I, no. 3) p.10, c4.

7507 R. G. WILLIAMS *to* **n.n. [from the** *Emancipator***] 9 August 1835. Tennessee.** Describes the beating of a slave by his master and the separation of family members sold to different masters; laments the sad state of the country and the lack of justice. September 1835 (vol. I, no. 3) p.10, c4.

7508 THOMAS NAPIER *to* **GENTLEMEN OF THE LAW FIRM OF LEGARE, O'HEAR AND LEGARE. [from the** *Charleston Mercury***] 3 September 1835. Northampton, Ma.** Refutes the charge that he is an abolitionist; declares that he is entirely opposed to abolitionism. October 1835 (vol. I, no. 4) p.15, c2.

7509 WILLIAM LLOYD GARRISON *to* **n.n. [from the** *Boston Liberator***] 25 October 1835. Boston.** Gives an account of the disruption of a meeting of the Boston Female AS by a mob of about a thousand; reports that pro-slavery sentiment had been stirred by local papers and that he barely escaped with his life. December 1835 (vol. I, no. 6) p.1, c1.

[1836]

7510 REV. DAVID NELSON *to* **CONGREGATION AT DANVILLE, KY. n.d. n.p.** Offers advice to parishioners from his deathbed; uses biblical arguments to convince his congregation that slavery is wrong; argues that blacks cannot learn the gospel while they are enslaved; urges parishioners not to condemn sinners who could become converts. January 1835 [1836] (vol. I, no. 7) p.3, c4.

7511 GEORGE STORRS *to* **MR. KIMBALL. [from** *Herald of Freedom***] n.d. n.p.** Reports an unsuccessful attempt by a mob to disrupt speeches and abduct Storrs at a meeting of the Dover Young Men's AS. February 1836 (vol. I, no. 8) p.2, c2.

7512 WM. R. BUFORD *to* **n.n. [from the** *Northampton* **(Ma.)** *Hampshire Gazette***] n.d. n.p.** A former slaveholder proposes that each slaveholder free his slaves and set an example for the eventual emancipation of all slaves. April 1836 (vol. I, no. 10) p.1, c1.

7513 JOHN GREEN *to* **THE EDITOR. 1 March 1836. Lincoln, Ky.** Reports on attitudes towards slavery in Kentucky; feels that abolitionists' views are too drastic for many who would prefer another plan for ending slavery. May 1836 (vol. I, no. 11) p.1, c1.

7514 E. *to* **MR. EDITOR. n.d. n.p.** Relates account of the removal of respectable colored persons from a stage at the insistence of white passengers who did not seem disturbed when a drunken white woman took the vacated place. May 1836 (vol. I, no. 11) p.1, c4.

7515 PHEBE BROWNRIGG *to* **EMILY BROWNRIGG. 13 September 1835. Edenton, N.C.** Bids farewell to her daughter and grandchildren before moving to Alabama with her master. May 1836 (vol. I, no. 11) p.2, c1.

7516 EMILY BROWNRIGG *to* **PHEBE BROWNRIGG. 12 February 1836. Edenton, N.C.** Replies to her mother's letter, informing her that she had married, but her husband was soon afterwards sold to another family. May 1836 (vol. I, no. 11) p.2, c1.

7517 S. CROTHERS *to* **n.n. [from the** *Philanthropist*] **n.d. n.p.** Notes the hypocrisy of Christians who uphold slavery; reminds that God punished first the Egyptians and then the Jews for keeping slaves. May 1836. (vol. I, no. 11) p.4, c3.

7518 REV. ROBERT RUTHERFORD *to* **BROTHER WELD. 25 December 1834. n.p.** Discusses a group of former slaves who settled at Brush Creek Camps in Ohio with an allotment of only ten acres of swampland each; relates that although they were surrounded by unscrupulous whites who tried to cheat them at every opportunity, they remained peaceable and industrious. August 1836 (vol. II, no. 2) p.3, c1.

7519 H. PANGBURN *to* **n.n. 1834. Brown County.** Discusses the former slaves of Samuel Gist, settled on swampland by Gist's agents after his death; notes that they are illiterate, sometimes intemperate, yet apparently no less honest than whites. August 1836 (vol. II, no. 2) p.3, c2.

7520 JOSIAH MOORE *to* **n.n. 28 December 1834. Sardinia.** Discusses the settlement of former slaves at Brush Creek in Ohio; notes that they are at times immoral, but feels this is due to the influence of the immoral whites nearby; adds that they must seek work in Cincinnati, because their land is too poor to farm. August 1836 (vol. II, no. 2) p.3, c2.

7521 ABRAHAM PETTYJOHN (PRESBYTERIAN ELDER) *to* **n.n. n.d. n.p.** Declares that the 500 former slaves who settled sixteen years earlier at Brush Creek have since conducted themselves as well as or better than whites in the area. August 1836 (vol. II, no. 2) p.3, c2.

7522 S. J. M., NEW ENGLAND CLERGYMAN *to* **n.n. n.d. n.p.** Expresses horror at his first view of slavery; relates story of a plantation owner who moved to the city, fired his overseers and turned the plantation over to his slaves, who have run it successfully ever since. September 1836 (vol. II, no. 3) p.2, c3.

7523 L. G. HAMILTON *to* **E. WRIGHT, JR. 6 September 1836. Port-Au-Prince (Hayti).** Describes religious practices and the lack of color prejudice in Haiti to members of the AAS. October 1836 (vol. II, no. 4) p.2, c2.

7524 ROBERT PURVIS *to* **THE EDITOR OF THE** *LIBERATOR* **[W. L. GARRISON]. n.d. n.p.** Mourns the death of Thomas Shipley, "friend of the oppressed colored man." October 1836 (vol. II, no. 4) p.3, c4.

[1837]

7525 JAMES G. BIRNEY *to* **PASTORS AND OTHERS WHO CONTROL CHURCHES IN CINCINNATI. [from the** *Philanthropist*] **n.d. n.p.** Requests that one of the Cincinnati churches allow him to lecture on abolition, in order to convince the churches and community of the justice of the anti-slavery movement. January 1837 (vol. II, no. 7) p.2, c3.

7526 JOHN G. WHITTIER *to* **GARRISON. [from the** *Liberator***] 2 December 1836. Haverhill.** Urges circulation of anti-slavery petitions in Massachusetts, in order to convince timid congressmen to support the anti-slavery bill introduced in the senate. January 1837 (vol. II, no. 7) p.4, c3.

7527 DR. W. G. SMITH *to* **MR. EDITOR. [extract] 20 November 1836. Port-Au-Prince.** A former American declares that the Haitians, if more "indolent" than the Europeans, are "less vicious and friendlier"; notes effective government, peaceful conditions, and rise in the population of Haiti since the revolution. March 1837 (vol. II, no. 9) p.1, c4.

7528 H. WILSON *to* **SIR. 26 January 1837. Toronto.** Poses questions to a member of the Society of Canada concerning the loyalty, morality, work habits, and economic conditions of the 600 former slaves residing there. March 1837 (vol. II, no. 9) p.4, c4.

7529 R. G. DUNLAP *to* **HIRAM WILSON. 27 January 1837. Toronto.** A member of the House of Assembly discusses ex-slaves residing in Canada, declaring that no people in Canada are more loyal, industrious, friendly, or moral than they, and that he hopes for God's grace for the Negroes. March 1837 (vol. II, no. 9) p.4, c4.

7530 W. L. MACKENZIE *to* **H. WILSON. 30 January 1837. Toronto.** Replies to Wilson's inquiries concerning the colony of ex-slaves living in Canada; affirms their loyalty, temperance, industriousness, and honesty; notes that they oppose union with the United States. March 1837 (vol. II, no. 9) p.4, c4.

7531 JOHN H. DUNN *to* **H. WILSON. 28 January 1837. Toronto, Canada.** Answers inquiry by Wilson, affirming the loyalty, morality, temperance, and good behavior of the 600 former slaves residing in Canada. March 1837 (vol. II, no. 9) p.4, c4.

7532 REV. DR. WILSON *to* **n.n. 5 December 1836. Coldenham.** Believes that there are no slaves who prefer their condition to freedom. April 1837 (vol. II, no. 10) p.4, c2.

7533 SUSAN E. WATTLES *to* **THE EDITOR OF** *HUMAN RIGHTS***. 26 February 1837. St. Mary's.** Reports on a young woman who taught a colored school in Brown County "at the risk of her life," and the burning of that school. April 1837 (vol. II, no. 10) p.4, c1.

7534 W. H. J. *to* **THE EDITOR OF THE** *NATIONAL ENQUIRER***. 18 July 1837. Buckingham, Pa.** Feels that more people need to see and acknowledge the realities of slavery; reports the arrest of a free Negro as a runaway slave. August 1837 (vol. III, no. 2) p.1, c3.

7535 REV. WILLIAM DICKEY *to* **EDITOR. n.d. n.p.** Reports that Lilburn Lewis, the nephew of T. Jefferson and a resident of Livingston, Kentucky, murdered one of his slaves with an ax, was subsequently deserted by family and friends, and later committed suicide. August 1837 (vol. III, no. 2) p.4, c1.

7536 D. I. ROBINSON *to* **THE EDITOR OF THE** *HERALD OF FREEDOM***. n.d. n.p.** States that Rev. Richard Watson estimated that 59 million slaves had been taken from Africa, and Robinson calculates over 40 million murders have resulted from the slave trade; cites births out of wedlock, theft of wages, and cruelty as the evils of slavery. September 1837 (vol. III, no. 3) p.2, c1.

7537 WM. H. PRITCHARD *to* **EDITORS OF THE** *CONSTITUTIONALIST***. 20 December 1836. Aiken, S.C.** Refutes a coroner's report concerning a runaway slave, which claimed that a minimum of force was used in his apprehension. September 1837 (vol. III, no. 3) p.4, c2.

7538 ELIJAH P. LOVEJOY *to* **FRIENDS OF THE** *ALTON OBSERVER*. **n.d. n.p.**
Reports that the *Observer*'s office was entered and ransacked, and its equipment destroyed; asks old subscribers to pay up, new customers to subscribe, and others to donate toward the $1500 needed to start publishing the paper again. October 1837 (vol. III, no. 4) p.4, c4.

[1838]

7539 JAMES S. BULLOCH *to* **THE EDITOR OF THE** *SAVANNAH GEORGIAN*. **n.d. n.p.** A former Southerner describes the "injustice" and unfriendliness encountered in Connecticut during the trial for the freedom of Nancy Jackson, his former slave. February 1838 (vol. III, no. 7) p.1, c3.

7540 B. GIRARD *to* **n.n. n.d. n.p.** A Frenchman recalls the egalitarian treatment of colored persons at the Royal College of Marseilles; notes that his classmate, Chapus, a mulatto from Martinique, was selected to address the Duke d'Angouléme upon his visit to the Royal College. March 1838 (vol. III, no. 9) p.2, c4.

7541 MATTHEW FORSTER *to* **E. WRIGHT, JR. 10 May 1838. Newcastle-upon-Tyne.** Reports on progress in British abolitionism. June 1838 (vol. III, no. 12) p.3, c1.

7542 DR. J. BOWRING *to* **HIS WIFE. [extract] 2 December 1837. Grand Cairo.** Reports on war in Egypt and Egyptian slave trade. June 1838 (vol. III, no. 12) p.3, c2.

7543 F. H. ELMORE *to* **JAS. G. BIRNEY. 16 February 1838. Washington City.** Encloses a list of questions on the ASS concerning the number of societies, jurisdiction, publications, and finances. June 1838 (vol. III, no. 12) p.5, c1.

7544 JAMES G. BIRNEY *to* **HON. F. H. ELMORE. 8 March 1838. New York.** Answers Elmore's inquiries, noting the existence of over 1400 auxiliary ASS, 112,480 members, and societies in Canada, France, Great Britain, and Haiti. June 1838 (vol. III, no. 12) p.5, c2.

St. Louis/Alton *Observer*

Figure 5. Elijah Parish Lovejoy

Elijah Parish Lovejoy

[Editor, *Alton Observer*]

The Rev. Elijah Parish Lovejoy was the eldest of nine children, five of whom survive, three in Alton and two in Maine. His father was from Marblehead, and was aided in his preparation for College by the Rev. Elijah Parish, D.D., of Byfield, Mass. Hence the name of his first born, conferred in token, not of relationship but of gratitude. Elijah, at a very early age, gave evidence of uncommon talents and courage. At the age of nineteen he commenced his preparatory studies for a public education. In May, 1827, he left home, an adventurer for the great West. He found his way to St. Louis, taught a school a year or more, and became editor of the *St. Louis Times*. We now have it on good authority that he never was admitted to the bar and also that he was never an *infidel*, but that, on the contrary, he published in his political paper an able refutation of the sentiments advanced by Robert Dale Owen. In January, 1832, he became a Christian under the preaching of the Rev. David Nelson. Immediately renouncing his prospects of worldly advancement, he devoted his life to the gospel ministry. After some time spent in the study of theology at the Presbyterian Seminary, at Princeton, N.J., he was licensed to preach the gospel, and preached for some months in the Spring-street church in [New York], during the absence of the pastor, Mr. Ludlow. He also preached at Hartford, Connecticut. But his home was in the West, and in November, 1833, he returned to St. Louis, whither he had been called to edit the "*St. Louis Observer*."

This paper he conducted with great energy and ability. It became noted for its controversy with the papists, in which its editor engaged by way of self-defence. He was a warm colonizationist at the commencement of his editorial career, and, of course, while under that flag, gave no offence to slaveholders. Indeed, he seems to have been as popular as it was possible for a protestant religious editor to be, in the State of Missouri. Some of his brethren in that State, however, urged him to study more seriously and attentively the subject of slavery. His inquiries were quickened by the riots in [New York], in July 1834. A week after the news of these outrages, he said, "Slavery, as it now exists among us, must cease to exist. It is useless for us who live in slaveholding states, to shut our eyes to this fact. Meanwhile, as long as this evil shall continue, we maintain that they [the slaves] must be taught the truths of the Bible so far that they may secure the salvation of their souls. Here we take our stand, and sooner than be driven from it, we would even—a sad alternative—*go over on to abolition ground*."

Mr. Lovejoy continued to speak out occasionally on slavery, especially to develope facts, and as his interest increased, his articles grew more conspicuous in length, and more decisive in tone. Still he by no means identified himself with the immediate abolitionists. So much, however, had he excited attention, that when in June, 1836, Judge *Lawless* charged the Grand Jury in relation to the burning of McIntosh, he directed the attention of the inquest to the *St. Louis Observer* as having stirred up the colored people to arrogance, and excited them to deeds which would necessarily bring upon them popular vengeance similar to that which had fallen upon poor McIntosh. To this extraordinary and infamous charge,

Mr. Lovejoy replied through his paper as became a man and a Christian. In consequence of this, a mob of about twenty ruffians attacked his printing office, upset the press, and scattered the types in the street. This was done on the 21st July, 1836.

In a few days Mr. Lovejoy removed his press to Alton, twenty-two miles above on the Illinois side of the Mississippi. As soon as it was discharged from the boat, the press was broken to pieces, and the type scattered upon the wharf. This was very justly considered by many of the people of Alton as a disgrace to their rising city, and a public meeting was held for the reestablishment of the press.

It is pretended that Mr. Lovejoy, at this meeting, gave a pledge that he would not agitate the subject of slavery in his paper. This matter is set in its true light by an extract from the proceedings of the public meeting at Alton, a few days before the riot, as reported in the *Alton Telegraph*. Mr. Hogan had represented Mr. Lovejoy's conduct as a violation of his pledge, when he was thus replied to:

"The Rev. F. W. Graves asked Mr. Hogan, 'whether Mr. Lovejoy did not at the time referred to, distinctly state that he yielded none of his rights to discuss any subject which he saw fit.' Mr Hogan replying in the *affirmative*, Mr. G. proceded to remark, that when Mr. Lovejoy arrived in this city, he entertained the views attributed to him by the gentleman who had just taken his seat; [viz. that it was not his duty to advocate emancipation in a free State,] that a change had subsequently taken place in his opinions, and that at a certain meeting of the friends of the *Observer*, he (Mr. Lovejoy) had made known this alteration in his sentiments, and asked advice whether it was best to come out in public on the subject. That, under the circumstances of the case, it was deemed most proper to let the paper go on—there then being no excitement in the public mind. Mr. G. next alluded to the present excited state of popular feeling; and said that the friends of the *Observer* had lately received communications from all parts of the country, and even from Kentucky, Missouri, and Mississippi, urging the necessity of re-establishing the press."

The publication of the *Alton Observer* was commenced about the 1st of October, 1836. It was not till some months after this, that Mr. Lovejoy ranked himself with immediate abolitionists. From the first, however, he made free with the "delicate subject." Though his paper was not exclusively, or for the greater part, occupied with that subject, he at length spoke so decidedly, that on the 21st of August, 1837, his press and types were again destroyed by a mob. Another press was obtained, which was also destroyed immediately on its landing. Measures were promptly taken to procure a third press, which was landed on the morning of the 7th of November 1837, and in the evening of the same day its proprietor was murdered.

CHARACTER.

Mr. Lovejoy, though decided, fearless, zealous, and immoveable, except by the power of argument, was, both as a man and an editor, gentle, courteous, and kind. His attacks were open and magnanimous; and his treatment of those who differed from him was marked with the utmost liberality. He did not fight from behind an editorial shelter, but gave his adversaries a fair field in his own columns. If he was shown to be mistaken in his facts, he made the most ingenuous and candid retraction. His spirit was not in the least discernible degree vindictive; he dealt not at all in rancorous personalities or abusive epithets.

Indeed, if the mob were to appoint a *Bartholemew's eve* for all the editors who have sinned as much in this respect as Mr. Lovejoy, we believe not one of the whole corps would escape to tell the tale. Often have we admired the calm blandness of his temper while the legions of his enemies were dipping their arrows in poison. There are few men who, in his circumstances, would not either have retired in disgust, or given loose to revenge. He was not a man who delighted in violence, nor did he counsel it. The people of Hannibal, Missouri, had invited Dr. Nelson to preach to them. At the appointed time, a mob from *Palmyra* was on the ground, with arms, to suppress the sermon! To a letter from Hannibal, expressing the indignation of the people of that place for this outrageous interference, Mr. Lovejoy appends the following remarks:—

"Feel indignant! and so they well may; yet we trust their indignation will be kept within proper bounds. Let not violence be repelled by violence, except in actual and necessary self-defence.

We may hope, however, that the people of Hannibal will henceforth know how to sympathize with those who for years now, have held their rights, civil, personal, and religious, at the mercy of the mob."—*Alton Observer, May* 15, 1837 . . . .

The truth is, that Mr. Lovejoy was highly esteemed and exceedingly popular, as an editor, *before* he began to discuss the subject of slavery; his popularity waned as he verged towards abolitionism, and upon his adopting the doctrine of immediate emancipation and renouncing colonization, like all other men who have had reputation to lose with the advocates and apologists of slavery, he lost the whole. It matters not how high a man has stood in public opinion, the moment he takes the stand that our national declaration of rights is *practically* applicable *to all*, he becomes a rash, fanatical, disorganizing man!

Human Rights, New York,
January 1838, p.1, c1
[Some paragraph indentions added.]

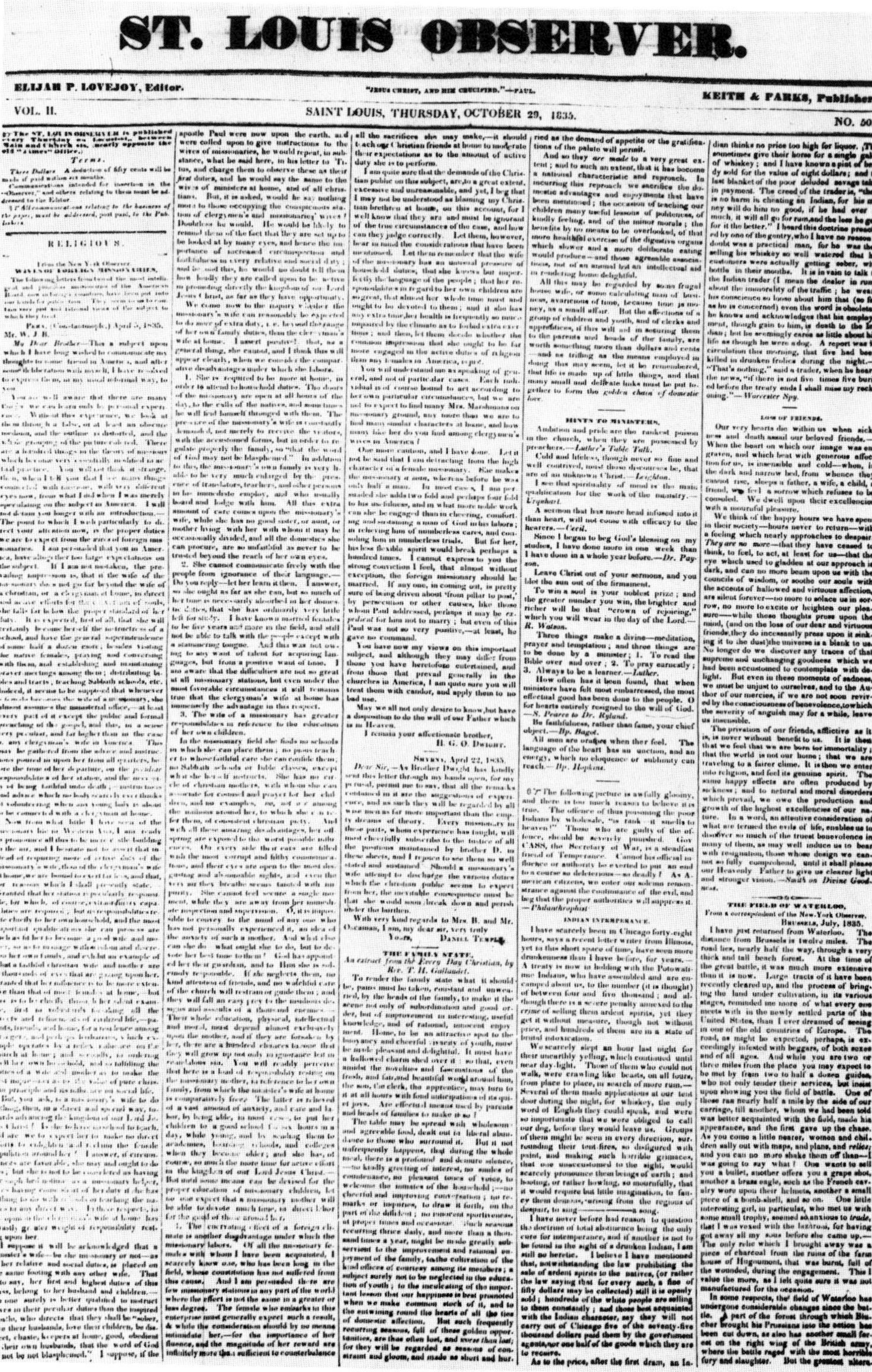

ST. LOUIS OBSERVER.

ELIJAH P. LOVEJOY, Editor.

"JESUS CHRIST, AND HIM CRUCIFIED."—PAUL.

KEITH & PARKS, Publishers

VOL. II.   SAINT LOUIS, THURSDAY, OCTOBER 29, 1835.   NO. 50.

RELIGION.

Figure 6

Journal Data

TITLE: *St. Louis Observer* (1835?–10 Aug. 1836); *Alton Observer* (8 Sept. 1836–1838?)

MOTTO: "Jesus Christ, and Him Crucified."—Paul (1835–10 Aug.1837)

INCLUSIVE DATES OF PUBLICATION: 1835?–1838?

PLACES OF PUBLICATION: St Louis, Mo. (by 3 Sept. 1835–21 July 1836); Alton, Il. (10 Aug. 1836–10 Aug. 1837); Cincinnati, Oh. (28 Dec. 1837–1838?)

FREQUENCY OF PUBLICATION: Weekly (irregular)

DAY OF WEEK WHEN PUBLISHED: Thursday

AVERAGE NUMBER OF PAGES PER ISSUE: 4

SIZE: varied

NUMBER OF COLUMNS PER PAGE: 5–6

EDITOR(s): Elijah Parish Lovejoy (1835–10 Aug. 1837); Elisha W. Chester (28 Dec. 1837–1838?)

PUBLISHER(s): Keith and Parks (3 Sept. 1835–5 Nov. 1835); Keith (19 Nov. 1835–26 Nov. 1835); Keith and Ostrander (26 Nov. 1835–?); Elisha W. Chester (28 Dec. 1837–1838?)

SPECIAL FEATURES: Advertisements; Illustrations

PRICE: Annual Subscription $3.00

CIRCULATION FIGURES (per issue): approx. 1,000 subscribers as of 8 Sept. 1836; approx. 1,700 as of 16 Mar. 1837

PERSPECTIVE: Anti-slavery, temperance, missionary

MISCELLANEOUS Elisha W. Chester assumed editorial duties on 28 Dec. 1837 after Elijah Parish Lovejoy was murdered on 7 Nov. 1837 by a violent mob which also destroyed his press.

REPOSITORY: Illinois State Historical Society. 3 Sept. 1835–19 Apr. 1838.

Editor's Address

Recent well-known occurrences in this city, and elsewhere, have, in the opinion of some of my friends, as well as my own, made it my duty to address myself to you personally. And, in so doing, I hope to be pardoned for that apparent egotism which, in such an address, is more or less unavoidable.—I hope also to write in that spirit of meekness and humility that become a follower of the Lamb, and at the same time with all that boldness and sincerity of speech, which should mark the language of a freeman and a Christian minister. It is not my design or wish to offend any one, but simply to maintain my rights as a republican citizen, free-born, of these United States, and to defend, fearlessly, the cause of TRUTH AND RIGHTEOUSNESS.

It is confidently reported through the State, and the charge is distinctly made in a paper of this city, that I am an abolitionist. And this is made use of to excite against me the public mind, and threats of personal violence are coming to my ears daily. Under almost any circumstances I should consider it a matter altogether too unimportant to trouble the public with, as to what I did or did not believe; what I was or was not. But inasmuch as the public have thought otherwise, I feel myself bound to give them every explanation possible.

In the first place, therefore, I declare that I *am not* an Abolitionist. By abolitionist I understand one who wishes to have the slaves amongst us *immediately* set free. Not only do I not desire such an event, but I should deplore it as one of the greatest evils that could afflict our community—injurious greatly to masters and slaves, but chiefly to the latter. The columns of the *Observer* will testify that such have ever been my sentiments, repeatedly and emphatically expressed. I have witnessed with grief and pain the erroneous views of many good men on this point, & I have repeatedly assured our abolition brethren at the East and North, that they mistook entirely the true remedy for the evils of slavery. And even now, if they would hear the voice of one who has lived, for years, in the midst of slavery, and who writes and publishes this at the peril of his life, I would conjure them to give up the unwise, the altogether impracticable notion of immediate abolition.—Alas! I have too much reason to fear that, while here, at home, I am threatened with violence and death, because I dare to advocate, in any way, the cause of the oppressed, abroad I shall, in many cases, fail to obtain the sympathies of my brethren, for the reason that both my judgment and conscience refuse to sanction their ultra measures.

As the term abolitionist, therefore, is understood, I am not one; and to charge me with being such, not only in the absence of all proof to sustain the charge, but also in the face of abundant evidence to the contrary, is a slanderous calumny.

But with equal frankness, I declare to you, my fellow citizens, that I am an *emancipationist.* I am, and while I exist, whether on earth or in heaven, I expect to be, opposed to the system of slavery. I believe it to be one of the greatest moral and political evils that could possibly be inflicted on any people. Consequently, I ardently desire to see some system devised and put into operation, by which the removal of this evil may be effected, in such a way as shall best consult for the good of the whole *community,* including in this word both master and slave. I do not for a moment admit the idea that slavery is to be perpetual or that the Bible sanctions it. But of this I shall have more to say by and by.

I come now to the specific charge made in one of the city papers, that I circulated abolition pamphlets, such as *Human Rights,* &c, by sending them in a box of Bibles to Jefferson

City. This charge was made in terms the most unkind and offensive. All the malignity and bitterness that so strikingly manifested themselves in him who wrote the article—I know not and wish not to know who it was—I freely forgive. And I not only forgive, but sincerely pity, the blundering error of that well meaning, but weak-minded and misguided brother, who, in reference to the same subject, in another number of the paper suffered his officious vanity to get the better of his charity and candor.

The facts are simply these. In the discharge of my official duty, I sent to the order of the Cole County Bible Society, a quantity of Bibles. In putting them into the box obtained for the purpose, I found that the box was not filled. I therefore gathered together the loose papers in the office, together with some obtained from the *Herald* office below stairs, put them, promiscuously, into the box, nailed it up and sent it off. Not long afterward, I received from my friend, Capt. Hart, of Jefferson City, a letter informing me that amongst the newspapers sent in the box was a copy of the *Emancipator,* and adding, moreover, that some persons there were disposed to believe that I had sent it purposely. To this letter I immediately replied stating the facts as here given, & assuring Capt. Hart that, until informed by him, I could not have told the title of a single one of all the newspapers sent in the box. I added an expression of my regret that the circumstance should have happened in connection with the sending of the Bibles, inasmuch as I should, above all things, desire to keep the Bible Society from any suspicion of intermeddling with other objects than the great one for which it was instituted. And this expression of regret I here renew.

I do not exchange with the *Emancipator,* nor is that paper regularly or generally received at this office. It so happened that two or three numbers of the paper did come here about the time referred to—the time they were sent, in such numbers, to the South. They were thrown aside among the other papers of the office, and thus, as have been explained, one of them, purely accidentally, found its way to Jefferson City.

Let this statement, fellow-citizens, show you the impropriety and the danger of putting the administration of justice into the hands of a mob. I am assured that had I been in the city, at the time when the charge here referred to, was first circulated, I should surely have suffered the penalty of the whipping post or the tar-barrel, if not both! I understand that a Christian brother was one of those who brought the report here from Jefferson City, and was among the most active in circulating it, and declaring his belief in my criminality. If this meets his eye, he is assured that I forgive him with all my heart.

And now, fellow-citizens, having made the above explanation, for the purpose of undeceiving such of you as have honestly supposed me in error; truth and candor require me to add that had I desired to send a copy of the *Emancipator* or of any other newspaper to Jefferson City, I should not have taken the pains to box it up. I am not aware that any law of my country forbids my sending what document I please to a friend or citizen. I know, indeed, that *mob-law* has decided otherwise, and that it has become fashionable in certain parts of the country, to break open the Post Office, and take from it such documents as the mob should decide ought not to pass *unburned.* But I had never imagined there was a sufficiency of respectability attached to the proceeding, to recommend it for adoption to the good citizens of my own State. And grievously and sadly shall I be disappointed to find it otherwise.

In fine, I wish it to be distinctly understood that I have never, knowingly, to the best of my recollection, sent a single copy of the *Emancipator* or any other abolition publication to a single individual in Missouri or elsewhere; while yet I claim the *right* to send ten thousand of them if I choose, to as many of my fellow-citizens. Whether I will *exercise* that right or not, is for me, and not for the *mob,* to decide. The right to send publications of any sort to slaves, or in any way to communicate with them, without the *express permission* of their masters, I freely acknowledge that I have not. Nor do I wish to have it. It is with the master alone, that I would have to do, as one freeman with another; and who shall say me nay?

I come now to the proceedings had at the late meetings of our citizens. And in discussing them I hope not to say a single word that shall wound the feelings of a single individual concerned. It is with principles I have to do, and not with men. And with canvassing them, freely, openly, I do but exercise a right secured by the solemn sanction of the constitution to the humblest citizen of this republic—a right that, so long as life lasts, I do not expect to relinquish.

I freely acknowledge the respectability of the citizens who composed the meetings referred to. And were the questions under consideration, to be decided as mere matters of opinion, it would become me, however much I might differ from them, to bow in humble silence to the decisions of such a body of my fellow-citizens. But I cannot surrender my principles, though the whole world besides should vote them down—I can make no compromise between truth and error, even though my life be the alternative.

Of the first resolution passed at the meeting of the 24th Oct., I have nothing to say, except that I perfectly agree with the sentiment, that the citizens of the non-slaveholding states have no right to interfere with the domestic relations between master and slave.

The second resolution, strictly speaking, neither affirms or denies any thing, in reference to the matter in hand. No man has a *moral* right to do any thing improper. Whether, therefore, he has the moral right to discuss the question of slavery, is a point with which human legislation or revolutions have nothing to do. The true issue to be decided is, whether he has the *civil*, the political right, to discuss it, or not. And this is a mere question of fact. In Russia, in Turkey, in Austria, nay, even in France, this right most certainly does not exist. But does it exist in Missouri? We decide this question by turning to the Constitution of the State. The 16th section, Article 13th, of the Constitution of Missouri, reads as follows:

"That the free communication of thoughts and opinions is one of the invaluable rights of man, and that every person may freely speak, write, and print ON ANY SUBJECT, being responsible for the abuse of that liberty."

Here, then, I find my warrant for using, as Paul did, all freedom of speech. If I abuse that right I freely acknowledge myself amenable to the laws.—But it is said that the right to hold slaves is a constitutional one, and therefore not to be called in question. I admit the premise, but deny the conclusion. To put a strong case by way of illustration. The Constitution declares that this shall be a perpetual republic, but has not any citizen the right to discuss, under that constitution, the comparative merits of despotism and liberty? And if he has eloquence and force of argument sufficient, may he not persuade us all to crown him our king? Robert Dale Owen came to this city, and Fanny Wright followed him, openly proclaiming the doctrine that the institution of marriage was a curse to any community, and ought to be abolished. It was, undoubtedly, an abominable doctrine, and one which, if acted out, would speedily reduce society to the level of barbarism and the brutes; yet who thought of denying Mr. Owen and his disciple the perfect right of avowing such doctrines, or who thought of mobbing them for the exercise of this right? And yet, most surely, the institutions of slavery are not more interwoven with the structure of our society, than those of marriage.

See the danger, and the natural and inevitable result to which the first step here will lead.—To-day a public meeting declares that you shall not discuss the subject of slavery, in any of its bearings, civil or religious. Right or wrong, the press must be silent. To-morrow, another meeting decides that it is against the peace of society, that the principles of Popery shall be discussed, and the edict goes forth to muzzle the press. The next day it is, in a similar manner, declared that not a word must be said against distilleries, dram shops, or drunkenness. And so on to the end of the chapter. The truth is, my fellow-citizens, if you give ground a single inch, there is no stopping place. I deem it, therefore, my duty to take my stand upon the Constitution. Here is firm ground—I feel it to be such. And I do most respectfully, yet decidedly, declare to you my fixed determination to maintain this ground. We have slaves, it is true, but *I* am not one. I am a citizen of these United States, a citizen of Missouri, free-born; and having never forfeited the inestimable privileges attached to such a condition, I cannot consent to surrender them. But while I maintain them, I hope to do it with all that meekness and humility that become a Christian, and especially a Christian minister. I am ready, not to fight, but to suffer, and if need be, to die for them. Kindred blood to that which flows in my veins, flowed freely to water the tree of Christian liberty, planted by the Puritans on the rugged soil of New England. It flowed as freely on the plains of Lexington, the heights of Bunker Hill, and fields of Saratoga. And freely, too, shall mine flow, yes, as freely as if it were so much water, ere I surrender my right to plead the cause of truth and righteousness, before my fellow-citizens, and in the face of it all their opposers.

Of the 3d resolution I must be allowed to say, that I have never seen the least evidence, whatever, that the Abolitionists, with all their errors, have ever desired to effect an amalgamation of the two races, black and white. I respectfully ask of the individuals composing the meeting that adopted this resolution, if they have ever seen any such evidence? They have formally, solemnly and officially denied it. It is certainly an abhorrent thing even in theory, & a thousand times more so in *practice*. And yet, unless my eyes deceive me as I walk the streets of our city, there are some among us who venture to put it into practice. And in the appointment of the numerous committees of vigilance, superintendance, &c., methinks that not one of them all was more needed than a Committee whose business it should be to ferret out from their secret "chambers of iniquity," these practical *amalgamationists*. If He who said to the woman taken in adultery, "Go and sin no more," had stood in the midst of the meeting at our Court House, I will not say that he would there have detected a single *amalgamator*; but I am sure that if a poor Abolitionist were to be stoned in St. Louis for holding this preposterous notion, and the same rule were to be applied that our Savior used in the case referred to, there are at least some amongst us who could not cast a pebble at the sinner's head.

What shall I, what can I, say of the 4th resolution? It was adopted, in a large assemblage of my fellow-citizens, with but a few dissenting voices. Many of our most respectable citizens voted for it—Presbyterians, Methodists, Baptists, Episcopalians, Roman Catholics; those who believe the Bible is the Word of God and those who do not, all united in voting for the resolution that the Bible sanctions slavery as it now exists in the United States. If the sentiment had been that the Bible sanctions the continuance of the system until proper measures can be taken to remove it, I too could adopt it.

If I have taken my neighbor's property and spent it, and afterwards repent of my sin, and wish to restore what I had unjustly taken, but have not the means, the Bible no longer holds me as a thief, but *sanctions* my withholding the money from my neighbor, until I can, by use of the best means of my power, obtain it and restore it. And although, meanwhile, my neighbor in consequence of my original crime may be deprived of his rights, and his family made to suffer all the evils of poverty and shame, the Bible would still enjoin it upon him to let me alone, nay, to forgive me, and even to be content in the abject condition to which I had reduced him. Even so the Bible now says to our slaves, as it said in the days of the Apostles, "Servants, (or slaves) obey in all things your masters according to the flesh; not with eye-service, as men-pleasers; but in singleness of heart, fearing God." But then it also adds "Masters, give unto your servants that which is just and equal." What is meant by "just and equal" we may learn from the Savior himself—"All things whatsoever ye would that men should do to you, do ye even so to them: for this is the LAW of the prophets." Thus far the Bible. And it will be seen, that in no case does it sanction, but that rather absolutely forbids, all insurrectionary, all seditious, all rebellious acts on the part of the slaves. But be it remembered, that, with equal decision and authority, it says to the master, "Undo the heavy burden, and let the oppressed go FREE." If either disobey these injunctions, then it bids us leave the whole matter with that GOD who declares, "Vengeance is mine, I will repay, saith the Lord."

But I am not at liberty so to understand the resolution. From the preamble, and from conversation with several who voted for it, I am compelled to understand the meeting as voting that the Bible—the blessed Savior, and his holy Apostles—sanctions the *principle* of slavery—the system itself, as such, as it now exists amongst us. Fellow citizens! I mean not to be disrespectful to you, but I declare before you all, I have not words to express my utter abhorrence of such a sentiment. My soul detests it, my heart sickens over it; my judgment, my understanding, my conscience, reject it with loathing and horror. What is the system of slavery "as it now exists in the United States?" It is a system of buying and selling immortal beings for the sake of gain; a system which forbids to man and woman the rights of husband and wife, sanctioning the dissolution of this tie at the mere caprice of another; a system which tolerates the existence of a class of men whose professed business it is to go about from house to house, tearing husband and wife, parent and child asunder, chaining their victims together, and then driving them with a whip, like so many mules, to a distant market, there to be disposed of to the highest bidder. And then the nameless pollutions, the unspeakable abominations that attend this unfortunate class in their cabins.—But I spare the details. And this is the system sanctioned by the Prince of Mercy and Love, by the God of Holiness and Purity! Oh God!—In the language of one of the Patriarchs to whom the meeting in their resolution refer, I say, "O my soul, come not thou into their secret, unto their assembly mine honor be not thou united!"

The fifth resolution appoints a Committee of Vigilance consisting of seven for each ward, twenty for the suburbs and seven for each township in the county—in all EIGHTY THREE persons—whose duty it shall be to report to the Mayor or the other civil authorities, all persons *suspected* of preaching abolition doctrines, &c., and should the civil authorities fail to deal with them, *on suspicion*, why then the Committee are to call a meeting of the citizens and execute their decrees—in other words, to *lynch* the suspected persons.

Fellow citizens; where are we, and in what age of the world do we live? Is this the land of Freedom or Despotism? Is it the ninth or nineteenth century? Have the principles of the *Lettres de Cachet*, driven from Europe, crossed the Atlantic and taken up their abode in Missouri? Lewis the XIV sent men to the Bastile on suspicion; we, more humane, do but whip them to death, or nearly so. But these things cannot last long. A few may be made the innocent victims of lawless violence, yet be assured there is a moral sense in the Christendom of the nineteenth century, that will not long endure such odious transactions. A tremendous reaction will take place. And remember, I pray you, that as Phalaris was the first man roasted in the brazen bull he constructed for the tyrant of Sicily, so the inventor of the guillotine was by no means the last whose neck had practical experience of the keenness of its edge.

I turn, for a moment, to my fellow-Christians, of all Protestant denominations.

Respected and beloved fathers and brethren. As I address myself to you, my heart is full, well-nigh to bursting, and my eyes overflow.—It is indeed a time of trial and rebuke. The enemies of the cross are numerous and bold and malignant, in the extreme. From the situation in which the Providence of God has placed me, a large portion of their hatred, in this quarter, has concentrated itself on me.—You know that, now for nearly two years, a constant stream of calumnies and personal abuse of the most viperous kind, has been poured upon me, simply because I have been your organ through which—I refer now more especially to my Presbyterian brethren—you have declared your sentiments. You know, also, that I have never, in a single instance, replied to or otherwise noticed these attacks. And now not only is a fresh attack, of ten-fold virulence, made upon my character, but violence is threatened to my person. Think not that it is because I am an abolitionist that I am so persecuted. They who first started this report knew and still know better. In the progress of events slavery has doubtless contributed its share, though a very small one, to the bitterness of hatred with which the *Observer*, and I as connected with it, are regarded. But the true cause is the open and decided stand which the paper has taken against the encroachments of Popery. This is not only my own opinion, but that of others, and indeed of nearly or quite all with whom I have conversed on the subject, & among the rest, as I learn, of a French Catholic. And here I take leave to remark—what, indeed, I have, in substance, once before publicly stated—that in no portion of our citizens is there, deservedly, more confidence to be placed, than in those of French origin. As a class, they are eminently men of peace and order, respecting the laws themselves and desirous of seeing them respected by others. Whatever they may have thought or felt respecting the course which a sense of duty has impelled me to pursue, in speaking of the principles of that religion of which most of them are at least the nominal professors, I do not believe that any of them ever harbored the idea of opposing the *Observer* by other than moral weapons. So far from fearing personal violence from them, there is no portion of my fellow-citizens to whose keeping I would sooner commit my person or my life, were they in danger. And it has not been among the least painful incidents of my course, that in yielding to the imperative calls of duty, I had to run the risk of wounding the feelings of a class of citizens I so highly respected—or at the least of being misunderstood by them.

I repeat it, then, the real origin of the cry, "Down with the *Observer*," is to be looked for in its opposition to Popery. The fire that is now blazing and crackling through this city, was kindled on Popish altars, and has been assiduously blown up by Jesuit breath. And now, dear brethren, the question is, shall we flee before it, or stay and abide its fury, even though we perish in the flames? For one, I cannot hesitate. The path of duty lies plain before me, and I must walk therein, even tho' it lead to the whipping-post, the tar-barrel, or even the stake. I was bold and dauntless in the service of sin; it is not fitting that I should be less so in the service of my Redeemer. He sought me out when there was none to help; when I was fast sinking to eternal ruin, he raised me up and placed me on the Rock of Ages; and now shall I forsake him when he has so few friends and so many enemies, in St. Louis? I cannot, I dare not, and, His grace sustaining me, *I will not.*

Some of you I know are with me in feeling, in sympathy, and in prayer. And this knowledge is, indeed, a cordial to my heart. We have wept and prayed together in the midst of our present afflictions, and we have risen from our knees, refreshed and cheered by a sense of God's presence and his approving smile. And indeed, but for this,—but that I have felt the upholding hand of God supporting me, I had long since fallen. "I had fainted, unless I had believed to see the goodness of the Lord in the land of the living." And the heaviest blows have been those which I have received from the hands of some of my brethren. May the Lord forgive them, as freely and heartily as I do.

But, O my brethren, what shall I say to those of you who recorded your votes in favor of the resolution that the Bible sanctions slavery? It is not for me to reproach you; nor have I the least disposition to utter one unkind word. I only wish that I could make you sensible of the feelings I experienced when I first read that resolution as sanctioned by you. It did seem to me as though I could perceive a holy horror thrilling though all heaven, at such a perversion of the principles of the gospel of the Son of God. O my brethren, may I not entreat you to pray over this subject, to ask for the wisdom of heaven to lead you into the truth? Depend upon it, you are wrong, fearfully wrong. Not for all the diadems of all the stars of heaven, though each were a world like this, would I have such a vote, unrepented of, to answer for at the bar of God, my Judge.

O, were the Church united at such a crisis as this, what a triumph we might achieve! But it never can be united, until you come over to us. Did you ever hear of a Christian, once holding the contrary doctrine, giving it up for yours? Never, I venture to say it, unless at the same time he gave up his Christianity with it. But there are instances, daily, of conversions from your side to ours. Come over then, brethren—O, come over. Let us unitedly take our stand upon the principles of truth and RIGHTEOUSNESS. Standing by them we cannot be moved. Even the heathen could say of the just man, that he would remain undismayed tho' the heavens should fall around him. How much more, then, may it be said of the Christian? In the midst of every assault, when foes are gathered around him on every side, in the calm, yet exulting confidence of faith, he can look upward and exclaim—"The LORD is my light and my salvation; whom shall I fear? the LORD is the strength of my life; of whom shall I be afraid."

A few words more, and I have done.

Fellow-citizens of St. Louis; above you have my sentiments, fully and freely expressed, on the great subjects now agitating the public mind. Are they such as render me unworthy of that protection which regulated Society accords to the humblest of its members? Let me ask you, why is it that this storm of persecution is directed against me? What have I done? Have I libelled any man's person or character? No. Have I been found in gambling-houses, billiard rooms or tippling shops? Never. Have I ever disturbed the peace and quiet of your city by midnight revellings, or riots in the streets? It is not pretended. Have I ever, by word or deed, directly or indirectly, attempted or designed to incite your slaves to insubordination? God forbid. I would as soon be guilty of arson and murder. And here you must permit me to say that the conduct of those who so fiercely accuse me here, strongly reminds me of the scene which took place between Ahab and the prophet Elijah. You remember that in a time of great drouth, which Elijah had predicted, and which God sent upon the land for the wickedness of Ahab and Israel, when Ahab met Elijah, he said to him, in great wrath, "Art though he that troubleth Israel?" But the prophet boldly, and in conscious innocence, replied, "I have not troubled Israel, but thou and thy father's house" &c. Elijah did not bring the drouth and the famine upon Israel, he simply announced what God had determined to do in punishment of their sins. The drouth would have come, though there had been no prophet to announce it. Yet so far as he had any personal agency in the matter, he may well be supposed to have been actuated by kind motives towards Ahab and his countrymen, inasmuch as by forewarning them of the evil, he gave them an opportunity to prepare for it at least, if not to avert it by a speedy repentance.

Even so, my fellow-citizens, is it unreasonable and unjust to charge upon those who, applying to the case the maxims of the Bible, of experience, and history, foresee and foretell to you the evil effects of the continuance of slavery, the crime of having introduced those very consequences. And here let me say, that in my opinion the proceedings of the late meetings in this city, and the agitation consequent upon them, have done more to disquiet and render uneasy and restless and discontented, the minds of the slaves, than all that the *Observer* could or would have said in an hundred years.

I again, therefore, ask you what I have done, that I am to be made an object of popular vengeance? From the time that I published the account of the consecration of the Cathedral, threats have been constantly coming to my ears that I was to be mobbed, and my office torn down. Is it to be borne, that a citizen in the peaceable exercise of those rights secured to him solemnly by charter, is thus to be hunted down and proscribed? If in any thing I have offended against the laws of my country, or its constitution, I stand ready to answer. If I have not, then I call upon those laws and that constitution and those who revere them to protect me.

I *do*, therefore, as an American citizen, and Christian patriot, and in the name of Liberty, and Law, and RELIGION, solemnly PROTEST against all these attempts, howsoever or by whomsoever made, to frown down the liberty of the press and forbid the free expression of opinion. Under a deep sense of my obligations to my country, the church, and my God, I declare it to be my fixed purpose to submit to no such dictation. *And I am prepared to abide the consequences.* I have appealed to the constitution and laws of my country; if they fail to protect me I APPEAL TO GOD, and with Him I cheerfully rest my cause.

Fellow citizens; they told me that if I returned to the city, from my late absence, you would surely lay violent hands upon me, and many of my friends besought me not to come. I disregarded their advice, because I plainly saw, or thought I saw, that the LORD would have me come. And up to this moment that conviction of duty has continued to strengthen, until now I have not a shadow of doubt that I did right. I have appeared openly amongst you, in your streets and market places, and now I openly and publicly throw myself into your hands.—I can die at my post, but I cannot desert it.

I have one request to make, and but one. The original proprietors of the *Observer*, have, as you know, disclaimed all responsibility in its publication. So far as depends upon them, nothing would appear in the paper on the subject of slavery. I am sure, therefore, that you will see the propriety of refraining from any act which would inflict injury upon them, either in person or property. I alone am answerable and responsible for all that appears in the paper, except when absent from the city. A part of the office also belongs to the young men who print the paper: and they are in no way responsible for the matter appearing in its columns. For the sake of both these parties I do, therefore, earnestly entreat you that, whatever may be done to me, the property of the office may be left undisturbed. If the popular vengeance needs a victim, I offer myself a willing sacrifice. To any assault that may be made upon me, I declare it my purpose to make no resistance. There is, I confess, one string tugging at my heart, that sometimes wakes it to mortal agony. And yet I cannot, dare not, yield to its influence. For my Master has said, "if any man come to me, and hate not his father, and mother, and WIFE, and children, and brethren, and sisters, yes, and his own life also, he cannot be my disciple."

Humbly entreating all whom I have injured, whether intentionally or otherwise, to forgive me; in charity with all men; freely forgiving my enemies, even those who thirst for my blood, and with the blest assurance, that in life or death nothing can separate me from my Redeemer, I subscribe myself,

Your fellow citizen,

ELIJAH P. LOVEJOY

Alton Observer, Alton, Il.,
5 November 1835, Vol. II, no. 51, p. 2

[1835]

7545 B. *to* **BRETHREN. 4 July. Cattskill [sic].** A Methodist minister describes a method used to stop smoking and chewing tobacco. 3 September 1835. p.1, c2.

7546 T. *to* **SIR. n.d. n.p.** Regrets the amount of gambling observed aboard the boat on which he is travelling; urges respectable men to express their disgust with this practice. 3 September 1835. p.2, c1.

7547 n.n. *to* **THE** *ST. LOUIS OBSERVER.* **[extract] 4 August 1835. Courtland, Al.** Reports unusually good prospects for a large cotton crop; describes its effect on religion in Courtland. 3 September 1835. p.2, c1.

7548 n.n. *to* **MR. OVERTON. n.d. Miami University.** A student of the ministry requests repayment with interest on the sum owed his uncle, Mr. Overton's master, as part of the price of his freedom. 3 September 1835. p.2, c2.

7549 REV. PHINEAS COOKE *to* **n.n. nd. Lebanon, N.H.** Describes a revival in Lebanon; observes that most converts are of pious families. 3 September 1835. p.2, c2.

7550 Z. J. *to* **n.n. [from the** *Morning Star***] n.d. n.p.** A minister reports good health resulting from one year as a non-smoker. 3 September 1835. p.2, c3.

7551 n.n. *to* **n.n. [extract] n.d. London.** A Frenchman conveys his disapproval of "fancy fairs" held to raise money for charities; observes that women act flirtatiously to attract strange men to their booths. 3 September 1835. p.2, c3.

7552 n.n. *to* **SIR. [from the** *Missouri Intelligencer***] 26 August. Fayette.** Gives an eye-witness account of the shooting of General Owen by Joseph Davis; sympathizes with Davis. 3 September 1835. p.2, c3.

7553 LORD NELSON *to* **MURRAY. [from the** *London Atheneum***] n.d. n.p.** "If it is midnight, I shall not go to dinner till you come." 3 September 1835. p.2, c3.

7554 n.n. *to* **n.n. [continued from unspecified date] n.d. Rome** Attempts to demonstrate similarities between practices of current Roman Catholicism and Roman paganism. 3 September 1835. p.4, c1.

7555 A MISSISSIPPI COTTON PLANTER *to* **THE EDITOR. [from the** *Cumberland Presbyterian***] n.d. n.p.** Encloses prose by a slaveholder and asks, like the slaveholder, why it is so difficult to revive religion among his slaves. 10 September 1835. p.1, c3.

7556 n.n. *to* **n.n. [extract from the** *Christian Advocate and Journal***] 5 July. Royalton, Vt.** Presents details of a large meeting chaired by Rev. Mr. Burchard in Royalton; feels encouraged by the proceedings and the number of people attending. 10 September 1835. p.1, c4.

7557 REV. A. SABIN *to* **n.n. [extract from the** *Vermont Telegraph* **via the** *New York Evangelist***] n.d. n.p.** Describes a revival in Barnston, Lower Canada, at which the Rev. Abial Moulton delivered a sermon; discusses his lectures in that region, and a Freewill Baptist meeting in East Hatley. 10 September 1835. p.1, c5.

7558 n.n. *to* **n.n. [from the** *Charleston Courier***] n.d. Tyger Bayou, Madison County, Ms.** Details violence in neighboring counties, especially in the towns of Livingston and Madison, resulting from the widespread suspicion of conspiracy to urge Negroes to revolt. 10 September 1835. p.3, c1.

7559 n.n. *to* **n.n. [extract from the** *Philadelphia Evening Star* **via the** *St. Louis Herald***]** **n.d. n.p.** A visitor to Missouri describes unfavorable agricultural and economic conditions near St. Louis; lists representative figures and prices. 10 September 1835. p.3, c3.

7560 n.n. *to* **n.n. [extract from the** *Baltimore American***]** **16 August. Charlestown, Md.** Reports that a stranger from New Orleans was jailed for conversing with Negroes in Charlestown, and that the entire town is in an uproar. 10 September 1835. p.3, c4.

7561 n.n. *to* **n.n. [continued from 3 September 1835] n.d. Rome.** Attempts to demonstrate essential similarity between present-day Roman Catholicism and ancient Roman paganism. 10 September 1835. p.4, c1.

7562 MR. HOTCHKISS *to* **n.n. [extract from the** *Missionary Herald***]** **5 April 1835. Clear Creek.** A missionary among the Choctaw Indians relates difficulties of the past winter; describes the death of a particularly religious and faithful young Indian; expresses hope for the future. 17 September 1835. p.1, c1.

7563 MR. WOOD *to* **n.n. [extract from the** *Missionary Herald***]** **26 February 1835. n.p.** Discusses plans for missionary work among the Choctaw Indians; reports that enthusiasm among Indians is so great that he expects to preach no more than once monthly in any one place. 17 September 1835. p.1, c1.

7564 REV. A. K. BUELL *to* **n.n. [extract from the** *Home Missionary***] n.d. St. Catharines, Upper Canada.** A missionary, presumably among the Choctaws, is pleased with the results of a recent meeting and expects at least twenty converts; describes destruction by lightning of a recently built meeting house. 17 September 1835. p.1, c2.

7565 REV. O. MINER *to* **n.n. [extract from the** *Home Missionary***] n.d. Peru, N. Y.** Expresses gratitude for money to build a stone meetinghouse which was dedicated 18 June; reports many conversions and success with the temperance cause. 17 September 1835. p.1, c2.

7566 ASA A. STONE *to* **BROTHER LEAVITT [THE EDITOR OF THE** *NEW YORK EVANGELIST***]. 1 June 1835. Natchez.** Reports that it is very common for slaves to be poorly dressed or even naked in Louisiana; observes that the occurrence of nudity among adults and children, as well as labor on the Sabbath, increases as one moves further South. 17 September 1835. p.2, c1.

7567 L. CLARK *to* **n.n. [extract from the** *New York Evangelist***] n.d. Dryden, Tompkins County, N. Y.** A pastor joyously reports the conversion of fifty to seventy people since last January. 17 September 1835. p.2, c2.

7568 D. N. MERRITT *to* **BROTHER LEAVITT. 7 August 1835. Marion, Wayne County, N. Y.** Reports ten to fifteen conversions during a period of two to three weeks. 17 September 1835. p.2, c2.

7569 REV. P. CHASE *to* **MR. EDITOR. [extract from the** *Vermont Telegraph***] 27 July 1835. Franklin.** Rejoices in the successful conversion of about seventy people during a seventeen-day meeting in Enosburgh, Vermont; attributes success to "an unusual spirit of *laboring prayer*." 17 September 1835. p.2, c3.

7570 S. KELLOGG *to* **n.n. [from the** *Vermont State Journal***] 8 August 1835. n.p.** Reports on protracted meetings in Berlin, Worchester, and Barre; predicts special efforts to win converts in the region. 17 September 1835. p.2, c3.

7571 A FRIEND OF LIBERTY *to* **BROTHER LOVEJOY. n.d. n.p.** Criticizes those who consider the man who donated money to the Bible Society a fool. 17 September 1835. p.2, c3.

7572 J. B. BOOTH *to* **THE MANAGER OF THE N. ORLEANS THEATRE. 27 July 1835. Baltimore, Md.** States his intention to break his acting engagement at the New Orleans Theatre because of a municipal law which undermines the interests of gamblers, whom the writer regards as his patrons. 17 September 1835. p.2, c4.

7573 n.n. *to* **n.n. [extract from the** *Commercial Advertiser***] n.d. Vicksburgh.** Describes an armed battle between Mr. Sharkey, cousin of the state chief justice, and several men of Madison County who were angry over a decision Sharkey had made as magistrate. 17 September 1835. p.3, c2.

7574 n.n. *to* **n.n. [continued from 10 September 1835] n.d. Rome** Attempts to demonstrate the essential similarity between present-day Roman Catholicism and ancient Roman paganism. 17 September 1835. p.4, c1.

7575 CHARLES GUTZLAFF *to* **REV. DR. REED. 20 January 1835. Macao.** A missionary to China reports on his present labors and his hopes for the future. 24 September 1835. p.1, c3.

7576 n.n. *to* **n.n. [continued from 17 September 1835] n.d. Rome.** Attempts to demonstrate the essential similarity between present-day Roman Catholicism and ancient Roman paganism. 24 September 1835. p.1, c5.

7577 THE REV. MR. SCHAUFFLER *to* **THE AMERICAN TRACT SOCIETY. [from the** *New York Observer***] n.d. n.p.** A missionary to the Jews in Turkey declares his faith in God and his confidence in the eventual success of his missionary venture. 24 September 1835. p.2, c2.

7578 A CITIZEN OF DUBUQUE, M. T. *to* **THE EDITOR OF THE** *N. W. GAZETTE***. [from the** *Galena Advertiser***] 7 September 1835. Dubuque.** Reports the murder of Woodbury Massey, an esteemed citizen, by two ruffians now in custody. 24 September 1835. p.3, c4.

7579 n.n. *to* **THE EDITOR [ELIJAH P. LOVEJOY]. n.d. n.p.** A minister forwards a journal of his trip from St. Louis to a camp meeting in Belview, Washington County. 1 October 1835. p.2, c5.

7580 EDWIN F. HATFIELD. *to* **MESSRS. EDITORS. [from the** *New York Observer***] 8 September 1835. n.p.** Refutes remarks by the Roman Catholic bishop of St. Louis that Protestant ministers fled the area during a recent epidemic, and that many converts were gained in the Catholic church. 8 October 1835. p.1, c2.

7581 n.n. *to* **THE EDITOR [ELIJAH P. LOVEJOY]. 23 September 1835. n.p.** Discusses the numbers who have professed faith in Jesus Christ at six successive camp meetings. 8 October 1835. p.2, c4.

7582 n.n. *to* **n.n. [extract] 17 August 1835. Guyama, Porto Rico.** Reports the devastating effects of a recent hurricane. 8 October 1835. p.3, c4.

7583 HIERONYMUS *to* **MR. EDITOR. [from the** *Journal of Commerce***] n.d. n.p.** A Southern slaveholder appeals to Americans to do all that they honestly can for the preservation of the Union; denounces deceptions propagated by extremist factions on both sides of the slavery issue. 8 October 1835. p.4, c1.

7584 D. *to* **MR. EDITOR [ELIJAH P. LOVEJOY]. n.d. Jacksonville, Il.** Discusses the importance of a classical education. 15 October 1835. p.1, c1.

7585 MISSISSIPPI *to* **MR. LOVEJOY. September. Dubuque.** Asserts the duty of Christian Americans to counteract Roman Catholicism by building Protestant churches and schools. 15 October 1835. p.1, c1.

7586 THE PROPRIETORS OF THE *ST. LOUIS OBSERVER to* **THE PUBLIC. 21 October 1835. n.p.** Determine that nothing should appear in the paper to fuel excitement over the issue of slavery; oppose the "mad schemes" of the abolitionists and regret the threats of violence to the *Observer* office. 22 October 1835. p.3, c1.

7587 n.n. *to* **SIR. 12 June 1835. Leeds.** Quotes an extract of a speech delivered before the House of Commons, declaring that moderation is not always a virtue, particularly regarding alcoholic drink. 22 October 1835. p.4, c2.

7588 n.n. *to* **n.n. n.d. St. Petersburgh.** Discusses the sale of tracts on temperance, profanity, and the Sabbath in Russia, Estonia, Livonia, Sweden, and Finland. 22 October 1835. p.4, c2.

7589 H. G. O. DWIGHT *to* **MR. W. J. B. [from the** *New York Observer***] 5 April 1835. Constantinople.** Comments on the duties of the wives of foreign missionaries, who commonly have too many demands made upon them. 29 October 1835. p.1, c1.

7590 DANIEL TEMPLE *to* **SIR [from the** *New York Observer***] 22 April 1835. Smyrna.** Concurs with H. G. O. Dwight's letter concerning the duties of the wives of foreign missionaries. 29 October 1835. p.1, c3.

7591 n.n. *to* **MR. AND MRS. HUTCHINGS. n.d. Oodooville, Jaffna.** A girl at the boarding school at Oodooville tells of her committment to Christ. 29 October 1835. p.2, c2.

7592 ELIZABETH McFARLANE *to* **THE REV. SAMUEL HUTCHINGS. n.d. Oodooville, Jaffna.** A young woman in the boarding school at Oodooville tells of her resolve to "live in the Lord all my life." 29 October 1835. p.2, c2.

7593 SILENCE HAYWOOD *to* **MR. AND MRS. HUTCHINGS. n.d. Oodooville, Jaffna.** A student at the girl's boarding school at Oodooville tells of her conversion to Christ, and her resolve to continue in this way. 29 October 1835. p.2, c2.

7594 n.n. *to* **THE REV. S. HUTCHINGS. n.d. Oodooville, Jaffna.** A school girl at Oodooville writes of her religious experience following Hutchings' visit to the school. 29 October 1835. p.2, c2.

7595 E. CARPENTER *to* **SIR [THE REV. S. HUTCHINGS]. n.d. Oodooville, Jaffna.** Expresses joy in her new knowledge of Jesus Christ. 29 October 1835. p.2, c2.

7596 LOUISA PAYSON *to* **THE REV. S. HUTCHINGS. n.d. Oodooville, Jaffna.** A student at the boarding school at Oodooville expresses love for God and thanks to Hutchings. 29 October 1835. p.2, c2.

7597 CAROLINE H. MURFREES *to* **MR. AND MR. HUTCHINGS. n.d. Oodooville, Jaffna.** A student at the boarding school at Oodooville requests prayers in her behalf in order that she might be faithful to Christ to the end. 29 October 1835. p.2, c2.

7598 n.n. *to* **SISTER. n.d. Oodooville, Jaffna.** A student at Oodooville tells of her experience of grace. 29 October 1835. p.2, c3.

7599 n.n. *to* **SIR [S. HUTCHINGS]. n.d. Oodooville, Jaffna.** A student of the girl's school at Oodooville speaks of her happiness in finding Christ. 29 October 1835. p.2, c3.

7600 n.n. *to* **SIR [S. HUTCHINGS]. n.d. Oodooville, Jaffna.** A student at the Oodooville school affirms her faith in God and is therefore unafraid to die. 29 October 1835. p.2, c3.

7601 ELIJAH P. LOVEJOY *to* **FELLOW CITIZENS. n.d. n.p.** Declares that he is not an abolitionist in the sense in which the term is commonly understood, for he does not advocate immediate emancipation; declares that he will not desert his post as editor despite injuries inflicted upon him, and that he alone should be held responsible for the material appearing in the *Observer.* 5 November 1835. p.2, c3.

7602 T. *to* **THE EDITOR OF THE** *ST. LOUIS OBSERVER* **[ELIJAH P. LOVEJOY]. 4 November 1835. Cincinnati.** Relates the particulars of recent meetings of the Young Men's City Temperance Society and the Young Men's Bible Society. 26 November 1835. p.1, c1.

7603 HENRY KROH *to* **BROTHER. [from the** *Chambersburg* **(Pa.)** *Messenger***] September 1835. n.p.** Forwards extracts from a journal kept on a recent journey westward through Pennsylvania, Illinois, and Missouri. 26 November 1835. p.1, c3.

7604 n.n. *to* **MR. EDITOR. [from the** *London Christian Observer***] n.d. n.p.** Encloses and criticizes a portion of a decree of Pope Gregory VII regarding the extent of papal authority. 26 November 1835. p.1, c4.

7605 C. *to* **THE EDITOR OF THE** *OBSERVER* **[ELIJAH P. LOVEJOY]. n.d. n.p.** Encloses a copy of a poem written by Mrs. Sigourney upon viewing an American copy of a painting by Leonardo Da Vinci. 26 November 1835. p.4, c1.

[1835]

7606 T. *to* **REV. MR. LOVEJOY. 7 November 1835. Cincinnati.** Relates particulars of the anniversary meeting of the western branch of the American Home Missionary Society. 3 December 1835. p.1, c2.

7607 A FRIEND TO MORALITY *to* **BROTHER LOVEJOY. 13 August 1835. Cane Hill, Washington County.** Opposes theatrical exhibitions, which "tend to dissipate the mind, and to render it indisposed for all sober, useful, or spiritual employment"; quotes from Plato, Aristotle and Tillotson. 3 December 1835. p.1, c4.

7608 THE REV. M. HOBART SEYMOUR *to* **THE BISHOP OF LONDON. [extract from the** *London Record***] n.d. Ballinrobe, County Mayo, Ireland.** Reports three instances of persecution of Protestants in Ireland. 3 December 1835. p.2, c1.

7609 A. E. GRIMKE *to* **n.n. [extract] n.d. n.p.** Exhorts Christians to be prepared to endure persecution for the cause of emancipation. 3 December 1835. p.2, c3.

7610 T. L. *to* **REV. E. P. LOVEJOY. 23 November 1835. Alton, Il.** Forwards resolutions of a 15 October meeting of the Synod of Illinois; comments upon two of the resolutions. 3 December 1835. p.3, c1.

7611 S. Z. H. *to* **FRIENDS. 24 July 1835. Laprarie.** Declares his conversion to faith in Jesus Christ. 10 December 1835. p.1, c2.

7612 NO HYPOCRITE *to* **MR. EDITOR [ELIJAH P. LOVEJOY]. n.d. Dubuque.** Comments upon an enclosed report of the founding of a Roman Catholic church in Galena; criticizes Catholics for breaking the Sabbath by selling and drinking "dram." 10 December 1835. p.1, c3.

7613 THE RT. REV. DANIEL WILSON *to* **THE REV. DR. MILNOR. 15 April 1835. Calcutta.** The Anglican bishop of Calcutta reports on the mission situation in India, and appeals for Episcopal missionaries from the United States. 10 December 1835. p.1, c5.

7614 S. L. *to* **MR. EDITOR. [from the** *Boston Recorder***]** **n.d. n.p.** Discusses atonement and God's law. 10 December 1835. p.2, c1.

7615 JOHN RANDOLPH *to* **THE REV. JOHN H. RICE. 8 September 1835. Roanoke.** Expresses gratitude for reading materials; affirms his faith in another and better world. 10 December 1835. p.4, c3.

7616 A NATIVE AMERICAN *to* **FELLOW CITIZENS. n.d. n.p.** Discusses the potentially fatal mistake of considering Roman Catholicism a religious and not a political organization. 17 December 1835. p.1, c3.

7617 n.n. *to* **BROTHER [ELIJAH P. LOVEJOY]. [extract] 16 November 1835. n.p.** Expresses sympathy for Lovejoy's views. 17 December 1835. p.2, c3.

7618 n.n. *to* **ELIJAH P. LOVEJOY. [extract] 21 November 1835. n.p.** States his support for Lovejoy's sentiments. 17 December 1835. p.2, c3.

7619 n.n. *to* **BROTHER LOVEJOY. [extract] 20 November 1835. n.p.** Sympathizes with Lovejoy in his trials regarding unpopular opinions; prays that God may help him to endure. 17 December 1835. p.2, c3.

7620 n.n. *to* **ELIJAH P. LOVEJOY. [extract] 20 November 1835. n.p.** Declares her enthusiastic support for Lovejoy. 17 December 1835. p.2, c3.

7621 n.n. *to* **ELIJAH P. LOVEJOY. [extract] n.d. n.p.** Concurs with the editorial opinions of Lovejoy's *Observer*. 17 December 1835. p.2, c3.

7622 n.n. *to* **BROTHER LOVEJOY. [extract] 30 November 1835. n.p.** Admires Lovejoy's stand regarding emancipation. 17 December 1835. p.2, c3.

7623 n.n. *to* **ELIJAH P. LOVEJOY. [extract] 7 December 1835. n.p.** Reports widespread support for Lovejoy's position regarding emancipation. 17 December 1835. p.2, c4.

7624 n.n. *to* **ELIJAH P. LOVEJOY. [extract] n.d. n.p.** Sends the names of new subscribers to the *Observer*, persuaded by Lovejoy's stand for emancipation. 17 December 1835. p.2, c4.

7625 THERON BALDWIN *to* **BRO. LOVEJOY. 11 December 1835. Jacksonville.** Clarifies his speech before the Home Missionary Society, reported in the 3 December issue of the *Observer*. 17 December 1835. p.3, c3.

7626 TRAVELER *to* **BRO. LOVEJOY. n.d. n.p.** Encloses an extract from his journal concerning a trip to Kentucky, emphasizing the poor religious instruction of slaves. 24 December 1835. p.1, c1.

7627 A NATIVE AMERICAN *to* **FELLOW CITIZENS. [continued from 17 December 1835] n.d. n.p.** Discusses the potentially fatal mistake of considering Roman Catholicism a religious and not a political organization. 24 December 1835. p.1, c3.

7628 W. H. THOMAS *to* **THE EDITOR. [from the** *Register and Library of Medical and Chirurgical Science***]** **16 September 1835. Bristol.** Cites the apparent suicide of a captive adder as evidence of the "existence of intellect, unquestionably bestowed in various modifications on the lower animals of the creation." 24 December 1835. p.1, c5.

7629 G. B. DAVIS *to* **BROTHER LOVEJOY. 15 December 1835. Alton.** Reports on resolutions passed at the annual meeting of the Illinois Bible Society. 24 December 1835. p.2, c1.

7630 T. L. *to* **BROTHER [ELIJAH P. LOVEJOY]. December 1835. Alton.** Reports on various meetings at the annual gathering of the Illinois Bible Society. 24 December 1835. p.2, c1.

7631 BARON STOW *to* **REV. W. A. HALLOCK. 6 November 1835. Boston.** Praises the *Memoir of Harlan Page*, and states that he has put several copies in circulation. 24 December 1835. p.2, c2.

7632 ENOCH POND *to* **BRO. CUMMINGS. [extract] 21 November 1835. Bangor, Me.** Reports on contributions received for the Bangor Theological Seminary. 24 December 1835. p.2, c5.

7633 A. *to* **REV. MR. CUMMINGS. 23 November 1835. Hallowell.** Discusses baptism, his attendance at a ceremony in Old South Church, and Doddridge's exposition of I Corinthians 15:29. 24 December 1835. p.3, c1.

7634 ROBERT N. ANDERSON *to* **JOSHUA LEAVITT. [from the** *New York Evangelist***] November 1835. Cumberland, Va.** Denounces abolitionist theology and urges that no further copies of the *Evangelist* be sent to him. 24 December 1835. p.4, c3.

7635 A NATIVE AMERICAN *to* **FELLOW CITIZENS. [continued from 24 December 1835] n.d. n.p.** Discusses the potentially fatal mistake of considering Roman Catholicism a religious and not a political organization. 31 December 1835. p.1, c2.

7636 n.n. *to* **ELIJAH P. LOVEJOY. [extract] 3 December 1835. Missouri.** Praises Lovejoy's editorial stand and expresses the sentiment that every true-hearted Presbyterian is behind Lovejoy. 31 December 1835. p.2, c2.

7637 n.n. *to* **ELIJAH P. LOVEJOY. [extract] 3 December 1835. Missouri.** Commends Lovejoy's published positions and assures him of widespread support. 31 December 1835. p.2, c2.

7638 n.n. *to* **ELIJAH P. LOVEJOY. [extract] 10 December 1835. Missouri.** Expresses satisfaction with Lovejoy's published self-defense. 31 December 1835. p.2, c2.

7639 n.n. *to* **BROTHER LOVEJOY. [extract] 16 December 1835. Missouri.** Assures Lovejoy of his support. 31 December 1835. p.2, c2.

7640 n.n. *to* **BROTHER LOVEJOY. [extract] 24 December 1835. Missouri.** Expresses support for Lovejoy and the *Observer*. 31 December 1835. p.2, c2.

7641 n.n. *to* **ELIJAH P. LOVEJOY. [extract] 10 December 1835. Illinois.** Assures Lovejoy of the sympathies and prayers of many Christian friends as he faces the trials brought about by unpopular editorializing. 31 December 1835. p.2, c2.

7642 n.n. *to* **ELIJAH P. LOVEJOY. [extract] 14 December 1835. Illinois.** Pledges moral and financial support for Lovejoy. 31 December 1835. p.2, c3.

7643 n.n. *to* **ELIJAH P. LOVEJOY. [extract] 20 December 1835. Illinois.** Voices approval of the principles set forth in the *Observer*. 31 December 1835. p.2, c3.

7644 n.n. *to* **ELIJAH P. LOVEJOY. [extract] 2 December 1835. Cincinnati, Oh.** Supports Lovejoy's stand against slavery. 31 December 1835. p.2, c3.

7645 WM. WRIGHT AND MR. BLAKLEY *to* **JNO. M'KEE. 7 December 1835. Palmyra, Mo.** Discusses the real estate ventures of the Rev. E. S. Ely, whose transactions have been beyond reproach. 31 December 1835. p.3, c2.

[1836]

7646 A NATIVE AMERICAN *to* **FELLOW CITIZENS. [continued from 31 December 1835] n.d. n.p.** Discusses the potentially fatal mistake of considering Roman Catholicism a religious and not a political organization. 7 January 1836. p.1, c2.

7647 JOSIAH F. GOODHUE *to* **MESSRS. RICHARDS AND TRACY. [from the** *Vermont Chronicle*] **7 November 1835. Shoreham.** Gives notice of a protracted revival meeting in progress at Shoreham, where the Rev. J. Burchard is preaching. 7 January 1836. p.1, c3.

7648 J. JEWETT *to* *ZION'S ADVOCATE.* **[extract] 5 November 1835. Knox, Me.** Reports that the local Baptist church has doubled its membership within the past several months. 7 January 1836. p.1, c3.

7649 REV. WILLIAM DAY *to* *ZION'S ADVOCATE.* **[extract] 26 October 1835. Belfast, Me.** Relates the circumstances surrounding a protracted revival meeting in the local Baptist church. 7 January 1836. p.1, c3.

7650 n.n. *to* **n.n. [from the** *National Intelligencer*] **28 November 1835. Florida.** Gives an account of a duel between Captain Everett White and Col. A. Bellamy, which proved fatal to both parties. 7 January 1836. p.2, c2.

7651 ROBERT OLDHAM *to* **BRO. SMITH. [from the** *Cumberland Presbyterian*] **15 November 1835. Tuscaloosa, Al.** Describes an interdenominational communion service which moved the writer greatly. 7 January 1836. p.3, c2.

7652 GERRIT SMITH *to* **DR. COX. [extract] n.d. n.p.** States that the immediate emancipation of slaves, which he advocates, does not entail immediate elevation of slaves to "our level of social and political rights." 7 January 1836. p.3, c2.

7653 n.n. *to* **BROTHER [ELIJAH P. LOVEJOY]. 19 December 1835. Upper Alton.** Encourages Lovejoy to stand fast in the face of public opposition to his views on emancipation; urges Lovejoy to take consolation in the support and prayers of many who are sympathetic to the same cause. 14 January 1836. p.2, c4.

7654 A FRIEND *to* **MR. LOVEJOY. n.d. n.p.** Encloses a ten-dollar contribution to the *Observer*; exalts the principle of free speech. 14 January 1836. p.2, c4.

7655 CHARLES GUTZLAFT *to* **THE SECRETARY OF THE AMERICAN TRACT SOCIETY. 20 December 1835. Macao.** States that in the past year some ten thousand tracts have been circulated in China; expresses hope that the annual number will reach one million. 14 January 1836. p.3, c1.

7656 REV. IRA TRACY *to* **n.n. [extract] 26 April 1835. Singapore.** Comments on the distribution of tracts in a Chinese hospital; notes that tracts are printed at the rate of 3,000 pages a day. 14 January 1836. p.3, c1.

7657 THOMAS WALLACE *to* **BRETHREN. [from the** *Western Christian Advocate*] **21** December 1835. Fayette, Mo. Announces that he has obtained fifteen new subscribers for the *Western Christian Advocate*. **14 January 1836. p.3, c2.**

7658 J. B. FINLEY AND R. O. SPENCER *to* **BRETHREN. [from the** *Western Christian Advocate*] **n.d. n.p.** Enclose the names of thirty-five new subscribers to the *Western Christian Advocate*. 14 January 1836. p.3, c2.

7659 n.n. *to* **MR. EDITOR. [from the** *Philadelphian*] **n.d. n.p.** Quotes from Cecil's *Remains* on the subject of justification by the imputed righteousness of Christ. 14 January 1836. p.3, c2.

7660 n.n. *to* **n.n. [extract] 7 November 1835. Saline County, Ms.** Quotes the local prices of mules, cattle, Negro men, and pork. 21 January 1836. p.3, c4.

7661 n.n. *to* **n.n. [extract] 26 November 1835. Monticello, Al.** Laments the death of Capt. Edward White, which resulted from a duel with Col A. Bellamy. 21 January 1836. p.3, c5.

7662 A CORRESPONDENT *to* **THE** *NEW YORK OBSERVER*. **October 1835. England.** Discusses political affairs in England: the results of voter registration; prospects for reform in the House of Lords; support for O'Connell, the Irish agitator; the moral poverty of the *London Times*; the trial of Dr. Beecher. 28 January 1836. p.2, c1.

7663 DR. JOHN GODFREY BUTTNER *to* **THE EVANGELICAL PROTESTANT CHURCHES. January 1836. St. Louis.** Requests aid for the construction of a German Protestant church. 28 January 1836. p.2, c4.

7664 THERON BALDWIN *to* **BRO. LOVEJOY. 15 January 1836. Jacksonville.** Discusses his efforts on behalf of the cause of home missions, stressing the importance of maintaining ministers in America's young communities. 28 January 1836. p.3, c2.

7665 WM. KIRBY *to* **BROTHER LOVEJOY. 9 January 1836. Fairfield, Adams County.** Announces the formation of a new Congregational church in Round Prairie. 28 January 1836. p.3, c3.

7666 MR. MONOD *to* **n.n. n.d. n.p.** A French evangelical pastor contends "that the Bible alone, without other means, is sometimes blessed to the conversion of souls," and offers a case study in support of this. 28 January 1836. p.4, c1.

7667 GEORGE DASHIELL *to* **BENEFACTRESSES [BALTIMORE FEMALE MITE SOCIETY]. 20 March 1835. Batticotta, Ceylon.** A student in a missionary school informs of his studies, activities, religious faith, and intention to join the church. 4 February 1836. p.2, c5.

7668 G. B. DAVIS *to* **BROTHER LOVEJOY. 16 January 1836. n.p.** Comments on his recent trip to Marion County, where he received generous financial contributions and organized three new Bible associations. 4 February 1836. p.3, c2.

7669 CAPT. J. MOUNTFORT *to* **n.n. [from the** *New Orleans Bulletin*] **1 January 1836. Fort Brooks, Fl.** Gives an account of an Indian war skirmish in Florida during which over 100 soldiers were killed. 4 February 1836. p.3, c3.

7670 THE REV. MR. DICKINSON *to* **ELIJAH P. LOVEJOY. 8 January 1836. Berlin, Oh.** Reports good results in gaining converts at various revival meetings in Ohio. 11 February 1836. p.1, c4.

7671 n.n. *to* **THE SABBATH SCHOOL CHILDREN IN WOLFSBORO, N.H. [extract from** *S. S. Treasury*] **n.d. n.p.** Relates an anecdote concerning a little boy in India who learns about Jesus Christ. 11 February 1836. p.1, c5.

7672 n.n. *to* **SIR. [extract] 2 January 1836. Charleston, S.C.** Describes a gun battle on the streets of Charleston between several young gentlemen of Columbia College. 11 February 1836. p.1, c5.

7673 J. S. *to* **THE EDITOR OF THE** *N. O. OBSERVER.* **30 December 1835. Mobile, Al.** Reports on the city of Mobile, discussing its history, economy, churches, schools, and organizations. 18 February 1836. p.2, c2.

7674 THOS. V. BROCKING *to* **THE EDITOR. [from the** *Southern Temperance Star*] **17 November 1835. Richmond.** Presents a case study of a man who embraced temperance. 18 February 1836. p.2, c3.

7675 RICHARD PETER *to* **MR. GORDON. [from the** *Southern Temperance Star*] **n.d. n.p.** A deaf child demonstrates how intemperance leads to disgrace. 18 February 1836. p.2, c3.

7676 n.n. *to* **n.n. [from the** *Jacksonville Patriot*] **2 February 1836. Beardstown.** Records brisk commerce on the Illinois River, enclosing a list of goods exported over the past season. 18 February 1836. p.3, c3.

7677 JOHN RANKIN *to* **BROTHER BRAINERD. [from the** *Journal and Luminary*] **n.d. n.p.** Answers at length the charge that the free states do not have the right to interfere with slavery. 18 February 1836. p.4, c1.

7678 SARAH L. SMITH *to* **n.n. [from the** *Connecticut Observer*] **31 April 1835. Jerusalem.** A minister's wife on a trip to the Holy Land describes the sights of Jerusalem. 25 February 1836. p.1, c1.

7679 SARAH L. SMITH *to* **n.n. 31 April 1835. Jerusalem.** A minister's wife describes the various sights she encounters on a trip to Jerusalem. 25 February 1836. p.1, c1.

7680 G. B. DAVIS *to* **BROTHER LOVEJOY. 17 February 1836. Alton.** Discusses his travels, his work to establish and strengthen Bible societies, and the money he raised for Bible distribution. 25 February 1836. p.2, c1.

7681 n.n. *to* **n.n. [extract] n.d. n.p.** A postmaster in Cook County, Illinois, complains of the irregularity of mail delivery at his office. 25 February 1836. p.3, c3.

7682 C. *to* **MR. EDITOR [ELIJAH P. LOVEJOY]. n.d. n.p.** Questions an article in the *Observer* of 18 February on "The Scriptural View of Divine Influence as Opposed to Pelagian and Other Views." 3 March 1836. p.1, c1.

7683 DAVID PORTER *to* **MESSRS. BAIRD, ELLIOT AND HAYNES. [from the** *Pittsburgh Christian Herald*] **26 January 1836. Pittsburgh.** Observes the pernicious effects of tobacco on the mind. 3 March 1836. p.1, c4.

7684 F. C. W. *to* **THE** *NEW YORK EVANGELIST.* **n.d. n.p.** Encloses an extract of a letter from Patrick Henry, late Governor of Virginia. 3 March 1836. p.2, c2.

7685 PATRICK HENRY *to* **SIR. [extract] n.d. n.p.** Characterizes the institution of slavery as abhorrent and anticipates the era of its abolition. 3 March 1836. p.2, c2.

7686 J. EDWARDS *to* **THE EDITORS OF ALL PAPERS, FRIENDLY TO THE CAUSE OF TEMPERANCE AND HUMANITY. n.d. n.p.** Appeals to American merchants to abstain from dealing in alcoholic drinks, and especially from sending them abroad. 3 March 1836. p.2, c3.

7687 n.n. *to* **J. EDWARDS. 29 October 1835. Smyrna.** Notes the number of American vessels arriving at Smyrna laden with rum; informs that, ironically, some of the vessels are owned by advocates of temperance. 3 March 1836. p.2, c3.

7688 J. B. MARTIN *to* **THE EDITOR OF THE** *ST. LOUIS OBSERVER* **[ELIJAH P. LOVEJOY]. 25 February 1836. New Madrid.** Informs the editor that two local subscribers have moved away, and that a third wishes his subscription terminated. 3 March 1836. p.2, c5.

7689 MR. PARKER *to* **n.n. [extract from the** *Missionary Herald*] **17 August 1835. Green River.** Reports on his missionary work among the Sioux; appeals for young men to take up the cross and join in teaching Christianity to the Indians. 3 March 1836. p.2, c5.

7690 JAMES E. WELSH *to* **n.n. [extract from the** *American Baptist*] **14 December 1835. Huntsville, Al.** Comments on his journey through Tennessee and his discovery of a heretical sect which believes that the Devil is an eternal being; asserts the need for Baptist ministers. 3 March 1836. p.2, c5.

7691 ANDREW JACKSON *to* **THE SENATE AND THE HOUSE OF REPRESENTA-TIVES. n.d. n.p.** Announces that he has accepted the offer of Great Britain to mediate the dispute between the United States and France. 3 March 1836. p.3, c3.

7692 n.n. *to* **n.n. [from the** *Louisville Journal*] **29 January 1836. Columbus, Ga.** A soldier reports from the site of recent Indian hostilities. 3 March 1836. p.3, c4.

7693 ROBINSON *to* **BROTHER STEVENS. [from the** *Cross and Journal*] **n.d. n.p.** Considers the nature and duty of prayer. 10 March 1836. p.1, c2.

7694 GARDINER SPRING *to* **THE** *NEW YORK OBSERVER*. **January 1836. New York.** Announces that he has requested the removal of his name from the list of recommendations to the college under the care of the Rev. Dr. Junkin. 10 March 1836. p.3, c1.

7695 EDWIN F. HATFIELD *to* **BRO. LEAVITT. [from the** *New York Evangelist*] **17 February 1836. New York.** Conveys news of a current revival at which Br. James Gallagher is preaching. 10 March 1836. p.3, c2.

7696 A. BULLARD *to* **REV. ELIJAH P. LOVEJOY. 23 February 1836. Walnut Hills.** Encloses an extract from a letter of the Rev. C. Kingsbury. 10 March 1836. p.3, c3.

7697 REV. C. KINGSBURY *to* **A. BULLARD. n.d. Harmony Mission, Osage River.** Expresses hope that funds may be obtained to open a school on the Osage. 10 March 1836. p.3, c3.

7698 N. M. ROTHCHILD *to* **MESSRS. J. L. AND S. JOSEPH AND CO. OF NEW YORK. [extract] 6 January 1835. London.** Announces that the recent message of the American president has had a favorable effect on the French government, to the benefit of American stocks and securities. 10 March 1836. p.3, c4.

7699 THE REV. BENJAMIN CHASE *to* **n.n. [extract] n.d. Natchez, Ms.** States that he has received a letter expressing the deep concern of some twenty students at Oakland College for the salvation and glory of God. 10 March 1836. p.4, c2.

7700 G. B. DAVIS *to* **BRO. LOVEJOY. 15 March 1836. St. Louis.** Encloses a note for publication which he believes may prove inspirational to others. 17 March 1836. p.3, c2.

7701 A FRIEND TO THE BIBLE CAUSE *to* **G. B. DAVIS. 14 March 1836. St. Louis.** Offers a contribution to the cause of Bible distribution, suggesting that a sum equal to one dollar for every inhabitant of St. Louis might be raised. 17 March 1836. p.3, c2.

7702 ZEBULON BUTLER *to* **THE EDITOR OF THE** *NEW ORLEANS OBSERVER*. **26 January 1836. Port Gibson.** Describes the reception of twelve young men into communion with the church at Bethel. 17 March 1836. p.3, c3.

7703 J. *to* **MR. EDITOR [ELIJAH P. LOVEJOY]. n.d. n.p.** Responds to an article in the *Observer* of 11 February, taking issue with its conclusion that while slavery is a sin, it need not be abolished immediately. 24 March 1836. p.1, c1.

7704 n.n. *to* **MR. EDITOR [ELIJAH P. LOVEJOY]. n.d. Illinois College, Jacksonville.** Encloses a letter he believes may be of interest to Lovejoy's readers. 24 March 1836. p.2, c5.

7705 TIME *to* **SON. 3 May 1836. London.** Addresses a student of Illinois College on the subject of prudence. 24 March 1836. p.2, c5.

7706 n.n. *to* **n.n. [extract] 16 February 1836. Indian Key, Fl.** A soldier discusses the Indian War in Florida, reporting movement of troops and noting that little else of interest has occurred recently. 24 March 1836. p.3, c3.

7707 L. F. LINN *to* **MR. DAVIS. 1 February 1836. Washington City.** Comments on a petition from the people of Wayne County, Missouri, and a memorial from the legislature of the Territory of Arkansas; requests an appropriation to remove obstructions to the navigation of the White, Big Black, and St. Francis rivers. 24 March 1836. p.4, c1.

7708 MR. STEVENS *to* **HIS BROTHER. [extract from the** *New York Evangelist*] **2 November 1835. Lintin [China].** Reports on the travel route of a missionary expedition in which he is engaged. 31 March 1836. p.2, c1.

7709 n.n. *to* **BRO. LOVEJOY. 18 March 1836. Marion College.** Reports that a revival in the past month has led to several open professions of faith; recounts the death of a young man who "spoke with humble confidence of his hope in God through the merits of Jesus Christ." 31 March 1835. p.2, c2.

7710 C. *to* **THE EDITOR [ELIJAH P. LOVEJOY]. [extract] n.d. n.p.** Reports plans for obtaining a library for a Sabbath School; discusses the contention that Missouri receives less than an equal share of the charities of the New England church; comments on the immorality of tobacco use. 31 March 1836. p.3, c2.

7711 n.n. *to* **THE EDITOR OF THE** *NEW YORK EVANGELIST*. **[extract] 23 February 1836. n.p.** Reports on a protracted revival meeting in his area which he believes has done much good for the church. 31 March 1836. p.3, c3.

7712 DANIEL SHARP *to* **MR. EDITOR. [from the** *Boston Christian Watchman*] **n.d. n.p.** Defends the American Bible Society's making appropriations for new versions of the Scriptures and encloses a letter on the subject. 7 April 1836. p.1, c1.

7713 DANIEL SHARP *to* **REV. J. GOING, D.D. 8 December 1835. Boston.** Contends that the American Bible Society funds should not be used to aid in the distribution of new foreign translations of the Scriptures unless the English version in common use is the basis of the new translation. 7 April 1836. p.1, c1.

7714 DANIEL SHARP AND FRANCIS WAYLAND, JR. *to* **n.n. 4 March 1836. Boston.** Affirm the sentiments expressed in Sharp's preceding letter, concerning the American Bible Society. 7 April 1836. p.1, c4.

7715 J. HAWES *to* **THE VERMONT AS. 7 February 1836. Hartford.** Declares that slaveholding is sinful and should be abolished immediately; believes that the cause of freedom will eventually triumph. 7 April 1836. p.1, c4.

7716 X.Y.Z. *to* **THE EDITOR OF THE** *QUEBEC GAZETTE.* **12 February 1836. Quebec.** Comments on the quantity of land held by religious communities in Canada prior to the British conquest. 7 April 1836. p.2, c3.

7717 LUTHER HALSEY *to* **n.n. [extract from the** *New York Observer*] **n.d. n.p.** A professor at Pittsburgh Theological Seminary seeks to establish the denominational principles of the Presbyterian church affiliated with the General Assembly in the United States. 7 April 1836. p.4, c1.

7718 A CORRESPONDENT OF THE *CINCINNATI JOURNAL to* **n.n. n.d. n.p.** Comments on the Rev. Mr. Wolff's missionary work. 14 April 1836. p.3, c3.

7719 L. F. LINN *to* **THE EDITOR OF THE** *MISSOURI ARGUS.* **12 March 1836. Washington City.** Forwards for publication a system of mail routes for the state of Missouri. 14 April 1836. p.3, c3.

7720 H. CHAMBERLAIN, A. B. CAMPBELL, AND WM. SPENCER *to* **THE GENERAL ASSEMBLY OF THE PRESBYTERIAN CHURCH TO BE CONVENED AT PITTSBURGH ON MAY, 1836. 22 October 1835. Marion College, Mo.** Protest several acts passed by the Presbyterian Synod of Missouri at a recent meeting. 14 April 1836. p.4, c1.

7721 H. CHAMBERLAIN, A. B. CAMPBELL, P. CAYCE, B. R. WARDLAW, AND WM. SPENCER *to* **THE GENERAL ASSEMBLY OF THE PRESBYTERIAN CHURCH TO BE CONVENED AT PITTSBURGH ON MAY, 1836. 22 October 1835. Marion College, Mo.** Protest further the proceedings of a recent meeting of the Presbyterian Synod of Missouri. 14 April 1836. p.4, c1.

7722 DOCTOR WILLIAMSON *to* **n.n [extract from the** *Missionary Herald*] **15 October 1835. Lac qui Parle.** A missionary to the Dakota Indians reports on his work and requests the aid of a man who might act as interpreter and translator. 21 April 1836. p.1, c2.

7723 DOCTOR WILLIAMSON *to* **n.n. [extract from the** *Missionary Herald*] **13 November 1836. Lac qui Parle.** Reports further on missionary work among the Dakotas, focussing on the school. 21 April 1836. p.1, c2.

7724 DOCTOR WILLIAMSON *to* **n.n. [extract from the** *Cincinnati Journal*] **20 November 1835. Lac qui Parle.** Discusses his missionary work among the Dakotas and the tribe's habits and manner of life. 21 April 1836. p.1, c2.

7725 HENRY STARR AND A. W. COREY *to* **THE FRIENDS OF SABBATH SCHOOLS IN THE STATE OF ILLINOIS. 20 March 1836. Cincinnati.** Announce the establishment by the American Sunday School Union of a western board of agency; inform that Starr and Corey were appointed to cooperate with friends of the Sunday School cause in Illinois. 21 April 1836. p.1, c4.

7726 RICHARD WILLIAMS *to* **THE BOARD OF DIRECTORS OF THE TOMPKINS COUNTY BIBLE SOCIETY. 18 January 1836. Ithaca.** Reports on his progress to assure that all families in the county possess a Bible. 21 April 1836. p.1, c5.

7727 JOSIAH BREWER *to* **THE EDITOR OF THE** *JOURNAL OF COMMERCE.* **1 April 1836. Off the Hook.** Expresses gratitude on the occasion of his departure on a missionary journey. 21 April 1836. p.2, c4.

7728 REV. J. GREENLEAF *to* **THE AMERICAN TRACT SOCIETY. n.d. n.p.** Proposes a plan to provide American seamen with religious reading materials; estimates the number of volumes and the cost involved in providing the ships with small libraries. 21 April 1836. p.3, c1.

7729 REV. STEPHEN PEET *to* **[THE AMERICAN TRACT SOCIETY]. [extract] n.d. n.p.** Encloses resolutions of the Sailor's and Boatmen's Friend Society requesting the appropriation of volumes by the American Tract Society and pledging to dispose of the volumes properly by establishing libraries on American vessels. 21 April 1836. p.3, c1.

7730 n.n. *to* **n.n. [extract] 24 March 1836. Picolata, Fl.** Gives an account of an Indian ambush on a company of American soldiers. 21 April 1836. p.3, c2.

7731 GEO. C. WOOD *to* **BROTHER LOVEJOY. 8 April 1836. Salem Grove.** Encloses for publication a copy of the minutes of the latest meeting of the Presbytery of St. Charles. 28 April 1836. p.2, c1.

7732 A SECRETARY OF THE AMERICAN BOARD OF COMMISSIONERS FOR FOREIGN MISSIONS *to* **THE REV. DAVID ABEEL. n.d. n.p.** Discusses the origin and ecclesiastical connections of the American Board of Commissioners for Foreign Missions. 5 May 1836. p.1, c1.

7733 I. J. ROBERTS *to* **MR. EDITOR [ELIJAH P. LOVEJOY]. 5 April 1836. Clinton, Ms.** Affirms his religious conviction at the start of a missionary journey to China. 5 May 1836. p.1, c2.

7734 JOSIAH BREWER *to* **THE EXECUTIVE COMMITTEE OF THE AMERICAN SUNDAY SCHOOL UNION. 22 March 1836. Philadelphia.** Appeals for funds to prepare and circulate translations of the Scriptures in the missions of the Mediterranean and near eastern countries. 5 May 1836. p.1, c5.

7735 Y. *to* **MR. EDITOR [ELIJAH P. LOVEJOY]. 18 March 1836. n.p.** Describes a journey by boat from Alton to Louisville. 5 May 1836. p.2, c5.

7736 A SECRETARY OF THE AMERICAN BOARD OF COMMISSIONERS FOR FOREIGN MISSIONS *to* **THE REV. DAVID ABEEL. n.d. n.p.** States that his organization is not an ecclesiastical body or a voluntary association in the common sense, but nonetheless possesses the advantages attributed to both forms of association. 12 May 1836. p.1, c1.

7737 G. DE F. *to* **n.n. [from the** *New York Observer***] 11 January 1836. Bolbec (Lower Seine).** Gives an account of a revival at Binningen, near Bale, Switzerland. 12 May 1836. p.1, c2.

7738 n.n. *to* **THE** *NEW ORLEANS BULLETIN.* **n.d. Texas.** Reports that Nacodoches has been abandoned, the Mexican army has become allied with Indians of the North, and hundreds of families are fleeing for their lives. 12 May 1836. p.3, c3.

7739 HENRY B. STANTON *to* **n.n. n.d. n.p.** Reports that a church in western New York was burned because of an abolitionist lecture delivered there. 12 May 1836. p.3, c4.

7740 A SECRETARY OF THE AMERICAN BOARD OF COMMISSIONERS FOR FOREIGN MISSIONS *to* **THE REV. DAVID ABEEL. n.d. n.p.** Expresses confidence in the future proceedings of his organization. 19 May 1836. p.1, c1.

7741 TRAVELER *to* **MR. EDITOR. [from the** *Buffalo Spectator*] **26 April 1836. n.p.** Favors the "immediate and total abolition" of profane swearing. 19 May 1836. p.2, c1.

7742 H. C. *to* **MR. EDITOR [ELIJAH P. LOVEJOY]. 3 May 1836. Independence, Mo.** Notes that letters from Ohio inform him that the Mormons are arming and moving towards Missouri; adds that travelers confirm this, and that the people in Jackson and the surrounding countries "will be found at their post in the hour of trial." 19 May 1836. p.3, c2.

7743 A SECRETARY OF THE AMERICAN BOARD OF COMMISSIONERS FOR FOREIGN MISSIONS *to* **THE REV. DAVID ABEEL. n.d. n.p.** Explains why his organization has its headquarters in Boston; states that it continues to exist only by keeping the confidence of various churches; comments on the feasibility of a union between the Presbyterian, Reformed Dutch, and Congregational denominations. 26 May 1836. p.1, c1.

7744 W. L. J. *to* **MR. EDITOR [ELIJAH P. LOVEJOY]. n.d. n.p.** Upholds Christian unity and supports the American Bible Society. 26 May 1836. p.3, c1.

7745 W. G. *to* **MR. EDITOR. [from a New York paper] n.d. n.p.** Announces the availability to Americans of an unfermented wine which, if it is adopted for communion services, should settle the dispute over the question of alcoholic beverages at the Lord's table. 2 June 1836. p.2, c1.

7746 GENERAL ASHLEY *to* **THE EDITORS OF THE** *REPUBLICAN.* **3 June 1836. House of Representatives.** Announces that both houses of Congress have passed a bill providing for the extension of the western boundary of Missouri to the Missouri River. 16 June 1836. p.3, c5.

7747 A. B. *to* **MR. MARSH. n.d. n.p.** Opposes the license law, which authorizes the sale of liquor; maintains that the state should not become a patron of intemperance and crime. 23 June 1836. p.4, c3.

7748 A CORRESPONDENT OF THE *NEW YORK OBSERVER to* **GENTLEMEN. 3 May 1836. London.** Reports on the annual meetings of four organizations in London: the Sunday School Society, the Lord's Day Society, the Society for the Prevention of Cruelty to Animals, and the Wesleyan Missionary Society. 30 June 1836. p.1, c1.

7749 n.n. *to* **E. 29 August 1821. n.p.** A clergyman addresses a dying friend, urging him to repent of his sins and believe in the Lord Jesus Christ. 30 June 1836. p.4, c1.

7750 n.n. *to* **BROTHER. [from the** *New York Evanglist*] **30 May 1836. Troy.** Reports on a revival in Troy, where 115 persons have joined the church on profession; discusses the history of Bethel Church, where the revival is taking place. 7 July 1836. p.2, c3.

7751 JOHN BLAIN *to* **THE EDITOR OF THE** *CHRISTIAN WATCHMAN.* **n.d. Providence.** Comments on the effects of a revival in Providence where it is estimated that some 400 persons have been "born of the Spirit." 7 July 1836. p.2, c4.

7752 T. L. *to* **BROTHER [ELIJAH P. LOVEJOY]. 4 May 1836. Columbia, Pa.** Relates details of his journey from Louisville to Pennsylvania. 14 July 1836. p.1, c1.

7753 T. L. *to* **BROTHER [ELIJAH P. LOVEJOY]. 17 May 1836. New York.** Describes his travels through the Pennsylvania countryside en route to New York. 14 July 1836. p.2, c5.

7754 T. L. *to* **BROTHER [ELIJAH P. LOVEJOY]. 24 May 1836. Philadelphia.** Relates particulars of an anniversary meeting of the American Tract Society. 21 July 1836. p.1, c1.

7755 T. L. *to* **BROTHER [ELIJAH P. LOVEJOY]. 30 May 1836. Boston.** Reports on an anniversary meeting of Sunday school advocates in Philadelphia; reflects on his trip to Boston and the changes that have taken place in that city over the past twenty years. 21 July 1836. p.1, c2.

7756 H. B. W. *to* **BROTHER. n.d. n.p.** Urges a Sunday school teacher to pray earnestly for the salvation of his students' souls. 21 July 1836. p.3, c4.

7757 T. L. *to* **SIR [ELIJAH P. LOVEJOY]. 31 May 1836. Boston.** Opposes those who deny demonstrations of the existence of God; describes the inauguration of Isaac Hill as governor of New Hampshire. 21 July 1836. p.3, c5.

7758 ELIJAH P. LOVEJOY *to* **THE *ALTON TELEGRAPH*. 27 July 1836. Alton, Il.** Gives an account of how a mob entered the office of the *St. Louis Observer* and destroyed most of the property there. 10 August 1836. [extra] p.1, c1.

7759 ADELPHUS *to* **BROTHER LOVEJOY. n.d. n.p.** Questions the contention that impenitent sinners ought to offer prayers to God. 8 September 1836. p.1, c1.

7760 PROTESTANT LAYMAN *to* **VISCOUNT MELBOURNE. n.d. n.p.** Asserts that England has always prospered under Protestant sovereigns and withered under Roman Catholic sovereigns. 8 September 1836. p.1, c4.

7761 [illegible] *to* **MR. BAIRD. [from the *Pittsburgh Christian Herald*] n.d. n.p.** Comments negatively on the official opinion of the General Assembly of the Presbyterian Church; believes that it had no power to act in relation to slavery and that it is the moral duty of the South to educate the slaves and prepare them for freedom. 8 September 1836. p.1, c5.

7762 L. *to* **MR. LOVEJOY. 13 July 1836. Dubuque.** Describes the ceremonial laying of the cornerstone of the first Presbyterian church in the Wisconsin Territory. 8 September 1836. p.3, c2.

7763 REV. DR. PHILIP *to* **THE AMERICAN TRACT SOCIETY. [extract] 2 November 1835. Cape Town, South Africa.** Notes the need for tracts in the Dutch language. 8 September 1836. p.3, c2.

7764 T. L. *to* **BROTHER [ELIJAH P. LOVEJOY]. 24 June 1836. Steamboat *New England*, Kennebec River.** Reports on his visit to a church conference in Maine, and a Fourth of July celebration and Sabbath school visit in Hartford. 29 September 1836. p.1, c2.

7765 J. A. C. *to* **SIR [ELIJAH P. LOVEJOY]. 18 June 1836. Westport.** Reports on missions among the Pawnees; emphasizes the poverty of the Indians during the past winter. 29 September 1836. p.1, c4.

7766 MAX. ISNARD *to* **THE HON. L. WINTHROP. 15 April 1836. Boston.** Discusses the cultivation of the sugar beet and the method of manufacturing sugar from it. 29 September 1836. p.4, c1.

7767 J. M. STURTEVANT *to* **BRO. LOVEJOY. 27 September 1836. Illinois College.** Encloses for publication a program of the recent commencement exercises at Illinois College. 13 October 1836. p.1, c2.

7768 REV. SAMUEL DYER *to* **SIR [ELIJAH P. LOVEJOY]. n.d. n.p.** A missionary to China gives his assessment of the ways in which China is open to the Gospel and the ways in which it is not. 13 October 1836. p.1, c2.

7769 JOHN TILSON, JR. *to* **MESSRS. MOORE, MORTON AND CO. [LAND AGENTS]. 9 August 1836. New York.** An agent of the New York and Boston Illinois Land Company announces a list of two thousand quarter sections of land, which will soon be printed with the conditions of sale. 13 October 1836. p.2, c4.

7770 TIMOTHY TURNER *to* **FRIEND. [from the** *Illinois Temperance Herald*] **20 September 1836. Griggsville.** Forwards extracts from the journal of a circuit-riding temperance agent. 13 October 1836. p.3, c1.

7771 n.n. *to* **SIR. n.d. n.p.** Describes how a certain carpenter, prone to drunkenness, reformed himself. 13 October 1836. p.4, c4.

7772 n.n. *to* **THE** *JOURNAL OF COMMERCE.* **7 September 1836. New Orleans.** Gives an account of a mob's attempt to threaten a judge and the ensuing fight which left two of the mob dead and one wounded. 20 October 1836. p.2, c3.

7773 n.n. *to* **THE** *JOURNAL OF COMMERCE.* **8 September 1836. n.p.** Reports that excitement over the events of the past week [an attempted lynching of an alleged criminal and an assault on a judge] has diminished. 20 October 1836. p.2, c3.

7774 A LAYMAN *to* **MR. EDITOR [ELIJAH P. LOVEJOY]. n.d. n.p.** Laments the present state of Christendom; asserts that Christians are divided because they have neglected the faith once handed to the apostles and concerned themselves with innovations of men. 20 October 1836. p.3, c1.

7775 CYRUS HAYNES *to* **MR. EDITOR. [from the** *Cumberland Presbyterian*] **n.d. n.p.** States that he has attended five camp meetings and four sacramental meetings in the past season at which there have been more than fifty professions of religion. 20 October 1836. p.3, c2.

7776 G. W. KENNEDY *to* **BROTHER. [from the** *Philadelphia Observer*] **30 August 1836. Lebanon, Ky.** Reports that he is in the midst of a protracted meeting, where twenty to thirty persons have found Christ and over 100 are "anxiously inquiring what they must do to be saved." 20 October 1836. p.3, c3.

7777 n.n. *to* **MR. FESSENDEN. [from the** *New England Farmer*] **July 1836. Charlestown.** Advises on the successful way to raise chickens. 20 October 1836. p.4, c1.

7778 SAMUEL M. POND *to* **MR. EDITOR [from the** *Maine Temperance Herald*] **17 August 1836. Bucksport.** Gives an account of the death of a drunkard by "spontaneous combustion." 20 October 1836. p.4, c2.

7779 n.n. *to* **n.n. 1 October 1836. Mission Station, Lake Harriet.** Describes a mission station near Fort Snelling. 27 October 1836. p.2, c2.

7780 JOHN D. PEERS *to* **BRO. LOVEJOY. 18 October 1836. Farmington, Mo.** Reports on meetings at Brazeau and Apple Creek; requests that Lovejoy attend a meeting of the presbytery the following month and assist in an ordination ceremony. 27 October 1836. p.3, c1.

7781 T. TURNER *to* **FRIEND. [from the** *Illinois Temperance Herald***]** **27 October 1836. Carlyle.** Forwards extracts from the journal of a circuit-riding temperance agent. 3 November 1836. p.2, c3.

7782 R. J. BRECKENRIDGE *to* **DR. WARDLAW. 20 August 1836. Paris.** Argues that evils equal to American slavery exist in Britain. 24 November 1836. p.1, c1.

7783 THERON BALDWIN *to* **BROTHER LOVEJOY. 14 November 1836. Steamboat** *Vermont,* **Ohio River.** Gives an account of a trip to Cincinnati where he attended the anniversary meetings of the Home Missionary, Sunday School, Emigrant's Friend, and Foreign Missionary societies. 24 November 1836. p.3, c1.

7784 COUNTRY FRIENDS *to* **MR. EDITOR [ELIJAH P. LOVEJOY]. n.d. n.p.** Urges that the anniversary meetings of the Bible, Sunday School, Temperance, and Tract societies, scheduled to be held in Alton in early evening, be re-scheduled to an earlier time for the benefit of those who live beyond the limits of the city. 24 November 1836. p.3, c4.

7785 REV. R. TURNBULL *to* **THE** *CHRISTIAN SECRETARY.* **[extract] 29 September 1836. Detroit.** Reports on the formation of a Baptist State Convention in Michigan; gives particulars of an anniversary meeting of the Michigan Baptist Association. 24 November 1836. p.3, c4.

7786 H. HAWTHORN *to* **BROTHER STEVENS. [from the** *Cross and Journal***]** **12 October 1836. Barberville, Al.** Reports on a meeting of the Alabama Baptist Association where the participants were divided on the question of missions. 24 November 1836. p.3, c4.

7787 n.n. *to* **MR. EDITOR [ELIJAH P. LOVEJOY]. n.d. n.p.** Encloses a poem for publication. 24 November 1836. p.3, c4.

7788 NOAH WEBSTER *to* **n.n. [extract] n.d. n.p.** Addresses the topic of education, concluding that any system which limits instruction to the arts and sciences, and rejects religion, is defective. 1 December 1836. p.1, c1.

7789 n.n. *to* **MR. LOVEJOY. n.d. n.p.** Submits a letter for publication concerning ministers who have violated the Sabbath. 1 December 1836. p.1, c3.

7790 B. *to* **MR. EDITOR [ELIJAH P. LOVEJOY]. n.d. n.p.** Denounces the actions of four Presbyterian ministers who, in the author's opinion, violated the fourth commandment by travelling on Sunday. 1 December 1836. p.1, c3.

7791 A TRAVELLER *to* **MR. EDITOR [ELIJAH P. LOVEJOY]. n.d. n.p.** Recounts a scene, observed in Kentucky, of a master brutally beating a female slave. 1 December 1836. p.1, c5.

7792 PAUL *to* **MESSRS. EDITORS. [from the** *New York Observer***] n.d. n.p.** Asserts the necessity for churches to provide adequate means of support for their ministers. 1 December 1836. p.2, c2.

7793 GEO. C. WOOD *to* **REV. ELIJAH P. LOVEJOY. 13 October 1836. Salem Grove.** Requests publication of the minutes of a recent meeting of the Presbytery of St. Charles. 1 December 1836. p.3, c2.

7794 A. D. EDDY *to* **REV. MR. ARMSTRONG. [from the** *New York Evangelist***] 10 October 1836. Newark, N.J.** Announces the affiliation of the First Presbyterian Church of Newark with the American Board of Commissioners for Foreign Missions. 1 December 1836. p.3, c2.

7795 n.n. *to* **BROTHER BRECKENRIDGE. [extract from the** *Western Presbyterian Herald*] **8 November 1836. Columbia, Ky.** Reports on a protracted meeting of 18 days, at which 130 persons made professions of faith in Jesus Christ. 1 December 1836. p.3, c3.

7796 CAROLUS *to* **MR. HOLMES. [from the** *Maine Farmer*] **n.d. n.p.** Discusses the vigorous occupation of farming and advises farmers on ways to improve the quality of their produce and livestock. 1 December 1836. p.4, c1.

7797 E. MATTOON *to* **PHILIP SCHUYLER. 7 October 1835. Amherst, Ma.** Provides an eyewitness account of the Battle of Saratoga. 1 December 1836. p.4, c4.

7798 n.n. *to* **GERRIT SMITH. [extract from the** *Friend of Man*] **20 September 1836. n.p.** Discusses the state of the British West Indies after two years of emancipation, maintaining that conditions there counter certain arguments of Americans who oppose emancipation. 8 December 1836. p.1, c1.

7799 ANTI TOBACCO *to* **MR. BAIRD. [from the** *Pittsburgh Christian Herald*] **n.d. n.p.** Criticizes ministers who use tobacco, drawing illustrations from a recent meeting of a presbytery. 8 December 1836. p.1, c4.

7800 n.n. *to* **n.n. [extract] 1 November. Indian Key, Fl.** Reports on an Indian attack in Florida which was made on a schooner lying at anchor. 8 December 1836. p.2, c4.

7801 JOHN F. COWAN *to* **BROTHER LOVEJOY. 24 November 1836. Potosi, Washington County, Mo.** Reports on several recent revival meetings in which he has participated 8. December 1836. p.2, c6.

7802 HUGH CAMPBELL *to* **THE** *LONDON TIMES.* **19 September 1836. Petonville.** Reports on the extent of the famine in the Western Isles of Scotland. 8 December 1836. p.3, c3.

7803 WESLEY LINTHICUM *to* **WILLIAM GWYNN. n.d. n.p.** Requests publication of an enclosed letter. 8 December 1836. p.3, c4.

7804 WESLEY LINTHICUM *to* **MESRS. M'GILL, WASON, GUYNN, FISHER, ELLICOTT, BELL, VANSANT, HARWOOD, HOPE, SUTTON, KEENE, FOUNTAIN, EVANS, G. A. THOMAS, DUVALL, J. B. THOMAS, AND GEORGE. 12 November 1836. Elk Ridge, Md.** Announces his intention to come to Annapolis to take his place in the Electoral College; invites his colleagues to meet him there, rescinding their prior resolution of secession from that body. 8 December 1836. p.3, c4.

7805 ALEX. IZNARD *to* **MR. W. HOLLAND. [from the** *Hampshire Republican*] **5 October 1836. Boston.** Discusses the cultivation of beet root and the manufacturing of sugar from its juice. 8 December 1836. p.4, c1.

7806 A. SENAKERIM DEG MANASIAN *to* **THE FRIENDS OF CHRIST IN THE UNITED STATES OF AMERICA. 16 July 1836. Constantinople.** An Armenian convert to Christianity expresses gratitude to American Christians for their missionary efforts. 15 December 1836. p.1, c1.

7807 NEW ENGLAND *to* **MR. EDITOR [ELIJAH P. LOVEJOY]. n.d. n.p.** Defends the quality of life in the West against an anonymous quote from *Abbot's Religious Magazine.* 15 December 1836. p.2, c6.

7808 GEO. CHAMPION *to* **MISS E. J. A. 7 March 1836. Port Natal.** Provides an account of his missionary work. 15 December 1836. p.3, c2.

7809 MARION *to* **MESSRS. CHARLESS AND PASCHAL. [from the** *Missouri Republican***]** **22 November 1836. Palmyra.** Criticizes the paper for printing an article which was designed to discourage American cultivation of the sugar beet; insists that such an enterprise would prove profitable. 15 December 1836. p.4, c1.

7810 n.n. *to* **THE EDITOR OF THE** *LONDON MIRROR.* **n.d. n.p.** Describes the Russian mode of making butter. 15 December 1836. p.4, c2.

7811 HENRY YOST *to* **THE EXECUTIVE COMMITTEE OF THE ILLINOIS STATE TEMPERANCE SOCIETY. [from the** *Temperance Herald***]** **28 November 1836. Fancy Farm, Franklin County, Il.** Requests fifteen copies of the *Temperance Herald* and two dozen "Almanacks." 15 December 1836. p.4, c2.

7812 NATHAN GOULD [SEC'Y.] *to* **BROTHER GRAVES. [from the** *Temperance Herald***]** **22 November 1836. Union Grove.** Forwards a report on the Putnam County Temperance Society to the secretary of the Illinois Temperance Society. 15 December 1836. p.4, c2.

7813 JOHN M. WEBSTER *to* **REV. MR. GRAVES. [from the** *Temperance Herald***]** **2 November 1836. Carlyle, Il.** Discusses an address given by Mr. Turner, an agent of the Illinois State Temperance Society, which was effective in convincing many of the evils of intemperance. 15 December 1836. p.4, c3.

7814 WM. P. REYNOLDS, MOSES DEARBON, L. W. BROOKS *to* **MR. EDITOR. [from the** *Temperance Herald***]** **22 November 1836. La Harpe.** Enclose a resolution of the La Harpe Temperance Society stating its intention to become auxiliary to the Illinois Temperance Society. 15 December 1836. p.4, c3.

7815 EDWARD C. DELAVAN *to* **R. H. WALWORTH. 23 September 1836. Farmington.** Reports on a state-wide temperance convention in Connecticut. 15 December 1836. p.4, c3.

7816 JOHN RANDOLPH *to* **n.n. [from the** *Southern Literary Messenger***]** **25 August 1818. Roanoke, Va.** Discusses his conversion to faith in Jesus Christ. 22 December 1836. p.1, c5.

7817 JOHN RANDOLPH *to* **FRIEND. [from the** *Southern Literary Messenger***]** **25 September 1818. Roanoke, Va.** Discusses his conversion, his reading of the Bible, and his disdain for religious tyranny in any form; notes avarice as the motivation for the slave trade. 22 December 1836. p.1, c6.

7818 JOHN RANDOLPH *to* **n.n. [from the** *Southern Literary Messenger***]** **January 1821. Washington.** Comments on his illness, his friends in Washington, and a biography of John Wesley. 22 December 1836. p.2, c1.

7819 P. H. *to* **THE EDITOR OF THE** *FARMER'S REGISTER.* **n.d. n.p.** Submits for publication an article on the general principles governing the selection and breeding of livestock. 22 December 1836. p.4, c1.

7820 WM. SPENCER *to* **THE** *CROSS AND JOURNAL.* **26 September 1836. Mechanicsville, Oh.** Encloses for publication a copy of an indulgence issued in 1772 by Pope Clement XIV, addressing those Roman Catholics who must live among heretics. 29 December 1836. p.1, c4.

7821 CH. GUTZLAFF *to* **THE SECRETARY OF THE AMERICAN TRACT SOCIETY. 13 October 1835. Macao.** Reports on the composition of pamphlets in the Chinese language; hopes to have a printing press soon, and trusts that God will aid him in his missionary work. 29 December 1836. p.2, c3.

7822 F. A. RAUCH *to* **n.n. [extract from the** *New York Observer*] **n.d. n.p.** Praises the Swiss reformer Zwingli. 29 December 1836. p.3, c3.

7823 REV. IRA TRACY *to* **n.n. [extract from the** *New York Observer*] **April 1836. Singapore.** Reports on the distribution of a large number of tracts at a Chinese festival of the tombs. 29 December 1836. p.3, c3.

[1837]

7824 WILLIAM E. CHANNING *to* **JAMES G. BIRNEY. [from the** *Philanthropist*] **1 November 1836. Boston.** Denounces the moral outrage of slavery; comments on the abolitionists, whose methods of promoting emancipation are open to censure; condemns those who do violence to abolitionists. 5 January 1837. p.2, c3.

7825 R. L. McABEE *to* **BRO. LOVEJOY. 20 December 1836. Columbia, Mo.** Encloses for publication the official decision of the Presbytery of Missouri in the case of Common Fame versus Rev. Hiram Chamberlain. 12 January 1837. p.1, c4.

7826 n.n. *to* **BROTHER LEAVITT. [from the** *New York Evangelist*] **5 December 1836. Boston.** Relates account of a ceremony of dedication for missionaries departing for Hawaii; quotes speech, discusses present missions in Hawaii. 12 January 1837. p.1, c5.

7827 THE POSTMASTER AT ROCK SPRING, ILLINOIS *to* **THE** *ALTON OBSERVER*. **[extract] n.d. n.p.** Advises the editor of irregularities in delivery when the papers are sent by the eastern mail. 12 January 1837. p.2, c6.

7828 T. BALDWIN *to* **BRO. LOVEJOY. 2 January 1837. Jacksonville.** Encloses a letter for publication; discusses travelling on the Sabbath; relates a situation concerning a man who writes and distributes his own tracts on various subjects. 12 January 1837. p.3, c2.

7829 J. W. *to* **BROTHER BALDWIN. 15 December 1836. Tremont, Tazewell County, Il.** Relates his experience of travelling West with his family via river boat; discusses the penalties for those who would not travel on the Sabbath. 12 January 1837. p.3, c2.

7830 W. *to* **MR. EDITOR. [ELIJAH P. LOVEJOY]. n.d. n.p.** Comments on the "rapid and almost unparalleled progress" of the cause of temperance in Alton. 12 January 1837. p.3, c3.

7831 A SOUTHERN SUBSCRIBER *to* **THE EDITOR OF THE** *AFRICAN REPOSITORY*. **n.d. n.p.** Encloses a notice of the death of an aged slave in Virginia, taken from the *National Intelligencer*; maintains that the affectionate terms in which the notice is couched counter certain assertions by Northern abolitionists regarding the inhuman manner in which slaves are regarded in the South. 12 January 1837. p.3, c5.

7832 CHARLES POYEN *to* **MR. EDITOR. [from the** *Providence Journal*] **n.d. n.p.** Refers to an experiment in "animal magnetism." 12 January 1837. p.4, c2.

7833 CHARLES POYEN *to* **MR. EDITOR [from the** *Providence Daily Journal*] **n.d. n.p.** Relates facts surrounding a public experiment in "animal magnetism" which took place several days before and was referred to in the preceding letter. 12 January 1837. p.4, c3.

7834 TRUE BENEVOLENCE *to* **BROTHER LOVEJOY. n.d. n.p.** Discusses the proper way to build a church; notes that construction should be free of useless expenditures that only adorn the house of worship in a "fashionable" manner. 19 January 1837. p.3, c2.

7835 THE EDITOR OF THE *ZION'S ADVOCATE* *to* **n.n. [from the** *Zion's Advocate*] **n.d. n.p.** Discusses the peculiar views of Mr. Daniel Parker, a Baptist pamphleteer in Indiana. 19 January 1837. p.3, c4.

7836 CHARLES GUTZLAFF *to* **n.n. 16 May 1836. Macao.** Comments on his Japanese tract on the life of Christ. 26 January 1837. p.1, c3.

7837 A CORRESPONDENT OF THE *ST. CHARLES CLARION to* **SIR. 16 January 1837. Jefferson City.** Discusses the proceedings of the Missouri legislature, its leadership, and current bills under consideration. 26 January 1837. p.2, c3.

7838 ANDREW JACKSON *to* **EMILY DONELSON. 27 November 1836. Washington.** Expresses hope that she will be restored to perfect health; relates particulars of his own illness; reflects on the loving kindness of God and the duty of mortals to live in such a state that they may daily be prepared to die. 26 January 1837. p.2, c5.

7839 A HEARER *to* **MR. EDITOR [ELIJAH P. LOVEJOY]. n.d. n.p.** Reviews a sermon preached by the Rev. Mr. De Pui, who interpreted the Book of Genesis in light of modern geology. 26 January 1837. p.2, c6.

7840 WM. KIRBY *to* **BRO. LOVEJOY. 28 November 1836. Fairfield.** Requests publication of an abstract on the affairs of the Illinois Congregational Association's recent meeting in Fairfield. 26 January 1837. p.2, c6.

7841 CHARLES ROBINSON *to* **n.n. 8 March 1836. Bangkok, Siam.** Criticizes the opinion that men of popular talents should remain at home and not go to the mission fields; calls for more volunteers to do missionary work in Siam. 26 January 1837. p.3, c3.

7842 n.n. *to* **n.n. [extract] 26 December 1836. Louisville, Ky.** Reports on the appearance of General Santa Anna en route to Washington. 26 January 1837. p.3, c4.

7843 ELIJAH DECKERT *to* **THE SECRETARY OF THE PENNSYLVANIA TEMPER-ANCE SOCIETY. n.d. n.p.** Reports on the advance of the cause of temperance in Berks County, Pennsylvania. 26 January 1837. p.4, c3.

7844 WILLIAM SMITH *to* **THE** *ALTON OBSERVER.* **24 November 1836. Lynnville, Morgan County, Il.** Advocates African colonization as the proper remedy for slavery and a means of securing trade for the United States. 2 February 1837. p.1, c1.

7845 OBSTA PRINCIPILS *to* **MESSRS. EDITORS. [from the** *New York Journal of Commerce***] n.d. n.p.** Encloses two letters of the Roman Catholic Bishop of New York, whom he criticizes for opposing efforts of Catholic laymen to form a society for the promotion of religious knowledge. 2 February 1837. p.1, c4.

7846 JOHN, BISHOP OF NEW YORK *to* **THE EDITOR OF THE** *TRUTH TELLER.* **October 1836. n.p.** States that he has read a notice in the *Catholic Diary* of the formation of a New York Catholic Society, whose intent is to promote religious knowledge; urges the editor of the *Truth Teller* not to publish such a notice. 2 February 1837. p.1, c4.

7847 JOHN, BISHOP OF NEW YORK *to* **THE EDITOR OF THE** *CATHOLIC DIARY.* **n.d. n.p.** Condemns the announcement of the formation of the New York Catholic Society, a laymen's society for the promotion of religious knowledge. 2 February 1837. p.1, c5.

7848 B. *to* **SIR. [from the** *Alton Spectator***] n.d. n.p.** Discusses two bills before the Illinois legislature, one concerning revenues and the other proposing a convention to amend the state constitution. 2 February 1837. p.2, c3.

7849 A CORRESPONDENT OF THE *ST. CHARLES CLARION to* **SIR. 22 January 1837. Jefferson City.** Discusses a controversial bank bill before the Missouri legislature. 2 February 1837. p.2, c4.

7850 R. D. DAWSON *to* **THE EDITOR OF THE** *ALTON OBSERVER* **[ELIJAH P. LOVEJOY]. 25 January 1837. Jefferson City, Mo.** A state senator returns a pamphlet dissuading the passage of a law prohibiting the distribution of abolitionist materials. 2 February 1837. p.2, c4.

7851 ABRAHAM BYRD *to* **SIR [ELIJAH P. LOVEJOY]. 26 January 1837. Jefferson City, Mo.** A state senator denounces Lovejoy; refers to a pamphlet distributed among Missouri lawmakers. 2 February 1837. p.2, c5.

7852 A TEETOTALLER *to* **MR. EDITOR [ELIJAH P. LOVEJOY]. n.d. n.p.** Discusses the progress of the cause of temperance in Alton. 2 February 1837. p.3, c2.

7853 T. BALDWIN *to* **BRO. LOVEJOY. n.d. n.p.** Addresses churches which cannot immediately support a minister, suggesting how available funds might be put to good use. 2 February 1837. p.3, c2.

7854 F. W. GRAVES *to* **THE EDITOR OF THE** *OBSERVER* **[ELIJAH P. LOVEJOY]. n.d. n.p.** Encloses for publication a letter from the Rev. Robert Stewart. 2 February 1837. p.3, c3.

7855 ROBERT STEWART *to* **BRO. GRAVES. 23 January 1837. Canton, Fulton County, Il.** Reports highly successful results of the visit of Mr. Turner, a temperance agent, to the town of Canton. 2 February 1837. p.3, c3.

7856 J. M. PECK. *to* **REV. F. W. GRAVES. 11 January 1837. Rock Spring, Il.** Encloses the minutes of a meeting of a temperance society in Lebanon, Pennsylvania, expressing his hope for frequent meetings in the future. 2 February 1837. p.4, c2.

7857 JUSTIN PERKINS *to* **REV. WM. J. HALLOCK. 8 July 1836. Oormiah, Persia.** Expresses gratitude for funds to support his mission work among the Nestorians in Persia. 9 February 1837. p.1, c1.

7858 A. M. HUNTER *to* **BROTHER LOVEJOY. 27 January 1837. Mission Institute.** Encloses for publication a letter written by D. Nelson to his congregation in Missouri. 9 February 1837. p.1, c2.

7859 D. NELSON *to* **[MEMBERS OF HIS CONGREGATION]. n.d. n.p.** Comments on the teaching of Christ, asserting that his true followers will be hated by the world. 9 February 1837. p.1, c2.

7860 THOMAS BUCHANAN *to* **THE MONTHLY CONCERT OF PRAYER OF THE REFORMED DUTCH CHURCH OF PHILADELPHIA. n.d. n.p.** The governor of the Bassa Cove Colony in Africa appeals to American Christians to work for an end to the African slave trade. 9 February 1837. p.1, c6.

7861 n.n. *to* **THE** *RELIGIOUS HERALD.* **n.d. n.p.** Announces that henceforth he would like five papers delivered to him instead of one, on the grounds that "a few dollars . . . cannot be spent more profitably than in the diffusion of religious knowledge." 9 February 1837. p.2, c2.

7862 n.n. *to* **MESSRS. HALE AND HALLOCK. [from the** *Journal of Commerce***] 13 January 1837. New York.** The physician of a New York man who recently died of hydrophobia offers some particulars of the case. 9 February 1837. p.2, c3.

7863 n.n. *to* **SIR. [from the** *St. Charles Clarion***] 29 January 1837. Jefferson City, Mo.** Discusses several bills currently before the Missouri legislature. 9 February 1837. p.2, c5.

7864 ELIJAH P. LOVEJOY *to* **THE REV. ASA CUMMINGS. n.d. n.p.** Takes issue with several points in an article by Cummings in the *Christian Mirror* of 29 December. 9 February 1837. p.2, c6.

7865 n.n. *to* **MR. EDITOR [ELIJAH P. LOVEJOY]. [extract] 25 January 1827. Palmyra, Mo.** Expresses joy in the revivals recently held at Marion College. 9 February 1837. p.3, c2.

7866 B. *to* **MR. EDITOR [ELIJAH P. LOVEJOY]. n.d. n.p.** Expresses disgust at those who violate the Sabbath, particularly females who ride on horseback for pleasure "during the time devoted to religious service." 9 February 1837. p.3, c3.

7867 JAMES DELL *to* **THE EDITOR. [from the *Jacksonville Courier*] n.d. n.p.** Relates the particulars surrounding the capture of eleven of Mr. B. M. Dell's Negroes by a party of Indians. 9 February 1837. p.3, c4.

7868 CHARLES DELL *to* **UNCLE. 8 January [1837]. Black Creek.** Reports on a party in pursuit of the Indians who captured Mr. B. M. Dell's Negroes. 9 February 1837. p.3, c4.

7869 JUSTIN PERKINS *to* **THE SABBATH SCHOOLS IN AMHERST AND AN-DOVER, MA. [from the *Sabbath School Visitor*] February 1835. Oormiah, Persia.** Comments on his travels in Persia, where he is a missionary. 9 February 1837. p.4, c3.

7870 A CITIZEN *to* **MR. EDITOR. [from the *Illinois Temperance Herald*] n.d. n.p.** Gives an account of a drunken brawl witnessed in Alton; informs of subsequent appeal for enforcement of temperance legislation. 9 February 1837. p.4, c4.

7871 TIMOTHY TURNER *to* **SIR. [from the *Illinois Temperance Herald*] 20 January 1837. Peoria.** A travelling temperance agent offers an account of his recent activities. 9 February 1837. p.4, c4.

7872 W. O. *to* **MR. EDITOR [ELIJAH P. LOVEJOY]. n.d. n.p.** Criticizes a lecture by a doctor of divinity who gave undue importance to the cause of home missions at the expense of the cause of foreign missions. 16 February 1837. p.1, c3.

7873 B. HARVEY *to* **BROTHER. [extract from the *United Brethren's Missionary Intelligencer*] 2 December 1836. St. John's, Antigua.** Reports that after four months of freedom in the West Indies, the emancipated slaves "continue to improve in character as an orderly and industrious people." 16 February 1837. p.3, c1.

7874 n.n. *to* **MR. HAWLEY. [from the Hampshire *Gazette*] n.d. n.p.** Suggests molasses as an effective remedy for whooping-cough. 16 February 1837. p.3, c1.

7875 n.n. *to* **MR. EDITOR [ELIJAH P. LOVEJOY]. n.d. n.p.** Comments on the wealth of both natural and human resources in Alton. 16 February 1837. p.3, c2.

7876 F. *to* **MR. LOVEJOY. n.d. n.p.** Criticizes William Smith, who advocated African colonization as a solution to slavery and a means of securing trade for the United States. 23 February 1837. p.1, c1.

7877 UNUS *to* **MESSRS. EDITORS. [from the *Western Christian Advocate*] n.d. n.p.** Refutes the contention that the use of tobacco is acceptable from the standpoint of biblical Christianity. 23 February 1837. p.2, c1.

7878 PETER PARKER *to* **THE SABBATH SCHOOL OF THE FIRST CHURCH IN HARTFORD. [extract] n.d. n.p.** Provides an account of the various practices associated with the Chinese New Year; appeals for persons to dedicate themselves to missionary work. 23 February 1837. p.2, c2.

7879 JOHN WESLEY *to* **n.n. 26 February 1791. London.** In the last letter written before his death, Wesley denounces American slavery as the "vilest that ever saw the sun," and bids his friend to persevere in the struggle against it. 23 February 1837. p.2, c3.

7880 n.n. *to* **SIR [ELIJAH P. LOVEJOY]. 16 January 1837. Missouri.** Relates news of his region of Missouri, noting the low ebb of Presbyterianism, the evil of Western settlers who are desirous of too much liberty and thus disregard the commands of God, and his own attempt to sustain a Sabbath school. 23 February 1837. p.3, c4.

7881 H. HAWLEY *to* **SIR. [from the** *Cultivator***] 10 October 1836. Alton.** Discusses the beneficial effects of producing beet sugar in America and the desirability of establishing agriculture as a distinct branch of learning in higher educational institutions. 23 February 1837. p.4, c1.

7882 n.n. *to* **n.n. [extract from the** *Christian Witness***] n.d. n.p.** Contrasts the moral, intellectual, and industrial achievements of South America and New England, concluding that the latter's vast superiority is attributable to its religious foundation on the Bible, as opposed to the popish tyranny prevalent in South America. 2 March 1837. p.1, c6.

7883 ANDREW JACKSON *to* **THE HON. J. C. CALHOUN. 7 February 1837. Washington.** Denies charges that he stands to profit personally from the passage of a bill currently before the Congress; bids Calhoun either to place these charges before the House of Representatives or to withdraw them. 2 March 1837. p.2, c3.

7884 n.n. *to* **BROTHER LOVEJOY. n.d. n.p.** Praises the land and people of Illinois. 2 March 1837. p.3, c1.

7885 L. *to* **MR. EDITOR [ELIJAH P. LOVEJOY]. n.d. n.p.** Defends the Protestant Episcopal church against the popular charge that it is simply a child of the Church of Rome. 2 March 1837. p.3, c2.

7886 E. JENNEY *to* **BROTHER LOVEJOY. 23 February 1837. Jacksonville.** Acknowledges the receipt of sums for the Foreign Missionary Society of the Valley of Mississippi. 2 March 1837. p.3, c3.

7887 E. JENNEY *to* **ELIJAH P. LOVEJOY. [extract] 23 February 1837. Jacksonville.** Reports favorable results of his preaching at Winchester. 2 March 1837. p.3, c3.

7888 n.n. *to* **MR. LOVEJOY. n.d. n.p.** Requests publication of two enclosed letters. 2 March 1837. p.3, c3.

7889 B. K. HART AND GEO. T. M. DAVIS *to* **H. HAWLEY, ESQ. 27 February 1837. Alton.** Offer thanks on behalf of the vestry and congregation of St. Paul's Church, Alton, for Hawley's donation of a lot for the purpose of building a church. 2 March 1837. p.3, c3.

7890 H. HAWLEY *to* **MESSRS. HART AND DAVIS, COM. 1 March 1837. Alton.** Expresses appreciation for their kind wishes, stipulating that a church should be erected in "a reasonable time, say within three years." 2 March 1837. p.3, c3.

7891 S. B. S. *to* **THE** *BUFFALO SPECTATOR***. [extract] 27 January 1837. Darien, N.Y.** Reports sixty souls converted to God as a result of recent preaching efforts. 2 March 1837. p.3, c4.

7892 E. M. BEEDE *to* **THE** *ZION'S HERALD***. [extract] 18 January [1837]. Ipswich.** Reports twelve conversions resulting from a series of meetings just ended. 2 March 1837. p.3, c4.

7893 ROBERT STEWART *to* **BROTHER [ELIJAH P. LOVEJOY]. 7 February 1837. Canton.** Reports the death of Nancy Hood. 2 March 1837. p.3, c5.

7894 n.n. *to* **THE** *NEW YORK DAILY EXPRESS.* **12 February [1837]. Washington.** Reports on the fight in the House of Representatives, led by J. Q. Adams, to recognize the right to petition slaves. 9 March 1837. p.2, c2.

7895 n.n. *to* **THE** *NEW YORK DAILY EXPRESS.* **14 February [1837]. Washington.** Comments on the appropriation bills before the House and Senate. 9 March 1837. p.2, c2.

7896 n.n. *to* **THE** *NEW YORK DAILY EXPRESS.* **16 February [1837]. Washington.** Reports congressional debate on a bill which would increase the size of the regular army and reorganize its staff. 9 March 1837. p.2, c2.

7897 AUREY BALLARD *to* **ELIJAH P. LOVEJOY. n.d. Iowa Mission, Northwest Missouri.** Discusses his missionary work among the Iowa tribe. 9 March 1837. p.2, c5.

7898 E. STRONG, W. SMITH, AND P. GOODRICH *to* **SIR [ELIJAH P. LOVEJOY]. 20 February 1837. Dupage.** Extend thanks, on behalf of the church in Dupage, to the Church of Christ in Cazenovia, New York, for its gift of church furniture. 9 March 1837. p.2, c5.

7899 A. O. *to* **MR. EDITOR [ELIJAH P. LOVEJOY]. n.d. n.p.** Laments the state of progress in the contemporary world, particularly the breakdown of authority in the family and the church, and the lack of respect shown to the older generation. 9 March 1837. p.2, c5.

7900 A FRIEND OF MISSIONS *to* **BRO. LOVEJOY. n.d. n.p.** Criticizes the judgement of correspondent "W.O.," who claimed that America has "rejected the offer of eternal life long enough to justify the church in turning from its inhabitants to another people who will hear and obey it." 9 March 1837. p.2, c6.

7901 C. *to* **MR. LOVEJOY. n.d. n.p.** Encloses for publication a letter from a friend, for the purpose of illustrating the delinquencies of mail contractors in the northern part of Illinois. 9 March 1837. p.3, c3.

7902 n.n. *to* **SIR. 3 February 1837. Pittsfield, Il.** States that his area has been without mail for five weeks, due to ice on the Illinois River. 9 March 1837. p.3, c3.

7903 WILLIAM SMITH *to* **THE EDITOR [ELIJAH P. LOVEJOY]. 28 February 1837. Lynnville, Morgan County, Il.** Responds to correspondent "F.," who maintained that Smith's scheme of African colonization was neither practical nor moral. 16 March 1837. p.1, c1.

7904 G. *to* **BROTHER LOVEJOY. 28 February 1837. Jacksonville.** Exhorts fellow Christians to take up the cause of Sabbath schools, with the recommendation that a depository of books be established at Alton. 16 March 1837. p.2, c4.

7905 A FRIEND OF MISSIONS *to* **BRO. LOVEJOY. n.d. n.p.** Refutes earlier letter of "W.O." which claimed that the peculiar sin of the primitive church was a neglect to preach the gospel to the Gentiles. 16 March 1837. p.2, c4.

7906 H. HAWLEY *to* **REV. CHARLES HOWARD. 4 March 1837. Alton.** Donates two lots for the construction of a church and a school. 16 March 1837. p.2, c6.

7907 TIMOTHY TURNER *to* **REV. F. W. GRAVES. [from the** *Illinois Temperance Herald*] **4 March 1837. n.p.** Encloses extracts from the journal of a travelling temperance agent. 16 March 1837. p.2, c6.

7908 T. L. *to* **MR. EDITOR [ELIJAH P. LOVEJOY]. n.d. n.p.** Comments on the necessity of Sabbath schools. 16 March 1837. p.4, c2.

7909 F. *to* **MR. LOVEJOY. n.d. n.p.** Denies the assertion that, in the event of emancipation, the Northern people are under a moral obligation to pay the Southern people for their slaves. 23 March 1837. p.1, c1.

7910 S. B. H. *to* **MR. EDITOR [ELIJAH P. LOVEJOY]. n.d. St. Charles, Mo.** Recommends, especially to youthful readers, *Pike's Persuasives to Early Piety.* 23 March 1837. p.1, c3.

7911 N. JONES *to* **SIR [ELIJAH P. LOVEJOY]. n.d. n.p.** In the first of an intended series of "thoughts on the faith once delivered to the saints," the author contends that the Christian should not use tobacco. 23 March 1837. p.1, c3.

7912 HOWARD *to* **BROTHER LOVEJOY. n.d. n.p.** Asserts that church members have an obligation to serve their Lord with their substance, as much as with their bodies and spirits. 23 March 1837. p.1, c4.

7913 L. *to* **MR. EDITOR [ELIJAH P. LOVEJOY]. n.d. n.p.** Gives a humorous delineation of the character of dyspepsia. 23 March 1837. p.3, c1.

7914 JUSTICE *to* **MR. LOVEJOY. 7 March 1837. Quincy.** Criticizes the common practice of taking wood from another person's land, which he believes is clearly an act of theft to be condemned by Christian people. 23 March 1837. p.3, c1.

7915 MOSES E. MORRELL *to* **SIR [ELIJAH P. LOVEJOY]. 4 February 1837. Texas Army, Headquarters, Camp Independence, on La Bacca River.** A soldier in the Texas army offers a sketch of the military situation in Texas, as well as his opinion of the country. 23 March 1837. p.3, c2.

7916 L. D. DEWEY *to* **MESSRS. EDITORS. [from the** *New York Observer***] n.d. n.p.** Requests publication of an enclosed notice regarding a $1,000 prize offered by the American Peace Society for an essay on a Congress of Nations; notice (signed by John Quincy Adams, James Kent and Daniel Webster) states that none of the essays submitted proved decidedly superior to the rest, and that a prize would not be awarded. 23 March 1837. p.3, c5.

7917 THE EDITOR OF THE *HERALD OF FREEDOM to* **THE CORRESPONDING SECRETARY OF THE AAS. 7 December 1836. St. Thomas, West Indies.** Describes St. Thomas: its topography, population, slavery, and free labor. 23 March 1837. p.4, c4.

7918 T. *to* **MR. LOVEJOY. n.d. n.p.** Argues that slaveholders are not entitled to compensation for their slaves in the event of emancipation. 30 March 1837. p.1, c2.

7919 N. JONES *to* **SIR [ELIJAH P. LOVEJOY]. [continued from 23 March 1837] n.d. n.p.** Contends that it is "the duty of all that use tobacco, to lay it totally aside, from the fact that they are so offensive to the temperate." 30 March 1837. p.1, c6.

7920 D. L. CHILD *to* **GEO. KIMBALL, ESQ. 9 January 1837. Arras.** Examines the manufacture and profitability of beet sugar. 30 March 1837. p.2, c1.

7921 n.n. *to* **MR. SMITH. [from the** *Cumberland Presbyterian***] n.d. n.p.** Discontinues his subscription to the paper. 30 March 1837. p.2, c5.

7922 n.n. *to* **REVT. SIR. [from the** *Lutheran Observer***] n.d. n.p.** Requests termination of his subscription. 30 March 1837. p.2, c5.

7923 n.n. *to* **ELIJAH P. LOVEJOY. [extract] 17 March 1837. Southern Missouri.** Praises Lovejoy and the *Observer*. 30 March 1837. p.2, c5.

7924 Y. *to* **REV. MR. EDITOR [ELIJAH P. LOVEJOY]. n.d. n.p.** Denies that after the conversion, one need do nothing more in regard to the cultivation of personal holiness. 30 March 1837. p.2, c6.

7925 n.n. *to* **n.n. [extract] 15 January 1837. Carthage, Hancock County, Il.** Complains of the poor mail delivery in the area, stating that he has received a letter which would have travelled at the rate of ten miles per day. 30 March 1837. p.3, c2.

7926 n.n. *to* **n.n. [extract] 1 March 1887 [*sic*]. Monmouth, Warren County, Il.** Writes in order to illustrate the poor mail delivery in the area, stating that Monmouth has just received mail for the first time in four weeks. 30 March 1837. p.3, c2.

7927 P. *to* **F. W. GRAVES. [from the *Illinois Temperance Herald*] 9 February 1837. Jacksonville.** Demonstrates the consequences of selling ardent spirits to others by relating the story of a gentleman who almost received a beating from his drunken son, intoxicated by rum bought at his father's store. 30 March 1837. p.4, c3.

7928 n.n. *to* **REV. MR. LOVEJOY. n.d. n.p.** Compares American slavery with that of the commonwealth of Israel and the Roman empire; questions whether the commands and duties of masters and servants proscribed in the Old and New Testaments are applicable to Americans in the present age. 6 April 1837. p.2, c4.

7929 n.n. *to* **BRO. LEAVITT. 15 March 1837. Philadelphia.** Reports many conversions as the result of a protracted meeting in progress at the Rev. James Patterson's church. 6 April 1837. p.2, c5.

7930 n.n. *to* **THE *BUFFALO SPECTATOR*. [extract] 27 January 1837. Darien, N.Y.** Reports sixty conversions as the result of a preaching mission by Brother Judson of Stafford. 6 April 1837. p.2, c5.

7931 J. PEARSALL *to* **MESSRS. EDITORS. [from the *Christian Advocate and Journal*] 2 February 1837. Tyrone, N.Y.** Reports over 100 conversions at a revival in Wayne, Steuben County, N.Y. 6 April 1837. p.2, c5.

7932 M. *to* **MR. EDITOR [ELIJAH P. LOVEJOY]. n.d. n.p.** Discusses the late Mr. Samuel Gooch, of whom it is said, "He was all that he professed to be"; admonishes professors of religion to be all that they profess to be. 6 April 1837. p.3, c2.

7933 REV. MR. JANSEN *to* **THE *PROVIDENCE HERALD*. n.d. Chepachet, R.I.** Reports that a four-year-old boy died as a result of drinking rum which his father had purchased for his own use. 6 April 1837. p.4, c3.

7934 A SLAVEHOLDER *to* **THE EDITOR OF THE *CHARLESTON OBSERVER*. n.d. n.p.** Asserts that the evil of dram shops will not be cured by refusing to grant licenses to those guilty of irregularities, but rather by granting no licenses at all. 6 April 1837. p.4, c3.

7935 AN AMERICAN *to* **THE *ALTON OBSERVER*. n.d. n.p.** Refutes an earlier letter by "T," which claimed that a slaveholder is not entitled by moral right to financial compensation in the event of emancipation. 13 April 1837. p.1, c1.

7936 W. O. *to* **A FRIEND OF MISSIONS. n.d. n.p.** Replies to articles in the *Observer* which criticized his views on home and foreign missions. 13 April 1837. p.1, c3.

7937 NEHEMIAH WEST *to* **BROTHER LOVEJOY. 28 March 1837. Knoxville.** Encloses for publication a letter from Dr. Grant, a missionary in Persia, to his son. 13 April 1837. p.2, c5.

7938 A. GRANT *to* **HASTINGS [GRANT]. 26 June 1836. Oormiah, Persia.** Describes conditions in Persia, where he is a missionary. 13 April 1837. p.2, c6.

7939 DR. HUMPHREY *to* **n.n. [extract from the** *New York Observer***] n.d. n.p.** Discusses the various Protestant sects in Ireland. 13 April 1837. p.3, c3.

7940 n.n. *to* **n.n. [extract from the** *Charleston Observer***] 7 February 1837. Washington, Arkansas.** Reports that a Presbyterian church has been organized at Spring Hill and is the only one within 150 miles. 13 April 1837. p.3, c3.

7941 THE REV. EZRA KELLER *to* **n.n. [extract from the** *Lutheran Observer***] n.d. n.p.** Reports on the condition of Germans in Beardstown, Illinois; notes that the church is not so well attended as the game field, and that many profane the Sabbath by working. 13 April 1837. p.3, c3.

7942 GEO. C. WOOD *to* **BROTHER LOVEJOY. 17 April 1837. Paris.** Encloses for publication the minutes of a recent meeting of the Presbytery of St. Charles. 4 May 1837. p.1, c1.

7943 HYPO-DORIAN *to* **MR. EDITOR [ELIJAH P. LOVEJOY]. n.d. n.p.** Introduces twelve wide-ranging theses concerning civil and religious matters. 4 May 1837. p.1, c1.

7944 N. JONES *to* **SIR [ELIJAH P. LOVEJOY]. n.d. n.p.** Continues his remarks on tobacco; seeks to show some of the evil effects which this practice has on different communities. 4 May 1837. p.1, c2.

7945 n.n. *to* **n.n. [extract] n.d. n.p.** A minister in a slave state condemns the institution of slavery as a "national degradation," but hesitates to call for absolute and immediate emancipation. 4 May 1837. p.2, c3.

7946 SPENCER MERRILL *to* **THE EDITOR OF THE** *ALTON OBSERVER* **[ELIJAH P. LOVEJOY]. 22 April 1837. Petersburg, Il.** Requests cancellation of his subscription after having received his first copy of the *Observer*. 4 May 1837. p.2, c3.

7947 J. S. *to* **BROTHER [ELIJAH P. LOVEJOY]. 15 April 1837. Quincy, Adams Co., Il.** Describes the town of Quincy, including its location, business establishments, churches, and mission institute. 4 May 1837. p.2, c4.

7948 E. B. P. *to* **SIR [ELIJAH P. LOVEJOY]. 29 April [1837]. Upper Alton.** Announces a Sunday school jubilee on the second Sunday of May; encloses particulars of the event; requests publication of the hymns that will be sung there. 4 May 1837. p.2, c5.

7949 THE COUNCIL OF THE PARISH OF GABERELE *to* **LOUIS PHILLIPPE. 10 January 1837. Ergue Gaberle.** Addresses the King of France, stating that the year 1836 was unfortunate both for him and for Ergue Gaberle; hopes for a better year to come. 4 May 1837. p.3, c4.

7950 TIMOTHY TURNER *to* **THE EXECUTIVE COMMITTEE OF THE ILLINOIS STATE TEMPERANCE SOCIETY. [from the** *Illinois Temperance Herald***] n.d. n.p.** Reports on his labors for the cause of temperance in Illinois. 4 May 1837. p.4, c3.

7951 F. *to* **MR. LOVEJOY. n.d. n.p.** Claims that his remarks were distorted in an earlier communication to the *Observer* from "An American"; seeks to demonstrate that the founding fathers were opposed to slavery; reasserts his claim that the South is not morally entitled to pecuniary compensation in the event of emancipation. 11 May 1837. p.1, c1.

7952 n.n. *to* **n.n. [extract from the** *Liberator***] n.d. n.p.** Warns colored citizens to beware of slaveholding ministers from the South who will be in Northern cities for anniversary meetings and might seek to kidnap colored citizens to sell in the South. 11 May 1837. p.2, c3.

7953 REV. W. H. NORRIS *to* **THE** *CHRISTIAN ADVOCATE AND JOURNAL***. [extract] n.d. n.p.** Reports a growing interest in the doctrine of evangelical holiness among Methodists in Maine; considers this interest to be an encouraging sign. 11 May 1837. p.2, c5.

7954 STEAMBOAT *MADISON to* **n.n. [extract] 24 April 1837. New Orleans.** Reports to a commercial house in Illinois that commerce has stopped suddenly in New Orleans and that the West will feel the economic effects. 11 May 1837. p.3, c1.

7955 A MISSISSIPPIAN *to* **MR. EDITOR. [from the** *Cold Water Man***] n.d. n.p.** Reports on two new towns in Mississippi, Sharon and Claibournville, both founded on the principle of total abstinence. 11 May 1837. p.4, c2.

7956 AN AMERICAN *to* **F. n.d. n.p.** Responds to F.'s communication in the 27 April *Observer*; refutes F.'s method of argument, his proposition concerning the principle of law by which land is held, his proposition regarding tariffs, and his contention that the South would not be entitled to pecuniary compensation in the event of emancipation. 18 May 1837. p.1, c1.

7957 C. A. F. *to* **BROTHER. [from the** *Western Messenger***] 3 April 1837. Alton, Il.** Gives an account of a revival held the preceding February; pays special attention to a riotous meeting at the Methodist church. 18 May 1837. p.1, c5.

7958 n.n. *to* **n.n. [extract from the** *Baltimore Patriot***] n.d. Washington.** Reports on a newly invented telegraph system. 18 May 1837. p.1, c6.

7959 GEORGE CHURCHILL *to* **REV. E. P. LOVEJOY. 13 May 1837. Ridge Prairie, Il.** The postmaster explains why an issue of the *Observer* failed to reach the Ridge Prairie post office. 18 May 1837. p.2, c3.

7960 n.n. *to* **n.n. [extract from the** *New York Observer***] n.d. n.p.** Discusses the sale of bound volumes of the American Tract Society, which has reached a total of some 43,500. 18 May 1837. p.2, c4.

7961 C. L. WATSON *to* **BROTHER LOVEJOY. 4 May 1837. Bloomington, Il.** Corrects errors in an obituary published in a previous issue of the *Observer*. 18 May 1837. p.2, c4.

7962 AN AMERICAN *to* **F. n.d. n.p.** Responds to F's letter in the 11 May *Observer*; challenges his assertions about the Northern delegates who ratified the Constitution, and his interpretation of Northern sentiment regarding the slave trade. 18 May 1837. p.2, c5.

7963 B. *to* **THE EDITOR OF THE** *ALTON OBSERVER* **[ELIJAH P. LOVEJOY]. n.d. n.p.** Defends the General Assembly of the Presbyterian Church and the General Conference of the Methodist Episcopal Church against derogatory statements made by a writer in a previous issue of the *Observer*. 18 May 1837. p.2, c6.

7964 NATHAN WILD *to* **MR. COOKE. [from the** *Silk Grower and Agriculturalist***] 20 March 1837. Chesterfield.** Reports on his experimentation in the cultivation of potatoes. 18 May 1837. p.4, c1.

7965 W. O. *to* **MR. EDITOR [ELIJAH P. LOVEJOY]. n.d. n.p.** Compares and contrasts slavery in ancient Egypt with slavery in the United States. 25 May 1837. p.1, c1.

7966 BENEVOLENS *to* **MESSRS. EDITORS. [from the** *New York Observer***] n.d. n.p.** Addresses questions to those who will speak at forthcoming anniversary meetings concerning the decline of benevolent causes in contemporary society. 25 May 1837. p.2, c2.

7967 INQUIRER *to* **BRO. LOVEJOY. n.d. n.p.** Discusses theological education and the amount of time involved in preparing for the ministry. 25 May 1837. p.2, c5.

7968 M. VAN BUREN *to* **MESSRS. ISAAC S. HONE, JAS. W. BRYAN, BENJ. LODER, ELEX. B. McALPIN, JOHN A. UNDERWOOD, THOMAS TILESTON, MEIGS D. BENJAMIN, ELISHA LEWIS, AND SIMEON DRAPER, JR. 4 May 1837. Washington.** The president of the United States responds to a written document by a committee of merchants established for the purpose of representing the commercial distress of New York City and the United States and to request repeal of the treasury circular. 25 May 1837. p.3, c2.

7969 F. *to* **MR. LOVEJOY. n.d. n.p.** Continues debate with "An American"; discusses principles upon which man's duty and government are to be founded; concludes that the slaveholder is not entitled by moral right to compensation in the event of emancipation. 1 June 1837. p.1, c1.

7970 ANTI TOBACCO *to* **MR. EDITOR. [from the** *Pittsburgh Christian Herald***] n.d. n.p.** Laments that the use of tobacco was not discussed at a recent meeting of the Total Abstinence Society. 1 June 1837. p.1, c4.

7971 H. C. WRIGHT *to* **BROTHER. [from the** *Liberator***] 10 May 1837. New York.** Reports on the fourth anniversary meeting of the AAS. 1 June 1837. p.2, c1.

7972 HORATIO NEWHALL, A. B. CAMPBELL, JEREMIAH BETTES *to* **THE COR. SEC. OF THE A. H. M. S. [from the** *Home Missionary***] 18 March 1837. Galena, Il.** Inform the American Home Mission Society that the First Presbyterian Church in Galena has voted in favor of a resolution stating that they can and ought to support their own minister; assert that they no longer need the assistance of the society. 1 June 1837. p.2, c2.

7973 D. NELSON *to* **BROTHER LOVEJOY. 25 May 1837. Mission Institute, Il.** Responds to various inquiries about the Mission Institute. 1 June 1837. p.2, c4.

7974 INQUIRER *to* **BROTHER LOVEJOY. n.d. n.p.** Argues that men are not deterred from the ministry by the proscribed course of study so much as by the "fastidiousness and love of novelty" in the churches. 2 June 1837. p.2, c5.

7975 J. N. PIGGOTT *to* **SIR [ELIJAH P. LOVEJOY]. 8 May 1837. Newbern, Greene County.** At the request of the coroner, transmits the description of an unidentified corpse found near the town of Grafton. 1 June 1837. p.3, c1.

7976 n.n. *to* **n.n. [extract] 25 April 1837. New Orleans.** Writes to his brother in New York about the deplorable conditions in Texas, where there are scarce provisions and exorbitant prices. 1 June 1837. p.3, c3.

7977 A. B. *to* **MR. EDITOR [ELIJAH P. LOVEJOY]. 24 May [1837]. Lynville, Morgan Co., Il.** Denounces slavery for injuring society by violating man's inherent right to liberty and equality. 8 June 1837. p.1, c1.

7978 INQUIRER *to* **BRO. LOVEJOY. n.d. n.p.** Discusses the influences that deter individuals from entering the ministry; emphasizes the temptation to worldliness. 8 June 1837. p.1, c3.

7979 GERRIT SMITH *to* **MR. EDITOR. [from the** *New York Evangelist***] n.d. n.p.** Encloses for publication a letter he wrote to Edward C. Delavan and Mr. Delavan's response. 8 June 1837. p.1, c4.

7980 GERRIT SMITH *to* **EDWARD C. DELAVAN. 10 April 1837. Peterboro.** Seeks to enroll Delavan as a member of the AAS. 8 June 1837. p.1, c4.

7981 EDWARD C. DELAVAN *to* **FRIEND [GERRIT SMITH]. 10 May 1837. Ballston Centre, Saratoga County. N.Y.** Responds to Smith's effort to enroll him in the AAS, announcing that he has already joined. 8 June 1837. p.1, c6.

7982 J. TUCKER *to* **BRO. CUMMINGS. [from the** *Christian Mirror***] 12 April 1837. Bingham.** Reports the opening of a new church in Bingham. 8 June 1837. p.2, c1.

7983 n.n. *to* **[ELIJAH P. LOVEJOY]. [extract] n.d. Missouri.** Advocates the establishment of separate churches for those who favor slavery and those who oppose it. 8 June 1837. p.2, c3.

7984 JOHN GREEN *to* **SIR. [from the** *Cincinnati Journal and Luminary***] 1 March 1836. Lincoln, Ky.** States that the consensus in Kentucky is that abolition has hurt the cause of gradual emancipation. 8 June 1837. p.2, c3.

7985 F. W. GRAVES *to* **BROTHER [ELIJAH P. LOVEJOY]. 12 May 1837. New York.** Describes his mood at the close of a week of anniversary meetings; feels both joyful and melancholy; notes that many active friends of certain benevolent institutions have fallen away. 8 June 1837. p.2, c5.

7986 F. W. GRAVES *to* **BROTHER [ELIJAH P. LOVEJOY]. 16 May 1837. Philadelphia.** Reports on the opening session of the General Assembly of the Presbyterian Church in Philadelphia. 8 June 1837. p.2, c5.

7987 F. *to* **MR. LOVEJOY. n.d. n.p.** Summarizes his argument with "An American"; responds to his opponent's letter in the 18 May issue. 15 June 1837. p.1, c1.

7988 FRIEND OF HUMAN RIGHTS *to* **MR. EDITOR [ELIJAH P. LOVEJOY]. n.d. Missouri.** Encloses a 1687 speech by Sidi Mahomet Ibrahim, a member of the divan of Algiers, opposing a petition by the sect called Erika, or Purists, who advocated the abolition of piracy and slavery; quotes Dr. Franklin as saying that this speech shows "that men's interests operate . . . with surprising similarity in all ages and countries, whenever they are under similar circumstances." 15 June 1837. p.1, c3.

7989 n.n. *to* **n.n. [extract from the** *Palmyra* **(Mo.)** *Examiner***] n.d. n.p.** Threatens violence to Lovejoy and Dr. Nelson in the event that either should visit Marion County, Missouri. 15 June 1837. p.2, c3.

7990 INQUIRER *to* **BRO. LOVEJOY. n.d. n.p.** Argues that instead of devising a new and speedier method of educating ministers, the Church should make better use of its existing manpower, much of which is wasted due to unnecessary denominational divisions. 15 June 1837. p.2, c3.

7991 E. H. PHELPS *to* **SIR [ELIJAH P. LOVEJOY]. 31 May 1837. Princeton, Il.** The secretary of the Princeton AS encloses for publication the proceedings of a recent meeting of that organization. 15 June 1837. p.2, c6.

7992 n.n. *to* **BRO. LOVEJOY. 1 June 1837. Whitehall, Green County.** Describes a method for keeping apple trees free of worms. 15 June 1837. p.2, c6.

7993 FRANCIS ASBURY *to* **FRIENDS. 14 September 1836. Madura.** A native of India writes to American Sunday school children about his country's pagan religious practices; appeals to them to live Christian lives. 15 June 1837. p.4, c3.

7994 AN AMERICAN *to* **F. n.d. n.p.** Reflects on their debate thus far, defends himself against charges of employing "error, sophistry, and deceit," and maintains that immediate emancipation, with no financial compensation to the slave states, is unjust. 22 June 1837. p.1, c1.

7995 n.n. *to* **n.n. [extract from the *Journal of Commerce*] 10 May 1837. Natchez.** A gentleman in Mississippi writes to his friend in Washington about a steamboat disaster; notes that among approximately 300 passengers, about fifty survived, one of whom was the author. 22 June 1837. p.1, c5.

7996 WILLIAM KINNEY, M. McCONNEL, ELIJAH WILLARD, M. K. ALEX-ANDER, J. WRIGHT, AND E. PECK *to* **JOSEPH DUNCAN. 5 June 1837. Vandalia, Illinois.** Forward the semi-annual report of the Board of Public Works to the governor of Illinois. 22 June 1837. p.2, c1.

7997 n.n. *to* **n.n. 31 May [1837]. Philadelphia.** A correspondent of the *New York Observer* reports on the proceedings of the General Assembly of the Presbyterian Church in Philadelphia, where "It has become obvious to all that the Presbyterian Church is in fact two bodies; the only perplexity is, how to get them apart." 22 June 1837. p.2, c3.

7998 E. S. *to* **MR. EDITOR [ELIJAH P. LOVEJOY]. 24 May 1837. Desplain.** Discusses the problem of reconciling the discipline in the Presbyterian church with the words of Christ in Matthew 18:15–18. 22 June 1837. p.2, c4.

7999 LEVI HILLS *to* **MR. LOVEJOY. 5 June 1837. Lisbon, LaSalle County, Il.** The postmaster at Lisbon advises Lovejoy of the irregularity of the arrival of the *Alton Observer* at his office. 22 June 1837. p.2, c4.

8000 INQUIRER *to* **BRO. LOVEJOY. n.d. n.p.** Warns, once again, against lowering intellectual standards in order to increase the number of ministers; reminds readers of the many valuable services laymen can perform. 22 June 1837. p.2, c6.

8001 n.n. *to* **SIR [ELIJAH P. LOVEJOY]. [extract] 14 June 1837. Griggsville.** Requests that his name be entered on the *Observer*'s subscription list. 22 June 1837. p.3, c1.

8002 J. *to* **MR. LOVEJOY. n.d. n.p.** Asserts the duty of Sabbath school superintendents to visit the families of children under their care and the duty of teachers to pray with their classes. 22 June 1837. p.3, c1.

8003 n.n. *to* **THE EDITOR OF THE *CHARLESTON OBSERVER*. [extract] 15 May 1837. Selma, Al.** Reports that the churches in the area are "languishing under the withering influence of the mammon of unrighteousness." 22 June 1837. p.3, c1.

8004 A SUBSCRIBER *to* **SIR [ELIJAH P. LOVEJOY]. n.d. n.p.** Submits for publication a poem on the subject of slavery written by the Rev. Charles Wilcox. 22 June 1837. p.4, c1.

8005 W. E. C. *to* **BROTHER LOVEJOY. 14 June 1837. Alton.** Submits for publication a poem written by himself on the subject of keeping the Sabbath. 22 June 1837. p.4, c1.

8006 n.n. *to* **n.n. [extract from the** *Journal of Commerce***] 13 May 1837. Jamaica.** Laments the system of overtrading and wild speculation in America; reports basic economic stability in Jamaica. 22 June 1837. p.4, c1.

8007 C. W. P. *to* **n.n. n.d. n.p.** Upholds the obligation of ministers to devote themselves wholly to the duties of their office, to live by the pecuniary support of their congregations, and to remain free of secular vocations. 22 June 1837. p.2, c5.

8008 C. W. P. *to* **BRO. LOVEJOY. n.d. n.p.** States that ministers of the gospel are not objects of charity and ought not to be treated as such by their congregations; asserts that they are talented men performing vital services. 29 June 1837. p.1, c1.

8009 n.n. *to* **n.n. [extract] n.d. Buffalo.** Reports that many revivals are being held near Buffalo. 29 June 1837. p.2, c1.

8010 n.n. *to* **the** *CINCINNATI JOURNAL AND LUMINARY.* **6 June [1837]. Philadelphia.** Reports on the proceedings of the General Assembly of the Presbyterian Church, notably a speech by W. S. Plummer which displeased the audience. 29 June 1837. p.2, c2.

8011 n.n. *to* **THE** *CINCINNATI JOURNAL AND LUMINARY.* **n.d. n.p.** Observes the extent of Southern control over debate at the Presbyterian General Assembly. 29 June 1837. p.2, c2.

8012 JOS. M. SADD *to* **THE** *ALTON OBSERVER.* **n.d. n.p.** Explains, in response to his dismissal from the St. Louis Presbytery, why he has had no direct communication with that body in the past two years. 29 June 1837. p.2, c4.

8013 MARY A. C. RIGGS *to* **MRS. GILMAN. 10 June 1837. Lake Harriet.** Gives an account of her journey from Alton to the mission station at Lake Harriet. 29 June 1837. p.2, c5.

8014 N. GOULD *to* **BRO. LOVEJOY. n.d. n.p.** Discusses the potential split in the General Assembly of the Presbyterian Church and the problem of dividing church property in that event; proposes that individual churches make their own division of property. 29 June 1837. p.3, c2.

8015 NO TREE *to* **BROTHER MANLY. [from the** *Southern Watchman***] n.d. n.p.** Refers to "sappy religion" which "in the winter runs down the tree and the top dies; but when spring comes, it runs up again, and the whole tree is lively." 29 June 1837. p.4, c4.

8016 C. W. P. *to* **n.n. n.d. n.p. [continued from 29 June 1837].** Stresses the duty of a congregation to pay its minister punctually. 6 July 1837. p.1, c1.

8017 N. GOULD *to* **MR. EDITOR [ELIJAH P. LOVEJOY]. n.d. n.p.** Criticizes tobacco chewers at the recent General Assembly of the Presbyterian Church at Philadelphia. 6 July 1837. p.1, c2.

8018 n.n. *to* **MR. EDITOR [ELIJAH P. LOVEJOY]. 1837. Winchester, Morgan County, Il.** Describes at length the town of Winchester. 6 July 1837. p.1, c2.

8019 W. SMITH *to* **ELIJAH P. LOVEJOY. [extract] 14 June 1837. n.p.** Reports on a protracted but successful meeting in his parish; offers thanks to God for the beneficial results obtained. 6 July 1837. p.2, c2.

8020 A. P. B. *to* **THE FRIENDS OF EQUITY IN THE PRESBYTERIAN CHURCH. n.d. n.p.** Discusses the division in the Presbyterian church, entreating the "new school" presbyteries and synods not to withdraw from the General Assembly, but rather to send full delegations to the next assembly and "try once more for justice." 6 July 1837. p.2, c4.

8021 DAVID NELSON *to* **THE PRESBYTERIAN MINISTERS OF TENNESSEE, KENTUCKY, AND MISSOURI. 20 June 1837. Mission Institute.** Forwards nine points of general advice to ministers. 6 July 1837. p.2, c4.

8022 S. P. *to* **MR. LOVEJOY. 11 June 1837. Griggsville, Il.** Describes the town of Griggsville; upholds Lovejoy's stand against slavery and for freedom of opinion. 6 July 1837. p.2, c5.

8023 THE REV. JOHN P. LANNEAU *to* **n.n. n.d. n.p.** Reports on the effects of an earthquake which took place in Syria on 1 January 1837. 6 July 1837. p.3, c3.

8024 F. *to* **MR. LOVEJOY. n.d. n.p.** Considers the moral character of slaveholding in light of what he defines as the first principles of God's government. 13 July 1837. p.1, c1.

8025 WILLARD KEYES *to* **BRO. LOVEJOY. 26 June 1837. Quincy, Il.** Encloses for publication an abstract from the records of a meeting of the Adams County AS. 13 July 1837. p.1, c3.

8026 C. W. P. *to* **n.n. n.d. n.p.** Attacks the apathy of professed Christians who fail to contribute their share to the cause of Christ's kingdom. 13 July 1837. p.1, c4.

8027 MR. HOMES *to* **n.n. [extract from the** *Missionary Herald***] 29 December 1836. Constantinople.** Comments on the morality and temperance of the Moslems of Broosa. 13 July 1837. p.1, c5.

8028 JOHN EDGAR *to* **REV. JOSHUA LEAVITT. [from the** *New York Evangelist***] 18 May 1837. Belfast.** Forwards a letter from himself to the members of American churches. 13 July 1837. p.1, c6.

8029 JOHN EDGAR *to* **THE MEMBERS OF AMERICAN CHURCHES. [from the** *New York Evangelist***] n.d. n.p.** Admonishes American Christians to work for emancipation. 13 July 1837. p.1, c6.

8030 LYMAN BEECHER *to* **MR. McKNIGHT. [from the** *Philadelphia Observer***] 29 May 1837. Cincinnati.** Claims misrepresentation in a story published in the *Philadelphia Presbyterian* concerning an alleged conversation between Beecher and Mr. Musgrave of Philadelphia. 13 July 1837. p.2, c1.

8031 A CITIZEN OF MISSOURI *to* **MR. EDITOR [ELIJAH P. LOVEJOY]. 28 June 1837. Southern Missouri.** Praises the terrain and the people of Southern Missouri; finds slavery the only distasteful aspect of the area; urges emigrants from the free states to settle in Missouri. 13 July 1837. p.2, c4.

8032 A SUBSCRIBER *to* **SIR [ELIJAH P. LOVEJOY]. n.d. n.p.** Poses questions concerning the Christian millennium, which the author believes to be only thirty-five years away. 13 July 1837. p.2, c6.

8033 TEMPERANCE *to* **MR. EDITOR [ELIJAH P. LOVEJOY]. n.d. n.p.** Describes the Fourth of July celebration in Upper Alton, which was "in a sober, rational, and patriotic manner; no intoxication . . . befalling those who partook in the festivities of the day." 13 July 1837. p.2, c6.

8034 SAMUEL H. DAVIS *to* **THE EDITOR OF THE** *ST. LOUIS COMMERCIAL BULLETIN.* **4 July 1837. Catteese.** The editor of the *Peoria Register* and *Northwestern Gazetteer* reports hostile feelings among the Sac and Fox Indians on the Ioway due to the government's failure to provide them with the horses promised in the Ioway Treaty of 1836. 13 July 1837. p.3, c3.

8035 MARTHA DUDLEY *to* **MR. WELD. 27 March 1837. New York Asylum.** A former Matron of the American Asylum recalls certain experiences with Julia Brace, a deaf, dumb, and blind student at the asylum who possessed remarkable talents. 13 July 1837. p.4, c5.

8036 AN AMERICAN *to* **F. n.d. n.p.** Asserts, once again, that the South should not be left to bear the economic burden of emancipation without help since the North has shared in the sin of slavery and profited from it. 20 July 1837. p.1, c1.

8037 DAVID NELSON *to* **BRO. LOVEJOY. 1 July 1837. Mission Institute.** Accuses Lovejoy of printing only half the story in a recent account of a revival and of reporting the conversions without the news of wisepsread apostasy in the region. 20 July 1837. p.1, c3.

8038 I. J. ROBERTS *to* **MR. EDITOR [ELIJAH P. LOVEJOY]. 17 February 1837. Batavia, Java.** A misssionary conveys his impressions of China following his first month there. 20 July 1837. p.1, c4.

8039 JOSEPH DUNCAN *to* **THE SENATE AND HOUSE OF REPRESENTATIVES [OF ILLINOIS]. 11 July 1837. Vandalia, [Il.].** The governor of Illinois addresses the state legislature regarding the economic problem resulting from the instability of American currency. 20 July 1837. p.2, c1.

8040 n.n. *to* **the** *ALTON OBSERVER.* **[extract] n.d. n.p.** Expresses enthusiastic support for the proposed anti-slavery convention. 20 July 1837. p.2, c5.

8041 n.n. *to* **THE** *ALTON OBSERVER.* **[extract] n.d. n.p.** Displays confidence in the success of an anti-slavery convention. 20 July 1837. p.2, c5.

8042 n.n. *to* **THE** *ALTON OBSERVER.* **[extract] n.d. n.p.** Calls for an anti-slavery convention, preferably in Jacksonville. 20 July 1837. p.2, c5.

8043 n.n. *to* **ELIJAH P. LOVEJOY. n.d. Vermillionville.** Comments on the late arrival of the *Observer* at Vermillionville. 20 July 1837. p.2, c6.

8044 T. GALT *to* **BROTHER LOVEJOY. n.d. n.p.** Reports on various measures adopted at the recent General Assembly of the Presbyterian Church. 20 July 1837. p.3, c2.

8045 AN EXPUNGED PRESBYTERIAN *to* **MR. EDITOR [from the** *Ohio Observer***] n.d. n.p.** Suggests a meeting of all Presbyterian synods expelled by the previous General Assembly. 20 July 1837. p.3, c3.

8046 STEPHEN R. RIGGS *to* **BRO. COREY. [from the** *Illinois Temperance Herald***] 2 June 1837. Fort Snelling.** A missionary relates the effects of intemperance in his area, particularly among the Indians. 20 July 1837. p.4, c2.

8047 n.n. *to* **n.n. [from the** *U. S. Gazette***] March 1837. London.** Describes docks and other monuments to commerce in London. 20 July 1837. p.4, c3.

8048 J. *to* **MR. LOVEJOY. n.d. n.p.** Examines the current division within the Presbyterian church; inquires into the first principles of church order. 27 July 1837. p.1, c1.

8049 E. *to* **MR. EDITOR. 1 July 1837. Missouri.** Criticizes the common practice, when preaching the gospel, of emphasizing human evil to an extraordinary degree. 27 July 1837. p.1, c2.

8050 WILLARD KEYES *to* **BRO. LOVEJOY. 17 July 1837. Quincy.** Forwards for publication the proceedings of a meeting of the Adams County AS. 27 July 1837. p.1, c3.

8051 H. *to* **BROTHER LEAVITT. [from the** *New York Evangelist***] 30 June 1837. Portland, Me.** Reports on the anniversary meeting of the General [Methodist] Conference of Maine. 27 July 1837. p.1, c5.

8052 MR. BROWN *to* **n.n. [extract from the** *Baptist Magazine***] 23 June 1836. Burmah.** Rejoices to learn that a certain Mr. Bruce has ceased to sell ardent spirits; criticizes the common practice in India of securing the goodwill of native leaders through gifts of intoxicants. 27 July 1837. p.2, c1.

8053 MR. BROWN *to* **n.n. [extract from the** *Baptist Magazine***] 2 July 1836. Burmah.** A Baptist missionary writes of the discovery of excellent places where tea might be cultivated; describes a good location for a mission. 27 July 1837. p.2, c1.

8054 MR. BROWN *to* **n.n. [extract from the** *Baptist Magazine***] 11 July 1836. Burmah.** Describes a painful death resulting from opium addiction. 27 July 1837. p.2, c1.

8055 MR. BROWN *to* **n.n. [extract from the** *Baptist Magazine***] n.d. Burmah.** Proposes that Christian names be given to the natives who are beneficiaries of Friends in America. 27 July 1837. p.2, c1.

8056 ELIAS BOND *to* **BROTHER [ELIJAH P. LOVEJOY]. 28 June 1837. Hallowell, Me.** Anticipates the eventual triumph of the anti-slavery cause in the Church of Christ; discloses the scandalous example of a slaveholding minister; reports on the anniversary meeting of the Maine Methodist Conference. 27 July 1837. p.2, c4.

8057 W. K. *to* **BRO. LOVEJOY. 17 July 1837. Quincy.** Encloses a contribution to the American Board of Commissioners for Foreign Missions. 27 July 1837. p.2, c5.

8058 A. HALE *to* **BRO. LOVEJOY. 18 July 1837. Jacksonville.** Echoes an appeal for immediate contributions in behalf of the Home Missionary Society. 27 July 1837. p.2, c5.

8059 P. *to* **BRO. LOVEJOY. n.d. n.p.** Proposes, as a solution to the current division in the Presbyterian church, that the "new school" Presbyterians break away from the "ultras" and form their own association. 27 July 1837. p.2, c6.

8060 n.n. *to* **MR. EDITOR [ELIJAH P. LOVEJOY]. July 1837. Carlinville.** Describes the journey from Alton to Carlinville and Pleasant Grove. 27 January 1837. p.2, c6.

8061 A. KENT *to* **BROTHER [ELIJAH P. LOVEJOY]. 13 July 1837. Galena.** The captain of the *Olive Branch* expresses regret that the vessel travelled on the Sabbath; explains that the incident occurred in his absence. 27 July 1837. p.2, c6.

8062 W. *to* **MR. EDITOR [ELIJAH P. LOVEJOY]. n.d. n.p.** Praises the "Mansion House" in Alton for its comfortable accommodations and temperance principles. 27 July 1837. p.3, c1.

8063 CHARLES GUTZLAFF *to* **THE PRESIDENT OF THE ROBERTS' FUND AND CHINA MISSION SOCIETY OF THE MISSISSIPPI VALLEY. March 1837. Macao.** Expresses gratitude upon being made a member of the newly formed organization; refers to his long-standing desire to see a mission society formed expressly to aid China. 27 July 1837. p.3, c2.

8064 GIDEON B. SMITH *to* **THE EDITOR OF THE** *GENNESSEE FARMER.* **n.d. n.p.** Advises on the establishment of a mulberry orchard. 27 July 1837. p.4, c2.

8065 A PATRON *to* **THE EDITOR OF THE** *NEW ENGLAND FARMER.* **n.d. n.p.** Requests information on how to kill lice on a horse. 27 July 1837. p.4, c2.

8066 DR. WOODS *to* **REV. G. N. JUDD [extract] n.d. n.p.** Denies that he gave counsel in favor of the action which expelled four synods at the last General Assembly of the Presbyterian Church. 10 August 1837. p.2, c2.

8067 J. HEDRICK *to* **ELIJAH P. LOVEJOY. [extract] n.d. Burlington, Wisconsin Territory.** Cancels his subscription to the *Observer*; denies the existence of hell. 10 August 1837. p.2, c2.

8068 F. W. GRAVES *to* **BROTHER [ELIJAH P. LOVEJOY]. 19 July 1837. Painted Post, N. Y.** Expresses his desire to be back home in Illinois; remarks upon the beauty of New England and New York; announces his intention to attend the Auburn convention of synods and Presbyterians expelled from the late Presbyterian General Assembly. 10 August 1837. p.2, c6.

8069 n.n. *to* **MR. LOVEJOY. 1837. Putnam County, Il.** Laments the theft of land from the Indians; praises the beauty of Peoria; describes his journey to Princeton. 10 August 1837. p.3, c1.

8070 JAY HATHEWAY *to* **JUDGE BELL. [from the** *Albany Cultivator***] June 1837. Rome.** Reports the discovery of a plant which may serve as a substitute for mulberry in raising silk worms. 10 August 1837. p.4, c1.

8071 n.n. *to* **BROTHER CHESTER. [extract] 8 November 1837. n.p.** Recounts the events surrounding the murder of Elijah P. Lovejoy. 28 December 1837. p.1, c5.

8072 n.n. *to* **THE** *CINCINNATI JOURNAL.* **[extract] n.d. n.p.** Discusses the events preceding the mob violence and murder of Elijah P. Lovejoy; describes the proceedings of a public meeting held three days prior to the incident. 28 December 1837. p.1, c6.

8073 THOMAS BRAINERD *to* **MR. CHESTER. 12 December [1837]. Philadelphia.** Expresses his moral outrage at the murder of Elijah P. Lovejoy. 28 December 1837. p.2, c4.

8074 n.n. *to* **THE** *BALTIMORE CHRONICLE.* **21 December 1837. Washington.** Reports on an unsuccessful attempt by Southern delegates in the House of Representatives to promote a resolution that all abolition petitions be tabled upon receipt. 28 December 1837. p.3, c1.

8075 MR. HAMMOND *to* **THE** *GAZETTE.* **[extract] 21 December 1837. Columbus.** Reports on a debate between pro- and anti-slavery factions in the Ohio legislature over a bill subjecting townships, towns, and cities to the payment of property damage perpetrated by mobs. 28 December 1837. p.3, c1.

8076 n.n. *to* **THE** *LOUISVILLE CITY GAZETTE.* **[extract] n.d. n.p.** Gives a report concerning the business of the Kentucky legislature. 28 December 1837. p.3, c1.

8077 n.n. *to* **THE** *CINCINNATI JOURNAL.* **[extract] n.d. Alton.** Discusses certain members of the CS who were auxiliaries to the mob in Alton [which murdered Lovejoy]. 28 December 1837. p.3, c2.

8078 JOHN RANKIN *to* **BROTHER CHESTER. n.d. n.p.** Challenges an assertion by the editor of the *New York Observer* that abolitionists "have gone on the false principle that it is right to crush individual opinion by the weight of public opinion." 4 January 1838. p.1, c3.

8079 J. C. *to* **MR. CHESTER. n.d. n.p.** Discusses various prayer meetings in Cincinnati. 4 January 1838. p.1, c3.

8080 E. W. CHESTER *to* **FRIEND. 1 January 1838. Cincinnati.** The superintendent writes to members of the Sunday school of the Second Presbyterian Church in Cincinnati admonishing them to live a holy life, and requesting each student's signature on the seven enclosed resolutions. 4 January 1838. p.2, c6.

8081 n.n. *to* **n.n. [extract from the *National Intelligencer*] 20 December 1837. Milledgeville, Ga.** Discusses recent votes on resolutions before the Georgia legislature. 4 January 1838. p.3, c2.

8082 n.n. *to* **n.n. [extract from the *National Intelligencer*] n.d. Florida.** Notes the high cost of the Florida military campaign. 4 January 1838. p.3, c2.

8083 n.n. *to* **n.n. [extract from the *National Intelligencer*] 25 December 1837. New York.** Reports that Dr. Richard K. Frost was found guilty on a charge of manslaughter in the fourth degree in connection with the death of Tiberius G. French. 4 January 1838. p.3, c2.

8084 n.n. *to* **MR. CHESTER. 15 February 1838. n.p.** Criticizes a previously published article concerning one "Aunt Charity" whom the author believes bears a strong resemblance to herself. 22 February 1838. p.1, c1.

8085 J. C. *to* **n.n. n.d. n.p.** Addresses the religious conversion of children; discusses the problem of children's maintaining faith. 22 February 1838. p.1, c1.

8086 D. C. *to* **BROTHER CHESTER. 2 February 1838. Cincinnati.** Encloses contribution to the American Board of Commissioners for Foreign Missions. 22 February 1838. p.2, c3.

8087 n.n. *to* **MR. E. W. CHESTER. 1 February 1838. South Carolina.** Requests cancellation of his subscription due to Chester's anti-slavery stand. 22 February 1838. p.2, c3.

8088 J. C. *to* **n.n. n.d. n.p.** Attempts to answer the question, "Why does God give revivals?" 22 February 1838. p.2, c5.

8089 O. C. *to* **THE COMMON COUNCIL OF CINCINNATI. 14 February 1838. Cincinnati.** Comments on the aggregate evils of the present liquor license system in Cincinnati. 22 February 1838. p.2, c5.

8090 COMMON SCHOOLS *to* **MR. EDITOR [E. W. CHESTER]. 15 February [1837].** **Cincinnati.** Responds to Chester's statement that music should be taught in the common schools; informs Chester that music is in fact taught in six of the ten districts; requests that he publish the *Report of Mr. Lewis* regarding education. 22 February 1838. p.2, c6.

8091 THORNTON A. MILLS *to* **MR. CHESTER. 12 February 1838. Cincinnati.** Discusses the organization and present condition of the Third Presbyterian Church of Cincinnati. 22 February 1838. p.2, c6.

8092 n.n. *to* **n.n. 13 February 1838. Ripley, Oh.** Comments on the Presbyterian Church of Ripley, their minister, who is currently laboring for the AAS, and a revival held in the fall. 22 February 1838. p.3, c2.

8093 n.n. *to* **n.n. [extract] 29 January 1838. Fort Pierce, Fl.** Relays news of a battle between General Jessup's forces and the Indians. 22 February 1838. p.3, c3.

8094 n.n. *to* **n.n. [extract] 1 February 1838. Fort Pierce, Fl.** An army officer gives an account of a battle between General Jessup's forces and the Indians, in which the Indians were completely routed. 22 February 1838. p.3, c3.

8095 n.n. *to* **MR. EDITOR [extract from the** *New York Evangelist***] n.d. n.p.** Discusses the publication of the minutes of the last General Assembly of the Presbyterian Church; adds that part of the minutes has been withheld from the public. 22 February 1838. p.4, c4.

8096 J. C. *to* **n.n. n.d. n.p.** Introduces a series of letters to children, urging parents and teachers to encourage their children to read them and resolve to seek the Lord. 1 March 1838. p.1, c1.

8097 CHILDREN'S MINISTER *to* **MY YOUNG FRIENDS. n.d. n.p.** Urges children to try to find Jesus through prayer and reading the New Testament. 1 March 1838. p.1, c1.

8098 J. C. *to* **n.n. n.d. n.p.** Cautions parents to utilize careful discrimination in judging the character of their children; explains that the converted child could be rashly and injuriously judged as unconverted. 1 March 1838. p.1, c2.

8099 n.n. *to* **MR. CHESTER. 22 February 1837. Bowling Green, Ky.** Encloses money for his delinquent account. 1 March 1838. p.2, c4.

8100 VISITOR *to* **n.n. 24 February 1838. n.p.** Summarizes a lecture of Dr. [Lyman] Beecher to the Artisans of Cincinnati, in which he attempted to demonstrate the republican tendencies of the Old Testament; encloses a letter written by another to Dr. Beecher pertaining to a previous lecture. 1 March 1838. p.2, c5.

8101 A JOURNEYMAN MECHANIC *to* **REV. DR. BEECHER. 20 February 1838. Cincinnati.** Challenges the historical authenticity of the New Testament. 1 March 1838. p.2, c5.

8102 AUSTIN BRYANT AND JUSTIN H. OLD *to* **E. W. CHESTER, n.d. n.p.** Enclose resolutions of a meeting of the citizens of Bureau County held "for the purpose of a united expression of views on the freedom of speech and the press, and especially in its practical application to the late Alton outrage." 1 March 1838. p.2, c6.

8103 S. *to* **SIR [E. W. CHESTER]. n.d. n.p.** Suggests religious tracts to aid the West in its religious instruction; informs readers of a tract society in Philadelphia; gives an address for inquiries. 1 March 1838. p.2, c6.

8104 B. W. CHIDLAW *to* **BROTHER CHESTER. 17 January 1838. Paddy's Run, Oh.** Reports on the state of his own congregation, which has lately been blessed with thirty new members. 1 March 1838. p.3, c1.

8105 n.n. *to* **BROTHER CHESTER. 14 February 1838. Marietta.** Reports on a meeting of the Society of Inquiry at Marietta College; encloses the order of exercises. 1 March 1838. p.3, c1.

8106 n.n. *to* **n.n. [extract from the** *National Intelligencer***] 15 February 1838. New York.** Comments on the low rate of foreign exchange. 1 March 1838. p.3, c4.

8107 n.n. *to* **n.n. [extract from the** *National Intelligencer***] 17 February 1838. New York.** Examines the gloomy economic state of the nation. 1 March 1838. p.3, c4.

8108 J. C. *to* **n.n. n.d. n.p.** Elaborates on the harm that may be inflicted on a converted child by his parents if they do not apply the proper set of criteria when judging the quality of the child's conversion. 8 March 1838. p.1, c1.

8109 CHILDREN'S MINISTER *to* **FRIENDS. n.d. n.p.** Stresses the urgency of seeking Christ; urges children to commence the search without delay. 8 March 1838. p.1, c2.

8110 R. *to* **J. G. n.d. n.p.** Answers the "Thirty-nine Questions for Peace Men," published in the *Cincinnati Journal* of 15 February and signed by J. G. 8 March 1838. p.4, c1.

8111 WM. CLARK *to* **THE PASTORS, ELDERS, AND MEMBERS OF THE PRESBYTERIAN CHURCHES IN OHIO, KENTUCKY, AND INDIANA. 23 February 1838. Cincinnati.** Appeals for funds on behalf of the American Tract Society. 8 March 1838. p.4, c1.

8112 n.n. *to* **n.n. 9 February 1838. Upper Alton, Il.** Comments on a letter by Mr. O. Lovejoy, in the late edition of the *Journal of Commerce*, and certain rebukes contained therein. 8 March 1838. p.4, c2.

8113 n.n. *to* **n.n. [extract] 2 February 1838. Northwood, N.H.** A clergyman notifies his daughter of a series of revival meetings which have resulted in numerous conversions. 8 March 1838. p.4, c3.

8114 B. W. CHIDLAW *to* **BROTHER. 28 February 1838. Paddy's Run, Oh.** A clergyman writes concerning new members received into his parish. 8 March 1838. p.4, c3.

8115 REV. THERON BALDWIN *to* **n.n. [extract] 24 February 1838. Alton, Il.** Reports that a revival is in progress in the city. 8 March 1838. p.4, c3.

8116 REV. S. COWLES *to* **THE EDITORS OF THE** *HOME MISSIONARY.* **[extract] n.d. Ellicottville, Chautauque County,** N.Y. Reports numerous religious conversions in his area. 8 March 1838. p.4, c3.

8117 REV. C. SMITH *to* **THE EDITORS OF THE** *HOME MISSIONARY.* **[extract] n.d. Bolton, Warren County, N.Y.** Informs of a great revival in his area, where as many as 100 souls have been converted. 8 March 1838. p.4, c3.

8118 n.n. *to* **THE EDITORS OF THE** *NEW YORK OBSERVER.* **[extract] 5 February 1838. Rochester, N.Y.** Reports over 100 conversions in a local church. 8 March 1838. p.3, c3.

8119 VIATOR *to* **BROTHER CHESTER. n.d. n.p.** Describes his visit to the Granville Female Academy. 15 March 1838. p.1, c1.

8120 CHILDREN'S MINISTER *to* **FRIENDS. n.d. n.p.** Discusses various sins which are obstructions to finding God. 15 March 1838. p.1, c1.

8121 J. C. *to* **MR. CHESTER. n.d. n.p.** Encloses for publication an ancient passage regarding the prohibition of commerce on the Sabbath; poses questions arising from the passage. 15 March 1838. p.2, c5.

8122 A. POMEROY *to* **BROTHER CHESTER. 21 February 1838. Lacon, Putnam County, Il.** Reports on the great success of a revival in his parish. 15 March 1838. p.2, c6.

8123 n.n. *to* **SIR [E. W. CHESTER]. 29 January 1838. Galesburg, Knox County, Il.** Forwards for publication a set of resolutions passed by a group of citizens in Alton honoring the memory of Elijah P. Lovejoy and expressing approbation of the principles for which he died. 15 March 1838. p.2, c6.

8124 JULIA *to* **THE** *CINCINNATI JOURNAL* **AND** *ALTON OBSERVER.* **21 February 1838. Jacksonville, Il.** Encloses for publication a poem entitled "Alton" which neither paper in Jacksonville would print. 15 March 1838. p.4, c1.

8125 CHILDREN'S MINISTER *to* **FRIENDS. n.d. n.p.** Discusses the love between God and man, and how the signs of such a relationship are manifest. 22 March 1838. p.1, c1.

8126 WM. KIRBY AND JOHN B. CHITTENDEN. 24 February 1838. Adams County, Il. Enclose for publication the minutes of a meeting of the Congregational Association of Illinois. 22 March 1838. p.1, c2.

8127 EASTERN FRIEND *to* **BROTHER CHESTER. 7 March 1838. New York.** Reports on New England revivals in Hartford, West Hartford, Farmington, Berlin, Southington, and Northington. 22 March 1838. p.1, c3.

8128 W. T. ROGERS *to* **BROTHER [E. W. CHESTER]. [extract from the** *Cincinnati Journal***] 10 May 1837. Sabathu.** A missionary to India offers an extensive account of his work and surroundings. 22 March 1838. p.2, c3.

8129 J. C. *to* **n.n. n.d. n.p.** Asserts that the converted child cannot be expected to maintain a penitent frame of mind without the assistance of others. 22 March 1838. p.2, c5.

8130 T. B. MASON *to* **MR. CHESTER. n.d. n.p.** Corrects an inaccuracy, in a previous issue of the paper, which ascribed the authorship of a report exclusively to Mason. 22 March 1838. p.2, c6.

8131 J. C. *to* **n.n. n.d. n.p.** Asserts that it is because parents expect their children, if converted, to maintain a Christian character without the aid of adults that the children so often regress and disappoint the parents. 29 March 1838. p.1, c1.

8132 CHILDREN'S MINISTER *to* **FRIENDS. n.d. n.p.** Warns of the danger of resisting the Holy Spirit. 29 March 1838. p.1, c2.

8133 A JOURNEYMAN MECHANIC *to* **REV. DR. BEECHER. 12 February 1838. Cincinnati.** Challenges the historical integrity of the New Testament narrative. 29 March 1838. p.1, c6.

8134 J. S. *to* **n.n. n.d. n.p.** Advises ministers to "preach small" and communicate the gospel with simplicity. 29 March 1838. p.2, c6.

8135 J. S. *to* **n.n. n.d. n.p.** Reports on the fate of four individuals who were responsible for breaking up a Sabbath school. 29 March 1838. p.3, c1.

8136 D. *to* **n.n. n.d. n.p.** Notes that the party which had the majority at the last convention is equally zealous to secure a majority at the next Presbyterian General Assembly; urges various presbyteries to take measures to avoid this unhappy state. 29 March 1838. p.3, c1.

8137 J. G. *to* **n.n. n.d. n.p.** Queries why there was no publication of the pledge obtained from the clerks of the last Presbyterian General Assembly concerning the commissions of delegates to the next assembly; suspects that the action was unconstitutional. 29 March 1838. p.3, c1.

8138 T. *to* **MR. CHESTER. n.d. n.p.** Encloses an extract from the *S.S. Journal* pertaining to the American Sunday School Union; explains that the publishing of books is a secondary operation which excludes ultimate profit. 29 March 1838. p.3, c1.

8139 n.n. *to* **n.n. n.d. n.p.** Discusses the extensive circulation of volumes of the American Tract Society in Berkshire County, Massachusetts, resulting from the labors of Rev. R. S. Cook. 29 March 1838. p.3, c2.

8140 n.n. *to* **n.n. n.d. n.p.** A gentleman in Pittsburgh solicits contributions to the American Tract Society for the purpose of distributing tracts in eight or ten states in the South and West. 29 March 1838. p.3, c2.

8141 n.n. *to* **THE EDITOR OF THE** *CHRISTIAN MIRROR*. **[extract] n.d. Hampshire County, Ma.** Reports on a series of revivals in Hampshire County, Massachusetts. 29 March 1838. p.4, c1.

8142 BROTHER MORGAN *to* **n.n. n.d. Uniontown, Pa.** Reports on revival meetings in Uniontown, Pennsylvania. 29 March 1838. p.4, c1.

8143 J. C. *to* **n.n. n.d. n.p.** Cites two additional causes of "religious declension" among children: the attempt, for insufficient reasons, to "tear away hope from the child," and the practice of excluding children from participating in the privileges of the Church. 5 April 1838. p.1, c1.

8144 CHILDREN'S MINISTER *to* **FRIENDS. n.d. n.p.** Examines the question of how a Christian knows that his heart has been changed. 5 April 1838. p.1, c2.

8145 WOODWARD COLLEGE *to* **n.n. n.d. n.p.** Offers examples of modern writers who have borrowed from classical sources. 5 April 1838. p.1, c2.

8146 Z. Y. *to* **THE EDITOR OF THE** *SOUTHERN RELIGIOUS TELEGRAPH*. **n.d. n.p.** Believes that the "Abolition Act of 1818," an anti-slavery measure adopted by the Presbyterian General Assembly in that year, should be repealed. 5 April 1838. p.1, c4.

8147 THOMAS SHORE *to* **J. W. PEGRAM. [extract from the** *Petersburg Intelligencer***] 8 February 1838. Petersburg, Md.** Encloses an anti-slavery article from the *Baltimore Religious and Literary Magazine*, with the recommendation that it be publicly burned. 5 April 1838. p.2, c1.

8148 J. W. PEGRAM *to* **THOMAS SHORE. [extract from the** *Petersburg Intelligencer***] 9 February 1838. Petersburg, Md.** The justice of the peace issues the opinion that the article brought to his attention in the *Baltimore Literary and Religious Magazine* does in fact violate an act of assembly of the state of Maryland. 5 April 1838. p.2, c1.

8149 JOHN SCUDDER *to* **BROTHER HALLOCK. 12 August 1837. Madras, India.** A missionary appeals to the American Tract Society for funds to set his idle presses in motion. 5 April 1838. p.2, c1.

8150 MR. WINSLOW *to* **n.n. [extract] 16 August 1837. n.p.** Requests that the American Tract Society make a strong effort in behalf of southern India. 5 April 1838. p.2, c1.

8151 CYMRO *to* **n.n. 22 March 1838. Paddy's Run, Oh.** Announces the publication of a new monthly periodical, the *Cyfaill*, printed for Welsh immigrants in the Welsh language. 5 April 1838. p.3, c3.

8152 J. C. *to* **n.n. n.d. n.p.** Considers why it is desirable to labor for early conversions. 12 April 1838. p.1, c1.

8153 CHILDREN'S MINISTER *to* **FRIENDS. n.d. n.p.** Considers what it means to grow in grace, and offers some practical advice concerning prayer. 12 April 1838. p.1, c2.

8154 WM. FITHIAN, GEORGE THOMPSON, A. G. FIELD, JOHN RENDALL, O. KENDALL *to* **n.n. n.d. Mission Institute, Il** Offer advice on how to erect a mission institute, which they maintain is a fairly simple task. 12 April 1838. p.1, c3.

8155 AHAB JENKS *to* **SIR [E. W. CHESTER]. 1 March 1838. Galena.** Reports extensively on a protracted revival in the church at Kingston. 12 April 1838. p.1, c3.

8156 J. G. *to* **FRIEND R. 26 March 1838. n.p.** Refutes R's earlier letter which advocated absolute non-resistance. 12 April 1838. p.1, c4.

8157 B. D. *to* **SIR [E. W. CHESTER]. n.d. n.p.** Believes that ministers should give themselves wholly to their work and not be distracted by outside activities such as farming. 12 April 1838. p.1, c5.

8158 J. *to* **n.n. n.d. n.p.** Discusses the standards by which a minister ought to be judged. 12 April 1838. p.1, c5.

8159 G. F. *to* **MR. CHESTER. n.d. n.p.** Praises the church in Lacon, Illinois, which is setting a noble example in its devotion to the cause of education. 12 April 1838. p.2, c5.

8160 J. C. *to* **n.n. n.d. n.p.** Opposes the distribution of milk on the Sabbath. 12 April 1838. p.2, c6.

8161 n.n. *to* **THE** *BALTIMORE SUN.* **[extract] 28 March 1838. Washington.** Reports on the vote of the U.S. House of Representatives requiring the Cherokee Indians to migrate west of the Mississippi; discusses the unfortunate consequences which could follow. 12 April 1838. p.2, c6.

8162 n.n. *to* **n.n. [extract] 12 February 1838. Antigua.** A Connecticut merchant residing in the West Indies reports on the favorable economic conditions in the aftermath of emancipation. 12 April 1838. p.3, c2.

8163 JUSTICE *to* **MR. EDITOR. [from the** *Watchman***] n.d. n.p.** Discusses the difficulties of sustaining a religious newspaper. 12 April 1838. p.4, c3.

8164 THE EDITOR OF THE *MARYLAND REPUBLICAN* *to* **EDITORS. n.d. n.p.** Discusses Thomas Galany, a young man in search of his sisters who supposedly set sail to America from Ireland four years ago, having no acquaintance with the country; requests information concerning their whereabouts. 12 April 1838. p.4, c3.

8165 J. C. *to* **n.n. n.d. n.p.** Discusses the "increased amount of good" which may be expected to result from the child's conversion. 19 April 1838. p.1, c1.

8166 CHILDREN'S MINISTER *to* **FRIENDS. n.d. n.p.** Presents some recommendations regarding daily devotions. 19 April 1838. p.1, c2.

8167 n.n. *to* **n.n. n.d. n.p.** Comments on the Marietta Female Seminary. 19 April 1838. p.1, c3.

8168 ISAAC J. BIGELOW *to* **BROTHER CHESTER. 24 March 1838. Putnam.** Comments on the seminary at Putnam. 19 April 1838. p.1, c4.

8169 n.n. *to* **n.n. n.d. n.p.** Discusses the facilities of Jefferson College in Canonsburg, Pennsylvania. 19 April 1838. p.1, c4.

8170 P. B. *to* **n.n. n.d. n.p.** Urges the patronage of steamboats which operate on temperance principles. 19 April 1838. p.1, c4.

8171 M. *to* **n.n. n.d. n.p.** Argues against a recent editorial in the *Presbyterian*, which asserts that "The Presbyteries, which in defiance of the Assembly's order, have still retained the Congregational members—will probably find themselves excluded [from the next Assembly] by their own act." 19 April 1838. p.3, c2.

8172 L. G. BINGHAM *to* **n.n. n.d. n.p.** The corresponding secretary of the Western Education Society acknowledges a number of donations to that organization. 19 April 1838. p.3, c2.

8173 J. C. *to* **BROTHER CHESTER. n.d. n.p.** Calls for a clear and able exposition of the scriptural passage commonly referred to as "The Golden Rule." 19 April 1838. p.3, c2.

8174 WILLIAM CLARK *to* **MR. CHESTER. 12 April 19836. Cincinnati.** The general agent of the American Tract Society acknowledges a number of donations to that organization. 19 April 1838. p.3, c2.

8175 REV. ARCHER B. SMITH *to* **n.n. [extract from the** *Church Watchman***] n.d. Lynchburgh, Va.** Reports successful results of several revivals in Virginia. 19 April 1838. p.3, c3.

8176 BROTHER HAWTHORN *to* **n.n. [extract from the** *Christian Index***] n.d. Alabama.** Reports on the baptism of 132 persons since August; states that "The Lord has wonderfully blessed us . . . with an outpouring of the Holy Spirit." 19 April 1838. p.3, c3.

8177 WILLARD GLOVER *to* **n.n. [extract from the** *Religious Herald***] 13 February 1838. Spencer, Ma.** Reports that a revival is taking place in Spencer. 19 April 1838. p.3, c3.

Index of Correspondents